Oran's Dictionary of the Law

http://www.wld.com/conbus/oran/Welcome.asp

A searchable legal dictionary.

Virtual Law Libraries

Find Law
http://www.findlaw.com

Includes laws, cases, and codes, legal practice materials, legal news, dictionaries, and more.

The 'Lectric Law Library
http://www.lectlaw.com

An excellent collection of on-line legal materials and resources.

WashLaw Web
http://www.washlaw.edu

A great site with lots of links. Offered by Washburn University School of Law.

The World Wide Web Virtual Library—Law Section
http://www.law.indiana.edu/v-lib/

Run by Indiana University School of Law–Bloomington, the WWW Virtual Library offers searches by topic or type of information.

Law Journals on the World Wide Web

Alabama Law Review
http://www.law.ua.edu/lawreview

Provides full-text reproductions of its articles via the Internet.

American University International Law Review
http://www.wcl.american.edu/pub/ilr/home.htm

An international law journal produced by law students at American University.

American University Law Review
http://www.wcl.american.edu/pub/journals/lawrev/aulrhome.htm

The oldest and the largest journal at the American University Washington College of Law. The range of articles *The Law Review* publishes is not limited to one particular area of law. Full text of some articles is available.

Cardozo Law Review
http://www.cardozo.yu.edu/cardlrev/index.html

An on-line version of the Cardozo Law Review, a student-edited publication of the Benjamin N. Cardozo School of Law at Yeshiva University. Full-text articles are provided.

Coalition of Online Law Journals
http://www.urich.edu/~jolt/e-journals

Provides information about the on-line availability of law journals.

Florida State University Law Review
http://www.law.fsu.edu/journals/lawreview/index.html

Published by the FSU College of Law, the journal provides Adobe PDF versions of its articles on-line.

Indiana Law Journal
http://www.law.indiana.edu/ilj/ilj.html

Published quarterly by students of the Indiana University School of Law–Bloomington. Full-text articles of selected volumes are available on-line.

Mercer Law Review
http://www.review.law.mercer.edu/issueindex.cfm

Published by students at the Walter F. George School of Law of Mercer University (Georgia). Full-text articles from recent issues are available on-line.

Murdoch University Electronic Journal of Law
http://www.murdoch.edu.au/elaw

An Australian law journal available entirely on-line.

New England Law Review
http://www.nesl.edu/lawrev/lawrev.htm

Published on the Web by the New England School of Law.

Stanford Law & Policy Review
http://www.stanford.edu/group/SLPR

An academic journal concentrating on issues of law and public policy, published twice a year by the law students of Stanford Law School.

University Law Review Project
http://www.lawreview.org

Perform a full-text search of law journals and of law journal abstracts.

Washington and Lee Law Review
http://www.wlu.edu/~lawrev

Published quarterly by students of the Washington and Lee University School of Law. Full-text articles are available on-line.

Web Journal of Current Legal Issues
http://webjcli.ncl.ac.uk

Published by the University of Newcastle upon Tyne (U.K.) in association with Blackstone Press, Ltd.

Law-Related Web Search Tools

All Law
http://www.alllaw.com

Permits a search of the All Law site itself, as well as targeted searches of federal and state law.

American Law Sources On-line (ALSO)
http://LawSource.com/also

Provides a comprehensive, uniform, and useful compilation of links to all on-line sources of American law that are available without charge.

Find Law
http://www.findlaw.com
Permits searching of many law-related topics, including case law, legal practice materials, law schools, legal subjects, dictionaries, and libraries.

Law Crawler
http://www.lawcrawler.com
Allows plain English and Boolean searches for legal information within individual country domains and state and federal government servers.

Law Guru
http://www.lawguru.com/multisearch/multimenu.html
The multiple-resource legal research tool at Law Guru is a parallel search engine that allows you to search more than 500 legal search engines and tools at one time.

Law Runner
http://www.lawrunner.com
Provides for the use of predefined intelligent agents in conjunction with the well-known Web index, AltaVista™.

Laws Online
http://www.lawsonline.com
Allows searches of federal and state legal databases, as well as searches of all federal and many state courts.

Virtual Chase
http://www.virtualchase.com/resources/index.shtml
The Legal Research Guide section of Virtual Chase permits searches of case law, state and local law, international law, legal reference materials, and more.

Courts Resources

Conference of State Court Administrators (COSCA)
http://cosca.ncsc.dni.us
COSCA was organized in 1953 and is dedicated to the improvement of state court systems. Its membership consists of the state court administrator in each of the fifty states, the District of Columbia, Puerto Rico, American Samoa, and the Virgin Islands.

Courts Net
http://www.courts.net
A site that provides directory listings for courts across the United States.

Federal Judiciary
http://www.uscourts.gov
Home page of the Administrative Office of the U.S. Courts.

National Center for State Courts
http://www.ncsc.dni.us
The National Center for State courts is an independent, nonprofit organization dedicated to the improvement of justice.

U.S. Court of Appeals for the Armed Forces
http://www.armfor.uscourts.gov
Appellate court empowered to review court-martial cases.

U.S. Court of Appeals, First Circuit
http://www.ca1.uscourts.gov/opinions/main.php

U.S. Court of Appeals, Second Circuit
http://www.law.pace.edu/lawlib/legal/us-legal/judiciary/second-circuit

U.S. Court of Appeals, Third Circuit
http://pacer.ca3.uscourts.gov

U.S. Court of Appeals, Fourth Circuit
http://www.law.emory.edu/4circuit

U.S. Court of Appeals, Fifth Circuit
http://www.ca5.uscourts.gov

U.S. Court of Appeals, Sixth Circuit
http://pacer.ca6.uscourts.gov/opinions/main.php

U.S. Court of Appeals, Seventh Circuit
http://www.ca7.uscourts.gov

U.S. Court of Appeals, Eighth Circuit
http://www.ca8.uscourts.gov/index.html

U.S. Court of Appeals, Ninth Circuit
http://www.ca9.uscourts.gov

U.S. Court of Appeals, Tenth Circuit
http://www.kscourts.org/ca10

U.S. Court of Appeals, Eleventh Circuit
http://www.ca11.uscourts.gov/opinions.htm

U.S. Court of Appeals, D.C. Circuit
http://www.cadc.uscourts.gov

U.S. Court of Appeals, Federal Circuit
http://www.fedcir.gov

U.S. Supreme Court
http://www.supremecourtus.gov
Round-the-clock access to the U.S. Supreme Court. This site provides public access to the Court's decisions, argument calendar, schedules, rules, visitors' guides, building photos, and bar admission forms. Although dockets have also been available by phone, this is the first venture onto the Internet for the nation's highest court. It has decision texts available on-line by noon on the day they are announced (which always occurs at 10 A.M. ET).

Sentencing/Capital Punishment

ACLU's Death Penalty Page
http://www.aclu.org/issues/death/hmdp.html
The ACLU's Execution Watch page offers comprehensive resources on activism against the death penalty in the United States. It includes a link to the ACLU's death penalty briefing paper and the ACLU Abolitionist.

Criminal Law Today

AN INTRODUCTION WITH CAPSTONE CASES

Second Edition

FRANK SCHMALLEGER, PH.D.

Professor Emeritus, University of North Carolina at Pembroke

Upper Saddle River, NJ 07458

Library of Congress Cataloging-in-Publication Data
Schmalleger, Frank.
    Criminal law today : an introduction with capstone cases / Frank Schmalleger.—2nd ed.
      p. cm.
    Includes bibliographical references and index.
    ISBN 0-13-092204-8
    1. Criminal law—United States. 2. Criminal law—United States—Cases. I. Title.
KF9219 .S36 2001
345.73—dc21   2001021564

Publisher: Jeff Johnston
Executive Assistant & Supervisor: Brenda Rock
Executive Acquisitions Editor: Kim Davies
Editorial Assistant: Sarah Holle
Development Editor: Ohlinger Publishing Services, Inc.
Managing Editor: Mary Carnis
Production Management: Carlisle Communications, Ltd.
Production Editor: Lori Dalberg
Production Liaison: Adele M. Kupchik
Interior Design: Wanda España
Director of Manufacturing and Production: Bruce Johnson
Manufacturing Buyer: Cathleen Petersen
Manufacturing Manager: Ilene Sanford
Creative Director: Cheryl Asherman
Cover Design Coordinator: Miguel Ortiz
Director of Marketing Communication and New Media: Frank Mortimer, Jr.
Marketing Manager: Ramona Sherman
Marketing Coordinator: Adam Kloza
Printer/Binder: Courier Westford
Copy Editor: Lorretta Palagi
Proofreader: Chris Feldman
Cover Design: Kevin Kall
Cover Illustration: Leza Anthenien
Cover Printer: Phoenix Color

Pearson Education LTD.
Pearson Education Australia PTY, Limited
Pearson Education Singapore, Pte. Ltd.
Pearson Education North Asia Ltd.
Pearson Education Canada, Ltd.
Pearson Educación de Mexico, S.A. de C.V.
Pearson Education—Japan
Pearson Education Malaysia, Pte. Ltd.

Prentice
Hall

10 9 8 7 6 5 4 3
ISBN 0-13-092204-8

DEDICATION

This book is dedicated to champions of justice and to students of the law everywhere. May you find what you need between these covers.

ADVISORY PANEL

K. Lee Derr, J.D., *The Senate of Pennsylvania*

Thayne D. Gray, J.D.,
Assistant Prosecuting Attorney, Clinton County, Ohio

Dennis Murphy, J.D., Ph.D., *Armstrong Atlantic State University*

Marty McAuliffe, J.D., *University of Phoenix*
Staff Counsel, Academic Legal Services

Cliff Roberson, J.D., L.L.M., Ph.D., *Washburn University*

Michael A. Sullivan, J.D.,
Assistant County Prosecutor, Cuyahoga County, Ohio

Reece Trimmer, J.D., *The North Carolina Justice Academy*

David J. W. Vanderhoof, L.L.M.,
Criminal Justice Studies, University of North Carolina at Pembroke

Summary Contents

Contents

CHAPTER 6:   Excuses as Defenses   **184**

CHAPTER 7:   The Defense of Insanity   **242**

CHAPTER 8: **Legal and Social Dimensions of Personal Crime: Homicide** — **278**

CHAPTER 9: **Legal and Social Dimensions of Personal Crime: Assault, Battery, and Other Personal Crimes** — **318**

CHAPTER 10:   Legal and Social Dimensions of Property and Computer Crimes   364

CHAPTER 11:   Offenses Against Public Order and the Administration of Justice   428

CHAPTER 12: **Offenses Against Public Morality**   **482**

CHAPTER 13: **Victims and the Law**   **536**

CHAPTER 14: **Punishment and Sentencing**　　　　**586**

The publisher and the author of this book jointly donate a portion of proceeds from all sales to research in the field of crime and justice.

Preface

My purpose in writing this textbook has been to provide students with an appreciation for the fundamental nature of law, an overview of general legal principles, and a special understanding of the historical development of criminal law and its contemporary form and function in today's American society. Stories from real life, the critical placement of photographs illustrating cogent contemporary issues, and the use of end-of-chapter Capstone Cases are all meant to bring the law to life.

My approach has been strongly influenced by my belief that the law has always been, and remains, a vital policy-making tool. As a topic for study and discussion, the nature and life of the law is more important today than ever before. The challenges that face the law as it continues to adapt to the needs of a complex and rapidly changing society are highlighted in this text and serve to emphasize for readers the contemporary relevance of our ever-evolving American criminal law.

A central feature of this textbook can be found in its Capstone Cases, placed at the end of each chapter, which provide actual court opinions illustrating important themes in the law. Capstone Cases afford significant insights into the everyday workings of American jurisprudence, and they illustrate the logic by which appellate decisions are made. Law on the Books and Criminal Law in the News boxes, placed throughout the text, illustrate the multiplicity of legal perspectives found at federal, state, and local levels and make students aware of jurisdictional differences in the law. Marginal quotations, found alongside the text column throughout the book, serve to illustrate the inevitable link between matters of the criminal law and contemporary social issues.

Unlike most other criminal law textbooks, *Criminal Law Today* draws on the latest technology to facilitate learning. The World Wide Web site (http://www.prenhall.com/schmalleger) that supports *Criminal Law Today* provides a wealth of resources, activities, and ideas for both students and professors. Special end-of-chapter Legal Resources on the World Wide Web sections refer students to the *Criminal Law Today* home page, which is regularly updated, and to other important Criminal Law Resources on the Internet.

Finally, *Criminal Law Today* is the only criminal law textbook that I am aware of which is supported by a full-featured student study guide. The guide, written by noted attorney and educator Cliff Roberson of Washburn University, allows students to integrate the ideas presented in the text and facilitates the learning of what might otherwise be difficult concepts. The guide also provides a useful self-paced review and allows self-testing for students wishing to delve more deeply into the subject matter of this text.

Like any author, lost in the proverbial forest of words, it is sometimes difficult for me to get a clear view of how my books will be received. As the first edition of this book neared completion, however, I felt satisfied that I had achieved what I set out to do. That feeling came as I glanced over the observations of one reviewer who had painstakingly read through this book as it was under development. His final comment, after months of review, accompanied by well-placed suggestions, read as follows: "This textbook presents criminal law, which is as ancient as human society itself, in a fresh, modern format . . . one which will bring criminal law to life for students everywhere." That's just what I intended!

Frank Schmalleger
The Justice Research Association

NOTE: *Court opinions, statutes, and other quoted materials have occasionally been slightly edited for clarity.*

Acknowledgments

Criminal Law Today owes much to the efforts of many people. Members of the Advisory Panel, who reviewed drafts of this text as it developed and showered me with comments and suggestions, deserve a special thanks. Advisory Panel members include attorneys K. Lee Derr, Thayne D. Gray, Marty McAuliffe, Dennis Murphy, David P. O'Neil, Cliff Roberson, Michael A. Sullivan, Reece Trimmer, and David J. W. Vanderhoof.

Others who have contributed to this text, and to whom I am very grateful, are Lance Parr of California's Grossmont College, and Mike Gray at Maryland's Eastern Shore Criminal Justice Academy. Thanks also to Morgan Peterson at California's Palomar College for assistance in tracking down thorny permissions issues, and to Richard Guymon at Missouri's Maplewoods Community College for his ideas, encouragement, and support. I am indebted to Cliff Roberson of Washburn University, my very capable supplements author, who has striven to bring the law to life for students working with the entire learning package.

This new edition has benefited substantially from the suggestions and ideas provided by these reviewers: Ellen Cohn, Florida International University (Miami); Frank L. Fischer, Kankakee Community College; Stephen Landuyt, Culver-Stockton College; Christine Ludowise, Georgia Southern University; Allison McKenney Brown, Witchita State University; and Kathryn K. Russell, University of Maryland.

The court opinions that are reprinted in this text come from a variety of online sources, and are reprinted with the permission of those sources. Sources include Cal Law (http://www.callaw.com), Versus Law (http://www.versuslaw.com), and WESTLAW (http://www.westlaw.com). I am especially thankful for the assistance of Donna Gies at WESTLAW, Allyson Quibell at Cal Law, and Valerie Sanford at Versus Law in helping me to obtain reprint permissions. Thanks also to Elena A. Cappella at the American Law Institute for help in wending my way through the process necessary to obtain permission to reprint selected portions of the Model Penal Code.

I am especially indebted to the fine folks at the Legal Information Institute at Cornell Law School (including co-directors Thomas R. Bruce and Peter W. Martin), which offers United States Supreme Court opinions under the auspices of the Court's electronic-dissemination Project Hermes.

Last but not least, I wish to thank the staffs at Prentice Hall and Carlisle Communications—professionals all—who have made this book the quality product that it is. Many thanks to Cheryl Asherman, Mary Carnis, Theresa J. Curtis, Lori Dalberg, Kim Davies, Marianne Frasco, Sarah Holle, Adele Kupchik, Craig Marcus, Frank Mortimer, Jr., Miguel Ortiz, Lorretta Palagi, Ilene Sanford, Patrick Walsh, and many other staffers (some of whom remain anonymous) who have brought this book to fruition. Thank you, each and every one!

About the Author

Frank Schmalleger, Ph.D., is Director of The Justice Research Association, a private consulting firm and "think tank" focusing on issues of law, crime, and justice. The Justice Research Association, which is based in Hilton Head Island, South Carolina, serves the needs of the nation's civil and criminal justice planners, administrators, and educators through workshops, conferences, and grant-writing and program evaluation support. Its most significant project to date is the Criminal Justice Distance Learning Consortium (CJDLC). CJDLC can be found on the Web at http://www.cjcentral.com/cjdlc.

Dr. Schmalleger holds degrees from the University of Notre Dame and Ohio State University, having earned both a master's (1970) and doctorate (1974) from Ohio State University with a special emphasis in criminology. From 1976 to 1994, he taught criminal justice courses at the University of North Carolina at Pembroke. For the last sixteen of those years, he chaired the university's Department of Sociology, Social Work, and Criminal Justice. He was named Professor Emeritus at the University of North Carolina at Pembroke in 2001. As an adjunct professor with Webster University in St. Louis, Missouri, Schmalleger helped develop the university's graduate program in security administration and loss prevention. He taught courses in that curriculum for more than a decade. Schmalleger has also taught in the New School for Social Research's online graduate program, helping to build the world's first electronic classrooms in support of distance learning through computer telecommunications. An avid Web surfer, Schmalleger is also the creator of a number of award-winning World Wide Web sites, including one that supports this textbook (http://www.prenhall.com/schmalleger).

Frank Schmalleger is the author of numerous articles and many books, including the widely used *Criminal Justice Today* (Prentice Hall, 2001); *Criminology Today* (Prentice Hall, 2002); *Criminal Justice: A Brief Introduction* (Prentice Hall, 2002); *Crime and the Justice System in America: An Encyclopedia* (Greenwood Publishing Group, 1997); *Computers in Criminal Justice* (Wyndham Hall Press, 1991); *Career Paths: A Guide to Jobs in Federal Law Enforcement* (Regents/Prentice Hall, 1994); *Criminal Justice Ethics* (Greenwood Press, 1991); *Finding Criminal Justice in the Library* (Wyndham Hall Press, 1991); *Ethics in Criminal Justice* (Wyndham Hall Press, 1990); *A History of Corrections* (Foundations Press of Notre Dame, 1983); and *The Social Basis of Criminal Justice* (University Press of America, 1981). Schmalleger is also founding editor of the journal *The Justice Professional*.

A Note to Students

This textbook references a wealth of Web-based resources, including chapter-specific Web Extras!; end-of-chapter Legal Resources; and a list of recommended Web sites that you will find printed on the inside covers. Web Extras!, which are listed in the margins of this textbook, can be found at the Web site that supports this textbook. Visit http://www.prenhall.com/schmalleger and click on the textbook's cover. Look for Web Extras! by chapter. Accessing Web Extras! through the Web site that supports this book insures that the Web locations to which they point are always up to date.

End-of-chapter Legal Resources frequently provide specific URLs (Uniform Resource Locators) pointing to Web sites described there. Similarly, the recommended Web sites that are listed on this text's inside covers are printed along with their associated URLs. As anyone who uses the Internet on a regular basis knows, URLs change frequently. You can keep up with changing URLs for all of the sites listed in this text by visiting Dr. Frank Schmalleger's Cybrary (cyber library) of Crime and Justice Links at http://www.talkjustice.com/cybrary.asp. The Cybrary, which is known on the Internet as the World's Crime and Justice Directory, is fully searchable and lists many thousands of crime, justice, and law-related sites.

Let reverence for the laws,
be breathed by every American mother,
to the lisping babe, that prattles on her lap;
let it be taught in schools, in seminaries, and in colleges;
let it be written in Primers, spelling books, and in Almanacs;
let it be preached from the pulpit, proclaimed in legislative halls,
and enforced in courts of justice.
And, in short, let it become the political religion of the nation;
and let the old and the young, the rich and the poor, the grave and the gay,
of all sexes and tongues, and colors and conditions,
sacrifice unceasingly upon its altars.

—ABRAHAM LINCOLN (1838)

The Nature and History of Criminal Law

Law is the art of the good and the fair.

—Ulpian, Roman judge (circa A.D. 200)

[D]ue process . . . embodies a system of rights based on moral principles so deeply embedded in the traditions and feelings of our people as to be deemed fundamental to a civilized society as conceived by our whole history. Due process is that which comports with the deepest notions of what is fair and right and just.

—Justice Hugo Black (1886–1971)[1]

The law is that which protects everybody who can afford a good lawyer.

—Anonymous

CHAPTER OUTLINE

AFTER READING THIS CHAPTER YOU SHOULD:

▷ Appreciate the difference between "crime" and "deviance."

▷ Understand the terms "law" and "criminal law."

▷ Know that while laws offer a fair degree of predictability, the law is dynamic and ever-changing.

▷ Understand the importance of the "rule of law" and "due process of law."

▷ Understand distinctions between different types of crime.

▷ Realize that laws can be the end product of organized efforts undertaken by special interest groups.

INTRODUCTION

In June 2000 Larico Garrett, 22, of Manchester, Connecticut, was arrested for car theft after he pulled the stolen vehicle he was driving into a convenience store parking lot to ask a police officer for directions to a nearby street.[2] Although he answered the man's questions, Officer Robert Johnson found the 2 A.M. encounter suspicious and ran a radio check of the license plate on the Cadillac that Garrett was driving. When dispatchers reported the vehicle stolen, Johnson summoned help and drove to the street where Garrett was headed. Garrett was arrested and charged under Connecticut law with taking a vehicle without the owner's permission, a misdemeanor punishable by less than a year in jail.

WHAT IS CRIMINAL LAW?

Although most people would agree that it is not very smart for a car thief to ask directions from a police officer, it is not a crime to be stupid. Car theft, of course, is

CRIMINAL LAW IN THE NEWS

Man in Stolen Car Asks Cop for Directions

Officer Runs Plates, Nabs Suspect at His Destination

MANCHESTER, Conn.—A man driving a stolen car was shown the way to jail after he stopped and asked a police officer for directions, authorities said today.

Larico Garrett, 22, was driving on Main Street around 2 A.M. Wednesday when he pulled into a convenience store parking lot to ask Officer Robert Johnson for directions to a nearby street, police said.

Garrett, who lives in the neighboring town of Vernon, questioned the officer's directions, which the officer found suspicious, police said.

The officer then ran a check of the license plate on the Cadillac that Garrett was driving and learned it was reported stolen from Bridgeport, police said.

Johnson and other officers went to the street where Garrett was headed and found the stolen car parked outside a home.

Faces a year in jail

A woman in a third-floor apartment said Garrett was not there, Officer Hank Minor said. Minor, meanwhile, climbed a fire escape and peeked through a window to find Garrett scurrying behind a dresser in the woman's apartment. The other officers then entered the apartment and arrested the alleged car thief, Minor said.

Officers are puzzled as to why Garrett stopped to ask a police officer for directions since he had been to the woman's home earlier, Minor said.

"Not a smart man," Minor said. "We win one every once in a while."

Garrett was charged with taking a vehicle without the owner's permission, a misdemeanor punishable by less than a year in jail, police said.

He was released on his own recognizance following his arraignment in Manchester Superior Court and is next scheduled to appear in court on July 14, a court spokeswoman said.

Source: Richard Zitrin, "Man in Stolen Car Asks Cop for Directions; Officer Runs Plates, Nabs Suspect at His Destination," APB News. June 22, 2000. Reprinted with permission.

LAW
that which is laid down, ordained, or established . . . a body of rules of action or conduct prescribed by controlling authority, and having binding *legal* force.[3]

NORMS
unwritten rules that underlie and are inherent in the fabric of society.

MORES
unwritten, but generally known, rules that govern serious violations of the social code.

MORALS
ethical principles, or principles meant to guide human conduct and behavior; principles or standards of right and wrong.

"Law" is a solemn expression of the will of the supreme power of the state.
—Montana Code Annotated, Section 1-1-101

Law is whatever is boldly asserted and plausibly maintained.
—Aaron Burr (1756–1836)

---

another matter, and most forms of theft (which are discussed in greater detail in Chapter 10) violate the law. *Black's Law Dictionary,* an authoritative source of legal terminology, defines the word *law* as follows: "that which is laid down, ordained, or established . . . a body of rules of action or conduct prescribed by controlling authority, and having binding *legal* force."[4]

However, not all rules are laws, fewer still are criminal laws, and not all have "binding legal force." Sociologists, for example, distinguish between **norms** and **mores,** while philosophers and ethicists talk of **morals** and morality. Morals are ethical principles, and moral behavior is that which conforms to some ethical principle or moral code. Norms refer to rules that underlie and are inherent in the fabric of society. So, for example, it is regarded as inappropriate to belch in public. Anyone who intentionally violates a social norm may be seen as inadequately socialized (others might call them "uncivilized"), offensive, and even dangerous (if the violation is a serious one) to an accepted way of life. When social norms are *unintentionally* violated (as may be the case with a belch at the dinner table), a mere request to be excused generally allows social interaction to proceed with little or no interruption. Mores, on the other hand, are rules that govern serious violations of the social code, including what social scientists call "taboos." For example, during the 1995 criminal trial of former football superstar O. J. Simpson, defense attorneys believed it necessary to describe the language Los Angeles police detective Mark Fuhrman was known to have frequently used in describing black people. Although witnesses testified that Fuhrman had voiced the word "nigger" on many occasions, attorneys called the word an "epithet" and would themselves not pronounce it in court—preferring to use the phrase "the N-word" in its place. Members on both sides of the case apparently considered the "N-word" itself taboo—especially in open court (where the proceedings were being nationally televised). No doubt they also feared that use of the word "nigger" might offend jurors, most of whom were black.

Social norms can often be violated with relative impunity, while violations of the criminal law carry potentially far more serious consequences. Here platinum-haired Chicago Bulls' basketball superstar Dennis Rodman, dressed as a bride, poses for photographers at a Manhattan bookstore. Rodman was promoting his book, Bad As I Wanna Be. (Photo by Mark Lennihan, courtesy of AP/Wide World Photos.)

Violations of both mores and norms are forms of deviance and can properly be called "deviant behavior." Even so, few violations of social norms are illegal, and fewer still are crimes. Since laws have not been enacted against quite a large number of generally recognized taboos, it is possible for behavior to be contrary to accepted principles of social interaction and even immoral—but still legal. As you read through this book, it is important to remember that *only human conduct that violates the criminal law can properly be called "criminal."* While other forms of nonconformist behavior may be undesirable or even reprehensible, they are not crimes.[5]

The practice of law depends on the application of clear and concise definitions. Hence, before proceeding further, it is appropriate that the notion of "crime" be clarified. An early, but influential, definition of crime read as follows: "A crime or misdemeanor is an act committed or omitted, in violation of a public law either forbidding or commanding it."[6] The **Model Penal Code**, an important document intended to guide state legislators in formulating statutory provisions, defines the term *crime* as "[a]n offense defined by this Code or by any other statute of this State, for which a sentence of [death or of] imprisonment is authorized."[7] A popular criminal law textbook of a few years ago offered this definition of crime: "Crime is any social harm defined and made punishable by law."[8] All three definitions, while their emphases vary, implicitly recognize the role played by government in defining exactly what a crime is. Hence, a more useful (and comprehensive) definition of the word *crime* (and the one we use in this book) might be "any act or omission prohibited by public law, committed without defense or justification, and made punishable by the state in a judicial proceeding in its own name."

The criminal law . . . is an expression of the moral sense of the community.

—*United States* v. *Freeman*,
357 F.2d 606 (2d Cir. 1966)

Web Extra! 1–1

Britannica online: principles of criminal law

MODEL PENAL CODE

a model code of criminal laws intended to standardize general provisions of criminal liability, sentencing, defenses, and the definitions of specific crimes between and among the states. The Model Penal Code was developed by the American Law Institute.

CRIME

any act or omission prohibited by public law, committed without defense or justification, and made punishable by the state in a judicial proceeding in its own name.

Law is born from despair of human nature.

—José Ortega y Gasset

Web Extra! 1–2

Britannica online:
crime

Web Extra! 1–3:

Britannica online:
the concept of crime

CRIMINAL LAW

that body of rules and regulations that defines and specifies punishments for offenses of a public nature, or for wrongs committed against the state or society; also called **penal law.**

Crimes can be distinguished from other legal transgressions by the fact that they are essentially offenses against the community or the public. Edwin Sutherland, a famous criminologist of the early twentieth century, put it this way: "the essential characteristic of crime is that it is behavior which is prohibited by the State as an injury to the State and against which the State may react, at least as the last resort, by punishment."[9] Sir William Blackstone (1723–1780), the great British jurist, described the principles of the common law in his voluminous *Commentaries on the Laws of England,* published in 1769. Blackstone's *Commentaries,* which was to guide American judges and lawyers struggling to build an American legal system after the Revolution, described the "public" feature of crimes in this now famous passage: "The distinction of public wrongs from private, of crimes and misdemeanors from civil injuries, seems principally to consist of this: that private wrongs, or civil injuries, are an infringement or privation of the civil rights which belong to individuals, considered merely as individuals; public wrongs, or crimes and misdemeanors, are a breach and violation of the public rights and duties due to the whole community, considered as a community . . . treason, murder, and robbery are properly ranked among crimes; since besides the injury done the individual, they strike at the very being of society; which cannot possibly subsist where actions of this sort are suffered to escape with impunity."[10]

Criminal law can be understood, then, as that body of rules and regulations that defines and specifies punishments for offenses of a public nature, or for wrongs committed against the state or society. Criminal law is also called **penal law** and is usually embodied in the penal codes of various jurisdictions. In short, criminal law defines certain activities as illegal, and violations of the criminal law are referred to as crimes.

Types of Crime

TREASON

violation of allegiance toward one's country or sovereign, esp. the betrayal of one's own country by waging war against it or by consciously and purposely acting to aid its enemies.[12]

FELONY

a serious crime, generally one punishable by death or by incarceration in a state or federal prison facility as opposed to a jail.

MISDEMEANOR

a minor crime; an offense punishable by incarceration, usually in a local confinement facility, for a period of which the upper limit is prescribed by statute in a given jurisdiction, typically limited to a year or less.

Further distinctions can be drawn between types of crimes, such as (in descending order of seriousness) treason, felonies, misdemeanors, and infractions.[11] A crucial feature that distinguishes one type of crime from another is the degree of punishment. Hence, **treason** and **felonies** are thought of as serious crimes for which at least a year in prison is a possible punishment. **Misdemeanors** are less serious offenses, generally thought of as punishable by less than a year's incarceration. The Texas Penal Code, for example, defines a felony as "an offense so designated by law or punishable by death or confinement in a penitentiary." A misdemeanor, according to the Texas Code, "means an offense so designated by law or punishable by fine, by confinement in jail, or by both fine and confinement in jail."

Other states use similar definitions. The California Penal Code describes a felony as "a crime which is punishable with death or by imprisonment in the state prison." "Every other crime," reads the California Code, "or public offense is a misdemeanor except those offenses that are classified as infractions." Continuing with its emphasis on degree of punishment as a distinguishing feature between felonies and misdemeanors, California law reads: "Except in cases where a different punishment is prescribed by any law of this state, every offense declared to be a misdemeanor is punishable by imprisonment in the county jail not exceeding six months, or by fine not exceeding one thousand dollars ($1,000), or by both." In California, "[a]n infraction is not punishable by imprisonment." Some jurisdictions refer to **infractions** as "ticketable offenses," to indicate that such minor crimes usually result in the issuance of citations, which are often payable through the mail.

Another important distinction can be drawn between crimes that are completed and those that are attempted or are still in the planning stage. The term "inchoate,"

Web Extra! 1–4

Britannica online:
common law
and code law

which means partial or unfinished, is applied to crimes such as conspiracy to commit a criminal act, solicitation of others to engage in criminal acts, and attempts to commit crimes. Inchoate crimes are discussed in greater detail later in this book.

Crimes can also be classified as either *mala in se* or *mala prohibita*. *Mala in se* crimes are those that are regarded, by tradition and convention, as wrong in themselves. Such acts are said to be inherently evil and immoral and are sometimes called "acts against conscience." *Mala in se* crimes, such as murder, rape, and other serious offenses, are almost universally condemned and probably would be so even if strictures against such behaviors were not specified in the criminal law.[13] Clarence Ray Jeffery, a sociologist of law, says that just as there is a natural law, there are also "natural crimes." "The notion of natural crime," says Jeffery, as "a crime against a law of nature rather than against a legal law, was present in the criminal law at its inception. This led to the definition of crimes as *mala in se,* acts bad in themselves, and *mala prohibita,* acts which are crimes mainly because they are prohibited by positive law."[14]

As Jeffery observed, *mala prohibita* crimes (*malum prohibitum* is the singular term that refers to one such crime) are considered "wrongs" only because there is a law against them. Without a statute specifically proscribing them, *mala prohibita* offenses might *not* be regarded as "wrong" by a large number of people. *Mala prohibita* offenses often include the category of "victimless crimes," such as prostitution, drug use, and gambling, in which a clear-cut victim is difficult to identify, and whose commission rarely leads to complaints from the parties directly involved in the offense.

Many other distinctions can be drawn between types of crimes, but space does not permit discussion of them all. One final division should be mentioned however—the traditional classification of offenses into four types: (1) **property crimes,** (2) **personal crimes,** (3) **public order offenses,** and (4) **morals offenses.** The distinction between property and personal crimes is of special importance in most state penal codes, and official reports on the incidence of crime, such as the FBI's Uniform Crime Reports (UCR), are structured along such a division. Crimes against property (which are discussed in Chapter 10) include burglary, larceny, arson, criminal mischief (vandalism), property damage, motor vehicle theft, passing bad checks, commission of fraud or forgery, and so on. Personal crimes, or offenses against persons (discussed in Chapters 8 and 9), include criminal homicide, kidnapping and false imprisonment, various forms of assault, and rape. Personal crimes are also termed "violent crimes." Public order offenses (discussed in Chapter 11) are sometimes called "crimes against the public order" and include offenses such as fighting, breach of peace, disorderly conduct, vagrancy, loitering, unlawful assembly, public intoxication, obstructing public passage, and (illegally) carrying weapons. Finally, morals offenses (discussed in Chapter 12) denote a category of unlawful conduct that was criminalized originally to protect the family and related social institutions. The "morals offense" category includes lewdness, indecency, sodomy, and other sex-related offenses, such as seduction, fornication, adultery, bigamy, pornography, obscenity, cohabitation, and prostitution.

Types of Law

Just as distinctions can be drawn between types of crime, so too can various kinds of law be described. Criminal law is just one type of law, although it is the form of law with which this book is primarily concerned. Useful distinctions can be drawn between other major categories of law, such as substantive law and procedural law; case law and statutory law; and civil law and criminal law.

INFRACTION
sometimes called a **summary offense;** a violation of a state statute or local ordinance punishable by a fine or other penalty, but not by incarceration.

The purpose of all law, and the criminal law in particular, is to conform conduct to the norms expressed in that law.
—*United States v. Granada,*
565 F.2d 922, 926 (5th Cir. 1978)

MALA IN SE
acts that are regarded, by tradition and convention, as wrong in themselves.

MALA PROHIBITA
acts that are considered "wrongs" only because there is a law against them.

The first requirement of a sound body of law is that it should correspond with the actual feelings and demands of the community, whether right or wrong.
—Oliver Wendell Holmes, Jr.
(*The Common Law,* 1881)

PROPERTY CRIME
a crime committed against property, including (according to the FBI's UCR program) burglary, larceny, auto theft, and arson.

PERSONAL CRIME
also called **violent crime;** a crime committed against a person, including (according to the FBI's UCR program) murder, rape, aggravated assault, and robbery.

PUBLIC ORDER OFFENSE
an act that is willfully committed and that disturbs public peace or tranquillity. Included are offenses such as fighting, breach of peace, disorderly conduct, vagrancy, loitering, unlawful assembly, public intoxication, obstructing public passage, and (illegally) carrying weapons.

MORALS OFFENSES
a category of unlawful behavior that was originally created to protect the family and related social institutions. Included are crimes such as lewdness, indecency, sodomy, and other sex-related offenses, such as seduction, fornication, adultery, bigamy, pornography, obscenity, cohabitation, and prostitution.

SHOULD CROSS BURNINGS BE PROTECTED AS A FORM OF FREE SPEECH?

While some forms of activity may be clearly obnoxious and offensive to a large number of citizens, the U.S. Supreme Court has found that, when it is not otherwise threatening or destructive, such behavior may be protected under First Amendment guarantees. As the wording of the Court's decision shows, however, the purpose of legislation may be as important as the object of that legislation.

R.A.V. v. City of St. Paul, Minnesota
U.S. Supreme Court, 1992
505 U.S. 377

Justice Scalia delivered the opinion of the Court.

In the predawn hours of June 21, 1990, petitioner and several other teenagers allegedly assembled a crudely made cross by taping together broken chair legs. They then allegedly burned the cross inside the fenced yard of a black family that lived across the street from the house where petitioner was staying. Although this conduct could have been punished under any of a number of laws, one of the two provisions under which respondent, City of St. Paul, chose to charge petitioner (then a juvenile) was the St. Paul Bias-Motivated Crime Ordinance, St. Paul, Minn. Legislative Code Section 292.02 (1990), which provides:

> *Whoever places on public or private property a symbol, object, appellation, characterization, or graffiti, including, but not limited to, a burning cross or Nazi swastika, which one knows or has reasonable grounds to know arouses anger, alarm, or resentment in others on the basis of race, color, creed, religion, or gender, commits disorderly conduct and shall be guilty of a misdemeanor.*

Petitioner moved to dismiss this count on the ground that the St. Paul ordinance was substantially overbroad and impermissibly content-based and therefore facially invalid under the First Amendment. The trial court granted this motion, but the Minnesota Supreme Court reversed. . . .

The First Amendment generally prevents government from proscribing speech, see, e.g., *Cantwell* v. *Connecticut*, 310 U.S. 296, 309-311

(1940), or even expressive conduct, see, e.g., *Texas* v. *Johnson*, 491 U.S. 397, 406 (1989), because of disapproval of the ideas expressed. Content-based regulations are presumptively invalid. *Simon & Schuster, Inc.* v. *Members of N. Y. State Crime Victims Bd.*, 502 U.S. 105 (1991) . . . *Consolidated Edison Co. of N. Y.* v. *Public Serv. Comm'n of N. Y.*, 447 U.S. 530, 536 (1980); *Police Dept. of Chicago* v. *Mosley*, 408 U.S. 92, 95 (1972). From 1791 to the present, however, our society, like other free but civilized societies, has permitted restrictions upon the content of speech in a few limited areas, which are "of such slight social value as a step to truth that any benefit that may be derived from them is clearly outweighed by the social interest in order and morality." *Chaplinsky*, 315 U.S., at 572. We have recognized that "the freedom of speech" referred to by the First Amendment does not include a freedom to disregard these traditional limitations. See, e.g., *Roth* v. *United States*, 354 U.S. 476 (1957) (obscenity); *Beauharnais* v. *Illinois*, 343 U.S. 250 (1952) (defamation); *Chaplinsky* v. *New Hampshire, supra,* ("fighting words"). . . .

Our cases surely do not establish the proposition that the First Amendment imposes no obstacle whatsoever to regulation of particular instances of such proscribable expression, so that the government "may regulate [them] freely,". . . . That would mean that a city council could enact an ordinance prohibiting only those legally obscene works that contain criticism of the city government or, indeed, that do not include endorsement of the city government. Such a simplistic, all-or-nothing-at-all approach to First Amendment protection is at odds with common sense and with our jurisprudence as well. It is not true that "fighting words" have at most a "*de minimis*" expressive content or that their content is in all respects "worthless and undeserving of constitutional protection," . . . sometimes they are quite expressive indeed. We have not said that they constitute "no part of the expression of ideas," but only that they constitute "no essential part of any exposition of ideas." *Chaplinsky, supra,* at 572. . . .

The proposition that a particular instance of speech can be proscribable on the basis of one feature (e.g., obscenity) but not on the basis of another (e.g., opposition to the city government) is commonplace and has found application in many contexts. We have long held, for example, that nonverbal expressive activity can be banned because of the action it entails, but not because of the ideas it expresses "so that burning a flag in violation of an ordinance against outdoor fires could be punishable, whereas burning a flag in violation of an ordinance against dishonoring the flag is not" . . . Similarly, we have upheld reasonable "time, place, or manner" restrictions, but only if they are "justified without reference to the content of the regulated speech". . . .

In other words, the exclusion of "fighting words" from the scope of the First Amendment simply means that, for purposes of that Amendment, the unprotected features of the words are, despite their verbal character, essentially a "nonspeech" element of communication. Fighting words are thus analogous to a noisy sound truck: each is, as Justice Frankfurter recognized, a "mode of speech," *Niemotko* v. *Maryland,* 340 U.S. 268, 282 (1951) (Frankfurter, J., concurring in result); both can be used to convey an idea; but neither has, in and of itself, a claim upon the First Amendment. As with the sound truck, however, so also with fighting words: the government may not regulate use based on hostility or favoritism towards the underlying message expressed. . . .

To illustrate: A State might choose to prohibit only that obscenity which is the most patently offensive in its prurience—i.e., that which involves the most lascivious displays of sexual activity. But it may not prohibit, for example, only that obscenity which includes offensive political messages. . . .

Applying these principles to the St. Paul ordinance, we conclude that, even as narrowly construed by the Minnesota Supreme Court, the ordinance is facially unconstitutional. Although the phrase in the ordinance, "arouses anger, alarm or resentment in others," has been limited by the Minnesota Supreme Court's construction to reach only those symbols or displays that amount to "fighting words," the remaining, unmodified terms make clear that the ordinance applies only to "fighting words" that insult, or provoke violence, "on the basis of race, color, creed, religion, or gender." Displays containing abusive invective, no matter how vicious or severe, are permissible unless they are addressed to one of the specified disfavored topics. Those who wish to use "fighting

words" in connection with other ideas—to express hostility, for example, on the basis of political affiliation, union membership, or homosexuality—are not covered. The First Amendment does not permit St. Paul to impose special prohibitions on those speakers who express views on disfavored subjects. . . .

What we have here, it must be emphasized, is not a prohibition of fighting words that are directed at certain persons or groups (which would be facially valid if it met the requirements of the Equal Protection Clause); but rather, a prohibition of fighting words that contain (as the Minnesota Supreme Court repeatedly emphasized) messages of "bias-motivated" hatred and in particular, as applied to this case, messages "based on virulent notions of racial supremacy." 464 N. W. 2d, at 508, 511. One must wholeheartedly agree with the Minnesota Supreme Court that "[i]t is the responsibility, even the obligation, of diverse communities to confront such notions in whatever form they appear," *ibid.,* but the manner of that confrontation cannot consist of selective limitations upon speech. . . .

The First Amendment cannot be evaded that easily. It is obvious that the symbols that arouse "anger, alarm, or resentment in others on the basis of race, color, creed, religion, or gender" are those symbols that communicate a message of hostility based on one of these characteristics. St. Paul concedes in its brief that the ordinance applies only to "racial, religious, or gender-specific symbols"—such as "a burning cross, Nazi swastika, or other instrumentality of like import." Brief for Respondent 8. Indeed, St. Paul argued in the Juvenile Court that "[t]he burning of a cross does express a message and it is, in fact, the content of that message which the St. Paul Ordinance attempts to legislate." Memorandum from the Ramsey County Attorney to the Honorable Charles A. Flinn, Jr., dated July 13, 1990, in *In re Welfare of R. A. V.,* No. 89-D-1231 (Ramsey Cty. Juvenile Ct.), p. 1, reprinted in App. to Brief for Petitioner C-1. . . .

St. Paul has not singled out an especially offensive mode of expression—it has not, for example, selected for prohibition only those fighting words that communicate ideas in a threatening (as opposed to a merely obnoxious) manner. Rather, it has proscribed fighting words of whatever manner that communicate messages of racial, gender, or religious intolerance.

(continued)

LAW IN PRACTICE

Selectivity of this sort creates the possibility that the city is seeking to handicap the expression of particular ideas. That possibility would alone be enough to render the ordinance presumptively invalid, but St. Paul's comments and concessions in this case elevate the possibility to a certainty. . . .

Let there be no mistake about our belief that burning a cross in someone's front yard is reprehensible. But St. Paul has sufficient means at its disposal to prevent such behavior without adding the First Amendment to the fire.

The judgment of the Minnesota Supreme Court is reversed, and the case is remanded for proceedings not inconsistent with this opinion.

It is so ordered.

What do *you* think?

1. Summarize the decision of the U.S. Supreme Court in this case. In a few words, explain why the Court overturned the decision of the Minnesota Supreme Court.

2. Does this decision leave any avenues open by which behavior such as cross-burning might be criminalized without running afoul of First Amendment guarantees? If so, what might they be?

3. If you were a city council member wishing to pass an ordinance against cross-burnings, how might you proceed? How would you word such an ordinance to make it consistent with *R.A.V. v. City of St. Paul, Minnesota*?

NOTE: Many of the cases referred to by the U.S. Supreme Court in this opinion are available as Capstone Cases throughout this book.

Web Extra! 1–5
Britannica online:
substantive
criminal law

SUBSTANTIVE LAW
that part of the law that creates and defines fundamental rights and duties.

SUBSTANTIVE CRIMINAL LAW
that part of the law that defines crimes and specifies punishments.

PROCEDURAL LAW
that aspect of the law that specifies the methods to be used in enforcing substantive law.

STATUTORY LAW
law in the form of statutes or formal written strictures, made by a legislature or governing body with the power to make law.

CASE LAW
the body of previous decisions, or precedents, that has accumulated over time and to which attorneys refer when arguing cases and that judges use in deciding the merits of new cases.

Substantive law refers to that part of the law that creates and defines fundamental rights and duties. Substantive law includes criminal law as well as contract law, tort law, and other forms of the law that specify rules which must be followed in social life. **Substantive criminal law,** which defines crimes and specifies punishments, can be found in the penal codes of the various states and the federal government. **Procedural law,** on the other hand, specifies the methods to be used in enforcing substantive law. Laws of criminal procedure enumerate acceptable steps to be undertaken during the investigation, arrest, trial, and sentencing of criminal defendants. One judge described the difference between substantive and procedural criminal law this way: "Substantive law is that which declares what acts are crimes and describes the punishment therefor; whereas procedural law is that which provides or regulates the steps by which one who violates a criminal statute is punished."[15]

Most procedural laws in jurisdictions within the United States today are statutory in nature—that is, they are formal written rules of procedure. Hence, another major distinction is that made between case law and statutory law. **Statutory law** exists in the form of statutes or formal written strictures and is made by a legislature or governing body with the power to make law. **Case law** is sometimes called "judge-made law" and refers to the body of previous decisions, or precedents, that have accumulated over time and to which attorneys refer when arguing cases and which judges use in deciding the merits of new cases. Central to case law is the principle of *stare decisis. Stare decisis* literally means "standing by decided matters" and forms the basis of our modern law of precedent. The principle of *stare decisis* requires that courts be bound by their own earlier decisions, and by those of higher courts having jurisdiction over them, regarding subsequent cases on similar issues of law and fact. The U.S. Supreme Court has ruled that "*Stare decisis* is of fundamental importance to the rule of law."[16]

Case law and statutory law make for predictability in the law. Criminal defendants and their attorneys entering a modern courtroom can generally gauge with a fair degree of accuracy what the law will expect of them. In the words of the Court: "acknowledgments of precedent serve the principal purposes of *stare decisis,* which are to protect reliance interests and to foster stability in the law."[17] In a strongly worded acknowledgment of the importance of *stare decisis,* the majority opinion of the U.S. Supreme Court in the 1986 case of *Vasquez* v. *Hillary*[18] says that *stare decisis* "permits society to presume that bedrock principles are founded in the law rather than in the proclivities of individuals, and thereby contributes to the integrity of our constitutional system of government, both in appearance and in fact." Even so, a number of Justices have, in various cases, recognized that *stare decisis* "is not an imprisonment of reason."[19] In other words, while *stare decisis* is a central guiding principle in Western law, it does not dictate blind obedience to precedent.

Many cases, of course, are not subject to *stare decisis* because they are unlike previous cases. They may deal with new subject matter or novel situations, raise unusual legal questions, or fall outside of the principles established by earlier decisions. Even when cases are apparently similar, it is possible for courts to **distinguish** a new case from earlier ones. When a case is distinguished, a court finds that prior cases are sufficiently dissimilar to the one under review that previous precedents do not apply.

Criminal law, which was defined earlier as that form of law whose violation is an offense against the state or against the nation, must be distinguished from civil law. **Civil law** governs relationships between parties. Civil codes regulate contracts of all sorts, including marriages, divorces, and many other forms of personal and business relationships, such as inheritance and adoption. A private or civil wrong or injury is referred to as a **tort.** A tort can be more formally defined as "the unlawful violation of a private legal right other than a mere breach of contract, express or implied. A tort may also be the violation of a public duty if, as a result of the violation, some special damage accrues to the individual."[20] An individual or business that commits a tort is called a **tort-feasor.**

A tort may give rise to civil liability, under which the injured party may sue the person or entity who caused the injury and ask that the offending party be ordered to pay damages directly to them. Civil law, however, is more concerned with assessing liability than it is with intent. Accidents, as in cases of airline or automobile crashes, may result in huge civil settlements, even though the defendant did not intend the crash to occur.

Parties to a civil suit are referred to as the plaintiff and the defendant and, as with criminal cases, the names of civil suits take the form *Named Plaintiff* v. *Named Defendant.* Unlike criminal cases, in which the state routinely prosecutes wrongdoers, most civil suits are brought by individuals. On occasion, however, the plaintiff in a civil suit may be the state or a government office or agency. Hence, the state may bring a suit to revoke an attorney's right to practice law or a doctor's right to practice medicine. Similarly, the state may bring antitrust cases and initiate other types of civil action. In contrast to the criminal law, however, no civil action will be undertaken that is not initiated by the injured party.

Damage awards in civil cases, when they occur, may be both compensatory—in which the amount to be paid directly compensates the injured party for the amount of damage incurred—and punitive—in which the award serves to punish the defendant for some especially wrongful or treacherous act. In 1996, for example, thirty-seven-year-old Alex Hardy, an Alabama man who had been seriously injured when his Chevrolet Blazer flipped over, received a $150 million award from a civil jury.[22] One-third of the award, or $50 million, was in the form of compensatory damages intended to provide medical care for Hardy, who was left partially paralyzed. The other $100 million came in the form of punitive damages, with the jury accepting Hardy's claim that General Motors knew that the door latches on Blazers were defective and that the latches might allow the doors to open in crashes. Although Hardy had been thrown from his vehicle, GM claimed the door latches were safe and that Hardy had fallen asleep and was not wearing a seat belt at the time of the accident.

It is important to realize that violations of the criminal law can also lead to civil actions—even though the defendant may not be convicted of the criminal charges. In 1996, for example, Bernhard Goetz, also known as the "subway vigilante," was

---

STARE DECISIS
the legal principle that requires that courts be bound by their own earlier decisions and by those of higher courts having jurisdiction over them regarding subsequent cases on similar issues of law and fact. The term literally means "standing by decided matters."

Courts of law follow precedent, on the general theory that experience is more than just individual decision. Precedent, however, tends to carry forward the ignorance and injustice of the past. Mankind is constantly learning, getting new views of truth, seeing new values in social justice. Precedent clogs this advance.

—Frank Crane (1919)

DISTINGUISH
to argue or to find that a rule established by an earlier appellate court decision does apply to a case currently under consideration even though an apparent similarity exists between the cases.

CIVIL LAW
that form of the law that governs relationships between parties.

TORT
a private or civil wrong or injury. The unlawful violation of a private legal right other than a mere breach of contract, express or implied.[21]

TORT-FEASOR
an individual, business, or other legally recognized entity that commits a tort.

Stare decisis is ordinarily a wise rule of action. But it is not a universal, inexorable command. The instances in which the court has disregarded its admonition are many.

—Justice Louis D. Brandeis, dissenting in *Washington* v. *W. C. Dawson & Co.,* 264 U.S. 219, 238 (1924)

While Justice Cardozo pointed out with great accuracy that the power of the precedent is only "the power of the beaten track"; still the mere fact that a path is a beaten one is a persuasive reason for following it.

—Robert H. Jackson (1945)

Web Extra! 1–6

The Law Dictionary

Web Extra! 1–7

Plain English Legal
Dictionary

ordered to pay $43 million in damages to Darrell Cabey, one of four young black men he shot on a New York City subway train in 1984. Goetz did not deny that he shot the men, but claimed that they were trying to rob him. After the shooting, Goetz was acquitted of attempted murder and assault charges at a criminal trial, but served eight months in prison on weapons charges. Immediately after the civil award Goetz filed for bankruptcy, listing $17,000 in assets and $60 million in liabilities.

Perhaps the most famous example of such an instance, however, was the wrongful death suit filed against O. J. Simpson by Fredric Goldman, father of murder victim Ronald Goldman, and Kimberly Goldman (Ronald's sister). The suit demanded monetary damages for what the plaintiffs claimed was Simpson's role in the wrongful death of Ronald Goldman, and it alleged that Simpson (and possibly other unknown defendants) caused Goldman's death. In 1997 Simpson was ordered to pay $33.5 million to the family of Ron Goldman and to Nicole Simpson's estate, after a California civil jury found that he was responsible for their deaths. An appeal of the award was denied by California Superior Court Judge Hiroshi Fujisaki—who had also presided over the trial.[23]

Because criminal law and civil law are conceptually distinct, both in function and process, a person can be held accountable under both types of law for the same instance of misbehavior without violating constitutional guarantees of double jeopardy.

EXHIBIT 1–A

EXCERPTS FROM THE CIVIL ACTION FILED BY THE GOLDMANS AGAINST O. J. SIMPSON

On May 4, 1995, after "not guilty" verdicts in the double murder trial of O. J. Simpson, Fred Goldman and his daughter Kimberly Goldman filed a civil suit against Simpson claiming that he (and possibly a number of unknown other persons referred to in the suit as "Does 1 to 10") wrongfully and maliciously killed Ronald Goldman. Goldman was the man discovered murdered along with Nicole Brown Simpson on June 12, 1994. In 1997, a California civil jury found Simpson responsible in Goldman's death, and the court ordered that he pay more than $33 million to surviving family members and to the estate of Nicole Brown Simpson. Excerpts from the civil complaint filed against Simpson by the Goldmans follow.

SUPERIOR COURT OF THE STATE OF CALIFORNIA FOR THE COUNTY OF LOS ANGELES

FREDRIC GOLDMAN, an individual, and KIMBERLY ERIN GOLDMAN, an individual, Plaintiffs, vs.
ORENTHAL JAMES SIMPSON, an individual, and DOES 1 through 10, inclusive, Defendants.

CASE NO. SC036340
Complaint for Damages for Wrongful Death (Jury Trial Demanded)

Plaintiffs, FREDRIC GOLDMAN and KIMBERLY ERIN GOLDMAN, allege:

- Plaintiffs are informed and believe and based thereon allege that defendant Orenthal James Simpson (hereinafter referred to as "defendant Simpson") brutally murdered the decedent on June 12, 1994, at a location known as 875 South Bundy Drive, in an area of the City of Los Angeles known as "Brentwood," which area is located in the West District of this Court, and, in doing so, was guilty of a felony as defined in California Penal Code, Section 187. . . .

- The true names, identities, and capacities for the individuals, associates, corporate co-conspirators, or otherwise of defendant DOES 1 through 10, inclusive, are

(continued)

presently unknown to plaintiffs herein who therefore sue said defendants by such fictitious names. Plaintiffs will seek leave of the Court to amend this complaint to show the true names and capacities of said defendants when the same has been ascertained. Plaintiffs are informed and believe and based thereon allege that each of said fictitiously named defendants is a person, firm, or corporation in some way legally responsible for the wrongful death of decedent as well as the damages alleged herein.

- Plaintiffs are informed and believe and based thereon allege that on June 12, 1994, defendant Simpson and Does 1 through 10, inclusive, and each of them, negligently, carelessly, unlawfully, willfully, wantonly, and maliciously threatened to kill decedent. Immediately thereafter on the same date defendant Simpson and Does 1 through 10, inclusive, and each of them, negligently, unlawfully, willfully, wantonly, and maliciously killed decedent.

- Plaintiffs are informed and believe and based thereon allege that by reason of the conduct of defendant Simpson and Does 1 through 10, inclusive, as herein above alleged, and the acts and commission of acts of omission of these defendants, as alleged aforesaid, and as a direct and legal result thereof, decedent died on or about June 12, 1994.

- By reason of the death of decedent, which plaintiffs are informed and believe and based thereon allege was legally and proximately caused by the conduct of defendant Simpson and Does 1 through 10, inclusive, as herein alleged, plaintiff Fredric Goldman has sustained pecuniary loss resulting from the losses of the company, presence, companionship, society, comfort, attention, services, guidance, and support of decedent.

- By reason of the death of decedent, which plaintiffs are informed and believe and based thereon allege was legally and proximately caused by the conduct of defendant Simpson and Does 1 through 10, inclusive, as herein alleged, plaintiff Kimberly Erin Goldman has sustained pecuniary loss resulting from the losses of the company, presence, companionship, society, comfort, attention, services, guidance, and support of decedent.

- By reason of the death of decedent, which plaintiffs are informed and believe and based thereon allege was legally and proximately caused by the conduct of defendant Simpson and Does 1 through 10, inclusive, as herein alleged, plaintiff Fredric Goldman has suffered economic compensatory damages in the amount to be proven at trial.

- By reason of the death of decedent, which plaintiffs are informed and believe and based thereon allege was legally and proximately caused by the conduct of defendant Simpson and Does 1 through 10, inclusive, as herein alleged, plaintiff Kimberly Erin Goldman has suffered economic and compensatory damages in an amount to be proven at trial.

- The conduct of defendant Simpson and Does 1 through 10, inclusive, as herein above alleged was willful, wanton, and outrageous beyond the ability of ordinary human beings to comprehend and such conduct was intended by said defendants to and did actually cause the death of decedent such that the conduct of defendant Simpson and Does 1 through 10, inclusive, was oppressive and malicious as those terms are defined in California Civil Code, Section 3294(d). The imposition of substantial punitive and exemplary damages will in this case be both justified and necessary in order to send out a message from this Court to all persons in the United States and throughout the world that such vicious and outrageous savagery inflicted by one human being upon another shall be met with the severest of civil penalties.

(continued)

WHEREFORE, plaintiffs pray for judgment against defendants, and each of them, as follows:

1. For general damages, according to proof;

2. For special damages, according to proof;

3. For reimbursement of funeral expenses and costs of burial;

4. For interest on all sums awarded, according to proof;

5. For punitive and exemplary damages, according to proof;

6. For costs of suit incurred herein;

7. For such other and further relief as to the Court may be just and proper.

DATED: May 4, 1995
TOURTELOT & BUTLER, PLC
ROBERT H TOURTELOT
LAURIE J BUTLER
Attorneys for Plaintiffs
FREDRIC GOLDMAN and
KIMBERLY ERIN GOLDMAN

THE PURPOSE OF LAW

Max Weber (1864–1920), an eminent sociologist of the early twentieth century, said that the primary purpose of law is to regulate the flow of human interaction.[24] Without laws of some sort modern society probably could not exist, and social organization would be unable to rise above the level found in primitive societies (where mores and norms are the primary regulatory forces). Laws make for predictability in human events by using the authority of government to insure that socially agreed-on standards of behavior will be followed and enforced. They allow people to plan their lives by guaranteeing a relative degree of safety to well-intentioned individuals, while constraining the behavior of those who would unfairly victimize others. Laws provide a stable foundation for individuals wishing to join together in a legitimate undertaking by enforcing rights over the control and ownership of property. They also provide for individual freedoms and personal safety by sanctioning the conduct of anyone who violates the legitimate expectations of others. Hence, the first, and most significant, purpose of the law can be simply stated: laws support social order.

To many people, a society without laws is unthinkable. Were such a society to exist, however, it would doubtless be ruled by individuals and groups powerful enough to usurp control over others. The personal whims of the powerful would rule, and less powerful persons would live in constant fear of attack. The closest we have come in modern times to lawlessness can be seen in war-torn regions of the world. The genocidal activities of warring parties in Bosnia-Herzegovina, Croatia, and Rwanda, and the wholesale looting of homes, offices, and businesses, and the frequent sexual attacks on Kuwaiti women by Iraqi troops during the Gulf War provide a glimpse of what can happen when the rule of law breaks down.

Crime is a technical word. It is the law's name for certain acts which it is pleased to define and punish with a penalty.

—Melville D. Post (1897)

Web Extra! 1–8

Pound's "Jural Postulates"

Moral Enterprise

Because the law can exert powerful control over human conduct, some have suggested that it can be purposefully used as a tool to intentionally shape society. This approach, known as "social engineering," found its best expression in the writings of Roscoe Pound (1870–1964). Pound served as dean of Harvard Law School from 1916 to 1936 and authored a number of influential works on the law, including the book, *Spirit of the Common Law* (1921). Pound distilled his ideas into a set of **jural postulates,** or rules. Such postulates, claimed Pound, form the basis of all law, because they reflect shared needs. In 1942 Pound published his postulates in the form of five propositions, as follows[25]:

JURAL POSTULATES

rules that, according to former Harvard Law School dean Roscoe Pound, reflect shared needs common to the members of society and form the basis of all law in advanced societies.

1. In civilized society, men [and women] must be able to assume that others will commit no intentional aggressions upon them.

2. In civilized society, men [and women] must be able to assume that they may control for beneficial purposes what they have discovered and appropriated to their own use, what they have created by their own labor, and what they have acquired under the existing social and economic order.

3. In civilized society, men [and women] must be able to assume that those with whom they deal in the general intercourse of society will act in good faith and hence:

   Will make good reasonable expectations which their promises or other conduct will reasonably create;

   Will carry out their undertakings according to the expectations which the moral sentiment of the community attaches thereto;

   Will restore specifically or by equivalent what comes to them by mistake or unanticipated or [via a] not fully intended situation whereby they receive at another's expense what they could not reasonably have expected to receive under the circumstances.

4. In civilized society, men [and women] must be able to assume that those who are engaged in some course of conduct will act with due care not to cause an unreasonable risk of injury upon others.

5. In civilized society, men [and women] must be able to assume that those who maintain things likely to get out of hand or to escape and do damage will restrain them or keep them within their proper bounds.

In later writings, Pound modified his concept of jural postulates to reflect the fact that laws cannot equally meet the interests of all social groups in any particular society—especially one as diverse as the United States. Pound used the concept of a "**jurisprudence** of interest" to show that one of the basic purposes of law in a free society is to satisfy as many claims or demands of as many people as possible.

Other writers have gone beyond Pound in showing that laws are the result of active enterprise, and they reflect the philosophical, moral, and economic perspectives of their creators. As such, laws enforce the values of the powerful and uphold established patterns of social privilege. In 1963 Howard Becker used the term **moral enterprise** to refer to the activities of moral crusaders through which new laws are created, and he used the phrase **moral entrepreneurs** to refer to those who work to enact desired legislation. In Becker's words: "Rules are not made automatically. Even though a practice may be harmful in an objective sense to the group in which it occurs, the harm needs to be discovered and pointed out. People must be made to feel that something ought to be done about it. Someone must call the public's attention to these matters, supply the push necessary to get things done, and direct such energies as are aroused in the proper direction to get a rule created."[26]

JURISPRUDENCE

the philosophy of law; the science and study of the law.

MORAL ENTERPRISE

the activities of moral crusaders through which new laws are created.

MORAL ENTREPRENEURS

those who work to enact desired legislation.

We can have as much or as little crime as we please, depending on what we choose to count as criminal.

—Herbert L. Packer (1968)

Examples of contemporary moral enterprise can be seen in the activities of interest groups that have influenced recent passage of three-strikes legislation and specific statutes, such as "Megan's Law." Three-strikes legislation, which was passed in California in 1994 amid much fanfare, and since has been enacted in various forms in a number of other states, requires criminal offenders to be sentenced to lengthy prison terms after their third felony conviction. California's law, which is retroactive (in that it counts offenses committed before the date the legislation was signed), requires a twenty-five-year-to-life sentence for three-time felons with convictions for two or more serious or violent prior offenses. Criminal offenders facing a "second strike" can receive up to double the normal sentence for their most recent offense. Parole consideration is not available until at least 80 percent of the sentence has been served. (Chapter 14 discusses the California three-strikes law in greater detail.) Three-strikes provisions continue to find much public support, and the federal Violent Crime Control and Law Enforcement Act of 1994 also contains a three-strikes provision, which mandates life imprisonment for federal criminals convicted of three violent felonies or drug offenses.

Megan's Laws, first enacted in New Jersey, require public notification whenever previously convicted sex offenders move into neighborhoods. The 1994 rape and murder of Megan Kanka, a seven-year-old New Jersey girl, by Jesse K. Timmendequas, a twice-convicted sex offender living across the street from her home, provided the impetus for the New Jersey legislation. Timmendequas, whose criminal history had been unknown to the Kankas, was sentenced to death on June 20, 1997, for Megan's murder. Long before sentence was imposed on Timmendequas, however, Megan's case had attracted national attention. On May 17, 1996, President Clinton signed into law a federal version of Megan's Law. The legislation requires federal criminal justice agencies to notify local law enforcement officials and members of the public when known sex offenders move into their communities. As of this writing, forty-five states and the federal government have enacted Megan's Laws.

An entrepreneurial organization that has had a considerable amount of impact on recent legislation is Handgun Control Inc. (HCI), founded in 1974 by Republican businessman Pete Shields (whose twenty-three-year-old son was murdered that year) and others. HCI began in partnership with the National Coalition to Ban Handguns (NCBH), which was formed about the same time. The NCBH changed its name to the Coalition to Stop Gun Violence in 1990. In the early 1980s, the murder of John Lennon helped spark interest in gun control and led to substantial success in fund-raising activities for most gun control organizations.

Since starting operations, HCI has been primarily involved in national and state lobbying efforts to control the sale and spread of handguns. Sarah Brady, wife of James Brady, Ronald Reagan's press secretary, who was seriously injured in the 1981 assassination attempt against the president, has headed HCI since 1989. HCI, affiliated with the Center to Prevent Handgun Violence, has been successful in the enactment of gun control measures in Congress and in many states. HCI's major victory to date came in the form of the so-called "Brady Law," formally known as the Brady Handgun Violence Prevention Act, which was signed into law by President Clinton in 1994. The Brady Law provided for a five-day waiting period before the purchase of a handgun[27] and for the establishment of a national instant criminal background check system to be contacted by firearms dealers before the transfer of any handgun.[28]

> A decided case is worth as much as it weighs in reason and righteousness; and no more.
>
> —*Adams Express Co. v. Beckwith,*
> 100 Ohio St. 348, 126 N.E. 300 (1919)

The Role of Criminal Law

Like laws in general, the criminal law has a variety of purposes. Some say that the primary purpose of the criminal law is to "make society safe for its members, and to punish and rehabilitate those who commit offenses."[29] Others contend that the basic purpose of the criminal law is "to declare public disapproval of an offender's conduct by means of public trial and conviction and to punish the offender by imposing a penal sanction."[30]

The criminal law also serves to restrain those whom society considers dangerous, often through imprisonment, home confinement, or other means. It deters potential offenders through examples of punishments applied to those found guilty of crimes, and it protects honest and innocent citizens by removing society's most threatening members. In short, criminal law protects law-abiding individuals while maintaining social order through the conviction and sentencing of criminals. A more complete list shows that criminal law functions to:

- Protect members of the public from harm
- Preserve and maintain social order
- Support fundamental social values
- Distinguish criminal wrongs from civil wrongs[31]
- Express communal condemnation of criminal behavior
- Deter people from criminal activity
- Stipulate the degree of seriousness of criminal conduct
- Establish criteria for the clear determination of guilt or innocence at trial
- Punish those who commit crimes
- Rehabilitate offenders
- Assuage victims of crime.

Before the law can do any of these things, however, it must first identify those to whom it most intimately applies. That is, the criminal law has the job of defining precisely what may not be done, by whom, and of imposing penalties on those who do that which it prohibits.

Once a criminal law has been enacted, and crimes defined, the criminal justice system comes into play. The justice system emphasizes crime reporting, criminal investigation, the apprehension and arrest of suspects, trials and plea bargaining with the resulting conviction or acquittal of suspects, and, finally, punishment and sentencing. Punishment is intricately tied to criminal sentencing, and the imposition of punishments on those convicted of violating the criminal law is discussed in considerable detail in Chapter 14.

The Rule of Law

In 1739, David Hume asked the following question:

> Here are two persons who dispute for an estate; of whom one is rich, a fool, and a bachelor; the other poor, a man of sense, and has a numerous family. The first is my enemy; the second my friend. To whom should the estate be awarded?[32]

To Hume, the morally correct decision would have been to award the estate based on principles of law without regard to personal passions, individual motives, or the economic power or social positions of those involved. By following this course of action, we are adhering to the "rule of law," not the "rule of man."

The **"rule of law,"** sometimes also referred to as "the supremacy of law," involves the belief that an orderly society must be governed by established principles and known codes, which are applied uniformly and fairly to all of its members. Under the rule of law no one is above the law, and those who enforce the law must abide by it.

The rule of law has been called "the greatest political achievement of our culture,"[33] for without it few other human achievements—especially those which require the efforts of a large number of people working together—would be

Web Extra! 1–9
Principles of
Criminal Law

RULE OF LAW
also, the **supremacy of law.** The maxim that an orderly society must be governed by established principles and known codes that are applied uniformly and fairly to all of its members.

King John of England signs the Magna Carta on June 15, 1215, at Runnymede, under threat of civil war. Clause 39 of the Magna Carta, or "Great Charter," stated that "no free man shall be . . . imprisoned or disseised [dispossessed] . . . except by the lawful judgment of his peers or by the law of the land." Hence, the Magna Carta enshrined the rule of law, and proclaimed that even kings must be bound by law. (Courtesy of Bettmann/CORBIS.)

Web Extra! 1–10

The Rule of Law

possible. The American Bar Association (ABA) defines the rule of law to include the following[34]:

- Freedom from private lawlessness provided by the legal system of a politically organized society
- A relatively high degree of objectivity in the formulation of legal norms and a like degree of evenhandedness in their application
- Legal ideas and juristic devices for the attainment of individual and group objectives within the bounds of ordered liberty
- Substantive and procedural limitations on governmental power in the interest of the individual for the enforcement of which there are appropriate legal institutions and machinery.

DUE PROCESS OF LAW

those procedures that effectively guarantee individual rights in the face of criminal prosecution; the due course of legal proceedings according to the rules and forms that have been established for the protection of private rights; formal adherence to fundamental rules for fair and orderly legal proceedings. Due process of law is a constitutional guarantee.

As the ABA definition indicates, the rule of law also includes the notion that **due process of law,** or those procedures that effectively guarantee individual rights in the face of criminal prosecution, is necessary prior to the imposition of any punishments on law breakers. Due process of law can be defined as "the due course of legal proceedings according to the rules and forms which have been established for the protection of private rights,"[35] or as formal adherence to fundamental rules for fair and orderly legal proceedings. Due process means that laws may not be created or enforced in arbitrary or unreasonable fashion.

Due process guarantees are found in the Fifth, Sixth, and Fourteenth amendments to the U.S. Constitution. The Fourteenth Amendment states the due process requirement of the rule of law rather succinctly in these words: "No State shall make or enforce any law which shall abridge the privileges or immunities of citizens of the United States; nor shall any State deprive any person of life, liberty, or property,

DOES THE RULE OF LAW APPLY TO FORMER HEADS OF STATE?

The rule of law is a principle that stands for equality before the law. It holds that any fair society must be governed by laws, not by individual proclivities or favoritism. As the following story illustrates, however, the rule of law may have special meaning under some circumstances—especially those involving former heads of state.

In October 1998, the British government arrested former Chilean dictator General Augusto Pinochet on a warrant from a Spanish magistrate who asked that Pinochet be extradited to stand trial in Spain. Pinochet was wanted on charges involving the murder or "disappearances" of 3,178 people, including Spanish citizens, in Chile during the period from 1973 to 1990.[1] The eighty-two-year-old Pinochet, who had ruled Chile during that period, resigned as commander of the Chilean armed forces in March 1998. Before he left Chile, Pinochet had surrendered his power after receiving absolute immunity from prosecution in his home country under a new national constitution drafted by his own government prior to his leaving office. At the time the Spanish warrant was issued, Pinochet was in England for medical treatment. He was arrested at an English clinic where he was recovering from back surgery.

Still a Chilean senator and holder of a diplomatic passport, Pinochet was detained by Scotland Yard on Spanish claims that he had violated the European Convention on Terrorism. Britain's Lord Chief Justice, Lord Bingham, and two judges sitting with him on England's High Court, quashed (invalidated) the Spanish warrant on October 28, 1998, ruling that Pinochet was "entitled to immunity as a former sovereign from the criminal and civil process of the English courts." A short time later, however, England's highest court, the five-judge panel known as the "Law Lords" of the House of Lords, reinstated the warrant. Interestingly, at the time of the proceedings against Pinochet, no head of state who had stepped down voluntarily had ever been criminally sanctioned by another nation, particularly (as in this case) over the objections of his own country.[2]

In March 2000, following a series of strokes that Pinochet suffered, British Home Secretary Jack Straw declared that the former dictator could not receive "a fair trial in any country" due to mental frailty. Straw allowed Pinochet to return to his home

Former Chilean dictator General Augusto Pinochet ruled Chile from 1973 to 1999. After Pinochet relinquished power, opponents insisted that he stand trial for crimes against humanity. No political or social status, they claimed, could be sufficient to shield a person from answering to the rule of law. (Photo by Santiago Llanqun, courtesy of AP/Wide World Photos.)

in Chile. Despite his release, the proceedings against Pinochet raised interesting questions regarding the rule of law.

What do *you* think?

1. Should Pinochet have been punished for murders or other atrocities that it could be proven he ordered or permitted while he was in office?

2. If Pinochet had indeed violated the law, shouldn't he have been punished like any other citizen?

3. Might allowing Pinochet to go unpunished establish a double standard and encourage other dictators to engage in similar practices while in office? Alternatively, might punishing Pinochet have encouraged other dictators to cling to power at all costs if they might otherwise be snatched and tried by any country that could lay hands on them?

4. Did the British comply with the rule of law in this case?

5. How would you have ruled in the case? Would your answer be different if it could have been proven that Pinochet ordered the execution of thousands of Chilean citizens after he took power, or that he ordered the killings on U.S. soil of American dissidents protesting his terrorist tactics during the late 1970s?

6. How does the rule of law apply in this case, if at all?

NOTES:

1. "The Pinochet Case: Timeline" and "Legal Lessons of Pinochet Case," BBC News World Service on-line. Posted at http://newswww.bbc.net.uk/hi/english/special_report/1998/10/98/the_pinochet_file/newsid_600000/600617.stm.

2. Stuart Taylor, Jr., "Bad Effects of Feel-Good Laws," *Texas Lawyer,* November 9, 1998.

without due process of law; nor deny to any person within its jurisdiction the equal protection of the laws." Although that amendment applies primarily to state governments, the Fifth Amendment imposes due process requirements upon the federal government as well. The Fifth Amendment reads: "No person shall be held to answer for a capital, or otherwise infamous crime . . . nor shall any person be subject for the same offence to be twice put in jeopardy of life or limb; nor shall be compelled in any criminal case to be a witness against himself, nor be deprived of life, liberty, or property, without due process of law. . . ."

HISTORICAL SOURCES OF TODAY'S LAW

NATURAL LAW

rules of conduct inherent in human nature and in the natural order, which are thought to be knowable through intuition, inspiration, and the exercise of reason without the need for reference to man-made laws.

Criminal laws in the United States have been shaped by a number of historical antecedents and philosophical perspectives (Table 1.1). Important roots of the law include arguments from nature (**natural law**), the Old and New Testaments, religious belief and practice, early Roman law, English common law, and our nation's Constitution and Bill of Rights. Each of these important historical sources is discussed in the pages that follow. Other sources of the criminal law include constitutions (state and federal), executive orders, quasi-legislative administrative rules and regulations, court precedent, opinions of attorneys general, and various historical treaties and codes.

Natural Law

One historical source of today's law is natural law. Natural law adherents claim that some laws are fundamental to human nature and discoverable by human reason, intuition, or inspiration, without the need for reference to man-made laws. Such people believe that an intuitive and rational basis for many of our criminal laws can be found in immutable moral principles or some identifiable aspects of the natural order.

One authoritative source has this to say about natural law: "This expression, 'natural law,' or *jus naturale,* was largely used in the philosophical speculations of the Roman jurists of the Antonine age, and was intended to denote a system of rules and principles for the guidance of human conduct which, independently of enacted law or the systems peculiar to any one people, might be discovered by the rational intelligence of man, and would be found to grow out of and conform to his *nature,* meaning by that word his whole mental, moral, and physical constitution."[36]

TABLE 1.1

HISTORICAL SOURCES OF TODAY'S LAW

Nature (natural law)
The Old and New Testaments
Religious belief and practice
Early Roman law
English common law
U.S. Constitution and Bill of Rights

Ideally, say natural law advocates, man-made laws should conform to principles inherent in natural law. The great theologian Thomas Aquinas (1225–1274), for example, wrote in his *Summa Theologica* that any man-made law that contradicts natural law is corrupt in the eyes of God.[37]

Natural law principles continue to be influential in many spheres. The modern debate over abortion, for example, relies on the use of natural law arguments to support both sides in the dispute. Prior to the 1973 U.S. Supreme Court decision of *Roe v. Wade*,[38] abortion was a crime in most states (although abortions were sometimes permitted in cases of rape or incest or when the mother's life was in danger). In *Roe* the Justices held that: "State criminal abortion laws . . . that except from criminality only a life-saving procedure on the mother's behalf without regard to the stage of her pregnancy and other interests involved violate the Due Process Clause of the Fourteenth Amendment, which protects against state action the right to privacy, including a woman's qualified right to terminate her pregnancy." The Court set limits on the availability of abortion, however, when it said that although "the State cannot override that right, it has legitimate interests in protecting both the pregnant woman's health and the potentiality of human life, each of which interests grows and reaches a 'compelling' point at various stages of the woman's approach to term." Natural law supporters of the *Roe* standard argue that abortion must remain a "right" of any woman because she is naturally entitled to be in control of her own body. "Pro-choice" advocates claim that the legal system must continue to protect this "natural right" of women.

In contrast, antiabortion forces—sometimes called "pro-lifers"—claim that the unborn fetus is a person and that he or she is entitled to all the protections that can reasonably and ethically be given to any living human being. Such protection, they suggest, is basic and humane and lies in the natural relationship of one human being to another. If antiabortion forces have their way, abortion will one day again be outlawed.

Natural law became an issue in confirmation hearings conducted for U.S. Supreme Court Justice nominee Clarence Thomas in 1991. Because then-judge Thomas had mentioned natural law and natural rights in speeches given prior to his nomination to the Court, Senate Judiciary Committee Chairman Joseph Biden (and others) grilled him about the concept. Biden suggested that natural law was a defunct philosophical perspective, no longer worthy of serious consideration, and said that the duty of a U.S. Supreme Court Justice was to follow the American Constitution. Thomas responded by pointing out that natural law concepts contributed greatly to the principles underlying the Constitution. It was the natural law writing of John Locke, Thomas suggested, that inspired the Framers to declare: "All men are created equal." A brief portion of Thomas's confirmation hearing, highlighting the role natural law played in them, is reproduced in the accompanying Law in Practice feature.

> Natural law provides a basis in human dignity by which we can judge whether human beings are just or unjust, noble or ignoble.
>
> —Justice Clarence Thomas (1987)

Web Extra! 1–11

Excerpts from Blackstone's *Commentaries*

Early Codes

Early criminal codes provide another source of contemporary law. The development of criminal codes can be traced to the Code of Hammurabi, an ancient set of laws inscribed on a stone pillar near the ancient city of Susa around the year 1750 B.C. The Hammurabi Code, named after the Babylonian King Hammurabi (1792–1750 B.C.), specified a number of property rights and crimes and associated punishments. Hammurabi's laws spoke to issues of ownership, theft, sexual relationships, and interpersonal violence. Although Hammurabi's code specified a variety of corporal punishments, and even death, for named offenses, its major contribution was that it routinized the practice of justice in Babylonian society by

Web Extra! 1–12

The Code of Hammurabi

LAW IN PRACTICE

THE ROLE OF NATURAL LAW IN THE CONFIRMATION HEARINGS OF U.S. SUPREME COURT JUSTICE CLARENCE THOMAS

During the 1991 U.S. Senate confirmation hearings for Supreme Court Justice Clarence Thomas (a Bush nominee), natural law became a critical issue. Thomas's opponents claimed that his adherence to a natural law philosophy indicated a judge who was out of step with the times and dangerously independent from accepted forms of legal reasoning. Reproduced below is a portion of a statement made during the hearings by Representative Craig Washington (D.–Texas):

Thursday, September 19, 1991, Afternoon Session

REP. WASHINGTON: Mr. Chairman and members, I thank you for the privilege and honor of speaking before you today. We truly appreciate this opportunity to express our views on a vitally important nomination.

I speak in opposition to the nomination of Judge Clarence Thomas. My opposition to Judge Thomas has nothing at all to do with his personal political views. It has nothing at all to do with the politics that results in his nomination, but rather is based upon a scientific objective reason and calm analysis of Judge Thomas' legal writings, legal opinions, editorial opinions, remarks, and speeches.

I have concluded at least the following: Judge Thomas has a disturbingly paradigmatic disdain and disregard for legal precedents and *stare decisis*. In fact, I don't think he knows what "*stare decisis*" means. Judge Thomas has shown a previous long-standing disrespect for the civil

liberties of groups. Judge Thomas has espoused as a fulcrum of his legal thought the concept of natural law, and Judge Thomas has shown a lack of respect for the rule of law.

We have reached these and other conclusions only after much research and analysis. As you know, it is often difficult to take a stand that would seem to be unpopular. It is our duty, however, as elected officials to speak against the nomination of Judge Clarence Thomas based upon the facts. Our position is clearly based upon just that: the fact that the elevation of Judge Clarence Thomas to the Supreme Court of the United States is dangerous for all Americans.

The quintessential underpinning of Anglo-Saxon jurisprudence is that if you have a case with similar facts, similar evidence, and similar legal predicates, you should reach a similar outcome. *Stare decisis*, which in Latin, as you know, means "standing by decided matters," is a doctrine of following rules of principles laid down in previous judicial decisions. . . .

The most blatant example of Judge Thomas' disregard for legal precedent came when Judge Thomas was Chairman of the Equal Employment Opportunity Commission. As Chairman of the EEOC, Judge Thomas spoke out against the Supreme Court's approval of racially and sexually defined employment goals and time tables. Judge Thomas states that he considered those goals and time tables to be a weak and limited weapon against forms of discrimination. There have been at least four Supreme Court decisions on race-conscious remedies in which the Supreme

lending predictability to punishments. Prior to the code, captured offenders often faced the most barbarous and capricious of punishments, frequently at the hands of revenge-seeking victims, no matter how minor their offenses had been. As Marvin Wolfgang has observed, "In its day, 1700 B.C., the Hammurabi Code, with its emphasis on retribution, amounted to a brilliant advance in penal philosophy mainly because it represented an attempt to keep cruelty within bounds."[39]

Although it is of considerable archeological importance, the Code of Hammurabi probably had little impact on the development of Western legal traditions. Roman law, however, appears to have influenced our own legal tradition in many ways. Roman law derived from the Twelve Tables, which were written about 450 B.C. The Tables, a collection of basic rules related to family, religious, and economic life, ap-

Court has approved them. They are, as you know: *United States* v. *Paradise*; *Local 28 Sheetmetal Workers* v. *the EEOC*; *Local 93 Firefighters* v. *Cleveland*; and *Johnson* v. *Transportation Agency Santa Clara County, California.*

There are times when we all disagree with the law. Rules and regulations make our society stable. If we all agree that, for better or worse, the rule is that privates salute generals and that we should drive the speed limit as established by the legislatures of our various states, then we should obey those rules and regulations. I might not like the person wearing the uniform of the general, but if I'm a private and he or she is a general, I am bound to respect the rank of the general. . . .

Moreover, the Bill of Rights and other amendments were intended to protect those who are similarly situated from the tyranny of government. Natural law has as much to do with judicial opinion as voodoo has to do with the practice of medicine. An example of the application of natural law would be to take the example I used earlier about driving the speed limit. Under the theory of natural law, the majority of the people have agreed that we should drive the speed limit. If one were to adhere to a natural law philosophy, however, one could state: Since I've paid for my car and I've paid part of the taxes to build this highway, I can drive as fast as I wish. I'm not bound by mere legal opinion; I'm bound only by myself. The logical extension to such a philosophy is that we would have no law, no order, and no rules to govern our society.

During Judge Thomas' tenure at the EEOC, he refused to process cases of age discrimination in spite of the fact he had been ordered to do so by several governmental bodies. Instead, Judge

Thomas allowed 13,000 age discrimination cases to expire and go unresolved. It was Judge Thomas' duty to file these cases. It did not matter that he disagreed with the law. He, like others, was bound to respect and follow the law regardless of whether he liked it or not. I oppose Judge Thomas based upon these aforementioned facts. Choice based upon my evidence and that of Congressional Black Caucus colleagues is that Judge Thomas is not a worthy successor to Justice Marshall. The difference that we have is that Judge Thomas' [decisions] did not stem from merely reasonable and understandable differences over particular cases or remedies. Rather, Judge Thomas repudiates the fundamental role of the Supreme Court as a guardian of the constitutional freedoms and rejects the legacy of Judge Marshall.

On behalf of twenty-five of the twenty-six members of the Congressional Black Caucus, we respectfully urge you to reject the nomination of Judge Clarence Thomas. At the appropriate time, I'll be happy to respond to your questions.

What do *you* think?

1. Representative Washington says that Justice Thomas doesn't understand the principle of *stare decisis*. Would you say, from the example of natural law given by Rep. Washington, that he (Washington) understands the concept of natural law? Why or why not?

2. How does Rep. Washington's interpretation of *stare decisis* compare to Justice Marshall's position, cited earlier in this chapter, that *stare decisis* "is not an imprisonment of reason"?

3. Based on what Rep. Washington says about Judge Thomas, do you think Thomas would make a good U.S. Supreme Court justice? Why or why not?

pear to have been based on common and fair practices generally accepted among early tribes that existed prior to the establishment of the Roman republic. Roman law was codified under the Emperor Justinian I, who ruled between A.D. 527 and 565. In its complete form, the Justinian Code consisted of three lengthy legal documents: (1) the Institutes, (2) the Digest, and (3) the Code itself. Justinian's code distinguished between two major legal categories: public laws and private laws. Public laws dealt with the organization of the Roman state, its senate, and governmental offices. Private law concerned itself with contracts, personal possessions, the legal status of various types of persons (citizens, free persons, slaves, freedmen, guardians, husbands and wives, etc.) and injuries to citizens. The Emperor Claudius conquered England in the mid-first century, and Roman authority over

"Britannia" was consolidated by later rulers who built walls and fortifications to keep out the still-hostile Scots. Roman customs, law, and language were forced on the English population during the succeeding three centuries under the *Pax Romana*—a peace imposed by the military might of Rome.[40]

Common Law

Web Extra! 1–13

The Common Law

COMMON LAW

law originating from use and custom rather than from written statutes. The term refers to nonstatutory customs, traditions, and precedents that help guide judicial decision making.

The common law of England is not to be taken in all respects to be that of America. Our ancestors brought with them its general principles, and claimed it as their birthright; but they brought with them and adopted only that portion which was applicable to their situation.

—*Van Ness v. Pacard,* 27 U.S. (2 Pet.) 137, 144 (1829)

Common law is an especially important historical source of many of our modern laws. English legal practices prior to A.D. 1000 were influenced by both Roman legal principles and the laws of invading Germanic tribes, known as Anglo-Saxons, who conquered England around the year A.D. 400. When William the Conqueror invaded England in 1066, he declared Saxon law absolute and announced that he was "the guardian of the laws of Edward," his English predecessor. William, however, in seeking to add uniformity to the law, lent impetus to the development of common law by ordering that judicial decisions be recorded and disseminated. Under William's decrees, significant decisions were distributed to judges throughout the country, leading to the development and application of common principles of jurisprudence. Enumeration of the various kinds of offenses for which punishment could be meted out led to acknowledgment of "common law crimes" throughout England. Eventually, a **common law** arose out of prevailing customs, rules, and social practices that found support in an ever-evolving body of judicial decisions. Common law was the result of precedent and tradition, and its authority rested primarily on usage and custom rather than on any official decree or statutory enactment. As Clarence Ray Jeffery observes, "It was during the reign of Henry II (1154–1189) that the old tribal-feudal system of law disappeared and a new system of common law emerged in England."[41] By the year 1200, common law was firmly entrenched in England.

Because it depended so heavily on judicial interpretation, common law has often been referred to as "judge-made" law. As Howard Abadinsky observed, "Common law involved the transformation of community rules into a national legal system. The controlling element (was) precedent."[42]

Common law crimes and the common law legal tradition were transferred to the English colonies in North America, and today they form the basis of much statutory and case law in this country. The influence of common law on contemporary criminal law is so great that it has often been called *the* major source of modern criminal law. The American frontier provided an especially fertile ground for the acceptance of common law principles. The scarcity of churches and infrequent visits by traveling ministers prompted many territories to recognize common law marriages and to recognize that a meeting of minds constituted a valid contract in most areas of human endeavor.

Web Extra! 1–14

Britannica online: codes of law

The strength of the common law tradition in early America was highlighted in 1811, when the famous English prison reformer and jurist Jeremy Bentham wrote a letter to President James Madison in which he offered to codify the law of the United States in its entirety. Bentham told Madison that the case-by-case approach of the common law, based solely on precedent, was too "fragmented, flexible, and uncertain" to support the continued economic and social development of the country. Madison, however, rejected the offer and directed John Quincy Adams to reply to Bentham, telling him "[either] I greatly overrate or [Bentham] greatly underrates the task . . . not only of digesting our Statutes into a concise and clear system, but [of reducing] our unwritten to a text law." A short time later Madison also rejected federal use of the written legal code developed by the American Benthamite Edward Livingston.[43]

By the late 1800s, however, common law principles were giving way across America to written civil and penal codes. The Married Women's Property Act of 1875, for example, which provided a model for state legislatures of the period, gave married women control over wages earned independently of husbands. The act effectively dissolved the older common law doctrine of unity of husband and wife, a principle that had given husbands control over their wives' wages and property. About the same time the nineteenth-century jurist David Dudley Field drafted what came to be known as the "Field Code"—a set of proposed standardized criminal and civil procedures and uniform criminal statutes that were adopted by the state of New York and served as a model for other states seeking to codify their laws.

Although modern American substantive and procedural criminal law is largely codified, some states still explicitly acknowledge the common law roots of contemporary penal legislation. The Florida Criminal Code, for example, provides that "The common law of England in relation to crimes, except so far as the same relates to the modes and degrees of punishment, shall be of full force in this state where there is no existing provision by statute on the subject."[44] With regard to "punishment of common law offenses," the Florida Code says "When there exists no such provision by statute, the court shall proceed to punish such offense by fine or imprisonment, but the fine shall not exceed $500, nor the imprisonment 12 months."[45] Arizona Revised Statutes contain a similar provision, which reads "The common law only so far as it is consistent with and adapted to the natural and physical conditions of this state and the necessities of the people thereof, and not repugnant to or inconsistent with the Constitution of the United States or the constitution or laws of this state, or established customs of the people of this state, is adopted and shall be the rule of decision in all courts of this state."

Occasionally individuals are arrested and tried under common law when appropriate statutory provisions are not in place. In 1996, for example, euthanasia advocate Dr. Jack Kevorkian was arrested and tried in Michigan on charges of violating the state's common law against suicide. After Kevorkian was acquitted, jury foreman Dean Gauthier told reporters, "We felt there was a lack of evidence regarding the interpretation of the common law."[46] In 1999, however, after Michigan enacted statutory legislation outlawing physician-assisted suicide, Kevorkian was convicted of a number of crimes and sentenced to ten to twenty-five years in prison. Evidence against Kevorkian came largely from a videotape aired on CBS's *60 Minutes,* showing the doctor giving a lethal injection to fifty-two-year-old Thomas Youk, who suffered from Lou Gehrig's disease.

No one, sir, is above the law. No one.

—Kevorkian Judge, Jessica Cooper

While Florida and a few other states have passed legislation officially institutionalizing common law principles, most states today—even those which have not done so—remain **common law states.** Common law states are jurisdictions in which the principles and precedents of common law continue to hold sway, although they have been greatly augmented with many statutory provisions. In contrast, a handful of states, called **code jurisdictions,** have enacted legislation that says something to the effect that "no conduct constitutes an offense unless it is a crime or violation under this Code or another statute of this State."[47] Even in most code jurisdictions, however, the principles and strictures of common law are generally reflected in statutes. Similarly, code jurisdictions continue to accept defenses that were traditionally available at common law.

Although common law crimes that have not been codified may be difficult to successfully prosecute today, the American legal system still bears many important characteristics of English common law. Among them are (1) application of the common law principle of *stare decisis,* (2) guarantees of "due process of law," (3) recognition of "the rule of law," and (4) the use of juries in important cases in most jurisdictions. Given the continuing significance of each of these principles in the legal system of the United States, our nation remains, in many significant ways, a common law country.

COMMON LAW STATES

jurisdictions in which the principles and precedents of common law continue to hold sway.

CODE JURISDICTIONS

those states that have enacted legislation recognizing as criminal only that conduct specifically prohibited by statute.

LAW ON THE BOOKS

COMMON LAW REFERENCES IN STATE CRIMINAL CODES

Compare with Model Penal Code, Section 1.05.

FLORIDA CRIMINAL CODE

Chapter 775, Section 1. The common law of England in relation to crimes, except so far as the same relates to the modes and degrees of punishment, shall be of full force in this state where there is no existing provision by statute on the subject.

ARIZONA REVISED STATUTES

Title 1, Section 201. Adoption of common law; exceptions.

The common law only so far as it is consistent with and adapted to the natural and physical conditions of this state and the necessities of the people thereof, and not repugnant to or inconsistent with the Constitution of the United States or the constitution or laws of this state, or established customs of the people of this state, is adopted and shall be the rule of decision in all courts of this state.

UTAH CODE ANNOTATED

Section 76-1-105 Common law crimes are abolished and no conduct is a crime unless made so by this code, other applicable statute or ordinance.

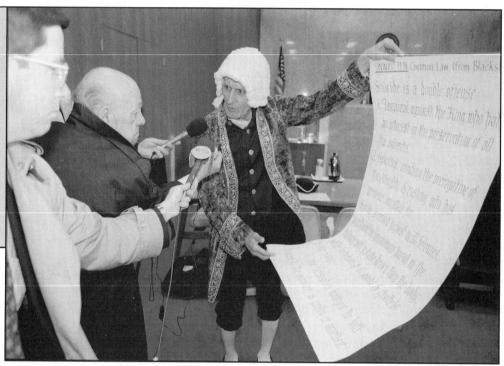

At his third assisted suicide trial, Dr. Jack Kevorkian, dressed in a colonial-style costume, unfurled a scroll containing snippets of English common law. "I'm dressed for the part now," said Kevorkian, as he faced trial under Michigan's common law prohibiting suicide. Although Kevorkian was acquitted in the 1996 trial, the state later enacted a law criminalizing assisted suicide. As a consequence of his continuing activities he was convicted in 1999 of a number of offenses and sentenced to ten to twenty-five years in prison. (Photo courtesy of AP/Wide World Photos.)

The U.S. Constitution

BILL OF RIGHTS
the first ten amendments to the U.S. Constitution; made part of the Constitution in 1791.

The U.S. Constitution and **Bill of Rights** provide other important sources of today's laws. Because it embodies many of the ideals, principles, and beliefs on which American society is based, the spirit of the Constitution has frequently guided and shaped the creation of today's statutory law.

Statutory law varies considerably from state to state. For example, although tattooing is rapidly becoming popular among some young people, a mishmash of laws, some of them criminal, regulate the tattooing of minors. Nineteen states make it a crime to tattoo a minor without parental consent, a few prohibit all tattooing, and others allow only physicians or nurses to tattoo or supervise the tattooing process. Florida requires that tattooing be supervised by a dentist, while New Hampshire permits any form of tattooing except at carnivals, circuses, fairs, or other temporary gatherings. (Photo courtesy of AP/Wide World Photos.)

The Constitution, however, is not so much a source of specific laws or criminal prohibitions (although it does define treason as a crime), as it is a constraint on government **police powers.** The Constitution sets limits on the nature and extent of criminal law that the government can enact. It guards personal liberties by restricting undue government interference in the lives of individuals and by ensuring personal privacy.

The Constitution can be seen as the sole piece of legislation by which all other laws and legislation are judged acceptable or nonacceptable. For example, the Constitution enshrines the notion that persons should only be held accountable for that which they do or do not do (omissions), rather than for what they think or believe. Hence, if a state legislature were to enact a law prohibiting thoughts of a seditious or carnal nature, such a law would likely be overturned should it ever come before the U.S. Supreme Court, which serves as our nation's constitutional interpreter.

Constitutional provisions determine the nature of criminal law by setting limits on just what can be **criminalized,** or made illegal. Generally speaking, constitutional requirements hold that criminal laws can only be enacted where there is a compelling public need to regulate conduct. The U.S. Supreme Court has held that "to justify the exercise of police power the public interest must require the interference, and the measures adopted must be reasonably necessary for the accomplishment of the purpose."[48]

As mentioned earlier in this chapter, the Constitution also demands that anyone accused of criminal activity be accorded due process. Similarly, the Constitution helps ensure that accused persons are provided with the opportunity to offer a well-crafted defense.

POLICE POWER
the authority of a state to enact and enforce a criminal statute. *Jacobson* v. *Massachusetts*, 197 U.S. 11 (1905).

CRIMINALIZE
to make criminal. To declare an act or omission to be criminal or in violation of a law making it so.

The U.S. Constitution—an enduring source of today's legal precepts. Other sources of contemporary American law include early Roman law, English common law, religious belief and practice, and arguments from natural law. (Photo by Jon Feingersh, courtesy of Stock Boston.)

The Constitution imposes a number of specific requirements and restrictions on both the state and federal governments, and it protects individual rights in the area of criminal law. Most of the restrictions, requirements, protections, and rights inherent in the Constitution, as they relate to criminal law, are discussed elsewhere in this textbook. For now, we should recognize that they include:

- Limits on the government's police power
- Limits on strict liability crimes
- Protection against *ex post facto* laws
- Protection against laws that are vague and unclear
- Protection of free thought and free speech
- Protection of the right to keep and bear arms
- Freedom of religion
- Freedom of the press
- Freedom to assemble peaceably
- Due process requirements
- Prohibitions against unreasonable searches and seizures
- Protection against warrants issued without probable cause
- Protection against double jeopardy in criminal proceedings
- Privilege against self-incrimination
- Right to a speedy and public trial before an impartial jury
- Right to be informed of the nature of the charges
- Right to confront witnesses
- Right to the assistance of defense counsel
- Prohibition of excessive bail
- Prohibition of excessive fines
- Prohibition against cruel and unusual punishments
- Guarantees of equal protection of the laws.

THE FEDERAL SYSTEM

The U.S. Constitution provides the basis of a federal system of government with significant implications for American criminal law. The system is known as federalism. Unfortunately, however, when federalism is discussed confusion frequently arises over use of the term "federal government." Federalism embraces both national and state governments, and under a federal system of government both state and national governments are technically part of "federal government." The fact that our nation's central government is popularly referred to as the "federal government" appears to be largely the result of historical accident. To avoid confusion, in this brief section we will use the terms "national government" or "central government" rather than "federal government."

"A federal system of government is one in which two governments have jurisdiction over the inhabitants."[49] Under federalism a central government coexists with various state and local governments. Each governing body has control over activities that occur within its legal sphere of influence. The Constitution gives our national government control over activities such as interstate and international commerce, foreign relations, warfare, immigration, bankruptcies, and certain crimes committed on the high seas and against the "law of nations" (or international law). Individual states are prohibited from entering into treaties with foreign governments, from printing their own money, from granting titles of nobility (as is the central government), and various other things. States retain the power, however, to make laws regulating or criminalizing activity within their boundaries. Like the national government, states may also levy sanctions against those who violate the laws they create. This system is sometimes referred to as dual sovereignty, although the phrase can be misleading since under American federalism the Constitution imposes limits on both forms of government and therefore neither is truly "sovereign." The Tenth Amendment makes clear the very precise limits on the powers of both national and state governments. It reads "The powers not delegated to the United States by the Constitution, nor prohibited by it to the states, are reserved to the states respectively, or to the people."

One way to distinguish between state and national governments is to recognize that the most important responsibility of the national government is to ensure that the rights guaranteed to the people under the Constitution are not curtailed by the states. States, on the other hand, have an interest in protecting their powers (sometimes called "states' rights") and in keeping the national government from unlawfully interfering in their activities.

Limits on the federal power to criminalize what might otherwise be undesirable activity can be seen in the 1995 U.S. Supreme Court case of *U.S.* v. *Lopez*.[50] In *Lopez*, the Court held that Congress had overstepped its bounds in passing the 1990 Gun-Free School Zones Act. The legislation made it a crime to possess a firearm in a school zone. Congressional authority for the legislation was said to reside in the Commerce Clause of the Constitution, which gives Congress the authority to regulate interstate commerce. Attorneys for the government defended the act, arguing that, among other things, guns in schools have a negative impact on education, which in turn has an adverse effect on citizens' productivity. Hence, they claimed, interstate commerce would be negatively impacted by allowing guns to be carried in school zones. The Supreme Court disagreed and invalidated the law, finding that the legislation exceeded Congress's authority to regulate commerce among the states.

Similarly, in 2000, the U.S. Supreme Court overturned the federal arson conviction of a man who had firebombed his cousin's home.[51] The defendant had been arrested and prosecuted under Section 844 of Title 18 of the United States Code, which makes it a federal crime to maliciously damage or destroy, by means of fire or an explosive, any building used in interstate or foreign commerce or in any activity affecting interstate or foreign commerce. The Court found that this particular instance of arson could not be prosecuted under the law because the residence was not *used* in interstate or foreign commerce. In its ruling, the Court rejected the government's argument that the Indiana residence involved in this case was constantly used in at least three activities affecting commerce: (1) it was "used" as collateral to obtain and secure a mortgage from an Oklahoma lender, who, in turn, "used" it as security for the loan; (2) it was "used" to obtain from a Wisconsin insurer a casualty insurance policy, which safeguarded the interests of the homeowner and the mortgagee; and (3) it was "used" to receive natural gas from sources outside Indiana.

Practically speaking, American federalism has resulted in the creation of fifty state criminal codes, the creation of a separate United States criminal code, and numerous city and local ordinances detailing many types of violations. As a consequence, crimes can have different descriptions and associated penalties depending on the **jurisdiction** involved. Still, considerable commonality exists in practice, because all state codes criminalize serious misconduct such as murder, rape, robbery, assault and battery, burglary, and theft. Although statutory terminology may differ from state to state, and although particular crimes themselves may even be given different names, commonalities can be found among almost all of the states in terms of the types of behavior they define as criminal. The Model Penal Code, discussed in the next section, represents one attempt to standardize American criminal law between jurisdictions.

JURISDICTION

(1) the geographical district or subject matter over which the authority of a government body, especially a court, extends; (2) the authority of a court to hear and decide an action or lawsuit.

THE MODEL PENAL CODE

The Model Penal Code (MPC), referred to briefly earlier in this chapter, deserves special mention. The MPC is not law, but a proposed model, which states can use in developing or revising their statutory codes. The MPC was published as a "Proposed Official Draft" by the American Law Institute (ALI) in 1962, after having undergone thirteen previous revisions and represented the culmination of efforts that had been ongoing since the ALI's inception.

The American Law Institute was organized in 1923, after a study was conducted by a group of prominent American judges, lawyers, and teachers who were known as "The Committee on the Establishment of a Permanent Organization for the Improvement of the Law."[52] A report of the committee highlighted two chief defects in American law—uncertainty and complexity—which had combined to produce a "general dissatisfaction with the administration of justice" throughout the country. According to the committee, uncertainty of the law, as it then existed, was due to:

Web Extra! 1–15

The American Law Institute

1. A lack of agreement among the fundamental principles of the common law
2. A "lack of precision in the use of legal terms"
3. "Conflicting and badly drawn statutory provisions"
4. "The great volume of recorded decisions" and
5. "The number and nature of novel legal questions."

The law's complexity, on the other hand, was attributed in significant part to its "lack of systematic development" and to its numerous variations within the different jurisdictions of the United States.

The committee recommended that a lawyers' organization be formed to improve the law and its administration. That recommendation led to the creation of the ALI. The institute's charter stated its purpose to be "to promote the clarification and simplification of the law and its better adaptation to social needs, to secure the better administration of justice, and to encourage and carry on scholarly and scientific legal work." ALI founders included Chief Justice and former President William Howard Taft, future Chief Justice Charles Evans Hughes, and former Secretary of State Elihu Root; Judges Benjamin N. Cardozo and Learned Hand were among its early leaders. The ALI remains active today, with 3,000 elected members including judges, lawyers, and law professors from all areas of the United States as well as some foreign countries.

Although just one of many projects of the ALI, the Model Penal Code remains one of its most significant. The MPC had many contributors, but its leading author was Herbert Weschsler, a prominent legal theorist of the first half of the twentieth century. Weschsler was a prominent figure in the ALI and focused much of his effort on attempts to standardize the laws of the fifty states and other U.S. jurisdictions.

The MPC serves today as a suggested model for the creation and revision of state criminal laws. It is divided into four parts: general provisions, definitions of specific crimes, treatment and correction, and the organization of correction. A fundamental standard underlying the MPC is "the principle that the sole purpose of the criminal law [is] the control of harmful conduct . . ." instead of punishment, as many had previously believed. Because the code's authors believed that "faultless conduct should be shielded from punishment,"[53] the MPC limited criminal liability for a number of law violators—especially those who served merely as accomplices or who acted without an accompanying culpable mental state.

Although no state has adopted the MPC in its entirety, aspects of the MPC have been incorporated into the penal codes of nearly all the states. Moreover, in 1966, the U.S. Congress established the National Commission on Reform of Federal Criminal Laws. The commission eventually produced a recommended revision of Title 18 of the United States Code (which contains the bulk of federal criminal laws), in part based on MPC provisions. A number of recommended revisions have since been enacted into law. As the great legal scholar Sanford Kadish once said, the MPC has "permeated and transformed" the body of American criminal law.[54]

The MPC is an important document, not only because it attempts to achieve standardization in American criminal law and has served as a model for many state criminal statutes, but also because it contains legal formulations created by some of the most cogent thinkers in American jurisprudence. As a consequence, we frequently contrast MPC provisions with existing state statutes throughout the various chapters of this book—presenting opportunities for comparison in a variety of "Law on the Books" boxes. One area in which such a contrast is not possible, however, is the area of high-technology and computer crimes. The MPC, originally drafted more than thirty years ago, makes no specific mention of high-technology crime, crimes committed with the use of computers, and other crimes involving advanced technology.

SUMMARY

- Law is a body of rules of action or conduct prescribed by a controlling authority, and having binding *legal* force.

- Laws derive from many different sources. The development of criminal law in the United States was strongly influenced by English common law. Central to common law is the principle of *stare decisis,* which demands that judges recognize precedents, or earlier decisions, in their rulings.

- While much contemporary criminal law can be found in the form of statutes or penal codes, the principle of *stare decisis* continues to influence the interpretation of written codes by the courts.

- Criminal law is but one type of law. It can be distinguished from other forms of the law in that violations of the criminal law are considered to be offenses against the state, the community, and the public. Moreover, it is the power of the state that is brought to bear against criminal offenders when crimes are investigated, when suspected offenders are tried, and when those convicted of violating criminal statutes are punished.

- Criminal law defines crimes according to the nature of the proscribed conduct and distinguishes among crimes by degree of seriousness. Felonies are serious crimes for which offenders may be sentenced to lengthy prison terms or (for crimes like murder) may be put to death. Misdemeanors are less serious offenses for which offenders may be fined, placed on probation, or sentenced to brief terms of incarceration.

- Two important forms of the criminal law are substantive and procedural. Substantive criminal law defines crimes and specifies punishments for violations of the law. Procedural criminal law specifies the methods to be used in enforcing substantive law.

- Another major category of the law is civil law. Civil laws regulate private relations among individuals, businesses, and other legal entities, such as corporations.

- All laws, including criminal and civil law, facilitate predictable social interaction and guarantee a relative degree of safety to members of society.

- Laws of all kinds can be used as tools to build a given vision of society, and laws are often the result of efforts by organized groups to have their interests and moral sense formally legislated.

QUESTIONS FOR DISCUSSION

1. What is the purpose of law? What is the purpose of criminal law? What would a society without laws be like?
2. What is the difference between criminal law and other forms of the law? How do laws of criminal procedure differ from substantive criminal laws?
3. What is *stare decisis?* From where does the principle of *stare decisis* derive?
4. What is "judge-made law?" How does judge-made law differ from other types of law?
5. How can the law be used as a tool for social engineering? If you were in a position to enact laws, what kind of social engineering might you undertake? Why?
6. What is meant by the "rule of law?" Why is due process an integral part of the rule of law?

LEGAL RESOURCES ON THE WORLD WIDE WEB

To access sites and links that are related to the material covered in this chapter, point your Web browser at http://www.prenhall.com/schmalleger. Once there, you can click on the cover of your textbook, then "chapters," then "Chapter 1," to explore materials and sites of relevance to this chapter. A chat feature and e-mail discussion list allow you to exchange opinions and ideas with others using the Internet, and electronic homework can be submitted directly to your instructor via e-mail. As you read through this book, remember that you can access other chapters the same way.

Legal research involves the ability to fully and authoritatively explore all aspects of a question of law. It includes ascertaining the current status of relevant law in the proper jurisdiction, finding all cross-references and parallel case citations necessary to properly analyze a question as well as to analyze the arguments of the opposing side, finding relevant law in the proper format and context—including annotations and history, and verifying that the law the researcher has uncovered is still valid and has not been replaced or overruled. Proprietary electronic databases, which are available either online or as stand-alone software tools, offer fantastic and complete resources for legal research. Primary among such databases are Lexis® and Westlaw®, both of which are available on a fee-paid basis. For anyone undertaking serious legal research, a subscription to one or both of those services (or others like them) is probably mandatory.

The World Wide Web, which is expanding at a phenomenal rate, now offers a limited ability to perform some aspects of legal research—although the quality and availability of free materials on the Web may never be a replacement for proprietary legal databases. This is so because most free Web-based materials are not subject to peer review and may contain gaps and delays in the availability of crucial subject matter. Similarly, few free materials allow for easy cross-referencing and comprehensive analysis.

Nonetheless, a number of readily available Web-based resources in the legal area can give students of the law a sense of the issues involved in legal research, and they permit anyone with the requisite computer equipment and necessary skills to access a wealth of potentially useful information. To build on those resources, each chapter in this book contains a section like this one titled "Legal Resources on the World Wide Web." A variety of Web-based legal resources and law-related services are highlighted in the chapters that follow, and issues pertaining to Web-based legal resources are discussed. A number of legal research links that you may find useful as starting points in any research effort include the following:

Web Extra! 1–16

Learn About Legal Research

Web Extra! 1–17

Basic Legal Citation

The Annotated Guide to Resources for Legal Professionals
http://www.virtualchase.com/resources
Excellent resource for those involved in Web-based legal research.

Cornell University's Legal Information Institute
http://www.law.cornell.edu
An excellent starting point for online legal research.

FedLaw
http://www.legal.gsa.gov
Outstanding resource for online legal research. Though available to the public, the site was developed "to see if legal resources on the Internet could be a useful and cost-effective research tool for federal lawyers."

FindLaw.com
http://www.findlaw.com
Extensive collection of legal information. Ranges from links to state and federal court cases and statutes, to analysis of the U.S. Constitution and Bill of Rights with case law annotations.

The Internet Legal Research Compass
http://vls.law.vill.edu/compass
The site offers federal and state legal research tools as well as legal research guides.

The Internet Legal Resource Guide
http://www.ilrg.com
A great resource for Internet legal research. Links to journals, cases, statutes, and more. This site was established to serve as a comprehensive resource of the information available on the Internet concerning law and the legal profession.

Law Guru

http://www.lawguru.com

Offers the ability to do extensive legal research using more than 500 legal search engines, tools, and databases.

Law Research

http://www.lawresearch.com

Everything from style manuals to research links.

Laws.com

http://www.laws.com

Good site with links to Web-based legal resources. Maintained by a private lawyer.

Legal Research Using the Internet

http://www.lib.uchicago.edu/~llou/mpoctalk.html

Overview of Internet legal research with links to useful sites.

Lexis One

http://www.lexisone.com

A free resource from the Lexis-Nexis Group. Lexis One provides free case law research, free legal forms, the Legal Internet Guide, and more.

Mega Law

http://www.megalaw.com

A rich resource; useful as a starting point for Web-based legal research.

Nolo's Legal Encyclopedia

http://www.nolo.com/encyclopedia

Excellent resource for lawyers and nonlawyers alike.

Versus Law

http://www.versuslaw.com

Subscription-based service allowing search of federal and state case law.

Virtual Chase

http://www.virtualchase.com

An online legal research site that began as an effort to disseminate articles and teaching aids to law librarians and other instructors of Internet research. Today the site offers more than 500 pages of information pertaining to Internet resources and research strategies.

Check the *Criminal Law Today* Web site for URLs that may have changed.

SUGGESTED READINGS AND CLASSIC WORKS

P. S. Atiyah and R. S. Summers, *Form and Substance in Anglo-American Law: A Comparative Study in Legal Reasoning, Legal Theory, and Legal Institutions* (Oxford: Oxford University Press, 1987).

Howard S. Becker, *Outsiders: Studies in the Sociology of Deviance* (New York: The Free Press, 1963).

Edward Eldefonso and Alan R. Coffey, *Criminal Law: History, Philosophy, Enforcement* (New York: Harper & Row, 1981).

Lawrence M. Friedman, *A History of American Law* (New York: Simon and Schuster, 1973).

George P. Fletcher, *Basic Concepts of Legal Thought* (New York: Oxford University Press, 1996).

Kermit L. Hall, *Crime and Criminal Law: Major Historical Interpretations* (New York: Garland, 1987).

Herbert Lionel Adolphus Hart, Penelope A. Bulloch, and Joseph Raz, *The Concept of Law,* 2nd ed. (Milltown, NJ: Clarendon Press, 1994).

Henry Sumner Maine, *Ancient Law: Its Connection with the Early History of Society and Its Relation to Modern Ideas* (Tucson, AZ: University of Arizona Press, 1986).

William E. Nelson, *Americanization of the Common Law: The Impact of Legal Change on Massachusetts Society, 1760–1830* (Cambridge, MA: Harvard University Press, 1975).

William Seagle, *The Quest for Law* (New York: Alfred A. Knopf, 1941).

Sir James Fitzjames Stephen, *History of the Criminal Law of England* (New York: Macmillan, 1883).

William Graham Sumner, *Folkways* (New York: Dover, 1906).

James Q. Wilson, *The Moral Sense* (New York: The Free Press, 1993).

HOW TO BRIEF A CASE

CAPSTONE CASE

Most of the chapters in this book conclude with "Capstone Cases." Capstone Cases, as the term is used here, are actual court opinions that bring to life the concepts discussed in the chapters where they are found. Your professor may ask that you prepare a brief of any or all of the Capstone Cases, or that you brief other cases that may be assigned—including those found on the *Criminal Law Today* Web site.

Generally speaking, two types of briefs are used within the legal profession. The first is an extensive kind that summarizes cases, statutes, regulations, and related legal materials that are pertinent to a legal issue that is under consideration. It is usually offered to a judge or to the court in support of the position of the submitting party.

A second type of brief—the kind with which we are concerned here—is simply a concise summary of the relevant facts of a single case. A brief of this sort is prepared in order to analyze a case and to present needed information in an abbreviated format that is convenient for use in class or as part of legal research. To prepare a brief for use in class, you need to read the court's written opinion and take notes on the case, being careful to arrange them in a certain format. A case brief, which may be only one or two pages in length, generally includes seven parts: (1) the case **citation,** (2) a short statement of the **facts** of the case, (3) a brief procedural **history** of the case, (4) a summation of the **issue** or issues involved, (5) the court's **decision,** (6) an overview of the **rationale** provided by the court for its decision, and (7) **notes** to yourself about the case. Each of these parts is briefly discussed below.

CITATION: The citation includes the name of the case (usually found italicized or underlined at the top of the page in a case reporter or in large boldfaced type at the beginning of an opinion published online), conventional information needed to find the case through legal research, a reference to the court that issued the opinion, and the date of the case. A typical citation might look like this:

> *State* v. *Smith,* 58 So. 2d 853 (Ala. Crim. App. 1997)

In this instance "58" refers to the volume number of the reporter in which the case is published, while "So. 2d" is the name of the reporter—in this case the second series of the Southern Reporter. The number "853" refers to the page number in the reporter where the decision begins; "Ala. Crim. App." references the court issuing

the decision (in this case, the Alabama Court of Criminal Appeals); and "1997" refers to the year in which the case was decided. Often court names are not given, since one familiar with legal citation can deduce the court from the name of the reporter. In that case, a citation may look like this:

People v. *Versaggi*, 83 N.Y.2d 123 (1994)

Practiced legal researchers will probably understand that "N.Y." in this citation refers to the New York Court of Appeals. Anyone not sure can check the reporter referenced by the citation, in which the court's entire name is given.

The citation format used in this book follows the convention of italicizing the names of the plaintiff (in this case the state, or the "People") and the defendant. Note that the "v.," which appears between the names of the parties (and stands for "versus") is not italicized. Other formats may differ. If you want to learn more about legal citations, you might want to consult a printed guide, such as *A Uniform System of Citation*,[55] known in the legal profession as the *"Bluebook."*[56] The *Bluebook* is the result of the collaborative efforts of The Columbia Law Review Association, The Harvard Law Review Association, The University of Pennsylvania Law Review, and the Yale Law Review. As an alternative, you might also survey the appropriate format for legal citations through an online service, such as Boston College's Law Library (visit the *Criminal Law Today* site on the World Wide Web for the current link to this site).[57]

Relational electronic databases now under development will soon allow rapid online retrieval of case opinions by employing technologically advanced computerized search capabilities. Newly emerging citation styles, necessary to take full advantage of the capabilities of such electronic case databases, may augment the standard citation format in years to come.

In recognition of just such a possibility, the sixteenth edition of the *Bluebook* addresses citability of opinions found on the Internet. It suggests that "When citing the materials found on the Internet, provide . . . the title or top level heading of the material being cited, and the Uniform Resource Locator (URL). The URL is the electronic Internet address of the material and should be given in brackets. . . . Point citations should refer to the paragraph number if available."[58] An example might be:

LLR No. 9405161.PA, P10 [http://www.versuslaw.com]

In this example, from the Versus Law site on the World Wide Web, "LLR" refers to "Lawyer's Legal Research"—an electronic citation format created by the Versus Law staff. The number after the LLR designator refers to a specific case (in this instance, a 1994 Pennsylvania Supreme Court case, *Commonwealth* v. *Berkowitz*), and the letters after the period reference the jurisdiction (Pennsylvania). "P10" refers to the fact that the tenth paragraph in the case is being referred to, and the URL for Versus Law is provided in brackets.

On August 6, 1996, in an effort to further standardize case citations, the ABA's House of Delegates passed a motion to recommend a universal citation system to the courts. The resolution recommends that courts adopt a universal citation system using sequential decision numbers for each year and internal paragraph numbers within the decision. The numbers should be assigned by the court and included in the decision at the time it is made publicly available by the court. The standard form of citation, shown for a decision in a federal court of appeals, would be:

Smith v. *Jones*, 1996 5Cir 15, ¶ 18, 22 F.3d 955

"1996" is the year of the decision; "5Cir" refers to the United States Court of Appeals for the 5th Circuit; "15" indicates that this citation is to the fifteenth decision released by the court in the year; "18" is the paragraph number where the material referred to is located, and the remainder is the parallel citation to the volume and page in the printed case report, where the decision may also be found.

FACTS: The facts of a case, for purposes of a legal brief, refer to only those facts that are *essential* to the court's decision. Facts should be presented in the form of a story and should relate what happened that led to the arrest of the defendant(s).

> *The defendant, Robert Versaggi, who worked for Eastman Kodak Corporation as a computer technician at the time of his arrest, was charged with two counts of computer tampering in the second degree (under New York Penal Law § 156.20). Authorities alleged that Versaggi intentionally altered two computer programs designed to provide uninterrupted telephone service to the offices of Eastman Kodak Corporation. It was also alleged that, as a result of Versaggi's actions, approximately 2,560 of the lines at the Kodak Park Complex were shut down and use of another 1,920 impaired for approximately an hour and a half on October 10, 1986, before company employees were able to restore service. As a result, a substantial number of the employees working at that large industrial complex, with the potential for dangerous chemical spills and accidents, were unable to receive calls, to call outside the complex, or to call 911 or similar emergency services. On November 19, 1986, a second interruption occurred. Essentially all service at the State Street office of Kodak was shut down for four minutes before the computer reactivated itself. As a result all outside telephone calls, from the company's customers and offices worldwide, were disconnected. Evidence against Versaggi consisted of telephone company and computer records showing that he accessed Kodak computers from his home computer at the time of both incidents and had instructed them to shut down.*

HISTORY: The legal history of a case describes what has already happened before the case reached its current level. Legal history should consist of a rendering of who was arrested, what they were charged with, and the findings of trial and appellate courts. In the case cited above, for example, the words of the New York Court of Appeals provide a concise legal history:

> *Charged with two counts of computer tampering, [the defendant was found guilty by] Rochester City Court . . . of two counts of computer tampering in the second degree. [The court determined] that [the defendant] intentionally altered two computer programs designed to provide uninterrupted telephone service to the offices of the Eastman Kodak Corporation. The County Court affirmed.*

ISSUE: The question before the court, or the legal issue that the court is being asked to resolve, should be plainly stated. It will always be a question about the law, application of a specific law, or about a general legal principle. Sometimes there is more than one issue. Even so, the issue can often be stated in one or two sentences, although occasionally a statement of the issue (or issues) requires more detail. Keep in mind that questions have been concisely stated if they can be answered with a "yes" or a "no." Frequently, the court states the issue itself in language such as "the issue before the court is . . ." and such a statement can be incorporated directly into the brief. Continuing with the case of *People* v. *Versaggi,* for example, we might say:

> Does merely entering commands without changing any programs or computer code constitute tampering or altering within the meaning of

the statute? *The defendant argued that he could not be guilty under New York law of tampering with a computer program because he did not alter or change any programs. He claimed that he merely entered commands, which allowed the disconnect instructions of each program to function. Hence, the issue for the court became deciding whether the defendant's conduct was encompassed within the language of the tampering statute.*

DECISION (OR HOLDING):   What did the court rule? How did it answer the question before it? You should remember that the decision of the court can always be stated in "yes" or "no" fashion and that an appellate court may affirm or reverse the decision of a lower court. Appellate courts may also send a case back to a lower court for review or retrial. In the case we have been using as an example:

> Yes. *The appellate court affirmed the judgment of the lower court and upheld the defendant's conviction.*

RATIONALE: In their written opinions, courts explain the reasons they had for reaching their decision. It may be that the court applied or interpreted a particular statute, that it analyzed previous cases and decided the present one within the context of such historical decisions, or that the court chose to create a new precedent based on the majority's sense of justice and fairness. Summaries of such rationales, especially as they are stated in the written opinion of the court, should be contained in your brief. Hence, an analysis of this case might conclude:

> *The court reasoned that although the word "alter," as contained within the New York computer tampering statute means "to change or modify," the legislature had "attached expansive language to the verb" stating that the crime consisted of altering a computer program "in any manner." The term "computer program" had not been defined by the statute, but the court reasoned that a "computer program" consists of "an ordered set of instructions" given to a computer telling it how to function. Hence, according to the court's interpretation, the defendant modified the computer's programming by sending it instructions via his modem and thereby violated the computer tampering statute.*

NOTES: For purposes of further study you should take notes for your own use. You might want to outline what you think about the case. Do you agree or disagree with the conclusion reached by the court? Why? Might the court have used a different rationale in reaching its decision? If so, what might it have been? Perhaps you will want to make note of dissenting or concurring opinions. Finally, you might want to note what lessons you learned from a review of the case.

> *In 1986, the New York state legislature modified the state penal code to include five new crimes: unauthorized use of a computer (Penal Law § 156.05); computer trespass (Penal Law § 156.10); computer tampering (Penal Law §§ 156.20 and 156.25); unlawful duplication of computer-related material (Penal Law § 156.30); and criminal possession of computer-related material (Penal Law § 156.35). Versaggi could not logically be indicted for the crimes of unauthorized use of a computer, since he had lawful access to the computer whose services he disrupted. Moreover, he had not duplicated any computer-related materials, nor had he in his possession any computer-related materials that he had not been authorized to possess. Hence, he was charged with the crime of "computer trespass."*

NOTES

1. *Solesbree* v. *Balkcom,* 339 U.S. 9 (1950).

2. Richard Zitrin, "Man in Stolen Car Asks Cop for Directions," APBNews online, June 22, 2000. Posted at http://www.apbnews.com/newscenter/breaking news/2000/06/22/driver0622_01.html.

3. Joseph R. Nolan and Jacqueline M. Nolan-Haley, *Black's Law Dictionary: Definitions of the Terms and Phrases of American and English Jurisprudence, Ancient and Modern,* 6th ed. (St. Paul, MN: West Publishing Co., 1990). Italics added.

4. Ibid.

5. Although they may be subject to civil, administrative, and other sanctions.

6. Sir William Blackstone, *Commentaries on the Laws of England* (Oxford: Clarendon Press, 1765–69).

7. American Law Institute, *Model Penal Code,* Part 1, Section 1.04(1).

8. Rollins M. Perkins and Ronald N. Boyce, *Criminal Law,* 3rd ed. (Mineola, NY: Foundation Press, 1982), p. 12.

9. Edwin Sutherland, *White Collar Crime* (New York: Holt, Rinehart and Winston, 1949).

10. Blackstone, *Commentaries.*

11. "Infractions" are not considered crimes under the Model Penal Code.

12. *The American Heritage Dictionary and Electronic Thesaurus* (New York: Houghton Mifflin, 1987).

13. See, for example, James Q. Wilson, *The Moral Sense* (New York: The Free Press, 1993).

14. Clarence Ray Jeffery, "The Development of Crime in Early English Society," *Journal of Criminal Law, Criminology, and Police Science,* Vol. 47 (1957), 647–666.

15. *State* v. *Hutchinson,* 228 Kan. 279, 615 P.2d 138, 145 (1980).

16. *Welch* v. *Texas Highways and Public Transp. Dept.,* 483 U.S. 468, 494 (1987).

17. *Itel Containers International Corp.* v. *Huddleston,* 507 U.S. 60 (1993).

18. *Vasquez* v. *Hillary,* 474 U.S. 254, 265–266 (1986).

19. *Guardians Assn.* v. *Civil Service Comm'n of New York City,* 463 U.S. 582, 618 (1983); *United States* v. *International Boxing Club of New York, Inc.,* 348 U.S. 236, 249 (1955); and *Payne* v. *Tennessee,* 501 U.S. 808 (1991).

20. General Statutes of Georgia, 51-1-1.

21. Ibid.

22. Carrie Dowling, "Jury Awards $150 Million in Blazer Crash," *USA Today,* June 4, 1996, p. 3A.

23. Jane E. Allen, "Simpson Appeal Rejected," *USA Today,* April 29, 1997, p. 1A.

24. Max Rheinstein (Ed.), *Max Weber on Law in Economy and Society* (Cambridge, MA: Harvard University Press, 1954).

25. Roscoe Pound, *Social Control Through the Law: The Powell Lectures* (Hamden, CT: Archon, 1968), pp. 113–114.

26. Howard S. Becker, *Outsiders: Studies in the Sociology of Deviance* (New York: The Free Press, 1963), p. 162.

27. The five-day waiting period was phased out after a national instant background checking system became fully operational.

28. A portion of the Brady Handgun Violence Prevention Act, requiring the "chief law enforcement officer" of each local jurisdiction to conduct background checks and perform related tasks on an interim basis until a national checking system became operative, was struck down by the U.S. Supreme Court as unconstitutional in 1997. The Court, in *Printz-Mack v. United States*, 521 U.S. 98 (1997), held that the constitutional principle of "dual sovereignty" prohibited direct federal control over state officers.

29. British Columbia Superior Courts home page, http://www.courts.gov.bc.ca/LegalCompendium/Chapter9.htm.

30. A. Ashworth, "Punishment and Compensation: Victims and the State," *Oxford Journal of Legal Studies*, Vol. 6 (1986), p. 89.

31. See M. Findlay, S. Odgers, and S. Yeo, *Australian Criminal Justice*, 2nd ed. (Oxford: Oxford University Press, 1999).

32. The question has been edited to make it easier to read. Taken from David Hume, *A Treatise of Human Nature*, Vol. II, Book III, "Of Morals," Sec. VI, "Some Further Reflections Concerning Justice and Injustice," as found in Clarence Morris (Ed.), *The Great Legal Philosophers: Selected Readings in Jurisprudence* (Philadelphia: University of Pennsylvania Press, 1959).

33. John S. Baker, Jr., Daniel H. Benson, Robert Force, and B. J. George, Jr., *Hall's Criminal Law: Cases and Materials*, 5th ed. (Charlottesville, VA: The Michie Company, 1993), p. 3.

34. American Bar Association Section of International and Comparative Law, *The Rule of Law in the United States* (Chicago, IL: American Bar Association, 1958).

35. Bureau of Justice Statistics, *Dictionary of Criminal Justice Data Terminology*, 2nd ed. (Washington, D.C.: U.S. Government Printing Office, 1982).

36. *Black's Law Dictionary*, p. 1026.

37. Thomas Aquinas, *Summa Theologica* (Notre Dame, IN: University of Notre Dame Press, 1983).

38. See *Roe v. Wade*, 410 U.S. 113 (1973).

39. Marvin Wolfgang, *The Key Reporter* (Phi Beta Kappa), Vol. 52, No. 1.

40. Roman influence in England had ended by A.D. 442, according to Crane Brinton, John B. Christopher, and Robert L. Wolff, in *A History of Civilization*, 3rd ed., Vol. 1 (Englewood Cliffs, NJ: Prentice Hall, 1967), p. 180.

41. Jeffery, "The Development of Crime."

42. Howard Abadinsky, *Law and Justice* (Chicago: Nelson-Hall, 1988), p. 6.

43. See William D. Bader, 20 Vermont L. Rev. 5,7 (1995).

44. Florida Criminal Code, Chapter 775, Section 1.

45. Ibid, Section 2.

46. Todd Nissen, "Suicide Advocate Kevorkian Acquitted for Third Time," Reuter online, May 14, 1996.

47. Model Penal Code, Section 1.05(1).

48. *California Reduction Company v. Sanitary Reduction Works*, 199 U.S. 306 (1905), citing *Lawton v. Steele*, 152 U.S. 133 (1894).

49. Clarence B. Carson, "The Meaning of Federalism," September 20, 2000. Posted at http://www.libertyhaven.com/politicsandcurrentevents/governmentreformitsrealrole/federalism.html.

50. *U.S. v. Lopez*, 514 U.S. 549 (1995).

51. *Jones v. U.S.*, No. 99-5739. Decided May 22, 2000.

52. Some of the material in this section, as well as wording, is taken from "About the American Law Institute," at the American Law Institute's home page on the World Wide Web.

53. Stephen A. Saltzburg, John L. Diamond, Kit Kinports, and Thomas H. Morawetz, *Criminal Law: Cases and Materials* (Charlottesville, VA: The Michie Company, 1994), p. 53.

54. Ibid.

55. *A Uniform System of Citation,* 16th ed. (Cambridge, MA: Harvard Law Review Association, 1996).

56. *Bluebook* format requires that the "v." between parties be italicized.

57. Visit the *Criminal Law Today* home page at http://www.prenhall.com/ schmalleger.

58. *A Uniform System of Citation,* Section 17.3.3.

2

Criminal Liability and the Essence of Crime

The love of justice is, in most men, nothing more than the fear of suffering injustice.

—François, Duc de La Rochefoucauld (1613–1680)

Who thinks the Law has anything to do with Justice? It's what we have because we can't have Justice.

—William McIlvanney (b. 1936)

CHAPTER OUTLINE

KEY CONCEPTS

actual possession

actus reus

adversarial system

advocacy model

burden of proof

clear and convincing
  evidence

concurrence

conduct

constructive possession

criminal liability

criminal negligence

elements of crime

general intent

general intent crimes

intentional action

jury instructions

knowing behavior

knowing possession

mens rea

mere possession

motive

omission to act

preponderance of the
  evidence

reasonable doubt

reasonable doubt standard

reckless behavior

scienter

specific intent

specific intent crimes

strict liability

AFTER READING THIS CHAPTER YOU SHOULD:

▷ Understand the nature of the advocacy model and the adversarial system of criminal trial practice.

▷ Be familiar with standards of proof, such as reasonable doubt and preponderance of the evidence.

▷ Be able to describe the various elements of crime.

▷ Know the different levels of *mens rea.*

▷ Understand the concept of strict liability.

▷ Be familiar with the idea of legal cause.

INTRODUCTION

Near the close of the California double-murder trial of O. J. Simpson, Judge Lance Ito began his final instructions to the jury with these words: "All right, ladies and gentlemen of the jury, you have heard all the evidence, and it is now my duty to instruct you on the law that applies to this case. . . . The law requires that I read these instructions to you here in open court. Please listen carefully." Judge Ito's instructions to the jury that day included the following:

> No person may be convicted of a criminal offense unless there is some proof of each element of the crime independent of any admission made by him outside of this trial. . . .
>
> A defendant in a criminal action is presumed to be innocent until the contrary is proved, and in case of a reasonable doubt whether his guilt is satisfactorily shown, he is entitled to a verdict of not guilty. This presumption places upon the prosecution the burden of proving him guilty beyond a reasonable doubt. . . .
>
> The prosecution has the burden of proving beyond a reasonable doubt each element of the crimes charged in the information and that the defendant was the perpetrator of any such charged crimes. The defendant is not required to prove himself innocent or to prove that any other person committed the crimes charged. . . .
>
> The defendant is accused in counts one and two of having committed the crime of murder, a violation of Penal Code, Section 187. Every person who unlawfully kills a human being with malice aforethought is guilty of the crime of

JURY INSTRUCTIONS
directions given by a judge to a jury concerning the law of the case.

murder, in violation of Section 187 of the California Penal Code. In order to prove such crime, each of the following elements must be proved: one, a human being was killed; two, the killing was unlawful; and, three, the killing was done with malice aforethought. . . .

All killing that is perpetrated by any kind of willful, deliberate and premeditated killing, with express malice aforethought, is murder of the first degree. . . . Murder of the second degree is the unlawful killing of a human being with malice aforethought, where there is manifested an intention unlawfully to kill a human being, but the evidence is insufficient to establish deliberation and premeditation. Murder is classified into two degrees and if you should find the defendant guilty of murder, you must determine and state in your verdict, whether you find the murder to be of the first or second degree. . . .

The purpose of the court's instructions is to provide you with the applicable law so that you may arrive at a just and lawful verdict. . . .

THE ADVERSARIAL SYSTEM

ADVERSARIAL SYSTEM

in-court arrangements that pit the prosecution against the defense in the belief that truth can best be realized through effective debate over the merits of the opposing sides.

ADVOCACY MODEL

a perspective that holds that the greatest number of just and equitable resolutions of all criminal cases occurs when both sides are allowed to argue their cases effectively and vociferously before a fair and impartial jury.

Bluster, sputter, question, cavil; but be sure your argument is intricate enough to confound the court.

—William Wycherley, English dramatist (1640-1716)

Criminal trials, such as the O. J. Simpson double-murder trial, occur within the context of an **adversarial system** that pits the prosecution against the defense. The adversarial system has its origins in the ancient practice of trial by combat.[1] Trial by combat pitted two armed contestants with conflicting claims against one another, with a neutral party serving as referee. The winner had his claim validated and was exonerated, if accused of a criminal offense. In the modern-day practice of criminal law, the judge serves the role of referee, while defense and prosecution attorneys assume the role of contestants.

Central to the adversarial system is the **advocacy model,** which holds that the greatest number of just and equitable resolutions of all criminal cases will occur when both sides are allowed to argue their cases effectively and vociferously before a fair and impartial jury. In other words, the advocacy model is built on the premise that truth is the ultimate goal of any criminal trial and that truth can best be realized through effective debate over the merits of opposing perspectives. One modern source explains it this way:

> The theory behind the adversary system is that a fair and impartial jury will be best able to arrive at a truthful verdict if each side . . . is given an opportunity to present evidence and to cross-examine the evidence submitted by the opposing party. In this system, each side has an equal chance to present its proof and thereby persuade the jury of the merits of its position, and each side has the opportunity to attack the opponent's proof and thereby expose its deficiencies.[2]

The adversarial system requires that advocates for both sides do their utmost, within the boundaries set by law and professional ethics, to protect and advance the interests of their clients (that is, the defendant and the state). Hence, even defense attorneys who are convinced that their client is guilty are still exhorted to offer the best possible defense and to counsel their client as effectively as possible.

Needless to say, expectations of vigorous representation, even on behalf of clients who are extremely unpopular in the public eye, or who seem to be clearly guilty of reprehensible crimes, often lead to practical and ethical dilemmas for criminal defense attorneys. As one training manual for attorneys puts it:

All sides in a trial want to hide at least some of the truth.

—Alan M. Dershowitz (b. 1938)

> The trial context raises its own unique variety of ethical issues because of the nature of the trial itself. The trial is fundamentally an exercise in which the lawyers for each of the opposing sides attempt to present fact images about an event, circumstance, or condition that occurred outside the courtroom. The fidelity and accuracy of the in-court fact presentations are vital to the integrity of the process. . . . The tension between effective presentation of facts from the

standpoint of a client's interest and the presentation of the facts in an objectively accurate fashion is ever present. Each case is likely to involve two versions of what really happened. It is rare that both versions are objectively true. And the presentation process itself can involve deception and tactics that may seem unfair.[3]

To guide the behavior of all attorneys (including defense attorneys, judges, and prosecutors) the American Bar Association (ABA) has created a number of ethical codes. Among them are the Model Code of Professional Responsibility and the Model Rules of Professional Conduct. Although ABA standards may provide general guidelines, the ABA has no official authority and cannot actively discipline attorneys. Each state bar, however, has adopted codes of professional responsibility, many of them modeled after ABA codes, to which attorneys in the state must adhere or risk discipline. State bars may publicly reprimand unethical attorneys, suspend them from the practice of law, or disbar them. Attorneys, whatever their role, must abide by the standards of their state bar association or risk being officially sanctioned.

Zealous advocacy can sometimes even lead to criminal charges against an attorney. Such was the case in 1995 when Donald L. Ferguson, a former federal prosecutor who became a defense attorney, pleaded guilty to illegally aiding Colombian cocaine traffickers. Ferguson was accused of obstructing justice by preparing false affidavits on behalf of members of the Cali drug cartel, of delivering drug profits to other attorneys to pay the legal fees of cartel members, and of providing warnings to the drug traffickers of pending investigations and charges.[4]

Web Extra! 2–1

American Bar Association

Standards of Proof

As Judge Ito informed the jury in the Simpson case, "No person may be convicted of a criminal offense unless there is some proof of each element of the crime . . . A defendant in a criminal action is presumed to be innocent until the contrary is

A disagreement between attorneys at a criminal trial. Under our adversarial system of justice, prosecutors and defense attorneys are duty bound to present the best possible case— within ethical and legal boundaries. (Photo courtesy of PhotoEdit.)

STEPHEN J. SUNDVOLD

Web Extra! 2–2

American Bar Association's Criminal Justice Section

BURDEN OF PROOF

the mandate, operative in American criminal courts, that an accused person is assumed innocent until proven guilty. The prosecution is required to prove the defendant's guilt beyond a reasonable doubt.

REASONABLE DOUBT

(in legal proceedings) an actual and substantial doubt arising from the evidence, from the facts or circumstances shown by the evidence, or from the lack of evidence.[5] Also, that state of the case which, after the entire comparison and consideration of all the evidence, leaves the minds of the jurors in such a condition that they cannot say they feel an abiding conviction of the truth of the charge.[6]

REASONABLE DOUBT STANDARD

the standard of proof necessary for conviction in criminal trials.

> A reasonable doubt is nothing more than a doubt for which reasons can be given. The fact that one or two men out of twelve differ from the others does not establish that their doubts are reasonable.
>
> —Quintin Hogg, nineteenth-century British statesman

PREPONDERANCE OF THE EVIDENCE

a standard for determining legal liability that requires a probability of just over 50 percent that the defendant did what is claimed.

CLEAR AND CONVINCING EVIDENCE

the level of factual proof used in civil cases involving issues of personal liberty. The standard requires greater certainty than "more probable than not," but is not as demanding as "no reasonable doubt."[10]

proved, and in case of a reasonable doubt whether his guilt is satisfactorily shown, he is entitled to a verdict of not guilty. This presumption places upon the prosecution the burden of proving him guilty beyond a reasonable doubt. . . . The prosecution has the burden of proving beyond a reasonable doubt each element of the crimes charged in the information and that the defendant was the perpetrator of any such charged crimes. The defendant is not required to prove himself innocent or to prove that any other person committed the crimes charged. . . ."

Under the American system of criminal justice, as these jury instructions reveal, an accused person is assumed innocent until proven guilty. Hence, in any criminal trial, the prosecution is tasked with proving the defendant's guilt. The defense, on the other hand, need not prove innocence but may raise doubt that the defendant is guilty. Since the defendant does not have to prove his or her innocence, there is no requirement that he or she testify or that the defense call witnesses, cross-examine prosecution witnesses, or present evidence. In any case, the **burden of proof** requirement, by which American criminal courts operate, mandates that for a guilty verdict to be returned in a given case a defendant's guilt must be established beyond a **reasonable doubt.** Although the **reasonable doubt standard** is intertwined with the burden of proof requirement, the difference between the two is important. One is an *obligation* imposed on the prosecution; the other is a *criterion* that must be met if a conviction is to be obtained.

In 1970, the majority opinion of the U.S. Supreme Court in the case of *In re Winship*[7] held that "[t]he reasonable-doubt standard plays a vital role in the American scheme of criminal procedure. . . . The standard provides concrete substance for the presumption of innocence—that bedrock 'axiomatic and elementary' principle whose 'enforcement lies at the foundation of the administration of our criminal law.' " The Court went on to say, "It is critical that the moral force of the criminal law not be diluted by a standard of proof that leaves people in doubt [about] whether innocent men are being condemned."[8]

The U.S. Supreme Court, however, has not precisely defined "reasonable doubt"—leaving it to the states to communicate the essence of the concept to juries. The opening paragraphs of this chapter referenced reasonable doubt, in the form of a standard California jury instruction, read by Judge Lance Ito during the double-murder trial of O. J. Simpson. In his charge to the jury, Judge Ito defined reasonable doubt as follows: "It is not a mere possible doubt, because everything relating to human affairs is open to some possible or imaginary doubt. It is that state of the case which, after the entire comparison and consideration of all the evidence, leaves the minds of the jurors in that condition that they cannot say they feel an abiding conviction of the truth of the charge."

Other states define the concept differently. A Nebraska jury instruction, for example, that was held to be constitutional by the U.S. Supreme Court in 1994, explains reasonable doubt this way: "A reasonable doubt is an actual and substantial doubt arising from the evidence, from the facts or circumstances shown by the evidence, or from the lack of evidence."[9]

In contrast to criminal cases, where the reasonable doubt standard prevails, a lesser standard of proof is needed in civil cases. A finding for the plaintiff in a civil case requires only the determination that a **preponderance of the evidence** shows that the defendant should be held accountable. A preponderance of the evidence can mean a probability of just over 50 percent that the defendant did what is claimed. Following the criterion of the preponderance of the evidence, a judge or jury can find for the plaintiff if they conclude that it is more likely than not that the allegations against the defendant are true.

A third standard of proof, which requires **clear and convincing evidence,** falls somewhere between the standards of proof beyond a reasonable doubt and preponderance of the evidence. Clear and convincing evidence establishes the reasonable certainty of a claim. The clear and convincing evidence standard requires less than proof "beyond a reasonable doubt" but more than a preponderance of the evidence. Oklahoma jury instructions on clear and convincing evidence, for example, read as follows: "By requiring proof by clear and convincing evidence, I mean that you must be persuaded, considering all the evidence in the case, that each of these elements is highly probable and free from serious doubt."[11]

Web Extra! 2–3

Commonwealth v. Webster (1850)

LAW IN PRACTICE

WHAT CONSTITUTES REASONABLE DOUBT?

Jury instructions equating guilt beyond a reasonable doubt with moral certainty have their origin in an 1850 decision of the Massachusetts Supreme Judicial Court. In that early case, Commonwealth v. Webster, *Chief Justice Lemuel Shaw defined reasonable doubt as a mental state in which jurors "cannot say they feel an abiding conviction, to a moral certainty, of the truth of the charge." Justice Shaw's description was to later be incorporated into the jury instructions given to criminal trial juries in many states and came to be known as the Webster charge.*

Commonwealth v. Webster
Massachusetts Supreme Judicial
Court, 1850
59 Mass. 295, 320

[W]hat is reasonable doubt? It is a term often used, probably pretty well understood, but not easily defined. It is not mere possible doubt; because every thing relating to human affairs, and depending on moral evidence, is open to some possible or imaginary doubt. It is that state of the case, which, after the entire comparison and consideration of all the evidence, leaves the minds of jurors in that condition that they cannot say they feel an abiding conviction, to a moral certainty, of the truth of the charge. The burden of proof is upon the prosecutor.

All the presumptions of law independent of evidence are in favor of innocence; and every person is presumed to be innocent until he is proved guilty. If upon such proof there is reasonable doubt remaining, the accused is entitled to the benefit of it by an acquittal. For it is not sufficient to establish a probability, though [it be] a strong one arising from the doctrine of chances, that the fact charged is more likely to be true than the contrary; but the evidence must establish the truth of the fact to a reasonable and moral certainty; a certainty that convinces and directs the understanding, and satisfies the reason and judgment, of those who are bound to act conscientiously upon it. This we take to be proof beyond reasonable doubt.

This 1850 definition later became the basis for the reasonable doubt jury instruction now in use by the state of California (and many other states). In 1994, in the case of Sandoval v. California, *the U.S. Supreme Court upheld the constitutionality of the California instruction, but indicated its displeasure with the use of the phrase "moral certainty." Hence, California courts (and the courts of most other states) now generally use the reasonable doubt instruction printed in the opening paragraphs of this chapter—from which that phrase is noticeably absent.*

What do **you** think?

1. Why do you think the U.S. Supreme Court objected to the phrase "moral certainty" in the California jury instruction about reasonable doubt?

2. Can you think of any way in which reasonable doubt might be better defined or clarified? If so, how would you define it?

Criminal Liability

One who violates the criminal law, and whose illegal activity is discovered, becomes a defendant—subject to investigation, arrest, and prosecution. Brought before the court, defendants in a criminal case may then become liable to criminal sanctions specified by the law unless they can offer a good defense, or otherwise show cause why they should not be held accountable. The term **criminal liability** can be used to describe the degree of blameworthiness assigned to the defendant after processing by a court, and the concomitant extent to which the defendant is subject to penalties prescribed by the criminal law. Hence, the primary purpose of any criminal trial is the determination of the defendant's degree of criminal liability, if any.

In the example of the O. J. Simpson criminal case, which opened this chapter, two murder charges were brought against Simpson, and the jury was instructed that it could find Simpson guilty of either first- or second-degree murder on each charge, or that it could acquit him entirely on one or both charges. A conviction on two counts of first-degree murder obviously carries far more criminal liability than, say, conviction on only one charge of second-degree murder. Of course, Simpson was found "not guilty" of all charges, absolving him of any criminal liability and removing the possibility that he would face any criminal sanction.

As later chapters show, although a defendant may have committed an action in violation of the criminal law and may even admit doing so, criminal liability may be reduced or entirely eliminated by his or her ability to successfully raise a defense. With this in mind, the concept of criminal liability can be expressed by the following formula:

Degree of Criminal Liability **equals** *Violation(s) of the Criminal Law* **minus** *Defenses or Justifications*

In discussing criminal liability, it is important to recognize the crucial distinction between legal guilt and factual guilt. Factual guilt deals with the issue of whether or not the defendant is actually responsible for the crime of which he or she stands accused. If the defendant "did it" (i.e., performed the act), then he or she is, *in fact*, guilty. Legal guilt is not so clear. Legal guilt is established only when the prosecutor presents evidence that is sufficient to convince the judge (where the judge determines the verdict) or jury that the defendant is guilty as charged. The distinction between legal guilt and factual guilt is crucial, because it points to the burden of proof requirement that rests with the prosecution, and it indicates the possibility that defendants who are factually guilty may, nonetheless, be found legally "not guilty."

THE BASIC ELEMENTS OF CRIME

From the perspective of Western jurisprudence all crimes can be said to share certain features, or elements, and the notion of crime itself can be said to rest on such general principles. Taken together, these features comprise the legal essence of the concept of crime. They are referred to in legal parlance as the **elements of crime** and describe the most essential aspects of criminal conduct. All crimes can be said to have these general elements in one form or another. They may be defined by statute in various ways—depending on the jurisdiction.

These fundamental or basic elements of criminal activity in general must be distinguished from the distinct elements defined by statute for *specific crimes*. Because statutes differ between jurisdictions, the specific elements of a particular crime,

---

CRIMINAL LIABILITY

the degree of blameworthiness assigned to a defendant by a criminal court and the concomitant extent to which the defendant is subject to penalties prescribed by the criminal law.

Commonly we say a judgment falls upon a man for something in him we cannot abide.

—John Seldon (1584–1654)

ELEMENTS OF CRIME

(1) the basic components of crime; (2) in a specific crime, the essential features of that crime as specified by law or statute.

O. J. Simpson expresses relief as jury verdicts are read in his criminal trial on double-murder charges. The primary task of a criminal trial is assessing criminal liability. (Photo courtesy of Corbis/Sygma.)

such as murder, may vary. To convict a defendant of a particular crime prosecutors must prove to a judge or jury that all the required statutory elements are present.[12] If even one element of an offense cannot be established beyond a reasonable doubt criminal liability will not have been demonstrated, and the defendant will be found not guilty. Later chapters examine the material elements of *specific* crimes as well as defenses to charges of criminal liability. For now, we will turn our attention to the most fundamental features of crime in general.

Conventional legal wisdom holds that the conceptual essence of crime consists of three conjoined and essential elements: (1) the criminal act (which, in legal parlance, is termed the *actus reus*), (2) a culpable mental state (*mens rea*), and (3) a concurrence of the two. Hence, as is discussed in the remaining pages of this chapter, the essence of criminal conduct consists of a concurrence of a criminal act with a culpable mental state. The critical issue of concurrence is what distinguishes murder from homicide committed in self-defense, for example, or rape from consensual sex.

It is important to recognize that some legal scholars add the concept of harm, or a harmful result, to the list of elements that conceptually constitute the essence of crime. We do not do so here, however, because—as we shall later see—some crimes do not involve a clear-cut harm, while others can be effectively committed before actual harm occurs.

Through years of effort, legal scholars have refined considerably each of the elements that comprise the conceptual essence of criminality. Some suggest that a number of additional elements are inherent in the concept. These additional elements are (1) causation, (2) a resulting harm (as mentioned above), (3) the principle of legality, and (4) necessary attendant circumstances. In the remainder of this chapter, we discuss the three essential elements of crime. In Chapter 3, we describe the remaining four elements as they relate to contemporary understandings of criminality.

Before beginning our discussion of the essential elements of crime, however, it is necessary to point out that when attorneys speak of *conduct*, they routinely mean more than mere behavior or action. The term **conduct,** as it is used in the discussion that follows, encompasses both the behavior and the mental state that were present at the time of the behavior.

CONDUCT
in the criminal law, behavior and its accompanying mental state.

A purse snatching in progress. Central to most crimes is the criminal act, or actus reus. (Photo by Richard Hutchings, courtesy of PhotoEdit.)

The Criminal Act

ACTUS REUS

an act in violation of the law; a guilty act.

Generally, a person must commit some act before they are subject to criminal sanctions, and a necessary first feature of most crimes is some act in violation of the law. Such an act is termed the *actus reus* of a crime. The term (which, like much other legal terminology, is Latin) means a "guilty act." For purposes of the criminal law the word *act* is often said to mean a performance, a deed, or a movement as distinguished from remaining at rest. In keeping with common law tradition, Arizona law, for example, couches the idea of an act squarely in terms of physical conduct. The "definitions" section of the Arizona Revised Statutes says, quite simply, " 'Act' means a bodily movement."[13] The same words are found in Part I, Article 1, Section 1.13(2) of the Model Penal Code (see Appendix B).

Some bodily movements may appear relatively minor, even though they result in considerable criminal liability. An individual who hires someone to kill another person, for example, may move only their tongue, but he or she is still liable to a criminal charge. Hence, words are acts in the sense that term is used by the criminal law. In this same regard, given technology, it takes little bodily movement to actually kill someone—merely the pull of a finger on the trigger of a gun.

Thinking Is Not Doing Some religious traditions hold that evil or bad thoughts are sins. But thoughts are not actions in the sense of an *actus reus*. Hence, although people might feel guilty about their own thoughts, even to the point of considerable mental anguish, one cannot be arrested merely for thinking something. The philosophical basis of this principle may lie in the belief that "thoughts are not susceptible of proof except when demonstrated by outward action."[14] Moreover, there are people who think all kinds of things, but never act on their thoughts. Hence, people may more easily control their actions than their thoughts, and it is, after all, their actions that cause harm to others.[15]

Although the notion of bodily movement or physical activity has formed an integral part of the notion of *actus reus* in most jurisdictions for quite a long time, technological advances may one day mandate changes in the concept. A few years ago, for example, a popular science fiction movie featured a fighter airplane that responded to its pilot's thoughts. In the movie, the futuristic airplane was controlled by computers that responded to brainwaves—a necessity because the "g-forces" generated by the plane made physical movement of the pilot all but impossible, and human reaction times were unable to keep pace with the rapidity of ultrasonic flight. Although that movie was science fiction, machines on the market today reveal the possibility of bringing about physical result through mere thought. Biofeedback devices, for example, sense the user's brainwaves or blood pressure and produce an audible or physical response—allowing the user to gain control over subtle aspects of the body not generally thought of as bodily movements. Since, biologically speaking, muscles respond to electrical impulses generated by the brain, it is not too far fetched to imagine a scenario in which a mechanical device becomes an effective extension of the human body (as some artificial limbs already are) capable of physical movement and directed by the wearer's thoughts.

Given the possibility that such imaginary scenarios may one day border on reality, the notion of an act may be more appropriately conceived of as "the external manifestation of an actor's will" than a physical movement. After all, bodily movements themselves are manifestations of the actor's will.

Being and Doing Are Two Different Things

To *be something* is not a crime—to *do something* may be. Persons who admit (perhaps on a TV talk show) that they are drug users, for example, cannot be arrested on that basis (see, for example, the Capstone Case of *Robinson* v. *California* at the end of Chapter 12). However, a police detective who heard the admission might begin gathering evidence to prove some specific law violation in that person's past or perhaps they may watch that individual for future conduct in violation of the law. An arrest might then occur. If it did, it would be based on a specific action in violation of the law pertaining to controlled substances.

> If there were no bad people there would be no good lawyers.
> —Charles Dickens, English novelist (1812–1870)

Voluntary Acts

Some forms of human action are inherently noncriminal. The laws of most jurisdictions specify that a person's actions must be voluntary for them to carry criminal liability. The Indiana Code, for example, reads: "A person commits an offense only if he voluntarily engages in conduct in violation of the statute defining the offense. However, a person who omits to perform an act commits an offense only if he has a statutory, common law, or contractual duty to perform the act."[16] Similarly, Title 2 of the Texas Penal Code reads: "(a) A person commits an offense only if he voluntarily engages in conduct, including an act, an omission, or possession."[17] Hence, involuntary or reflex actions, or actions undertaken during sleep, under anesthesia, under hypnosis, or otherwise unwittingly undertaken, would not be considered criminal under Texas law even if they resulted in harm or appeared to constitute violations of the criminal law. Similarly, where a person's actions are forced by another, as when one's hand is forced down onto a button that activates a destructive device, criminal liability should not result.

Because the laws of most jurisdictions, like that of Texas, require action to be voluntarily undertaken before criminal liability can accrue, a person who kills another during a "bad dream" or while sleepwalking may not be criminally liable for his or her actions. In 1988, in just such a case, twenty-four-year-old Kenneth Parks was acquitted by a Canadian jury of second-degree murder charges after he admittedly drove fourteen miles to his mother-in-law's home and beat her to death with a tire iron.[18] Parks claimed he was sleepwalking while he committed the killing. During the trial, friends of Parks said he had a history of sleepwalking, and doctors testified that about thirty cases of murder committed by sleepwalkers are known to exist in medical literature.[19]

In 1999, however, Scott Falater, 43, of Phoenix, Arizona, was convicted in Maricopa County Superior Court of first-degree murder after a jury refused to believe his claim that he stabbed his wife forty-four times, dragged her to a backyard swimming pool, and held her head under water until she died—all while he was sleepwalking.[20]

Falater admitted that he must have killed his wife of twenty years, and later removed his bloodstained clothes and hid them and the knife used in the slaying in his Volvo. But, he said, he was asleep at the time of the 1997 killing, and had no memory of his actions. Although two sleep experts cited a family history of sleepwalking, job stress, and lack of recent sleep as explanations for Falater's supposedly violent sleepwalking episode, jurors sided with prosecutors who said that Falater's actions were too deliberate to constitute sleepwalking.

Possession Possession is generally considered to be another form of action. Possession, like any other act, may not always be voluntary. According to the Texas Penal Code, "[P]ossession is a voluntary act if the possessor knowingly obtains or receives the thing possessed or is aware of his control of the thing for a sufficient time to permit him to terminate his control."[21] In like manner, Title 13 of the Arizona Revised Statutes says that " 'Possession' means a voluntary act if the defendant knowingly exercised dominion or control over property." Arizona law also says that the word " '[p]ossess' means knowingly to have physical possession or otherwise to exercise dominion or control over property."[22]

As can be inferred from these laws, most jurisdictions draw a distinction between **knowing possession** and **mere possession.** A person who knowingly possesses something is well aware of what he or she has and has probably taken steps to obtain it. Someone who merely transports something for another, on the other hand, may be unaware of what he or she possesses. Similarly, a person on whom drugs are "planted," and who remains unaware of their presence, cannot be found guilty of drug possession. Nonetheless, both knowing possession and mere possession constitute **actual possession,** meaning that the person is actually in direct physical control of the object in question.

An individual may also exercise **constructive possession** over property and objects. Constructive possession means that, at a given time, a person may not have actual physical custody of the material in question, but is still able to control or influence it. Hence, objects that are in my desk drawer or in my safe deposit box are still effectively under my constructive possession, although I may not have them in my immediate presence. So, for example, I may still be in possession of controlled substances, for purposes of the law, even though the drugs are hidden in a vacation house that I own and I am sitting in my university office.

A Failure to Act In times past, persons could be routinely arrested for doing nothing at all. Vagrancy laws, for example, were popular in the early part of the twentieth century, but they have generally been invalidated by the courts because they did not specify what act violated the law. In fact, the *less* a person did, the more vagrant they were.

An **omission to act,** or a failure to act, however, may be criminal where the person in question is required by law to do something; that is, where the law specifies

KNOWING POSSESSION
possession with awareness (of what one possesses).

MERE POSSESSION
possession in which one may or may not be aware of what he or she possesses.

ACTUAL POSSESSION
possession in which one has direct physical control over the object or objects in question.

CONSTRUCTIVE POSSESSION
the ability to exercise control over property and objects, even though they are not in one's physical custody.

OMISSION TO ACT
an intentional or unintentional failure to act, which may impose criminal liability if a duty to act under the circumstances is specified by law.

a duty to act. Classic examples of such offenses include the failure to file a tax return or to register for military drafts. More recently, child-neglect laws, which focus on parents and child guardians who do not live up to their responsibilities for caring for their children, have received considerable attention. Similarly, intentionally withholding needed medication from a critically ill individual might constitute the basis for a charge of homicide.

In a real-life example, Ginger and David Twitchell were convicted in 1990 of involuntary manslaughter after their two-year-old son Robyn died of a bowel obstruction that could have been easily treated surgically.[23] The Twitchells, members of the Christian Science Church,[24] believed in the efficacy of "scientific prayer" as the sole way to treat illness and refused medical treatment for their son. Their conviction was overturned in 1993, however, when the Massachusetts Supreme Court ruled that the Twitchells should have been allowed to argue at trial that they believed they were within their parental rights to choose spiritual treatment.

Finally, we should note that *reasonable* failures to act may be noncriminal, even when serious harm results. Hence, the captain of a passenger airplane may decide to avoid a rapid landing to save the life of a heart attack victim if doing so might endanger the airplane and its other passengers.

Threatening to Act While most forms of speech are protected by the first amendment to the U.S. Constitution, threatening to act can be a criminal offense. Telling someone "I'm going to kill you" might result in an arrest for the offense of "communicating threats." Similarly, threatening the president of the United States may be a crime under federal law and is taken seriously by the Secret Service, which regularly arrests individuals for boasting about planned violence directed at the president.[25]

Part II, Article 2, Section 211.3, of the Model Penal Code provides for the offense of "terroristic threat" and says: "A person is guilty of a felony of the third degree if he threatens to commit any crime of violence with purpose to terrorize another or to cause evacuation of a building, place of assembly, or facility of public transportation,

LAW ON THE BOOKS

"ACT" DEFINED

Compare with Model Penal Code, Section 1.13.

ARIZONA REVISED STATUTES

Title 13, Section 105. Definitions.
In this title, unless the context otherwise requires:
1. "Act" means a bodily movement.

TEXAS PENAL CODE

Title 1, Chapter 1, Section 1.07. Definitions.
(a) In this code: (1) "Act" means a bodily movement, whether voluntary or involuntary, and includes speech. (2) "Actor" means a person whose criminal responsibility is in issue in a criminal action. Whenever the term "suspect" is used in this code, it means "actor."

OREGON REVISED STATUTES

Chapter 161, Section 161.085. Definitions with respect to culpability.
As used in chapter 743, Oregon Laws 1971, and ORS 166.635, unless the context requires otherwise:
(1) "Act" means a bodily movement.
(2) "Voluntary act" means a bodily movement performed consciously and includes the conscious possession or control of property.
(3) "Omission" means a failure to perform an act the performance of which is required by law.
(4) "Conduct" means an act or omission and its accompanying mental state.
(5) "To act" means either to perform an act or to omit to perform an act.

or otherwise to cause serious public inconvenience, or in reckless disregard of the risk of causing such terror or inconvenience." Threats made for the purpose of illegally acquiring money or other things of value are described separately in most state penal codes as extortion and blackmail.

State of Mind

MENS REA
The specific mental state operative in the defendant at the time of a crime; a guilty mind.

Web Extra! 2–4
*Britannica online:
mens rea*

Mens rea is the second general element of crime. The term literally means "guilty mind" and refers to the specific mental state operative in the defendant at the time the behavior in question was being enacted. The importance of *mens rea* as a component of crime cannot be overemphasized, which can be seen in the fact that some courts have held that "[a]ll crime exists primarily in the mind."[26]

In legal usage, *mens rea* can encompass notions of (1) a guilty mind, (2) a wrongful purpose, and (3) criminal intent. The extent to which a person can be held criminally responsible for his or her actions generally depends on the nature of the mental state under which he or she was laboring at the time of the offense. Even activity that seriously harms others may *not* be criminal if *mens rea*, or a culpable mental state, is lacking during the time the proscribed behavior is undertaken. It is only when an act, in the sense of a bodily movement, and a culpable mental state come together in violation of the law that criminal conduct can be said to have occurred.

As mentioned earlier, the concepts of *actus reus* and *mens rea* are conjoined in the legal notion of *conduct*. Arizona law, for example, which generally follows Model Penal Code conventions, defines the word "conduct" to mean "an act or omission and its accompanying culpable mental state." Texas law, reflecting Model Penal Code language, holds that "a person does not commit an offense unless he intentionally, knowingly, recklessly, or with criminal negligence engages in conduct as the definition of the offense requires."[27]

As the Texas statute indicates, four levels or types of *mens rea* can be distinguished: (1) purposeful (or intentional), (2) knowing, (3) reckless, and (4) negligent. *Mens rea* is most clearly present when a person acts purposefully and knowingly, but *mens rea* sufficient for criminal prosecution may also result from reckless or negligent behavior. Pure accident, however, which involves no recklessness or negligence, cannot serve as the basis for either criminal or civil liability. "Even a dog," once wrote the famous Supreme Court Justice Oliver Wendell Holmes, "distinguishes between being stumbled over and being kicked."[28]

Nonetheless, *mens rea* is said to be present when a person *should have known better,* even if the person did not directly intend the consequences of his or her action. A person who acts negligently, and thereby endangers others, may be found guilty of a crime when harm occurs, even though no negative consequences were intended. For example, a mother who left her twelve-month-old child alone in the tub can later be prosecuted for negligent homicide if the child drowns.[29] It should be emphasized, however, that negligence in and of itself is not a crime. Negligent conduct can be evidence of crime only when it falls below some acceptable standard of care. That standard is today applied in criminal courts through the fictional creation of a *reasonable person.* The question to be asked in a given case is whether or not a reasonable person, in the same situation, would have known better, and acted differently, than the defendant. The reasonable person criterion provides a yardstick for juries faced with thorny issues of guilt or innocence. Returning to Arizona statutes, we find this definition of **criminal negligence**[30]: " 'Criminal negligence' means, with respect to a result or to a circumstance described by a statute defining an offense, that a person fails to perceive a substantial and unjustifiable risk that the result will occur or that the circumstance exists. The risk must be of such nature and degree that the failure to perceive it constitutes a *gross* deviation from the standard of care that a reasonable person would observe in the situation."[31]

Purposeful or **intentional action,** in contrast to negligent action, is that which is undertaken to achieve some goal. Sometimes the harm that results from intentional action may be quite unintended—and yet fail to reduce criminal liability. The doctrine of transferred intent, for example, which operates in all U.S. jurisdictions, would hold a person guilty of murder even if he took aim and shot at an intended victim but missed, killing another person instead. The philosophical notion behind the concept of transferred intent is that the killer's intent to kill, which existed at the time of the crime, transferred from the intended victim to the person who was struck by the bullet and died. It is also possible to distinguish between **general intent** and **specific intent.** General intent refers to an actor's physical conduct and is that form of intent that can be assumed from the defendant's behavior. Hence, if one person intentionally strikes another, he generally intends assault—an act prohibited by law. When a crime requires proof only of general intent, the judge or the jury may reasonably infer the defendant's intent from his or her conduct. **General intent crimes** are those particular forms of voluntary behavior that are prohibited by law.

Specific intent, on the other hand, refers to a thoughtful, conscious intention to perform a specific act *in order to achieve a particular result.* The term is often used to describe the intention of a person to commit a particular crime or prohibited act. If a person strikes another *with intent to kill,* for example, he commits a specific intent offense. Similarly, in order to convict a defendant of attempted murder, the prosecutor must show that he or she specifically intended to kill the victim.

Specific intent crimes usually involve a secondary purpose—that is, the perpetrator commits one crime with the intent to commit another. General intent crimes do not contain a lesser included offense, and if a defendant is found "not guilty" of

CRIMINAL NEGLIGENCE
(1) behavior in which a person fails to reasonably perceive substantial and unjustifiable risks of dangerous consequences; (2) negligence of such a nature and to such a degree that it is punishable as a crime; (3) flagrant and reckless disregard for the safety of others, or willful indifference to the safety and welfare of others.

INTENTIONAL ACTION
that which is undertaken volitionally to achieve some goal.

GENERAL INTENT
that form of intent that can be assumed from the defendant's behavior. General intent refers to an actor's physical conduct.

GENERAL INTENT CRIMES
those particular forms of voluntary behavior that are prohibited by law.

SPECIFIC INTENT
a thoughtful, conscious intention to perform a specific act *in order to achieve a particular result.*

SPECIFIC INTENT CRIMES
literally, crimes that require a specific intent. Generally speaking, specific intent crimes involve a secondary purpose.

a general intent crime, he or she will be set free. On the other hand, specific intent crimes may involve lesser degrees, and a person found "not guilty" of assault with intent to kill may still be found "guilty" of assault.

KNOWING BEHAVIOR
action undertaken with awareness.

Knowing behavior is action undertaken with awareness. Hence a person who acts purposefully always acts knowingly, although a person may act in a knowingly criminal way but for another purpose. The airline captain who allows a flight attendant to transport cocaine aboard an airplane may do so in order to gain sexual favors from the attendant—but without having the purpose of drug smuggling in mind. Arizona statutes contain these definitions: " 'Intentionally' or 'with the intent to' means, with respect to a result or to conduct described by a statute defining an offense, that a person's objective is to cause that result or to engage in that conduct.... 'Knowingly' means, with respect to conduct or to a circumstance described by a statute defining an offense, that a person is aware or believes that his or her conduct is of that nature or that the circumstance exists."

SCIENTER
knowledge; guilty knowledge.

The term **scienter** is sometimes used to signify a defendant's knowledge or "guilty knowledge." Some criminal laws require that the prosecution must prove that the defendant had knowledge of a given matter in order to obtain a conviction. In 1994, for example, the Illinois Supreme Court validated a state law making it a felony to knowingly expose uninformed others to HIV through sexual contact.[32] Under the law, persons who are aware that they are infected with HIV must avoid sexual contact with persons unaware of their condition or risk felony prosecution. The court held that the law had been properly applied in two cases: that of a woman who knew she was infected with HIV when she had sex with a man without telling him, and a case involving a man with HIV infection who was charged with raping a woman. In neither case, however, was the purpose of sexual intercourse to intentionally transmit the disease-causing agent.

> The trial court is the most important agency of the judicial branch of the government precisely because on it rests the responsibility of ascertaining the facts.
>
> —Jerome N. Frank, *United States* v. *Forness*, 125 F.2d 928, 942-43 (2d Cir. 1942)

Knowing behavior involves near certainty. Hence, if the flight attendant in the example above carries cocaine aboard the airplane, it *will* be transported; and if an HIV-infected individual has unprotected sexual intercourse with another person, that person *will* be exposed to the virus.

RECKLESS BEHAVIOR
activity that increases the risk of harm.

Reckless behavior, in contrast, is activity that increases the risk of harm. Although knowledge may be a part of such behavior, it exists more in the form of probability than certainty. So, for example, Elton John's song about Princess Diana says "you lived your life like a candle in the wind." The wind is, of course, a risky place to keep a lighted candle—and doing so increases the likelihood that its flame will be extinguished. But there is no certainty that the flame will be blown out or, if so, when it might happen. As a practical example, reckless driving is a common charge in many jurisdictions and is generally brought when a driver engages in risky activity that endangers others. Arizona law states that " '[r]ecklessly' means, with respect to a result or to a circumstance described by a statute defining an offense, that a person is aware of and consciously disregards a substantial and unjustifiable risk that the result will occur or that the circumstance exists. The risk must be of such nature and degree that disregard of such risk constitutes a gross deviation from the standard of conduct that a reasonable person would observe in the situation. A person who creates such a risk but is unaware of such risk solely by reason of voluntary intoxication also acts recklessly with respect to such risk." Hence, in Arizona, as in most other jurisdictions, intoxication is no bar to prosecution of reckless behavior undertaken while intoxicated.

Web Extra! 2–5
Mental State and Criminal Liability

Although most statutes defining criminal activity specify a requisite *mens rea*, a few (discussed shortly) do not. "When the law defining an offense prescribes the kind of culpability that is sufficient for the commission of an offense . . ." reads the Model Penal Code, "such provision shall apply to all the material elements of the offense. . . ."[33] This rule, generally followed in all jurisdictions as a matter of course, means that if a statute specifies elements of an offense, such as a specific result or harm, then a successful prosecution has to show a fusion of *mens rea* and each of those additional elements, as well as the more commonplace link between the act and a culpable state of mind (for additional insight into this principle, see the Capstone Case in this chapter that discusses the New York case of *People* v. *Ryan*).

A person's state of mind during the commission of an offense can rarely be known directly, unless the person confesses. Hence, *mens rea* is generally inferred from a person's actions and from all the circumstances surrounding those actions.

It is important to note that *mens rea,* even in the sense of intent, is not the same thing as **motive.** A motive refers to a person's reason for committing a crime. Although evidence of motive may be admissible during a criminal trial in order to establish other elements that are essential, motive itself is not an essential element of a crime. As a result, we cannot say that a bad or immoral motive makes an act a crime.

MOTIVE
a person's reason for committing a crime.

Strict Liability and *Mens Rea* A special category of crimes, called **strict liability** offenses, requires no culpable mental state and presents a significant exception to the principle that all crimes require a conjunction of action and *mens rea.* Strict liability offenses (also called "absolute liability offenses") make it a crime simply to *do* something, even if the offender has no intention of violating the law. Strict liability is based philosophically on the presumption that causing harm is in itself blameworthy, regardless of the actor's intent.

STRICT LIABILITY
liability without fault or intention. Strict liability offenses do not require *mens rea.*

Routine traffic offenses are generally considered "strict liability" offenses that do not require intent and may even be committed by someone who is consciously unaware of what they are doing. A driver commits minor violations of his or her state motor vehicle code simply by doing that which is forbidden. Hence, driving sixty-five miles per hour in a fifty-five-mile-per-hour zone is a violation of the law, even though the driver may be listening to music, thinking, or simply going with the flow of traffic—entirely unaware that his or her vehicle is exceeding the posted speed limit.

LAW ON THE BOOKS

INDIANA DEFINES *MENS REA.*

Compare with Model Penal Code, Sections 2.01-2.02

INDIANA CODE 35-41-2

Section 1. (a) A person commits an offense only if he voluntarily engages in conduct in violation of the statute defining the offense. However, a person who omits to perform an act commits an offense only if he has a statutory, common law, or contractual duty to perform the act.

(b) If possession of property constitutes any part of the prohibited conduct, it is a defense that the person who possessed the property was not aware of his possession for a time sufficient for him to have terminated his possession.

Section 2. (a) A person engages in conduct "intentionally" if, when he engages in the conduct, it is his conscious objective to do so.

(b) A person engages in conduct "knowingly" if, when he engages in the conduct, he is aware of a high probability that he is doing so.

(c) A person engages in conduct "recklessly" if he engages in the conduct in plain, conscious, and unjustifiable disregard of harm that might result and the disregard involves a substantial deviation from acceptable standards of conduct.

(d) Unless the statute defining the offense provides otherwise, if a kind of culpability is required for commission of an offense, it is required with respect to every material element of the prohibited conduct.

LAW IN PRACTICE

SHOULD MEDICAL MISDIAGNOSIS BE A CRIME?

In 1995, a spate of criminal indictments were brought against physicians charged with negligence in the deaths of patients. In the first case, a Wisconsin inquest jury recommended negligent homicide charges against technicians and a physician who misread Pap smears, causing cancer treatments to be delayed for Karin Smith and Dolores Geary. Both women later died of cervical cancer. A medical expert testified at the inquest hearing that, in both instances, laboratory personnel repeatedly missed unmistakable signs of cancer, which had been present for years before the women's deaths. The case marked the first time in Wisconsin's history that criminal charges were considered for a fatal medical misdiagnosis.

Also in 1995, New York physician Dr. Gerald Einaugler was ordered to spend fifty-two weekends in jail for reckless endangerment after he mistook a dialysis tube for a feeding tube and pumped food into the abdomen of a nursing home patient. About the same time, Denver anesthesiologist Dr. Joseph J. Verbrugge, Sr., was charged with reckless manslaughter after he apparently fell asleep during ear surgery on an eight-year-old boy and the child died.

Reacting to the notion that criminal charges could be filed against physicians who lose patients through negligence, Kirk Johnson, general counsel for the American Medical Association, said that it is very unusual for doctors or technicians to be indicted for homicide when mistakes are made. The usual punishment, said Johnson, is for licensing boards to take away their credentials. "They're basically just banished from their profession. It's a pretty serious sanction," he said. Johnson also questioned the need for criminal charges without willful misconduct. "It seems to me, you have a state medical board . . . designed to deal with this very kind of thing. If you can find this element of willfulness and knowledge, obviously a criminal case can be made," he said. "It sounds like what you have here is very bad practice or negligence and you have a pretty effective remedy" in lifting doctors' licenses.

What do *you* think?

1. Do you agree with AMA general counsel Johnson's implication that "if you can find this element of willfulness and knowledge" murder charges can be brought against physicians whose patients die, but that instances of medical misdiagnosis are best handled through professional sanctions rather than criminal action?

2. Do you think that someone who does not intend harm—indeed, someone who intends to heal, as in the case of a physician—should be held criminally liable if serious harm results through negligence due to overwork or inattention? Why?

3. If physicians can be indicted for homicide and other crimes due to negligence, what other professions can you think of whose members might be liable for similar charges?

4. If you were a member of a jury hearing a case of negligent homicide against a physician for a medical misdiagnosis, would you have any preconceptions about either the law or the medical profession that might influence your verdict? If so, what might they be?

SOURCE: James A. Carlson, "Cancer Inquest," Associated Press online, April 10, 1995.

> It is better that ten guilty persons escape than one innocent suffer.
>
> —Sir William Blackstone (1723–1780)

Statutory rape provides another example of the concept of strict liability.[34] The crime of statutory rape generally occurs between two consenting individuals and requires only that the offender have sexual intercourse with a person under the age of legal consent. Statutes describing the crime routinely avoid any mention of a culpable mental state. California law, for example, contains the crime of "unlawful sexual intercourse," which reads: "Unlawful sexual intercourse is an act of sexual intercourse accomplished with a person who is not the spouse of the perpetrator, if the person is a minor. For the purposes of this section, a 'minor' is a person under the age of 18 years."[35] The law goes on to say: "Any person who engages in an act of unlawful sexual intercourse with a minor who is not more than three years older

LAW ON THE BOOKS

AN EXAMPLE OF SCIENTER

Sexual penetration as felony.

MICHIGAN PUBLIC HEALTH CODE, SECTION 5210

Sec. 5210. (1) A person who knows that he or she has or has been diagnosed as having acquired immunodeficiency syndrome or acquired immunodeficiency syndrome related complex, or who knows that he or she is HIV infected, and who engages in sexual penetration with another person without having first informed the other person that he or she has acquired immunodeficiency syndrome or acquired immunodeficiency syndrome related complex or is HIV infected, is guilty of a felony.

(2) As used in this section, "sexual penetration" means sexual intercourse, cunnilingus, fellatio, anal intercourse, or any other intrusion, however slight, of any part of a person's body or of any object into the genital or anal openings of another person's body, but emission of semen is not required.

CRIMINAL LAW IN THE NEWS

Prosecutors Offer Inmates DNA Testing

Exams May Exonerate or Link Them to Other Crimes

SAN DIEGO—In what may be the first effort of its kind in the nation, San Diego prosecutors are reviewing hundreds of old cases to see if longtime prison inmates can be cleared by DNA evidence.

If evidence is found, the San Diego County District Attorney's office will have it tested for free if an inmate agrees.

But there's a catch that may prevent guilty people from clogging up the system: the inmate's DNA will end up in a national database where it may be used to solve other unsolved crimes.

Prosecutors are looking at a total of 560 criminal cases.

"We have the responsibility to see that justice is done in every case," said Deputy District Attorney William "Woody" Clarke, who is overseeing the project. "This gives us the opportunity to ensure that we don't have any innocent men or women in prison."

Law students to present findings

The prosecutors began the project ear-

lier this year. Late this week, Clarke's partner made a presentation about the project at a Justice Department law enforcement conference in Washington, D.C.

Law students are reviewing the files of all criminals who were prosecuted by the county before 1992 and remain in prison. They include murderers and others convicted of serious crimes such as multiple sexual assaults.

After 1992, local officials began to routinely use DNA during investigations, said Clarke, who is nationally known for his work in the O.J. Simpson case.

The law students will present their findings to prosecutors, who will examine each case.

"An opportunity to say no"

Cases will be reopened if prosecutors discover that there is biological evidence that may clear the inmate, Clarke said.

Inmates will decide whether the testing will go forward.

"We're going to give them an opportunity to say no," he said. "It wouldn't surprise me if one or more would refuse the testing."

That's because the inmate's DNA will be added to a national database, where it may be matched to DNA from other crimes, Clarke said. "There's a potential that we will solve heretofore unsolved crime. I don't know if that's going to happen or not."

So far, prosecutors have reviewed about 40 cases. They are only pursuing one, a sexual assault case in which it's not even clear that there is biological evidence, Clarke said.

He expects about 10 of the 560 cases will be eligible for DNA review.

Orange County contacting inmates

Meanwhile, another California county is also looking for innocent inmates, although it's taking a different approach.

Orange County, located between San Diego and Los Angeles, plans to contact inmates and their attorneys *(continued)*

Prosecutors Offer Inmates DNA Testing

Exams May Exonerate or Link Them to Other Crimes

to let them know that prosecutors are interested in reopening old cases if forensic evidence is available, county District Attorney spokeswoman Tori Richards said.

If DNA or fingerprints or other evidence is found, prosecutors will de-termine if testing is warranted, Richards said.

"Unlike San Diego, we are not go-ing to go trolling through hundreds of old cases," she said. "The burden is on the defense lawyer or the defen-dant to come to us and give us the ev-idence, notify us that it exists."

The outreach to inmates should be-gin in about two months, Richards said.

Source: Randy Dotinga, "Prosecutors Offer In-mates DNA Testing; Exams May Exonerate or Link Them to Other Crimes," APB News. July 28, 2000. Reprinted with permission.

Web Extra! 2–6

Proving Guilty Knowledge

or three years younger than the perpetrator, is guilty of a misdemeanor," and "[a]ny person who engages in an act of unlawful sexual intercourse with a minor who is more than three years younger than the perpetrator is guilty of either a misde-meanor or a felony, and shall be punished by imprisonment in a county jail not ex-ceeding one year, or by imprisonment in the state prison."

In many jurisdictions, it matters little in the crime of statutory rape that the "per-petrator" knew the exact age of the "victim," or that the "victim" lied about his or her age or may have given consent, since such laws are "an attempt to prevent the sexual exploitation of persons deemed legally incapable of giving consent."[36] They assume that such persons are "too innocent and naïve to understand the implica-tions and nature of [the sexual] act."[37]

Some legal experts maintain that strict liability offenses can never be "true crimes" because they require no mental element. In fact, most strict liability offenses are violations of regulatory statutes, such as those that declare it a violation to sell misbranded items, possess a motor vehicle with an altered serial number, or oper-ate a car with a burned-out taillight. Since violations of health regulations can cause considerable harm to a large number of people, even though the violator neither in-tends harm nor knowingly violates the law, courts may assess liability according to a principle articulated years ago by the U.S. Court of Appeals for the Third Circuit, which held: "Where the offenses prohibited and made punishable are capable of in-flicting widespread injury, and where the requirement of proof of the offender's guilty knowledge and wrongful intent would render enforcement of the prohibition difficult if not impossible . . . the legislative intent to dispense with *mens rea* as an el-ement of the offense has justifiable basis."[38] Under the Model Penal Code and some state codes, strict liability offenses are termed "violations" rather than crimes and are punishable only by fines or forfeiture.

Web Extra! 2–7

Morissette v.
United States

Some laws require a culpable mental state *and* contain strict liability provisions that may increase criminal liability when other elements can be demonstrated. In an interesting 1996 Missouri Supreme Court case,[39] for example, the drug-dealing con-victions of two men, Lamar Hatton and Richard Troy, Jr., were upheld, although the men claimed that the state statute under which they were convicted was a strict li-ability statute. The statute in question read: "A person commits the offense of dis-tribution of a controlled substance near public housing or other governmental as-sisted housing if he . . . unlawfully distribute[s] or deliver[s] any controlled substance to a person in or on, or within one thousand feet of the real property com-prising public housing or other governmental assisted housing." The appellants ad-mitted that they had sold drugs but contended that they were unaware of the fact that they were close to a public housing project. Their attorney claimed that "be-cause the language of [the statute] contains no *mens rea* or knowledge requirement (i.e., it is a 'strict liability' statute according to appellants), . . . a conviction is easier to obtain, and a criminal defendant left more vulnerable than he would be otherwise, when the prosecution is relieved of a major obstacle—the burden of proving defendant's bad intent."

In finding against the men, the Missouri court held that the state law under which they were convicted "is not a strict liability statute." The words "within 1000 feet . . . of public housing" are merely a punishment-enhancement provision and do not create a separate crime, said the court. "Appellants' real complaint," said the court, "is that they did not know they were within one thousand feet of public housing when they carried out their plan to sell crack cocaine. This ignorance is not a product of appellants' inability to understand the statute. It is the result of their failure to determine the existence of and their distance from public housing. The burden of ascertaining those facts lies with appellants under the statute. The due process clause simply does not require that the state prove appellant's knowledge of his proximity to public housing, nor does it require the state prove appellant's knowledge that the property is classified as public housing, before it will allow the state to enhance the punishment for a crime appellant intentionally committed."

LAW IN PRACTICE

ARE STRICT LIABILITY CRIMES CONSTITUTIONAL?

Some people claim that strict liability statutes violate due process because they hold a person criminally liable without the need to show criminal intent or criminal mens rea. As the following excerpt from a Michigan court of appeals decision shows, however, strict liability offenses may legitimately encompass even felonies to which potentially severe penalties are attached.

People v. Trotter
Michigan Court of Appeals (1995)
530 N.W.2d 516

Defendant's two-year-old nephew was attacked and killed by defendant's two pit bull terriers. Defendant pleaded *nolo contendere* to involuntary manslaughter under the dangerous animals act, MCL [Michigan Compiled Laws] 287.323(1); MSA [Michigan Statutes Annotated] 12.545(23)(1), and was sentenced to thirty-six months' probation. She appeals as of right. We affirm.

At issue in this case is the validity of MCL 287.323(1); MSA 12.545(23)(1), which provides: The owner of an animal that meets the definition of a dangerous animal in section 1(a) [MCL 287.321a; MSA 12.545(21)(1)] that causes the death of a person is guilty of involuntary manslaughter, punishable under [MCL 750.321; MSA 28.553]. MCL 287.321a; MSA

12.545(21)(1) defines "dangerous animal" as follows:

(a) *"Dangerous animal" means a dog or other animal that bites or attacks a person, or a dog that bites or attacks and causes serious injury to another dog while the other dog is on the property or under the control of its owner. However, a dangerous animal does not include any of the following:*
  (i) *An animal that bites or attacks a person who is knowingly trespassing on the property of the animal's owner.*
  (ii) *An animal that bites or attacks a person who provokes or torments the animal.*
  (iii) *An animal that is responding in a manner that an ordinary and reasonable person would conclude was designed to protect a person if that person is engaged in a lawful activity or is the subject of an assault.*
  (iv) *Livestock.*

Defendant contends that MCL 287.323(1); MSA 12.545(23)(1) violates due process because it holds the owner of a dangerous animal strictly liable for involuntary manslaughter,

(continued)

LAW IN PRACTICE

a felony punishable by up to fifteen years' imprisonment, without a showing of criminal intent or criminal *mens rea*. We disagree.

While the wisdom of excluding the element of knowledge or intent from the definition of a crime has been questioned, the United States Supreme Court has recognized as a general matter that the Constitution does not preclude the enactment of even strict liability criminal statutes. *People* v. *Quinn*, 440 Mich. 178, 185; 487 N.W.2d 194 (1992), citing *Lambert* v. *California*, 355 US 2251 78 S. Ct. 240; 2 L. Ed. 2d 228 (1957). It is also

well settled in Michigan that true strict liability crimes are proper under some circumstances. *Quinn, supra*, pp. 188–189. . . .

What do you think?

1. Do you agree with the court that strict liability offenses do not violate a defendant's due process rights? Why or why not?

2. The court says that "the wisdom of excluding the element of knowledge or intent from the definition of a crime has been questioned. . . ." When might statutes that exclude such elements be wise, if ever?

Concurrence

CONCURRENCE

the simultaneous coexistence of an act in violation of the law and a culpable mental state.

The concurrence of an unlawful act and a culpable mental state provides the third fundamental aspect of crime. **Concurrence** requires that the act and the mental state occur together in order for a crime to take place. If one precedes the other, the requirements of the criminal law are not met. A person may intend to kill a rival, for example. As she carefully drives to the intended victim's house, gun in hand, fantasizing about how she will commit the murder, the unrecognized victim may be crossing the street on the way home from grocery shopping. If the two accidentally collide, and the intended victim dies, there has been no concurrence of act and intent—even though the driver may later rejoice in her "good fortune" at having killed her enemy without incurring criminal liability.

Some jurisdictions make the need for concurrence a clear part of their legal codes. The California Penal Code, for example, requires that: "In every crime or public offense there must exist a union, or joint operation of act and intent, or criminal negligence."[40]

> Lest there remain any doubt about the constitutional stature of the reasonable-doubt standard, we explicitly hold that the Due Process Clause protects the accused against conviction except upon proof beyond a reasonable doubt of every fact necessary to constitute the crime with which he is charged.
>
> —Justice William J. Brennan, Jr., *In re Winship*, 397 U.S. 358, 364 (1970)

SUMMARY

- Criminal trials in America occur within the context of an adversarial system. Central to the adversarial system is the advocacy model, which pits opposing sides against one another (i.e., prosecution and defense, or the people against the defendant). The advocacy model is based on the belief that truth can best be achieved through effective debate in open court.

- Under the American system of criminal justice an accused person is assumed innocent until proven guilty. The burden of proof requirement mandates that for a guilty verdict to be returned in a given case a defendant's guilt must be established beyond a reasonable doubt.

- The concept of criminal liability refers to the extent to which an offender can be held responsible for the commission of a crime. Even if a defendant violates a criminal statute, he or she may not be criminally liable if an effective defense can be offered.

- The legal essence of crime consists of three essential elements: *actus reus* (an act in violation of the law), *mens rea* (a guilty mind), and the concurrence of an act in violation of the law and a culpable mental state. Some scholars suggest that another four elements are also inherent in the concept of crime: causation, a resulting harm, the principle of legality, and necessary attendant circumstances.

- In contrast to the elements common to all crimes, particular offenses are statutorily defined in terms of specific statutory elements. To convict a defendant of a given crime, prosecutors must prove to a judge or jury that all of the statutory elements of a crime are present. If even one statutory element of an offense cannot be established beyond a reasonable doubt, criminal liability will not have been demonstrated, and the defendant will be found not guilty.

- Degrees of culpability, or types of *mens rea,* can be distinguished. Today the four most commonly specified levels of culpability are purposeful, knowing, reckless, and negligent.

- It is important to note that *mens rea* is not the same thing as motive. A motive refers to a person's reason for committing a crime. *Mens rea* refers to the offender's mental state at the time the crime was committed. Strict liability offenses, which are based on the presumption that causing harm in itself is blameworthy, represent an exception to general understandings of the nature of crime since they require no accompanying culpable mental state.

QUESTIONS FOR DISCUSSION

1. Do you believe that the adversarial system is the best way to achieve "justice" in American criminal courts? Within the context of this question, and keeping the limits of the adversarial system in mind, what does "justice" mean?

2. What alternatives to the adversarial system can you envision? List the advantages and disadvantages of each relative to our present system.

3. What is the difference between the reasonable doubt standard and the burden of proof requirement? Why should the prosecution carry the burden of proof rather than the defense? Can you think of any circumstances under which the burden of proof (perhaps on specific issues) should lie with the defendant?

4. What is meant by reasonable doubt? How does reasonable doubt differ from a preponderance of evidence? Which is the better standard for use in criminal court? Why?

5. What are the three "constituent elements" of crime? How is each central to the concept of crime?

6. What is *mens rea?* How many different levels or types of *mens rea* does this chapter identify? What are they? Might there be others? If so, what might they be?

7. What is strict liability? Why are some crimes punished solely on the basis of strict liability? Are strict liability offenses as worthy of "blame" as other offenses that require *mens rea?* Why or why not?

LEGAL RESOURCES ON THE WORLD WIDE WEB

Law dictionaries can be especially useful to students using this textbook and to anyone beginning the study of law. A few are listed in the margin of Chapter 1 as Web

Extra! features. Quite a few other legal dictionaries are available on the World Wide Web. Among them are the following:

1 L Dictionary
http://www.law.harvard.edu/library/research_guides/one_l_dictionary.htm
A Harvard Law School Library dictionary designed to assist new law students during the first few days of their law school experience.

Court TV Glossary of Legal Terms
http://www.courttv.com/legalterms/glossary.html
A comprehensive glossary of legal terms with built-in hyperlinks.

Duhaime's Law Dictionary
http://www.duhaime.org/diction.htm
Plain language definitions of legal terms. Maintained by a private attorney.

Everybody's Law Dictionary
http://www.nolo.com/dictionary
A plain English law dictionary of hundreds of legal terms from Nolo Press.

International Law Dictionary
http://august1.com/pubs/dict
A good resource for international criminal and civil law definitions. Some with links to more information.

Jurist's Legal Dictionary
http://jurist.law.pitt.edu/dictionary.htm
A dictionary of basic U.S. legal terminology with a focus on legal procedure. The dictionary includes hyperlinks to relevant Web sites.

Law.com Dictionary
http://dictionary.law.com
A "real life dictionary of the law."

Merriam-Webster's Dictionary of the Law
http://dictionary.findlaw.com
A service of FindLaw.com.

Oran's Dictionary of the Law
http://www.wld.com/conbus/orans
A searchable legal dictionary.

Check the *Criminal Law Today* Web site for URLs that may have changed.

SUGGESTED READINGS AND CLASSIC WORKS

American Law Institute, *Model Penal Code and Commentaries* (Philadelphia: American Law Institute, 1985).

Lawrence M. Friedman, *A History of American Law* (New York: Simon and Schuster, 1973).

Jerome Hall, *General Principles of Criminal Law,* 2nd ed. (Indianapolis: Bobbs-Merrill, 1960).

Peter Murray, *Basic Trial Advocacy* (Boston: Little, Brown, 1995).

Herbert L. Packer, *The Limits of the Criminal Sanction* (Palo Alto, CA: Stanford University Press, 1968).

Dennis Patterson, *Law and Truth* (New York: Oxford University Press, 1996).

Rollin M. Perkins and Ronald N. Boyce, *Criminal Law,* 3rd ed. (Mineola, NY: Foundation Press, 1982).

Scott Turow, *Presumed Innocent* (New York: Farrar Straus Giroux, 1987).

CAN A STATUTE THAT DOES NOT CONTAIN A *MENS REA* REQUIREMENT BE CONSTITUTIONAL?

CAPSTONE CASE

People v. *Jensen*
Michigan Court of Appeals, 1998
No. 210655

Following a jury trial, defendant was convicted of three counts of knowing that she was HIV positive and engaging in sexual penetration without informing her partner of her HIV status, MCL 333.5210; MSA 14.15(5210). Thereafter, the trial court sentenced defendant to concurrent terms of two years and eight months to four years' imprisonment on each of the three counts. On appeal, this Court affirmed her convictions. *People v Jensen*, 222 Mich App 575; 564 NW2d 192 (1997). Defendant filed her application for leave to appeal with the Supreme Court. Pursuant to MCR 7.302(F)(1) and in lieu of granting leave, the Supreme Court entered the following order:

> We VACATE in part the judgment of the Court of Appeals and REMAND this case to the Court of Appeals for further consideration and decision on the merits of the question whether MCL 333.5210; MSA 14.15(5210) is constitutional. In all other respects, leave to appeal is DENIED, because the Court is not persuaded that the questions presented should be reviewed by this Court.

On remand, we find that the HIV notice statute is neither unconstitutionally overbroad nor violative of defendant's rights to privacy or against compelled speech.

I

Initially, we incorporate by reference the extended recitation of facts set forth in the original *Jensen, supra* at 577–579.

First, defendant asserts that MCL 333.5210; MSA 14.15(5210), which makes it a crime to fail to inform a sexual partner that one has AIDS or is HIV positive, is unconstitutionally overbroad because it (1) includes both consensual and nonconsensual sexual acts and (2) fails to require an intent to cause harm. We believe that defendant's constitutional challenges on these grounds fail.

A

MCL 333.5210; MSA 14.15(5210) states as follows:

> A person who knows that he or she has or has been diagnosed as having acquired immunodeficiency syndrome or acquired immunodeficiency syndrome related complex, or who knows that he or she is HIV infected, and who engages in sexual penetration with another person without having first informed the other person that he or she has acquired immunodeficiency syndrome or acquired immunodeficiency syndrome related complex or is HIV infected, is guilty of a felony.

As used in this section, "sexual penetration" means sexual intercourse, cunnilingus, fellatio, anal intercourse, or any other intrusion, however slight, of any part of a person's body or of any object into the genital or anal openings of another person's body, but emission of semen is not required. . . .

B

Defendant . . . argues that the statute is unconstitutional because it does not contain an intent, or *mens rea*, requirement. More specifically, defendant asserts that because the statute does not require a specific intent to harm, one who does not understand

or appreciate the consequences of his or her acts can be found criminally responsible. We disagree.

In light of defendant's repeated argument that mentally deficient individuals will be prosecuted under this statute, we reiterate and remind defendant that, even though the evidence in the instant case does not support this factual scenario, if a "person lacks substantial capacity either to appreciate the wrongfulness of his conduct or to conform his conduct to the requirements of the law," he or she will be found lacking in criminal responsibility under the legal insanity defense statute, MCL 768.21a(1); MSA 28.1044(1)(1).

With respect to defendant's *mens rea* argument, we note that fewer than half the states have criminal statutes penalizing the exposure of others to the HIV virus, and only a few of those contain an explicit *mens rea* requirement. See Idaho Code § 39-608 ("Any person who exposes another in any manner with the *intent to infect* or knowing that he or she is or has been afflicted with . . . [AIDS, ARC, or HIV] transfers or attempts to transfer any of his or her body fluid, body tissue or organs to another person is guilty of a felony"); Okla Stat title 21 § 1192.1 (it is unlawful for a person who knows he or she has AIDS or HIV "and with *intent to infect* another" to engage in sexual penetration with another where the other person did not consent to the penetration or had not been informed of the AIDS or HIV virus); ND Cent Code § 12.1-20-17 (a person with HIV or AIDS who "willfully transfers" any of that person's body fluid to another person is guilty of a felony unless the risk was fully disclosed and an "appropriate prophylactic device" was used). The others, including Michigan's statute, are silent on this topic except to require that the defendant know of his or her HIV or AIDS infection and fail to reveal it before donating blood, engaging in sexual penetration, or engaging a prostitute. Unfortunately, neither *Russell, supra,* nor any of the other states with similar statutes have resolved this *mens rea* dispute.

Notably, however, in *People* v. *Lardie,* 452 Mich 231, 256; 551 NW2d 656 (1996), our Supreme Court recently upheld the constitutionality of the statute that criminalizes causing death by operating a vehicle while intoxicated. The statute was challenged after the trial court held that it unconstitutionally precluded the jury from determining the defendant's mental state or intent, but this Court upheld the statute as creating a "strict liability, public welfare offense" without requiring the prosecutor to prove *mens rea. Lardie, supra,* at 235-236.

In upholding the constitutionality of this statute, our Supreme Court, *id.* at 239-241, 246, made the following observations:

> In order to determine whether a statute imposes strict liability or requires proof of a mens rea, *that is, guilty mind, this Court first examines the statute itself and seeks to determine the Legislature's intent.* People v Quinn, *440 Mich 178, 185; 487 NW2d 194 (1992). In interpreting a statute in which the Legislature has not expressly included language indicating that fault is a necessary element of a crime, this Court must focus on whether the Legislature nevertheless intended to require some fault as a predicate to finding guilt.* Id. *In this statute, the Legislature did not expressly state that a defendant must have a criminal intent to commit this crime.*
>
> Criminal intent is ordinarily an element of a crime even where the crime is created by statute. People v Rice, *161 Mich 657, 664; 126 NW 981 (1910). Statutes that create strict liability for all of their elements are not favored.* Quinn, supra *at 187. Nevertheless, a state may decide under its police power that certain acts or omissions are to be punished irrespective of the actor's intent.* Id. *at 186–187;* People v Hatinger, *174 Mich 333, 335; 140 NW 648 (1913). Many of the crimes that impose strict liability have been termed "public welfare regulation."* Quinn, supra *at 187; see also* Morissette v United States, *342 US 246, 255; 72 S Ct 240; 96 L Ed 288 (1952) (public-welfare offenses). . . .*
>
> Specific intent is defined as a particular criminal intent beyond the act done, whereas general intent is merely the intent to perform the physical act

itself. People *v* Beaudin, *417 Mich 570, 573–574; 339 NW2d 461 (1983);* People *v* Langworthy, *416 Mich 630, 639, 644; 331 NW2d 171 (1982). For a strict liability crime, the people need only prove that the act was performed regardless of what the actor knew or did not know.* Quinn, supra *at 188. On this basis, the distinction between a strict-liability crime and a general intent crime is that, for a general-intent crime, the people must prove that the defendant purposefully or voluntarily performed the wrongful act, whereas, for a strict-liability crime, the people merely need to prove that the defendant performed the wrongful act, irrespective of whether he intended to perform it. Under MCL 257.625(4); MSA 9.2325(4), the distinction is important only in the rare circumstances where a defendant was driving when he honestly did not know he had consumed alcohol, which subsequently caused him to be intoxicated, or where he was forced to drive for some reason despite his intoxication. . . . Where a statute is a codification of the common law and that common-law crime includes a* mens rea *as an element, this Court will interpret that statute to require a* mens rea *even if the statute is silent regarding knowledge as a necessary element. See* Quinn, supra *at 185–186.*

Where the offense in question does not codify the common law and omits reference to the element of intent, this Court will examine the Legislature's intent in enacting the legislation to determine whether there is a *mens rea* requirement. *Quinn, supra* at 196.

Our Supreme Court in *Lardie* concluded that the Legislature intended to eliminate the gross negligence requirement that attended common-law involuntary manslaughter, the crime with which intoxicated drivers who killed were charged before the statute was enacted. *Id.* at 250–251. Rather, the Legislature essentially presumed that voluntarily driving while one knows he or she could be intoxicated is gross negligence as a matter of law. *Id.* Nevertheless, the Court believed that the Legislature presumably intended to require proof of a criminal intent for the criminal act of intoxicated driving. *Id.* "[W]e conclude that the statute requires the people to prove that a defendant, who kills someone by driving while intoxicated, acted knowingly in consuming an intoxicating liquor or a controlled substance, and acted voluntarily in deciding to drive after such consumption." *Id.* at 256.

Applying the rationale of *Lardie* to the case at bar, we believe it likely that the Legislature intended to require some type of intent as a predicate to finding guilt under MCL 333.5210; MSA 14.15(5210), but that here the requisite intent is inherent in the HIV-infected person's socially and morally irresponsible actions. *Lardie, supra.* Moreover, the Legislature could reasonably have presumed that it is grossly negligent for an HIV-infected person to engage in *any* sexual penetration with another person without full disclosure of his or her HIV infection. What does nondisclosure achieve? Only further dissemination of a lethal, incurable disease in order to gratify the sexual or other physical pleasures of the already infected individual. Disclosure would permit the other person to either refuse sexual contact or consent with knowledge of the risks he or she is taking. We also believe that the Legislature's primary concern is stemming the spread of HIV and AIDS throughout the population (similar to curtailing people from voluntarily driving while under the influence, as in *Lardie, supra*). Failure to disclose not only places the unwitting participant but also that participant's other sexual partners at serious risk of premature death. Indeed, the probable results accompanying nondisclosure are fairly predictable: death to innocent third parties.

Moreover, in *Lardie, supra* at 264, 267, our Supreme Court also found that the death caused by intoxicated driving statute required a "causal relationship" between the defendant's culpable state of mind, i.e., intentionally driving while intoxicated, and the other person's resulting death. Here, the same causal connection exists despite the variety of methods by which one may contract AIDS or HIV or a myriad of other diseases that could end one's life. Knowingly engaging in sexual conduct capable of transmitting the AIDS virus or HIV without telling a partner

about one's HIV positive status, is the culpable state of mind that can cause the partner's resulting infection and eventual death. Accordingly, although the MCL 333.5210; MSA 14.15(5210) contains no express *mens rea* requirement, we presume that the Legislature intended to require that the prosecution prove that the defendant had a general intent to commit the wrongful act, i.e., to engage in sexual penetration with another person while withholding the defendant's positive AIDS or HIV status. See *Lardie, supra* at 267. Thus, the statute does not require strict liability because if the defendant explains his or her HIV status and the other person consents to the physical contact despite the risks associated with such contact, there is no criminal liability. Finally, the statute requires that the culpable mental state have a causal relationship to the harm that the statute seeks to prevent, *id.,* i.e., requiring disclosure of one's HIV status will reduce the unwitting spread of AIDS and HIV-related diseases. We therefore find that MCL 333.5210; MSA 14.15(5210) is not unconstitutionally infirm on the basis that it lacks an explicit *mens rea* requirement. . . .

II

We therefore affirm the constitutionality of MCL 333.5210; MSA 14.15(5210) and defendant's convictions pursuant to the statute.

WHAT DO *YOU* THINK?

1. What kinds of crimes require intent? Which do not?
2. What is the difference between specific intent and general intent? Is either concept relevant in this case? Why?
3. Why does the court find that the statute on which this case is based "does not require strict liability"?
4. Some people argue that the kind of law discussed in this case turns a personal status (being infected with the AIDS virus) into a crime. Do you agree or disagree? Why?
5. Do you agree with the court's ruling in this case? Why or why not?

CAPSTONE CASE

DOES A DEFENDANT WHO BELIEVES THAT THE FEDERAL INCOME TAX IS UNLAWFUL, AND THUS DOES NOT PAY HIS TAXES, WILLFULLY VIOLATE THE LAW?

Cheek v. *United States*
U.S. Supreme Court, 1991
498 U.S. 192

JUSTICE WHITE delivered the opinion of the Court.

Title 26, 7201 of the United States Code provides that any person "who willfully attempts in any manner to evade or defeat any tax imposed by this title or the payment thereof" shall be guilty of a felony. Under 26 U.S.C. 7203, "[a]ny person required under this title . . . or by regulations made under authority thereof to make a return . . . who willfully fails to . . . make such return" shall be guilty of a misdemeanor. This case turns on the meaning of the word "willfully" as used in 7201 and 7203.

I.

Petitioner John L. Cheek has been a pilot for American Airlines since 1973. He filed federal income tax returns through 1979, but thereafter ceased to file returns. He also claimed an increasing number of withholding allowances, eventually claiming 60 allowances by mid-1980—and for the years 1981 to 1984 indicated on his W-4 forms that he was exempt from federal income taxes. In 1983, petitioner unsuccessfully sought a refund of all tax withheld by his employer in 1982. Petitioner's income during this period at all times far exceeded the minimum necessary to trigger the statutory filing requirement.

As a result of his activities, petitioner was indicted for 10 violations of federal law. He was charged with six counts of willfully failing to file a federal income tax return for the years 1980, 1981, and 1983 through 1986, in violation of 26 U.S.C. 7203. He was further charged with three counts of willfully attempting to evade his income taxes for the years 1980, 1981, and 1983 in violation of 26 U.S.C. 7201. In those years, American Airlines withheld substantially less than the amount of tax petitioner owed because of the numerous allowances and exempt status he claimed on his W-4 forms. The tax offenses with which petitioner was charged are specific intent crimes that require the defendant to have acted willfully.

At trial, the evidence established that, between 1982 and 1986, petitioner was involved in at least four civil cases that challenged various aspects of the federal income tax system. In all four of those cases, the plaintiffs were informed by the courts that many of their arguments, including that they were not taxpayers within the meaning of the tax laws, that wages are not income, that the Sixteenth Amendment does not authorize the imposition of an income tax on individuals, and that the Sixteenth Amendment is unenforceable, were frivolous or had been repeatedly rejected by the courts. During this time period, petitioner also attended at least two criminal trials of persons charged with tax offenses. In addition, there was evidence that, in 1980 or 1981, an attorney had advised Cheek that the courts had rejected as frivolous the claim that wages are not income.

Cheek represented himself at trial and testified in his defense. He admitted that he had not filed personal income tax returns during the years in question. He testified that, as early as 1978, he had begun attending seminars sponsored by, and following the advice of, a group that believes, among other things, that the federal tax system is unconstitutional. Some of the speakers at these meetings were lawyers who purported to give professional opinions about the invalidity of the federal income tax laws. Cheek produced a letter from an attorney stating that the Sixteenth Amendment did not authorize a tax on wages and salaries, but only on gain or profit. Petitioner's defense was that, based on the indoctrination he received from this group and from his own study, he sincerely believed that the tax laws were being unconstitutionally enforced and that his actions during the 1980–1986 period were lawful. He therefore argued that he had acted without the willfulness required for conviction of the various offenses with which he was charged.

In the course of its instructions, the trial court advised the jury that, to prove "willfulness," the Government must prove the voluntary and intentional violation of a known legal duty, a burden that could not be proved by showing mistake, ignorance, or negligence. The court further advised the jury that an objectively reasonable good-faith misunderstanding of the law would negate willfulness, but mere disagreement with the law would not. The court described Cheek's beliefs about the income tax system, and instructed the jury that, if it found that Cheek "honestly and reasonably believed that he was not required to pay income taxes or to file tax returns," App. 81, a not guilty verdict should be returned.

After several hours of deliberation, the jury sent a note to the judge that stated in part: " 'We have a basic disagreement between some of us as to if Mr. Cheek honestly & reasonably believed that he was not required to pay income taxes. . . . [the relevant jury instruction] discusses good faith misunderstanding & disagreement. Is there any additional clarification you can give us on this point?' "

The District Judge responded with a supplemental instruction containing the following statements:

> "[A] person's opinion that the tax laws violate his constitutional rights does not constitute a good faith misunderstanding of the law. Furthermore, a

person's disagreement with the government's tax collection systems and policies does not constitute a good faith misunderstanding of the law."

At the end of the first day of deliberation, the jury sent out another note saying that it still could not reach a verdict because "[w]e are divided on the issue as to if Mr. Cheek honestly & reasonably believed that he was not required to pay income tax." When the jury resumed its deliberations, the District Judge gave the jury an additional instruction. This instruction stated in part that "[a]n honest but unreasonable belief is not a defense, and does not negate willfulness," and that "[a]dvice or research resulting in the conclusion that wages of a privately employed person are not income or that the tax laws are unconstitutional is not objectively reasonable, and cannot serve as the basis for a good faith misunderstanding of the law defense." The court also instructed the jury that "[p]ersistent refusal to acknowledge the law does not constitute a good faith misunderstanding of the law." Approximately two hours later, the jury returned a verdict finding petitioner guilty on all counts. Petitioner appealed his convictions, arguing that the District Court erred by instructing the jury that only an objectively reasonable misunderstanding of the law negates the statutory willfulness requirement. The United States Court of Appeals for the Seventh Circuit rejected that contention, and affirmed the convictions. 882 F.2d 1263 (1989). In prior cases, the Seventh Circuit had made clear that good-faith misunderstanding of the law negates willfulness only if the defendant's beliefs are objectively reasonable; in the Seventh Circuit, even actual ignorance is not a defense unless the defendant's ignorance was itself objectively reasonable. See, e.g., *United States* v. *Buckner*, 830 F.2d 102 (1987). In its opinion in this case, the court noted that several specified beliefs, including the beliefs that the tax laws are unconstitutional and that wages are not income, would not be objectively reasonable. Because the Seventh Circuit's interpretation of "willfully" as used in these statutes conflicts with the decisions of several other Courts of Appeals, see, e.g., *United States* v. *Whiteside*, 810 F.2d 1306, 1310–1311 (CA5 1987); *United States* v. *Phillips*, 775 F.2d 262, 263–264 (CA10 1985); *United States* v. *Aitken*, 755 F.2d 188, 191–193 (CA1 1985), we granted certiorari. . . .

II

The general rule that ignorance of the law or a mistake of law is no defense to criminal prosecution is deeply rooted in the American legal system. See, e.g., *United States* v. *Smith*, 5 Wheat. 153, 182 (1820) (Livingston, J., dissenting); *Barlow* v. *United States*, 7 Pet. 404, 411 (1833); *Reynolds* v. *United States*, 98 U.S. 145, 167 (1879); *Shevlin-Carpenter Co.* v. *Minnesota*, 218 U.S. 57, 68 (1910); *Lambert* v. *California*, 355 U.S. 225, 228 (1957); *Liparota* v. *United States*, 471 U.S. 419, 441 (1985) (WHITE, J., dissenting); O. Holmes, The Common Law 47–48 (1881). Based on the notion that the law is definite and knowable, the common law presumed that every person knew the law. This common law rule has been applied by the Court in numerous cases construing criminal statutes. See, e.g., *United States* v. *International Minerals & Chemical Corp.*, 402 U.S. 558 (1971); *Hamling* v. *United States*, 418 U.S. 87, 119–124 (1974); *Boyce Motor Lines, Inc.* v. *United States*, 342 U.S. 337 (1952).

The proliferation of statutes and regulations has sometimes made it difficult for the average citizen to know and comprehend the extent of the duties and obligations imposed by the tax laws. Congress has accordingly softened the impact of the common law presumption by making specific intent to violate the law an element of certain federal criminal tax offenses. Thus, the Court almost 60 years ago interpreted the statutory term "willfully" as used in the federal criminal tax statutes as carving out an exception to the traditional rule. This special treatment of criminal tax offenses is largely due to the complexity of the tax laws. In *United States* v. *Murdock*, 290 U.S. 389 (1933), the Court recognized that:

"Congress did not intend that a person, by reason of a bona fide misunder-standing as to his liability for the tax, as to his duty to make a return, or as to the adequacy of the records he maintained, should become a criminal by his mere failure to measure up to the prescribed standard of conduct."

The Court held that the defendant was entitled to an instruction with respect to whether he acted in good faith based on his actual belief. In *Murdock,* the Court interpreted the term "willfully" as used in the criminal tax statutes generally to mean "an act done with a bad purpose," or with "an evil motive."

Subsequent decisions have refined this proposition. In *United States* v. *Bishop,* we described the term "willfully" as connoting "a voluntary, intentional violation of a known legal duty," *id.,* at 360, and did so with specific reference to the "bad faith or evil intent" language employed in *Murdock.* Still later, *United States* v. *Pomponio* . . . addressed a situation in which several defendants had been charged with willfully filing false tax returns. The jury was given an instruction on willfulness similar to the standard set forth in *Bishop.* In addition, it was instructed that "[g]ood motive alone is never a defense where the act done or omitted is a crime." The defendants were convicted, but the Court of Appeals reversed, concluding that the latter instruction was improper because the statute required a finding of bad purpose or evil motive.

We reversed the Court of Appeals, stating that "the Court of Appeals incorrectly assumed that the reference to an 'evil motive' in *United States* v. *Bishop,* supra, and prior cases," *ibid.,* "requires proof of any motive other than an intentional violation of a known legal duty." As "the other Courts of Appeals that have considered the question have recognized, willfulness in this context simply means a voluntary, intentional violation of a known legal duty." We concluded that, after instructing the jury on willfulness, "[a]n additional instruction on good faith was unnecessary." Taken together, *Bishop* and *Pomponio* conclusively establish that the standard for the statutory willfulness requirement is the "voluntary, intentional violation of a known legal duty."

III

Cheek accepts the *Pomponio* definition of willfulness . . . , but asserts that the District Court's instructions and the Court of Appeals' opinion departed from that definition. In particular, he challenges the ruling that a good-faith misunderstanding of the law or a good-faith belief that one is not violating the law, if it is to negate willfulness, must be objectively reasonable. We agree that the Court of Appeals and the District Court erred in this respect.

A

Willfulness, as construed by our prior decisions in criminal tax cases, requires the Government to prove that the law imposed a duty on the defendant, that the defendant knew of this duty, and that he voluntarily and intentionally violated that duty. We deal first with the case where the issue is whether the defendant knew of the duty purportedly imposed by the provision of the statute or regulation he is accused of violating, a case in which there is no claim that the provision at issue is invalid. In such a case, if the Government proves actual knowledge of the pertinent legal duty, the prosecution, without more, has satisfied the knowledge component of the willfulness requirement. But carrying this burden requires negating a defendant's claim of ignorance of the law or a claim that, because of a misunderstanding of the law, he had a good-faith belief that he was not violating any of the provisions of the tax laws. This is so because one cannot be aware that the law imposes a duty upon him and yet be ignorant of it, misunderstand the law, or believe that the duty does not exist. In the end, the issue is whether, based on all the evidence, the Government has proved that the defendant was aware of the duty at issue, which cannot be true if the

jury credits a good-faith misunderstanding and belief submission, whether or not the claimed belief or misunderstanding is objectively reasonable.

In this case, if Cheek asserted that he truly believed that the Internal Revenue Code did not purport to treat wages as income, and the jury believed him, the Government would not have carried its burden to prove willfulness, however unreasonable a court might deem such a belief. Of course, in deciding whether to credit Cheek's good-faith belief claim, the jury would be free to consider any admissible evidence from any source showing that Cheek was aware of his duty to file a return and to treat wages as income, including evidence showing his awareness of the relevant provisions of the Code or regulations, of court decisions rejecting his interpretation of the tax law, of authoritative rulings of the Internal Revenue Service, or of any contents of the personal income tax return forms and accompanying instructions that made it plain that wages should be returned as income.

We thus disagree with the Court of Appeals' requirement that a claimed good-faith belief must be objectively reasonable if it is to be considered as possibly negating the Government's evidence purporting to show a defendant's awareness of the legal duty at issue. Knowledge and belief are characteristically questions for the factfinder, in this case the jury. Characterizing a particular belief as not objectively reasonable transforms the inquiry into a legal one, and would prevent the jury from considering it. It would of course be proper to exclude evidence having no relevance or probative value with respect to willfulness, but it is not contrary to common sense, let alone impossible, for a defendant to be ignorant of his duty based on an irrational belief that he has no duty, and forbidding the jury to consider evidence that might negate willfulness would raise a serious question under the Sixth Amendment's jury trial provision. Cf. *Francis* v. *Franklin,* U.S. 307 (1985); *Sandstrom* v. *Montana,* 442 U.S. 510 (1979); *Morissette* v. *United States,* 342 U.S. 246 (1952). It is common ground that this Court, where possible, interprets congressional enactments so as to avoid raising serious constitutional questions. . . .

It was therefore error to instruct the jury to disregard evidence of Cheek's understanding that, within the meaning of the tax laws, he was not a person required to file a return or to pay income taxes and that wages are not taxable income, as incredible as such misunderstandings of and beliefs about the law might be. Of course, the more unreasonable the asserted beliefs or misunderstandings are, the more likely the jury will consider them to be nothing more than simple disagreement with known legal duties imposed by the tax laws, and will find that the Government has carried its burden of proving knowledge.

B

Cheek asserted in the trial court that he should be acquitted because he believed in good faith that the income tax law is unconstitutional as applied to him, and thus could not legally impose any duty upon him of which he should have been aware. Such a submission is unsound, not because Cheek's constitutional arguments are not objectively reasonable or frivolous, which they surely are, but because the *Murdock-Pomponio* line of cases does not support such a position. Those cases construed the willfulness requirement in the criminal provisions of the Internal Revenue Code to require proof of knowledge of the law. This was because in "our complex tax system, uncertainty often arises even among taxpayers who earnestly wish to follow the law" and " '[i]t is not the purpose of the law to penalize frank difference of opinion or innocent errors made despite the exercise of reasonable care.' " *United States* v. *Bishop,* 412 U.S. 346, 360–361 (1973). . . .

Claims that some of the provisions of the tax code are unconstitutional are submissions of a different order. They do not arise from innocent mistakes caused by the complexity of the Internal Revenue Code. Rather, they reveal full knowledge of the provisions at issue and a studied conclusion, however wrong, that those provisions are invalid and unenforceable. Thus, in this case, Cheek paid his taxes for years, but after attending various seminars and based on his own study, he concluded that the income tax laws could not constitutionally require him to pay a tax.

We do not believe that Congress contemplated that such a taxpayer, without risking criminal prosecution, could ignore the duties imposed upon him by the Internal Revenue Code and refuse to utilize the mechanisms provided by Congress to present his claims of invalidity to the courts and to abide by their decisions. There is no doubt that Cheek, from year to year, was free to pay the tax that the law purported to require, file for a refund and, if denied, present his claims of invalidity, constitutional or otherwise, to the courts. See 26 U.S.C. 7422. Also, without paying the tax, he could have challenged claims of tax deficiencies in the Tax Court, 6213, with the right to appeal to a higher court if unsuccessful. 7482(a)(1). Cheek took neither course in some years, and, when he did, was unwilling to accept the outcome. As we see it, he is in no position to claim that his good-faith belief about the validity of the Internal Revenue Code negates willfulness or provides a defense to criminal prosecution under 7201 and 7203. Of course, Cheek was free in this very case to present his claims of invalidity and have them adjudicated, but, like defendants in criminal cases in other contexts who "willfully" refuse to comply with the duties placed upon them by the law, he must take the risk of being wrong.

We thus hold that, in a case like this, a defendant's views about the validity of the tax statutes are irrelevant to the issue of willfulness, need not be heard by the jury, and if they are, an instruction to disregard them would be proper. For this purpose, it makes no difference whether the claims of invalidity are frivolous or have substance. It was therefore not error in this case for the District Judge to instruct the jury not to consider Cheek's claims that the tax laws were unconstitutional. However, it was error for the court to instruct the jury that petitioner's asserted beliefs that wages are not income and that he was not a taxpayer within the meaning of the Internal Revenue Code should not be considered by the jury in determining whether Cheek had acted willfully.

IV

For the reasons set forth in the opinion above, the judgment of the Court of Appeals is vacated, and the case is remanded for further proceedings consistent with this opinion. It is so ordered.

JUSTICE SOUTER took no part in the consideration or decision of this case.

JUSTICE SCALIA, concurring in the judgment.
I concur in the judgment of Court because our cases have consistently held that the failure to pay a tax in the good-faith belief that it is not legally owing is not "willful." I do not join the Court's opinion because I do not agree with the test for willfulness that it directs the Court of Appeals to apply on remand.

As the Court acknowledges, our opinions from the 1930s to the 1970s have interpreted the word "willfully" in the criminal tax statutes as requiring the "bad purpose" or "evil motive" of "intentional[ly] violat[ing] a known legal duty." See, e.g., *United States* v. *Pomponio*, 429 U.S. 10, 12 (1976); *United States* v. *Murdock*, 290 U.S. 389, 394–395 (1933). It seems to me that today's opinion squarely reverses that long-established statutory construction when it says that a good-faith erroneous belief in the unconstitutionality of a tax law is no defense. It is quite impossible to say that a statute which one believes unconstitutional represents a "known legal duty." See *Marbury* v. *Madison*, 1 Cranch 137, 91 Cranch 177–178 (1803).

Although the facts of the present case involve erroneous reliance upon the Constitution in ignoring the otherwise "known legal duty" imposed by the tax statutes, the Court's new interpretation applies also to erroneous reliance upon a tax statute

in ignoring the otherwise "known legal duty" of a regulation, and to erroneous reliance upon a regulation in ignoring the otherwise "known legal duty" of a tax assessment. These situations as well meet the opinion's crucial test of "reveal[ing] full knowledge of the provisions at issue and a studied conclusion, however wrong, that those provisions are invalid and unenforceable," ante, at 205-206. There is, moreover, no rational basis for saying that a "willful" violation is established by full knowledge of a statutory requirement, but is not established by full knowledge of a requirement explicitly imposed by regulation or order. Thus, today's opinion works a revolution in past practice, subjecting to criminal penalties taxpayers who do not comply with Treasury Regulations that are in their view contrary to the Internal Revenue Code, Treasury Rulings that are in their view contrary to the regulations, and even IRS auditor pronouncements that are in their view contrary to Treasury Rulings. The law already provides considerable incentive for taxpayers to be careful in ignoring any official assertion of tax liability, since it contains civil penalties that apply even in the event of a good-faith mistake, see, e.g., 26 U.S.C. 6651, 6653. To impose in addition criminal penalties for misinterpretation of such a complex body of law is a startling innovation indeed.

I find it impossible to understand how one can derive from the lonesome word "willfully" the proposition that belief in the nonexistence of a textual prohibition excuses liability, but belief in the invalidity (i.e., the legal nonexistence) of a textual prohibition does not. One may say, as the law does in many contexts, that "willfully" refers to consciousness of the act, but not to consciousness that the act is unlawful. See, e.g., *American Surety Co. of New York* v. *Sullivan*, 7 F.2d 605, 606 (CA2 1925) (L. Hand, J.); cf. *United States* v. *International Minerals and Chemical Co.*, 402 U.S. 558, 563-565 (1971). Or alternatively, one may say, as we have said until today with respect to the tax statutes, that "willfully" refers to consciousness of both the act and its illegality. But it seems to me impossible to say that the word refers to consciousness that some legal text exists, without consciousness that that legal text is binding, i.e., with the good-faith belief that it is not a valid law. Perhaps such a test for criminal liability would make sense (though in a field as complicated as federal tax law, I doubt it), but some text other than the mere word "willfully" would have to be employed to describe it—and that text is not ours to write.

Because today's opinion abandons clear and long-standing precedent to impose criminal liability where taxpayers have had no reason to expect it, because the new contours of criminal liability have no basis in the statutory text, and because I strongly suspect that those new contours make no sense even as a policy matter, I concur only in the judgment of the Court.

JUSTICE BLACKMUN, with whom JUSTICE MARSHALL joins, dissenting.

It seems to me that we are concerned in this case not with "the complexity of the tax laws," but with the income tax law in its most elementary and basic aspect: Is a wage earner a taxpayer and are wages income?

The Court acknowledges that the conclusively established standard for willfulness under the applicable statutes is the "voluntary, intentional violation of a known legal duty." See *United States* v. *Bishop*, 412 U.S. 346, 360 (1963), and *United States* v. *Pomponio*, 429 U.S. 10, 12 (1976). That being so, it is incomprehensible to me how, in this day, more than 70 years after the institution of our present federal income tax system with the passage of the Revenue Act of 1913, 38 Stat. 166, any taxpayer of competent mentality can assert as his defense to charges of statutory willfulness the proposition that the wage he receives for his labor is not income, irrespective of a cult that says otherwise and advises the gullible to resist income tax collections. One might note in passing that this particular taxpayer, after all, was a licensed pilot for one of our major commercial airlines; he presumably was a person of at least minimum intellectual competence.

The District Court's instruction that an objectively reasonable and good-faith misunderstanding of the law negates willfulness lends further, rather than less, protection to this defendant, for it added an additional hurdle for the prosecution to overcome. Petitioner should be grateful for this further protection, rather than be opposed to it.

This Court's opinion today, I fear, will encourage taxpayers to cling to frivolous views of the law in the hope of convincing a jury of their sincerity. . . . While I may not agree with every word the Court of Appeals has enunciated in its opinion, I would affirm its judgment in this case. I therefore dissent.

WHAT DO *YOU* THINK?

1. What does the term "willfully" mean to you? Does this decision change your views as to the meaning of the term?
2. Which opinion—majority, concurring, or dissenting—do you agree with? Why?
3. Why does Justice Blackmun think that this decision will encourage taxpayers to cling to frivolous views of the law?

MUST A DEFENDANT KNOW A CONTROLLED SUBSTANCE'S WEIGHT IN ORDER TO BE CONVICTED UNDER A STATE LAW THAT GRADES THE OFFENSE OF DRUG POSSESSION BY BOTH TYPE OF SUBSTANCE AND WEIGHT?

CAPSTONE CASE

People v. *Ryan*
Supreme Court of New York, 1993
82 N.Y.2d 497, 626 N.E.2d 51, 605 N.Y.S.2d 235

OPINION

Penal Law § 220.18(5) makes it a felony to "knowingly and unlawfully possess . . . six hundred twenty-five milligrams of a hallucinogen." The question of statutory interpretation before us is whether "knowingly" applies to the weight of the controlled substance. We conclude that it does and that the trial evidence was insufficient to satisfy that mental culpability element. . . .

Viewed in a light most favorable to the People (*People* v. *Contes,* 60 NY2d 620, 621), the trial evidence revealed that on October 2, 1990, defendant asked his friend David Hopkins to order and receive a shipment of hallucinogenic mushrooms on his behalf. Hopkins agreed and, adhering to defendant's instructions, placed a call to their mutual friend Scott in San Francisco and requested the "usual shipment." Tipped off to the transaction, on October 5, State Police Investigator Douglas Vredenburgh located the package at a Federal Express warehouse in Binghamton. The package was opened (pursuant to a search warrant) and resealed after its contents were verified. The investigator then borrowed a Federal Express uniform and van and delivered the package to Hopkins, the addressee, who was arrested upon signing for it.

Hopkins explained that the package was for defendant and agreed to participate in a supervised delivery to him. In a telephone call recorded by the police, Hopkins notified defendant that he got the package, reporting a "shit load of mushrooms in there." Defendant responded, "I know, don't say nothing." At another point Hopkins referred to the shipment as containing two pounds. The men agreed to meet later that evening at the firehouse in West Oneonta.

At the meeting, after a brief conversation, Hopkins handed defendant a substitute package stuffed with newspaper. Moments after taking possession, defendant was arrested. He was later indicted for attempted criminal possession of a controlled substance in the second degree. . . .

The case proceeded to trial, where the evidence summarized above was adduced. Additionally, the police chemist testified that the total weight of the mushrooms in Hopkins' package was 932.8 grams (about two pounds), and that a 140-gram sample of the package contents contained 796 milligrams of psilocybin, a hallucinogen. . . . He did not know, however, the process by which psilocybin appears in mushrooms, whether naturally, by injection, or some other means. Nor was there any evidence as to how much psilocybin would typically appear in two pounds of mushrooms.

At the close of the People's case, defendant moved to dismiss for insufficient proof that he knew the level of psilocybin in the mushrooms, and also requested a chargedown to seventh degree attempted criminal possession, which has no weight element. Both applications were denied, defendant was convicted as charged, and he was sentenced as a second felony offender to ten-years-to-life.

The Appellate Division affirmed. The court held that a defendant must know the nature of the substance possessed and acknowledged that the weight of the controlled substance is an element of the crime. The court declined, however, to read the statute as requiring that a defendant have actual knowledge of the weight. Instead, the court held that "the term 'knowingly' should be construed to refer only to the element of possession and not the weight requirement. . . ."

Finding ample evidence that defendant intended and attempted to possess psilocybin while knowing the nature of the substance, and that the weight of the psilocybin ultimately proved to be more than 625 milligrams, the Appellate Division sustained the conviction. Similarly, because there was no reasonable view of the evidence that the weight of the psilocybin in the mushrooms was less than 625 milligrams, the court rejected the argument that the trial court erred in refusing the charge-down.

We now reverse.

Although the present case involves an attempt, analysis begins with the elements of the completed crime, second-degree criminal possession of a controlled substance. Penal Law § 220.18(5) provides:

> *A person is guilty of criminal possession of a controlled substance in the second degree when he knowingly and unlawfully possesses . . . six hundred twenty-five milligrams of a hallucinogen.*

It is undisputed that the knowledge requirement of the statute applies to the element of possession . . . , and that defendant must also have "actual knowledge of the nature of the possessed substance" (*People* v. *Reisman,* 29 NY2d 278, 285). At issue is whether defendant must similarly know the weight of the material possessed. That is a question of statutory interpretation, as to which the Court's role is clear: our purpose is not to pass on the wisdom of the statute or any of its requirements, but rather to implement the will of the Legislature as expressed in its enactment.

In effectuating legislative intent, we look first of course to the statutory language. Read in context, it seems evident that "knowingly" does apply to the weight element. Indeed, given that a defendant's awareness must extend not only to the fact of possessing something ("knowingly . . . possesses") but also to the nature of the material possessed ("knowingly . . . possesses . . . a hallucinogen"), any other reading would be strained. Inasmuch as the knowledge requirement carries through to the end of the sentence (see *People* v. *Reisman,* 29 NY2d at 285), eliminating it from the intervening element—weight—would rob the statute of its obvious meaning. We conclude, therefore, that there is a *mens rea* element associated with the weight of the drug.

That reading is fortified by two rules of construction ordained by the Legislature itself. First, a "statute defining a crime, unless clearly indicating a legislative intent to impose strict liability, should be construed as defining a crime of mental culpability" (Penal Law § 15.15[2]). If any material element of an offense lacks a *mens rea* requirement, it is a strict liability crime (Penal Law § 15.10). Conversely, a crime is one of "mental culpability" only when a mental state "is required with respect to every material element of an offense" (*id.*).

By ruling that a defendant need not have knowledge of the weight, the Appellate Division in effect held, to that extent, that second-degree criminal possession is a strict liability crime (see Penal Law § 15.10). That is an erroneous statutory construction unless a legislative intent to achieve that result is "clearly indicat[ed]" (Penal Law § 15.15[2]).

In a similar vein, the Legislature has provided in Penal Law §15.15(1):

> *Construction of statutes with respect to culpability requirements.*
> *1. When the commission of an offense defined in this chapter, or some element of an offense, requires a particular culpable mental state, such mental state is ordinarily designated in the statute defining the offense by use of the terms "intentionally," "knowingly," "recklessly" or "criminal negligence," or by use of terms, such as "with intent to defraud" and "knowing it to be false," describing a specific kind of intent or knowledge. When one and only one of such terms appears in a statute defining an offense, it is presumed to apply to every element of the offense unless an intent to limit its application clearly appears.*

Accordingly, if a single *mens rea* is set forth, as here, it presumptively applies to all elements of the offense unless a contrary legislative intent is plain.

We discern no "clear" legislative intent to make the weight of a drug a strict liability element, as is required before we can construe the statute in that manner (Penal Law §§ 15.15 [1], [2]). Moreover, the overall structure of the drug possession laws supports the view that a defendant must have some knowledge of the weight.

There are six degrees of criminal possession of a controlled substance, graded in severity from a class A misdemeanor (Penal Law § 220.06 [seventh degree]) up to an A-I felony (Penal Law § 220.21 [first degree]). The definition of each begins identically: "A person is guilty of criminal possession of a controlled substance in the _____ degree when he knowingly and unlawfully possesses. . . ." The primary distinctions between one grade or another relate to the type and weight of the controlled substance and, in some instances, the existence of an intent to sell (e.g., Penal Law § 220.16[1]) or intent to sell combined with a prior drug conviction (e.g., Penal Law § 220.09[13]).

Taking hallucinogens as an example, knowing and unlawful possession of any amount, even a trace (see *People v. Mizell*, 72 NY2d 651, 655) is seventh-degree possession (Penal Law § 220.03); 25 milligrams or more, fourth-degree (Penal Law § 220.09[6]); 125 milligrams or more, third-degree (Penal Law § 220.16[10]; and 625 milligrams, second-degree (Penal Law § 220.18[5]). The maximum penalty for these crimes ranges from one year's incarceration to a life sentence, yet the only statutory difference relates to the weight of the drugs. To ascribe to the Legislature an intent to mete out drastic differences in punishment without a basis in culpability would be inconsistent with notions of individual responsibility and proportionality prevailing in the Penal Law (see, e.g., Penal Law 1.05[4]). . . .

In sum, the plain language of the statute, rules of construction, the format of the drug possession laws, and our cases all lead to the conclusion that the Appellate Division erred in holding that there is no *mens rea* requirement associated with the weight of a controlled substance. . . .

With the foregoing principles in mind, we consider whether there was sufficient evidence to convict defendant of attempted second-degree possession, an A-II felony.

Certainly there was sufficient evidence from which the jury could conclude, beyond a reasonable doubt, that defendant attempted and intended to possess a two-pound box of hallucinogenic mushrooms. It is also undisputed that, upon testing, the mushrooms in the particular box defendant attempted to possess—the one sent to Hopkins by Scott—contained more than 650 milligrams of psilocybin. The issue we must decide, however, is whether sufficient evidence was presented at trial from

which it could be inferred that defendant had the requisite knowledge of the weight. We disagree with the People's suggestion that the evidence of defendant's knowing attempt to possess two pounds of mushrooms, without more, could satisfy their burden of proof. The controlled substance here is psilocybin; had defendant ordered a specific quantity of that drug, plainly that would satisfy the knowledge element. But defendant attempted to possess two pounds of mushrooms, only a small portion of which was pure psilocybin.

Although in these circumstances defendant could properly be convicted of attempting to possess the amount of psilocybin that would typically appear in two pounds of hallucinogenic mushrooms, there was no evidence linking psilocybin weight to mushroom weight. Indeed, there was no evidence indicating whether psilocybin grows naturally or is injected into the mushrooms, or of the usual dose of the drug—matters not within the ken of the typical juror. We thus conclude on this record that there was insufficient evidence to satisfy the knowledge requirement within the meaning of the statute.

That deficiency does not absolve defendant of all criminal liability. There is sufficient evidence to sustain a conviction for the lesser-included offense of attempted criminal possession of a controlled substance in the seventh degree (Penal Law § 220.03), which does not have a weight element. . . .

Accordingly, the order of the Appellate Division should be reversed and the indictment dismissed with leave to the People to institute such proceedings as they deem appropriate respecting the lesser-included offense of attempted criminal possession of a controlled substance in the seventh degree.

WHAT DO *YOU* THINK?

1. Do you agree with the New York court that a defendant must *know* the weight of a controlled substance in order to be guilty of possession of such a substance under New York law?
2. Generally speaking, do people dealing in controlled substances "know" how much of the controlled substance is in their possession?
3. If you were a New York state legislator, would you feel the need to rewrite the state's law on possession of controlled substances? If so, how might you reword it?

NOTES

1. See Howard Abadinsky, *Law and Justice* (Chicago: Nelson Hall, 1988), p. 21.
2. Patrick L. McCloskey and Ronald L. Schoenberg, *Criminal Law Deskbook* (New York: Matthew Bender, 1988), p. 1–1.
3. Peter Murray, *Basic Trial Advocacy* (Boston: Little, Brown, 1995), p. 20.
4. David Stout, "Defense Lawyer Pleads Guilty to Aiding Colombian Drug Smugglers," *The New York Times,* July 14, 1995.
5. *Victor* v. *Nebraska*, 114 S. Ct. 1239, 127 L. Ed. 2d 583 (1994).
6. As found in California Jury Instructions.
7. *In re Winship*, 397 U.S. 358 (1970).
8. Although the main thrust of *Winship* was in the area of the rights of juveniles facing adjudication by the juvenile court, the case has been held applicable to adult defendants facing criminal prosecution as well. See, for example, *Victor* v. *Nebraska*, 511 U.S. 1 (1994).
9. Ibid.
10. Committee on Psychiatry and Law, Group for the Advancement of Psychiatry, *The Mental Health Professional and the Legal System* (Washington, D.C.: American Psychiatric Press, 1992).

11. Oklahoma Uniform Jury Instructions—Civil, No. 3.2 (2nd ed., 1993).

12. Common law crimes, of course, are not based on statutory elements.

13. Arizona Revised Statutes, Title 13, Section 105.

14. Wayne R. LaFave and Austin W. Scott, Jr., *Criminal Law* (St. Paul, MN: West Publishing Co., 1986).

15. Recent studies, however, which appear to demonstrate the efficacy of prayer, and certain "New Age" and Eastern beliefs in "thought manifestation" are not subsumed under this principle.

16. Indiana Code, Title 35, Article 41, Chapter 2, Section 1.

17. Texas Penal Code, Title 2, Section 6.01.

18. The woman, Barbara Woods, was also stabbed.

19. "Sleepwalker Acquitted in Mother-in-Law Slaying," *San Francisco Examiner*, May 28, 1988, p. 1.

20. Matt Kelley, "Jury Convicts Husband in Sleepwalking Murder Trial," Associated Press online, June 27, 1999. Posted at http://www.trib.com/HOME-NEWS/WASH/SleepwalkTrial.html.

21. Texas Penal Code, Title 2, Section 6.01.

22. Arizona Revised Statutes, Title 13, Section 105, paragraphs 30 and 31.

23. For additional information see Fred Bayles, "Spiritual Healing," Associated Press online, November 27, 1993.

24. The Boston-based church is officially known as "The First Church of Christ, Scientist."

25. The free speech clause of the First Amendment may allow one to say that the president deserves to die. But to actually threaten the president is an offense under Title 18, Chapter 41, Section 871, of the federal criminal code.

26. *Gordon* v. *State*, 52 Ala. 3008, 23 Am. Rep. 575 (1875).

27. Texas Penal Code, Title 2, Section 6.02.

28. Oliver Wendell Holmes, *The Common Law*, Vol. 3 (1881).

29. But not for more serious degrees of homicide, since leaving a young child alone in a tub of water, even if intentional, does not necessarily mean that the person who so acts intends the child to drown.

30. All Arizona definitions in this section are taken from Arizona Revised Statutes, Title 13, Section 105.

31. Italics added.

32. Gregory Tejeda, "Supreme Court Backs State Law Making Knowing HIV Transmission a Crime," United Press online, January 20, 1994.

33. Model Penal Code, Part I, Article 2, Section 2.02 (4).

34. There is disagreement, however, among jurists as to whether or not the crime of statutory rape is a strict liability offense. Some jurisdictions treat it as such, and will not accept a reasonable mistake about the victim's age. Others, however, do accept such a mistake as a defense.

35. California Penal Code, Part 1, Title 9, Chapter 1, Section 261.5.

36. *State* v. *Stiffler*, 763 P.2d 308 (Idaho App. 1988).

37. *People* v. *Hernandez*, 393 P.2d 673 (Cal. 1964).

38. *U.S.* v. *Greenbaum*, 138 F.2d 437 (3d Cir. 1943).

39. *Missouri* v. *Hatton*, No. 78277 (consolidated with) *Missouri* v. *Richard Troy, Jr.*, No. 78278 (Missouri Supreme Court cases).

40. California Penal Code, Preliminary Provisions, Section 20.

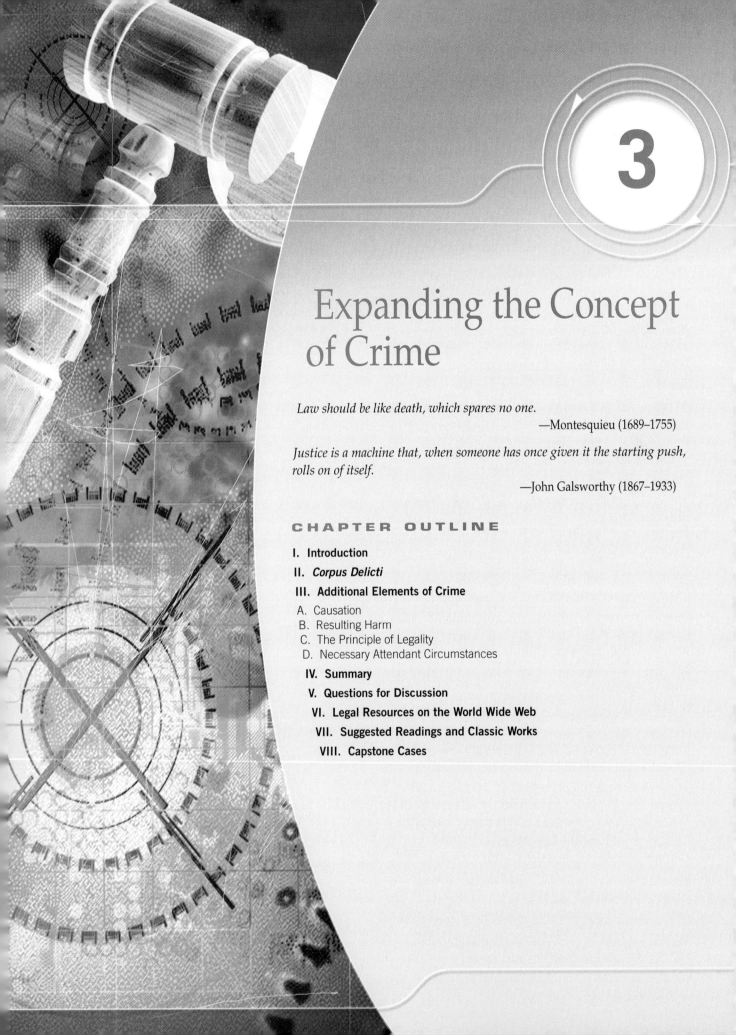

Expanding the Concept of Crime

Law should be like death, which spares no one.

—Montesquieu (1689–1755)

Justice is a machine that, when someone has once given it the starting push, rolls on of itself.

—John Galsworthy (1867–1933)

CHAPTER OUTLINE

AFTER READING THIS CHAPTER YOU SHOULD:

▷ Understand the *corpus delicti* of a crime.

▷ Be familiar with the idea of legal cause.

▷ Be able to describe the various kinds of causation.

▷ Be able to explain the principle of legality.

▷ Be able to describe the nature of "victimless crimes" and explain the harms they produce.

INTRODUCTION

On March 30, 1992, David Smith's double-wide mobile home in Orangeburg County (South Carolina) suffered damage from a fire. Investigators determined the fire started in the kitchen and was the result of cooking oil igniting after being heated in a deep-fat fryer for at least an hour. Although no accelerant was discovered, investigators found evidence that the house had been "sterilized" prior to the fire. Outside the trailer, a trash can filled with children's toys was found. In a pump house adjacent to the trailer, personal items were discovered in two suitcases, one bearing an identification tag with David Smith's name on it. The items included photo albums, love notes, costume jewelry, and "sex toys." Moreover, the back door—a sliding glass door—was open three inches. One investigator opined that the door had been left open to provide an oxygen supply that would facilitate the burning of the fire.

Before the trial, defense counsel moved the trial court to conduct an evidentiary hearing out of the presence of the jury for the purpose of determining whether sufficient evidence of the ***corpus delicti*** existed to proceed to trial. Counsel argued that "the government must establish the incendiary nature of the fire before it can get into the issue of statements or admissions." The trial court agreed and conducted a hearing at which two arson investigators testified. At the conclusion of the hearing, the trial court held that: "In order for the State to establish *corpus delicti* in this case, it must provide evidence that the burning was by a wilful act and not a result of natural or accidental causes. There has been no testimony whatsoever to suggest that this fire was the result of a wilful act; that any criminal agency was involved whatsoever; that these defendants had any connection whatsoever with the fire that resulted. . . . There was no testimony that would even support the theory of circumstantial evidence, wherein if employed it would have to exclude every other reasonable hypothesis, except point toward the guilt of these defendants."

The trial court then dismissed the arson charges against all three defendants.

CORPUS DELICTI
the "body of crime." Facts which show that a crime has occurred.

An arson fire in progress. The corpus delicti of the crime of arson requires a showing of (1) an illegal burning, (2) willfully caused, (3) by a person. (Photo by Scott Weersing/ The Enterprise, courtesy of Liaison Agency, Inc.)

CORPUS DELICTI

These chapter-opening paragraphs are taken from the 1996 South Carolina appellate case of *State* v. *Williams*.[1] They highlight the importance of ***corpus delicti*** in the judicial process and give some insight into the nature of the concept itself.

The term "*corpus delicti*" literally means "body of crime." The term is often confused with statutory elements of a crime (which will be discussed in future chapters) or taken literally to mean the body of a murder victim or some other physical results of criminal activity. The concept actually means something quite different. One way to understand the concept of *corpus delicti* is to realize that a person cannot be tried for a crime unless it can first be shown that the offense has occurred. In other words, to establish the *corpus delicti* of a crime, the state has to demonstrate that a criminal law has been violated and that someone violated it. Hence, there are only two components of the *corpus delicti* of an offense: (1) that a certain result has been produced, and (2) that a person is criminally responsible. As one court said, "[c]orpus delicti consists of a showing of: (1) the occurrence of the specific kind of injury and (2) someone's criminal act as the cause of the injury."[2] So, for example, the crime of larceny requires proof that the property of another has been stolen—that is, taken unlawfully with the intent to permanently deprive the owner of its possession.[3] Hence, evidence offered to prove the *corpus delicti* in a trial for larceny is insufficient when the evidence fails to prove that property has been stolen from another, or when property found in the accused's possession cannot be identified as having been stolen. Similarly, "[i]n an arson case, the *corpus delicti* consists of (1) a burned building or other property, and (2) some criminal agency which caused the burning. . . . In other words, the *corpus delicti* includes not only the fact of burning, but it must also appear that the burning was by the wilful act of some person, and not as a result of a natural or accidental cause. . . ."[4]

Another court described the concept this way: "The rule in criminal cases is that the coincidence of circumstances tending to indicate guilt, however strong and numerous they may be, avails nothing unless the *corpus delicti*, the fact that the crime has been actually perpetrated, be first established. So long as the least doubt exists

A trial is still an ordeal by battle. For the broadsword there is the weight of evidence; for the battle-ax, the force of logic; for the sharp spear, the blazing gleam of truth; for the rapier, the quick and flashing knife of wit.

—Lloyd Paul Stryker

as to the act there can be no certainty as to the criminal agent."[5] As a general rule, *corpus delicti* must be established beyond a reasonable doubt.

Here's how one court, in a pocket-picking case, explained the central role played by *corpus delicti:* "We conclude that the government failed to prove beyond a reasonable doubt that Zanders and Harris took the wallets from the immediate actual possession of Dr. Sokolov and Mr. Routson, or from their persons, or that a pickpocketing even took place. There was no direct evidence that Zanders and Harris took the wallets, and no expert testimony as to the methods used by pickpockets to remove wallets from the clothing of individuals, or the amount of force necessary to pick a pocket. Hence, there was neither direct nor indirect evidence of a taking of property from Dr. Sokolov or Mr. Routson by anyone, much less by Zanders or Harris. . . . The evidence presented is just as consistent, at least on a reasonable doubt standard, with both victims having lost their wallets and the defendants having found them and having used the credit cards without authority. In short, the government failed to establish the *corpus delicti* of the offense of robbery. In other words, the government failed to show, that the victims were dispossessed of their wallets by some person or persons by stealth or other means."[6]

We might add to the requirement to establish the *corpus delicti* of a crime before a successful prosecution can occur, the identity of the perpetrator is not an element of the *corpus delicti* of an offense. Hence, the fact that a crime has occurred can be established without one's having any sense of who committed it. In a Montana case this principle was clearly enunciated by the Montana Supreme Court when it said that "the identity of the perpetrator is not an element of the *corpus delicti.* In *State* v. *Kindle* (1924) . . . we stated that '[i]n a prosecution for murder, proof of the *corpus delicti* does not necessarily carry with it the identity of the slain nor of the slayer' . . . The essential elements of the *corpus delicti* are . . . establishing the death and the fact that the death was caused by a criminal agency, nothing more."[7]

Confessions present an especially thorny area when the *corpus delicti* of a crime cannot be independently established. Generally speaking, the **corpus delicti** rule holds that a criminal conviction cannot be based solely on the uncorroborated confession or admission of the accused. As one court explains it: "It is a settled principle of law that a mere extrajudicial confession, uncorroborated by other facts, is insufficient to show the *corpus delicti* and cannot support a conviction." A person may, for example, confess to a crime—but if there is no independent evidence showing that such a crime has even taken place, the individual making the confession can't be prosecuted. If a person confesses to a murder, but the supposed murder victim is found alive and in good health, no charge of murder can be brought. The problem of demonstrating the *corpus delicti* of a crime is more difficult when a person confesses to murder, but the murder victim's remains cannot be found. Most states do not permit a confession to stand alone as the basis of a criminal charge, without independent corroborating evidence. As the Indiana Supreme Court held: "A defendant's extrajudicial confession may be introduced into evidence only if the State establishes the *corpus delicti* of the crime by independent evidence.[8] . . . This rule is designed to 'reduce the risk of convicting a defendant based on his confession for a crime that did not occur,' prevent coercive interrogation tactics, and encourage thorough criminal investigations."[9] A Texas court put it this way: "The wisdom of this rule lies in the fact that no man should be convicted of a crime, the commission of which he confesses, unless the state shows, by testimony other than the accused's confession, that the confessed crime was in fact committed."[10]

A determination of the *corpus delicti* of a crime is important for another reason: a crime will generally be prosecuted in the location where it was committed; that is, where the *corpus delicti* of the crime exists. Following this principle, the Wyoming Constitution,[11] for example, provides in part: "When the location of the offense cannot be established with certainty, venue may be placed in the county or district where the *corpus delicti* is found. . . ."

CORPUS DELICTI RULE
a principle of law that says that an out-of-court confession, unsupported by other facts, is insufficient to support a criminal conviction.

Life and liberty can be as much endangered from illegal methods used to convict those thought to be criminals as from the actual criminals themselves.

—Chief Justice Earl Warren, writing for the majority
Spano v. *New York*, 360 U.S. 315 (1959)

Finally, federal courts and a few state courts have abandoned the requirement of establishing the *corpus delicti* of a crime because doing so is not always possible. Attempted crimes, some high-technology crimes, conspiracies, and crimes like income tax evasion make the *corpus delicti* requirement difficult, if not impossible, to meet.

ADDITIONAL ELEMENTS OF CRIME

Web Extra! 3–1

Britannica online: elements of crime

Many scholars contend that the three features of crime (which we outlined in the last chapter), *actus reus, mens rea,* and concurrence, are sufficient to describe the essence of the legal concept of crime. Other scholars, however, see modern Western law as more complex. They argue that consideration of four additional principles is necessary to fully appreciate contemporary understandings of crime. As mentioned earlier, these principles include: (1) causation, (2) a resulting harm, (3) the principle of legality, and (4) necessary attendant circumstances. Each of these is discussed in the pages that follow.

Causation

Causation refers to the fact that the concurrence of a guilty mind and a criminal act must produce or *cause* harm. While some statutes criminalize only conduct, others subsume the notion of concurrence under causality and specify that a causal relationship is a necessary element of a given crime. They require that the offender *cause* a particular result before criminal liability can be incurred. In wording reflective of the Model Penal Code, for example, the Texas Penal Code definition of homicide says: "A person commits criminal homicide if he intentionally, knowingly, recklessly, or with criminal negligence causes the death of an individual."[12] If there is no death of a human being *caused* by another person, the statute cannot apply.

While the Texas statute seems clear enough, the word *causes* may be open to a number of interpretations. Does a person, for example, cause the death of another if he or she fires a weapon at someone intending to kill them, but misses and the targeted person drops dead from fright? Does a person cause the death of another if he or she shoots them, but they die six months later in the hospital from pneumonia—never having fully recovered from the gunshot wound? Does a person cause the death of another if he or she contracts with a witch doctor to curse that individual, and that individual soon dies in an accident or from disease?

When discussing a specific ultimate harm, such as "death," which is referred to in homicide statutes, it is necessary to recognize the difference between **causation in fact** and **proximate cause.** If there is an actual link between the actor's conduct and the resulting harm, causation in fact exists. Even so, a cause in fact cannot be said to be the sole cause, or even the primary cause, of a particular event. If a person fires a gun, for example, and the bullet strikes a building, causing it to ricochet and hit a person standing next to the shooter, it can be said that the person who fired the weapon shot the bystander, or at the very least, *caused* him to be shot. In this case, other causes clearly contributed to the event, including the presence and movements of the bystander who was struck, the choices made by the designers of the building as to which materials to use and how to position the structure when it was built, and perhaps even weather conditions (a gust of wind or a particular barometric pressure may have affected the course of the bullet). Each of these features of the event may be said to be causes in fact, for without each being present the harm in question would not have occurred.

CAUSATION IN FACT
an actual link between an actor's conduct and a result.

PROXIMATE CAUSE
the primary or moving cause that plays a substantial part in bringing about injury or damage. It may be a first cause that sets in motion a string of events whose ultimate outcome is reasonably foreseeable.

Factual causality can be determined through the *sine qua non* test, which holds, in effect, that "without this, that would not be." The *sine qua non* test is also referred to as the "had not test" and as the **but for rule,** because it means that some injury would not have happened *but for* the conduct of the accused. In the example above, the bystander would not have been shot but for the actions of the shooter. Similarly, he would not have been shot but for the fact that someone had chosen to build a wall out of, say, steel-reinforced concrete, which caused the bullet fired by the shooter to ricochet. Even where factual cause can be demonstrated, however, it might not provide the basis for a criminal prosecution, because the government must then prove that it is also a legally recognized cause. Hence, proof of factual cause may be *necessary* for a conviction, but it alone is not *sufficient* for a conviction to result.

The idea of proximate cause is a more useful legal concept than factual cause. Proximate cause holds individuals criminally liable for causing harm when it can logically be shown that the harm caused was reasonably foreseeable from their conduct. Proximate cause can also be thought of as the first cause in a string of events that ultimately produced the harm in question. If, for example, a woman poisons her husband's dinner, intending to kill him, but he stays late at the office and she puts the meal in the refrigerator, she may still be held liable for the crime of homicide if a boarder staying in the house gets up in the middle of the night, eats the meal, and dies. In this case, the actions of the woman who intended to cause the death of her husband become the proximate cause of the death of the boarder. Proximate cause exists for two reasons: first, the woman set in motion a chain of events with potentially deadly consequences; and, second, the boarder's consumption of food in the refrigerator was a reasonably foreseeable event, and his death was therefore a foreseeable consequence of the woman's actions. Hence, even though the wrong person died, the death should have been reasonably foreseeable from the defendant's actions. As a result, legal liability exists.

A proximate cause is also a primary cause. The U.S. Supreme Court observed that " 'proximate cause' requires some direct relation between the injury asserted and the injurious conduct alleged."[13] If, for example, one person assaults another and chases him out of a building and through a driving rainstorm, the assault cannot be said to be the proximate cause of the victim's death if he is struck by lightning (the primary cause of the death) and killed during the pursuit—even though one might argue that, but for the initial assault, he would not have been exposed to the elements and would therefore have lived. This is so because the lightning strike was not related to the assault, that is, not brought on by it in the same sense that an infection might be produced by a gunshot wound. The bolt of lightning, in this instance, was independent of any harm caused by the assailant and could not have been reasonably foreseen.

To clarify the issue of causation, the American Law Institute suggests use of the term **legal cause** rather than proximate cause in order to emphasize the notion of a legally recognizable cause and to preclude any assumption that such a cause must be close in time and space to the result it produces. Legal causes can be distinguished from those causes that may have produced the result in question but which may not provide the basis for a criminal prosecution because they are too complex, too indistinguishable from other causes, not knowable, or not provable in a court of law.

Resulting Harm

The need for some identifiable **harm** as an actual or potential consequence of culpable activity is often cited as a general feature of crime. If an action held no potential

---

BUT FOR RULE
a method for determining causality which holds that "without this, that would not be," or *but for* the conduct of the accused, the harm in question would not have occurred."

LEGAL CAUSE
a legally recognizable cause. The type of cause that is required to be demonstrated in court in order to hold an individual criminally liable for causing harm.

HARM
also **resulting harm.** Loss, disadvantage, or injury or anything so regarded by the person affected, including loss, disadvantage, or injury to any other person in whose welfare he is interested.

LAW ON THE BOOKS

PENNSYLVANIA DEFINES "CAUSATION."

Compare with Model Penal Code, Section 2.03

PENNSYLVANIA CONSOLIDATED STATUTES

Title 18, Section 303. Casual relationship between conduct and result.

(a) General rule.—Conduct is the cause of a result when:

(1) it is an antecedent but for which the result in question would not have occurred; and

(2) the relationship between the conduct and result satisfies any additional causal requirements imposed by this title or by the law defining the offense. . . .

NORTH DAKOTA DEFINES "CAUSATION."

NORTH DAKOTA CRIMINAL CODE

Title 12.1, Section 02-05. Causal relationship between conduct and result.

Causation may be found where the result would not have occurred but for the conduct of the accused operating either alone or concurrently with another cause, unless the concurrent cause was clearly sufficient to produce the result and the conduct of the accused clearly insufficient.

to cause harm, it would make little sense to pass a law prohibiting it. Personal crimes, such as murder and rape, cause specific harm to nameable individuals, while other offenses, such as attempts, may have harm as their goal, but fail to achieve it. Still other crimes, such as those against the environment, cause a more general and diffuse kind of harm, the impact of which might be fully felt only in later generations.

A special offense category, however, sometimes called "social order offenses" or "victimless crimes," denotes a type of criminal law violation in which parties to the crime willfully (even joyfully) participate and in which the element of harm seems remote. Victimless crimes, which will be discussed in detail in Chapter 12, include offenses such as prostitution, gambling, homosexuality, "crimes against nature" (sexual deviance), and illegal drug use. People involved in such crimes argue that, if anyone is being hurt, it is only they. What these offenders fail to recognize, say legal theorists, is the social harm caused by their conduct. Areas afflicted with chronic prostitution, drug use, sexual deviance, and illegal gambling usually find property values falling, family life disintegrating, and other, more traditional crimes increasing as money is sought to support the "victimless" activities, and law-abiding citizens flee the area. As Joel Feinberg, a well-known contemporary analyst of the law, says, "it is legitimate for the state to prohibit conduct that causes . . . harm to important public institutions and practices."[14] Feinberg's dictum agrees with our conclusion, reached in Chapter 1, that "crimes can be distinguished from other law violations by the fact that they are essentially offenses against the community or the public."

An important point to remember, however, is that from a legal perspective, "the question is not whether in some sense, ethical or sociological, the defendant has committed a harm. Rather, the question is whether the defendant's conduct has caused the harm, which the law in question sought to prevent."[15] In a criminal prosecution, it is rarely necessary to prove harm as a separate element of a crime, since it is subsumed under the notion of a guilty act. In the crime of murder, for example, the "killing of a human being" brings about a harm, but is, properly speaking, an act, which, when done with the requisite *mens rea*, becomes a crime. A similar type

All laws are an attempt to domesticate the natural ferocity of the species . . . We can't stop a banker from stealing a widow's money, but we can make it harder for him to steal.

—John W. Gardner, *San Francisco Examiner*, July 3, 1974

of reasoning applies to the criminalization of attempts, and some writers have used the example of throwing rocks at blind people to illustrate that behavior need not actually produce harm for it to be criminal. One could imagine a scenario in which vandals decide to throw rocks at visually impaired individuals but, because of bad aim, the rocks never hit anyone and the intended targets remain blissfully unaware that anyone is trying to harm them. In such a case, shouldn't throwing rocks provide a basis for criminal liability? As one authority on the subject observes, "[c]riticism of the principle of harm has . . . been based on the view that the harm actually caused may be a matter of sheer accident and that the rational thing to do is to base the punishment on the *mens rea,* and the action, disregarding any actual harm or lack of harm or its degree."[16] Similarly, the prominent contemporary legal scholar George P. Fletcher says, "The emphasis on intention as the core of crime [highlights] the offender's attitude as the essence of criminality."[17] This is why we have said that the essence of criminality consists only of three things: (1) an *actus reus,* (2) *mens rea,* and (3) a concurrence of an illegal act and a culpable mental state.

Although the need for an identifiable harm is sometimes specified by law as an element of an offense, at other times degree of harm increases the seriousness of an offense. Indiana law, for example, allows greater punishment for the crime of product tampering when harm results. The law reads: "A person who: (1) recklessly, knowingly, or intentionally introduces a poison, a harmful substance, or a harmful foreign object into a consumer product; or (2) with intent to mislead a consumer of a consumer product, tampers with the labeling of a consumer product that has been introduced into commerce, commits consumer product tampering, a class D felony. However, the offense is a class C felony if it results in harm to a person, and it is a class B felony if it results in serious bodily injury to another person."[18]

Where a particular result *is* specified by law as a necessary element of a given crime, however, a successful prosecution requires both a concurrence of *mens rea* and the act, as well as of *mens rea* and the resulting harm. When the harm that results from criminal activity is different in *degree* from the intended harm, the concurrence requirement is still met. Hence, if I shoot someone, intending only to wound them, but the person dies, I may still be liable for homicide. If, on the other hand, the resulting harm is of a different *kind* than that intended, the needed concurrence may be lacking. If I leave a getaway car whose engine is running parked in the garage under an apartment in the middle of the night while I break into a nearby bank, and the person sleeping in the apartment above the car dies from carbon monoxide poisoning, I would not be guilty of homicide, even though my actions may have caused a person's death.

LAW ON THE BOOKS

INDIANA DEFINES "HARM."
INDIANA CODE 35-41-1

Section 13. "Harm" means loss, disadvantage, or injury or anything so regarded by the person affected, including loss, disadvantage, or injury to any other person in whose welfare he is interested.

NORTH DAKOTA DEFINES "HARM"
NORTH DAKOTA CRIMINAL CODE 12.1-01-04.

General definitions. As used in this title, unless a different meaning plainly is required:

14. "Harm" means loss, disadvantage, or injury to the person affected, and includes loss, disadvantage, or injury to any other person in whose welfare he is interested.

A "john" discusses terms with a prostitute. Not all crimes produce readily identifiable harms. (Photo by Adam Scull/Rangefinders, courtesy of Globe Photos, Inc.)

The felony murder rule, however, is an exception to the general notion that criminal liability does not accrue when the harm that results is different in kind from the harm intended. Felony murder statutes hold a person involved in the commission of a felony responsible for homicide if another person dies during the offense, even though the death may have been unintentional. Hence, if two armed robbers enter a bank, and one is shot by security guards, the surviving robber may be guilty of homicide even though he never fired his weapon or pointed it at anyone. Some jurisdictions have even prosecuted surviving drug users under felony murder statutes when a friend's death resulted from an overdose brought on by the sharing of drugs.

The Principle of Legality

PRINCIPLE OF LEGALITY
an axiom that holds that behavior cannot be criminal if no law exists that defines it as such.

The **principle of legality** reflects the fact that behavior cannot be criminal if no law exists that both defines it as illegal and prescribes a punishment for it. It is all right to drink beer, if you are of "drinking age," because there is no statute "on the books" prohibiting it. During Prohibition, of course, the situation was quite different. (In fact, some parts of the United States are still "dry," and the sale, purchase, or public consumption of alcohol can be a violation regardless of age.) The need for a specified punishment is also part of the principle of legality. Larceny, for example, would not be a crime if the law simply said, "It is illegal to steal." Punishment needs to be specified by law so that if a person is found guilty of violating the law, sanctions can be lawfully imposed. Two legal dicta capture the role of state-sanctioned punishment in the principle of legality. The first is *nullen crimen, nulla poena, sine lege,* which means "there is no crime, there is no punishment, without law." The second is *nullum crimen sine poena,* which means "no crime without punishment."

The principle of legality also includes the notion that a law cannot be created tomorrow that will hold a person legally responsible for something he or she does today. These are called *ex post facto* laws. Following an express provision in the U.S. Constitution, laws are binding only from the date of their creation or from some future date at which they are specified as taking effect.[19] Of course, a jurisdiction can change its laws in such a way as to *reduce* the criminality of specified conduct. Doing so would not be a violation of the legality principle.

Another aspect of the principle of legality is the constitutional void-for-vagueness principle. The U.S. Supreme Court gave voice to the **void-for-vagueness** principle in an early ruling in which it held: "a statute which either forbids or requires the doing of an act in terms so vague that men of common intelligence must necessarily guess at its meaning and differ as to its application, violates the first essential of due process of law." Statutes are void when vague because their enforcement would require after-the-fact judicial interpretations of what the law means—an activity akin to *ex post facto* rule creation.

In 1999, in *Chicago* v. *Morales,*[20] for example, the U.S. Supreme Court held that a city ordinance that prohibited criminal street gang members from loitering in public places was unconstitutionally vague and an arbitrary restriction on personal liberties. The Court found that "because the ordinance fails to give the ordinary citizen adequate notice of what is forbidden and what is permitted, it is impermissibly vague."[21] The term "loiter," said the Court, "may have a common and accepted meaning, but the ordinance's definition of that term—'to remain in any one place with no apparent purpose'—does not." The Court reasoned that "It is difficult to imagine how any Chicagoan standing in a public place with a group of people would know if he or she had an 'apparent purpose'. " The ordinance, under which 42,000 people had been arrested,[22] was also found to lack sufficient minimal standards to guide law enforcement officers because it failed to provide any gauge by which police officers could judge whether an individual "has an 'apparent purpose'. " The Court concluded that "this vagueness about what loitering is covered and what is not, dooms the ordinance." The majority opinion in *Morales* can be found in a Capstone Case at the end of this chapter.

Shortly after the *Morales* decision, the Chicago City Council passed a new anti-gang ordinance intended to meet Supreme Court objections.[23] The city's new ordinance permits police officers to arrest suspected gang members or drug dealers if they disregard an order to leave a corner or block that the police have identified as a gang "hot spot." The ordinance also requires police officers to have a "reasonable belief that gang or drug activity is taking place." The law only permits the jailing of suspects until they can be fingerprinted, and does not allow them to be held longer unless they are found to be in possession of guns or drugs. As of this writing, the new ordinance has not faced a court challenge. A serious weakness of the ordinance, however, may lie in the fact that "hot spots" are not currently being disclosed by the police department—and can only be figured out by gang members after arrests have been made.

Game is game, and he who finds may kill. That has been the law in these mountains for forty years, to my certain knowledge; and I think one old law is worth two new ones.

—James Fenimore Cooper
(The Pioneers, 1823)

EX POST FACTO
formulated, enacted, or operating retrospectively. Literally, "after the fact."

VOID-FOR-VAGUENESS
a constitutional principle that refers to a statute defining a crime that is so unclear that a reasonable person of at least average intelligence could not determine what the law purports to command or prohibit.

CRIMINAL LAW IN THE NEWS

Ban on Secret Nude Videotaping Lifted

Wis. High Court Strikes Down Law as Too Broad

MADISON, Wis.—It is no longer a crime to videotape an unsuspecting person who is nude, but prosecutors say they will work to ensure a state Supreme Court decision striking down the law does not give a green light to Peeping Toms and pornographers.

In a 5–2 vote Wednesday, the high court ruled the 4-year-old law making it a felony to depict nudity without the subject's consent was unconstitutional. As a result, as many as 20 cases involving video voyeurs could be dismissed statewide, prosecutors said.

The court, ruling on a 1997 case involving a man who filmed his ex-girlfriend in the nude without her knowledge, found the law violated legitimate First Amendment rights.

"The statute not only properly prohibits [Scott] Stevenson's surreptitious videotaping of his former girlfriend in the nude, but also improperly prohibits all visual expression of nudity without explicit consent including political satire and newsworthy images," wrote Justice Ann Walsh Bradley for the court.

"Open season for Peeping Toms"?

Prosecutors said they were disappointed with the decision and had hoped the court would choose to narrow the interpretation of the law rather than throw it out entirely.

"We thought it would have been perfectly appropriate for the court to take a narrow interpretation of the law in order to protect legitimate First Amendment expression," said Jim Haney, a spokesman for state Attorney General Jim Doyle.

Haney said he hopes the decision does not "give the green light" to voyeurs.

"We hope this is not open season for Peeping Toms," he said. "There are other statutes to go after people who behave this way."

But Haney conceded most of the other prosecutorial options involve offenses such as disorderly conduct or trespassing, which are often misdemeanors.

Other cases in jeopardy

The ruling could mean that at least two other cases in Waukesha County court involving similar offenses might be thrown out, said Waukesha County prosecutor Paul Bucher, who estimated another 20 similar cases would be reviewed statewide.

"They may be dismissed. We may have a look at other statutes [under which to charge the individuals]," said Bucher. "I can assure you we are not going to let this conduct go unaddressed."

Stevenson's attorney, Daniel Fay, who agreed with the judge's description of his client's behavior as "abhorrent," called the ruling a victory for artists and the news media.

"We did this on behalf of others whose conduct should be protected," Fay said. "So artists don't have to take the chance and be arrested."

"Too far reaching"

Free speech proponents condemned both the defendant's actions and the law under which he was prosecuted.

"The law was overbroad and too far reaching," said Chris Ahmuty, executive director of the American Civil Liberties Union of Wisconsin, which opposed the law when it was proposed in 1996. "Everybody agrees it's repulsive behavior, but the court was right to go down the route of narrowly constructing the statute."

Ahmuty said the state Legislature must draft a bill that better strikes the balance between protecting privacy and First Amendment rights.

"This should remind legislators to give consideration to all interests when drafting legislation," he said.

Wisconsin's nudity law, one of an estimated three similar state laws, was enacted after it was revealed a couple had been filming exchange students in the bathroom of their home for years.

The Legislature will likely consider a new bill early next year, Haney said.

Source: Amy Worden, "Ban on Secret Nude Videotaping Lifted; Wis. High Court Strikes Down Law as Too Broad," APB News. June 29, 2000. Reprinted with permission.

Necessary Attendant Circumstances

ATTENDANT CIRCUMSTANCES
the facts surrounding an event.

Finally, statutes defining crimes may specify that additional elements, called **attendant circumstances,** be present for a conviction to be obtained. Attendant circumstances refer to the "facts surrounding an event,"[24] and include such things as time and place. Attendant circumstances specified by law as necessary elements of an offense are sometimes referred to as "necessary attendant circumstances" to indicate the fact that the existence of such circumstances is required in order for all of the elements of the crime to be met.

LAW IN PRACTICE

EX POST FACTO LAWS

The principle of ex post facto rule creation is illustrated by the 1993 New Hampshire Supreme Court case of State v. Reynolds, excerpts from which read as follows:

State v. Reynolds
Supreme Court of New Hampshire, 1993
642 A.2d 1368

In 1986, the defendant, Anne Marie Reynolds, pled guilty to second degree murder. On the date of her crime, RSA 651:20 (1986) (the old law) permitted prisoners to petition for sentence suspension every two years. Reynolds filed such a petition in January 1990, without success.

In 1992, the legislature amended the old law, effective January 1, 1993, to preclude violent offenders, such as Reynolds, from petitioning for sentence suspension more often than every four years. Laws 1992, 254:13 (codified at RSA 651:20, I(a) (Supp. 1993)) (the new law). In April 1993, Reynolds filed the pending petition. The State objected to it as premature under the new law. Reynolds responded that application of the new law to her petition would violate the state and federal constitutional prohibitions against *ex post facto* laws. . . .

Both Article 1, Section 10 of the Federal Constitution and part I, article 23 of the New Hampshire Constitution forbid *ex post facto* penal laws . . . . Part I, article 23 proclaims: "Retrospective laws are highly injurious, oppressive, and unjust. No such laws, therefore, should be made, either for the decision of civil causes, or the punishment of offenses." The latter portion of this article, concerning retrospective application of penal laws, is a prohibition against *ex*

post facto laws. . . . A law or an application of a law is *ex post facto* if it "makes an action done before the passing of the law, and which was innocent when done, criminal, and punishes such action; or . . . aggravates a crime, and makes it greater, than it was when committed; or . . . changes the punishment, and inflicts greater punishment, than the law annexed to the crime when committed. . . ." Reynolds argues that application of the new law to her petition for sentence suspension would violate part I, article 23, because it "inflicts greater punishment" for her crime than the old law. . . .

We hold that application of the new law to Reynolds' petition would violate part I, article 23, because the new law could operate to keep her in prison longer than the old law. The new law reduces the frequency of opportunities a violent offender has to petition for sentence suspension. Without an opportunity to petition, an offender's sentence cannot be suspended. . . . For such an inmate, any delay in the chance to petition translates into more time in prison. The imposition of extra prison time is plainly an infliction of greater punishment. If a delay in the chance to petition is caused by a retrospective application of a penal law, such an application violates part I, article 23. . . .

Remanded.

What do *you* think?

1. Do you agree with the court? That is, do you think the law in question is an *ex post facto* law? Why or why not?

2. Should restrictions on *ex post facto* laws apply to administrative procedures, such as parole hearings, or should they only apply to laws that define crimes themselves? Why?

Florida law, for example, makes it a crime to "Knowingly commit any lewd or lascivious act in the presence of any child under the age of sixteen years. . . ."[25] In this case, the behavior in question might not be a crime if committed in the presence of persons older than sixteen. Also, curfew violations are being increasingly criminalized by states shifting liability for a minor's behavior to his or her parents. To violate a curfew, it is necessary that a juvenile be in a public place between specified times (such as 11 P.M. or midnight, and 5 or 6 A.M.). In those states which hold parents liable for the behavior of their children, parents can be jailed or fined if such violations occur.

DEGREE

the level of seriousness of an offense.

Sometimes attendant circumstances increase the **degree,** or level of seriousness, of an offense. Under Texas law, for example, the crime of burglary has two degrees, defined by state law as follows: burglary is a "(1) state jail felony if committed in a building other than a habitation; or (2) felony of the second degree if committed in a habitation." Hence, the degree of the offense of burglary changes depending on the nature of the place burglarized.

Similarly, Florida law specifies a number of degrees of "sexual battery," depending on the amount of force used to commit the crime, the age of the victim, and whether or not more than one perpetrator was involved in the commission of the offense.[26] The relevant statute reads: "The penalty . . . shall be increased as provided in this subsection if it is charged and proven by the prosecution that, during the same criminal transaction or episode, more than one person committed an act of sexual battery on the same victim." Florida law also increases the degree of sexual battery (and associated penalties) "[w]hen the victim is physically helpless to resist . . . ; [w]hen the offender, without the prior knowledge or consent of the victim, administers or has knowledge of someone else administering to the victim any narcotic, anesthetic, or other intoxicating substance, which mentally or physically incapacitates the victim . . . ; [w]hen the victim is mentally defective and the offender has reason to believe this or has actual knowledge of this fact . . . ; [w]hen the victim is physically incapacitated. . . ; when the offender is a law enforcement officer, correctional officer, or correctional probation officer. . . ;" and under other circumstances.

Circumstances surrounding a crime can also be classified as aggravating or mitigating, and may, by law, be used to lessen or increase the penalty that can be imposed on a convicted offender. Aggravating and mitigating circumstances are not elements of an offense, because they are primarily relevant at the sentencing stage of a criminal prosecution and are therefore discussed in a later chapter.

SUMMARY

- The term *corpus delicti* literally means "body of crime." To prove the *corpus delicti* of a crime is to show that a crime has in fact occurred. Doing so requires the state to demonstrate that a criminal law has been violated and that someone violated it.

- The *corpus delicti* rule holds that a criminal conviction cannot be based solely on the uncorroborated confession or admission of an accused; i.e., a confession, uncorroborated by other facts, is insufficient to show the *corpus delicti* of a crime and cannot support a conviction.

- In addition to the three fundamental elements of crime (*actus reus, mens rea,* and concurrence) discussed in the last chapter, four additional principles are necessary to fully appreciate contemporary understandings of crime: (1) causation, (2) a resulting harm, (3) the principle of legality, and (4) necessary attendant circumstances.

- Causation refers to the fact that the concurrence of a guilty mind and a criminal act may produce or *cause* harm. While some statutes criminalize only conduct, others subsume the notion of concurrence under causality and specify that a causal relationship is a necessary element of a given crime.

- If there is an actual link between the actor's conduct and the resulting harm, causation in fact is said to exist. The "but for rule" is another way of determining causation and looks to see whether some injury would not have happened *but for* the conduct of the accused.

- A "proximate cause" is a primary or moving cause that plays a substantial part in bringing about injury or damage. It may be a first cause that sets in motion a string of events whose ultimate outcome is reasonably foreseeable. A "legal cause," on the other hand, is simply one which is legally significant.

- While all crimes can be said to result in harm, some crimes, such as victimless crimes or public order offenses, denote a type of criminal law violation in which the parties to the offense willfully participate. Even so, most such crimes still produce identifiable harms—although they may be more of a public than a private sort.

- The principle of legality mirrors the fact that behavior cannot be criminal if no law exists that both defines it as such and prescribes punishment for it.

- The principle of legality also includes the notion that a law cannot be created tomorrow that will hold a person legally responsible for something he or she does today. Such laws are called *ex post facto* laws, their primary feature being that they are retroactive. *Ex post facto* laws are illegal under the U.S. Constitution.

- Statutes defining some crimes specify that additional elements, called attendant circumstances, be present in order for a conviction to be obtained. Attendant circumstances refer to the "facts surrounding an event" and include such things as time and place. Sometimes attendant circumstances increase the degree, or level of seriousness, of an offense.

QUESTIONS FOR DISCUSSION

1. Explain the concept of *corpus delicti*. How does the *corpus delicti* of a crime differ from the elements of a crime?

2. Sometimes people mistakenly say that the body of a murder victim provides the *corpus delicti* of the crime of murder. What actually constitutes the *corpus delicti* of murder?

3. What is the difference between causation in fact and proximate cause? What is meant by "but for" causation? By "legal cause?" Give an example of each.

4. What are victimless crimes? Why are they sometimes called social order offenses? Do you think that such law violations are truly victimless? Why or why not?

5. What is felony murder? How does it differ from other forms of murder?

6. What is an *ex post facto* law? Why is the creation of *ex post facto* laws regarded as impermissible in our legal system?

LEGAL RESOURCES ON THE WORLD WIDE WEB

A number of electronic discussion groups (or "newsgroups") are accessible through the Internet for anyone studying criminal law. The easiest way to participate in these discussions is through the use of newsreader software. A few of the law-related newsgroups available at the time this book went to press were:

    clari.usa.law
    clari.usa.law.supreme
    law.court.federal

A focused discussion group is available to users of this textbook. Called "lawtoday," it can be accessed through ListBot.com at the following Web address: http://lawtoday.listbot.com. You may use that address to subscribe to the list, or you can subscribe via e-mail by sending mail to <u>LAWTODAY-subscribe@listbot.</u> <u>com</u>. Be sure to send mail from the address you want to use to receive list postings. Once subscribed, you may post messages to the lawtoday discussion list for other students and professors using this textbook to read.

A directory of law-related discussion groups is available on the Web at <u>http://www.law.ou.edu/lists</u>. It contains information on approximately 200 Internet-based law-related discussion groups and links to seventy archive sites.

Some discussion groups require those wishing to subscribe to send an e-mail message to the computer serving the group—commonly known as a listserver. The syntax of the message may vary from group to group, but in general it takes this form:

"subscribe listname firstname lastname"

To subscribe to a group named "criminallaw," for example, you might type:

subscribe criminallaw John Doe

The listserver reads your e-mail address from your e-mail message and adds you to the list. Messages will be sent to the e-mail address from which you sent your message to the listserver. Some discussion groups are private and entry may require you to provide additional information about yourself.

Remember to use only plain ASCII text when sending messages directly to a listserver. If your e-mail software automatically attaches a signature block to your messages you should disable this feature when corresponding with the listserver. Once your subscription has been accepted, you will want to be sure and save the initial messages that are automatically sent to you from the listserver because they contain the information you need to discontinue receiving messages from the server. Additional "listserv" commands are described at: <u>http://www.lsoft.com/info/default.</u> <u>asp?item=manuals</u>.

Check the *Criminal Law Today* Web site for URLs or newsgroup names that may have changed.

SUGGESTED READINGS AND CLASSIC WORKS

Howard Abadinsky, *Law and Justice* (Chicago: Nelson-Hall, 1988).

David L. Bazelon, *Questioning Authority: Justice and Criminal Law* (New York: Knopf, 1989).

George P. Fletcher, *Rethinking Criminal Law* (Boston: Little, Brown, 1978).

Jerome Frank, *Law and the Modern Mind* (Garden City, NY: Anchor Books, 1970). Originally published in 1930.

Charles W. Thomas and Donna M. Bishop, *Criminal Law: Understanding Basic Principles* (Newbury Park, CA: Sage, 1987).

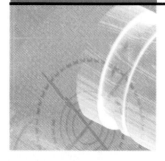

CAPSTONE CASE

WHAT CONSTITUTES THE *CORPUS DELICTI* OF AN OFFENSE?

Johnson v. *State*
Supreme Court of Indiana, 1995
653 N.E.2d 478

OPINION

On appeal is the sole issue of whether the trial court erred in determining that independent evidence established the *corpus delicti* for robbery and that evidence of extrajudicial confessions by the defendant was thereby admissible. We affirm.

I.

Seventy-four year old Florence Hoke called her niece, Nancy Whiteman, at 8:30 A.M. on April 10, 1990, and told Whiteman that she was going to get license plates for her car. At 12:30 P.M., Whiteman called Hoke twice, but Hoke did not recognize her. Whiteman went to Hoke's apartment, where she discovered Hoke sitting in a chair holding her head. Whiteman called "911." [R. 233] Richard Bourdon, a paramedic, arrived and observed that Hoke was disoriented and unable to communicate. He observed a small bruise and a bump on the back of Hoke's head. At the hospital later that day, Whiteman observed bruises on Hoke's knees and on one elbow.

Hoke was diagnosed as suffering a subdural hematoma, "a collection of blood that forms under the external cover of the brain." The treating physician testified that subdural hematomas are caused by trauma, which could result from "a blow to the head, a fall, [or] any type of force." Doctors performed a craniotomy, but Hoke never regained consciousness, and died approximately two months later from pneumonia and infection. Hoke's new license plates were found in her apartment, but her purse was missing. A leather bow resembling one that was on Hoke's purse was found on the ground near where Hoke's car was parked.

On April 10, 1990, Margaret Jackson resided with Homer Frison. Andre D. Johnson visited that morning and left with Frison. The two told Jackson that when they returned they "would either have some money or would have a way of making some money." When Frison and Johnson later met up with Jackson, they had a purse and a wallet containing credit cards belonging to Hoke. The trio went shopping, Jackson purchased cigarettes with the credit cards, and the trio sold the cigarettes to obtain money to purchase drugs.

Following a jury trial, Johnson was convicted of robbery, a class A felony, and of being an habitual offender. The trial court sentenced Johnson to fifty years for the robbery conviction, to be served concurrently with the sentence imposed for an unrelated offense. For the habitual offender conviction, the trial court sentenced Johnson to twenty-five years, to be served consecutive to the robbery sentence.

II.

At issue in this case is whether the trial court erred in admitting the testimony of four witnesses, Odie Miller, Anthony Taylor, Darrell Vaughn, and Detective Sergeant Michael Swanson, regarding confessions made by Johnson. A defendant's extrajudicial confession may be introduced into evidence only if the State establishes the *corpus delicti* of the crime by independent evidence.[1] *Willoughby* v. *State* (1990), Ind., 552 N.E.2d 462, 466. *Corpus delicti* consists of a showing of "1) the occurrence of the specific kind of injury and 2) someone's criminal act as the cause of the injury." *Id.*

In particular, at trial Miller responded to the question "what did [Johnson] tell you about Florence Hoke?" by stating that Johnson had told Miller that "he and Homer were trying to find a way to get some money to buy some drugs and that they came around the corner and they seen [Hoke] walking down the sidewalk and they got out of the car to snatch her purse and she fell and he said a couple of months later that he read in the newspaper" that Hoke had died. [R. 384–85]

Taylor testified that he and Johnson were watching a "Crime Stoppers" show featuring an elderly woman being robbed of her purse. Taylor testified that Johnson told him "that what was on T.V., that he had done with someone else." Specifically, Taylor claimed that Johnson said that he and Frison were near the mall, that they saw a lady, and that he jumped out of a car. "He ran towards the lady and when he tried to get the purse from her, she struggled and then that's when he hit her with a forearm and from that point, the other individual came up and took the purse and they fled the scene." [R. 409–10]

Vaughn testified that Johnson confided in him that he and Frison "snatched" an elderly woman's purse, and that the woman was in the hospital. Johnson allegedly

said that it went "kind of crazy" because "the old lady tried to hold on and Homer hit her–not Homer–Johnson hit her." [R. 439] Detective Sergeant Swanson testified that he interrogated Johnson as part of his investigation into the Hoke case. Johnson told him that he would not "go on tape. I will talk to you and I will just tell you that Homer and I did it." Detective Sergeant Swanson also testified that Johnson stated "Homer and I had did it and you guys can't prove it anyway." [R. 469]

As Johnson virtually concedes, the *corpus delicti* for the crime of theft exists based upon Johnson's possession of Hoke's purse, wallet, and credit cards. Johnson contends, however, that no *corpus delicti* exists for the crime which he was convicted of, namely, robbery.[2] Essentially he argues that the independent evidence does not adequately demonstrate that someone took Hoke's purse by force or threat of force or by putting Hoke in fear. Regarding Hoke's physical injuries, Johnson argues that it is possible that Hoke fell by accident, thus causing the subdural hematoma and other bruises.[3]

We have held that "[t]he independent evidence need not be shown beyond a reasonable doubt nor demonstrate *prima facie* proof as to each element of the charged offense, but must support an inference that the crime was committed." *Willoughby,* 552 N.E.2d at 467. In this case, the evidence does not conclusively establish that Hoke's purse was taken forcibly from her. The evidence does, however, support an inference that she was robbed.[4] We specifically reject Johnson's contention on appeal that "[t]here is no evidence here of violent injury." In the most analogous Indiana case, the defendant was convicted of murder committed during the commission of a "purse-grab" robbery of an eighty-two-year-old woman. *Hayden* v. *State* (1964), 245 Ind. 591, 199 N.E.2d 102, *cert. denied,* 384 U.S. 1013 (1966). The victim was found lying on the ground near her apartment with blood flowing from her mouth, ears, and nose. *Id.* at 596. This Court noted that the victim's "body had many marks of violence upon it. Evidence from police and medical authorities indicated that the victim could have been assailed and pushed against the door of the apartment building, thus causing the injuries and marks of violence. The woman later died of these injuries." *Id.* at 596–97. Additional independent evidence showed that the victim had a purse with money and personal items on her person prior to the alleged attack, and that the purse, without the money, was later found in a nearby alley. *Id.* at 597. We determined that because ordinary people "might reasonably conclude that the deceased did not die of natural causes and that the injuries from which she died were inflicted in the course of a robbery," the *corpus delicti* for a robbery-murder charge existed. *Id.* at 597. Significantly, the evidence in *Hayden* tended only to show that the victim "could have" been assailed, not that her injuries could have only been caused by force exerted during a robbery. Even though, as in *Hayden,* the independent evidence here does not conclusively establish the cause of Hoke's injuries, this does not preclude a *corpus delicti* for robbery since a reasonable person could conclude that Hoke's injuries were the product of a robbery.

Johnson's reliance upon *Parker* v. *State* (1949), 228 Ind. 1, 88 N.E.2d 556, is misplaced. In that case, this Court reversed the defendant's conviction for murder in the second degree based upon the absence of *corpus delicti.* Parker confessed to killing the alleged victim, dismembering her, and burying her in three different places. *Id.* at 5. Police discovered human remains in the places designated, but could not identify the remains as the missing person's or determine the cause of death. *Id.* at 10. As such, the only evidence that the alleged victim had been murdered aside from Parker's extrajudicial confession was the alleged victim's disappearance. *Id.* This Court deemed the independent evidence insufficient to establish the *corpus delicti* for murder. *Id.*

Parker is wholly different from the instant case because here evidence identifies Hoke as the victim of theft and demonstrates that Hoke incurred injuries caused by force. Whether Johnson caused the injuries or another force was at work is a question different in kind and degree than whether unidentifiable human remains adequately prove that a particular missing person was murdered.

We thus reject Johnson's argument that the State failed to prove the *corpus delicti* and that the trial court erred in admitting the testimony of Miller, Taylor, Vaughn, and Swanson into evidence. We affirm the judgment of the trial court.

Footnotes
1. This rule is designed to "reduce the risk of convicting a defendant based on his confession for a crime that did not occur," prevent coercive interrogation tactics, and encourage thorough criminal investigations. *Willoughby,* 552 N.E.2d at 466. We previously observed, however, that the rule's efficacy in meeting these objectives has been seriously questioned. *Id.;* see generally 1 *McCormick on Evidence* 145, at 563 (John W. Strong ed., 4th ed. 1992).
2. By statute, a person who knowingly or intentionally takes property from another person or from the presence of another person: (1) by using or threatening the use of force on any person; or (2) by putting any person in fear; commits robbery, a class C felony. However, the offense is a class B felony if it is committed while armed with a deadly weapon or results in bodily injury to any person other than a defendant, and a class A felony if it results in serious bodily injury to any person other than a defendant. Ind. Code Ann. 35–42–5–1 (West 1986).
3. Johnson observes that Hoke "could have slipped or tripped or lost her balance. She could have fallen on the stairs or on the sidewalk or at the license bureau or in the parking lot getting into or out of her car." Additionally Johnson points out that it is possible that Hoke did not sustain the head trauma and the bruises contemporaneously.
4. The independent evidence supporting the *corpus delicti* need not preclude every possible explanation of the circumstances. For example, one court held that a *corpus delicti* for attempted armed robbery existed when evidence showed that a person was shot to death at 1 A.M. and that the shooter fled, even though other explanations, such as a dispute between the two persons, were possible, since the independent evidence "sufficiently corroborated the defendant's confession of attempted armed robbery." *People* v. *Montes,* 549 N.E.2d 700, 705 (Ill. App. Ct. 1989).

WHAT DO *YOU* THINK?
1. How can the *corpus delicti* of robbery be demonstrated? Of theft?
2. Why did the court conclude that: "In this case, the evidence does not conclusively establish that Hoke's purse was taken forcibly from her. The evidence does, however, support an inference that she was robbed"?

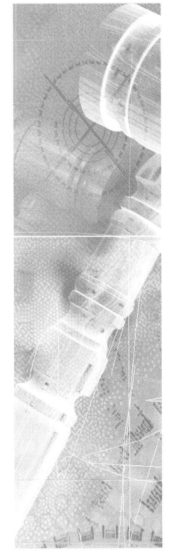

CAN AN ANTI-LOITERING STATUTE BE VAGUE EVEN IF IT PURPORTS TO DEFINE "LOITERING"

CAPSTONE CASE

Chicago v. *Morales*
Supreme Court of the United States, 1999
No. 97–1121

OPINION
In 1992, the Chicago City Council enacted the Gang Congregation Ordinance, which prohibits "criminal street gang members" from "loitering" with one another or with other persons in any public place. The question presented is whether the Supreme Court of Illinois correctly held that the ordinance violates the Due Process Clause of the Fourteenth Amendment to the Federal Constitution.

I
Before the ordinance was adopted, the city council's Committee on Police and Fire conducted hearings to explore the problems created by the city's street gangs, and more particularly, the consequences of public loitering by gang members. Witnesses

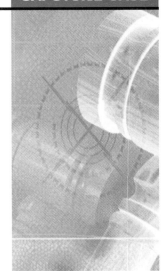

included residents of the neighborhoods where gang members are most active, as well as some of the aldermen who represent those areas. Based on that evidence, the council made a series of findings that are included in the text of the ordinance and explain the reasons for its enactment.

The council found that a continuing increase in criminal street gang activity was largely responsible for the city's rising murder rate, as well as an escalation of violent and drug related crimes. It noted that in many neighborhoods throughout the city, "the burgeoning presence of street gang members in public places has intimidated many law abiding citizens." 177 Ill. 2d 440, 445, 687 N.E. 2d 53, 58 (1997). Furthermore, the council stated that gang members "establish control over identifiable areas . . . by loitering in those areas and intimidating others from entering those areas; and . . . [m]embers of criminal street gangs avoid arrest by committing no offense punishable under existing laws when they know the police are present. . . ." *Ibid.* It further found that "loitering in public places by criminal street gang members creates a justifiable fear for the safety of persons and property in the area" and that "[a]ggressive action is necessary to preserve the city's streets and other public places so that the public may use such places without fear." Moreover, the council concluded that the city "has an interest in discouraging all persons from loitering in public places with criminal gang members." *Ibid.*

The ordinance creates a criminal offense punishable by a fine of up to $500, imprisonment for not more than six months, and a requirement to perform up to 120 hours of community service. Commission of the offense involves four predicates. First, the police officer must reasonably believe that at least one of the two or more persons present in a "public place" is a "criminal street gang membe[r]." Second, the persons must be "loitering," which the ordinance defines as "remain[ing] in any one place with no apparent purpose." Third, the officer must then order "all" of the persons to disperse and remove themselves "from the area." Fourth, a person must disobey the officer's order. If any person, whether a gang member or not, disobeys the officer's order, that person is guilty of violating the ordinance. *Ibid.* . . .

The Illinois Supreme Court . . . held "that the gang loitering ordinance violates due process of law in that it is impermissibly vague on its face and an arbitrary restriction on personal liberties." 177 Ill. 2d, at 447, 687 N.E. 2d, at 59. . . .

In support of its vagueness holding, the court pointed out that the definition of "loitering" in the ordinance drew no distinction between innocent conduct and conduct calculated to cause harm. "Moreover, the definition of 'loiter' provided by the ordinance does not assist in clearly articulating the proscriptions of the ordinance." *Id.,* at 451–452, 687 N.E. 2d, at 60–61. Furthermore, it concluded that the ordinance was "not reasonably susceptible to a limiting construction which would affirm its validity."

We granted certiorari, 523 U.S. _____(1998), and now affirm. Like the Illinois Supreme Court, we conclude that the ordinance enacted by the city of Chicago is unconstitutionally vague.

III

. . . vagueness may invalidate a criminal law for either of two independent reasons. First, it may fail to provide the kind of notice that will enable ordinary people to understand what conduct it prohibits; second, it may authorize and even encourage arbitrary and discriminatory enforcement. See *Kolender* v. *Lawson,* 461 U.S., at 357. Accordingly, we first consider whether the ordinance provides fair notice to the citizen and then discuss its potential for arbitrary enforcement.

IV

"It is established that a law fails to meet the requirements of the Due Process Clause if it is so vague and standardless that it leaves the public uncertain as to the conduct it prohibits. . . ." *Giaccio* v. *Pennsylvania,* 382 U.S. 399, 402–403 (1966). The Illinois

Supreme Court recognized that the term "loiter" may have a common and accepted meaning, 177 Ill. 2d, at 451, 687 N.E. 2d, at 61, but the definition of that term in this ordinance—"to remain in any one place with no apparent purpose"—does not. It is difficult to imagine how any citizen of the city of Chicago standing in a public place with a group of people would know if he or she had an "apparent purpose." If she were talking to another person, would she have an apparent purpose? If she were frequently checking her watch and looking expectantly down the street, would she have an apparent purpose?

Since the city cannot conceivably have meant to criminalize each instance a citizen stands in public with a gang member, the vagueness that dooms this ordinance is not the product of uncertainty about the normal meaning of "loitering," but rather about what loitering is covered by the ordinance and what is not. The Illinois Supreme Court emphasized the law's failure to distinguish between innocent conduct and conduct threatening harm. Its decision followed the precedent set by a number of state courts that have upheld ordinances that criminalize loitering combined with some other overt act or evidence of criminal intent. However, state courts have uniformly invalidated laws that do not join the term "loitering" with a second specific element of the crime.

The city's principal response to this concern about adequate notice is that loiterers are not subject to sanction until after they have failed to comply with an officer's order to disperse. "[W]hatever problem is created by a law that criminalizes conduct people normally believe to be innocent is solved when persons receive actual notice from a police order of what they are expected to do." We find this response unpersuasive for at least two reasons.

First, the purpose of the fair notice requirement is to enable the ordinary citizen to conform his or her conduct to the law. "No one may be required at peril of life, liberty or property to speculate as to the meaning of penal statutes." *Lanzetta* v. *New Jersey*, 306 U.S. 451, 453 (1939). Although it is true that a loiterer is not subject to criminal sanctions unless he or she disobeys a dispersal order, the loitering is the conduct that the ordinance is designed to prohibit. If the loitering is in fact harmless and innocent, the dispersal order itself is an unjustified impairment of liberty. If the police are able to decide arbitrarily which members of the public they will order to disperse, then the Chicago ordinance becomes indistinguishable from the law we held invalid in *Shuttlesworth* v. *Birmingham,* 382 U.S. 87, 90 (1965). Because an officer may issue an order only after prohibited conduct has already occurred, it cannot provide the kind of advance notice that will protect the putative loiterer from being ordered to disperse. Such an order cannot retroactively give adequate warning of the boundary between the permissible and the impermissible applications of the law.

Second, the terms of the dispersal order compound the inadequacy of the notice afforded by the ordinance. It provides that the officer "shall order all such persons to disperse and remove themselves from the area." App. to Pet. for Cert. 61a. This vague phrasing raises a host of questions. After such an order issues, how long must the loiterers remain apart? How far must they move? If each loiterer walks around the block and they meet again at the same location, are they subject to arrest or merely to being ordered to disperse again? As we do here, we have found vagueness in a criminal statute exacerbated by the use of the standards of "neighborhood" and "locality." *Connally* v. *General Constr. Co.*, 269 U.S. 385 (1926). We remarked in *Connally* that "[b]oth terms are elastic and, dependent upon circumstances, may be equally satisfied by areas measured by rods or by miles." *Id.,* at 395.

Lack of clarity in the description of the loiterer's duty to obey a dispersal order might not render the ordinance unconstitutionally vague if the definition of the forbidden conduct were clear, but it does buttress our conclusion that the entire ordinance fails to give the ordinary citizen adequate notice of what is forbidden and what is permitted. The Constitution does not permit a legislature to "set a net large

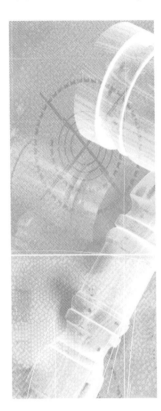

enough to catch all possible offenders, and leave it to the courts to step inside and say who could be rightfully detained, and who should be set at large." *United States v. Reese*, 92 U.S. 214, 221 (1876). This ordinance is therefore vague "not in the sense that it requires a person to conform his conduct to an imprecise but comprehensible normative standard, but rather in the sense that no standard of conduct is specified at all." *Coates* v. *Cincinnati*, 402 U.S. 611, 614 (1971). . . .

VI

. . . We recognize the serious and difficult problems testified to by the citizens of Chicago that led to the enactment of this ordinance. "We are mindful that the preservation of liberty depends in part on the maintenance of social order." *Houston* v. *Hill,* 482 U.S. 451, 471–472 (1987). However, in this instance the city has enacted an ordinance that affords too much discretion to the police and too little notice to citizens who wish to use the public streets.

Accordingly, the judgment of the Supreme Court of Illinois is Affirmed.

WHAT DO *YOU* THINK?

1. Why did the court find the city ordinance in this case to be unconstitutional?
2. What does the Court mean when it says that "The term 'loiter' may have a common and accepted meaning, but the ordinance's definition of that term—'to remain in any one place with no apparent purpose'—does not."?
3. What did the city mean in its rejoinder that loiterers are not subject to criminal sanction until after they have disobeyed a dispersal order? Why did the Court not accept that argument?

NOTES

1. *State* v. *David C. Williams,* South Carolina Supreme Court, Opinion No. 24403. Filed March 25, 1996. LLR 1996.SC.17.
2. *Willoughby* v. *State* (1990), Ind., 552 N.E.2d 462, 466.
3. See *Maughs* v. *Commonwealth,* 181 Va. 117, 120, 23 S.E.2d 784, 786 (1943).
4. *Williams,* South Carolina Supreme Court, LLR 1996.SC17; and *State* v. *Blocker,* 205 S.C. 303, 31 S.E.2d 908 (1944).
5. *Poulos* v. *Commonwealth,* 174 Va. 495, 500, 6 S.E.2d 666, 667 (1940).
6. *Zanders* v. *U.S.,* No. 91-CF-1394 & Nos. 91-CF-1465 & 94-CO-1558, District of Columbia Court of Appeals.
7. *State* v. *Arrington* (Mont. 1993). *Bluebook,* 16th ed., citation format for electronic citations via the World Wide Web: 1993.MT.7 (http://www.versuslaw.com).
8. *Willoughby,* 552 N.E.2d 784, 786.
9. *Willoughby,* 555 N.E.2d, at 466.
10. *East* v. *State,* 146 Tex. Crim. 396, 175 S.W.2d 603 (1942).
11. Article 1, Section 10.
12. Texas Penal Code, Title 5, Chapter 19, Section 1.
13. *Holmes* v. *Securities Investor Protection Corporation,* 503 U.S. 258 (1992).
14. Joel Feinberg, *Harm to Others* (Oxford: Oxford University Press, 1984).
15. John S. Baker Jr., Daniel H. Benson, Robert Force, and B. J. George, Jr., *Hall's Criminal Law: Cases and Materials,* 5th ed. (Charlottesville, VA: The Michie Company, 1993), p. 135.
16. Ibid., p. 138.

17. George P. Fletcher, *Basic Concepts of Criminal Law* (New York: Oxford University Press, 1998), p. 178.

18. Indiana Code, Article 45, Chapter 8, Section 3.

19. The same is not true for procedures within the criminal justice system, which can be modified even after a person has been sentenced and, hence, become retroactive. See, for example, the U.S. Supreme Court case of *California Department of Corrections* v. *Morales*, 514 U.S. 499 (1995), which approved of changes in the length of time between parole hearings, even though those changes applied to offenders already sentenced.

20. *Chicago* v. *Morales*, 527 U.S. 41, 56–57 (1999).

21. See, e.g., *Coates* v. *Cincinnati*, 402 U.S. 611, 614 (1971).

22. Pam Belluck, "Chicago Anti-Loitering Law Aims to Disrupt Gangs," *New York Times* online, August 31, 2000. Posted at http://www.nytimes.com/library/national/083100gangs-law.html.

23. Ibid.

24. Joseph R. Nolan and Jacqueline M. Nolan-Haley, *Black's Law Dictionary: Definitions of the Terms and Phrases of American and English Jurisprudence, Ancient and Modern,* 6th ed. (St. Paul, MN: West Publishing Co., 1990), p. 127.

25. The statute also says, "A mother's breastfeeding of her baby does not under any circumstance violate this section."

26. Florida Statutes, Section 794.011.

4

Extending Criminal Liability: Inchoate Offenses and Parties to Crime

Intent to commit a crime is not itself criminal. There is no law against a man's intending to commit a murder the day after tomorrow. The law only deals with conduct.

—Oliver Wendell Holmes (*The Common Law*, 1881)

If there are still any citizens interested in protecting human liberty, let them study the conspiracy laws of the United States.

—Clarence Darrow (*The Story of My Life*, 1932)

CHAPTER OUTLINE

KEY CONCEPTS

abandonment	dangerous proximity test	principal in the first degree
accessory	impossibility	principal in the second
accessory after the fact	inchoate crime	degree
accessory before the fact	last act test	renunciation
accomplice	mere preparation	strict liability crimes
accomplice liability	misprision of felony	substantial step
complicity	parties to crime	vicarious liability
criminal conspiracy	physical proximity test	Wharton's Rule
criminal solicitation	plurality requirement	

AFTER READING THIS CHAPTER YOU SHOULD:

▷ Know what inchoate crimes are.

▷ Understand the concept of a "substantial step."

▷ Be able to describe the required intent for attempted crimes.

▷ Be able to explain the proximity approach in criminal attempts and the problems associated with using that approach.

▷ Be able to list the alternatives to the proximity approach for criminal attempts.

▷ Understand the defenses to crimes of attempt, conspiracy, and solicitation.

▷ Know the required elements of the offenses of attempt, conspiracy, and solicitation.

▷ Understand the doctrine of complicity.

▷ Understand Wharton's Rule.

▷ Be able to describe the various parties to criminal misconduct.

INTRODUCTION

Melvin Lee Davis was convicted in federal court in 1982 and was sentenced to prison. A release date was set for October 2011. In late 1990, while incarcerated at the Federal Correctional Institute in Summers, Connecticut (FCIS), Melvin was an inmate trustee and worked as a law library clerk. On October 18 of that year the warden's office at FCIS received, through inter-office mail, two official-looking documents describing changes in Davis' case. The first, a letter written on letterhead stationery from the "U.S. Department of Justice, Federal Bureau of Prisons, Community Programs Office, Boston, Massachusetts," said that Virginia Department of Corrections officials had dropped an administrative hold on Davis and indicated that Davis' release date had been changed to January 8, 1991. The second document appeared to be an official U.S. Government memorandum instructing prison officials to release Davis' on January 8, 1991. Authorities at FCIS became suspicious and called the offices from which the letters appeared to originate. After learning that both written communiqués were fraudulent, further investigation revealed Davis' fingerprints on both documents. Davis was charged with attempted escape from a

Web
EXTRA!

Web Extra! 4–1
U.S. v. *Davis* (1993)

federal institution, and the U.S. District Court for the District of Connecticut held that his making and passing of two false documents in an attempt to move his release date up by twenty years constituted the offense of attempted escape. The court's decision was upheld by the U.S. Court of Appeals for the Second Circuit.[1]

Inchoate crimes are incipient crimes "which generally lead to other crimes."[2] "Inchoate" means imperfect, partial, or unfinished. They are also referred to as *anticipatory offenses.* Inchoate crimes traditionally include: (1) attempts, (2) solicitation, and (3) conspiracies. While language favoring punishment of inchoate misconduct can be found in fourteenth-century judicial opinions, most inchoate crimes were not recognized until the late eighteenth century. Until then, prevailing legal wisdom often held that "a miss is as good as a mile."[3]

A conceptual difficulty with inchoate crimes is that the earlier the police intervene to arrest someone for a crime, the greater the possibility that the person will be arrested for conduct that may appear suspicious but which is actually innocent. On the other hand, the longer the police abstain from intervening in what may be a planned crime, the greater the likelihood that the crime will be successfully completed and victims will suffer harm.

There are some crimes that are often thought of as complete crimes, which are actually inchoate crimes in disguise.[4] Most of these crimes are discussed in other chapters. Burglary, which is discussed in Chapter 10, is one such offense. In most jurisdictions, the crime of burglary is defined as the entering of a building with the intent to commit a theft or a felony. Technically speaking, the crime of burglary is completed with an illegal entry of a building, although the crime for which the entry was made may never be completed. Other offenses that fall into this nebulous category include possession of burglary tools and stalking.

INCHOATE CRIME

an unfinished crime that generally leads to another crime. Also, a crime that consists of actions that are steps toward another offense. Sometimes referred to as an anticipatory offense.

CRIMINAL ATTEMPT

Web Extra! 4–2
Britannica online:
attempt

Joshua Dressler suggests that it takes six steps for a person to intentionally commit a crime.[5] First, according to Dressler, the individual conceives an idea of the crime. Second, the individual then evaluates the idea. Third, he or she forms the intention to go forward. Fourth, he or she prepares to commit the crime. Fifth, he or she commences the acts necessary to complete the crime, and, sixth, the individual finishes the actions defined by law as necessary to complete the crime. Dressler notes that a person is not punished during the first three stages of the process. In the first two stages, the individual lacks a *mens rea* (intent). In addition, since people are not punished for thoughts alone, there is no crime until there is an *actus reus.* According to Dressler, it is the activity in the middle range (the fourth and fifth stages), which comes after the formation of the *mens rea* but before the attainment of the criminal goal, that is legally considered inchoate or incomplete conduct.[6]

Statutory definitions of the crime of attempt are generally brief and often fail to provide a complete understanding as to what constitutes an attempt.[7] New York, for example, describes the crime of attempt as follows: "A person is guilty of an attempt to commit a crime when, with the intent to commit a crime, he engages in conduct which tends to effect the commission of such crime."[8] In California, the statute on criminal attempts provides: "A person commits an attempt when, with the intent to commit a specific offense, he does any act which constitutes a substantial step toward the commission of that offense."[9] Illinois takes an approach similar to California's. According to the Illinois statute on attempts, a criminal attempt occurs when a person, with the intent to commit an offense, performs any act that constitutes a **substantial step** toward the commission of that offense.[10] Federal courts[11] and the Model Penal Code[12] also acknowledge the substantial step principle.

SUBSTANTIAL STEP

significant activity undertaken in furtherance of some goal. An act or omission that is a significant part of a series of acts or omissions, constituting a course of conduct planned to culminate in the commission of a crime. Also, an important or essential step toward the commission of a crime that is considered sufficient to constitute the crime of criminal attempt. A substantial step is conduct that is strongly corroborative of the actor's criminal purpose. According to one court, a substantial step is "behavior of such a nature that a reasonable observer, viewing it in context, could conclude beyond a reasonable doubt that it was undertaken in accordance with a design to violate the statute."

Preparing to commit a crime. A criminal attempt occurs when a person, with the intent to commit an offense, performs any act that constitutes a substantial step toward the commission of that offense. Mere preparation is not sufficient. (Photo by Marc Bove, courtesy of Pearson Education/PH College.)

As these definitions note, attempt is a specific intent crime. For an individual to commit the crime of attempted murder (criminal homicide), for example, the individual must specifically intend to commit murder. On the other hand, an individual may commit murder without necessarily intending to do so, as in the case of felony murder (which is discussed in Chapter 8). Hence, in some cases there is a substantial difference in the culpable mental state required for the completed crime and the attempt. Speaking generally, then, the crime of attempt can be said to have two elements:

- Specific intent to commit a criminal offense, and
- A substantial step undertaken toward the commission of the intended offense.

The Act Requirement

Attempted criminal activity encompasses a broad area. Almost any crime that can be envisioned can be attempted, and under the penal codes of most states, any crime defined by statute has as its adjunct an attempt to commit that crime. Florida law, for example, says that "a person who attempts to commit an offense prohibited by law and in such attempt does any act toward the commission of such offense, but fails in the perpetration or is intercepted or prevented in the execution thereof, commits the offense of criminal attempt. . . ."[13] The Model Penal Code,[14] sounding much like the examples from California and Illinois cited earlier, requires a substantial step to corroborate intent. Its suggested wording is also reflected in Alaska law, which reads: "A person is guilty of an attempt to commit a crime if, with intent to commit a crime, the person engages in conduct which constitutes a substantial step toward the commission of that crime."[15] Hence, under the laws of most states, for the crime of homicide there is the corresponding crime of attempted homicide, for the crime of rape there is the corresponding crime of attempted rape, and so on.

For an attempt to be charged, an act of some sort is necessary. But what kinds of acts are sufficient to constitute attempts? Generally speaking, courts have held that **mere preparation** to commit an offense is not sufficient to support a charge of attempted criminal activity, and that some specific action must be taken toward the actual completion of the intended offense. Consider, for example, Title 5, Chapter 22, Section 8 of the Texas Penal Code, which describes the crime of "aiding suicide" with these words: "A person commits an offense if, with intent to promote or assist the commission of suicide by another, he aids or attempts to aid the other to commit or attempt to commit suicide."

Just what constitutes "an attempt to aid?" On that issue, the Texas statute is silent. Texas law, however, says that a person is generally guilty of attempted criminal activity if "he does an act amounting to more than mere preparation that tends but fails to effect the commission of the offense intended." Under Texas law, then, would a person be guilty of attempting to aid another to commit suicide if he or she purchased a copy of the book *Final Exit*,[16] which describes various methods of suicide and tells readers how to enact them, and gave the book to the person contemplating suicide? That is, would they have gone beyond "mere preparation" in the provision of aid? Similarly, if they requested literature from the Hemlock Society, an association of suicide rights activists, would that be an act beyond mere preparation? If they feigned symptoms to a physician in order to obtain tranquilizers that could be used in a suicide, would that be more than mere preparation? What if they provided such pills to the person seeking to die? Read the Capstone Case at the end of this chapter that provides various interpretations of the idea of a "substantial step" that goes beyond mere preparation in order to answer these questions.

MERE PREPARATION

an act or omission that may be part of a series of acts or omissions constituting a course of conduct planned to culminate in the commission of a crime, but which fails to meet the requirements for a **substantial step**. Also, preparatory actions or steps taken toward the completion of a crime that are remote from the actual commission of the crime.

Your verdict will be "Guilty" or "Not Guilty." Your job is not to find innocence.

—Judge Russell R. Leggett, Westchester County (N.Y.) Court

Preparation

Mere preparation to commit a crime is generally insufficient to constitute the crime of criminal attempt. As mentioned, the Model Penal Code provides that conduct is not an attempt unless it involves a substantial step toward the commission of the offense and is strongly corroborative of the actor's criminal purpose.[17] A central issue becomes one of deciding when the conduct in question is no longer considered to be "mere preparation" and becomes an attempt within the meaning of an applicable statute. The U.S. Court of Appeals for the Fifth Circuit, in *Mims* v. *United States*,[18] recognized the difficulty involved in resolving the issue, and observed that "[m]uch ink has been split in an attempt to arrive at a satisfactory standard for telling where preparation ends and attempt begins."

In the oft-cited case of *People* v. *Rizzo*,[19] four defendants were cruising the streets of New York searching for a victim they knew as Charles Rao. Rao was a payroll clerk, and the defendants felt certain that he would be walking from a bank carrying a deposit bag, which they thought would be full of money to meet an upcoming payroll at the company where Rao worked. One of the defendants, Charles Rizzo, told the others that he would be able to identify Rao and would point him out to them before the robbery. Although the defendants never found Rao, their suspicious activity attracted the attention of police. They were arrested and charged with attempted robbery. At trial all four defendants were convicted of attempted first-degree robbery and sentenced to prison. Rizzo appealed his conviction, arguing that he had not legally attempted the crime of robbery, since he never came close to carrying out the offense. The New York Court of Appeals agreed and reversed Rizzo's conviction. The appellate court based its decision, in large part, on an earlier court's finding that "acts constituting an attempt" are those which come "very near to the accomplishment of the crime."[20] Holding that the actions of the defendants constituted "mere preparation," the appeals court asked:

> Did the acts above described come dangerously near to the taking of Rao's property? Did the acts come so near to the commission of robbery that there was reasonable likelihood of its accomplishment but for the interference (of the police)? Rao was not found; the defendants were still looking for him; no attempt to rob him could be made, at least until he came in sight. . . . There was no man there with the payroll for the United Lathing Company whom these defendants could rob. Apparently no money had been drawn from the bank for the payroll by anybody at the time of the arrest. In a word, these defendants had planned to break into a building and were arrested while they were hunting about the streets for the building, not knowing where it was. Neither would a man be guilty of an attempt to commit murder if he armed himself and started out to find the person whom he had planned to kill but could not find him. So here these defendants were not guilty of an attempt to commit robbery in the first degree when they had not found or reached the presence of the person they intended to rob.

"For these reasons," concluded the court, "the judgment of conviction of this defendant appellant must be reversed."[21]

Formulations that courts have used to distinguish between preparation and a substantial step include:

- The last act test, which asks whether the conduct completed is dangerously close to completing the crime itself.
- The notion that the more serious the threatened harm, the more justified the court would be in examining acts further back in the series of acts that would lead to crime completion.
- The idea that the clearer the intent to commit the offense is, the less proximate the acts need to be to the completion of the crime to constitute the crime of attempt.

Proximity Approach The proximity approach was the traditional test used at common law.[22] Under this approach, acts remotely leading toward the commission of the offense are not considered as attempts to commit the crime, but acts immediately connected with it are. The proximity test was based on the **last act test.**

The last act test originated from the frequently cited English case of *Regina* v. *Eagleton.*[23] The defendant in *Eagleton* was a baker who was hired by the welfare office to provide bread for the poor. He was to receive credit vouchers from the poor for each loaf of bread that he provided them and was then to take the vouchers to the welfare office, which would then credit him for his efforts. He was to be paid later, based on the number of vouchers submitted. Soon, however, the baker was charged with attempting to obtain money by false pretenses for having delivered underweight loafs and for turning in the credit vouchers he had received for them.

Eagleton defended himself on the grounds that turning the tickets into the welfare office earned him credit, not money. In effect, he argued that his activity did not amount to an attempt to obtain money, only credits. He was, nonetheless, convicted based on the fact that, after he turned in the vouchers to the welfare office, he was not required to perform any other act in order to be paid. Hence, the court reasoned, he had completed the last act necessary for payment.

The last act test required that the accused has taken the last step or act and has performed all that he intended to do and was able to do in an attempt to commit the crime, but for some reason the crime was not completed. Using this test in a murder by shooting situation, for example, an attempt would not be completed until the accused fired the weapon. The last act test was popular in England during the latter part of the nineteenth century,[24] but was eventually abandoned amidst charges that

LAST ACT TEST
in the crime of attempt, a test that asks whether the accused had taken the last step or act toward commission of the offense and had performed all that he intended to do and was able to do in an attempt to commit the crime, but for some reason, the crime was not completed.

PHYSICAL PROXIMITY TEST

a test traditionally used under common law to determine whether a person was guilty of attempted criminal activity. The physical proximity test requires that the accused has it within his or her power to complete the crime almost immediately.

the test made it virtually impossible for law enforcement personnel to prevent the commission of a substantive crime.

In an effort to reduce the strict provisions of the last act test, the **physical proximity test** was developed. Under the physical proximity test, the substantial step need not be the last act, but it must approach sufficiently near to it in order to stand as a substantial step in the direct movement toward commission of the intended crime.[25] Under the physical proximity test, which was well-articulated in the 1948 Pennsylvania case of *Commonwealth* v. *Kelly*,[26] the required substantial step is not held to have been completed until the accused has it within his or her power to enact the crime almost immediately. Under this test, for example, in order to be found guilty of attempted rape the accused would need to have the victim under his control and have started taking the necessary steps to force the victim to have sexual relations with him. In the *Kelly* case cited above, two men intending to trick a victim out of his money convinced him to go to the bank to withdraw funds. The men were arrested at the bank, but before the potential victim withdrew the funds. The men were arrested at the bank, but before the potential victim withdrew the funds. The court held that their conduct did not amount to criminal attempt since the money had not actually been removed from the intended victim's account.

DANGEROUS PROXIMITY TEST

a test for assessing attempts, under which a person is guilty of an attempt when his or her conduct comes dangerously close to success.

Justice Oliver Wendell Holmes developed the **dangerous proximity test.** This test incorporates the physical proximity standard but is more flexible. According to the dangerous proximity test, a person is guilty of an attempt when his or her conduct is in "dangerous proximity" to success. According to Holmes, courts should consider three factors: the nearness of completion, the degree of intended harm, and the degree of apprehension felt by the intended victim.[27] For example, a drug-dealing defendant intending to buy a large quantity of cocaine in an illegal transaction from a wholesaler may meet with the higher-level dealer, examine the goods, and then reject the drugs for quality reasons. Under the dangerous proximity test, however, the defendant could still be found guilty of attempted possession of a controlled substance with intent to sell since the acts that were undertaken were dangerously close to completing the targeted offense.

Alternatives to the Proximity Approach Alternatives to the proximity approach include the "indispensable element test," the "unequivocally test," and the "probable desistance test." Under the indispensable element test, the accused is not guilty of an attempt if he or she has yet to obtain control of an indispensable feature of the crime. For example, an accused who intends to commit armed robbery is not guilty of an attempted armed robbery prior to obtaining a weapon that is an indispensable element of armed robbery. Criticism of the indispensable element test says that it does little to consider an actor's actual degree of culpability.

Web Extra! 4–3

Commonwealth v. *Kelly* (1948)

We hold that the reckless disregard for human life implied in knowingly engaging in criminal activity known to carry a grave risk of death represents a highly culpable mental state....

—Justice Sandra Day O'Connor, writing on accomplice liability
Tison v. *Arizona*, 481 U.S. 137 (1987)

Under the unequivocally test, an act does not become an attempt until it ceases to be equivocal.[28] This test requires that an act or acts committed by the defendant must unequivocally manifest his or her criminal intent in order to constitute an attempt. Conduct that may indicate *either* noncriminal *or* criminal intent is not sufficient to demonstrate attempt. This test has been criticized on the grounds that there is no act that is completely unequivocal, since all human behavior is open to interpretation.

A third alternative is the probable desistance approach. Under this approach, the defendant's conduct constitutes an attempt if it has gone beyond the point where the defendant is likely to *voluntarily* stop short of completing the offense. This test has been criticized on the grounds that it is difficult to determine whether a defendant is likely to stop a course of action.

Model Penal Code Approach As noted earlier, the Model Penal Code approach uses the substantial step test. The Model Penal Code approach is used in most states and in the federal courts. This approach incorporates aspects of both the proximity test and the unequivocally test. Any conduct that meets any of the variations of either test is sufficient to constitute an attempt, since it constitutes a substantial step toward crime completion. Under this approach, an attempt will be found to have occurred in many cases where the defendant does not move very far along the path toward consummation of the intended offense.

The Model Penal Code approach is reflective of a continuing trend during the past thirty years toward a broadening of attempt liability. The Model Penal Code lists the following examples of activity that might meet the substantial step criterion, providing that the behavior in question is thought to corroborate the defendant's criminal purpose[29]:

- Lying in wait or searching for or following the contemplated victim[30];
- Enticing or seeking to entice the contemplated victim of the crime to go to the place contemplated for its commission;
- Reconnoitering the place contemplated for the commission of the crime;
- Unlawful entry of a structure, vehicle, or enclosure in which it is contemplated that the crime will be committed;
- Possession of materials to be employed in the commission of the crime, which are specially designed for such unlawful use or which can serve no lawful purpose of the actor under the circumstances;
- Possession, collection, or fabrication of material to be employed in the commission of the crime, at or near the place contemplated for its commission, where such possession, collection, or fabrication serves no lawful useful purpose of the actor under the circumstances;
- Soliciting an innocent agent to engage in conduct constituting an element of the crime.

Defenses

During the Vietnam conflict, Father Phillip Berrigan and another prisoner in a federal correctional institution were charged with attempting to violate a federal statute prohibiting the sending of letters into and out of a federal institution without the warden's consent. Both were apprehended as they attempted to mail the letters. In presenting evidence in the case, an assistant U.S. attorney established that, unknown to the defendants, the warden had been aware that the letters were being prepared and were about to be sent. Apparently the warden let the conduct leading up to the actual mailing of the letters occur in order to help the government build a case against the defendants.[31] In this situation, Father Phillip clearly did all that he intended to do in order to commit the targeted crime.

Berrigan was convicted by a trial court of an attempt violation, but his conviction was overturned by a federal appellate court, which ruled that although the priest's conduct amounted to more than mere preparation, it was legally impossible for him to commit the crime because the warden had, in effect, consented to the conduct when he did not interfere with it. Although Berrigan's case may have been unusual, anyone charged with an attempt may generally raise two defenses: abandonment and impossibility.

Abandonment or Renunciation The defense of **abandonment** claims that the defendant voluntarily decided to renounce continued attempts to commit the crime. Indiana law reads: ". . . it is a defense that the person who engaged in the

RENUNCIATION (ABANDONMENT)

the voluntary and complete abandonment of the intent and purpose to commit a criminal offense. Renunciation (abandonment) is a defense to a charge of attempted criminal activity.

prohibited conduct voluntarily abandoned his effort to commit the underlying crime and voluntarily prevented its commission."[32] In some jurisdictions, the term **renunciation** is used instead of abandonment. Texas law, for example, states: "It is an affirmative defense to prosecution . . . that under circumstances manifesting a voluntary and complete renunciation of his criminal objective the actor avoided commission of the offense attempted by abandoning his criminal conduct. . . ."

Similarly, Florida law reads: "It is a defense to a charge of criminal attempt, criminal solicitation, or criminal conspiracy that, under circumstances manifesting a complete and voluntary renunciation of his criminal purpose, the defendant: (a) abandoned his attempt to commit the offense or otherwise prevented its commission; (b) after soliciting another person to commit an offense, persuaded such other person not to do so or otherwise prevented commission of the offense; or (c) after conspiring with one or more persons to commit an offense, persuaded such persons not to do so or otherwise prevented commission of the offense."[33]

Arguments in favor of allowing abandonment or renunciation as a defense include: (1) it encourages desistance, (2) indicates a lack of dangerousness on the part of the offender, and (3) indicates a lack of intent on the part of the defendant to carry the crime to completion. On the other hand, arguments against allowing the use of this defense include suggestions that: (1) it has little deterrent effect, (2) it fails to indicate whether the defendant will not prove dangerous in the future, and (3) the accused has already completed the crime of attempt. Even so, courts in most American jurisdictions today recognize the abandonment defense.

The Model Penal Code also allows for the defense of abandonment. The code provides "it is an affirmative defense that the defendant has abandoned his effort to commit the crime or otherwise prevented its commission. . . ."[34] Virtually all jurisdictions require that abandonment be voluntary. Postponement of the crime in anticipation of a possibly better time for its commission, the defendant's deciding to find a different victim, or disappointment in the anticipated fruits of the crime are not considered to constitute voluntary abandonment. Involuntary abandonment is not a bar to prosecution since a defendant may be forced to abandon attempts to commit a crime because of police intervention, inclement weather, a debilitating accident, or some other inability to continue. Even when the defense is successful, it does not affect the criminal liability of an accomplice who does not join in such abandonment or renunciation.

IMPOSSIBILITY

a defense to a charge of attempted criminal activity that claims the defendant could not have factually or legally committed the envisioned offense even if he or she had been able to carry through the attempt to do so. It is, for example, factually impossible to kill someone who is already dead.

Impossibility Impossibility, the second defense to a charge of attempted criminal activity, may be of either the factual or legal variety. Factual impossibility, which is rarely successful as a defense, claims that the defendant could not have committed the envisioned offense even if he or she had been able to carry through the attempt to do so. It is factually impossible, for example, to rob a person who has no possessions, even though a robbery might be attempted; and it is similarly impossible to kill someone who is already dead (although an attempt might be made by someone who lacks knowledge of the person's death[35]). Another example of factual impossibility is that of a pickpocket who tries to pick an empty pocket. Even though the intended victim had nothing in his or her pockets, the would-be thief could still be charged with an attempt to steal. A final example might be that of a person who attempts to shoot another, only to find that the gun is not loaded.

Legal impossibility, a much different type of impossibility, generally precludes prosecution in most jurisdictions. The defense of legal impossibility claims that the attempted offense is really no offense at all, either because there is no law against the imagined crime or because the actions in question do not meet the requirements of the law for a crime to have occurred. So, for example, a person who sells powdered sugar, believing that it is cocaine, may not be prosecuted under a statute that makes "trafficking in controlled substances" illegal, since powdered sugar is not a controlled substance. Likewise, although receiving stolen goods is a crime in most jurisdictions, someone who receives nonstolen goods, believing them to be stolen, will rarely face prosecution.

It is important to realize, however, that some jurisdictions accept neither claims of factual nor legal impossibility as a bar to prosecution. The Alaska Penal Code, for example, reads: "In a prosecution under this section, it is not a defense that it was factually or legally impossible to commit the crime which was the object of the attempt if the conduct engaged in by the defendant would be a crime had the circumstances been as the defendant believed them to be." Although the intent of the provision is no doubt to allow prosecution of cocaine dealers who sell powdered sugar (often knowingly) and the like, it raises some interesting possibilities under which one could imagine the prosecution of a person who attempts a crime that exists only in the imagination of the actor.

Completed Offense

In most jurisdictions, if a defendant is charged with a substantive crime but evidence indicates that she only completed an attempt, she may be found guilty only of the *lessor included offense* of an attempt. If the crime is completed, however, then the attempt is usually considered to have merged into the completed offense—and the defendant would be guilty only of the substantive offense, and *not* of both the substantive offense *and* an attempt to complete that offense.

Suppose, however, that the defendant is charged *only* with an attempt but evidence establishes that she actually completed the offense. Could she then be found guilty of the substantive crime? The answer is "no," since virtually all jurisdictions hold that a defendant may not be found guilty of a greater offense than the one with which he or she is charged. On the other hand, the fact that the substantive crime was actually committed cannot be used as a defense to a charge of attempt to commit that crime.

Punishment

At common law, all attempts were punishable as misdemeanors. Accordingly, offenders convicted of attempt were punished less severely than they would have been had the contemplated crime been completed. Over the years, legislatures in this country have struggled to establish appropriate punishments for criminal attempts.

Noted jurist H. L. A. Hart reasoned that attempts should be punished because "there must be many who are not completely confident that they will succeed in their criminal objective, but will be prepared to run the risk of punishment if they can be assured that they have to pay nothing for attempts which fail; whereas if unsuccessful attempts were also punished, the price might appear to them to be too high. Again, there must be many cases where men might with good or bad reason believe that if they succeed in committing some crime they will escape, but if they fail they may be caught."[36]

Today, punishment schemes relating to offenses are usually closely related to the grading system established for the intended offense, and in many states the punishment for an attempt is one classification below that for the intended offense itself. The Model Penal Code, on the other hand, provides the same punishment for attempts that it does for completed crimes (except in cases of crimes punishable by life imprisonment or death). Supporters of the Model Penal Code approach argue that the same *mens rea* exists in an offender's mind when a crime is attempted as when it is completed—and that, consequently, the same punishment is justified. For purposes of punishment, they say, it matters little whether the attempted crime actually occurred or failed for some reason to be completed. According to commentaries on the Model Penal Code, an appropriate sentence can best be determined by the antisocial *disposition* of the offender, and by the demonstrated *need for a corrective sanction*. Therefore, in most instances, it makes little difference when applying sanctions whether the offender was able to consummate the attempted criminal activity or not.[37]

CRIMINAL CONSPIRACY

CRIMINAL CONSPIRACY

an agreement between two or more persons to commit or to effect the commission of an unlawful act, or to use unlawful means to accomplish an act that is not unlawful.

A **criminal conspiracy** is an agreement between two or more persons to commit or to effect the commission of an unlawful act, or to use unlawful means to accomplish an act that is not unlawful. The notion of conspiracy was first formulated by the English Star Chamber in 1611. Under English common law the term had much the same meaning as it does today. However, while conspiracy was generally considered to be a misdemeanor under common law, most states and the federal government today classify it as a felony.

Florida law says that "A person who agrees, conspires, combines, or confederates with another person or persons to commit any offense commits the offense of criminal conspiracy. . . ."[38] The Commentaries on the Model Penal Code state: "Conspiracy as an offense has two different aspects, reflecting the different functions it serves in the legal system. In the first place, conspiracy is an inchoate crime, complementing the provisions dealing with attempt and solicitation in reaching preparatory conduct before it has matured into commission of a substantive offense. Second, it is a means of striking against the special danger incident to group activity, facilitating prosecution of the group, and yielding a basis for imposing added penalties when combination is involved."

According to legal commentator Paul Marcus, striking changes in criminal conspiracy prosecutions during the past two decades include an enormous growth in the number of cases involving many defendants, an increase in the prevalence of complex evidentiary issues, and increasingly complicated charges brought against defendants in conspiracy cases.[39] Cases he cites as examples include: (1) *United States* v. *Casamento* (1989),[40] involving 21 defendants, 275 witnesses, and 40,000 pages of transcripts; (2) *United States* v. *Ianniello* (1989),[41] a thirteen month-long trial with 11 defendants; (3) *United States* v. *Kopituk* (1982),[42] a case that had 12 defendants and 130 witnesses; and (4) *United States* v. *Martino* (1981),[43] with 20 defendants and more than 200 witnesses. Many of today's conspiracy cases involve drug trafficking, in which several people agree to work in concert to manufacture, transport, and distribute controlled substances.

Doctrine of Complicity

Conspiracy is a complex and controversial crime. Some judges and legal scholars have advocated its reform or abolition.[44] Criticisms of the crime of conspiracy include charges that it provides the state with a potent, and possibly unfair, weapon because it gives prosecutors extraordinary latitude in prosecuting behavior that would not otherwise be criminal. Similarly, prosecutors pursuing conspiracy cases have available to them a number of procedural advantages that are not available in other cases. Procedural advantages favoring the prosecution include the use of joint

A criminal conspiracy develops. A criminal conspiracy is an agreement between two or more persons to commit or to effect the commission of an unlawful act, or to use unlawful means to accomplish an act that is not unlawful. (Photo by Michael Newman, courtesy of PhotoEdit.)

trials, admission of hearsay evidence, and the fact that venue (place of trial) may be in any jurisdiction in which any element of the offense occurred. Other criticisms include the charge that the crime of conspiracy is so vague that it defies definition and the claim that the offense of conspiracy is predominantly mental in composition—resulting in prosecutions based more on thought than on activity.

Because conspiracy statutes give prosecutors a broad authority to charge individuals for what often appear to be rather nebulous offenses, Justice Learned Hand once described the crime of conspiracy as "the darling of the modern prosecutor's nursery."[45] Justice Hand noted that the crime of conspiracy is fundamentally "formless" and therefore serves as a powerful tool of prosecutors. Many contend that because of conspiracy's emphasis on *mens rea* and its corresponding de-emphasis of conduct, there is a greater risk that persons will be punished for what they say or think rather than for what they do. In a famous English case, for example, the House of Lords upheld a conviction for "conspiracy to corrupt public morals."[46] Defendants had been convicted based on an agreement made between them to publish a directory listing prostitutes and their services (the agreement was regarded as illegal because it had the intention of promoting immoral acts). The publishing of the directory never occurred. If it had, however, it would not in itself have been a crime.

Elements of the Crime

The elements of the crime of conspiracy are as follows:

- An agreement between two or more persons.
- To carry out an act that is unlawful or one that is lawful but is to be accomplished by unlawful means.
- A culpable intent on the part of the defendants.

When a conspiracy unfolds, the ultimate act that it aims to bring about does not have to occur for the parties to the conspiracy to be arrested. When people plan to bomb a public building, for example, they can be legally stopped before the bombing. As soon as they take steps to "further" their plan, they have met the requirement for an act. Buying explosives, telephoning one another, or drawing plans of the building may all be actions in "furtherance of the conspiracy."

Plurality Requirement

PLURALITY REQUIREMENT

the logical and legal requirement that a conspiracy involve two or more parties.

The essence of the crime of conspiracy is an *agreement* for the joint purpose of unlawful ends. Since conspiracy is defined in terms of an agreement, it necessarily involves two or more persons. This aspect of the offense is called the **plurality requirement.**

The required agreement does not, however, need to be a "meeting of the minds," such as is required to create an enforceable contract. All that is needed for the crime of conspiracy to occur is that the parties communicate to each other in some way their intentions to pursue a joint and criminal objective, or to pursue a joint objective in a criminal manner.[47]

Any implied agreement is sufficient for prosecution under most conspiracy statutes. One party may, for example, by his or her actions indicate to another party that he or she will pursue a joint venture. Courts are generally very liberal as to the types of proof that may be used to prove an agreement. In *Williams* v. *United States,* the government was allowed to prove an agreement by circumstantial evidence that strongly suggested that there must have been a common plan. In *United States* v. *James,* defendants were convicted of a conspiracy to assault a federal officer based on the fact that they attended drills designed to train for an anticipated attack by law enforcement personnel. Defendants who were present for some of the drills, but were not present at the shoot-out, were found guilty of conspiracy because attendance at the drills established that they must have been part of the agreement to attack the officer.[48]

Wharton's Rule Some crimes, by their very nature, require two or more criminal participants for their commission. Adultery, for example, requires at least two persons (generally a man and a woman, one of whom must be married to someone else). Other crimes may be committed by solitary offenders but sometimes involve more than one criminal participant. Murder, for example, requires only one person—the murderer—for its commission. The crime of conspiracy to commit murder, however, involves at least two persons.

WHARTON'S RULE

a rule applicable to conspiracy cases that holds that, when the targeted crime by its very nature takes more than one person to commit, there can be no conspiracy when no more than the number of persons required to commit the offense participate in it.

Wharton's Rule provides that where the targeted crime by its very nature takes more than one person to commit, then there can be no conspiracy when no more than the number of persons required to commit the offense participate in it. In the crime of adultery, for example, there can be no conspiracy to commit adultery unless more than two people are involved in the offense (as when a married couple conspires to lure others into adulterous relationships).[49] Wharton's Rule was named after Francis Wharton, the criminal law author who first articulated it. The rationale behind the rule is that where the crime requires more than one person to commit it, the legislature presumably factored into the prescribed punishment for the offense the dangers stemming from group criminality.

Wharton's Rule does not apply to those situations where the crime is defined so as to require two or more persons to commit, but where only one of the offenders is punishable under the targeted crime statute. The rule is irrelevant, for example, in the case of a statute that punishes the selling of liquor during certain hours of the day but which prescribes a punishment only for the seller. In some jurisdictions and under federal law, Wharton's Rule is only a presumption that does not apply if it is clear that the legislature did not intend to bar convictions for conspiracy.[50]

Similarly, Wharton's Rule has not been incorporated into the Model Penal Code. According to Code Commentaries, the fact that an offense inevitably requires concert is no reason to immunize criminal preparation to commit it. The Code does indicate that in those situations where the minimum number of participates required to commit the crime are involved, those offenders may not be convicted of both the substantive crime and the conspiracy to commit it.[51]

Web Extra! 4–4

People v. Powell
(1875)

Required Intent

As noted earlier, the essence of the crime of conspiracy is an agreement to commit an illegal activity or to commit some legal activity via illegal means. Accordingly, there must be some intent on the part of the conspirators to reach an agreement, and there must be an intent to achieve the objective.

Some states require a "corrupt motive" to establish conspiracy. In the well-known case of *People v. Powell*,[52] for example, the defendants were charged with conspiracy to violate a statute requiring municipal officials to advertise for bids before buying supplies for the city. The defendants had offered a substantial discount to the city, if the city would forgo the bidding process. The defendants were successful in arguing that they could not be convicted of a conspiracy, since they acted in good faith ignorance of the bidding requirement. The court held that they could not be convicted unless there was proof that the defendants acted with "an evil purpose." Most states and the Model Penal Code, however, emphasize the responsibility of potential conspirators to know the law relevant to their actions and do not require a "corrupt motive" for proof of conspiracy.

> If a man intentionally adopts certain conduct in certain circumstances known to him; and that conduct is forbidden by the law under those circumstances, he intentionally breaks the law in the only sense in which the law ever considers intent.
>
> —Justice Oliver Wendell Holmes, Jr., *Ellis* v. *United States*, 206 U.S. 246, 257 (1907)

Parties to a Conspiracy

When people participate in a conspiracy, the law does not require that each party form an agreement with all of the other parties involved. In complex conspiracies, for example, the parties may not all know one another and may not even be aware of the involvement of all of the other parties. This is particularly true in cases involving organized crime, drug dealing and distribution, illicit gambling, and organized prostitution.

Elaborate conspiracies, in which the parties to the conspiracy may not all be aware of one another's identity or even involvement, are sometimes described as "wheel" or "chain" conspiracies. In "wheel" conspiracies, the conspirators deal only with a ring leader and not with each other. The leader of the conspiracy can be thought of as a hub around which each of the others—like spokes on a wheel—revolve. To establish whether a wheel conspiracy is a single conspiracy or a series of conspiracies for purposes of the law, courts have developed a "community of interests" test. A single conspiracy exists if: (1) each "spoke" knows that other "spokes" exist, although they need not know the precise identity of the other "spokes," and (2) the various "spokes" have a community of shared interests. In one early case where such a test was applied, a woman was convicted of conspiracy to perform illegal abortions as part of a wheel conspiracy. The convicted woman had referred pregnant women to a doctor (who was also a defendant) in violation of the law. In declaring that a wheel-type of conspiracy existed, the trial court held that the

LAW ON THE BOOKS

ALASKA DEFINES "CONSPIRACY."

Compare with Model Penal Code, Section 5.03

ALASKA PENAL CODE

Section 11.31.120. CONSPIRACY. (a) An offender commits the crime of conspiracy if, with the intent to promote or facilitate a serious felony offense, the offender agrees with one or more persons to engage in or cause the performance of that activity and the offender or one of the persons does an overt act in furtherance of the conspiracy.

(b) If an offender commits the crime of conspiracy and knows that a person with whom the offender conspires to commit a serious felony offense has conspired or will conspire with another person or persons to commit the same serious felony offense, the offender is guilty of conspiring with that other person or persons to commit that crime whether or not the offender knows their identities.

(c) In a prosecution under this section, it is a defense that the defendant was merely present at the time that two or more other persons agreed to engage in or cause the performance of a serious felony offense.

(d) In a prosecution under this section, it is not a defense that a person with whom the defendant conspires could not be guilty of the crime that is the object of the conspiracy because of:

1. Lack of criminal responsibility or other legal incapacity or exemption;
2. Belonging to a class of persons who by definition are legally incapable in an individual capacity of committing the crime that is the object of the conspiracy;
3. Unawareness of the criminal nature of the conduct in question or of the criminal purpose of the defendant; or,
4. Any other factor precluding the culpable mental state required for the commission of the crime.

(e) If the offense that the conspiracy is intended to promote or facilitate is actually committed, a defendant may not be convicted of conspiring to commit that offense with another person for whose conduct the defendant is not legally accountable under AS 11.16.120(b).

(f) In a prosecution under this section, it is an affirmative defense that the defendant, under circumstances manifesting a voluntary and complete renunciation of the defendant's criminal intent, either:

1. Gave timely warning to law enforcement authorities; or,
2. Otherwise made proper effort that prevented the commission of the crime that was the object of the conspiracy. Renunciation by one conspirator does not affect the liability of another conspirator who does not join in the renunciation.

(g) Notwithstanding AS 22.10.030, venue in actions in which the crime of conspiracy is alleged to have been committed may not be based solely on the location of overt acts done in furtherance of the conspiracy.

(h) Conspiracy is:

1. An unclassified felony if the object of the conspiracy is murder in the first degree;
2. A class A felony if the object of the conspiracy is a crime punishable as an unclassified felony other than murder in the first degree;
3. A class B felony if the object of the conspiracy is a crime punishable as a class A felony;
4. A class C felony if the object of the conspiracy is a crime punishable as a class B felony.

(i) In this section,

1. "Overt act in furtherance of the conspiracy" means an act of such character that it manifests a purpose on the part of the actor that the object of the conspiracy be completed;
2. "Serious felony offense" means an offense (A) against the person under AS 11.41, punishable as an unclassified or class A felony; or (B) involving controlled substances under AS 11.71, punishable as an unclassified, class A, or class B felony.

defendant had been aware that others were also referring pregnant women to the same doctor for illegal abortions.[53]

The second type of conspiracy, the "chain" conspiracy, involves a sequence of individuals. Conspiracies of the chain-type are often found in illegal drug distribution schemes (in which controlled substances move sequentially from importer, to wholesaler, to retailer, and, ultimately, to the consumer) and in other activities associated with racketeering. The community interest test may also be used to determine if a chain-type of conspiracy consists of a single conspiracy or a group of conspiracies. Under both the wheel and the chain-type conspiracies, the precise identity of the other conspirators is not important, so long as it can be demonstrated that charged conspirators had knowledge of the fact that others were involved in the scheme and that they acted in terms of a shared interest.

Web Extra! 4–5
U.S. v. *Alvarez*
(1980)

Duration of Conspiracy

For purposes of the law, the duration of a conspiracy may be a critical issue. The longer a conspiracy continues, for example, the greater the chances of successful prosecution, since most statutes of limitation do not begin measuring time until a crime is complete. Also, in most jurisdictions, declarations of conspirators are admissible against other conspirators if the declarations are made while the conspiracy is still in progress.

Generally speaking, a conspiracy can be said to continue until the crime it anticipates is either completed or is abandoned by all of the parties involved. If a crime involves multiple conspirators, and a single conspirator withdraws, the conspiracy continues for purposes of the law so long as two or more parties continue to be involved in it. It is often important to establish when an individual conspirator withdrew for a variety of purposes, including: (1) prosecution under a statute of limitations, (2) defense challenges to declarations made by other conspirators after withdrawal, and (3) defense claims of nonliability for crimes committed by others

---

CRIMINAL LAW IN THE NEWS

Teacher Held in Conspiracy to Kill Judge

Allegedly Sought Hit Man on Behalf of Childhood Friend

SAN ANTONIO, TEXAS—A well respected high school soccer coach and social studies teacher is being held on $40,000 bail, charged with conspiring with a childhood buddy to arrange for the slaying of a state judge, authorities said.

Authorities say 38-year-old Carroll Parker, arrested Monday, was the moneyman behind a scheme to hire a paid assassin to kill state District Court Judge Mark Luitjen.

The social studies teacher and soccer coach had agreed to collect cash for his childhood friend, Robert E. Lee, who is serving a 25-year sentence for conspiracy to commit murder, authorities said. Lee planned to use the money to pay for a hit on Luitjen, a judge who had opposed his bid for parole, authorities said.

Agents go undercover
Investigators got wind of the scheme several weeks ago after a local newspaper received a tip and passed it along, a spokesman for the State Department of Criminal Justice confirmed today.

Investigators for the department and the state Department of Public Safety went undercover, some posing as hit men, and foiled the scheme, authorities said.

On Monday, they arrested Parker, who had collected an undisclosed amount of cash for the scheme, as he ate lunch at a San Antonio restaurant.

Parker was being held Monday at a state prison in Beeville, charged with solicitation to commit capital murder. Lee, who has reportedly been a close friend of Parker's since the sixth grade, faces the same charge.

Source: Seamus McGraw, "Teacher Held in Conspiracy to Kill Judge; Allegedly Sought Hit Man on Behalf of Childhood Friend," APB News. August 1, 2000. Reprinted with permission.

after the date of a defendant's withdrawal. To effectively constitute withdrawal, however, the individual withdrawing generally must give notice of having withdrawn to other conspirators or to law enforcement officials. Intent to withdraw is not the same as withdrawal. For a defense based on withdrawal to be successful under Model Penal Code guidelines, the defendant must show that withdrawal was voluntary and that the "success of the conspiracy" was "thwarted."[54] A withdrawal motivated by fear of immediate detection is not considered voluntary.

CRIMINAL SOLICITATION

CRIMINAL SOLICITATION
the encouraging, requesting, or commanding of another person to commit a crime.

Under common law, **criminal solicitation** occurs when one person requests or encourages another to perform a criminal act. Consider the following scenario: Jerry

LAW IN PRACTICE

WHAT ARE THE ESSENTIAL ELEMENTS OF A CRIMINAL CONSPIRACY?

The case summary provided in this box illustrates the essential elements of the crime of criminal conspiracy and shows how the agreement may be established.

United States v. Matta-Ballesteros
United States Court of Appeals,
Ninth Circuit (1995)
71 F.3d 754.

Juan Ramon Matta-Ballesteros had been convicted in a jury trial in a United States District Court of conspiring to kidnap a federal agent engaged in official duties, kidnapping a federal agent engaged in official duties, and other crimes. The case involved the infamous kidnapping and torture death of American DEA Special Agent Enrique Camarena. Camarena disappeared on February 7, 1985, after leaving the DEA office in Guadalajara, Mexico. His mutilated body was later discovered by Mexican police.

After his conviction, Matta-Ballesteros argued, among other things, that the evidence against him was insufficient to support his conviction on charges of conspiracy, prompting the U.S. Supreme Court to outline the elements needed to prove conspiracy under federal law. The majority opinion held: "The essential elements of a conspiracy are (1) an agreement to accomplish an illegal objective, (2) the commission of an overt act in furtherance of the conspiracy, and (3) the

requisite intent necessary to commit the underlying offense. . . ." The Court continued, saying, "An agreement may be inferred from the defendant's acts pursuant to the scheme, or other circumstantial evidence, and a defendant's proximity to the scene of illicit activity may support an inference when viewed in context with other evidence. . . . Once the existence of a conspiracy is shown, the government need only prove a slight connection between the defendant and the conspiracy. . . . A defendant's knowledge of and participation in a conspiracy may be inferred from circumstantial evidence and from evidence of the codefendants' actions. Acts which seem otherwise innocent, when viewed in the context of the surrounding circumstances, may justify an inference of complicity."

What do *you* think?

1. The Court stated that once the existence of a conspiracy is shown, the government need only prove a slight connection between the defendant and the conspiracy. Do you think the Court is saying that, on this aspect of the crime, the prosecution is not required to establish guilt beyond a reasonable doubt? Why or why not?

2. Do you think that the prosecution in conspiracy cases should be required to establish the existence of an agreement beyond a reasonable doubt since an agreement is an essential element of the crime of criminal conspiracy? Why or why not?

Jones's daughter has been dating Tim Collins, but Jones does not like Collins. Soon Jones learns that his neighbor, William White, is an important organized crime figure. Jones conceals this knowledge from White. He also knows that Collins is one of White's employees and is apparently involved in illegal activity. During a casual conversation with his neighbor, Jones tells White that Collins is a police informant. Could Jones be charged with solicitation to commit murder?[55] Although this is a question with no clear answer, if a jury were to find that Jones' purpose in disclosing that information was to encourage White to commit a crime, then the crime of criminal solicitation has been committed.

All states have codified the crime of criminal solicitation. Florida law, for example, reads: "A person who solicits another to commit an offense prohibited by law and in the course of such solicitation commands, encourages, hires, or requests another person to engage in specific conduct which would constitute such offense or an attempt to commit such offense commits the offense of criminal solicitation. . . ."[56] Most states consider it immaterial whether or not the solicitee agrees to perform the act solicited.

Consider a second scenario in which Joe asks Jim to kill his wife, Joyce. Since criminal solicitation consists of the requesting or encouraging of another to commit a crime, Joe's request clearly constitutes the crime of solicitation. The crime is completed upon the transmission of the request or the encouragement. If Jim agrees to the request, generally both parties will be guilty of conspiracy when an overt act is taken in furtherance of the conspiracy (such as Jim buying a gun to be used to kill Joe's wife). If Jim does in fact kill Joyce, then both Joe and Jim would be guilty of murder. While solicitation is, in effect, an attempted conspiracy, it is possible to have a conspiracy without a prior solicitation.

Criminal solicitation, unlike conspiracy, requires no overt act. It does, however, require a mental state such that the defendant must have intended to induce the other person to perform the crime, and a successful prosecution must establish that the defendant had the mental state required for the completed crime. Hence, in the above example, Joe must have intended to induce Jim to kill Joyce, and must in fact have intended that Joyce be murdered.

It is not necessary that the solicitor intend that the person he or she solicits commit the crime. It would, for example, also be criminal solicitation for Joe to ask Jim to find someone else to kill Joyce. Similarly, solicitation does not need to be addressed to one person and may also be addressed to members of a group. A *communication* to a large and *undefined* group will not normally, however, be considered a solicitation.[57]

Consider another possible scenario: Joe calls Jim's home, but Jim is not at home and Joe leaves a message on Jim's answering machine asking for help in killing his wife. Before Jim receives the message, Jim's wife turns it over to the police. Has Joe committed the crime of criminal solicitation? In some states the answer would be "no," since these jurisdictions require that the solicitation be communicated before the crime can be considered to have been completed. Other states, however, and the Model Penal Code declare it irrelevant that the defendant failed to communicate with the person who was the object of the solicitation so long as the defendant's conduct was designed to produce such a communication.[58] In this scenario, leaving the message on the answering machine was evidence of conduct designed to produce communication. Hence, under the Model Penal Code, Joe would be guilty of criminal solicitation.

Finally, no jurisdiction in the United States defines the use of an innocent person in the commission of an offense as criminal solicitation. If, for example, Joe requests that Bill bring him his briefcase that is lying on the table in the hotel lounge, but, unbeknownst to Bill, the briefcase does not in fact belong to Joe, then no criminal solicitation (for the crime of theft) occurs. Joe may, however, be guilty of an attempted larceny by trying to commit the offense with the use of an innocent instrumentality.

PARTIES TO CRIME

PARTIES TO CRIME

all persons who take part in the commission of a crime, including those who aid and abet and who are therefore criminally liable for the offense.

PRINCIPAL IN THE FIRST DEGREE

a person whose acts directly result in the criminal misconduct in question.

PRINCIPAL IN THE SECOND DEGREE

any person who was present at the crime scene and who aided, abetted, counseled, or encouraged the principal.

ACCESSORY BEFORE THE FACT

anyone who aides and abets in the commission of a crime, but who was not present at the crime scene.

ACCESSORY AFTER THE FACT

a person who did not participate in a crime, but who furnished post-crime assistance to keep the offender from being detected or from being arrested.

Common law developed a fairly complex scheme of labeling persons involved in a crime according to their relationship to the criminal act. It distinguished between those who actually committed the crime and other who assisted the perpetrator either before, during, or after the crime had been committed. Common law categories included: (1) the **principal in the first degree;** that is, the individual who actually committed the crime; (2) the **principal in the second degree;** or any person who was present at the crime scene and who aided, abetted, counseled, or encouraged the principal in the commission of the crime; (3) an **accessory before the fact,** who, like the principal in the second degree, aided and abetted in the preparation for the crime but was not present at the crime scene; and, finally, (4) an **accessory after the fact,** or a person who did not participate in the crime, but knew that the crime had been committed and furnished post-crime assistance to keep the criminal from being detected or from being arrested. Common law also took note of whether a principal in the second degree assumed a "constructive presence," as in the case of a lookout who stayed outside of the building in which a crime was being committed, or an "actual presence," as in the case of a person who more directly assisted in the actual commission of the offense.

Under common law, such distinctions were quite important, because an indictment charging a defendant as an accessory would not allow his or her conviction as a principal and vice versa. Additionally, an accessory could not be tried until the principal was first convicted. Such rules no longer exist in the United States today, and any participant in a crime may be tried and convicted even if the individual who actually committed the crime has not yet been apprehended.

Relationship of Complicity

A trend in modern American law has been to eliminate distinctions between principals and accessories before the fact. Most jurisdictions within the United States, and the Model Penal Code, no longer distinguish between the principal in the first or second degree or an accessory before the fact. The degree of a person's criminal liability today is rarely dependent on his or her presence or absence at the crime scene, and most jurisdictions draw distinctions only between principals and accessories—recognizing an **accessory** only as one who assists the felon after the crime has been committed.

ACCESSORY

one who knowingly gives assistance to a person who has committed a felony for the purpose of helping that individual avoid apprehension or detection. An accessory is liable for separate, lesser offenses following a crime.

The old common law categories of principal in the first degree, principal in the second degree, and the accessory before the fact are now often legislatively combined into our modern understanding of "principal." Federal law, for example, says "(a) Whoever commits an offense against the United States or aids, abets, counsels, commands, induces or procures its commission, is punishable as a principal. (b) Whoever willfully causes an act to be done which if directly performed by him or another would be an offense against the United States, is punishable as a principal."[59] (Also see the Law on the Books feature "Parties to Crime" in this chapter.)

This section of the U.S. Code makes clear the legislative intent to punish as a principal not only one who directly commits an offense, as well as one who "aids, abets, counsels, commands, induces or procures" another to commit an offense, but also anyone who *causes* the doing of an act that, if done by him or by her directly, would render him or her guilty of an offense against the United States. It removes all doubt that one who puts in motion or assists in the illegal enterprise, and thus causes the commission of an indispensable element of the offense by another agent or instrumentality, is guilty as a principal even though he or she intentionally refrained from the direct act that constituted the completed offense.

Accomplice Liability

Generally, one who assists in the commission of a crime, but does not commit the *actus reus,* is called an **accomplice.** Unlike a mere accessory, an accomplice is often present or directly aids in the commission of the crime. The relationship between the person who commits the crime and his or her accomplice is one of **complicity.** The principle of **accomplice liability** is based on the notion that any individual who aids, abets, encourages, or assists another person to commit a crime should share in the criminal liability that accrues under law.

Although we often think of an accomplice as playing a central role in the commission of a crime, words alone may be sufficient to establish accomplice liability if the words constitute approval or encouragement and thus further the actions that constitute the offense. Generally, however, mere presence at the scene of the crime is not, by itself, sufficient to render one an accomplice because it would not make sense to charge mere bystanders with a crime. Likewise, one who is present at the scene when a crime was committed and who then flees from the scene cannot, on that basis alone, be charged with an offense. Only if an individual is present at the crime scene for the purpose of approving, encouraging, or assisting in the commission of the crime may the person be charged under the principle of accomplice liability. Furthermore, to be liable as an accomplice, a defendant must: (1) know what the criminal is trying to do, (2) intentionally aid or encourage another person to commit a crime, and (3) believe that the aid or encouragement would make the criminal's success likely.[60] For his or her actions to be considered intentional, the defendant must have intended to: (1) commit the acts which in fact gave aid or encouragement, and (2) bring about the other party's commission of the offense by committing those acts.

As noted in the preceding section, under the law of most jurisdictions today, an accomplice may share in the same charge and punishment as the principal criminal.

Accessory

As previously mentioned, the emphasis in substantive and procedural laws in most American jurisdictions today is to distinguish between those who are involved in crime as principals or as accessories. The contemporary concept of a person as an accessory to criminal activity evolved from the common law idea of an accessory after the fact. Hence, the crime of being accessory after the fact remains on the books in most states. Under the laws of most jurisdictions today, one who knowingly gives assistance to a person who has committed a felony for the purpose of helping that individual avoid apprehension or detection is guilty as an accessory. For example, the United States Code says that: "Whoever, knowing that an offense against the United States has been committed, receives, relieves, comforts or assists the offender in order to hinder or prevent his apprehension, trial or punishment, is an accessory after the fact."[61] (Also see the Law on the Books feature "Parties to Crime" in this chapter, which defines "accessory" under California law in a similar fashion.)

Proving an accessory's guilt requires a showing that: (1) a crime has been completed, (2) the defendant knew that the crime had been committed, (3) the defendant knew that the crime was committed by the individual who was being assisted, and (4) assistance must have been personally given by the defendant to the individual who committed the crime. A person who is coerced or forced into giving assistance to a criminal offender, however, will not generally be charged as an accessory after the fact since the assistance was given unwillingly. Such would be the case where an innocent bystander is forced to drive a getaway car at gunpoint and later released.

ACCOMPLICE
a person who, with intent to promote or facilitate the commission of a crime, gives assistance or encouragement to the principal. An accomplice is liable as a principal before and during a crime.

COMPLICITY
involvement in crime either as principal or accomplice. The term also refers to the activities of conspirators, and may therefore be taken to mean the conduct on the part of a person that is intended to encourage or aid another person in the commission of a crime, assist in an escape, or avoid prosecution.

ACCOMPLICE LIABILITY
the degree of criminal blameworthiness that accrues to one who aids, abets, encourages, or assists another person in the commission of a crime.

Web Extra! 4–6
Britannica online: degrees of participation

It is not necessary that an accessory be aware of the precise details of the crime in order to be charged. In one example, a defendant was found guilty as an accessory after the fact in an aggravated assault case for providing assistance to an individual who had attacked a prison guard. Although the accessory knew that an assault had occurred, he did not know that the person who had been assaulted was a prison guard (which, under state law, raised the level of seriousness of the offense and resulted in the accessory receiving a higher sentence). His conviction and sentence were later upheld by an appellate court.[62]

Some states no longer charge persons with the offense of accessory after the fact, but have instead codified new crimes of aiding and abetting, aiding a felon, aiding an escape, interference with a police officer, and so on.

MISPRISION OF FELONY

the failure to report a known crime; concealment of a crime.

At common law, the failure to report a known crime was considered a **misprision of felony** and was chargeable as such. In most jurisdictions today, however, no such crime exists and, in order to be charged as an accessory after the fact, a defendant must have taken affirmative acts to hinder the felon's arrest or detection. Mere failure to inform authorities of an offender's presence or failure to come forward and provide authorities with suspicions about a person's guilt is not sufficient unless a legal duty to inform exists (as is the case in many jurisdictions with child-protection personnel, physicians, nurses, and other medical personnel who know of cases of child abuse). A few states, however, have created the statutory crime of compounding a felony. This offense is basically an agreement not to prosecute or inform on one who has committed a crime in return for the payment of money or in return for having received some benefit from the criminal.

A getaway car driver preparing to speed off after a robbery. The principle of accomplice liability is based on the concept that any individual who aids, abets, encourages, or assists another person (the principal) to commit a crime should share in the criminal liability that accrues under law. (Photo by Marc Bove, courtesy of Pearson Education/PH College.)

LAW ON THE BOOKS

"PARTIES TO CRIME" UNDER THE CALIFORNIA PENAL CODE.

Title 2 of the California Penal Code classifies and defines parties to a crime. Relevant sections of that Title, and other relevant provisions, are shown in this box.

Section 30. The parties to crimes are classified as:
1. Principals; and
2. Accessories.

Section 31. [Principals defined] All persons concerned in the commission of a crime, whether it be felony or misdemeanor, and whether they directly commit the act constituting the offense, or aid and abet in its commission, or, not being present, have advised and encouraged its commission, and all persons counseling, advising, or encouraging children under the age of fourteen years, lunatics, or idiots, to commit any crime, or who, by fraud, contrivance, or force, occasion the drunkenness of another for the purpose of causing him to commit any crime, or who, by threats, menaces, command, or coercion, compel another to commit any crime, are principals in any crime committed.

Section 32. [Accessories defined.] Every person who, after a felony has been committed, harbors, conceals, or aids a principal in such felony, with the intent that said principal may avoid or escape from arrest, trial, conviction, or punishment, having knowledge that said principal has committed such felony or has been charged with such felony or convicted thereof is an accessory to such felony.

Section 33. [Punishment as an accessory.] Except in cases where a different punishment is prescribed, an accessory is punishable by a fine not exceeding five thousand dollars ($5,000), or by imprisonment in the state prison, or in a county jail not exceeding one year, or by both such fine and imprisonment.

Section 971. [Abrogation of distinction between accessories and principals.] The distinction between an accessory before the fact and a principal, and between principals in the first and second degree is abrogated; and all persons concerned in the commission of a crime, who by the operation of other provisions of this code are principals therein, shall hereafter be prosecuted, tried and punished as principals and no other facts need be alleged in any accusatory against any such person than are required in an accusatory pleading against a principal.

Section 972. [Accessory; prosecution without regard to prosecution of principal.] An accessory to the commission of a felony may be prosecuted, tried, and punished, though the principal may be neither prosecuted nor tried, and though the principal may have been acquitted.

The Criminal Liability of Corporations

Can a corporation be a party to a crime? In 1999 aircraft maintenance company SabreTech was convicted in federal court in Miami of eight counts of causing the air transportation of hazardous materials and of one count of failing to provide training in the handling of hazardous materials. The charges resulted from actions by the company's employees in improperly packaging oxygen canisters blamed for an airplane cargo hold fire that caused the 1996 crash of ValuJet Flight 592 in the Florida Everglades. One hundred and ten people died in the crash. The case marked the first time that a maintenance company faced criminal charges in connection with an air disaster in the United States. SabreTech, which went out of business, was also charged in state court with numerous counts of murder and manslaughter stemming from the crash. "This is the first criminal homicide prosecution involving a passenger aircraft tragedy in the United States," said Florida state attorney Katherine Fernandez-Rundle.[63]

As a matter of legal development, it has taken time to establish criminal liability for a corporation and not merely for its agents. In the late 1700s, for example, the famous jurist Sir William Blackstone wrote in his *Commentaries* that "a corporation

Web Extra! 4–7

Vaughn and Sons v. *State* (1983)

cannot commit treason or felony or other crimes in its corporate capacity, though its members may in their distinct individual capacities."[64] Blackstone reasoned that a corporation could not commit a criminal act because it has no physical body, and because it cannot form the necessary *mens rea* required by many serious crimes since it is literally a mindless organization.

Times change, however,[65] and the history of federal food and drug legislation in the United States illustrates the elaborate phraseology that was deemed necessary as little as 100 years ago to fasten criminal liability on corporations. Section 12 of the Food and Drugs Act of 1906, for example, provided that "the act, omission, or failure of any officer, agent, or other person acting for or employed by any corporation, company, society, or association, within the scope of his employment or office, shall in every case be also deemed to be the act, omission, or failure of such corporation, company, society, or association as well as that of the person." By the mid-twentieth century, legal understanding and practice had come to categorize corporate legal entities as "persons" for purposes of the law, rendering them liable for a variety of crimes in most jurisdictions.[66]

The modern trend is to hold corporations criminally liable for illegal acts performed by agents acting on behalf of businesses. This is especially true for **strict liability crimes** and minor offenses. (The concept of strict liability is also discussed in Chapter 2.) In most cases, punishments for the strict liability crimes of corporations are limited to fines, since organizations cannot be imprisoned. In some cases, the charter or right of the organization to operate in the state where the crime was committed may be officially rescinded.

STRICT LIABILITY CRIMES

violations of law for which one may incur criminal liability without fault or intention. Strict liability offenses do not require *mens rea*.

The legal philosophy determining which corporations can be held criminally liable is still developing. This is especially true in the realm of large multinational corporations that, for the most part, are a product of twentieth-century industry and free enterprise. As one legal scholar observes, "There has been a gradual expansion in the . . . law of corporate criminal liability, both of the range of offenses a corporation is capable of committing and in the means by which an offense is imputed to a corporation. There are now very few offenses which a corporation cannot commit. . . ."[67]

Criminal fault can be imputed to corporations based on two legal theories: (1) the principle of vicarious liability and (2) the identification doctrine. The principle of vicarious liability grew out of the idea of the liability a master (or employer) holds for the actions of his servant (or employee). The principle of vicarious liability has mostly been used to hold a corporate body accountable for violations of regulatory offenses. Under the identification model, however, a corporation can be held responsible for more serious criminal offenses—including those which require a mental element, or *mens rea* for their commission. The identification doctrine builds on the principle that a corporation is an abstract entity with no mind of its own—but which is actively directed by its officers and senior officials, whose initiatives can be *identified* with those of the company. Identification liability stops at wrongdoing in the boardroom, whereas vicarious liability extends corporate responsibility to the acts of all employees.[68]

Although the general principle that a company can be prosecuted for a criminal offense is generally well-accepted, the question of whether a particular statute imposes such liability is rarely, if ever, spelled out. Although some criminal statutes explicitly state that corporations can be treated, for purposes of the law, as persons, others are less clear. Hence, in this still-emerging area of the criminal law, it is often up to the courts to decide whether a company can be held criminally liable for violation of a particular statute.[69]

The Model Penal Code[70] provides that a corporation may be held criminally liable if:

1. The offense is a violation (minor offense) and the conduct was performed by an agent acting on the corporation's behalf within the scope of the agent's employment.

A Ford Explorer following an accident that may have been caused by tires manufactured by Bridgestone/Firestone, Inc. In the fall of 2000, a rash of such accidents prompted calls for a criminal investigation of the tire manufacturer, after questions arose about what Firestone officials knew about tire defects before recalling many of its all-terrain tires. The principle of corporate criminal liability is a well-established doctrine of American jurisprudence. (Photo by J. Michael Short/Laredo Morning Times, courtesy of Corbis/Sygma.)

2. The offense is defined by other statutes and made applicable to corporations.

3. The offense consists of a failure to perform a specific duty imposed on the corporation by law, for example, failing to file a tax return.

4. The criminal acts were approved, authorized, permitted, or recklessly tolerated by the board of directors or a high management official acting on behalf of the corporation and within the scope of his or her employment.

Some U.S. jurisdictions take the approach that a corporation may be held criminally liable for crimes committed by any employee who has been given the power and duty, or responsibility and authority, to act on behalf of the corporation. This approach is based on the belief that it should be incumbent on boards of directors and high management officials to be sufficiently informed so as not to condone criminal misconduct on behalf of the corporation. An example, from Pennsylvania law, is provided in a Law on the Books feature in this section.

Some of the better known recent cases in which corporations have been held criminally liable include Ford Motor Corporation's conviction in 1978 on three counts of reckless homicide in the deaths of three teenage girls in a Ford Pinto whose gas tank exploded in a crash; Exxon Corporation's agreement to pay $100 million in criminal fines (and more than $1 billion in civil damages) in charges stemming from the Exxon Valdez oil spill in Alaska in 1989; General Electric Corporation's 1990 conviction on charges of defrauding the U.S. Army; and a $20,000 fine paid by a Wisconsin corporation after it was found guilty of two counts of reckless homicide in the misreading of Pap smears that led to the deaths of two women in 1996.

Vicarious Liability

Vicarious liability is a concept that is related to strict liability. Vicarious liability imposes criminal liability on one party for the criminal acts of another party. It is generally associated only with regulatory crimes, and the most common form of vicarious liability is that of an employer who is held liable for the criminal acts of employees. Similarly, an automobile owner may be criminally liable for the acts of

VICARIOUS LIABILITY
the criminal liability of one party for the criminal acts of another party.

LAW ON THE BOOKS

THE CRIMINAL LIABILITY OF CORPORATIONS UNDER PENNSYLVANIA LAW.

Compare with Model Penal Code, Section 2.07

PENNSYLVANIA CONSOLIDATED STATUTES

Title 18, Section 307. Liability of organizations and certain related persons. (a) Corporations generally—A corporation may be convicted of the commission of an offense if:

1. The offense is a summary offense or the offense is defined by a statute other than this title in which a legislative purpose to impose liability on corporations plainly appears and the conduct is performed by an agent of the corporation acting in behalf of the corporation within the scope of his office or employment, except that if the law defining the offense designates the agents for whose conduct the corporation is accountable or the circumstances under which it is accountable, such provisions shall apply;
2. The offense consists of an omission to discharge a specific duty of affirmative performance imposed on corporations by law; or
3. The commission of the offense was authorized, requested, commanded, performed or recklessly tolerated by the board of directors or by a high managerial agent acting in behalf of the corporation within the scope of his office or employment.

(b) Corporations, absolute liability—When absolute liability is imposed for the commission of an offense, a legislative purpose to impose liability on a corporation shall be assumed, unless the contrary plainly appears.

LAW ON THE BOOKS

THE CRIMINAL LIABILITY OF CORPORATIONS UNDER DELAWARE LAW.

Compare with Model Penal Code, Section 2.07

DELAWARE CODE UNANNOTATED

Title 11, Section 281. Criminal liability of corporations.

A corporation is guilty of an offense when:

1. The conduct constituting the offense consists of an omission to discharge a specific duty of affirmative performance imposed on corporations by law; or
2. The conduct constituting the offense is engaged in, authorized, solicited, requested, commanded or recklessly tolerated by the board of directors or by a high managerial agent acting within the scope of employment and in behalf of the corporation; or
3. The conduct constituting the offense is engaged in by an agent of the corporation while acting within the scope of employment and in behalf of the corporation and:
   a. The offense is a misdemeanor or a violation; or
   b. The offense is one defined by a statute which clearly indicates a legislative intent to impose such criminal liability on a corporation.

an individual to whom she lends her automobile. So, for example, a person who loans a vehicle to an individual who parks it in a fire zone may find themselves responsible for paying the fine associated with the illegal parking.

Those who advocate holding offenders responsible under the concept of vicarious liability argue that doing so is necessary for the effective enforcement of important regulatory schemes, such as pure food and drug regulations, child labor laws, alcoholic beverage control laws, and so on. Those who oppose the concept of vicarious liability argue that it is inconsistent with the basic principles of criminal law, and that individuals should only be held accountable when they are clearly and morally blameworthy.

In most cases, the criminal liability that is created under the concept of vicarious liability is punishable only by a fine. An exception to this rule may occur when a statute places an affirmative duty on a person to perform a specified act. In the case of *United States* v. *Parks*,[71] for example, a federal court upheld the conviction and one-year prison sentence of a company president for the shipment of adulterated foods. The FDA statute under which the official had been prosecuted placed an affirmative duty on company officers to ensure that no adulterated food was shipped. Even though, in this case, employees shipped adulterated food without the knowledge of their company's president, his conviction under this vicarious liability statute was upheld by the U.S. Supreme Court.

It is, however, important to distinguish between accomplice liability and vicarious liability. Accomplice liability is based on affirmative participation in a crime, whereas vicarious liability is based solely on a recognizable relationship between the defendant and the perpetrator. Hence, as in the above example, vicarious liability may be imposed when the defendant is made legally accountable by statute for the crimes committed by others, even though he or she lacked any knowledge of the crime's commission.[72]

Most states require that before vicarious liability may be imposed on an individual, the individual must have control over the perpetrator. Accordingly, in those states vicarious liability is limited to employer–employee relationships and similar situations.[73] Precedent appears to limit vicarious liability to situations where the potential for punishment is not extreme. This "punishment limitation" is based on the fact that although there are social interests in imposing some degree of vicarious liability, anyone who lacks knowledge of an offense should not be too severely punished because of it, even when technically liable for its preventions.[74]

While strict liability and vicarious liability are both forms of liability without fault, they dispense with the fault requirement in entirely different ways. Strict liability is imposed in situations where the *mens rea* requirement has been eliminated. Vicarious liability, on the other hand, may be imposed in situations where the act requirement has been eliminated.

SUMMARY

- Inchoate offenses are incipient crimes that generally lead to other crimes. "Inchoate" means imperfect, partial, or unfinished. Inchoate crimes include: (1) attempts, (2) solicitation, and (3) conspiracies.

- Almost any crime that can be envisioned can be attempted, and under the penal codes of most states, any crime defined by statute has as its adjunct an attempt to commit that crime.

- To constitute an attempt, an act of some sort is necessary. Mere preparation to commit an offense is not sufficient to support a charge of attempted criminal activity.

- The crime of attempt is a specific intent crime. It has two elements; first, the specific intent to commit a criminal offense and, second, a substantial step toward the commission of the intended offense.

- In most jurisdictions, anyone charged with an attempt may raise the defenses of abandonment and impossibility. In some jurisdictions, the term "renunciation" is used in place of abandonment. Virtually all jurisdictions require that the abandonment be a voluntary one. The defense does not affect the criminal liability of an accomplice who does not join in such abandonment or renunciation.

- Impossibility may be of either the factual or legal variety. Factual impossibility, which is rarely useful as a defense, means that a person could not commit the envisioned offense even if he or she were successful in the attempt. Legal impossibility means that the attempted offense is really no offense at all, perhaps because there is no law against the imagined crime, or because the actions in question do not meet the requirements of the law for a crime to have occurred. Legal impossibility generally precludes prosecution in most jurisdictions.

- At common law, all attempts were punishable as misdemeanors. Today, punishments for attempts are usually based on the punishments specified for the intended offense. Many state statutes punish attempts by referring to the level of punishment specified for the intended crime, and then reducing it by some degree. Except for crimes punishable by life imprisonment or death, the Model Penal Code provides the same punishment for attempts as for the crimes attempted.

- The common law crime of conspiracy is an agreement between two or more persons to commit an unlawful act or a lawful act by unlawful means. At common law, conspiracy was a misdemeanor. However, in most states today, and under federal jurisdiction, conspiracy is classified as a felony.

- The elements of the crime of conspiracy are: (1) an agreement between two or more persons, (2) to carry out an act that is unlawful or lawful but which is to be accomplished by unlawful means, and (3) a culpable intent on the part of the defendants.

- For persons to be charged with a conspiracy, it is not necessary that each party form an agreement with all other parties involved in the conspiracy. In complex conspiracies, the parties may not know each other and may not even be aware of what other parties are involved. This is particularly true in cases involving organized crime.

- Under common law, criminal solicitation occurs when one requests or encourages another to perform a criminal act. Criminal solicitation, unlike conspiracy, requires no overt act. The required mental state is one in which the defendant must have intended to induce the other person to perform the crime. In addition, a successful prosecution must establish that the defendant possessed the mental state required for the completed crime.

- Under common law, a fairly complex scheme was developed for labeling persons involved in a felony according to their relationship to the criminal act. Offenders could be classified as: (1) a principal in the first degree, (2) a principal in the second degree, or as (3) an accessory before the fact, or (4) an accessory after the fact.

- States have abolished the distinction between principal in the second degree and an accessory before the fact. The degree of an offender's criminal liability is today assessed independently of the individual's presence or absence at the crime scene. Generally, one who assists in the commission of a crime, but does not commit the *actus reus*, or the actual crime itself, is considered to be an accomplice. The individual who commits the *actus reus* is considered to be the principal.

- To be held guilty as an accomplice, a defendant must have intentionally aided or encouraged another person to commit a crime. Intentionally in this instance means that: (1) the defendant must have intended to commit the acts that in fact give aid or encouragement; and (2) by committing those acts, the defendant must have intended to bring about the other party's commission of the offense.

- One who knowingly gives assistance to a person who has committed a felony for the purposes of helping that individual avoid apprehension or detection is guilty as an accessory after the fact.

QUESTIONS FOR DISCUSSION

1. Why is it necessary to require a "substantial step" before mere plans become a criminal attempt?

2. Why are courts hesitant to punish a person for "evil thoughts" alone?

3. What is the difference between conspiracy and criminal solicitation?

4. Why is it easier for prosecutors to build a case when they are not required to establish whether the defendant is a principal in the first degree, or in the second degree, or an accomplice?

5. When is a corporation liable for the acts of its officers?

6. Under the statutes of many states, a bar owner is criminally liable when an employee-bartender sells liquor to juveniles. What if the bar owner instructs the bartender not to sell liquor to juveniles, but the bartender disregards those instructions and sells to juveniles anyway? Should the owner then be held criminally liable? Why or why not?

LEGAL RESOURCES ON THE WORLD WIDE WEB

A variety of law-related associations, such as the American Bar Association and the National Lawyers Associations, can be reached via the World Wide Web. Some associations of interest to students of criminal law are:

American Bar Association (ABA)
http://www.abanet.org
Home page of the largest and most influential national association of attorneys. Information about the positions taken by the association and model rules of ethics are available at this site.

American Bar Association's Criminal Justice Section
http://www.abanet.org/crimjust/home.html
The mission of the ABA's Criminal Justice Section is to improve the criminal justice system. The site offers publications and press releases.

Association of Federal Defense Attorneys
http://www.afda.org
Members' Web site (though visitors are allowed) for attorneys that represent defendants in federal criminal actions.

Association of Trial Lawyers of America (ATLA)
http://www.atlanet.org
Web site of the largest national association of attorneys involved in criminal defense and personal injury litigation.

National Association of Criminal Defense Lawyers (NACDL)
http://www.criminaljustice.org
The preeminent organization in the United States advancing the mission of the nation's criminal defense lawyers to ensure justice and due process for persons accused of crime or other misconduct.

National Association of Sentencing Advocates (NASA)
http://www.sentencingproject.org/nasa
A professional membership organization of sentencing advocates and defense-based mitigation specialists.

National District Attorneys Association (NDAA)
http://www.ndaa.org
NDAA offers local prosecutors the opportunity to network with fellow prosecutors throughout the nation to enhance their knowledge and skills.

National Lawyers Association (NLA)
http://www.nla.org
A national bar association organized to improve the image of the legal profession, to advance legal institutions and respect for the law, and to educate the public on such matters.

Check the *Criminal Law Today* Web site for URLs that may have changed.

SUGGESTED READINGS AND CLASSIC WORKS

Thurmon Arnold, "Criminal Attempts: The Rise and Fall of an Abstraction," *Yale Law Journal,* Vol. 90 (1930), p. 53.

Andrew Ashworth, "Criminal Attempts and the Role of Resulting Harm Under the Code and the Common Law," *Rutgers Law Journal,* Vol. 19 (1988), p. 725.

John W. Curran, "Solicitation: A Substantive Crime," *Minnesota Law Review,* Vol. 17 (1933), p. 499.

Robert A. Duff, "The Circumstances of an Attempt," *Cambridge Law Journal,* Vol. 50 (1991), p. 100.

Phillip E. Johnson, "The Unnecessary Crime of Conspiracy," *California Law Review,* Vol. 61 (1973), p. 1137.

Sanford H. Kadish, "Complicity, Cause and Blame," *California Law Review,* Vol. 73 (1985), p. 323.

David Moriarty, "Extending the Defense of Renunciation," *Temple Law Review,* Vol. 62 (1989), p. 1.

Francis B. Syre, "Criminal Conspiracy," *Harvard Law Review,* Vol. 35 (1922), p. 393.

CAPSTONE CASE

FOR PURPOSES OF CRIMINAL ATTEMPT, WHAT CONSTITUTES A "SUBSTANTIAL STEP" TOWARD COMMISSION OF THE TARGETED OFFENSE?

Tennessee v. *Reeves*
Supreme Court of Tennessee, 1996
917 S.W.2d 825

FACTS: The defendant, Tracie Reeves, appeals from the Court of Appeals' affirmance of the trial court's order designating her a delinquent child. The trial court's delinquency order, which entered following a jury trial, was based on the jury's finding that the defendant had attempted to commit second degree murder—a violation of Tenn. Code Ann. Section(s) 39-12-101. The specific issue for our determination is whether the defendant's actions constitute a "substantial step," under Section(s) 39-12-101(a)(3), toward the commission of that crime. For the following reasons, we hold that they do, and therefore affirm the judgment of the Court of Appeals.

FACTS AND PROCEDURAL HISTORY: On the evening of January 5, 1993, Tracie Reeves and Molly Coffman, both twelve years of age and students at West Carroll Middle School, spoke on the telephone and decided to kill their homeroom teacher, Janice Geiger. The girls agreed that Coffman would bring rat poison to school the following day so that it could be placed in Geiger's drink. The girls also agreed that they would thereafter steal Geiger's car and drive to the Smoky Mountains. Reeves then contacted Dean Foutch, a local high school student, informed him of the plan, and asked him to drive Geiger's car. Foutch refused this request.

On the morning of January 6, Coffman placed a packet of rat poison in her purse and boarded the school bus. During the bus ride Coffman told another student, Christy Hernandez, of the plan; Coffman also showed Hernandez the packet of rat poison. Upon their arrival at School Hernandez informed her homeroom teacher, Sherry Cockrill, of the plan. Cockrill then relayed this information to the principal of the school, Claudia Argo.

When Geiger entered her classroom that morning she observed Reeves and Coffman leaning over her desk; and when the girls noticed her, they giggled and ran back to their seats. At that time Geiger saw a purse lying next to her coffee cup on top of the desk. Shortly thereafter Argo called Coffman to the principal's office. Rat poison was found in Coffman's purse and it was turned over to a Sheriff's Department investigator. Both Reeves and Coffman gave written statements to the investigator concerning their plan to poison Geiger and steal her car.

Reeves and Coffman were found to be delinquent by the Carroll County Juvenile Court, and both appealed from that ruling to the Carroll County Circuit Court. After a jury found that the girls attempted to commit second degree murder in violation of Tenn. Code Ann. Section(s) 39-12-101, the "criminal attempt" statute, the trial court affirmed the juvenile court's order and sentenced the girls to the Department of Youth Development for an indefinite period. Reeves appealed from this judgment to the Court of Appeals, which affirmed the judgment of the trial court. Reeves then applied to this Court for permission to appeal pursuant to Tenn. R. App. P. 11. Because we have not addressed the law of criminal attempt since the comprehensive reform of our criminal law undertaken by the legislature in 1989, we granted that application.

PRIOR AND CURRENT LAW OF CRIMINAL ATTEMPT: Before the passage of the reform legislation in 1989, the law of criminal attempt, though sanctioned by various statutes, was judicially defined. In order to submit an issue of criminal attempt to the jury, the State was required to present legally sufficient evidence of: (1) an intent to commit a specific crime; (2) an overt act toward the commission of that crime; and (3) a failure to consummate the crime. *Bandy* v. *State*, 575 S.W.2d 278, 281 (Teen. 1979); *Gervin* v. *State*, 212 Tenn. 653, 371 S.W.2d 449, 451 (1963); *Dupuy* v. *State*, 204 Tenn. 624, 325 S.W.2d 238, 240 (1959).

Of the elements of criminal attempt, the second, the "overt act" requirement, was by far the most problematic. By attempting to draw a sharp distinction between "mere preparation" to commit a criminal act, which did not constitute the required overt act, and a "direct movement toward the commission after the preparations had been made," *Dupuy*, 325 S.W.2d at 239, 240, which did, Tennessee courts construed the term "overt act" very narrowly. The best example of this extremely narrow construction occurred in *Dupuy*. In that case, the Memphis police sought to lay a trap for a pharmacist suspected of performing illegal abortions by sending a young woman to request these services from him. After the woman had made several attempts to secure his services, he finally agreed to perform the abortion. The pharmacist transported the young woman to a hotel room, laid out his instruments in preparation for the procedure, and asked the woman to remove her clothes. At that point the police came into the room and arrested the pharmacist, who then admitted that he had performed abortions in the past. The defendant was convicted under a statute that made it illegal to procure a miscarriage, and he appealed to this Court.

A majority of this Court reversed the conviction. After admitting that the defendant's "reprehensible" court of conduct would doubtlessly have resulted in the commission of the crime "had he not been thwarted in this efforts by the arrival of the police," *Dupuy*, 325 S.W.2d at 239, the majority concluded that: "While the defendant had completed his plan to do this crime the element of attempt [overt act]

does not appear in this record. The proof shows that he did not use any of the instruments and did not touch the body of the girl in question. Under such facts we do not think that the defendant is guilty under the statute." *Dupuy*, 325 S.W.2d at 240. To support its holding, the *Dupuy* court quoted a treatise passage concerning actions that constituted "mere preparation," as opposed to actions that would satisfy the overt act requirement:

"In a general way, however, it may be said that preparation consists in devising or arranging the means or measures necessary for the commission of the offense and that the attempt [overt act] is the direct movement toward the commission after the preparations are made. Even though a person actually intends to commit a crime, his procurement of the instrumentalities adapted to that end will not constitute an attempt to commit the crime in the absence of some overt act. *Id.* (quoting 14 Am. Jur. Section(s) 68 (1940)). To further illustrate the foregoing principle, the majority provided the following example: "the procurement by a prisoner of tools adapted to breaking jail does not render him guilty of an attempt to break jail." *Id.*"

As indicated above, the sharp differentiation in *Dupuy* between "mere preparation" and "overt act," or the "act itself," was characteristic of the pre-1989 attempt law. See, e.g., *Gervin v. State*, 212 Tenn. 653, 371 S.W.2d 449 (1963) (criminal solicitation does not constitute an attempt); *McEwing v. State*, 134 Tenn. 649, 185 S.W. 688 (1915) (conviction for attempted rape affirmed because defendant actually laid hands on the victim). In 1989, however, the legislature enacted a general criminal attempt statute, Tenn. Code Ann. Section(s) 39-12-101, as part of its comprehensive overhaul of Tennessee's criminal law. In that statute, the legislature did not simply codify the judicially created elements of the crime, but utilized language that had up to then been entirely foreign to Tennessee attempt law. Section 39-12-101 provides, in pertinent part, as follows:

> a. *A person commits criminal attempt who, acting with the kind of culpability otherwise required for the offense:*
>
> > 1. *Intentionally engages in action or causes a result that would constitute an offense if the circumstances surrounding the conduct were as the person believes them to be;*
> > 2. *Acts with intent to cause a result that is an element of the offense, and believes the conduct will cause the result without further conduct on the person's part; or*
> > 3. *Acts with intent to complete a course of action or cause a result that would constitute the offense, under the circumstances surrounding the conduct as the person believe them to be, and the conduct constitutes a substantial step toward the commission of the offense.*
>
> b. *Conduct does not constitute a substantial step under subdivision (a)(3) unless the person's entire course of action is corroborative of the intent to commit the offense....*

THE SUBSTANTIAL STEP ISSUE: As stated above, our task is to determine whether the defendant's actions in this case constitute a "substantial step" toward the commission of second degree murder under the new statute. The "substantial step" issue has not yet been addressed by a Tennessee court in a published opinion, and the question is made more difficult by the fact that the legislature declined to set forth any definition of the term, preferring instead to "leave the issue of what constitutes a substantial step [to the courts] for determination in each particular case." Section(s) 39-12-101, Comments of Sentencing Commission.

In addressing this issue, we first note that the legislature, in enacting Section(s) 39-12-101, clearly looked to the criminal attempt section set forth in the Model Penal Code. That section provides, in pertinent part, as follows:

1. *Definition of attempt. A person is guilty of an attempt to commit a crime if, acting with the kind of culpability otherwise required for commission of the crime, he:*
    a. *purposely engages in conduct which would constitute the crime if the attendant circumstances were as he believes them to be; or*
    b. *when causing a particular result is an element of the crime, does or omits to do anything with the purpose of causing or with the belief that it will cause such result, without further conduct on his part; or*
    c. *purposely does or omits to do anything which, under the circumstances as he believes them to be, is a substantial step in a course of conduct planned to culminate in his commission of the crime.* (Model Penal Code, Section 5.01.)

The State argues that the striking similarity of Tenn. Code Ann. 39-12-101 and the Model Penal Code evidences the legislature's intention to abandon the old law of criminal attempt and instead adopt the Model Penal Code approach. The State then avers that the model code contains examples of conduct which, if proven, would entitle, but not require, the jury to find that the defendant had taken a "substantial step;" and that two of these examples are applicable to this case. The section of the model code relied upon by the State, Section(s) 5.01(2), provides, in pertinent part, as follows:

1. *Conduct which may be held substantial step under paragraph (1)(c). Conduct shall not be held to constitute a substantial step under paragraph (1)(c) of this Section unless it is strongly corroborative of the actor's criminal purpose. Without negating the sufficiency of other conduct, the following, if strongly corroborative of the actor's criminal purpose, shall not be held insufficient as a matter of law. . . .*
    e. *possession of materials to be employed in the commission of the crime, which are specially designed for such unlawful use or which can serve no lawful purpose of the actor under the circumstances;*
    f. *possession, collection, or fabrication of materials to be employed in the commission of the crime, at or near the place contemplated for its commission, where such possession, collection, or fabrication serves no lawful purpose of the actor under the circumstances;*

The State concludes that, because the issue of whether the defendant's conduct constitutes a substantial step may be a jury question under the model code, the jury was justified in finding her guilty of attempting to commit second-degree murder.

The defendant counters by arguing that despite the similarity of Tenn. Code Ann. Section(s) 39-12-101 and the Model Penal Code's attempt provision, the legislature intended to retain the sharp distinction between "more preparation" and the "act itself" characteristic of such decisions as *Dupuy*. She supports this assertion by pointing out that although the legislature could have easily included the examples set forth in Section(s) 5.01(2) of the model code, the Tennessee statute does not include the examples. The defendant concludes that the new statute did not substantially change Tennessee attempt law and that her conviction must be reversed because her actions constitute "mere preparation" under *Dupuy*.

Initially, we cannot accept the argument that the legislature intended to explicitly adopt the Model Penal Code approach, including the examples set forth in Section(s) 5.01(2). Although Section(s) 39-12-101 is obviously based on the model code, we agree with the defendant that the legislature could have, if it had so desired, simply included the specific examples in the Tennessee statute. That it did not do so prohibits us from concluding that the legislature explicitly intended to adopt the model code approach in all its particulars.

This conclusion does not mean, however, that the legislature intended to retain the distinction between "mere preparation" and the "act itself." Moreover, while

we concede that a strong argument can be made that the conviction conflicts with *Dupuy* because the defendant did not place the poison in the cup, but simply brought it to the crime scene, we also are well aware that the *Dupuy* approach to attempt law has been consistently and effectively criticized. One persistent criticism of the endeavor to separate "mere preparation" from the "act itself" is that the question is ultimately not one of kind but of degree[1]; the "act itself" is merely one of the termini on a continuum of criminal activity. Therefore, distinguishing between "mere preparation" and the "act itself" in a principled manner is a difficult, if not impossible, task.[2] See *United States* v. *Dworken*, 855 F.2d 12, 19 (1st Cir. 1988); *United States* v. *Brown*, 604 F.2d 347, 350 (5th Cir. 1979); Levenbook, Prohibiting Attempts and Preparations, 49 U.M.K.C. L. Rev. 41 (1980); Hall, Criminal Attempt: A Study of Foundations of Criminal Liability, 40 Yale L. J. 789, 821–22 (1940).

The other principal ground of criticism of the *Dupuy* approach bears directly on the primary objective of the law—that of preventing inchoate crimes from becoming full-blown ones. Many courts and commentators have argued that failing to attach criminal responsibility to the actor—and therefore prohibiting law enforcement officers from taking action—until the actor is on the brink of consummating the crime endangers the public and undermines the preventative goal of attempt law. See *People* v. *Terrell*, 459 N.E.2d 1337, 1341 (Ill. 1984); *United States* v. *Prichard*, 781 F.2d 179, 182 (10th Cir. 1986); *United States* v. *Stallworth*, 543 F.2d 1038, 1040 (2d Cir. 1976). See generally Wechsler, Jones, & Korn, The Treatment of Inchoate Crimes in the Model Penal Code of the American Law Institute: Attempt, Solicitation, and Conspiracy, 61 Colum. L. Rev. 571, 586–611 (1961).

The Shortcomings of the *Dupuy* rule with respect to the goal of prevention are particularly evident in this case. As stated above, it is likely that under *Dupuy* no criminal responsibility would have attached unless the poison had actually been placed in the teacher's cup. This rigid requirement, however, severely undercuts the objective of prevention because of the surreptitious nature of the act of poisoning. Once a person secretly places a toxic substance into a container from which another person is likely to eat or drink, the damage is done. Here, if it had not been for the intervention of the teacher, she could have been rendered powerless to protect herself from harm.

After carefully weighing considerations of *stare decisis* against the persuasive criticisms of the *Dupuy* rule, we conclude that this artificial and potentially harmful rule must be abandoned. We hold that when an actor possesses materials to be used in the commission of a crime, at or near the scene of the crime, and where the possession of those materials can serve no lawful purpose of the actor under the circumstances, the jury is entitled, but not required, to find that the actor has taken a "substantial step" toward the commission of the crime if such action is strongly corroborative of the actor's overall criminal purpose.[3] For the foregoing reasons, the judgment of the Court of Appeals is affirmed. . . .

Footnotes

1. Judge Holmes noted this point by stating: "Preparation is not an attempt. But some preparations may amount to an attempt. It is a question of degree." *Commonwealth* v. *Peaslee*, 177 Mass. 267, 272, 59 N.E. 55, 56 (1901).
2. This conclusion was drawn long ago by Judge Learned Hand, who stated that "the decisions [addressing when preparation has become attempt] are too numerous to cite, and would not be much help anyway, for there is, and obviously can be, no definite line." *United States* v. *Coplon*, 185 F2d 629, 633 (2d Cir. 1950). Interestingly, Judge Hand also rejected the defendant's argument that no attempt responsibility attached until the moment of consummation of the criminal act, stating that "[t]o divide 'attempt' from 'preparation' by the very instant of consummation would be to revert to the old [rejected English] doctrine." *Id.*
3. This decision is limited to the facts of this case; we do not specifically adopt any of the examples set forth in Section(s) 5.01(2) of the Model Penal Code, but simply agree with the reason-

ing underlying subsections (e) and (f). However, we do note that several courts charged with the responsibility of defining "substantial step" have adopted or applied the examples in the Model Penal Code. . . .

WHAT DO *YOU* THINK?

1. Do you agree that the girls had taken a substantial step toward the commission of a targeted offense? What test does the court establish for Tennessee to determine if a substantial step has been taken?
2. Would your answer be different if Tennessee used the "last step" test or the "physical proximity" test? If so, how?
3. Do you think that the court, in using common law rules of construction, modifies the legislative enactment? Is the court using its judgment to replace that of the drafters of the statute?

DOES THE CONDUCT OF THE DEFENDANT IN MEETING WITH A SELLER THAT INVOLVES DISCUSSING PRICES FOR VARIOUS TYPES OF MARIJUANA CONSTITUTE A SUBSTANTIAL STEP?

CAPSTONE CASE

New Hampshire v. *Allcock*
Supreme Court of New Hampshire, 1993
629 A.2d 99

FACTS: The defendant, Cecile Allcock, was convicted of attempted possession of a controlled drug, marijuana, with intent to dispense, RSA 318-B:26, I(c)(5) (1984 & Supp. 1992); RSA 629:1 (1986), after a jury trial in Superior Court (Barry, J.). On appeal, she argues that there was insufficient evidence for the jury to find that she took a "substantial step" towards commission of the crime. Because there is ample evidence on the record to support the jury's verdict, we affirm.

The defendant was the target of an undercover operation conducted by Detective Carl Patten, Jr., of the Keene Police Department. On August 3, 1989, Patten contacted a drug dealer, Marc Pelow, and asked about purchasing a quarter pound of marijuana. Pelow phoned the Allcock home, and the two men later purchased marijuana from Christina Allcock, the defendant's daughter. On August 22, 1989, Patten again contacted Pelow and asked him to find a buyer for several pounds of marijuana. Pelow indicated that the defendant would take "a couple" pounds of marijuana, and told Patten to call back. Patten called Pelow on the following day and Pelow told him that the defendant wanted two pounds. On August 24, 1989, Patten called Pelow and told him he had the marijuana and asked where they should meet. During this conversation, Pelow informed Patten that the defendant only wanted one pound.

Patten drove to Pelow's house, where Pelow called the defendant and told her they would meet her shortly. The two men used Pelow's car to drive to Cold River Road in Walpole, and waited for the defendant. When the defendant arrived, she asked to meet at a more secluded spot. Pelow drove about a quarter of a mile from where they had originally stopped, and the defendant followed and parked behind Pelow's vehicle.

Pelow introduced Patten to the defendant, and Patten showed her the marijuana he had for sale. Patten was authorized to wear an electronic transmitter to monitor and record the transaction with the defendant. See RSA chapter 570-A (1986 & Supp. 1992). The defendant commented on the color of the marijuana and was apparently displeased that Patten had brown marijuana instead of green marijuana. The defendant said, "I'm sitting with two pounds of this stuff [brown marijuana] I can't

get rid of. He promised me green." She also stated that the marijuana smelled different. Patten had three bags of marijuana and asked what price the defendant would pay for all of it. The defendant responded that she would give him "eleven." Patten then asked how much the defendant would pay for two bags of marijuana. She again indicated that she wished the marijuana was green and that she wished she had the "magic touch to make it green." The defendant conceded that Patten's marijuana was not the same kind of brown marijuana she already had, but noted that it did not matter because brown marijuana "just won't move." Patten made another offer, and the defendant said she could not accept because she would not have money to buy green marijuana if she bought Patten's marijuana. She told Patten that she expected green marijuana to be available soon, and that she could get it for about $1,200 per pound. She also said that she could make a "couple hundred bucks" on green marijuana. Patten stated that he needed money, and again asked the defendant how much she would give him for a bag of marijuana. The defendant stated that if she had extra money, she could buy the marijuana, but all she could afford was a pound of green marijuana at $1,800. Patten then offered to sell all of the marijuana he had with him for $1,800, and the defendant again said she would not buy it because she could not get rid of it.

Patten next asked the defendant the price of green marijuana. She told him it averaged between $1,500 and $1,600 a pound, but that she had one source who could get it for $600 to $700 a pound. Patten asked when the defendant next expected to buy green marijuana, and she said she hoped it would not be longer than a week since her supply had dried up. She again indicated that she wished Patten had green marijuana, which she could "get rid of" in an hour, but concluded that she could not purchase the brown marijuana. Patten made one last offer to reduce the price of the brown marijuana, but the defendant declined.

Patten ended the conversation by asking if the defendant wanted him to call her if he could get green marijuana. She indicated that he should call her. When Patten asked if the defendant could sell five pounds of green marijuana, she responded, "if you get five, I can move five pounds within three weeks. That's nothing for me." Patten told her he would know whether he could get green marijuana in a few days. She responded by asking him to contact her as soon as he obtained it and said she would see what she could do with it. Both the defendant and Patten left the scene, and the defendant was ultimately arrested on September 26, 1989.

OPINION

The jury convicted the defendant of attempted possession of marijuana with intent to dispense. RSA 629:1 (1986) provides:

> *"I. A person is guilty of an attempt to commit a crime if, with a purpose that a crime be committed, he does or omits to do anything which, under the circumstances as he believes them to be, is an act or omission constituting a substantial step toward the commission of the crime.*
>
> *II. As used in this section, 'substantial step' means conduct that is strongly corroborative of the actor's criminal purpose."*

During trial, the defendant testified that she did not have the intent to possess the marijuana, and claimed she was doing private "undercover" work to learn about Patten and give the police evidence to use against him. On appeal, she argues that there was insufficient evidence to prove that she took a substantial step towards commission of the crime.

In order to prevail on her claim that there was insufficient evidence to convict, the defendant must show "that no rational trier of fact could have found guilt be-

yond a reasonable doubt." *State* v. *Baker,* 135 N.H. 447, 449, 606 A.2d 309, 310 (1992) (quotation omitted). The defendant bears a heavy burden on appeal in that the "evidence and reasonable inferences drawn therefrom will be viewed in the light most favorable to the State." *Id.* The defendant argues that meeting with Patten and discussing prices for green and brown marijuana does not amount to a substantial step. She notes that she did not produce any money to purchase marijuana, and that she refused to purchase the marijuana that Patten offered for sale.

The proper focus of the inquiry is whether the defendant's conduct "strongly corroborate[s] clear criminal intent." *United States* v. *Dworken,* 855 F.2d 12, 19 (1st Cir. 1988). The act of taking a substantial step towards the commission of a crime has been described as behavior "of such a nature that a reasonable observer, viewing it in context could conclude beyond a reasonable doubt that it was undertaken in accordance with a design to violate the statute." *Id.* at 19-20 (quotation omitted). The defendant agreed to meet with Pelow and his source, Patten, to purchase one pound of marijuana. She met the men and requested to move to a more secluded spot. She inspected the marijuana, smelled it, and voiced her displeasure that it was brown. She repeatedly stated that she wanted to buy green marijuana, although she valued the brown marijuana at $1,100. She evidenced familiarity with other dealers and the market price for green marijuana, stated her ability and intent to resell or "move" marijuana, and asked Patten to contact her if he obtained green marijuana.

Viewed in the light most favorable to the State, there was ample evidence from which the jury could find that the defendant had the intent to violate the law, and that she took a substantial step towards that aim. In light of all this evidence, the mere fact that the defendant refused to purchase the marijuana offered by Patten does not satisfy her burden on appeal. The failure to go through with the sale "means only that the purchase was not consummated, not that there was no attempt to purchase." *United States* v. *Rivera-Sola,* 713 F.2d 866, 870 (1st Cir. 1983). The defendant's conduct was "strongly corroborative of [her] criminal purpose," RSA 629:1, II (1986), and thus constituted a substantial step towards commission of the crime.

The defendant relies on a factually similar case, *United States* v. *Joyce,* 693 F.2d 838 (8th Cir. 1982), to support her claim that she did not commit the crime of attempt. In *Joyce,* the court held that the defendant abandoned his intent to procure cocaine before he took a substantial step towards commission of the crime. *Id.* at 841. The defendant here, however, did not raise the affirmative defense of voluntary renunciation or abandonment at trial, see *State* v. *Patten,* 126 N.H. 227, 489 A.2d 657 (1985); RSA 629:1, III (1986). Accordingly, we do not rely on *Joyce* as support for the defendant's argument and therefore affirm the conviction.

Affirmed.

[footnotes omitted]

WHAT DO *YOU* THINK?

1. What test does this court use to determine if the conduct amounts to a substantial step?
2. In this case and the one preceding it, are the courts in agreement regarding what constitutes a substantial step? Explain the differences.
3. Would these cases be decided any differently using the Model Penal Code approach? The last act test?
4. See if you can formulate a more precise test regarding when an individual has moved from planning to the crime of an attempt.
5. Does the statutory statement that a "substantial step means conduct that is strongly corroborative of the actor's criminal purpose" provide any guidance in determining if a substantial step has been taken in this case?

WHAT ACTIONS ARE NECESSARY TO ESTABLISH ACCOMPLICE LIABILITY?

State v. *Kobel*
Missouri Appellate Court, Western District, 1996
927 S.W.2d 455

Appellant Jeffrey H. Kobel was charged with and tried for first-degree assault and armed criminal action as an accomplice in an assault upon a bouncer outside a Kansas City bar in December, 1993. The jury convicted Mr. Kobel of second-degree assault, for which he was sentenced to two years in prison, and armed criminal action, for which he was sentenced to four years in prison.

Mr. Kobel appeals the convictions on the bases of insufficiency of the evidence, failure to submit an instruction on a lesser included offense, and erroneous exclusion from evidence of a prior inconsistent statement. We find no reversible error and affirm both convictions.

FACTUAL AND PROCEDURAL BACKGROUND: The testimony supporting the verdict is as follows: Two vehicles, including Mr. Kobel's, were moving together along Main Street near Eighteenth Street in downtown Kansas City in the early morning hours of December 13, 1993. Both vehicles stopped in front of a bar called "Illusions" shortly after closing time. Illusions was known as a bar frequented by homosexuals. Mr. Kobel and another male were in his car. A total of five males, including Mr. Kobel, exited the two vehicles and began crossing the street towards the bar at approximately the same time. Mr. Kobel was carrying a can of Mace™. One of the other males, Christopher Anderson, carried a metal bar used to lock an automotive steering wheel into place. All five males, including Mr. Kobel, were yelling hostile and derogatory remarks concerning sexual orientation to a group of women near the entrance of the bar. At the direction of Robert Tucker, a "bouncer" at Illusions, the women took refuge in the bar while Mr. Tucker stood guard outside the door.

Mr. Kobel, Mr. Anderson, and the other males surrounded Mr. Tucker. Mr. Anderson assaulted Mr. Tucker by hitting him twice in the head with the metal steering wheel bar. A few seconds thereafter Mr. Kobel sprayed Mace™ in Mr. Tucker's face. Mace™ is a substance that is designed to cause temporary incapacitation when sprayed near a person's face. After being maced, Mr. Tucker fell to the ground. All five males left the scene at the same time and drove off in the same direction.

Mr. Tucker suffered a cracked rib, considerable bleeding, extensive stitches, and temporarily burning eyes as a result of the attack.

Mr. Kobel denied the accuracy of most of the above evidence in his testimony at trial. He characterized his presence outside of the bar on the night in question merely as a "chance involvement." More specifically, he testified that he had not associated with Mr. Anderson on the night in question. Rather, Mr. Kobel testified, he had been driving alone around downtown Kansas City, an area unfamiliar to him in an effort to locate a bar called "The Deep" where he was supposed to pick up his brother-in-law. Unable to locate the bar in question, he said, he stopped in front of Illusions and got out of the car to ask directions. By bad luck, he did so just as Mr. Anderson confronted Mr. Tucker. Mr. Kobel further testified he sprayed the Mace™ in self-defense, because he thought Mr. Tucker was charging towards him with an empty beer bottle.

OPINION

The jury apparently did not believe Mr. Kobel's story, for it convicted him of second-degree assault and armed criminal action. On appeal, Mr. Kobel alleges that:

(1) the State failed to prove he acted as an accomplice of Mr. Anderson; (2) the State failed to prove use of a dangerous instrument; (3) the court erred in failing to instruct on the lesser included offense of assault in the third degree; and (4) the court erred in exclusion of the prior inconsistent statement of a witness. Mr. Kobel also asserts ineffective assistance of counsel in failing to ask for a lesser included offense instruction and in failing to call Mr. Anderson as a witness. We address each contention in turn. . . .

ACCOMPLICE LIABILITY: Mr. Kobel first claims on appeal that there was insufficient evidence to support a finding that he was an accomplice to Mr. Anderson's assault on Mr. Tucker. Missouri law is clear that anyone who in any way aids, abets, or encourages another in the commission of a crime by any form of affirmative participation with a common intent and purpose is guilty to the same extent as the principal offender even though the accomplice did not personally commit every element of the principal offense. See, e.g., *State* v. *Gaines*, 807 S.W.2d 678, 679 (Mo. App. 1991).

Mr. Kobel admits his presence at the scene of the crime but notes that such presence alone is insufficient to make one an accomplice. It is, however, a relevant indicia of affirmative participation in the crime. Other relevant indicia of accomplice liability include acting as part of a "show of force" in the commission of the crime, flight after the crime, and association with others before, during, or after commission of the crime. *State* v. *Roper,* 819 S.W.2d 384, 386 (Mo. App. 1991); *Gaines,* 807 S. W.2d at 679. Each of these indicia are present here.

Thus, the evidence was that the two vehicles arrived together in front of the bar. There was evidence that, as they pulled up in front of the bar, all five males displayed a truculent attitude towards homosexuals by yelling derogatory epithets at the people congregating outside of the bar. All five males got out of their vehicles at the same time and quickly crossed the street towards the bar together as a group. Both Mr. Kobel and Mr. Anderson carried objects—Mace™ and the metal bar, respectively, which were then used to assault the victim.

At the time of the assault, Mr. Kobel was in very close physical proximity to the victim and the principal attacker, Mr. Anderson. Mr. Kobel and the other males surrounded Mr. Tucker. Mr. Kobel sprayed Mace™ at the victim's face within seconds after Mr. Anderson struck the victim twice in the head with a metal bar. All five males then immediately returned to their vehicles and abruptly left the crime scene together, heading in the same direction.

These facts, taken together, constitute evidence of presence at the scene, participation in a show of force, association during the attack, and flight. This evidence also supports the inference that the Mace™ was sprayed to incapacitate Mr. Tucker, so as to allow Mr. Anderson and the others to leave the crime scene without restraint or further identification of the attacker or his vehicle. The evidence is fully sufficient to support the jury's finding that Mr. Kobel was an accomplice in acting with Mr. Anderson with a common intent and purpose. As an accomplice, Mr. Kobel is guilty to the same extent that Mr. Anderson is guilty. . . .

For the reasons stated above, the judgments of conviction are affirmed.

[footnotes omitted]

WHAT DO *YOU* THINK?
1. What is required under Missouri law to establish accomplice liability?
2. While mere presence at the scene when the crime is committed is insufficient to make one an accomplice, how was the defendant's presence used by the court in reaching the conclusion that the defendant was an accomplice?
3. What factors did the court use to establish the defendant's liability as an accomplice?

CAPSTONE CASE

WHEN IS A PERSON LEGALLY ACCOUNTABLE FOR THE CONDUCT OF ANOTHER?

People v. *Eubanks*
Appellate Court of Illinois, First District, Second Division, 1996
669 N.E.2d 678

FACTS: Defendant was convicted in the Circuit Court of Cook County (Edward M. Fiala, Judge) of aggravated battery with a firearm and armed robbery. Defendant appealed. Appellate Court (P. J. Hartman, Judge) held that: (1) defendant was accountable for armed robbery; (2) defendant was accountable for shooting by codefendant; (3) evidence was sufficient to find essential elements of crimes; (4) defendant's use of Ventolin (albuterol) did not require fitness hearing because Ventolin was not psychotropic drug, (5) sentence was not disparate with codefendant's as they were not similarly situated; and (6) sentence was not excessive.

Affirmed.

Presiding Justice Hartman delivered the opinion of the court:

Defendant, Vernal Eubanks, codefendant Brian Robinson, and two others were charged with the numerous offenses resulting from the robbery and shooting of Leonard Macon. Defendant and Robinson were tried before two separate juries, and the other two suspects pled guilty. A jury found defendant guilty of aggravated battery with a firearm and armed robbery, but acquitted him of attempted murder. Defendant appeals, raising as issues whether (1) he was proved guilty of the charges beyond a reasonable doubt; (2) the circuit court erred in failing to conduct a fitness hearing; and (3) the circuit court erred in sentencing him.

Leonard Macon testified that on December 17, 1992, at 3:00 P.M., he was walking along Fourteenth Place when a gray car with four occupants stopped about fifteen yards from him. Brian Robinson, who Macon knew from the neighborhood, exited the car and went into a house adjacent to an alley. Robinson returned to the car and pulled up alongside Macon. The four occupants, identified by Macon as Robinson, defendant, Gerald Taylor, and Sammy "Shine" McGruder, approached him. Robinson pulled out a .38-caliber handgun and asked Macon where his roommate George "Butch" Addison was; Macon responded that he did not know. Defendant then punched Macon on the side of the face, knocking off his eyeglasses. Robinson spoke of killing Macon, but instead told him to hand over his money. Macon responded that he had no money. Robinson then demanded his leather jacket. Macon took off his jacket, and McGruder took it. Taylor and defendant stood near McGruder.

The four men then took Macon through a vacant lot to an alley located north of Fourteenth Place. Robinson had his gun pointed at Macon the entire time. In the presence of defendant and the other two, Robinson directed Macon to go into a vacant garage, which Macon entered. Macon started walking briskly when he saw a door in the back of the garage, but halfway through, Macon heard three gunshots and felt two shots hit him in the back. Macon ran out of the garage door towards Fourteenth Place. When Macon saw the four perpetrators running through the vacant lot, he turned around and ran to his home on Fourteenth Street, north of the alley. Once inside his house, Macon saw the perpetrators drive past his home. When they were gone he ran to his neighbor Shirley Brown's home, where he fell to the floor.

She called the police and the paramedics. Macon provided information to the police and was taken to the hospital. Macon admitted that he had been convicted for forgery, for which he received twenty-four months' probation.

On cross-examination, Macon stated, among other things, that defendant was not carrying a gun.

Chicago police officer Thomas Newton testified that on December 17, 1992, he responded to a report of a shooting. There he saw Macon lying on the floor of Brown's home. Newton saw blood and noticed that Macon had been shot. Macon said that Robinson shot him. Newton went to the garage where the shooting occurred and found a trail of blood.

Chicago police officer Andre Hasan testified that on December 20, 1992, he arrested defendant and took his photographs. These were shown to Macon along with other random photos, and he identified defendant.

At the conclusion of the State's case-in-chief, defendant testified that he has a twin brother, Benal, and they both have the nickname "Atwin." He knew Robinson, McGruder, Taylor, Macon, and Addison from the neighborhood. On December 17, 1992, at 3:00 P.M., outside of a liquor store with some friends, he was talking to his girlfriend on the telephone when he heard gunshots coming from somewhere between Fourteenth Place and Fourteenth Street. He and his friends went to Fourteenth Place and Ashland, where he saw a car speed away, but did not see any of the passengers.

Defendant stated that on the day of the shooting, he had not been getting along with McGruder because McGruder had shot at him. He denied planning with McGruder or Robinson to shoot someone. Defendant denied punching Macon, or knocking off his glasses, or entering Robinson's car on the day of the shooting, or being present when Macon was held at gunpoint. He denied seeing Macon or Robinson on the day of the shooting.

Defendant spoke to a detective at the police station during the early morning hours of December 21, 1992, but denied telling him he was in an alley with Robinson December 17, or that he was standing five feet from Robinson while Robinson pointed a gun at Macon.

Chicago police officer Deborah Dorken testified that when she talked to Macon at Brown's home and the hospital, the only name he gave was the shooter Robinson.

In rebuttal, Chicago police detective Michael Hughes testified that at 2 A.M. on December 21, 1992, he interviewed defendant, in custody, who admitted he was in an alley near Fourteenth Place with Taylor at 3 P.M. on December 17, 1992. He was about five feet from Robinson, who was pointing a gun a Macon. Defendant told Robinson not to shoot Macon.

At the close of the evidence and after closing argument, the jury was instructed upon the theory of accountability and found defendant not guilty of attempted murder but guilty of aggravated battery with a firearm and armed robbery. The circuit court sentenced him to twelve years' imprisonment for aggravated battery with a firearm and, concurrently, twelve years for armed robbery. Defendant timely filed a notice of appeal.

OPINION

1.

Defendant first contends that he was not proved guilty beyond a reasonable doubt of aggravated battery with a firearm and armed robbery.

The standard of review for challenging the sufficiency of evidence is whether, after viewing all the evidence in the light most favorable to the prosecution, any rational trier of fact could have found the essential elements of the crime beyond a reasonable doubt, *Jackson* v. *Virginia,* 443 U.S. 307, 99 S. Ct. 2781, 61 L. Ed. 2d 560 (1979); *People* v. *Collins,* 106 Ill. 2d 237, 261, 87 Ill. 2d 910, 478 N.E.2d 267 (1985). The determination of the trier of fact will not be set aside on review unless the proof is so unsatisfactory, improbable or implausible as to justify a reasonable doubt as to defendant's guilt. *People* v. *Slim,* 127 Ill. 2d 302, 307, 130 Ill. Dec. 250, 537 N.E.2d 317 (1989).

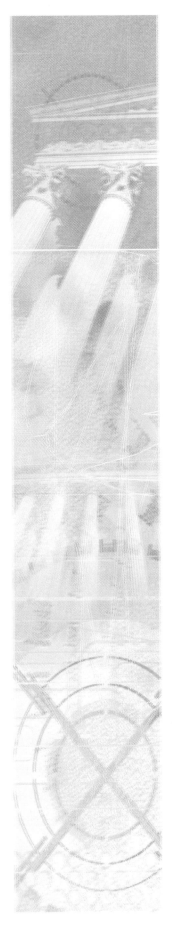

Under Illinois law, a person is legally accountable for the conduct of another if "either before or during the commission of an offense, and with the intent to promote or facilitate such commission, he solicits, aids, abets, agrees or attempts to aid, such other person in the planning or commission of the offense." 720 ILCS 5/5-2(c) (West 1992). In *People* v. *Taylor*, 164 Ill.2d 131, 140–41, 207 Ill. Dec. 1, 646 N.E.2d 567 (1995), our supreme court explained:

> *The mere presence of a defendant at the scene of a crime does not render one accountable for the offense. Moreover, presence at the scene plus knowledge that a crime was being committed, without more, is also insufficient to establish accountability. Nevertheless, active participation has never been a requirement for the imposition of criminal guilt under an accountability theory. One may aid and abet without actively participating in the overt act.*
>
> *A defendant may be deemed accountable for acts performed by another if there was a common criminal plan or purpose. Words of agreement are not necessary to establish a common purpose to commit a crime. The common design can be inferred from the circumstances surrounding the perpetration of the unlawful conduct. Proof that defendant was present during the perpetration of the offense, that he maintained a close affiliation with his companions after the commission of the crime, and that he failed to report the crime are all factors that the trier of fact may consider in determining the defendant's legal accountability. Defendant's flight from the scene may also be considered in determining whether defendant is accountable.*

With the foregoing as frames of reference, defendant's specific arguments will be considered.

A.

Defendant maintains that he cannot be held accountable for armed robbery where he had no interest in the coat taken, was not armed, said nothing to Macon, and was merely present.

Armed robbery occurs when a person, while armed with a dangerous weapon, takes property from the person or presence of another by the use of force or by threatening the imminent use of force. 720 ILCS 5/182(a) (West 1992).

Viewing the evidence in the fight most favorable to the prosecution, the jury could have believed that defendant, Robinson, Taylor, and McGruder were in a car together and pulled up next to Macon as he walked along the street. They approached Macon, and Robinson pulled out a gun. When Macon said he did not know the whereabouts of his roommate Butch, defendant punched him in the face. Robinson, at gunpoint, then told Macon to hand over his money and jacket. Defendant stood by and said nothing. McGruder took Macon's jacket, the four offenders led Macon to the vacant garage, and he was shot.

A rational trier of fact could conclude that defendant aided his conconspirators in the commission of the armed robbery. Defendant, along with the three others, created an atmosphere of coercion and intimidation. It was he who punched Macon, stood by and remained with the group after the coat was taken, was present at and fled from the scene after the shooting, and never reported the crime to the police. All the foregoing factors could have been considered in determining that defendant was accountable for the actions of his cohorts. See *Taylor*, 164 Ill. 2d at 140–41, 207 Ill. Dec. 1, 646 N.E.2d 567.

Defendant was proved guilty beyond a reasonable doubt of armed robbery.

B.

Defendant asserts that he was not accountable for aggravated battery with a firearm where the facts indicate he was not armed, he had no agreement with Robinson to shoot anyone and, according to Detective Hughes, he told Robinson not to shoot Macon.

Aggravated battery with a firearm occurs when a person, in committing a battery, knowingly causes any injury to another by means of the discharging of a firearm. 720 ILCS 5/12-4.2(a) (West 1992).

Here, the evidence, when viewed in the light most favorable to the prosecution, showed that the four offenders directed Macon into a vacant garage near the alley. As Macon was led into the alley, he glanced back and saw Robinson pointing the gun at him and also saw defendant walking along with them. When near the garage, Macon did not turn around, but heard voices. Defendant evidently anticipated a shooting because he claims to have told Robinson not to shoot Macon. Nevertheless, Robinson told Macon to walk into the vacant garage and, shortly thereafter, Macon was shot. Thereafter, Macon escaped through the garage door and saw the four offenders ran away. Later, he saw them drive by his home.

Defendant cites three cases to support his argument that he was not accountable for Macon's shooting. In *People* v. *Green,* 74 26 Ill. App. 3d 662, 668, 325 N.E.2d 316, *affd. in part rev'd in part,* 62 Ill.2d 146, 340 N.E.2d 9 (1975), the court concluded, with little analysis, that defendant could not be convicted of murder under an accountability theory where he and two others attempted to rob a passenger on a train and, as they were preparing to leave the train, one of the cohorts shot the passenger as he ran by them [Note: defendant was found guilty of murder under the felony murder rule]. . . . In *People* v. *Lincoln,* 157 Ill. App. 3d 700, 109 Ill. Dec. 958, 510 N.E. 9d 1026 (1987), defendant went into the bedroom of his neighbor looking for a man named Mitchell, while his codefendants shot a man who was sitting in the living room. The court held that defendant was not accountable for murder because his plan was "to get" Mitchell, and defendant was not present during the events that led to killing. In *People* v. *Estrada,* 243 Ill. App. 3d 177, 178–180, 183 Ill. Dec. 415, 611 N.E. 2d 1063 (1993), defendant was riding in a car with three fellow gang members, knowing that one of them was carrying a semi-automatic weapon. They pulled up to a street corner and exchanged gang signs with members of an opposing gang. After defendant exited the car with a tire iron, someone in the car fired two shots. Defendant chased one of the opposing gang members and shattered a window of the building where the individual entered. The court held that defendant was not accountable for the murder of the individual killed by gunfire because when defendant left the car brandishing a tire iron, he was not aware that one of his companions would shoot the gun. *Estrada,* 243 Ill. App. 3d at 185, 183 Ill. Dec. 415, 611 N.E.2d 1063. Here, defendant punched Macon, stood by as he was robbed, helped coerce him into the garage, knew there would be a shooting, fled with the other offenders after the shooting, and failed to notify the authorities. In addition, Macon was held at gunpoint the entire time, and Robinson threatened to kill him, but defendant said nothing.

The State refers to *People* v. *Terry,* 99 Ill. 2d 508, 515, 77 Ill. Dec. 442, 460 N.E.2d 746 (1984), where the court held that defendants could be held accountable for the murder of another, although their sole intent may have been to beat the victim, since they knew that a third companion brought a knife and intended to kill the victim. In *Terry,* the court explained the "common-design rule," which is incorporated in the accountability statute and provides that where two or more persons engage in a common criminal design or agreement, any acts in furtherance thereof committed by one party are considered to be the acts of all parties to the common design and all are equally responsible for the consequences of such further acts. 99 Ill. 2d at 514, 77 Ill. Dec. 442, 460 N.E.2d 746.

The *Terry* court discussed *Brennan* v. *People,* 15 Ill. 511 (1854), where the common design rule was applied. In *Brennan,* a group of persons pursued a man named Story to a barn and killed him, although it was not clear who or why they killed him. In holding defendants guilty of murder, the court stated:

> The [defendants] may be guilty of murder, although they neither took part in
> the killing, nor assented to any arrangement having for its object the death of

Story. It is sufficient that they combined with those committing the deed to do an unlawful act, such as to beat or rob Story; and that he was killed in the attempt to execute the common purpose. If several persons conspire to do an unlawful act, and death happens in the prosecution of the common object, all are alike guilty of the homicide." Brennan 15 Ill. at 516–17, quoted in Terry, 99 Ill. 2d at 514, 77 Ill.. Dec. 442, 460 N.E.2d 746.

Defendant was accountable for the actions of Robinson. As in *Brennan,* where defendants chased Story into a barn, defendant and his companions here led Macon into an empty garage for an unknown purpose. Whatever their reason for taking Macon to the garage at gunpoint, it was unlawful. Defendant's own evidence suggests that he knew of an impending shooting. The fact that Macon was shot during the execution of the common purpose is sufficient to hold defendant accountable for the shooting. A rational trier of fact could have concluded that defendant was accountable for the shooting of Macon.

The cases cited by defendant are distinguishable. In *Green,* defendants were leaving the train, having already attempted to rob the victim, when one of the defendants shot the victim as he ran by. In *Lincoln,* the plan was to get Mitchell. Any consequence to Mitchell resulting from their plan to get him would have been attributable to defendant, but the death of a bystander went beyond the plan. In *Estrada,* there was no evidence that defendant had advance knowledge of the plan to kill the opposing gang member. 243 Ill. App. 3d at 185, 183 Ill. Dec. 415, 611 N.E.2d 1063. Because defendant exited the car brandishing a tire iron, there was not evidence that he and his cohort were in concert with respect to their thoughts or actions. Here, defendant stood by Robinson the entire time Macon was held at gunpoint.

Under the evidence produced in the present case, defendant was proved guilty beyond a reasonable doubt of aggravated battery with a firearm. . . .

For the reasons set forth above, there are no bases for disturbing the circuit court proceedings and, accordingly, we affirm.

Affirmed.

[footnotes omitted]

WHAT DO *YOU* THINK?

1. On what legal principle did the court hold the defendant guilty of armed robbery?
2. Would it have mattered if the defendant had established that he did not intend for the victim to be robbed?
3. What is the "common-design" rule?
4. Explain what the court meant by the statement that "active participation has never been a requirement for imposition of criminal guilt under an accountability theory?"
5. What is the difference in legal accountability or liability between the cases cited by the defendant and the present case?

CAPSTONE CASE

CAN A PRIVATE CORPORATION BE HELD LIABLE FOR THE CRIME OF HOMICIDE?

Commonwealth v. *McIlwain School Bus Lines*
Superior Court of Pennsylvania, 1980
283 Pa. Super. 1, 423 A.2d 413

This is an appeal by the Commonwealth from an order quashing an information. The principal issue is whether a private corporation may be held criminally liable for homicide by vehicle. On April 3, 1978, a school bus owned by the McIlwain School Bus Lines, Inc. [hereinafter, the corporation] and operated by one of its employees, ran over and killed 6-year-old Lori Sharp; she had just gotten off the bus and was walking in front it when she was run over. On May 26, 1978, the corporation was charged with homicide by vehicle. The corporation waived its right to a preliminary hearing, but subsequently filed a motion to quash the information against it. One ground of the motion was that the statute defining the offense of homicide by vehicle did not apply where the particular regulation allegedly violated involved the equipment required on a vehicle (its front and rear view mirrors) and not the operation of the vehicle. A second ground of the motion was that by definition, the offense could only be committed by a natural person, not by a corporation. By order filed on March 16, 1979, the lower court granted the corporation's motion to quash. The court did not rule on the first ground of the motion. Instead, the court held, *sua sponte,* that the information issued against the corporation was insufficient. The court did not rule on the second ground of the motion, and held, as argued by the corporation, that the offense of homicide by vehicle could not be committed by a corporation. . . .

The criminal law has not always regarded a corporation as subject to criminal liability. Indeed, it was once widely accepted that a corporation was incapable of committing a criminal offense.

This doctrine of non-liability for crime arose from the theory that a corporation, being an intangible entity, [*New York Cent. & H. River R. Co. v. United States,* 212 U.S. 481, 29 S. Ct. 304, 53 L. Ed. 613; *Sutton's Hospital Case,* 10 Coke 23, 32], could neither commit a crime nor be subjected to punishment, because any illegal act of a corporate agent was done without authority of the corporation and ultra vires. [*Music Box, Inc. v. Mills,* 10 La. App. 6765, 121 S. 196] [10 *Fletcher Cyc. Corp.* § 4942 (Perm. Ed. 1978) p. 620.]

Today, however, it is generally recognized that a corporation may be held criminally liable for criminal acts performed by its agents on its behalf. See, e.g., *United States v. Wise,* 370 U.S. 405, 82 S. Ct. 1354, 8 L. Ed. 2d 590 (1962) (conspiracy, violation of Sherman Act); *United States v. Johns-Manville Corporation,* 231 F. Supp. 690 (E. D. Pa. 1964) (antitrust, conspiracy); *People v. Schomig,* 74 Cal. App. 109, 239 P. 413 (1925) (violation of legislation regulating real estate brokerages); *West Valley Estates, Inc. v. Florida,* Fla. App., 286 So. 2d 208 (1973) (violation of statute proscribing dredging of lands); *Southern Ry. Co. v. State,* 125 Ga. 287, 54 S.E. 160 (1906) (violation of state penal code re: operation of passenger cars); *State v. Adjustment Dept. Credit Bureau, Inc.,* 94 Idaho 156, 483 P.2d 687 (1971) (extortion); *People v. Duncan,* 363 Ill. 495, 2 N.E.2d 705 (1936) (violation of Motor Fuel Tax Act); *Golden Guernsey Farms v. State,* 223 Ind. 606, 63 N.E.2d 699 (1945) (violation of Uniform Food, Drug & Cosmetic Act); *G. & H. Cattle Co. v. Commonwealth,* 312 Ky. 315, 227 S.W.2d 420 (1950) (nuisance, pollution); *Telegram Newspaper Co. v. Commonwealth,* 172 Mass. 294, 52 N.E. 445 (1898) (criminal contempt); *State v. Worker's Socialist Pub. Co.,* 150 Minn. 406, 185 N.W. 931 (1921) (criminal syndicalism); *Department of Health of State of New Jersey v. Borough of Fort Lee,* 108 N. J. Eq. 139, 154 A. 319 (1931) (criminal contempt); *People v. Canadian Fur Trappers' Corp.,* 248 N.Y. 159, 161 N.E. 455 (1928) (larceny); *Hardeman King Co. v. State,* 29 Okl. Cr. 319, 233 P. 792 (1925) (violation of laws re: selling agricultural seeds); *Commonwealth v. American Baseball Club of Philadelphia,* 290 Pa. 136, 138 A. 497 (1927) (violation of Sunday laws); *Love v. Nashville Agricultural & Normal Institute,* 146 Tenn. 550, 243 S.W. 304 (1922) (nuisance); *Postal Tel. Cable Co. v. City of Charlottesville,* 126 Va. 800, 101 S.E. 357 (1919) (violation of intrastate telegraph laws); *Vulcan Last Co. v. State,* 194 Wis. 636, 217 N.W. 412 (1928) (attempt to influence votes of employees in referendum election).

As early as the 1860s Pennsylvania courts have recognized that a corporation may be subject to criminal liability. Corporations in Pennsylvania have been indicted or

convicted of maintaining public nuisances, unlawful manufacture or possession of intoxicating liquors, violation of Sunday laws, and violation of the Unlawful Collection Agency Practices Act. For a time, the Pennsylvania courts were unwilling to extend corporate criminal liability to crimes involving specific intent or homicide. In *Commonwealth v. Punxsutawney*, 24 Pa. C. C. 25, 48 Pittsb. Leg. J. 42 (1900), the court of common pleas of Jefferson County refused to hold a street railway company criminally liable for the crime of assault in ejecting a passenger.

Some courts have shown a tendency to enlarge on the criminal liability of corporations but no court has gone as far as we are urged to go in this case. Hence, not a single case is to be found to sustain this indictment. We should make haste slowly when it is in the direction of holding either an individual or a corporation criminally liable for a crime committed by an employee without his or its knowledge or consent. Moreover, the criminal act here alleged is so far ultra vires as to contravene all the accepted rules in the criminal law for making it the act of the principal. 48 P.L.J. at 42.

And in *Commonwealth v. Peoples Natural Gas Co.*, 102 P.L.J. 348 (1954), the court of common pleas of Allegheny County granted a corporation's motion to quash an indictment charging involuntary manslaughter, then the common law offense; the court reasoned that the phrase, "the killing of another," implied that the killer had to be of the same nature as the killed ("another"). Courts in other jurisdictions, however, have abandoned this limitation.

For example, the Supreme Court of New Jersey has held that a corporation may be held criminally liable for involuntary manslaughter. In *State v. Lehigh Valley R. Co.*, 90 N.J.L. 372, 103 A. 685 (1917), in denying a corporation's motion to quash an indictment for involuntary manslaughter, the court said:

"It has long been settled in this state that a corporation aggregate may in a proper case be held criminally for acts of malfeasance as well as for nonfeasance. *State v. Morris and Essex Railroad Co.*, 23 N. J. Law 360; *State v. Passaic County Agricultural Society*, 54 N. J. Law 260, 23 Atl. 680. So well settled is the general rule that in the later cases it has not even been questioned. *States [State] v. Erie Railroad Co.*, 83 N. J. Law 231, 84 Atl. 698; *Id.* 84 N. J. Law 661, 87 Atl. 141, 46 L.R.A. 117, *State v. Lehigh Valley Railroad Co.*, 89 N. J. Law 48, 97 Atl. 786; *Id.* 90 N. J. Law 340, 100 Atl. 167. [90 N. J. Law at 373, 103 A. at 685.]"

The court went on to say that "[w]e can think of no reason why it [the corporation] should not be held for the criminal consequences of its negligence or its nonfeasance." 90 N. J. Law at 374, 103 A. at 686. In *United States v. Van Schaick et al.*, 134 F.592 (C.C.S.D.N.Y. 1904), the court held that a corporate owner of a steam vessel could be guilty of manslaughter for "fraud, connivance, misconduct or violation of the law" resulting in loss of life. The charge was that as owner, the corporation had failed to equip the vessel with life preservers and fire fighting equipment. In *People v. Ebasco Services, Incorporated et al.*, 77 Misc. 2d 784, 354 N.Y.S.2d 807 (1974), the Supreme Court of New York (Queens County) held that a corporation could be guilty of negligent homicide. The court held that although the statute's use of the word "person" in referring to the victim of a homicide naturally meant a human being, the statute did not require that the "person" committing the act of homicide also be a human being.

There is, however, no manifest impropriety in applying the broader definition of "person" to a corporation in regard to the commission of a homicide particularly in view of the statement by the *Court of Appeals in People v. Rochester Railway & Light Co.* (*supra*) that the Legislature is empowered to impose criminal liability upon a corporation for a homicide. Accordingly, the court concludes that although a corporation cannot be the victim of a homicide, it may commit that offense and be held to answer therefore. [77 Misc. 2d at 787, 354 N.Y.S.2d at 811.]

The law of Pennsylvania has developed in a manner consistent with these New Jersey and New York decisions. With the enactment of the Crimes Code, Act of Dec.

6, 1972, P.L. 1482, No. 334, § 1 *et seq.*, eff. June 6, 1973, 18 Pa. C.S.A. § 101 *et seq.*, the criminal liability of corporations was codified, as follows:

> (a) *Corporations generally.—A corporation may be convicted of the commission of an offense if:*
> (1) *the offense is a summary offense or the offense is defined by a statute other than this title in which a legislative purpose to impose liability on corporations plainly appears and the conduct is performed by an agent of the corporation acting in behalf of the corporation within the scope of his office or employment, except that if the law defining the offense designates the agents for whose conduct the corporation is accountable or the circumstances under which it is accountable, such provisions shall apply;*
> (2) *the offense consists of an omission to discharge a specific duty of affirmative performance imposed on corporations by law; or*
> (3) *the commission of the offense was authorized, requested, commanded, performed or recklessly tolerated by the board of directors or by a high managerial agent acting in behalf of the corporation within the scope of his office or employment.*
>
> (b) *Corporations, absolute liability.—When absolute liability is imposed for the commission of an offense, a legislative purpose to impose liability on a corporation shall be assumed, unless the contrary plainly appears. 18 Pa.C.S.A. § 307(a) and (b).*

We recently had occasion to apply this provision, in *Commonwealth v. J. P. Mascaro and Sons, Inc.*, 266 Pa. Super. 8, 402 A.2d 1050 (1979), where we held that under subsection (a)(3) of section 307, a corporation could be convicted of theft by deception, deceptive business practices, and unsworn falsification to authorities arising out of false reports pertaining to rubbish hauled pursuant to a contract between the corporation and a county. Cases such as *Commonwealth v. Punxsutawney*, supra, and *Commonwealth v. Peoples Natural Gas Co.*, supra, therefore no longer have any precedential value.

When section 307 of the Crimes Code is applied to the present case, it is apparent that the critical words are that "[a] corporation may be convicted of the commission of an offense if: (1) the offense is . . . defined by a statute other than this title in which a legislative purpose to impose liability on corporations plainly appears. . . ." 18 Pa. C.S.A. § 307(a)(1). Here, the offense—homicide by vehicle—is "defined by a statute other than [the Crimes Code]"; it is defined by the Vehicle Code, Act of June 17, 1976, P.L. 162, No. 81, § 1, eff. July 1, 1977, 75 Pa. C.S.A. § 3732. The question that we must decide, therefore, is whether from that definition "a legislative purpose to impose liability on corporations plainly appears."

The statute provides that homicide by vehicle may be committed by "[a]ny person who unintentionally causes the death of another person while engaged in the violation of . . . [etc.]." (Emphasis added.) Section 102 of the Vehicle Code defines "person" as "[a] natural person, firm, co-partnership, association or corporation." 75 Pa. C.S.A. § 102. It therefore "plainly appears" that homicide by vehicle may be committed by a corporation. This conclusion is made even more plain by the opening paragraph of Section 102, which provides:

"Subject to additional definitions contained in subsequent provisions of this title which are applicable to specific provisions of this title, the following words and phrases when used in this title shall have, unless the content clearly indicates otherwise, the meanings given to them in this section [75 Pa. C.S.A. § 102.]"

"Person" is one of the "following words" thus referred to. There are no "additional definitions" of "person" in Section 3732, defining homicide by vehicle. Therefore, "unless the content [of Section 3732] clearly indicates otherwise [emphasis

added]," the meaning given "person" in Section 3732 shall be the meaning given it in Section 102, i.e., as including a corporation.

The lower court acknowledged that Section 102 defined "person" as including a corporation, but held, nevertheless, that as used in Section 3732, "person" did not include a corporation. Said the court:

"If 'person' was to include a corporation, Section 3732 semantically and grammatically should have read 'any person who or which unintentionally causes the death. . . .' In modern usage *who* refers to actual persons (human beings). *Which* refers to the unnatural, artificial or inanimate as a corporation. [Webster's Collegiate 5th Edition Dictionary.]

The Latin 'qui' means *who* referring to the natural or human, and 'quod' means *which* referring to the unnatural, artificial or inanimate. (The New Century Dictionary Foreign Words and Phrases) [Slip op. at 3.]"

We are not persuaded by this reasoning. Initially, it may be noted that the argument from Latin is not persuasive, for reference to another language would have shown that the word for "who" and the word for "which" may be the same. Nor is the argument from grammar persuasive; indeed, it cuts just the other way. The phrase, "any person who or which," is not only extremely awkward but sounds wrong, for in ordinary usage, "person" refers only to a natural person and therefore takes only "who," not "which." Accordingly, no legislative draftsman wants to resort to the phrase, "any person who or which." Instead, the draftsman will make a choice. One choice is to avoid definitions. With respect to the Vehicle Code, that would mean that throughout the statute there would appear the phrase, "Any natural person, firm, co-partnership, association or corporation who or which . . . [does one of the many acts proscribed by the Code]." This is clear but cumbersome. A second choice, therefore, is to avoid being cumbersome by using one word instead of many, and still be clear by giving that one word a definition that includes the many. This is the choice usually made when the statute in question is long and divided into many sections. Here, the draftsman of the Vehicle Code made this second choice. Having done so, he wished to be grammatical, and not offend the reader with an awkward phrase. He therefore said, "Any person who . . . ," knowing that by reference to the definitions in Section 102, the reader could learn what "person" referred to, and did not say, "Any person who or which . . . ," which would not only be awkward and sound wrong, but because of Section 102, was unnecessary.

Other jurisdictions have similarly applied criminal statutes defining the word "person" as including corporation. For example, in *Vulcan Last Co. v. State,* 194 Wis. 636, 217 N.W. 412 (1928), the Supreme Court of Wisconsin held that a corporation is liable to prosecution under a statute prohibiting any "person" from attempting to influence a voter, where the statute provided that "person" included a corporation. In *State v. Workers' Socialist Pub. Co.,* 150 Minn. 406, 185 N.W. 931 (1921), the Supreme Court of Minnesota held that a corporation was criminally liable under a statute prohibiting "any person" from advocating violence to gain political ends, where the statute provided that the word "person" included a corporation. See also *State v. Adjustment Dept. Credit Bureau, Inc.,* 94 Idaho 156, 483 P.2d 687 (1971); *Paragon Paper Co. v. State,* 19 Ind. App. 314, 49 N.E. 600 (1898).

The lower court also gave the following reasons for its decision:

"The Homicide by Vehicle Section 3732 nowhere contains the word corporation: no Pennsylvania courts have applied this section to corporations; the penalty of the section providing jail is not corporately oriented; the revocation of one's license is not corporately applicable; and the section (as with the entire Vehicle Code Serious Offense Section 3731 to 3734, inclusive) is strictly natural person solely operational driver oriented. [Slip op. at 2.]"

It is true that Section 3732 does not use the word "corporation." However, given the definition of the word "person", there is no need for it to do so. It is also true—

at least so far as we know—that no court in Pennsylvania has applied Section 3732 to a corporation; the present case appears to be of first impression. However, given the fact that the section did not become effective until July 1, 1977, the fact that no case other than this one has been brought against a corporation for homicide by vehicle is hardly conclusive proof that the section may not be so applied. Neither are we persuaded by the next two reasons of the lower court—that since a corporation cannot be put in jail or have its license revoked, Section 3732 does not apply to corporations.

The offense of homicide by vehicle is a misdemeanor of the first degree. 75 Pa. C.S.A. § 3732. It is true that one of the punishments that may be imposed for committing a misdemeanor of the first degree is a term of imprisonment:

A person who has been convicted of a misdemeanor may be sentenced to imprisonment for a definite term which shall be fixed by the court and shall be not more than:

"(1) Five years in the case of a misdemeanor of the first degree. [18 Pa. C.S.A. § 1104.]"

It is also true that another possible punishment for homicide by vehicle is the revocation of one's driving license:

The department shall revoke the operating privilege of any driver for one year upon receiving a certified record of the driver's conviction of any of the following offenses: . . . Section 3732 (relating to homicide by vehicle). 75 Pa. C.S. 1532(a)(3).

However, a third possible punishment is the imposition of a fine:

"A person who has been convicted of any offense may be sentenced to pay a fine not exceeding:

(1) . . . .

(2) . . . .

(3) $ 10,000, when the conviction is of a misdemeanor of the first degree. [18 Pa. C.S.A. § 1101.]"

Where alternate punishments are provided for a crime, the court may in appropriate circumstances impose the fine only:

"Fine only.—The court may, as authorized by law, sentence the defendant only to pay a fine, when, having regard to the nature and circumstances of the crime and to the history and character of the defendant, it is of the opinion that the fine alone suffices. [18 Pa. C.S. § 1326(a).]"

In *United States* v. *Hougland Barge Line, Inc.*, 387 F. Supp. 1110 (W. D. Pa. 1974), the court held that a statute requiring any "person in charge" of a vessel to notify the United States Coast Guard of oil discharges from the vessel applied to corporations as well as individuals, and that when applied to a corporation, only a fine may be imposed:

"The defendant also argues that as a corporation it cannot be imprisoned, and therefore, this would indicate that it [the statute in question] was not intended to apply to corporations. Innumerable federal penal statutes prohibit certain activities, including business entities, and provide penalties for violation of such prohibited acts. Both individuals and corporations are penalized even though a corporation may not be imprisoned. Thus, as illustrated by antitrust cases and Internal Revenue cases, where a statute calls for imprisonment, when imposed against a defendant corporation, only the fine portion of the penalty may be imposed. *United States* v. *Hilton Hotel [Hotels] Corporation, supra* [467 F.2d [1000] (9th Cir. 1972) *cert. Denied*, 409 U.S. 1125, [93 S. Ct. 938, 35 L. Ed. 2d 256] (1973)]; *United States* v. *Swift & Company*, 189 F. Supp. 885(D. C. Ill. 1960), affirmed, 367 U.S. 909, 81 S. Ct. 1918, 6 L. Ed. 2d 1249 (1961). [387 F. Supp. at 1114.]"

Courts in other jurisdictions have similarly applied this principle, recognizing that to do otherwise would in effect confer upon the corporation immunity for its criminal acts. Thus, the Supreme Court of Illinois has said:

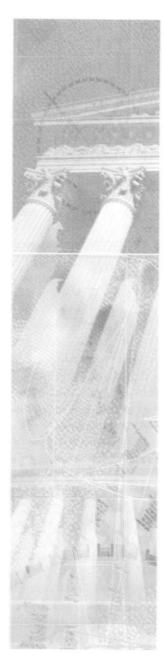

"Where the statutory penalty is both fine and imprisonment, the corporate offender can be punished by imposing a fine, inasmuch as the two penalties are independent. *United States* v. *Union Supply Co.,* [215 U.S. 50, 30 S. Ct. 15, 54 L. Ed. 87] *supra;* 7 R.C.L. § 784. The theory is that a court shall apply the appropriate penalty in such instances as far as possible, in order that the corporate defendant shall not escape all punishment. [*People* v. *Duncan,* 363 Ill. 495, 2 N.E.2d 705 (1936).]"

The Supreme Court of North Carolina has said:

"It is true that, when the statute imposes a penalty of a fine or imprisonment, only the fine can be placed upon a corporation. But this is no reason why that should not be imposed. The corporation should not be wholly exempted from punishment, because it cannot be imprisoned. . . . *State* v. *Ice & Fuel Co.,* 166 N.C. 366, 369, 81 S.E. 737, 738 (1914)."

And in *United States* v. *Van Schaick et al., supra,* the Circuit Court for the Southern District of New York reached a similar conclusion:

"But it is said that no punishment can follow conviction. This is an oversight in the statute. Is it to be concluded, simply because the given punishment cannot be enforced, that Congress intended to allow corporate carriers by sea to kill their passengers through misconduct that would be a punishable offense if done by a natural person?"

A corporation can be guilty of causing death by its wrongful act. It can with equal propriety be punished in a civil or criminal action. It seems a more reasonable alternative that Congress inadvertently omitted to provide suitable punishment for the offense when committed by a corporation, than it intended to give the wrongdoer impunity simply because it happened to be a corporation. 134 F. at 602.

Finally, we are unable to accept the lower court's conclusion that Section 3732 "is strictly natural person solely operational driver oriented." For the reasons we have given, it appears to us equally to include corporations.

Reversed.

[footnotes omitted]

WHAT DO *YOU* THINK?

1. In this case, Mcilwain School Bus Lines, Inc., argued that the offense of homicide by vehicle could not be committed by a corporation. On what grounds did the corporation base its arguments?
2. Why did the court conclude that a corporation was a "person" for purposes of the law? How was such a conclusion reached?
3. What are the potential legal ramifications of granting the status of "person" to a corporation?

NOTES

1. *United States* v. *Davis,* 8 F.3d 923 (2d Cir. 1993).

2. Joseph R. Nolan and Jacqueline M. Nolan-Haley, *Black's Law Dictionary: Definitions of the Terms and Phrases of American and English Jurisprudence, Ancient and Modern,* 6th ed. (St. Paul, MN: West Publishing Co., 1990), p. 761.

3. Jerome Hall, *General Principles of Criminal Law,* 2nd ed. (Charlottesville, VA: Michie, 1960).

4. Joshua Dressler, *Understanding Criminal Law,* 2nd ed. (Boston: Matthew Bender, 1995), p. 351.

5. Ibid.

6. Ibid, p. 347.

7. Stanford H. Kadish and Stephen J. Schulhofer, *Criminal Law and Its Processes,* 6th ed. (Boston: Little, Brown and Company, 1995), p. 581.

8. N.Y. Penal Law, Section 110.0.

9. California Penal Code, Section 664.

10. Illinois Ann. Stat. Ch. 38, Section 8-4.

11. See *United States* v. *Mandujano,* 499 F.2d 370, 376 (5th Cir. 1974), cert. denied, 419 U.S. 1114, 95 S. Ct. 792, 42 L. Ed. 2d 812 (1975).

12. Model Penal Code, Section 5.01(2).

13. Florida Penal Code, Chapter 777, Section 4, paragraph 1.

14. Model Penal Code, Section 5.01(2).

15. Alaska Statutes, Sec. 11.31.100.

16. Derek Humphry, *Final Exit* (New York: Dell, 1992).

17. Model Penal Code, Section 5.01(2).

18. *Mims* v. *United States*, 373 F.2d 135, 148 (5th Cir. 1967).

19. *People* v. *Rizzo*, 246 N.Y. 334, 158 N.E. 888 (1927).

20. *Commonwealth* v. *Peaslee,* 177 Mass. 267, 59 N.E. 55 (Sup. Judicial Ct. of Mass. 1901).

21. *People* v. *Rizzo*, 246 N.Y. 334, 158 N.E. 888.

22. *Commonwealth* v. *Peaslee,* 177 Mass. 267, 59 N.E. 55.

23. *Regina* v. *Eagleton.* 6 Cox Criminal Cases 559 (Eng. 1855).

24. Ibid.

25. *Commonwealth* v. *Kelly,* 58 A.2d 375 (Pa. Super. Ct. 1948).

26. Ibid, p. 377.

27. *People* v. *Rizzo*, 246 N.Y. 334, 158 N.E. 888.

28. *King* v. *Barker,* 1924 N.Z.L.R. 865 (N.Z. 1924).

29. Model Penal Code, Sections 5.01(2)(a) through (g).

30. Note this example would overrule the case of *People* v. *Rizzo* discussed earlier.

31. *United States* v. *Berrigan,* 482 F.2d 171 (3d Cir. 1973).

32. Indiana Code, Title 35, Article 41, Chapter 3, Section 10.

33. Florida Penal Code, Chapter 777, Section 4, paragraph 5.

34. Model Penal Code, Section 5.01(4).

35. See, for example, *People* v. *Dlugash,* 363 N.E.2d 1155 (N.Y. 1977).

36. H. L. A. Hart, *Punishment and Responsibility,* (London: Oxford University Press, 1968), p. 130.

37. Model Penal Code and Commentaries, Comment to Section 5.05 at 490 (1985).

38. Florida Penal Code, Chapter 777, Section 4, paragraph 3.

39. Paul Marcus, "Criminal Conspiracy Law: Time to Turn Back From An Ever Expanding, Ever More Troubling Area," *Bill of Rights Journal,* Vol. 1, (1992), pp. 8–11.

40. *United States* v. *Casamento,* 887 F.2d 1141 (2d Cir. 1989).

41. *United States* v. *Ianniello,* 866 F.2d 540 (2d Cir. 1989).

42. *United States* v. *Kopituk,* 690 F.2d 1289 (11th Cir. 1982).

43. *United States* v. *Martino,* 648 F.2d 367 (5th Cir. 1981).

44. Dressler, 1995:393.

45. *Harrison v. United States*, 7 F.259 (2d Cir. 1925).

46. *Shaw v. Director of Public Prosecutions*, A.C. 220 at page 294 (1962).

47. *Williams v. United States*, 218 F.2d 276 (4th Cir. 1954).

48. *United States v. James*, 528 F.2d 999 (5th Cir. 1976).

49. *Gebardi v. United States*, 287 U.S. 112 (1932).

50. *Iannelli v. United States*, 420 U.S. 770 (1975).

51. Model Penal Code, Section 1.07(1)(b).

52. *People v. Powell*, 63 N.Y. 88 (1875).

53. *Anderson v. Superior Court*, 177 P.2d 315 (Cal. Super. Ct. 1947).

54. Model Penal Code, Section 5.03(6).

55. This problem is an adaptation of a hypothetical point made by Kent Greenawalt in "Speech and Crime," *American Bar Foundation Research Journal* (1980), p. 662.

56. Florida Penal Code, Chapter 777, Section 4, paragraph 2.

57. *People v. Quentin*, 296 N.Y.S.2d 443 (Sup. Ct. 1968).

58. Model Penal Code, Section 5.02(2).

59. U.S. Code, Title 18, Section 2.

60. *United States v. Ortega*, 44 F.3d 505 (7th Cir. 1995).

61. U.S. Code, Title 18, Section 3.

62. *United States v. Hobson*, 519 F.2d 765 (9th Cir. 1975).

63. "SabreTech Charged with Murder in ValuJet Crash," CNN.com online, July 13, 1999. Posted at http://fyi.cnn.com/US/9907/13/valujet.indictments.03.

64. Sir William Blackstone, *Commentaries on the Law of England*, Chap. 18, Sec. 12 (Oxford, England: Clarendon Press, 1765–69).

65. As early as 1886 the U.S. Supreme Court held that a corporation is a "natural person" and thus entitled to equal protection of the laws as guaranteed by the Fourteenth Amendment to the U.S. Constitution [see *Santa Clara County v. Southern Pacific Railroad*, 118 U.S. 394 (1886)].

66. See, for example, *United States v. Dotterweich*, 320 U.S. 277, 64 S. Ct. 134, 88 L. Ed. 48 (1943).

67. Celia Wells, "The Millennium Bug and Corporate Criminal Liability," *Journal of Information, Law and Technology* on-line, No. 2, 1999. Posted at http://elj.warwick.ac.uk/jilt/99-2/wells.html.

68. Ibid.

69. Ibid.

70. Model Penal Code, Section 2.07.

71. *United States v. Parks*, 421 U.S. 658 (1975).

72. *United States v. Dotterweich*, 320 U.S. 277 (1943).

73. *People v. Forbath*, 5 Cal. App. 2d 767 (1935).

74. *Commonwealth v. Koczwara*, 155 A.2d 825 (Pa. 1959).

Justifications as Defenses

If someone comes to kill you, rise up and kill him first.

—The Talmud, *Sanhedrin 72A*

The end must justify the means.

—Matthew Prior (1664–1721)

Men use thought only to justify their wrongdoings.

—Voltaire [François Marie Arouet] (1694–1778)

AFTER READING THIS CHAPTER YOU SHOULD:

▷ Understand the nature of legal defenses.

▷ Know the difference between justifications and excuses.

▷ Be able to explain an "affirmative defense."

▷ Be able to list and describe the various kinds of justifications that may serve as defenses to a criminal charge.

▷ Know the circumstances under which a person may claim self-defense, and understand the requirements of "perfect self-defense."

▷ Understand the concept of reasonable force, and know when the use of deadly force may be reasonable.

INTRODUCTION

The case of Bernhard Goetz, the demure white electronics technician who shot four black youths on a New York City subway train in 1984 after they demanded money, made headlines for years afterward. In 1996, amid continuing debate over whether the shooting was justified, Goetz lost a civil suit brought against him by one of the men he shot—forcing him to file for bankruptcy.

The facts of the original criminal case brought against Goetz were well-summarized by the New York Court of Appeals, which found: "On Saturday afternoon, December 22, 1984, Troy Canty, Darryl Cabey, James Ramseur, and Barry Allen boarded an IRT express subway train in the Bronx and headed south toward lower Manhattan. The four youths rode together in the rear portion of the seventh car of the train. Two of the four, Ramseur and Cabey, had screwdrivers inside their coats, which they said were to be used to break into the coin boxes of video machines.

"Defendant Bernhard Goetz boarded this subway train at Fourteenth Street in Manhattan and sat down on a bench towards the rear section of the same car occupied by the four youths. Goetz was carrying an unlicensed .38-caliber pistol loaded with five rounds of ammunition in a waistband holster. The train left the Fourteenth Street station and headed towards Chambers Street.

"It appears from the evidence before the grand jury that Canty approached Goetz, possibly with Allen beside him, and stated 'give me five dollars.' Neither Canty nor any of the other youths displayed a weapon. Goetz responded by standing up, pulling out his handgun and firing four shots in rapid succession. The first shot hit Canty in the chest; the second struck Allen in the back; the third went

Web Extra! 5–1
Defenses

The case of Bernhard Goetz, who shot four black youths after they demanded money on a New York City subway train in 1984, continues to remain controversial. Goetz claimed self-defense and was only convicted of a weapons charge. In 1996, however, he lost a civil suit brought against him by one of the men he shot—forcing him to file for bankruptcy. Here Goetz arrives at a New York court for a 1987 hearing. (Photo by David Bookstaver, courtesy of AP/Wide World Photos.)

through Ramseur's arm and into his left side; the fourth was fired at Cabey, who apparently was then standing in the corner of the car, but missed, deflecting instead off of a wall of the conductor's cab. After Goetz briefly surveyed the scene around him, he fired another shot at Cabey, who then was sitting on the end bench of the car. The bullet entered the rear of Cabey's side and severed his spinal cord.

"All but two of the other passengers fled the car when, or immediately after, the shots were fired. The conductor, who had been in the next car, heard the shots and instructed the motorman to radio for emergency assistance. The conductor then went into the car where the shooting occurred and saw Goetz sitting on a bench, the injured youths lying on the floor or slumped against a seat, and two women who had apparently taken cover, also lying on the floor. Goetz told the conductor that the four youths had tried to rob him.

"While the conductor was aiding the youths, Goetz headed towards the front of the car. The train had stopped just before the Chambers Street station and Goetz went between two of the cars, jumped onto the tracks and fled. Police and ambulance crews arrived at the scene shortly thereafter. Ramseur and Canty, initially listed in critical condition, [recovered fully]. Cabey remains paralyzed, and has suffered some degree of brain damage."[1]

Before Goetz stood trial, a New York court dismissed attempted murder charges that had been brought against him, finding that Goetz believed his life was in danger, and that he had acted in self-defense at the time of the shooting. Goetz was later convicted at trial on a charge of carrying an unlicensed concealed weapon. He was sentenced to one year in jail, but served only eight months of that sentence before being released.[2]

DEFENSE
evidence and arguments offered by a defendant and his or her attorney(s) to show why that person should not be held liable for a criminal charge.

TYPES OF DEFENSES

A **defense** consists of evidence and arguments offered by a defendant and his or her attorneys to show why that person should not be held liable for a criminal charge.

Defenses are built on four bases: (1) alibi, in which it is argued that the defendant could not have committed the crime in question, and in which witnesses or evidence may be presented to prove the claim; (2) inability of the prosecution to prove all of the elements necessary for conviction; (3) **justifications,** in which the defendant admits committing the act in question, but claims it was necessary in order to avoid some greater evil; and (4) **excuses,** whereby the defendant claims that some personal condition or circumstance at the time of the act was such that he or she should not be held accountable under the criminal law. This chapter concerns itself with justifications, while the two chapters that follow examine excuses.

As the well-known jurist Jerome Hall says, " '[j]ustification' and 'excuse' are very old concepts. Indeed these words have long been parts of everyday speech; Anglo-American law has used them for centuries. . . . What is common to both concepts is that an injury or damage has been caused by a human being. The difference is that in the former, the actor did the right thing in the circumstances, e.g., he defended himself against an assailant or destroyed property to save life; while in 'excuse' the rectitude of the actor or his action is simply irrelevant. What is relevant in excuse, i.e., relevant to penal law, is that for reasons either of incapacity or of extreme pressure, such as the threat of immediate death, the actor should not be held criminally liable; instead he is excused."[3]

Another author explains the difference between justification and excuse this way: "A justified actor engages in conduct that is not culpable because its benefits outweigh the harm or evil of the offense; an excused actor admits the harm or evil but nonetheless claims an absence of personal culpability. . . ."[4]

Generally speaking, conduct that a person believes is necessary to avoid a harm or evil to himself or herself, or to avoid harm to another, is justifiable if the harm or evil to be avoided is greater than that which the law defining the offense seeks to avoid. Hence, justifications may apply when people find themselves facing a choice between a "lesser of two evils." The correct choice will, of course, be the morally correct one. The "right choice" may then reduce or eliminate criminal liability for the act in question. A frequently used example is that of a fireman who sets a controlled fire in order to create a firebreak to head off a conflagration threatening a community. While intentionally setting a fire may constitute arson, doing so in order to save a town may be justifiable behavior in the eyes of the community *and* in the eyes of law.

An excuse, in contrast, does not claim that the conduct in question is justified—but claims that the actor who engaged in it was, at the time, not legally responsible for his or her actions. So, for example, a person who assaults a police officer thinking that the officer is really a disguised "space alien" who has come to abduct him may be found "not guilty" of the charge of assault by reason of insanity. Actions for which excuses are offered do not morally outweigh the wrong committed, but criminal liability may still be negated on the basis of some personal disability of the actor, or because of some special circumstances surrounding the situation. Some excuses, however, as in the case of insanity, may not entirely eliminate the need for restraint, and may result in further handling by agencies of control—as anyone who habitually assaults police officers thinking they are aliens from outer space will soon learn.

As we begin our discussion of justifications and excuses, it is important to realize that not all states have codified defenses, and those that have do not necessarily address all of the defenses that are discussed here. As the Model Penal Code explains, "The main aim of a criminal code is to differentiate conduct that warrants criminal sanctions from conduct that does not. If it is clear that conduct will not be subject to criminal sanctions, the effort to establish precisely in each case whether that conduct is actually justified or only excused does not seem worthwhile."[5]

JUSTIFICATIONS
a category of legal defenses in which the defendant admits committing the act in question but claims it was necessary in order to avoid some greater evil.

EXCUSES
a category of legal defenses in which the defendant claims that some personal condition or circumstance at the time of the act was such that he or she should not be held accountable under the criminal law.

He who excuses himself accuses himself.
—William Shakespeare, *King John*

THE NATURE OF DEFENSES

AFFIRMATIVE DEFENSE
an answer to a criminal charge in which a defendant takes the offense and responds to the allegations with his or her own assertions based on legal principles. Affirmative defenses must be raised and supported by the defendant independently of any claims made by the prosecutor, and include justifications and excuses.

Justifications and excuses are **affirmative defenses.** That is, they must be raised or asserted by the defendant independently of any claims made by the prosecutor. The nature of affirmative defenses is that they do not negate any element of the crime charged, but rather build on new matters that would excuse or justify the defendant's behavior. Once raised, it may be incumbent on the defendant to provide further proof of his or her claim. Some jurisdictions, however, require defendants raising certain defenses to produce only initial evidence that the claim is valid. From that point onward it becomes the responsibility of the prosecutor to show that the defense is without merit. Hence, in many jurisdictions, once a defendant raises an insanity claim, it becomes the task of the prosecution to prove sanity. Affirmative defenses essentially attack the moral and *legal authority* of the state to bring a criminal charge against the defendant, although they do not dispute the truth of the prosecution's claim that a law was broken.

A successfully raised defense may have the effect of completely exonerating the defendant of any criminal liability. At times, however, the defense raised is less than perfect—that is, the defendant is unable to meet all of the requirements necessary to demonstrate that a particular justification or excuse should be entirely accepted in his or her case. When claims offered by the defendant are not sufficient for a "not guilty" verdict, they may still mitigate the defendant's liability and result in a lesser punishment.

Since most criminal cases are complex, it is difficult to be certain whether or not a specific defense will be accepted by a judge or jury in a given instance where criminal activity is charged. Moreover, those charged with crimes may be particularly inventive in their efforts to "bend" traditional defenses in order to apply them to their cases. Other defendants may offer creative excuses, the particular form of which may not have been previously heard in American courts. Still others may attempt to apply traditionally accepted defenses under novel circumstances. All this makes it difficult to generalize about the applicability of any particular defense to a given set of circumstances.

JUSTIFICATION AS A DEFENSE

Conduct that violates the law may be justifiable. A person who kills another in self-defense, for example, may be completely innocent of criminal homicide. Justifications include: (1) self-defense, (2) defense of others, (3) defense of home and property, (4) necessity, (5) consent, and (6) resisting unlawful arrest. We shall discuss each of these defenses in the pages that follow. Keep in mind that the applicability of any particular defense may vary between jurisdictions, and that some jurisdictions have codified a wide number of defenses while others continue to follow common law tradition in the acceptability of some defenses.

Necessity

NECESSITY
a defense to a criminal charge that claims that it was necessary to commit some unlawful act in order to prevent or to avoid a greater harm.

Strictly speaking, the concept of **necessity** forms the basis of all justifications. A defendant offering the defense of necessity makes the claim that it was necessary to commit some unlawful act in order to prevent or to avoid a greater harm. Sometimes the harm avoided is one that otherwise would accrue to oneself, sometimes it is a harm that would affect others. In a third type of situation, both the person taking the necessary action and others whom he or she is acting to protect might be harmed.

The Model Penal Code (MPC) says that the principle of necessity "is essential to the rationality and justice of the criminal law," and official commentaries on the Code recognize specific instances in which necessity may provide an effective defense to a criminal charge, including the need for emergency vehicles to pass through traffic lights; the jettisoning of cargo to save a sinking ship; breaking and entering in order to find shelter by those lost in a blizzard; and the dispensing of medication by a pharmacist without a prescription in an emergency situation.

A number of state laws refer specifically to the defense of necessity (see, for example, the Law on the Books feature in this section), while the Model Penal Code contains a "choice of evils" provision under which necessity is subsumed.[6] MPC Section (3.02), which is entitled "Justifications Generally: Choice of Evils," reads:

> "Conduct that the actor believes to be necessary to avoid a harm or evil to himself or to another is justifiable, provided that: (a) the harm or evil sought to be avoided by such conduct is greater than that sought to be prevented by the law defining the offense charged," and the actor was not negligent or reckless "in bringing about the situation requiring a choice of harms or evils in appraising the necessity for his conduct. . ."[7]

As the Model Penal Code points out, necessity can only be claimed where the "evil" to be avoided is less than the harm caused. A person who throws luggage overboard in order to save a falling aircraft and its passengers will be far more justified in his actions in the eyes of the law than one, say, who kills another in order to avoid a financial loss.

One of the earliest and best known cases involving a necessity defense is that of *Regina* v. *Dudley and Stephens*.[8] The case began in 1884 when an English ship sunk in a squall about 1,600 miles off the Cape of Good Hope. Three seamen, Thomas Dudley, Edward Stephens, and a man named "Brooks," found themselves in a lifeboat with a seventeen-year-old cabin boy named Richard Parker. Although none of the four had sustained serious injuries in the sinking of their vessel, little food had been stowed away on the lifeboat. After twelve days adrift the men ran out of food, and eight days later Dudley and Stephens decided to kill and eat the cabin boy—which they did. The men ate the boy's flesh and drank his blood. Brooks did not participate in the killing, and four days later, the three surviving seamen were rescued by a passing ship. Dudley and Stephens were arrested and charged with murder. At trial they offered the defense of necessity, saying that it had been necessary to kill the cabin boy in order that at least some of those on the lifeboat might survive.

The court found that "the prisoners were subject to terrible temptation, to sufferings which might break down the bodily power of the strongest man, and try the conscience of the best." Moreover, the court continued, "if the men had not fed upon the body of the boy they would probably not have survived," and "the boy being in a much weaker condition was likely to have died before them." Nonetheless, the court ruled: " . . . the deliberate killing of this unoffending and unresisting boy was clearly murder, unless the killing can be justified by some well-recognized excuse admitted by law . . . in this case there was no such excuse, unless the killing was justified by what has been called 'necessity'. . . ." The court continued: "Though law and morality are not the same, and many things may be immoral which are not necessarily illegal, yet the absolute divorce of law from morality would be of fatal consequence; and such divorce would follow if the temptation to murder in this case were to be held by law an absolute defense of it. It is not so. To preserve one's life is generally speaking a duty, but it may be the plainest and the highest duty to sacrifice it. War is full of instances in which it is a man's duty not to live but to die. The

Every jurisdiction recognizes that special circumstances can justify conduct that otherwise would be an offense.

—Paul H. Robinson, Northwestern University Law School

LAW ON THE BOOKS

"NECESSITY" UNDER THE TEXAS PENAL CODE.

Compare with Model Penal Code, Section 3.02

TEXAS PENAL CODE

Sec. 9.22. NECESSITY. Conduct is justified if:

1. the actor reasonably believes the conduct is immediately necessary to avoid imminent harm;
2. the desirability and urgency of avoiding the harm clearly outweigh, according to ordinary standards of reasonableness, the harm sought to be prevented by the law proscribing the conduct; and
3. a legislative purpose to exclude the justification claimed for the conduct does not otherwise plainly appear.

New York Police Department officers Richard Murphy (left), Kenneth Boss, and Edward McMellon. In February 2000, they were acquitted of all charges after being tried for the 1999 killing of unarmed African immigrant Amadou Diallo. Diallo died when the policemen fired forty-one bullets at him as he stood in the doorway of his Bronx apartment building. The officers claimed that they had acted in self-defense, thinking that Diallo's actions, after they approached him, indicated that he had a gun and made them fear for their lives. Not shown is officer Sean Carroll who was also acquitted. (Photo by David Karp, courtesy of AP/Wide World Photos.)

duty, in case of shipwreck, of a captain to his crew, of the crew to the passengers, of soldiers to women and children; these duties impose on men the moral necessity, not of the preservation, but of the sacrifice of their lives for others. . . . It is not correct, therefore, to say that there is any absolute or unqualified necessity to preserve one's life." Found guilty of murder, Dudley and Stephens were sentenced to die—a sentence that was later commuted by the Queen to six months' imprisonment.

As a defense, necessity has generally been far more effective in protecting defendants facing grave physical threats that are immediately present than it has been in protecting defendants who are facing economic or psychological necessity from criminal liability. So, for example, a person who destroys a house to stop a fire advancing on a town is far less likely to incur criminal liability than one who steals because of hunger, or another who breaks into a pharmacy in order to acquire the drugs needed to feed a powerful addiction.

Self-Defense

Defense of self has long been accepted as justification for activities which might otherwise confer criminal liability. **Self-defense** is based on the recognition that a person has an inherent right to self-protection and that to reasonably defend oneself from unlawful attack is a "natural" response to threatening situations. Similarly, it can be argued that one who acts in self-defense lacks the requisite *mens rea* for the commission of a crime. That is, the person who kills an attacker does not have as his or her primary purpose the taking of a life—but rather the preservation of his or her own.

As a Law on the Books feature later in this section shows, Texas law reads: "A person is justified in using force against another when and to the degree he reasonably believes the force is immediately necessary to protect himself against the other's use or attempted use of unlawful force." The wording of the Model Penal Code is similar. It reads: "The use of force upon or toward another person is justifiable when the actor believes that such force is immediately necessary for the purpose of protecting himself against the use of unlawful force by such other persons on the present occasion."[9] A significant difference between the two, however, is the *reasonableness requirement* of the Texas law—a requirement also found in the laws of many other states. In judging the validity of a claim of self-defense, the Model Penal Code asks us to decide whether or not the defendant *subjectively* believed that the use of force was necessary; while Texas law judges the actor's decision *objectively*—that is, from the point of view of a reasonable person. The difference can be a crucial one.

As we shall see in Chapter 6, the requirement that the use of force in self-defense be reasonable mandates that the accused behave as a reasonable person would under the same circumstances. The concept of a **reasonable person** envisions a person who acts with common sense and who has the mental capacity of an average, normal, sensible human being. In judging any activity, the reasonable person criterion requires that the assumptions and ideas on which a defendant acted must have been objectively reasonable, in that the circumstances as they appeared to the defendant

SELF-DEFENSE
a defense to a criminal charge that is based on the recognition that a person has an inherent right to self-protection and that to reasonably defend oneself from unlawful attack is a "natural" response to threatening situations.

REASONABLE PERSON
a person who acts with common sense and who has the mental capacity of an average, normal, sensible human being. The reasonable person criterion requires that the assumptions and ideas on which a defendant acted must have been reasonable, in that the circumstances as they appeared to the defendant would have created the same beliefs in the mind of an ordinary person.

CRIMINAL LAW IN THE NEWS

Killing of Burglars May Be Ruled Self-Defense

N.C. Homeowner Shot Two Men in His Driveway

LENOIR, N.C.—Authorities say that a homeowner who shot two suspected burglars to death appears to have acted in self-defense.

Caldwell County District Attorney David Flaherty said today that no charges would likely be filed against Keith Nadeau, 44, for killing John Wesley Dula Jr., 36, and Danny Koonce Jr., 34. But he emphasized that no final decision has been made.

"Until we get the complete investigation done, we're not going to make that call," Flaherty said.

Two burglaries in one day
Nadeau and his wife, Linda, told investigators that they returned to their home near Collettsville Sunday afternoon and found a window broken and a television set and VCR missing, said Capt. Danny Barlow of the Caldwell County Sheriff's Department.

Several hours later, as they returned from a neighbor's house, they saw a red Geo pull into their driveway. Two men then got out and entered the house and came out with a microwave and another VCR.

Nadeau said he was in the driveway when the car came up, and he hid in the bushes, Barlow said. His wife told investigators that she was walking up the driveway with a flashlight that she shined on the car.

Nadeau then fired through an open car window, killing both men, Barlow said.

Was safety at stake?
Investigators have evidence that Koonce and Dula committed the first break-in, Barlow said, but the missing items have not been recovered.

Flaherty said the issue is whether Nadeau had reason to fear for his own safety in the confrontation.

Source: Frances Ann Burns, "Killing of Burglars May Be Ruled Self-Defense; N.C. Homeowner Shot Two Men in His Driveway," APB News. August 15, 2000. Reprinted with permission.

Once someone uses the term "reasonable person," it's awfully hard to define it.

—Richard J. Bartlett, former Dean, Albany Law School, Union University

APPARENT DANGER

that form of imminent danger that is said to exist when the conduct or activity of an attacker makes the threat of danger obvious.

When you are surrounded by four people, one of them smiling, taunting, demanding, terrorizing, you don't have a complete grasp or perfect vision.

—Bernhard Goetz (March 1985)

REASONABLE FORCE

a degree of force that is appropriate in a given situation and is not excessive. The minimum degree of force necessary to protect oneself, one's property, a third party, or the property of another in the face of a substantial threat.

DEADLY FORCE

force likely to cause death or great bodily harm.

would have created the same beliefs in the mind of an ordinary person. Hence, anyone motivated by special needs or driven by psychological forces not routinely present in the average person may find that the claim of self-defense would not be available to them in jurisdictions that impose the reasonableness requirement.

Apparent danger is another concept associated with self-defense. Apparent danger exists when the conduct or activity of an attacker makes the threat of danger obvious. Danger, for example, becomes apparent when a threatening individual draws a gun or a knife and approaches another person in a menacing fashion. The emphasis on "immediacy" and "present occasion" found in many state codes classifies forceful activities undertaken in self-defense as justifiable only when they occur within the context of a face-to-face encounter. Hence, while one who uses force to fight off an unlawful attack is justified in doing so, one who stalks and kills a potential attacker in a preemptive strike would be hard pressed to claim self-defense. Likewise, a person who "takes the law into their own hands" and exacts vengeance on a person who has previously victimized her, cannot be said to be acting in self-defense. In short, "the victim had it coming" is not a valid self-defense justification.

"Force," as the term is used within the context of self-defense, means physical force, and does not extend to emotional, psychological, economic, psychic, or other forms of coercion. A person who turns the tables on a robber and assaults him during the robbery attempt, for example, may be able to claim self-defense, while the business person who assaults a financial rival to prevent a hostile takeover of her company will have no such recourse.

Individuals may also protect themselves in the face of threats, where the threat implies that danger is present in a given situation even though the precise nature of that danger may not be immediately apparent. Situations involving present danger include circumstances where the threatened individual can anticipate the danger that he or she is about to face. So, for example, if a threatening individual says, "I am going to kill you!" and advances on another while reaching into his pocket, the threatened individual can reasonably assume that the attacker is reaching for a weapon and can act on that basis. Difficulties may arise, however, when defensive force is used on an attacker who may be incapable of carrying out the threat. Someone who says "I'm going to kill you," for example, while searching for lost keys to a locked gun cabinet would appear to represent a less immediate danger than one who has keys in hand. Most jurisdictions recognize, however, that a reasonable amount of force can be used to protect oneself in the face of threats that seem to clearly imply that the use of unlawful force is imminent.

The amount of force used by one who seeks to defend oneself from unlawful attack must be proportionate to the amount of force or perceived degree of threat that one is seeking to defend against. Hence, **reasonable force** is that degree of force that is appropriate in a given situation and is not excessive. Reasonable force can also be thought of as the minimum degree of force necessary to protect oneself, one's property, a third party, or the property of another in the face of a substantial threat.

Deadly force, the highest degree of force, is considered reasonable only when used to counter an immediate threat of death or great bodily harm. Deadly force cannot be used against nondeadly force. If a lesser degree of injury can be anticipated, or if a lesser degree of force affords an effective defense, it must be used. Similarly, once danger has been averted the use of force must cease. A person who overcomes an attacker, for example, leaving him incapable of further attack, is unjustified in then taking the attacker's life. Once a threat has been deterred it is improper for a person who has successfully defended himself to continue using force. Doing so effectively reverses the role of attacker and victim. So, for example, a person walking home alone at night might be accosted by a robber who beats him. If the would-be victim turns the tables on the robber by using a can of "pepper spray," which disables and temporarily blinds the robber, he would be unjustified if he then picked up a rock and smashed the skull of the incapacitated robber.

In 1997, a Bluffton, South Carolina woman was arrested after trying to run over a man who allegedly raped her repeatedly just minutes before. The woman told police that the suspect, twenty-four-year-old Charles Edward Hayward, broke into her house at night while she was alone and sleeping. Hayward apparently forced his way into the woman's bedroom, beat her severely, took what money she had in the home, and raped her twice. He then forced her out of the home and into her car, ordering her to drive him out of the area. The woman, however, jumped quickly into the car and locked the doors before the suspect could enter. As a detective put it the following morning: "She was fortunate enough to jump in the car and lock the doors. She started the vehicle up and tried her damnedest to run over him. In doing so, she ended up stuck in the ditch by a neighbor's house."[10] The woman blew the car horn, waking neighbors who called 911. She was taken to a local hospital where she was arrested on charges of assault with a deadly weapon.

In like manner, one who is facing assault cannot exceed the bounds of necessary force in repelling an attack. If a large and robust person is struck by an unarmed small and weak—but angry—individual, for example, it would be unreasonable for the much stronger person to break the smaller person's neck if merely restraining him would have been possible.

The claim of self-defense is usually unavailable to those who precipitate or incite an attack on themselves. In other words, one who initiates a confrontation cannot later be reasonably afforded the protection of a self-defense claim. A verbally and physically abusive person, for example, cannot claim self-defense if the person being abused responds with force and the situation escalates into a brawl or leads to a homicide. Under such circumstances the law recognizes the inherent validity of the claim often heard in childhood of "He started it!" As the U.S. Court of Appeals for the Second Circuit explained it in the 1994 case of *United States* v. *Thomas*[11]: "The defense of self-defense is not available to one who acts as the aggressor, and commits his aggression threatening deadly force, even though the intended victim responds with deadly force so that the original aggressor will be killed if he does not first kill. It has long been accepted that one cannot support a claim of self-defense by a self-generated necessity to kill. The right of homicidal self-defense is granted only to those free from fault in the difficulty; it is denied to slayers who incite the fatal attack, encourage the fatal quarrel, or otherwise promote the necessitous occasion for taking life. . . . In sum, one who is the aggressor in a conflict culminating in death cannot invoke the necessities of self-preservation."

Most jurisdictions impose a **retreat rule** upon those who would claim self-defense. Those jurisdictions require that the person being attacked retreat in order to avoid the necessity of using force, if retreat can be accomplished with "complete safety." Jurisdictions that follow a retreat rule, however, often specify that an actor is not obliged to retreat from specific locations, such as his or her home or place of work, before responding forcefully when threatened or assailed. Actors who do not retreat may be judged according to other criteria, such as whether the amount of force with which they responded was reasonable and proportionate to the threat at hand. Some jurists argue that a person who is under attack should have no obligation to retreat since he or she has a natural right to resist an unprovoked attack under any circumstances.

A number of jurisdictions, like North Carolina, have developed the notion of **perfect self-defense.** When deadly force is used, perfect self-defense is established "when the evidence, viewed in the light most favorable to the defendant, tends to show that at the time of the killing it appeared to the defendant and she believed it to be necessary to kill the decedent to save herself from imminent death or great bodily harm. That belief must be reasonable, however, in that the circumstances as they appeared to the defendant would create such a belief in the mind of a person of ordinary firmness. Further, the defendant must not have been the initial aggressor provoking the fatal confrontation. A killing in the proper exercise of the right of

> We cannot lightly . . . allow the perpetrator of a serious crime to go free simply because that person believed his actions were reasonable and necessary to prevent some perceived harm.
>
> —Judge Sol Wachtler, N.Y. State Court of Appeals, ruling in the case of Bernhard Goetz (July 8, 1986)

RETREAT RULE

a rule operative in many jurisdictions that requires that a person being attacked retreat in order to avoid the necessity of using force against the attacker, if retreat can be accomplished with "complete safety."

PERFECT SELF-DEFENSE

a claim of self-defense that meets all of the generally accepted legal conditions for such a claim to be valid. Where deadly force is used, perfect self-defense requires that, in light of the circumstances, the defendant reasonably believed it to be necessary to kill the decedent to avert imminent death or great bodily harm and that the defendant was neither the initial aggressor or responsible for provoking the fatal confrontation.

perfect self-defense is always completely justified in law and constitutes no legal wrong."[12] Imperfect self-defense may exist when any of the conditions required for perfect self-defense are lacking. In jurisdictions where the concepts of perfect and imperfect self-defense are employed, imperfect self-defense may lower criminal liability, but not eliminate it.

In the case of Bernhard Goetz, with which this chapter opened, it seems clear that Goetz's actions fell short of perfect self-defense. It is true that Goetz had no easy path of retreat when approached by four youths demanding money. A moving subway car effectively seals any reasonable escape route. The question in the Goetz case, however, was not one of retreat—but whether Goetz was ever in any real danger, and if he was, whether he should have waited for his assailants to draw a weapon or to use obvious physical force against him before he defended himself with potentially deadly force. In other words, were the young men who confronted Goetz bent on robbing him, or were they merely panhandling? And what duty did Goetz have to clearly determine what their intent was before acting? Moreover, we might ask, can judgments as to the intentions of others be fairly based on stereotypical characteristics, such as age, sex, race, and mode of dress?

The law of self-defense generally provides that a person is justified in acting to defend himself under circumstances in which a reasonable person would believe themselves to be in danger. In Goetz's case, the nation was divided over whether Goetz was ever in fact in danger, or if he acted too quickly without waiting to discover the true intentions of the youths who surrounded him. The *Goetz* case points out the significance of a subjective standard in assessing reasonableness. Goetz attempted to convince the court that his personal experience of being robbed and of a beating at the hands of black youths and his knowledge of the fact that a doorman at his apartment complex had recently been seriously beaten by black youths made his actions reasonable for *him*. A more objective assessment of reasonableness, however, might involve no such personal biases.

Since the shooting, a plethora of commentators have given voice to widely varying opinions. Among them, however, is the observation that riders on New York subway trains rarely speak to one another, that those who initiate conversation are often regarded as dangerous or threatening, and that young black inner-city youths

Web Extra! 5–2

Britannica online:
self-defense

LAW ON THE BOOKS

"SELF-DEFENSE" UNDER TENNESSEE LAW.
Compare with Model Penal Code, Section 3.04

TENNESSEE CODE

Section 39-2-101. LAWFUL RESISTANCE—BY WHOM MADE.

Lawful resistance to the commission of a public offense may be made by the party about to be injured, or by others.

Section 38-2-102. RESISTANCE BY PARTY ABOUT TO BE INJURED.

Resistance sufficient to prevent the offense may be made by the party about to be injured to prevent an:

   (1) Offense against the party's person; or
   (2) Illegal attempt by force to take or injure property in the party's lawful possession.

Section 38-2-103. RESISTANCE BY OTHERS.

Any other person, in aid or defense of the person about to be injured, may make resistance sufficient to prevent the offense.

are perceived as dangerous by both middle-class blacks and whites. Marvin Wolfgang, an eminent University of Pennsylvania criminologist, observed around the time of the Goetz shootings that black rates of crime were more than ten times higher than white rates, and suggested that: "The expectation that four young black males are going to do you harm is indeed greater than four young whites."[13] Wolfgang concluded: "I can understand the black position that this is a racist attitude, but it's not realistic."

LAW ON THE BOOKS

"SELF-DEFENSE" UNDER THE TEXAS PENAL CODE.

Compare with Model Penal Code, Section 3.04

TEXAS PENAL CODE

Section 9.31. SELF-DEFENSE.

a. Except as provided in Subsection (b), a person is justified in using force against another when and to the degree he reasonably believes the force is immediately necessary to protect himself against the other's use or attempted use of unlawful force.

b. The use of force against another is not justified:

(1) in response to verbal provocation alone;

(2) to resist an arrest or search that the actor knows is being made by a peace officer, or by a person acting in a peace officer's presence and at his direction, even though the arrest or search is unlawful, unless the resistance is justified under Subsection (c);

(3) if the actor consented to the exact force used or attempted by the other;

(4) if the actor provoked the other's use or attempted use of unlawful force, unless:

(A) the actor abandons the encounter, or clearly communicates to the other his intent to do so reasonably believing he cannot safely abandon the encounter; and

(B) the other nevertheless continues or attempts to use unlawful force against the actor; or

(5) if the actor sought an explanation from or discussion with the other person concerning the actor's differences with the other person while the actor was:

(A) carrying a weapon in violation of Section 46.02; or

(B) possessing or transporting a weapon in violation of Section 46.05.

c. The use of force to resist an arrest or search is justified:

(1) if, before the actor offers any resistance, the peace officer (or person acting at his direction) uses or attempts to use greater force than necessary to make the arrest or search; and

(2) when and to the degree the actor reasonably believes the force is immediately necessary to protect himself against the peace officer's (or other person's) use or attempted use of greater force than necessary.

d. The use of deadly force is not justified under this subchapter except as provided in Sections 9.32, 9.33, and 9.34.

Section 9.32. DEADLY FORCE IN DEFENSE OF PERSON.

a. A person is justified in using deadly force against another:

(1) if he would be justified in using force against the other under Section 9.31;

(2) if a reasonable person in the actor's situation would not have retreated; and

(3) when and to the degree he reasonably believes the deadly force is immediately necessary:

(A) to protect himself against the other's use or attempted use of unlawful deadly force; or

(B) to prevent the other's imminent commission of aggravated kidnapping, murder, sexual assault, aggravated sexual assault, robbery, or aggravated robbery.

b. The requirement imposed by Subsection (a)(2) does not apply to an actor who uses force against a person who is at the time of the use of force committing an offense of unlawful entry in the habitation of the actor.

CRIMINAL LAW IN THE NEWS

Man Charged in Death of Naked Neighbor

Accused of Manslaughter for Shooting Intruder Eight Times

UPPER GWYNEDD, Pa. —A local man has been charged with manslaughter for shooting and killing a naked neighbor whom he allegedly mistook for a burglar.

Paul Bellina, 52, is free on $30,000 bail following his appearance in county court Tuesday to answer charges of voluntary manslaughter and reckless endangerment in connection with the Sept. 13 shooting death of a next-door neighbor, 31-year-old Craig Holtzman.

Bellina allegedly shot Holtzman eight times with a 9 mm semi-automatic handgun after an intoxicated Holtzman, following a night of drinking, apparently went outside to urinate around 4:30 A.M. He became disoriented and tried to get into the wrong townhouse through a basement sliding-glass door, authorities said. His townhouse and Bellina's share a common wall, authorities said.

Bellina was legally justified in shooting Holtzman in the chest and arm after he entered Bellina's home, but Bellina allegedly overreacted by following the naked, wounded man outside and shooting him six more times, including twice in the back and three times in the head, according to a court affidavit.

The final shot to the head was a "coup de grace" as Holtzman was lying on his side with his head against the ground, according to the affidavit.

Found man outside door

Bellina, who was awakened by a burglar alarm, went downstairs with his gun and first saw the naked neighbor standing outside of his basement door, according to the court document.

Holtzman walked away when he could not open the door, but Bellina allegedly unlocked it, removed the security bar, cocked the hammer on his pistol, walked outside and, pointing the gun at Holtzman, told him to put his hands up.

He complied, but refused Bellina's order to lie face down on the ground, according to the affidavit.

Holtzman then allegedly approached Bellina as he retreated into his home. Bellina told authorities the unclothed man opened and closed his fists as he approached him and entered his basement, which is when he began to open fire, according to the affidavit.

Holtzman's body ended up 8 to 10 feet from Bellina's basement sliding door, according to the affidavit.

Suspect confident of acquittal

Bellina today defended his actions.

"Well, part of the problem is that when something like this starts inside the house, that's a natural thing," he told APBnews.com, referring to following Holtzman outside and shooting him. "All the details will come out and people, I'm sure, will be much clearer about everything at the trial."

"What the D.A. has in effect done is try to put this case with only the facts that he wants known at this time out there," Bellina said. "There's a lot of missing information, and that will all come out at the trial. It's great to be an armchair quarterback and sit back and look at only some of the information and make a judgment, but that's not a good thing to do."

Bellina, who lives in this Philadelphia suburb with his companion and her 10-year-old daughter, said he clearly believed the nude man, whom he said he didn't recognize, was trying to break into his home.

"This has taken its toll, of course, but I'm sure that we won't have any problem in the courts," he said.

Source: Richard Zitrin, "Man Charged in Death of Naked Neighbor; Accused of Manslaughter for Shooting Intruder Eight Times," APB News. September 27, 2000. Reprinted with permission.

Resisting Unlawful Arrest

All jurisdictions today have laws making it illegal for a person to resist a lawful arrest. Under common law, however, it was lawful to use force to resist an unlawful arrest. Following common law tradition, some jurisdictions today continue to consider resistance in the face of an unlawful arrest justifiable, and many have codified statutory provisions detailing the limits imposed on such resistance and the conditions under which it can be used. The Texas statute cited in the preceding section, for example, makes it clear that a person may use a reasonable amount of force, other than deadly force, to resist an unlawful arrest or an unlawful search by a law enforcement officer if the officer "uses or attempts to use greater force than necessary to make the arrest or search," and "when and to the degree the actor reasonably believes the force is immediately necessary to protect himself against the peace officer's use or attempted use of greater force than necessary." A provision of the law makes it inapplicable to cases where the defendant is the first to resort to force, and deadly force to resist arrest is not justified unless the law enforcement officer resorts to deadly force when it is not called for.

On the other hand, some states require a person to submit to any arrest by an authorized law enforcement officer acting on official business. That's because resisting arrest can be a dangerous undertaking for all the parties involved, and because the complexities of today's law may make it difficult for those on the scene to decide at the moment of arrest whether an arrest is lawful or not. Moreover, in contrast with common law days, the ready availability of defense counsel makes it unlikely that anyone unlawfully arrested will spend much time in jail. The offense of resisting arrest is discussed in more detail in Chapter 11.

Most jurisdictions provide statutory protections to law enforcement officers who find it necessary to use force to effect an arrest or to prevent persons who are in their custody from escaping. Such statutes provide an **execution of public duty defense,** and preclude the possibility of arresting officers being prosecuted on charges of assault or battery (if force is needed to effect the arrest or to maintain custody) so long as the officers acted in a lawful manner. Requirements of a lawful arrest typically include: (1) making the purpose of the arrest known to the person arrested and (2) the use of a valid arrest warrant (if the arrest is to be made on the authority of a warrant—something not necessary if the crime is committed in the officer's presence). Execution of public duty statutes also protect anyone carrying out the order of a lawful court or tribunal, anyone performing the duties or functions of a public officer, and anyone lawfully involved in the execution of legal processes defined by law. Blanket statutes of this sort legitimize the behavior of public servants, government employees, and elected officials when lawfully undertaken.

The use of deadly force by law enforcement officers is of special concern. Prior to the U.S. Supreme Court case of *Tennessee v. Garner* (1985),[14] which specified the conditions under which deadly force could be used in the apprehension of suspected felons, most law enforcement departments throughout the United States operated under the **fleeing felon rule.** The fleeing felon rule permitted officers to shoot a suspected felon who attempted to flee from a lawful arrest. In *Garner,* however, the Court ruled that "the use of deadly force to prevent the escape of all felony suspects, whatever the circumstances, is constitutionally unreasonable."[15] According to *Garner,* deadly force may be applied only to prevent death or the threat of serious injury to the public, or to protect the law enforcement officer from a defendant who resorts to the use of deadly force. Because *Garner* was a civil case, however, the actions of police officers, while they might violate criteria established by *Garner,* may still not be criminal.

Defense of Others

The use of force to defend oneself has generally been extended to permit the use of reasonable force to defend others who are or appear to be in imminent danger. Simply put, when another person is being victimized, you can stand in the shoes of the victim and can use whatever force the victim could use in that person's defense.

The defense of others, however, sometimes called "defense of a third person," is circumscribed in some jurisdictions by the **alter ego rule.** The alter ego rule holds that a person can only defend a third party under circumstances and only to the degree that the third party could act. Hence, a person who aids a third party whom he sees being accosted may become criminally liable if the third party initiated the

EXECUTION OF PUBLIC DUTY DEFENSE
a defense to a criminal charge (such as assault) that is often codified and that precludes the possibility of police officers and other public employees from being prosecuted when lawfully exercising their authority.

When the suspect poses no immediate threat to the officer and no threat to others, the harm resulting from the failing to apprehend him does not justify the use of deadly force to do so.

—Justice Bryan R. White,
writing for the majority
Tennessee v. *Garner*, 471 U.S. 1, 11 (1985)

Web Extra! 5–3
Tennessee v. *Garner*
(1985)

FLEEING FELON RULE
a now defunct law enforcement practice that permitted officers to shoot a suspected felon who attempted to flee from a lawful arrest.

ALTER EGO RULE
a rule of law that, in some jurisdictions, holds that a person can only defend a third party under circumstances and only to the degree that the third party could act on their own behalf.

attack, or if the assault on the third party is a lawful one—i.e., is being made by a law enforcement officer conducting a lawful arrest of a person who is resisting.

Jurisdictions, such as Texas (see the Law on the Books feature in this section), which follow Model Penal Code conventions, however, do not recognize the alter ego rule, and allow a person to act in defense of another if "the actor reasonably believes that his intervention is immediately necessary to protect the third person." Even though a person may misperceive a situation, if he or she acts in defense of a third party, thinking that they are in immediate danger, the requisite *mens rea* that might otherwise make the action a crime is lacking.

Defense of others cannot be claimed by an individual who joins an illegal fight merely in order to assist a friend or family member. Likewise, one who intentionally aids an offender in an assault, even though the tables have "turned" and the offender is losing the battle, cannot claim the defense of defense of others. In other words, defense of third persons always requires that the defender be free from fault and that he or she act to aid an innocent person who is in the process of being victimized. Restrictions that apply to self-defense also apply to defense of a third party. Hence, a defender must only act in the face of an immediate threat to another person, cannot use deadly force against less than deadly force, and must only act to the extent and use only the degree of force needed to repel the attack.

Finally, force may be used against another to prevent them from hurting themselves. As the box on Texas law in this section shows, "protection of life or health" may sometimes require that a person be forced to do something they don't want to do. A mother may be pulled from a burning building, which is about to collapse, by a fireman, for example, even though she may be trying frantically to locate her children who remain inside. A weapon may be wrested from the hand of a suicidal person, just as someone about to jump from a high building may be tackled and saved from death.

LAW ON THE BOOKS

"DEFENSE OF THIRD PERSON" UNDER THE TEXAS PENAL CODE.

Compare with Model Penal Code, Section 3.05

TEXAS PENAL CODE

Section 9.33. DEFENSE OF THIRD PERSON. A person is justified in using force or deadly force against another to protect a third person if:

1. Under the circumstances as the actor reasonably believes them to be, the actor would be justified under Section 9.31 or 9.32 in using force or deadly force to protect himself against the unlawful force or unlawful deadly force he reasonably believes to be threatening the third person he seeks to protect; and
2. The actor reasonably believes that his intervention is immediately necessary to protect the third person.

Section 9.34. PROTECTION OF LIFE OR HEALTH.

a. A person is justified in using force, but not deadly force, against another when and to the degree he reasonably believes the force is immediately necessary to prevent the other from committing suicide or inflicting serious bodily injury to himself.
b. A person is justified in using both force and deadly force against another when and to the degree he reasonably believes the force or deadly force is immediately necessary to preserve the other's life in an emergency.

Defense of Home and Property

Defense of property, also called protection of property, can apply in the following situations: (1) protection of personal property, (2) defense of home or habitation, (3) defense of another's property, and (4) use of a mechanical device to protect property.

In most jurisdictions the owner of property can justifiably use reasonable *nondeadly* force to prevent others from unlawfully taking or damaging it. As a general rule, however, the preservation of human life outweighs protection of property, and the use of deadly force to protect property is not justified unless the perpetrator of the illegal act may intend to commit, or is in the act of committing, a violent act against another human being. A person who shoots a trespasser, for example, could not claim as a defense the defense of property in order to avoid criminal liability, but one who shoots and kills an armed robber while being robbed can. The difference is that a person facing an armed robber has a right to protect his or her property but is also in danger of death or serious bodily harm. An unarmed trespasser represents no such serious threat.[16]

In 1999, for example, North Augusta, Georgia businessman Richard H. Mathis, 34, was arrested and charged with assault and battery with intent to kill after he opened fire on two burglars at his mobile home dealership.[17] After the dealership had been repeatedly burglarized, Mathis decided to spend the night at the business protecting his property. On hearing a break-in, Mathis surprised two alleged burglars and fired shots in their direction with a semiautomatic assault rifle. One burglar, twenty-seven-year-old Douglas M. West, was slightly wounded on the face and neck by flying shrapnel. West was charged with second-degree burglary and, if convicted, could receive up to fifteen years in prison. Mathis, on the other hand, could receive up to twenty years on the assault charges. As of this writing both cases remain unresolved.

The use of mechanical devices to protect property is a special area of law. Since, generally speaking, deadly force is not permitted in defense of property, the setting of booby traps, such as spring-loaded shotguns, electrified grates, explosive devices, and the like, is generally not permitted to protect property that is unattended and unoccupied. Of course, another problem may arise in the use of such devices, and that is the death or injury of an innocent person. Booby-trapped property may

A man guards his home. The right to defend one's home is deeply rooted in Western legal tradition. (Photo by Frank Siteman, courtesy of Index Stock Imagery, Inc.)

be entered by children trying to recover a baseball, by firemen called to extinguish a fire, or by law enforcement officers with a lawful search warrant. If an individual is injured as a result of a mechanical device intended to cause death or injury in the protection of property, criminal charges may be brought against the person who set the device. These principles were well summarized by the Supreme Court of California in the case of *People* v. *Ceballos* (1974),[18] when it observed: "In the United States, courts have concluded that a person may be held criminally liable under statutes proscribing homicides and shooting with intent to injure, or civilly liable, if he sets upon his premises a deadly mechanical device and that device kills or injures another. . . . However, an exception to the rule that there may be criminal and civil liability for death or injuries caused by such a device has been recognized where the intrusion is, in fact, such that the person, were he present, would be justified in taking the life or inflicting the bodily harm with his own hands. . . ."[19]

On the other hand, acts which would otherwise be criminal may carry no criminal liability if undertaken to protect one's home. For purposes of the law, one's "home" is one's dwelling, whether owned, rented, or merely "borrowed." Hotel rooms, rooms onboard vessels, and rented rooms in houses belonging to others are all considered, for purposes of the law, one's "dwelling." The retreat rule, referred to earlier, which requires a person under attack to retreat when possible before resorting to deadly force, is subject to what some call the castle exception. The **castle exception** can be traced to the writings of the sixteenth-century English jurist Sir Edward Coke, who said, "A man's house is his castle—for where shall a man be safe if it be not in his house?"[20] The castle exception generally recognizes that a person has a fundamental right to be in his or her home and also recognizes the home as a final and inviolable place of retreat (that is, the home offers a place of retreat from which a person can be expected to retreat no further). Hence, it is not necessary for one to retreat from one's home in the face of an immediate threat, even where such retreat is possible, before resorting to deadly force in protection of the home. A number of court decisions have extended the castle exception to include one's place of business, such as a store, office, or other place of business.

The law describing defense of home, however, is far from clear. Part of the problem comes from the fact that anyone defending their home against intrusion is of-

CASTLE EXCEPTION
an exception to the retreat rule that recognizes a person's fundamental right to be in his or her home and also recognizes the home as a final and inviolable place of retreat. Under the castle exception to the retreat rule it is not necessary to retreat from one's home in the face of an immediate threat, even where retreat is possible, before resorting to deadly force in protection of the home.

ten acting out of self-defense or defense of family. Another problem arises from the fact that not all states have codified the conditions under which the use of force in defense of the home is justifiable. Some states follow the old common law rule that permits the use of deadly force to prevent an unlawful entry of any kind into the home. Other states, however, especially those that have enacted statutes designed to give the weight of legal authority to defense of one's home, qualify the use of deadly force by authorizing it only for purposes of preventing a felony. Under such statutes a person would be authorized in using force against a burglar who has illegally entered his or her home with the intent to steal, but would not be authorized in using force against someone who mistakenly or lawfully enters the residence.

Finally, property in the possession of a third person, or the home of a third person, may be protected by one who assists that person to the same degree and in the same manner that the owner of the property or the home would have been privileged to act.

LAW ON THE BOOKS

"PROTECTION OF PROPERTY" UNDER THE TENNESSEE CRIMINAL CODE.
Compare with Model Penal Code, Section 3.06

TENNESSEE CRIMINAL CODE

39-11-614. Protection of property.
(a) A person in lawful possession of real or personal property is justified in threatening or using force against another when and to the degree it is reasonably believed the force is immediately necessary to prevent or terminate the other's trespass on the land or unlawful interference with the property.
(b) A person who has been unlawfully dispossessed of real or personal property is justified in threatening or using force against the other when and to the degree it is reasonably believed the force is immediately necessary to reenter the land or recover the property if the person threatens or uses the force immediately or in fresh pursuit after the dispossession; and:
  (1) The person reasonably believes the other had no claim of right when the other dispossessed the person; and
  (2) The other accomplished the dispossession by threatening or using force against the person.
(c) A person is not justified in using deadly force to prevent or terminate the other's trespass on real estate or unlawful interference with personal property.

39-11-615. Protection of third person's property.

A person is justified in threatening or using force against another to protect real or personal property of a third person if, under the circumstances as the person reasonably believes them to be, the person would be justified under 39-11-614 in threatening or using force to protect the person's own real or personal property.

39-11-616. Use of device to protect property.
(a) The justification afforded by §§ 39-11-614 and 39-11-615 extends to the use of a device for the purpose of protecting property only if:
  (1) The device is not designed to cause or known to create a substantial risk of causing death or serious bodily harm;
  (2) The use of the particular device to protect the property from entry or trespass is reasonable under the circumstances as the person believes them to be; and
  (3) The device is one customarily used for such a purpose or reasonable care is taken to make known to probable intruders the fact that it is used.
(b) Nothing in this section shall affect the law regarding the use of animals to protect property or persons.

LAW ON THE BOOKS

"PROTECTION OF PROPERTY" UNDER THE TEXAS PENAL CODE.

Compare with Model Penal Code, Section 3.06

TEXAS PENAL CODE

Section 9.41. PROTECTION OF ONE'S OWN PROPERTY.

a. A person in lawful possession of land or tangible, movable property is justified in using force against another when and to the degree the actor reasonably believes the force is immediately necessary to prevent or terminate the other's trespass on the land or unlawful interference with the property.

b. A person unlawfully dispossessed of land or tangible, movable property by another is justified in using force against the other when and to the degree the actor reasonably believes the force is immediately necessary to reenter the land or recover the property if the actor uses the force immediately or in fresh pursuit after the dispossession and:

   (1) The actor reasonably believes the other had no claim of right when he dispossessed the actor; or

   (2) The other accomplished the dispossession by using force, threat, or fraud against the actor.

Section 9.42. DEADLY FORCE TO PROTECT PROPERTY. A person is justified in using deadly force against another to protect land or tangible, movable property:

   1. If he would be justified in using force against the other under Section 9.41; and

   2. When and to the degree he reasonably believes the deadly force is immediately necessary:

   (A) to prevent the other's imminent commission of arson, burglary, robbery, aggravated robbery, theft during the nighttime, or criminal mischief during the nighttime; or

   (B) to prevent the other who is fleeing immediately after committing burglary, robbery, aggravated robbery, or theft during the nighttime from escaping with the property; and

   3. He reasonably believes that:

   (A) the land or property cannot be protected or recovered by any other means; or

   (B) the use of force other than deadly force to protect or recover the land or property would expose the actor or another to a substantial risk of death or serious bodily injury.

Section 9.43. PROTECTION OF THIRD PERSON'S PROPERTY. A person is justified in using force or deadly force against another to protect land or tangible, movable property of a third person if, under the circumstances as he reasonably believes them to be, the actor would be justified under Section 9.41 or 9.42 in using force or deadly force to protect his own land or property and:

   1. The actor reasonably believes the unlawful interference constitutes attempted or consummated theft of or criminal mischief to the tangible, movable property; or

   2. The actor reasonably believes that:

   (A) the third person has requested his protection of the land or property;

   (B) he has a legal duty to protect the third person's land or property; or

   (C) the third person whose land or property he uses force or deadly force to protect is the actor's spouse, parent, or child, resides with the actor, or is under the actor's care.

Section 9.44. USE OF DEVICE TO PROTECT PROPERTY. The justification afforded by Sections 9.41 and 9.43 applies to the use of a device to protect land or tangible, movable property if:

   1. The device is not designed to cause, or known by the actor to create a substantial risk of causing, death or serious bodily injury; and

   2. Use of the device is reasonable under all the circumstances as the actor reasonably believes them to be when he installs the device.

Consent

Consent is the final justification discussed in this chapter. The defense of **consent** makes the claim that the person suffering an injury either: (1) agreed to sustain the injury or (2) that the possibility of injury in some activity was agreed to before that activity was undertaken. In either case, consent must be voluntarily and legally given if the defense is to be useful. It is also important to note that consent is only available as a defense if lack of consent is an element of the crime (as it is, for example, in the crime of rape).

Consent is inherent in some situations. As one author says, "The act of one who grabs another by the ankles and causes him to fall violently to the ground may result in a substantial jail sentence under some circumstances, but receive thunderous applause if it stops a ball carrier on the gridiron."[21] A person injured in an athletic contest cannot under most circumstances bring a charge of battery against another player, since both consented to participate in the game. Of course, some sporting events are much more likely to produce injuries than others, and some involve far more personal contact than others. Football players, for example, are routinely expected to tackle one another, while tennis players are not. If an assault continues beyond the point permitted by the rules of the sport it may become illegal. Fistfights between basketball players, even though they occur on court, provide an example of such illegal activity. Similarly, violent sports that are not recognized as legitimate by government authorities may leave the participants liable to a criminal charge. Contestants in bare-knuckle or street fighting, for example, can be charged with assault, even though the "contest" may have been informally arranged by the "local community" and sanctioned by numerous observers.

Sexual activity is another area where the defense of consent is frequently employed. A man might claim in defense to a charge of rape, for example, that a woman consented to his sexual advances and therefore agreed to sexual intercourse. Consent to one thing (sexual advances), however, does not constitute consent to another (sexual intercourse). Problems may arise when one of the parties to a sexual act wrongly believes that the other has consented, and proceeds to engage in sexual activity on the basis of that belief. In 1988, for example, twenty-one-year-old Robert Chambers pled "guilty" to a charge of first-degree manslaughter after eighteen-year-old Jennifer Levin died during what Chambers called consensual "rough sex." Levin, said Chambers, had injured his testicles causing him to strike out at her in pain, resulting in her death. More recently, in 1993, the "condom rapist" Joel Valdez was found guilty of rape after a jury in Austin, Texas, rejected his claim that the act became consensual once he complied with his victim's request to use a condom. Valdez, who was drunk and armed with a knife at the time of the attack, claimed that his victim's request to use a condom amounted to consent. The woman pledged not to resist, and in fact did not resist, in exchange for his agreeing to use a condom. From that point forward, claimed Valdez, "we were making love."

Although cases like those of the "condom rapist" may be easy to decide, clear consent in cases involving sexual activity may be difficult to establish. The reason is that much sexual activity proceeds on the basis of nonverbal cues, which require a fair degree of subjective interpretation, and both the cues and the manner of their interpretation are the products of strong cultural influences. Members of certain subcultures, for example, believe that a woman is required to offer at least a modicum of resistance to a man's sexual advances even though she may intend to engage in sexual intercourse with him. Men in such subcultures may inaccurately gauge the degree of persistence required to overcome a woman's "resistance," or may force an encounter by misinterpreting a woman's intentions. Some of the same difficulties may accrue in judging the willingness of homosexual partners, or in assessing a man's degree of consent to sexual intercourse when a woman is the aggressor.

To address these issues, some have advocated requiring **express consent**. Express consent is a verbally expressed willingness to engage in a specified activity, and in the heterosexual arena generally places the burden of ensuring that consent has been obtained on the man. In 1990, for example, Antioch College instituted a requirement of "willing and verbal consent for each individual sexual act." The Antioch policy requires express consent from both partners at each stage as the level of sexual activity

CONSENT
a justification that claims that the person suffering an injury either agreed to sustain the injury or that the possibility of injury in some activity was agreed to before that activity was undertaken; offered as a defense to a criminal charge.

EXPRESS CONSENT
verbally expressed willingness to engage in a specified activity.

increases. Although the college's statute does not carry the force of law, it is indicative of the complexities involved in determining consent.

Because the public has an interest in the protection of its citizens, consent is generally not available as a defense in cases of homicide or where the injury inflicted causes serious bodily harm. Reflecting such concerns, consent, or lack thereof, is not an element specified by laws contravening homicide and many other crimes. A killer who shoots another person, for example, after being told "There's the gun. Go ahead and shoot me!" cannot effectively offer a consent defense, even though the victim's comments may be substantiated by witnesses.[22] Likewise, a person who complies with the request of a panhandler and cuts off the beggar's hand in order to make him appear more needy can still be prosecuted for battery. Similarly, most jurisdictions do not permit one to consent to one's own death, and consent is not a valid defense in cases of euthanasia—especially where the defendant played an *active* role in the decedent's death, or directly caused the death.

Consent cannot be claimed in cases of intimidation or fraud. A person cannot, for example, be forced to give consent. Intimidation or the threatened use of force to obtain consent invalidates the consent given and may result in charges of extortion or blackmail against the threat-maker. Similarly, a person tricked into giving consent may later bring charges of fraud against the trickster. Likewise, one who is mentally incompetent, unconscious, or otherwise incapable of giving consent is protected by the law in most matters.

SUMMARY

- A defense consists of evidence and arguments offered by a defendant and his or her attorneys to show why that person should not be held liable for a criminal charge. A successful defense may have the effect of completely exonerating the defendant of any criminal liability.

- Defenses may be built upon four bases: (1) alibi, (2) inability of the prosecution to prove all of the elements necessary for conviction, (3) justifications, and (4) excuses.

- Conduct that a person believes is necessary in order to avoid a harm or evil to him- or herself, or to avoid harm to another, is justifiable if the harm or evil to be avoided is greater than that which the law defining the offense seeks to avoid.

- An excuse does not claim that the conduct in question is justified—but suggests instead that the actor who engaged in it was, at the time, suffering under some defect of personality or circumstance so as to not be legally responsible for his or her actions.

- Justifications and excuses are affirmative defenses. They must be raised or asserted by the defendant independently of any claims made by the prosecutor.

- Justifications include: (1) self-defense, (2) defense of others, (3) defense of home and property, (4) necessity, (5) consent, and (6) the defense of resisting unlawful arrest.

- The defense of necessity claims that it was necessary to commit some unlawful act in order to prevent or to avoid a greater harm. The defense of necessity has generally been far more effective in the face of grave physical threats that are immediately present than it has been in protecting defendants facing economic or psychological necessity from criminal liability.

- Self-defense is based on the recognition that a person has an inherent right to self-protection and that to defend oneself from unlawful attack is a "natural" response to threatening situations. The "law" of self-defense generally holds that the use of force upon or toward another person is justifiable when the actor believes that such force is immediately necessary for the purpose of protecting himself against the unlawful use of force by the other person.

- Deadly force, the highest degree of force, can only be used to counter an immediate threat of death or great bodily harm.

- Resistance in the face of an unlawful arrest is considered justifiable in almost all jurisdictions. Many states have codified statutory provisions detailing the limits imposed on such resistance and the conditions under which it can be used.

- Most states also provide statutory protections to law enforcement officers who find it necessary to use force to effect an arrest or to prevent persons who are in their custody from escaping. Such statutes provide an execution of public duty defense, and preclude the possibility of arresting officers being prosecuted on charges of assault or battery (if force is needed to effect the arrest or to maintain custody), so long as the officer acts in a lawful manner.

- The use of force to defend oneself has generally been extended to permit the use of reasonable force to defend others who are or appear to be in imminent danger. Property in the possession of a third person, or the home of a third person, may be protected by one who assists that person to the same degree and in the same manner that the owner of the property or the home would have been privileged to act.

- The defense of consent makes the claim that the person suffering an injury either agreed beforehand to sustain the injury, or that the possibility of injury in some activity was agreed to before that activity was undertaken. Sexual activity is an area where the defense of consent is frequently employed, since lack of consent is an element of many sex crimes. Consent, however, is generally not available as a defense where the victim's lack of consent is not a statutory element of the offense.

QUESTIONS FOR DISCUSSION

1. What is the purpose of a defense to a criminal charge? What is an "affirmative defense"?
2. What is the difference between justifications and excuses? Give examples of each type of defense.
3. What fundamental claim is raised by the defense of necessity? When are claims of necessity most successful?
4. When may force be used in self-defense? When may deadly force be used?
5. Explain the "execution of public duty" defense. When and by whom might such a defense be employed?

LEGAL RESOURCES ON THE WORLD WIDE WEB

Some Web sites are virtual law libraries and provide a wealth of links to statutes, important documents, and court opinions. Some of the best such sites include these:

Find Law
http://www.findlaw.com
Includes laws, cases, and codes, legal practice materials, legal news, dictionaries, and more.

The 'Lectric Law Library
http://www.lectlaw.com
An excellent collection of online legal materials and resources.

WashLaw Web
http://www.washlaw.edu
A great site with lots of links. Offered by the Washburn University School of Law.

The World Wide Web Virtual Library—Law Section
http://www.law.indiana.edu/v-lib
Run by Indiana University School of Law–Bloomington, the WWW Virtual Library offers searches by topic or type of information.

Check the *Criminal Law Today* Web site for URLs that may have changed.

SUGGESTED READINGS AND CLASSIC WORKS

Michael Louis Corrado, *Justification and Excuse in the Criminal Law: A Collection of Essays* (New York: Garland, 1994).

Alan M. Dershowitz, *The Best Defense* (New York: Random House, 1983).

George Fletcher, "Justification," in Sanford H. Kadish (Ed.), *Encyclopedia of Crime and Justice*, Vol. 3 (New York: Free Press, 1983), pp. 941–946.

Leo Katz, *Bad Acts and Guilty Minds: Conundrums of the Criminal Law* (Chicago: University of Chicago Press, 1987).

Paul H. Robinson, *Criminal Law Defenses,* 2 vols. (St. Paul, MN: West Publishing Co., 1984).

CAPSTONE CASE

CAN A PERSON WHO INITIATES THE USE OF DEADLY FORCE CLAIM SELF-DEFENSE?

United States v. *Thomas*
United States Court of Appeals for the Second Circuit, 1994
34 F.3d 44

OPINION

BACKGROUND: On October 30th, 1990, Wallie Howard, a Syracuse police officer working undercover for the Federal Drug Enforcement Administration (DEA), was shot and killed during a cocaine "buy-bust" taking place in the parking lot of "Mario's Big M Market" in Syracuse.

According to the testimony adduced at trial, Davidson was the head and supplier of a cocaine conspiracy that had begun in Syracuse in or around 1988. The conspiracy allegedly sold between ten thousand and fifty thousand dollars of cocaine weekly, with Davidson supplying the cocaine and receiving the bulk of the proceeds. The testimony indicated that Parke was a chief lieutenant of Davidson's, and that Parke and Morales frequently delivered cocaine to customers who had called them on their beepers to place orders. Lawrence was a seller at one of the conspiracy's drug apartments; he also functioned as "muscle" for the conspiracy. Stewart had dealt cocaine for the conspiracy in the past, and he owed the group a debt for cocaine he had purchased three weeks earlier, which turned out to be "bad." He was invited to participate in the events of the thirtieth as a means of paying off the debt he owed to the conspiracy for this cocaine.

On October 18, 1990, Agent Howard and confidential informant Luther Gregory purchased three ounces of cocaine from Morales for $2,700. While the deal took place in Gregory's apartment, Parke walked around the apartment house, apparently conducting countersurveillance. On October 22, Howard and Gregory purchased another four ounces of cocaine from Morales. Parke waited in the car outside while Morales delivered the cocaine and collected the money. At that purchase, Howard and Gregory inquired about the possibility of buying an additional one and one-half kilograms of cocaine. Morales indicated that he would be able to supply that amount, and the transaction was scheduled for October 29. Because Parke and Morales did not arrive with the cocaine on the twenty-ninth, the sale was rescheduled for the thirtieth. On the morning of October 30, the DEA drug task force met to schedule the buy-bust. Because more than $40,000 in cash was to change hands, the agents were concerned about the possibility of a robbery and attempted to arrange the purchase in a public location. Their fears were well-founded; Davidson had made plans to rob Gregory, because he felt Gregory had robbed him in the past.

The defendants also met the morning of the thirtieth,[1] and Davidson laid out his plan to rob Gregory of the money. Parke supplied Lawrence with a .357-caliber revolver, and Stewart was armed with a .22-caliber handgun. Morales was to negotiate the deal and act as the driver, and Lawrence and Stewart were to conduct the actual robbery. Davidson and Parke remained behind as the others left to meet Gregory.

Morales met with Agent Howard and Gregory at Gregory's apartment, and they agreed to do the deal in the parking lot of Mario's Big M. When the buyers arrived at the parking lot, Morales told Gregory to come with him to Morales' apartment to check the quality of the cocaine. When they arrived at Morales' apartment, Lawrence and Stewart emerged with guns drawn. They bound and gagged Gregory, breaking his wrist in the process. Morales, Lawrence, and Stewart then returned to Mario's Big M. While Morales waited in his car, Lawrence and Stewart, both armed, approached Gregory's vehicle, where Agent Howard was seated in the passenger seat. Stewart proceeded to the driver's side and got in the driver's seat, while Lawrence went around the back of the vehicle to the passenger side. The following conversation was recorded on the agent's equipment:

> *Stewart: What the f____'s up?*
> *Howard: Huh?*
> *Lawrence: Open up the door.*
> *Stewart: Tell me where the money is.*
> *Howard: What money?*
> *Lawrence: Hey, hey, hey . . .*
> *Stewart: Hey, don't shut . . .*
> *Lawrence: Open the door, man.*

At that point, conversation ceased and background noises are heard on the recording. According to trial testimony, Stewart had the loaded .22 in his hand and tried to shoot, but was unsuccessful because no round had been placed in the chamber. Agent Howard got three shots off, one of which struck Stewart in the shoulder. From behind Howard, Lawrence, who was standing at the rear passenger side of the vehicle, fired the .357 at Agent Howard, striking him in the rear of the head and killing him. Stewart was arrested seconds later, slumped against a wall with the .22 nearby. Morales and Lawrence attempted to flee but were both apprehended within moments; the murder weapon was recovered from the floor of Morales' vehicle. Both Morales and Stewart waived their *Miranda* rights, made admissions, and signed confessional affidavits.

At trial, in addition to the detailed confessions, the government presented significant testimony that established the facts underlying the longstanding cocaine ring. Daryl Gibbs, a cooperating co-conspirator, testified at length about the operation of the conspiracy. He also testified that the conspirators had planned to rob someone who had robbed Davidson in the past. Gibbs also testified that he saw Davidson after the shooting, and Davidson had stated that he had told his men, "if the guy [Gregory] was with someone, don't rob him." Other witnesses confirmed

various aspects of the conspiracy. Additionally, bystander witnesses described seeing one man [Stewart] holding a gun stagger backwards and fall, lying there until apprehended by the police, and another man [Lawrence] standing by the rear passenger side of the car, holding a smoking gun and uttering expletives.

In his confession, Morales recounted the events of the day largely as outlined above. He stated that seated in his car in the parking lot, he saw Stewart draw a gun and get shot by Howard. He further testified that Lawrence then shot Howard in the head, threw his gun into Morales' car, and started to run.

Stewart's confession was largely consistent with that of Morales'. However, he stated that it was Lawrence who brandished a handgun, whereas he had kept his gun in his pocket until the shooting began. Stewart testified that he asked, "Where is the money" and that when Howard appeared to be reaching for a gun, Stewart threw his own gun away and started out of the car. He stated that he then felt a sharp pain in his back and fell to the ground. He was apprehended, with the .22 a few feet away from him.

At trial, the defendants-appellants were found guilty as charged. All of the defendants were sentenced to life terms on Counts I, VI, and VII, for narcotics conspiracy, felony murder committed in furtherance of a robbery, and intentional killing of a federal agent, respectively, to be served concurrently, plus five years on the firearms charge. Certain of the defendants also received two or four twenty-year terms on counts involving distribution of cocaine.[2] Final judgment was entered on July 1, 1993.

DISCUSSION: The appellants make various claims of error. None justifies reversal of their convictions.

I. Self-Defense

The defendants contend that the district court erred in not specifically charging the jury that it was the government's obligation to prove the absence of self-defense beyond a reasonable doubt. The government generally has the burden of disproving self-defense beyond a reasonable doubt once it is raised by a defendant. *United States* v. *Alvarez*, 755 F.2d 830, 842–43 (11th Cir. 1985), *cert. denied*, 474 U.S. 905 (1985). For reasons not clear, Judge McCurn agreed to give only a portion of the requested self-defense charge (which was taken virtually verbatim from Leonard B. Sand et al., *Modern Federal Jury Instructions*, 1993). He declined to give the last two paragraphs of the requested charge, which expressly placed the burden on the government to prove beyond a reasonable doubt that the defendants did not act in self-defense. The defendants claim that this omission was error.

Some circuit courts have held that the failure to provide a separate instruction explaining that the government bears the burden of proof on self-defense can constitute reversible error. See, e.g., *Government of Virgin Islands* v. *Smith*, 949 F.2d 677, 686 (3d Cir. 1991); *Guthrie* v. *Warden, Maryland Penitentiary*, 683 F.2d 820, 824–26 (4th Cir. 1982); *United States* v. *Corrigan*, 548 F.2d 879, 883–84 (10th Cir. 1977). These courts have held that the failure specifically to so instruct the jury suggests the incorrect inference that, although the government must prove the elements of the offense beyond a reasonable doubt, the defendant must prove self-defense.

The government contends that the charge, taken as a whole, correctly placed the burden on the government. See *Virgin Islands*, 949 F.2d at 682–83 n.4; *Corrigan*, 548 F.2d at 882. We need not rule on this contention because, even if the charge failed to place the burden on the government, there was no reversible error in this case. That is because the defendants were not entitled, as a matter of law, to rely on the defense of self-defense.

The defense of self-defense is not available to one who acts as the aggressor, and commits his aggression threatening deadly force, even though the intended victim responds with deadly force so that the original aggressor will be killed if he does not first kill.

It has long been accepted that one cannot support a claim of self-defense by a self-generated necessity to kill. The right of homicidal self-defense is granted only to those free from fault in the difficulty; it is denied to slayers who incite the fatal attack, encourage the fatal quarrel or otherwise promote the necessitous occasion for taking life. . . . In sum, one who is the aggressor in a conflict culminating in death cannot invoke the necessities of self-preservation. *United States* v. *Peterson*, 483 F.2d 1222, 1231 (D.C. Cir.), *cert. denied*, 414 U.S. 1007 (1973) (footnotes omitted); see also *Melchior* v. *Jago*, 723 F.2d 486, 493–94 (6th Cir. 1983), *cert. denied*, 466 U.S. 952 (1984).

Under this principle, the defendants had no entitlement to any self-defense charge. The unrebutted evidence showed that with guns drawn, Lawrence, Stewart, and Morales bound and gagged Gregory, breaking his wrist in the process; they then returned to the parking lot where Stewart and Lawrence, armed with a .22 and a .357 respectively, approached Howard's car from two opposite sides; Lawrence banged on the window, and they demanded the money Howard was carrying. At least Lawrence, and possibly both Lawrence and Stewart, had their guns drawn as they confronted Howard and demanded the $40,000. Moreover, in finding the defendants guilty of felony murder under Count VI, the jury necessarily found that the killing was done in the attempted perpetration of a robbery. Upon this evidence, it is clear that Lawrence and Stewart were the aggressors, and that their felonious aggression was accompanied at the outset by the threat of deadly force. There was no evidence to the effect that Howard menaced Stewart and Lawrence prior to their assault on him. Even if one believes Stewart's contention that he did not draw his gun until Howard drew on him, that claim would not alter the uncontested evidence that Lawrence menaced Howard with his gun while Lawrence and Stewart approached him. Thus, even on Stewart's asserted facts, the defendants were the first to threaten deadly force. They therefore did not raise an issue of fact calling for an instruction on self-defense.

The charge was therefore unnecessarily favorable to the defendants in that it offered the jury the option to acquit by reason of self-defense. The judge's failure to make clear that the burden on the issue of self-defense rests on the government cannot have prejudiced the defendants when they had no right to have the jury consider the issue at all.

II. Felony murder and malice aforethought under 18 U.S.C. § 1111.

Defendants next contend that the district court erred by failing to instruct that first-degree felony murder under 18 U.S.C. § 1111 requires both a finding of malice aforethought and either a premeditated killing or a killing committed during the perpetration of an enumerated crime, such as a robbery. The contention is without merit. . . .

We have examined the defendants' remaining contentions and they are without merit. Some are discussed in a separate summary order.

CONCLUSION: The judgments of conviction are affirmed.

Footnotes
1. Gwendolyn Morrow testified that she was Lawrence's girlfriend and that on the morning of October 30th, all of the defendants-appellants met in her apartment.
2. Count I charged Davidson, Parke, Lawrence, Morales, and Stewart with conspiracy to distribute cocaine, in violation of 21 U.S.C. § 846. Counts II and III charged Davidson with distributing cocaine, and Counts IV and V charged Davidson, Parke, and Morales with distributing cocaine in violation of 21 U.S.C. § 841(a)(1) and 18 U.S.C. 2. Count VI charged Davidson, Parke, Lawrence, Morales, and Stewart with murdering Agent Howard in the attempt to perpetrate a robbery, in violation of 18 U.S.C. § 1111, 1114, and 2. Count VII charged Davidson, Parke, Lawrence, Morales, and Stewart with murdering Agent Howard during the commission of and in furtherance of the conspiracy to distribute cocaine, in violation of 21 U.S.C. § 848(e)(1)(B) and 18 U.S.C. 2. Count VIII charged Davidson, Parke, Lawrence, Morales, and Stewart with using, or aiding, abetting, and causing the use of, a firearm in a drug trafficking crime, in violation of 18 U.S.C. § 924(c)(1) and (2).

WHAT DO *YOU* THINK?

1. Lawrence fired at Agent Howard and killed him after Howard had already drawn his weapon and fired. Why was Lawrence unable to claim self-defense in the shooting? Do you think he should have been able to successfully raise such a claim? Why or why not?

2. In this case the U.S. Court of Appeals for the Second Circuit says that: "It has long been accepted that one cannot support a claim of self-defense by a self-generated necessity to kill." What is the logic behind such a principle? Do you agree with it? Why or why not?

3. Under what circumstances, if any, might the defendants have been justified in using force against Agent Howard? Under what circumstances might they have been justified in using deadly force?

CAPSTONE CASE   **CAN ONE CONSENT TO ONE'S OWN MURDER?**

Edinburgh v. *State*
Oklahoma Court of Criminal Appeals, 1995
896 P.2d 1176

OPINION

David Duane Edinburgh, Appellant, was charged by Information in the District Court of Canadian County in Case No. CRF-90-212 with the crime of malice aforethought murder, in violation of 21 O.S.Supp.1989, 701.7. A jury trial was held before the Honorable Edward C. Cunningham. The jury returned a verdict of guilty and recommended punishment at life imprisonment. The trial court sentenced appellant in accordance with the jury's verdict. From this judgment and sentence, appellant has perfected this appeal.

FACTS: In January, 1990, Dean Plummer was diagnosed with terminal cancer–multiple myeloma involving his kidneys, lymph system, and bone marrow. His wife, Maxine Plummer, was also in poor health, having suffered a heart attack. Dean asked Maxine's son, David Edinburgh, to quit his job and move in with them to help take care of them. David did so, and spent the next five months taking care of Dean, Maxine, and the family greyhound business.

Prior to his death, Dean had deteriorated greatly in health. He lost over 100 pounds and two inches in height. His kidneys also failed, forcing him to go in for dialysis three to four times per week. He was in almost constant pain and spent a lot of time in the hospital. Finally, the doctors decided that the cancer treatments were not doing any good and decided to discontinue all but the dialysis. In May, they told him that he had approximately two weeks to live.

On May 27, 1990, David Edinburgh shot Dean Plummer in the head with a .22 rifle. He testified that in late March or early April, Dean brought up the subject of suicide and asked David to help him. David refused. The subject was brought up again, but David still refused to go through with it. On the day in question, Dean and Maxine had just returned from visiting his sister. According to appellant, he was waiting for Dean to get home in order to check with him about putting down a sick greyhound. In anticipation, he had the .22 loaded. When he asked Dean about the dog, Dean begged David to kill him instead of the dog. He told David that he was in great pain, and [he] cried while he asked David to end his life as humanely as David would kill the dog.

David testified that he put the gun up to Dean's head, and Dean told him to just do it and then looked away. David, however, claims that he does not remember pulling the trigger and that he did not know right from wrong when he pulled the trigger. After shooting Dean, David went and got his mother from the barn. He told her what had happened and then took her to the neighbor's house to call the sheriff. When the police came, he told his mother that he was going to jail and emptied out his pockets.

The State put on testimony from several witnesses tending to show evidence of premeditation by appellant. Jamie Lindsey, the registered nurse who administered dialysis treatment to Mr. Plummer, testified about her conversations with Mr. Plummer wherein he talked about his future plans to open a barbecue restaurant. Lonnie Craighead also testified about his conversations with Mr. Plummer about opening a barbecue restaurant and buying a new pick-up truck.

Witness Paul O'Daniel testified that he mowed the grass for Mr. Plummer. He recalled an occasion in May, 1990, when he had a conversation with appellant wherein appellant related that he was tired of taking care of sick people, that it was dragging his life down, and that he wished "they" would go on and die and have it over with. Another witness, Billy Wood, testified that appellant and Mr. Plummer "couldn't get along" and "were at each other all of the time." He further testified that approximately two weeks prior to the incident in question, Appellant related, "One of these days I'll kill the old bastard and I'll own the whole place down there." In his first proposition of error, appellant asserts that he was deprived of his constitutional rights to due process, to a fair trial, and to a trial by jury when the trial court refused or failed to issue appropriate instructions on lesser included offenses which he claims the evidence clearly warranted. . . .

Appellant claims that, although not requested, instructions on second-degree (felony) murder and on aiding and abetting suicide were warranted by the evidence and should have been given. . . .

A. First-Degree (Heat of Passion) Manslaughter, First-Degree Manslaughter, and Second-Degree (Depraved Mind) Murder

This Court has repeatedly held that an instruction on a lesser included offense need only be given when there is evidence that tends to prove the lesser included offense was committed. Absent such evidence, an instruction should not be given . . . first-degree (heat of passion) manslaughter, first degree manslaughter, and second-degree (depraved mind) murder all include a similar element: a showing that there was no premeditated design to effect death. Here, appellant placed the gun against the victim's head and pulled the trigger. There could be no other intent than to effect death. As such, the trial court properly refused appellant's requested instructions for second-degree (depraved mind) murder, first-degree (heat of passion) manslaughter, and second-degree (culpable negligence) murder. Instructions on negligent homicide were also not properly given for the same reasons.

B. Aiding Suicide

This is a case of first impression for Oklahoma. Title 21 O.S.1981, Section 813, Aiding Suicide, makes it a crime for anyone "who willfully, in any manner, advises, encourages, abets, or assists another person in taking his own life." Section 814, Furnishing Weapon or Drug, makes it a crime for anyone "who willfully furnishes another person with any deadly weapon or poisonous drug, knowing that such person intends to use such weapon or drug in taking his own life, is guilty of aiding suicide, if such person thereafter employs such instrument or drug in taking his own life."

Appellant takes the position that the mere fact that the legislature passed "two separate statutes makes it clear that the Oklahoma Legislature intended the crime of aiding suicide to apply to either positive euthanasia or passive euthanasia." Specifically, appellant focuses on the alternative "or" in Section 813, thus making it separate crimes to either: (1) advise, (2) encourage, (3) abet, or (4) assist another in taking his own life. In this case, Appellant holds that he assisted the suicidant who, "while mentally able to decide his own fate, is too debilitated to be physically able to perform the overt act of self-killing and must depend upon his assistant to perform that

act at his request." Appellant offers the fact that he took steps to ensure that Dean Plummer's death was immediately reported to the authorities, thus demonstrating any lack of intent of a murder cover-up.

Thirty states currently have laws imposing criminal sanctions for aiding, assisting, causing, or promoting suicide. An additional five states impose criminal penalties under case law. However, as no other states, including Oklahoma,[1] seem to have statutes either criminalizing or condoning active euthanasia, our legal analysis centers on case law interpreting criminal homicide statutes. Many states have distinguished between the direct killing involved in euthanasia and conduct characterizing mere suicide assistance:

> *[The Oregon assisted suicide] statute does not contemplate active participation by one in the overt act directly causing death. It contemplates some participation in the events leading up to the commission of the final overt act, such as furnishing the means for bringing about death—the gun, the knife, the poison. . . . But where a person actually performs, or actively assists in performing, the overt act resulting in death, such as shooting or . . . administering the poison . . . his act constitutes murder. . . ." State v. Bouse, 264 P.2d 800, 812 (Or. 1953), overruled on other grounds by State v. Fisher, 376 P.2d 418 (Or. 1962).*

In *Aven v. State,* 277 S.W. 1080, 1083 (Tx. Crim. App.1925), the court held that where the defendant placed the poison in the mouth of a suicide, with knowing intent to help victim complete suicide, he is guilty of murder. Thus, where the defendant only furnishes the means by which the victim kills herself, he has merely assisted suicide. But, where the defendant proximately causes the defendant's death, he can be held liable for homicide.

In addition, the victim's request is usually irrelevant in criminal prosecutions. "The victim's invitation and consent to the perpetration of a crime does not constitute a defense, adequate excuse, or provocation." *Martin v. Commonwealth,* 37 S.E.2d 43, 47 (Va. 1946). In *Turner v. State,* 108 S.W. 1139, 1140 (Tenn. 1908), the defense contended that the accused's conduct was not murder since the victim requested it. However, the Tennessee Supreme Court stated:

"Murder is no less murder because the homicide is committed at the desire of the victim. He who kills another upon another's desire or command is, in the judgment of the law, as much a murderer as if he had done it merely of his own head." *Id.* at 1141.

In *People v. Matlock,* 336 P.2d 505 (Cal. 1959), the California Supreme Court affirmed, stating that: "Where a person actually performs, or actively assists in performing, the overt act resulting in death . . . it is wholly immaterial whether this act is committed pursuant to an agreement with the victim. . . ."

Also, other state courts do not recognize the defendant's motive as an element or defense to euthanasia. *People v. Conley,* 411 P.2d 911, 918 (Cal. 1966) (Intentionally engaging in a legally proscribed killing constitutes the necessary malice aforethought for murder. Malice had nothing to do with motive.); *People v. Cleaves,* 280 Cal. Rept. 145, 151 (Cal. Ct. App. 1991) (Court refused to fashion a new manslaughter category for a killing performed at the victim's request after defendant killed a friend suffering from AIDS.); *Gilbert v. State,* 487 So. 2d 1185, 1190 (Fla. Dist. Ct. App.1986) (In killing of wife with advanced Alzheimer's disease, the court held that euthanasia was not a defense to first-degree murder.).

Accordingly, we hold that Section 813 does not embrace "positive" (active) euthanasia. Thus, the trial court did not err in failing to instruct on aiding suicide. . . . For the foregoing reasons, the Judgment and Sentence are AFFIRMED.

Footnote

1. However, 63 O.S.Supp.1992, 3101.2(C) contains the following language: "The Oklahoma Rights of the Terminally Ill or Persistently Unconscious Act does not condone, authorize, or approve mercy killing, assisted suicide or euthanasia."

WHAT DO *YOU* THINK?

1. Do you agree with the opinion of the Oklahoma Supreme Court that Edinburgh is guilty of murder? Why or why not? Is your personal opinion based on the law or on philosophical and ethical considerations?

2. Do you agree with the logic of the law, cited in this case, that "The victim's invitation and consent to the perpetration of a crime does not constitute a defense, adequate excuse, or provocation"? Why or why not?

3. Do you agree with the statement cited by the court in this case that "Murder is no less murder because the homicide is committed at the desire of the victim. He who kills another upon another's desire or command is, in the judgment of the law, as much a murderer as if he had done it merely of his own head"? Why or why not?

4. Why does the defendant in this case ask the court to distinguish between suicide and euthanasia? Why might differences between the two be important?

NOTES

1. *People* v. *Goetz*, 68 N.Y.2d 96, 497 N.E.2d 41 (1986).

2. For additional information, see George P. Fletcher, *A Crime of Self-Defense: Bernhard Goetz and the Law on Trial* (Chicago: University of Chicago Press, 1991).

3. Jerome Hall, "Comments on Justification and Excuse," *American Journal of Comparative Law,* Vol. 24 (1976), pp. 638–640.

4. Paul H. Robinson, "Criminal Law Defenses: A Systematic Analysis," *Columbia Law Review,* Vol. 82 (1982), pp. 190, 203–204.

5. Model Penal Code, Article 3, Commentary.

6. The "Codification of a Principle of Necessity" is discussed in Part I of the Code's Commentaries.

7. Model Penal Code, Section 3.02.

8. 14 Q.B.D. 273 (1884).

9. Model Penal Code, Section 3.04 (1).

10. Carolyn Grant, "Police: Victim Aimed Car at Attacker," *The Island Packet* (newspaper), January 23, 1997, p. 1A.

11. *United States* v. *Thomas,* U.S. Court of Appeals for the Second Circuit (1994).

12. *State* v. *Norman,* 324 N.C. 253, 378 S.E.2d 8 (1989).

13. Joseph Berger, "Goetz Case: Commentary on Nature of Urban Life," *The New York Times,* June 18, 1987, B6.

14. *Tennessee* v. *Garner,* 471 U.S. 1, 9–10 (1985).

15. Berger, "Goetz Case."

16. The exception, of course, is that of a trespasser who trespasses in order to commit a more serious crime.

17. "Man Charged in Shooting of Burglars," *The Island Packet* (newspaper), February 7, 1999, p. 3A.

18. *People* v. *Ceballos,* 12 Cal. 3d 470, 526 P.2d 241 (1974).

19. At common law, exceptions were made in instances of attempted arson and attempted burglary of a dwelling house.

20. Sir Edward Coke, *Third Institute,* p. 162.

21. Rollin M. Perkins and Ronald N. Boyce, *Criminal Law,* 3rd ed. (Mineola, NY: Foundation Press, 1982), p. 1075.

22. See, for example, *State* v. *Fransua,* 85 N.M. 173, 510 P.2d 106, 58 A.L.R. 3d 656 (Ct. App. 1973).

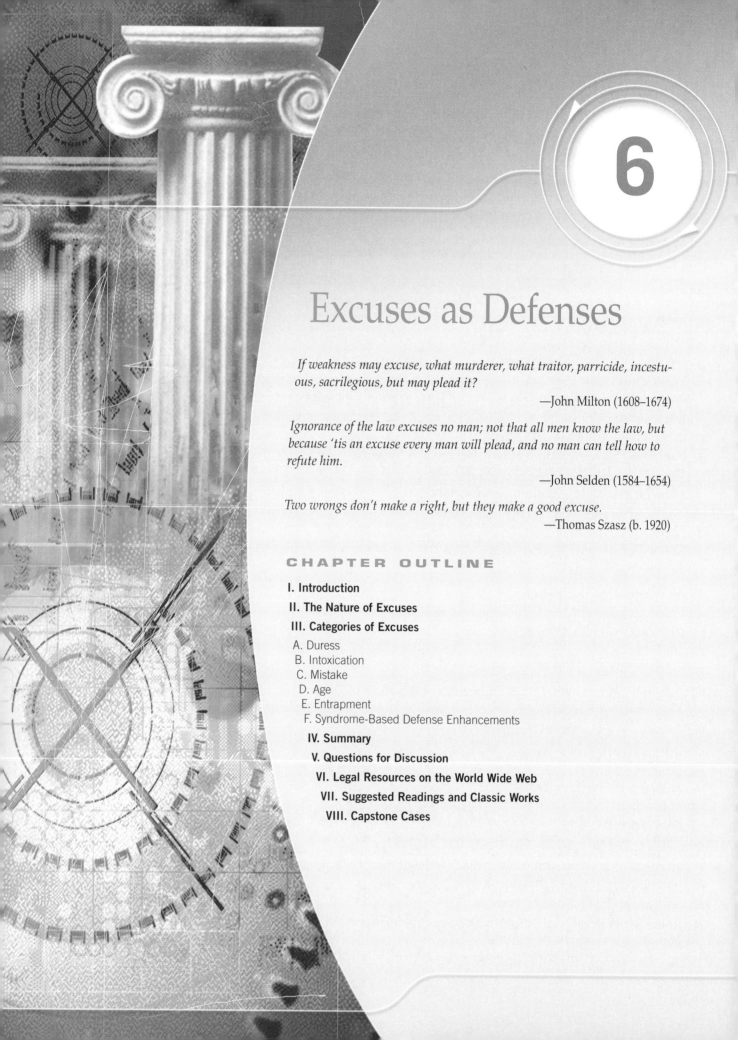

6

Excuses as Defenses

If weakness may excuse, what murderer, what traitor, parricide, incestuous, sacrilegious, but may plead it?

—John Milton (1608–1674)

Ignorance of the law excuses no man; not that all men know the law, but because 'tis an excuse every man will plead, and no man can tell how to refute him.

—John Selden (1584–1654)

Two wrongs don't make a right, but they make a good excuse.

—Thomas Szasz (b. 1920)

AFTER READING THIS CHAPTER YOU SHOULD:

▷ Understand the personal and subjective nature of excuse defenses.

▷ Know the seven types of excuses recognized by law.

▷ Understand the defense of duress and the limitations surrounding it.

▷ Know the difference between voluntary and involuntary intoxication, and be able to explain when each may be a defense to a criminal charge.

▷ Know the difference between mistake of fact and mistake of law, and be able to explain when each may be a defense to a criminal charge.

▷ Understand the defense of entrapment, and be able to explain the difference between subjective and objective assessments of the entrapment defense.

▷ Be able to explain how the use of syndromes may enhance defenses against criminal liability, and be able to list and explain various syndrome-based defense enhancements.

INTRODUCTION

After midnight on February 17, 1992, Alice Mahaffey told police officer Ronald Wright, paramedic Venetia Giger, and neighbor William Tice that Horace Pope had beaten her, stabbed her, and kicked her in the head repeatedly with his cowboy boots. She added that he took her car keys, left her for dead, and drove away in her car with his eighteen-year-old niece Marsha Pope. After Pope and Marsha left, Alice managed to drag herself across the street to William Tice's residence where she lay slumped on his sofa, covered in blood, until the police and paramedics arrived. She died in the hospital eight days after surgery for her wounds and an ensuing infection.

Marsha was an eyewitness to the attack by Pope which she described as follows: She was alone in her parents' home on February 16, 1992, when Pope and Alice, both alcoholics, arrived in Alice's car. Both had been drinking and, while Alice was placing beer in the kitchen, Pope and Marsha were left alone in the living room. Pope, at this time, told Marsha that he was going to kill Alice for her car and money. Thinking Pope was drunk and not to be taken seriously, Marsha retired to her bedroom, leaving Pope and Alice in her parents' bedroom. Later, Pope summoned Marsha and forced her to watch him beat, kick, and stab Alice. Marsha witnessed Pope beat Alice's head against the sink and wall while Alice was sitting on the toilet, after which he pushed her off the toilet and stomped on her head and back with his boots. While Alice was lying face down on the floor, Pope straddled and stabbed her. When Marsha tried to escape, Pope threatened to kill her if she attempted to leave. Pope then left Alice lying on the bathroom floor and went to the kitchen to wash his hands, after telling Marsha to see if Alice was dead. In order to prevent Pope from inflicting further violence, Marsha confirmed that Alice was dead. Marsha then left with Pope in Alice's car. After being threatened again with death, Marsha persuaded Pope to drop her off at a friend's house, at which time she immediately called 911. After dropping Marsha off, Pope drove to the trailer where his brother's family was staying and attempted to borrow money. Upon being refused, he made the following statement: "Well, I've killed a woman in your house and your bathroom's in a mess." Pope then drove away in Alice's car and was apprehended by the police, at which time he made two spontaneous statements. He said calmly, "I hope I killed the bitch" and, as the officers were discussing Alice's condition, Pope said loudly, "I hope I didn't go through all that for nothing. I hope she's dead as a doornail."

The trial court found that at the time he attacked Ms. Mahaffey, Pope was intoxicated to the point that his capacity to appreciate the criminality of his conduct or to conform his conduct to the requirements of law was substantially impaired and he was suffering from extreme mental or emotional disturbance. In making these findings, the court considered the fact that Pope was an alcoholic who generally consumed two six packs to a case of beer per day and who had consumed at least a half case of beer prior to attacking Ms. Mahaffey. The court also considered Pope's family history of mental illness and extreme alcoholism as well as expert opinion that was based in part on that history.

Although Pope refused to be evaluated by the defense's mental health expert, the expert interviewed members of Pope's family and reviewed the facts of the murder. According to the mental health expert, given his history of chronic alcohol abuse and the amount of alcohol he consumed on the night of the murder, Pope's behavior was impaired such that his impulse control was decreased and his aggression increased and his ability to appreciate the criminality of his conduct or to conform his conduct to the law was impaired.[1]

This is a true story, and the wording in these opening paragraphs is taken directly from an opinion by the Florida Supreme Court.[2] You might ask yourself the following questions: (1) Do you think the fact that the defendant was drunk at the time he committed the crimes should excuse him of responsibility for his actions, or reduce his degree of criminal liability? (2) Do you think the fact that Alice Mahaffey did not die until eight days until after she was attacked and that she succumbed to infection while in the hospital should reduce the defendant's degree of criminal liability? You should know that Pope was found guilty of first-degree murder and robbery and acquitted of kidnapping. He was sentenced to death for the homicide and to a consecutive life term for robbery with a deadly weapon. The Florida Supreme Court upheld his convictions. As you read through this chapter you will learn about the nature of excuses, and you will see why voluntary intoxication is rarely a successful defense to a criminal charge.

THE NATURE OF EXCUSES

EXCUSES

(also defined in Chapter 5); a category of legal defenses in which the defendant claims that some personal condition or circumstance at the time of the act was such that he or she should not be held accountable under the criminal law

As discussed in Chapter 5, "justification declares the allegedly criminal act legal; excuse admits the act's criminality, but declares the allegedly criminal actor not to be worthy of blame."[3] **Excuses** admit that the action committed by the defendant was wrong and that it violated the criminal law, but claim that the defendant should be excused from criminal liability by virtue of special conditions or circumstances which suggest that the actor is not or was not responsible for his or her deeds. The majority of excuses are personal in nature—that is, they claim that the defendant acted on the basis of some disability or some abnormal condition, such as intoxication, insanity, or immaturity. Even where a defendant suffers from a disability, however, that disability alone is not sufficient to excuse him or her of criminal responsibility. Only when the disability has the effect of in some way contributing to the criminal activity in question will the actor be excused. Like justifications, excuses are affirmative defenses and must be raised by the defendant.

> Oftentimes excusing of a fault doth make the fault the worse by the excuse.
> —William Shakespeare, *King John*

CATEGORIES OF EXCUSES

Paul H. Robinson says that "society is generally willing to excuse an actor under four types of conditions,"[4] and he lists those conditions as follows:

1. When the conduct constituting the offense is simply not the product of the actor's voluntary effort or determination (e.g., the actor is having a seizure);

2. When the conduct is the product of the actor's voluntary effort or determination, but he does not accurately perceive the physical nature or consequences of the conduct (e.g., the actor thinks a gun is a paintbrush, or accurately sees the physical characteristics of the gun but does not know that the gun shoots bullets that injure people);

3. When the actor accurately perceives and understands the physical nature of the conduct, its physical results, and physical surroundings, but he does not know that the conduct or its results are wrong or criminal (e.g., the actor thinks God has ordered him to sacrifice a neighbor for the good of mankind, or believes, because of paranoid delusions, that the man waiting for a bus is about to assault him); or

4. When the actor perceives the conduct accurately and fully, understands its physical consequences, and knows its wrongfulness or criminality, but the actor lacks the ability to control his conduct (e.g., because of an insane compulsion or duress) to such an extent that it is no longer proper to hold him accountable for it.

To this list we might add:

5. When the conduct constituting the offense is the product of the actor's voluntary effort or determination, and the wrongfulness of the conduct is properly understood by the actor, but the illegal action is initiated by the government or by agents of enforcement (i.e., entrapment); and

6. When the conduct constituting the offense is the unavoidable consequence of the actor's previous life experiences, deviant socialization, or victimization (i.e., the "abuse excuse").

Other authors[5] reduce the six categories of excuse just listed to three general types. The first type of excuse, they suggest, is that of involuntary actions, in which the actor has no voluntary control over bodily movements. The second type of excuse might be termed "deficient but reasonable actions," or actions which are voluntary but are undertaken by mistake or under threat of harm. The third type of excuse can be found in "irresponsible actions" brought about by some mental or physical limitation, such as insanity or age. As Sanford Kadish and Stephen Schulhofer observe: "[These] three categories of legal excuses . . . suggest the common rationale behind them both in the law and in everyday moral judgments; namely, that justice precludes blame where none is deserved. In the first category, people are not to blame because they have no control over their movements; in the second, because they acted in circumstances so constraining that most people would have done the same; in the third, because they suffer from a fundamental deficiency of mind and are therefore not responsible moral agents."[6]

Subsumed under these broad categories are specific excuses recognized by the law, including: (1) duress, (2) involuntary intoxication, (3) mistake, (4) age, (5) entrapment, (6) insanity, and (7) diminished responsibility. The first five of these excuses are discussed in this chapter, while insanity and diminished responsibility are covered in Chapter 7. Also discussed in this chapter is the special area of syndrome-based defenses, a form of excuse that has recently entered the legal limelight.

Duress

The Model Penal Code says: "It is an affirmative defense that the actor engaged in the conduct charged to constitute an offense because he was coerced to do so by the use of, or a threat to use, unlawful force against his person or the person of another, which a person of reasonable firmness in his situation would have been unable to resist."[7]

DURESS
also known as **compulsion;** a condition under which one is forced to act against one's will.

The defense of **duress,** sometimes also called **compulsion,** is based on the belief that people do not willfully engage in acts they are compelled or coerced to perform. Hence, the mother forced to rob a bank by someone holding her children hostage, the captured military officer compelled to provide secrets to an enemy under threat of torture, and the pilot of an airplane who flies off course after her plane has been commandeered by terrorists are all forced to commit acts they would not otherwise perform.

In an interesting 1997 case, fifty-three-year-old Jose Fernandez Pupo, a thirty-year veteran of Cuba's military intelligence and police services, was acquitted by a federal jury in Tampa, Florida, on charges stemming from the hijacking of a small Cuban plane to U.S.-controlled territory.[8] He admitted having commandeered a Cuba Aero Taxi flight over the eastern part of Cuba on July 7, 1996, and forcing it to divert to the U.S. Naval Base at Guantanamo Bay. He also admitted having been armed with two firearms at the time of the hijacking and did not contest allegations that he fired one of the weapons out of an open cockpit window to show that he "meant business." Arrested on federal charges of air piracy, Fernandez Pupo offered a duress defense, saying that he had no alternative to breaking the law because Cuban authorities had become aware that he headed an underground anti-Castro movement and were about to arrest him. A colleague, he said, had told him that a warrant had been issued for his arrest. Torture and death, he claimed, would likely follow. At the trial, U.S. District Judge Joyce Hens Green informed the jury that Fernandez Pupo could not be held criminally responsible for his act if jury members agreed that it was carried out "under duress." She said the hijacking could be excused if the defense could prove that Fernandez Pupo acted on the "reasonable belief" that he "would suffer immediate injury or death if he did not commit the crime." The jury concluded the defense met that standard.

> Things in law tend to be black and white. But we all know that some people are a little bit guilty, while other people are guilty as hell.
>
> —Donald Cressey, University of California, Santa Barbara

Some legal scholars say that duress may qualify as either a justification or an excuse. The main difference, they point out, is that necessity (which, as a "justification" for unlawful behavior, was discussed in the last chapter) is brought about by acts of nature or natural events, whereas duress is imposed by one human being on another. Whenever a person is forced to act in violation of the law, whether by reason of human or natural "pressure," they are probably convinced that such action is necessary.

In most jurisdictions, effective use of the duress defense must be based on a showing that the defendant feared for his or her life, or was in danger of great bodily harm—or that he or she was acting so as to prevent the death or bodily harm of another.[9] Likewise, the threat under which the defendant acted must have been immediate, clear, and inescapable and must not have arisen from some illegal or immoral activity of the defendant. The Model Penal Code states that the defense of duress is "unavailable if the actor recklessly placed himself in a situation in which it was probable that he would be subjected to duress." Such a clause, found in many state statutes that codify the defense of duress, is called the "at fault exception." So, for example, one who joins a street gang cannot later claim that the gang "forced" him to engage in illegal acts against his will. Similarly, a prostitute ordered to shoplift by her "pimp" under the threat of being denied drugs to support her habit would be hard pressed to claim duress as a defense to a larceny charge.

Generally speaking, duress is a defense only where the crime committed is less serious than the harm avoided. Some jurisdictions limit the applicability of the duress defense to less serious crimes (see the Law on the Books box on Texas law in this section), others state that it cannot be used as a defense to a charge of homicide, and still others broaden the ban to all crimes of personal violence. The California Penal Code limits the applicability of duress defenses to noncapital crimes in which the actor's life was threatened. It reads: "All persons are capable of committing crimes except . . . [p]ersons (unless the crime be punishable with death) who committed the act or made the omission charged under threats or menaces sufficient to show that they had reasonable cause to and did believe their lives would be endangered if they refused."

States that have not codified the defense of duress generally adhere to common law requirements that the alleged coercion involve "a use or threat of harm which is present, imminent, and pending, and of such a nature as to induce a well grounded apprehension of death or serious bodily harm if the act is not done."[10]

Although widely recognized today as a useful defense to a criminal charge, the well-known nineteenth-century English jurist J. Stephen suggested that duress should be an ameliorating factor when punishment is considered but that it should not eliminate criminal liability. Stephen wrote: "It is, of course, a misfortune for a man that he should be placed between two fires, but it would be a much greater misfortune for society at large if criminals could confer impunity upon their agents by

LAW ON THE BOOKS

"DURESS" UNDER THE TEXAS PENAL CODE.
Compare with Model Penal Code, Section 2.09

TEXAS PENAL CODE

Section 8.05. DURESS.
   a. It is an affirmative defense to prosecution that the actor engaged in the proscribed conduct because he was compelled to do so by threat of imminent death or serious bodily injury to himself or another.
   b. In a prosecution for an offense that does not constitute a felony, it is an affirmative defense to prosecution that the actor engaged in the proscribed conduct because he was compelled to do so by force or threat of force.
   c. Compulsion within the meaning of this section exists only if the force or threat of force would render a person of reasonable firmness incapable of resisting the pressure.
   d. The defense provided by this section is unavailable if the actor intentionally, knowingly, or recklessly placed himself in a situation in which it was probable that he would be subjected to compulsion.
   e. It is no defense that a person acted at the command or persuasion of his spouse, unless he acted under compulsion that would establish a defense under this section.

threatening them with death or violence if they refused to execute their commands." As an example, Stephen says, "The law says to a man intending to commit murder, if you do it I will hang you. Is the law to withdraw its threat if someone else says, if you do not do it I will shoot you?"

Intoxication

The story that opened this chapter described how an alcoholic, Horace Pope, severely beat and then stabbed a woman named Alice Mahaffey, who later died. Although mental health experts testified at trial that Pope had a history of chronic alcohol abuse and that his ability to control his behavior on the night of the assault had been severely impaired by the large amount of alcohol he had consumed, he was nonetheless convicted of murder and sentenced to die.

The verdict in the *Pope* case is consistent with the application of the intoxication defense in most jurisdictions. A claim of intoxication is generally not regarded as an effective defense even where the intoxication results from alcoholism, and laws which codify the defense (such as the Indiana law shown in a Law on the Books box in this section) usually mandate strict limits on the use of the intoxication defense. Intoxication is not a useful defense because most intoxicated individuals are responsible for their impaired state, and the law generally holds that a person who voluntarily puts himself in a condition so as to have little or no control over his actions must be held to have intended whatever consequences ensue. In some jurisdictions and for certain crimes, however, voluntary intoxication may lessen criminal liability. Such is the case where a high level of intoxication makes it impossible for a person to form the *mens rea* necessary for a given offense (see the Law in Practice box in this section). For example, while first-degree murder requires premeditation, a defense showing that a defendant was highly intoxicated while committing homicide—and therefore unable to think clearly—may result in a second-degree murder or manslaughter conviction.

In *People* v. *Walker*,[11] for example, California Jury Instruction Number 4.21 was read to the jury as follows:

> In the crime of attempted murder of which the defendant is accused in count 1 of the information, a necessary element is the existence in the mind of the defendant of the specific intent to kill. If the evidence shows that the defendant was intoxicated at the time of the alleged crime, you should consider that fact in determining whether defendant had such specific intent. If from all the evidence you have reasonable doubt whether the defendant formed such specific intent, you must find that he did not have such specific intent.

The essence of any defense based on intoxication can be found in the effect that an intoxicating substance has on the mental state of the defendant. Of course, intoxication may make it impossible to commit a crime. A man charged with rape, for example, could conceivably use expert testimony to support his contention that it was impossible for him to achieve an erection because of his highly intoxicated condition at the time of the alleged offense. Such a claim, however, does not reference the mental state of the defendant, but relies instead on the assertion that the crime in question did not actually occur because the defendant was too intoxicated to commit it. This kind of a defense is far different from the claim that the requisite mental state needed to commit an offense was lacking.

The difference between these two types of claims points out the important distinction between voluntary and involuntary intoxication. The California Penal Code says that "**voluntary intoxication** includes the voluntary ingestion, injection, or taking by any other means of any intoxicating liquor, drug, or other substance."[12]

There is never a deed so foul that something couldn't be said for the guy; that's why there are lawyers.

—Melvin Belli

VOLUNTARY INTOXICATION

willful intoxication; intoxication that is the result of personal choice. Voluntary intoxication includes the voluntary ingestion, injection, or taking by any other means of any intoxicating liquor, drug, or other substance.

A fraternity party in New York state. Although the consumption of alcoholic beverages is relatively common in America, drunkenness—because it is generally self-induced—is rarely an acceptable defense to a criminal charge. (Photo by Andrew Lichtenstein, courtesy of The Image Works.)

Involuntary intoxication, in contrast, generally results from the unknowing ingestion of an intoxicating substance.

Involuntary intoxication may result from secretly "spiked" punch, LSD-laced desserts, from following medical advice, and from situations in which an individual is tricked or forced into consuming an intoxicating substance. Recently, for example, the Drug Enforcement Administration reported on the growing use of the drug Rohypnol® (flunitrazepam) by young men who secretly put the substance into women's drinks in order to lower their inhibitions. Rohypnol® is a powerful sedative whose side effects are not entirely known.

Involuntary intoxication is difficult to demonstrate in the case of alcohol, since the taste and effects of alcohol are both widely known in our culture, and it can be

INVOLUNTARY INTOXICATION

intoxication that is not willful.

LAW ON THE BOOKS

"INTOXICATION" UNDER THE INDIANA PENAL CODE.

Compare with Model Penal Code, Section 2.08

INDIANA PENAL CODE

Chapter 3, Section 5.

a. It is a defense that the person who engaged in the prohibited conduct did so while he was intoxicated, if the intoxication resulted from the introduction of a substance into his body:
   (1) without his consent; or
   (2) when he did not know that the substance might cause intoxication.

b. Voluntary intoxication is a defense only to the extent that it negates an element of an offense referred to by the phrase "with intent to" or "with an intention to".

LAW IN PRACTICE

CAN STATE LAW PRECLUDE CONSIDERATION OF THE EFFECTS OF VOLUNTARY INTOXICATION ON *MENS REA* AT TRIAL?

Like the law in many states, Montana law does not permit voluntary intoxication to be used as a defense in criminal proceedings. In the U.S. Supreme Court opinion that is summarized in this box, that restriction was challenged on the basis that a defendant might be so intoxicated as to be unable to form the mens rea *needed for a specific crime. Attorneys for the defendant argued that the right of due process requires that defendants be given the opportunity to present "all relevant evidence to rebut the State's evidence on all elements of the offense charged."*

Montana v. Egelhoff
Supreme Court of the United States, 1996
116 S. Ct. 2013

Justice Scalia delivered the opinion of the Court.

I.

In July 1992, while camping out in the Yaak region of northwestern Montana to pick mushrooms, respondent made friends with Roberta Pavola and John Christenson, who were doing the same. On Sunday, July 12, the three sold the mushrooms they had collected and spent the rest of the day and evening drinking, in bars and at a private party in Troy, Montana. Some time after 9 P.M., they left the party in Christenson's 1974 Ford Galaxy station wagon. The drinking binge apparently continued, as respondent was seen buying beer at 9:20 P.M. and recalled "sitting on a hill or a bank, passing a bottle of Black Velvet back and forth" with Christenson. 272 Mont. 114, 118, 900 P.2d 260, 262 (1995).

At about midnight that night, officers of the Lincoln County, Montana, sheriff's department, responding to reports of a possible drunk driver, discovered Christenson's station wagon stuck in a ditch along U.S. Highway 2. In the front seat were Pavola and Christenson, each dead from a single gunshot to the head. In the rear of the car lay respondent, alive and yelling obscenities. His blood-alcohol content measured .36 percent over one hour later. On the floor of the car, near the brake pedal, lay respondent's .38-caliber handgun, with four loaded rounds and two empty casings; respondent had gunshot residue on his hands.

Respondent was charged with two counts of deliberate homicide, a crime defined by Montana law as "purposely" or "knowingly" causing the death of another human being. Mont. Code Ann. Section(s) 45-5-102 (1995). . . . Respondent's defense at trial was that an unidentified fourth person must have committed the murders; his own extreme intoxication, he claimed, had rendered him physically incapable of committing the murders, and accounted for his inability to recall the events of the night of July 12. Although respondent was allowed to make this use of the evidence that he was intoxicated, the jury was instructed, pursuant to Mont. Code Ann. Section(s) 45-2-203 (1995), that it could not consider respondent's "intoxicated condition . . . in determining the existence of a mental state which is an element of the offense." App. to Pet. for Cert. 29a. The jury found respondent guilty on both counts, and the court sentenced him to eighty-four years' imprisonment.

The Supreme Court of Montana reversed. It reasoned: (1) that respondent "had a due process right to present and have considered by the jury all relevant evidence to rebut the State's evidence on all elements of the offense charged . . . ," and (2) that evidence of respondent's voluntary intoxication was "clear[ly] . . . relevant to the issue of whether [respondent] acted knowingly and purposely . . ." Because Section(s) 45-2-203 prevented the jury from considering that evidence with regard to that issue, the court concluded that the State had been "relieved of part of its burden to prove beyond a reasonable doubt every fact necessary to constitute the crime charged . . . ," and that respondent had therefore been denied due process. We granted certiorari. . . .

II.

The cornerstone of the Montana Supreme Court's judgment was the proposition that the due process clause guarantees a defendant the right to present and have considered by the jury "*all relevant evidence* to rebut the State's evidence on *all elements* of the offense charged." 272 Mont. at 125, 900 P.2d, at 266 (emphasis added). . . .

The State Supreme Court's proposition that the due process clause guarantees the right to introduce all relevant evidence is indefensible. See, e.g., *Taylor* v. *Illinois*, 484 U.S. 400, 410; Fed. Rule Evid. 403; Fed. Rule Evid. 802. The clause does place limits upon restriction of the right to introduce evidence, but only where the restriction "offends some principle of justice so rooted in the traditions and conscience of our people as to be ranked as fundamental." See *Patterson* v. *New York*, 432 U.S. 197, 201–202. Respondent has failed to meet the heavy burden of establishing that a defendant's right to have a jury consider voluntary intoxication evidence in determining whether he possesses the requisite mental state is a "fundamental principle of justice." The primary guide in making such a determination, historical practice, gives respondent little support. It was firmly established at common law that a defendant's voluntary intoxication provided neither an "excuse" nor a "justification" for his crimes; the common law's stern rejection of inebriation as a defense must be understood as also precluding a defendant from arguing that, because of his intoxication, he could not have possessed the *mens rea* necessary to commit the crime. The justifications for this common-law rule persist to this day and have only been strengthened by

modern research. Although a rule allowing a jury to consider evidence of a defendant's voluntary intoxication where relevant to *mens rea* has gained considerable acceptance since the nineteenth century, it is of too recent vintage and has not received sufficiently uniform and permanent allegiance to qualify as fundamental, especially since it displaces a lengthy common-law tradition which remains supported by valid justifications. . . .

None of this Court's cases on which the Supreme Court of Montana's conclusion purportedly rested undermines the principle that a state can limit the introduction of relevant evidence for a "valid" reason, as Montana has. The due process clause does not bar states from making changes in their criminal law that have the effect of making it easier for the prosecution to obtain convictions. See *McMillan* v. *Pennsylvania*, 477 U.S. 79, 89, n. 5. . . .

The judgment is reversed.

What do *you* think?

1. How does a claim that (a) an intoxicated defendant should not be held responsible for his or her criminal activity because of the inability to form the requisite *mens rea* for a specific crime differ from the claim that (b) an intoxicated defendant should be excused because he or she had lowered inhibitions and impaired judgment as a consequence of ingesting alcohol? Do both claims carry the same *moral* weight? Why or why not?

2. Do you believe that, as a matter of fundamental due process rights, a defendant should be given the opportunity to present "all relevant evidence to rebut the State's evidence on all elements of the offense charged"? Why or why not?

3. Do you think that, in circumstances such as those described in this box, voluntary intoxication should completely exonerate a defendant of criminal liability because of its impact on the defendant's mental state? Why or why not?

assumed that most people who consume the substance are aware of its effects. Involuntary intoxication, however, may also result from the use of prescription or over-the-counter drugs containing substances with which the user is unfamiliar. One recent case,[13] for example, involved a hunter who assaulted other members of his hunting party. Expert witnesses testified that, at the time of the assaults, the man was suffering from toxic psychosis brought on by the excessive use of cough drops containing the chemical dextromethorphan hydrobromide (he had consumed twelve boxes of the cough drops in a twenty-four-hour period preceding the attacks), and the defendant was acquitted by a trial court.

Finally, involuntary intoxication can also result from a rare biological condition under which a person's body ferments food. The internal fermentation process, which takes place in the intestines, is caused by the yeast *Candida albicans* and can result in drunkenness, even though the afflicted individual has not consumed alcohol.

Involuntary intoxication may serve as a defense if it creates in the defendant an incapacity either to appreciate the criminality of his or her conduct or creates an incapacity to conform his or her behavior to the requirements of the law.

Mistake

In 1992, sixteen-year-old Japanese exchange student Yoshihiro Hattori was shot to death in Baton Rouge, Louisiana, by homeowner Rodney Peairs when he went to the wrong house looking for a Halloween party. Hattori, whose command of the English language was very poor, continued to approach Peairs' home when ordered to stop by an armed Peairs. Peairs was acquitted of manslaughter charges after claiming that he mistakenly thought the student was an intruder.

An honest **mistake of fact** will generally preclude criminal liability in instances where the actions undertaken would have been lawful had the situation been as the person acting reasonably believed them to be. An *honest* mistake means one that is genuine and sincere and not a pretext offered merely to hide criminal intent. A decade ago, for example, many questions were raised when fashion model Jerry Hall was arrested after she picked up a marijuana-filled suitcase in a public baggage claim area at an airport in Barbados. Hall, girlfriend of the rock musician Mick Jagger, claimed that she mistakenly grabbed the bag because it looked just like one she owned. She was released after convincing authorities that the mistake was genuine and after spending a night in jail.

A *reasonable* mistake is one that might be made by a typically competent person acting under the same set of circumstances. A man who forces a woman whom he does not know to accompany him on a journey she does not want to take may, for example, be guilty of kidnapping even though he believed she acquiesced to his requests that she go with him. In just such a case, the Indiana Supreme Court found a defendant guilty of kidnapping a woman who offered no physical resistance out of fear of the defendant—although she expressed verbal reservations. Any reasonable man, under the same circumstances, said the court, would have realized that she did not want to go with him. In the words of the court:

> Appellant's assertion that he did not 'force' the victim out of the laundromat provides some evidence that he honestly so believed. It is, however, no evidence of the reasonableness of that belief. . . . Apart from this statement, we find nothing in the record to suggest that a reasonable man in appellant's position would have interpreted the victim's actions as indicative of her free consent to accompany appellant. By appellant's own version of the encounter the facts are such that no reasonable person could have believed as appellant alleges he did.[14]

MISTAKE OF FACT
misinterpretation, misunderstanding, or forgetfulness of a fact relating to the subject matter at hand; belief in the existence of a thing or condition that does not exist.

Ignorance of the law is no excuse in any country. If it were, the laws would lose their effect, because it can always be pretended.

—Thomas Jefferson (1787)

Web Extra! 6–1
Britannica online: ignorance and mistake

Mistake as to fact should be distinguished from **ignorance of fact.** Ignorance of fact refers to a lack of knowledge of some fact relating to the subject matter at hand, while mistake of fact refers to a misinterpretation or misunderstanding of the facts at hand. Both can be defenses to a criminal charge. As a defense, both ignorance of fact and mistake of fact may negate the *mens rea* required for a specific offense. As one court said, "[t]he criminal intention being of the essence of crime, if the intent is dependent on a knowledge of particular facts, a want of such knowledge, not the result of carelessness or negligence, relieves the act of criminality. . . ."[15]

Some mistakes do not relieve a defendant of criminal liability. A drug dealer who mistakenly purchases heroin, thinking it is cocaine, will still be found guilty of trafficking in a controlled substance.[16] Likewise, when a person intends to commit one crime but actually commits another, his or her mistake will be no defense. So, for example, a burglar who breaks into the wrong house seeking money he has heard is hidden under a mattress will still be guilty of the crime of burglary even though he is unable to locate the cash.

Another form of mistake is **mistake of law.** Generally speaking, however, courts have held that neither **ignorance of the law** (where one does not know a law exists) nor a misunderstanding of the law (i.e., misinterpretation of existing law) provides for an acceptable defense, and criminal proceedings assume that "every one capable of acting for himself knows the law."[17] This assumption does not mean, of course, that everyone is actually familiar with each and every law, but it effectively compels people to learn the standards set by the law in their sphere of activity. In effect, ignorance of the law is a kind of **culpable ignorance,** in which an individual's failure to exercise ordinary care to acquire knowledge of the law may result in criminal liability.

Although quite rare in practice, ignorance or mistake of law may be a defense where a given offense requires specific intent or where mistake of law negates the *mens rea* required by a statute. Recently, for example, in the case of *Ratzlaf* v. *United States* (1994),[18] the U.S. Supreme Court ruled that no one can be convicted of trying to evade specific federal bank reporting requirements that mandate "wilfullness" unless it can be shown that they knew they were violating the law. Federal law requires a domestic bank involved in a cash transaction exceeding $10,000 to file a report with the Secretary of the Treasury; makes it illegal to "structure" a transaction—that is, to break up a single transaction above the reporting threshold into two or more separate transactions "for the purpose of evading the reporting requiremen[t];" and sets out criminal penalties for "[a] person *wilfully* violating" the antistructuring provision.

Waldemar Ratzlaf was found guilty of violating the antistructuring provision of the law after he made a number of cash withdrawals just below the $10,000 threshold in order to pay off gambling obligations. He appealed his conviction, claiming that the "wilfulness" requirement of the law made it necessary for the government to prove that he acted with knowledge that his structuring activities were illegal. The U.S. Supreme Court agreed, ruling that "[t]o give effect to [the statute's] 'wilfulness' requirement, the Government must prove that the defendant acted with knowledge that the structuring he or she undertook was unlawful, not simply that the defendant's purpose was to circumvent a bank's reporting obligation." The Court ruled that "the lower courts erred in treating the 'wilfulness' requirement essentially as words of no consequence." The fact that currency structuring is not necessarily an inherently immoral activity bolstered Ratzlaf's contention that the government had to prove his "wilfulness" in violating the law. In the words of the Court:

> "Because currency structuring is not inevitably nefarious, this Court is unpersuaded by the United States' argument that structuring is so obviously 'evil' or inherently 'bad' that the 'wilfullness' requirement is satisfied irrespective of the

IGNORANCE OF FACT
lack of knowledge of some fact relating to the subject matter at hand.

MISTAKE OF LAW
a misunderstanding or misinterpretation of the law relevant to a situation at hand.

IGNORANCE OF THE LAW
a lack of knowledge of the law or of the existence of a law relevant to a situation at hand.

CULPABLE IGNORANCE
the failure to exercise ordinary care to acquire knowledge of the law or of facts that may result in criminal liability.

Web Extra! 6–2
Ratzlaf v. *U.S.* (1994)

defendant's knowledge of the illegality of structuring," as it might be, for example, in cases of rape or murder.

The Court continued:

> The interpretation adopted in this case does not dishonor the venerable principle that ignorance of the law generally is no defense to a criminal charge, for Congress may decree otherwise in particular contexts, and has done so in the present instance.[19]

⌐ Ignorance of the law may also be an excuse where the law is not adequately published, or is incapable of being known. An individual who violates a federal law by "knowingly making false statements" by placing his or her signature on a complicated government form may, for example, raise just such a defense. In one such case, a defendant signed a federal form required to obtain a firearm, but the form contained references to federal statutes by numbered sections and subsections, without explaining the content or purpose of the law it cited. Although the defendant was technically in violation of the law (he was a convicted felon, and the laws referred to on the form prohibited a convicted felon from purchasing a gun), he claimed that he did not knowingly make a false statement because he was ignorant of what the legal nomenclature on the form meant. Although convicted, a federal appeals court reversed his conviction saying that "many lawyers would not have understood"[20] the language of the form and that it was therefore unreasonable to expect a layman to understand it.

Finally, mistake of law may be a valid defense to a criminal charge if made in good faith under circumstances involving a bona fide attempt to ascertain the meaning of the law through reliance on a public official who is in a position to interpret the statute, or through the use of appropriate legal counsel. In some jurisdictions, a defendant may effectively raise such a defense where "before engaging in the conduct, the defendant made a bona fide, diligent effort, adopting a course and resorting to sources and means at least as appropriate as any afforded under our legal system, to ascertain and abide by the law, and where he acted in good faith reliance upon the results of such effort."[21]

> The man who has maimed, let him be maimed. The man who has killed, let him be killed.
>
> —Anonymous

LAW ON THE BOOKS

"MISTAKE OF LAW" UNDER THE TEXAS PENAL CODE.

Compare with Model Penal Code, Section 2.04

TEXAS PENAL CODE

Section 8.03. MISTAKE OF LAW.
 a. It is no defense to prosecution that the actor was ignorant of the provisions of any law after the law has taken effect.
 b. It is an affirmative defense to prosecution that the actor reasonably believed the conduct charged did not constitute a crime and that he acted in reasonable reliance upon:
   (1) an official statement of the law contained in a written order or grant of permission by an administrative agency charged by law with responsibility for interpreting the law in question; or
   (2) a written interpretation of the law contained in an opinion of a court of record or made by a public official charged by law with responsibility for interpreting the law in question.
 c. Although an actor's mistake of law may constitute a defense to the offense charged, he may nevertheless be convicted of a lesser included offense of which he would be guilty if the law were as he believed.

LAW IN PRACTICE

MISTAKE OF FACT EXONERATES MURDER DEFENDANT OF KIDNAPPING CHARGE

Mistake of fact can be asserted by a defendant to show that, based on the defendant's belief at the time of the illegal activity, no crime occurred because the requisite mens rea *was lacking. In* People v. Tolbert, *56 Cal. Rptr. 2d 604 (1996), a California appellate court case, the court held that a reasonable but mistaken belief in a victim's death prior to movement of that person by the defendant precludes conviction for kidnapping. In* Tolbert, *the defendant shot the victim (Killingbeck) in the right eye with a shotgun at close range—but the victim didn't die. Since the defendant, thinking the victim was dead, then transported the still living body of his victim, he was charged with kidnapping. At trial, Tolbert was found guilty and sentenced on three counts. On count 4 (felon in possession of a firearm) the trial court sentenced him to two years in prison; on count 1 (second-degree murder), the trial court imposed an indeterminate term of twenty-four years to life, to be served consecutively; on count 3, kidnapping for robbery, it imposed an additional life term, plus four years on a personal firearm use enhancement, also to be served consecutively. Tolbert appealed the kidnapping conviction and sentence, claiming that the fact that he believed the victim was dead at the time he transported the body meant he lacked the* mens rea *needed for the crime of kidnapping. The appellate court agreed. Excerpts from the court's opinion follow.*

People v. Tolbert
California Court of Appeals, Fourth Appellate District, 1996
56 Cal. Rptr. 2d 604

[California] Penal Code, Section 26, recites, generally, that one is incapable of committing a crime who commits an act under a mistake of fact disproving any criminal intent. Penal Code Section 20 provides, "In every crime . . . there must exist a union, or joint operation of act and intent, or criminal negligence." The word "intent" in Section 20 means "wrongful intent." "So basic

is this requirement [of a union of act and wrongful intent] that it is an invariable element of every crime unless excluded expressly or by necessary implication." (*People* v. *Mayberry, supra,* 15 Cal. 3d at p. 154, quoting *People* v. *Vogel* (1956) 46 Cal. 2d 798, 801, 801, fn. 2.)

The kidnapping statute "neither expressly nor by necessary implication negate[s] the continuing requirement that there be a union of act and wrongful intent. The severe penalties imposed for th[is] offense . . . and the serious loss of reputation following conviction make it extremely unlikely that the Legislature intended to exclude as to th[is] offense the element of wrongful intent." (*Id.* at p. 155.)

Mistake of fact is an affirmative defense. The defendant therefore has the burden of producing evidence that "he had a *bona fide* and reasonable belief that the [victim] consented to the movement. . . ." (*People* v. *Mayberry, supra,* 15 Cal. 3d at p. 157.) The Supreme Court has since held that this burden may be met with evidence supplied by the prosecution. (*People* v. *Williams* (1992) 4 Cal. 4th 354, 361.) However, because wrongful intent is an element of the crime, the ultimate burden of persuasion is on the people; the defendant is "only required to raise a reasonable doubt as to whether he had such a belief." (*People* v. *Mayberry, supra,* 15 Cal. 3d at p. 157; cf. *People* v. *Curtis* (1994) 30 Cal. App. 4th 1337, 1353 [burden of proving defenses of justification and excuse].)

We find ourselves unable to distinguish a mistake of fact about whether the kidnapping victim consents from a mistake of fact about whether the kidnapping victim is alive. If the victim is dead, he or she is no longer a "person" who can be kidnapped, precisely because he or she can no longer give or withhold consent to the asportation. (Cf. *People* v. *Kelly* (1992) 1 Cal. 4th 495, 524 [it is legally impossible to rape a dead body because "[a] dead body cannot consent to or protest a rape . . ."]; *People* v. *Thompson* (1993) 12 Cal. App. 4th 195, 201 ["the crime of rape requires a live victim, because it requires nonconsensual sexual intercourse."]; *People* v. *Sellers* (1988) 203 Cal. App. 3d 1042, 1050

(continued)

LAW IN PRACTICE

["Rape must be accomplished with a person, not a dead body. It must be accomplished against a person's will. A dead body cannot consent to or protest a rape. . . ."], fn. omitted.) It does appear that under *Mayberry*, knowledge that the victim was alive is not an element of the crime of kidnapping, which the prosecution must prove in all cases; but if there is any evidence that the defendant honestly and reasonably believed the victim was dead, the people must prove beyond a reasonable doubt that the defendant lacked such a belief. . . .

Here, there was ample evidence that defendant reasonably believed Killingbeck was dead before the asportation began. Indeed, it seems amazing that Killingbeck stayed alive for any time at all. He had been shot in the right eye by a shotgun held six to twelve inches away; there was an exit wound behind his right ear. Some of the pellets left through the exit wound, but "lots of them" remained inside. The force was sufficient to leave his head "slightly deformed." He was rendered unconscious instantly; the wound was inevitably fatal. The pathologist testified that Killingbeck was able to live for a little while because the left side of his brain was uninjured, but this would hardly have been obvious to a layman. The fact that defendant believed Killingbeck was dead is further evidenced by his comment to Tim that there was "a dead body" in the car, even though Killingbeck actually was still alive at the time.

Thus, it is inferable that defendant reasonably believed Killingbeck died immediately after he was shot. On the other hand, there is no evidence that

defendant did not reasonably believe Killingbeck died immediately. Certainly one could imagine all sorts of scenarios in which defendant could have realized Killingbeck was still alive; he might have noticed that Killingbeck was still breathing before he closed the trunk; or he might have stopped the car at some point and opened the trunk to check on Killingbeck. "But speculation is not evidence, less still substantial evidence." (*People* v. *Berryman* (1993) 6 Cal. 4th 1048, 1081.). . . .

The only sufficient asportation here consisted of the movement of the car around Rubidoux with Killingbeck in the trunk. There was substantial evidence that at this point defendant honestly and reasonably believed Killingbeck was dead; there was no substantial evidence to the contrary. Accordingly, the kidnapping for robbery conviction must be reversed. Retrial is barred by double jeopardy. . . .

The kidnapping for robbery conviction is reversed, and the case is remanded for resentencing. In all other respects, the judgment is affirmed.

[footnotes omitted]

What do *you* think?

1. Should mistake of fact exonerate a defendant who, through criminal activity, brings about a situation (as in this case) that causes him to mistake the facts?

2. How does the court's reasoning that "a dead woman cannot be raped" support its position in this case? Do you agree with such reasoning? Why or why not?

Age

INFANCY DEFENSE

also **immaturity defense;** a defense that makes the claim that certain individuals should not be held criminally responsible for their activities by virtue of youth.

Defenses based on age, also called **infancy** or **immaturity defenses,** make the claim that certain individuals should not be held criminally responsible for their activities by virtue of youth. The defense of infancy has its origin in early Christian teachings, which held that children under the age of seven were incapable of rational thought and planned action. Under common law, children below the age of seven were presumed to be without criminal capacity—that is, to be incapable of forming the *mens rea* needed for criminal activity. Today that rule still holds, and in most states children below the age of seven cannot be charged even with juvenile offenses, no matter how serious their actions. However, in a startling 1994 case, prosecutors in Cincinnati, Ohio, charged a twelve-year-old girl with murder after she confessed to

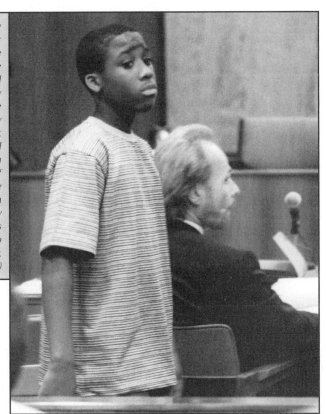

Youthful status has traditionally limited criminal responsibility. Under common law, children under the age of seven were considered to be incapable of rational thought and planned action. Most states today limit the liability of anyone under the age of eighteen by refusing to try juveniles as adults. In 1999, however, thirteen-year-old Nathaniel Abraham, shown here, was tried as an adult and convicted of the murder of an eighteen year old—a crime committed in 1997 when Abraham was only eleven years old. Many people saw Abraham's conviction as indicative of a changing trend. (Photo by The Oakland Press/Jose Jaurez, courtesy of AP/Wide World Photos.)

drowning her toddler cousin ten years earlier—when the girl was only two years old! The cousin, thirteen-month-old Lamar Howell, drowned in 1984 in a bucket of bleach mixed with water. Howell's drowning had been ruled an accidental death until his cousin confessed. In discussing the charges with the media, Hamilton (Ohio) County prosecutor Joe Deters admitted that the girl could not be prosecuted. "Frankly," he said, "anything under seven cannot be an age where you form criminal intent. . . ."[22] The prosecution's goal, claimed one of Deters' associates, was simply to "make sure she gets the counseling she needs."

Another rationale for the defense of infancy questions the assertion that children are too young to form the *mens rea* required for a criminal act and is based instead on the belief that children—although they may act wilfully—are too young to "know any better." As one writer says: "The reason society holds minors free from criminal liability is not because they are too young to form a criminal intent, but because they are presumed to be too young to make a conscious, moral choice between doing good and doing evil."[23]

Most jurisdictions today do not impose full criminal culpability on children under the age of eighteen, while a number of states set the age of responsibility at sixteen, and some at seventeen. In an effort to avoid stigmatization that might follow them throughout life, children who violate the criminal law are officially referred to as **juvenile offenders** rather than as "criminals." Juvenile offenders may be adjudicated "delinquent," but they are not "found guilty."

Children under the age of criminal responsibility are subject to juvenile court jurisdiction, rather than to the jurisdiction of adult criminal courts, although almost all states allow for a transfer of older children to criminal court jurisdiction if the crimes they are charged with are especially serious, or if the children are habitually in trouble with the law. Transfer to adult court requires a showing by the prosecution that the child was able to "appreciate the wrongfulness of their conduct," that

JUVENILE OFFENDER
a child who violates the criminal law, or who commits a status offense. Also, a person subject to juvenile court proceedings because a statutorily defined event caused by the person was alleged to have occurred while his or her age was below the statutorily specified age limit of original jurisdiction of a juvenile court.

the child had "a guilty knowledge of wrongdoing," or that the child was "competent to know the nature and consequences of his conduct and to know that it was wrong." Some states specify that juvenile courts have no jurisdiction over certain excluded offenses. Delaware, Louisiana, and Nevada, for example, allow no juvenile court jurisdiction over children charged with first-degree murder.

In a hearing that made headlines some years ago, Cameron Kocher, a ten-year-old Pennsylvania youngster, was arraigned as an adult for the murder of his seven-year-old neighbor Jessica Carr.[24] Cameron, who was only nine years old at the time of the crime, was alleged to have used his father's scope-sighted hunting rifle to shoot the girl from a bedroom window while she was riding on a snowmobile in a neighbor's yard. The two had argued earlier over who would get to ride on the vehicle. The case was resolved in 1992, when the Pennsylvania Supreme Court overturned Kocher's arraignment as an adult, and the boy was placed on juvenile probation.

The defense of infancy is based on the chronological age of the defendant, and has not been successful when based upon claims of *mental* immaturity. Courts have held that persons who have passed the chronological age necessary for criminal responsibility cannot raise the defense of infancy based upon psychological determinations of mental immaturity because "if by reason of mental disease or defect a particular individual has not acquired [the ability to observe legal requirements] his remedy is a defense based on idiocy or insanity."[25] The following Law on the Books section contains a section of the Texas Penal Code highlighting the relationship between age and criminal responsibility in that state.

LAW ON THE BOOKS

"AGE AFFECTING CRIMINAL RESPONSIBILITY" UNDER THE TEXAS PENAL CODE.

Compare with Model Penal Code, Section 4.10

TEXAS PENAL CODE

Section 8.07. AGE AFFECTING CRIMINAL RESPONSIBILITY.
   a. A person may not be prosecuted for or convicted of any offense that he committed when younger than fifteen years of age except:
      (1) perjury and aggravated perjury when it appears by proof that he had sufficient discretion to understand the nature and obligation of an oath;
      (2) a violation of a penal statute cognizable under Chapter 302, Acts of the 55th Legislature, Regular Session, 1957 (Article 67011-4, *Vernon's Texas Civil Statutes*),
      (3) a violation of a motor vehicle traffic ordinance of an incorporated city or town in this state;
      (4) a misdemeanor punishable by fine only, other than public intoxication;
      (5) a violation of a penal ordinance of a political subdivision; OR
      (6) a violation of a penal statute that is, or is a lesser included offense of, a capital felony, an aggravated controlled substance felony, or a felony of the first degree for which the person is transferred to the court under Section 54.02, Family Code, for prosecution if the person committed the offense when fourteen years of age or older.
   b. Unless the juvenile court waives jurisdiction under Section 54.02, Family Code, and certifies the individual for criminal prosecution or the juvenile court has previously waived jurisdiction under that section and certified the individual for criminal prosecution, a person may not be prosecuted for or convicted of any offense committed before reaching seventeen years of age except an offense described by subsections (a)(1)-(5). No person may, in any case, be punished by death for an offense committed while he was younger than seventeen years.

CRIMINAL LAW IN THE NEWS

Ruling Defines Limits of Online Sex Stings

Pedophile Suspect Entrapped by Overeager Investigators

NEW YORK—Finding would-be pedophiles on the Internet is easy. Convicting them is harder—even when they're caught walking into a hotel room on the promise of having sex with three underage girls.

That's the lesson from a federal appeals court ruling this week, which overturned the conviction of a Florida man who was arrested under just those circumstances as a result of a police sting. The court ruled that Mark Poehlman was entrapped by the task force involving FBI, Navy and county officials, and his 10-year prison sentence was set aside.

The ruling, say experts, will further define how such law enforcement operations can be handled—and perhaps give those looking to engaging in child pornography tips on how to avoid getting caught.

"This is a question of civil rights and due process," said Parry Aftab, executive director of Cyberangels.org, a volunteer organization that works with law enforcement on matters of Internet safety, including child pornography and stalking.

"It is so hard to do this right," Aftab said of cyber-stings. "Many local police haven't been trained in how to do it right, and often they end up letting pedophiles go free. The key is not to cross the line between being a victim and entrapment."

Travelers and transmitters

Catching sexual predators online has become a regular feature of law enforcement. Many local, county and state agencies have set up their own task forces, and more than a few civilians have engaged in the practice on their own.

To make these arrests properly, said Pete Gulotta of the FBI's Innocent Images task force, a would-be pedophile must first be identified and then caught committing a criminal act. "There are two kinds of predators," said Gulotta. "We call them travelers and transmitters."

Travelers are those who physically go on the road to meet a child on the promise of sex; transmitters are those who send pornographic images of children over the Internet. Arrests of transmitters outnumber those of travelers 3-to-1, said Gulotta, mostly because there are a lot more of them out there.

"It usually gets very graphic"

But travelers, because they present a physical threat to children, are the FBI's chief targets.

"Our agents pose as a young boy or a young girl in 'predicated chat rooms,' " he said, defining those as sites that have blatant signs of serving adults looking for children for sexual purposes.

"Sometimes it's obvious just from their names—like 'older men looking for younger boys.' In a short period of time the agent is contacted by an individual, and it usually gets very graphic."

The agent then begins an online relationship with the suspect.

"A meeting is set up in which the individual travels from one state to another," he said.

"We meet him there, and he is arrested and charged."

Must be suspect's idea

The problem in the California case, according to the 9th Circuit Court of Appeals, happened well before Poehlman was arrested and charged. The court ruled that Poehlman was induced to commit the crime by law enforcement, and that he would not have committed it without those suggestions.

"U.S. law," said Aftab, "allows you to be a victim—a very attractive victim—but not to entice someone into doing something they ordinarily might not do. You can't go first.

"It's like when we were kids. You have to be able to say 'It was his idea.' "

Gulotta, while stressing he was not familiar with the Poehlman case and could not comment on it, summed it up similarly: "In layman's terms, whose idea is this, anyway?"

If it's not the idea of the suspect, then the case is in trouble.

Investigator made suggestion

That was what transpired in the Poehlman case, according to the appeals court ruling.

The case dates back to 1995, when Poehlman—recently divorced, just retired from the Air Force and living in Florida—began frequenting Internet chat rooms and discussion groups for "alternative lifestyles."

He received a response from a woman named Sharon—really an undercover law enforcement agent—who explained that she was a divorced mother of three young girls who needed "someone to help with their special education."

Poehlman replied that he was seeking "a long-term relationship leading to marriage" with a woman who would not be bothered by his "unique needs"—dressing up like a woman and a sexual attraction to feet.

"If you don't mind me wearing your hose and licking your toes," he wrote to Sharon, "then I am open for anything."

He also said that, although he was uncertain what she meant by "special teacher," he would willingly teach the girls—ages 7, 10 and 12—"proper morals and give support to them where it is needed."

"Tell me more"

But that, apparently, wasn't what Sharon had in mind. She wrote back,

(continued)

CRIMINAL LAW IN THE NEWS

Ruling Defines Limits of Online Sex Stings

Pedophile Suspect Entrapped by Overeager Investigators

asking that Poehlman "let me know what you have in mind for the darlings," and to "tell me more about how their first lesson will go."

"I do like to watch, though," she wrote to him. "I hope you don't think I'm too weird."

Sharon also talked of her own "special teacher"—"I still get goose bumps thinking about it"—and that her daughters were "very excited" about having their own special teacher.

"Poehlman finally got the hint," wrote Judge Alex Kozinski in the majority opinion, and he began sending Sharon graphic descriptions of sexual acts he would perform with the children—"acts too tasteless to mention," wrote the judge.

State and federal charges

After months of correspondence, Poehlman eventually traveled to California and met in a hotel room with an agent posing as Sharon. She offered him some child pornography magazines, which he accepted, and led him into an adjoining room where daughters Karen, Bonnie and Abby were to be waiting for their first lesson.

Instead, Poehlman was met by FBI and Naval Criminal Investigation agents and Los Angeles County sheriff's officers. He was arrested and charged with attempted lewd acts with a minor, to which he pleaded no contest in return for time served in county jail.

Two years after his release, however, Poehlman was arrested again and charged with federal crimes arising from the same incident. This time he received 10 years in federal prison.

"It's just not right"

Poehlman's attorney in the federal case, Edward M. Robinson, said the second indictment came as a shock.

"It's absurd what happened to Mark, it's just not right," said Robinson. "We never considered settling the case because legally it lacked merit."

The court, on appeal, agreed.

"Had Sharon merely responded enthusiastically to a hint from Poehlman that he wanted to serve as her daughters' sexual mentor, there certainly would have been an inducement," Kozinski wrote. "But Sharon did much more than that."

The court wrote that Poehlman was "harmlessly cruising the Internet looking for an adult relationship; the idea of sex with children had not entered his mind."

The court was especially harsh on the task force that arrested Poehlman.

"There is surely enough real crime in our society that it is unnecessary for our law enforcement officials to spend months luring an obviously lonely and confused individual to cross the line between fantasy and criminality," Kozinski wrote.

A lesson for investigators

"This appears to be a classic case of bait-and-switch," said Jim Dempsey of the Center for Democracy and Technology, a privacy and civil liberty advocacy group in Washington. "It sounds as if the government was out of line with this one. The only surprising thing is that the task force could've gone this far down the line with the case."

Dempsey called the decision "a healthy one" that should not have a great effect on pedophile investiga-

tions—except to make them better by serving as a lesson.

"The government has made a lot of good cases," he said, "this one was a bad scenario, a losing scenario."

The U.S. attorney's office for the Central District of California, which argued the case, would not offer any specific comment on the ruling, releasing only this statement: "We are disappointed by the court's decision, but we understand that the court has spoken."

A warning for pedophiles

For the FBI's Gulotta, the case might also serve as warning to other sexual predators.

"The people who commit these crimes against children are bright people," he said. "Many of them are above-average intelligence, with more money than most professionals. We've arrested elementary school principals, military officers, computer programmers, attorneys, accountants, even a Broadway producer.

"They read the paper and learn from these things. The next time they'll be more careful."

Gulotta also knows about sexual predators first hand. He said he once intercepted a phone call meant for his daughter—and it turned out to be a pedophile to whom she'd given out the phone number.

He realized then, he said, how easy it was to prey on children.

"That hit home with me," he said.

Source: Kenneth Pringle, "Ruling Defines Limits of Online Sex Stings; Pedophile Suspect Entrapped by Overeager Investigators," APB News. June 29, 2000. Reprinted with permission.

Entrapment

A box[26] in this section describes how the conviction[27] of accused Internet pedophile Mark Poehlman was overturned when a federal judge ruled that he had been illegally entrapped by law enforcement agents. The defense of **entrapment** is built on the assertion that, in some situations, were it not for government instigation, no crime would occur. Entrapment defenses may be raised where public law enforcement officials or persons acting on their behalf induce or encourage an otherwise law-abiding person to engage in illegal activity. In effect, the defense of entrapment claims that law enforcement officers are guilty of manufacturing a crime where none would otherwise exist.

Entrapment activities may include a number of inducements to crime, but the two most common are: (1) false representation by agents of enforcement that are calculated to induce the belief that the illegal behavior is not prohibited, and (2) the use of inducements to crime that are so strong that a person of average will and good intent cannot resist.

The judge in Poehlman's case found that agents had improperly induced the defendant to commit the crime. "Had Sharon merely responded enthusiastically to a hint from Poehlman that he wanted to serve as her daughters' sexual mentor, there certainly would have been an inducement," the judge wrote. "But Sharon did much more than that. . . . [She] did not merely invite Poehlman to have a sexual relationship with her minor daughters, she made it a condition of her own continued interest in him." The court concluded that, at the time he encountered Sharon, Poehlman had been "harmlessly cruising the Internet looking for an adult relationship; the idea of sex with children had not entered his mind."

Entrapment cannot be effectively raised as a defense, however, where government employees "merely afford opportunities or facilities for the commission of the offense," or where law enforcement officers or their representatives engage in the "mere fact of deceit."[28] In other words, an undercover "sting" operation set up by the government to lure burglars and thieves wanting to sell stolen goods would be legal, while government enticements to steal might not be.

U.S. Supreme Court cases have differentiated between a "subjective approach" to gauging entrapment and an "objective approach," which developed later. The subjective approach excludes from criminal liability persons "otherwise innocent, who have been lured to the commission of the prohibited act through the Government's instigation."[29] The subjective approach attempts to distinguish between those who are blameworthy and those who are not, by asking whether a person "caught" by the government was predisposed to commit the crime in question. In doing so, it distinguishes "unwary criminals" ready and willing to commit the offense when presented with a favorable opportunity, from those who are not. Some courts have held that predisposition can be established by demonstrating a defendant's: (1) prior convictions for similar crimes, (2) reputation for committing similar crimes, or (3) readiness to engage in a crime suggested by the police.[30] The subjective test for entrapment uses the criterion of "origin of intent," and asks "[d]id the criminal intent start in the mind of the officers, or was the defendant 'predisposed' to commit the offense when the officer first appeared on the scene?"[31] Hence, following the subjective approach, traps may be legitimately laid by the government only for those who are already bent on crime.

The objective approach to entrapment is based on "the belief that the methods employed on behalf of the Government to bring about conviction cannot be countenanced."[32] If government agents have acted in such a way as is likely to instigate or create a criminal offense, regardless of the predisposition to crime of a particular defendant, then—according to the objective approach to assessing entrapment—the

ENTRAPMENT
an improper or illegal inducement to crime by agents of enforcement. Also, a defense that may be raised when such inducements occur.

Web Extra! 6–3
Sorrells v. *U.S.* (1932)

CRIMINAL LAW IN THE NEWS

Wiretap Ruling May Tame 'Carnivore'

Privacy Experts Say FBI Surveillance System Too Intrusive

WASHINGTON—Privacy advocates say an appeals court decision limiting government wiretap capabilities will have far-reaching implications, among them delivering a severe blow to the future of the FBI's controversial Internet surveillance system known as Carnivore.

In its ruling Tuesday, the U.S. Court of Appeals for the District of Columbia threw out sections of rules adopted by the Federal Communications Commissions to enforce the 1994 electronic wiretap law. The provisions gave federal authorities access to all phone numbers called by the subject of a wiretap.

The measure was designed to help authorities track suspects who use 1-800 numbers, calling cards, or phone cards, which allow them to remain anonymous, officials said.

"The decision says that government agencies cannot cut constitutional corners," said James Dempsey, director of the Center for Democracy and Technology, a privacy advocacy group. "They have to meet the highest Fourth Amendment standard, which is the obtaining of a search warrant on probable cause."

Privacy vs. effectiveness

But federal authorities said the kind of wiretap currently under scrutiny is essential to 21st-century crime fighting efforts.

"In the analog world before phone cards, there was no problem [establishing a direct connection] from drug dealer X to drug dealer Y," said Assistant Attorney General Stephen Colgate. "In the new world, someone can go to 1-800-CALL ATT and all we'll get is the network phone number."

Privacy rights advocates said the decision supports their belief that the e-mail surveillance system Carnivore is too intrusive. The system, which has the ability to scan vast amounts of e-mail traffic via Internet Service Providers, has been criticized by members of Congress and private sector groups.

"It darkens the shadow of doubt over the legality of Carnivore," said Dempsey. "[The FBI] is getting access to information it is not authorized to see just because they promise they won't read it."

He said that, while the decision may not kill Carnivore, "in the short run," it is "another strike against the system."

Too soon to declare victory

But FBI and Justice Department officials said it is too early to determine the implications of the court ruling.

"[The privacy groups] may be rushing out to call it a victory, but we are still reviewing what it means," said FBI spokesman Paul Bresson.

Colgate said the Justice Department would include the case in its ongoing review of Carnivore.

FBI officials are meeting with the Justice Department today to discuss the case, even as they respond to an order from Attorney General Janet Reno to select an independent academic institution to review Carnivore, Bresson said.

Need for new standards

Dempsey said the decision also raises questions about the FCC and whether it is fulfilling its regulatory role.

"It is setting a precedent," he said. "Can the FBI come in and dictate design standards? Will the FCC back them up or constrain them? The court said the role of the FCC should be to scrutinize [FBI] demands."

Colgate said he does not view the court's ruling as a win–lose situation. "It instructed the FCC about what needed to be addressed in order for them to reissue the standards that were vacated."

In the meantime, he said, there will be a delay in issuing such wiretaps until "we get the standards reintroduced."

Source: Amy Worden, "Wiretap Ruling May Tame 'Carnivore'; Privacy Experts Say FBI Surveillance System Too Intrusive," APBNews. August 16, 2000. Reprinted with permission.

OUTRAGEOUS GOVERNMENT CONDUCT

a kind of entrapment defense based on an objective criterion involving "the belief that the methods employed on behalf of the Government to bring about conviction cannot be countenanced."[33]

defendant could successfully raise the defense of entrapment. The objective approach to assessing entrapment is sometimes separately referred to as the defense of **outrageous government conduct.**

Definitive federal cases in the area of the entrapment defense include *Sorrells* v. *United States* (1932)[34], *Sherman* v. *United States* (1958)[35], and *Jacobson* v. *United States* (1992)[36]. In *Jacobson* v. *United States*[37], the U.S. Supreme Court ruled that, "In their zeal to enforce the law . . . government agents may not originate a criminal design, implant in an innocent person's mind the disposition to commit a criminal act, and then induce commission of the crime so that the government may prosecute." (See the Capstone Case at the end of this chapter.) However, since the decisions by the U.S. Supreme Court in the area of entrapment defense are not based on constitu-

LAW ON THE BOOKS

"ENTRAPMENT" UNDER PENNSYLVANIA LAW.

Compare with Model Penal Code, Section 2.13

PENNSYLVANIA CONSOLIDATED STATUTES

Title 18, Section 313. ENTRAPMENT.
  a. General rule.—A public law enforcement official or a person acting in cooperation with such an official perpetrates an entrapment if for the purpose of obtaining evidence of the commission of an offense, he induces or encourages another person to engage in conduct constituting such offense by either:
     (1) making knowingly false representations designed to induce the belief that such conduct is not prohibited; or
     (2) employing methods of persuasion or inducement which create a substantial risk that such an offense will be committed by persons other than those who are ready to commit it.
  b. Burden of proof.—Except as provided in subsection (c) of this section, a person prosecuted for an offense shall be acquitted if he proves by a preponderance of evidence that his conduct occurred in response to an entrapment.
  c. Exception.—The defense afforded by this section is unavailable when causing or threatening bodily injury is an element of the offense charged and the prosecution is based on conduct causing or threatening such injury to a person other than the person perpetrating the entrapment.

tional principles, they are not binding on the states. Nonetheless, all states recognize the defense of entrapment, and some have codified it (as the above box on Pennsylvania law shows). Most states follow a subjective approach in assessing claims of entrapment raised by a defendant. A dozen states, on the other hand, follow an objective approach. No jurisdiction permits the excuse of entrapment to serve as a defense to serious crimes, such as murder and rape.

Syndrome-Based Defense Enhancements

In 1997, sixteen-year-old Jarred Viktor of Escondido, California, was arrested and charged with the brutal murder of his step-grandmother, fifty-three-year-old Elizabeth "Betty" Carroll. Carroll, who was killed in the hallway of her home, was slashed and stabbed sixty-one times in a vicious killing that sent shockwaves through the local community. At the time of the murder, Viktor, a troubled teen, had been studying at home after being kicked out of high school. He was arrested hours after the killing, along with his girlfriend, when he crashed his grandmother's stolen Mustang in which the two had been riding. Following the crash, Viktor confessed to the murder. In an interesting twist, however, defense attorney Jeff Martin tried to show jurors that Viktor—because of his use of a powerful antidepressant called Paxil, and his intense involvement in the popular Nintendo game called *Zelda: Link to the Past*—was unable to form the intent required for a murder conviction. In *Zelda,* players arm themselves with a "master sword," and then repeatedly stab at obstacles blocking their progress to higher levels. According to attorney Martin, "He played, excessively, these role-playing video games, for hours at a time. And it's my understanding that *Zelda* is a game where you progress through it by stabbing, and being rewarded for that." Martin's gambit was unsuccessful, and Viktor—convicted of first-degree murder—was sentenced to life in prison without the possibility of parole.

The Viktor case, however, remains characteristic of new and innovative defense strategies that make use of enhancements to traditional defenses—with varying degrees of success. Primary among such strategies has been the use of claimed syndromes to broaden the scope of existing defenses. Some defense attorneys, for example, have attempted to employ BWS, or battered woman's syndrome, in an effort to show how battered wives who kill their abusive husbands were really acting in self-defense. Others have used syndrome-based defense enhancements to lessen the degree of an offender's criminal liability, where some accountability remains.

Other claimed "syndromes" used for such purposes include battered child's syndrome, rape trauma syndrome, sexual abuse syndrome, urban survival syndrome, and black rage syndrome. Syndromes, because they refer to personal abnormalities, generally supplement defenses based on excuses rather than those claiming justifications. "[A]bnormalities are usually excusing conditions that bear on the accused's responsibility, rather than objectively justifying conditions that make otherwise wrongful conduct right under the circumstances."[38]

SYNDROME

a complex of signs and symptoms presenting a clinical picture of a disease or disorder.[39]

In the medical literature, a **syndrome** is defined as "a complex of signs and symptoms presenting a clinical picture of a disease or disorder."[40] If it can be demonstrated that a person charged with a crime was "suffering" from a known syndrome at the time that the crime was committed, such a showing may lower or eliminate criminal liability in at least three ways: (1) it may help support the applicability of a traditional defense (including a justification), (2) it may expand the applicability of traditional defenses (including justifications) to novel or unusual situations, or to situations where such defenses might not otherwise apply, or (3) it may negate the *mens rea* needed to prove the offense, leading the jury or trial judge to conclude that a crucial element necessary to prove the crime with which the defendant is charged is missing. Some suggest a fourth possibility, however, and that is "the creation of new affirmative defenses,"[41] in which novel and unique defenses, beyond those now recognized by law, would take their place alongside of other more traditional defenses, such as duress, mistake, self-defense, and so on. Defenses predicated on, or substantially enhanced by, the acceptability of syndrome-related claims are termed **syndrome-based defenses.**

SYNDROME-BASED DEFENSE

a defense predicated on, or substantially enhanced by, the acceptability of syndrome-related claims.

As a matter of constitutional law, any defendant is entitled to introduce evidence that might disprove any element of the crime with which he or she is charged. As a consequence, many efforts to employ syndromes as defenses have built on the supposed worth of syndrome-based defenses to demonstrate that, at the time of the crime, the defendant was unable to form the *mens rea* required by law for commission of the offense. Convincing arguments of this sort, however, have been difficult to make because few syndromes are medically well-documented, and fewer still have found an established place within American legal tradition.

Although courts have been reluctant to recognize the claim that syndromes negate *mens rea*, the use of syndromes in expanding the applicability of traditional defenses has met with greater success. In such a role, syndromes—in and of themselves—provide neither a justification nor an excuse for otherwise criminal behavior. Syndromes may be called on, however, to explain why a given individual in a particular situation should be held to a different set of standards than those to which a typical "reasonable person" is held. Should the actions of a battered woman, for example, be judged according to the criterion of a "reasonable battered woman" rather than that of a reasonable nonbattered person? If so, the fact that a woman suffering from a history of spousal abuse chose to kill her husband might be defensible under the doctrine of self-defense, even though an otherwise "reasonable" person (with no history of spouse abuse) might have been expected to leave the marital relationship rather than kill. Defenses that might be "expanded" by syndromes include self-defense and diminished responsibility (discussed in the next chapter).

Finally, some suggest that syndrome-based defenses should be recognized as new affirmative defenses, and that their legitimacy should be predicated on the widely accepted legal principle that only those who are morally responsible should be punished for their acts. Western jurisprudence has generally held that where moral responsibility does not exist, for whatever reason, it is unjust to punish one who violates the criminal law. Advocates of such wholesale adoption of syndrome-based defenses suggest a "totality of circumstances" approach, which would allow a defendant to present any evidence that may have some bearing on his motivation. Under this approach, juries would be faced with deciding the question of whether the individual acted "voluntarily" or whether, instead, his behavior was a quasi-automatic product of forces beyond his control.

Battered Woman's Syndrome Battered woman's syndrome (BWS) is the best known of the syndromes on which today's innovative defenses are based. BWS, sometimes also referred to as "battered spouse syndrome" or "battered person's syndrome," entered contemporary awareness with the 1979 publication of Lenore Walker's book, *The Battered Woman*. Defense attorneys were quick to use Walker's slogan of "learned helplessness" to explain why battered women were unable to leave abusive situations, and why they sometimes found it necessary to resort to violence to free themselves from it. Walker helped popularize the syndrome in legal circles by testifying at a number of trials as an expert witness. **Battered woman's syndrome** has been defined by the New Jersey Supreme Court as "a series of common characteristics that appear in women who are abused physically and psychologically over an extended period of time by the dominant male figure in their lives; a pattern of psychological symptoms that develop after somebody has lived in a battering relationship; or a pattern of responses and perceptions presumed to be characteristic of women who have been subjected to continuous physical abuse by their mate[s]."[43]

As is the case with syndromes generally, BWS is not in itself a defense. It is a *condition* said to characterize women who live in abusive relationships. BWS may, however, provide additional justification for a woman who kills a battering spouse during an episode of battering—when the threat of serious bodily harm or death is imminent. As an excuse for killings that do not occur within the context of an immediate threat, however, BWS has proven less effective in eliminating criminal liability, although it may lessen it (resulting, for example, in a manslaughter conviction rather than one of first-degree or second-degree murder).

An oft-cited example of BWS is the 1989 North Carolina case of *State v. Norman*. The case illustrates some of the difficult issues involved in any defense invoking a BWS claim. In *Norman*, the defendant, Judy Norman, was arrested and tried in 1987 for the first-degree murder of her husband, J.T. Norman, whom she shot three times in the back of the head as he slept. Judy and J.T.'s twenty-five years of marriage had been stormy and fraught with violence. As the state's supreme court later observed:

> The defendant presented evidence tending to show a long history of physical and mental abuse by her husband due to his alcoholism. . . . The defendant testified that her husband had started drinking and abusing her about five years after they were married. His physical abuse of her consisted of frequent assaults that included slapping, punching and kicking her, striking her with various objects, and throwing glasses, beer bottles and other objects at her. The defendant described other specific incidents of abuse, such as her husband putting her cigarettes out on her, throwing hot coffee on her, breaking glass against her face, and crushing food on her face . . . The defendant's evidence also tended to show other indignities inflicted upon her by her husband. Her evidence tended to show that her husband did not work and forced her to make money by prostitution, and that he made humor of the fact to family and friends. He would beat her if she

BATTERED WOMAN'S SYNDROME also **battered person's syndrome;** a condition characterized by a history of repetitive spousal abuse and learned helplessness—or the subjective inability to leave an abusive situation. BWS has been defined by California courts as "a series of common characteristics that appear in women who are abused physically and psychologically over an extended period of time by the dominant male figure in their lives; a pattern of psychological symptoms that develop after somebody has lived in a battering relationship; or a pattern of responses and perceptions presumed to be characteristic of women who have been subjected to continuous physical abuse by their mate[s]."[42]

The common characteristics of a battered wife [include] her inability to leave despite . . . constant beatings; her "learned helplessness," her lack of anywhere to go; her feelings that if she tried to leave, she would be subjected to even more merciless treatment; her belief in the omnipotence of her battering husband; and sometimes her hope that her husband will change his ways.

—Chief Justice Robert N. Wilentz, New Jersey Supreme Court *State v. Kelly*, 478 A.2d 364 (1984) resisted going out to prostitute herself or if he was unsatisfied with the amounts of money she made. He routinely called the defendant 'dog,' 'bitch' and 'whore,' and on a few occasions made her eat pet food out of the pet's bowls and bark like a dog. He often made her sleep on the floor. At times, he deprived her of food and refused to let her get food for the family. During those years of abuse, the defendant's husband threatened numerous times to kill her and to maim her in various ways.[44]

On the day of the killing, J.T. Norman had again beaten his wife, and when nighttime came ordered her to sleep on the bedroom floor, telling her "that's where dogs sleep." Mrs. Norman found that she couldn't sleep, walked to a neighboring house to find pain pills, but discovered a pistol instead. She took the weapon back to her home and shot her husband in the back of the head as he slept. After the first shot had been fired, she felt her husband's chest and, after determining that he was still breathing, shot him twice more in the head.

Two expert witnesses in forensic psychiatry examined Mrs. Norman after the shooting and testified at trial that the defendant fit the profile of a battered woman. The condition, they testified, "is characterized by such abuse and degradation that the battered wife comes to believe she is unable to help herself and cannot expect help from anyone else." A psychologist testified that Mrs. Norman believed it was reasonably necessary for her to shoot her husband because she thought herself doomed to "a life of the worst kind of torture and abuse . . . [and] that it would only get worse, and that death was inevitable."

At the close of trial, Mrs. Norman's attorneys asked the jury to acquit her of all charges because, they claimed, given her circumstances, the killing of her husband had been an act of reasonable self-defense. The jury, however, returned a verdict of "guilty" on one charge of voluntary manslaughter, and Mrs. Norman was sentenced to six years' imprisonment. She appealed, saying that the trial court should have more fully considered her claim of self-defense based on BWS. The North Carolina Court of Appeals granted a new trial, ruling that the trial court should have instructed the jury of the possibility of returning a "not guilty" verdict based on the claim of self-defense. The court of appeals reasoned that "when there is evidence of battered wife syndrome, neither an actual attack nor threat of attack by the husband at the moment the wife uses deadly force is required to justify the wife's killing of him in . . . self-defense." The appellate court concluded that "to impose such requirements would ignore the 'learned helplessness,' meekness, and other realities of battered wife syndrome and would effectively preclude such women from exercising their right of self-defense." In the words of the court: "A jury, in our view, could find that decedent's sleep was but a momentary hiatus in a continuous reign of terror by the decedent, that defendant merely took advantage of her first opportunity to protect herself, and that defendant's act was not without the provocation required for perfect self-defense."

Eventually the *Norman* case reached the North Carolina Supreme Court. That court overruled the appellate court's decision, finding that an immediate threat to the defendant was lacking because of the nonconfrontational circumstances surrounding the killing. A valid claim of self-defense, the supreme court ruled, can only be based on evidence "tending to show that, at the time of the killing, the defendant reasonably believed herself to be confronted by circumstances which necessitated her killing her husband to save herself from imminent death or great bodily harm." The term "imminent," said the court, can be defined as "immediate danger, such as must be instantly met, such as cannot be guarded against by calling for the assistance of others or the protection of the law. . . ." Since no imminent harm was about to befall the defendant at the time she shot her husband, the court reasoned, the claim of self-defense was not justified.

In this case, the North Carolina Supreme Court judged the actions of Mrs. Norman according to traditionally accepted standards of self-defense. As mentioned in

Chapter 5, such standards rely on the *objective* criterion of what a "reasonable person" would do under the same circumstances. Although the appellate court was willing to modify the standards for a claim of self-defense by allowing a *subjective* evaluation of reasonableness—that is, that an habitually battered woman might reason differently than would an average, normal, and sensible human being—the state's supreme court was not.

BWS is an area of the law which is still in flux. Some states, such as California, specifically permit expert testimony regarding BWS concerning "the physical, emotional, or mental effects upon the beliefs, perceptions, or behavior of victims of domestic violence . . .,"[45] while others make no specific provision for the admissibility of BWS testimony. Such testimony, however, when it is available, may help juries better understand claims of self-defense made by battered women. As one Kansas court explained: "Expert testimony on the battered woman syndrome would help dispel the ordinary lay person's perception that a woman in a battering relationship is free to leave at any time. The expert evidence would counter any 'common sense' conclusions by the jury that if the beatings were really that bad the woman would have left her husband much earlier. Popular misconceptions about battered women would be put to rest, including the beliefs the women are masochistic and enjoy the beatings and that they intentionally provoke their husbands into fits of rage."[46] At the same time, defense initiatives based on a view of BWS *as a syndrome* may one day effectively extend the role of BWS beyond that of merely expanding self-defense claims and into the role of an excuse, such as duress or diminished capacity.

Efforts at clarification continue. Section 40507 of the Violent Crime Control and Law Enforcement Act of 1994 requires the U.S. Attorney General and the Secretary of Health and Human Services to undertake a study of battered women's syndrome and to "transmit to the House Committee on Energy and Commerce, the Senate Committee on Labor and Human Resources, and the Committees on the Judiciary of the Senate and the House of Representatives a report on the medical and psychological basis of" the syndrome "and on the extent to which evidence of the syndrome has been considered in criminal trials." The report is to include "(1) medical and psychological testimony on the validity of battered women's syndrome as a psychological condition; (2) a compilation of State, tribal, and Federal court cases in which evidence of battered women's syndrome was offered in criminal trials; and (3) an assessment by State, tribal, and Federal judges, prosecutors, and defense attorneys of the effects that evidence of battered women's syndrome may have in criminal trials." The report is available as a Web Extra! at the Web site supporting this book.

Other Syndromes BWS was one of the first syndromes to be raised as a defense enhancement in American courtrooms. Many others have since followed. Among them are[47] adopted child syndrome, false memory syndrome, premenstrual syndrome (PMS), holocaust survival syndrome (see, for example *Werner* v. *State*[48]), attention deficit disorder (raised in defense of Michael Fay, the teenager "caned" a few years ago in Singapore), black rage defense (created by William Kunstler, and offered in defense of Colin Ferguson, the Long Island Railroad shooter), elder abuse syndrome, fetal alcohol syndrome (a variation of which was used in defense of Eric Smith, the fourteen-year-old who killed and sodomized a four-year-old neighborhood boy), Gulf War syndrome, Munchausen-by-proxy syndrome (wherein a caregiver injures his or her children to gain attention), nicotine withdrawal syndrome, repressed memory syndrome (used by California prosecutors to convict George Franklin, Sr., of the rape-murder of his eight-year-old daughter's friend twenty years after the killing), rotten social background, parental abuse syndrome (employed by Erik and Lyle Menendez), post-traumatic stress disorder, rape trauma syndrome (see, for example, *State* v. *Marks*[50]), ritual abuse syndrome (abuse at the hands of Satanic and other cults), UFO survivor syndrome, urban survival syndrome (used to

Web Extra! 6–4

Emerging defenses

Web Extra! 6–5

Report to Congress: *Battering and its Effects*

We've been abused! The citizens have been abused by abusive excuses! We've been abused by the "dumb excuse syndrome," and because of that we're not responsible . . . as a society . . .

—Gregory Kould, *Stand to Reason* Commentary

Nicole Brown Simpson displaying bruises allegedly inflicted by husband O.J. Simpson before she was brutally murdered in 1994. Battered woman's syndrome (BWS), which may enhance claims of self-defense, has been defined by California courts as "a series of common characteristics that appear in women who are abused physically and psychologically over an extended period of time by the dominant male figure in their lives; a pattern of psychological symptoms that develop after somebody has lived in a battering relationship; or a pattern of responses and perceptions presumed to be characteristic of women who have been subjected to continuous physical abuse by their mate[s]."[49] (Photo courtesy of AP/Wide World Photos.)

defend Texas killer Daimian Osby), and Vietnam syndrome (see, for example, *State v. Kenneth J. Sharp, Jr.*[51]). One especially recent syndrome to be discussed in the medical literature is Internet addiction disorder (IAD). Specialists studying this disorder say that IAD is as real as alcoholism. People with IAD tend to lose control over their daily activities and crave the use of the Internet. They even have withdrawal symptoms when forced to forego access to the Internet for any extended period of time.

Since syndromes are clinically viewed as diseases or disorders, we might anticipate the development of defenses based on other disorders, including hypoglycemia, senility, Alzheimer's disease, sleep disorders, postpartum disorders, preexisting genetic conditions, alcoholism, and drug addiction. Proponents of defenses based on chronic alcoholism, for example, suggest that the overpowering nature of addiction is such that alcoholics are unable to control their drinking, and that any criminal behavior that follows from a lessening of personal control induced by the consumption of alcohol should be excused because it is the result of disease rather than willful choice. Others make the same argument for those addicted to drugs.

Independent of such arguments, defenses based on syndromes, diseases, and disorders (other than "insanity," which is discussed in the next chapter) have yet to meet with widespread success. Even so, the use of "syndrome" -type defense enhancements is increasing. In 1991, for example, a Fairfax, Virginia, judge dismissed drunk-driving charges against Dr. Geraldine Richter, an orthopedic surgeon, who cited the role PMS played in her behavior.[52] Dr. Richter admitted to drinking four glasses of wine and allegedly kicked and cursed a state trooper who stopped her car because it was weaving down the road. A breathalyzer test showed a blood-alcohol level of 0.13 percent—higher than the 0.10 percent needed to meet the requirement for drunken driving under Virginia law. A gynecologist who testified as an expert witness on Dr. Richter's behalf, however, said that the behavior she exhibited is characteristically caused by PMS, and asserted that PMS "explained away" what would otherwise have been unacceptable behavior on the part of the surgeon.

The defense of PMS has met with greater success in England, where a 1980 case resulted in a "not guilty" verdict against Christine English, who had killed her live-in lover when he threatened to leave her. An expert witness at the trial, Dr. Katharina Dalton, testified that English had been the victim of PMS for more than a decade. According to Dr. Dalton, PMS had left Ms. English "irritable, aggressive, . . . and confused, with loss of self-control."[53]

Problems with Syndrome-Based Defense Enhancements

One of the central problems with all defenses based on syndromes is that there is no syndrome that includes homicide, or any other law-breaking behavior, as a symptom or as an *inevitable result* of the syndrome. In other words, according to most specialists, most people suffering from syndromes are as capable of controlling their behavior as anyone else.[54] In fact, most do. Speaking loosely, for every one hundred persons afflicted with some "syndrome," ninety-nine do not violate the criminal law, and far fewer kill.[55] Most women suffering from PMS, for example, are unlikely to attack a highway patrol officer. At the same time, almost everyone, if we were to dig hard enough, probably has something in his or her background that could be pointed to in an effort to mitigate responsibility for any particular act. That is to say, at one time or another, we have probably all suffered experiences that have left "negative" impressions that could serve as excuses for otherwise irresponsible behavior.

To conclude that the mere existence of a syndrome supports a legal excuse, claims Stephen J. Morse, is "fundamental psycholegal error."[56] **Psycholegal error,** says Morse, refers to "the mistaken belief that if we identify a cause for conduct, including mental or physical disorders, then the conduct is necessarily excused." "Causation," continues Morse, "is not an excuse, nor is a cause identical to compulsion, which may be an excuse." It is not enough, says Morse, that a syndrome be identified as part of the causal chain that led to the commission of a crime; rather the syndrome needs to produce some excusing condition before the defendant can be lawfully excused. Morse concludes: "[S]hould the use of syndromes to excuse be expressed doctrinally by the creation of new, discrete excuses for each new syndrome, or by the use of new syndrome evidence simply to support existing excuses?" "I strongly favor the latter approach," says Morse, "because the former—the creation of a new excuse based on the syndrome—suggests confusingly that it is simply the presence of the syndrome in the causal chain that somehow itself excuses."[58]

Another problem with syndrome-like excuses is that, in a fundamental sense, they seem to rely on a tactic of *blame shifting,* in which the victim of crime is made to seem less like a victim and more like a criminal in hopes that a jury will side with the defendant. Blame shifting attempts to convince the jury that the victim "had it coming" and builds on such notions as a history of abuse that can actually justify homicide. Famed trial lawyer Alan M. Dershowitz, in his book *The Abuse Excuse,*[59] says: "At bottom, the subtle message of these abuse-excuse defenses is that the *real* criminal is the dead victim and the defendant performed a public good by dispatching him. Thus, the abuse excuse places the *victim* of the killing or maiming on trial—generally in absentia—and if the defense lawyer can persuade the jury that he or she 'had it coming,' there is a chance that the jury will disregard the established rules of self-defense and take the law into its own hands by acquitting the defendant or reducing the charges."[60]

This kind of thinking quickly became clear in arguments raised by defense attorneys on behalf of Erik and Lyle Menendez, the California brothers who were recently convicted (in a second trial) of murdering their parents. "Good parents do not get shotgunned by their kids. Period," said defense attorney Leslie Abramson.[61]

If they [the accused] didn't have a moral obligation to do right because of their bad circumstances, why do we have a moral obligation to understand their bad circumstances and exercise leniency?

—Gregory Kould, *Stand to Reason* Commentary

PSYCHOLEGAL ERROR
the mistaken belief that if we identify a cause for conduct, including mental or physical disorders, then the conduct is necessarily excused.[57]

Taken to this extreme, cautions Dershowitz, abuse excuses are "lawless invitation[s] to vigilantism, both on the part of abuse victims and on the part of jurors who sympathize more with them than with those whom they have killed or maimed."[62]

The Future of Syndrome-Based Defense Enhancements Although their use has met with some limited success, syndrome-based defense enhancements continue to face an uphill battle for courtroom acceptability against an entrenched legal tradition that has long guided American jurisprudence. A growing tendency among courts in recent years to accept an expansion of criminal defenses based on syndromes reflects an increased willingness by other social institutions to accept sophisticated excuses (especially "scientifically" supported ones) for wrongdoing of all kinds. As a direct result of this society-wide intellectual revolution, says U.S. Supreme Court Justice Clarence Thomas, "[m]any began questioning whether the poor and minorities could be blamed for the crimes they committed. Our legal institutions and popular culture began identifying those accused of wrongdoing as victims of upbringing and circumstances. The point was made that human actions and choices, like events in the natural world, are often caused by factors outside of one's control. No longer was an individual identified as the cause of a harmful act. Rather, societal conditions or the actions of institutions and others in society became the responsible causes of harm. The external causes might be poverty, poor education, a faltering family structure, systemic racism or some other forms of bigotry, and spousal or child abuse, just to name a few. The consequence of this new way of thinking about accountability and responsibility—or lack thereof," wrote Thomas, "was that a large part of our society could escape being held accountable for the consequences of harmful conduct. The law punishes only those who are responsible for their actions; and in a world of countless uncontrollable causes of aggression or lawlessness, few will have to account for their behavior."[63] Thomas concludes: "An effective criminal justice system—one that holds people accountable for harmful conduct—simply cannot be sustained under conditions where there are boundless excuses for violent behavior and no moral authority for the state to punish. . . . How can we teach future generations right from wrong if the idea of criminal responsibility is riddled with exceptions. . . ?"[64]

Alan Dershowitz phrases the same sentiments succinctly. Dershowitz says, "The most profound danger posed by the proliferation of abuse and other excuses is that it may be a symptom of a national abdication of personal responsibility."[65]

Others, however, feel that it is time for syndrome-based excuses to be accorded legitimacy. As one author puts it: "Once it is recognized that excuses are based on notions of justice, and show the law's consideration for the defendant's predicament in particular circumstances, it becomes obvious that the list of excuses need not be regarded as closed. Our judges are so costive in their attitude to defenses that there is perhaps no immediate hope of a change of attitude on their part; but if the call for new defenses is made insistently enough it may be heeded eventually."[66]

SUMMARY

- This chapter discusses excuses, the second major category of defenses. The other major category, justifications, was discussed in Chapter 5. Excuses admit that the law-breaking actions committed by a defendant were wrong and that they violated the criminal law, but excuses claim that the defendant should nonetheless be excused from criminal liability because of special circumstances.

- The majority of excuses are personal in nature—that is, they claim that the defendant acted on the basis of some disability or some abnormal condition, such as intoxication, insanity, or immaturity, and that the defendant should not be held responsible for his or her actions.

- Where a defendant suffers from a known disability, that disability alone is not sufficient to excuse him or her of criminal responsibility. Only when the disability has the effect of in some way producing or contributing to the criminal activity in question will the actor be excused.

- Excuses recognized by law include: (1) duress, (2) intoxication, (3) mistake, (4) age, (5) entrapment, (6) insanity, (7) diminished capacity, and to a limited degree, (8) various "syndromes."

- The defense of duress, sometimes also called compulsion, is based on the notion that people do not willfully engage in acts that they are compelled or coerced to perform. In most jurisdictions, effective use of the duress defense must be based upon a showing that the defendant feared for his or her life, or was in danger of great bodily harm—or that he or she was acting so as to prevent the death or bodily harm of another. Likewise, for the duress defense to be effective, the threat under which the defendant acted must have been immediate, clear, and inescapable and must not have arisen from some illegal or immoral activity of the defendant.

- Voluntary intoxication is generally not a defense because these individuals are responsible for their impaired state, and the law generally holds that a person who voluntarily puts himself in a condition so as to have little or no control over his actions must be held to have intended whatever consequences ensue.

- Involuntary intoxication may serve as a defense if it creates in the defendant an incapacity either to appreciate the criminality of one's conduct or creates an incapacity to conform one's behavior to the requirements of the law.

- Mistake of fact will preclude criminal liability in instances where the actions undertaken would have been lawful had the situation been as the acting person reasonably believed them to be. Mistake of law, or ignorance of the law, however, rarely provides an effective defense.

- Infancy, or immaturity, defenses make the claim that certain individuals should not be held criminally responsible for their activities by virtue of youth. Most jurisdictions do not impose full criminal culpability on children under the chronological age of eighteen, while a number of states set the age of responsibility at sixteen, and some at seventeen.

- The entrapment defense is built on the assertion that, in some situations, were it not for government instigation, no crime would occur. Two approaches to assessing entrapment can be found in the law: the subjective and the objective. The subjective approach excludes from criminal liability persons, otherwise innocent, who have been lured to the commission of the prohibited act through the government's instigation. The objective approach to entrapment, also referred to as the "outrageous government conduct defense," is based on the claim that methods employed by the government to bring about a conviction in the case are offensive to moral sensibilities.

- In recent years, a number of new and innovative defense strategies based on the use of "syndromes" have been proposed—with varying degrees of success. Among the syndromes through which claims for the expansion of traditional defenses have been made are battered woman's syndrome, premenstrual syndrome, sexual abuse syndrome, urban survival syndrome, and black rage syndrome.

- Although courts have been reluctant to recognize the claim that syndromes negate *mens rea,* the use of syndromes in expanding the applicability of traditional defenses has met with greater success. Nonetheless, the future of syndrome-based defenses remains very much in doubt.

QUESTIONS FOR DISCUSSION

1. What is the difference between a justification and an excuse? What are the main distinguishing features of each?

2. What are the conditions needed for the defense of duress to be successfully employed? Why is the defense inapplicable in cases of serious law violations, such as murder and rape?

3. Why is voluntary intoxication usually not accepted as a defense to criminal liability? Should it be? Why or why not?

4. At what age do you think persons should be held criminally liable for their actions? Should there be a minimum age and a maximum age for determining culpability?

5. What is the difference between the subjective and the objective approaches to assessing entrapment? Which do you think is most useful? Why?

6. Is a syndrome an excuse, a justification, or an explanation? Should syndromes be best viewed as potentially negating *mens rea*, as widening traditional defenses, or as justifying behavior for a particular class of people? Why?

LEGAL RESOURCES ON THE WORLD WIDE WEB

A large number of law schools maintain World Wide Web sites. Law school sites serve a variety of purposes. They provide admissions information to prospective students, list the credentials of law school faculty, and often include at least limited facilities for legal research, as well as links to law libraries. The sites listed here allow you to find schools in which you might be interested.

American Bar Association Approved Law Schools
http://www.abanet.org/legaled/approvedlawschools/approved.html
Includes 184 institutions searchable by state and via a clickable map.

Association of American Law Schools
http://www.aals.org/members.html
Provides a list of 162 member schools.

New York University School of Law
http://www.law.nyu.edu/library/lawsch.html
Provides a directory of law school directories, including some of those listed here.

The Open Directory Project Law Schools List
http://dmoz.org/Reference/Education/Colleges_and_Universities/Post_
    Graduate_Education/Law_School/Law_Schools
Lists most law schools in the United States.

Rominger Legal Services Law School Directory
http://www.romingerlegal.com/lawschools.htm
An alphabetical listing of law schools. A state-by-state directory is also provided.

Washburn University School of Law, Law School Directory
http://www.washlaw.edu/lawschools.html
A thorough listing of American and foreign law schools.

The Washington, D.C., Regional Legal Directory
http://www.dclegal.com/us_law_schools.htm
Provides a nationwide listing of law schools.

Check the *Criminal Law Today* Web site for URLs that may have changed.

SUGGESTED READINGS AND CLASSIC WORKS

D. Bazelon, *Questioning Authority: Justice and Criminal Law,* reprint ed. (New York: New York University Press, 1990).

Alan M. Dershowitz, *The Abuse Excuse* (Boston: Little, Brown, 1994).

Alan M. Dershowitz, *Reasonable Doubts: The O.J. Simpson Case and the Criminal Justice System* (New York: Simon and Schuster, 1996).

J. Roland Pennock and John Chapman, *Due Process* (New York: New York University Press, 1977).

Judge Harold J. Rothwax, *Guilty: The Collapse of Criminal Justice* (New York: Random House, 1996).

CAN A DEFENDANT WHO LIES ABOUT HER ROLE IN SPOUSAL HOMICIDE STILL RAISE A "BATTERED WOMAN'S" DEFENSE?

CAPSTONE CASE

State v. *Evans*
Appellate Court of Illinois, Third Division, 1994
631 N.E.2d 281

OPINION

Justice Rizzi delivered the opinion of the court: Defendant, Gwendolyn Evans (Gwen), killed her husband Jerry Evans (Jerry), and was found guilty of first degree murder by a jury. She was sentenced to 20 years imprisonment. On appeal, she contends that: (1) the State failed to prove beyond a reasonable doubt that she was not acting in self-defense, (2) the trial court erred in failing to instruct the jury that her conduct could be considered self-defense even though Jerry was not armed, and (3) that her constitutional right to due process was violated because of the wording of the Illinois Pattern Jury Instruction on second degree murder that was given to the jury. We reverse the judgment of conviction for the reason that the State failed to prove beyond a reasonable doubt that Gwen was not acting in self-defense. Gwen was 39 at the time of the homicide. She graduated from grade school and attended Du Sable High School for three years. At the time of her arrest she was unemployed and receiving public aid for food and any medical attention that she needed. Although Jerry worked, he spent his money on himself and did not give Gwen the money needed to support the household on a regular basis. Jerry was six foot, two hundred thirty pounds, and physically well-developed. Gwen is five foot, eight inches and one hundred thirty-five pounds.

At close to midnight on December 10, 1988, Gwen stabbed Jerry with a kitchen knife that she had been using earlier in the day to peel potatoes. There was a stab wound to Jerry's lower chest about four inches long. There was another stab wound in his upper left chest area about an inch long, and there was a stab wound to his left upper arm. The stab wounds were consistent with the premise that they were inflicted by a person who was right-handed and shorter than the decedent; Gwen is right-handed. Jerry died from the wounds on December 11, 1988.

Gwen and Jerry were married in July of 1980. The two of them and Gwen's daughter lived in Chicago. About a year after the marriage, Jerry began drinking heavily, going out alone, and staying out late. He was getting drunk every weekend. Also, he would come home drunk and start arguments and fights with Gwen.

As a result of the many fights while Jerry was drunk, Gwen suffered numerous physical injuries. On separate occasions, Jerry hit her with a variety of objects,

including a baseball bat, a skillet, and a shovel. On other occasions, he beat her with his fists and slapped her, and he spit on her and threw objects at her. Gwen was also verbally brutalized continuously by Jerry. Jerry would tell her: "F___ you bitch." He would also call her names such as "mother-f___ing ass" and "bitch," and "red-assed bitch." In one incident, Jerry slapped Gwen's face while he was drunk, and she threatened to call the police. As Gwen was running upstairs to her girlfriend's apartment to use the telephone, Jerry grabbed a snow shovel from the hallway closet and said: "You old red bitch." He then hit Gwen in the leg with the shovel. A couple of days later, due to the intensive pain, Gwen went to Michael Reese Hospital. Gwen's leg was so swollen that she could not walk. The parties stipulated to the testimony of Jenny Stevens, a nurse at Michael Reese Hospital. Her testimony corroborates the testimony about Gwen's visit to the hospital for the injury.

In another incident, Jerry hit Gwen on the left shoulder with a piece from a broken baseball bat. Gwen was taken to Michael Reese Hospital, where an orthopedic surgeon found that she had a hairline fracture to the tip of her right shoulder, and Gwen's arm was put in a sling for three or four weeks.

On another day, Jerry slapped Gwen and continuously hit her until she fell on the couch. He then slapped and hit her again. He beat her continuously until her tooth came out and she swallowed it.

On another occasion, Jerry became angry and told Gwen: "F___ you, bitch." He then threw a glass peanut butter jar at her. Gwen ducked her head and threw her hand up. The jar hit a cabinet and broke, but a piece of glass cut Gwen's finger. The finger was bleeding, and when the bleeding would not stop, Gwen went to Michael Reese Hospital, where she was treated for a serious cut on one of the fingers of her left hand.

On the day after one of Gwen's birthdays, Jerry called Gwen a "red-assed bitch." He beat her and slapped her so hard that it sounded like a gunshot. He then ran out of the house and did not come back until the next morning. When he returned he was drunk. Gwen was lying in bed, wearing a nightgown. Jerry came in, threw Gwen out of the house, and locked the door.

Gwen went across the hall to a neighbor's apartment and telephoned the police. She then went back to her apartment and began knocking on the door. The police never came. But, after awhile Jerry let her back in the apartment. Gwen was having sharp pains in her neck and shoulders, as well as shortness of breath, due to Jerry's beating the night before. As a result, Gwen asked Jerry to take her to a hospital. He took her to Michael Reese Hospital, where it was found that Gwen had a swollen area on her forehead and tenderness in her neck and shoulders.

There were other specific incidents of physical and mental abuse while Jerry was drunk. One day he came home drunk and began throwing pots, pans, and catsup, mustard, and mayonnaise jars at Gwen. He then picked up a cocktail table and threw it in the middle of the floor and it broke in half. Also, he threw a skillet which skimmed Gwen's head. Every time Gwen tried to get out the door, she would get hit by Jerry.

Eventually, Gwen was able to escape and she ran down the street to see a friend. Gwen returned to her apartment with the friend, who asked Jerry to "cool out." Jerry replied: "Okay, man. I ain't got nothing else to throw at the old red bitch so I guess I'll just go on and cool out." He then fell asleep at the kitchen table.

One winter, Gwen and Jerry were outside making a snowman. Jerry wanted to drag Gwen through the snow, but Gwen refused. Jerry grabbed Gwen and dragged her through the snow against her will. As he dragged her, Gwen's jacket was pushed upward, and rocks and glass scratched her back. Gwen kicked and screamed until he finally let her go. Gwen then ran to her sister's apartment. Jerry followed, and banged on the door and tried to get into the apartment. Jerry yelled through the door that he was going to drag Gwen through the snow again, and he called her a "red-assed bitch," and said that he was going to beat her "mother-f___ing ass." He also told her that he was going to "f___" her up. Finally, Jerry left, and Gwen spent the night with her sister.

Around August of 1988, Gwen learned that Jerry had a girlfriend. Gwen found out about the girlfriend because the girlfriend would telephone the apartment asking for Jerry, mostly on weekends. Gwen asked Jerry to tell her to stop calling. Jerry told Gwen that he had gotten drunk and given the telephone number to the other woman but he did not mean to give her the telephone number. Jerry said that he would tell her to stop calling.

On the morning of December 10, 1988, Jerry was home. After answering a telephone call, Jerry told Gwen that he was going to the store, and he left the apartment. As he left, Gwen asked Jerry if he would bring back some chicken wings for her to eat for lunch. Gwen waited for Jerry to return, but at noon she started to peel some potatoes with a kitchen knife because she was hungry. There was no other food in the house. The kitchen knife that Gwen used to peel the potatoes was the knife that was later used in the homicide.

Later in the day, Jerry returned with the chicken wings, and a bag of food from a Cub Foods mart. Jerry put the Cub Foods bag on the couch, and the telephone rang. After answering the telephone call, Jerry said that he had some place to go and left the apartment. Gwen then noticed the Cub Foods bag and said to herself: "He must have took his friend out to Cubs and I've been asking J.D.—I wanted to go shopping too, you know." Gwen looked in the bag to see what was inside, but left the bag on the couch.

Gwen then began sweeping the living room floor, and her friend Shirley stopped by to visit; Shirley lived in the same apartment building as Gwen. Later, at about 4 P.M., Gwen went to Earl Scott's house. Earl Scott was a friend of both Jerry and Gwen. Gwen had heard Jerry mention Earl Scott's name on the telephone earlier, and she thought that Jerry might be there.

Earl Scott was not home when Gwen arrived, but his uncle was there and Gwen stayed and talked with him. Earl Scott testified that he was not home at the time because Jerry had come to his house that afternoon, and the two of them went out drinking. Earl Scott testified that Jerry was drinking beer and Bacardi rum, and that they had "quite a lot to drink that day." When Earl Scott came home, he told Gwen that Jerry just dropped him off and was on his way home. Gwen, therefore, telephoned her home to tell Jerry that she was on her way home. When Jerry answered the telephone, he told Gwen: "You can keep your red ass over there. You ain't been here all day. What you want to come here now for." Gwen knew from the conversation that Jerry was drunk, and after she hung up the phone, she asked Earl Scott to walk her home. Earl Scott walked Gwen to the front steps of her apartment, but he did not walk her upstairs. When Gwen got home, it was close to midnight.

After she entered the apartment, she saw Jerry. He was standing in the living room and he "looked like a wild man." His eyes were "bugged" and he had sweat on his face, with his hair standing straight up. He looked mad. He said: "Bitch, you finally brought your ass home, huh?" Gwen said: "I see you took your girlfriend to Cub's, huh?" Jerry said: "I'm a grown-assed man. I can take anybody anywhere I want them. That is my goddamn car. I pay the car note. I work hard for that mother-f___ing car. I do what I want to do. Yeah, I took her to Cub's Food." Gwen thought Jerry was going to hit her, so she started running to the bedroom. She was trying to go around a table to get to the bedroom, but Jerry cut her off. Gwen testified as follows:

> I went across. I did not go to him. I went across to the other side of the couch because I know he was going to start hitting me, to try to go running to the bedroom, and before I can get over there, he ran over there and he started hitting me in my face with the paper bag. I took the bag and snatched it and threw it on the floor. That's when he come down to my face and he started saying, if you all don't like what the f___ I do, you can get your mother-f___ing ass out of here.

When he was in my face, he started spitting in my face. I said, J.D., get out of my face. Stop spitting on my face. He say, you don't tell me what to do. He started to spit—a whole lot of spit started coming on my face.

So I took his forehead, that is when he hit me in the back of my head and kept on hitting, kept on hitting. I had my head down.

I was closing my eyes, I looked down on the floor, and I seen that knife down there. So I picked the knife up and I just started stabbing and I was just stabbing at him and stabbing and just kept on swinging my arms, kept swinging my arms back there, and he kept on hitting me.

Then he said, you old red bitch, you done stabbed me. I'm going to break your mother-f___ing neck. So I dropped the knife. That is when I ran down the back steps.

He was chasing me down the back steps. He was chasing me. He was chasing behind me and then he started hollering, Gwen. I ran downstairs and I ran behind the garbage can that was down there on the first floor.

He kept saying, Gwen, Gwen. I wouldn't answer. I had did that one time, and when I came out, he really beat me up. I said, I ain't going to answer. I did not know if I had stabbed the knife for real or not anyway.

Then I heard something say "boom." So then I started tippy toes out because I didn't know if he was going to jump out of somewhere or what. I ain't seen him over there where the steps was at, and then I looked over that way and that is the garage over there, the roof, and he was laying over there.

I said, J.D., J.D. He said, Gwen, Gwen. So I climbed over. You got to kind of like climb over there. I climbed over there, and that is when I put his head in my lap.

I said, J., J. He said, Gwen, Gwen. I said, J., you're hurt. I'm going to call the police. I'm going to get you some help. I'll be right back.

When I ran into the house, I ran—It was raining outside, rain and snow. Then the bedroom is right there. He was getting wet and everything. I snatched a blanket off the bed and I ran back out there and covered him up. Then I ran back in there, and I called the police.

I called Earl first. Then I called the police and I went back out there with J.D. and put J.D.'s head back on my lap and I sat out there with him and I seen out front the flashing lights so I assumed that was the police and I was saying, back here, help, help, help. They heard me. I said come in the back, come in the back. They came around the back and. . . . Then Earl had came up and I climbed back over and Earl said, what happened. I said, we got to fighting. He said, don't tell the police nothing, you know. He said, he'll be all right, you know. We thought he was going to be all right.

The ambulance came, and they dragged him down the steps. They couldn't pick him up. The man was too small. He bumped his head going down the steps.

I told him to wait a minute, let me hold his head. I caught his head down the last couple of steps and they put him in the ambulance and me and Earl were standing there and I asked, could I sit in. They told me, no, there is no room, you know.

I told them that I was his wife and this was his best friend and could we sit in there with him and they said, no. By that time Ricky had pulled up—my brother, Ricky, was coming over to spend some time with us. He asked, what happened. After I explained to him, he said, well, you can ride with me to the police—to the hospital so—

Q: Did you go to the hospital with him?

A: We rode behind the ambulance to the hospital and—

Q: Was J.D. dead?

A: When I got to the hospital, that is when the police, the lady officer, came over and said, you're under arrest, and she read me my rights and took me down to the 51st Street Police Station.

Q: Gwen, when you called 911, you told them some dudes stabbed your husband?
A: Yes. I figured if I said that they would hurry up and come fast because they know it was a bad neighborhood and they know a lot of times you can get stuck-up and a lot of peoples got messed up around there and they know there is an whole lot of thugs over there. If I tell them it was some dudes, you know, that robbed him and stabbed him, they will hurry up and come. Because if you just say, I cut my husband, they may just take their time, you know. They think it's just—
Q: A domestic?
A: Yeah and wasn't nothing, you know. They take a long time to come. In order to get an ambulance to come, you have to tell them—you have to stretch it real hard.
Q: When you saw the police later, you told them you stabbed him?
A: Yes.

In addition, Gwen testified as follows:

Q: How come you picked up that knife?
A: Because when J.D. told me he was going to break my neck, I thought he was going to break my neck. When he hit me last time and I thought my neck was broken, I went to Michael Reese Hospital. They thought it was broke. He told me, he said, next time, I'm going to break your mother-f___ing neck if you ever, you know, put your hands on me. So when I pushed him in his face and he say he was going to f___ me up, I figured he was going to try to break my neck because he kept hitting me all behind my head. He was hitting harder and harder. I didn't want my neck broken. I was trying to keep him from stop hitting me.
Q: Gwen, did you kill him because he had a girlfriend?
A: No. We didn't even get into about the girlfriend. It was because he was—I had no intention to kill him. I wanted him to stop. I stabbed him because he was hitting me. He kept hitting me harder, and I know he was going to break my—All I can think about is he is going to break your neck, he's going to break your neck. You'd better stop him. If he breaks your neck, you're dead, you know. I was trying to stop him from breaking my neck.
Q: How do you feel about J.D.?
A: I still love J.D. I miss him. I wish he was still alive. I wish I was still his wife, and he was still with me.

Paramedics and the police arrived on the scene shortly after the occurrence. Gwen told one of the police officers at the scene that "my husband left the apartment to get some cigarettes, he got to the alley, and then ran back upstairs holding his chest yelling 'Gwen, Gwen.' " Gwen testified that she told the police officer that because, "I didn't think it was their business to know exactly what happened, at that time." She said, "I just wanted to hurry up and get my husband to the hospital." Later, when she was at the police station, she told the police that she stabbed her husband and gave an account of what occurred.

In the meantime, a police officer at the scene went up the back stairs and into the second-floor rear apartment. There was blood splattered all over the wall above the couch in the front room, which would indicate a violent struggle preceded the homicide. The blood that had been splattered was "leading toward the kitchen." There was also blood on the kitchen floor.

Another investigating police officer who was at the scene testified that he went to the apartment and looked in a dresser that was near the couch. He testified that in the top drawer of the dresser he saw a black fur scarf or muffler, and under the garment was the knife that was involved in the homicide. The knife was a "standard kitchen knife," about nine inches long overall, with a six-inch blade. The knife still

had blood on the blade from the homicide. In addition, another investigating police officer testified that he found a pair of blood-stained blue jeans in the apartment. The blood-stained blue jeans were found in open view on the bed in the bedroom near the kitchen.

Gwen was arrested at Michael Reese Hospital and taken to Area 1 police station. The Felony Review Unit of the State's Attorney's office was called into the case, and an assistant State's Attorney took an oral statement from Gwen at the police station. No tape recording was used. The assistant State's Attorney made a handwritten summary of Gwen's oral statement, which was signed by Gwen. The handwritten summary by the assistant State's Attorney provides:

> *I explained to Gwendolyn Evans I am an assistant State's Attorney, a lawyer working with the police and not her lawyer. I gave Gwendolyn Evans the above rights which she indicated she understood. Gwendolyn then agreed to give the following statement, which is a summary and not verbatim. My name is Gwendolyn Evans. I also use Gwendolyn Knight. I am thirty-nine years old. I live at 1243 East Forty-sixth Street. Jerry Evans is my husband. We have been married for nine years. I call Jerry J.D.*
>
> *On Saturday, 10 December '88 Jerry and I got up around eleven o'clock in the morning. Jerry went out to get some chicken wings. When he came back he had a Cub Food's bag. Jerry dropped the stuff off and left. I stayed in the house all day. I knew Jerry had been out a long time. Jerry had a girlfriend for about three months. Jerry had given her our phone number. Jerry said it was a mistake. She kept calling. Around twelve o'clock I had one or two drinks. Around four o'clock Shirley came up and we finished the chicken wings. When it started getting dark, I went to A.D.'s house. A.D. (the initials) is Earl's uncle. I was hoping J.D. would come by. Earl came home and said J.D. just dropped him off. I called home and talked to J.D. Then I went home. When I came in J.D. was in the living room. J.D. and I got into a fight about him taking his girlfriend to Cub Foods. J.D. said he was a grown man and could do whatever he wants or can do whatever he wants. We kept arguing. J.D. hit me with his hand. He went around the table. I saw the knife on the table, picked it up and stabbed him. I don't know how many times I stabbed him. I just chopped at him. Then I ran. J.D. ran after me. He fell on the back porch by the steps. J.D. was calling Gwen, Gwen. J.D. was bleeding. I went back and said get up, get up. J.D. didn't get up. I ran in the house and got the blanket. I put his head on my lap. That is how I got the blood on my jeans. J.D.'s eyes started rolling.*
>
> *I went and called Earl and the police. After I stabbed J.D. I dropped the knife. The knife has a wooden handle. The police and State's Attorney had treated me okay. No threats or promises were made to me to get me to make this statement. I am telling this because it is the truth.*
>
> *The first story I told the police wasn't true. I didn't say I stabbed J.D. because I was scared. I have had cigarettes and coffee. I was allowed to go to the bathroom. I can read and write English. I am not under the influence of alcohol or drugs.*

The paramedics who were at the scene took Jerry to Michael Reese Hospital, where he was later pronounced dead by a physician. Dr. Kalelkar performed an autopsy of the decedent. He noted in his autopsy report that Jerry had a blood alcohol level of .243, almost two and a half times the legal level for a finding of intoxication. See 625 ILCS 5/11-501 (West 1992). Dr. Kalelkar also testified that Jerry had an enlarged liver, which would be consistent with chronic alcoholism.

The facts in this case leave no room for doubt that Gwen was a battered woman imbued with all of the psychological and emotional impairments of what we all know and commonly call battered woman's syndrome. Thus, we need not waste time or paper attempting to legally define or expound the symptoms of battered woman's syndrome and its application to this case. Paraphrasing the classic statement of Justice Potter Stewart: "Perhaps we could never succeed in intelligibly defining the kinds of matter we understand to be embraced within the shorthand description of battered woman's syndrome. But we know it when we see it, and what we have in this case is precisely that." See *Jacobellis* v. *Ohio* (1963), 378 U.S. 184, 197, 12 L. Ed. 2d 793, 804, 84 S. Ct. 1676, 1683 (Stewart, J., concurring).

When the defendant is a victim of battered woman's syndrome in a case involving the homicide of her husband, and the homicide was committed during the course of another beating, the law can no longer ignore the fact that in reality what occurred involved two victims. Moreover, because of the nature of the event and the present-day sociolegal problems that are involved in domestic violence cases, a crucible for justice exists when a woman is both the victim of battered woman's syndrome and the killer of her husband during the course of another beating.

Thus, the law must finally step up to the times and itself comprehend the reality of domestic violence cases, which involve victims of battered woman's syndrome. If the law does not keep up with the times in this area, a system whose *raison d'être* is justice will mete out injustice under the guise of unenlightened rationalizations.

As a start in the right direction, the law must make it absolutely clear that when the defendant is a victim of battered woman's syndrome, that fact must be taken into account with all the other facts if the homicide occurs while her husband is imposing another beating. In addition, in reviewing such cases, judges must examine the record with the discerning eye and cool judgment of a Talmudic Exegete. The present case demonstrates the need for such exacting care.

In its brief, the State states unequivocally that "the people's theory of the case was that defendant killed Jerry because she was jealous about his girlfriend." The problem with the State's theory is that while there may be evidence that Gwen was "jealous about his girlfriend," there is no evidence that she killed Jerry because she was jealous of his girlfriend. Merely establishing the existence of jealousy by a party in a homicide scenario is not the same as establishing the reason for the homicide. It is very important to bear this distinction in mind when there is a homicide committed by a battered woman who kills her husband not in any prearrangement but rather in an attempt to stop another beating.

Here, it is virtually indisputable that Jerry started the incident while he was drunk and that he was the aggressor. The evidence is that he hit Gwen before he was stabbed, and that before he was stabbed he was in the midst of imposing a physical beating of Gwen as he had done repeatedly in the past. It follows that while jealousy may have precipitated the argument, jealousy was not the predetermination for the stabbing. Rather, what was involved in the moment was a beating and an attempt to stop it. Jerry was not killed because Gwen was jealous of his girlfriend. He was killed because Gwen was attempting to stop an unlawful beating.

To support its argument that Gwen killed Jerry because she was jealous of Jerry's girlfriend, the State states in its brief:

"Defendant told Officer Dwyer that she stabbed Jerry because they had an argument about his girlfriend." The fact is, however, that the supplemental record plainly establishes that Gwen did not make that statement. Rather, the supplemental record shows that Officer Dwyer, a witness for the State, volunteered the statement in what appears to be a procrustean attempt to support the State's theory of the case. It was Officer Dwyer's own statement which the State attributes to Gwen.

The supplemental record provides that the following occurred during the cross-examination of Officer Dwyer:

DEFENSE COUNSEL:
Q: During this conversation that you had with Miss Evans, you talked about what happened that night?

A: Yes, ma'am.

Q: You did not talk to her about her marriage with J.D., did you?

A: No, ma'am.

Q: You did not ask her what her relationship was like with him, did you?

A: No, ma'am.

Q: You didn't ask Miss Evans how J.D. treated her, did you?

A: She did mention that he went out for chicken wings for lunch for her.

Q: No. I mean in the past, detective.

A: No, ma'am.

Q: Detective, when she told you that she stabbed him, you didn't ask her how she felt when she stabbed him?

A: No, ma'am.

Q: You didn't ask her how she felt when he hit her?

A: No, ma'am.

Q: You didn't really ask her why she stabbed him?

A: She told me why she stabbed him.

Q: Because he was hitting her?

A: They had an argument about his girlfriend.

Q: Detective, you show me in this report where it says that she stabbed him because of the argument with his girlfriend.

PROSECUTOR: Objection.

THE COURT: Basis?

PROSECUTOR: Improper impeachment.

THE COURT: It is sustained as to that.

DEFENSE COUNSEL:

Q: Detective, did you put in your report that she told you she stabbed him because of his girlfriend?

A: She told me that they had an argument about his girlfriend, and she stabbed him.

Q: She didn't tell you why she stabbed him?

PROSECUTOR: Objection.

THE COURT: It is sustained.

Q: You didn't ask her why she stabbed him?

PROSECUTOR: Objection.

THE COURT: It has been asked and answered.

DEFENSE COUNSEL: It has not been answered, your Honor, if I may.

THE COURT: You may pursue another line, but as to that particular question, it will be sustained.

DEFENSE COUNSEL: Detective, Miss Evans told you they had an argument about J.D.'s girlfriend?

PROSECUTOR: Objection.

THE WITNESS: Yes.

PROSECUTOR: I will withdraw that.

THE COURT: All right.

DEFENSE COUNSEL: And later in that conversation she told you she stabbed him?

PROSECUTOR: Objection. Asked and answered.

DEFENSE COUNSEL: Judge, I have one more question.

PROSECUTOR: I will withdraw it for the sake of brevity.

DEFENSE COUNSEL: And later in that conversation she told you that she stabbed him?

A: Yes, ma'am.

Q: She did not specifically tell you, detective, that she stabbed him because of his girlfriend?

PROSECUTOR: Objection. Asked and answered.

THE COURT: Overruled. It is a different question. You may answer it.

THE WITNESS: She told me about the argument and later told me that she stabbed him.
DEFENSE COUNSEL: You are making the connection that she stabbed him because of his girlfriend?
PROSECUTOR: Objection.
THE WITNESS: Of course.

Plainly, the supplemental record does not support the State's claim that: "Defendant told Officer Dwyer that she stabbed Jerry because they had an argument about his girlfriend." The State's claim is clearly unfounded and misleading.

In another effort to support its argument that Gwen killed Jerry because she was jealous of his girlfriend, the State states in its brief: "Defendant also included in her statement given to an assistant State's Attorney, '(Jerry) and I got into a fight about him taking his girlfriend to Cub Foods.' " The record clearly shows, however, that the State has taken the statement out of context and distorted the meaning of what was said. The statement attributed to Gwen does not support the State's argument that she killed Jerry because she was jealous of his girlfriend.

Initially, it should be noted that the statement is part of a written summary by the assistant State's Attorney as to what Gwen said without benefit of counsel being present. The part of the summary statement that is pertinent here provides that Gwen said:

> *Earl came home and said J.D. just dropped him off. I called home and talked to J.D. Then I went home. When I came in J.D. was in the living room. J.D. and I got into a fight about him taking his girlfriend to Cub Foods. J.D. said he was a grown man and could do whatever he wants or can do whatever he wants. We kept arguing. J.D. hit me with his hand. He went around the table. I saw the knife on the table, picked it up and stabbed him. I don't know how many times I stabbed him. I just chopped at him. Then I ran. J.D. ran after me. He fell on the back porch by the steps. J.D. was calling Gwen, Gwen. J.D. was bleeding. I went back and said get up, get up. J.D. didn't get up. I ran in the house and got the blanket. I put his head on my lap. That is how I got the blood on my jeans. J.D.'s eyes started rolling. I went and called Earl and the police. After I stabbed J.D. I dropped the knife.*

It is clear from the textual content of the summary statement that Gwen did not say or imply that she stabbed Jerry because she was jealous of Jerry's girlfriend. Rather, she said and implied that she stabbed Jerry only after he hit her and that he was coming around the table to continue the beating. It is a distortion of the summary statement to claim that Gwen said she stabbed Jerry because she was jealous of Jerry's girlfriend.

The State also argues: "It is clear from the record that defendant used an unreasonable and unnecessary amount of force in allegedly protecting herself from her husband and, therefore, killed him without lawful justification." The record, however, does not substantiate that thesis.

In examining the State's contention, we first address the fact that Jerry was not armed. On this point, the law does not require that the aggressor be armed in order that the use of a deadly weapon to stop the attack be justified as self-defense. Where it is clear that the aggressor is capable of inflicting serious bodily harm on the defendant without the use of a deadly weapon, and it appears that he intends to do so, then it is not necessary that the aggressor be armed for the defendant to employ deadly force in self-defense. *People* v. *Estes* (1984), 127 Ill. App. 3d 642, 652, 469 N.E.2d 275, 283.

In the present case, it is clear that Jerry was capable of inflicting serious bodily harm on Gwen without the use of a deadly weapon, and it appears that he intended to do so. Thus, the fact that Jerry was not armed does not mean that Gwen used an unreasonable or unnecessary amount of force when she stabbed him to stop the attack.

Next, we specifically address whether Gwen used an unreasonable and unnecessary amount of force in protecting herself from the attack. When a woman is threatened with violence by a physically larger man, she does not have time to muse about how much force is reasonable or necessary to quell the attack, subdue the attacker, and provide for her escape. Moreover, the attack may escalate. We must also bear in mind that she is not involved in a sporting event where there are umpires or referees and a "time-out" may be called so that a reassessment of the threat may be made.

As a result, the law does not require that a woman exercise infallible judgment when she uses deadly force to repel her attacker if she has reasonable grounds to believe that she is in danger of suffering great bodily injury or losing her life. Rather, the law only requires that she use reasonable judgment under the existing circumstances. Moreover, reasonable judgment under the existing circumstances means that a woman's right of self-defense arises before she is caused to spout blood. *People* v. *Estes* (1984), 127 Ill. App. 3d 642, 653, 469 N.E.2d 275, 284; *People* v. *White* (1980), 87 Ill. App. 3d 321, 323, 409 N.E.2d 73, 75.

Thus, the question in a case such as this is whether the deadly force used by the woman was necessary and reasonable taking into account such facts as: (1) the attacker's apparent mental state and sobriety, (2) the woman's apparent mental state and sobriety, (3) the difference between the physical attributes and apparent strengths of the attacker and the woman, (4) whether the attacker has physically or verbally abused and threatened the woman on prior occasions and to what extent the threats were carried out, (5) whether the attacker was the apparent aggressor, (6) what recourse and what options were readily available to the woman to quell the attack during the course of the attack, and to escape, (7) the nature and extent of the attack, (8) the weapon that was used by the woman to stop the attack, (9) the apparent escalation or diminishment of the attack at the time the woman resorted to deadly force, and (10) the reasonable apprehension of the woman at the time the deadly force was used, which encompasses the fact that she is a victim of battered woman's syndrome.

When these ten factors are applied to the facts in the present case there is no question that the deadly force that was used by Gwen was necessary and reasonable to save herself from serious bodily harm or from a serious threat of her life. Jerry was six foot, two hundred thirty pounds, and physically well-developed. Gwen is four inches shorter and almost one hundred pounds lighter. When Gwen came home on the night of the occurrence, it was close to midnight. Jerry was standing in the living room and he looked like a wild man. His eyes were bugged, he was sweating, and his hair was standing straight up. He looked mad.

In addition, Jerry was drunk. The fact that he was drunk at the time cannot be disputed or even doubted. The autopsy report provides that he had a blood alcohol level of .243, which is substantially above the level for intoxication under the law. See 625 ILCS 5/11-501 (West 1992). The police testified that Gwen was not drunk.

Moreover, Jerry was following a pattern of verbal and physical abuse and threats. For years, Jerry would verbally brutalize and physically beat Gwen. He would tell her, "f___ you bitch," and he would repeatedly call her a "bitch" and a "mother-f___ing ass." He told her that he was going to "break her mother-f___ ing neck." He hit her with such objects as a shovel, a baseball bat, and a skillet. He beat her with his fists and spit on her. He also threw objects at her. As a result of the physical abuse by Jerry, Gwen suffered physical injuries, such as a broken shoulder, a "punched-out" tooth that was swallowed, and a leg injury and back abrasions. After one particular beating, she thought her neck was broken and went to Michael Reese Hospital. These facts demonstrate that Gwen was a victim of battered woman's syndrome and that Jerry had the apparent potential to carry out his threats.

At trial, Gwen testified that on the night of the occurrence Jerry kept spitting in her face, and that he hit her in the back of the head and "kept on hitting, kept on hitting." She also testified:

> *I had my head down. I was closing my eyes, I looked down on the floor, and I seen that knife down there. So I picked the knife up and I just started stabbing and I was just stabbing at him and stabbing and just kept on swinging my arms, kept swinging my arms back there, and he kept on hitting me.*

Surely, at the time of the occurrence the attack on Gwen was escalating, and she had a reasonable apprehension that she was in immediate danger of serious bodily injury and that her life was in jeopardy. Also, it is plain that the entire matter was spontaneous, and the grabbing and use of the knife reasonably appears to have been Gwen's only recourse to stop the beating and escape. Under the circumstances, it is clear that the deadly force used by Gwen was not unreasonable or unnecessary.

Although there are some discrepancies between Gwen's trial testimony and the initial statements that she made following the occurrence, the discrepancies do not negate the fact that she did not use an unreasonable or unnecessary amount of force to stop the attack. Thus, the State's contention on this point is unavailing.

The State next argues that "another indication that defendant did not kill her husband in self-defense is her initial attempt to cover up the crime." In this context, the State states: "Defendant lied when she told the 911 operator that, 'some dudes stabbed her husband.' Later, defendant lied again when she told Officer Cosgrove, 'my husband left the apartment to get some cigarettes, he got to the alley, and then ran back upstairs holding his chest yelling 'Gwen, Gwen.' " When the statements relied upon by the State are read in their context as set forth in the factual text of our discussion of this case, it is clear that the statements are insignificant or of minuscule significance, at best, with respect to whether Gwen was acting in self-defense at the time she stabbed her husband.

The State also states: "Defendant attempted to hide the bloodstained knife in a dresser drawer. Defendant attempted to conceal her involvement in the crime by changing out of her bloodsoaked blue jeans before the police arrived. These actions would be illogical and unnecessary for someone who believed she took another life in self-defense." The problem with what is stated by the State is that it is nothing more than hyperbole founded upon pure tendentious speculation.

Although the bloodstained knife was found in a dresser drawer by the police, there is no evidence that Gwen was attempting to hide the knife. Gwen had not "cleansed" the knife or wiped it for fingerprints before the police arrived. Moreover, Gwen had not been asked the whereabouts of the knife before it was found by the police. The State's claim is untenable.

The State's contention that Gwen attempted to conceal her involvement in the crime by changing out of her bloodsoaked blue jeans before the police arrived is also untenable. The fact that the blue jeans were bloodsoaked is itself ample reason to change out of them. In addition, the bloodsoaked blue jeans were found by the police on the bed in open view while Gwen was on her way to the hospital. Under the circumstances, to say that Gwen was attempting to conceal her involvement in the crime by changing out of her bloodsoaked blue jeans is nonsense.

On this same point, the State says: "Finally, at the police station, defendant told the detectives the truth when she stated that she stabbed Jerry because 'they had an argument about his girlfriend.' " We have already discussed the fact that what the State quotes as being said by Gwen was not a statement made by Gwen, but rather, it was Officer Dwyer's own statement. The State's repeated attempt to use the statement of Officer Dwyer as if it was a statement made by Gwen reflects poorly upon the State's handling of this case.

In its last thrust to demonstrate that it proved beyond a reasonable doubt that Gwen was not acting in self-defense, the State says:

> Finally, defendant's testimony at trial was not credible. Her testimony concerning her actions in picking up the knife and how the stab wounds occurred was not consistent with Dr. Kalelkar's testimony about how the stab wounds would have had to occur with regard to the position of defendant in relation to Jerry and the thrust of the knife at a 'downward angle.' Defendant said in her statement, 'I saw the knife on the table,' but later testified she 'saw the nine-inch knife on the floor.' There is testimony defendant 'swept the floor' earlier in the day, but somehow the knife apparently remained on the floor. One would think defendant would remember where she obtained the knife she supposedly used to protect herself.

The State does not refer to a record page with respect to its reference to the testimony of Dr. Kalelkar. Dr. Kalelkar was called as a witness by the State. The record reflects that he testified on direct examination as follows:

Q: Doctor, what type of angle was this wound, the upper right hand corner, the one in the upper chest?
A: The angle is from left to right of the deceased and in a downward motion.
Q: And what type of a cutting action would be caused by the wounds in the center of this photograph?
A: The action is that the knife or the weapon is plunged into the body and then when it is removed from the body is dragged along the skin. That is why there is a slash mark on the lower corner of that stab wound.
Q: Is that wound also a downward angle?
A: Yes.
Q: And the far right hand corner of the photograph, which is the deceased's left arm, is there any discernible angle to that wound?
A: It is the same angle again, downward, probably downward angle because there is a slash mark again at the bottom of it.
Q: Doctor, do you have an opinion based on a reasonable degree of medical and scientific certainty as to the cause of the death of Jerry Evans?
A: Yes, I do.
Q: Can you please tell us what that is?
A: Yes. In my opinion Mr. Evans died as a result of multiple stab wounds.
Q: And do you have an opinion as to the manner of death?
A: Yes.
Q: What is that?
A: Homicide.

On cross-examination, Dr. Kalelkar, testified as follows:

Q: You stated that the stab wounds had a downward angle and a left to right?
A: Right.
Q: Left to right would be consistent with the person using the knife on Mr. Evans as being right-handed?
A: Correct.
Q: And the downward angle would be consistent with the person using the knife being shorter?
A: Well, yes, that is consistent with the person being shorter because that person is reaching up.
Q: Would you explain what a slash wound is?
A: We don't usually describe a wound as slash wound. We call it an incised wound. An incised wound is longer on the skin surface that it is deeper.

Q: That would be consistent with someone reaching up and making a move like this (indicating), is that correct?

THE COURT: Do you want to state for the record?

A: I am showing my right arm, moving from an upward to downward or sideward angle.

Q: The injury on the arm, what kind of injury—it was a stab wound. Was it also consistent with a slashing motion?

A: Yes, it was because there is a mark at the bottom of the stab wound which shows that the knife was pulled against the skin.

Q: And the other injuries on the chest, do those also show signs of a slash?

A: Yes, particularly the wounds on the middle of the chest.

Q: And the scrape that he has on his face and on his shoulders, that might be consistent with falling on the ground?

A: Yes.

Q: So at best you cannot say exactly where his arms were or what he was doing at the time he was being stabbed?

A: That is correct.

We have set forth above all of the pertinent testimony and opinions testified to by Dr. Kalelkar. The pertinent testimony of Gwen is as follows:

> *When he was in my face, he started spitting in my face. I said, J.D., get out of my face. Stop spitting on my face. He say, you don't tell me what to do. He started to spit—a whole lot of spit started coming on my face. So I took his forehead, that is when he hit me in the back of my head and kept on hitting, kept on hitting. I had my head down.*
>
> *I was closing my eyes, I looked down on the floor, and I seen that knife down there. So I picked the knife up and I just started stabbing and I was just stabbing at him and stabbing and just kept on swinging my arms, kept swinging my arms back there, and he kept on hitting me.*
>
> *Then he said, you old red bitch, you done stabbed me. I'm going to break your mother-f___ing neck. So I dropped the knife. That is when I ran down the back steps.*
>
> *Then I heard something say boom. So then I started tippy toes out because I didn't know if he was going to jump out of somewhere or what. I ain't seen him over there where the steps was at, and then I looked over that way and that is the garage over there, the roof, and he was laying over there.*

Plainly, the record belies the State's contention that Gwen's "testimony concerning her actions in picking up the knife and how the stab wounds occurred was not consistent with Dr. Kalelkar's testimony about how the stab wounds would have had to occur with regard to the position of defendant in relation to Jerry and the thrust of the knife at a 'downward angle.' " The State's contention is not only unfounded, it is also misleading.

In addition, the State's reference to whether the knife was on the table or on the floor, and the reference to the floor having been swept are insignificant references within the assemblage of facts and circumstances that are involved. Surely, it makes no difference in this case whether the knife was on the table and fell to the floor and grabbed by Gwen, or whether it was grabbed off the table by Gwen. This case involved a real-life highly volatile set of facts and emotions. Under the circumstances, pinpoint accuracy and precise recollection of the mercurial moments cannot and in reality should not be expected.

Lastly, as part of its argument that Gwen's testimony at trial was not credible, the State states in its brief: "Defendant lied to the Illinois Department of Public Aid in order to receive $154 a month." What the defendant said to or did with the Illinois Department of Public Aid has absolutely no bearing on whether her testimony at

trial was credible or on whether the State proved beyond a reasonable doubt that she was not acting in self-defense.

The State's reference to defendant's receipt of public aid to discredit her trial testimony makes us mindful of the penumbral circumstances that perhaps may be an integral part of this case. Gwen is an economically poor African-American who lived in a part of the community that may appropriately be described as the "low-end." Based on the record here, it is a high crime area where the police may not always respond to telephone calls reporting domestic violence.

The public services that are provided in the area are apparently demonstrated by what occurred when the paramedics proceeded to remove Jerry from the scene to take him to a hospital in an effort to save his life. A paramedic dragged Jerry down the steps with his head repeatedly bouncing on the steps as he was being taken from the scene, although he was bleeding and near death. Moreover, the incident occurred at about midnight on December 10, 1988, and Jerry was pronounced dead in the early morning hours on December 11, 1988. Within hours, on December 11, 1988, a complaint was filed charging Gwen with first-degree murder.

These kind of circumstances place a heavy burden on judges to make sure that our system of justice gives equal treatment to defendants coming from the "low-end" as they do for defendants coming from more affluent areas. This is just an added reason why the record in this case must be scrutinized befitting a biblical exegete.

When the record is carefully scrutinized and all of the evidence that is gleaned is taken together as a whole, neither the State's theory nor its contentions and arguments can bear water. At best, the State's theory, contentions, and arguments leave far too much room for doubt.

We are cognizable of the principle that a reviewing court must view the evidence in the light most favorable to the prosecution when a conviction is challenged on the basis that the State did not prove the defendant guilty beyond a reasonable doubt. *People v. Collins* (1985), 106 Ill. 2d 237, 261, 478 N.E.2d 267, 277. We are also aware, however, that on the issue of self-defense, a reviewing court has a duty to reverse the conviction when the evidence is so unsatisfactory as to raise a serious doubt as to the defendant's guilt. See *People v. Estes* (1984), 127 Ill. App. 3d 642, 651-53, 469 N.E.2d 275, 282-84; *People v. Reeves* (1977), 47 Ill. App. 3d 406, 409, 362 N.E.2d 9, 12.

Self-defense is an affirmative defense and, once it has been raised, the State has the burden of disproving it beyond a reasonable doubt. The test to be applied is whether the facts and circumstances would induce a reasonable apprehension of serious bodily harm or threat of life and whether the force used was reasonable and necessary. See *People v. Goodman* (1979), 77 Ill. App. 3d 569, 574-75, 396 N.E.2d 274, 277; *People v. Moore* (1976), 43 Ill. App. 3d 521, 527, 357 N.E.2d 566, 570.

Here, considering all of the evidence taken together as a whole and in the light most favorable to the prosecution, the State did not prove beyond a reasonable doubt that Gwen's use of deadly force was unreasonable or that the force she employed was unreasonable or unnecessary. Clearly, the evidence is so unsatisfactory as to raise a serious doubt of her guilt. The conviction must therefore be reversed. *People v. Estes,* 127 Ill. App. 3d 642, 653–55, 469 N.E.2d 275, 284–85; *People v. Reeves,* 47 Ill. App. 3d 406, 412, 362 N.E.2d 9, 14. Since the conviction is reversed, we do not consider the alleged trial errors that are raised.

Accordingly, the judgment of conviction is reversed. REVERSED.

ADDENDUM: Our opinion was filed on March 9, 1994. After the opinion was filed, we learned for the first time that Gwen had died on March 16, 1993, while she was in prison for her conviction of first-degree murder. Under the circumstances, rather than reversing the judgment of conviction, we remand the case to the circuit court to vacate the judgment of conviction and to dismiss the indictment.

[footnotes omitted]

WHAT DO *YOU* THINK?

1. The Illinois appellate court, citing a U.S. Supreme Court Justice, says that "Perhaps we could never succeed in intelligibly defining the kinds of matter we understand to be embraced within the shorthand description of battered woman's syndrome." Why not? Would you be able to formulate an effective legal description of "battered woman's syndrome"? If so, what would it be?
2. What important differences exist between the facts of this case, and the 1989 North Carolina case of *State* v. *Norman,* discussed earlier in this chapter? Why are those differences significant?
3. In this opinion, the Illinois court says: " . . . the law must finally step up to the times and itself comprehend the reality of domestic violence cases which involve victims of battered woman's syndrome. If the law does not keep up with the times in this area, a system whose *raison d'être* is justice will mete out injustice under the guise of unenlightened rationalizations." What is the court saying? Do you think it may have had the *Norman* case in mind when that portion of the opinion was written?
4. How do you think that the appellate court that heard the *Evans* case would have decided a case like *Norman?* Why?
5. How would the ten factors listed in *Evans,* as to "whether the deadly force used by the woman was necessary and reasonable" apply to *Norman?* Consider each.

WHAT CONSTITUTES ENTRAPMENT BY GOVERNMENT AGENTS?

CAPSTONE CASE

Jacobson v. *United States*
U.S. Supreme Court, 1992
503 U.S. 540

Justice White delivered the opinion of the Court.

On September 24, 1987, petitioner Keith Jacobson was indicted for violating a provision of the Child Protection Act of 1984, Pub. L. 98-292, 98 Stat. 204 (Act), which criminalizes the knowing receipt through the mails of a "visual depiction [that] involves the use of a minor engaging in sexually explicit conduct. . . ." 18 U.S.C. § 2252(a)(2)(A). Petitioner defended on the ground that the Government entrapped him into committing the crime through a series of communications from undercover agents that spanned the twenty-six months preceding his arrest. Petitioner was found guilty after a jury trial. The Court of Appeals affirmed his conviction, holding that the Government had carried its burden of proving beyond reasonable doubt that petitioner was predisposed to break the law and hence was not entrapped.

Because the Government overstepped the line between setting a trap for the "unwary innocent" and the "unwary criminal," *Sherman* v. *United States,* 356 U.S. 369, 372 (1958), and as a matter of law failed to establish that petitioner was independently predisposed to commit the crime for which he was arrested, we reverse the Court of Appeals' judgment affirming his conviction.

I.

In February 1984, petitioner, a fifty-six-year-old veteran-turned-farmer who supported his elderly father in Nebraska, ordered two magazines and a brochure from

a California adult bookstore. The magazines, entitled *Bare Boys I* and *Bare Boys II,* contained photographs of nude preteen and teenage boys. The contents of the magazines startled petitioner, who testified that he had expected to receive photographs of "young men eighteen years or older." Tr. 425. On cross-examination, he explained his response to the magazines:

PROSECUTOR: [Y]ou were shocked and surprised that there were pictures of very young boys without clothes on, is that correct?
JACOBSON: Yes, I was.
PROSECUTOR: Were you offended? . . .
JACOBSON: I was not offended because I thought these were a nudist type publication. Many of the pictures were out in a rural or outdoor setting. There was—I didn't draw any sexual connotation or connection with that. *Id.* at 463.

The young men depicted in the magazines were not engaged in sexual activity, and petitioner's receipt of the magazines was legal under both federal and Nebraska law. Within three months, the law with respect to child pornography changed; Congress passed the Act illegalizing the receipt through the mails of sexually explicit depictions of children. In the very month that the new provision became law, postal inspectors found petitioner's name on the mailing list of the California bookstore that had mailed him *Bare Boys I* and *II.* There followed over the next two-and-one-half years repeated efforts by two Government agencies, through five fictitious organizations and a bogus pen pal, to explore petitioner's willingness to break the new law by ordering sexually explicit photographs of children through the mail.

The Government began its efforts in January 1985 when a postal inspector sent petitioner a letter supposedly from the American Hedonist Society, which in fact was a fictitious organization. The letter included a membership application and stated the Society's doctrine: that members had the "right to read what we desire, the right to discuss similar interests with those who share our philosophy, and finally that we have the right to seek pleasure without restrictions being placed on us by outdated puritan morality." Record, Government Exhibit 7. Petitioner enrolled in the organization and returned a sexual attitude questionnaire that asked him to rank on a scale of one to four his enjoyment of various sexual materials, with one being "really enjoy," two being "enjoy," three being "somewhat enjoy," and four being "do not enjoy." Petitioner ranked the entry "[p]re-teen sex" as a two, but indicated that he was opposed to pedophilia. *Ibid.*

For a time, the Government left petitioner alone. But then a new "prohibited mail specialist" in the Postal Service found petitioner's name in a file, Tr. 328-331, and in May 1986, petitioner received a solicitation from a second fictitious consumer research company, "Midlands Data Research," seeking a response from those who "believe in the joys of sex and the complete awareness of those lusty and youthful lads and lasses of the neophite [*sic*] age." Record, Government Exhibit 8. The letter never explained whether "neophite" referred to minors or young adults. Petitioner responded: "Please feel free to send me more information, I am interested in teenage sexuality. Please keep my name confidential." *Ibid.*

Petitioner then heard from yet another Government creation, "Heartland Institute for a New Tomorrow" (HINT), which proclaimed that it was "an organization founded to protect and promote sexual freedom and freedom of choice. We believe that arbitrarily imposed legislative sanctions restricting *your* sexual freedom should be rescinded through the legislative process." *Id.* Defendant's Exhibit 102. The letter also enclosed a second survey. Petitioner indicated that his interest in "[p]reteen sex-homosexual" material was above average, but not high. In response to another question, petitioner wrote: "Not only sexual expression but freedom of the press is under attack. We must be ever vigilant to counterattack right-wing fundamentalists who are determined to curtail our freedoms." *Id.* Government Exhibit 9.

"HINT" replied, portraying itself as a lobbying organization seeking to repeal "all statutes which regulate sexual activities, except those laws which deal with violent behavior, such as rape. HINT is also lobbying to eliminate any legal definition of 'the age of consent'." *Id.* at Defendant's Exhibit 113. These lobbying efforts were to be funded by sales from a catalog to be published in the future "offering the sale of various items which we believe you will find to be both interesting and stimulating." *Ibid.* HINT also provided computer matching of group members with similar survey responses; and, although petitioner was supplied with a list of potential "pen pals," he did not initiate any correspondence.

Nevertheless, the Government's "prohibited mail specialist" began writing to petitioner, using the pseudonym "Carl Long." The letters employed a tactic known as "mirroring," which the inspector described as "reflect[ing] whatever the interests are of the person we are writing to." Tr. 342. Petitioner responded at first, indicating that his interest was primarily in "male-male-items." Record, Government Exhibit 9A. Inspector "Long" wrote back:

> "My interests too are primarily male-male items. Are you satisfied with the type of VCR tapes available? Personally, I like the amateur stuff better if its [sic] well produced as it can get more kinky and also seems more real. I think the actors enjoy it more." Id. Government Exhibit 13.

Petitioner responded:

> "As far as my likes are concerned, I like good looking young guys (in their late teens and early 20's) doing their thing together." Id. Government Exhibit 14.

Petitioner's letters to "Long" made no reference to child pornography. After writing two letters, petitioner discontinued the correspondence.

By March 1987, thirty-four months had passed since the Government obtained petitioner's name from the mailing list of the California bookstore, and twenty-six months had passed since the Postal Service had commenced its mailings to petitioner. Although petitioner had responded to surveys and letters, the Government had no evidence that petitioner had ever intentionally possessed or been exposed to child pornography. The Postal Service had not checked petitioner's mail to determine whether he was receiving questionable mailings from persons—other than the Government—involved in the child pornography industry. Tr. 348.

At this point, a second Government agency, the Customs Service, included petitioner in its own child pornography sting, "Operation Borderline," after receiving his name on lists submitted by the Postal Service. *Id.* at 71–72. Using the name of a fictitious Canadian company called "Produit Outaouais," the Customs Service mailed petitioner a brochure advertising photographs of young boys engaging in sex. Record, Government Exhibit 22. Petitioner placed an order that was never filled. *Id.* Government Exhibit 24.

The Postal Service also continued its efforts in the Jacobson case, writing to petitioner as the "Far Eastern Trading Company Ltd." The letter began:

> "As many of you know, much hysterical nonsense has appeared in the American media concerning 'pornography' and what must be done to stop it from coming across your borders. This brief letter does not allow us to give much comments; however, why is your government spending millions of dollars to exercise international censorship, while tons of drugs, which makes yours the world's most crime ridden country, are passed through easily." Id. Government Exhibit 1.

The letter went on to say:

> "[W]e have devised a method of getting these to you without prying eyes of U.S. Customs seizing your mail. . . . After consultations with American

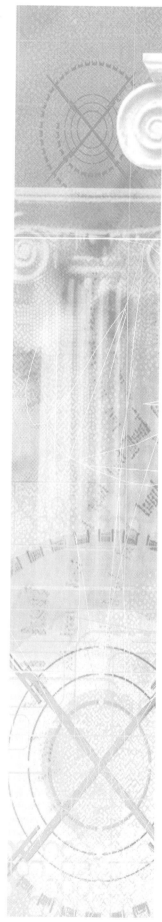

solicitors, we have been advised that once we have posted our material through your system, it cannot be opened for any inspection without authorization of a judge." Ibid.

The letter invited petitioner to send for more information. It also asked petitioner to sign an affirmation that he was "not a law enforcement officer or agent of the U.S. Government acting in an undercover capacity for the purpose of entrapping Far Eastern Trading Company, its agents, or customers." Petitioner responded. *Ibid.* A catalogue was sent, *Id.* Government Exhibit 2, and petitioner ordered *Boys Who Love Boys, Id,* Government Exhibit 3, a pornographic magazine depicting young boys engaged in various sexual activities. Petitioner was arrested after a controlled delivery of a photocopy of the magazine.

The prosecution's evidence of predisposition falls into two categories: evidence developed prior to the Postal Service's mail campaign, and that developed during the course of the investigation. The sole piece of preinvestigation evidence is petitioner's 1984 order and receipt of the *Bare Boys* magazines. But this is scant, if any, proof of petitioner's predisposition to commit an illegal act, the criminal character of which a defendant is presumed to know. It may indicate a predisposition to view sexually oriented photographs that are responsive to his sexual tastes; but evidence that merely indicates a generic inclination to act within a broad range, not all of which is criminal, is of little probative value in establishing predisposition.

Furthermore, petitioner was acting within the law at the time he received these magazines. Receipt through the mails of sexually explicit depictions of children for noncommercial use did not become illegal under federal law until May 1984, and Nebraska had no law that forbade petitioner's possession of such material until 1988. Neb. Rev. Stat. § 28-813.01 (1989). Evidence of predisposition to do what once was lawful is not, by itself, sufficient to show predisposition to do what is now illegal, for there is a common understanding that most people obey the law even when they disapprove of it. This obedience may reflect a generalized respect for legality or the fear of prosecution, but for whatever reason, the law's prohibitions are matters of consequence. Hence, the fact that petitioner legally ordered and received the Bare Boys magazines does little to further the Government's burden of proving that petitioner was predisposed to commit a criminal act. This is particularly true given petitioner's unchallenged testimony was that he did not know until they arrived that the magazines would depict minors.

The prosecution's evidence gathered during the investigation also fails to carry the Government's burden. Petitioner's responses to the many communications prior to the ultimate criminal act were at most indicative of certain personal inclinations, including a predisposition to view photographs of preteen sex and a willingness to promote a given agenda by supporting lobbying organizations. Even so, petitioner's responses hardly support an inference that he would commit the crime of receiving child pornography through the mails [note omitted]. Furthermore, a person's inclinations and "fantasies . . . are his own and beyond the reach of government. . . ." *Paris Adult Theatre I* v. *Slaton,* 413 U.S. 49, 67 (1973); *Stanley* v. *Georgia,* 394 U.S. 557, 565–566 (1969).

On the other hand, the strong arguable inference is that, by waving the banner of individual rights and disparaging the legitimacy and constitutionality of efforts to restrict the availability of sexually explicit materials, the Government not only excited petitioner's interest in sexually explicit materials banned by law but also exerted substantial pressure on petitioner to obtain and read such material as part of a fight against censorship and the infringement of individual rights. For instance, HINT described itself as "an organization founded to protect and promote sexual freedom and freedom of choice" and stated that "the most appropriate means to accomplish [its] objectives is to promote honest dialogue among concerned individuals and to continue its lobbying efforts with State Legislators." Record, Defendant's

Exhibit 113. These lobbying efforts were to be financed through catalogue sales. *Ibid.* Mailings from the equally fictitious American Hedonist Society, *Id.* Government Exhibit 7, and the correspondence from the nonexistent Carl Long, *Id.* Defendant's Exhibit 5, endorsed these themes.

Similarly, the two solicitations in the spring of 1987 raised the specter of censorship, while suggesting that petitioner ought to be allowed to do what he had been solicited to do. The mailing from the Customs Service referred to "the worldwide ban and intense enforcement on this type of material," observed that "what was legal and commonplace is now an 'underground' and secretive service," and emphasized that "[t]his environment forces us to take extreme measures" to insure delivery. *Id.* Government Exhibit 22. The Postal Service solicitation described the concern about child pornography as "hysterical nonsense," decried "international censorship," and assured petitioner, based on consultation with "American solicitors" that an order that had been posted could not be opened for inspection without authorization of a judge. *Id.* Government Exhibit 1. It further asked petitioner to affirm that he was not a government agent attempting to entrap the mail order company or its customers. *Ibid.* In these particulars, both Government solicitations suggested that receiving this material was something that petitioner ought to be allowed to do.

Petitioner's ready response to these solicitations cannot be enough to establish beyond reasonable doubt that he was predisposed, prior to the Government acts intended to create predisposition, to commit the crime of receiving child pornography through the mails. See *Sherman,* 356 U.S. at 374. The evidence that petitioner was ready and willing to commit the offense came only after the Government had devoted two-and-one-half years to convincing him that he had or should have the right to engage in the very behavior proscribed by law. Rational jurors could not say beyond a reasonable doubt that petitioner possessed the requisite predisposition prior to the Government's investigation and that it existed independent of the Government's many and varied approaches to petitioner. As was explained in *Sherman,* where entrapment was found as a matter of law, "the Government [may not] pla[y] on the weaknesses of an innocent party and beguil[e] him into committing crimes which he otherwise would not have attempted." *Id.* at 376.

Law enforcement officials go too far when they "implant in the mind of an innocent person the *disposition* to commit the alleged offense and induce its commission in order that they may prosecute." *Sorrels,* 287 U.S. at 442 (emphasis added). Like the *Sorrels* court, we are "unable to conclude that it was the intention of the Congress in enacting this statute that its processes of detection and enforcement should be abused by the instigation by government officials of an act on the part of persons otherwise innocent in order to lure them to its commission and to punish them." *Id.* at 448. When the Government's quest for convictions leads to the apprehension of an otherwise law-abiding citizen who, if left to his own devices, likely would have never run afoul of the law, the courts should intervene.[1]

Because we conclude that this is such a case and that the prosecution failed, as a matter of law, to adduce evidence to support the jury verdict that petitioner was predisposed, independent of the Government's acts and beyond a reasonable doubt, to violate the law by receiving child pornography through the mails, we reverse the Court of Appeals' judgment affirming the conviction of Keith Jacobson.

It is so ordered.

Footnote

1. The jury was instructed:

"As mentioned, one of the issues in this case is whether the defendant was entrapped. If the defendant was entrapped he must be found not guilty. The government has the burden of proving beyond a reasonable doubt that the defendant was not entrapped.

If the defendant before contact with law-enforcement officers or their agents did not have any intent or disposition to commit the crime charged and was induced or persuaded by law-enforcement officers o[r] their agents to commit that crime, then he was entrapped. On the other hand, if the defendant before contact with law-enforcement officers or their agents did have an intent or disposition to commit the crime charged, then he was not entrapped even though law-enforcement officers or their agents provided a favorable opportunity to commit the crime or made committing the crime easier or even participated in acts essential to the crime." App. 11–12.

WHAT DO *YOU* THINK?

1. Do you think that, in this case, "the Government overstepped the line between setting a trap for the 'unwary innocent' and the 'unwary criminal' "? Why or why not?
2. How does the U.S. Supreme Court define entrapment in this case? Do you agree with the definition? Why or why not?

CAPSTONE CASE

HOW CAN A DEFENDANT RAISING THE DEFENSE OF ENTRAPMENT ESTABLISH THAT HE LACKED THE PREDISPOSITION NECESSARY TO ENGAGE IN DRUG TRAFFICKING?

State v. *Day*
Appellate Court of Illinois, Third District, 1996
665 N.E.2d 867

OPINION

Defendant Dana Day was indicted by a Will County grand jury on two counts of unlawful delivery of a controlled substance within 1,000 feet of a public park and one count of unlawful delivery of a controlled substance within 1,000 feet of a school, and three counts of unlawful delivery of a controlled substance. 720 ILCS 570/401(c)(2); 720 ILCS 570/407(b)(1) (West 1994). Defendant pled not guilty and raised the affirmative defense of entrapment. 720 ILCS 5/7–12 (West 1994). Following a jury trial, he was convicted and sentenced to concurrent terms of seven years' incarceration.

The issue presented for our review is whether the evidence adduced during the State's case in chief was sufficient to rebut the defense of entrapment beyond a reasonable doubt. For the reasons set forth below, we hold that the State's evidence did not rebut the defense of entrapment beyond a reasonable doubt and that the defendant was entrapped as a matter of law. Accordingly, the conviction is reversed.

The Metropolitan Area Narcotics Squad (MANS) launched a police investigation called Operation Cooperation Two. The investigation utilized undercover police officers to assist neighboring police agencies by making controlled buys of crack cocaine and other drugs outside of the undercover officer's home jurisdiction. Joliet police officer Anthony White was a MANS officer who assisted the city of Bolingbrook police department with Operation Cooperation Two.

In the early summer of 1994, Marla Nobles, a former gang member, approached police authorities to discuss becoming a paid informant. Nobles was referred to special MANS agent Jeff Lockard who recommended she become a confidential source working on Operation Cooperation Two. Nobles was paid $100 for each introduction she made between an undercover officer and an alleged drug dealer.

In May of 1994, twenty-two-year-old defendant Dana Day returned home to Bolingbrook for the summer from the University of Wyoming. Day and Nobles met coincidentally at a J.J. Pepper's gas and convenience store in Bolingbrook where they exchanged telephone numbers to resume an eighth-grade acquaintanceship. One week later Day was at a friend's home in Bolingbrook when Nobles arrived. Day and Nobles were speaking about going out on a date when she asked him to get her cocaine. Day refused, telling Nobles he "had nothing to do with it, I didn't want to take part in it." A few days later he ran into Nobles and she again asked him to obtain cocaine for her. Day told Nobles, "I couldn't get any drugs for her, that I wasn't engaged in anything like that." Day and Nobles also spoke on the telephone and, on at least three occasions, Nobles asked Day to obtain drugs and he again stated he could not. Day testified he was romantically interested in Nobles and they went on a date. While on their date Nobles persistently requested drugs. This time Day stated, "I don't know, I'll see what I can do. I can ask somebody, but I don't know."

On June 23, 1994, a few days after their date, Nobles paged Day at 10:10 P.M. and said she and her girlfriend wanted to meet with him and his friend Jeff Arnold at the Speedway gas station at the corner of Boughton and Schmidt roads to "go out and do something." Day and Arnold drove in Arnold's car to the Speedway gas station and Nobles arrived unexpectedly with her friend "Tony" (Officer White). Nobles asked Day to get some drugs for her or her friend "Tony." Day asked his friend Arnold if he knew anyone who could get drugs and Arnold replied that he knew someone in Cicero.

Nobles asked Day to get an "eight ball." Day asked what an eight ball was and was told an eight ball is an eighth of an ounce of cocaine. Nobles claimed the cocaine was for her friend "Tony" who needed the cocaine as a favor. Day asked "Tony" to come to Cicero to get the cocaine. "Tony" declined to accompany Day saying he did not know and trust him well enough to travel to Cicero. Day requested money for the cocaine, but "Tony" said he would pay for the drugs when Day returned. When Day and Arnold returned to the Speedway gas station, Day gave "Tony" the cocaine and received $160, earning a ten-dollar profit on the $150 eight ball of cocaine. Although the indictment alleged this delivery occurred within 1,000 feet of a public park, trial testimony revealed the delivery did not occur within the requisite 1,000 feet. Consequently, the State dismissed this charge at trial.

Agent Lockard and other Bolingbrook police officers were engaged in a mobile surveillance of the drug transaction. Agent Lockard followed Arnold's car from the Speedway to a J.J. Pepper's gas station where Day and Arnold bought gasoline. Agent Lockard then instructed Officer Hild to make a traffic stop on the car, if at all possible, to positively identify the car's occupants. Officer Hild stopped the car for speeding and obtained identification verifying Jeff Arnold and the defendant as the car's occupants.

A few days later, White paged Day and asked for more drugs. Day stated "it was possible, but I don't know. I have to make some phone calls and ask some people." White said he would travel to Bolingbrook and contact Day from the Speedway gas station. When Day received White's page, he ignored it and did not return White's call. Nobles then spoke with Day and conveyed White's distress at Day's inability to "come through for him."

On July 12, 1994, at 6:15 P.M., Officer White paged Day several times and Day finally responded to the page. White requested an eight ball and Day agreed to meet with White at the Speedway gas station located at Boughton and Schmidt roads in Bolingbrook. At approximately 6:40 P.M., Day arrived with several other people and requested that White follow him. Day stopped at a cul-de-sac on Norman Road in Bolingbrook and delivered the cocaine to White. This delivery took place within 1,000 feet of Winston Woods, a public park. After the drugs were delivered, Day requested $150 for the cocaine, admitting he had received too much money on June 23, 1994. During the transaction Day asked White if he was a police officer wearing a "wire." White lifted his shirt to reveal he was not wearing a listening device.

Between July 12 and July 29, 1994, Officer White paged Day several times and Day agreed to meet him at a Popeye's chicken restaurant. While there, White requested cocaine but Day refused saying, "I just couldn't. I mean, the other times I did it was just like luck. I just knew people that may know somebody that can get drugs." White told Day, "if you can't get the dope, just let me know and I will get it from somewhere else." Day then requested White "do some dope" to prove he was not a police officer. White testified he resisted Day's suggestion by feeding Day "a script, a line . . . [about how] I got enough problems, I am getting divorced and I got to pay child support, I don't need to be strung out."

White testified Day then stated he was a college athlete who did not do drugs and had a four-year football scholarship to lose if he went to prison for selling drugs.

After their meeting at Popeye's, Day testified Officer White contacted him frequently and finally, at 5:20 P.M. on July 29, 1994, Day responded to White's page. White told Day he wanted two eight balls of cocaine. At White's suggestion the delivery site was a Taco Bell restaurant at the intersection of Bolingbrook Drive and Barbers Corner located within 1,000 feet of a school, Children's World preschool. White arrived at the Taco Bell and paged the defendant. Day was across the street at a Wendy's restaurant making arrangements to obtain the drugs. At 7:30 P.M., Day delivered two eight balls of cocaine to White at the Taco Bell. This drug transaction was captured on videotape by a MANS surveillance team.

At the end of the summer Day transferred to a Missouri college and returned to school. In October of 1994, an arrest warrant was issued for his arrest. Upon his return to Illinois, Day pled not guilty and requested a trial by jury. He gave the State notice of his intent to utilize the entrapment defense at trial. At trial, the State called Officer White and Agent Lockard to testify about the June 23, 1994; July 12, 1994; and July 29, 1994 drug transactions. Day testified on his behalf as did several character witnesses during the defense's case in chief. The State presented no rebuttal evidence. The jury was properly instructed on the entrapment defense and rendered a verdict of guilty. Day filed a timely notice of appeal.

Day argues the evidence adduced at trial established entrapment as a matter of law and requests that the jury verdict be set aside and that his conviction be reversed. The defense of entrapment is found in Section 7–12 of the Criminal Code of 1961, which states: "[a] person is not guilty of an offense if his conduct is incited or induced by a public officer or employee, or agent of either, for the purpose of obtaining evidence for the prosecution of such person. However, this Section is inapplicable if a public officer or employee, or agent of either, merely affords to such person the opportunity or facility for committing an offense in furtherance of a criminal purpose, which such person has originated." 720 ILCS 5/7–12 (West 1994).

Entrapment occurs when governmental officials originate a criminal design, implant the disposition to commit the offense in the mind of an innocent person, and induce the commission of the offense in order to obtain evidence for use in prosecuting that person. *People v. Chism*, 248 Ill. App. 3d 804, 617 N.E.2d 1333 (1993). Thus, when a defendant puts forth evidence showing: (i) the State improperly induced him to commit the crime, and (ii) a lack of predisposition to commit the crime, the defendant has established the entrapment defense. *Chism*, 248 Ill. App. 3d at 811, 617 N.E.2d at 1338.

A defendant who raises entrapment as an affirmative defense to a criminal charge necessarily admits to committing the crime, albeit because of improper governmental inducement. *People v. White*, 249 Ill. App. 3d 57, 63, 618 N.E.2d 889, 894 (1993). Once a defendant presents some evidence, however slight, to support an entrapment defense, the State bears the burden to rebut the entrapment defense beyond a reasonable doubt. *People v. Alcala*, 248 Ill. App. 3d 411, 618 N.E.2d 497 (1993); *White*, 249 Ill. App. 3d 57, 618 N.E.2d 889. Once raised, the question of entrapment is to be determined by the trier of fact. *People v. Tipton*, 78 Ill. 2d 477, 401 N.E.2d 528

(1980). The trier of fact's determination of entrapment will not be set aside unless entrapment as a matter of law exists. *People* v. *Saindon,* 239 Ill. App. 3d 554, 605 N.E.2d 1121 (1992). Thus, the appellate standard used to review the trier of fact's resolution of the entrapment defense is whether, upon viewing the evidence in the light most favorable to the prosecution, any rational trier of fact could have found the elements essential to the criminal conviction beyond a reasonable doubt. *People* v. *Lambrecht,* 231 Ill. App. 3d 426, 595 N.E.2d 1358 (1992).

Day first argues the State did not, beyond a reasonable doubt, rebut uncontroverted defense evidence that Day was induced by the government and its agents to commit the crimes for which he was convicted. We find the record consistently demonstrates that Day was repeatedly approached to obtain drugs by MANS confidential source Nobles and Officer White from approximately May of 1994 to July 29, 1994. Thus, the record supports the defense argument that the initial idea to obtain and sell drugs originated with the government. In the similar case of *People* v. *Fisher,* the defendant's drug conviction was reversed when uncontradicted defense testimony established that the idea to commit the offense did not originate with the defendant. *People* v. *Fisher,* 74 Ill. App. 3d 330, 334, 392 N.E.2d 975, 978–79 (1979).

Day's testimony remained uncontradicted that he resisted Noble's requests for drugs until June 23, 1994, and refused to respond to White's pages for drugs on numerous occasions. As in Fisher, this unrebutted defense testimony strongly indicates that the idea to commit a drug offense did not originate with Day and further establishes Day did not actively encourage the government's solicitations for drugs. Rather, the record reveals Nobles and White cultivated relationships with the defendant exclusively designed to induce Day to obtain drugs. We acknowledge entrapment does not exist as a matter of law merely because a government agent initiates a relationship leading to a drug transaction. *People* v. *Dennis,* 94 Ill. App. 3d 448, 418 N.E.2d 479 (1981). However, we find the course of criminal conduct for which the defendant was convicted initially originated in the mind of a paid government agent who, for no reason apparent from the record, arbitrarily engaged in a relationship with the defendant and purposely encouraged its growth as an inducement to obtain drugs. See *People* v. *Poulos,* 196 Ill. App. 3d 653, 659-60, 554 N.E.2d 448, 452 (1990).

It became incumbent upon the State to rebut Day's uncontradicted testimony that he did not originate the idea to engage in drug trafficking and was induced to commit the crime through improper governmental influence. Upon a review of the record, we find the State failed to proffer evidence rebutting defense evidence that Day was subjected to improper governmental inducement. In this regard, we find it significant the State did not call Nobles to testify during its case in chief or in rebuttal. While the State was under no obligation to produce Nobles to testify at trial, its failure to do so gives rise to an inference against the State. *Poulos,* 196 Ill. App. 3d at 661, 554 N.E.2d at 453. We therefore hold the State's evidence failed to rebut this prong of the entrapment defense beyond a reasonable doubt.

Day next argues the State failed to rebut defense evidence that established he lacked the predisposition necessary to commit the charged crimes. Predisposition is determined through a factual analysis of the case. *People* v. *Katsigiannis,* 171 Ill. App. 3d 1090, 526 N.E.2d 508 (1988). Factors to be analyzed include: (1) defendant's initial reluctance or ready willingness to commit the crime; (2) defendant's familiarity with drugs and willingness to accommodate the needs of drug users; (3) defendant's willingness to make a profit from the illegal act; (4) defendant's prior or current use of illegal drugs; (5) defendant's participation in testing or cutting the drugs; (6) defendant's engagement in a course of conduct involving similar offenses; (7) defendant's ready access to a drug supply; and (8) defendant's subsequent activities. *White,* 249 Ill. App. 3d at 64, 618 N.E.2d at 895.

We find Day put forth sufficient evidence to demonstrate the factors necessary to establish that he lacked the predisposition necessary to engage in drug trafficking.

The State argues the evidence adduced during its case in chief was sufficient to rebut, beyond a reasonable doubt, defense evidence demonstrating the absence of such a predisposition. However, upon a review of the record we find the State merely presented some evidence which, when viewed in the light most favorable to the prosecution, reveals Day's passing familiarity with drugs and a limited willingness to accommodate White's needs as a drug user.

For example, White testified that on June 23, 1994, Day knew an eight ball was an eighth of an ounce of cocaine and used the drug trade term "fronted" when requesting money to purchase drugs. Additionally, the State argues Day's inquiries of whether White was a police officer and if he wore a "wire" indicate predisposition. As a further indication of predisposition, the State points to Day's willingness to establish a line of communication with White by establishing a code so Day would be aware of White's incoming pages. The State also argues Day engaged in counter-surveillance techniques during several of the drug transactions. However, even when these examples are viewed in a light most favorable to the prosecution, they do not outweigh the substantial remainder of unrebutted defense evidence, which tended to demonstrate Day lacked the predisposition to commit the drug offenses with which he was charged and convicted.

Using the factors listed above to establish predisposition we find Day was not inclined to commit a criminal offense. Further, although Day made a ten-dollar profit on June 23, 1994, from his sale to White, Day voluntarily lowered the price on the two subsequent sales to his actual cost for the drugs. Testimony also established Day did not use drugs. Additionally, no evidence was presented to establish Day cut or tested the drugs sold to White. Further, the State's evidence did not satisfactorily establish Day had a ready source of drugs. Rather, Day had to rely on his friend's knowledge of a drug source in Cicero. Moreover, White was kept waiting for two eight balls of cocaine for over two hours on July 29, 1994, despite White's testimony that an eight ball was a small amount of crack cocaine relatively easy to purchase within Will County. Finally, there was no evidence that Day had a prior criminal history of any type, but especially of drug use or drug sales, in Illinois or Wyoming.

We find the evidence, when viewed in the light most favorable to the prosecution, overwhelmingly established that Day lacked the predisposition necessary to commit the drug offenses for which he was convicted. The evidence adduced during the State's case in chief was therefore insufficient to rebut, beyond a reasonable doubt, the second prong of the entrapment defense.

For the foregoing reasons, the judgment of the Circuit Court of Will County is reversed.

Judgment reversed.

[footnotes omitted]

WHAT DO *YOU* THINK?

1. How does the Illinois Criminal Code define entrapment? What two issues must a defendant in Illinois prove in order to establish the entrapment defense?
2. Earlier in this chapter we discussed two approaches to determining whether entrapment had, in fact, occurred: the objective and the subjective. Which approach is used by the court in this case?
3. The Illinois appellate court cited eight factors to be analyzed to determine whether the defendant had or lacked the predisposition necessary to commit the crimes charged. How do each of the eight apply in this case?

NOTES

1. *Pope* v. *State*, 679 So. 2d 710 (1996).

2. Ibid.

3. Sanford H. Kadish and Stephen J. Schulhofer, *Criminal Law and Its Processes: Cases and Materials,* 6th ed. (New York: Little, Brown, 1995), p. 821.

4. Paul H. Robinson, "Criminal Law Defenses: A Systematic Analysis," *Columbia Law Review,* Vol. 82 (1982), pp. 119, 203–204.

5. Kadish and Schulhofer, *Criminal Law,* pp. 893–896.

6. Ibid, p. 896.

7. Model Penal Code, Section 2.09.

8. George Gedda, "Cuba Hijacker Acquitted for Duress," Associated Press wire services, July 26, 1997.

9. Some jurisdictions specify that the "other" must be an immediate family member.

10. *State* v. *Toscano*, 74 N.J. 421, 378 A.2d 755 (1977).

11. *People* v. *Walker,* 18 Cal. Rptr. 2d 431 (1993).

12. California Penal Code, Section 22.

13. See, *People* v. *Low,* 732 P.2d 622 (Colo. 1987).

14. *Davis* v. *State*, 265 Ind. 476, 355 N.E.2d 836 (1976).

15. *Gordon* v. *State,* 52 Ala. 308, 23 Am. Rep. 575 (1875).

16. Although one who purchases baking powder thinking it is heroin may suffer only from his own mistake, since actual possession of a controlled substance is an element of most trafficking offenses.

17. *Gordon,* 52 Ala. 308, 23 Am. Rep. 575.

18. *Ratzlaf* v. *United States,* 114 S. Ct. 655, 126 L. Ed. 2d 615 (1994).

19. *Ratzlaf,* syllabus.

20. *United States* v. *Squires,* 440 F.2d 859 (2d Cir. 1971).

21. *Long* v. *State,* 44 Del. 262, 65 A.2d 489 (1949).

22. "Girl Charged," Associated Press online, northern edition, February 28, 1994.

23. Ira Mickenberg, "A Pleasant Surprise: The Guilty But Mentally Ill Verdict Has Both Succeeded in Its Own Right and Successfully Preserved the Traditional Role of the Insanity Defense," *University of Cincinnati Law Review,* Vol. 55, (1987), pp. 943, 987–991.

24. "Ten-Year-Old Faces Murder Trial as Adult," *The Fayetteville Observer-Times* (North Carolina), August 27, 1989, p. 5A.

25. *In re Ramon M.,* 22 Cal. 3d 419, 584 P.2d 524, 149 Cal. Rptr. 387 (1978).

26. Details for this story are taken from Carl S. Kaplan, "Court Says Agents Went Too Far in Online Sting," *The New York Times online,* July 7, 2000. Posted at http://www.nytimes.com/library/tech/00/07/cyber/cyberlaw/07law.html.

27. In violation of 18 U.S.C., Section 2423(b).

28. *United States* v. *Russell,* 411 U.S. 423 (1973).

29. Ibid.

30. *Cruz* v. *State,* 465 So. 2d 516, 518 (Fla. 1985).

31. Rollin M. Perkins and Ronald N. Boyce, *Criminal Law,* 3rd ed. (Mineola, NY: Foundation Press, 1982), p. 1167.

32. Ibid.

33. Ibid.

34. *Sorrells* v. *United States,* 287 U.S. 435 (1932).

35. *Sherman* v. *United States,* 356 U.S. 369 (1958).

36. *Jacobson* v. *United States,* 503 U.S. 540 (1992).

37. Ibid.

38. Stephen J. Morse, "The 'New Syndrome Excuse Syndrome,' " *Criminal Justice Ethics* (Winter/Spring 1995), p. 7.

39. C. F. Chapman, *Barron's Medical Dictionary for the Non-Professional* (New York: Barron's Educational Series, 1984).

40. Ibid.

41. Morse, "The 'New Syndrome Excuse Syndrome,' " p. 3.

42. *People* v. *Romero,* 8 Cal. 4th 728, 735 (1994), and *People* v. *Dillard,* 96 C.D.O.S. 3869 (1996).

43. *State* v. *Kelly,* 97 N.J. 178 (N.J. 1984).

44. *State* v. *Norman,* 324 N.C. 253, 378 S.E.2d 9 (1989).

45. California Evidence Code, Section 1107.

46. *State* v. *Hodges,* 716 P.2d 563, 567 (Kan. 1986), *supra,* 716 P.2d at p. 567, citing Lenore Walker, *The Battered Woman* (New York: Harper and Row, 1979) pp. 19–31.

47. This list is drawn from Alan M. Dershowitz, *The Abuse Excuse: And Other Cop-Outs, Sob Stories, and Evasions of Responsibility* (Boston: Little, Brown, 1994), pp. 321–341; Richard G. Singer and Martin R. Gardner, *Crimes and Punishment: Cases, Materials, and Readings in Criminal Law,* 2nd ed. (New York: Matthew Bender, 1996), pp. 903–920; and Stephen J. Morse, "The 'New Syndrome Excuse Syndrome,' " *Criminal Justice Ethics* (Winter/Spring 1995), p. 3.

48. *Werner* v. *State,* 711 S.W.2d 639 (Tex. Crim. App. 1986), in which the son of a Nazi concentration camp survivor claimed that Holocaust syndrome caused him to be overly assertive in confrontational situations. The court hearing the case disallowed the claim.

49. *Romero,* 8 Cal. 4th, and *Dillard,* 96 C.D.O.S.

50. *State* v. *Marks,* 647 P.2d 1292 (Kan. Supreme Ct., 1982), in which expert testimony about rape trauma syndrome was allowed to counter a consent defense.

51. *State* v. *Kenneth J. Sharp, Jr.,* 418 So. 2d 1344 (La. Sup. Ct., 1982).

52. "Drunk Driving Charge Dismissed: PMS Cited," *The Fayetteville Observer-Times* (North Carolina), June 7, 1991, p. 3A.

53. As reported in Arnold Binder, *Juvenile Delinquency: Historical, Cultural, Legal Perspectives* (New York: Macmillan, 1988), p. 494.

54. See, for example, Dershowitz, *The Abuse Excuse,* pp. 30–31.

55. These numbers are not meant to be exact, but are only exemplary.

56. Morse, "The 'New Syndrome Excuse Syndrome,' " p. 7.

57. Ibid.

58. Ibid, p. 9.

59. Dershowitz, *The Abuse Excuse.*

60. Ibid, pp. 20–21.

61. *Time,* September 27, 1993, p. 32.

62. Dershowitz, *The Abuse Excuse,* p. 27.

63. Clarence Thomas, "Crime and Punishment—and Personal Responsibility," *The National Times,* September 1994, p. 31.

64. Ibid.

65. Dershowitz, *The Abuse Excuse,* p. 41.

66. G. Williams, "The Theory of Excuses," *Criminal Law Review,* Vol. 19 (1982), pp. 732, 741–742.

7

The Defense of Insanity

Ever since our ancestral common law emerged out of the darkness of its early barbaric days, it has been a postulate of Western civilization that the taking of life by the hand of an insane person is not murder.
—Justice Felix Frankfurter[1] (1882–1965)

It is not because crazy people are caused to do what they do that they are excused; rather, crazy people are excused because they are crazy.
—Michael Moore[2]

No man is sane who does not know how to be insane on proper occasions.
—Henry Ward Beecher (1813–1887)

CHAPTER OUTLINE

AFTER READING THIS CHAPTER YOU SHOULD:

▷ Know the difference between competency to stand trial and the defense of insanity.

▷ Understand the difference between legal understandings of insanity and medical and psychiatric perspectives on mental disorder.

▷ Appreciate the history of the insanity defense, and know the various legal criteria for determining sanity.

▷ Be able to explain the likely consequences to the defendant of a finding of "not guilty by reason of insanity."

▷ Be able to explain the consequences to the defendant of a finding of "guilty but mentally ill."

▷ Know the difference between the defense of diminished capacity and the insanity defense.

INTRODUCTION

On November 15, 1989, Pamela Pearson, Carolyn Sullivan, and Willis Thrasher were murdered at the Crosstown intersection in Tupelo, Mississippi. According to the various witnesses who testified during the trial, at approximately 4 P.M. that afternoon, Joseph Lynn Westbrook stopped his white Oldsmobile vehicle behind a blue vehicle at a red light at the Crosstown intersection. Westbrook then got out of his vehicle and walked to the driver's window of the car stopped directly in front of his. He then fired shots into the car. Witnesses to the crime said that after Westbrook shot into the car, he fired a fifth shell, which was discharged on the ground. At that point, Westbrook walked back to his vehicle and drove away.

At trial, several witnesses who observed the shootings testified and identified Westbrook as the perpetrator. In addition, law enforcement officials described the scene and Westbrook's subsequent arrest. Expert witnesses testified to establish the cause of death, the fact that the fingerprints taken from the shotgun were Westbrook's, and that the five spent shells were fired from the shotgun that was recovered.

Westbrook did not take the stand or otherwise contradict the state's evidence. Instead, the defense sought to establish Westbrook's insanity by calling psychological experts. Dr. L.D. Hutt testified that Westbrook suffered from major depression and also from a condition known as borderline personality disorder, wherein a person alternates between neurosis and psychosis and is otherwise out of touch with reality. Hutt also stated that Westbrook engaged in instances of explosive, violent behavior, a symptom of the diagnosed condition. Hutt testified that Westbrook's relationship with Pamela Pearson was a "major stressor" and that his fear of abandonment attributed greatly to his borderline personality disorder. Hutt also said that, in his opinion, Westbrook was suffering from the conditions of his mental

Web Extra! 7–1

Westbrook v. *State* (1995)

defect at the time of the crime, so that he was unaware of the nature and quality of his actions. In addition, Hutt stated that, during the times he interviewed and observed Westbrook, the defendant was in a condition whereby he could not distinguish right from wrong.

The defense also called Dr. Jan E. Kloek, who testified that at the time of the crime Westbrook was incompetent due to the nature of his condition and that at the time of the shootings he may have been in a dissociative state. Further, Kloek stated that the defendant's mental condition preempted him from understanding or knowing the nature and quality of his actions and from distinguishing right from wrong.

The state, on rebuttal, called Dr. Reb McMichael, who in a written report noted that Westbrook was mentally fit to assist counsel with the preparation of his defense. McMichael ultimately opined that he believed that Westbrook was sane, knew what he was doing, and was aware that his actions were wrong at the time the shootings occurred.

The state also called Dr. Helen Robertson, employed as a clinical psychologist for the State Mental Hospital. Robertson testified that she observed Westbrook while he was housed at the state hospital, and it was her opinion that he was "able to understand and appreciate the nature and quality of his actions on that day." Robertson discussed the basis of her opinion, including the interviews, tests performed, and case history, and also opined that appellant was not psychotic at the time of the shootings. The jury returned a verdict of guilty on all three murder counts.

The wording in this chapter-opening story is adapted from the 1995 Mississippi Supreme Court case of *Westbrook* v. *State*.[3] The story illustrates a central principle of criminal law: A defendant who was insane at the time the offense was committed is generally immune from criminal liability. Moreover, an insane person cannot be tried, convicted, or sentenced for a crime; and a person who becomes insane after sentencing may not be executed if convicted of a capital offense and sentenced to die.[4]

It is important to realize, however, that the terms "insanity" and "insane" are strictly legal terms and have no place in the medical or psychiatric literature. Nonetheless, "insanity" sometimes becomes an issue in legal proceedings, and the defense of insanity is an affirmative defense that can be subsumed under the category of excuses. All United States jurisdictions create a presumption of sanity at trial. In the absence of evidence or claims to the contrary, an accused person is assumed sane for all legal purposes. When a claim of insanity is made, however, some jurisdictions require the defendant to provide proof of his or her claimed condition, while others require the prosecution to prove sanity once the defense of insanity has been raised by the defendant.

COMPETENCY TO STAND TRIAL

COMPETENT TO STAND TRIAL
a finding by a court, when a defendant's mental competency to stand trial is at issue, that the defendant has sufficient present ability to consult with his lawyer with a reasonable degree of rational understanding and that he has a rational as well as factual understanding of the proceeding against him.

Due process requirements prohibit the government from prosecuting a defendant who is legally incompetent to stand trial. Competency to stand trial may become an issue when a defendant appears to be incapable of understanding the proceedings against him or is unable to assist in his own defense due to mental disease or defect. Conversely, a person is **competent to stand trial** if he or she, at the time of trial, has sufficient present ability to consult with his or her lawyer with a reasonable degree of understanding, and a rational as well as factual understanding of the proceedings against him or her.[5]

In 1996, for example, lawyers for multimillionaire chemical heir John E. du Pont successfully argued at a pretrial hearing that their client was psychotic and, as a consequence, was unable to work effectively with lawyers in preparing a defense to murder charges. Du Pont was accused of shooting and killing David Schultz, an Olympic wrestler and 1984 gold medalist who had trained on du Pont's estate near Philadelphia. After the shooting, du Pont was declared schizophrenic by news commentators, pop psychologists, and his own attorneys. His delusions of being the Dalai Lama, Jesus, and "heir to the Third Reich" were all publicized in the national media. "He's not faking it. It's real. He's psychotic," Dr. Robert Sadoff, an expert witness hired by the defense, testified at the pre-trial hearing.[6]

Even a psychotic person, however, may be competent to stand trial—although he or she may later be relieved of criminal responsibility if tried and found not guilty by reason of insanity. Hence, prior to trial prosecutors pointed out that du Pont appeared competent, since he answered to his own name, showed no psychosis while in jail, and signed his own name on court documents—not that of Jesus Christ or the Dalai Lama. He also continued to run his huge estate, dubbed "Foxcatcher," and handle his financial affairs through telephone calls to his staff from jail. "The defendant is able to conduct his affairs, both financial and legal,"[7] assistant district attorney Joseph McGettigan told the court. Delaware County Common Pleas Judge Patricia Jenkins sided with du Pont's attorneys, however, declaring that du Pont "is actually psychotic," and ordered him held in a mental hospital for treatment until doctors could decide that he would be able to assist his lawyers in preparing his defense. In 1997, after half a year of treatment with antipsychotic drugs, a judge ruled that du Pont's competency had been restored. He was then tried and found guilty of third-degree murder in the killing of Schultz, and he was sentenced to thirteen to thirty years in prison or a mental hospital (the place of detention to be decided by Pennsylvania correctional authorities).

Competency to stand trial focuses on the defendant's condition at the time of trial, rather than at the time of the crime. The U.S. Supreme Court has held that "[f]undamental principles of due process require that a criminal defendant who is legally incompetent shall not be subjected to trial."[8] In *Pate* v. *Robinson* (1966)[9] the Court held that a failure to observe procedures adequate to protect a defendant's right not to be tried or convicted while incompetent to stand trial deprives the defendant of the right to a fair trial. The federal test to determine whether a defendant is competent to stand trial was set forth in *Dusky* v. *United States* (1960),[10] in which the Supreme Court held that the "test must be whether he has sufficient present ability to consult with his lawyer with a reasonable degree of rational understanding—and whether he has a rational as well as factual understanding of the proceedings against him."

Section 4241 of Title 18 of the United States Code is entitled, "Determination of Mental Competency to Stand Trial," and reads:

> If . . . the court finds by a preponderance of the evidence that the defendant is presently suffering from a mental disease or defect rendering him mentally incompetent to the extent that he is unable to understand the nature and consequences of the proceedings against him or to assist properly in his defense, the court shall commit the defendant to the custody of the Attorney General. The Attorney General shall hospitalize the defendant for treatment in a suitable facility.[11]

Once sanity has been recovered, the defendant may be brought to trial.

In 1996 the U.S. Supreme Court, in *Cooper* v. *Oklahoma* (1996),[12] ruled that states must let criminal defendants avoid trials if it's more likely than not that they are incompetent. Until *Cooper*, Oklahoma defendants (and defendants in Pennsylvania, Connecticut, and Rhode Island) were required to provide clear and convincing evidence that they were mentally incompetent and therefore unable to participate in their own trials in a meaningful way. As discussed in Chapter 2, clear and convincing evidence is that which establishes the reasonable certainty of a claim, although

Web Extra! 7–2

Cooper v. *Oklahoma* (1996)

the standard requires less than proof "beyond a reasonable doubt." In *Cooper,* the Court held that the clear and convincing evidence standard was too strict and ruled that criminal defendants must be allowed to avoid trials if they show by a preponderance of the evidence that they are mentally unfit. As also pointed out in Chapter 2, proof by a preponderance of the evidence means that the defendant must only convince the court that it is more likely than not that the defendant is mentally incompetent and unable to participate in his or her own trial. Most states and all federal courts[13] were already using the preponderance of the evidence standard to determine competency to stand trial at the time of the *Cooper* ruling.

Once the issue of incompetency is raised, some states and the federal government require the defendant to prove lack of competency in order to avoid trial, while other states require that the prosecution prove the defendant competent before trial can proceed. Arizona is typical of how many states handle competency hearings. Following guidelines set down in *Dusky,* Arizona law says that the term **"incompetent to stand trial** means that, as a result of a mental illness, defect, or disability, a defendant is unable to understand the nature and object of the proceeding or to assist in the defendant's defense." The Arizona law continues, saying: "The presence of a mental illness, defect, or disability alone is not grounds for finding a defendant incompetent to stand trial." In the state of Arizona, at "any time after the prosecutor charges a criminal offense by complaint, information, or indictment, any party or the court on its own motion may request in writing that the defendant be examined to determine the defendant's competency to stand trial, to enter a plea, or to assist the defendant's attorney. . . . Within three working days after a motion is filed . . . the parties shall provide all available medical and criminal history records to the court," and the "court may request that a mental health expert assist the court in determining if reasonable grounds exist for examining a defendant."

Arizona law also says that "[w]ithin thirty days after the report is filed, the court shall hold a hearing to determine a defendant's competency to stand trial. The parties involved may introduce other evidence regarding the defendant's mental condition or may submit the matter by written stipulation on the expert's report. . . . If the court finds that the defendant is competent to stand trial, the proceedings . . . continue without delay." Arizona law specifies that "[i]f the court initially finds that the defendant is incompetent to stand trial, the court shall order treatment for the restoration of competency unless there is clear and convincing evidence that the defendant will not be restored to competency within fifteen months. The court may extend the restoration treatment by six months if the court determines that the defendant is making progress toward the goal of restoration."

When competency cannot be restored, Arizona law stipulates as follows: "If the court finds that a defendant is incompetent to stand trial and that there is no substantial probability that the defendant will regain competency within twenty-one months after the date of the original finding of incompetency, any party may request that the court: (1) Remand the defendant to the custody of the department of health services for the institution of civil commitment proceedings. . . . (2) Appoint a guardian . . . (3) Release the defendant from custody and dismiss the charges against the defendant. . ."[14]

In like manner, all capital punishment jurisdictions require that a person about to be executed understand the situation he or she faces before execution can occur. Continuing with Arizona law, for example, we find that it provides that: "Prisoners who are sentenced to death are presumed competent to be executed. A prisoner may be found incompetent to be executed only on clear and convincing evidence of incompetency." If a condemned prisoner is found to be incompetent, he or she must be sent to a state hospital, and "shall remain confined at the state hospital until the prisoner becomes competent to be executed."[15]

INCOMPETENT TO STAND TRIAL

a finding by a court that, as a result of a mental illness, defect, or disability, a defendant is unable to understand the nature and object of the proceeding against him or to assist in the preparation of his own defense.

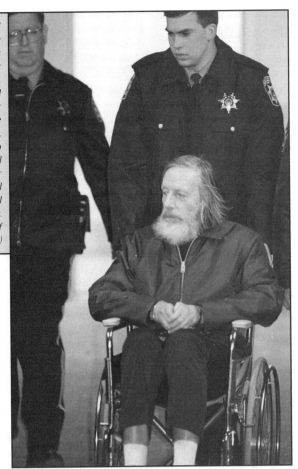

Both competency to stand trial and the legal defense of insanity became issues in criminal proceedings against multimillionaire murder suspect John E. du Pont. Before trial, du Pont, shown here, was portrayed by defense attorneys as psychotic and unable to cooperate in the preparation of an effective defense. Although found incompetent to stand trial in 1996, he was tried and found guilty of third-degree murder in 1997 following a six-month period of forced hospitalization and treatment with antipsychotic drugs. (Photo by Chris Gardner, courtesy of AP/Wide World Photos.)

LAW IN PRACTICE

WAS JOHN SALVI COMPETENT TO STAND TRIAL?

A finding of incompetency to stand trial means that as a result of a mental illness, defect, or disability a defendant is unable to understand the nature and object of legal proceedings or to assist in defense efforts. In 1995, competency to stand trial became an issue in the case of abortion clinic shooter John Salvi III. At the time, Salvi stood accused of killing receptionists Lee Ann Nichols, 38, and Shannon Lowney, 25, and of wounding five other people in two separate attacks on Brookline, Massachusetts, clinics. The attacks occurred on December 30, 1994.

During four days of testimony in July 1995, four psychiatrists argued the issue of Salvi's competency. Three psychiatrists testifying for the defense (Dr. Phillip Resnick, Dr. Ronald Shouten, and Dr. Robert Kinscherff) concluded that Salvi was mentally ill and unfit to stand trial. Dr. Joel Haycock, a psychiatrist for the prosecution, agreed that Salvi suffered from a mental disorder but insisted that the condition would not undermine his ability to participate in a trial. A portion of the hearing transcripts, containing an exchange between Dr. Resnick, a professor of psychiatry at Case Western Reserve University School of Medicine, and defense counsel is reproduced here.

Following the hearing Salvi was found competent and ordered to stand trial. He was convicted of the shootings and sentenced to life in prison without parole. In November 1996 Salvi was found dead in his cell in the state's maximum security prison. Officials said he was

(continued)

LAW IN PRACTICE

Abortion clinic shooter John Salvi. Salvi was convicted in 1995 of the shooting deaths of two people in separate attacks on abortion clinics in Brookline, Massachusetts, in 1994. Salvi, for whom competency to stand trial had been an important issue, later committed suicide in prison. (Photo by Steve Senne, courtesy of AP/Wide World Photos.)

under his bed with a plastic bag tied around his head, while his hands and feet were bound with laces. His death was ruled a suicide.

Q. Now, based on all of the information that you have received and read, and based upon your interviews of Mr. Salvi on those two occasions, and based on our observation of the interaction between Mr. Salvi and one of his attorneys on the second visit, do you have an opinion based on reasonable medical certainty as to whether Mr. Salvi is suffering from a mental disease, disorder, or impairment, sir?

A. Yes, I do.

Q. And what is that opinion, sir?

A. It's my opinion that Mr. Salvi is suffering from a mental disease.

Q. Can you tell us, sir, what mental disease it is in your opinion he is suffering from?

A. Yes. In my opinion Mr. Salvi is suffering from schizophrenia, undifferentiated . . .

Q. Sir, could you tell us what the basis is for your opinion Mr. Salvi is suffering from schizophrenia of an undifferentiated type?

A. Yes. Mr. Salvi shows a number of characteristic symptoms of schizophrenia. The first of these involve delusions, and a delusion is a fixed false belief that cannot be changed by logic. And Mr. Salvi's delusions, there actually are a number of them. He believes that the members of the Catholic Church are being systematically discriminated against and they are losing their jobs. He uses the phrase "financial holocaust" that Catholics are undergoing, and he is very anxious to unite Catholics. Particularly, he has a plan, which he has been discussing for more than a year, of allowing persons charged with counterfeiting to be released from state prisons to be employed by the Vatican to print money. . . . Other examples of delusions that Mr. Salvi has expressed include a belief that frequently adult male Catholics are sterile because of a conspiracy in which their scrotums were injected with a spermicidal agent when they were infants. He also has expressed concern that there is a conspiracy of Free Masons who may blind and kill him. That the Mafia has been after him. That his car has been bugged. . . .

Q. Between the first interview you had and the second interview you had, which were a number of months apart, are you aware of Mr. Salvi becoming aware of his counsel's questions with regard to his competency?

A. Yes. I first raised the issue of competence to Mr. Salvi during my January 15 interview and he made it clear to me that he wanted to be competent to stand trial, did not believe he had a mental illness. Felt that might take away from the message it was important to him to deliver, and so it is entirely possible that he would be less forthcoming with ideas that others would view as psychiatric because he did not want a diagnosis of mental illness. . . .

Q. Do you have some special expertise in the area of malingering?

A. Yes. I have written a number of book chapters and articles on the topic of detecting malingering of mental illness, and I teach workshops around the country on that topic.

Q. Do you have an opinion based on reasonable medical certainty as to whether Mr. Salvi was faking a mental illness at the time that you saw him in January—or in June?

A. My opinion is that Mr. Salvi is not faking mental illness. . . .

Q. In addition to what you just told us, is a history of bizarre and perhaps psychotic behavior indicative of lack of malingering as well?

A. Yes. The more someone had been shown to act in a bizarre manner, say strange things, earlier in their life, that would, that would give weight to the legitimacy of illness, as opposed to someone who said I was fine until two o'clock on a Sunday and now I have had the strange belief since then. That would be more suspicious.

Q. Did you have historical evidence of psychosis in this case?

A. Yes. I had a number of pieces of historical evidence which were consistent with earlier onset of psychosis. . . .

Q. Now, sir, moving on from your diagnosis with regard to mental illness, what is your understanding, sir, of the legal standard in Massachusetts for competency to stand trial?

A. My understanding of the precise legal standard in Massachusetts comes from a case called *Dusky* v. *United States*, and the test is whether Mr. Salvi has sufficient present ability to consult with his lawyer with a reasonable degree of rational understanding and whether he has a rational as well as factual understanding of the proceedings against him.

Q. And in conducting an evaluation to determine competency to stand trial, other than determining whether the individual has some kind of mental illness, could you tell us what is involved in making that evaluation?

A. Yes. In making an evaluation of competent to stand trial as an examiner, I would want to look at those various aspects of things to show whether Mr. Salvi did or did not have a true understanding of the proceedings against him, whether he was able to rationally cooperate with counsel. And ability to cooperate with counsel would include such issues as (1) ability to testify relevantly, (2) has ability to give a valid account of what happened, (3) has ability to understand his legal jeopardy, (4) has an understanding of whether he trusts counsel, and (5) is willing to cooperate in making decisions, such as whether to accept a sanity defense or not. So there would be a number of different areas that would go into that leg of the test regarding ability to rationally cooperate with counsel.

Q. Now sir, based on your, the information that you had accumulated with regard to Mr. Salvi,

your interviews with him in January and June, are you able to form an opinion . . . with reasonable certainty as to whether Mr. Salvi is competent to stand trial at this time?

A. Yes, I am.

Q. And what is that opinion, sir?

A. It's my opinion with reasonable medical certainty that at the present time Mr. Salvi is not competent to stand trial.

Q. Would you tell us, sir, the basis of your opinion?

A. Yes. First I should indicate that there are a number of things which Mr. Salvi is capable of doing. At times he is capable of holding rational conversations. In many areas, he does understand the proceedings against him and the specific charges against him. So I'm not suggesting that he's so ill that he is totally without this ability. However, in my opinion the number of serious deficits are so great that he cannot receive a fair trial in the sense of his ability to cooperate with counsel and his lack of rational understanding of the proceedings against him because of the failure to appreciate his jeopardy.

Q. And do you have an opinion on why he cannot do so, sir?

A. Yes. Specifically, there are four areas which I consider significant in Mr. Salvi's inability to cooperate with his counsel. The first is that Mr. Salvi is so preoccupied with getting out his schizophrenic delusional message, this is the major purpose for his living. That supersedes his own desire to avoid conviction and if necessary receive the death penalty. I understand that the death penalty does not exist in Massachusetts, but he nonetheless has sought it if he were convicted. Specifically, I found when I observed Mr. Salvi and Miss Basil for a 25-minute period in my second interview, where she was going over with him some very important aspects of legal issues, he was distracted, he kept coming back to "have you released my statement, have you released my statement, when are you going to release my statement," and was so preoccupied with that he was unable to attend to the critical issues where his attorney was trying to gain information from him and get him to understand certain legal issues.

Other examples of how important getting the psychiatric message is that he made the statement to me, quote, "My main concern is that
(continued)

LAW IN PRACTICE

if they do away with the case," and that referred to being found not competent to stand trial, "no one will be able to buy, sell, trade," close quotes. So this is an example of his persecution delusions, the credit card, mark of the beast, the need to get out that message which he sees as so important. That is more important than whether or not he goes to trial or the outcome of the trial.

Another example of how important that message is, is that he wrote a letter to the FBI unbeknownst to his attorneys seeking to plea bargain for the death penalty under federal charges where the death penalty is possible and the FBI then turned over the letter to his attorneys, and when Miss Basil confronted him with why were you writing to the FBI about plea bargaining, why weren't you working with me to accomplish that, his response was to not give a good answer and refocus on release of the statement. So here's an example, again, where the importance of the statement supersedes whether he gets good representation or not.

When I ask him "If you could have different attorneys who were willing to release the statement," and I'm referring to those as containing psychotic material, because that is my view, "If you could have attorneys who would be less qualified but would be willing to release the statement, would that, would you be willing to accept less good attorneys who would release the statement," and his answer was, "Yes." Another example of how getting out the psychiatric material is more important than protecting his own jeopardy in court. . . .

And it's also my understanding that in May he had like a minor scene in a courtroom where he was trying to release the statements, and even though he was admonished to be quiet by the judge, he was focused on releasing his statements.

The second area of why he is not able to cooperate with counsel has to do with the fact that Mr. Salvi has not revealed his account of events during the crime, where he was for those two or three days, what his state of mind was, any potential witnesses to call, and he also declines to answer any questions about earlier psychiatric symptoms. So when both his attorney and I have approached Mr. Salvi and said, "Cindy Lockshire says you talked about an angel and demon on your shoulder, is that true or not," his answer is that is

a private matter, or no comment, or I won't discuss that, or that is not relevant. So in terms of building a mental illness defense, which is a critical issue potentially in this trial, his unwillingness to discuss any past psychiatric symptoms is, along with his unwillingness to give an account of the crime, is a critical issue because effectively that causes him to waive the benefits of counsel. If he is unwilling to tell counsel what happened, his counsel cannot rationally decide what affirmative defense might be offered, what plea bargain should or should not be entered into if the counsel does not know what happened and what his state of mind was.

Mr. Salvi also told me, and has told his attorneys, and told Dr. Haycock numerous times that he plans a defense of silence and when he's questioned about that, first of all when his attorneys say, there is no such thing as defense of silence, you know there are certain affirmative defenses, a defense of silence is not valid defense, he nonetheless persists, as he does in other delusional beliefs. And when I pressed him on this he said, quote, "I would rather not acknowledge the prosecution," close quote. That rigid kind of thinking, rather than acknowledge the prosecution, again, suggests he does not fully appreciate the jeopardy he is in because he is also fixed in his ideas.

I also found out, supporting the idea that he doesn't fully appreciate his legal jeopardy, the fact that he is unrealistically optimistic in spite of what I have been told is overwhelming evidence that he did the crime with regard to fingerprints, ballistic evidence, eyewitnesses, he still is unrealistically optimistic that he will not be convicted simply using a defense of silence.

Dr. Haycock in his examination of him made the statement he does not show any anxiety regarding his legal issues. Most people facing life in prison do show some anxiety regarding their legal situation. And when his attorneys press him for information and say, Mr. Salvi I can't defend you, you know, I can't provide a good defense if you don't provide this information. Mr. Salvi's repeated response is, quote, "What will be, will be," close quote. So in other words, there is a kind of acceptance of whatever will happen to him because his principal goal is getting out the message. And again if you can understand this from his psychotic vantage point, if he believes as he said on the video tape that if Catholics will read his message and rise up and stop being persecuted and start printing money, he would have a chance to create a [chance of] saving the homes and the lives and the better health and financial well-being of millions of people, compared to that psychotic goal which he unrealistically believes may occur by simply releasing his statement, his own jeopardy, or going to prison, or being executed is small potatoes in his mind next to his psychotic goal. . . .

Q. With respect to Mr. Salvi's competence, did you consider whether or not Mr. Salvi would be able to evaluate and cooperate with his counsel in selecting relevant defenses, for example, a defense of not guilty by reason of insanity?

A. Yes, I did consider that.

Q. And would he be able to do something like that, is he able to?

A. It's my opinion that this is another area in which Mr. Salvi is not able to cooperate with counsel in a rational manner. Mr. Salvi has no insight into the fact that he is mentally ill. He believes he has no mental illness whatsoever and since a possible insanity defense may be critical in a trial in which a man has a serious disturbance in his thinking, and in which there is strong evidence that he committed a crime, his ability to consider an insanity defense would be important, and Mr. Salvi has been counseled about this by Dr. Haycock, seems to have some trouble understanding the distinction between competent to stand trial and sanity at the time of the act in spite of repeated explanations and, separate from confusion about it, categorically rejects an insanity defense not for rational reasons, such as I would rather be in a prison than a psychiatric hospital, or I don't want the stigma of being in a psychiatric hospital, but simply because he has no insight in the fact that he is seriously mentally ill, so he's rejecting it for irrational reasons and that could seriously interfere with his attorney's ability to gather relevant information about insanity defense and work with him towards his presentation without so antagonizing him that he would become even less cooperative.

Q. Did you consider whether or not Mr. Salvi would be able to testify relevantly in his own behalf?

A. Yes. I did consider that issue carefully, and I considered that part of what would be necessary to cooperate with counsel.

Q. And in your opinion is he able to do so?

A. It's my opinion that Mr. Salvi would not be able to take the stand and testify relevantly. This is in part due to his idiosyncratic, rigid, over elaborative disorganized speech. It's also because of the preeminent importance of getting out his psychotic message that rather than answer questions relevantly on direct or cross he would use such a forum to convey to Catholics the importance of his psychotic message about Catholics being persecuted. And I believe he would refuse to answer some questions, as he has repeatedly for me, Dr. Haycock, and his attorneys and that he would use this defense of silence, which again is not rationally made, and the second video clip illustrates briefly from my first interview an example of how I am trying to gather data from him and he is not answering my questions. . . .

Q. Dr. Resnick . . . I now ask you whether you formed an opinion whether Mr. Salvi rationally understands the proceedings against him?

A. Yes. It's my opinion that Mr. Salvi, although [he] does understand some areas, has some serious defects in his rational understanding of the proceedings against him.

Q. Would you tell us what those serious defects are and your perception about them?

A. I don't think that Mr. Salvi fully appreciates the adversarial nature of the proceedings. Let me give an example of this. In talking about selection of juries, at one point he said "I think that juries can be quick to jump on a Christian," suggesting he was concerned about a fair trial.

Then we talked about what kind of jurors he might want, he said he would like one juror from each different denomination and a juror who is a KKK [member], a juror who is a Free Mason, one juror represents one denomination within Christianity. And when I tried to clarify this because he gave quite a rambling response, I tried to clarify this, he said that that would be a fair trial and it wouldn't be fair if he was able to get twelve Christians.

The point here is that rather than understanding the adversarial nature of the fact that the prosecution may seek jurors who are not favorable to the defense, and vice versa, he felt a need to create fairness in the jury to the extent that he could control it, failing to appreciate the adversarial nature of the proceedings.

(continued)

LAW IN PRACTICE

Q. Are there additional factors that you took into consideration?

A. Yes. As I mentioned earlier, he is unrealistically optimistic and I think therefore does not appreciate the full jeopardy he's in, and when weighing the death penalty decision, he said to Dr. Haycock that he made the decision, quote, based on, quote "finances, time, and Catholic tax dollars." And I think that is an example of where he's allowing his psychotic belief system, more concerned about Catholics, and Catholic tax dollars than he is about protecting his own interests about whether he views the death penalty as a good decision for himself. It ties in with his psychotic thinking about persecution of Catholics. So that globally I think his decision making ability is influenced by the psychotic belief systems so that even though he might intellectually be able to say here's what a judge does, here's what I am charged with, and he can do that for the most part, except in some very small areas. But globally I think that his psychotic, delusional, peculiar idiosyncratic over-elaborative concrete thinking does not allow him to fully and rationally appreciate his own danger in the current situation. . . .

Mr. LaChance: Thank you, Doctor. I have no further questions.

What do you think?

1. What is meant by "competency to stand trial?" Based on the testimonial materials contained here, would you conclude that Mr. Salvi was competent to stand trial? Why or why not?

2. Is there enough information here to make the determination called for in the previous question? If not, what other information would you like to have?

3. Do you think that, based on the materials presented here, Mr. Salvi had "sufficient present ability to consult with his lawyer with a reasonable degree of rational understanding" and had "a rational as well as factual understanding of the proceedings against him"?

4. Do you think Mr. Salvi's assertion that he wanted to use a "defense of silence" was a sign that he was not competent to stand trial? Why or why not? Do you think his claim that "[w]hat will be, will be," and his "acceptance of whatever will happen to him because his principal goal is getting out the message" are signs of insanity? Why or why not?

When the hearing concluded, the hearing judge found Salvi competent to stand trial. At trial, the jury found him guilty of two counts of criminal homicide. In 1996 Salvi received a mandatory sentence of life in prison without parole. Had he been found innocent by reason of insanity, he would have been confined to a state mental hospital, but could have been released when and if authorities found that he had recovered his sanity. He committed suicide a few months later.

PURPOSE OF THE INSANITY DEFENSE

While the question of competency to stand trial may be vitally important to defendants who claim insanity at the time of trial, the court hearing the *Westbrook* case (with which this chapter opened) faced a different issue: the need to determine whether a criminal defendant was insane at the time the crime was committed. It is that question with which we will be concerned throughout the remainder of this chapter.

The insanity defense, like other defenses that have found a place in our legal system, exists because, as the famed jurist David Bazelon once observed, "the criminal law [is] an embodiment of society's moral vision." Therefore, says Bazelon, "[f]inding a defendant guilty is not only a factual judgment; it also constitutes a moral condemnation of the person. In our tradition, moral blame cannot attach where an act was not the result of a free choice. The verdict of not guilty by reason of insanity is nothing more than an expression of that moral intuition."[16]

LAW IN PRACTICE

CAN MENTAL DISEASE OR DISORDER NEGATE *MENS REA?*

Insanity may be a defense to a crime, but the existence of mental disease or disorder can also negate the mens rea necessary for a crime to occur. When that happens, a defendant may be found "not guilty" (rather than "not guilty by reason of insanity"), since the prosecution will be unable to prove that all of the needed elements were in place at the time the offense was committed. Consider, in the following case, whether or not the requisite mens rea for charges of impersonating a federal officer was present in the mind of the defendant.

United States **v. Westcott**
United States Court of Appeals,
Eleventh Circuit, 1996
83 F.3d 1354

Defendant Westcott was charged with two counts of falsely representing himself to be a United States Secret Service agent, in violation of 18 U.S.C. Section 912. The incidents giving rise to the charges occurred on January 5 and 6, 1994. . . .

On March 9, 1994, the district court held a hearing on pending motions. . . . Defendant proffered the testimony of Dr. Ernest Miller, a psychiatrist retained by defendant for the purpose of examining defendant. Dr. Miller testified that defendant suffered from bipolar disorder and that, due to altered brain chemistry, defendant believed himself to be a United States Secret Service agent. When examined by defense counsel, Dr. Miller testified [as follows]:

Q. Now, Mr. Westcott's accused of representing himself to be a Secret Service agent back in January 5th and January 6th of this year and attempting to have motel clerks accept his personal check for payment of a motel room. . . . [D]oes his representation that he was a Secret Service agent, does that relate in any way to his mental condition at the time?
A. Yes. In my opinion it was a—this misidentification of himself, which I think he truly believed himself to be a member of the Secret Service, was a product of the altered brain chemistry which is associated with this genetically

related metabolic defect, the—which causes what we, what we have labeled bipolar disorder to manifest itself. He—he saw himself as a Secret Service agent only because his brain chemistry alters his ability to perceive himself correctly.
Q. Are you saying that Mr. Westcott did not know that he was lying? Assuming that he's not a Secret Service agent. He's not. Are you saying that Mr. Westcott didn't understand, didn't know that he really wasn't a Secret Service agent?
A. In my opinion, the patient believed himself to be a Secret Service agent and connected in some manner with the government, the Treasury Department and/or Secret Service. . . .
Q. Could a person suffering from Mr. Westcott's mental disease, in the condition he was at the time of the charged acts, be able to form or to have what the law refers to as criminal intent in your opinion?
A. No. My opinion—his mental condition was such that he could not form the intent.
Q. Could a person, such a person suffering from the disease Mr. Westcott suffered and the condition he was in at the time, be said to knowingly and willfully commit the crime that he's charged with committing?
A. No.
Q. Could you briefly explain to the Court why not?
A. He truly believed himself to be a representative of the United States government in one of those agencies which I mentioned. He believed this because of a state involuntarily placed upon him by way of his genetics and other features which factor into the development of bipolar disorder. As a result of this, he was under the illusion, slash, delusion that he was a representative of the United States government, and the representations he made, he truly believed and did not—that these were not fabrications or, or designs on his part in order to manipulate others to gain a profitable end, or something of that sort.

Dr. Miller was questioned by the trial judge:

The Court: All right. Assume for the purpose of my next question then that the term "insanity" means a severe mental disease or defect as a

(continued)

LAW IN PRACTICE

result of which one is unable to appreciate the wrongfulness of his acts.

The Witness: Yes, sir.

The Court: All right. How does that definition of "insanity" differ, if at all, from the opinions you have given here concerning Mr. Westcott's mental state on or around January 5, 1994?

The Witness: There is no bottom-line difference as I perceive it, Your Honor.

On the basis of Dr. Miller's testimony, defendant requested that the jury be instructed that defendant's mental condition could be considered in determining whether the government had proven the required element of specific intent and that no instruction be given as to the affirmative defense of insanity. On March 21, 1994, prior to the time opening statements were to be given, the district court ruled that Dr. Miller's proffered testimony constituted evidence of insanity, as defined by the Insanity Defense Reform Act, 18 U.S.C. Section(s) 17. . . .

What do _you_ think?

1. If the expert witness's testimony is to be believed, it would appear that the defendant believed himself to be a Secret Service agent. Would such a belief negate the _mens rea_ needed to prove a charge of impersonating a federal officer? Why or why not?

2. Dr. Miller testified that the defendant in this case suffered from "bipolar disorder," which produced altered brain chemistry. How does the psychiatric notion of bipolar disorder relate to legal notions of insanity, if at all?

Insanity can impact criminal liability in two ways: (1) it may result in a finding that the _mens rea_ required for a specific crime was lacking, leading the court to conclude that no crime occurred, or (2) it may lead to a showing that although the requisite _mens rea_ was present at the time of the crime, the defendant should be excused from legal responsibility because of mental disease or defect. The first perspective allows that a given mental condition may negate an element of an offense, while the latter recognizes that a crime took place but excuses the perpetrator due to a lack of moral blameworthiness. If _mens rea_ cannot be proven by the prosecution, a "not guilty" finding should result. If the defendant possessed the necessary _mens rea_ but is able to successfully raise the defense of insanity, a **"not guilty by reason of insanity" (NGRI)** verdict should be returned. In short, _as a defense,_ insanity recognizes that some persons, by virtue of mental disease or mental defect, cannot morally and justly be held accountable for their actions.

THE INSANITY DEFENSE— A COMMON MISUNDERSTANDING

A prevalent misconception in the criminal law, even among some attorneys, is the belief that _mens rea_ is _automatically_ lacking in an insane defendant and that the purpose of the insanity defense is to advance such a claim. The famed jurist Jerome Hall, for example, once wrote: "If the defendant was insane at the time of the conduct in issue, the requisite _mens rea_ was lacking and no crime was committed."[17] Hall believed that a culpable mental state could not be shown to exist in an insane defendant. Similarly, the Court TV World Wide Web site tells visitors: "In the eyes of the law, a defendant is legally insane if he or she is unable, because of a mental problem, to form a _mens rea,_ a Latin term meaning a guilty mind. Because the law only punishes people who are mentally responsible for their actions, most states allow juries to find a defendant not guilty if he or she was insane at the time a crime was committed. At the heart of an insanity defense is the notion that, because of mental illness, either the defendant could not understand the difference between right and wrong or could not keep from doing the wrong act."[18]

The ability to distinguish between moral good and evil is, however, quite a different issue than that of demonstrating a culpable *mens rea*, when *mens rea* is understood as purposeful or intentional behavior. A person suffering from mental illness may still act purposefully, even though they may not, due to mental disease, be able to fully appreciate the moral implications of their behavior. The difference between intent or purpose and lack of moral sense can be seen in some of the actions of children. Children often act purposefully and intentionally, and they may also act selfishly. A child whose behavior harms another may have intended the behavior, and may even have intended harm, but may not—by virtue of immaturity—have been able to fully realize the moral implications (that is, the "wrongfulness") of their actions.[19]

If children can act purposefully, but are unable to fully appreciate the consequences of their actions, a similar claim can be made for those who are insane at the time they commit a crime. As one court held: "Even the most psychiatrically ill have the capacity to form intentions, and the existence of intent usually satisfies any *mens rea* requirement."[20] Whether we speak of children or the insane, it would be unjust for society to punish those who lack the capacity to understand the moral consequences of their behavior, however intentional it may have been. Children and the insane are not responsible for their behavior not because they don't intend it, but because to hold them responsible given their lack of moral appreciation is fundamentally unfair. In the one case, that of children, the law distinguishes the immature person from the bad one; in the other case, that of the mentally ill, the law distinguishes the bad from the sick.

WHAT *IS* INSANITY?

Just what constitutes "insanity?" The authoritative *Black's Law Dictionary* warns that the term **"insanity"** is "a social and legal term rather than a medical one" and goes on to define the concept as "a condition which renders the affected person unfit to enjoy liberty of action because of the unreliability of his behavior with concomitant danger to himself and others."[22] *Black's* continues, saying that the term "is used to denote that degree of mental illness which negates the individual's legal responsibility or capacity." In other words, mental illness and mental abnormalities, in whatever form they may appear, are not necessarily the same as legal insanity. A person may be mentally ill or mentally abnormal and yet be legally sane.

Moreover, while the term "insanity" may have a relatively specific legal meaning, and a somewhat less specific social one, it does not refer to a particular mental condition recognized by psychiatrists. As *Black's* observes, the term "insanity" has no place in the medical literature—which speaks instead of "mental disorders"—a term also used in some statutes. The definitive work on mental disorders is the *Diagnostic and Statistical Manual of Mental Disorders*[23] published by the American Psychiatric Association. The *Manual*, now in its fourth edition, is referred to as **DSM-IV** and was last revised in 1994. It lists twelve major categories of mental disorders, which are presented in Table 7–1. As the table shows, researchers have identified many different mental illnesses of varying severities and complexities. From a psychiatric perspective, it is far too simplistic to describe a severely mentally ill person merely as "insane." In fact, the vast majority of people with a mental illness would be judged "sane" if current legal tests for insanity were applied to them.[25] Hence, while mental illness may explain a person's behavior, it seldom excuses it.

INSANITY
an affirmative defense to a criminal charge; a social and legal term (rather than a medical one) that refers to "a condition which renders the affected person unfit to enjoy liberty of action because of the unreliability of his behavior with concomitant danger to himself and others."[21] Also, a finding by a court of law.

Web Extra! 7–3

Britannica online: insanity

The insane, like young infants, lack one of the essential attributes of personhood—rationality.

—M. Moore, *California Law Review* (1985)

DSM-IV
the fourth edition of the *Diagnostic and Statistical Manual of Mental Disorders*,[24] published by the American Psychiatric Association. The DSM-IV lists twelve major categories of mental disorder.

TABLE 7.1

MEDICAL CATEGORIES OF MENTAL DISORDERS

Organic Mental Disorders: Psychological or behavioral abnormalities associated with temporary or permanent dysfunction of the brain. Causes include aging, disease, injury, and drugs. Delirium and dementia are subcategories.

Schizophrenia: Characterized by symptoms such as disordered thought processes and delusions or hallucinations. Symptoms must exist for more than six months for a diagnosis of schizophrenia to be made. Catatonic and paranoid schizophrenia are subtypes.

Dissociative Disorder: Characterized by a splitting or dissociation of normal consciousness. Included here are multiple personalities, psychogenic amnesia, and psychogenic fugue.

Delusional Disorders: Central feature is the presence of a dominant delusion (for example, the belief that the person is being persecuted). Delusions may also be associated with schizophrenia.

Personality Disorders: Chronic, inflexible, and maladaptive personality patterns that are generally resistant to treatment. Antisocial personality disorder is one subtype.

Psychosexual Disorders: Characterized by sexual arousal via unusual objects (fetishism) or situations, or by sexual dysfunctions.

Impulse Control Disorders: Characterized by an inability to control impulses, and to act impulsively. Included are kleptomania, pyromania, and pathological gambling. Addictions, including drug addiction, alcoholism, and food additions may also fall into this category.

Psychoactive Substance Use Disorders: Produced by excessive and long-term use of mind-altering substances, such as stimulants, barbiturates, cocaine, heroin, and alcohol.

Mood Disorders: Also known as affective disorders, they are characterized by emotional extremes. Major depression and manic-depressive (bipolar) disorders are included.

Anxiety Disorders: Characterized by apprehension, dread, and fear, and sometimes associated with particular situations or types of situations, but which may also exist independently of such situations. Phobias, generalized anxiety disorder, panic attacks, and obsessive-compulsive disorders are subtypes.

Somatoform Disorders: Physical symptoms, such as paralysis, without biological explanation. Hypochondriasis, conversion disorder, and somatization disorder are subtypes.

Disorders Evident in Infancy, Childhood, or Adolescence: Disorders characterized by early onset, including mental retardation, attention-deficit disorder, hyperactivity, anorexia, bulimia, stuttering, sleep-walking, and bedwetting.

SOURCE: Adapted from American Psychiatric Association, *Diagnostic and Statistical Manual of Mental Disorders*, 4th ed. (Washington, D.C.: American Psychiatric Association, 1994).

Psychiatric understandings of mental disorder focus on conditions that produce problems in living and are built on therapeutic models. Such understandings are clearly amenable to societal pressures and influences. For example, although the American Psychiatric Association had at one time classified homosexuality as a disorder, a powerful gay rights movement during the 1980s led to the exclusion of sexual preferences from the current list of medically recognized mental disorders.

Even though the term "insanity" is a legal and not a psychiatric one, legal insanity, as a concept, is still predicated upon a disease or disability of the mind. As one judge observed: "It is not enough, to relieve from criminal liability, that the prisoner is morally depraved. It is not enough that he has views of right and wrong at variance with those that find expression in the law. The variance must have its origin in some disease of the mind."[26]

HISTORY OF THE INSANITY DEFENSE

The insanity defense has its modern roots in the 1843 case of Daniel M'Naughten, a woodcutter from Glasgow, Scotland. M'Naughten appears to have suffered from what today might be called paranoia or delusions of persecution. He believed that he was in some way being persecuted by Robert Peel, who was then prime minister of England. M'Naughten traveled to London with the intention of assassinating Peel and would have succeeded but for the fact that Peel chose to ride in the carriage of Queen Victoria (who did not take part in the procession) rather than in his own. Peel's carriage was occupied by Edward Drummond, Peel's secretary, and it was Drummond whom M'Naughten killed—believing him to be Peel. Upon his arrest, M'Naughten told police that he had come to London to kill the prime minister because "[t]he Tories in my city follow and persecute me wherever I go, and have entirely destroyed my peace of mind. [T]hey do everything in their power to harass and persecute me; in fact they wish to murder me."

Early English common law tests for determining sanity stressed the defendant's ability "to discern the difference between moral good and evil,"[27] and the defendant's knowledge of the nature of the act.[28] The *M'Naughten* case formalized both tests and brought them together, although it almost led in an entirely new direction. In the course of a lengthy trial, M'Naughten's defense counsel claimed that their client was insane, relying in large part on a new and innovative work by Dr. Isaac Ray, entitled the *Medical Jurisprudence of Insanity*. Dr. Ray's text foreshadowed much of what we know today as modern psychiatry. Jurors in the *M'Naughten* trial, for example, were told that "the human mind is not compartmentalized and . . . a defect in one aspect of the personality could spill over and affect other areas."[29] Seen this way, Ray's thinking represented an enlightened movement away from then-prevalent conceptions, such as "phrenology" and "monomania,"[30] which saw the personality as a compartmentalized structure whose various characteristics were in large part determined by the shape of the skull and physical features of the brain. Lord Chief Justice Tindal, obviously impressed with the new perspective on insanity, undertook a clear movement away from established tradition when he charged the *M'Naughten* jury with these words: "The question to be determined is whether at the time the act in question was committed, the prisoner had or had not the use of his understanding, so as to know that he was doing a wrong or wicked act. If the jurors should be of opinion that the prisoner was not sensible, at the time he committed it, that he was violating the laws both of God and man, then he would be entitled to a verdict in his favour; but if, on the contrary, they were of the opinion that when he committed the act he was in a sound state of mind, then their verdict must be against him." *M'Naughten,* found to be insane, was acquitted.

The *M'Naughten* Rule—Knowing Right from Wrong

As one judge observed, "M'Naughten's case could have been the turning point for a new approach to more modern methods of determining criminal responsibility."[31] The *M'Naughten* verdict, however, caused much public outcry and angered Queen Victoria, who herself had been the recent target of an assassination attempt. In an effort to bolster traditional common law interpretations of insanity, the leadership of the House of Lords called judges from across the country to a special session. Under strong political pressure, the assembled judges were led to reaffirm the old

M'NAUGHTEN RULE
a rule for determining insanity that asks whether the defendant knew what he was doing or whether he knew that what he was doing was wrong.

right–wrong test and to reject emerging medical understandings of insanity. Lord Chief Justice Tindal responded to questions by members of the House on behalf of the gathered judges. A portion of his remarks are reproduced in the following Law in Practice box. Hence, as one author observed, "By an accident of history, the rule of M'Naughten's case froze [those primitive] concepts [of phrenology and mono-mania] into the common law just at a time when they were becoming obsolete"[32] in the medical community. "In this manner," one court wrote, "Dr. Ray's insights were to be lost to the common law for over one hundred years except in the small state of New Hampshire."[33]

> M'Naughten and its antecedents can, in many respects, be seen as examples of the law's conscientious efforts to place in a separate category, people who cannot be justly held 'responsible' for their acts.
>
> —*United States v. Freeman*, 357 F.2d 606 (2d Cir. 1966)

Problems with *M'Naughten* The *M'Naughten* Rule includes two possibilities: (1) a lack of *mens rea* (the person didn't know what he was doing) and (2) an acceptable legal excuse (the person didn't know that it was wrong). *Either* alternative provides an acceptable defense under *M'Naughten*.

LAW IN PRACTICE

LORD CHIEF JUSTICE TINDAL ANSWERS QUESTIONS ON THE INSANITY DEFENSE

The verdict of "not guilty by reason of insanity" in the 1843 trial of Daniel M'Naughten broke new ground by bringing legal conceptualizations of insanity closer to emerging medical understandings of mental illness. The verdict so enraged Queen Victoria, however, that she called a special session of the House of Lords to clarify English common law understandings of insanity. Judges from across the country were required to attend. The atmosphere of the session was fraught with strong political pressure to reject the reasoning of the M'Naughten court and to reinforce traditional understandings of insanity. Lord Chief Justice Tindal answered questions on behalf of the assembled judges. The following key passage from Lord Tindal's testimony embodies what has come to be known as the M'Naughten Rule, and was to guide English and American courts on issues of insanity for the better part of a century. Many jurisdictions still adhere to the M'Naughten Rule.

Lord Chief Justice Tindal:

. . . Your Lordships are pleased to inquire of us. . . "What are the proper questions to be submitted to the jury, where a person alleged to be afflicted with insane delusions respecting one or more particular subjects or persons, is charged with the commission of a crime (murder, for example), and insanity is set up as a defence?"

. . . We have to submit our opinion to be, that the jurors ought to be told in all cases that every man is to be presumed to be sane, and to possess a sufficient degree of reason to be responsible for his crimes, until the contrary be proved to their satisfaction; and that to establish a defence on the ground of insanity, it must be clearly proved that, at the time of the committing of the act, the party accused was labouring under such a defect of reason, from disease of the mind, as not to know the nature and quality of the act he was doing; or, if he did know it, that he did not know he was doing what was wrong. . .

Note: 8 Eng. Rep. 718 (1843).

What do *you* think?

1. How does Lord Tindal's formulation of the insanity defense compare with contemporary understandings? How is it similar to the Pennsylvania statutes that are reprinted in the Law on the Books box on page 263? How is it similar to the charge Lord Tindal gave the jury in the *M'Naughten* case? How is it different?

2. If Daniel M'Naughten had been tried under the criteria expressed in this box, how do you think he would have fared? Would he have been convicted of murder, or found "not guilty by reason of insanity?" Give reasons for your position.

Central to the second alternative provided by the *M'Naughten* Rule is the possibility that a defendant may be able to demonstrate insanity by showing that, while he knew what he was doing, he did not know that his behavior was "wrong." The wrongfulness test has been at the center of controversy since its inception. The **Insanity Defense Reform Act (IDRA)** of 1984, the Model Penal Code, the American Psychiatric Association's model standard on legal insanity, and most state penal codes, all contain some form of the wrongfulness test, and all make use of the word "wrong" or "wrongfulness" in attempting to assess a defendant's mental condition at the time of the crime.

Considerable disagreement exists, however, over whether the word "wrong" refers to the defendant's ability to appreciate the *legal* or the *moral* wrongfulness of his or her act. For a defendant to know that an act was legally wrong, all that is required is that he or she be aware of the fact that the act in question is against the law. Defendants who, by reason of mental disease or defect (Alzheimer's disease, for example), are not so aware, would be insane from a legal point of view. On the other hand, according to the second school of thought, if a defendant knows that his or her activity is illegal, but believes that it is morally acceptable or even righteous, then he or she might be legally insane.

In the case of John Salvi, for example, whose competency hearing is the subject of a Law in Practice box in this chapter, it seems clear that Salvi knew that the killing of abortion clinic workers was against the law, but the actions were justified in his mind because he saw them as necessary to prevent a greater holocaust (the deaths of numerous unborn babies). He may even have believed that, in killing workers at abortion clinics, he was carrying out God's will. As one precedent-setting case held: "If . . . there is an insane delusion that God has appeared to the defendant and ordained the commission of a crime, we think it cannot be said of the offender that he knows the act to be wrong."[34]

In addition to legal and moral perspectives, the ability to *appreciate* or to *know* the wrongfulness of conduct can be interpreted from a psychiatric point of view. Psychiatrically speaking, the ability to appreciate wrongfulness can involve much more than either a legal or moral sense. A deeper appreciation of the wrongfulness of one's actions can be had when a well-integrated personality experiences both emotional as well as cognitive and intellectual awareness that give rise to a sense of right and wrong.

Given the complexities of the issues involved, some jurisdictions attempt to solve the question of whether a defendant *knew* his or her action was *wrong* by instructing juries that a defendant must have the capacity to understand the nature of the act. Other jurisdictions leave it up to the jury's common sense to decide what such terms mean.

By the early 1900s, it was generally accepted that strict application of the *M'Naughten* Rule "deprives the trier of fact of many of the insights yielded by modern psychiatry." As a result, other proposals for assessing legal insanity were made—primary among them the irresistible impulse test, the American Law Institute test, and the *Durham* Rule. Each will be discussed in the pages that follow.

INSANITY DEFENSE REFORM ACT (IDRA) part of the 1984 Crime Control and Prevention Act, the IDRA mandated a comprehensive overhaul of the insanity defense as it operated in the federal courts, making insanity an affirmative defense to be proved by the defendant by clear and convincing evidence and creating a special verdict of "not guilty by reason of insanity."

Control Rules—The Irresistible Impulse Test

The wrongfulness component of the *M'Naughten* Rule has been criticized for the fact that it focuses only on the cognitive component of the personality. In other words, to *know* that one's actions are wrong requires the ability to think and to judge. Moreover, the *M'Naughten* Rule does not allow for degrees of insanity.

[The insanity defense] invokes the deepest questions about our society's willingness to pay the price of our moral principles...
—Judge David Bazelon (D.C. Cir.)

Under the rule, either a person knows what he or she is doing, and knows that it is wrong, or he or she does not. There is no middle ground. Recognizing this, some authors have said: "The essence of *M'Naughten* is that for mental disease or defect to incapacitate, it must be of such a degree as to leave the person irrational—that is, no rational person lacks criminal capacity by reason of insanity."[35] It is possible to imagine a situation, however, in which a person knows what they are doing, knows that it is wrong, and still is unable to stop doing it. A famous potato chip commercial of a few years ago, for example, challenged viewers with the phrase "You can't eat just one!" The advertisement made the claim that once a person tasted one of the seller's chips, they would be unable to resist having more.

Although there is nothing legally or morally "wrong" with eating potato chips, it may be that some people find it equally impossible to control other forms of behavior that are against the law. During the 1920s, in the belief that some forms of behavior could not be controlled, many states modified the *M'Naughten* Rule to permit "irresistible impulse" defenses. **Irresistible impulse defenses** claim that, at the time the crime was committed, a mental disease or disorder prevented the defendant from controlling his or her behavior. Some jurisdictions that use the irresistible impulse provision employ a "policeman at the elbow" jury instruction. Jurors are told that "if the accused would not have committed that act had there been a policeman present, he cannot be said to have acted under irresistible impulse."

Critiques of the irresistible impulse defense point out that it may be impossible to really know who can and who cannot control their behavior in specific situations, and that such an excuse might apply to all who commit crimes. In the case of the second claim, the inability to control one's impulses might be a general characteristic of criminal personalities, making it possible to argue that all criminal offenders engage in illegal behavior because of lessened behavioral controls. Were it not for such a lack of control ability, proponents of such a perspective would suggest, criminals would be law-abiding citizens.

IRRESISTIBLE IMPULSE TEST

a test for insanity that evaluates defense claims that, at the time the crime was committed, a mental disease or disorder prevented the defendant from controlling his or her behavior in keeping with the requirements of the law.

The *Durham* Rule—Crime as a Product of Mental Disease

Web Extra! 7–4

Durham v. *U.S.* (1972)

In 1954, in the case of *Durham* v. *United States* (1954),[36] the U.S. Court of Appeals for the District of Columbia concluded that all existing tests to determine legal sanity were flawed. The court then went on to develop its own standard, stating that the rule "is simply that an accused is not criminally responsible if his unlawful act was the *product* of mental disease or mental defect." The **Durham Rule,** also known as the **"product rule,"** built on the court's belief that an inability to distinguish right from wrong is merely a symptom of mental disease, and that behavior resulting from the disease is a more apt determinant of legal insanity.

DURHAM RULE

also known as the **product rule;** holds that an accused is not criminally responsible if his or her unlawful act was the product of mental disease or mental defect.

Unfortunately, however, few mental health professionals could be found who expressed the relationship between mental illness and behavior as the court did. As a result, the *Durham* Rule was quickly criticized by those who said that it was out of touch with medical reality. Others claimed that it was far too vague, and provided little guidance to the jury, resulting in potentially far too many acquittals. As one federal appellate court held: "The most significant criticism of *Durham* . . . is that it fails to give the fact-finder any standard by which to measure the competency of the accused."[37]

In 1972 the District of Columbia court that had offered the *Durham* rule eighteen years earlier finally rejected it[38] in favor of a "prevailing community standards" approach to assessing criminal liability. In *United States* v. *Brawner,*[39] the court held that "a defendant is not responsible if at the time of his unlawful conduct his mental or emotional processes or behavior controls were impaired to such an extent that he cannot *justly* be held responsible for his act." The *Brawner* ruling effectively defined insanity in terms of social justice, rather than in terms of established legal or psychiatric notions.

The ALI Test—Substantial Capacity

In an effort to clarify standards for assessing legal insanity, the American Law Institute (ALI) incorporated a **substantial capacity test** into the Model Penal Code. In doing so, the ALI noted that "[n]o problem in the drafting of a penal code presents larger intrinsic difficulty than that of determining when individuals whose conduct would otherwise be criminal ought to be exculpated on the ground that they were suffering from mental disease or defect when they acted."[41]

The ALI substantial capacity test is a modernized version of the *M'Naughten* Rule, blended with control rules. It reads: "A person is not responsible for criminal conduct if at the time of such conduct, as a result of mental disease or defect, he lacks substantial capacity either to appreciate the criminality [wrongfulness] of his conduct or to conform his conduct to the requirements of the law."[42]

The ALI test substitutes the word *appreciate* for *know* in the original *M'Naughten* formulation and recognizes the role of impulse through use of the phrase "conform his conduct to the requirements of the law." The test is also written so as to better recognize modern psychiatric knowledge through use of the word *substantial*, which acknowledges that although portions of a defendant's personality might be affected by mental disease in such a way as to render him or her legally insane, some mental capacity might still remain.

> **SUBSTANTIAL CAPACITY TEST**
> a test developed by the American Law Institute and embodied in the Model Penal Code. The test holds that "a person is not responsible for criminal conduct if at the time of such conduct as a result of mental disease or defect he lacks substantial capacity either to appreciate the criminality [wrongfulness] of his conduct or to conform his conduct to the requirements of the law."[40]

> It is not because their mental disease causes the insane to commit crimes that we excuse them, no more than it is because an infant's lack of rationality causes him to do bad that we excuse him. Rather, in both cases, we excuse because the actors lack the status of moral agents.
>
> —M. Moore, *California Law Review* (1985)

Guilty But Mentally Ill (GBMI)

A definitive moment in the history of the insanity defense in this country came in 1982—with a NGRI verdict in the trial of John Hinckley, a young man enamored of actress Jodie Foster, who admitted trying to assassinate President Ronald Reagan for the delusional purpose of proving his love for the actress. After weeks of conflicting testimony by a parade of expert witnesses for both the defense and prosecution, the judge in the *Hinckley* trial instructed jurors to weigh the issue of insanity in terms of the Model Penal Code approach and to return a verdict of "not guilty" unless they could agree "beyond a reasonable doubt" that Hinckley was sane. Since the expert witnesses the jury heard from could not agree among themselves as to Hinckley's sanity, the jury instruction virtually assured the NGRI verdict—and one was promptly returned.

Public outcry at the *Hinckley* verdict led as many as half of all the states to rewrite their "insanity" statutes, with many returning to *M'Naughten*–like standards. Before *Hinckley*, the Model Penal Code definition of insanity had been adopted by ten of the eleven federal courts of appeals and by more than half of all the states. After *Hinckley*, a few states (Idaho, Montana, and Utah among them) abolished the insanity defense except insofar as insanity could be shown to impact the specific *mens rea* required by statute for a particular crime. Also in response, the U.S. Congress passed the 1984 Crime Control and Prevention Act, which included the Insanity Defense Reform Act (IDRA) of 1984[43]—mentioned briefly earlier in this chapter. With the IDRA, Congress mandated a comprehensive overhaul of the insanity defense as it operated in the federal courts. The IDRA made insanity an affirmative defense to

> At bottom, the determination whether a man is or is not held responsible for his conduct is not a medical but a legal, social, or moral judgment.
>
> —*United States* v. *Freeman*, 357 F.2d 606 (2d Cir. 1966)

be proven by the defendant by clear and convincing evidence and created a special verdict of "not guilty by reason of insanity" (NGRI).[44] Through the IDRA, Congress intended to prohibit the presentation of evidence of mental disease or defect, short of insanity, to excuse conduct.[45]

The IDRA does not, however, prohibit psychiatric evidence that may be relevant to proving whether or not a crime occurred. If a subjective state of mind is an element of a crime, for example, evidence regarding the existence or absence of that state of mind becomes relevant to whether a crime was in fact committed. As federal courts have ruled: "Psychiatric evidence which negates *mens rea* . . . negates an element of the offense rather than constituting a justification or excuse"[46] and may be admitted at trial for that purpose. As in federal courts, the use of psychiatric evidence is admissible in all state jurisdictions today to negate *mens rea* where the evidence presented focuses on the defendant's specific state of mind at the time the offense was committed.

The IDRA also created a comprehensive civil commitment procedure under which a defendant found NGRI is held in custody pending a court hearing. The hearing must occur within forty days of the verdict. At the conclusion of the hearing, the court determines whether the defendant should be hospitalized or released.

A second type of response to the *Hinckley* verdict found ten states adopting statutes that permitted findings of **"guilty but mentally ill" (GBMI).** All of the states patterned their laws after a 1975 Michigan statute that created the possibility of GBMI verdicts in Michigan criminal trials. GBMI statutes require that, when the insanity defense is raised at trial, judges must instruct juries that four verdicts are possible: (1) guilty, (2) not guilty, (3) not guilty by reason of insanity, and (4) guilty but mentally ill. A jury must return a finding of "guilty but mentally ill" if: (1) every element necessary for a conviction has been proven beyond a reasonable doubt, (2) the defendant is found to have been *mentally ill* at the time the crime was committed, and (3) the defendant was *not* found to have been *legally insane* at the time the crime was committed. The difference between mental illness and legal insanity is a crucial one, as a Law in Practice box in this chapter points out.

A finding of GBMI is equivalent to a finding of "guilty," and the court will sentence the defendant just as a person found guilty of the crime in question would be sentenced. A GBMI verdict establishes that "the defendant, although mentally ill, was sufficiently in possession of his faculties to be morally blameworthy for his acts."[48] As one author says, "[t]he most obvious and important function of the GBMI verdict is to permit juries to make an unambiguous statement about the factual guilt, mental condition, and moral responsibility of a defendant."[49]

Once sentenced, GBMI offenders are evaluated to determine whether hospitalization or psychiatric treatment is needed. If the offender is hospitalized, he or she will join the "regular" prison population on release from the treatment facility. Time spent in the hospital and in prison both count toward sentence completion, and the offender will be released from custody after the sentence has been served—even if he or she still suffers from mental disease.

GUILTY BUT MENTALLY ILL (GBMI) equivalent to a finding of "guilty," a GBMI verdict establishes that "the defendant, although mentally ill, was sufficiently in possession of his faculties to be morally blameworthy for his acts."[47]

DIMINISHED CAPACITY

DIMINISHED CAPACITY also **diminished responsibility;** a defense based on claims of a mental condition, which may be insufficient to exonerate a defendant of guilt but that may be relevant to specific mental elements of certain crimes or degrees of crime.

The defense of **diminished capacity,** also called **diminished responsibility,** is available in some jurisdictions. However, "the terms 'diminished responsibility' and 'diminished capacity' do not have a clearly accepted meaning in the courts."[50] Some defendants who offer diminished capacity defenses do so in recognition of the fact that such claims may be based on a mental condition that would not qualify as mental disease or mental defect, nor be sufficient to support the affirmative defense of insanity—but which might still lower criminal culpability. According to Peter

LAW ON THE BOOKS

"GBMI" AND "INSANITY" UNDER PENNSYLVANIA LAW.

Compare with Model Penal Code, section 4.01

PENNSYLVANIA CONSOLIDATED STATUTES

Title 18, Section 314. Guilty but mentally ill.

a. General rule.—A person who timely offers a defense of insanity in accordance with the Rules of Criminal Procedure may be found "guilty but mentally ill" at trial if the trier of facts finds, beyond a reasonable doubt, that the person is guilty of an offense, was mentally ill at the time of the commission of the offense, and was not legally insane at the time of the commission of the offense.

b. Plea of guilty but mentally ill—A person who waives his right to trial may plead guilty but mentally ill. No plea of guilty but mentally ill may be accepted by the trial judge until he has examined all reports prepared pursuant to the Rules of Criminal Procedure, has held a hearing on the sole issue of the defendant's mental illness at which either party may present evidence, and is satisfied that the defendant was mentally ill at the time of the offense to which the plea is entered. If the trial judge refuses to accept a plea of guilty but mentally ill, the defendant shall be permitted to withdraw his plea. A defendant whose plea is not accepted by the court shall be entitled to a jury trial, except that if a defendant subsequently waives his right to a jury trial, the judge who presided at the hearing on mental illness shall not preside at the trial.

c. Definitions—For the purposes of this section and 42 Pa. C.S., section 9727, (relating to disposition of persons found guilty but mentally ill):

1. "Mentally ill." One who as a result of mental disease or defect, lacks substantial capacity either to appreciate the wrongfulness of his conduct or to conform his conduct to the requirements of the law.

2. "Legal insanity." At the time of the commission of the act, the defendant was laboring under such a defect of reason, from disease of the mind, as not to know the nature and quality of the act he was doing or, if he did know it, that he did not know he was doing what was wrong.

d. Common law *M'Naughten's* Rule preserved—Nothing in this section shall be deemed to repeal or otherwise abrogate the common law defense of insanity (*M'Naughten's* Rule) in effect in this Commonwealth on the effective date of this section.

Title 18, Section 315. Insanity.

a. General rule—The mental soundness of an actor engaged in conduct charged to constitute an offense shall only be a defense to the charged offense when the actor proves by a preponderance of evidence that the actor was legally insane at the time of the commission of the offense.

b. Definition—For purposes of this section, the phrase "legally insane" means that, at the time of the commission of the offense, the actor was laboring under such a defect of reason, from disease of the mind, as not to know the nature and quality of the act he was doing or, if the actor did know the quality of the act, that he did not know that what he was doing was wrong.

Arenella, "The defense [of diminished responsibility] was first recognized by Scottish common law courts to reduce the punishment of the 'partially insane' from murder to culpable homicide, a non-capital offense."[51]

The diminished capacity defense is similar to the defense of insanity in that it depends on showing that the defendant's mental state was impaired at the time of the crime. As a defense, diminished capacity is most useful where it can be shown that, because of some defect of reason or mental shortcoming, the defendant's capacity to form the *mens rea* required by a specific crime was impaired. Unlike an insanity defense, however, which can result in a finding of "not guilty," a diminished capacity defense is built on the recognition that "[m]ental condition, though insufficient to

Web Extra! 7–5

Britannica online: diminished responsibility

Andrew Goldstein (left), sentenced to twenty-five years to life in prison after being convicted of murder for throwing a stranger (thirty-two-year-old Kendra Webdale, right) to her death in front of a speeding subway train in New York City in 1999. Jurors concluded that Goldstein, a paranoid schizophrenic who had been in and out of mental institutions for years, knew right from wrong at the time of the crime. (Photo(a) by Marth Lederhandler, courtesy of AP/Wide World Photos. Photo(b) courtesy of AP/Wide World Photos.)

exonerate, may be relevant to specific mental elements of certain crimes or degrees of crime."[52] So, for example, defendants might present evidence of mental abnormality in an effort to reduce first-degree murder to second-degree murder, or second-degree murder to manslaughter when a killing occurs under extreme emotional disturbance. Similarly, in some jurisdictions very low intelligence will, if proved, serve to reduce first-degree murder to manslaughter.[53]

The Model Penal Code limits applicability of diminished capacity to cases in which capital punishment might be imposed, saying: "Whenever the jury or the Court is authorized to determine or to recommend whether or not the defendant shall be sentenced to death or imprisonment upon conviction, evidence that the capacity of the defendant to appreciate the criminality [wrongfulness] of his conduct or to conform his conduct to the requirements of law was impaired as a result of mental disease or defect is admissible in favor of sentence of imprisonment."[54]

As is the case with the insanity defense, some jurisdictions have entirely eliminated the diminished capacity defense. The California Penal Code, for example, provides: "The defense of diminished capacity is hereby abolished . . .,"[55] and adds that "[a]s a matter of public policy there shall be no defense of diminished capacity, diminished responsibility, or irresistible impulse in a criminal action or juvenile adjudication hearing."[56] Although California law limits the use of certain excuses that might be raised to negate *mens rea*, however, a showing that the required *mens rea* was in fact lacking can still lead to acquittal. California does allow that ". . . evidence of diminished capacity or of a mental disorder may be considered by the court at the time of sentencing or other disposition or commitment."[57]

HOW WIDELY USED IS THE INSANITY DEFENSE?

> We have an insanity plea that would have saved Cain.
>
> —Mark Twain (1872)

The insanity defense is not widely used. According to a 1991 eight-state study, which was funded by the National Institute of Mental Health and reported in the

Bulletin of the American Academy of Psychiatry and the Law,[58] the insanity defense was used in less than 1 percent of the cases that came before county-level courts. The study showed that only 26 percent of all insanity pleas were argued successfully and further found that 90 percent of those who employed the defense had been previously diagnosed with a mental illness. As the American Bar Association says, "[t]he best evidence suggests that the mental nonresponsibility defense is raised in less than 1 percent of all felony cases in the United States and is successful in about a fourth of these."[59] In most cases where a defendant is acquitted on a NGRI finding, it is because the prosecution and the defense have agreed on the appropriateness of the plea before trial. The implication, according to the American Psychiatric Association, is that the insanity defense is rarely used by "fakers."[60]

Other studies show similar results. *Myths and Realities: A Report of the National Commission on the Insanity Defense,* for example, found that in 1982 only 52 of 32,000 adult defendants represented by the Public Defender's office in New Jersey—less than .2 percent—entered an insanity plea; and, of those, only 15 were successful.[61] Similar studies of New York City courts reveal that an insanity plea is entered, on average, in only 1 in 600 or 700 criminal cases.[62]

When entered, however, insanity pleas may be used in a wide variety of cases. The eight-state study found that approximately half of those pleading insanity had been indicted for violent crimes, although less than 15 percent had been charged with murder. The "other" 50 percent of insanity pleas were entered in robbery, property damage, and minor felony cases.

CONSEQUENCES OF AN INSANITY FINDING

Few defendants found "not guilty by reason of insanity" or "guilty but mentally ill" are immediately released, as would be a person who is acquitted of a crime—although nondangerous defendants may not by law be kept longer than necessary to assess their condition. Generally, those found "not guilty by reason of insanity" or "guilty but mentally ill" are subject to a hearing to determine whether or not they are still mentally ill and dangerous to themselves or others, and whether or not confinement in a treatment facility is justified.[63] Most are so confined, and studies show that persons found NGRI are, on average, held at least as long as persons found guilty and sent to prison.[64] After a period of time, a person so confined may request a hearing to determine if he or she is no longer a danger to self or others and is eligible to be released. At such a hearing, in order for confinement to continue, the state must demonstrate by clear and convincing evidence that the person poses a danger to self or others and requires continued confinement.

In *Foucha* v. *Louisiana* (1992),[65] the U.S. Supreme Court held that it is unconstitutional to put the burden of proving that confinement is no longer justified on the defendant. In *Foucha,* the Court overturned Louisiana's blanket procedure of incarcerating in mental facilities those acquitted of crimes by reason of insanity. The state's scheme, which resulted in the detention of acquitted defendants who were no longer insane, required detainees to prove that they were not "dangerous" before they could be released. In contrast, the Court concluded that acquitted defendants no longer suffering from mental disease should be released, and held that an assessment of "dangerousness" that is not based on a clear showing of mental illness does not provide a legal justification for detention. In the words of the Court:

> . . . the State asserts that, because Foucha once committed a criminal act and now has an antisocial personality that sometimes leads to aggressive conduct, a disorder for which there is no effective treatment, he may be held indefinitely. This

rationale would permit the State to hold indefinitely any other insanity acquittee not mentally ill who could be shown to have a personality disorder that may lead to criminal conduct. The same would be true of any convicted criminal, even though he has completed his prison term. It would also be only a step away from substituting confinements for dangerousness for our present system which, with only narrow exceptions and aside from permissible confinements for mental illness, incarcerates only those who are proved beyond a reasonable doubt to have violated a criminal law.[66]

After *Foucha,* other courts found it acceptable for states to require offenders found NGRI, and who are no longer deemed mentally ill at the conclusion of trial, to participate in outpatient treatment programs through which they can be monitored.[67]

Today, most persons found NGRI are confined after trial, since they continue to be mentally ill. As a result, defense attorneys generally request that juries be in-

---

CRIMINAL LAW IN THE NEWS

Congress OKs Mental Health Courts

Bill Seeks Treatment, Not Jail for Ill Inmates, Sponsors Say

WASHINGTON—A bill on its way to the White House for approval would create 100 mental health courts nationwide to focus on treatment or rehabilitation of the mentally ill or retarded who have ended up in the criminal justice system.

The legislation, sponsored by two Ohio congressmen, would seek up to $10 million a year to fund the new courts, which would be created by 2005.

The attorney general would be responsible for providing grants to states to set up the specialized courts. Under the plan, prisoners suspected of mental afflictions would be diverted from the criminal justice system into the mental health courts, which would work in cooperation with local community-based programs offering treatment, counseling, education and health care.

"As a prosecutor in my home of Greene County, Ohio, I learned that our state and local penal facilities have become way stations for far too many of our nation's mentally ill," said Sen. Mike DeWine, R–Ohio, in a statement.

DeWine said the legislation is intended to relieve law enforcement and corrections officials from handling people whose actions may have been influenced by forces out of their control.

Penal institutions are designed to incarcerate hardened criminals and are not necessarily the best places for treating and caring for those with mental illnesses, he said.

Broad support

Rep. Ted Strickland, D–Ohio, a psychologist, co-sponsored the bill with DeWine, and it now awaits action by President Clinton.

The measure was supported by several governmental, corrections and mental health organizations, including the National Mental Health Association.

NMHA spokesman Ralph Ibson said prisons have become "mental health warehouses" and welcomed the concept of the mental health courts, which he characterized as a pilot program that has not been tested nationwide.

A growing problem

Currently, mental health courts exist only in Alaska, California, Florida, Indiana, New York, Ohio, Oregon, and Washington.

But Ibson stressed the measures in the legislation are not the only solutions to a growing problem in U.S. jails and prisons.

"If there are not appropriate and quality treatment programs to which to divert offenders who have mental illnesses, you haven't helped the system in any significant way" by merely creating a court, Ibson said.

If Clinton signs the bill, the new courts will need to be evaluated to see if they really work as desired, he said.

Similar to drug courts

DeWine compared the mental health courts to the drug courts that have sprouted up in many communities in recent years. Those courts have been expected to relieve some of the congestion in criminal courts by dealing solely with drug offenses, and assigning and monitoring treatment, rehabilitation, and punitive actions.

Ibson said he saw potential overlap between the two specialized court systems, because many inmates who are mentally ill are also substance abusers. "Integrated care" could tangle the parallel, specialized judicial systems at times, he said.

Congress voted to approve the bill late Tuesday as it steams toward a possible Friday recess for the session.

Source: James Gordon Meek, "Congress OKs Mental Health Courts; Bill Seeks Treatment, Not Jail for Ill Inmates, Sponsors Say," APB News. October 25, 2000. Reprinted with permission.

Most defendants found 'not guilty by reason of insanity' are sent to mental institutions until they are no longer considered a danger to themselves or to others. (Photo by John Zillioux, courtesy of Liaison Agency, Inc.)

formed of the likely consequences of a NGRI verdict. Attorneys want to ensure that the jury doesn't assume a potentially dangerous or unstable defendant will be immediately released back into the community if an NGRI verdict is returned. In *Shannon* v. *United States* (1994),[68] however, the U.S. Supreme Court held that federal courts are not required to instruct a jury regarding the potential consequences to the defendant of a verdict of NGRI. Most state courts have still to rule on the issue.

ABOLISHING THE INSANITY DEFENSE

Because of the difficulties associated with assessing insanity from a legal perspective, some scholars advocate a strict *mens rea* approach to insanity. That approach would amount to a wholesale elimination of the insanity defense and its replacement with a test to assess the presence or absence of a culpable mental state in a defendant who is thought to be suffering from mental disease or defect.

As mentioned earlier, three states—Montana, Utah, and Idaho—have already moved in just such a direction. Frustration over the inability of medical and legal professionals to agree on the nature of exculpatory insanity, plus the difficulties that attend the application of legal tests for insanity, led to the abolishment of the insanity defense *as an excuse* in those jurisdictions. The Idaho criminal code, for example, succinctly states: "Mental condition shall not be a defense to any charge of criminal conduct."[69] While states such as Iowa no longer allow defendants to raise the insanity defense as an excuse to a criminal charge, defendants in all jurisdictions may still claim that the presence of mental disease at the time of the crime left them unable to form the *mens rea* needed for criminal activity. In states such as Iowa (and elsewhere), a successful showing that a culpable mental state was lacking would lead a judge or jury to conclude that no crime occurred.

Rather than focusing on the elements necessary for crime, other authorities suggest that claims of insanity should only be considered at the sentencing phase of a criminal proceeding—once guilt has already been established. Some states do just that and use bifurcated trials, involving two stages. In the first stage, the state attempts to prove the defendant's guilt without reference to claims of insanity. If the trier of fact determines that the defendant committed the offense in violation of the law, a second stage then follows in which attention turns to psychiatric testimony and the offender's claim that he or she should be sentenced differently, due to mental problems, than others found guilty of the same offense.

SUMMARY

- Insanity is a social and legal term rather than a medical one. Psychiatrists speak of mental disorders and do not use the term "insanity," making it difficult to fit expert psychiatric testimony into legal categories. Nonetheless, the legal concept of insanity still has its basis in some disease of the mind.

- Competency to stand trial focuses on the defendant's condition at the time of trial, rather than at the time of the crime. The U.S. Supreme Court has held that "[f]undamental principles of due process require that a criminal defendant who is legally incompetent shall not be subjected to trial."

- Competency to stand trial exists when a defendant has sufficient present ability to consult with his or her lawyer with a reasonable degree of rational understanding and has a rational as well as factual understanding of the proceedings against him or her. Defendants found incompetent to stand trial may later be brought to trial if competency is recovered.

- The purpose of the insanity defense is to remove legal culpability from a mentally ill defendant under circumstances where it would not be morally right to hold him or her criminally responsible. The insanity defense recognizes that some persons, by virtue of mental disease or mental defect, cannot morally and justly be held accountable for their actions.

- Insanity can impact criminal liability in two ways: (1) it may result in a finding that the *mens rea* required for a specific crime was lacking at the time the crime was committed or (2) it may lead to a showing that although the requisite *mens rea* was present at the time of the crime, the defendant should be excused from legal responsibility because of mental disease or defect.

- The defense of insanity is an affirmative defense and must be raised by the defendant. If successful, an insanity defense results in a verdict of "not guilty by reason of insanity" (NGRI).

- The *M'Naughten* Rule, an early test, held that a person was insane if he or she "was laboring under such a defect of reason, from disease of mind, as not to know the nature and quality of the act he was doing; or if he did know it, that he did not know he was doing what was wrong."

- The claim of irresistible impulse is a defense in some jurisdictions. The irresistible impulse test asks if, at the time the crime was committed, a mental disease or disorder prevented the defendant from controlling his or her behavior.

- The *Durham* Rule, also known as the product rule, holds that an accused is not criminally responsible if his unlawful act was the *product* of mental disease or mental defect.

- The American Law Institute's substantial capacity test, which is incorporated into the Model Penal Code, says that a person is not responsible for criminal conduct if at the time of such conduct, and as a result of mental disease or defect, he lacks substantial capacity either to appreciate the criminality of his conduct or to conform his conduct to the requirements of the law.

- A guilty but mentally ill (GBMI) verdict establishes that a defendant, although mentally ill, was sufficiently in possession of his faculties to be morally blameworthy for his acts.

- The defense of diminished capacity, also called diminished responsibility, is available in some jurisdictions. It is based on claims that a defendant's mental condition at the time of the crime, although not sufficient to support the affirmative defense of insanity, might still lower criminal culpability. A finding of diminished capacity may result in a verdict of "guilty" to lessened charges.

- The insanity defense is not widely used and is raised in only about 1 percent of all criminal cases. Defendants found "not guilty by reason of insanity" are rarely set free, but are instead committed to a mental hospital until confinement is no longer deemed necessary.

- Because of the difficulties associated with assessing insanity from a legal perspective, a number of jurisdictions have eliminated the insanity defense. While some states no longer allow defendants to raise the insanity defense *as an excuse* to a criminal charge, defendants in all jurisdictions may still claim that the presence of mental disease at the time of the crime left them unable to form the *mens rea* needed for criminal activity.

QUESTIONS FOR DISCUSSION

1. How does the legal notion of "insanity" differ from psychiatric conceptions of "mental disorder?" What is the significance of such differences from a legal perspective?

2. How is competency to stand trial assessed? How might defendants who are truly incompetent be best distinguished from those who are "faking it?"

3. What is the difference in a finding that, as a result of mental disease or defect, a defendant may lack the specific *mens rea* required for a given crime, and a finding that a defendant is insane?

4. What is the difference between a finding of NGRI and one of GBMI?

5. Compare and contrast the various legal "tests" for assessing insanity that are discussed in this chapter. Which do you think is the most useful? Why?

6. Some jurisdictions have eliminated the insanity defense. Why do you think they did so? Do you agree with such reasoning? Why or why not?

LEGAL RESOURCES ON THE WORLD WIDE WEB

Some Web sites provide powerful search engines that can help you find topics of interest, including particular statutes, important documents, and court opinions. Some of the best known legal search engines on the Internet include these:

All Law
http://www.alllaw.com
Permits a search of the All Law site itself, as well as targeted searches of federal and state law.

American Law Sources Online (ALSO)
http://lawsource.com
Provides a comprehensive, uniform, and useful compilation of links to all online sources of American law that are available without charge.

Find Law
http://www.findlaw.com
Permits searching of many law-related topics, including case law, legal practice materials, law schools, legal subjects, dictionaries, and libraries.

Law Crawler
http://www.lawcrawler.com
Allows plain English and Boolean searches for legal information within individual country domains and state and federal government servers.

Law Guru
http://www.lawguru.com/multisearch/multimenu.html
The multiresource legal research tool at Law Guru is a parallel search engine that allows you to search more than 500 legal search engines and tools at one time.

Law Runner
http://www.lawrunner.com
Provides for the use of predefined intelligent agents in conjunction with the well-known Web index, AltaVista™.

Laws Online
http://www.lawsonline.com
Allows searches of federal and state legal databases, as well as searches of all federal and many state courts.

Virtual Chase
http://www.virtualchase.com/resources/index.shtml
The Legal Research Guide section of Virtual Chase permits searches of case law, state and local law, international law, legal reference materials, and more.

Information on how to choose a Web search engine can be found at http://www.virtualchase.com/Search_Engines/index.html. Remember to check the *Criminal Law Today* Web site for URLs that may have changed.

SUGGESTED READINGS AND CLASSIC WORKS

Bruce A. Arrigo, *The Contours of Psychiatric Justice: A Postmodern Critique of Mental Illness, Criminal Insanity, and the Law* (Hamden, CT: Garland, 1996).

Michael Bavidge, *Mad or Bad?* (New York: St. Martins Press, 1989).

Carl Elliott, *The Rules of Insanity: Moral Responsibility and the Mentally Ill Offender* (Binghamton, NY: State University of New York Press, 1996).

Norman Finkel, *Insanity on Trial* (New York: Plenum, 1988).

Seymour L. Halleck, "The Assessment of Responsibility in Criminal Law and Psychiatric Practice," in David N. Weisstub (Ed.), *Law and Mental Health: International Perspectives* (New York: Pergamon, 1987).

Harlow M. Huckabee, *Lawyers, Psychiatrists and Criminal Law: Cooperation or Chaos?* (Springfield, IL: Charles C. Thomas, 1980).

Michael Moore, *Law and Psychiatry: Rethinking the Relationship* (New York: Cambridge University Press, 1985).

Richard Moran (Ed.), *The Annals of the American Academy of Political and Social Science: The Insanity Defense* (London: Sage Publications, 1985).

Norval Morris, *Madness and the Criminal Law* (Chicago: University of Chicago Press, 1982).

Donald Paull, *Fitness to Stand Trial* (Springfield, IL: Charles C. Thomas, 1993).

Daniel N. Robinson, *Wild Beasts and Idle Humours: The Insanity Defense from Antiquity to the Present* (Cambridge, MA: Harvard University Press, 1996).

Rita Simon and David Aaronson, *The Insanity Defense: A Critical Assessment of Law and Policy in the Post-Hinckley Era* (New York: Praeger, 1988).

Henry J. Steadman, Margaret A. McGreevy, and Joseph P. Morrisey, *"Before and After Hinckley: Evaluating Insanity Defense Reform* (New York: Guilford Press, 1993).

Thomas Szasz, *Psychiatric Justice* (Syracuse, NY: Syracuse University Press, 1989).

IS THERE A MEANINGFUL DIFFERENCE BETWEEN "INSANITY" AND "TEMPORARY INSANITY"?

CAPSTONE CASE

Miller v. *State*
Supreme Court of Nevada, 1996
991 P.2d 1183

FACTS: On May 8, 1993, Robyn Goring (Goring) was stabbed to death in the apartment she shared with appellant John Kilioi Miller (Miller) and their two children. Maria Jordan (Jordan), an officer on the Las Vegas police force, lived in the apartment directly below Goring and Miller's apartment. Jordan heard loud noises in the apartment above her on May 8, 1993. When Jordan went to the upstairs apartment, Miller opened the door and stated something to the effect that "I blew it" or "I lost it." Jordan noticed blood on Miller's clothes, two children in the apartment's living room, and the body of a young woman on the kitchen floor.

Officers responded to a 911 call by Jordan and observed Goring's body on the kitchen floor with a knife protruding from her torso. While being transported to the police station, Miller stated that he did not deserve to be treated nicely. Before and after Miller was informed of his *Miranda* rights, he volunteered incriminating statements. Miller stated, "I lost control and I just picked her up," and "I'm sorry. I don't want to live anymore. Shoot me." Also, Miller's shirt and the bottom of his pants appeared to be bloodstained.

The medical examiner's office found a total of forty-two stab wounds, many superficial, inflicted upon Goring's body. On June 10, 1993, Miller was charged with first-degree murder with the use of a deadly weapon. At trial, Goring's mother and sister testified that Goring lived with Miller for twelve years but was planning to leave Miller because he oppressively controlled Goring's life and was physically violent toward her.

Thomas Bittker (Bittker), an expert in psychiatry, testified regarding Miller's history of seizures and other symptoms that are indicative of depression. Bittker noted that Miller's medical history "conspicuously lacked" any evidence of amnesia or a violent episode associated with a specific seizure. Bittker concluded that no clear evidence existed to connect Miller's seizure disorder with the killing of Goring. The parties stipulated that if Bittker was recalled as a witness, he would conclude that Miller was sane at the time of the murder.

Norton Roitman (Roitman), a certified psychiatrist, diagnosed Miller as suffering from organic aggressive and delusional behavior, a seizure condition that was first recognized by dysfunctional brain-wave activity when Miller was twenty-two years old. Miller's aggressive outbursts started early in his life and resulted in rage that was totally out of proportion to the stimuli. According to Roitman,

Miller's personality condition is directly related to his seizure activity. But for this condition, Roitman concluded that the attack on Goring would not have occurred. Roitman also concluded that when Miller stabbed Goring, he could not appreciate the nature of his acts and could not recognize the difference between right and wrong. Also, according to Roitman, Miller can only understand what he is doing before the violence is triggered, whereupon his outburst is not structured but has a flaring, slashing quality. Remorse then sets in when the violent outburst subsides. In conclusion, Roitman stated that Miller was not sane at the time of the stabbing.

Austin Moody (Moody), a certified neurologist, testified for the defense and agreed with Roitman regarding Miller's abnormal brain activity and personality disorder. Moody believed that Miller suffers from an aggressive brain disorder whereby violence can be triggered quickly and end quickly, immediately followed by remorse. Moody concluded that before the stabbing of Goring, Miller was sane; but during the stabbing, Miller could not appreciate the nature of his actions and was insane.

Dr. Jack Jurasky, a psychiatrist who testified for the prosecution, concluded that Miller's outburst was of such a violent nature that he could not have appreciated the nature of his actions when he stabbed Goring.

Miller's sister, Annie Pedro (Pedro), testified that on one occasion, Miller hit their brother ten times in an outburst that ended as abruptly as it began. Afterwards, Miller was very remorseful. On another occasion, according to Pedro, Miller struck her numerous times and immediately apologized, not knowing why he hit her. Miller's father testified that Miller did not remember attacking Goring and that there were a lot of things his son did not remember.

At the close of the guilt phase of the trial, the jury found Miller guilty of first-degree murder with the use of a deadly weapon. At the penalty hearing, Miller was sentenced to life in prison without the possibility of parole.

Miller raises five contentions in this appeal: (1) whether the district court properly refused to give Miller's proffered jury instructions regarding the insanity defense, (2) whether the prosecution's and the district court's comments regarding temporary insanity unduly prejudiced Miller, (3) whether the prosecution's penalty phase argument for sympathy for the victim unduly prejudiced Miller, (4) whether the district court properly admitted hearsay statements of the victim, and (5) whether the district court properly admitted evidence of Miller's prior bad acts. Because we conclude that the denial of Miller's proffered instructions, coupled with the subsequent comments of the State and the district court regarding temporary insanity, confused the jury and unduly prejudiced Miller's trial, this opinion does not address Miller's latter three contentions.

DISCUSSION: The *M'Naughten* test for insanity has been applied in Nevada since 1889. *State* v. *Lewis*, 20 Nev. 333, 22 P.241 (1889). To prove a defendant is insane under the *M'Naughten* test, the defense must show that the defendant labors under such a mental defect that the defendant cannot understand the nature of his or her actions, or cannot tell the difference between right and wrong. See *Kuk* v. *State*, 80 Nev. 291, 298–99, 392 P.2d 630, 634 (1964) (explaining the holding of Lewis). Because a finding of criminal liability requires a conclusion that a defendant's culpable mental state existed contemporaneously with a culpable act, a successful insanity defense must show the elements of *M'Naughten* existed at the time of the act. See *United States* v. *Fox*, 95 U.S. 670, 671 (1877).

In the trial described here, Miller's defense theory was that he was sane before and after killing Goring, but was insane during the actual killing. Three medical experts testified that his mental condition made him prone to fall into violent seizures while completely sane. Further testimony showed that Miller could then act extremely violent with no ability to appreciate the nature of his actions, but would come out of the seizure acting deeply remorseful upon realizing the nature of his conduct. Miller presented evidence that on May 8, 1993, he fell into a violent seizure, stabbed Goring forty-two times, and then came out of the seizure consumed with remorse. Three medical experts concluded that Miller satisfied the *M'Naughten* insanity test during the period in which he stabbed Goring.

At the close of evidence in the trial, the district court instructed the jury to determine whether Miller was legally insane when he killed Goring. The district court also instructed the jury that a finding of insanity required proof that at the time Miller killed Goring, he was laboring under a defect of the mind that caused him not to understand the nature or quality of his actions, or that what he was doing was wrong. Finally, the district court instructed the jury to consider Miller's mental condition before and after the killing to throw light on what Miller's mental condition was at the time of the killing.

Concerned that the jury was confused about the time duration component of the insanity defense, Miller proffered two jury instructions. The first proffered instruction was entitled "temporary insanity" and stated that "[r]egardless of its duration, legal insanity which existed at the time of the commission of the crime is a defense to the crime." The second proffered instruction stated that when evidence shows that at times the defendant was legally insane and at other times he was legally sane, he has the burden of proving by a preponderance of the evidence that he was legally insane at the time of the commission of the act. The district court denied Miller's proffered instructions, ruling that the instructions described temporary insanity and that temporary insanity is not a defense in Nevada.

On two occasions during closing arguments in the guilt phase of Miller's trial, the prosecutor told the jury that temporary insanity is not a recognized defense in Nevada. On one occasion, the prosecutor stated that "[o]n defense's closing you heard about organic aggressive syndrome in relation to temporary insanity or insanity in general. Again, there's no such thing as temporary insanity in this state. It does not exist." The district court endorsed the prosecutor's statements by overruling Miller's objections to the statements and proclaiming, "He [the prosecutor] can argue that it's not a defense under the law."

The district court based its denial of Miller's proffered instructions, and its allowance of the prosecutor's statements regarding temporary insanity, on this court's decisions in *Fox* v. *State*, 73 Nev. 241, 316 P.2d 924 (1957), and *Singleton* v. *State*, 90 Nev. 216, 522 P.2d 1221 (1974).

In *Fox*, the defendant sought a jury instruction that evidence of a mental defect could lessen his degree of guilt even though he could not satisfy the *M'Naughten* test for insanity. *Fox*, 73 Nev. at 242–43, 316 P.2d at 925. In essence, *Fox* was requesting a diminished capacity defense. *Id.* at 243, 316 P.2d at 925. The *Fox* court denied the use of diminished capacity as a justification for a lesser degree of guilt. *Id.* at 245, 316 P.2d at 926. However, in so ruling, the *Fox* court characterized Fox's defense as that of "temporary insanity." *Id.* at 242, 316 P.2d at 925.

In *Singleton*, this court cited to *Fox* and stated that "[a] mental disorder less than insanity does not itself destroy the capacity to premeditate or to entertain the requisite intent." *Singleton*, 90 Nev. at 220, 522 P.2d at 1223. Like *Fox*, the defense proffered in *Singleton* was not insanity for a temporary interval of time. *Id.*

We conclude that *Fox* and *Singleton* considered only the diminished capacity defense, a condition that can be present only in the absence of *M'Naughten* insanity. The diminished capacity defense, in states where it is recognized, requires only a showing of a mental illness that is partially responsible for the defendant's conduct. See *State* v. *Wilcox*, 436 N.E.2d 523 (Ohio 1982). The diminished capacity defense does not require a showing that the defendant could not appreciate the nature of his acts or determine whether his acts were right or wrong. *Id.*

Accordingly, we conclude that any implication drawn from the reference in *Fox* and *Singleton* to temporary insanity is misplaced and the spawning ground for

substantial confusion. Clearly, a person can benefit from the *M'Naughten* insanity defense if he shows he was insane during the temporal period that coincides with the time of the crime. *Flowers* v. *State,* 139 N.E.2d 185, 196 (Ind. 1957). Technically and semantically, such a finding is temporary insanity. Therefore, if a defendant presents evidence of insanity during the interval that coincides with the commission of the crime charged, that defendant is entitled to a correct and complete instruction that insanity on a temporary basis can be a defense to the crime.

We conclude that the district court properly denied Miller's instructions when they were offered. The instructions given by the district court addressed the contemporaneous requirement of the *M'Naughten* rule. In two places, the instructions stated that the sanity of the defendant had to be determined at the time of the commission of the offense or crime. As such, the essence of Miller's proffered instructions were contained in the instructions given by the district court. See *Collins* v. *State,* 88 Nev. 168, 170, 494 P.2d 956, 957 (1972).

However, after the instructions were given, the district court and the prosecutor told the jury that "temporary insanity" is not a defense. Even though the jury instructions stated that insanity must be present at the time of the commission of the offense, the jury was not told that the duration of the insanity does not matter. The jury was not told that the insanity defense applied even if the evidence showed Miller to be legally insane at some time and yet legally sane at others.

We conclude that allowing the prosecutor to comment that "temporary insanity is not a defense" materially confused the jury. The jury was then faced with the dilemma of distinguishing between whether insanity existed "for the time interval" that coincides with the time of the criminal act or for a "temporary" time. While Miller's proffered instructions could have alleviated the jury's confusion, the district court refused to offer those instructions to the jury. Therefore, the denial of Miller's proffered instructions, coupled with the comments of the State and the district court regarding temporary insanity, prejudicially confused the jury.

CONCLUSION: In this case, Miller presented competent evidence that he was insane when he killed Goring but was sane before and after the killing. Accordingly, Miller was entitled to a correct and complete instruction that excusable insanity, even for a short period, could be a defense to the crime. Moreover, comments of the prosecutor and the district court regarding the unavailability of temporary insanity as a defense in Nevada hopelessly confused the jury.

Accordingly, Miller's judgment of conviction is reversed and this matter is remanded for a new trial.[1]

Footnote
1. The legislature revised NRS 174.035 in 1995, thereby replacing the plea of not guilty by reason of insanity with the plea of guilty but mentally ill. 1995 Nev. Stat., Ch. 637, Section(s) 5 at 2450. The amendment will not affect Miller's prosecution because the amendatory provisions are applicable only to offenses committed on or after October 1, 1995. *Id.* Section(s) 61 at 2485.

WHAT DO *YOU* THINK?
1. Dr. Norton Roitman, a psychiatrist, diagnosed the defendant, John Kilioi Miller, as suffering from an "organic aggressive delusional" disorder. What else does Roitman say about Miller's mental condition?
2. According to Roitman, when Miller killed Robyn Goring he "could not appreciate the nature of his acts and could not recognize the difference between right and wrong." If Roitman was correct, what legal test for insanity would Miller have met?
3. Dr. Jack Jurasky, a psychiatrist who testified for the prosecution, concluded that Miller's outburst was of such a violent nature that he could not have appreciated the nature of his actions when he stabbed Goring. If Jurasky was correct, what legal test for insanity would Miller have met?

4. Miller claimed to be sane before and after the killing, but insane during the time the crime was committed. His attorneys asked that, at the close of trial, the jury be instructed on the issue of temporary insanity, and that they be told that "regardless of its duration, legal insanity that existed at the time of the commission of the crime is a defense to the crime." Why do you think that the trial court refused to give the jury instructions regarding the insanity defense, which the defendant wished to have communicated?

5. In this case, the appellate court reversed the defendant's conviction and remanded the case for a new trial. On what basis was that decision reached? Do you agree that the appellate court should have reached such a decision? Why or why not?

6. What does this case have to tell us about the difference between insanity and temporary insanity? Are differences between the two terms significant in cases such as this one? Why or why not?

NOTES

1. As quoted in Alan M. Dershowitz, *The Abuse Excuse: And Other Cop-Outs, Sob Stories, and Evasions of Responsibility.* (Boston: Little, Brown, 1994), p. 9.

2. Michael Moore, "Causation and Excuses," *California Law Review,* Vol. 73 (1985), pp. 1091, 1137–1139.

3. *Westbrook* v. *State,* 658 So. 2d 847 (Miss. 1995).

4. See *Ford* v. *Wainwright,* 477 U.S. 399 (1986).

5. *United States* v. *Taylor,* 437 F.2d 371 (4th Cir. 1971).

6. "Experts Testify du Pont 'Psychotic,'" Associated Press, September 22, 1996.

7. Aliah Wright, "Du Pont Incompetent," Associated Press, September 24, 1996.

8. *Pate* v. *Robinson* (1966), 383 U.S. 375, 86 S. Ct. 836, 15 L. Ed. 2d 815.

9. Ibid.

10. *Dusky* v. *United States* (1960), 362 U.S. 402, 80 S. Ct. 788, 789, 4 L. Ed. 2d 824, 825.

11. 18 U.S.C. Section 4241, subsection C.

12. *Cooper* v. *Oklahoma,* 116 S. Ct. 1373, 134 L. Ed. 2d 498 (1996).

13. See 18 U.S.C. Section 4241.

14. Arizona Penal Code, Sections 13-4501; 13-4503; 13-4507; 13-4510.

15. Arizona Penal Code, Section 13-4022.

16. D. Bazelon, *Questioning Authority: Justice and Criminal Law,* reprint ed. (New York: New York University Press).

17. Jerome Hall, *General Principles of Criminal Law,* 2nd ed. (Indianapolis, IN: Bobbs-Merrill, 1960), p. 449.

18. Court TV, World Wide Web site, September 21, 1996.

19. Note that this is quite a different question than assuming that children under the age of seven cannot form the *mens rea* needed for criminal liability.

20. *United States* v. *Pohlot,* 827 F.2d 889 (3d Cir. 1987).

21. Joseph R. Nolan and Jacqueline M. Nolan-Haley, *Black's Law Dictionary: Definitions of the Terms and Phrases of American and English Jurisprudence, Ancient and Modern,* 6th ed. (St. Paul, MN: West Publishing Co., 1990).

22. Ibid.

23. American Psychiatric Association, *Diagnostic and Statistical Manual of Mental Disorders,* 4th ed. (Washington, D.C.: American Psychiatric Association, 1994).

24. Ibid.

25. American Psychiatric Association, World Wide Web site, September 20, 1996.

26. *People* v. *Schmidt,* 110 N.E. 945, 949 (N.Y. 1915).

27. *Ferrers' Case,* 19 How. St. Tr. 886 (1760).

28. *Hadfield's Case,* 27 How. St. Tr. 1282 (1800).

29. Much of the material in this section is taken from *United States* v. *Freeman,* 357 F.2d 606 (2d Cir. 1966), which provides an excellent summation of the *M'Naughten* case and of the development of the M'Naughten Rule.

30. Phrenology was the study of the shape of the human skull in an attempt to assess personality characteristics. Monomania is a theory that holds "a disorder affected only one compartment of the mind without affecting the mind as a whole." See Rollin M. Perkins and Ronald N. Boyce, *Criminal Law,* 3rd ed. (Mineola, NY: Foundation Press, 1982), p. 964, citing earlier sources.

31. Ibid.

32. Ibid.

33. Ibid.

34. *Schmidt,* 110 N.E., at 945, 949.

35. Perkins and Boyce, *Criminal Law.*

36. *Durham* v. *United States,* 94 U.S. App. D.C. 228; 214 F.2d 862, 874–75 (1954).

37. *United States* v. *Freeman,* 357 F.2d 606, 618–622 (2d Cir. 1966).

38. *United States* v. *Brawner,* 153 U.S. App. D.C. 1, 471 F.2d 969, 998–1002 (1972).

39. Ibid.

40. Model Penal Code, Section 4.01(1).

41. Model Penal Code, *Commentary,* Comment on Section 4.01 at 156–160 (Tentative Draft No. 4, 1955).

42. Model Penal Code, Section 4.01(1).

43. 18 U.S.C. Section 17.

44. 18 U.S.C. Sections 17 and 4242(b).

45. See, for example, *United States* v. *Pohlot,* 827 F.2d 889, 897 (3d Cir. 1987), cert. denied, 484 U.S. 1011, 108 S. Ct. 710, 98 L. Ed. 2d 660 (1988).

46. *United States* v. *Cameron,* 907 F.2d 1051, 1065 (11th Cir. 1990).

47. Ira Mickenberg, "A Pleasant Surprise: The Guilty But Mentally Ill Verdict Has Both Succeeded in Its Own Right and Successfully Preserved the Traditional Role of the Insanity Defense," *University of Cincinnati Law Review,* Vol. 55 (1987), pp. 943, 987–991.

48. Ibid.

49. Ibid.

50. *Pohlot,* 827 F.2d, at 889.

51. Peter Arenella, "The Diminished Capacity and Diminished Responsibility Defenses: Two Children of a Doomed Marriage," *Columbia Law Review,* Vol. 77 (1977), p. 830.

52. *United States* v. *Brawner,* 471 F.2d 969 (1972).

53. *Black's Law Dictionary,* p. 458.

54. Model Penal Code, Section 4.03.

55. California Penal Code, Section 25 (a).

56. California Penal Code, Section 28 (b).

57. California Penal Code, Section 25 (c).

58. *Bulletin of the American Academy of Psychiatry and the Law,* Vol. 19, No. 4, 1991.

59. American Bar Association Standing Committee on Association Standards for Criminal Justice, *Proposed Criminal Justice Mental Health Standards* (Chicago: ABA, 1984).

60. American Psychiatric Association, World Wide Web site, September 20, 1996, from which much of the material in this section is derived.

61. Ibid.

62. Ibid.

63. Even those who have committed no crime can be confined under civil procedures if found dangerous to themselves or others. See, for example, *Kansas v. Hendricks*, U.S. Supreme Court, No. 95-1649. Decided June 23, 1997.

64. American Psychiatric Association, World Wide Web site, September 20, 1996.

65. *Foucha v. Louisiana*, 504 U.S. 71 (1992).

66. Ibid.

67. See, for example, *People v. Beck*, 96 C.D.O.S. 5794 (California's First Appellate District, 1996).

68. *Shannon v. United States*, 114 S. Ct. 2419, 129 L. Ed. 2d 459 (1994).

69. Idaho Code, 18-207 (1).

8

Legal and Social Dimensions of Personal Crime: Homicide

"Murder" is never more than a shortening of life; if [a] defendant's culpable act has significantly decreased [the] span of human life, the law will not hear him say that [the] victim would thereafter have died in any event.
—People *v.* Phillips, 64 Cal. 2d 574, 414 P.2d 353 (Cal. 1966).

The typical murderer is a young man in his 20s who kills another man only slightly older.

—Marvin Wolfgang[1]

CHAPTER OUTLINE

KEY CONCEPTS

accidental death

accidental killing

adequate cause

adequate provocation

affirmative act

aggravated murder

brain death

capital murder

criminal homicide

criminal negligence

criminally negligent
   homicide

depraved heart murder

excusable homicide

felony murder rule

first-degree murder

gross negligence

homicide

inherently dangerous

involuntary manslaughter

justifiable homicide

malice

malice aforethought

manslaughter

murder

negligent homicide

ordinary negligence

premeditated murder

premeditation

reasonable provocation

second-degree murder

sudden passion

Uniform Determination of
   Death Act (UDDA)

vehicular homicide

voluntary manslaughter

year and a day rule

AFTER READING THIS CHAPTER YOU SHOULD:

▷ Know the different types of homicide.

▷ Be able to describe how criminal homicide differs from noncriminal homicide.

▷ Understand the *corpus delicti* of criminal homicide.

▷ Know the elements of the crimes of murder and manslaughter.

▷ Understand the felony murder rule, and know when it applies.

▷ Understand the problems involved in defining "life" and "death."

▷ Be able to explain the meaning of "proximate cause" and "malice aforethought."

▷ Be able to explain when a murder may be punishable by a sentence of death.

▷ Be able to explain the difference between voluntary and involuntary manslaughter.

▷ Appreciate the current status of assisted suicide laws in various jurisdictions.

INTRODUCTION

Most homicide cases are heart-wrenching, but few are as difficult to come to terms with emotionally as that of thirty-one-year-old Farinoosh "Roya" Dalili.[2] Officials claim that on March 3, 1997, Dalili jumped from the tenth floor of the Marriott Hotel in Torrence, California, holding her three-year-old daughter, Nagen, in her arms in a suicide attempt. Although badly injured, the mother survived. Her daughter did not. Prosecutors charged Dalili with first-degree murder in her daughter's death.

Dalili attended the three-week-long trial that ensued while lying prone in the courtroom in a hospital-style bed, with more than 200 pins holding her broken bones together. During testimony she blamed the suicide attempt on depression brought on by spousal abuse. Her husband denied the allegation.

Describing the events that led up to the death of her daughter, Dalili said, "There was a rush and a voice that was telling me, 'Do it. Do it.' . . . I don't remember jumping." Dalili also testified that she recalled being alone on the window ledge just before jumping, and could see her daughter in a stroller in the hotel room. Prosecutors

Farinoosh 'Roya' Dalili and her three-year-old daughter, Nagen Natalie. In 1997 Dalili apparently attempted suicide by jumping from the tenth floor of the Marriott Hotel in Torrence, California, while holding her young daughter in her arms. Although badly injured, the mother survived. Her daughter did not. Originally charged with first-degree murder, Dalili was convicted of involuntary manslaughter in her daughter's death. (Photos courtesy of CBS News.)

revealed to jurors, however, that the woman told investigators she cradled her daughter in her arms as she jumped. "I know that now, that I took her with me," Dalili had said. Defense attorneys countered with claims that the child probably saw her mother jump, and followed her out of the window.

Jurors refused to find Dalili guilty of first-degree murder, convicting her instead of involuntary manslaughter. Although prosecutor Alex Karkanen had sought a prison term, she was sentenced to a year of house arrest and five years of probation. "The victim is dead," Karkanen told reporters, "because of what the defendant did."

In February 2000, Dalili again tried to take her life by driving her car off Palos Verdes Drive East in San Pedro, California. She was apparently distraught over a pending civil suit filed her by ex-husband charging her with the wrongful death of the couple's daughter.[3] A guardrail foiled the attempt.

ACCIDENTAL DEATH
a death that is caused by unexpected or unintended means.

ACCIDENTAL KILLING
a death that is the result of a purposeful human act lawfully undertaken in the reasonable belief that no harm would result.

HOMICIDE
the killing of a human being by the act, procurement, or omission of another human being.

JUSTIFIABLE HOMICIDE
(1) homicide that is permitted under the law. (2) A killing justified for the good of society. (3) The killing of another in self-defense when danger of death or serious bodily harm exists. (4) The killing of a person according to one's duties or out of necessity but without blame.

CRIMINAL HOMICIDE

Some deaths are accidental. Others are caused by human intent, recklessness, or negligence. An **accidental death,** or one which is caused by unexpected or unintended means, can be distinguished from an **accidental killing,** which is the result of a purposeful human act lawfully undertaken in the reasonable belief that no harm will result.

Homicide is the killing of one human being by another human being (by definition, suicides are not included). More precisely, homicide can be defined as "the killing of one human being by the act, procurement, or omission of another human being." There are three basic types of homicide: justifiable, excusable, and criminal. **Justifiable homicides** are those that are permitted under law, as in the case of a state-ordered execution or a military killing of an enemy soldier in the line of duty. A death caused by the legitimate use of self-defense is sometimes called a justifiable homicide, although it may also be termed an "excusable homicide."

Excusable homicides are those homicides that may involve some fault but not enough for the act to be considered criminal. A death caused by a vehicular accident in which the driver was not negligent, for example, would probably be excusable. The term **criminal homicide** refers only to those homicides to which criminal liability may attach. Generally speaking, any homicide that is not classified as justifiable or excusable may be considered criminal homicide.

Common law distinguished between two types of criminal homicide: **murder** and **manslaughter.** Later, both murder and manslaughter were subdivided into graded offenses. Some distinctions made were those between voluntary manslaughter and involuntary manslaughter, and between first-degree and second-degree murder. Each of these grades will be discussed in greater detail later in this chapter. Most states today have taken the Model Penal Code approach and have passed laws recognizing three types of criminal homicide: (1) murder (of which there may be various degrees), (2) manslaughter (of which there may be various kinds), and (3) **negligent homicide** (which some consider to be a variety of involuntary manslaughter). This chapter is structured in terms of these three categories. In general, the circumstances surrounding the killing and the mental state of the actor at the time the killing occurs determine the type (or degree) of criminal homicide that can be charged. The terminology applied to different categories and subcategories of homicide, however, varies considerably between jurisdictions.

Corpus Delicti

The *corpus delicti* of a criminal homicide consists of the death of a human being and of the fact that the death was caused by a criminal act or agency of another person. (See Chapter 3 for a detailed discussion of the concept of *corpus delicti.*) Included within this definition is the requirement that the victim's death was the natural and probable consequence of another person's unlawful conduct.[4]

At common law, an individual could not be convicted of any grade of criminal homicide unless the body of the deceased or at least portions of it were found and sufficiently identified to establish the fact of the victim's death. This requirement has since been modified in most states. Today, in order to conduct a successful prosecution on a charge of criminal homicide, the state must establish the *corpus delicti* of the crime of homicide—that is, the prosecution must establish the cause of death and show that death was caused by the criminal act of another.

Although discovery of the body of the murder victim may not be necessary to prove criminal homicide in courts today, a conviction requires prosecutors to prove that the death in question was caused "by the act, agency, procurement, or omission of the accused."[5] In *Williams* v. *State,*[6] for example, the defendant was convicted after he confessed to shooting the victim at close range with a shotgun, although the victim's body was never recovered. In addition, several witnesses testified that they helped the defendant dispose of the body and that the victim was dead. A Texas appellate court, which upheld Williams's conviction, ruled that the state had successfully established that the victim was dead, even though no body had been found, and that the state had established that the victim's death was caused by the criminal act of the accused—thus meeting the requirements for proving criminal homicide under state law.

Taking of a Life

During the final stage of labor, Californian Mary Chavez walked into her bathroom and sat on the toilet. Her baby dropped from her womb into the bowl and drowned.

EXCUSABLE HOMICIDE
killing in a manner that the criminal law does not prohibit. Also, homicide that may involve some fault but is not criminal homicide.

CRIMINAL HOMICIDE
the purposeful, knowing, reckless, or negligent causing of the death of one human being by another. Also, that form of homicide for which criminal liability may be incurred. Criminal homicide may be classified as murder, manslaughter, or negligent homicide.

MURDER
the unlawful killing of a human being, carried out with malice or planned in advance. According to common law, the killing of one human being by another with malice aforethought.

MANSLAUGHTER
the unlawful killing of a human being without malice. Manslaughter differs from murder in that malice and premeditation are lacking.

NEGLIGENT HOMICIDE
the killing of a human being by criminal negligence, or by the failure to exercise reasonable, prudent care. Also, a criminal offense commited by one whose negligence is the direct and proximate cause of another's death

---

Oh dear, I never realized what a terrible lot of explaining one has to do in a murder!

—Agatha Christie (*Spider's Web*, 1956)

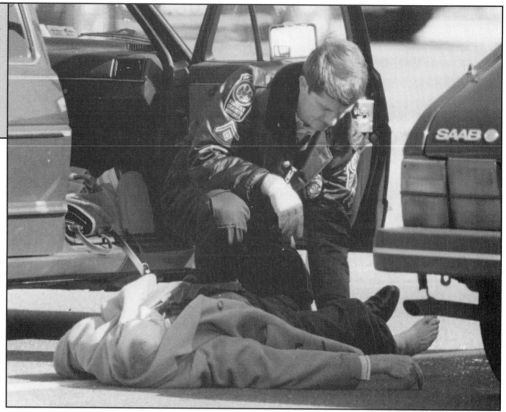

A homicide victim. Homicide is the killing of one human being by another human being. Not all homicides violate the criminal law. The term 'criminal homicide' refers only to those homicides to which criminal liability may attach. (Photo by Bruce Young/Reuters, courtesy of Corbis-Bettmann.)

The baby never had a chance to cry, and evidence later showed that the umbilical cord had not been cut before its death. Evidence also indicated that the baby had breathed for a brief period of time after its head emerged but that it was probably dead before the birth process was completed. Ms. Chavez was convicted of murder, but appealed, claiming that she had not killed a "human being," since her baby had not yet become a fully functioning independent entity at the time of its death. A California court of appeals, however, in upholding her murder conviction, ruled that "a viable child in the process of being born is a human being within the meaning of the homicide statutes whether or not the birth process has been fully completed."[7]

At common law, an essential element of homicide was the "killing of a human being." By definition, the victim must have been alive before the homicidal act occurred. Hence, under common law, the killing of an unborn child was not chargeable as homicide because the fetus was not considered "alive" in the sense of a "walking, breathing, human being." As one court noted: "Where the birth process has not begun, the courts are reluctant to consider the fetus a human being for homicide purposes."[8] If, however, the fetus was born alive and then died as the result of an act committed against the mother prior to the birth of the fetus (as, for example, where the mother was shot, but gave birth to the child after the shooting), then the fetus' death could be considered criminal homicide. Most states still follow that common law rule. Texas, for example, requires that a person "cause the death of an individual" before the crime of murder can be said to have occurred.[9] Since causing of the death of a living individual is a requirement for the act of murder, the act of decapitating a dead body is not considered homicide.[10]

The "alive" requirement has been modified in some states, where the killing of a fetus is now considered homicide. California's penal code, for example, was changed a few years ago to read: "Murder is the unlawful killing of a human being, or a fetus, with malice aforethought."[11] The change in the California law came in the case of *Keeler* v. *Superior Court*,[12] in which a California court held that the killing of

Murder is not the crime of criminals, but that of law-abiding citizens.

—Emmanuel Teney, Professor of Psychiatry
Wayne State University

an unborn fetus is not murder, since "a killing cannot be a criminal homicide unless the victim is a living human being."[13] By 1996, following California's lead, thirteen states had amended the wording of their homicide statutes to include the term "viable fetus" under the notion of a living human being. For purposes of such statutes, the term "viable" is said to mean that if the fetus had been born prematurely at the time it was killed, it would have had at least a 75 percent chance of survival for at least a limited period of time outside of the womb. Four states (California, Minnesota, Massachusetts, and South Carolina) have adopted even more stringent statutes, which say that, except for legal abortions, the killing of any fetus constitutes homicide.

In some states, illegal abortions may be chargeable as murder, and all jurisdictions have statutes prohibiting abortion except as permitted by therapeutic abortion laws. It is generally a felony to either solicit or to perform an illegal abortion. California Penal Code, Section 274 says, for example, that every person who provides, supplies, or administers to any woman, or procures any woman to take any medicine, drug, or substance, or uses or employs any instrument or other means, with intent to procure the miscarriage of the woman, except as provided for in the state's Therapeutic Abortion Act, is punishable by imprisonment in a state prison. In addition, Section 275 of California's code makes it a crime for a woman to solicit any person to perform an illegal abortion.

Defining "Death"

A central issue in criminal homicide cases is the definition of death—which is needed before criminal prosecution begins in order to establish that death has actually occurred. The Model Penal Code provides no definition of death, and the Code's *Commentary* cites two reasons for this failure: (1) contemporary scientific understandings of death were not available when the code was first drafted, making death difficult to define at the time; and (2) the delicate contemporary interplay between criminal law and advances in medical science is still too nebulous to reduce to statutory formulation.[14]

LAW ON THE BOOKS

CALIFORNIA DEFINES "MURDER."

Compare with Model Penal Code, Section 210.2

CALIFORNIA PENAL CODE

Section 187. Murder defined; death of fetus.
  a. Murder is the unlawful killing of a human being, or a fetus, with malice aforethought.
  b. This section shall not apply to any person who commits an act which results in the death of a fetus if any of the following apply:
    (1) The act complied with the Therapeutic Abortion Act. . . .
    (2) The act was committed by a holder of a physician's and surgeon's certificate, as defined in the Business and Professions Code, in a case where, to a medical certainty, the result of childbirth would be death of the mother of the fetus or where her death from childbirth, although not medically certain, would be substantially certain or more likely than not.
    (3) The act was solicited, aided, abetted, or consented to by the mother of the fetus. . . .

BRAIN DEATH

death determined by a "flat" reading on an electroencephalograph (EEG), usually after a twenty-four-hour period, or by other medical criteria.

UNIFORM DETERMINATION OF DEATH ACT (UDDA)

a standard supported by the American Medical Association, the American Bar Association, and the National Conference of Commissioners on Uniform State Laws, which provides that "An individual who has sustained either: (1) irreversible cessation of circulatory and respiratory functions, or (2) irreversible cessation of all functions of the entire brain, including the brain stem, is dead."[19] The UDDA provides a model for legislation and has been adopted in various forms by many states.

The common law rule was that death, or "cessation of life," occurs when a person's heartbeat and respiration cease.[15] In 1968, a report defining the characteristics of a permanently nonfunctioning brain was published by a committee of the Harvard Medical School and became the basis for the concept of **brain death.**[16] Brain death is used today by some courts to establish the death of homicide victims. Under the standard of brain death, death is said to occur when a blood flow test, called a cerebral angiogram, or an EEG (electroencephalogram), produces no evidence of physiological or electrical brain activity for a given period of time (usually twelve hours). Brain death can occur even though the victim's heart continues to beat and respiration persists.[17]

Many jurisdictions have adopted the **Uniform Determination of Death Act**[18] **(UDDA),** which provides that "An individual who has sustained either: (1) irreversible cessation of circulatory and respiratory functions, or (2) irreversible cessation of all functions of the entire brain, including the brain stem, is dead."[20] The UDDA, an evolutionary formulation of the Uniform Brain Death Act originally proposed by the National Conference of Commissioners on Uniform State Laws, is supported by the American Medical Association, the American Bar Association, and the national conference itself. The National Conference of Commissioners on Uniform State Laws is a nonprofit association comprised of state commissions on uniform laws from each state, the District of Columbia, the Commonwealth of Puerto Rico, and the U.S. Virgin Islands.[21] California's version of the UDDA is reproduced in a Law on the Books box in this chapter.

Today more than thirty states have adopted a "cessation of brain function" approach to defining death—established either through statute or a state supreme court ruling. Even so, there is "deep disagreement" even among physicians as to "whether brain death is synonymous with death," since "[d]eath of the brain is not the same as death in a traditional sense."[22] EEG measurements of brain function, the primary criteria by which brain death is assessed today, are capable of recording only the brain's surface electrical activity and not other electrical activity, which may be occurring deeper in the brain.

Moreover, the UDDA accepts two separate, readily distinguishable clinical situations as death, both of which can be manifested successively in the same individual. Complicating matters still further from both legal and medical perspectives is the fact that a pregnant woman meeting the criteria for brain death can often be sustained on life support systems until the fetus sufficiently matures to be able to live outside of the womb.

LAW ON THE BOOKS

THE TEXAS BRAIN DEATH LAW.

TEXAS HEALTH AND SAFETY CODE

Section 671.001. Standard used in determining death.

a. A person is dead when, according to ordinary standards of medical practice, there is irreversible cessation of the person's spontaneous respiratory and circulatory functions.

b. If artificial means of support preclude a determination that a person's spontaneous respiratory and circulatory functions have ceased, the person is dead when, in the announced opinion of a physician, according to ordinary standards of medical practice, there is irreversible cessation of all spontaneous brain function. Death occurs when the relevant functions cease.

c. Death must be pronounced before artificial means of supporting a person's respiratory and circulatory functions are terminated. . . .

LAW ON THE BOOKS

CALIFORNIA'S UNIFORM DETERMINATION OF DEATH ACT.

CALIFORNIA HEALTH AND SAFETY CODE, SECTION 7180

Section 7180. (a) An individual who has sustained either (1) irreversible cessation of circulatory and respiratory functions, or (2) irreversible cessation of all functions of the entire brain, including the brain stem, is dead. A determination of death must be made in accordance with accepted medical standards . . . (c) This article may be cited as the Uniform Determination of Death Act.

Time of Death

Sometimes victims of homicidal acts suffer injuries but do not die immediately. Death may occur some time after the fatal injury. In such cases, homicide prosecutions under common law required the death of the victim within a year and a day from the time that the ultimately fatal act took place. The requirement was termed the **year and a day rule.** The rule was based on the belief that proof of causation (i.e., the ability to show that actions by the accused were the cause of the victim's death) becomes ever more difficult with the passage of time—resulting in potentially unjustified prosecutions and convictions.[23]

The year and a day rule is still influential in some parts of the country. In 1991, for example, Guilford County (North Carolina) Superior Court Judge Peter M. McHugh cited the rule in dismissing a murder indictment against Terry Dale Robinson.[24] Evidence in the case plainly showed that Robinson had brutally beaten his estranged wife, Gina Robinson, with his hands, feet, and a shotgun that he used as a club. After the beating he ran her over several times with an automobile. Mrs. Robinson did not die immediately, but remained comatose from the time of the assault until her death—almost three years later. After Mrs. Robinson's death, prosecutors sought to indict her former husband on murder charges, but the defendant's lawyer moved to dismiss the indictment citing the fact that the victim's death occurred more than a year and a day after the assault. Although the trial court agreed with the attorney, the state challenged the ruling. Upon appeal, the North Carolina Court of Appeals reinstated the indictment and ordered that Robinson be tried for murder. The appellate court said, "We hold, on the facts before us, that the relevant date of Mrs. Robinson's murder . . . is the date upon which she died."[25]

Today only a few jurisdictions still follow the year and a day rule, although others, like California, have extended the time limit. In California, in order for homicide prosecutions to proceed, the victim's death must occur within three years and a day from the time of the act.[26]

YEAR AND A DAY RULE a common law requirement that homicide prosecutions could not take place if the victim did not die within a year and a day from the time that the fatal act occurred.

Some people are alive simply because it is illegal to kill them.
—Anonymous

Proximate Cause and Homicide

Criminal homicide must be the result of an **affirmative act,** an omission to act, or criminal negligence. For criminal liability to accrue, the cause of death must not be so remote as to fail to constitute natural and probable consequences of the defendant's act. In other words, for charges of homicide to be successfully brought, a person's death must be the proximate result of a human act. Proximate cause is

AFFIRMATIVE ACT voluntary conscious conduct. An affirmative act is not an omission or failure to act.

discussed in greater detail in Chapter 3. Suffice it to say here that, in homicide cases, a determination of proximate cause requires that death be a natural and probable consequence of the act in question. A test that is frequently used can be stated this way: "If the original act had not occurred, would the victim have died?" If, for example, a victim is shot by the accused, resulting in a nonfatal wound, but the victim later dies on the operating table as a result of shock, the shooting is considered to constitute the proximate cause of death.[27] Similarly, in *People* v. *Moan*,[28] a victim who was already very ill suffered an injury that accelerated his death. Nonetheless, the injury was considered the "proximate cause" of death. Hence, an act that is determined to be the proximate cause of death need not be the only or sole cause of a person's death.[29]

Where concurring causes contribute to a victim's death, an accused may be held criminally liable by reason of his own conduct, which directly contributes to the fatal result. In one case, for example, the removal of artificial life-support systems from a homicide victim after all electrical activity in the brain had ceased was not found to be an independent, intervening cause of death so as to relieve the defendant of criminal responsibility.[30] Similarly, in an Illinois case, the defendant raped and severely beat an eighty-five-year-old woman. Following the incident, the victim was moved to a nursing home. She became depressed and refused to eat. Because of injuries sustained during the beating, the victim could not be fed through a nasal tube, and a broken rib sustained in the beating limited her lung capacity, leaving her unable to expel food accidentally aspirated into her windpipe by nurses who were trying to feed her. The woman consequently died of asphyxiation during an attempted feeding. The rapist was convicted of homicide, and an appellate court, upholding the conviction, stated that his criminal acts had set in motion a series of events that eventually caused the victim's death.[31]

Other courts have held that delays in medical treatment, whether avoidable or not, are not in fact intervening forces and cannot legally be considered superseding causes of death that would relieve murder defendants from criminal responsibility.[32] An accused cannot be found guilty of criminal homicide, however, in a case where death is brought about by grossly erroneous medical or surgical treatment rather than by the wound inflicted by the accused. Finally, when the conduct of two or more persons concurrently contributes to the death of a human being, the conduct of each person can be viewed as a proximate cause regardless of the extent to which each contributed to the death.[33]

MURDER

Murder is the first of the three types of criminal homicide. The elements of the crime of murder are:

- an unlawful killing,
- of a human being,
- with malice.

In most states, murder is divided into two categories: first degree and second degree. Generally speaking, **first-degree murder** includes any willful, deliberate, and premeditated killing. The term **premeditation** (which is discussed in greater detail later in this chapter) means the act of deliberating or meditating on, or planning, a course of action (i.e., a crime). For purposes of the criminal law, premeditation requires the opportunity for *reflection* between the time the intent to act is formed and the act itself is committed. Hence, murder is clearly first degree when it is committed through the use of poison, or by lying in wait, or when it involves torture. First-degree murder is usually punishable by death, or by life in prison.

LAW ON THE BOOKS

"MURDER" UNDER PENNSYLVANIA LAW.

Compare with Model Penal Code, Section 210.2

TITLE 18, PENNSYLVANIA CONSOLIDATED STATUTES

Section 2502. Murder.

a. Murder of the first degree.—A criminal homicide constitutes murder of the first degree when it is committed by an intentional killing.

b. Murder of the second degree.—A criminal homicide constitutes murder of the second degree when it is committed while defendant was engaged as a principal or an accomplice in the perpetration of a felony.

c. Murder of the third degree.—All other kinds of murder shall be murder of the third degree. Murder of the third degree is a felony of the first degree. . . .

In states where only two degrees of murder are recognized, all murders other than first degree are said to constitute **second-degree murder.** Some states, such as Pennsylvania (see accompanying Law on the Books box), recognize three or more degrees of murder. Where three degrees of murder are found they usually include: (1) murders that are committed wilfully and deliberately, and are premeditated; (2) murders committed during the perpetration or attempted perpetration of an enumerated felony, such as arson, rape, robbery, or burglary; and (3) all other types of murder.

SECOND-DEGREE MURDER
depending upon jurisdiction, either (1) murders committed during the perpetration or attempted perpetration of an enumerated felony, such as arson, rape, robbery, or burglary, or (2) all murder not classified by statute as first-degree murder.

Malice Aforethought

An essential element of the crime of murder is malice. At common law, the "grand criterion" that "distinguished murder from other killing" was malice on the part of the killer, and this malice was not necessarily "malevolent to the deceased particularly" but "any evil design in general; the dictate of a wicked, depraved, and malignant heart."[34] As a contemporary legal term, **malice** refers to the intentional doing of a wrongful act without just cause or legal excuse. Malice encompasses the intentional carrying out of a hurtful act without cause, and hostility of one individual toward another. In cases of homicide, the term means "an intention to kill."

First-degree murder is often described as requiring **malice aforethought**—a historical term that connotes a malicious design to kill or injure. In early English history, "aforethought" required that a person think about, envision, plan, or premeditate homicide before the time of the killing. Hence, *malice aforethought* and *premeditation* were essentially equivalent terms.

Since then, however, the term "malice aforethought" has undergone considerable evolution, and today it includes several states of mind. It may, for example, encompass the causing of death during the commission of specified felonies, whether or not the offender premeditated the killing. The authors of a now classic work put it best when they said that "malice aforethought is an unjustifiable, inexcusable, and unmitigated person-endangering state of mind."[36] In contemporary murder statutes, the term "malice aforethought" is generally understood to mean a killing while in possession of any one of the following five mental states: (1) an intent to kill, (2) an intent to inflict great bodily injury, (3) an intent to commit a felony (as in felony murder), (4) an intent to resist a lawful arrest, or (5) an awareness that one is engaged in

MALICE
a legal term that refers to the intentional doing of a wrongful act without just cause or legal excuse. In cases of homicide the term means "an intention to kill."

MALICE AFORETHOUGHT
an unjustifiable, inexcusable, and unmitigated person-endangering state of mind.[35]

DEPRAVED HEART MURDER
(1) unjustifiable conduct that is
extremely negligent and results
in the death of a human being,
or (2) the killing of a human
being with extreme atrocity.

Every unpunished murder takes away
something from the security of every
man's life.

—Daniel Webster (1830)

conduct that carries with it a high risk of someone else's death. The fifth mental state, which describes unjustifiable conduct that is extremely reckless, is sometimes called **depraved heart murder** when it results in the death of a human being.[37]

Although, technically speaking, malice aforethought is planned malice, emphasis today is on the "malice" aspect of the term rather than on any kind of planning that includes the opportunity for reflection. Hence, in modern context, the term can be understood as "the intention to kill, actual or implied, under circumstances which do not constitute excuse or justification or mitigate the offense to manslaughter."[38] It is important to realize that neither malice nor malice aforethought require an ill will or hatred of the victim.

Other distinctions can also be drawn. When an accused consciously desires to cause death, for example, the intent to kill is *actual* or *express*. It is *implied* when the defendant intends to cause great bodily harm, or where the natural tendency of his or her behavior is to cause death or great bodily harm. California law, for example, says that "malice may be express or implied. It is expressed when there is manifested a deliberate intention unlawfully to take away the life of a fellow creature. It is implied, when no considerable provocation appears, or when the circumstances attending the killing show an abandoned and malignant heart."[39]

Malice may exist where the killing is unpremeditated, and malice may be inferred from surrounding circumstances. Pointing a firearm at an individual and firing it, for example, creates the presumption that the defendant actually intended to kill the victim. Malice may also be established by proving that the defendant intended to inflict serious bodily injury, even though he or she did not consciously desire the death of the victim.[40]

As mentioned above, under some circumstances a defendant may be guilty of murder if he or she acts in a manner that creates an unusually high risk of another's death, and that results in death. Driving over 100 miles per hour in a school zone while young children are present, for example, could establish malice in the form of a "depraved mind" or an "abandoned and malignant heart." A similar situation could exist where a newborn baby, although alive and well at the time, is put in a trash bin and covered up, or where the defendant fires a weapon into a passing automobile. In *Commonwealth* v. *Malone*,[41] the accused was found guilty of murder when he killed the victim while playing a game of "Russian roulette." The game involved loading a pistol with one round and, after spinning the chamber, placing the gun to the victim's head and pulling the trigger. In holding the defendant criminally responsible, the court ruled that the defendant had acted with the awareness that his conduct created an extremely high risk of death to the victim. There is, however, disagreement as to whether a defendant must have been actually aware of the high risk involved, or whether it is enough that his or her conduct created that risk. Most states require a subjective realization of the risk, on the theory that anything less is too removed from the notion of an "intent to kill" to justify a charge of murder.

Capital Murder

CAPITAL MURDER
murder for which the death
penalty is authorized by law.

Thirty-eight states and the federal government presently authorize the death penalty for some types of murder. In some states, murders for which the death penalty is authorized are treated as a separate class of murder called **capital murder**. In Florida, Georgia, Idaho, Louisiana, Mississippi, Missouri, Nebraska, New Hampshire, New Mexico, North Carolina, Tennessee, and Wyoming, all murders in the first degree fall into the capital crimes category. The most common statutory requirement of first-degree murder is that the killing had to have been *premeditated* and *deliberate*.

The concepts "premeditation" and "deliberation" are attempts to encapsulate the mental state of the offender at the time of the crime. The idea that only persons who kill with clear intention, or who envision killing before the commission of their crimes, should be subject to capital punishment is well-supported by decisions of the U.S. Supreme Court. In the case of *Edmund* v. *Florida*[42] (1982), for example, the Court held that the Eighth Amendment prohibition against cruel and unusual punishment prohibits the use of the death penalty on a defendant who does not himself kill, attempt to kill, or intend that a killing take place or that lethal force be employed. In *Edmund,* the defendant waited in a getaway car while two accomplices went into a farmhouse and murdered an elderly couple who lived there. Since Edmund was guilty of murder only by a combination of the felony-murder rule and rules on accomplice liability, the Court stated it would be cruel and unusual punishment for him to be treated the same as if he had intentionally caused the harm.

The Court, however, did allow application of the death penalty in *Tison* v. *Arizona*[43] (1987). In *Tison,* the accomplice knew that the principal (his brother) might kill in furtherance of a joint plan designed to help their father escape from prison. The Court noted that the brothers possessed the mental state required for murder under Arizona law, in that they exhibited an extreme indifference to the value of human life. Taken together, the *Edmund* and *Tison* cases demonstrate that an accomplice to murder can be given the death penalty if he or she had the requisite mental state for capital murder, but not if he or she was merely an accomplice with no desire that deadly force be used or that a killing take place. *Tison* and *Edmund*, along with another case, *Coker* v. *Georgia*[44] (1977), led to the conclusion that the U.S. Supreme Court will not allow imposition of the death penalty for crimes other than unlawful homicides committed with murderous intent. In *Coker,* for example, the Court held that the death penalty could not be imposed for the brutal rape of an adult woman. (Chapter 14 contains a detailed discussion of capital punishment–related issues.) The court, however, left open the question of whether someone who rapes a child can receive the death penalty.

Premeditated murder is murder in which the intent to kill is formed pursuant to preexisting reflection, rather than as the result of a sudden impulse or heat of passion. The word "premeditated" (which was defined earlier in this chapter) means that the defendant must have considered his or her act before the killing. As noted in one court case, premeditated means "formed or determined upon as a result of careful thought and weighing of considerations for and against the proposed course of conduct." In that case, the court stated that the true test of premeditation was not the duration of time available for thought but the extent of reflection.[45]

Following the lead of the Model Penal Code, some states have rejected premeditation and deliberation as the basis for identifying a murder as one that deserves the death penalty. Those states have legislatively defined capital murder as murder plus one or more specific aggravating factors, constituting what is sometimes called **aggravated murder.** The term "aggravated murder" is found in the statutes of some states (such as Utah, Washington, and Ohio), although other states depict capital murder as "first-degree murder with aggravating factors" or with "special circumstances." Illinois law, for example, defines capital murder as first-degree murder with any one of fifteen aggravating circumstances, while capital murder in Ohio consists of "aggravated murder with one of eight aggravating circumstances."[46] The Texas capital murder statute, which is reprinted in the box on the next page, is a typical aggravated murder law.

Essentially, the concept of aggravated murder encompasses the notion that certain identifiable factors surrounding the circumstances of a particular murder may so enhance the culpability of the murderer that punishment of the first degree is warranted. While the term aggravated murder is used to describe murders that are punishable by death in most jurisdictions, the term can also refer to murders punishable by life imprisonment in jurisdictions where the death penalty is lacking. (See Chapter 14 for more information on capital punishment.)

PREMEDITATED MURDER
murder that was planned in advance (however briefly) and wilfully carried out.

Web Extra! 8–1
Britannica online: murder

AGGRAVATED MURDER
murder plus one or more aggravating factors as specified by law. Aggravated murder is generally capital murder.

LAW ON THE BOOKS

TEXAS DEFINES "CAPITAL MURDER."

Compare with Model Penal Code, Sections 210.2(2) and 210.6

TEXAS PENAL CODE

Section 19.03. Capital Murder.

a. A person commits an offense [capital murder] if he commits murder as defined under Section 19.02(b)(1) [intentionally or knowingly causes the death of an individual] and:

(1) the person murders a peace officer or firefighter who is acting in the lawful discharge of an official duty and who the person knows is a peace officer or firefighter;

(2) the person intentionally commits the murder in the course of committing or attempting to commit kidnapping, burglary, robbery, aggravated sexual assault, arson, or obstruction or retaliation;

(3) the person commits murder for remuneration or the promise of remuneration or employs another to commit murder for remuneration or the promise of remuneration;

(4) the person commits the murder while escaping or attempting to escape from a penal institution;

(5) the person, while incarcerated in a penal institution, murders another:

(a) who is employed in the operation of the penal institution; or

(b) with the intent to establish, maintain, or participate in a combination or in the profits of a combination;

(6) the person:

(a) while incarcerated for an offense under this section or Section 19.02 [murder] murders another; or

(b) while serving a sentence of life imprisonment or a term of 99 years . . . murders another;

(7) the person murders more than one person:

(a) during the same criminal transaction; or

(b) during different criminal transactions, but the murders are committed pursuant to the same scheme or course of conduct; or

(8) the person murders an individual under six years of age.

b. An offense under this section is a capital felony.

c. If the jury or, when authorized by law, the judge does not find beyond a reasonable doubt that the defendant is guilty of an offense under this section, he may be convicted of murder or any other lesser included offense.

Felony Murder

In early summer of 1999, forty-five-year-old Miami taxi driver Webert St. Jean died of a heart attack while being robbed of $12. His alleged assailants, twenty-two-year-old Alex Marrero and an unidentified second man, were apparently unarmed at the time, but threatened to harm the cabbie if he resisted. St. Jean was forced from his cab and ran to a nearby home to call for help, but collapsed and died before police arrived. St. Jean suffered from high blood pressure and had been on blood pressure medication. Following his death, police put out an arrest warrant for Marrero and his accomplice, charging them with first-degree murder. "They murdered him just as surely as if they stabbed him or shot him," said Miami police spokesperson Lt. Bill Schwartz. "If a criminal act places someone in such a stressful enough situation that their body can't handle it and as a result that person dies, the persons committing the crime are culpable."[47] Marrero surrendered to police shortly after the warrant was issued, but his accomplice remained at large.

At common law, a defendant was guilty of murder if, while perpetrating a felony, or in the attempt to perpetrate a felony, another person died as a consequence of the crime or as a consequence of the attempt. Even if the other person's death was not intentional or foreseen, as in the case of a kidnapping victim who inadvertently suffocated or drowned, the offender could still be found guilty of murder, and was often hanged. The **felony murder rule** was abolished by England in 1957, and it never existed in France or Germany.

Even though the felony murder rule has been widely criticized, it is still retained (in various forms) in most of the states today, where felony murder is often synonymous with first-degree murder. Defenders of the rule contend that it reaffirms the sanctity of human life and say that the rule reflects society's judgment that the commission of a felony resulting in death is more serious and deserving of greater punishment than the commission of a felony that does not result in death. The felony murder rule is also intended to deter negligent and accidental killings during the commission of a felony. Critics of the rule complain that an unintended act cannot be effectively deterred, and they point out that deaths during the commission of felonies—the crimes "targeted" by felony murder laws—are quite rare.[48]

In most states, a death that results from the commission of an enumerated felony, i.e., arson, rape, robbery, or burglary, constitutes first-degree murder. If the death results from the commission of a felony that is not listed or enumerated in the jurisdiction's felony murder statute, then the murder is either second-degree murder or manslaughter as per the state statute.

Because the felony murder rule applies whether the defendant kills the victim intentionally, recklessly, negligently, accidentally, or unforeseeably (rather than purposefully or intentionally), it creates a form of strict criminal liability for any death that results from the intentional commission of a felony. Courts have struggled with the felony murder rule, because a murder conviction under the rule does not require malice or intent. Generally speaking, courts have justified felony murder rules in two ways: (1) by holding that the rule dispenses with the requirement for malice, and (2) by holding that malice is implied from the intentional commission of a felony.

At common law, all felonies were subject to the felony murder rule. Over the past 100 years or so, however, the felony murder rule has generally become more limited in scope in most jurisdictions. Every state has numerous statutory felonies that were unknown at common law, and most pose virtually no unusual threat of death. Accordingly, the felony murder rule is today applied only to certain felonies. Generally there are three schemes for identifying those felonies to which the rule applies, including those acts that: (1) are inherently dangerous to life or health, (2) are held to be *malum in se,* and (3) were felonies at common law. *Malum in se* acts, for purposes of the felony murder rule, include "all felonies, all breaches of public order, injuries to person or property, outrages upon public decency or good morals, and breaches of official duty, when done wilfully or corruptly."[49] Most jurisdictions use an **inherently dangerous** test in order to decide when the felony murder rule applies. Felonies are inherently dangerous when, by their very nature or by the nature of their commission, they may result in death or serious bodily harm to a person. Also, the rules of proximate cause discussed earlier generally apply in felony murder situations, since the felony murder rule requires a causal relationship between the felony and the death. It is not sufficient that a death merely occurs at the same time as the felony. In some way, the felony must give rise to the killing.

In a noteworthy 1997 trial that may give new direction to felony murder prosecutions, a Winston-Salem, North Carolina, district attorney asked for the death penalty in a case involving a drunk driving defendant who had caused the deaths of two nineteen-year-old sorority sisters.[50] The defendant, forty-year-old Richard Jones, had consumed both prescription painkillers and beer before crashing into a car carrying six Wake Forest University coeds. At the time of the crash, Jones had two prior convictions for driving while impaired, and a third charge was pending. Although he was sentenced to life in prison without parole, and not death, the case may lead to other similar prosecutions of drunk drivers across the country.

FELONY MURDER RULE
a rule that establishes murder liability for a defendant if another person dies during the commission of certain felonies.

There are four kinds of homicide: felonious, excusable, justifiable, and praiseworthy, but it makes no great difference to the person slain whether he fell by one kind or another—the classification is for the advantage of the lawyers.

—Ambrose Bierce (*The Devil's Dictionary*, 1911)

INHERENTLY DANGEROUS
describes an act or course of behavior (usually a felony), which by its very nature is likely to result in death or serious bodily harm to either the person involved in the behavior or to someone else.

MANSLAUGHTER

Manslaughter is the second of the three general types of criminal homicide discussed in this chapter. Manslaughter is the unlawful killing of a human being without malice. Manslaughter differs from murder in that malice and premeditation are lacking. Hence, the elements of manslaughter are:

- an unlawful killing,
- of a human being,
- without malice.

Voluntary Manslaughter

VOLUNTARY MANSLAUGHTER

the unlawful killing of a human being, without malice, which is done intentionally during a sudden quarrel or in the heat of passion. Also, a killing committed without lawful justification, wherein the defendant acted under a sudden and intense passion resulting from adequate provocation.

ADEQUATE PROVOCATION

provocation is said to be "adequate if it would cause a reasonable person to lose self-control." Adequate provocation is also termed **reasonable provocation.**

ADEQUATE CAUSE

(as in instances of **voluntary manslaughter**) a cause that would commonly produce a degree of anger, rage, or terror in a person of ordinary temper, sufficient to render the mind of the defendant incapable of objective reflection.

SUDDEN PASSION

(as in instances of **voluntary manslaughter**) passion directly caused by and rising out of provocation by the victim or of another acting with the victim. Includes the understanding that the passion arises at the time of the killing and is not solely the result of former provocation.

Manslaughter occurs without deliberation, planning, or premeditation and may be voluntary or involuntary. "**Voluntary manslaughter** is the unlawful killing of a human being, without malice, which is done intentionally upon a sudden quarrel or in the heat of passion."[51] In other words, voluntary manslaughter is a homicide associated with a sudden fit of rage or passion. Such a killing, although intentional, is not premeditated nor motivated by a basic evil intent (that is, by malice). Voluntary manslaughter would otherwise be murder, except that it is committed in response to **adequate provocation** (as when a person finds his or her spouse in bed with another). Provocation is said to be "adequate" if it would cause a reasonable person to lose self-control.[52] Adequate provocation is also termed **reasonable provocation.** Under common law, only a limited set of circumstances fell into the category of "reasonable provocation." Among them were mutual combat, serious assault or battery, an unlawful arrest, the commission of a crime against a close relative or family member, and the witnessing of one's spouse in an act of adultery. Provocative words alone did not provide adequate provocation to reduce a wilful killing to manslaughter.

Voluntary manslaughter can be more formally defined as a killing committed without lawful justification, wherein the defendant acted under a sudden and intense passion resulting from serious provocation. Although the provocation may have been made by the person who was killed, voluntary manslaughter can also be charged when someone other than the person who incites the killer's passion dies. When a defendant, for example, endeavors to shoot an adulterous spouse caught in the act, but kills a bystander who tries to prevent the shooting instead, he or she may still be charged with voluntary manslaughter.

Voluntary manslaughter is usually committed with one of the states of mind required for malice aforethought, but the presence of adequate provocation negates the state of mind—resulting in a lesser charge, or a lowered sentence. The Texas law that defines murder, for example, reads: "At the punishment stage of a trial, the defendant may raise the issue as to whether he caused the death under the immediate influence of *sudden passion* arising from an *adequate cause.* [Emphasis added.] If the defendant proves the issue in the affirmative by a preponderance of the evidence, the offense is a felony of the second degree [voluntary manslaughter]."[53] As used here, **adequate cause** means a cause that would commonly produce a degree of anger, rage, or terror in a person of ordinary temper, sufficient to render the mind of the defendant incapable of objective reflection. **Sudden passion** means passion directly caused by and rising out of provocation by the victim or of another acting with the victim, and includes the understanding that the passion arises at the time of the killing and is not solely the result of former provocation. In Texas, as in other jurisdictions that follow similar conventions, the burden is on the defendant to establish the existence of the necessary factors to reduce the crime from murder to voluntary manslaughter.

LAW ON THE BOOKS

"VOLUNTARY MANSLAUGHTER" UNDER PENNSYLVANIA LAW.

Compare with Model Penal Code, section 210.3

TITLE 18, PENNSYLVANIA CONSOLIDATED STATUTES

Section 2503. Voluntary manslaughter.

a. General rule.—A person who kills an individual without lawful justification commits voluntary manslaughter if at the time of the killing he is acting under a sudden and intense passion resulting from serious provocation by:

(1) the individual killed; or

(2) another whom the actor endeavors to kill, but he negligently or accidentally causes the death of the individual killed.

b. Unreasonable belief killing justifiable.—A person who intentionally or knowingly kills an individual commits voluntary manslaughter if at the time of the killing he believes the circumstances to be such that, if they existed, would justify the killing under Chapter 5 of this title (relating to general principles of justification), but his belief is unreasonable.

c. Grading.—Voluntary manslaughter is a felony of the first degree.

To reduce what would otherwise be murder to voluntary manslaughter in the state of Texas, four requirements must be met: (1) the defendant must have acted in response to a provocation that would be sufficient to cause a reasonable person to lose self-control, (2) the defendant must have acted in a "heat of passion," (3) any lapse of time between the provocation and the killing must not have been great enough that a reasonable person would have "cooled off" or regained control of themselves, and (4) the defendant must not, in fact, have "cooled off" by the time of killing. As the last three requirements indicate, provocation must occur close in time to the killing for a lesser degree of murder to be charged. A murder that occurs six months after an incident of provocation, for example, would probably not be reduced to voluntary manslaughter in most jurisdictions.

The Model Penal Code approach to voluntary manslaughter is similar except for the lack of a "sudden passion" requirement. Section 210.3 (b) of the code says: "Criminal homicide constitutes manslaughter when . . . (b) a homicide which would otherwise be murder is committed under the influence of extreme mental or emotional disturbance for which there is reasonable explanation or excuse. The reasonableness of such explanation or excuse shall be determined from the viewpoint of a person in the actor's situation under the circumstances as he believes them to be."

Involuntary Manslaughter

In December 1999, forty-five-year-old John Mickle was attacked and killed by two pit bull dogs as he walked through a Winnsboro, South Carolina, neighborhood at 3 o'clock in the morning.[54] Mickle was attacked about 200 yards from the dogs' home. Bitten more than 1,000 times, Mickle's windpipe was also crushed. His body was discovered around sunrise by a patrolling sheriff's deputy. A few days later, the dog's owner, Frank Paul Speagle, 22, was charged with involuntary manslaughter. Authorities said he should have known the animals were dangerous and should have kept them confined or leashed. A jury acquitted Speagle in September, 2000, when witnesses to the attack could not be found.

Involuntary manslaughter is an unlawful homicide that is unintentionally caused, and which is either: (1) the result of an unlawful act other than a dangerous felony (or of a lawful act done in an unlawful way), or (2) which occurs as the result of criminal negligence or recklessness. The central distinguishing feature between voluntary and involuntary manslaughter is the absence, in involuntary manslaughter, of the intention to kill or to commit any unlawful act that might reasonably produce death or great bodily harm. In other words, in cases of voluntary manslaughter, killing is intentional, while it is unintentional in instances of involuntary manslaughter. Pennsylvania law, for example, says: "A person is guilty of involuntary manslaughter when, as a direct result of the doing of an unlawful act in a reckless or grossly negligent manner, or the doing of a lawful act in a reckless or grossly negligent manner, he causes the death of another person."[55] An "unlawful act other than a dangerous felony" generally refers to a misdemeanor involving danger of injury.

Unlawful Act An involuntary manslaughter conviction may be based on an accidental death caused by the defendant during the commission of an unlawful act. The unlawful act may be any misdemeanor or felony that is not included under the felony murder rule. In some states, when death occurs as the result of an unlawful act that is a misdemeanor involving danger of injury, a charge of misdemeanor manslaughter may be brought under what is known as the "misdemeanor-manslaughter" rule—still operative in about a dozen states. Whether the unlawful act is a felony or a misdemeanor, there must be a causal relationship between the act and the death of the victim. In those situations where the wrongful act is a serious felony, however, the requirement of proximate cause is generally suspended. The Model Penal Code[56] does not define manslaughter in relationship to other unlawful behavior except to say generally that, "Criminal homicide constitutes manslaughter when (a) it is committed recklessly. . . ." The Model Penal Code does recognize the fact that the act that causes death is unlawful, and that this may have an evidentiary bearing on whether it is reckless.

Criminal Negligence Unintentional killings may constitute involuntary manslaughter when they result from criminal negligence—which in itself may be unlawful—or from gross negligence. Some state laws describe a special category of involuntary manslaughter called **criminally negligent homicide.** Although the definition may sound a bit circular, criminally negligent homicide is usually defined as homicide resulting from criminal negligence. The Code of Alabama, for example, says: "A person commits the crime of criminally negligent homicide if he causes the death of another person by criminal negligence."[57]

Criminal negligence is negligence of such a nature and to such a degree that it is punishable as a crime. Criminal negligence is defined by statute in most jurisdictions, and consists of flagrant and reckless disregard of the safety of others, or of wilful indifference to the safety and welfare of others. Whether criminal negligence is present depends on all the circumstances surrounding an act or a failure to act. Criminal negligence is usually regarded as a form of **gross negligence**—which is a conscious disregard of one's duties, resulting in injury or damage to another. However, when the defendant uses an object or undertakes a course of action that is inherently dangerous, courts are generally more willing to find him or her criminally negligent, even though the negligence may not be gross. This is especially true in cases involving automobiles and firearms. Gross negligence goes well beyond the purview of what is sometimes termed ordinary negligence. **Ordinary negligence** is said to be "the want of ordinary care," or negligence that could have been avoided if one had exercised ordinary, reasonable, or proper care. Ordinary negligence is not wilful or purposeful, but rather, unthinking. It is based on the idea that the actor should have known the results or consequences of his or her actions, whereas gross

An involuntary manslaughter conviction may result from an accidental death caused by the defendant during the commission of an unlawful act—such as driving while intoxicated or speeding. In 1997, North Carolina prosecutors sought the death penalty in a trial involving Thomas Richard Jones (shown here on the stand) for having caused the deaths of two nineteen-year-old sorority sisters while driving with a combination of alcohol and painkillers in his system. The prosecution based its arguments on the felony murder rule. Jones was eventually sentenced to life in prison without parole. (Photo courtesy of AP/Wide World Photos.)

negligence rests upon the belief that the actor was in fact cognizant of the results of his or her acts.

For an unintentional killing to constitute involuntary manslaughter, gross negligence or criminal negligence is required. In addition, there is generally the requirement that a very substantial danger of serious bodily harm or death have existed at the time of the offense. The Model Penal Code, and a minority of jurisdictions, require that the defendant has acted "recklessly," and the code defines "recklessly" as a "gross deviation from the standard of conduct that a law-abiding person would observe in the defendant's situation."[58]

The courts appear to be in disagreement as to whether a defendant is liable for manslaughter if he or she is unaware of the risk imposed by his or her conduct. In one case in Washington State, the defendant was found guilty of manslaughter for the death of her infant even though she did not realize that the infant's abscessed tooth had become gangrenous, which led to his death.[59] The Model Penal Code, in contrast, requires an actual knowledge by its definition of "recklessness." Under the code, a person acts recklessly only when he or she "consciously disregards" a substantial and unjustified risk.[60]

There must, of course, be a causal link between the defendant's criminal negligence and the ensuing death. The defendant's conduct must not only be the cause in fact of the death, but also the proximate cause of the death. For example, if the defendant is speeding through a residential area and hits a parked car, which secretly contains explosives, the defendant will not be liable for the death of an individual a block away who is killed by flying glass. In this situation, the fact that the car contained explosives was not reasonably foreseeable, nor was the fact that an individual a block away would be killed.

Unlike civil law, the contributory negligence of the victim is not a defense to an involuntary manslaughter charge. It may, however, have a bearing on whether the defendant was grossly negligent or whether the defendant's conduct was the proximate cause of the death of the victim.

NEGLIGENT HOMICIDE

Negligent homicide is the third of the three general types of criminal homicide discussed in this chapter. Negligent homicide does not exist in the codes of all jurisdictions, but in many states, deaths resulting from degrees of negligence below that required for a charge of manslaughter may give rise to prosecutions for the crime of negligent homicide. Negligent homicide is quite separate from the crime of involuntary manslaughter (discussed previously), with which it is easily confused. The confusion stems from the fact that negligence may characterize both offenses. However, while involuntary manslaughter charges may be based on criminal negligence or gross negligence, the offense of negligent homicide, in contrast, allows for prosecution where the defendant's conduct was negligent, but where the degree of negligence involved did not amount to gross or criminal negligence, or recklessness. Hence, negligent homicide can be defined as the killing of a person without intent to kill, when the killing takes place while the offender is performing a negligent act, or when the offender fails to exercise reasonable, prudent care.

A number of states and the Model Penal Code have established the crime of negligent homicide, and the Code provides that: "Criminal homicide constitutes negligent homicide when it is committed negligently. In cases of negligent homicide, the failure of the defendant to perceive the risk involved is not a defense."[61] Under the Model Penal Code and the codes of some states, negligent homicide is a third-degree felony, and it is considered less serious than manslaughter.

Vehicular Homicide

VEHICULAR HOMICIDE
the killing of a human being by the operation of a motor vehicle by another in a reckless manner likely to cause the death of, or great bodily harm to, another.

Many unintentional deaths involve automobile accidents, in which at least one surviving driver may have been to blame. Because of the difficulty of obtaining involuntary manslaughter convictions in such cases, some states have created the lesser offense of **vehicular homicide,** which, like negligent homicide, requires a substantially lower degree of negligence than involuntary manslaughter. As Florida law says, "Vehicular homicide is the killing of a human being by the operation of a motor vehicle by another in a reckless manner likely to cause the death of, or great bodily harm to, another."[62]

Additionally, many states have enacted statutes creating the crime of "causing a death while driving intoxicated." Unlike vehicular homicide, which is generally a lesser included offense of involuntary manslaughter, causing a death by driving while intoxicated frequently results in the imposition of greater punishment than would an involuntary manslaughter conviction.

SUICIDE

Because suicide involves the intentional death of a human being, and because it is sometimes brought about with the assistance of another person, it deserves special mention in this chapter. At early common law, suicide was murder, and anyone who assisted another in committing suicide was a party to murder. Generally, the modern position is that suicide is not murder because of the requirement that a murderous killing must be that of another individual. Thirty-five states, however, have created the statutory crime of aiding or assisting suicide. Section 401 of the California Penal Code, for example, provides that any person who deliberately aids, advises, or encourages another to commit suicide is guilty of a felony. Nine states criminalize assisted suicide through common law,[63] although successful prosecutions based on common law may be difficult to obtain (as in the 1996 common law prosecution of assisted suicide advocate Dr. Jack Kevorkian, which is discussed in Chapter 1). Three states have abolished common law crimes and do not have statutes criminalizing assisted suicide. Only one state (Oregon), however, permits physician-assisted suicide.

Most statutes regarding the crime of aiding suicide refer only to passive action, and one who takes active steps to end the life of another is guilty of murder, even if the actions were taken at the request of the victim. It has been difficult for the courts to determine when the defendant crosses the line between aiding suicide and committing murder. If, for example, the defendant buys potentially deadly drugs for the victim to take, such conduct is generally considered only to constitute aiding. If, however, the defendant actually gives the drugs to the victim, such an action is generally considered to be active conduct and, therefore, murder.

Suppose, for example, that a young couple makes a suicide pact. To accomplish the suicides, the defendant, with his girlfriend in the front seat, drives his automobile off a cliff. The defendant survives, but his girlfriend dies. In such a case the defendant would most likely be charged with murder. If, however, the girlfriend lives and the driver of the automobile dies, then she would probably be guilty only of aiding or encouraging the suicide, since she was not actively involved in the attempt to commit it.

On June 26, 1997, the U.S. Supreme Court upheld the constitutionality of two assisted suicide laws. In *Vacco* v. *Quill*,[64] plaintiffs claimed that a New York law banning physician-assisted suicide violated the Fourteenth Amendment's equal protection clause (Excerpts from the majority opinion are reproduced in a Law in Practice box in this chapter). The claim rested on the observation that New York law allows persons wishing to hasten their own deaths to do so by directing the removal of life-support systems, but it does not permit terminally ill persons to self-administer prescribed lethal drugs to end their lives. The Court disagreed and upheld the New York ban.

The other 1997 case was that of *Washington* v. *Glucksberg*.[65] In *Glucksberg*, the Court upheld a state of Washington law that makes "[p]romoting a suicide attempt" a felony and provides that: "A person is guilty of [that crime] when he knowingly causes or aids another person to attempt suicide." Respondents in the case were four Washington physicians who occasionally treated terminally ill patients. In papers filed with the Court, the physicians declared that they would assist such patients in ending their lives were it not for the state's assisted suicide ban. They, along with three gravely ill plaintiffs and a nonprofit organization that counsels people considering physician-assisted suicide, filed suit against the state seeking a declaration that the Washington ban is unconstitutional. The basis of their action rested on the claim that the Fourteenth Amendment's Due Process Clause establishes a liberty interest that extends to a personal choice by a mentally competent, terminally ill adult to commit physician-assisted suicide. The Supreme Court disagreed, ruling that Washington's prohibition against causing or aiding a suicide does not violate the due process clause. In the words of the Court: "An examination of our Nation's history, legal traditions, and practices demonstrates that Anglo-American common law has punished or otherwise disapproved of assisting suicide for over seven hundred years; that rendering such assistance is still a crime in almost every State; that such prohibitions have never contained exceptions for those who were near death; that the prohibitions have in recent years been re-examined and, for the most part, reaffirmed in a number of States; and that the President recently signed the Federal Assisted Suicide Funding Restriction Act of 1997, which prohibits the use of federal funds in support of physician-assisted suicide." The Court concluded that: "In light

Web Extra! 8–2

Euthanasia information

Web Extra! 8–3

The Hemlock Society

CRIMINAL LAW IN THE NEWS

Mom May Be Charged in Baby's Sweating Death

Infant Was Bundled in Snowsuit, Left on Heated Waterbed

LITTLETON, Colo.—Two weeks after a 3-month-old baby sweated to death on a heated waterbed, the county sheriff's department has recommended criminal neglect charges be pressed against the boy's mother, authorities said.

Kylee Mortensen, 23, allegedly wrapped her son, Case Welch, in a snowsuit on March 18 and put him to sleep overnight on a heated waterbed set at 85 degrees, officials said. He was found dead the next morning, his snowsuit drenched in sweat.

David Berrett, attorney for the woman, insisted Mortensen was a good mother who never meant her baby harm. He said that she frequently wrapped the infant in a snowsuit to get him to fall asleep faster.

Sheriff Patrick Sullivan Jr., however, said that Mortensen should have known better than to make her baby so warm, and that the death was the result of criminal negligence.

"I don't think she was thinking right," he said, "She was negligent, so we decided she should be charged."

Autopsy shows baby died of hyperthermia Sullivan said the baby was left in the bed for about 12 hours. He said Mortensen checked the infant once during the night and found him to be all right, but at about 9:15 A.M. she found him dead and called authorities, he said.

Initially investigators thought the baby may have died of Sudden Infant Death Syndrome, but an autopsy later determined it was hyperthermia.

Berrett said he and Mortensen met with prosecutors today in an effort to prevent charges from being filed, but no decision has yet been made. The Arapahoe County prosecutors could not be reached for comment.

"The coroner ruled this case was an accident, and that's what we think happened here—this was an accident," Berrett said. "I don't think anything that happened rose to the level of criminal neglect."

Source: Todd Venezia, "Mom May Be Charged in Baby's Sweating Death; Infant Was Bundled in Snowsuit, Left on Heated Waterbed," APB News. March 31, 2000. Reprinted with permission.

---

of that history, this Court's decisions lead to the conclusion that respondents' asserted 'right' to assistance in committing suicide is not a fundamental liberty interest protected by the Due Process Clause."

Mercy killings, in which a person actively seeks to end the life of someone who is suffering, are frequently prosecuted as homicides. In February 2000, for example, Kim Kevin Howell, 43, of Queen Creek, Arizona, was arrested and charged with murder after allegedly ending the life of his terminally ill friend, James Leon Scott.[66] The forty-three-year-old Scott lay dying of bladder cancer at the Jerry L. Pettis Memorial Veterans' Medical Administration Medical Center in Loma Linda, California, when Howell allegedly pulled a ventilator tube from his neck. Howell told authorities that he had a long-standing pact with Scott in which both men agreed that if one friend ever lingered on life support, the other would pull the plug. Unbeknownst to Howell, however, his friend's family had already made the decision to stop blood pressure medication that was keeping Scott alive and had given doctors a do-not-resuscitate order. The order would have allowed Scott's blood pressure to drop naturally until he died. "I knew about their agreement," said Scott's mother. "Everybody knew about their agreement. But it never entered my mind he would really do it."[67]

LAW IN PRACTICE

DO STATE STATUTES AGAINST ASSISTED SUICIDE VIOLATE EQUAL PROTECTION GUARANTEES FOUND IN THE U.S. CONSTITUTION?

This box contains excerpts from the majority opinion in the 1997 U.S. Supreme Court case of Vacco v. Quill. *At issue were state laws against assisted suicide involving the terminally ill.*

Vacco v. Quill
U.S. Supreme Court (1997)
521 U.S. 793

Chief Justice Rehnquist delivered the opinion of the Court.

In New York, as in most States, it is a crime to aid another to commit or attempt suicide, but patients may refuse even lifesaving medical treatment. The question presented by this case is whether New York's prohibition on assisting suicide therefore violates the Equal Protection Clause of the Fourteenth Amendment. We hold that it does not.

Petitioners are various New York public officials. Respondents Timothy E. Quill, Samuel C. Klagsbrun, and Howard A. Grossman are physicians who practice in New York. They assert that although it would be "consistent with the standards of [their] medical practice[s]" to prescribe lethal medication for "mentally competent, terminally ill patients" who are suffering great pain and desire a doctor's help in taking their own lives, they are deterred from doing so by New York's ban on assisting suicide. Respondents, and three gravely ill patients who have since died, sued the State's Attorney General in the United States District Court. They urged that because New York permits a competent person to refuse life sustaining medical treatment, and because the refusal of such treatment is "essentially the same thing" as physician assisted suicide, New York's assisted suicide ban violates the Equal Protection Clause. *Quill* v. *Koppell,* 870 F. Supp. 78, 84–85 (SDNY 1994).

The District Court disagreed: "[I]t is hardly unreasonable or irrational for the State to recognize a difference between allowing nature to take its course, even in the most severe situations, and intentionally using an artificial death producing device." The court noted New York's "obvious legitimate interests in preserving life, and in protecting vulnerable persons," and concluded that "[u]nder the United States Constitution and the federal system it establishes, the resolution of this issue is left to the normal democratic processes within the State."

The Court of Appeals for the Second Circuit reversed. 80 F.3d 716 (1996). The court determined that, despite the assisted suicide ban's apparent general applicability, "New York law does not treat equally all competent persons who are in the final stages of fatal illness and wish to hasten their deaths," because "those in the final stages of terminal illness who are on life support systems are allowed to hasten their deaths by directing the removal of such systems; but those who are similarly situated, except for the previous attachment of life sustaining equipment, are not allowed to hasten death by self administering prescribed drugs." In the court's view, "[t]he ending of life by [the withdrawal of life support systems] is nothing more nor less than assisted suicide." (emphasis added) (citation omitted). The Court of Appeals then examined whether this supposed unequal treatment was rationally related to any legitimate state interests, and concluded that "to the extent that [New York's statutes] prohibit a physician from prescribing medications to be self administered by a mentally competent, terminally ill person in the final stages of his terminal illness, they are not rationally related to any legitimate state interest." We granted certiorari . . . and now reverse.

The Equal Protection Clause commands that no State shall "deny to any person within its jurisdiction the equal protection of the laws." This provision creates nonsubstantive rights. *San Antonio Independent School Dist.* v. *Rodriguez,* 411 U.S. 1, 33 (1973); *id.,* at 59 (Stewart, J., concurring). Instead, it embodies a general rule that States must treat like cases alike but may treat unlike cases accordingly. *Plyler* v. *Doe,* 457 U.S. 202, 216 (1982) (" '[T]he Constitution does not require things which are different in fact or opinion to be treated in law as though they were the same' ") (quoting *Tigner* v. *Texas,* 310 U.S. 141, 147 (1940)). If a legislative classification or distinction "neither burdens a fundamental right nor targets a suspect class, we will uphold [it] so

(continued)

LAW IN PRACTICE

long as it bears a rational relation to some legitimate end." *Romer* v. *Evans*, 517 U.S. ___, ___ (slip op. at 10) (1996).

New York's statutes outlawing assisting suicide affect and address matters of profound significance to all New Yorkers alike. They neither infringe fundamental rights nor involve suspect classifications. *Washington* v. *Glucksberg, ante,* at 15–24; see 80 F.3d, at 726; *San Antonio School Dist.,* 411 U.S., at 28 ("The system of alleged discrimination and the class it defines have none of the traditional indicia of suspectness"); *id.,* at 33–35 [courts must look to the Constitution, not the "importance" of the asserted right, when deciding whether an asserted right is "fundamental"). These laws are therefore entitled to a "strong presumption of validity." *Heller* v. *Doe,* 509 U.S. 312, 319 (1993).

On their faces, neither New York's ban on assisting suicide nor its statutes permitting patients to refuse medical treatment treat anyone differently than anyone else or draw any distinctions between persons. Everyone, regardless of physical condition, is entitled, if competent, to refuse unwanted lifesaving medical treatment; no one is permitted to assist a suicide. Generally speaking, laws that apply evenhandedly to all "unquestionably comply" with the Equal Protection Clause. *New York City Transit Authority* v. *Beazer,* 440 U.S. 568, 587 (1979); see *Personnel Administrator of Mass.* v. *Feeney,* 442 U.S. 256, 271–273 (1979) ("[M]any [laws] affect certain groups unevenly, even though the law itself treats them no differently from all other members of the class described by the law").

The Court of Appeals, however, concluded that some terminally ill people—those who are on life support systems—are treated differently than those who are not, in that the former may "hasten death" by ending treatment, but the latter may not "hasten death" through physician assisted suicide. 80 F.3d, at 729. This conclusion depends on the submission that ending or refusing lifesaving medical treatment "is nothing more nor less than assisted suicide." Unlike the Court of Appeals, we think the distinction between assisting suicide and withdrawing life sustaining treatment, a distinction widely recognized and endorsed in the medical profession and in our legal traditions, is both important and logical; it is certainly rational. See *Feeney, supra,* at 272 ("When the basic classification is rationally based, uneven effects

upon particular groups within a class are ordinarily of no constitutional concern").

The distinction comports with fundamental legal principles of causation and intent. First, when a patient refuses life sustaining medical treatment, he dies from an underlying fatal disease or pathology; but if a patient ingests lethal medication prescribed by a physician, he is killed by that medication. *See, e.g., People* v. *Kevorkian,* 447 Mich. 436, 470–472, 527 N.W.2d 714, 728 (1994), *cert. denied,* 514 U.S. 1083 (1995); *Matter of Conroy,* 98 N. J. 321, 355, 486 A.2d 1209, 1226 (1985) (when feeding tube is removed, death "result[s] . . . from [the patient's] underlying medical condition"); *In re Colyer,* 99 Wash. 2d 114, 123, 660 P.2d 738, 743 (1983) ("[D]eath which occurs after the removal of life sustaining systems is from natural causes"); American Medical Association, Council on Ethical and Judicial Affairs, *Physician Assisted Suicide,* 10 Issues in Law & Medicine 91, 92 (1994) ("When a life sustaining treatment is declined, the patient dies primarily because of an underlying disease").

Furthermore, a physician who withdraws, or honors a patient's refusal to begin, life sustaining medical treatment purposefully intends, or may so intend, only to respect his patient's wishes and "to cease doing useless and futile or degrading things to the patient when [the patient] no longer stands to benefit from them." Assisted Suicide in the United States, Hearing before the Subcommittee on the Constitution of the House Committee on the Judiciary, 104th Cong., 2d Sess., 368 (1996) (testimony of Dr. Leon R. Kass). The same is true when a doctor provides aggressive palliative care; in some cases, painkilling drugs may hasten a patient's death, but the physician's purpose and intent is, or may be, only to ease his patient's pain. A doctor who assists a suicide, however, "must, necessarily and indubitably, intend primarily that the patient be made dead." *Id.,* at 367. Similarly, a patient who commits suicide with a doctor's aid necessarily has the specific intent to end his or her own life, while a patient who refuses or discontinues treatment might not. *See, e.g., Matter of Conroy, supra,* at 351, 486 A.2d, at 1224 (patients who refuse life sustaining treatment "may not harbor a specific intent to die" and may instead "fervently wish to live, but to do so free of unwanted medical technology, surgery, or drugs"); *Superintendent of Belchertown State School* v. *Saikewicz,* 373 Mass. 728, 743, n. 11,

(continued)

LAW IN PRACTICE

370 N. E. 2d 417, 426, n. 11 (1977) ["[I]n refusing treatment the patient may not have the specific intent to die"]. . . .

What do you think?

1. Why did the Court of Appeals for the Second Circuit hold that "New York law does not treat

equally all competent persons who are in the final stages of fatal illness and wish to hasten their deaths"? On what basis did the U.S. Supreme Court disagree?

2. What important distinction did the U.S. Supreme Court draw between assisting suicide and withdrawing life sustaining treatment? Do you agree that the distinction is valid? Why or why not?

LAW IN PRACTICE

ASSISTED SUICIDE LAWS

Founded in 1980 by Derek Humphry, the Hemlock Society is the oldest and largest right-to-die organization in the United States. Members believe that people who wish to retain their dignity and choice at the end of lives should have the option of a peaceful, gentle, certain, and swift death in the company of their loved ones. The means to accomplish this, says the Hemlock Society, is with legally prescribed medication as part of the continuum of care between a patient and a doctor. The society advocates nationwide passage of laws allowing a dying patient to hasten his or her death with a doctor's help, with certain safeguards. Similarly, the society supports clear, enforceable laws governing physician aid to the dying. According to the society, the following guidelines offer protection for doctors, patients, and the public. The society says that while these points may vary somewhat, they are contained in some form or other in most of the "death with dignity" legislation that has been proposed in the United States and other countries since 1988.

A bill permitting physician aid in dying:

Pertains only to mentally competent, terminally ill adults.
- Requires that the patient be fully informed of all alternatives, including hospice care.
- Requires that only the patient make the decision and that the patient must exercise independent judgment and not be coerced.
- Defines terminal illness as one in which the patient has not more than six months to live.

- Requires that at least two independent physicians agree on the diagnosis and the prognosis.
- Requires a mental health consultation, which may be at the discretion of the physician, if the capacity of the patient is doubtful or if treatable depression is suspected.
- Requires the patient to make an enduring request verbally, usually on three occasions separated by waiting periods ranging from forty-eight hours to fifteen days.
- Requires that one of the requests be made in writing and be witnessed by uninvolved observers.
- Strongly encourages involvement of the family, with requests for the family to be notified and in agreement.
- May require that the patient be a resident of the state for at least six months.
- Allows multiple methods of communication in addition to verbal communication.
- Requires that the patient have multiple opportunities to withdraw his or her request at any time.
- Stipulates that any health care or administrative personnel not wishing to participate can decline with impunity, in which case a referral may/should be made to another physician or facility.
- May stipulate that the means of death can be by prescription only, or may provide for means mutually agreed on by the patient and the doctor.
- May require that the doctor be present when the prescription is administered.

(continued)

LAW IN PRACTICE

- May require video or audio taping of the requests.
- Stipulates that aid in dying may be offered by no one other than the physician whose aid has been requested orally and in writing.
- Requires that a report of assisted death, stating the underlying cause, be made to the County Health Department; the patient's name is not to be used.
- Stipulates that insurance benefits would not be affected.
- Provides civil and criminal immunity to physician, pharmacist, and people who are present to assist the patient. Criminal

penalties would attach if coercion were found or if the guidelines were not followed.

What do *you* think?

1. Do you agree with the Hemlock Society that "people who wish to retain their dignity and choice at the end of lives should have the option of a peaceful, gentle, certain, and swift death in the company of their loved ones"? If so, what kind of option do you envision?

2. Would you add any features to the society's proposed legislation? Would you delete any? If so, which ones? Why?

SOURCE: The Hemlock Society. Posted at http://www.hemlock.org. Reprinted with permission.

SUMMARY

- Homicide is the killing of a human being by another human being. Criminal homicides are those homicides for which criminal liability accrues. Generally any homicide that is not excusable or justifiable is considered criminal homicide.

- This chapter describes three general categories of homicide: murder, manslaughter, and negligent homicide.

- An essential element of criminal homicide is the killing of a human being. Accordingly, the victim must have been alive before the homicidal act occurred. The alive requirement has been modified in some jurisdictions.

- A major problem in homicide cases is in defining *death*. The common law rule was that death occurs when a person's heartbeat and respiratory functions cease.

- Many jurisdictions have adopted the Uniform Determination of Death Act (UDDA) in defining death. The UDDA says that death occurs when an individual has sustained either: (1) irreversible cessation of circulatory and respiratory functions, or (2) irreversible cessation of all functions of the entire brain, including the brain stem.

- Criminal homicides must be the result of an affirmative act, an omission to act, or criminal negligence. The act causing the death need not be the only cause of death.

- Murder is the unlawful killing of another person with malice aforethought. Hence, the statutory elements of the crime of murder are: (1) an unlawful killing, (2) of a human being, (3) with malice.

- Felony murders are deaths that result from the commission of a dangerous felony.

- Manslaughter is the unlawful killing of a human being without malice. Hence, the statutory elements of manslaughter are: (1) an unlawful killing, (2) of a human being, (3) without malice. Manslaughter may be of two types: voluntary or involuntary.

- Voluntary manslaughter is the unlawful killing of a human being, without malice, which is done intentionally upon a sudden quarrel or in the heat of passion. Voluntary manslaughter is homicide committed in response to adequate provocation.

- Provocation is said to be "adequate" if it would cause a reasonable person to lose self-control. Adequate provocation is also called reasonable provocation.
- Involuntary manslaughter is an unintended killing caused during the commission of an unlawful act not amounting to a dangerous felony or as the result of criminal negligence or recklessness.
- Criminal negligence is defined by statute in most jurisdictions, and it consists of flagrant and reckless disregard of the safety of others, or of wilful indifference to the safety and welfare of others.
- In many states, deaths resulting from degrees of negligence below that required for a charge of manslaughter may give rise to prosecutions for the crime of negligent homicide.
- Vehicular homicide is the killing of a human being by the operation of a motor vehicle in a reckless manner likely to cause the death of, or great bodily harm to, another.
- Many states have created the statutory crime of aiding suicide, although one who actually ends the life of a suicidal individual may be guilty of murder.

QUESTIONS FOR DISCUSSION

1. What distinguishes noncriminal homicide from criminal homicide?
2. What are the three types of criminal homicide?
3. Define *death.*
4. What causation problems characterize criminal homicide prosecutions?
5. Explain the concept of *corpus delicti* as it relates to criminal homicide.
6. Distinguish between murder and voluntary manslaughter.
7. What is meant by *malice aforethought?*
8. Explain the felony murder rule.
9. When a first-degree murder statute reads "wilful, deliberate, and premeditated" does the statute require anything more than that the killing be intentional? Why or why not?
10. The defendant took a pistol with him on a visit to the hospital to see his terminally ill father. At his father's request, he killed his father with a single shot to the head. What crime, if any, is the defendant guilty of? [See *State* v. *Forrest,* 362 S.E.2d 252 (N.C. 1987).]

LEGAL RESOURCES ON THE WORLD WIDE WEB

Some Web sites list law-related job opportunities. Although some jobs require a law degree, many employers are looking for candidates with undergraduate credentials to work in support roles.

Association of Trial Lawyers of America (ATLA)
http://www.atlanet.org/jobbank/openings.ht
The job bank at ATLA provides hundreds of listings at any one time.

Counsel Net
http://www.counsel.net/jobs
The career center at Counsel Net contains a series of free job posting boards for law firms and other businesses. An e-mail alert system, called JobAlert, notifies job hunters of legal jobs as they become available.

Emplawyer
http://www.emplawyernet.com
The site offers free career planning and contains a list of almost 6,000 law-related job openings.

Federal Judiciary Employment Opportunities
http://www.uscourts.gov/employment/opportunity.html
Includes information on a wide variety of federal government jobs in law-related fields.

Job Links for Lawyers
http://home.sprynet.com/~ear2ground
Not just for lawyers, this site provides jobs information for attorneys as well as law librarians, anyone in legal publishing, and those wanting to work in academia.

Law Info
http://jobs.lawinfo.com
The jobs page at Law Info allows attorneys and anyone involved with the law to post their resume. Also provides a list of jobs offered.

Lawyer's Weekly
http://www.lawyersweeklyjobs.com
The careers section of *Lawyer's Weekly* online includes job postings for attorneys, paralegals, legal secretaries, and other legal fields and specialties.

Check the *Criminal Law Today* Web site for URLs that may have changed.

SUGGESTED READINGS AND CLASSIC WORKS

Susan L. Brennan and Richard Delgado, "Death: Multiple Definitions or a Single Standard?" *Southern California Law Review,* Vol. 54 (1981), p. 1323.

Kevin Cole, "Killings During Crime: Toward a Discriminating Theory of Strict Liability," *American Criminal Law Review,* Vol. 28, (1990), p. 73.

David Crump and Susan Crump, "In Defense of the Felony Murder Doctrine," *Harvard Journal of Law and Public Policy,* Vol. 8 (Spring 1985), pp. 359–398.

H.L.A. Hart, *The Concept of Law* (London: Oxford University Press, 1961).

JoAnna K. Weinberg, "Whose Right Is It Anyway? Individualism, Community, and the Right to Die: A Commentary on the New Jersey Experience," *The Hastings Law Journal,* Vol. 40 (November 1988), p. 119.

CAPSTONE CASE

IS THE DEFENSE OF SELF-DEFENSE AVAILABLE IN FELONY MURDER CASES?

State v. *Amado*
Appellate Court of Connecticut, 1996
42 Conn. App. 348, 680 A.2d. 974

OPINION
Defendant Ford, J., was convicted upon jury verdict in the Superior Court, Judicial District of Fairfield, of two counts of murder, two counts of felony murder. . . . Defendant appealed. The Appellate Court, Heiman, J., held that the trial court properly instructed the jury that self-defense was not available as defense to a charge of felony murder.

Affirmed.

. . .Although the defendant raises a number of issues relating to the trial court's charge on self-defense, the dispositive issue in this appeal is whether self-defense . . . is available as a defense to a charge of felony murder. If self-defense is not available as a defense to felony murder, then the defendant's attack on the self-defense charge as it applies to his felony murder conviction would be unavailable, and, consequently, the felony murder conviction would [be supported]. . . . We do not address the defendant's attack on the self-defense charge as it applies to his intentional murder connections because, regardless of any impropriety in the self-defense charge as it applies to the intentional murder convictions, the felony-murder conviction would remain intact. . .

The jury could reasonably have found the following facts. On October 18, 1990, and for some time prior thereto, Eric Amado was living in an apartment in West Haven with Joanne Bailey and Hope Vaughn. Amado also stored cocaine that he was selling in bulk in the apartment. He stored the narcotics in a small safe and in a duffel bag, both of which were kept in the laundry room of the apartment.

On October 18, 1990, Vaughn called Anthony Young at his residence at 505 Williams Street in Bridgeport. Young came to the West Haven apartment, and he and Vaughn removed the duffel bag and the safe from the apartment and placed them in the truck of Young's red Toyota Celica. Before leaving the apartment, Vaughn and Young opened the window and knocked some items to the floor to make it appear that someone had broken into the premises. They left West Haven and went to 505 Williams Street. When they arrived in Bridgeport, Young telephoned Peter Hall, who then went to 505 Williams Street.

Some time during that same day, Amado returned to the apartment and found that a window had been opened and that items in the apartment had been knocked over. Amado had gone to the apartment to pick up a quantity of cocaine that he was going to deliver to a purchaser. When Amado went to the laundry room where his drugs had been stored, he discovered that the drugs were missing. Bailey also returned to the apartment and discovered the open window and items knocked to the floor. She left the premises and went to her sister's house in Bridgeport.

Later in the day, Amado picked up Bailey at her sister's house in Bridgeport. Amado was driving a white Mitsubishi. Amado was accompanied by Anthony Smalls. The group went to Norwalk to look for Vaughn to ascertain whether she knew who was responsible for the theft of the drugs. Amado, Bailey and Smalls met John Wideman, who joined in the search for Vaughn.

The group went to Stamford. They arrived at a house, and Bailey and Wideman waited in the car while Amado and Smalls entered the house. After about thirty minutes, Smalls emerged from the house. Fifteen minutes later, Amado came out of the house. Amado told the others that he had been visiting with a "voodoo man" who had told him that Vaughn and two others had stolen his drugs.

The group returned to Bridgeport and left Bailey at her sister's house. Amado told her to stay there until he returned. Amado, Smalls and Wideman left the house and returned about ten minutes later accompanied by David Bailey, who was driving a blue Volvo.

The group of five decided to look for Vaughn. Amado, Smalls, and Joanne Bailey rode in the white Mitsubishi, while Wideman and David Bailey rode in the blue Volvo. They first went to Vaughn's sister's house, and when they did not find Vaughn there, they proceeded to 505 Williams Street. The four men were armed with pistols. They arrived at 505 Williams Street about 9 P.M. and observed Vaughn standing on the porch with Young and Hall. Amado told Joanne Bailey to go to the porch and tell Vaughn that he wanted to talk with her, Vaughn came down from the porch and entered the white Mitsubishi. Amado asked Vaughn if she knew where his drugs were. Vaughn denied any knowledge of the theft or whereabouts of the missing cocaine. While questioning Vaughn, Amado was upset and talked loudly. Amado, Smalls, Vaughn, Wideman, David Bailey, and Joanne Bailey left Williams

Street and arrived at the West Haven apartment about 2:30 A.M. on October 19, 1990. The group remained there overnight.

About 10 A.M., Amado and Joanne Bailey went into the hallway to talk with neighbors. Amado wanted to determine whether the neighbors had observed anyone removing items from his apartment. After speaking with a neighbor across the hall, Amado told Vaughn that he had learned that she had taken his cocaine. Amado told Vaughn that the neighbor had seen her in a red Toyota Celica. Vaughn said that the vehicle belonged to Young.

Amado, Smalls, Vaughn, Wideman, David Bailey, and Joanne Bailey proceeded to 505 Williams Street. Amado, Smalls, Vaughn, and Joanne Bailey rode in the white Mitsubishi and the others rode in the blue Volvo. They arrived at the house at about 11 A.M., and everyone exited the vehicles. Amado and Smalls were both armed with handguns.

Amado, Vaughn and Joanne Bailey went to the porch of the house and rang the doorbell. When nobody answered, they knocked on the door. Young opened the door and Hall was standing beside him. Hall had a gun in the waistband of his pants. Amado accused Young and Hall of having his cocaine, and both Young and Hall denied having the drugs.

Young asked Amado if they could talk, and Amado began shooting. He fired five shots. Joanne Bailey was shot in the left thigh. Young was shot in the left groin area, and Hall was shot on the left side of the abdomen. Joanne Bailey went into the house, fell down, and crawled into the kitchen. Hall went into the kitchen and collapsed on the floor near the refrigerator. Young collapsed in the front hall near the doorway.

Amado, Smalls, Wideman, and David Bailey fled, leaving behind Vaughn and Joanne Bailey. Vaughn called 911 from a neighbor's house and EMTs responded to the call.

When the EMTs arrived at the house, the front door was locked and they were unable to enter. Vaughn returned and was screaming, "He's shot." She kicked in the window, entered the house and opened the front door for the EMTs.

Upon entering the house, the EMTs observed Young lying on the floor of the front hallway. He was unconscious and had sustained a gunshot wound. He was clutching a fully loaded magazine for an automatic weapon. Hall, also suffering from a gunshot wound, was sitting on the floor in the bedroom. He was unconscious, but his eyes were open. He held a small automatic pistol. The hammer of the pistol was cocked back, and his finger was on the trigger. The EMTs also found Joanne Bailey.

The Bridgeport police arrived. Officer John Galpin spoke with Young, who had regained consciousness, and asked him to name the person who had shot him. Young responded that Amado had shot him. Young and Hall were transported to Bridgeport Hospital. Both died as a result of gunshot wounds. Young died as a result of a gunshot wound to the groin area and Hall died as a result of a gunshot wound to the abdomen.

The police obtained a search warrant for 505 Williams Street, and a search of the basement resulted in the seizure of two large plastic bags containing rocky white powder. One of the plastic bags was inside a black duffel bag. In addition, the police found a strainer, a spoon, and a safe. The contents of the plastic bags tested positive for cocaine. The total weight of the two bags was about three and one half pounds, and the drugs had a bulk value of about $38,000.

An arrest warrant was issued for Amado (hereinafter the defendant), and he was arrested in Georgia as a fugitive from justice. Bridgeport authorities were notified of the defendant's arrest on March 21, 1992, and approximately ten months later he was returned to Bridgeport for trial.

The defendant testified at trial. He conceded that he had shot the victims, but asserted that he did so in self-defense. He admitted that he lived in the West Haven apartment with Joanne Bailey and that in October, 1990, he had been engaged in selling cocaine. He also conceded that the duffel bag containing the cocaine and the safe were his property. He claimed that on October 18, 1990, he discovered that these items were missing and that he and the others went to Bridgeport to find out about the disappearance of the items.

The defendant testified that upon arriving at 505 Williams Street, he walked up to the front door. He asserted that he did not display a weapon as he went to the door. He claimed that the first person that he observed in the doorway was Young. The defendant testified that he told Young that the house in West Haven had been "robbed" and that Young's car had been observed there. The defendant claimed that he asked Young whether he knew anything about the incident. According to the defendant, Young indicated that "he hadn't been up there" and that "he didn't have anything to do with it."

The defendant further testified that, as this conversation was taking place, Hall appeared in the doorway and stood to the rear of Young. The defendant stated that both Young and Hall were standing inside the house, while the defendant was standing on the porch. The defendant said that Smalls, who was standing to his rear, yelled at the men in the doorway, "Do you have our shit or don't you?" The defendant asserted that Young became upset and shouted back at Smalls. The defendant testified that, up to this point, neither Young nor Hall appeared to have a weapon.

According to the defendant, Young then took a step forward and the defendant took a step back. The defendant claimed that he then saw Hall reach for the waistband of his trousers and start to draw a gun. The defendant testified that he became frightened because he thought Hall was going to shoot him. The defendant claimed that he drew his gun and shot into the house several times because he saw Hall pull out a gun. The defendant asserted that following the shooting, he ran away. He testified that during the incident, he did not know that he had shot Young and Hall.

We now turn to the fifth claim advanced by the defendant, namely, that the trial court improperly instructed the jury that self-defense is not available as a defense to a charge of felony murder. As we have stated, if this claim is without merit, then, regardless of whether the self-defense instructions were improper as to the intentional murder convictions, the defendant's felony murder conviction would properly support his . . . conviction, and, consequently, the judgment must be affirmed. We recognize that this precise issue has not been addressed by our appellate courts. We are persuaded, however, that the trial court acted properly in instructing that self-defense is not available as a defense to a charge of felony murder.

We begin our analysis by recognizing that the defendant has a constitutionally guaranteed due process right to establish a defense. . . . The right to establish a defense, however, is not limitless. The defense sought to be established must be legally cognizable as a valid defense to the crime charged. . . . Thus, we must examine the nature of the crime charged in order to determine the applicability of a defense to that particular crime.

Our felony murder statute, "53a-54c, contains no *mens rea* requirement beyond that of an intention to commit the underlying felony upon which the felony murder charge is predicated. . . . In order to obtain a conviction for felony murder, the state must prove, beyond a reasonable doubt, all the elements of the statutorily designated underlying felony, and in addition, that a death was caused in the course of and in furtherance of that felony. . . . There is no requirement that the state prove an intent to cause death." (Citation omitted.) "Indeed, the felony murder statute does not require that the defendant commit the homicidal act. . . . A defendant may be liable if a death is caused by any participant in the underlying felony." (Citations omitted.)

Thus, the elements of felony murder differ markedly from those of intentional murder. Our Supreme Court has recognized this difference in determining that manslaughter is not a lesser included offense of felony murder. In *State v. Castro* . . . the court held: In both lessor degrees of manslaughter the state must prove that the defendant possessed a culpable state of mind. Manslaughter in the first degree

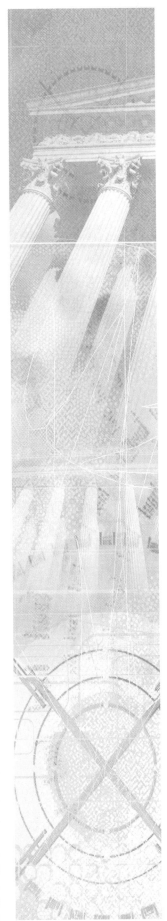

requires a showing that the defendant had the intent to cause serious physical injury. (General Statutes 53a-55.) Manslaughter in the second degree requires proof that a killing was committed recklessly. (General Statutes 52a.) "In contrast, the felony murder statute contains no such *mens rea* element. . . . Since both first-degree and second-degree manslaughter require the showing of a culpable state of mind, manslaughter is not a lesser included offense of felony murder." (Citations omitted.)

The purpose of the felony murder statute is to punish those whose conduct brought about an unintended death in the commission or attempted commission of a felony. . . . The felony murder rule includes accidental, unintended deaths. Indeed, our Supreme Court has noted that crimes against the person like robbery, rape, common-law arson, and burglary are, in common experience, likely to involve danger to life in the event of resistance by the victim. Robberies by armed robbers no doubt are even more likely to result in unintended deaths than are arsons. Often it is the victim of the robbery who is accidentally killed. The armed robber committing or attempting a robbery whose loaded gun is discharged accidentally when the robber and another person are struggling for the gun is guilty of felony murder when the victim is thus killed. . . . Moreover, the legislative history of 53a-54c indicates that the felony murder statute was enacted to provide prosecutors with a means of proving murder in cases where a homicide occurs during the commission of certain felonies, but specific intent to kill cannot be proven.

Courts often decline to allow a defendant to raise a claim of self-defense in a felony murder case. (See 2 P. Robinson, *Criminal Law Defenses.* (1984) 132, p. 99.) Having examined the language and the purpose of 53a-54c, we conclude that the trial court was correct in instructing that self-defense is not available as a defense to a charge of felony murder. In support of our conclusion, we next examine the opinions of courts of other jurisdictions that we find to be persuasive.

It has been held that the right to claim self-defense may be forfeited by one who commits an armed robbery, even if excessive force is used by the intended victim, or by any person intervening to prevent the crime or apprehend the robber. *Wilson v. State*, 473 P.2d 633, 636 (Alaska 1970). See *People v. Dillard*, 5 Ill. App. 3d 896, 284 N.E.2d 40 (1972) (robber has no right to kill his victim to save his own life). The United States Court of Appeals for the Second Circuit has determined that in a prosecution for felony murder under federal law, "One who commits or attempts a robbery armed with deadly force, and kills the intended victim when the victim responds with force to the robbery attempt, may not avail himself of the defense of self-defense." *United States v. Thomas*, 34 F.3d 44, 18 (2d Cir. 1994) *cert. denied*, 115 S. Ct. 1134, 130 L. Ed. 2d 1095 (1995). The court reasoned that "[i]t has long been accepted that one cannot support a claim of self-defense by a self-generated necessity to kill. The right of homicidal self-defense is . . . denied to slayers who incite the fatal attack. . . . In sum, one who is the aggressor in a conflict culminating in death cannot invoke the necessities of self-preservation." *Id.*, quoting *United States v. Peterson*, 483 F.2d 1222, 1231, *cert. denied.*, 414 U.S. 1007, 94 S. Ct. 367, 38 L. Ed. 2d 244 (1973). "Under this principle," the court held, "the defendants had no entitlement to any self-defense charge."

The California Court of Appeals, which has also discussed the inapplicability of self-defense to a charge of felony murder, held: "The purpose of the felony murder rule is to deter even accidental killings in the commission of designated felonies by holding the felon strictly liable for murder." *People v. Washington*, (1965) 62 Cal. 2d 777, 781. "When a burglar kills in the commission of a burglary, he cannot claim self-defense, for this would be inconsistent fundamentally with the very purpose of the felony murder rule." *People v. Arauz*, (1970) 5 Cal. App. 3d 523, 533.

The Supreme Court of Alaska has similarly explained that "authority clearly . . . indicates that a person who provokes a difficulty thereby forfeits his right to self-defense. This doctrine has been extended to preclude a person who commits a felony from claiming self-defense not only to the intended victim of the felony, but also to any person intervening in an attempt to prevent the crime or to apprehend the criminal." *Gray* v. *State,* 463 P.2d 897, 909 (Alaska 1970). Thus, the Alaska court held: "Where the defendant commits a felony which includes an immediate threat of violence, he has created a situation so fraught with peril as to preclude his claim of self-defense to any act of violence arising therefrom." *Id.,* at 910. Moreover, the Alaska court summarized its reasoning by stating that, in the felony murder situation at issue, "to permit appellants to justify their slaying of [the victim] by claiming self-defense . . . would be to fashion a rule of law unresponsive to society's need for protection against just such extraordinarily dangerous conduct. This would not, in our view, tend to facilitate decent and peaceful behavior by all. To bestow a privilege to slay would be manifestly unsound."

Finally, as the United States District Court for the District of Maryland has recognized, "when a defendant is charged under (the Maryland felony murder statute), the defense of self-defense is unavailable to him as a matter of law because he is an aggressor engaged in the perpetration of a felony. *Street* v. *State,* 26 Md. App. 336, 340; 338 A.2d 72 (1975). This . . . construction of the felony-murder statute comports with the general rule on the subject of the nonavailability of self-defense as a defense to felony murder. See *Smith* v. *State,* 209 Tenn. 499, 502, 54 S.W.2d 450, 452 (1961); *Wharton's Criminal Law and Procedure* 252 (19–57)."

We conclude that a bright line rule that self-defense is not available as a defense to a charge of felony murder in violation of 53a-54c is warranted. It is incongruous with the purpose of the felony murder statute to allow a defendant who causes a death, in the course of committing an enumerated felony, to mount a defense afterward asserting that he was merely defending himself. A defendant's invocation of self-defense under such circumstances gives new meaning to the word "chutzpah."

On the basis of the foregoing, we conclude that the trial court properly instructed the jury that self-defense is not available as a defense to felony murder. Because the defendant's two felony murder convictions, unsuccessfully attacked, properly support the defendant's conviction . . . we need not, and do not, discuss the defendant's other claims.

The judgment is affirmed. In this opinion, the other justices concurred.

[footnotes omitted]

WHAT DO *YOU* THINK?
1. Do you agree with the court that the defense of self-defense should not be available in cases involving felony murder?
2. What, according to the court, are the purposes of the felony murder rule? Do you see any additional rationales that might justify the rule?
3. What state of mind must the prosecution prove to establish guilt under a felony murder situation?
4. Why does the court conclude that manslaughter is not a lesser included offense to felony murder?

WHAT ARE THE DIFFERENCES BETWEEN MURDER AND INVOLUNTARY MANSLAUGHTER?

 **CAPSTONE CASE**

Johnson v. *Texas*
Texas Court of Appeals, 14th Judicial District, 1996
915 S.W.2d 653

Defendant was convicted of murder following jury trial in the 228th District Court, Harris County, Justice Ted Poe presiding. Defendant appealed. The Court of Appeals, Justice Fowler presiding held that: "Defendant was not entitled to jury

instructions on criminally negligent homicide, involuntary manslaughter, reckless conduct, or aggravated assault as lesser included charges to crime of murder. . . ."

Affirmed. Discretionary review refused on May 22, 1996.

OPINION

Justice Fowler: Following a jury trial, appellant was convicted of murder. The jury, finding two enhancement allegations to be true, sentenced appellant to seventy-five years in the Texas Department of Criminal Justice, Institutional Division. Appellant brings three points of error, alleging: (1) the trial court erred in overruling his request for lesser included offense charges; (2) he received ineffective assistance of counsel; and (3) the prosecutor engaged in prosecutorial misconduct. We affirm.

On March 25, 1994, appellant encountered Leon Freeman near an apartment complex. Lisa Freeman, who is married to Freeman's nephew, was walking through the area when she heard the two men talking. Apparently, the discussion was about drug money. When Lisa Freeman approached the two men, Freeman was telling appellant that he did not have his money, but when he got it, he would give it to appellant. Appellant yelled that he wanted his "goddamn" money, took out a pistol, and shot Freeman in the chest. Lisa Freeman, who was approximately three to four feet away, turned and ran.

Houston Police Officer Kevin Smith and his partner, Officer Thomas Wood, were patrolling the area when a child knocked on the car window and said someone had been shot. Officer Smith got out of the car and saw Freeman's body. When he approached the body, somebody pointed him toward the assailant's escape route. Ultimately, Officer Smith and a second officer apprehended appellant, who still had the gun in his hand.

In his first point of error, appellant claims the trial court erred in refusing his requested jury charges on the lesser included offenses of involuntary manslaughter, aggravated assault, criminally negligent homicide, and reckless conduct.

There is a two-pronged test to determine whether a jury must be charged on a lesser included offense. (Citations omitted.) This test has become known as the *"Royster"* or *"Royster-Aguilar"* test. First, the lesser included offense must be included in the proof necessary to establish the offense charged. Second, there must be some evidence that if the defendant is guilty, he is guilty only of the lesser included offense. In 1993, the Texas Court of Criminal Appeals modified the second prong to read "second, some evidence must exist in the record *that would permit a jury rationally to find* that if the defendant is guilty, he is guilty only of the lesser offense." The Court of Criminal Appeals noted, however, that it was not the intent of the court to change the substantive test of *Royster,* but only to interpret and clarify existing law.

When the reviewing court is asked to determine whether a lesser included offense charge should have been given, it must consider all of the evidence presented by the State and the defendant. Entitlement to a jury instruction on a lesser included offense must be made on a case-by-case basis according to the particular facts.

Appellant asked for a lesser included offense charge on involuntary manslaughter and criminally negligent homicide. Both of these offenses are lesser included offenses of murder. Thus, appellant has satisfied the first prong of the *Royster* test. We must now determine if the second prong has been met.

The distinction between murder, involuntary manslaughter, and criminally negligent homicide lies in the culpable mental state accompanying the defendant's act. . . . Section 19.07(a) of the Texas Penal Code provides that "[a] person commits an offense if he causes the death of an individual by criminal negligence." Tex. Code Ann. Section 19.07(a) (Vernon 1989). Section 6.03(d) of the Code defines criminally negligent conduct and states: "A person acts with criminal negligence, or is criminally negligent, with respect to circumstances surrounding his conduct, or the result of his conduct, when he ought to be aware of a substantial and unjustifiable risk that the circumstances exist or the result will occur. The risk must be of such a nature and degree that the failure to perceive it constitutes a gross deviation from the standard of care that an ordinary person would exercise under all the circumstances and viewed from the actor's standpoint." Tex. Code Ann. Section 6.03(d) (Vernon 1974). In other words, an actor is criminally negligent if he should have been aware of the risk surrounding his conduct but failed to perceive it.

Appellant requested an instruction on criminally negligent homicide based on his testimony that he knew Freeman often carried a gun, and he saw something "silver" in Freeman's hand. He also testified that Freeman cursed at him, grabbed him by the collar, and slapped him so that some of his teeth were knocked loose. Appellant claimed he was afraid Freeman would kill him. In other words, appellant claimed he shot Freeman in self-defense. He also testified that he did not intend to kill Freeman, he was "just intending to get him off of me." However, when determining whether appellant is entitled to a lesser included offense charge on criminally negligent homicide, we must look at all of the evidence.

Lisa Freeman testified that she saw appellant take out a gun and shoot Freeman at close range. She stated that Freeman did not make any moves toward appellant. Appellant testified that he routinely carried an unloaded gun. He stated that when Freeman slapped him, he loaded a clip into the gun and shot him because he was "scared" of him.

In *Thomas* v. *State,* the defendant requested an instruction on criminally negligent homicide based on his testimony that he did not intend to shoot the victim, that it was an accident, and that he shot the victim in self-defense. The court held that the defendant did not meet the second prong of the *Royster* test because his testimony did not show that he possessed the requisite culpable mental state so that if guilty, he was guilty only of criminally negligent homicide. The court reasoned: "Evidence that a defendant knows a gun is loaded, that he is familiar with guns and their potential for injury, and that he points a gun at another, indicates a person who is aware of a risk created by that conduct and disregards that risk."

Additionally, in *Navarro,* the court noted that the question in determining whether a homicide was criminal was whether the act was voluntary or involuntary, not whether the homicide was intentional or not. In this case, appellant was familiar with the gun and knew it was loaded. In fact, he loaded it just before he shot Freeman. He deliberately pointed the gun at Freeman and pulled the trigger "to get him off of me." These were voluntary actions. The thrust of appellant's defense, demonstrated through his own testimony, was self-defense, not an unawareness of risk in exhibiting a loaded gun under the circumstances. Appellant testified he was afraid of Freeman, knew he carried a gun, and that he was reacting to an assault by Freeman. This evidence does not raise the issue of criminally negligent homicide; therefore, the trial court did not err in refusing to give appellant's requested charge.

Appellant also requested a charge on involuntary manslaughter. A person commits involuntary manslaughter if he "recklessly causes the death of an individual." Tex. Code Ann. Section 19.05(a)(1) (Vernon 1989). Section 6.03(c) of the code provides: "A person acts recklessly, or is reckless, with respect to circumstances surrounding his conduct or the result of his conduct when he is aware of but consciously disregards a substantial and unjustifiable risk that the circumstances exist or the result will occur. The risk must be of such a nature and degree that its disregard constitutes a gross deviation from the standard of care that an ordinary person would exercise under all the circumstances as viewed from the actor's standpoint.

As already stated, involuntary manslaughter is a lesser included offense of murder, and thus, appellant has satisfied the first prong of the *Royster* test.

The specific intent to kill is not an element of the offense of involuntary manslaughter. "Recklessness" is satisfied by evidence showing that the defendant consciously disregarded a known substantial and unjustifiable risk that serious

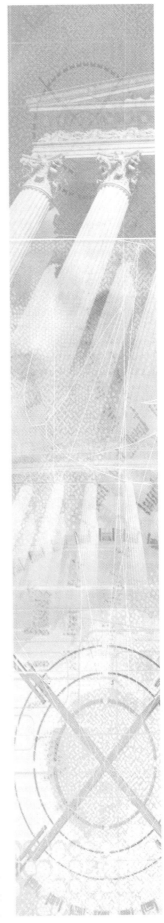

bodily injury would occur; a risk that if disregarded constitutes a gross deviation from the standard of care an ordinary person would exercise under the same circumstances. Here, the record does not reflect that appellant is guilty only of consciously disregarding a known substantial and unjustifiable risk that serious bodily injury would result. Appellant's claim that he did not intend to kill Freeman raises an issue as to his culpable mental state only if it is taken alone and out of context. The statement loses force when the evidence, including other statements by appellant, is viewed as a whole. A statement that a defendant did not intend to kill the victim cannot be "plucked out of the record and examined in a vacuum." Appellant's statement, when viewed along with the other evidence, is not evidence that would permit a jury rationally to find that if he is guilty, he is guilty only of involuntary manslaughter.

The other evidence at trial showed the following. Lisa Freeman testified that appellant demanded his money, and when he did not get it, he pulled out a gun and shot Freeman. Appellant testified that he habitually carried a gun. He claimed that Freeman was known to carry a gun, and that night, appellant saw something "silver" in Freeman's hand. He stated that he took five to seven seconds to load the gun, then shot Freeman. Appellant testified numerous times that he was in fear for his life; that he was afraid. Though appellant testified that he shot Freeman only to make Freeman get "off of him," this is not testimony that appellant's actions were anything other than deliberate. Moreover, appellant did not attempt to get help for Freeman or try to help Freeman himself; instead appellant fled the scene. Thus, the evidence as a whole does not support a rational inference that appellant was consciously disregarding the risk of death; rather, the evidence shows a deliberate, voluntary act by appellant, albeit in self-defense, if appellant is to be believed. The trial court did not err in refusing to instruct the jury on the lesser included offense of involuntary manslaughter.

Appellant also requested a charge on reckless conduct. A person commits the offense of reckless conduct if he recklessly engages in conduct that places another in imminent danger of serious bodily injury. Tex. Code Ann. Section 22.05(a) (Vernon 1989). The definition of "recklessly" entails an actor being aware of, but consciously disregarding, a substantial and unjustifiable risk that a result will occur. Recklessness and danger are presumed if the actor knowingly pointed a firearm at, or in the direction of, another. Tex. Code Ann. Section 22.05(b) (Vernon 1989). It is irrelevant whether or not the actor believed the firearm to be loaded.

Examination of the record, as demonstrated by the evidence detailed above, reveals that appellant's strategy at trial was to justify his act of shooting Freeman by relying upon his testimony that he fired because he was in fear for his own life, i.e., self-defense. Regardless of the veracity of appellant's theory, which was rejected by the jury, the consequence of appellant's intentional act of shooting Freeman went well beyond the mere act of placing another in imminent danger of serious bodily injury. Appellant did not say that the actual discharge of the gun was accidental; in fact, he said he deliberately fired the gun. One cannot accidentally or recklessly act in self-defense. The evidence clearly illustrates that appellant's intentional act of shooting Freeman, allegedly to protect himself, went beyond reckless conduct. Consequently, the record wholly fails to establish that appellant, if guilty, was guilty only of reckless conduct. As stated above, the statement by appellant that he did not intend to kill Freeman cannot be taken in a vacuum. That statement alone does not necessarily require an instruction on reckless conduct. Moreover, cases in which the Court of Criminal Appeals has found that an instruction on reckless conduct was required involved defendants whose guns had accidentally discharged or who testified that their guns accidentally discharged. In sum, the context of all of the evidence shows that appellant claimed he was acting in self-defense, and acted deliberately in shooting at Freeman from close range. Thus, the trial court did not err in refusing appellant's requested charge on reckless conduct. [Discussions on other points of error are omitted.]

[footnotes omitted]

WHAT DO *YOU* THINK?
1. Do you agree with the court's holding that the issue of criminally negligent homicide was not present in this case? Explain your answer.
2. Under what circumstances could involuntary manslaughter be a lesser included offense to murder?
3. Why can't a person act accidentally or recklessly in self-defense?

WHAT IS REQUIRED TO REDUCE A CHARGE OF MURDER TO VOLUNTARY MANSLAUGHTER?

CAPSTONE CASE

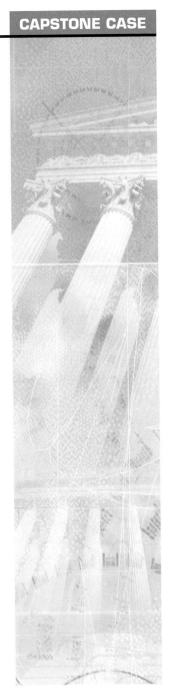

State v. *Thornton*
Supreme Court of Tennessee, 1987
730 S.W.2d 309

Appellant was convicted of murder in the first degree as a result of shooting his wife's paramour in the home of appellant and his wife on May 3, 1983. Appellant found his wife and the victim, Mark McConkey, engaged in sexual relations in the front bedroom of appellant's home. He fired a single shot which struck McConkey in the left hip. The victim died sixteen days later as the result of massive infection . . . from the bullet wound. . . .

Appellant and his wife had been married just under four years, and their three-year old son was in the home in an upstairs bedroom when the shooting occurred in a downstairs bedroom. Appellant and his wife had been separated for about six weeks, but no divorce action had been filed and appellant had been making a serious effort toward reconciliation with his wife. . . .

Appellant had never met McConkey and did not even know his name. Mrs. Thornton had met him four days before the homicide and had engaged in sexual relations with him in the home belonging to her and appellant every night since that time, including the night of the homicide. She testified that she thought that she told her husband that she might want to date someone else, that this, in modern society, indicated that she intended to have sexual relations. In that manner she sought to mitigate her infidelity and misconduct toward a husband who had never been unfaithful to her insofar as disclosed by the record. . . .

Appellant was slightly built, being only five feet, six inches in height and weighing about one hundred twenty-five pounds. McConkey was an athlete. . . . He was five feet, nine inches in height and weighed about one hundred eighty-two pounds. . . .

Appellant, according to uncontradicted testimony, was deeply disturbed over the separation of the parties. He had sought assistance from a marriage counselor, and had persuaded his wife to go with him to the marriage counselor on several occasions. . . . Appellant testified that the parties had agree to a separation of six months, and both he and the marriage counselor testified that the parties had agreed that they would not have sexual relations with each other or with anyone else during that period. Mrs. Thornton denied making that agreement. . . .

On the evening of May 3, appellant picked the wife and their child up at their home, and the three went to dinner. Again on that occasion, Mrs. Thornton reiterated that she thought that the marriage was over, and on this occasion, she told appellant that she planned to date someone else whom she had met. . . .

He returned his wife and child to their home at about 7:30 P.M. and then went to his apartment to study for a final examination. He called two close friends of the parties, however, and discussed his marital situation with them. . . . One of them advised him that his wife apparently did not believe his feelings about a reconciliation were sincere.

Acting on that suggestion, appellant returned to the home of the parties in his automobile, stating that he wanted to try once more to convince his wife that he was indeed sincere. When he arrived at the home he saw an automobile parked in the driveway. He did not recognize the car as being one belonging to any of his wife's friends. Accordingly, he parked around the corner and walked back to the house. Observing from the rear of the house, he saw his wife and McConkey in the kitchen with the child. He observed as Mrs. Thornton washed some laundry for McConkey and as they were eating dinner. Thereafter they sat and read. They drank wine and smoked some marijuana, and appellant saw them kissing.

He decided to go home to get his camera, but before doing so let the air out of one of the tires on McConkey's car. He went to his apartment, and obtained his camera and an old pistol which had belonged to his father. . . . He testified that he intended to take pictures for the purpose of showing them to the marriage counselor on the next day and possibly also for use in evidence if the divorce proceedings did ensue.

Appellant spent more than an hour in the backyard of his home observing his wife and McConkey in the den and kitchen. Thereafter they left the den area, but appellant remained behind the house, thinking that McConkey was about to leave. When he went around the house, however, he found that McConkey's car was still in the driveway and saw the drapes in the front guest bedroom downstairs had been closed. He listened near the window and heard unmistakable sounds of sexual intercourse. He then burst through the front door and into the bedroom where he found the nude couple and attempted to take some pictures. At that point, he testified that he thought McConkey was attempting to attack him. In all events, he drew his pistol and fired a single shot, striking McConkey in the left hip. . . . Appellant assisted in giving directions to enable an ambulance to bring aid to McConkey, and he remained at the house until the police arrived.

Appellant testified that he did not intend to kill McConkey, but simply to shoot him in order to disable him and also because of his outrage at the situation which he had found. The single shot was not aimed at a vital organ, but the victim ultimately died because of the spread of a massive infection from the wound. . . .

It has long been a well-settled legal principle that the commission of unlawful sexual intercourse with a female relative is an act obviously calculated to arouse ungovernable passion, and that the killing of the seducer or adulterer under the influence or in the heat of passion constitutes voluntary manslaughter, and not murder, in the absence of evidence of actual malice.

Appellant actually discovered his wife *in flagrante delicto* with a man who was a total stranger to him and at a time when appellant was trying to save his marriage and was deeply concerned about both his wife and his young child. He did not fire a shot or in any way harm the victim until he actually discovered the victim and his wife engaged in sexual intercourse in appellant's own home. In our opinion the passions of any reasonable person would have been inflamed and intensely aroused by this sort of discovery. Given the factual background of the case, this was a classic case of voluntary manslaughter and no more.

The conviction of murder in the first degree is set aside, and the cause will be remanded to the trial court for sentencing of the defendant for voluntary manslaughter.

[footnotes omitted]

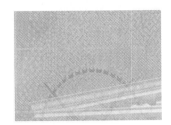

WHAT DO *YOU* THINK?

1. Opponents of the *provocation issue* contend that reasonable people do not kill, no matter how much they are provoked. Do you agree with the court or with its opponents on this issue? Why?
2. If the reason that provoked criminal homicide is punished is in order to deter people from committing the offense, then why not punish the offenders as murderers?
3. Many contend that the concept of voluntary homicide is a compromise, neither conceding the propriety of the act nor exacting the full penalty for it. Do you agree? Why or why not?

NOTES

1. Marvin Wolfgang, "A Sociological Approach to Criminal Homicide," *Federal Probation*, Vol. 23 (March 1961), p. 48.
2. See "Jumper Avoids Prison in Daughter's Death," Associated Press, July 15, 1998, and "Woman Testifies from Bed She Doesn't Remember Suicide Leap," Associated Press, May 26, 1998.
3. "Women's Second Suicide Attempt Foiled," Channel 2000, February 26, 2000. Posted at http://cbs2.com/news/stories/news-20000226-202413.html.
4. *Follis* v. *State*, 101 S.W.2d 242 (1947).
5. *Jones* v. *State*, 151 Tex. Crim. 114, 205 S.W.2d 603 (1947).
6. *Williams* v. *State*, 629 S.W.2d 791 (Tex. Ct. App. 5th Cir. 1981).
7. *People* v. *Chavez*, 176 P.2d 92 (Cal. App. 1947).
8. *Keeler* v. *Superior Court*, 470 P.2d 617 (Cal. 1970).
9. Texas Penal Code 19.02.
10. *Lovelady* v. *State*, 14 Tex. App. 545 (Tex. Ct. Crim. App. 1883).
11. Cal. Penal Code, Section 187.
12. *Keeler* v. *Superior Court*, 2 Cal. 3d 619, 87 Cal. Rptr. 481, 470 P.2d 617 (Cal. 1970).
13. Ibid.
14. *Commentary* to Model Penal Code, Section 210.1, p. 11.
15. *Thomas* v. *Anderson*, 215 P.2d 478, 96 Cal. App. 2d 371 (1950).
16. See Council on Ethical and Judicial Affairs. *Code of Medical Ethics: Current Opinions with Annotations* (Chicago: American Medical Association, 1995), and related publications.
17. *State* v. *Fierro*, 603 P.2d 74 (Ariz. 1979).
18. See National Conference of Commissioners on Uniform State Laws, *Uniform Determination of Death Act and Report* (1981).
19. Uniform Determination of Death Act, Uniform Law Ann., Chapter 12 (1981 Supp.), p. 187.
20. Ibid.
21. The National Conference of Commissioners on Uniform State Laws has worked for the uniformity of state laws since 1892. The conference promotes the principle of uniformity by drafting and proposing specific statutes in areas of the law where uniformity between the states is desirable. No uniform law is effective until a state legislature adopts it.
22. P.A. Byrne, S. O'Reilly, and P.M. Quay, "Brain Death—An Opposing Viewpoint," *JAMA*, Vol. 242 (1979), pp. 1985–1990.
23. See the dissenting opinion in *Commonwealth* v. *Ladd*, 166 A.2d 501 (Pa. 1960).

24. Guilford County (North Carolina), No. 91CRS20076, October 31, 1991.

25. North Carolina Court of Appeals, No. 9118SC1298, May 18, 1993.

26. Cal. Penal Code, Section 194.

27. *People v. Freudenberg,* 121 Cal. App. 2d 564 (1953).

28. *People v. Moan,* 65 Cal. 532 (1884).

29. *People v. Fowler,* 178 Cal. 657 (1918) and *People v. Lewis,* 124 Cal. 551 (1899).

30. *People v. Saldana,* 47 Cal. App. 3d 954 (1975).

31. *People v. Brackett,* 510 N.E.2d 877 (Ill. 1987).

32. *People v. McGee,* 31 Cal. 2d 229, 187 P.2d 706 (1947).

33. *People v. Vernon,* 89 Cal. App. 3d 853 (1979).

34. *Commonwealth v. Malone,* 47 A.2d 445 (Pa. 1946).

35. Rollin M. Perkins and Ronald N. Boyce, *Criminal Law,* 3rd ed. (Mineola, NY: Foundation Press, 1982), p. 75.

36. *People v. Vernon.*

37. In some jurisdictions the term "depraved heart murder" means the killing of a human being with extreme atrocity.

38. *People v. Morrin,* 187 N.W.2d 434 (Mich. 1971).

39. Cal. Penal Code, Section 188.

40. *People v. Geiger,* 159 N.W.2d 383 (Mich. 1968).

41. *Commonwealth v. Malone,* 47 A.2d. 445 (Pa. 1946).

42. *Edmund v. Florida,* 458 U.S. 782 (1982).

43. *Tison v. Arizona,* 107 S. Ct. 1676 (1987).

44. *Coker v. Georgia,* 433 U.S. 584 (1977).

45. *People v. Daniels,* 52 Cal. 3d 815 (1991).

46. Tracy L. Snell, "Capital Punishment 1995," Bureau of Justice Statistics *Bulletin,* December 1996.

47. Todd Venezia, "$12 Heist Nets Murder Charge," APB Online, May 5, 1999. Posted at http://www.apbonline.com/911/1999/05/07/taxi0507_01.html.

48. Statistically speaking, only about one half of one percent of all robberies involve homicide. (Joshua Dressler, *Understanding Criminal Law,* 2 ed (Boston: Matthew Bender, 1995), p. 451.).

49. Perkins and Boyce, *Criminal Law,* p. 109.

50. Richard Willing and Carol J. Castaneda, "Drinking Driver Gets Life in Prison, No Parole," *USA Today,* May 7, 1997, p. 1A; Richard Willing and Carol J. Castaneda, "A Message to Impaired Drivers: N.C. Case is a Sign of Stricter Times," *USA Today,* May 7, 1997, 3A.

51. Kan. Stat. Ann., Section 21-3403.

52. John Kaplan and Robert Weisberg, *Criminal Law: Cases and Materials,* 2nd ed. (Boston: Little, Brown, 1991), p. 248.

53. Texas Penal Code, Section 19.02.

54. "Pit Bull Owner Charged in Mauling of Neighbor," Associated Press, December 10, 1999.

55. Crimes Code of Pennsylvania, Section 2504(a).

56. Model Penal Code, Section 210.3.

57. Alabama Code, 13A-6-4.

58. Model Penal Code, Section 210.3(1)(b).

59. *State* v. *Williams*, 484 P.2d 1167 (Wash. App. 1971).

60. Model Penal Code, Section 2.02(2)(c).

61. Model Penal Code, Section 2.02(d).

62. Fla. Stat. Ann., Section 782.071.

63. As reported by Euthanasia.com. Posted at http://www.euthanasia.com/bystate.html. Accessed April 24, 2001.

64. *Vacco* v. *Quill*, 521 U.S. 793 (1997).

65. *Washington* v. *Glucksberg*, U.S. Supreme Court, No. 96-110. Decided June 26, 1997.

66. Todd Venezia, "Cops Say Mercy Killing Was Murder," APB News online, February 7, 2000. Posted at http://www.apbnews.com/newscenter/breakingnews.

67. "Family Upset After Man Pulls Plug on Dying Friend," Associated Press, February 13, 2000.

9

Legal and Social Dimensions of Personal Crime: Assault, Battery, and Other Personal Crimes

A battery committed by a person while in a state of voluntary intoxication is no less criminal by reason of his having been in such condition.
—Justice Traynor, in People v. Hood, 1 Cal. 3d 444 (1969)

Rape is nothing more or less than a conscious process of intimidation by which all men keep all women in a state of fear.
—Susan Brownmiller, Against Our Will, 1975

CHAPTER OUTLINE

KEY CONCEPTS

aggravated assault

aggravated battery

assault

battery

bodily injury

constructive touching

criminal sexual conduct

deviate sexual intercourse

effective consent

false arrest

false imprisonment

fellatio

forcible rape

kidnapping

mayhem

present ability

probative value

rape

rape shield laws

sexual assault

sexual battery

sexual contact

sodomy

spousal rape

stalking

statutory rape

transferred intent

AFTER READING THIS CHAPTER YOU SHOULD:

▷ Know the required elements of the various personal crimes.

▷ Understand the two different types of assault at common law.

▷ Understand the difference between assault and battery.

▷ Be able to describe the differences between mayhem and other assault crimes.

▷ Be able to discuss "force" and "consent" in rape crimes.

▷ Be able to explain the differences between kidnapping and false imprisonment.

INTRODUCTION

In 1996, Georgia resident Miguel Ortiz was convicted of rape, aggravated **sodomy**, incest, and battery—crimes committed against his fifteen-year-old niece.[1] The victim lived with Ortiz, his wife, and three children. Two of Ortiz's brothers and the victim's mother also lived in the household. One day, as the victim accompanied her uncle on some errands, Ortiz detoured, turned off on a rural road, and stopped his car. While on the isolated dirt road, Ortiz beat, raped, and sodomized his young niece. As they left the scene, Ortiz and the victim were involved in a single car accident in which their vehicle flipped over. The victim immediately ran from the car and sought assistance from the occupants of another vehicle, telling Trina Edwards and Ebony Reid that her uncle had just tried to rape her.

The victim's eye was swollen, she was not wearing any shoes, her clothing was unbuttoned, and she was crying and scared. She told Reid that her uncle had raped her, but then she claimed that he did not rape her, and then changed her story again, saying he "kind of raped" her. The victim was driven to a nearby house where medical and law enforcement personnel were summoned. She told Mattie Jo Duke, the responding EMT, that her uncle had raped her. The victim also told Investigator Lanny Dean that her uncle had raped her. After arrival at the hospital, medical personnel prepared a rape kit, and physical evidence gathered with the kit supported the victim's claim. Ortiz, a former offender, was sentenced to a lengthy prison term under Georgia's two-strikes law.

SODOMY
oral or anal copulation between persons of the same or different gender, or between a human being and an animal.

ASSAULT, BATTERY, AND MAYHEM

The emphasis in this chapter is on the legal and social dimensions of personal crimes, excluding homicide. As the chapter-opening story illustrates, there is often confusion—even in the victim's mind—over whether a crime should be reported and as to what the personal and social consequences of reporting may be. As we proceed, the reader should also note that there is considerable overlap between many of the crimes discussed here. A rape, for example, is also an aggravated form of a battery.

A good starting point for discussions involving personal crimes are the crimes of assault and battery. While the terms "assault" and "battery" are often used together or interchangeably, at common law they were different and distinct crimes. An **assault,** simply put, is an attempted or threatened battery. A **battery,** on the other hand, is a consummated assault. As one author succinctly explains it: "When we speak of an assault we usually have in mind a battery which was attempted or threatened. The attempt may have failed or it may have succeeded. If it failed, it constitutes an assault only. If it succeeded, it is an assault and battery."[3] Some state penal codes do not contain the word "assault," replacing it with the term "attempted battery."

Put more formally, an assault is a wilful attempt or wilful threat to inflict injury on another person. It may also include the act of intentionally frightening another person into fearing immediate bodily harm. Battery can be defined as unlawful physical violence inflicted on another without his or her consent, or as an intentional and offensive touching or wrongful physical contact with another without consent that results in some injury or offense to that person. Battery requires actual unauthorized contact with the victim. Generally, an assault is included in any actual battery—hence the crime of "assault and battery."

From an analytical viewpoint, however, one major difference between criminal assault and battery is that assault is a specific intent crime whereas battery is not. To commit an assault, a person must have intended to either commit a battery (attempted battery) or have intentionally frightened the victim into fearing immediate bodily harm. Battery is a general intent crime and may be the natural consequence of the commission of some other offense, or can result from gross negligence or recklessness. **Mayhem,** a third term of relevance here, is a battery that causes great bodily harm or disfigurement. Boxes in this chapter include representative laws on assault, battery, and mayhem from Texas and California.

ASSAULT
attempted or threatened battery. A wilful attempt or wilful threat to inflict injury upon another person. Also, the act of intentionally frightening another person into fearing immediate bodily harm. One statutory definition of assault reads "an unlawful attempt, coupled with a present ability, to commit a violent injury on the person of another."[2]

BATTERY
(1) unlawful physical violence inflicted upon another without his or her consent; (2) an intentional and offensive touching or wrongful physical contact with another without consent, that results in some injury or offends or causes discomfort.

MAYHEM
intentional infliction of injury on another that causes the removal of, seriously disfigures, or impairs the function of a member or organ of the body.

Assault

At common law, two types of assault could be distinguished: an attempted battery and a threatened battery. In an attempted battery–type of assault, a defendant *attempted* to commit a battery. The second type of assault, that of *threatened* battery, occurred when a defendant placed another in fear of imminent injury. The difference between the two is that the first was an actual attempt to commit a battery, whereas the latter criminalized conduct that made another person fear an assault. A number of states today, such as California, do not recognize the second type of assault. The common law elements of the attempted battery–type of assault are:

- an unlawful attempt,
- with present ability,
- to commit a battery.

Reflecting the influence of the common law, California statutes define assault as "an unlawful attempt, coupled with a present ability, to commit a violent injury on

LAW ON THE BOOKS

CALIFORNIA DEFINES "ASSAULT" AND "BATTERY."

Compare with Model Penal Code, Section 211.1

CALIFORNIA PENAL CODE

Section 240. An assault is an unlawful attempt, coupled with a present ability, to commit a violent injury on the person of another. . . .

Section 241.4. An assault is punishable by fine not exceeding one thousand dollars ($1,000), or by imprisonment in the county jail not exceeding six months, or by both. . . .

Section 242. A battery is any wilful and unlawful use of force or violence upon the person of another.

Section 243. (a) A battery is punishable by a fine not exceeding two thousand dollars ($2,000), or by imprisonment in a county jail not exceeding six months, or by both the fine and imprisonment. . . .

(d) When a battery is committed against any person and serious bodily injury is inflicted on the person, the battery is punishable by imprisonment in a county jail for a period of not more than one year or imprisonment in the state prison for two, three, or four years.

the person of another"[4] (see the accompanying box on California law). Each of these elements is discussed in what follows. It should be noted, however, that in an attempted battery–type assault, the victim need not be aware of the attempt. The victim, for example, may be unconscious at the time of the assault. To constitute assault, there must be an overt act from which the inference can be drawn that a violent injury was intended; mere words alone are insufficient.

Similarly, any attempt to commit an injury or an offensive touching must be unlawful. Accordingly, the attempt to inflict injury on a person in a valid self-defense situation is not an unlawful attempt. The use of force by law enforcement officers in effecting a valid arrest is also not unlawful. Nor is the reasonable use of force in a boxing match or football game. If, however, the force used or attempted to be used is not authorized or used in an unauthorized manner, it may be unlawful. Although fights and threatening gestures are a regular and expected part of professional boxing matches, for example, physical altercations are expected to remain within clearly specified bounds—and players who exceed those bounds may find themselves facing assault or battery charges. In a 1997 rematch for the World Boxing Association's heavyweight title, for example, Mike Tyson bit off part of defending champion Evander Holyfield's right ear. Following the match, the Nevada State Athletic Commission suspended Tyson indefinitely.

The **present ability** element of the crime of assault requires that the defendant be physically capable of carrying out the act that is attempted, and that the method he or she intends or threatens to use will in fact inflict an injury or offensive touching if carried out. Simply put, present ability, as used in assault statutes, means that the offender is physically capable of immediate battery. Present ability relates solely to the ability of the person attempting or threatening the unlawful injury or offensive touching. It does not, in most jurisdictions, refer to the fact that for some reason or condition unknown to and not controlled by the defendant, the intended injury cannot actually be inflicted. If, for example, the defendant fires a pistol at the intended victim who is riding in an automobile, but, unknown to the defendant, the automobile was specially constructed with bullet-proof glass and armor plating, then the defendant would still be guilty of assault.

PRESENT ABILITY
as used in assault statutes, a term meaning that the person attempting assault is physically capable of immediately carrying it out.

BODILY INJURY
in general use, the term refers to physical harm to a human being. In cases of assault and battery, however, the term refers to the unlawful application of physical force on the person of the victim—even when no actual physical harm results.

The term **bodily injury,** which appears in many assault and battery statutes, has a special meaning. It does not mean that the injury attempted must be a severe one or cause great physical pain. It means merely an unlawful application of physical force on the person of the victim. As one court noted, for assault crimes the terms "violence" and "force" are synonymous and include any application of force, even though it entails no pain or bodily harm and leaves no mark.[5]

Placing Another in Fear

The second type of assault at common law, the threatened battery–type, was the placing of another in fear of imminent injury. In some jurisdictions, the crime is described as "intentional-frightening assault." As noted earlier, not all jurisdictions recognize this form of assault. The threatened battery–type of assault requires that the defendant intend to create fear of imminent injury in the victim. As discussed previously, words alone do not suffice, and some overt act must occur before the crime can be said to have been committed. Telling a person, for example, "I am going to kill you!" is not an assault unless accompanied by some overt act, such as pointing a gun at the person.

Conditional Assaults

Either type of assault may be committed where the danger or threat is conditioned upon a meeting of the assailant's demands. For example, the statement "One false move and I'll shoot!" made to a victim during a bank robbery is a conditional assault.

To constitute an assault, the condition must be one that the defendant is not entitled to place on the victim. For example, the statement "Leave my property or I will throw you off!" made to a trespasser by a property owner who assumes a threatening stance is not an assault since the owner has a limited right to protect his or her property. If the condition is one that the defendant has no right to place on the victim, however, the actions constitute an assault. The statement "Hand me your money or I will shoot," for example, qualifies as such a condition, and may constitute an assault—especially when the person making it is armed or thought to be armed.

Aggravated Assaults

In most jurisdictions, a simple assault is one unaccompanied by aggravating circumstances. Simple assaults are classified as misdemeanors. All jurisdictions, however, have recognized various types of felonious assaults, terming them "aggravated." Aggravated assaults are generally assaults with intent to commit some other offense, such as rape or murder. As a result, aggravated assault is sometimes called "assault with intent," and indictments for specific offenses, such as "assault with intent to kill," are not unusual. Aggravated assault was not an offense under common law.

Special categories of assaults, such as those in which a dangerous weapon is employed or assault on a peace officer, assault on a school official or teacher, assault on a prison guard or correctional personnel, and so on, have also been classified in various jurisdictions as aggravated assault. Hence, the term **aggravated assault** may mean (1) an assault that is committed with the intention of committing an additional crime, or (2) an assault that involves special circumstances. To prove an aggravated assault, the prosecution would need to successfully show that an assault took place as part of another, more serious offense, or that an assault with an aggravating element specified by law occurred.

Where assault is considered to be aggravated when committed with a dangerous weapon, the weapons are usually said to be of two types: (1) those which are inherently dangerous or deadly (as a loaded gun would be), and (2) those which are not dangerous *per se*, but which can be used in a dangerous fashion (such as a rope used in a strangling). Some courts have held that a dog used in an attack is a dangerous weapon,[6] others have held that hands and fists can be deadly weapons (even if the person to whom they belong has not had martial arts or combat training),[7] and still others have held that human teeth are *not* deadly weapons.[8]

> **AGGRAVATED ASSAULT**
> an assault that is committed with the intention of committing an additional crime, such as assault with intent to commit a felony; assault with intent to murder; assault with intent to commit rape, sodomy, mayhem, robbery, or grand larceny; and assault with intent to commit any other felony. Also, an assault that involves special circumstances specified by law.

Attempted Assault

Although at common law assault was in most cases an attempted battery, the law pertaining to criminal attempts generally does not apply to assaults.[9] This is partially the result of historical exigencies, under which the common law on assaults developed earlier and independently of the common law on criminal attempts. As a result, a major difference between attempts and assaults, which continues to be recognized today, is that for a criminal assault to occur, a greater degree of proximity to completion of the offense is required than for a criminal attempt. The concept of *proximity to completion* refers to criminal attempt crimes in which the court looks at the nearness to completion of the intended crime in order to determine if a criminal attempt has taken place. More than one hundred years ago, the Ohio Supreme Court addressed the distinction this way: "An assault is an act done toward the commission of a battery; it must precede the battery, but it does so immediately. The next movement would, at least to all appearances, complete the battery . . . [A]n act constituting an attempt to commit a felony may be more remote. . . ."[10] A few courts have attempted to reconcile the law of attempts with the law on assault, creating the logically improbable term "attempted assault." In such cases, an attempt to assault means "an effort to accomplish a battery that had proceeded beyond the stage of preparation, but had not come close enough to completion to constitute an assault."

Another major difference between attempt and assault is that an accused may be convicted of a criminal attempt even if consummation of the primary offense is impossible to complete. An attempted battery–type of assault requires an unlawful attempt with the present ability to commit the battery. Accordingly, a defendant could be convicted of an attempted murder without committing the crime of assault with the intent to commit murder if the defendant's conduct constitutes a substantial step toward completion of the murder but the defendant lacks present ability to commit the murder. Similarly, a man who is physically unable to complete the act of intercourse might still be conceptually guilty of an attempt to commit an assault with intent to rape, were he to make unwanted physical advances under certain circumstances. In one case, a man went to his car to retrieve a gun with which he intended to threaten his wife at her place of work. When he returned to the building, however, his wife had locked the doors and he could not enter. He was convicted of attempt to commit an assault with a dangerous weapon.[11]

Antistalking Statutes

Web Extra! 9–1
Antistalking Web site

In 1997, forty-one-year-old Cheryl Vivier donned a beard, glasses, and baseball cap and posed as a fisherman.[12] With two handguns in her waistband, she entered the office of the Alligator Lakeside Inn in Saint Cloud, Florida. George Long, her forty-five-year-old ex-boyfriend and co-owner of the motel, was working behind the desk. A struggle ensued, and Long wrestled one of the guns away from Vivier before she pulled the other from her clothing and shot him four times in the chest. Long died at the scene, and Vivier shot herself soon afterward. The two had dated for several years before breaking up a few months earlier. After the breakup, Vivier had relentlessly pursued Long and had been arrested for trespassing and charged with aggravated stalking under Florida law.

The strict requirements needed to establish the crime of criminal assault have led many to believe that traditional criminal laws are not adequate to encompass the conduct of stalkers. Accordingly, many jurisdictions have extended the scope of their assault statutes to include intentional scaring or stalking. The first antistalking statute was enacted in California. California's statute reads as follows: "Any person who wilfully, maliciously, and repeatedly follows or harasses another person, and who makes a credible threat with the intent to place that person in reasonable fear of death or great bodily injury is guilty of the crime of **stalking**. . . ."[13] The statute defines *harasses* as "a knowing and wilful course of conduct directed toward a specific person which seriously harms, annoys, torments, or terrorizes that person, and which serves no legitimate purpose." *Credible threat* means a verbal or written threat implied by a pattern of conduct or a combination of verbal or written statements and conduct made with the intent and apparent ability to carry out the threat so as to cause the person who is the target of the threat to reasonably fear for his or her safety or the safety of his or her immediate family.[14] Stalking is punishable in California by a fine of up to $1,000 and imprisonment in a county jail for up to one year, or both.

STALKING
the intentional frightening of another through following, harassing, annoying, tormenting, or terrorizing activities.

Stalking activities now extend into cyberspace. Linda Fairstein, chief of the Sex Crimes Prosecution Unit of the Manhattan District Attorney's Office, recently noted that: "Cyberspace has become a fertile field for illegal activity. By the use of new technology and equipment which cannot be policed by traditional methods, cyberstalking has replaced traditional methods of stalking and harassment." In addition, said Fairstein, "cyberstalking has led to offline incidents of violent crime." Police and prosecutors, said Fairstein, "need to be aware of the escalating numbers of these events and devise strategies to resolve these problems through the criminal justice system.[15]

A 1999 report by the U.S. Attorney General's office says that "current trends and evidence suggest that cyberstalking is a serious problem that will grow in scope and complexity as more people take advantage of the Internet and other telecommunications technologies.[16] The report defines cyberstalking as "the use of the Internet, e-mail, or other electronic communications devices to stalk another person." It goes on to say that while cyberstalking shares important characteristics with offline stalking, there are major differences, including the following:

- Offline stalking generally requires the perpetrator and the victim to be located in the same geographic area; cyberstalkers may be located across the street or across the country.

- Electronic communications technologies make it much easier for a cyberstalker to encourage third parties to harass and/or threaten a victim (e.g., impersonating the victim and posting inflammatory messages to bulletin boards and in chat rooms, causing viewers of that message to send threatening messages back to the victim "author").

- Electronic communications technologies also lower the barriers to harassment and threats; a cyberstalker does not need to physically confront the victim.

Web Extra! 9–2
Attorney general's report on cyberstalking

Convicted cyberstalker Christian Hunold of Smithville, Missouri, is shown here prior to his arrest. In October, 2000, Hunold was sentenced to 15 years in prison after pleading guilty to three felony counts of attempted promotion of child pornography in the first degree and one misdemeanor count of harassment. The 19-year-old Hunold was arrested after he sent threats over the Internet to students and staff at a Massachusetts middle school. He was also charged under the laws of Massachusetts with producing, publishing and creating child pornography on the Internet and with using the Internet and telephone to frighten several individuals by threatening to kill them. Hunold sent the threats from his home computer after being partially paralyzed in a car crash when he was 16. (Photo by Julie Jacobsen, courtesy of The Kansas City Star.)

In many cases, the cyberstalker and his or her victims had prior relationships, and cyberstalking begins when the victim attempts to break off the relationship. However, there have also been many instances of cyberstalking by strangers. Given the enormous amount of personal information available through the Internet, a cyberstalker can easily locate private information about a potential victim with a few mouse clicks or key strokes.[17] Learn more about how the law sees stalking in the Capstone Case of *Clements* v. *State* at the end of this chapter.

Battery

As noted earlier, the crime of battery is the causing of either bodily injury, or the offensive touching of the person of another. According to Florida law, for example, "The offense of battery occurs when a person: (1) actually and intentionally touches or strikes another person against the will of the other; or (2) intentionally causes bodily harm to another person." Battery has three elements:

- the willful and unlawful,
- use of force, violence, or offensive contact,
- against the person of another.

Any unjustified offensive touching constitutes a battery. As one court noted: "No injury to the victim need occur; indeed the touching need not have left any mark at all upon the victim."[18] It is not necessary for the victim to actually fear physical harm as the result of the touching or the injury. The unwelcomed touching of the breast of a female, for example, is a battery. To determine if the touching is offensive, the court considers whether a reasonable person would be offended by the touching. In essence, the law against battery demands respect for the integrity of one's personal space.

Ruling Frightens Stalking Victims

They May Lose Protection, Convicts Could Go Free

KALAMAZOO, Mich.—A federal judge's ruling may mean Michigan stalking victims cannot count on state law to protect them from their tormentors anymore, and that 125 convicted stalkers now behind bars could soon be back on the street.

And these prospects have victims' rights advocates twisting in the wind while the decision is appealed.

U.S. District Judge Richard A. Enslen ruled against the state's 1993 anti-stalking law, declaring it "unconstitutionally overbroad" and said it "potentially criminalizes a substantial amount of conduct protected by the First Amendment."

The ruling stemmed from the case of Jerry Lee Staley, who was convicted of aggravated stalking in 1994 and appealed the case through state courts. After losing there, Staley sought to have his conviction overturned in federal court this year.

Enslen rejected some of Staley's arguments but agreed that the state law leaves too much wiggle room for prosecuting constitutionally protected behavior.

Reporters, neighbors as stalkers

An example of possible abuse of the statute's provisions, the judge said, could be a reporter prosecuted for repeatedly contacting a reluctant news source, or someone involved in a simple argument with a neighbor.

Michigan Attorney General Jennifer Granholm's office has appealed Enslen's ruling to the 6th U.S. Circuit Court of Appeals in Cincinnati.

Granholm's spokesman, Chris De Witt, said the judge's decision is just plain wrong. De Witt said there have been no cases of reporters jailed under the statute or other broad interpretations taken by prosecutors of the anti-stalking law.

"The people in prison in Michigan for stalking aren't in prison because they don't like their next-door neigh-

bor," De Witt told APB news.com. "This is not a matter of one person yelling across a hedge 'Hey, I'm going to kill you.' This goes well beyond that type of action."

Terror in eyes of beholder

Enslen was unavailable for comment today on his ruling, but Staley's attorney, David A. Dodge, said such assurances from the attorney general's office aren't good enough.

The argument relies on prosecutors to exercise good faith, he said.

"It's the prosecutor making a legislative determination of what comes under the statute and what doesn't," he said, "rather than the legislature having enough specificity in the provision."

Susan Howley, director of public policy at the National Center for Victims of Crime in Washington, said the constitutional concerns raised are moot because the Michigan law refers to whether a "reasonable person" feels his or her life or safety is threatened by someone.

"If a reasonable person heard their neighbor threaten them, if a jury found a reasonable person felt terrorized, that should be criminalized or stand up under the law," she said.

And that applies to pestering reporters who push the envelope of professionalism.

"If the news media makes somebody feel terrorized," she said, "they should be prosecuted."

"Victims will be fearful"

Enslen granted a two-week stay of his order at Granholm's request, and the state attorney general is seeking to delay it even longer to give the appeals court time to carefully consider the issues at stake.

Granholm also wants to avoid the release of Staley or any of the other 125 convicted stalkers who could potentially argue they never intended to

harm their victims and that their actions were protected by the First Amendment.

The suspense is nerve-wracking for some advocates who fear not only the loss of an important victims' rights law in Michigan, but the possible release of some of those convicted for what they view as serious crimes.

But De Witt said a mass release is not going to happen, even if the law is ultimately stricken. Many of those locked up for stalking in Michigan are in prison on other serious charges that would keep them behind bars regardless.

Still, that does little to reassure those who are faced with the prospect of the law being struck down.

"I certainly think victims will be fearful," said Angela Velasco, a program manager at the Michigan Coalition Against Domestic and Sexual Violence.

Two views from advocates

If Enslen's ruling is upheld, she said, the group will have to find creative ways to protect those it shelters and advises.

And it could set a dangerous precedent for other states where anti-stalking laws have been challenged in the courts, Velasco said.

Barbara Mills, who heads up the Kalamazoo YWCA's domestic assault program, said the law has been an effective tool for victims of stalking, but that disputes over its wording have become tedious and perhaps need to be clarified by the legislature.

"I don't think it's useful to have a law that is constantly challenged," Mills said.

But the ruling has incited venom in others who think the statute on the books works just fine.

"I think the language is very tight and the decision was outrageous,"

(continued)

CRIMINAL LAW IN THE NEWS

Ruling Frightens Stalking Victims

They May Lose Protection, Convicts Could Go Free

said Susan McGee of the Washtenaw County Domestic Violence Project.

McGee said the constitutional concerns raised by Enslen are preposterous.

"The statutes specifically talks about legal and constitutionally protected activity," she said.

"Extreme form of abuse"

The statute defines stalking as a "course of conduct involving repeated or continuing harassment of another individual that would cause a person to feel terrorized, frightened, intimi-

dated, threatened, harassed, or molested."

It stipulates that its definition "does not include constitutionally protected activity or conduct that serves a legitimate purpose"—such as newsgathering.

"It looks to me like the judge is incorrect, and I would expect the 6th Circuit to overturn that decision," said Susan Howley.

Michigan's anti-stalking law is unique because it does not require specific intent on the part of the perpetrator—the state doesn't have to

prove they intended to harm the victim.

If upheld, "it would be a setback for all that the criminal rights advocates have done to criminalize this extreme form of abuse," Howley said. "So many times, stalkers operate under the delusion or claim that they did not intend to terrorize a person."

Source: James Gordon Meek, "Ruling Frightens Stalking Victims; They May Lose Protection, Convicts Could Go Free," APB News. July 19, 2000. Reprinted with permission.

Battery consists of unlawful physical violence inflicted on another without his or her consent. Participants in sporting events, such as boxing matches, are generally immune to prosecution for the crime of battery so long as they adhere to the rules of the game. In a 1997 world heavyweight title rematch, shown here, Mike Tyson bit off part of defending champion Evander Holyfield's right ear. Following the match, Tyson was suspended indefinitely by the Nevada State Athletic Commission for unsportsmanlike conduct and prohibited from fighting in the state. (Photo by Jack Smith, courtesy of AP/Wide World Photos.)

Although in most cases battery is an intentional crime, it may also be committed recklessly or with criminal negligence.[19] The Texas Penal Code, for example, makes it a crime to "intentionally, knowingly, or recklessly [cause] bodily injury to another."[20]

The doctrine of **transferred intent** applies to the crime of battery. Accordingly, if an assailant intends to injure one person and by mistake or accident injures another, he or she is guilty of battery. If, for example, a defendant intended to hit his girlfriend with a baseball bat, but in swinging the bat accidentally hit her son instead, the defendant would be guilty of battery on the son (via transferred intent) and also guilty of an assault (attempted battery) on the girlfriend.

In some cases, a **constructive touching** is considered sufficient to sustain a battery charge. In one case, for example, a defendant was convicted of battery when he hit a horse that the "victim" was riding. In another case, a defendant was convicted of battery when he got a young female child to touch his penis. Constructive touching is touching that is implied by law to replace the touching requirement (for example, where the defendant gets the young female to do the touching, or the defendant touches a hat that the victim is wearing). Additionally, the force necessary to produce the touching can be applied indirectly, as where the defendant sets in motion a force or scheme that results in unwanted touching.[21]

In most jurisdictions, the crime of battery is a misdemeanor unless there are special conditions associated with it that aggravate the crime. The most common special conditions include battery on a peace officer, battery with the intent to inflict death or serious bodily injury, battery that results in serious bodily injury, and sexual battery. Serious bodily injury includes loss of consciousness, concussion, bone fracture, protracted loss or impairment of any bodily member or organ, a wound that requires extensive suturing, and disfigurement. **Sexual battery** occurs when a person unlawfully touches an intimate part of another person's body against that person's will and for the purpose of sexual arousal, gratification, or abuse. Section 243.4(a) of the California Penal Code says, for example, "Any person who touches an intimate part of another person while that person is unlawfully restrained by the accused or an accomplice, and if the touching is against the will of the person touched and is for the purpose of sexual arousal, sexual gratification, or sexual abuse, is guilty of sexual battery." Sexual battery may also include cases of forced intimate touching in which the victim is institutionalized for medical treatment and is seriously disabled or medically incapacitated.

The effective consent of the victim, also referred to as legal consent, or the defendant's reasonable belief that the victim legally consented to the conduct in question is a defense to the charge of battery if the conduct did not threaten to inflict or actually inflict serious bodily injury. **Effective consent** or legal consent is consent that has been obtained in a legal manner. The person giving consent must be of legal age and mentally capable of giving consent. Effective consent cannot be obtained by fraud or by force, or be given by a person who does not have the capacity to consent (i.e., to understandingly consent). No battery occurs, for example, when two people engage in friendly "horseplay," since both consent to physical interaction. A person cannot, however, effectively consent to the infliction of serious bodily injury. Hence the fact that a deathly ill "victim" begged another person to shoot him to put him out of his misery cannot be used as a defense if the other person obliges. Similarly, a child cannot effectively consent to sexual contact. Accordingly, sexual contact with a child is at least a battery (or sexual battery, depending on the wording used by the jurisdiction in which the activity occurs). A workable defense to a charge of battery might also be offered where it can be shown that the victim knew the conduct was a risk of his or her occupation, or that it was a recognized medical treatment, or a scientific experiment conducted by recognized methods.

It is important to note that, in contrast to common law and to the laws of many jurisdictions, the Model Penal Code defines assault to include both assault and battery. The code says, "A person is guilty of assault if he: (a) attempts to cause or pur-

TRANSFERRED INTENT

a legal construction by which an unintended act that results from intentional action undertaken in the commission of a crime may also be illegal.

CONSTRUCTIVE TOUCHING

a touching that is inferred or implied from prevailing circumstances. Also, a touching for purposes of the law.

SEXUAL BATTERY

the unlawful touching of an intimate part of another person against that person's will and for the purpose of sexual arousal, gratification, or abuse.

EFFECTIVE CONSENT

also termed **legal consent;** consent that has been obtained in a legal manner.

posely, knowingly, or recklessly causes bodily injury to another. . . . "[22] States, such as Texas, which follow the Model Penal Code, use similar wording in their statutes.

Aggravated Battery

As is the case with the crime of assault, some jurisdictions have specifically created the statutory crime of **aggravated battery.** Aggravated battery did not exist under common law. Like the crime of aggravated assault, aggravated battery may involve the use of a deadly weapon, may involve acts committed with the intention of committing another crime (i.e., rape or murder), or may include cases of battery that result in serious injury. In cases of serious injury, the degree of harm inflicted on the victim determines whether or not a crime is chargeable as simple or aggravated battery. Kansas law, for example, provides that aggravated battery is "[i]ntentionally causing great bodily harm to another person or disfigurement of another person."[23] Florida law says that a person commits aggravated battery if he or she: (1) intentionally or knowingly causes great bodily harm, permanent disability, or permanent disfigurement; or (2) uses a deadly weapon.[24] Although the definition of a deadly weapon may be open to dispute, some courts have held that hands can be deadly weapons, as can a simple pair of panty hose used in an attempt to strangle someone.[25]

A few states define the crime of aggravated battery to include the battery of special categories of persons, such as those who are pregnant or have a physical handicap, or who are teachers or emergency personnel operating in a professional capacity. (See the Law on the Books box below for an example of just such a law.) In some jurisdictions, battery is a misdemeanor, while aggravated battery is a felony.

AGGRAVATED BATTERY
a battery that is committed with the use of a deadly weapon, or that is committed with the intention of committing another crime, or a battery that results in serious injury.

LAW ON THE BOOKS

"AGGRAVATED BATTERY" UNDER ILLINOIS LAW.

ILLINOIS CRIMINAL CODE

Sec. 12-4. Aggravated Battery.

(a) A person who, in committing a battery, intentionally or knowingly causes great bodily harm, or permanent disability or disfigurement commits aggravated battery.

(b) In committing a battery, a person commits aggravated battery if he or she:

(1) Uses a deadly weapon other than by the discharge of a firearm;

(2) Is hooded, robed or masked, in such manner as to conceal his identity;

(3) Knows the individual harmed to be a teacher or other person employed in any school and such teacher or other employee is upon the grounds of a school or grounds adjacent thereto, or is in any part of a building used for school purposes;

(4) Knows the individual harmed to be a supervisor, director, instructor or other person employed in any park district and such supervisor, director, instructor or other employee is upon the grounds of the park or grounds adjacent thereto, or is in any part of a building used for park purposes;

(5) Knows the individual harmed to be a caseworker, investigator, or other person employed by the State Department of Public Aid, a County Department of Public Aid, or the Department of Human Services (acting as successor to the Illinois Department of Public Aid under the Department of Human Services Act [20 ILCS 1305/0.1 *et seq.*]) and such caseworker, investigator, or other person is upon the grounds of a public aid office or grounds adjacent thereto, or is in any part of a building used for public aid purposes, or upon the grounds of a home of a public aid applicant, recipient, or any

(continued)

LAW ON THE BOOKS

other person being interviewed or investigated in the employee's discharge of his duties, or on grounds adjacent thereto, or is in any part of a building in which the applicant, recipient, or other such person resides or is located;

(6) Knows the individual harmed to be a peace officer, a community policing volunteer, a correctional institution employee, or a fireman while such officer, volunteer, employee or fireman is engaged in the execution of any official duties including arrest or attempted arrest, or to prevent the officer, volunteer, employee or fireman from performing official duties, or in retaliation for the officer, volunteer, employee or fireman performing official duties, and the battery is committed other than by the discharge of a firearm;

(7) Knows the individual harmed to be an emergency medical technician-ambulance, emergency medical technician-intermediate, emergency medical technician-paramedic, ambulance driver or other medical assistance or first aid personnel engaged in the performance of any of his or her official duties, or to prevent the emergency medical technician-ambulance, emergency medical technician-intermediate, emergency medical technician-paramedic, ambulance driver, or other medical assistance or first aid personnel from performing official duties, or in retaliation for performing official duties;

(8) Is, or the person battered is, on or about a public way, public property or public place of accommodation or amusement;

(9) Knows the individual harmed to be the driver, operator, employee or passenger of any transportation facility or system engaged in the business of transportation of the public for hire and the individual assaulted is then performing in such capacity or then using such public transportation as a passenger or using any area of any description designated by the transportation facility or system as a vehicle boarding, departure, or transfer location;

(10) Knowingly and without legal justification and by any means causes bodily harm to an individual of 60 years of age or older;

(11) Knows the individual harmed is pregnant;

(12) Knows the individual harmed to be a judge whom the person intended to harm as a result of the judge's performance of his or her official duties as a judge;

(13) Knows the individual harmed to be an employee of the Illinois Department of Children and Family Services engaged in the performance of his authorized duties as such employee;

(14) Knows the individual harmed to be a person who is physically handicapped; or

(15) Knowingly and without legal justification and by any means causes bodily harm to a merchant who detains the person for an alleged commission of retail theft under Section 16A-5 of this Code [720 ILCS 5/16A-5]. In this item (15), "merchant" has the meaning ascribed to it in Section 16A-2.4 of this Code [720 ILCS 5/16A-2.4].

For the purpose of paragraph (14) of subsection (b) of this Section, a physically handicapped person is a person who suffers from a permanent and disabling physical characteristic, resulting from disease, injury, functional disorder or congenital condition.

(c) A person who administers to an individual or causes him to take, without his consent or by threat or deception, and for other than medical purposes, any intoxicating, poisonous, stupefying, narcotic, anesthetic, or controlled substance commits aggravated battery.

(d) A person who knowingly gives to another person any food that contains any substance or object that is intended to cause physical injury if eaten commits aggravated battery.

(e) Sentence. Aggravated battery is a Class 3 felony.

Mayhem

In 1993 John Wayne Bobbitt returned home and allegedly assaulted his wife, Lorena, sexually.[26] Later while he was sleeping, she cut off his penis with a kitchen knife. Mrs. Bobbitt, who admitted severing her husband's organ and throwing it out of a car window as she drove off, was charged with maiming her husband. Lorena Bobbitt soon became a media celebrity but was acquitted of all criminal charges in

1994, after expert witnesses testified that she was psychologically unable to resist the impulse to attack her husband.

Common law did not recognize aggravated forms of assault and battery. The crime of mayhem developed as an alternative, useful in punishing a perpetrator for a violent attack that did not end in death. To constitute mayhem, the injury suffered by the victim had to be serious and permanent. At early common law, the type of injury must have been one that lessened the ability of victims to defend themselves. Later, the types of injuries qualifying for prosecution under mayhem were broadened to include those that were disfiguring. In most jurisdictions today, mayhem requires an intent on the part of the defendant to cause an injury to, or death of, the victim. There are three elements to the crime of mayhem.[27] They are:

- an unlawful battery,
- involving maliciously inflicting or attempting to inflict violent injury, and
- one or more disabling or disfiguring injuries resulting from the illegal action.

California law says that "[e]very person who unlawfully and maliciously deprives a human being of a member of his body, or disables, disfigures, or renders it useless, or cuts or disables the tongue, or puts out an eye, or slits the nose, ear, or lip, is guilty of mayhem"[28] (see Law on the Books box on the following page). A more serious form of mayhem, that of aggravated mayhem, can be defined as "causing permanent disability or disfigurement of another human being, or depriving another human being of a limb, organ, or member of his or her body under circumstances manifesting extreme indifference to the physical or psychological well-being of that person."[29]

While most jurisdictions have enacted the common law crime of mayhem in their criminal statutes, the Model Penal Code does not recognize mayhem as a separate offense. Under the code it falls into the category of aggravated assault.[30] A few jurisdictions have enacted torture statutes, which may be closely related to mayhem laws. The California torture statute, for example, reads as follows: "Every person who, with the intent to cause cruel or extreme pain and suffering for the purpose of revenge, extortion, persuasion, or for any sadistic purpose, inflicts great bodily injury . . . upon the person of another, is guilty of torture."[31] Torture, in California, is punishable by imprisonment in the state prison for a term of life.

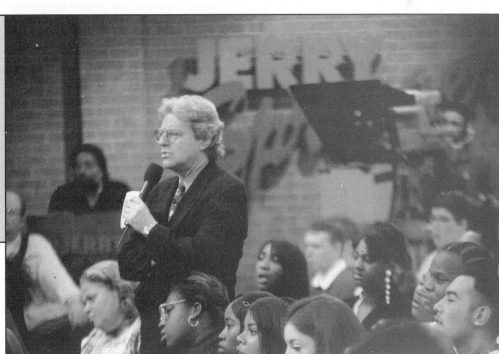

The Jerry Springer show. In 1999 TV talk show host Jerry Springer was summoned to appear before a Chicago City Council hearing to testify about his show's violent episodes. Council members insisted that, if the violence on the show was real, participants should be arrested and charged with battery. When asked about the violence, Springer replied, "It looks real to me." As a result of the hearings, the show's character changed to one that made greater use of verbal confrontations. (Photo by Todd Buchanan, courtesy of Black Star.)

LAW ON THE BOOKS

"MAYHEM" UNDER CALIFORNIA CODE.

CALIFORNIA PENAL CODE

Section 203. Every person who unlawfully and maliciously deprives a human being of a member of his body, or disables, disfigures, or renders it useless, or cuts or disables the tongue, or puts out an eye, or slits the nose, ear, or lip, is guilty of mayhem.

Section 204. Mayhem is punishable by imprisonment in the state prison for two, four, or eight years.

Section 205. A person is guilty of aggravated mayhem when he or she unlawfully, under circumstances manifesting extreme indifference to the physical or psychological well-being of another person, intentionally causes permanent disability or disfigurement of another human being or deprives a human being of a limb, organ, or member of his or her body. For purposes of this section, it is not necessary to prove an intent to kill. Aggravated mayhem is a felony punishable by imprisonment in the state prison for life with the possibility of parole.

SEX OFFENSES

Few areas of criminal law have attracted as much attention and controversy in the past twenty-five years as the attempt to place legislative controls on sexual behavior. Efforts to estimate the extent of sexual crime in our society also stirs controversy. One reason for the controversy is that in recent years attitudes about sexual relationships have become highly controversial and are themselves in a state of flux. People generally agree, however, that unwanted and nonconsensual sexual activity should be subject to criminal prosecution, and that sex with children under the age of legal consent should be criminalized. Statistics show that nonconsensual sexual behavior is relatively common. In one recent study, for example, researchers found that 27 percent of college-age women had been victims of rape or attempted rape, and that a number of the women had been victimized more than once.[32] **Criminal sexual conduct** is a gender-neutral term and is applied today to a wide variety of sex offenses, including rape, sodomy, criminal sexual conduct with children, and deviate sexual behavior.

CRIMINAL SEXUAL CONDUCT
a gender-neutral term, which is applied today to a wide variety of sex offenses, including rape, sodomy, criminal sexual conduct with children, and deviate sexual behavior.

Rape

Although the penal codes of many states today recognize that both males and females may be sexually assaulted, common law defined the crime of **rape** as "the carnal knowledge of a woman forcibly and against her will."[33] The term "carnal knowledge" meant sexual intercourse and has been replaced with the term "sexual intercourse" in many contemporary statutes. For centuries, courts required that a woman must "resist to the utmost of her ability," and that resistance must continue until the woman was physically overcome or until the offense was complete. No state adheres to the "utmost resistance" requirement today, although most continue to require some "reasonable resistance" on the part of a conscious victim, while recognizing that resistance can be overcome through threats.

At common law, any sexual penetration of the female vagina by the male penis was sufficient to complete the crime of rape. It was not necessary that emission oc-

RAPE
in common law, unlawful sexual intercourse with a female without her consent. Today, rape statutes in a number of jurisdictions encompass unlawful sexual intercourse between members of the same gender.

Rape is the only crime in which the victim becomes the accused.

—Freda Adler (*Sisters in Crime*, 1975)

cur or, as one English court put it, "the least penetration makes it rape . . . although there be no *emissio seminis*."[34] Common law convictions for the crime of rape required that the penetration be of the vagina, and penetration of the anus or mouth was referred to as **deviate sexual intercourse.** In contrast, the modern tendency is to term any nonconsensual sexually motivated penetration of any orifice of the victim's body "rape."

At common law a husband could not rape his wife, since it was believed that when a woman married she consented to sexual intercourse. This rule, called the "marital exemption," held that "a wife is irrebuttably presumed to consent to sexual relations with her husband, even if forcible and without consent."[35] New laws have been passed in most jurisdictions today, and spouses can now be prosecuted for the crime of **spousal rape.**[36] Even at common law, however, a husband could be guilty as an accomplice in the rape of his wife. A man who held his wife down while a friend raped her, for example, could be found guilty of rape.

In most jurisdictions today, the elements of the crime of rape are:

- sexual intercourse with a person not the spouse of the perpetrator,
- through force, the threat of force, or by guile, and
- without the lawful consent of the victim.

In the past, many rape statutes emphasized the role of force in the crime of rape, giving rise to the term **forcible rape.** Forcible rape is nonconsensual sexual intercourse, which is accomplished against a person's will by means of force, violence, duress, menace, or fear of immediate and unlawful bodily injury to the victim. Maryland law, for example, reads: "A person is guilty of rape in the second degree if the person engages in vaginal intercourse with another person (1) By force or threat of force against the will and without the consent of the other person. . . ."[37] In most jurisdictions, the crime of rape requires that the unlawful intercourse must be committed by force, fraud, or forcible compulsion—except for those situations where the victim is incapable of giving legal consent. Consent cannot be given by a victim who is a minor, who is mentally incompetent, or by one who is unconscious.

Over time, recognition grew in Western legal circles that force could exist without violence and that a rape victim might be compelled to submit to an assailant even though no overt force was employed. As one Maryland court reasoned:

> Force is an essential element of the crime and to justify a conviction, the evidence must warrant a conclusion either that the victim resisted and her resistance was overcome by force or that she was prevented from resisting by threats to her safety. But no particular amount of force, either actual or constructive, is required to constitute rape. Necessarily that fact must depend upon the prevailing circumstances. As in this case, force may exist without violence. If the acts and threats of the defendant were reasonably calculated to create in the mind of the victim—having regard to the circumstances in which she was placed—a real apprehension, due to fear, of imminent bodily harm, serious enough to impair or overcome her will to resist, then such acts and threats are the equivalent of force. . . . Since resistance is necessarily relative, the presence or absence of it must depend on the facts and circumstances in each case. . . . But the real test, which must be recognized in all cases, is whether the assault was committed without the consent and against the will of the prosecuting witness.[38]

As a result of such legal reasoning, contemporary rape laws in many jurisdictions give primacy to the fact that the intercourse forbidden by statute must be of a nonconsensual nature. As the Model Penal Code *Commentaries* observe, "The central element in the definition of rape is the absence of the female's consent."[39] Even so, state laws vary considerably in their description of the crime of rape. Utah law, for example, says simply, "A person commits rape when the actor has sexual intercourse with another person without the victim's consent."[40] Some states define rape to include both force and absence of consent. Still others require only force or coercion, and

DEVIATE SEXUAL INTERCOURSE
any contact between any part of the genitals of one person and the mouth or anus of another.

SPOUSAL RAPE
the rape of one's spouse.

FORCIBLE RAPE
rape that is accomplished against a person's will by means of force, violence, duress, menace, or fear of immediate and unlawful bodily injury to the victim.

> Certainly, then, a marriage license should not be viewed as a license for a husband to forcibly rape his wife with impunity. A married woman has the same right to control her own body as does an unmarried woman.
>
> —Sol Wachtler, *People* v. *Liberta*, 64 N.Y.2d 152, 164, 474 N.E.2d 567, 485 N.Y.S.2d 207 (1984).

LAW ON THE BOOKS

"RAPE" UNDER THE CALIFORNIA PENAL CODE.
Compare with Model Penal Code, Section 213.1

CALIFORNIA PENAL CODE

Section 261. Rape defined.

a. Rape is an act of sexual intercourse accomplished with a person not the spouse of the perpetrator, under any of the following circumstances:

(1) Where a person is incapable, because of a mental disorder or development or physical disability, of giving legal consent, and this is known or reasonably should be known to the person committing the act.

(2) Where it is accomplished against a person's will by means of force, violence, duress, menace, or fear of immediate and unlawful bodily injury on the person or another.

(3) Where a person is prevented from resisting by any intoxicating or anesthetic substance, or any controlled substance, and this condition was known or reasonably should have been known by the accused.

(4) Where a person is at the time unconscious of the nature of the act, and this is known to the accused.

(5) Where a person submits under the belief that the person committing the act is the victim's spouse, and this belief is induced by any artifice, pretense, or concealment practiced by the accused, with intent to induce the belief.

(6) Where the act is accomplished against the victim's will by threatening to retaliate in the future against the victim or any other person, and there is a reasonable possibility that the perpetrator will execute the threat. As used in this paragraph, threatening to retaliate means a threat to kidnap or falsely imprison, or to inflict extreme pain, serious bodily injury, or death.

(7) Where the act is accomplished against the victim's will by threatening to use the authority of a public official to incarcerate, arrest, or deport the victim or another, and the victim has a reasonable belief that the perpetrator is a public official. As used in this paragraph, public official means a person employed by a governmental agency who has the authority, as part of that position, to incarcerate, arrest, or deport another. The perpetrator does not actually have to be a public official.

Web Extra! 9–3
National Sexual
Violence Resource
Center

make little or no reference to consent. A few, like Utah, make no reference to force, requiring only a lack of consent. The example of California law, shown in the Law on The Books box above, outlines a variety of unlawful ways in which nonconsensual intercourse might be accomplished.

Most jurisdictions also distinguish between various degrees of rape. First-degree, or aggravated, rape is often defined to include one or more of the following: (1) an armed offender, (2) serious bodily injury to the victim, (3) an additional felony, where the rape occurs during the commission of some other crime, or (4) gang rape. The category of second-degree rape generally includes any other type of rape.

Lawful Consent As the boxes on California's rape law show, lawful consent can be lacking during sexual intercourse under any number of circumstances—ranging from the use of force or threats to achieve compliance with the offender's demands to intercourse with an unconscious or mentally incompetent individual. In individual cases, however, the question of whether intercourse occurred with or without the consent of the victim may be a difficult question to answer. If the victim is incapable of giving legally effective consent, then intercourse with the victim

LAW ON THE BOOKS

"SPOUSAL RAPE" UNDER THE CALIFORNIA PENAL CODE.

CALIFORNIA PENAL CODE

Section 262. Rape of a spouse.

b. Rape of a person who is the spouse of the perpetrator is an act of sexual intercourse accomplished under any of the following circumstances:

(1) Where it is accomplished against a person's will by means of force, violence, duress, menace, or fear of immediate and unlawful bodily injury on the person or another.

(2) Where a person is prevented from resisting by any intoxicating or anesthetic substance, or any controlled substance and this condition is known or reasonably should have been known by the accused.

(3) Where a person is at the time unconscious of the nature of the act, and this is known to the accused. As used in this paragraph, unconscious of the nature of the act means incapable of resisting because the victim meets one of the following conditions: was unconscious or asleep; was not aware, perceiving, or cognizant that the act occurred; or was not aware, knowing, perceiving, or cognizant of the essential characteristics of the act due to the perpetrator's fraud in fact.

(4) Where the act is accomplished against the victim's will by threatening to retaliate in the future against the victim or any other person, and there is a reasonable possibility that the perpetrator will execute the threat.

(5) Where the act is accomplished against the victim's will by threatening to use the authority of a public official to incarcerate, arrest, or deport the victim or another, and the victim has a reasonable belief that the perpetrator is a public official.

---

is rape even if he or she expressed words indicating consent. The fact that the victim consented to sexual foreplay does not mean that the victim consented to intercourse. Nor does the fact that the victim had in the past consented to intercourse with the defendant constitute consent on the present occasion. A difficult question arises in situations where the victim remains silent and offers no resistance to the act. Most jurisdictions require that the victim, if conscious and able to communicate, must in some manner manifest his or her objection to the act for it to constitute rape.

A lack of consent can be established by any acts of the victim that would lead a reasonable person to believe that he or she does not consent to the intercourse. In most jurisdictions, a reasonable mistake as to whether the victim consented is a defense to rape. In a case that made headlines during 1993, Joel Valdez, dubbed the "condom rapist," was found guilty of rape after a jury in Austin, Texas, rejected his claim that the act became consensual once he complied with his victim's request to use a condom. Valdez, who was drunk and armed with a knife at the time of the offense, claimed that his victim's request was a consent to sex. After that, he said, "we were making love."[41]

Statutory Rape All jurisdictions have laws defining **statutory rape.** Under such laws, anyone who has intercourse with a child below a certain specified age is guilty of statutory rape, whether or not the child consented. Statutory rape did not exist as a common law crime but was later enacted by statute in all American jurisdictions—giving rise to the "statutory" component of the term. Statutory rape, in most jurisdictions, is a strict liability crime. As mentioned earlier in this book, strict liability crimes can be committed when the offender engages in activity that is legally prohibited, even though the offender is unaware of breaking the law or did

STATUTORY RAPE
sexual intercourse, whether or not consensual, with a person under the "age of consent," as specified by statute.

not intend to do so. Hence, a man who has sexual intercourse with a consenting female under the age specified by statute can still be found guilty of statutory rape even though he thought she was older. Most jurisdictions hold that even a reasonable belief on the part of the defendant that the victim was over the age of consent at the time of the offense is no defense to a charge of statutory rape.[42] In some instances, men have been convicted of statutory rape even though they had been duped by a female below the age of consent into thinking that the girl was older. The Model Penal Code and a minority of jurisdictions, however, do allow the defense of reasonable mistake as to age.[43]

Same-Sex Rape

The common law definition of rape required both: (1) penetration, and (2) an unwilling *female* victim. Accordingly, it was generally held that there was no crime of homosexual rape at common law. Today, however, a majority of jurisdictions have rape statutes that are gender-neutral. In those jurisdictions, intercourse between persons of the same gender may be rape if all of the other elements of the crime are present. A few states, such as New York, have gender-neutral rape laws by virtue of court ruling, rather than statutory legislation.[44]

Similarly, a woman can be convicted of the rape of another woman when she forces a man to have nonconsensual sexual intercourse with a female victim. In a 1971 California case, for example, a female defendant who forced her husband to have intercourse with a young girl at gunpoint was convicted of rape.[45]

> Evidence that the victim has a bad reputation for chastity is inadmissible because consent is not an issue in a case involving statutory rape.
>
> —*State* v. *DeLawder*, 344 A.2d 212 (Md. Ct. Spec. App., 1975)

Rape Shield Laws

In the not too distant past, it was common practice in American courts for defendants charged with the crime of rape to cross-examine victims about prior acts of "unchastity." Evidence of this sort was allowed because it was believed to have bearing on the issue of consent. As one California court put it, in a 1970 instruction to a jury, "It may be inferred that a woman who has previously consented to sexual intercourse would be more likely to consent again. Such evidence may be considered by you only for such bearing as it may have on the question of whether or not she gave her consent to the alleged sexual act and in judging her credibility."[46]

During the past twenty or thirty years, many jurisdictions have passed **rape shield laws** intended to protect victims of rape. A typical rape shield provision requires that the relevancy of any evidence regarding the past sexual conduct of a rape victim be demonstrated before it can be presented in court. Whether a rape victim was a virgin, sexually experienced, or even a prostitute prior to the present instance of claimed rape, for example, may be irrelevant in a particular case. In some cases, however, such as where a defendant claims that the person charging him with rape is a prostitute and had actually consented to an act of prostitution, the victim's sexual history may be regarded as relevant.

Rape shield laws concern themselves more with appropriate courtroom procedure than they do with criminal behavior. In general, any evidence which has a tendency to prove or disprove the facts at issue is said to have **probative value.** Hence, rape shield laws mandate that the probative value, or worth, of any particular information about a woman's sexual history be demonstrated before such evidence can be presented in open court.

RAPE SHIELD LAWS statutes intended to protect victims of rape by limiting a defendant's in-court use of a victim's sexual history.

PROBATIVE VALUE the worth of any evidence to prove or disprove the facts at issue.

Sexual Assault

A recent trend in the United States is to combine all nonconsensual sexual offenses into one crime called **sexual assault** (which in some jurisdictions may also be termed "criminal sexual conduct" or "sexual abuse"). Where such broad laws exist, sexual assault encompasses far more than the common law crime of rape. Sexual assault (or criminal sexual conduct) may include the common law crimes of rape, deviate sexual intercourse, unlawful sexual contact, **fellatio** (oral stimulation of the male penis), and statutory rape. The Law on the Books box below reprints the Texas statute on sexual assault, which combines all sexual offenses into one crime. For purposes of law, deviate sexual intercourse, as mentioned earlier in this chapter, means any contact between any part of the genitals of one person and the mouth or anus of another person, or the penetration of the genitals or the anus of another person with an object. It can also include any form of sexual intercourse between a human being and an animal. **Sexual contact** means any touching of the anus, breast, or any part of the genitals of another person with intent to arouse or gratify the sexual desire of any person. Sexual contact generally means a touching short of intercourse.

Under Texas law, sexual assault becomes aggravated sexual assault (a felony in the first degree) if the offender: (1) causes serious bodily injury or attempts to cause the death of the victim or another person in the course of the same criminal episode; (2) by acts or words places the victim in fear that death, serious bodily injury, or kidnapping will be imminently inflicted on any person; (3) by acts or words occurring in the presence of the victim, threatens to cause the death, serious bodily injury, or kidnapping of any person; (4) uses or exhibits a deadly weapon in the course of the same criminal episode; or (5) acts in concert with another in perpetrating the offense. Sexual assault also falls into the "aggravated" category under Texas law if the victim is younger than fourteen years of age or is sixty-five years of age or older.

A few jurisdictions, and the Model Penal Code, give a much more limited meaning to the term "sexual assault." The Model Penal Code, for example, contains separate sections defining the crime of rape (Section 213.1), deviate sexual intercourse (Section 213.2), and statutory rape (213.3), but also contains a section (213.4) defining sexual assault. Under the code, sexual assault, which is classified as a misdemeanor, occurs whenever a person has sexual contact with another person (not his spouse) knowing that contact to be offensive to the other person. Sexual assault under the code also includes sexual contact that occurs when the victim is: (1) suffering from mental disease or defect that leaves him or her unable to consent; (2) unaware that a sexual act is being committed; (3) less than ten years old; (4) substantially impaired through actions of the offender, such as the administering of drugs; (5) less than sixteen years old and the actor is at least four years older; and (6) under a few other circumstances.

SEXUAL ASSAULT
a statutory crime that combines all sexual offenses into one offense (often with various degrees). It is broader than the common law crime of rape.

FELLATIO
oral stimulation of the penis.

SEXUAL CONTACT
any touching of the anus, breast, or any part of the genitals of another person with intent to arouse or gratify the sexual desire of any person.

LAW ON THE BOOKS

TEXAS DEFINES "SEXUAL ASSAULT."

Compare with Model Penal Code, Section 213.4

TEXAS PENAL CODE

Section 22.011. Sexual assault.

a. A person commits an offense [sexual assault] if the person:

(continued)

LAW ON THE BOOKS

    (1) intentionally or knowingly:

        (A) causes the penetration of the anus or female sexual organ of another person by any means, without that person's consent;

        (B) causes the penetration of the mouth of another person by the sexual organ or the actor, without that person's consent; or

        (C) causes the sexual organ of another person, without that person's consent, to contact or penetrate the mouth, anus, or sexual organ of another person, including the actor; or

    (2) intentionally or knowingly:

        (A) causes the penetration of the anus or female sexual organ of a child by any means;

        (B) causes the penetration of the mouth of a child by the sexual organ of the actor;

        (C) causes the sexual organ of a child to contact or penetrate the mouth, anus, or sexual organ of another person, including the actor; or

        (D) causes the anus of the child to contact the mouth, anus, or sexual organ of another person, including the actor.

b. A sexual assault under Subsection (a)(1) is without the consent of the other person if:

(1) the actor compels the other person to submit or participate by the use of physical force or violence;

(2) the actor compels the other person to submit or participate by threatening to use force or violence against the other person, and the other person believes that the actor has the present ability to execute the threat;

(3) the other person has not consented and the actor knows that the other person is unconscious or physically unable to resist;

(4) the actor knows that as a result of mental disease or defect the other person is at the time of the sexual assault incapable of appraising the nature of the act or of resisting it;

(5) the other person has not consented and the actor knows that the other person is unaware that the sexual assault is occurring;

(6) the actor has intentionally impaired the other person's power to appraise or control the other person's conduct by administering any substance without the other person's knowledge;

(7) the actor compels the other person to submit or participate by threatening to use force or violence against any person, and the other person believes that the actor has the ability to execute the threat;

(8) the actor is a public servant who coerces the person to submit or participate;

(9) the actor is a mental health services provider who causes the other person, who is a patient or former patient of the actor, to submit or participate by exploiting the other person's emotional dependency on the actor; or

(10) the actor is a clergyman who causes the other person to submit or participate by exploiting the other person's emotional dependency on the clergyman's professional character as spiritual adviser.

c. In this section:

(1) "Child" means a person younger than seventeen years of age who is not the spouse of the actor.

(2) "Spouse" means a person who is legally married to another.

d. It is a defense to prosecution under Subsection (a)(2) that the conduct consisted of medical care for the child and did not include any contact between the anus or sexual organ of the child and the mouth, anus, or sexual organ of the actor or third party.

e. It is an affirmative defense to prosecution under Subsection (a)(2) that the actor was not more than three years older than the victim, and the victim was a child of fourteen years of age or older.

f. An offense under this section is a felony of the second degree.

KIDNAPPING AND FALSE IMPRISONMENT

In early 1997, former New York City resident Joshua Torres, age twenty-three, began serving a sentence of fifty-eight years to life in prison for the 1995 kidnap-murder of twenty-year-old Kimberly Antonakos. Torres had been convicted a month earlier of abducting Antonakos from in front of her home and attempting to extort ransom money from her father. During the kidnapping, Antonakos had been grabbed and thrown into the trunk of a car, then driven to an abandoned house in Queens, where she was held for three days in an unheated basement—all the while gagged and tied to a pole.[47] After the young woman's father failed to respond to a $75,000 ransom demand because his answering machine did not record the kidnapper's call, Torres doused Antonakos with gasoline and burned her to death. Sentencing judge Thomas Demakos, who admitted being moved to tears by testimony in the case, said that the crime cried out for the death penalty, which was not in effect in New York State when the murder took place. Torres was sentenced instead to twenty-five years to life for murder, another twenty-five years to life for kidnapping, and eight to twenty-five years for arson—all to be served consecutively.

Kidnapping

Kidnapping and false imprisonment are crimes that intimately invade a person's privacy and take away his or her liberty—often in abrupt and forceful fashion. Kidnapping is generally defined as the unlawful removal of a person from the place where he or she is found, against that person's will, and through the use of force, fraud, threats, or some other form of intimidation.

At early common law, kidnapping consisted of the forcible abduction or stealing away of a person from his own country and into another. Somewhat later the requirement was modified to require involuntary movement merely from one county to another. Today most jurisdictions hold that any unlawful movement of the victim that is "substantial" is sufficient to satisfy the movement (asportation) requirement inherent in the crime of kidnapping. For courts today, the primary issue in kidnapping cases is whether a person is forcefully moved against his or her will and not the degree of movement or distance involved.[48] Even so, the movement involved must be "substantial"—meaning that merely forcing someone out of one's way, or pushing a person a few feet or even across the street would not constitute kidnapping within the meaning of the law.

Generally speaking, the elements of kidnapping are:

- an unlawful taking and carrying away,
- of a human being,
- by force, fraud, threats, or intimidation, and
- against the person's will.

In some jurisdictions, kidnapping may also be committed by the use of *deadly* force to confine the victim or by confining the victim for purposes of extortion, ransom, or sexual assault. "Kidnapping for ransom," or "aggravated kidnapping," as these crimes are sometimes called, are more serious forms of kidnapping and are usually punishable more severely than the crime of "simple kidnapping." The same may be true when state statutes specify that the release of a victim in a place that is not safe raises the degree of the crime committed.

KIDNAPPING
the unlawful removal of a person from the place where he or she is found, against that person's will, and through the use of force, fraud, threats, or some other form of intimidation. Also, an aggravated form of false imprisonment that is accompanied by either a moving or secreting of the victim.

The laws of some jurisdictions provide for more than one type of kidnapping. California law, for example, recognizes four different kidnapping offenses: (1) forcible kidnapping, (2) kidnapping with intent to commit certain specified felonies, (3) kidnapping with intent to take out of state, and (4) bringing a kidnapped victim into the state. California law also specifies penalty enhancements for kidnappings that are committed for the purposes of committing a sexual offense, ransom, extortion, or robbery, and for kidnapping a child under the age of fourteen.

Florida law, which is essentially an aggravated kidnapping law, defines kidnapping as follows: "The term 'kidnapping' means forcibly, secretly, or by threat confining, abducting, or imprisoning another person against his will and without lawful authority, with intent to: (1) Hold for ransom or reward or as a shield or hostage, (2) Commit or facilitate commission of any felony, (3) Inflict bodily harm upon or to terrorize the victim or another person, [or] (4) Interfere with the performance of any governmental or political function."[49] Were the law to end where the words "without lawful authority" appear, it would describe simple kidnapping.

In an effort to combat the abduction of children (as may happen in instances of contested divorce and child custody battles), which is sometimes called child stealing, Florida law also provides that "[c]onfinement of a child under the age of thirteen is against his will within the meaning of this subsection if such confinement is without the consent of his parent or legal guardian."[50]

Just as the laws of different jurisdictions vary as to what constitutes kidnapping, they also vary on how the confinement must be accomplished for the law to apply. A few jurisdictions do not classify an unwilling movement of an individual accomplished through fraud as kidnapping—holding instead that force, intimidation, or threat must be used for the offense to qualify as kidnapping. Similarly, if all of the elements are present except a substantial movement of the victim, then the offense may be an "attempted kidnapping." The general rule, however, is that movement or confinement accomplished by force or threat is sufficient to constitute the crime of kidnapping.[51] In some cases, the mere persuading of a minor or incompetent to remain in one place or to move is sufficient to constitute kidnapping. If a victim at first willingly accompanies the offender, the crime of kidnapping still occurs if force or restraint is later used to move the victim further.

In those situations where the movement of the victim is merely incidental to the commission of another crime, a few jurisdictions allow the prosecution of the defendant for both the intended crime and for kidnapping.[52] Some jurisdictions generally hold that a kidnapping has not been committed unless the forced movement substantially increases the risk to the victim beyond the risk created by the other crime.[53] In one Michigan case, for example, the defendant walked into a store, pulled a gun, and compelled the victim to go into another room in order to open a safe. Although the defendant was clearly guilty of armed robbery, a court held that he had not committed kidnapping—not because of the short distance involved in the forced movement, but because movement of the victim was merely incidental to commission of the armed robbery. Had the defendant used the victim as a shield as he left the scene of the robbery, however, it is likely that he would also have been guilty of kidnapping.

A federal kidnapping law, sometimes called the Lindbergh Law,[54] was created in response to the kidnapping of the infant son of Charles A. Lindbergh—the first person to make a nonstop solo trans–Atlantic flight. The Lindbergh baby was taken from the family's New Jersey home in 1932 by Bruno Richard Hauptmann. The child was later found dead, and Hauptmann was convicted of the crime and executed in 1936. Other federal laws make it a crime to take a hostage,[55] or to knowingly receive, possess, or dispose of any money or property that has been delivered as ransom on behalf of a victim of kidnapping.[56]

Gary Heidnik, convicted of kidnapping, false imprisonment, rape, and murder, arrives at court. Heidnik was executed in Pennsylvania in 1997. He had kept six women chained in the basement of his Philadelphia home, while repeatedly raping them over a period of four months. Heidnik electrocuted one of the women, starved another to death, and fed the victims' remains to imprisoned survivors. He was arrested when one of the surviving women managed to escape. (Photo by Pat Rogers, courtesy of AP/Wide World Photos.)

False Imprisonment

False imprisonment, which is basically the unlawful violation of the personal liberty of another, is similar to kidnapping except that it does not involve the "carrying away" of the victim. Not all states have false imprisonment statutes, and in those that do, it is usually classified as a misdemeanor. The elements of false imprisonment are:

- an unlawful restraint by one person,
- of another person's freedom of movement,
- without the victim's consent or without legal justification.

The defendant must have compelled the victim to remain or go where he or she did not want to go.[57] While the confinement must be accomplished by actual physical restraint, the application of force is not essential. Confinement may be accomplished by threats or by some other action of the defendant that restrains the victim's freedom of movement. One court, for example, found a defendant guilty of false imprisonment for intentionally driving a car too fast for his passenger to leave.[58]

In cases where the confinement is accomplished by threat, the victim must be aware of the threat. Similarly, it is not false imprisonment to prevent a person from

FALSE IMPRISONMENT
the unlawful restraint of another person's liberty. Also, the unlawful detention of a person without his or her consent. Sometimes called **false arrest.**

going in one direction, as long as the person may go in a different direction and is aware of this opportunity. Also, confinement must be unlawful in that there must be no legal authority for the confinement, and an arrest that is made without proper legal authority constitutes **false arrest** —a form of false imprisonment.

False imprisonment is essentially a lesser included offense of the crime of kidnapping. Some authors also note that kidnapping is also an aggravated form of false imprisonment—as this excerpt from Florida law reveals: "The term 'false imprisonment' means forcibly, by threat, or secretly confining, abducting, imprisoning, or restraining another person without lawful authority and against his will."[59] As with kidnapping, the statute also provides that "[c]onfinement of a child under the age of thirteen is against his will within the meaning of this section if such confinement is without the consent of his parent or legal guardian."[60] Federal law imposes a duty on states to enforce the child custody determinations made by other states under the Parental Kidnapping Prevention Act.[61] Some jurisdictions, which define false imprisonment simply as "restraining another unlawfully so as to interfere substantially with his liberty," would consider false imprisonment achieved through the use of force or threats as "aggravated false imprisonment."

At common law, both kidnapping and false imprisonment were misdemeanors. Today, however, kidnapping is generally regarded far more seriously, although false imprisonment remains a lesser crime. Florida law, for example, reads: "A person who kidnaps a person is guilty of a felony of the first degree, punishable by imprisonment for a term of years not exceeding life. . . ."[62]

SUMMARY

- Although the terms "assault" and "battery" are often used together or interchangeably, they should be distinguished for purposes of the criminal law. An assault is an attempted or threatened battery. A battery is a consummated assault. Mayhem is a battery that causes great bodily harm.

- At common law, two types of assault could be distinguished: an attempted assault and threats. In an *attempted* battery–type of assault a defendant attempted to commit a battery. The second type of assault, that of *threatened* battery, occurred when a defendant placed another in fear of imminent injury. The first was an actual attempt to commit a battery, whereas the latter criminalized conduct that made another person fear an assault.

- Some jurisdictions have combined assault and battery crimes into one offense called "assault."

- The present ability element of the crime of assault requires that the person attempting assault is physically capable of immediately carrying it out.

- The term aggravated assault may mean: (1) an assault that is committed with the intention of committing an additional crime, or (2) an assault that involves special circumstances.

- Many jurisdictions have enacted antistalking statutes designed to prevent the intentional harassing, annoying, or threatening of another person.

- The crime of battery is an intentional crime, but it may be committed through reckless or criminally negligent conduct. To constitute battery, the offense need cause no injury and the victim need not fear the force intended to be applied.

- Sexual battery occurs when a person unlawfully touches an intimate part of another person's body against that person's will and for the purpose of sexual arousal, gratification, or abuse.

- Traditionally, rape has been defined as unlawful sexual intercourse with a female without her effective consent. At common law, a husband could not rape his wife, since it was believed that when a woman married she consented to sexual intercourse. The rape statutes of an increasing number of jurisdictions today, however, are not gender specific and also permit charges of "spousal rape."

- Statutory rape is sexual intercourse, by an adult, with a child who has not yet reached the legal age of consent.

- Some jurisdictions have consolidated sexual offenses into one broad crime of sexual assault.

- Kidnapping is the unlawful removal of a person from the place where he or she is found, against that person's will, and through the use of force, fraud, threats, or some other form of intimidation.

- False imprisonment is the unlawful violation of the personal liberty of another. False arrest, or an arrest that is made without proper legal authority, is a form of false imprisonment.

QUESTIONS FOR DISCUSSION

1. What are the differences between the common law crimes of assault and battery?
2. What are the two types of common law assault, and what are the elements of each?
3. How does mayhem differ from other types of battery?
4. Explain the type or extent of injury to a victim required for the crime of battery.
5. Explain the difference between common law rape and modern statutes describing sexual assault. What does it mean to say that a rape statute is "not gender specific"?
6. Give an example of false imprisonment. How does false imprisonment differ from kidnapping? From false arrest?

LEGAL RESOURCES ON THE WORLD WIDE WEB

A growing number of Web sites provide the opportunity to participate in a variety of law-related simulations. iCourthouse, for example, allows participants to serve on virtual juries. iCourthouse cases are drawn from real life and permit virtual jury panel members to experience at least some of the ins and outs of jury service. iCourthouse and other similar services are listed here.

American Mock Trial Association (AMTA)
http://www.collegemocktrial.org
The AMTA sponsors annual mock trial tournaments for undergraduates. The organization seeks to help students understand the work of a trial attorney.

Court TV
http://www.courttv.com/games
The "games" section in Court TV features the software simulation "D.A. Pursuit of Justice" from Legacy Software,™ and allows visitors to play a limited version of the game.

iCourthouse
http://www.icourthouse.com
iCourthouse is "the courthouse for the Internet." iCourthouse is a greatly streamlined version of the real-world court system. The cases are real, the jurors are real, and the verdicts are real. iCourthouse is always in session.

Mock Trial Online
http://www.abc.net.au/mocktrial
An Australian site that conducts a full mock trial over the Internet. Mock Trial Online is a joint project involving the Law Society of New South Wales, ABC Online, and the British Council.

Check the *Criminal Law Today* Web site for URLs that may have changed.

SUGGESTED READINGS AND CLASSIC WORKS

Shana Alexander, *Anyone's Daughter* (New York: Viking Press, 1979).

Rene L. Augustine, "Marriage: The Safe Haven for Rapists," *Journal of Family Law,* Vol. 29 (1991), p. 559.

Vivian Berger, "A Not So Simple Rape," *Criminal Justice Ethics,* Vol. 7 (1988), p. 69.

John Diamond, "Kidnapping: A Modern Definition," *American Journal of Criminal Law,* Vol. 13 (Fall 1985), p. 1.

Susan Estrich, *Real Rape* (Cambridge: Harvard University Press, 1987).

John D. Harman, "Consent, Harm, and Marital Rape," *Journal of Family Law,* Vol. 22 (1983), p. 423.

Sanford H. Kadish, Ed., *Encyclopedia of Crime and Justice,* Vol. 3 (New York: The Free Press, 1983).

William Kirk and Richard Hawkins, "The Meaning of Arrest for Wife Assaulters," *Criminology,* Vol. 27 (February 1989), p. 163.

WHAT CONSTITUTES FELLATIO FOR PURPOSES OF THE LAW? WHAT CONSTITUTES FORCE IN SEXUAL CONDUCT WITH A CHILD?

CAPSTONE CASE

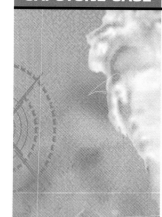

Note: Ohio is one of the states that have consolidated sex crimes into one offense, in this case, "rape."

State v. *Clark*
Ohio Court of Appeals for the Third District, 1995
106 Ohio App. 3d 426; 666 N.E.2d 308

OPINION

Defendant was convicted in the Common Pleas Court, Auglaize County, of rape, and he appealed. The Court of Appeals, Justice Hadley, held that: (1) to support rape conviction, there was no requirement of penetration into rape victim's mouth to commit fellatio; (2) evidence was sufficient to establish elements of rape beyond reasonable doubt; (3) there was sufficient evidence outside of defendant's confession to meet *corpus delicti* requirement of admitting confession; and (4) evidence that defendant held victim face down on his lap and subjected her to his erect penis was sufficient evidence to support element of force. Affirmed.

Defendant-appellant, Guy Clark (appellant), appeals from the judgment entry of conviction in the Auglaize County Court of Common Pleas for one count of rape in violation of R.C. 2907.02(A)(1)(b). His sentence was enhanced pursuant to R.C. 2907.02(B).

Appellant was indicted on August 12, 1994, for engaging in sexual conduct by force with his four-month-old granddaughter, Autumn. Autumn's mother, Angela, is appellant's daughter. Briefly, the incident occurred when appellant was watching Autumn while Angela went to a neighbor's home. Upon her return, Angela heard Autumn screaming. When she entered the trailer, Angela discovered Autumn's face down on appellant's lap. Angela grabbed Autumn and observed appellant's erect penis. On April 25, 1995, a jury found appellant guilty of rape by force. The trial court's judgment entry of conviction and imposition of sentencing was filed on April 25,1995.

It is from this judgment entry that appellant presents four assignments of error. . . . Assignment of Error No. 3: The trial court committed prejudicial error when it instructed the jury that fellatio is any stimulation of the penis by the mouth of another.

Since appellant is challenging the jury instruction regarding the definition of "fellatio," we address his third assignment of error prior to determining whether there was sufficient evidence to support a finding of fellatio. Appellant asserts that the common meaning of fellatio requires "that there be some penetration into the mouth."

R.C. 2907.02(A)(1)(b) states that "no person shall engage in sexual conduct" with an individual under the age of thirteen. Pursuant to R.C. 2907.01(A), sexual conduct includes fellatio. However, there is no definition of "fellatio" in the Revised Code.

In defining "fellatio," the Supreme Court of Ohio was guided by the common usage of the word and cited the following dictionary meaning, "The practice of obtaining sexual satisfaction by oral stimulation of the penis." *In re M.D.* (1988), 38 Ohio St. 3d 149, 152, 527 N.E.2d 286, 289, quoting Webster's Third New International Dictionary (1986) 836. In *State* v. *Long* (1989), 64 Ohio App. 3d 615, 618, 582 N.E.2d 626, 628, an appellate court found no error in the trial court's charge to "the jury that fellatio is committed by touching the male sex organ with any part of the mouth." Thus, the court found that no penetration was required. *Id.* See also, *State* v. *Turvey* (1992), 84 Ohio App. 3d 724, 748, 618 N.E.2d 214, 230 (holding that fellatio requires no penetration); *Black's Law Dictionary* (6 Ed-1990) 616 (defines "fellatio" as "[a] sexual act in which the mouth or lips come into contact with the penis"); *American Heritage Dictionary* (1985) 496 (defines fellatio as "oral stimulation of the penis").

Furthermore, "fellatio" is defined in four Ohio Jury Instructions (1994) 165, Section 507-02, as "a sexual act committed with the male sexual organ and the mouth."

In the instant case, the record shows that the trial court provided the jury with the instruction set forth in Ohio Jury Instructions. The jury requested additional instructions. Specifically, the jury asked, "May we be given a more detailed explanation of fellatio?" and "Does fellatio must have [sic] penetration of the penis into the mouth?" In response, the trial court instructed as follows: "You have already been given instructions concerning fellatio, and you should follow them. Fellatio is any stimulation of the penis by the mouth of another."

Upon our review, we conclude that there is no requirement of penetration to commit fellatio. The trial court, therefore, committed no error in its instruction and appellant's third assignment of error is overruled.

Assignment of Error No. 1: The conviction must be reversed because "there was insufficient evidence of fellatio, and thus the conviction was against the manifest weight of the evidence."

In view of the above analysis, we next examine appellant's first assignment of error. Appellant contends that "aside from appellant's statement to the police, the only evidence in support of the conviction came from Angela's statement that the baby's face was by [appellant's] private areas, and that appellant's penis was erect and exposed." Thus, appellant argues that his statement alone is insufficient to support a conviction.

When reviewing the weight and sufficiency of the evidence, an appellate court must inquire "whether, after viewing the evidence in a light most favorable to the prosecution, any rational trier of fact could have found the essential elements of the crime proven beyond a reasonable doubt." *State* v. *Jenks* (1991), 61 Ohio St. 3d 259; 574 N.E.2d 492. The reviewing court must remember that the jury heard the evidence and has the primary responsibility to consider the evidence and credibility of the witnesses. *State* v. *DeHass* (1967), 10 Ohio St. 2d 230, 39 Ohio St. 2d 366; 227 N.E.2d 212.

Again, the offense of rape results when a person engages in sexual conduct with an individual under the age of thirteen. R.C. 2907.02(A)(1)(b).

The trial transcript reveals the following testimony from Angela. Angela left Autumn with appellant while she walked to the neighbors. After a brief time, she returned to the trailer. As she was walking up the steps, she heard Autumn screaming. When questioned about the screaming, Angela stated it was different from a cry Autumn would make when she was hungry or needed to be changed. When she entered, she saw Autumn on appellant's "lap with her face down by his private areas." Appellant was reluctant to hand Autumn to Angela, but when he did, Angela observed appellant's erect penis. Angela then ran out of the house with the baby, screaming that "he did it." In a later conversation with Angela, appellant apologized and stated that he was getting help.

A detective testified that appellant, after changing his story, told him he had an urge to put his penis in Autumn's mouth. When the detective asked if he put his penis in Autumn's mouth, appellant responded "he didn't think so but maybe a little bit, and that it mostly brushed up against the outside." Towards the conclusion of the interview, appellant also signed a statement, written by the detective, regarding the incident. In his statement, appellant admitted that he had an urge to unzip his pants and see what Autumn would do with his penis. Again, appellant conceded that his penis may have gone into Autumn's mouth "a little, but mostly on the outside." In the statement, appellant, however, maintained that his penis was not erect during the incident.

Based upon the foregoing evidence, as well as the rest of the record, we find that there was evidence, if believed, by the jury to establish the elements of rape beyond a reasonable doubt. Appellant's first assignment of error, therefore, is overruled.

Assignment of Error No. 2: "The trial court committed prejudicial error in admitting appellant's confession because the *corpus delicti* of the offense had not been established before the statement was admitted."

Appellant submits that there was no evidence, apart from appellant's statement, to support the finding that there was sexual conduct. He further maintains that his confession, although violating no constitutional rights, was suggestive enough to apply the *corpus delicti* rule. Although some issues were raised regarding appellant's statement, there appears to be no specific *corpus delicti* issue raised at the trial level. We will, however, address his assignment of error.

The *corpus delicti* of a crime is composed of "the act and the criminal agency of the act" *State* v. *Van Hook* (1988), 39 Ohio St. 3d 256, 261, 530 N.E.2d 883, 888. The *corpus delicti* rule requires that the state present "some evidence outside of the confession that tends to prove some material element of the crime charged" in order to admit a confession. *Id.,* quoting *State* v. *MaMaranda* (1916), 94 Ohio St. 364, 114 N.E. 1088. Such evidence may be circumstantial. *State* v. *Nicely* (1988), 39 Ohio St. 3d 147, 154–155, 529 N.E.2d 1236, 1242–1243.

Upon a review of the record, we find sufficient evidence in appellant's confession to meet the *corpus delicti* requirement. As indicated by the previous references to the transcript, Angela heard Autumn screaming and upon entering the trailer saw Autumn face down on appellant's lap. Appellant was reluctant to give Autumn to Angela and when he did Angela observed his erect penis. Angela's testimony, as well as appellant's apology, claim of seeking help, and demeanor during the interview with the detective, meet the same evidence standard.

For the above stated reasons, appellant's second assignment of error is overruled.

Assignment of Error No. 4: "The conviction must be reversed because there was insufficient evidence that appellant used force in committing the offense."

Appellant argues that there was no force used in committing the act. Furthermore, he contends that "placing the baby on his lap is too attenuated from the rape itself to allow a finding that there was force." In analyzing appellant's assertions, we again apply the standard set forth in *State* v. *Jenks, supra.*

R.C. 2907.02(B) enhances the penalty for individuals convicted of raping a child under the age of thirteen by force or threat of force to life imprisonment. Force is defined in R.C. 2901.01(A) as "any violence, compulsion, or constraint physically exerted by any means upon or against a person or thing."

The Supreme Court of Ohio found that force "depends upon the age, size, and strength of the parties and their relation to each other." *State* v. *Eskridge* (1988), 38 Ohio St. 3d 56, 526 N.E.2d 304, paragraph one of the syllabus. *State* v. *Eskridge* involved a four-year-old child and was primarily based upon the inherent control a parent or other authority figure has upon a child. Obviously, this particular factor is not present when the victim is a four-month-old infant.

Nonetheless, in view of the above analysis and the statutory definition of "force," we find sufficient evidence to establish the use of force. In doing so, we conclude that an infant, because of its age, has no power to resist any adult actions. Simply, an adult's control is absolute. Thus, the compulsion or constraint needed to establish force when the victim is an infant is logically lessened.

Consequently, holding a four-month-old baby face down on the lap of an adult and subjecting it to an erect adult penis is clearly a physical compulsion or constraint. Based on this, as well as the rest of the record, we overrule appellant's fourth assignment of error.

Having found no error prejudicial to appellant, the judgment of the Auglaize County Court of Common Pleas is affirmed.

[footnotes omitted]

WHAT DO *YOU* THINK?

1. Since the victim was underage, what difference does it make that force was used in this sexual offense?
2. According to the court, what constitutes the *corpus delicti* of the common law crime of fellatio?
3. If you were the trial judge in this case, what type of punishment would you impose on the defendant?

WHAT CONSTITUTES "MOVEMENT" SUFFICIENT TO SUSTAIN A KIDNAPPING CONVICTION? WHAT FACTORS ARE USED TO DETERMINE WHETHER THERE HAS BEEN AN ASPORTATION OF THE VICTIM?

CAPSTONE CASE

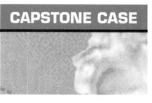

Illinois v. *Jackson*
Appellate Court of Illinois, First District, Fifth Division, 1996
281 Ill. App. 3d 759, 666 N.E.2d 854

OPINION

Defendant was convicted in the Circuit, Cook County, of murder and kidnapping, and he appealed.

The Appellant Court, Judge P.J. McNulty presiding: Defendant was found guilty of first-degree murder, felony murder, aggravated kidnapping, and kidnapping. The trial court merged the felony murder conviction into the first-degree murder conviction, and the kidnapping conviction into the aggravated kidnapping conviction. The trial court found defendant eligible for the death penalty but that mitigating factors precluded the imposition of the death penalty. The trial court sentenced defendant to natural life imprisonment for first-degree murder and a concurrent sentence of fifteen years' incarceration for aggravated kidnapping. We affirm the conviction.

FACTS: Illinois State Police Sergeant James Turner testified . . . that Cherise Watkins told him that when she last spoke to the victim, the victim stated that she was going to stay with friends at 127th Street. Sergeant Turner learned of an area called the "black bridge," which is an area adjacent to a residential neighborhood consisting of a large field leading to an abandoned railroad bridge that crosses the channel just east of Halsted. The channel flows from the black bridge to where the victim's body was found.

Sergeant Turner then conducted a door-to-door canvass of the neighborhood at 127th and Halsted and determined that the victim had been alive and in that area up to the beginning of April. Sergeant Turner spoke with Maurice Martin, whose name was on a piece of paper found on the victim, and he told the sergeant that he believed Venus Beckom, Daniel Butler, and Chezeray Moore had information regarding the victim's death.

On May 5, 1992, Sergeant Turner spoke with Venus Beckom and learned that Venus had last seen the victim at a bus stop in the area. The next day, Sergeant Turner interviewed Venus again and she gave him further information, which led him to Daniel and Cassandra Butler, Sharon Burke, and Lashonda Wilson. Interviews with these individuals led Sergeant Turner to arrest defendant and codefendants Chezeray Moore, Timothy Mobley, and Henry Lovett. Sergeant Turner ordered a search of the area of the black bridge, and a rock with hair and blood on it was recovered. It was discovered that a sewer cover was missing from a sewer hole approximately three hundred feet from the bridge. A sewer cover, weighing approximately one hundred fifty pounds, was recovered from the Cal-Sag Channel in the area of the black bridge. A green electrical wire was attached to the sewer cover. According to Sergeant Turner, the home of Cassandra and Daniel Butler, the home and garage of Chezeray Moore, the Nansin School Playground, and a Chicago Transit Authority bus stop are all located within a few blocks of the black bridge.

Dr. Robert Kirschner of the Cook County medical examiner's office performed an autopsy on the victim on April 26, 1992, and found that her hands had been tied behind her back with a rope and that her ankles had been bound with a plastic wire. He determined that the victim had been dead and submerged for many days. The victim had five lacerations to her head, four of which appeared to have been inflicted prior to her death. She had a stab wound to her lower left back inflicted before she died. Her left hand was broken, and the bruises to that hand were consistent with a defensive-type wound. She had a large bruise to the left knee and a smaller bruise to the right knee. Dr. Kirschner found "muddy materials fairly deep into the victim's lungs." In Dr. Kirschner's opinion, the cause of the victim's death was drowning in association with blunt trauma.

Daniel Butler testified that on about April 17, 1992, he arrived home around 7 P.M. and found a group of people in his basement, Butler could not recall if defendant was in the basement. Butler told the group to leave, and about ten to fifteen minutes later, he went to Moore's garage. Butler saw Weewee hit the victim. He could not remember whether defendant was in the garage.

When everyone left the garage, Butler walked to Nansin School with the victim, Venus, Weewee, and Poopoo. Moore and defendant arrived at the playground fifteen minutes later. Butler saw Venus and Poopoo hit the victim and the victim fall to the ground. Butler left the playground, and when he later returned, he did not see the victim, defendant, or Moore. Butler then went to the black bridge. When he reached the bridge twenty to twenty-five minutes later, he saw defendant walking away from the bridge. Butler saw the victim sitting or lying down near the bridge, but he did not know whether she was conscious or if her hands or feet were tied. As he was leaving the bridge, Butler saw defendant carrying what looked like a cover.

Butler and Poopoo then went to the bus stop at 127th and Lowe. A few minutes later, defendant, Moore, and Lovett joined them at the bus stop. Butler testified that he did not talk to them. Butler admitted that he had recently been convicted for felony delivery of a look-alike substance and had an unlawful-use-of-weapon-by-a-felon charge pending against him at the time of trial.

Butler admitted that he gave sworn testimony before the grand jury on May 8, 1992. According to his grand jury testimony, Butler stated that defendant, a Blackstone gang member, was also in Butler's basement with the victim. Defendant then left the basement with the victim and Moore. He then saw the victim, Venus, Weewee, and Poopoo in Moore's garage. As Butler walked from Moore's garage to the playground, he saw defendant, the victim, Venus, Poopoo, and Weewee walking toward the school. Later, as Butler was walking toward the black bridge, defendant walked toward him and said that he would be right back after he got a sewer cover.

In his testimony before the grand jury, Butler stated that as he got to the black bridge, he saw the victim lying on the ground with her hands and feet tied. Butler testified that he told Moore and Lovett, "This shit ain't right," and walked away. As Butler was leaving, he saw defendant approaching the bridge, carrying a sewer top. Butler saw defendant throw the sewer cover onto the bridge. Butler and Poopoo waited for a bus and then began walking toward 127th and Emerald. They ran into defendant, who told them he "sunk that bitch." When Butler asked him what he meant by that, defendant replied, "I sunk the whore." Butler testified at trial that he gave the grand jury testimony after the police told him what to say in order to avoid being charged with murder.

Lashonda Wilson, also known as Poopoo, testified that she saw the victim at Moore's garage. Weewee and the victim were arguing about the victim's involvement with Mendell Butler, and Weewee began striking the victim's hands and feet with a pipe. Venus then dragged the limping victim to the playground. Weewee and Venus started hitting the victim. The victim fell to the ground, and Venus began kicking her. Wilson saw defendant pick up the victim and walk with her east toward 127th and Halsted. Wilson left but then went back to the playground. When she got there, about thirty minutes after she first left, she decided to walk to the black bridge. While walking on a path to the bridge, Wilson saw defendant approach. Defendant appeared to be excited and happy and told her that he was going to get a sewer cover. Defendant walked off down the path. Moore told Wilson, that he "hit the bitch in the head with bricks, and she still wouldn't die." Wilson saw the victim lying on the bridge, curled up in a ball. Lovett told Wilson and Moore that, if they didn't want to see this, "[they] better leave." As Wilson walked away, she saw defendant returning to the bridge carrying a sewer cover over his head.

Wilson then walked to 127th and Halsted and waited for a bus. Defendant, Moore, and Lovett appeared. Moore was "joyful, kind of cheerful." Lovett was "sad" and defendant was "very excited." Defendant was "laughing, jumping up and down, talking out loud."

Wilson admitted that she had been charged with aggravated battery and unlawful restraint for her role in beating the victim at the playground. Wilson further admitted that in exchange for her testimony at defendant's trial, the state would recommend that she be sentenced to probation on those charges.

OPINION

Defendant claims on appeal that the evidence was insufficient to convict him and that errors by the trial court and prosecution denied him a fair trial. Defendant also claims that his sentence was excessive.

Defendant first contends that the State failed to prove beyond a reasonable doubt secret confinement and asportation, elements necessary to prove aggravated kidnapping. Defendant claims that these elements were not proved since the crime occurred in public view and any asportation or detention was merely inherent in the murder.

A reviewing court presented with a challenge to the sufficiency of the evidence should determine whether, after viewing the evidence in the light most favorable to the prosecution, any rational trier of fact could find the elements of the charged offense were proven beyond a reasonable doubt. . . . A person commits aggravated kidnapping when he knowingly by force or threat of force carries a victim from one place to another with the intent to secretly confine her against her will and, in doing so, inflicts great bodily harm upon the victim. . . . To determine whether an asportation or detention rises to the level of kidnapping as a separate offense, four factors must be considered: (1) the duration of the asportation or detention; (2) whether the asportation or detention occurred during the commission of a separate offense; (3) whether the asportation or detention that occurred is inherent in the separate offense; and (4) whether the asportation or detention created a significant danger to the victim independent of that posed by the separate offense. . . .

The victim in this case was not allowed to leave Cassandra Butler's house. Instead, she was forced to go to the basement, where Cassandra put a knife to her throat, cut her hair off, bound and gagged her, and stuffed her in a closet. . . . Defendant then picked the victim up off the ground, placed his arm around her and took her a few blocks away to the black bridge, a large field leading to an abandoned trestle that crosses the Cal-Sag Channel just east of Halsted. About thirty to fifty minutes after he had seen defendant take the victim from the playground, Daniel Butler saw defendant and the victim, whose hands and feet were bound, at the bridge.

We believe that these facts prove the elements of aggravated kidnapping as an offense distinct from murder. The asportation took place from the Nansin School playground to the black bridge, a distance of several blocks. In *People* v. *Riley* . . . the duration factor was satisfied where the asportation distance was approximately one [and] one-half blocks.

Second, the asportation of the victim occurred prior to her murder. At least thirty to fifty minutes had elapsed from the time defendant took the victim to the playground to the time Daniel Butler saw the bound victim lying on the bridge. During that time, the defendant escorted the victim from the playground, across a large field to the bridge, roped the victim's hands, and wired her ankles together. . . .

Third, the forced movement of a victim from one location to another is not inherent in the offense of murder. . . . Fourth, the asportation created a significant danger to the victim independent of the danger of murder by taking her from a public place to the abandoned bridge. . . .

The element of secret confinement was also satisfied by the fact that the victim was taken to the secluded bridge and bound. Secret confinement may be shown by proof of the secrecy of confinement or the place of confinement. . . . Although confinement usually means enclosure or confinement within something such as a house or car, it is not strictly limited to those types of places. . . .

Accordingly, for the reasons set forth above, we affirm defendant's conviction and sentence.

Affirmed.

[footnotes omitted]

WHAT DO *YOU* THINK?

1. What factors did the court use to determine that the elements of secret confinement and asportation were present to constitute the crime of aggravated kidnapping and not merely inherent to the murder?
2. Explain the rationale behind the defendant's contention that secret confinement did not occur because the crime occurred in public view?
3. According to the appellate court, what are the elements of aggravated kidnapping?
4. Do you agree with the court's holding that the element of secret confinement was established? Does it make any difference that the bridge was in a public place?
5. What factors should we look at to determine whether the kidnapping was merely inherent in the murder?

WHAT IS THE DIFFERENCE BETWEEN KIDNAPPING AND FALSE IMPRISONMENT?

CAPSTONE CASE

Schweinle v. *State*
Texas Court of Criminal Appeals, 1996
915 S.W.2d 17

OPINION
Defendant was convicted in the 351st District Court, Harris County, Judge Lupe Salinas presiding, of aggravated kidnapping, and he appealed. The Houston Court of Appeals, 893 S.W.2d 708, affirmed, and defendant petitioned for review. The Court of Criminal Appeals held that defendant was entitled to charge of false imprisonment as lesser included offense.

Reversed and remanded.

Appeal from 351st District Court, Harris County; Lupe Salinas, Judge.

A jury convicted appellant of aggravated kidnapping and assessed his punishment at confinement for fifteen years in the penitentiary. The conviction was affirmed. *Schweinle* v. *State*, 893 S.W.2d 708 (Tex. App.–Houston 1995). We granted discretionary review to determine whether evidence of extraneous offenses and expert testimony regarding "battered woman syndrome" was improperly admitted in the guilt-innocence phase, and whether a lesser included offense was raised by the evidence. Due to our disposition of the latter issue, which is raised in ground four of appellant's petition, we will not address grounds one, two, and three and will dismiss them without prejudice.

Appellant and the complainant became engaged after a brief courtship, and the complainant, who had formerly lived with her parents, moved into appellant's house. However, the couple began arguing, and the complainant moved back to her parents' house, although she would occasionally spend the night with appellant. On October 23, 1991, they had planned that appellant would pick up some food for dinner, and the complainant would meet appellant at his father's liquor store, where appellant worked. The complainant was alone at her parents' house changing clothes when she heard a door slam. Appellant came into the bedroom, enraged

because the complainant had not met him at the liquor store as planned. The complainant testified appellant told her she was coming with him, that he had some food in the car and she was going to eat every bite of it. He grabbed her by the arm, dragged her down the hall and slapped her. The complainant told appellant she did not want to go with him, but appellant insisted she was coming with him and walked her to the truck. As appellant was driving, he smeared a steak sandwich in the complainant's face and pointed a gun at her, telling her he would shoot her if she tried to escape. Appellant drove the truck to a subdivision near his house in which roads had been built but no houses constructed. There, he threw another sandwich at her and hit her in the stomach with his fist. He then drove to his house, where he continued to beat her with a belt and a rolled-up newspaper covered with duct tape. The next morning appellant took the complainant to her parents' house.

In ground four, appellant contends the Court of Appeals erred by holding that the lesser included offense of false imprisonment was not raised by the evidence. Whether a charge on a lesser included offense is required is determined by a two-pronged test. First, we must determine whether the offense constitutes a lesser included offense. Tex. Code Crim. Proc. Ann. art. 37.09 provides that an offense is a lesser included offense if, *inter alia:* "It is established by proof of the same or less than all the facts required to establish the commission of the offense charged." Second, the lesser included offense must be raised by the evidence at trial. In other words, there must be some evidence which would permit a rational jury to find that if guilty, the defendant is guilty only of the lesser offense. . . . Anything more than a scintilla of evidence from any source is sufficient to entitle a defendant to submission of the issue. . . .

Under V.T.C.A. Penal Code, Section 20.03, a person commits the offense of kidnapping if he intentionally or knowingly abducts another. " 'Abduct' means to restrain a person with intent to prevent his liberation by: (A) secreting or holding him in a place where he is not likely to be found; or (B) using or threatening to use deadly force." " 'Restrain' means to restrict a person's movements without consent, so as to interfere substantially with his liberty, by moving him from one place to another or by confining him. Restraint is 'without consent' if it is accomplished by force, intimidation, or deception. . . . " V.T.C.A. Penal Code, Section 20.01.

A person commits the offense of false imprisonment if he "intentionally or knowingly restrains another person." V.T.C.A. Penal Code, Section 20.02. Kidnapping is accomplished by abduction, which includes restraint, but false imprisonment is committed by restraint only. Thus, false imprisonment is a lesser included offense of kidnapping and aggravated kidnapping.

The next step of the analysis is to determine whether there was evidence that if guilty, appellant was guilty only of restraining the complainant, without intending to prevent her liberation by either secreting or holding her in a place where she was not likely to be found or using or threatening to use deadly force. The Court of Appeals held appellant was required to rebut or negate both theories of abduction which could have occurred anytime during the ongoing offense. It noted that appellant argued he needed only to refute that he pointed the gun at the complainant in the truck and that he kept her at his house. It held that keeping the complainant isolated at the undeveloped subdivision constituted restraint in a place where she was not likely to be found. It determined that the only evidence which refuted this theory was appellant's testimony that the complainant freely chose to go with him and stayed in the truck of her own free will. However, it reasoned that because this evidence refuted both abduction and restraint, appellant failed to show if guilty, he was guilty of *only* the lesser included offense. . . .

The Court of Appeals' analysis is flawed in two respects. First, the Court of Appeals determined that the subdivision where appellant stopped his truck to throw more food on the complainant and beat her was a place where she was not likely to be found, without considering whether a rational jury could have reached the opposite conclusion under the evidence. In *Saunders* v. *State*, 840 S.W.2d 390 (Tex. Cr. App.1992), this Court held that a lesser included offense may be raised if evidence either affirmatively refutes or negates an element establishing the greater offense, or the evidence on the issue is subject to two different interpretations, and one of the interpretations negates or rebuts an element of the greater. In the instant case, the Court of Appeals did not refer to any facts in the record which demonstrated that the subdivision was or was not a place where the complainant was not likely to be found.

Appellant testified that the complainant's parents lived on Woodforest, which was a main thoroughfare, and the subdivision where appellant lived was off Woodforest, two to three minutes away from the complainant's parents' house. Appellant described the area where he stopped his truck as a few blocks from his house and in his neighborhood. He testified he turned right off of Woodforest going into his neighborhood, and "as we got around the corner there, I had to make another left to cut down to go to my house." He testified the area where he stopped was very small, "two or three streets there, it's all cleaned out." He further explained, "It's developed, there is just no houses there. . . . It's not really what I would call secluded." The complainant testified that the area was "not very far off Woodforest, but it's just a little—just a little bit secluded. There is like some trees and it's right by the school." Pictures of this area were admitted into evidence. From this evidence, a rational jury could have believed that the street where appellant stopped his truck was not a place where the complainant was not likely to be found.

Secondly, by holding that appellant did not raise the lesser included offense because his testimony refuted both the greater and lesser offenses, the Court of Appeals erred under *Bignall*. In that case, this Court held that the defendant was entitled to submission of the lesser included offense of theft based on defense testimony that no one had a gun, despite his evidence showing he was not guilty of any offense. This Court held that a rational jury could have believed that part of the State's evidence that Bignall was involved in the theft, and that part of Bignall's evidence that no one had a gun, and concluded that appellant was guilty only of theft. We pointed out that the defendant's denial of committing any offense does not automatically foreclose submission of a lesser included offense. *Bignall*, 887 S.W.2d at 24.

Applying those principles to this case, a rational jury could have believed the complainant's testimony that she did not go freely with appellant. Appellant testified that he did not threaten to shoot the complainant, did not touch the gun during the drive from her parents' house to his, and did not point the gun at her at any time. He admitted that the gun was lying on the seat of his truck during the offense, but explained that he habitually carried the gun in his truck either on the seat next to him or on the floor next to the gearshift. He testified that when they reached his house, he retrieved the gun from the truck, took it inside as he always did, and placed it on his pinball machine where he often kept it. The complainant testified that she knew appellant kept a gun in his truck, and that it was not unusual for it to be lying on the seat. From this evidence, a rational jury could have found that despite the presence of a gun on the seat, appellant did not use or threaten to use deadly force to prevent the complainant's liberation.

Similarly, the jury could have believed that appellant held the complainant in his house against her will, but believed appellant's house was not a place where the complainant was not likely to be found. Evidence was presented that the complainant had a key to appellant's house, had formerly lived there, and had spent the night there the past three or four nights before the offense. In addition, the complainant's mother testified that when she came home on the night of the offense and found the house in disarray and her daughter missing, she became afraid for her daughter's safety and drove by appellant's house. From this evidence, a jury could have rationally concluded that the complainant was restrained at appellant's house, but his house was not a place where she was not likely to be found. In sum, the jury

could have found that appellant had restrained but not abducted the complainant, and thus was guilty only of false imprisonment. Therefore, the Court of Appeals erred by holding this lesser included offense was not raised by the evidence.

Accordingly, we reverse the judgment of the Court of Appeals and remand the case to that court to conduct a harm analysis pursuant to Tex. Code Crim. Proc. Ann. art. 36.19. Appellant's grounds for review one, two, and three are dismissed without prejudice.

McCormick, Presiding Judge, dissenting.

I dissent. The majority disagrees with the Court of Appeals' analysis on whether appellant was entitled to a jury instruction on false imprisonment. See *Schweinle* v. *State*, 893 S.W.2d 708, 714-15 (Tex. App.–Houston [1st Dist.] 1995). The issue in this case is whether there is some evidence in the record that would permit a jury rationally to find that appellant is guilty only of false imprisonment; or, in other words, whether there is some evidence in the record that would permit a jury rationally to find that appellant is guilty only of intentionally or knowingly restraining the victim, without her consent, so as to interfere substantially with her liberty, by moving her from one place to another or by confining her.

In support of its kidnapping theories, the State presented the victim's testimony, from which the jury reasonably could have inferred that appellant's act of restraining the victim was accompanied by a *specific intent* to prevent the victim's liberation either by secreting the victim in a place where she was not likely to be found or by using or threatening to use deadly force. See, e.g., *Mason* v. *State*, 905 S.W.2d 570, 579 (Tex. Cr. App.1995) (Clinton, J., dissenting) (to prove kidnapping, evidence need not show an actual secreting or use or threat of deadly force). The victim's testimony raised no fact issues on whether appellant was guilty only of false imprisonment. See, e.g., *Ramos* v. *State*, 865 S.W.2d 463, 465 (Tex. Cr. App. 1993).

The victim's testimony establishes appellant's guilt only of kidnapping because it shows appellant's specific intent to prevent her liberation either by secreting her in a place where she was not likely to be found or by using or threatening to use deadly force. The victim's testimony neither "refutes or negates other evidence establishing the greater offense" nor is it subject to "different interpretations" with regard to "every theory of kidnapping." See *Saunders* v. *State*, 840 S.W.2d 390, 391 (Tex. Cr. App.1992); *Schweinle*, 893 S.W.2d at 715.

In addition, appellant testified and claimed he committed no offense. He testified the victim willingly went with him and he never threatened her with the gun. Appellant did not testify that he "intentionally or knowingly restrained the victim, without her consent, so as to interfere substantially with her liberty, by moving her from one place to another or by confining her." See Sections 20.02 & 20.01(1). Appellant's testimony raised no fact issues on whether he was guilty only of false imprisonment. See *Ramos*, 865 S.W.2d at 465.

The majority apparently finds the victim's and appellant's testimony either "refutes or negates other evidence establishing the greater offense" or is subject to "different interpretations." The majority reasons that a rational jury could believe from the victim's and appellant's testimony "that the street where appellant stopped his truck" and appellant's "house" were not places "where the complainant was not likely to be found" thereby negating appellant's specific intent to prevent the victim's liberation by secreting her in a place where she was not likely to be found. Assuming this is true, this evidence does not "refute or negate" appellant's specific intent to prevent the victim's liberation by using or threatening to use deadly force. See *Schweinle*, 893 S.W.2d at 715 (requiring evidence refuting "every theory of kidnapping").

However, the majority decides "a rational jury could have believed the complainant's testimony that she did not go freely with appellant without believing that

Appellant threatened her with the gun." However, the victim's testimony was clear and positive that appellant threatened her with the gun. See *Schweinle*, 893 S.W.2d at 708 (victim testified appellant threatened her with the gun). The victim's testimony that appellant threatened her with the gun does not "refute or negate" appellant's specific intent to prevent her liberation by threatening to use deadly force nor is it subject to "different interpretations."

Under the majority's analysis, appellant would have been entitled to a jury instruction on false imprisonment *even had he not testified and denied threatening the victim with the gun.* However, simply because the jury could disbelieve part of the victim's testimony is not the same as "evidence which refutes or negates other evidence establishing the greater offense" or evidence that is subject to "different interpretations." See *Saunders*, 840 S.W.2d at 391; see also *Bignall v. State*, 887 S.W.2d 21, 24 (Tex. Cr. App. 1994) (a defendant is entitled to an instruction on a lesser included offense if evidence from any source "*affirmatively* raises the issue") (emphasis supplied) And, I do not believe this would be a close case had appellant not testified and denied threatening the victim with the gun. . . .

Because the majority's holding that appellant was entitled to a jury instruction on false imprisonment depends solely upon plucking a statement out of appellant's testimony and examining it in a vacuum, I dissent. See *Ramos*, 865 S.W.2d at 465; *Godsey*, 719 S.W.2d at 584.

[footnotes omitted]

WHAT DO *YOU* THINK?

1. What are the differences between false imprisonment and kidnapping?
2. Do you agree with the dissenting opinion that, under the facts, no reasonable person could have found the defendant guilty only of false imprisonment?
3. Of what importance is the issue of whether the victim was released in a safe place?
4. Based on the facts contained in the court's opinion, did the accused commit any offense other than kidnapping and false imprisonment? If so, what was it?

WHAT CONSTITUTES THE CRIME OF STALKING?   CAPSTONE CASE

Clements v. State
Court of Appeals for the First District of Texas
February 24, 2000
No. 01-99-00293

After a trial before the court, the trial judge sentenced appellant to 12 months probation for stalking. Appellant contends (1) the evidence is legally and factually insufficient to support his conviction for stalking, (2) the stalking statute is unconstitutional, (3) the trial court erred in admitting evidence about events occurring before the effective date of the stalking statute, and (4) the trial court erred in admitting evidence about events occurring on dates other than the date of the offense alleged in the information. We affirm.

FACTUAL BACKGROUND

Nathan and Jennifer Clements were married in September 1995, after a six-year courtship. Both were active members of the Christadelphian Church throughout their relationship. During the summer of 1996, Jennifer claims Nathan became possessive and controlling. Although he knew they frightened Jennifer, Nathan purchased guns and often left the guns on Jennifer's pillow. Nathan also scratched the name of one of Jennifer's male friends onto a bullet and told Jennifer that she could

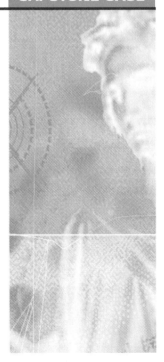

either give the bullet to her friend herself or Nathan would give it to him from the barrel of a gun. In November 1996, Nathan accused Jennifer of having affairs. Nathan stated that if he ever caught her with someone else, he would not hesitate to use one of his weapons.

In December 1996, Nathan told Jennifer she had 10 minutes to decide whether she would quit her job or be thrown out of their apartment. Jennifer then packed her things and left. Shortly after Jennifer left the apartment she began receiving phone calls from Nathan at her place of employment, Texas Instruments. From December 8, 1996, to January 1997, Jennifer received 26 phone messages from Nathan. Also during that time, Jennifer twice called Nathan to ask him to stop calling and harassing her. Jennifer testified that the telephone calls caused her to be in fear for her safety.

On December 18, 1996, Jennifer went to their apartment to retrieve her belongings. She hired a police officer to escort her because she was afraid for her safety. Although Nathan was not at the apartment, shortly after she left, Nathan left a message for Jennifer that he knew she brought a police officer with her to the apartment.

On December 19, 1996, Jennifer saw Nathan as she was leaving her new apartment. Nathan pulled next to her in his vehicle and began to honk his horn and yell at her. She drove to the Meadow Place police department because she was afraid Nathan would hurt her. At the police station, Nathan got out of his vehicle and began hitting Jennifer's window. Nathan could see Jennifer was in a hysterical state. Jennifer testified that she was afraid she would suffer bodily injury or death.

Because no one from the police station came out to offer assistance, Jennifer then drove to her place of employment because she knew there would be security personnel available. Nathan continued to follow Jennifer to Texas Instruments. Jennifer testified that Nathan was about an inch from her vehicle while she was driving and that he did not follow any traffic rules. Upon arriving at Texas Instruments, Nathan followed her around the parking lot at high rates of speed until Jennifer was able to contact a security officer.

Alice Wooten, a security officer at Texas Instruments, observed two vehicles traveling at high rates of speed in the Texas Instruments parking lot. When Wooten approached Jennifer she noticed Jennifer was crying, shaking, and appeared terrified. Jennifer told Wooten that her husband was following her. Nathan left Texas Instruments before Wooten could speak with him.

In January 1997, Nathan filed an answer to Jennifer's original petition for divorce. In his original answer to Jennifer's original petition for divorce, Nathan acknowledged Jennifer was in fear. Nathan also stated only death or the return of Christ would end their marriage.

On February 18, 1997, Jennifer saw Nathan at the gym where they both had memberships. Although Nathan did not speak to Jennifer, he stared at her for 30 minutes while she did aerobics. Jennifer testified that his actions caused her to be afraid. About a week later, Jennifer once again saw Nathan at the gym. Nathan again watched Jennifer, and it caused her to be afraid. Jennifer testified that Nathan arrived at the gym after she did because when she left, Nathan's car was parked directly beside hers, although his car was not there when she arrived. Jennifer also testified that Nathan did not regularly attend the gym and did not workout while he was there.

In March 1997, Jennifer and a male friend saw Nathan drive by the front of her apartment as they were leaving. When Nathan saw Jennifer he stopped and began to yell at Jennifer and her friend. Jennifer testified that this behavior also caused her to fear bodily injury or death.

Jennifer next saw Nathan on April 4, 1997, in the parking lot of her apartment. Nathan was running through the parking lot toward the swimming pool area of her apartment. Jennifer ran to her apartment and called the police because she was afraid Nathan would hurt her. Jennifer testified that this incident placed her in fear of bodily injury or death.

Throughout this time period Jennifer was aware that according to his faith, Nathan believed he would not be permitted to remarry until Jennifer died, even after they legally divorced. As a result of Nathan's actions, Jennifer requested that her employer transfer her to another location. Nathan was convicted of stalking in March 1999.

THE INFORMATION

The information alleged the following:

> *NATHAN BRIAN CLEMENTS, hereafter styled the Defendant heretofore on or about APRIL 4, 1997, . . . did then and there pursuant to the same scheme and course of conduct directed specifically at another person, to-wit: JENNIFER CLEMENTS, hereinafter referred to as complainant, knowingly engage in conduct, to-wit: following said complainant, and said defendant knew and reasonably believed said complainant regarded said conduct as threatening bodily injury and death for said complainant, and said conduct did cause said complainant to be placed in fear of bodily injury and death, and said conduct did cause a reasonable person to fear bodily injury and death for herself . . . pursuant to the same scheme and course of conduct directed specifically at another person, to-wit: JENNIFER CLEMENTS, hereinafter referred to as complainant, knowingly engage in conduct, to-wit: following said complainant, and said defendant knew and reasonably believed said complainant regarded said conduct as threatening bodily injury and death for said complainant, and said conduct did cause complainant to be placed in fear of bodily injury and death, and said conduct would cause a reasonable person to fear bodily injury and death for herself.*

THE STALKING STATUTE

The current stalking statute, under which appellant was prosecuted, provides:
(a) A person commits an offense if the person, on more than one occasion and pursuant to the same scheme or course of conduct that is directed specifically at another person, knowingly engages in conduct, including following the person, that:
    (1) the actor knows or reasonably believes the other person will regard as threatening:
        (A) bodily injury or death for the other person;
        (B) bodily injury or death for a member of the other person's family or household;
        or
        (C) that an offense will be committed against the other person's property;
    (2) causes the other person or member of the other person's family or household to be placed in fear of bodily injury or death or fear that an offense will be committed against the other person's property; and
    (3) would cause a reasonable person to fear:
        (A) bodily injury or death for herself;
        (B) bodily injury or death for a member of the person's family or household; or
        (C) that an offense will be committed against the person's property.
Tex. Penal Code Ann. §§ 42.072 (Vernon Supp. 1999). This statute became effective on January 23, 1997.

LEGAL SUFFICIENCY

In a legal sufficiency review, we examine the evidence in the light most favorable to the verdict. *Jackson v. Virginia*, 443 U.S. 307, 319, 99 S. Ct. 2781, 2789 (1979). We must determine whether a rational trier of fact could have found all essential elements of the crime beyond a reasonable doubt.

Appellant contends the evidence is legally insufficient for three reasons: (1) the information upon which the court proceeded to trial did not allege more than one occasion, (2) the trial court erroneously admitted and considered incidents that occurred on dates other than April 4, 1997, the date alleged in the information, and (3) even considering the evidence in a light most favorable to the prosecution, no rational trier of fact could have found Nathan guilty.

More Than One Occasion

First, Nathan argues that the information upon which the court proceeded to trial did not allege more than one occasion as required by the stalking statute. Tex. Penal Code Ann. §§ 42.072. However, any error in the charging instrument must be objected to prior to the date on which the trial on the merits commences. Tex. Code Crim. P. Ann. art. 1.14 (Vernon Supp. 1999) Thus, because Nathan did not raise the defect in the information until after the State rested its case-in-chief, the issue is waived and he is precluded from raising it on appeal.

Additionally, the State provided evidence that Nathan committed the offense of stalking on a number of different dates, including February 18, 1997, February 25, 1997, March 29, 1997, and April 4, 1997. All of these dates are after the effective date of the statute. . . .

Dates Other Than April 4, 1997

Secondly, Nathan contends the trial court erred in admitting and considering incidents that occurred prior to the date alleged in the information, April 4, 1997. We disagree. The State was required to prove Jennifer was placed in fear of bodily injury or death at the time of Nathan's conduct. Tex. Penal Code Ann. §§ 42.072. Therefore, the incidents that occurred prior to January 23, 1997, the effective date of the stalking statute, and April 4, 1997, the date alleged in the information, establish Jennifer's state of mind at the time of the offense. These events did not, however, establish the elements of the stalking statute. Only the events that occurred after the effective date of the statute established the elements of the offense.

The Evidence

Finally, Nathan argues that, even considering the evidence in a light favorable to the prosecution, no rational trier of fact could have found appellant guilty where: (1) Jennifer said Nathan did not follow her, as alleged in the information, (2) there is no evidence Nathan ever threatened to injure or kill Jennifer, (3) there is no evidence Nathan ever harmed Jennifer, (4) there is no evidence Jennifer ever communicated to Nathan, or that Nathan should have known his actions were regarded by Jennifer as threatening, (5) there is no evidence Nathan ever knew Jennifer was present on April 4, 1997, (6) there is no evidence that Nathan did anything to frighten Jennifer on April 4, 1997, and (7) there is no evidence Nathan's actions would cause a reasonable person to be placed in fear of injury or death.

Jennifer Said Nathan Did Not Follow Her, as Alleged in the Information

The current stalking statute does not define the term "follow," so we apply the plain meaning of the term. *Lane* v. *State*, 933 S.W.2d 504, 514 (Tex. Crim. App. 1996). We conclude that by repeatedly appearing at Jennifer's apartment when he did not reside there, and by causing himself to be where he knew Jennifer would be and engaging in conduct that he knew would cause Jennifer to be placed in fear, Nathan's conduct falls within the plain meaning of the term "follow."

There Is No Evidence Nathan Ever Harmed Jennifer

The stalking statute does not require that Jennifer be harmed by Nathan.

There Is Legally Sufficient Evidence Jennifer Communicated to Nathan, and that Nathan Knew His Actions Were Regarded by Jennifer as Threatening
On more than one occasion, Jennifer asked Nathan to stop harassing her. Additionally, in his response to Jennifer's petition for divorce, filed January 9, 1997, Nathan acknowledged Jennifer was in fear. Moreover, Nathan saw that Jennifer was hysterical, crying, and shaking after he followed her to the police department and to Texas Instruments. Finally, Nathan was aware that Jennifer hired a police officer to accompany her to remove her things from their apartment. This shows not only that Nathan should have known Jennifer regarded his actions as threatening, but that she communicated to him the threatening nature of his actions.

There Is Legally Sufficient Evidence Nathan Knew Jennifer Was Present on April 4, 1997
Jennifer testified that she observed Nathan running toward the swimming pool area next to her apartment on April 4, 1997. Because Nathan was running near the area in which her apartment was located, it is reasonable to assume he was aware that Jennifer was present and that he was trying to reach her.

There Is Legally Sufficient Evidence Nathan Frightened Jennifer on April 4, 1997
Jennifer testified that she saw Nathan run across the parking lot toward the swimming pool area near her apartment on April 4, 1997, and that this caused her to be in fear of bodily injury or death. Jennifer called the police upon returning to her apartment.

Jennifer also testified that she had seen Nathan several other times at her apartment complex, and on at least one of those occasions he yelled at her. Jennifer testified that on those other occasions, Nathan saw her become hysterical and cry and shake. As such, there is legally sufficient evidence that Nathan frightened Jennifer on April 4, 1997.

There Is Legally Sufficient Evidence Nathan's Actions Would Cause a Reasonable Person to Be Placed in Fear of Injury or Death
Considering the pattern of behavior Nathan exhibited, such as leaving numerous phone messages for Jennifer, appearing several times at her apartment and other places where he knew she would be, and engaging in conduct that he knew would frighten her, we find a reasonable person would also have been placed in fear of bodily injury or death.

We conclude a rational fact finder could have found all the essential elements of the crime of stalking beyond a reasonable doubt. As such, we find the evidence to be legally sufficient to support Nathan's conviction for stalking.

We overrule point of error one.

FACTUAL SUFFICIENCY
In a factual sufficiency review, we consider all the evidence giving deference to the fact finder's decision. *Clewis* v. *State*, 922 S.W.2d 126, 133 (Tex. Crim. App. 1996). We set aside the verdict only if it is so contrary to the overwhelming weight of the evidence as to be clearly wrong and unjust.

Nathan asserts the evidence is factually insufficient because he never threatened to harm Jennifer and never hurt her. He also contends there is no evidence Jennifer ever communicated to him that he frightened her. As such, Nathan argues there is no evidence that his actions caused Jennifer, or a reasonable person, to be in fear.

Having reviewed the entire record, we conclude Nathan's conviction for stalking is not contrary to the overwhelming weight of the evidence as to be clearly wrong and unjust. As such, we find the evidence to be factually sufficient to support Nathan's conviction.

We overrule point of error two.

CONSTITUTIONALITY OF STALKING STATUTE

In point of error three, Nathan contends the stalking statute is unconstitutional. Specifically, Nathan argues that the statute is unconstitutionally vague under the First Amendment and is overbroad and impinges upon protected speech and the marriage relationship.

In 1993, the Court of Criminal Appeals held the stalking statute in effect at that time was unconstitutionally vague on its face. *Long* v. *State*, 931 S.W.2d 285, 287 (Tex. Crim. App. 1996). Specifically, the court found the conduct requirement of the law was vague; the reasonable person standard could not be read into the statute; the report and threat requirements did not save the statute; and the statute could not be narrowly construed and legislative intent kept. The court provided several possible solutions to the legislature in order to correct the problems.

In 1997, with the *Long* decision in mind, the legislature enacted the stalking statute under which Nathan was convicted. Tex. Penal Code Ann. §§ 42.072. The legislature incorporated many of the suggestions made by the Court of Criminal Appeals in *Long* v. *State*. For example, the statute now contains a reasonable person standard. Additionally, the conduct provision, the language which the court found unconstitutionally vague, was stricken from the statute. Former Tex. Penal Code Ann. §§ 42.07(a)(7)(A) (Vernon 1994). Also, the 1997 statute requires the illegal conduct to be part of the same scheme or course of conduct, which satisfied the court's concern that there be a nexus between the threat and other, harassing conduct.

Vagueness

All laws carry a presumption of validity. *Ex parte Benavides*, 801 S.W.2d 535, 537 (Tex. App.–Houston [1st Dist.] 1990, *no pet.*). However, unless criminal laws are sufficiently clear, they are considered unconstitutionally vague. *Grayned* v. *City of Rockford*, 408 U.S. 104, 108–09, 92 S. Ct. 2294, 2298–99 (1972); *Long*, 931 S.W.2d at 287–88. The party challenging a statute has the burden to establish its unconstitutionality. *Ex parte Granviel*, 561 S.W.2d 503, 511 (Tex. Crim. App. 1978).

To pass a vagueness challenge, a criminal statute must give a person of ordinary intelligence a reasonable opportunity to know what is prohibited. *Grayned*, 408 U.S. at 108, 92 S. Ct. at 2298–99. Further, the law must establish guidelines for law enforcement. Where First Amendment freedoms are implicated, the law must be sufficiently definite to avoid chilling protected expression. If an act implicates First Amendment guarantees, the doctrine of vagueness demands a greater degree of specificity than in other contexts. A criminal law may be held facially invalid even though it may not be unconstitutional as applied to a defendant's conduct. *Gooding* v. *Wilson*, 405 U.S. 518, 521, 92 S. Ct. 1103, 1105 (1972).

The language of the 1997 statute is not unconstitutionally vague. We find this statute to thoroughly specify what conduct is prohibited and subject to prosecution. For example, one way in which a person can be convicted of stalking is by engaging in conduct he knows or reasonably believes will be regarded by the other person as threatening bodily injury or death. Tex. Penal Code Ann. §§ 42.072(a)(1)(A). It can also be an offense under the statute for a person to knowingly engage in conduct that would cause a reasonable person to fear bodily injury or death. Tex. Penal Code Ann. §§ 42.072(a)(3)(A). Therefore, the stalker is on notice of the prohibited conduct if he knows or believes the other person will regard that conduct as threatening bodily injury or death. As such, the previous vagueness problem no longer exists.

Overbreadth

A statute, even if clear and precise, is overbroad if in its reach it prohibits constitutionally protected conduct. *Grayned*, 408 U.S. at 114, 92 S. Ct. at 2302; *Rahmani v. State*, 748 S.W.2d 618, 621 (Tex. App.–Houston [1st Dist.] 1988, *pet. ref'd*). The broad statement of law, however, is tempered by the following two corollaries: (1) for a facial overbreadth challenge to succeed, the enactment must reach a substantial amount of protected conduct; and (2) even protected speech may be regulated to some degree by the State. *Rahmani*, 748 S.W.2d at 621.

Nathan argues the current stalking statute prohibits his constitutionally protected conduct of attempting to "save" his marriage. We disagree. The current stalking statute specifically prohibits conduct, such as conduct that causes another person to be placed in fear of bodily injury or death. "While conduct does not lose First Amendment protection merely because the actor intends to annoy the recipient, such conduct is much less likely to enjoy protection where the actor intends to place the recipient in fear of death or bodily injury. If the First Amendment can be removed from the arena, a stalking statute can be evaluated under more deferential due process standards, and is thus more likely to survive scrutiny." *Long*, 931 S.W.2d at 293. Here, Nathan was not engaged in constitutionally protected conduct because his conduct placed Jennifer in fear of bodily injury or death.

The court also suggested that there should be a nexus between the two or more instances of conduct so that the stalker is not denied notice of what is prohibited. The legislature addressed this concern by requiring that there be more than one isolated episode. Tex. Penal Code Ann. §§ 42.072. Specifically, the statute requires that the conduct occur on more than one occasion and pursuant to the same scheme or course of conduct.

The *Long* opinion also addresses the language in the 1993 statute "annoy" and "alarm." *Long*, 931 S.W.2d at 296. The *Long* court indicated that acts or speech that "annoys" and "alarms" another is often constitutionally protected. The legislature removed the terms "annoy" and "alarm" and replaced them with conduct that causes the other person to be placed in fear of death or bodily injury, thus removing the vague language. Tex. Penal Code Ann. §§ 42.072.

We hold the current stalking statute to be constitutional.

We overrule point of error three. . . . [Discussion on remaining points of error omitted.]

We affirm.

Michael H. Schneider, Chief Justice

WHAT DO *YOU* THINK?
1. What are the elements of the crime of stalking under the statute discussed in this case?
2. Do you agree with the court of appeals that the statute is not unconstitutionally vague?
3. Is the evidence in this case sufficient to support a "stalking" conviction?

NOTES

1. Adapted from *Ortiz* v. *State*, 470 S.E. 2d 874, 876 (Ga. 1996).
2. California Penal Code, Section 240.
3. Rollin M. Perkins and Ronald N. Boyce, *Criminal Law*, 3rd ed. (Mineola, NY: Foundation Press, 1982), p. 151, citing *State* v. *Jones*, 133 S.C. 167, 130 S.E. 747 (1925).
4. California Penal Code, Section 240.
5. *People* v. *James*, 9 Cal. App. 2d 162 (1935).
6. *State* v. *Bowers*, 239 Kan. 417, 721 P.2d 268 (1986).
7. *People* v. *Ross*, 831 P.2d 1310, 1314 (Colo. 1992).
8. *Commonwealth* v. *Davis*, 406 N.E.2d 417, 419 (Mass. App. Ct. 1980).
9. Joshua Dressler, *Understanding Criminal Law,* 2nd ed. (New York: Matthew Bender, 1995), p. 350.

10. *Fox* v. *State,* 34 Ohio St. 377, 380 (1878).

11. *State* v. *Wilson,* 218 Or. 575, 346 P.2d 115 (1959).

12. "Woman Kills Ex-Boyfriend, Self," Associated Press, January 22, 1997.

13. California Penal Code, Section 646.9.

14. Ibid.

15. *Cyberstalking: A New Challenge for Law Enforcement and Industry* (Washington, D.C.: U.S. Attorney General's Office, August 1999).

16. Ibid.

17. Ibid.

18. *Bowers,* 239 Kan. 417, 721 P.2d 268.

19. *Fish* v. *Michigan,* 62 F.2d 659 (6th Cir. 1933).

20. Texas Penal Code, Section 22.01, subparagraphs (1) and (3).

21. *State* v. *Monroe,* 28 S.E. 547 (N.C. 1897).

22. Model Penal Code, Section 211.1.

23. Kansas Statutes Annotated, 21-3414(a)(1)(A).

24. Florida Statutes, Section 784.045.

25. *Dixon* v. *State,* 1992 Fla. App. LEXIS 2401; 17 Fla. L. W. D. 700 (1992). The original decision was rendered by a three-member panel of the appellate court. The full court later ruled that "bare hands . . . are not deadly weapons for purposes of alleging or proving the crime of aggravated battery."

26. In November, 1993, a jury found Bobbitt not guilty of raping his wife.

27. Harvey Wallace and Cliff Roberson, *Principles of Criminal Law* (White Plains, NY: Longman, 1996) p. 164.

28. California Penal Code, Section 203.

29. California Penal Code, Section 205.

30. Model Penal Code, Section 211.1.

31. California Penal Code, Section 206.

32. Mary P. Koss, Christine A. Gidycz, and Nadine Wisniewski, "The Scope of Rape: Incidence and Prevalence of Sexual Aggression and Victimization in a National Sample of Higher Education Students," *Journal of Counseling and Clinical Psychology,* Vol. 55 (1987), p. 162.

33. Joseph R. Nolan and Jacqueline M. Nolan-Haley, *Black's Law Dictionary: Definitions of the Terms and Phrases of American and English Jurisprudence, Ancient and Modern,* 6th ed. (St. Paul, MN: West Publishing Co., 1990), p. 212.

34. East's Pleas of the Crown 436 (1803).

35. *State* v. *Bell,* 90 N.M. 134, 560 P.2d 925, 931 (1977).

36. Some legal scholars have noted that it is not the sexual component of spousal rape that is illegal, but the violence with which it is perpetrated.

37. Maryland Code, Art. 27, Section 463(a)(1).

38. *State* v. *Rusk,* 424 A.2d 720 (Md. 1981), citing *Hazel* v. *State,* 221 Md. 464, 157 A.2d 922 (1960).

39. American Law Institute, *Model Penal Code and Commentaries* (1985).

40. Utah Code Annotated, Section 76-402.

41. "Jury Convicts Condom Rapist," *USA Today,* May 14, 1993, p. 3A.

42. *State* v. *Randolph,* 528 P.2d 1008 (Wash. 1974).

43. Model Penal Code, Section 213.6 (1).

44. *People* v. *Liberta,* 474 N.E.2d 567 (N.Y. 1984).

45. *People* v. *Hernandez,* 18 Cal. App. 3d 651, 96 Cal. Rptr. 71 (1971).

46. *People* v. *Rincon-Pineda,* 14 Cal. 3d at 951–952.

47. "Judge Gives Max in Burned Alive Case," United Press, December 10, 1996.

48. *State* v. *Padilla,* 474 P.2d 821 (Ariz. 1970).

49. Florida Penal Code, Section 787.01.

50. Ibid.

51. Texas Penal Code, Section 20.01(1)(a).

52. *State* v. *Jacobs,* 380 P.2d 998 (Ariz. 1952).

53. *People* v. *Adams,* 192 N.W.2d 19 (Mich. 1971).

54. 18 U.S.C.A., Section 1201(a).

55. 18 U.S.C.A., Section 1203.

56. 18 U.S.C.A., Section 1202.

57. *People* v. *Agnew,* 16 Cal. 2d 655 (1940).

58. *Dupler* v. *Seubert,* 69 Wis. 2d 373, 230 N.W.2d 626, 631 (1975).

59. Florida Penal Code, section 787.02.

60. Ibid.

61. 28 U.S.C.A., Section 1738A.

62. Florida Penal Code, Section 787.01(2).

10

Legal and Social Dimensions of Property and Computer Crimes

It is not a crime to make a fool of another by delivering fewer goods than ordered.

—*Rex* v. *Wheatly*, 97 E.R. 746 (1761)

More money has been stolen at the point of a fountain pen than at the point of a gun.

—Woody Guthrie

As surely as the future will bring new forms of technology, it will bring new forms of crime. . . .

—Cynthia Manson and Charles Ardai[1]

CHAPTER OUTLINE

KEY CONCEPTS

acquisitive offenses

arson

asportation

blackmail

burglary

claim of right

compounding a crime

computer crime

computer fraud

computer tampering

computer trespass

constructive entry

conversion

crimes of misappropriation

criminal mischief

criminal simulation

criminal trespass

cybercrime

embezzlement

extortion

false pretenses

fixtures

forgery

identity theft

intangible property

intellectual property

larceny

looting

obtaining property by false
   pretenses

personal property

personal trespass by
   computer

real property

receiving stolen property

robbery

tangible property

theft

theft of computer services

trespassory taking

uttering

wrongful acquisition
   crimes

AFTER READING THIS CHAPTER YOU SHOULD:

▷ Be able to enumerate the various "acquisitive offenses," or theft crimes.

▷ Know the difference between larceny, embezzlement, robbery, and burglary.

▷ Know the difference between "possession" and "custody."

▷ Be able to explain the concept of a "trespassory taking" in larceny.

▷ Be able to explain the difference between tangible and intangible property.

▷ Understand the difference between possession, ownership, and mere custody (of property).

▷ Know the difference between embezzlement and the crime of false pretenses.

▷ Be able to explain the differences between forgery, uttering, and criminal simulation.

▷ Be able to explain the difference between robbery, extortion, and blackmail.

▷ Be able to explain the concept of identity theft and know how it relates to other acquisitive offenses.

▷ Understand the rationale behind the creation of consolidated theft statutes in some jurisdictions.

▷ Be able to explain the entry requirement and the concept of constructive entry in the crime of burglary.

▷ Be able to describe the five types of computer crime and list the elements of each.

INTRODUCTION

On July 29, 1999, Wisconsin resident Waverly C. Burns, 43, was sentenced to twenty-one months imprisonment and three years of supervised release by United States District Court Judge Barbara B. Crabb. Burns had pleaded guilty to identity theft,

CRIMINAL LAW IN THE NEWS

Police: Woman Had 350 Stolen Identities

Accused of Using Records to Charge Lavish Lifestyle

TAMPA, Fla.—A 28-year-old data entry clerk who had access to sensitive personal identification records has been accused of stealing the identities of more than 350 people in an effort to support a lavish lifestyle, police said.

Elnetta Denise Brown was arrested after trying to buy some goods with a fraudulent credit card at a Tampa-area Sears store. Inside her car, police found what they described as 350 "complete identities," including victim's names, addresses, Social Security numbers and dates of birth, authorities said.

Police said the former "confidential clerk" at a Tampa-area drug-testing lab may have used only about 20 of the identities to falsely obtain credit cards, though there may be more victims. Police said they do not know how much money was falsely charged.

"There's no telling how many people there are out there who have had their identity stolen," said Sgt. Rob Reder of the Tampa Police Department. "There's still more that's going to come of this."

A break in the case

The arrest Wednesday was the culmination of a more than two-year-long probe of identity thefts in the Tampa area, police said.

The big break in the case came in December of last year when Brown allegedly tried to buy a family Christmas portrait with a fraudulent credit card. Store workers who suspected the card was stolen noted Brown's license plate, which was emblazoned with her last name, and called police.

Reder said that while it is not known how much Brown stole, the car police found Brown at is a 2000 model Chevrolet minivan.

Brown was charged with 35 counts of fraudulently using an identity to get credit cards. She is free on $5,000 bail.

Source: Todd Venezia, "Police: Woman Had 350 Stolen Identities; Accused of Using Records to Charge Lavish Lifestyle," APB News. March 24, 2000. Reprinted with permission.

and was sentenced under the 1998 federal Identity Theft and Assumption Deterrence Act.[2] The law, which became effective October 30, 1998, criminalizes the unauthorized use of another person's identification with the intent to commit another crime. Under the law, anyone who obtains money or property valued at $1,000 or more over a one-year period can be sentenced to up to fifteen years in prison.

Burns had gained employment with Clean Power in Madison, Wisconsin, by using the identity of a man named James W. Clark. Through his job, Burns gained access to the Tenney Building, which houses the offices of the Wisconsin Supreme Court. On January 3, 1999, Burns entered the court's offices and took six computer monitors owned by the state of Wisconsin. His conviction resulted from an investigation conducted by the Social Security Administration's Office of Inspector General and the Wisconsin Capitol Police.

THEFT CRIMES

The modern concept of identity theft is very new, and laws specifically targeting it are only a few years old. On the other hand, the law of **theft** has a long and colorful history. Crimes of theft are generally property crimes, and this chapter discusses a variety of property crimes, including larceny, burglary, criminal trespass, arson, computer crimes involving misappropriation, and, of course, identity theft.

As one author notes, "Theft is a general term embracing a wide variety of misconduct by which a person is improperly deprived of his property. The purpose of theft law is to promote security of property by threatening aggressors with punishment."[3] For purposes of this chapter, we will change this definition of theft slightly, to read "a general term embracing a wide variety of misconduct by which a person is *unlawfully* deprived of his or her property."

THEFT
a general term embracing a wide variety of misconduct by which a person is unlawfully deprived of his or her property.

Crimes of theft are sometimes called **acquisitive offenses, wrongful acquisition crimes,** or **crimes of misappropriation,** since they involve the unlawful acquiring or appropriation of someone else's property. *Commentaries* to the Model Penal Code notes that laws defining theft as crime are the result of "a long history of expansion of the role of the criminal law in protecting property."[4] Although common law originally concerned itself only with crimes of violence, the law expanded, through application of the principle of trespass, "to cover all taking of another's property from his possession without his consent, even though no force was used."[5]

At first, only **larceny** was punished as a crime under common law. Larceny was defined as "the wrongful taking and carrying away by any person of the mere personal goods of another, from any place, with a felonious intent to convert them to his own use, and make them his own property, without the consent of the owner."[6] Larceny was a capital crime under common law.

Under early law, only personal belongings, such as tools, livestock, money, clothes, and household items, could be stolen. Real estate, in the sense of land and all that it naturally contained, was not thought subject to larceny, even though it could be temporarily "converted" for another's use. Squatters and those who trespassed on property that did not belong to them were dealt with under laws against poaching and laws against trespass—but were not said to have "stolen" the land. Even one who severed items (such as ore, trees, or crops) from the land of another and carried them away was not subject to prosecution for the crime of larceny. In contrast, once a crop had been harvested, or a tree cut down and made into lumber, then it was considered to be in the possession of its rightful owner, and any unlawful carrying away of the material constituted larceny.

Similarly, under common law, anyone who killed a wild animal on land belonging to another might be guilty of the crime of poaching but could not be convicted of larceny even if he carried the animal away—since the landowner did not have true possession of the animal before it was killed. The stealing of domestic animals, on the other hand, was larceny, since carrying them away removed them from the possession of their rightful owners. Early common law distinguished between the stealing of animals of a higher nature, such as cows, pigs, horses, and chickens (which was larceny) and the stealing of animals of a base nature, such as cats, dogs, and monkeys (which was not larceny). These distinctions were, of course, entirely artificial, but they served to limit use of the death penalty to more serious cases of theft.

The early law of theft rarely extended beyond larceny. Outright cheating and the misappropriation of goods entrusted into the care of another were not regarded as crimes, although civil remedies existed under common law by which proper ownership of misappropriated goods might be restored. Two hundred years ago, for example, one English court held that "[i]t is not a crime to make a fool of another by delivering fewer goods than ordered,"[7] even if the buyer trusts the seller and only later finds out that he or she has been duped. The watchword of the day was *caveat emptor,* or "buyer beware," and one who shortchanged another was generally not criminally liable under early common law.

Judged by today's standards, common law might seem inadequate. It should be understood, however, that at the time "business transactions were relatively few and comparatively simple. Individuals had time to make their own investigations and they usually did so, and it was not considered sound business or good common sense to rely on the mere oral statement of another."[8] In other words, in earlier times the burden of ensuring accurate transactions lay upon the purchaser, not the seller, and it was assumed that buyers would carefully watch any measuring process involved in the transaction, and that they would take the time to inspect the number and quality of goods they received before paying for them.

As commerce increased, criminal law expanded to punish new forms of theft. By then, however, the law regarding larceny had become so fixed that new crimes had

ACQUISITIVE OFFENSES
also **wrongful acquisition crimes,** and **crimes of misappropriation;** those that involve the unlawful acquiring or appropriation of someone else's property. Crimes of theft (larceny, extortion, embezzlement, false pretenses, robbery, and the receiving of stolen property).

LARCENY
the trespassory or wrongful taking and carrying away (asportation) of the personal property of another with intent to steal.

to be invented to fill the gaps. Crimes such as "embezzlement," "extortion," and "obtaining property by false pretenses" came to be recognized. A fundamental principle of common law crimes against property was that they concerned themselves with the wrongful acquisition of property, and the terms "wrongful acquisition crimes" and "acquisitive offenses" came into vogue.

Most acquisitive offenses, including larceny, embezzlement, false pretenses, robbery, and the receiving of stolen property, required such precise elements that early courts were slow to expand those crimes to cover novel and emerging situations. Even today, courts and legislatures have difficulty fitting certain offenses, such as computer and high-technology crimes, into the category of theft. The problem stems from the fact that it is sometimes difficult to demonstrate that something has been stolen when the "rightful" owner seems to still be in possession of it (as can happen with the theft of software). It is complicated by the fact that "in a commercial society no clear line can be drawn between greedy antisocial acquisitive behavior on the one hand, and on the other hand, aggressive selling, advertising, and other entrepreneurial activity that is highly regarded or at least commonly tolerated."[9]

The modern trend in some jurisdictions has been to consolidate all acquisitive crimes into the single crime of theft. In such jurisdictions, the consolidated crime of theft includes what had been the common law crimes of larceny, embezzlement, obtaining property by false pretenses, receiving stolen property, burglary, robbery, and extortion (sometimes called blackmail). Other jurisdictions treat each of these crimes separately, and we discuss each in turn.

Larceny

> I hate this "crime doesn't pay" stuff. Crime in the United States is perhaps one of the biggest businesses in the world today.
>
> —Peter Kirk, University of California

As discussed earlier, larceny was the first and most basic of the property crimes to develop at common law. Simply put, larceny is the wrongful taking of personal property from the possession of another. Under English common law, larceny initially consisted of the "unconsented to" taking of the property of another from that person's possession. As such, larceny was a crime against possession, not ownership, since the person from whom the item was stolen could still be said to have ownership, even if he or she was no longer in possession of the stolen property. A successful larceny resulted in *dispossessing* the rightful owner of something of value but did not terminate inherent rights of ownership—meaning that, once stolen property had been recovered, it could lawfully be returned to its rightful owner.

Possession and Custody Today larceny is generally understood as the:

- trespassory (wrongful) taking, and
- carrying away (asportation), of
- the personal property of another,
- with intent to steal.

Taken together, these four elements constitute the modern crime of larceny.

Almost all jurisdictions have divided larceny into two categories: petit (or petty) and grand. Grand larceny usually consists of the stealing of property that has a market value in excess of a certain specified amount, or the theft of certain statutorily listed property, such as firearms and cattle. Sections 486–487 of the California Penal Code, for example, read:

> Theft is divided into two degrees, the first of which is termed grand theft; the second, petty theft. . . . Grand theft is theft committed in any of the following cases: (a) When the money, labor, or real or personal property taken is of a value exceeding four hundred dollars ($400) . . . (b) Notwithstanding subdivision (a),

grand theft is committed in any of the following cases: (1) (A) When domestic fowls, avocados, olives, citrus or deciduous fruits, other fruits, vegetables, nuts, artichokes, or other farm crops are taken of a value exceeding one hundred dollars ($100). . . . (2) When fish, shellfish, mollusks, crustaceans, kelp, algae, or other aquacultural products are taken from a commercial or research operation which is producing that product, of a value exceeding one hundred dollars ($100). (3) Where the money, labor, or real or personal property is taken by a servant, agent, or employee from his or her principal or employer and aggregates four hundred dollars ($400) or more in any consecutive twelve-month period. (c) When the property is taken from the person of another. (d) When the property taken is an automobile, firearm, horse, mare, gelding, any bovine animal, any caprine animal, mule, jack, jenny, sheep, lamb, hog, sow, boar, gilt, barrow, or pig. . . .

Some states are very specific in defining just what constitutes grand larceny. Section 487e of the California Penal Code, for example, reads: "Every person who feloniously steals, takes, or carries away a dog of another which is of a value exceeding four hundred dollars ($400) is guilty of grand theft."[10]

Subject Matter of Larceny Under common law, only tangible personal property could be subject to the crime of larceny. **Tangible property** is property that has physical form and is capable of being touched. It is "movable" property in the sense that it can be taken and carried away. **Personal property** is anything of value that is subject to ownership that is not land or **fixtures** (that is, items that are permanently affixed to the land).[11] As mentioned earlier, under common law, crops and minerals were not considered to be personal property until they were severed from the land, but domestic animals were considered to be tangible personal property, and thus subject to larceny.

Such thinking leads to another principle, which is that in order to constitute larceny the thing stolen must have some value—however slight. This principle is generally recognized in societies around the globe. In some contemporary Islamic societies (such as Kuwait and Saudi Arabia), for example, it is not criminal to steal liquor, pigs, or pork, since such things are regarded as "unclean" under the Muslim *Koran* and are therefore without value.

Common law excluded **intangible property** from the realm of larceny. Intangible property is property that has no value in and of itself but that represents value. A deed to a piece of occupied land, for example, is a kind of intangible property. While a deed might be taken and carried away without the owner's consent, the rightful owner would still retain both legal ownership and possession of the land itself—that is, of the thing that had real value. The owner need merely to apply to the local courthouse for a new copy of the deed, while the person holding the stolen deed would find it to be of no value in trying to sell the land to someone else.

The distinction between tangible and intangible property was especially valid in early society, where populations were sparse and individuals and families were generally known to one another. In modern complex society, however, proof of ownership may be more difficult to establish. Hence, while most of today's larceny arrests are still made for the stealing of tangible property, larceny law has become much more complex. In many American jurisdictions today, goods and services, minerals, crops, fixtures, trees, utilities, software, intellectual and property rights, and other intangibles can all be stolen and are the subject of various laws designed to deter theft. Some jurisdictions have enacted larceny statutes designed to criminalize the misappropriation of property that, although it has value, cannot be touched. Texas law, for example, says quite succinctly: " 'Property' means: (A) **real property;** (B) tangible or intangible personal property, including anything severed from land; or (C) a document, including money, that represents or embodies anything of value."[12] The Model Penal Code, although a bit more complex, defines property as follows: " '[P]roperty' means anything of value, including real estate,

TANGIBLE PROPERTY
property that has physical form and is capable of being touched, such as land, goods, jewelry, furniture, and so forth. Movable property that can be taken and carried away.

PERSONAL PROPERTY
anything of value that is subject to ownership that is not land nor **fixtures.**

FIXTURES
items that are permanently affixed to the land.

INTANGIBLE PROPERTY
property that has no intrinsic value, but which represents something of value. Intangible personal property may include documents, deeds, records of ownership, promissory notes, stock certificates, computer software, and intellectual property.

REAL PROPERTY
land and fixtures.

tangible and intangible personal property, contract rights choses-in-action [things to which an owner has a contractual or legal right] and other interests in or claims to wealth, admission or transportation tickets, captured or domestic animals, food and drink, electric and other power."[13]

Under the Model Penal Code and the laws of a number of states, the theft of electricity from the company that generates it constitutes larceny, as would the theft of computer software, processing time, or the theft of proprietary information. Other jurisdictions have created special laws criminalizing the theft of intellectual property and other intangibles. The misappropriation of the fruits of high technology are discussed later in this chapter.

Trespassory Taking At common law, there could be no larceny unless there was a trespassory taking of property. Taking generally consists of a physical seizure by which one exercises dominion and control over the property in question.[14] To constitute larceny, however, the taking must also be trespassory. A **trespassory taking** is merely a taking without the consent of the victim. Consent induced by fraud may constitute trespassory taking. It is important to note that a "trespassory taking," as the term is used in conjunction with larceny cases, has no relationship to the idea of trespass where real estate or land is concerned. Under common law a trespassory taking was called *trespass de bonis asportatis* (trespass for goods carried away) to distinguish it from other forms of trespass.

As English society became more impersonal and more mercantile, the common law crime of larceny, based as it was on possession, became less and less adequate. Under early common law, if a defendant was already in possession of the property said to be stolen he or she could not be found guilty of larceny, since there would be no trespassory taking.[15] So, for example, a person entrusted with cargo could not be said to have taken it without the consent of the victim, even if he later diverted shipment of the cargo and sold it without delivering it to its planned destination. The need to stimulate commerce and to protect foreign merchants who might contract with carriers and haulers who, of necessity, were unknown to them, mandated modifications in the understanding of larceny. New rules were needed, and they came in the area of bailments—an aspect of the law concerned with the relationship between an owner and one to whom the owner had entrusted his property for purposes such as sale, storage, transport, repair, processing, or investment. Since bailments involved contractual arrangements, disagreements between owners and bailees had previously been the purview of civil law. Widespread economic changes, however, and the requirements they placed on the English judicial system soon brought bailments into the realm of criminal law.

The change came in an oft-cited 1473 case, commonly called the "Carrier's Case."[16] In the Carrier's Case, an English court struggled with the question of a carrier who was given possession of a wagon of goods to deliver for the owner. The carrier "broke the bulk" of the goods, or separated and stole items from the wagon. To bring such activities within the purview of larceny, the court hearing the case held that, although the carrier had rightful possession of the packaged goods, "constructive possession" returned to the owner as soon as he broke the bulk. The owner of the goods, said the court, had entrusted the carrier with bales, but not with the content of those bales. Accordingly, breaking bulk was a misappropriation and constituted a trespassory taking of possession. The carrier was found guilty of larceny.

The "breaking bulk" doctrine was later expanded to cover situations where the carrier or other bailee, such as a warehouse person, is given a quantity of bulk goods and appropriates some but not all of them. Some American jurisdictions continue to follow this doctrine, although others have enacted the statutory offense of "larceny by bailee."

TRESPASSORY TAKING
for purposes of crimes of theft, a taking without the consent of the victim.

A trespassory taking can also be understood as a taking of possession, even where the thief does not take physical possession of the stolen merchandise. If, for example, a person out playing tennis finds an unattended tennis racket and offers to sell it to a passerby, he is still guilty of larceny if the passerby consummates the transaction and walks off with the racket. In such a case, the unwary purchaser assumes that the person offering to sell the racket is the lawful owner, and the thief need never touch the racket in order for it to be stolen. If, on the other hand, the legitimate owner of the tennis racket returns before it can be carried off by the purchaser, the defendant may be guilty of receiving money under false pretenses, although he could not be found guilty of larceny.

Other issues arise when a person finds lost or mislaid property. If he or she takes the property and intends to keep it at the time it is carried away, he or she has committed a trespassory taking and is thus guilty of larceny. In 1997, for example, a Brinks armored truck overturned on Interstate 95 in the desperately poor Overtown section of Miami, Florida. The truck, loaded with an estimated $3.7 million, split open, dropping an unknown amount of money onto the highway, and spilling dollar bills, quarters, and fifty-pound bags of money onto a street below the overpass on which the accident happened. Money floated into trees, covered the highway, and showered down onto people, cars, and houses. Those on the scene said it seemed to be raining money. "People walking by, people driving by, anybody that was a witness got money," said Florida Highway Patrol spokesperson Lieutenant Ernesto Duarte.[17] "Things like this don't happen very often, and people are going to try to take advantage," said Duarte. "It's funny, but it's dangerous. People jumped out of cars and grabbed bags full of money. Residents all got money." Police estimated that about $550,000 disappeared before police arrived on the scene.

In the Miami incident, the rightful owner of the spilled cash was clearly known to the people who picked it up. Hence, people who took money and kept it committed larceny. Miami Police Lieutenant Bill Schwartz put it concisely when he said, "The money does not belong to them. It is theft, whether you picked up a quarter or $100,000. Collecting the quarters, nickels, and dimes will be hard," said Schwartz. "But the big bills, we'll be counting on people's consciences. . . ."[18] The detective also noted that previously poor people found suddenly "strutting the street with wads of cash" could be investigated.

On the other hand, if a finder of lost property does not know who the owner is and has no reason to believe that he or she can find the property's owner, then the finder may legally be considered the new owner of the property. If a person finds lost property, he or she may take possession of the lost item without incurring criminal liability if he or she intends to return it to the rightful owner. Hence, a person who discovers a lost wallet may lawfully take the wallet home with him if he intends to call the local "lost and found" bureau (or other authorities) and to return the wallet and all of its contents to its lawful owner.

Similar rules apply to one to whom property has been delivered by mistake. That is, a defendant who receives misdelivered property has a duty to return it and has no right to keep what was not intended for him. A person who receives misdelivered property is guilty of larceny if he or she realizes the mistake and intends to keep the property. Under the Model Penal Code, however, and the laws of some states, a defendant's intent at the time he or she receives the property is irrelevant, and the defendant becomes liable for theft if he or she, with the purpose to deprive the owner thereof, fails to take reasonable measures to restore the property to the person entitled to it.[19]

Carrying Away In most jurisdictions, to constitute larceny, the property that is "taken" must be "carried away." The technical term for "carrying away" is

Miami residents pick up money after a Brinks armored truck overturned on January 8, 1997, in the city's Overtown section—spilling thousands of dollars in coins, bills, and food stamps. An estimated half-million dollars in cash was quickly grabbed by people on the scene. As this chapter explains, the taking of property, where the owner is known or can be found, constitutes larceny. (Photo by WSVN, courtesy of AP/Wide World Photos.)

ASPORTATION

a trespassory taking and carrying away (as of personal property in the crime of larceny or of the victim in kidnapping).

asportation. Even the slightest movement of an object, if done in a "carrying away manner," is sufficient to constitute asportation.[20]

Objects may, however, be moved in a manner other than one consistent with a "carrying away" of those items. Jewelry on a jewelry counter, for example, might be picked up, turned over for examination, and even worn without "carrying away" movements. As soon as the object is concealed, however, as in the case of shoplifters who "palm" small items by hiding them in their closed hands, a carrying away movement can be said to have occurred. Similarly, a fallen bicycle may be picked off the ground, righted, and moved back into a bicycle stand by a good Samaritan. If the would-be do-gooder mounts the bicycle and begins to ride off, however, a "carrying away" movement occurs.

In many jurisdictions, the asportation requirement is viewed merely as a means of assuring that the defendant had dominion and control over the property in question. If, for example, a thief puts his hand into the pocket of an intended victim and begins to lift the victim's wallet, asportation sufficient for prosecution has occurred even though the wallet is not completely removed from the victim's pocket.

Some jurisdictions have eliminated the need that an object be "carried away" for a charge of larceny to be brought. The unlawful "taking" of the property of another with intent to steal constitutes larceny in those jurisdictions. Carrying away may not occur, for example, in cases of misdelivery, as when furniture is delivered to the wrong address. In such a case, taking delivery of misdelivered property may involve no physical movement of the property beyond the placement of the furniture by delivery persons. In such cases, larceny could still be said to have occurred without the need for legal fictions in support of the "carrying away" requirement.

Property of Another Larceny can only be committed against a person who has possession of the property in question. It is sometimes said that a person cannot be convicted of larceny if the property she carried away was her own. It is important, however, to draw distinctions between the concepts of: (1) ownership, (2) possession, and (3) custody. Because the crime of larceny builds on possession rather than ownership, it is possible, in at least some jurisdictions, for the rightful owner of property to unlawfully steal his or her own property when it is in the temporary possession or custody of another. As one well-known source puts it: "The phrase 'of another' in the definition of larceny has reference to possession rather than to title or ownership. . . . Even the owner himself may commit larceny by stealing his own goods if they are in the possession of another and he takes them from the possessor wrongfully with intent to deprive him of a property interest therein."[21]

When a demand of return is made, of course, property must be returned to its rightful owner unless some other condition exists that would lawfully preclude such a return. Conditions barring return of property might include a lien on the property, a contract granting possession of the property to another person for a specified period of time, or the fact that the property has been pawned or that it has been repaired and an outstanding repair bill must still be paid. A person who owns a car may, for example, sign a rental contract whereby he agrees to temporarily relinquish possession of the vehicle. If the owner then secretly steals the vehicle back when the renter is asleep, he may be guilty of larceny.

Property that is free and clear of all attachments, however, may still be stolen by its rightful owner if it is in the possession of another. Imagine, for example, that the owner of some property—say, gold jewelry—entrusts it into the care of another for safekeeping. If the owner were then to enter the place where the jewelry was being stored and secretly remove it (in order, perhaps, to later file a fraudulent insurance claim), she would then be guilty of larceny because she had unlawfully taken the property from another's possession.

Custody over an item is not the same thing as ownership or possession. A person who owns something may legally possess it but may also relinquish custody of it temporarily. A woman who hands her purse to a man, asking him to hold it while she goes on a ride at an amusement park, for example, has relinquished custody of her purse but is still the owner and maintains possession from a legal point of view. If she asks the man to hold her purse for safekeeping while she vacations for a few weeks, the man may be said to have both custody of the purse and temporary possession of it. He is still not the purse's owner, however. Assuming that the man complies with the woman's wishes and returns the purse when asked, no legal issues arise. If, however, he sells the purse to another, or gives it to his wife saying it is a present, he has taken possession of it—and has misappropriated the purse. Even so, he (or his wife) is still not the lawful owner of the purse.

At common law, a defendant who was a co-owner of the taken property could not be found guilty of larceny. A few jurisdictions, however, have changed this rule by statute.

Intent to Steal Larceny is a crime that can only be committed intentionally. It cannot be committed negligently or recklessly. If, for example, a defendant picks up a notebook computer on an airport luggage return rack, thinking that it is his, and walks off with it, he is not guilty of larceny. An unreasonable, but honest, belief in ownership or right to possession is sufficient to constitute a valid defense to larceny. Such a defense is called the **claim of right** and is recognized in most jurisdictions.

The "intent to steal" element of the crime of larceny is sometimes said to mean that the offender intends to permanently dispossess the rightful owner of the property in question. It would, however, be more accurate to say that the offender intends to wrongfully deprive one who lawfully has possession of an item (even though he or she may not be the owner) to the continued useful possession of that item. So, for example, a man could not be charged with larceny if he "borrows" a tie he finds on a restaurant coat stand upon learning that the restaurant has a "coat and tie" policy and then returns the tie when leaving the restaurant.[22] On the other hand, one who "borrows" a full can of paint and later returns it empty is guilty of

CLAIM OF RIGHT
a defense against a charge of larceny, consisting of an honest belief in ownership or right to possession.

larceny because he has deprived the legitimate owner of the value that had been inherent in the paint contained within the can.

The intent to steal requirement of the crime of larceny, however, often makes it difficult to obtain larceny convictions in "joy-riding" situations, since the "stolen" vehicle is only "borrowed" and may be returned even before the owner notices that it is missing. Accordingly, most jurisdictions have statutorily created the crime of "joy-riding," which involves the unauthorized use of a motor vehicle, even when no "intent to steal"—in the sense of permanently depriving the rightful owner of possession of the vehicle—can be demonstrated. The Model Penal Code, for example, provides that a person commits a misdemeanor if he or she operates another's automobile, airplane, motorcycle, or other motor-propelled vehicle without the consent of the owner.[23] Under the MPC, the crime is a misdemeanor.

Embezzlement

EMBEZZLEMENT
the misappropriation of property already in possession of the defendant. Also, the unlawful conversion of the personal property of another by a person to whom it has been entrusted by (or for) its rightful owner.

CONVERSION
unauthorized assumption of the right of ownership. Conversion is a central feature of the crime of embezzlement, as in the unlawful *conversion* of the personal property of another, by a person to whom it has been entrusted.

As mentioned earlier, larceny requires a trespassory *taking* of another's property. Under some circumstances, however, property may be misappropriated without the need for a trespassory taking. **Embezzlement** is the unlawful conversion of the personal property of another, by a person to whom it has been entrusted by, or for, its rightful owner. Embezzlement is fundamentally a violation of trust. Since an embezzler already has lawful possession of the property in question, embezzlement is not a crime against possession, but one against ownership. The central feature of the crime of embezzlement is unlawful **conversion.** Although the original "taking" of possession occurs legally, embezzled property is converted to an unauthorized use. If, for example, a woman's employer gives her money to take to the bank for deposit into the company's account, but the employee takes the money and spends it instead, she is guilty of embezzlement. One can be guilty of embezzlement only if the embezzled property belongs to another, since transferring ownership of an item to one who already owns it is not a crime. In some jurisdictions, embezzlement is known as "fraudulent conversion," since it involves the misappropriation of property entrusted into one's care.

False Pretenses

Web Extra! 10–2
Britannica online:
embezzlement

FALSE PRETENSES
knowingly and unlawfully obtaining title to, and possession of, the lawful property of another by means of deception, and with intent to defraud. Also known as **obtaining property by false pretenses.**

In cases of larceny, offenders gain possession of, but not title to, the property that is stolen. In the crime of embezzlement, offenders gain ownership of property they already possess through conversion. The crime of **obtaining property by false pretenses,** usually referred to as **false pretenses,** is a form of theft that also involves transfer of ownership or title—but that, in contrast to embezzlement, occurs when the transfer of ownership or the passing of title is brought about by an unlawful and false representation.

The crime of obtaining property by false pretenses can be defined as knowingly and unlawfully obtaining title to, and possession of, the lawful property of another by means of deception and with intent to defraud. False pretenses differs from the crime of "larceny by trick" (existent in some jurisdictions), in which the defendant, through trickery, gains only possession, not title, to the stolen property. If, for example, a defendant obtains a car from an automobile dealership, takes it for a test drive, and keeps the car, the defendant obtains only possession and not title—leading to a possible charge of larceny, or larceny by trick. If, however, the defendant obtains both the car and title to the vehicle by paying for the car with a worthless

LAW IN PRACTICE

WHO EMBEZZLES?

To be able to embezzle, an employee must occupy a position of financial trust and must be sufficiently familiar with company procedures to steal and to cover up his or her wrongdoings. As a consequence, most embezzlers appear to be law-abiding citizens until they are discovered. Embezzlers are sometimes called "white-collar criminals," because of the relatively prestigious positions they often occupy within the business world. Criminologists sometimes say that embezzlement is a crime that takes place where there is a meeting of desire and opportunity. Donald Cressy, for example, observed that most embezzlers are average middle-class employees, but that there are four events that may lead them to steal from their employers and violate the financial trust placed in them.[24] Those events coalesce into the crime of embezzlement when:

1. The embezzler-to-be is placed in a position of financial trust and he or she accepts this position with no intention of using it to steal.

2. The embezzler-to-be develops a personal problem that he or she is too embarrassed to share with anyone and that appears to be solvable by obtaining extra money.

3. The embezzler-to-be develops technical skills relating to his or her position, and in that learning process discovers the methods needed to secretly violate the trust placed in him or her.

4. The embezzler-to-be acquires the mind set that justifies embezzlement. Embezzlers routinely rationalize their conduct in order to maintain their self-image of being a trusted person. The embezzler may, for example, consider the embezzlement a form of borrowing or temporary taking of the money. Many embezzlers fully intend to return the money "someday."

> The rise of computer crime and armed robbery has not eliminated the lure of caged cash.
>
> —James Chiles

Cressy also noted that, since embezzlers must occupy positions of trust in order to steal, their positions insulate them from suspicion, often making them feel immune from detection.

Cressy's critics note that everyone has problems, many of which are financial, and that not everyone—even those in positions of trust—steal. Some critics note that the personal problems cited as leading to law violation by embezzlers who are apprehended may merely be explanations offered after the embezzler has been caught. Others say that an embezzler will always find a problem to justify his or her actions when caught because people have a natural ability to rationalize their bad actions.

Research on embezzlement cases shows that employees who embezzle tend to have higher levels of indebtedness, change jobs more frequently, and have lower incomes than employees in similar positions with other companies. Contract employees and those working on commission embezzle more often than other employees. A recent survey of ninety-seven embezzlers indicated that seventy-five of them were in financial difficulty at the time of their embezzlement. The next highest number of embezzlers were employees who perceived their income to be inadequate. One such employee who perceived his income to be inadequate had recently purchased a Lear jet and a $600,000 home.[25]

---

check, then the defendant has both committed a check offense and obtained property by false pretenses.

In the crime of false pretenses, the false representation must be material. That is, it must play an important role in a reasonable person's decision whether to enter into the fraudulent transaction. If the defendant attempts to deceive another through misrepresentation, but the real facts are known to the other at the time that ownership changes hands, then no crime of false pretenses has occurred. Such might be the case where a swindler attempts to gain ownership of a retiree's "nest egg," with the pretense of investing it on the other person's behalf. If friends of the retiree unmask the swindler's plans and make clear to the intended victim the defendant's purpose, but the defendant still willingly engages in the transaction, then the crime of false pretenses has not occurred. Similarly, if the defendant attempts to swindle another but fails, then he or she might be guilty of an *attempt* to gain property by false pretenses but not of the crime itself.

Although misrepresentation is often made vocally or in writing, it is also possible to misrepresent oneself and the facts surrounding a transaction merely by keeping quiet. Hence, if an offender says something without intending to mislead another but which is misunderstood, then he or she may be found guilty of false pretenses if the misunderstanding results in a transfer of ownership of something of value *and* the transfer was facilitated by the defendant's silence and lack of effort at correcting the misunderstanding. Finally, it is not an indictable offense for a person to use misrepresentation to obtain payments or property that are already due to him. So, for example, a person to whom a debt is owed may use deceit to obtain payment without violating any law.

As noted earlier, for the crime of false pretenses to be committed, title must also pass to the defendant. If sale of the property occurs, then title has passed. If the property is merely loaned or leased to the defendant, there has been no passing of title. An exception to this general rule exists where money is involved. When an individual loans money to another person because of false representation, it is generally not expected that the *same* money will be returned, and the crime of false pretenses may be charged.[26]

The three most common defenses to false pretenses are that: (1) the victim was too gullible and should have been more wary, (2) the victim suffered no pecuniary (monetary) loss, and (3) there was no intent to defraud. A few cases have allowed the defense that the representation, although false, was one that would not have deceived an ordinarily intelligent person. Most jurisdictions do not recognize such a defense, however, on the theory that one of the purposes of criminal law is to protect those who cannot protect themselves. Most jurisdictions also do not recognize the defense of no pecuniary loss.

If the defendant believes that his or her representation is true, he or she cannot be convicted of false pretenses even if the belief is unreasonable in the eyes of others. Accordingly, to constitute the crime of false pretenses there must an intentional deception. A false representation, however, may be made by a person who makes a statement alleging that a certain fact is true, when he or she does not know whether the statement is, in fact, true.

Forgery

The legal principles underlying the crime of false pretenses extend to many other illegal activities, including the writing of bad checks, credit card fraud, the unlawful altering of wills, counterfeiting, and any other crimes through which ownership of property is obtained by fraud. A number of such crimes, however, have been separately codified by legislative action and are worthy of separate mention.

One such offense is forgery. **Forgery** is the making of a false written instrument or the material alteration of an existing genuine written instrument. Forgery is complete when the perpetrator either makes or passes a false instrument with intent to defraud. The gist of the crime of forgery is the actual intent to defraud, and the act of defrauding is itself not required. The common law crime of forgery, however, included the act of *uttering* a forged document, and the crime was sometimes referred to as "forgery and uttering." **Uttering** is the offering, passing, or attempted passing of a forged document with knowledge that the document is false and with intent to

FORGERY

the making of a false written instrument or the material alteration of an existing genuine written instrument.

UTTERING

the offering, passing, or attempted passing of a forged instrument with knowledge that the document is false and with intent to defraud.

defraud. Today, most jurisdictions have separately established the statutory crime of uttering a forged document.[27]

The elements of forgery are:

- a false signature or material alteration,
- signed or altered without authority,
- of a writing or other instrument that, if genuine, would have legal significance,
- with intent to defraud.

The elements of the crime of uttering, passing, publishing, or attempting to pass are:

- possession or creation of a forged document that, if genuine, would have legal significance, and
- uttering, passing, publishing, or attempting to pass the forged document,
- with intent to defraud.

For an instrument to be subject to forgery, the instrument, were it to be genuine, must create some legal right or obligation with apparent legal significance. If the instrument has no legal significance, then it is not subject to forgery. Instruments said to have legal significance include checks, wills, college transcripts, college diplomas, insurance proof of loss forms, divorce decrees, badges, stamps, credit cards, credit card receipts, and trademarks.

A genuine document that has been materially altered is also considered to be a forged document. To constitute forgery, however, the alteration must be material and unauthorized. Changing the date on a check that has already been issued, for example, would not be a material alteration unless the change in date had some legal significance. To have legal significance, the alteration must result in some material change in the rights and obligations of the parties involved. If the document is only partially completed, for example, the completion of the document may be forgery if completed in an unauthorized manner. Filling the date in on a check that had been issued undated normally would not be forgery, nor would writing the correct amount into a signed but uncompleted charge card receipt left behind at the place of purchase. Modifying the amount for which a check has been written (i.e., by adding extra zeros), or altering a charge card receipt before submitting it for payment (as a waiter might do who adds a tip to a receipt that is untotaled), would be forgery if the action is secretly done and is unauthorized.

In cases involving forgery of a signature, the prosecution must establish that the defendant lacked the authority to sign the other person's name. Authority to sign may be implied from prior transactions. If, for example, one spouse regularly picks up the other spouse's pay checks and forges his or her name to the checks and cashes them, authority to sign may be implied by past actions. Accordingly, there would be no forgery. There are, however, situations where a person commits forgery even when he or she signs his or her own name to documents. If someone receives a check made out in his name, but he knows that the check was intended for another person by the same name, he commits forgery when he signs his name to the check and cashes it (uttering).

Many jurisdictions have enacted the statutory crime of **criminal simulation**.[28] Criminal simulation is different from forgery in that the item or document falsified does not need to have any apparent legal significance. Making a piece of furniture, for example, in a manner designed to allow its creator to pass it off as being antique would constitute the crime of criminal simulation. Criminal simulation, like forgery, requires an intent to defraud or harm another. It is generally a misdemeanor.

Laws against forgery and against criminal simulation are now undergoing sweeping changes as jurisdictions undertake modifications of existing laws in order to keep pace with the creation of valuable electronic documents. Such documents,

CRIMINAL SIMULATION
the making of a false document or object that does not have any apparent legal significance.

which may never be printed on paper, provide for critically needed authentication and identification during financial and other transactions conducted via computer and over telephone and radio communications. Emerging laws of relevance to such activities are discussed later in this chapter.

Receiving Stolen Property

Receiving stolen property is another form of theft. **Receiving stolen property** can be defined as knowingly taking possession of, or control over, property that has been unlawfully stolen from another. Simply put, it is the receiving of stolen property, knowing that it was stolen. "Receiving," for purposes of the law, means acquiring control over, taking possession of, or taking title to, any property.

At early common law, receiving stolen property was not a crime. Later, English statutes provided for accomplice liability for the act of receiving stolen property. It wasn't until 1827, however, that an English statute was passed making the receiving of stolen property a separate offense. Today, all American jurisdictions have the statutory crime of receiving stolen property, although in some jurisdictions, it is combined under a general theft statute. There are four elements to the crime of receiving stolen property[29]:

- receiving,
- stolen property,
- which the receiver knew was stolen, and
- where the property was received with the intent to deprive the rightful owner of its possession.

If the property in question is not stolen, then the crime of receiving stolen property cannot take place. Property that has been stolen and recovered can no longer be considered stolen property. Hence, if law enforcement officers recover stolen property and then attempt to entrap a person into receiving stolen property by selling it or delivering it to him, the crime of receiving stolen property cannot be charged. This conclusion is based on the principle that, once property is recovered by lawful authorities, it is no longer stolen.

Similarly, in almost all jurisdictions, the crime of receiving stolen property requires that the defendant know that the property was stolen. Such knowledge may be established by circumstantial evidence, as when a defendant pays an unreasonably low price for the merchandise in question. In a few jurisdictions, it is sufficient to show that a defendant should have been aware that there was a likelihood that the property in question was stolen (perhaps because the price asked for the item was unreasonably low), and he or she made no efforts to verify ownership. Under such circumstances the person buying the item would not be merely an innocent purchaser in the eyes of the law.

The crime of receiving stolen property is different from the theft of the property itself, and a defendant who steals property cannot be convicted of receiving the same property. That is to say, a thief cannot receive stolen property from himself.[30]

Robbery

The FBI classifies robbery as a violent, personal crime. We classify it here as a property crime, rather than as a personal crime, because the *object* of robbery is the unlawful acquisition of property—even though the property may be forcefully taken from the personal possession of another. From a definitional standpoint, **robbery** is the unlawful taking of property that is in the immediate possession of another by force or threat of force. Since an "unlawful taking" constitutes larceny, robbery can also be defined as a form of larceny, or as *larceny from a person by violence, intimidation, or by placing the person in fear.* From another point of view, robbery is simply an aggravated form of larceny and, in addition to the elements necessary to constitute larceny, the crime of robbery requires two more features: (1) that the property be taken from a person or removed from the victim's presence, and (2) that the taking occur through the use of force or by putting the victim in fear. As the last element indicates, actual force need not be used, and the threatened use of force suffices to constitute robbery. Hence, elements of the crime of robbery are:

ROBBERY
the unlawful taking of property that is in the immediate possession of another by force or threat of force. Also, larceny from a person by violence, intimidation, or by placing the person in fear.

- the felonious taking of personal property,
- from the person or immediate presence of another,
- against the will of the victim, and
- accomplished by means of force or by putting the victim in fear.

Some crimes, such as pocket picking and purse snatching, also involve the unlawful taking of property from the immediate possession of another person. They are crimes of larceny, however, and not robbery, because the stolen property is taken before the victim is aware of what is happening. No violence or intimidation is used in committing such crimes. If a purse snatcher or pickpocket misses his target on the first "grab," however, and a struggle ensues before the purse or wallet is taken, then the offender is guilty of robbery.

In cases of robbery it is generally easy to establish that property has been taken *from a person*—as happens in instances of armed robbery, where the robber demands a person's wallet or rings that he or she is wearing. Problems arise, however, when property is not taken from a person, but is merely removed *from the presence of the victim.* The test to determine if the property is taken from the *presence* of the victim is whether the victim, at the time of the offense, was in a location where he or she could have prevented the taking had he or she not been intimidated or forcibly restrained from doing so.

When property is stolen from a person who is unconscious or dead, the crime is larceny rather than robbery, because no force is used and the "victim" is not threatened. If, however, the person from whom valuables are stolen is unconscious at the time, and if the cause of unconsciousness was some intentional action on the part of the thief, then most courts would hold that robbery has occurred. On the other hand, if the person is in a state of voluntarily self-induced unconsciousness (as might happen with one who drinks too much), then stealing property from his or her person would likely be larceny. Courts have also held that one who kills another and then steals possessions from the deceased's body is guilty of robbery (as well as murder) if the passage of time between the killing and the robbery is not substantial. A murderer who returns to an undiscovered corpse a week after the killing, however, and steals items from the body of the victim would be committing larceny and not robbery.

It is important to note that robbery, in most jurisdictions, requires *either* the use or threatened use of force, *or* putting the victim in fear. One or the other will suffice. "Fear" means "intimidation." Some states use an objective standard in determining whether intimidation occurred—asking whether the circumstances were such that they would have induced fear in the mind of a reasonable person. Other states use a subjective standard and look to see whether the person robbed actually experienced fear. Accordingly, in such jurisdictions, if the victim is unusually timid, robbery can occur even though the average person would not have felt apprehensive under the same or similar circumstances.

Most jurisdictions recognize various degrees of robbery. First-degree robbery, for example, may be armed robbery—that is, robbery committed with the use of a dangerous or deadly weapon or robbery in which the victim is seriously injured. First-degree robbery is sometimes termed "aggravated robbery" (see the Texas statute defining aggravated robbery in the box below). Second-degree robbery may be robbery in which no weapon is used or where the victim is not seriously injured, sometimes called "strong arm robbery." Some states, like New York, make even finer distinctions and have established three or more statutorily defined degrees of robbery.

In deciding what degree of robbery a defendant can be charged with, it is important to know: (1) what constitutes a deadly weapon and (2) what constitutes a serious injury. Serious bodily injury has often been interpreted to mean an injury that requires medical treatment. The definition of a "deadly weapon" has proven more complex. Some state statutes specify that armed robbery is any robbery committed with a firearm, making the definition of a deadly weapon relatively straightforward. Most statutes, however, avoid use of the term "firearm," and refer instead to "deadly weapon" or "dangerous weapon." The dangerousness (or deadliness) of weapons has often been assessed on the basis of their construction and purpose, as well as the use to which they are put during the offense. Hence, guns, knives, screwdrivers, hammers, axes, clubs, sticks, and even dogs and high-heeled shoes and boots have been found to be "deadly weapons" within the meaning of robbery statutes. Some courts have gone so far as to conclude that a deadly weapon is anything that appears to be such from the point of view of the victim—meaning that even toy guns (and, in at least one case, a hairbrush hidden in a robber's pocket and held to look like a gun) can meet the criteria for a "deadly weapon." Finally, some courts have found that a robber in possession of a deadly weapon at the time of the robbery, such as a gun or a knife, has committed armed robbery even though the weapon remained concealed and was never "used" or brought to the attention of the victim.

Web Extra! 10–3

Britannica online:
extortion

Extortion

Some years ago, Vermont attorney John Harrington threatened to accuse Armand Morin of adultery unless Morin paid him $175,000. At the time of the threat, Har-

---

LAW ON THE BOOKS

TEXAS DEFINES "AGGRAVATED ROBBERY."

Compare with Model Penal Code, Section 222.1

TEXAS PENAL CODE

Sec. 29.03. Aggravated robbery.

a. A person commits an offense if he commits robbery as defined in Section 29.02, and he:

    (1) causes serious bodily injury to another;

    (2) uses or exhibits a deadly weapon; or

    (3) causes bodily injury to another person or threatens or places another person in fear of imminent bodily injury or death, if the other person is:

        (A) 65 years of age or older; or

        (B) a disabled person.

b. An offense under this section is a felony of the first degree.

c. In this section, "disabled person" means an individual with a mental, physical, or developmental disability who is substantially unable to protect himself from harm.

rington represented Morin's wife in divorce proceedings. Upon learning from Mrs. Morin that Mr. Morin routinely engaged in sexual relations with women staying alone at the couple's motel, Harrington arranged for a woman named Mrs. Mazza to register at Morin's motel and approach him in a friendly manner. Mrs. Mazza was instructed by the attorney to be "receptive and available," but not aggressive, so as to avoid any claims of entrapment. Shortly after she registered, Mr. Morin went to Mrs. Mazza's motel room. An hour later, attorney Harrington and a private investigator burst into the room and photographed Mr. Morin and Mrs. Mazza together in bed naked. Conversation between the two had also been secretly recorded by Mrs. Mazza and was later turned over to the attorney.

Armed with photographs and the recorded conversation, attorney Harrington sent a letter to Mr. Morin marked "personal and confidential," in which he proposed that his client would waive all alimony proceedings on receipt of $175,000. The letter also included a compromising photo showing Mr. Morin with Mrs. Mazza. Morin took the letter to the police, who then arrested the attorney and charged him with extortion. The relevant Vermont statute provided that a "person who maliciously threatens to accuse another of a crime or offense, or with an injury to his person or property, with intent to extort money or other pecuniary advantage, or with intent to compel the person so threatened to do an act against his will," is guilty of extortion. At trial, Harrington argued that he had been acting merely as an attorney, attempting to secure a divorce for his client "on the most favorable terms possible." Nonetheless, a jury found him guilty of extortion.

Harrington appealed, but the appellate court upheld his conviction, ruling that the attorney had threatened to accuse Morin of the *crime* of adultery—rather than attempting simply to negotiate a divorce settlement—thereby bringing his behavior under the purview of the state's extortion statute. In the words of the appellate court, "A demand for settlement of a civil action, accompanied by a malicious threat to expose the wrongdoer's criminal conduct, if made with intent to extort payment against his will, constitutes the crime alleged in the indictment."[31]

At early common law, **extortion** was the corrupt collection of an unlawful fee by a public officer under color of office, or the attempt to collect such a fee. It was then a misdemeanor. Today, almost all American jurisdictions have expanded the crime of extortion via statute to cover all persons using the threat of future actions to wrongfully obtain property or services. Hence, the contemporary crime of extortion can be defined as the taking of personal property by a threat of future harm. Statutory extortion is a felony in most jurisdictions.

Extortion differs from the crime of robbery in that robbery occurs when property is taken by force or threat of immediate violence. In extortion, the defendant obtains property by threat of *future* violence. The threat of violence can be to cause physical harm to the victim or to others whom the victim values. Some jurisdictions allow the threatened harm to extend to various other forms of injury, as in Vermont where threatened accusation of a crime will suffice. **Blackmail** is that form of extortion in which a threat is made to disclose a crime or other social disgrace. Even a threat to cause economic injury or social embarrassment may be sufficient to constitute extortion in most jurisdictions. A threat to bring a lawsuit or to take other official action, unless the property is given or returned to the defendant, may also constitute extortion. It is a defense under such circumstances, however, if the defendant honestly and lawfully claimed the property as restitution or indemnification for harm done, to which the lawsuit or other official action relates, or as compensation for property or other lawful services.[32]

Jurisdictions differ as to whether property must actually be received in order to complete the crime of extortion. In some states, like Kentucky, the uttering or issuing of the threat itself completes the offense. In others, the crime is not considered complete until the defendant receives the property—although "attempted extortion" or an "attempt to extort" may be charged.

EXTORTION
the taking of personal property by threat of future harm.

BLACKMAIL
a form of extortion in which a threat is made to disclose a crime or other social disgrace.

COMPOUNDING A CRIME
also known as **compounding a felony;** consists of the receipt of property or other valuable consideration in exchange for an agreement to conceal or not prosecute one who has committed a crime.[34]

It is worthwhile to note that extortion differs from the offense of **compounding a crime,** also known as "compounding a felony," which "consists of the receipt of property or other valuable consideration in exchange for an agreement to conceal or not prosecute one who has committed a crime."[33] Compounding usually involves a mutual agreement between parties, whereas extortion is based upon a qualified threat.

Identity Theft—A New Type of Theft

In July 2000, California Attorney General Bill Lockyer announced the arrest of six individuals for an alleged Medi-Cal fraud ring that bilked the state out of more

LAW ON THE BOOKS

CALIFORNIA DEFINES "EXTORTION."

Compare to Model Penal Code, Section 223.4

CALIFORNIA PENAL CODE

Section 518. Extortion is the obtaining of property from another, with his consent, or the obtaining of an official act of a public officer, induced by a wrongful use of force or fear, or under color of official right.

Section 519. Fear, such as will constitute extortion, may be induced by a threat, either:
 1. To do an unlawful injury to the person or property of the individual threatened or of a third person; or,
 2. To accuse the individual threatened, or any relative of his, or member of his family, of any crime; or,
 3. To expose, or to impute to him or them any deformity, disgrace, or crime; or,
 4. To expose any secret affecting him or them.

Section 520. Every person who extorts any money or other property from another, under circumstances not amounting to robbery or carjacking, by means of force, or any threat, such as is mentioned in Section 519, shall be punished by imprisonment in the state prison for two, three, or four years.

Section 521. Every person who commits any extortion under color of official right, in cases for which a different punishment is not prescribed in this Code, is guilty of a misdemeanor.

Section 522. Every person who, by any extortionate means, obtains from another his signature to any paper or instrument, whereby, if such signature were freely given, any property would be transferred, or any debt, demand, charge, or right of action created, is punishable in the same manner as if the actual delivery of such debt, demand, charge, or right of action were obtained.

Section 523. Every person who, with intent to extort any money or other property from another, sends or delivers to any person any letter or other writing, whether subscribed or not, expressing or implying, or adapted to imply, any threat such as is specified in Section 519, is punishable in the same manner as if such money or property were actually obtained by means of such threat.

Section 524. Every person who attempts, by means of any threat, such as is specified in Section 519 of this code, to extort money or other property from another is punishable by imprisonment in the county jail not longer than one year or in the state prison or by fine not exceeding ten thousand dollars ($10,000), or by both such fine and imprisonment.

Section 525. Upon conviction of a felony violation under this chapter, the fact that the victim was an elder or dependent adult, as defined in Section 368, shall be considered a circumstance in aggravation when imposing a term under subdivision (b) of Section 1170.

Blackmail is a form of extortion in which a threat is made to disclose a crime or other social disgrace. In 1997, twenty-two-year old Autumn Jackson (center) was convicted of attempting to extort $40 million from actor Bill Cosby. Jackson claimed to be Cosby's out-of-wedlock daughter and threatened to go public with her story unless Cosby met her demands. Cosby acknowledged an affair with Ms. Jackson's mother but denied that he was the woman's father. (Photo by Michael Schmelling, courtesy of AP/Wide World Photos.)

than $1.39 million dollars in a sophisticated identity theft scheme. A criminal complaint filed in Los Angeles County Superior Court accused the defendants of illegally obtaining physicians' medical licenses and other personal identification from Los Angeles-area hospitals. The defendants were also accused of submitting fraudulent applications to the California Department of Health Services under fraudulent doctors' names in order to request the Medi-Cal provider numbers needed to bill the state's Medi-Cal program. The defendants allegedly later obtained names and identifying information for several thousand hospital patients who were Medi-Cal beneficiaries without the knowledge or consent of the hospitals or the patients involved. According to Lockyer, the defendants then submitted fraudulent Medi-Cal claims representing that the victimized doctors had rendered services to these patients.

To mask their operations, the defendants allegedly established phony businesses and used mail drops to receive state checks (known in California as state "warrants"). Finally, using bogus identification, the defendants apparently opened bank accounts in the doctors' names and cashed the checks.[35]

Identity theft is rapidly becoming *the* most important new theft crime of the twenty-first century. It can be defined as the unauthorized use of another individual's personal identity to fraudulently obtain money, goods, or services, to avoid the payment of debt, or to avoid criminal prosecution.

At the federal level, the Federal Trade Commission (FTC) runs a clearinghouse for complaints by victims of identity theft. Although the FTC does not have the authority to bring criminal cases, the commission helps victims of identity theft by providing them with information to help resolve the financial and other problems that can result from such illegal activity. The FTC may also refer victim complaints to other appropriate government agencies and private organizations for action.

According to the FTC, many people have confronted, directly or through a third person, some form of identity theft.[36] Someone has either used their name to open up a credit card account or someone has used their identifying information—name,

Web Extra! 10–4
Identity theft

IDENTITY THEFT
the unauthorized use of another individual's personal identity to fraudulently obtain money, goods, or services, to avoid the payment of debt, or to avoid criminal prosecution.

Social Security number, mother's maiden name, or other personal information—to commit fraud or to engage in other unlawful activities.

Other common forms of identity theft include taking over an existing credit card account and making unauthorized charges to it (typically, the identity thief forestalls discovery by the victims by contacting the credit card issuer and changing the billing address on the account); taking out loans in another person's name; writing fraudulent checks using another person's name or account number; and using personal information to access and transfer money out of another person's bank or brokerage account. In extreme cases, the identity thief may completely take over his or her victim's identity—opening a bank account, getting multiple credit cards, buying a car, getting a home mortgage, and even working under the victim's assumed name.

Web Extra! 10–5

Internet Fraud Complaint Center (IFCC)

The FTC says that identity theft can be perpetrated based on simple, low-tech practices, such as stealing someone's mail or "dumpster diving" through his or her trash to collect credit card offers, or to obtain identifying information such as account numbers or Social Security numbers. Far more sophisticated practices are sometimes used, however. In a practice known as "skimming," identity thieves use computers to read and store the information encoded on the magnetic strip of an ATM or credit card when that card is inserted through either a specialized card reader or a legitimate payment mechanism (e.g., the card reader used to pay for gas at the pump in a gas station). Once stored, that information can be re-encoded onto any other card with a magnetic strip, instantly transforming a blank card into a machine-readable ATM or credit card identical to that of the victim.[37]

Web Extra! 10–6

National Fraud Information Center

The FTC also notes that the Internet has dramatically altered the potential impact of identity theft. Among other things, the Internet provides access to collections of identifying information gathered through both illicit and legal means. The global publication of identifying details, that were previously unavailable to most people, increases the potential misuse of that information. Similarly, the Internet expands exponentially the ability for a third party to disseminate the identifying information, making it available for others to exploit.[38]

In an effort to combat identity theft, the federal Identity Theft and Assumption Deterrence Act (also known as the Identity Theft Act)[39] was signed into law in 1998. The act, mentioned briefly at the start of this chapter, does not apply to thefts of less than $50,000, and makes it a federal offense to knowingly transfer or use, without lawful authority, a means of identification of another person with the intent to commit, or to aid or abet, any unlawful activity that constitutes a violation of federal law, or that constitutes a felony under any applicable state or local law.[40] The statute further defines "means of identification" to include "any name or number that may be used, alone or in conjunction with any other information, to identify a specific individual," including, among other things, name, address, Social Security number, driver's license number, biometric data, access devices (i.e., credit cards), electronic identification number or routing code, and telecommunications identifying information. Under the law, a conviction for identity theft carries a maximum penalty of fifteen years' imprisonment, and a possible fine and forfeiture of any personal property used or intended to be used to commit the crime.

Schemes to commit identity theft may also run afoul of other federal statutes, including those relating to credit card fraud, computer fraud, mail fraud, wire fraud, financial institution fraud, or Social Security fraud. Each offense under these statutes is a federal felony and carries substantial penalties—in some cases as much as thirty years in prison, combined with possible fines and criminal forfeiture.

Although identity theft is a relatively new crime, almost all states now have statutes specifically targeting the offense. The Law on the Books box on page 387 provides examples of two state laws criminalizing the fraudulent use of the personal identifying information of another individual.

Identity theft is the unauthorized use of another individual's personal identity to fraudulently obtain money, goods, or services, to avoid the payment of debt, or to avoid criminal prosecution. The theft of personal identities, which can occur when someone acquires the personal identifying information of another, has recently become a serious law enforcement concern. (Photo by Tony Freeman, courtesy of PhotoEdit.)

CRIMINAL LAW IN THE NEWS

Identity Theft Thrives in Cyberspace

Names, Numbers Easy to Find Online, Authorities Say

WASHINGTON—The information superhighway has become an express lane for identity theft, according to federal law enforcement agents.

The growth of the Internet, with its gigabytes of personal information floating around in cyberspace, has given criminals a quick and easy way to ferret out or even hack into computer systems to gather enough personal information to steal someone's identity.

That was the warning Tuesday from Gregory Regan, special agent in charge of the U.S. Secret Service's Finance Crimes Division, in testimony before the Senate Judiciary Committee Subcommittee on Technology, Terrorism and Government Information.

Identity theft occurs when someone gains access to a person's basic information, including name, addresses and credit card or Social Security numbers, and uses that information to open new charge and bank accounts, order merchandise or borrow money.

"As financial institutions and merchants become more cautious in their approach to hand-to-hand transactions, the criminals are looking for other venues to compromise," Regan said. "Today, criminals need look no further than the Internet."

Nurse works to clear name

Maureen Mitchell, an Ohio nurse, told the committee that someone was able to steal her identity even though she and her husband do no online buying. She is still unsure how the theft occurred, even though a suspect has been arrested.

The Mitchells have devoted hundreds of hours to sorting out their finances since they learned that some-

one had bought two vehicles and borrowed money in their names.

"We don't know if other accounts are still outstanding. This has a huge impact on your life," Mitchell told members of the subcommittee Tuesday.

Regan said a recent case investigated by the Secret Service and other federal agencies shows how easily Internet-savvy criminals can get personal information from public sources—in this case a promotion list of high-ranking military officers on a public Web site. In the past, published lists included the officers' Social Security numbers.

An over-friendly bank

Regan said that in this particular case, the financial institution, in an effort to operate in a consumer-friendly manner, issued credit over the Internet in less than a minute.

(continued)

CRIMINAL LAW IN THE NEWS

Identity Theft Thrives in Cyberspace

Names, Numbers Easy to Find Online, Authorities Say

"Approval for credit was granted after conducting a credit check for the applicant who provided a true name and matching true Social Security number," said Regan. "All other information provided, such as the date of birth, address and telephone number, which could have been used for further verification, was fraudulent. The failure of this bank to conduct a more comprehensive verification process resulted in substantial losses and more importantly a long list of high-ranking military officers who became victims of identity fraud."

Regan said the Internet offers the anonymity that criminals desire.

"In the past, fraud schemes required false identification documents and necessitated a face-to-face exchange of information and identity verification," Regan said. "Now with just a laptop and modem, criminals are capable of perpetrating a variety of financial crimes without identity documents through the use of stolen personal information."

Gauging the law's effectiveness

The hearing was held to gauge the effectiveness of the Identity Theft and Assumption Deterrence Act that was passed in 1998 to give law enforcement tools to stem this problem. Under the law, a conviction for identity theft carries a maximum penalty of 15 years'

imprisonment, a fine, and forfeiture of any personal property used or intended to be used to commit the crime.

Jodie Bernstein, director of the Federal Trade Commission's (FTC) Bureau of Consumer Protection, told the subcommittee that a brand new, toll-free FTC hot line to take identity theft calls is already logging 400 calls a week.

Bernstein said the agency is expecting the number of calls to increase to 200,000 annually.

The General Accounting Office reported that consumer inquiries to the Trans Union credit bureau's Fraud Victim Assistance Department increased from 35,235 in 1992 to 522,922 in 1997, and the Social Security Administration's Office of the Inspector General conducted 1,153 investigations of Social Security number misuse in 1997, compared with 305 in 1996.

In 1999, the telephone hot line established by the Social Security Administration's Office of the Inspector General received reports of almost 39,000 incidents of misuse of Social Security numbers.

Detecting fraud

Bernstein said that while law enforcement has been moving aggressively against the problem, there are steps that need to be taken to curtail the

trend, including "bringing together creditors and credit reporting agencies to develop mechanisms for detecting such fraud and thus heading off identity theft."

She said that victims run into numerous obstacles and bureaucratic hurdles in trying to resolve problems tied to identity theft. For example, many consumers must contact and re-contact creditors, credit bureaus and debt collectors, often with frustrating results.

Bernstein said that the ideal would be a system in which consumers could make a single telephone call to any of the three major credit bureaus or the FTC hot line to get fraud alerts placed on all of their credit reports.

"The success of such an effort depends on the cooperation of the major credit bureaus," she said.

Sen. John Kyl, R–Ariz., the chairman of the subcommittee and the sponsor of the identity theft law, said that since the law was enacted, a report from the inspector general of the Social Security Administration found that 81 percent of misuse of Social Security numbers relate to identity theft.

Source: David Noack, "Identity Theft Thrives in Cyberspace; Names, Numbers Easy to Find Online, Authorities Say," APB News. March 8, 2000. Reprinted with permission.

CONSOLIDATION OF THEFT CRIMES

Because of the complexities that can surround any given instance of theft, it has traditionally been difficult for prosecutors to know how to properly charge some defendants. The fine distinctions drawn by statutes, combined with the many statutory varieties of theft in some jurisdictions, have exacerbated the problem. As a result, suggestions arose some years ago to consolidate the crimes of larceny, embezzlement, and false pretenses. The suggestions were based on the belief that the misappropriation of property, whether by stealth, conversion, or deception, all rep-

LAW ON THE BOOKS

"IDENTITY THEFT" UNDER ARIZONA LAW.

ARIZONA CRIMINAL CODE

Section 2708. Taking identity of another person; classification.

   A. A person commits taking the identity of another person if the person knowingly takes the name, birth date or Social Security number of another person, without the consent of that other person, with the intent to obtain or use the other person's identity for any unlawful purpose or to cause loss to a person.

   B. Taking the identity of another person is a class 5 felony.

"IDENTITY THEFT" UNDER CONNECTICUT LAW.

CONNECTICUT PUBLIC ACT NO. 99-99

   A. A person is guilty of identity theft when such person intentionally obtains personal identifying information of another person without the authorization of such other person and uses that information for any unlawful purpose including, but not limited to, obtaining, or attempting to obtain, credit, goods, services or medical information in the name of such other person without the consent of such other person. As used in this section, "personal identifying information" means a motor vehicle operator's license number, Social Security number, employee identification number, mother's maiden name, demand deposit number, savings account number or credit card number.

   B. Identity theft is a class D felony.

resent different aspects of one general type of harm. The 1962 draft of the Model Penal Code (MPC) incorporated a consolidated theft provision (Section 223.1) that has since been adopted by many states. The MPC provision covers larceny, embezzlement, and false pretenses, as well as extortion, blackmail, and receiving stolen property. In effect, the MPC provision encompasses all nonviolent misappropriation of property crimes, while placing robbery (because it involves violence or the threat of violence) in a separate category.

   Today, in recognition of the common principles underlying theft offenses, a fair number of jurisdictions, including New York, Texas, and California, have statutorily consolidated all or most common law theft crimes under one heading. As is the case with the Model Penal Code, such laws generally combine two or more of the crimes of larceny, embezzlement, extortion, receiving stolen property, and false pretenses into one crime called "theft," or, as in New York, "larceny." The Law on the Books box on page 388 contains the New York consolidated theft statute. The New York law, in contrast to the consolidated theft statutes of some other states, does not include the crime of receiving stolen property, although it does incorporate the offense of "acquiring lost property."

BURGLARY

Jerry Gonzales was dating Krissi Caldwell. Her parents did not approve, and he was not permitted in their home. He and Krissi decided to kill her parents, and Krissi let Jerry into their home where he shot both of her parents several times. The father survived, but the mother died. Jerry was tried for the crime of murder committed in the course of committing a burglary. Jerry's attorney argued, in his defense, that the

LAW ON THE BOOKS

NEW YORK PENAL LAW DEFINES "LARCENY."

Compare With Model Penal Code, Section 223.1 (Consolidation of Theft Offenses)

NEW YORK PENAL LAW

Sec. 155.05 Larceny; defined.

1. A person steals property and commits larceny when, with intent to deprive another of property or to appropriate the same to himself or to a third person, he wrongfully takes, obtains or withholds such property from an owner thereof.

2. Larceny includes a wrongful taking, obtaining or withholding of another's property, with the intent prescribed in subdivision one of this section, committed in any of the following ways:

    (a) By conduct heretofore defined or known as common law larceny by trespassory taking, common law larceny by trick, embezzlement, or obtaining property by false pretenses;

    (b) By acquiring lost property.

A person acquires lost property when he exercises control over property of another which he knows to have been lost or mislaid, or to have been delivered under a mistake as to the identity of the recipient or the nature or amount of the property, without taking reasonable measures to return such property to the owner;

    (c) By committing the crime of issuing a bad check, as defined in section 190.05;

    (d) By false promise.

A person obtains property by false promise when, pursuant to a scheme to defraud, he obtains property of another by means of a representation, express or implied, that he or a third person will in the future engage in particular conduct, and when he does not intend to engage in such conduct or, as the case may be, does not believe that the third person intends to engage in such conduct.

In any prosecution for larceny based upon a false promise, the defendant's intention or belief that the promise would not be performed may not be established by or inferred from the fact alone that such promise was not performed. Such a finding may be based only upon evidence establishing that the facts and circumstances of the case are wholly consistent with guilty intent or belief and wholly inconsistent with innocent intent or belief, and excluding to a moral certainty every hypothesis except that of the defendant's intention or belief that the promise would not be performed;

    (e) By extortion.

A person obtains property by extortion when he compels or induces another person to deliver such property to himself or to a third person by means of instilling in him a fear that, if the property is not so delivered, the actor or another will:

        (i) Cause physical injury to some person in the future; or

        (ii) Cause damage to property; or

        (iii) Engage in other conduct constituting a crime; or

        (iv) Accuse some person of a crime or cause criminal charges to be instituted against him; or

        (v) Expose a secret or publicize an asserted fact, whether true or false, tending to subject some person to hatred, contempt or ridicule; or

        (vi) Cause a strike, boycott or other collective labor group action injurious to some person's business; except that such a threat shall not be deemed extortion when the property is demanded or received for the benefit of the group in whose interest the actor purports to act; or

        (vii) Testify or provide information or withhold testimony or information with respect to another's legal claim or defense; or

        (viii) Use or abuse his position as a public servant by performing some act within or related to his official duties, or by failing or refusing to perform an official duty, in such manner as to affect some person adversely; or

        (ix) Perform any other act which would not in itself materially benefit the actor but which is calculated to harm another person materially with respect to his health, safety, business, calling, career, financial condition, reputation, or personal relationships.

crime the boy committed was not burglary because the entry was made with Krissi's consent.

Burglary is another wrongful acquisition crime directed against property. Burglary involves more than theft, however, and at common law was considered to be a crime against habitation (or one's dwelling). At common law, burglary consisted of the breaking and entering of the dwelling house of another at night with intent to commit a felony. In most jurisdictions today, however, the crime of **burglary** is statutorily defined as the:

- breaking and,
- entering of,
- a building, locked automobile, boat, etc.,
- with the intent to commit a felony or theft.

BURGLARY
the breaking and entering of a building, locked automobile, boat, etc., with the intent to commit a felony or theft. Also, the entering of a structure for the purposes of committing a felony or theft offense.

Most jurisdictions divide the crime of burglary into burglary in the first and second degree, where burglary in the first degree is burglary of an inhabited dwelling and all other burglaries are second-degree burglaries. Some jurisdictions maintain the nighttime distinction, classifying burglaries of inhabited dwellings that occur at night as more serious than other burglaries.

The breaking requirement does not necessitate any damage to the property burglarized, although it is usually interpreted as requiring the use of actual or constructive force to create an opening in the thing burglarized. The forced opening of any part of a structure will suffice. It is sufficient that the defendant use only the slightest amount of force to create an opening. Hence, while an entry through an already open door is not sufficient to meet the "breaking" requirement of burglary in most jurisdictions, the simple act of opening a closed door, even one that is unlocked, is. Many jurisdictions hold that the application of force to enlarge an already existing opening also satisfies the breaking requirement, while other jurisdictions hold that enlargement is not sufficient.[41] Some years ago, one court explained the amount of force necessary to constitute a "breaking" this way: "The gist of burglarious breaking is the application of force to remove some obstacle to entry, and the amount of force employed is not material. The exercise of the slightest force is sufficient. The breaking consists of the removal by the intruder, by the exercise of force, of an obstruction which, if left untouched, would prevent entrance. Hence, the application of force to push further open an already partly open door or window to enable a person to enter a room or building, is a breaking sufficient to constitute burglary if the other essential elements of the offense are present."[42] In other words, although a "breaking" needs only the tiniest physical force, the concept of breaking requires more than merely passing over or through an imaginary line or threshold separating one defined space from another.

Obtaining entry by fraud, by threatening to use force against another person, entering through a chimney, and by having a co-conspirator open a door from within have all been held sufficient to constitute *constructive* breaking. Jurisdictions differ, however, on whether a defendant who has entered without a "breaking"—whether constructive or actual—commits the crime of burglary when he or she uses force to exit the structure—as when a person hides in a department store washroom before closing and breaks out of the store during the night with purloined merchandise. Most hold that the use of force merely to exit does not constitute burglary,[43] although a few follow an old common law rule that "breaking out of a building in making an exit is sufficient"[44] for the breaking requirement.

Generally speaking, breaking must be trespassory. Accordingly, a defendant who has permission to enter a structure cannot be found guilty of burglary in most jurisdictions.[45] Courts will examine any purported consent to determine whether the defendant in fact had permission to be on the premises at the time in question and to be in the particular part of the structure he or she entered. To constitute a defense, consent to enter must have been given by the owner of the structure entered or by a person legally authorized to act on behalf of the owner. Consent is not effective if given by a person the defendant knows is not legally authorized to provide it. In the Gonzales case, discussed earlier in this section, an appellate court held that Jerry Gonzales did not have effective consent to enter the Caldwell home and that a burglary charge (among other charges) was appropriate. The holding was based on the fact that Gonzales knew that Krissi Caldwell's parents did not want him in their home.[46]

In addition to "breaking," an actual or constructive *entry* into the structure is required for a burglary to occur. The slightest intrusion by the burglar or by any part of the burglar's body into the burglarized structure is sufficient to satisfy the requirement of an actual entry. Entry can also be accomplished by the insertion of a tool or other instrument into the structure burglarized. Drilling a hole into the floor of a granary, for example, in order to steal the grain that runs through the hole would be considered an entry for purposes of the crime of burglary.[47] A **constructive entry** occurs when the defendant causes another person (or a robot) to enter the structure to commit the crime or achieve the felonious purpose. Sending an innocent six-year-old child into a house, for example, to retrieve something for the burglar would be a constructive entry. In one early case, an individual was convicted of burglary when he sent his dog into a house to retrieve the desired object. All American jurisdictions recognize the concept of a constructive entry in burglary cases.

Courts have required that there be a causal relationship between the breaking and the entry. For example, in the case of *Regina* v. *Davis,* the defendant opened a window to crawl through. Before doing so, however, he noticed an open door and entered the structure through the door instead of the window. The court held that the defendant was not guilty of burglary because the breaking (raising the window) was not the means of entry.[48]

At common law, the burglarized structure had to be an occupied dwelling. Currently, in most jurisdictions, to constitute first-degree burglary the burglarized structure must be an occupied dwelling. Courts have generally held that as long as the structure that is burglarized is used to sleep in on a regular basis, it is an occupied dwelling for purposes of the law,[49] and it does not matter if the building is also used for business or other functions. During the temporary absence of the residents, an occupied dwelling is still considered "occupied," but ceases to be an occupied dwelling when the residents permanently move out.[50] All jurisdictions now recognize at least one form of burglary that does not require that the structure in question be a dwelling. Most still require, however, that it be a "building," although the definition of a building may be liberally interpreted. In one case, for example, a car wash, which was completely open on both ends, was considered to be a "building."[51] In many states, including California, even though an automobile is not a "building" in any reasonable sense of the word, a locked vehicle is also subject to being "burglarized."

Common law required that the breaking and entry had to occur during hours of darkness. It did not matter if the dwelling was brightly illuminated with artificial light. No jurisdictions presently limit breaking and entering offenses to nighttime hours, although in many jurisdictions, burglary during the hours between sunset and sunrise is a higher degree of burglary than one committed under the same circumstances during daylight.

Under common law, dictates against burglary were intended to protect owners of property and those dwelling therein. The target of burglary under common law, therefore, always had to be the property of *another*. The rule still applies, and one cannot burglarize one's own house. Even where individuals share living space, it is generally recognized as legally impossible for one occupant to commit burglary against the others. A more complicated situation exists, however, where a property

CONSTRUCTIVE ENTRY in the crime of burglary, one that occurs when the defendant causes another person to enter a structure to commit the crime or achieve a felonious purpose.

owner breaks into property rented to a tenant. In recognition of just such a possibility, the *Commentaries*[52] to the Model Penal Code say that the essential elements of burglary are:

- an unprivileged entry into,
- a building or occupied structure,
- with criminal purpose.

The commentary thus eliminates the need that the property be that of another, and dispenses with the necessity of a "breaking" as the term has been traditionally understood. The California burglary law, reproduced in an accompanying box, reflects a similar contemporary understanding of the essence of the crime of burglary (and the capstone case of *People* v. *Gauze,* at the end of this chapter, elaborates on it).

At common law, to constitute burglary the defendant must have intended to commit a felony at the time of the entry. Presently, most jurisdictions require that the defendant, at the time of entry, must have intended to commit a felony, such as rape, murder, or a theft offense. The theft offense, in many jurisdictions, may be a misdemeanor (e.g., petty theft). In some jurisdictions, all that is necessary is that the defendant intend to commit any crime, and in a few, it is not necessary that the burglar intend to commit that crime in the burglarized structure. Entering a structure in order to be a lookout or to hide until another crime can be completed elsewhere, for example, may constitute burglary in some jurisdictions. Intent, however, does not require that an identifiable offense actually be committed. Hence, one who breaks and enters someone else's house with murderous intent still commits burglary even if he or she is unable to find the intended victim.

The crime of burglary is completed when entry is made. A defendant who, for example, enters a building in order to steal something and then after entry changes his or her mind is still guilty of burglary. Generally, the crime of burglary is a felony, although most jurisdictions also recognize the statutory crimes of criminal trespass and looting.

Criminal trespass is a lesser included offense of burglary. Criminal trespass is the entering or remaining on the property or in the building of another when entry is forbidden, or failing to depart on having received notice to do so.[53] A similar statutory crime against property is **criminal mischief.** Criminal mischief is the intentional or knowing damage or destruction of the tangible property of another. It is committed by persons who deface or destroy property. In most jurisdictions, it is a misdemeanor. **Looting,** another crime against property, can be defined as burglary committed within an affected geographical area during an officially declared state of emergency, or during a local emergency resulting from an earthquake, fire, flood, riot, or other natural or manmade disaster. Some jurisdictions also criminalize the possession of burglary tools, that is, the possession of tools that serve a special purpose in breaking and entering a secured structure. The possession of burglary tools is only a crime when it can be shown that the possessor had the intent to use those tools for the purpose of burglary.

CRIMINAL TRESPASS
the entering or remaining on the property or in the building of another when entry was forbidden or, having received notice to depart, failing to do so.

CRIMINAL MISCHIEF
the intentional or knowing damage or destruction of the tangible property of another.

LOOTING
burglary committed within an affected geographical area during an officially declared state of emergency or during a local emergency resulting from an earthquake, fire, flood, riot, or other natural or manmade disaster.

ARSON

At common law, **arson** was the malicious burning of the dwelling of another. Hence, the crime was committed against habitation, not against property. The common law punishment for those convicted of arson, at least for a time, was death by burning. The modern trend has been to expand the scope of arson crimes to include many items other than "structures"—effectively transforming the crime into one against property. In the Washington State statute (see Law on the Books box), for example,

ARSON
the knowing and malicious burning of the personal property of another, or the burning of one's own property if the purpose is to collect insurance money.

LAW ON THE BOOKS

CALIFORNIA DEFINES "BURGLARY" AND "LOOTING."

Compare with Model Penal Code, Section 221.0–221.2

CALIFORNIA PENAL CODE

Section 459. Every person who enters any house, room, apartment, tenement, shop, warehouse, store, mill, barn, stable, outhouse or other building, tent, vessel, as defined in Section 21 of the Harbors and Navigation Code, floating home, as defined in subdivision (d) of Section 18075.55 of the Health and Safety Code, railroad car, locked or sealed cargo container, whether or not mounted on a vehicle, trailer coach, as defined in Section 635 of the Vehicle Code, any house car, as defined in Section 362 of the Vehicle Code, inhabited camper, as defined in Section 243 of the Vehicle Code, vehicle as defined by the Vehicle Code, when the doors are locked, aircraft as defined by Section 21012 of the Public Utilities Code, or mine or any underground portion thereof, with intent to commit grand or petit larceny or any felony is guilty of burglary. As used in this chapter, "inhabited" means currently being used for dwelling purposes, whether occupied or not. A house, trailer, vessel designed for habitation, or portion of a building is currently being used for dwelling purposes if, at the time of the burglary, it was not occupied solely because a natural or other disaster caused the occupants to leave the premises.

Section 460. (a) Every burglary of an inhabited dwelling house, vessel, as defined in the Harbors and Navigation Code, which is inhabited and designed for habitation, floating home, as defined in subdivision (d) of Section 18075.55 of the Health and Safety Code, or trailer coach, as defined by the Vehicle Code, or the inhabited portion of any other building, is burglary of the first degree.

(b) All other kinds of burglary are of the second degree. . . .

Section 461. Burglary is punishable as follows:

1. Burglary in the first degree: by imprisonment in the state prison for two, four, or six years.

2. Burglary in the second degree: by imprisonment in the county jail not exceeding one year or in the state prison.

Section 462. (a) Except in unusual cases where the interests of justice would best be served if the person is granted probation, probation shall not be granted to any person who is convicted of a burglary of an inhabited dwelling house or trailer coach as defined in Section 635 of the Vehicle Code, an inhabited floating home as defined in subdivision (d) of Section 18075.55 of the Health and Safety Code, or the inhabited portion of any other building.

(b) If the court grants probation under subdivision (a), it shall specify the reason or reasons for that order on the court record. . . .

Section 463. (a) Every person who violates Section 459, punishable as a second-degree burglary pursuant to subdivision 2 of Section 461, during and within an affected county in a "state of emergency" or a "local emergency" resulting from an earthquake, fire, flood, riot, or other natural or manmade disaster shall be guilty of the crime of looting, punishable by imprisonment in a county jail for one year or in the state prison. Any person convicted under this subdivision who is eligible for probation and who is granted probation shall, as a condition thereof, be confined in a county jail for at least 180 days, except that the court may, in the case where the interest of justice would best be served, reduce or eliminate that mandatory jail sentence, if the court specifies on the record and enters into the minutes the circumstances indicating that the interest of justice would best be served by that disposition. In addition to whatever custody is ordered, the court, in its discretion, may require any person granted probation following conviction under this subdivision to serve up to two hundred forty hours of community service in any program deemed appropriate by the court, including any program created to rebuild the community.

For purposes of this section, the fact that the structure entered has been damaged by the earthquake, fire, flood, or other natural or manmade disaster shall not, in and of itself, preclude conviction.

(b) Every person who commits the crime of grand theft, as defined in Section 487, except grand theft of a firearm, during and within an affected county in a "state of emergency" or a

(continued)

LAW ON THE BOOKS

"local emergency" resulting from an earthquake, fire, flood, riot, or other natural or unnatural disaster shall be guilty of the crime of looting, punishable by imprisonment in a county jail for one year or in the state prison. Every person who commits the crime of grand theft of a firearm, as defined in Section 487, during and within an affected county in a "state of emergency" or a "local emergency" resulting from an earthquake, fire, flood, riot, or other natural or unnatural disaster shall be guilty of the crime of looting, punishable by imprisonment in the state prison, as set forth in subdivision (a) of Section 489. Any person convicted under this subdivision who is eligible for probation and who is granted probation shall, as a condition thereof, be confined in a county jail for at least 180 days, except that the court may, in the case where the interest of justice would best be served, reduce or eliminate that mandatory jail sentence, if the court specifies on the record and enters into the minutes the circumstances indicating that the interest of justice would best be served by that disposition. In addition to whatever custody is ordered, the court, in its discretion, may require any person granted probation following conviction under this subdivision to serve up to one hundred sixty hours of community service in any program deemed appropriate by the court, including any program created to re-build the community.

(c) Every person who commits the crime of petty theft, as defined in Section 488, during and within an affected county in a "state of emergency" or a "local emergency" resulting from an earthquake, fire, flood, riot, or other natural or manmade disaster shall be guilty of a mis-demeanor, punishable by imprisonment in a county jail for six months. Any person convicted under this subdivision who is eligible for probation and who is granted probation shall, as a condition thereof, be confined in a county jail for at least ninety days, except that the court may, in the case where the interest of justice would best be served, reduce or eliminate that mandatory minimum jail sentence, if the court specifies on the record and enters into the min-utes the circumstances indicating that the interest of justice would best be served by that dis-position. In addition to whatever custody is ordered, the court, in its discretion, may require any person granted probation following conviction under this subdivision to serve up to eighty hours of community service in any program deemed appropriate by the court, including any program created to rebuild the community. . . .

(4) Consensual entry into a commercial structure with the intent to commit a violation of Section 470 [forgery], 476 [other forms of forgery], 476a [insufficient funds], 484f [use of counterfeit access card], or 484g [credit card fraud] of the Penal Code, shall not be charged as a violation under this section.

Section 464. Any person who, with intent to commit crime, enters, either by day or by night, any building, whether inhabited or not, and opens or attempts to open any vault, safe, or other secure place by use of acetylene torch or electric arc, burning bar, thermal lance, oxygen lance, or any other similar device capable of burning through steel, concrete, or any other solid sub-stance, or by use of nitroglycerin, dynamite, gunpowder, or any other explosive, is guilty of a felony and, upon conviction, shall be punished by imprisonment in the state prison for a term of three, five, or seven years.

arson includes the burning of hay, a bridge, a motor vehicle, and many other "things." To constitute arson in the contemporary sense of the offense, there is no requirement that an entire structure be burnt, or even that a "fire" in the normal sense of the word ensue. Arson occurs with even the slightest malicious burning, al-though a discoloration or blackening by heat or smoke would not be regarded as sufficient to constitute a "burning."

In almost all modern jurisdictions, arson requires the knowing and malicious burning of the fixture or personal property of another, and includes the burning of one's own property if the purpose is to collect insurance money. Arson cannot be committed by negligent or reckless conduct, and there is no felony arson rule, as there is in the case of felony murder. In determining the pecuniary loss in arson

LAW ON THE BOOKS

"ARSON" AS DEFINED BY THE STATE OF WASHINGTON.
Compare to Model Penal Code, Section 220.1

REVISED CODE OF WASHINGTON

Section 9A.48.020 Arson in the first degree.
1. A person is guilty of arson in the first degree if he knowingly and maliciously:
   (a) Causes a fire or explosion which is manifestly dangerous to any human life, including firemen; or
   (b) Causes a fire or explosion which damages a dwelling; or
   (c) Causes a fire or explosion in any building in which there shall be at the time a human being who is not a participant in the crime; or
   (d) Causes a fire or explosion on property valued at ten thousand dollars or more with intent to collect insurance proceeds.
2. Arson in the first degree is a class A felony.

Section 9A.48.030 Arson in the second degree.
1. A person is guilty of arson in the second degree if he knowingly and maliciously causes a fire or explosion which damages a building, or any structure or erection appurtenant to or joining any building, or any wharf, dock, machine, engine, automobile, or other motor vehicle, watercraft, aircraft, bridge, or trestle, or hay, grain, crop, or timber, whether cut or standing or any range land, or pasture land, or any fence, or any lumber, shingle, or other timber products, or any property.
2. Arson in the second degree is a class B felony.

cases, courts generally consider the fair market value of the property at the time it was destroyed or, in the case of damaged property, the cost of restoring it. Most states, like Washington, have divided arson into first and second degree, with first degree being the more aggravated form of arson.

Most jurisdictions also have statutes to punish persons who *recklessly start a fire*, or who *unlawfully cause a fire*. Such offenses differ from arson in that they may not include the "knowing and malicious" requirement necessary for the crime of arson. Section 452 of the California Penal Code, for example, provides that a person is guilty of unlawfully causing a fire when he or she recklessly sets fire to, or burns or causes to be burned, any structure, forest land, or other property. Accordingly, a person may be convicted of unlawfully causing a fire because of recklessness. Under California law the crime is a misdemeanor.

COMPUTER AND HIGH-TECHNOLOGY CRIMES

INTELLECTUAL PROPERTY
a form of creative endeavor that can be protected through patent, copyright, trade mark or other legal means. Intellectual property includes proprietary knowledge, trade secrets, confidentiality agreements, know-how, ideas, inventions, creations, technologies, processes, works of art and literature, and scientific discoveries or improvements.

COMPUTER CRIME
crime that employs computer technology as central to its commission and which could not take place without such technology.

The nature of criminal activity sometimes changes faster than laws can keep up with it. The burgeoning growth of technology, and especially computer technology, has brought with it new types of property crime. Many such crimes involve the theft of electronic forms of **intellectual property,** specifically the proprietary information stored in computers and digital devices, and on electromagnetic, optical, and other storage media. During the past twenty years all of the states, the federal government, and the District of Columbia have enacted **computer crime** statutes designed to facilitate the prosecution of high-technology and computer-related crimes.

Many traditional forms of crime, including fraud, drug dealing, theft, espionage, pornography, and extortion, can be committed using computers and the Internet.

The fact that computers can be used to commit crimes, however, does not necessarily make those crimes computer crimes.

Only crimes that employ computer technology as central to their commission, and that could not be committed without it, may properly be termed "computer crimes." Those that simply target computer machinery (such as the theft of computer equipment, the arson of computer facilities, and the like) or utilize computer facilities for the commission of more mundane crimes (such as theft, blackmail, and extortion) may be more appropriately prosecuted under other laws.

A few years ago, for example, FBI agents arrested a twenty-one-year-old Illinois man named Adam Quinn Pletcher and charged him with trying to extort $5.25 million from Microsoft founder and chairman Bill Gates. Pletcher,[54] a loner who spent hours in front of his computer, allegedly sent several letters to Gates demanding the money and threatening to kill him or his wife, Melinda, if he didn't respond to an America Online service known as "NetGirl." The service, an online dating forum, was to serve as a secure medium for the exchange of messages between Gates and the extortionist. FBI agents nabbed Pletcher after he sent a disk that held erased files still containing the names of Pletcher's parents to Gates. Some months earlier Pletcher had made headlines in Chicago when he was accused of running scams on his Internet Web page, including: (1) the sale of fake driver's licenses, telling people he could get them cars at bargain prices, and then pocketing their money; (2) running an illegal raffle that solicited ten-dollar chances to win an expensive automobile; and (3) offering "free" pagers that cost more than fifty dollars in service charges. By all accounts Pletcher was a hacker—a technologically sophisticated loner.

Although the attempt to extort money from Gates could easily have been prosecuted under "traditional" law, not all crimes committed with the use of computers can be so handled. The rapid growth in the number of crimes that took advantage of developing computer technology in the 1960s and 1970s—prior to the enactment of computer crime statutes—often forced prosecutors to use traditional tools in their arsenal and to charge computer criminals with larceny and other property crimes, even though the types of crimes being committed did not fit well with traditional understandings of crimes against property. As a consequence, it was not unusual to hear defendants argue, when charged with the larceny of software or

Web Extra! 10–7
Britannica online:
computer crime

A woman watches stock prices in the NASDAQ studio. Today's society is highly dependent on computer technology. That same technology provides fertile ground for criminals bent on stealing valuables, including cash, goods, and services, and intellectual property. (Photo courtesy of Impact Visuals Photo & Graphics, Inc.)

Web Extra! 10–8

The Secure Zone: The Computer Security Information Center

data, that nothing of substance had actually been "carried away" in a computer crime—since the allegedly stolen information generally remained on the computers from which it was said to have been stolen. Defendants and their attorneys typically argued that no crime had actually been committed since "property," under many larceny statutes of the time, meant only "tangible property" and electronic impulses, including computer programs and data, could not constitute tangible property.

In one exemplary case from the early 1960s, Robert F. Hancock, an employee of Dallas-based Texas Instruments Automatic Computers, was arrested and charged with stealing computer programs.[55] Hancock's story was fairly straightforward. In September of 1964, Hancock began sharing an apartment with a man named Smith. Hancock told Smith that his job was classified and said that he could not talk about it for security reasons. Nonetheless, Smith and Hancock frequently discussed computers, computer programming, and the impact of computerization on society. Eventually, Hancock told Smith that he was in possession of computer programs that would be of great value to Texaco, one of Texas Instrument's clients. Hancock asked Smith to go to Houston and approach executives at Texaco about buying the programs. He gave Smith a list of the programs that he had and also gave him one program on disk to verify the authenticity of those on the list. Smith made the trip and talked to two Texaco representatives, who told him that they could not enter into confidential negotiations.

A few days later, Hancock asked Smith to again contact Texaco executives, which he did. A man named Sims, who said he worked for Texaco, told Smith by telephone that his company was interested in the programs and asked Smith to bring them with him and be ready to discuss price. When he arrived in Houston, Smith was met at the airport by a man calling himself Don Sims, who said he worked with the computer department at Texaco. Sims looked at the index of programs presented by Smith, while Sims's companion examined the sample program. When Sims asked for a price, Smith offered the programs for $5 million. Sims then took all the materials from Smith and identified himself as an investigator, Dale Simpson. About the same time, a Texas Instruments security officer in Dallas was telling Hancock that he was being suspended for giving Smith the programs to sell.

Hancock was charged with felony theft under Texas law, tried, and convicted. He appealed his conviction, arguing, among other things, that computer programs are not corporeal property and are therefore not subject to theft. The appellate court, however, held that the Texas Penal Code defines "property," as related to the crime of theft, to include "all writings of every description, provided such property possesses any ascertainable value." The court wrote: "It is evident that the computer programs as alleged and the evidence in support thereof show that such property is included and comes within the meaning of the statutes defining the offenses of theft."[56]

As this example shows, computer crimes were not going unpunished before the enactment of a virtual plethora of computer crime statutes in the 1970s and 1980s. Because computer crimes generally violate traditional laws as well as laws specifically designed to combat them, many prosecutors successfully prosecuted early computer crimes under embezzlement, larceny, and fraud statutes. Federal prosecutors sometimes made use of existing wire fraud and mail fraud laws.

Early Computer Crime Cases

Not all computer crime prosecutions under existing laws were successful in the early days of high technology, as the 1972 Virginia case of *Lund* v. *Commonwealth*[57] shows. Charles Walter Lund was a graduate student in statistics at Virginia Technological University, and improperly used the university's computer to work on his doctoral thesis, billing the costs back to various departments. He was charged with grand larceny and larceny by false pretense for "stealing" computer time and computer services. Although convicted at trial, the Virginia Supreme Court reversed Lund's conviction, holding that computer time and services were not goods and chattels (personal property) within the meaning of the state's larceny statute. Since they could not be carried away, said the court, computer time and services were merely intangibles. In 1978, partially in reaction to the Lund case and others like it, the Virginia general assembly enacted penal code Section 18.2–98.1, which reads "Computer time or services or data processing services or information or data stored in connection therewith is hereby defined to be property which may be the subject of larceny under Section 18.2–95 or 18.2–96, or embezzlement under Section 18.2–111, or false pretenses under Section 18.2–178 [of the state's penal code]."

In another 1972 case, *Ward* v. *Superior Court*,[58] a California computer company employee was charged with grand theft of a trade secret belonging to another computer company. The trade secret was a computer program, valued by its owner at $5,000, which made it possible to provide a remote plotting service, through a switching attachment, over telephone lines to customers who had a specially designed plotter and transceiver unit. Because the program eliminated the need for an expensive transmitting unit, it gave its owner a substantial competitive advantage. Ward accessed and printed out the program from a terminal in his own company, using a third company's site and billing numbers. He was charged under two sections of the California Penal Code, one of which made it an offense to steal, take, or carry away any article representing a trade secret and the other of which made it an offense to mail a copy of any article representing a trade secret. Although the trial court reasoned that an article must be tangible in order for it to be possible that it be carried away and that electronic impulses transmitted over telephone lines are not tangible, it held that Ward had illegally copied an article that represented a trade secret.

Other courts were more reluctant to judicially create a new category of crime. In *People* v. *Weg*,[59] for example, the defendant—a computer programmer for the New York City Board of Education—allegedly stole data from the system he administered for his own commercial benefit. Although charged with theft of services under New York Penal Code Section 165.15(8), the court held that the Board of Education's computer was not "business" equipment. The court made clear that it felt that both the statutory context and the legislative history of the New York law clearly indicated that the legislature had meant to protect equipment in commercial use, but that the Board of Education's computers did not come under such a definition. If the legislature wanted to make unauthorized use of computers a crime, said the court, it could do so, as some other states had already had done at the time.

Although a number of early defendants in the computer crime arena were able to avoid criminal liability by playing on the shortcomings of traditional statutes defining property crimes, most were not. As the Electronic Frontier Foundation observes, "Without going into detailed discussion of [many] cases, we can make these general observations: (1) despite some ingenious defense arguments, most courts and prosecutors had little difficulty applying traditional concepts to computer offenses; (2) federal prosecutors frequently turned to wire fraud and mail fraud charges where state prosecutors would have charged fraud, larceny, or embezzlement; and (3) courts sometimes refused to apply traditional definitions to new offenses where there was no readily apparent loss by the victim."[60]

Computer Crime Laws

By 1990, all fifty states and the federal government had enacted computer crime statutes. The first state to pass a computer crime law was Florida, which passed

Kevin Mitnick, the FBI's most wanted hacker. Mitnick, nicknamed the "Billy-the-Kid of Computer Crime," was arrested a few years ago and charged with breaking into the computer systems of an Internet service provider in order to steal more than twenty thousand credit card numbers. (Photo by Bob Jordan, courtesy of AP/Wide World Photos.)

such a statute in 1978. The last state to enact a computer crime law was Massachusetts, which passed its statute in 1990. The first federal computer crime law, the Computer Fraud and Abuse Act, was enacted in October 1984.[61] A stop-gap measure, it has since been modified to incorporate recent computer-related developments. Central to federal law is a provision that makes it a federal crime to access, without authorization, any data processing system if the data processing system is involved in or used in relationship to interstate commerce. The act also makes it a crime to use a public telephone system to access, without authority, any data processing system, and the act prohibits those who have the authority to access a data processing system from using that authority in an unauthorized manner. Central to the law is the concept of a "protected computer," which is defined as "a computer (A) exclusively for the use of a financial institution or the United States Government, or, in the case of a computer not exclusively for such use, used by or for a financial institution or the United States Government and the conduct constituting the offense affects that use by or for the financial institution or the Government; or (B) which is used in interstate or foreign commerce or communication." Other federal statutes make it a felony to use, sell, or transfer counterfeit access devices that allow access to data processing systems.[62] Portions of the federal Computer Fraud and Abuse Act, as amended by the National Information Infrastructure Protection Act of 1996,[63] are reproduced in a Law on the Books box in this chapter.

Another relevant federal law is the 1997 No Electronic Theft Act (NET),[64] which makes it a crime to wilfully violate copyright, regardless of whether the infringement has a profit motive. The law was created in response to a 1994 case in which

David LaMacchia, a Massachusetts Institute of Technology student, distributed more than $1 million worth of copyrighted commercial software on an unauthorized MIT Internet bulletin board. LaMacchia couldn't be prosecuted under the federal Copyright Act because he didn't profit from the distribution. NET makes it a federal crime to distribute or possess unauthorized electronic copies of copyrighted materials valued at more than $1,000. Possessing ten or more illegal documents worth more than $2,500 carries a three-year prison term and a $250,000 fine.

Most computer crime laws—whether federal or state—criminalize unauthorized access, although penalties for simple access (or access without harm) are usually not harsh.[65] Most state computer crime laws are comprehensive statutes, and often take the form of an independent title in a state's criminal code called the "Computer Crimes Act" or the "Computer Crime Prevention Act."[66] In contrast, some states have created a patchwork quilt of modifications to existing laws to cover a variety of crimes, such as "computer trespass" and "theft with a computer." Ohio, for example, has inserted a series of computer crime definitions in its general theft statute, added one section on denying access to a computer, and placed computer systems, networks, and software used in committing any offense within its general definition of "contraband."[67] Many state computer crime statutes occupy a middle ground and can be found under other statutory categories, such as crimes against property, fraud, theft (as is the case in California), or business and commercial offenses. Arizona, for example, has placed its computer crime provisions under the section of its penal code entitled "Organized Crime and Fraud," while North Dakota places such legislation under its "Racketeer Influenced and Corrupt Organizations (RICO)" statute.

Due to the fact that legislatures often saw themselves creating new laws to deal with emerging and rapid social and technological changes, computer crime laws frequently set forth a number of definitions unique to such legislation. Typically defined by such laws are terms such as: (1) access, (2) computer, (3) computer network, (4) computer program, (5) computer software, (6) computer system, and (7) computer data. A few states have attempted to define specific terminology such as: (1) computer control language (Maryland), (2) computer database (Maryland), (3) computer hacking (South Carolina), (4) system hacker (Tennessee), (5) computer supplies (Wisconsin), (6) database (New Jersey and Pennsylvania), (7) private personal data (Connecticut and Delaware), and (8) supporting documentation (Wisconsin). The Pennsylvania computer crime law, which is fairly concise and similar in purpose to the computer crime laws of many other jurisdictions, is reproduced below (note the definition of the word "property" under the Pennsylvania law).

Web Extra! 10–9

Computer Crime Laws by State

LAW ON THE BOOKS

"COMPUTER CRIME" UNDER PENNSYLVANIA LAW.

TITLE 18, PENNSYLVANIA CONSOLIDATED STATUTES

Section 3933. Unlawful use of computer.
  a. Offense defined. A person commits an offense if he:
     (1) accesses, alters, damages, or destroys any computer, computer system, computer network, computer software, computer program or data base or any part thereof, with the intent to interrupt the normal functioning of an organization or to devise or execute any scheme or artifice to defraud or deceive or control property or services by means of false or fraudulent pretenses, representations, or promises;

(continued)

LAW ON THE BOOKS

(2) intentionally and without authorization accesses, alters, interferes with the operation of, damages, or destroys any computer, computer system, computer network, computer software, computer program, or computer data base or any part thereof; or

(3) intentionally or knowingly and without authorization gives or publishes a password, identifying code, personal identification number, or other confidential information about a computer, computer system, computer network, or data base.

b. Grading. An offense under subsection (a)(1) is a felony of the third degree. An offense under subsection (a)(2) or (3) is a misdemeanor of the first degree.

c. Definitions. As used in this section the following words and phrases shall have the meanings given to them in this subsection:

"Access." To intercept, instruct, communicate with, store data in, retrieve data from, or otherwise make use of any resources of a computer, computer system, computer network, or data base.

"Computer." An electronic, magnetic, optical, hydraulic, organic, or other high speed data processing device or system which performs logic, arithmetic, or memory functions and includes all input, output, processing, storage, software, or communication facilities which are connected or related to the device in a system or network.

"Computer network." The interconnection of two or more computers through the usage of satellite, microwave, line, or other communication medium.

"Computer program." An ordered set of instructions or statements and related data that, when automatically executed in actual or modified form in a computer system, causes it to perform specified functions.

"Computer software." A set of computer programs, procedures, and associated documentation concerned with the operation of a computer system.

"Computer system." A set of related, connected, or unconnected computer equipment, devices, and software.

"Data base." A representation of information, knowledge, facts, concepts, or instructions which are being prepared or processed or have been prepared or processed in a formalized manner and are intended for use in a computer, computer system, or computer network, including, but not limited to, computer printouts, magnetic storage media, punched cards, or data stored internally in the memory of the computer.

"Financial instrument." Includes, but is not limited to, any check, draft, warrant, money order, note, certificate of deposit, letter of credit, bill of exchange, credit or debit card, transaction authorization mechanism, marketable security, or any computer system representation thereof.

"Property." Includes, but is not limited to, financial instruments, computer software, and programs in either machine or human readable form, and anything of value, tangible or intangible.

"Services." Includes, but is not limited to, computer time, data processing, and storage functions.

(Dec. 2, 1983, P.L.248, No.67, eff. 60 days; Dec. 11, 1986, P.L.1517, No.164, eff. 60 days)

LAW ON THE BOOKS

"COMPUTER CRIME" UNDER FEDERAL LAW.

TITLE 18 UNITED STATES CODE

Section 1030. Fraud and related activity in connection with computers

(a) Whoever—

(1) having knowingly accessed a computer without authorization or exceeding authorized access, and by means of such conduct having obtained information that has been

(continued)

LAW ON THE BOOKS

determined by the United States Government pursuant to an Executive order or statute to require protection against unauthorized disclosure for reasons of national defense or foreign relations, or any restricted data, as defined in paragraph y of section 11 of the Atomic Energy Act of 1954, with reason to believe that such information so obtained could be used to the injury of the United States, or to the advantage of any foreign nation willfully communicates, delivers, transmits, or causes to be communicated, delivered, or transmitted, or attempts to communicate, deliver, transmit or cause to be communicated, delivered, or transmitted the same to any person not entitled to receive it, or willfully retains the same and fails to deliver it to the officer or employee of the United States entitled to receive it;

(2) intentionally accesses a computer without authorization or exceeds authorized access, and thereby obtains—

   (A) information contained in a financial record of a financial institution, or of a card issuer as defined in section 1602(n) of title 15, or contained in a file of a consumer reporting agency on a consumer, as such terms are defined in the Fair Credit Reporting Act (15 U.S.C. 1681 et seq.);

   (B) information from any department or agency of the United States; or

   (C) information from any protected computer if the conduct involved an interstate or foreign communication;

(3) intentionally, without authorization to access any nonpublic computer of a department or agency of the United States, accesses such a computer of that department or agency that is exclusively for the use of the Government of the United States or, in the case of a computer not exclusively for such use, is used by or for the Government of the United States and such conduct affects that use by or for the Government of the United States;

(4) knowingly and with intent to defraud, accesses a protected computer without authorization, or exceeds authorized access, and by means of such conduct furthers the intended fraud and obtains anything of value, unless the object of the fraud and the thing obtained consists only of the use of the computer and the value of such use is not more than $5,000 in any 1-year period;

(5)

   (A) knowingly causes the transmission of a program, information, code, or command, and as a result of such conduct, intentionally causes damage without authorization, to a protected computer;

   (B) intentionally accesses a protected computer without authorization, and as a result of such conduct, recklessly causes damage; or

   (C) intentionally accesses a protected computer without authorization, and as a result of such conduct, causes damage;

(6) knowingly and with intent to defraud traffics (as defined in section 1029) in any password or similar information through which a computer may be accessed without authorization, if—

   (A) such trafficking affects interstate or foreign commerce; or

   (B) such computer is used by or for the Government of the United States; or

(7) with intent to extort from any person, firm, association, educational institution, financial institution, government entity, or other legal entity, any money or other thing of value, transmits in interstate or foreign commerce any communication containing any threat to cause damage to a protected computer; shall be punished as provided in subsection (c) of this section.

(b) Whoever attempts to commit an offense under subsection (a) of this section shall be punished as provided in subsection (c) of this section.

(c) The punishment for an offense under subsection (a) or (b) of this section is—

   (1)

      (A) a fine under this title or imprisonment for not more than ten years, or both, in the case of an offense under subsection (a)(1) of this section which does not occur after a conviction for another offense under this section, or an attempt to commit an offense punishable under this subparagraph; and (B) a fine under this title or

(continued)

LAW ON THE BOOKS

imprisonment for not more than twenty years, or both, in the case of an offense under subsection (a)(1) of this section which occurs after a conviction for another offense under this section, or an attempt to commit an offense punishable under this subparagraph;

(2)

(A) a fine under this title or imprisonment for not more than one year, or both, in the case of an offense under subsection (a)(2), (a)(3), (a)(5)(C), or (a)(6) of this section which does not occur after a conviction for another offense under this section, or an attempt to commit an offense punishable under this subparagraph;

(B) a fine under this title or imprisonment for not more than 5 years, or both, in the case of an offense under subsection (a)(2), if—

(i) the offense was committed for purposes of commercial advantage or private financial gain;

(ii) the offense was committed in furtherance of any criminal or tortious act in violation of the Constitution or laws of the United States or of any State; or

(iii) the value of the information obtained exceeds $5,000; and

(C) a fine under this title or imprisonment for not more than ten years, or both, in the case of an offense under subsection (a)(2), (a)(3) or (a)(6) of this section which occurs after a conviction for another offense under this section, or an attempt to commit an offense punishable under this subparagraph; and (3)(A) a fine under this title or imprisonment for not more than five years, or both, in the case of an offense under subsection (a)(4), (a)(5)(A), (a)(5)(B), or (a)(7) of this section which does not occur after a conviction for another offense under this section, or an attempt to commit an offense punishable under this subparagraph; and

(B) a fine under this title or imprisonment for not more than ten years, or both, in the case of an offense under subsection (a)(4), (a)(5)(A), (a)(5)(B), (a)(5)(C), or (a)(7) of this section which occurs after a conviction for another offense under this section, or an attempt to commit an offense punishable under this subparagraph.

(d) The United States Secret Service shall, in addition to any other agency having such authority, have the authority to investigate offenses under subsections (a)(2)(A), (a)(2)(B), (a)(3), (a)(4), (a)(5), and (a)(6) of this section. Such authority of the United States Secret Service shall be exercised in accordance with an agreement which shall be entered into by the Secretary of the Treasury and the Attorney General.

(e) As used in this section—

(1) the term "computer" means an electronic, magnetic, optical, electrochemical, or other high speed data processing device performing logical, arithmetic, or storage functions, and includes any data storage facility or communications facility directly related to or operating in conjunction with such device, but such term does not include an automated typewriter or typesetter, a portable hand held calculator, or other similar device;

(2) the term "protected computer" means a computer—

(A) exclusively for the use of a financial institution or the United States Government, or, in the case of a computer not exclusively for such use, used by or for a financial institution or the United States Government and the conduct constituting the offense affects that use by or for the financial institution or the Government; or

(B) which is used in interstate or foreign commerce or communication;

(3) the term "State" includes the District of Columbia, the Commonwealth of Puerto Rico, and any other commonwealth, possession or territory of the United States;

(4) the term "financial institution" means—

(A) an institution, with deposits insured by the Federal Deposit Insurance Corporation;

(B) the Federal Reserve or a member of the Federal Reserve including any Federal Reserve Bank;

(C) a credit union with accounts insured by the National Credit Union Administration;

(D) a member of the Federal home loan bank system and any home loan bank;

(continued)

LAW ON THE BOOKS

(E) any institution of the Farm Credit System under the Farm Credit Act of 1971;

(F) a broker-dealer registered with the Securities and Exchange Commission pursuant to section 15 of the Securities Exchange Act of 1934;

(G) the Securities Investor Protection Corporation;

(H) a branch or agency of a foreign bank (as such terms are defined in paragraphs (1) and (3) of section 1(b) of the International Banking Act of 1978); and

(I) an organization operating under section 25 or section 25(a) of the Federal Reserve Act;

(5) the term "financial record" means information derived from any record held by a financial institution pertaining to a customer's relationship with the financial institution;

(6) the term "exceeds authorized access" means to access a computer with authorization and to use such access to obtain or alter information in the computer that the accesser is not entitled so to obtain or alter;

(7) the term "department of the United States" means the legislative or judicial branch of the Government or one of the executive departments enumerated in section 101 of title 5;

(8) the term "damage" means any impairment to the integrity or availability of data, a program, a system, or information, that—

(A) causes loss aggregating at least $5,000 in value during any 1-year period to one or more individuals;

(B) modifies or impairs, or potentially modifies or impairs, the medical examination, diagnosis, treatment, or care of one or more individuals;

(C) causes physical injury to any person; or

(D) threatens public health or safety; and

(9) the term "government entity" includes the Government of the United States, any State or political subdivision of the United States, any foreign country, and any state, province, municipality, or other political subdivision of a foreign country. . . .

The Electronic Frontier Foundation (EFF),[68] a San Francisco–based organization founded in 1990 and dedicated to protecting civil liberties on the World Wide Web, points out that "state statutes do not always give computer offenses specific names." The EFF notes that such laws "use a variety of descriptions to state exactly what they are prohibiting," and found that the following descriptive titles are among the most commonly used: (1) access to defraud, (2) access to obtain money, (3) computer fraud, (4) offenses against computer users, (5) offenses against intellectual property, (6) offenses against computer equipment and supplies, (7) unauthorized access, (8) and unauthorized or unlawful computer use.

Generally speaking, computer crimes laws attempt to apply the concept of common law trespass to computers. Hence, computer crimes are usually defined as unauthorized entry onto someone else's property. Where no criminal intent beyond curiosity or mischief exists, the crime may be a minor offense, such as "computer hacking." Where criminal intent exists, however, the laws of most jurisdictions allow prosecution for both the unauthorized access and some other crime—usually a fraud or theft, or an attempt to commit a fraud or theft. Similarly, most computer crime laws contain provisions making it illegal to interfere with another person's legitimate access to computer services or to information stored in a computer. Most states, however, provide for an affirmative defense of authorization when a reasonable belief that access was authorized can be demonstrated.

CRIMINAL LAW IN THE NEWS

Feds: Hacker Hosted Hackers on NASA Computers

N.Y. Man Accused of Cracking Jet Propulsion Lab

WHITE PLAINS, N.Y.—Federal authorities today arrested an alleged hacker who they say broke into NASA computers in 1998 and used one to host a chat room for other hackers.

Mary Jo White, the U.S. attorney for the Southern District of New York, indicted Raymond Torricelli, 20, aka "rolex," on five felony counts for credit card fraud, interception and unauthorized access to two National Aeronautics and Space Administration computers.

White alleged in court documents that Torricelli broke into two computers at the agency's Jet Propulsion Laboratory (JPL).

Prosecutors allege the hackers, part of a group called "#conflict," chatted about hacking, cracking, credit card fraud and how to "use their computers to alter the results of the annual MTV Movie Awards," White said in a statement.

Codes decrypted

Torricelli allegedly used the other JPL computer to place a "sniffer" program to intercept computer user names and passwords on networks.

Prosecutors said they discovered 76,000 such passwords on Torricelli's home computer—many of which had been decrypted.

Torricelli allegedly also cracked 800 other computers in his online sneaking spree.

Conviction on the credit card fraud and password possession charges could lead to 10 years in jail and a $250,000 fine. The password interception charge carries a possible five-year term and $250,000 fine, and the two charges for computer intrusion are punishable by a year in jail for each count.

Went home to mom

Torricelli's court-appointed attorney, Suzanne Brody of Federal Legal Aid, said she had not yet had a chance to discuss the case in depth with her client.

She said his computers were seized two years ago following the alleged activity, but Torricelli was not arrested then.

Before being released on $50,000 bond today, Torricelli was "understandably frightened" by the experience of being arrested by federal authorities, Brody said.

"We got him bailed out, and he went home to his mother," Brody said.

Torricelli is from New Rochelle.

Last December, another New Rochelle teenager was sentenced for hacking America Online's computer system after gaining knowledge of the Internet service provider working as a technical support volunteer for the company.

Source: James Gordon Meek, "Feds: Hacker Hosted Hackers on NASA Computers; N.Y. Man Accused of Cracking Jet Propulsion Lab," APB News. Reprinted with permission.

Types of Computer Crimes

CYBERCRIME

crime that employs computer technology as central to its commission and which could not occur without such technology. Another word for computer crime.

COMPUTER FRAUD

a statutory provision, found in many states, which makes it unlawful for any person to use a computer or computer network without authority and with the intent to: (a) obtain property or services by false pretenses; (b) embezzle or commit larceny; or (c) convert the property of another.

A contemporary term for computer crime is **cybercrime.** Simply put, cybercrime is crime committed with or through the use of computers. Generally speaking, there are five *types* of cybercrime found in today's law—although the names given each type vary considerably between jurisdictions. The five types are: (1) computer fraud, (2) computer trespass, (3) theft of computer services, (4) personal trespass by computer, and (5) special laws against the dissemination of computer viruses, worms, and Trojan Horses, best called "computer tampering."

Even though titles vary, each type of computer offense has distinguishable elements. Distilling the laws of a variety of jurisdictions, it can be said that the elements of **computer fraud** make it unlawful for any person to:

- use a computer or computer network,
- without authority, and
- with the intent to: (a) obtain property or services by false pretenses; (b) embezzle or commit larceny; or (c) convert the property of another.

The elements of **computer trespass** criminalize the activities of any person who:

- uses a computer or computer network,
- without authority, and
- with the intent to: (a) remove computer data, computer programs, or computer software from a computer or computer network; (b) cause a computer to malfunction; (c) alter or erase any computer data, computer programs, or computer software; (d) effect the creation or alteration of a financial instrument or of an electronic transfer of funds; (e) cause physical injury to the property of another; or (f) make or cause to be made an unauthorized copy of data stored on a computer, or of computer programs or computer software.

Laws against the **theft of computer services** make it unlawful for any person to:

- willfully use a computer or computer network,
- with intent to obtain computer services,
- without authority.

The elements of **personal trespass by computer** make it illegal for a person to:

- use a computer or computer network,
- without authority, and
- with the intent to cause physical injury to an individual.

Some states, depending on the seriousness of the behavior involved, or the degree of harm that results, define greater and lessor degrees of each type of offense.

Although many states deal with computer viruses, worms, and Trojan Horses (sometimes called "rogue programs") under laws against computer trespass, a number of states have now enacted special **computer tampering** legislation to deal with such threats. A number of such special laws were passed after the arrest of Robert Morris, whose November 1, 1988, release of an Internet "worm" that spread to computers throughout the country (and the world) in a matter of hours, slowing them down and necessitating special administrative measures, became a watershed event in the history of computing. Morris' experiment in malicious programming cost thousands of hours of operator time to repair and an untold amount of monetary damage. Following Morris' arrest and prosecution, California modified its computer crime legislation to specifically refer to both worms and viruses, calling them "computer contaminants."[70] Maine and Texas both changed their laws to include "computer viruses," while other states used terminology such as "destructive computer program" and "computer tampering" to describe the same phenomenon.

In 1994, under Title XXIX of the Violent Crime Control and Law Enforcement Act of 1994, the federal government enacted legislation targeting viruses and other rouge programs. The legislation, known as the Computer Abuse Amendments Act of 1994,[71] modified 18 U.S.C.A. 1030(a)(5) and came on the heels of a number of well-publicized attacks on computers throughout the country by hackers writing rogue programs.

Computer tampering has four elements. Laws against computer tampering make it illegal for a person to:

- insert or attempt to insert a "program" into a computer,
- while knowing or believing that,
- the "program" contains information or commands that,
- will or may damage or destroy that computer (or its data) or any other computer (or its data) accessing or being accessed by that computer, *or* that will or may cause loss to the users of that computer or the users of a computer that accesses or that is accessed by such "program."

Individual computer tampering statutes may define the terms "program" and "loss" more precisely, although they do not do so in all cases.[72]

COMPUTER TRESPASS the offense of using a computer or computer network without authority and with the intent to: (a) remove computer data, computer programs, or computer software from a computer or computer network; (b) cause a computer to malfunction; (c) alter or erase any computer data, computer programs, or computer software; (d) effect the creation or alteration of a financial instrument or of an electronic transfer of funds; (e) cause physical injury to the property of another; or (f) make or cause to be made an unauthorized copy of data stored on a computer or of computer programs or computer software.

THEFT OF COMPUTER SERVICES an offense in which a person wilfully uses a computer or computer network with intent to obtain computer services without authority.

PERSONAL TRESPASS BY COMPUTER an offense in which a person uses a computer or computer network without authority and with the intent to cause physical injury to an individual.

COMPUTER TAMPERING the illegal insertion or attempt to insert a "program" into a computer, while knowing or believing that the "program" contains information or commands that will or may damage or destroy that computer (or its data), or any other computer (or its data) accessing or being accessed by that computer, *or* that will or may cause loss to the users of that computer or the users of a computer that accesses or that is accessed by such "program."[69]

Web Extra! 10–10

Computer Crime and
Intellectual Property
Section, USDOJ

Federal Cybercrime Enforcement Agencies

A number of federal agencies are involved in the battle against computer crime. Primary among them are the Computer Crime and Intellectual Property Section (CCIPS) of the U.S. Department of Justice and the FBI's Infrastructure Protection and Computer Intrusion Squad (IPCIS). CCIPS was founded in 1991 as the Computer Crime Unit, but was elevated to "section" status within the Criminal Division of the U.S. Department of Justice in 1996.

The CCIPS staff consists of about two dozen lawyers who focus exclusively on the issues raised by computer and intellectual property crime. CCIPS staffers work closely on computer crime cases with assistant United States attorneys known as Computer and Telecommunications Coordinators (CTCs) in U.S. attorney's offices around the country.[73] CCIPS attorneys take a lead role in litigating some computer crime and intellectual property investigations, and a coordinating role in some national investigations. Section attorneys advise federal prosecutors and law enforcement agents, comment on and propose legislation, coordinate international efforts to combat computer crime, litigate cases, and train federal law enforcement groups.

The FBI's IPCIS is responsible for investigating unauthorized intrusions into major computer networks belonging to telecommunications providers, private corporations, U.S. government agencies, and public and private educational facilities.[74] The squad also investigates the illegal interception of signals (especially cable and satellite signal theft) and infringement of copyright laws related to software.

Internet-Based Crime

In February 2000, the President's Working Group on Unlawful Conduct on the Internet released a report entitled *The Electronic Frontier: The Challenge of Unlawful Conduct Involving the Use of the Internet.*[75] The group reported that "similar to the technologies that have preceded it, the Internet provides a new tool for wrongdoers to commit crimes, such as fraud, the sale or distribution of child pornography, the sale of guns or drugs or other regulated substances without regulatory protections, or the unlawful distribution of computer software or other creative material protected by intellectual property rights. In the most extreme circumstances, cyberstalking and other criminal conduct involving the Internet can lead to physical violence, abductions, and molestation."[76] Some criminal activities, the group observed, "employ both the product delivery and communications features of the Internet." Pedophiles, for example, "may use the Internet's file transfer utilities to distribute and receive child pornography, and use its communications features to make contact with children."

The group said that "although the precise extent of unlawful conduct involving the use of computers is unclear, the rapid growth of the Internet and e-commerce has made such unlawful conduct a critical priority for legislators, policymakers, industry, and law enforcement agencies."[77] One reason is the Internet's potential to reach vast audiences easily, meaning that the potential scale of unlawful conduct is often much wider in cyberspace than the same conduct would be in the offline world.

The group attempted to assess the extent to which existing federal laws adequately address unlawful conduct involving the use of the Internet. It developed four general principles to guide its analysis. Those principles, which can also serve as guidelines for future legislation at both the state and federal level, are as follows:

- *Online–offline consistency.* Substantive regulation of unlawful conduct (e.g., legislation providing for civil or criminal penalties for given conduct) should, as a rule, apply in the same way to conduct in the cyberworld as it does to conduct in the physical world. If an activity is prohibited in the physical world but not on the Internet, then the Internet becomes a safe haven for that unlawful activity. Similarly, conduct that is not prohibited in the physical world should not be subject to prohibition merely because it is carried out in cyberspace. Thus, unlawful conduct involving the use of the Internet should not be treated as a special form of conduct outside the scope of existing laws. For example, fraud that is perpetrated through the use of the Internet should not be treated any differently, as a matter of substantive criminal law, from fraud that is perpetrated through the use of the telephone or the mail. To the extent that existing laws treat online and offline conduct inconsistently, they should be amended to remove inconsistencies.

- *Appropriate investigatory tools.* To effectively enforce substantive laws that apply to online conduct, law enforcement authorities need appropriate tools for detecting and investigating unlawful conduct involving the Internet. To the extent that existing investigative authority is tied to a particular technology, for example, it may need to be modified or clarified so that it also applies to the Internet. Moreover, the Internet, like other new technologies before it, may justify new forms of investigative authority. Before the invention of the telephone, for example, law enforcement agencies had no need for wiretaps, but once it was clear that the telephone was being used to facilitate illegal activity, that new authority (circumscribed with protections for civil liberties and other societal interests) became necessary and appropriate. In like manner, features of the Internet that make it different from prior technologies may justify the need for changes in laws and procedures that govern the detection and investigation of computer crimes.

- *Technology neutrality.* To the extent that specific regulation of online activity may be necessary, any such regulation should be drafted in a technology-neutral way. Regulation tied to a particular technology may quickly become obsolete and require further amendment. In particular, laws written before the widespread use of the Internet may be based on assumptions regarding then-current technologies and thus may need to be clarified or updated to reflect new technological capabilities or realities. For example, regulation of "wire communications" may not account for the fact that communications may now occur through wireless means or by satellite. Technology-specific laws and regulations may also "lock in" a particular technology, hindering the development of superior technology.

- *Consideration of other societal interests.* Any government regulation of conduct involving the use of the Internet requires a careful consideration of different societal interests. In addition to society's strong interests in investigating and prosecuting unlawful conduct, society also has strong interests in promoting free speech, protecting children, protecting reasonable expectations of privacy, providing broad access to public information, and supporting legitimate commerce.

It is important to realize that the Internet presents new issues relating to online expectations of privacy and confidentiality that may or may not have analogs in the offline world. Accordingly, concluded the working group, "rules and regulations designed to protect the safety and security of Internet users should be carefully tailored to accomplish their objectives without unintended consequences, such as stifling the growth of the Internet or chilling its use as a free and open communication medium."[78]

The group concluded that existing substantive federal laws appear to be generally adequate to protect Internet users from unlawful conduct. As noted earlier in this chapter, many such laws generally do not distinguish between unlawful conduct committed through the use of the Internet and the same conduct committed through the use of other, more traditional means of communication. For example, laws governing fraud, such as credit card fraud, identity theft, securities fraud, and unfair and deceptive trade acts or practices, apply with equal force to both online as well as offline conduct. Similarly, laws prohibiting the distribution and possession of child pornography and the luring of minors across state lines for unlawful sexual activity have been used with success to prosecute and convict those who use the Internet to distribute such material or to communicate with child victims in violation of statutory prohibitions. Laws in other areas, including the sale of firearms, interstate transmission of gambling information, the sale of alcohol, securities fraud, and the theft of intellectual property, also generally apply to online as well as offline conduct.

One special problem associated with Internet activity noted by the working group, however, involves questions about jurisdiction. Although crimes on the Internet may victimize local populations, the medium over which these crimes are committed permits a defendant to be located anywhere in the world. The group noted that "in the physical world, one cannot visit a place without some sense of its geographic location. Whether a particular street address or an area of the world, human travel is spatially based." By contrast, the group said, "because one can access a computer remotely without knowing where, in physical space, that computer is located, many people have come to think of the collection of worldwide computer linkages as 'cyberspace'."

Significantly, cybercriminals are no longer hampered by the existence of national or international boundaries, because information and property can be easily transmitted through communications and data networks. As a result, a criminal no longer needs to be at the actual scene of the crime (or anywhere nearby) to prey on his or her victims. A computer server running a Web page designed to defraud senior citizens, for example, might be located in Thailand, and victims of the scam could be scattered throughout numerous countries. A child pornographer might distribute photographs or videos via e-mail making its way through the communications networks of several countries before reaching the intended recipients. Likewise, evidence of a crime can be stored at a remote location, either for the purpose of concealing the crime from law enforcement and others, or simply because of the design of the network. To clarify its point about jurisidictional issues, the working group gave this example: "A cyberstalker in Brooklyn, New York, may send a threatening e-mail to a person in Manhattan. If the stalker routes his communication through Argentina, France, and Norway before reaching his victim, the New York Police Department may have to get assistance from the Office of International Affairs at the Department of Justice in Washington, D.C., which, in turn, may have to get assistance from law enforcement in (say) Buenos Aires, Paris, and Oslo just to learn that the suspect is in New York." In this example, the working group points out, the perpetrator needs no passport and passes through no checkpoints as he commits his crime, while law enforcement agencies are burdened with cumbersome mechanisms for international cooperation—mechanisms that often derail or slow investigations.

The group adds that such jurisdictional issues do "not mean that traditional legal structures cannot be meaningfully applied to the Internet. Even though connections may be of short duration, computers are still physically located in particular places. The challenge to law enforcement is identifying that location and deciding which laws apply to what conduct." Some state computer crime statutes specifically provide that prosecution for computer crimes can take place in any jurisdiction where the computer used in the offense was located, in any area where an affected computer network functions, or in any jurisdiction "from which, to which, or through which any use of a computer or computer network was made, whether by wires, electromagnetic waves, microwaves, or any other means of communication."[79]

The report concludes by calling for increased interstate and federal–state cooperation. The fundamental question, says the group, is "how sovereign nations can meaningfully enforce national laws and procedures on a global Internet." Because the gathering of information in other jurisdictions and internationally will be crucial to investigating and prosecuting cybercrimes, the group concludes that "all levels of government will need to develop concrete and reliable mechanisms for cooperating with each other."

SUMMARY

- This chapter discusses property crimes, including larceny, burglary, criminal trespass, arson, and computer crimes involving misappropriation.
- Most property crimes are crimes of theft. Crimes of theft are sometimes called "acquisitive offenses," "wrongful acquisition crimes," or "crimes of misappropriation" because they involve the unlawful acquiring or appropriation of someone else's property.
- Larceny was the only form of theft originally punished under early common law. In early times, it was a capital offense.
- In most jurisdictions, the statutory crime of larceny today consists of the wrongful taking and carrying away (which is called "asportation") of the personal property of another with the intent to permanently deprive the owner of possession of the property.
- Almost all jurisdictions have divided larceny into "petit" and "grand." Grand larceny (also known as grand theft) usually consists of the theft of property that has a market value of more than a certain amount, or certain property listed in the statute, such as firearms and cattle.
- Embezzlement is the unlawful conversion of the personal property of another, by a person to whom it has been entrusted by (or for) its rightful owner. Embezzlement is fundamentally a violation of trust. Like larceny, one can be guilty of embezzlement only if the embezzled property belongs to another. Embezzlement is also known as fraudulent conversion.
- The crime of obtaining property by false pretenses, usually referred to simply as "false pretenses," occurs when the taking of property with the passing of title is predicated on a false representation of a material fact. The crime occurs when a person uses false pretenses to obtain both possession of, and title to, the property in question.
- Forgery is the making of a false instrument or the material alteration of an existing genuine instrument. Forgery is complete when one either makes or passes a false instrument with the intent to defraud. The gist of the crime of forgery is the intent to defraud.
- Uttering is the offering, passing, or attempted passing of a forged document with knowledge that the document is false and with intent to defraud. Today, most jurisdictions have separately established the statutory crime of uttering a forged document.
- Receiving stolen property is another form of theft. Receiving stolen property can be defined as knowingly taking possession of, or control over, property that has been unlawfully stolen from another. Simply put, it is the receiving of stolen property, knowing that it has been stolen.
- Robbery is an aggravated form of larceny. In addition to the elements necessary to constitute larceny, robbery involves two additional aspects: (1) the property must be taken from a person or removed from the presence of the victim, and (2) the taking must be by use of force or by putting the victim in fear.
- At early common law, extortion was the corrupt collection of an unlawful fee by a public officer under color of office. It was a misdemeanor. Almost all American

jurisdictions have expanded the crime of extortion to cover all persons using future threats to wrongfully obtain property. The contemporary crime of extortion can be defined as the taking of personal property by a threat of future harm. Statutory extortion is a felony in most jurisdictions.

- Blackmail is a form of extortion in which a threat is made to disclose a crime or other social disgrace. Even a threat to cause economic injury or social embarrassment may be sufficient to constitute blackmail in most jurisdictions.

- Identity theft, which is the unauthorized use of another individual's personal identity to fraudulently obtain money, goods, or services, is quickly becoming the most important new theft crime of the twenty-first century. Common forms of identity theft include taking over an existing credit card account and making unauthorized charges to it, taking out loans in another person's name, writing fraudulent checks using another person's name or account number, and using personal information to access and transfer money out of another person's bank or brokerage account.

- At common law, burglary was the breaking and entering of the dwelling house of another in the nighttime with the intent to commit a felony. In most jurisdictions today, however, the crime of burglary is statutorily defined as the: breaking and entering of a building, locked automobile, boat, and so on with the intent to commit a felony or theft. Many jurisdictions divide burglary into burglary in the first degree and burglary in the second degree, with burglary in the first degree being burglary of an inhabited dwelling and all other burglaries being in the second degree.

- Looting, another crime against property, can be defined as burglary committed within an affected geographical area during an officially declared state of emergency, or during a local emergency resulting from an earthquake, fire, flood, riot, or other natural or manmade disaster.

- At common law, arson was the malicious burning of a structure of another. The modern trend is to increase the types of items that may be subject to arson. In almost all jurisdictions today, arson is defined in terms of knowingly and maliciously causing a fire. Arson cannot be committed by negligent or reckless conduct.

- Computer crime is that form of crime that employs computer technology as central to its commission and that could not be committed without such technology. All fifty states and the federal government have enacted special laws, known as computer crime statutes, against cybercrime.

- Generally speaking, there are five *types* of cybercrime found in today's law. They are: (1) computer fraud, (2) computer trespass, (3) theft of computer services, (4) personal trespass by computer, and (5) special laws against the dissemination of computer viruses and worms, sometimes called computer tampering.

QUESTIONS FOR DISCUSSION

1. Explain the importance of the differences between larceny and embezzlement.
2. What are the rules regarding the keeping of found property?
3. What types of property were subject to the common law crime of larceny?
4. Explain the difference between embezzlement and false pretenses.
5. What was the nature of the historical "need" that led to formulation of the "breaking bulk" doctrine?

6. It is often stated that "Only persons you trust can embezzle from you." Do you agree or disagree with this statement? Explain your answer.

7. What advantages are there to the consolidation of the wrongful acquisition crimes into a single crime of theft? What disadvantages?

8. Explain the concept of "constructive entry" as applied to burglary crimes.

9. What test do the courts use in robbery cases to determine if property was taken from the presence of the victim?

10. How does extortion differ from robbery?

11. What are the five types of computer crime discussed in this chapter? What are the unique features of each?

LEGAL RESOURCES ON THE WORLD WIDE WEB

Some Web sites contain a wealth of material describing high-technology crime and computer crime—as well as descriptions of statutes intended to curb such activity.

The CERT Coordination Center
http://www.cert.org
The CERT home page. CERT focuses on computer security concerns for Internet users.

Computer Crime and Intellectual Property Section, U.S. Department of Justice (CCIPS)
http://www.cybercrime.gov
CCIPS is a central resource in the federal government's fight against cybercrime. A weekly e-mail newsletter is available through the site.

Computer Security Laboratory—UC Davis
http://seclab.cs.ucdavis.edu/Security.html
Web site for the Computer Security Laboratory at the University of California–Davis.

Lawrence Livermore National Laboratory Computer Security Technology Center (CSTC)
http://ciac.llnl.gov/cstc
Provides solutions to U.S. government agencies facing today's security challenges in information technology.

National Infrastructure Protection Center (NIPC)
http://www.nipc.gov
NIPC manages computer intrusion investigations at the federal level.

National Institute of Standards and Technology Computer Security Division
http://www.itl.nist.gov/div893
The mission of NIST's Computer Security Division is to improve information systems security by raising awareness; researching, studying, and advising; developing standards; and developing guidance to increase secure information technology planning, implementation, management, and operation.

National Institute of Standards and Technology Computer Security Resource Clearinghouse
http://csrc.nist.gov/welcome.html
NIST's Computer Security Resource Clearinghouse provides information on numerous security topics, as well as alerts about viruses and other security threats.

The Secure Zone: The Computer Security Information Center
http://www.securezone.com
Provides many links to sources of information and tools for computer and Internet
  security.

For additional links to Web sites focusing on Internet security and privacy visit
http://virtuallibrarian.com/legal. Remember to check the *Criminal Law Today* Web
site for URLs that may have changed.

SUGGESTED READINGS AND CLASSIC WORKS

American Law Institute, *Model Penal Code and Commentaries,* Vol. 2 (Philadelphia:
  American Law Institute, 1980).

Kathleen F. Brickley, "The Jurisprudence of Larceny: An Historical Inquiry and Interest Analysis," *Vanderbilt Law Review,* Vol. 33 (1980), p. 1101.

Donald Cressy, *Other People's Money* (Belmont, CA: Wadsworth, 1953).

George P. Fletcher, "The Metamorphosis of Larceny," *Harvard Law Review,* Vol. 89
  (1976), p. 469.

Thomas Gabor and Andre Normandeau, *Armed Robbery: Cops, Robbers, and Victims*
  (Springfield, IL: Charles C. Thomas, 1987).

Peter Goldberger, "Forgery," in Sanford Kadish, Ed., *Encyclopedia of Crime and Justice,* Vol. 2 (New York: The Free Press, 1983).

Jerome Hall, *Theft, Law, and Society,* 2nd ed. (Indianapolis, IN: Bobbs-Merrill, 1952).

David Icove, Karl Seger, and William VonStorch, *Computer Crime: A Crimefighter's
  Handbook* (Cambridge, MA: O'Reilly & Associates, 1995).

Cliff Roberson, *Preventing Employee Misconduct* (Lexington, MA: Lexington Books,
  1986).

Lloyd L. Weinreb, "Manifest Criminality, Criminal Intent, and the Metamorphosis
  of Larceny," *Yale Law Journal,* (1980), p. 294.

CAPSTONE CASE   ## WHAT CONSTITUTES A TRESPASSORY TAKING?

Commonwealth v. *Tluchak*
Supreme Court of Pennsylvania, 1950
70 A.2d 657

A husband and wife (appellants) separately appealed from their convictions for larceny. The lower appellate court overruled their motions for new trials and arrest of
judgment. The husband was sentenced to pay a fine of $50 and make restitution.
Sentence was suspended in the wife's case.

FACTS: The case arose out of a real estate transaction. By a written instrument appellants agreed to sell their farm to [complainant] and his wife. The agreement did
not include any personal property, but it did cover: "All buildings, plumbing, heat-
ing, lighting fixtures, storm sash, shades, blinds, awnings, shrubbery, and plants."
The purchasers took possession on June 14, 1946, and discovered that certain articles which had been on the premises at the time the agreement of sale was executed

were missing. They were a commode, which had never been attached and lay on the back porch in its shipping crate; an unattached washstand, which had been stored in a bedroom; a hay carriage used in the barn; an electric stove cord extending from the switch box in the cellar to the kitchen; and thirty or thirty-five peach trees. These articles were charged in the indictment as subjects of the larceny.

The Commonwealth contended that the articles that were not covered by the written contract had been sold by oral agreement between the parties. Appellants denied the oral agreement; denied the sale of the personal property; denied taking the trees; admitted they took the hay carriage; and as to all the articles that they took, they contended that they were taken under a claim of right and therefore not feloniously. The jury found against them and, although they contend that the evidence is not sufficient in law to sustain a conviction, we shall assume, for the purpose of this decision, that the testimony established a sale of the personal property by appellants to [complainant] and his wife. That is, that appellants sold but failed or refused to deliver the goods to the purchasers. Are sellers who refuse or fail to deliver goods sold to their purchasers guilty of larceny?

. . . Appellants had possession of the goods, not mere custody of them. The evidence indicates that they were allowed to retain possession without trick or artifice and without fraudulent intent to convert them. Presumably title passed upon payment of the purchase price; nevertheless appellants had lawful possession thereafter. One who is in lawful possession of the goods or money of another cannot commit larceny by feloniously converting them to his own use, for the reason that larceny, being a criminal trespass on the right of possession, cannot be committed by one who, being invested with that right, is consequently incapable of trespassing on it. (Citations omitted.)

An extensive research failed to uncover a Pennsylvania case in which the rule was applied to a factual situation similar to that at bar. But the principle has been recognized; e.g., in *Com. v. Quinn*, 144 Pa. Super. 400, 408, 19 A.2d 526, 530, this Court approved instructions to a jury wherein it was said:

> But a person may come into possession of somebody else's property in a legal way and if he, being so in possession of the property in a legal way converts it to his own use or withholds it from the owner so that the owner is deprived of the use thereof which he should have, then, though the defendant could not be guilty of larceny because he received it legally, he may be guilty of fraudulent conversion because after having received it he has deprived the owner of his use of it. . . .

As suggested, appellants may have been guilty of fraudulent conversion, or of larceny by bailee if the theory is accepted that a vendor retaining possession of goods sold by him becomes constructively a bailee of the purchaser, and criminally culpable for a failure to deliver them to his purchaser. Appellants were indicted for larceny only, and of that they clearly were not guilty. . . .

The judgments and sentences are reversed and appellants are discharged without delay.

[footnotes omitted]

WHAT DO *YOU* THINK?

1. If the defendants stole the property, why should it make any difference as to how they obtained possession of the property?
2. What crimes did the defendants commit?
3. How does this case highlight the need for a consolidated theft statute?
4. The court indicated that the defendants had possession of the goods, not mere custody of them. What difference does that make?

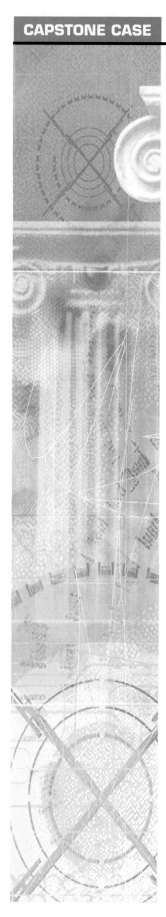

CAPSTONE CASE

WHAT IS THE MEANING OF THE WORD "STOLEN"?

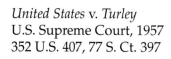

United States v. *Turley*
U.S. Supreme Court, 1957
352 U.S. 407, 77 S. Ct. 397

Mr. Justice Burton delivered the opinion of the Court.

This case concerns the meaning of the word "stolen" in the following provision of the National Motor Vehicle Theft Act, commonly known as the Dyer Act:

> *Whoever transports in interstate or foreign commerce a motor vehicle or aircraft, knowing the same to have been stolen, shall be fined not more than $5,000 or imprisoned not more than five years, or both.*

The issue before us is whether the meaning of the word "stolen," as used in this provision, is limited to a taking which amounts to common law larceny, or whether it includes an embezzlement or other felonious taking with intent to deprive the owner of the rights and benefits of ownership. For the reasons hereafter stated, we accept the broader interpretation.

In 1956, an information based on this section was filed against James Vernon Turley in the United States District Court for the District of Maryland. It charged that Turley, in South Carolina, lawfully obtained possession of an automobile from its owner for the purpose of driving certain of their friends to the homes of the latter in South Carolina, but that, without permission of the owner and with intent to steal the automobile, Turley converted it to his own use and unlawfully transported it in interstate commerce to Baltimore, Maryland, where he sold it without permission of the owner. The information thus charged Turley with transporting the automobile in interstate commerce knowing it to have been obtained by embezzlement rather than by common law larceny.

Counsel appointed for Turley moved to dismiss the information on the ground that it did not state facts sufficient to constitute an offense against the United States. He contended that the word "stolen" as used in the Act referred only to takings which constitute common law larceny and that the acts charged did not. The District Court agreed and dismissed the information. The United States concedes that the facts alleged in the information do not constitute common law larceny, but disputes the holding that a motor vehicle obtained by embezzlement is not "stolen" within the meaning of the Act.

Decisions involving the meaning of "stolen" as used in the National Motor Vehicle Theft Act did not arise frequently until comparatively recently. Two of the earlier cases interpreted "stolen" as meaning statutory larceny as defined by the State in which the taking occurred. The later decisions rejected that interpretation but divided on whether to give "stolen" a uniformly narrow meaning restricted to common law larceny, or a uniformly broader meaning inclusive of embezzlement and other felonious takings with intent to deprive the owner of the rights and benefits of ownership. The Fifth, Eighth, and Tenth Circuits favored the narrow definition while the Fourth, Sixth, and Ninth Circuits favored the broader one. We agree that in the absence of a plain indication of an intent to incorporate diverse state laws into a federal criminal statute, the meaning of the federal statute should not be dependent on state law.

We recognize that where a federal criminal statute uses a common law term of established meaning without otherwise defining it, the general practice is to give that term its common law meaning. But "stolen" (or "stealing") has no accepted common law meaning. On this point the Court of Appeals for the Fourth Circuit recently said:

But while "stolen" is constantly identified with larceny, the term was never at common law equated or exclusively dedicated to larceny. "Steal" (originally stale) at first denoted in general usage a taking through secrecy, as implied in stealth, or through stratagem, according to the Oxford English Dictionary. Expanded through the years, it became the generic designation for dishonest acquisition, but it never lost its initial connotation. Nor in law is "steal" or "stolen" a word of art. Blackstone does not mention "steal" in defining larceny—"the felonious taking and carrying away of the personal goods of another—" or in expounding its several elements.

Webster's New International Dictionary (2ed., 1953) likewise defines "stolen" as "Obtained or accomplished by theft, stealth, or craft." Black's Law Dictionary (4ed., 1951) states that " 'steal' may denote the criminal taking of personal property either by larceny, embezzlement, or false pretenses." Furthermore, "stolen" and "steal" have been used in federal criminal statutes, and the courts interpreting those words have declared that they do not have a necessary common law meaning coterminous with larceny and exclusive of other theft crimes. Freed from a common law meaning, we should give "stolen" the meaning consistent with the context in which it appears.

That criminal statutes are to be construed strictly is a proposition which calls for the citation of no authority. But this does not mean that every criminal statute must be given the narrowest possible meaning in complete disregard of the purpose of the legislature. It is, therefore, appropriate to consider the purpose of the Act and to gain what light we can from its legislative history.

By 1919, the law of most States against local theft had developed so as to include not only common law larceny but embezzlement, false pretenses, larceny by trick, and other types of wrongful taking. The advent of the automobile, however, created a new problem with which the States found it difficult to deal. The automobile was uniquely suited to felonious taking, whether by larceny, embezzlement, or false pretenses. It was a valuable, salable article which itself supplied the means for speedy escape. "The automobile [became] the perfect chattel for modern large-scale theft." This challenge could be best met through use of the Federal Government's jurisdiction over interstate commerce. The need for federal action increased with the number, distribution, and speed of the motor vehicles until, by 1919, it became a necessity. The result was the National Motor Vehicle Theft Act.

This background was reflected in the Committee Report on the bill presented by its author and sponsor, Representative Dyer. . . . This report, entitled "Theft of Automobiles," pointed to the increasing number of automobile thefts, the resulting financial losses, and the increasing cost of automobile theft insurance. It asserted that state laws were inadequate to cope with the problem because the offenders evaded state officers by transporting the automobiles across state lines where associates received and sold them. Throughout the legislative history Congress used the word "stolen" as synonymous with "theft," a term generally considered to be broader than "common-law larceny." To be sure, the discussion referred to "larceny" but nothing was said about excluding other forms of "theft." The report stated the object of the Act in broad terms, primarily emphasizing the need for the exercise of federal powers. No mention is made of a purpose to distinguish between different forms of theft, as would be expected if the distinction had been intended.

"Larceny" is also mentioned in *Brooks* v. *United States*. This reference, however, carries no necessary implication excluding the taking of automobiles by embezzlement or false pretenses. Public and private rights are violated to a comparable degree whatever label is attached to the felonious taking. A typical example of common law larceny is the taking of an unattended automobile. But an automobile is no less "stolen" because it is rented, transported interstate, and sold without the permission of the owner (embezzlement). The same is true where an automobile is purchased with a worthless check, transported interstate, and sold (false pretenses).

Professional thieves resort to innumerable forms of theft and Congress sought to meet the need for federal action effectively rather than to leave loopholes for wholesale evasion.

We conclude that the Act requires an interpretation of "stolen" which does not limit it to situations which at common law would be considered larceny. The refinements of that crime are not related to the primary congressional purpose of eliminating the interstate traffic in unlawfully obtained motor vehicles. The Government's interpretation is neither unclear nor vague. "Stolen" as used in 18 U.S.C. 2312, . . . includes all felonious takings of motor vehicles with intent to deprive the owner of the rights and benefits of ownership, regardless of whether or not the theft constitutes common law larceny.

Reversed and remanded.

[footnotes omitted]

Mr. Justice Frankfurter, whom Mr. Justice Black and Mr. Justice Douglas join, dissenting.

If Congress desires to make cheating, in all its myriad varieties, a federal offense when employed to obtain an automobile that is then taken across a state line, it should express itself with less ambiguity than by language that leads three Courts of Appeals to decide that it has not said so and three that it has. If "stealing" (describing a thing as "stolen") be not a term of art, it must be deemed a colloquial, everyday term. As such, it would hardly be used, even loosely, by the man in the street to cover "cheating."

Legislative drafting is dependent on treacherous words to convey, as often as not, complicated ideas, and courts should not be pedantically exacting in construing legislation. But to sweep into the jurisdiction of the federal courts the transportation of cars obtained not only by theft but also by trickery does not present a problem so complicated that the Court should search for hints to find a command. When Congress has wanted to deal with many different ways of despoiling another of his property and not merely with larceny, it has found it easy enough to do so, as a number of federal enactments attest. No doubt, penal legislation should not be artificially restricted so as to allow escape for those for whom it was with fair intendment designed. But the principle of lenity which should guide construction of criminal statutes, . . precludes extending the term "stolen" to include every form of dishonest acquisition. This conclusion is encouraged not only by the general consideration governing the construction of penal laws; it also has regard for not bringing to the federal courts a mass of minor offenses that are local in origin until Congress expresses, if not an explicit, at least an unequivocal, desire to do so.

I would affirm the judgment.

WHAT DO *YOU* THINK?
1. When you use the term "stolen," what do you mean by it? Would the Court, in this case, agree with you?
2. Do you agree with the Court's interpretation of the word "stolen?" Why or why not?
3. Should the manner of acquisition have any bearing on whether the defendant committed a violation of the Dyer Act?
4. Three of the nine justices dissented in this case. Do you see any conflicts between the majority and the minority opinions? If you do, with which opinion do you most agree? Why?

CAN A PERSON BURGLARIZE HIS OR HER OWN HOME?

People v. *Gauze*
California Supreme Court, 1975
542 P.2d 1365

Can a person burglarize his own home? That is the quandary which emerges in the case of James Matthew Gauze, who appeals from a judgment of conviction of assault with a deadly weapon (Pen.Code, Section 245, subd. (a)) and burglary (Pen.Code, Section 459).

Defendant shared an apartment with Richard Miller and a third person and thus had the right to enter the premises at all times. While visiting a friend one afternoon, defendant and Miller engaged in a furious quarrel. Defendant directed Miller to "Get your gun because I am going to get mine." While Miller went to their mutual home, defendant borrowed a shotgun from a neighbor. He returned to his apartment, walked into the living room, pointed the gun at Miller and fired, hitting him in the side and arm. Defendant was convicted of assault with a deadly weapon and burglary; the latter charge was predicated on his entry into his own apartment with the intent to commit the assault.

Common law burglary was generally defined as "the breaking and entering of the dwelling of another in the nighttime with intent to commit a felony." . . . The present burglary statute, Penal Code section 459, provides in relevant part that "Every person who enters any house, room, apartment . . . with intent to commit grand or petit larceny or any felony is guilty of burglary."

Facially the statute is susceptible of two rational interpretations. On the one hand, it could be argued that the Legislature deliberately revoked the common law rule that burglary requires entry into the building of another. On the other hand, the Legislature may have implicitly incorporated the common law requirement by failing to enumerate one's own home as a possible object of burglary. . . . No cases directly on point have been found. Therefore, in determining which statutory interpretation should be adopted it is necessary to examine the purposes underlying common law burglary and how they may have been affected by the enactment of the Penal Code.

Common law burglary was essentially an offense "against habitation and occupancy." By proscribing felonious nighttime entry into a dwelling house, the common law clearly sought to protect the right to peacefully enjoy one's own home free of invasion. In the law of burglary, in short, a person's home was truly his castle. . . . It was clear under common law that one could not be convicted of burglary for entering his own home with felonious intent. This rule applied not only to sole owners of homes, but also to joint occupants. . . . The important factor was occupancy, rather than ownership.

California codified the law of burglary in 1850. (Stats.1850, ch. 99, § 58, P. 235.) That statute and subsequent revisions and amendments preserved the spirit of the common law, while making two major changes. First, the statute greatly expanded the type of buildings protected by burglary sanctions. Not only is a person's home his castle under the statute, but so, *inter alia*, are his shop, tent, airplane, and outhouse. This evolution, combined with elimination of the requirement that the crime be committed at night, signifies that the law is no longer limited to safeguarding occupancy rights. However, by carefully delineating the type of structures encompassed under section 459, the Legislature has preserved the concept that burglary law is designed to protect a possessory right in property, rather than broadly to preserve any place from all crime.

The second major change effected by codification of the burglary law was the elimination of the requirement of a "breaking": Under the statute, every person who enters with felonious intent is a burglar. This means, at a minimum, that it no longer matters whether a person entering a house with larcenous or felonious intent does so through a closed door, an open door, or a window. The entry with the requisite intent constitutes the burglary.

The elimination of the breaking requirement was further interpreted in *People* v. *Barry* (1892) 94 Cal. 481, 29 P. 1026, to mean that trespassory entry was no longer a necessary element of burglary. In *Barry,* this court held [that] a person could be convicted of burglary of a store even though he entered during regular business hours. A long line of cases has followed the *Barry* holding. (Citations omitted.)

Barry and its progeny should not be read, however, to hold that a defendant's right to enter the premises is irrelevant. Indeed, the court in *Barry*, by negative implication, substantiated the importance of determining the right of an accused to enter premises. When the defendant thief in *Barry* argued he had a right to be in the store, the court could have replied that his right to enter the store was immaterial. Instead the court declared, "To this reasoning, we can only say a party who enters with the intention to commit a felony enters without an invitation. He is not one of the public invited, nor is he entitled, to enter. Such a party could be refused admission at the threshold, or ejected from the premises after the entry was accomplished," (*Id.,* 94 Cal. at p. 493, 29 P. at p. 1027.) Thus, the underlying principle of the *Barry* case is that a person has an implied invitation to enter a store during business hours for legal purposes only. The cases have preserved the common law principle that in order for burglary to occur, "The entry must be without consent. If the possessor actually invites the defendant, or actively assists in the entrance, e.g., by opening a door, there is no burglary."

Thus, section 459, while substantially changing common law burglary, has retained two important aspects of that crime. A burglary remains an entry which invades a possessory right in a building. And it still must be committed by a person who has no right to be in the building.

Applying the foregoing reasoning, we conclude that defendant cannot be guilty of burglarizing his own home. His entry into the apartment, even for a felonious purpose, invaded no possessory right of habitation; only the entry of an intruder could have done so. More importantly, defendant had an absolute right to enter the apartment. This right, unlike that of the store thief in Barry, did not derive from an implied invitation to the public to enter for legal purposes. It was a personal right that could not be conditioned on the consent of defendant's roommates. Defendant could not be "refused admission at the threshold" of his apartment, or be "ejected from the premises after the entry was accomplished." He could not, accordingly, commit a burglary in his own home.

The People argue, however, that a contrary conclusion is compelled by a dictum in *People* v. *Sears* (1965) 62 Cal. 2d 737, 44 Cal. Rptr. 330, 401 P.2d 938. In *Sears,* defendant was convicted of felony murder. For three years prior to the murder, defendant had slept in a garage nearby the cottage occupied by his wife. Then the spouses separated and defendant moved to a hotel. Three weeks later, he returned to the cottage, looking for his wife and hiding a reinforced steel pipe under his shirt. In an ensuing struggle, he killed his wife's daughter. This court reversed his conviction because a confession was improperly admitted, but for guidance upon retrial we declared valid a felony-murder instruction based on burglary—entering the cottage with intent to assault his wife as the felony. In answer to defendant's argument that he could not be guilty of burglary because he had a right to enter the house, the court replied, "One who enters a room, or building with the intent to commit a felony is guilty of burglary even though permission to enter has been extended to him personally or as a member of the public. The entry need not constitute a trespass. [citations omitted.] Moreover, since defendant had moved out of the family home three weeks prior to the crime, he could claim no right to enter the residence of another without permission. Even if we assume that defendant could properly enter the house for a lawful purpose, such an entry still constitutes burglary if accomplished with the intent to commit a felonious assault within it." (*Id.* at p. 746, 44 Cal. Rptr. at p. 336, 401 P.2d at P. 944.)

As the above quotation indicates, our opinion that Sears could be convicted of burglary was based on two separate considerations. First, Sears had no right to enter his wife's house; that fact alone supported the conviction. Second, even if he had a right to enter, the right was based on former section 157 of the Civil Code, which gave a person the right to enter the separate property of his or her spouse, subject to certain conditions. Thus Sears' "right" to enter his wife's house, like the "right" of the felon to enter the store in *Barry,* was at best conditional. An entry for anything but a legal purpose was a breach of his wife's possessory rights, in marked contrast to the entry in the present case.

Only if the *Sears* dictum is read in an expansive manner can it be used to support the prosecution theory that a person can burglarize his own home. Such a reading would be entirely inconsistent with the purposes of section 459. As aptly articulated by the Court of Appeal in *People* v. *Lewis* (1969) 274 Cal. App. 2d 912, 79 Cal. Rptr. 650, "Burglary laws are based primarily upon a recognition of the dangers to personal safety created by the usual burglary situation—the danger that the intruder will harm the occupants in attempting to perpetrate the intended crime or to escape, and the danger that the occupants will in anger or panic react violently to the invasion, thereby inviting more violence. The laws are primarily designed, then, not to deter the trespass and the intended crime, which are prohibited by their laws, so much as to forestall the germination of a situation dangerous to personal safety." Section 459, in short, is aimed at the danger caused by the unauthorized entry itself.

In contrast to the usual burglary situation, no danger arises from the mere entry of a person into his own home, no matter what his intent is. He may cause a great deal of mischief once inside. But no emotional distress is suffered, no panic is engendered, and no violence necessarily erupts merely because he walks into his house. To impose sanctions for burglary would in effect punish him twice for the crime he committed while in the house. In such circumstances it serves no purpose to apply section 459.

It has been urged that the purpose of burglary laws is to protect persons inside buildings because indoor crime is more dangerous than outdoor crime. . . . We have never categorized all indoor crimes to be more dangerous than all outdoor crimes. Nor would such a conclusion be relevant to the purposes of section 459. The statute protects against intruders into indoor areas, not persons committing crimes in their own homes.

To hold otherwise could lead to potentially absurd results. If a person can be convicted for burglarizing his own home, he would violate section 459 by calmly entering his house with intent to forge a check. A narcotics addict could be convicted of burglary for walking into his home with the intent to administer a dose of heroin to himself. Since a burglary is committed upon entry, both could be convicted even if they changed their minds and did not commit the intended crimes.

For the foregoing reasons, we conclude defendant cannot be guilty of burglarizing his own home, and the judgment of conviction for burglary must therefore be reversed. The judgment is reversed on count I (burglary) and affirmed on count II (assault with a deadly weapon).

[footnotes omitted]

WHAT DO *YOU* THINK?

1. Do you agree that the defendant is not guilty of burglarizing his own home? Why or why not?

2. Can you think of circumstances where a defendant might burglarize his own home? If so, what might they be?

3. Is the court creating a defense that was not intended by the legislature when the crime of burglary was modified by statute?

4. Do you agree with the court that a person has an unconditional right to enter his or her home, even when the reason for entering is to commit a violent crime against another person living in that home?

CAPSTONE CASE

WHAT CONSTITUTES THE CRIME OF COMPUTER TAMPERING?

People v. *Versaggi*
New York Court of Appeals, 1994
83 N.Y.2d 123

Rochester City Court has found defendant guilty of two counts of computer tampering in the second degree (Penal Law section 156.20), determining that he intentionally altered two computer programs designed to provide uninterrupted telephone service to the offices of the Eastman Kodak Corporation (see, 136 Misc. 2d 361, 518 N.Y.S.2d 553).[1] County Court affirmed, without opinion.

Defendant contends that he is not guilty of altering the programs because he did not change them; he merely activated existing instructions which commanded the computers to shut down. The People maintain that defendant is guilty because he changed the instructions being received by the computers and thereby prevented the computers from performing their intended functions. We agree and therefore affirm the judgment of conviction.

I.

The telephone system at Kodak is operated by two SL-100 computers. One, located at Kodak's State Street office in the City of Rochester, operates 7,000 lines and the other, at the Kodak Park Complex, operates 21,000 lines. On November 10, 1986, approximately 2,560 of the lines at the Kodak Park Complex were shut down and use of another 1,920 impaired for approximately an hour and a half before company employees were able to restore service. As a result, a substantial number of the employees working at this large industrial complex, with the potential for dangerous chemical spills and accidents, were unable to receive calls, to call outside the complex, or to call 911 or similar emergency services. On November 19, 1986, a second interruption occurred. Essentially all service at the State Street office of Kodak was shut down for four minutes before the computer reactivated itself. As a result, all outside telephone calls, from the company's customers and offices worldwide, were disconnected.

At the time of these incidents, defendant was employed by Kodak as a computer technician and was responsible for maintaining and repairing several telephone systems, though not the SL-100's. His job often required him to work from his home and for that purpose Kodak provided him with home computer equipment and a company telephone line which allowed him to connect his computer with the Kodak systems. All calls from defendant's home to Kodak appeared on the monthly New York Telephone Company bill as itemized long-distance calls. Defendant also had been given an "accelerator"—a security device which allowed him to access the Kodak systems.

Kodak maintained several computer systems and to reach a particular one from outside, a caller first accessed the Tellabs system and it then routed the call to the system desired. Security was maintained by requiring the use of an accelerator to access the systems and Tellabs also maintained a log of all calls in a script file. Once a caller had accessed another system by way of Tellabs, a monitor port recorded on a floppy disc everything that appeared on the user's screen. The monitor port thus performed a security function similar to a hidden bank camera. By using the printouts from the Tellabs system and the telephone bills for defendant's telephone line, company investigators determined that defendant had accessed the SL-100 systems on November 10 and November 19 and caused the phone lines to shut down. He was subsequently charged with two counts of computer tampering in the second degree.

II.

At defendant's trial, the People presented two witnesses who explained the mechanics of what defendant had done. David Nentarz, a Kodak employee who worked in the telecommunications department, testified that he had reviewed a printout of activity on the Tellabs system for November 10, 1986, and discovered that a user had accessed the SL-100 system and issued commands which caused the computer at Kodak Park to shut down. An hour and a half and some forty commands later, technicians were able to restore phone service.

Nentarz testified further that the printout for November 19, 1986, showed that a user had first accessed defendant's electronic mail—which required the use of a password chosen by defendant—and then accessed the SL-100 system at the State Street office. Once in the State Street SL-100 system, the user first issued commands which forced two parallel central processing units out of synchronization, i.e., disabled the back-up devices for the SL-100, and then issued commands which caused the program to shut down completely.

Joseph Doyle, supervisor of Kodak's Telecommunications Department, testified that without defendant's commands on November 10 and November 19, the telephone service would have run without interruption. In fact, he stated, it had done so for six years before the November incidents. Doyle testified that to direct the SL-100 to perform a function other than basic telephone service, [e.g.,] duties such as providing dial tones and placing telephone calls, specific commands had to be entered which activated a series of instructions directing the SL-100 off its existing operation. For example, to discontinue service on November 10 defendant had to confront a list of approximately fourteen questions asking him if he wished to continue with his destructive commands and to respond to each before proceeding, questions such as "Do you want to go ahead? Respond 'yes' or 'no' " [and] "Do you want to kill the program? Respond 'yes' or 'no'." In each case defendant answered "yes." On November 19, before shutting down the State Street computer, defendant had to respond to similar questions advising him that he was discontinuing the parallel functions of the synchronized Central Processing Units and that at his command, the system would shut down completely. In each instance defendant answered "yes," indicating that it was his intention to change the existing function of the programs.

There was no evidence of physical damage to Kodak's programs and expert testimony established that defendant did not delete or add to the programs which run the SL-100 systems. Rather, he selected and activated various options as they were presented by the programs.

At the close of evidence defendant moved to dismiss, insisting that his conduct did not constitute alteration of a computer program under Penal Law section 156.20. City Court denied the motion and found defendant guilty of both charges. It held that by "issuing commands to the software which changed the instructions to the hardware, taking it off its normal course of action and shutting down the phone lines," defendant had "altered" a computer program within the meaning of Penal Law section 156.20 (136 Misc. 2d 361, 368, 518 N.Y.S.2d 553, *supra*).

III.

In this Court, defendant renews his argument that he cannot be guilty of tampering because he merely entered commands which allowed the disconnect instructions of each program to function. In his view, he did not "alter" the "programs"; he used them. His appeal presents us with our first opportunity to construe the statute.

A.

In 1986, the New York State Legislature made significant changes to the Penal Law in an effort to control what a Task Force of the American Bar Association had described as the "frightening spectre" of increased computer crime in our society (see generally, June 1984 Report on Computer Crime, ABA Task Force on Computer Crime, at *iii;* see also, Donnino, Practice Commentary, McKinney's Cons. Laws of N.Y., Book 39, Penal Law art. 156, at 173). A program bill submitted by the Attorney-General sought to provide a "comprehensive statutory scheme" to allow for effective law enforcement in the area (Mem of Atty. Gen., Bill Jacket, L.1986, ch. 514, at 32). The breadth of the changes manifests the Legislature's intent to address the full range of computer abuses.

The Legislature proceeded in two ways. First, it added statutory definitions to the Penal Law which described "computer data" and a "computer program" as "property." Second, it added to the Penal Law new sections addressing specific computer crimes. The expansive definitions were intended to eliminate any doubt that computer data and programs are protected under Penal Law, article 145 ("Criminal Mischief and Related Offenses") and article 155 ("Larceny"). Additionally, to provide protection from electronic forgers, the Legislature included "computer data" and "computer program" within the definitions of written instruments and business records (Penal Law art. 170—"Forgery and Related Offenses"; Penal Law art. 175—"Offenses Involving False Written Statements").

However, the Legislature went beyond expanding the definitions of "property" and "written instrument" as applied by the more traditional criminal statutes; it also criminalized activity which constituted misuse of a computer but was difficult to categorize under the existing Penal Law. Specifically, the Legislature created the offenses of unauthorized use of a computer (Penal Law section 156.05); computer trespass (Penal Law section 156.10); computer tampering (Penal Law sections 156.20, 156.25); unlawful duplication of computer-related material (Penal Law section 156.30); and criminal possession of computer-related material (Penal Law section 156.35).

The crime of computer tampering involves the use of a computer or a computer service as the instrumentality of a crime (see Donnino, Practice Commentary, *op. cit.,* at 177). The defendant uses the computer to sabotage its intended operation in some way. The American Bar Association's Task Force on Computer Crime found in its survey that such tampering was the most prevalent means of computer abuse (June 1984 Report on Computer Crime, *op. cit.,* at 9). In contending that defendant was guilty of tampering in this case, the People sought to establish that he had altered two computer programs. The issue before the Court is whether defendant's conduct is encompassed within the language of the tampering statute.

B.

Interpretation begins with the language of the statute. The Legislature did not define "alter," however, and thus the Court must give the word its ordinary meaning (*Matter of Manhattan Pizza Hut* v. *New York State Human Rights Appeal Bd.,* 51 N.Y.2d 506, 511, 434 N.Y.S.2d 961, 415 N.E.2d 950). As commonly understood, "alter" means to change or modify. When something is altered it is made "different in some particular characteristic . . . without changing [it] into something else" (Webster's Third New International Dictionary 63 [Unabridged]). For an alteration to occur, the identity of the thing need not be destroyed, nor need an entirely new thing be substituted. It is sufficient if some of the "elements or ingredients or details" are changed (Black's Law Dictionary 103 [4th ed]). Significantly, the Legislature attached expansive language to the verb it used in section 156.20, stating that the crime consisted of altering a computer program "in any manner."

A program's function is to control the computer's activities. It does so by a series of instructions or statements prepared in order to achieve a certain result and input into a computer in a form acceptable to it (see, 1 Bender, Computer Law section 2.06[1], at 2-115). Notwithstanding this general definition, a program has been defined differently under various statutes as consisting of a single instruction (see, e.g., Montana Code Annot. section 45-2-101 [10]) or a set of instructions (see, e.g., Mo. Rev. Stat. section 569.093).

The New York statute defines a program as "an ordered set of data representing coded instructions or statements that, when executed by computer, cause the computer to process data or direct the computer to perform one or more computer operations" (Penal Law section 156.00[2]). A computer may contain several "sets" of "coded instructions," however, and, in that sense, a computer may contain more than one "program." Indeed, computers commonly contain both "system programs" and "application programs" (1 Bender, Computer Law section 2.06[2], at 2-117). A system program is generally provided by the computer manufacturer and is intended to make the computer function. "It is the collection of system programs (called the 'operating system') which converts the computer hardware . . . into a . . . functioning computer" *(ibid.)*. The application program "is the program with which the ultimate user directs the computer to perform [a] particular task" *(id.,* section 2.06[3], at 2-118.2).

There is nothing in the statutory language which compels an interpretation that the Legislature intended its definition of a "computer program" to include all of the instructions contained in a computer. If it considered the question at all, and the legislative history sheds no light on the question, the Legislature did not address it in the law as finally enacted. Thus, to the extent that the definition contained in Penal Law section 156.00(2) fails to specify whether a "computer program" includes all the input instructions, its language is ambiguous.

Defendant would resolve this ambiguity by confining the statutory definition to the total set of instructions which directs all the functions of a computer. As he interprets the statute, so long as the computer contains an existing set of coded instructions which allows it to perform a function, a user may never be convicted of computer tampering no matter how malevolent the user's purpose or how disastrous or unintended the result of activating those instructions may be to the owner. He fortifies his view by relying on the common law rule that penal statutes must be strictly construed.

There is no justification for defining the terms of the statute so narrowly. The Legislature has expressly declared that the provisions of the Penal Law be construed "according to the fair import of their terms to promote justice and effect the objects of the law" (Penal Law section 5.00; *People v. Ditta,* 52 N.Y.2d 657, 660, 439 N.Y.S.2d 855, 422 N.E.2d 515). While section 5.00 of the Penal Law does not allow imposition of criminal sanctions for conduct "beyond the fair scope of the statutory mandate" (*People v. Wood,* 8 N.Y.2d 48, 51, 201 N.Y.S.2d 328, 167 N.E.2d 736), "it does authorize a court to dispense with hypertechnical or strained interpretations of [a] statute" (Ditta, *supra,* 52 N.Y.2d at 660, 439 N.Y.S.2d 885, 422 N.E.2d 515; see also, *People v. Sansanese,* 17 N.Y.2d 302, 306, 270 N.Y.S.2d 607, 217 N.E.2d 660; *People v. Abeel,* 182 N.Y. 415, 420-421, 75 N.E. 307). Conduct that falls within the plain, natural meaning of the language of a Penal Law provision may be punished as criminal (Ditta, *supra,* 52 N.Y.2d at 660, 439 N.Y.S.2d 855, 422 N.E.2d 515). Indeed, given that the enactment of a criminal statute often "follow[s] in [the] wake"

of the activity it attempts to penalize, courts should not legislate or nullify statutes by overstrict construction (*People* v. *Abeel, supra,* 182 N.Y. at 421–422, 75 N.E. 307). Applying these rules of construction, and giving the language of the statute its ordinary meaning, we conclude that the interpretation applied by City Court comports with the legislative intention.

C.

The purpose of Kodak's computers was to provide telephone service and, absent instructions to the contrary, that is exactly what they did. By implementing the application programs, a set of coded instructions were executed by the computers which directed them to perform a computer operation. Those directions clearly came within the statutory definition of an "ordered set of . . . instructions" which, when executed, directed the computer "to perform one or more computer operations." Thus those instructions constituted a "computer program."

Defendant encountered the application programs when he entered the SL-100 systems. By disconnecting them and commanding the computers to shut down, he altered the programs in some manner. Whether defendant used existing instructions to direct the phone system offline or input new instructions accomplishing the same thing is legally irrelevant. He made the system "different in some particular characteristic . . . without changing [it] to something else" (see, Webster's Third New International Dictionary, *op. cit.*). His conduct differed only in degree from shutting down the system by executing a command to add or delete program material. In either event, the result would be the same. The intended purpose of the computer program is sabotaged. Defendant's conduct constituted tampering within the intendment of the statute because it altered the computer programs at Kodak's State Street office and Kodak Park Complex by interrupting the telephone service to those two facilities. Accordingly, the order of County Court should be affirmed. Order affirmed.

[footnotes omitted]

WHAT DO *YOU* THINK?

1. New York penal law distinguished among the crimes of: (1) unauthorized use of a computer, (2) computer trespass, (3) computer tampering, (4) unlawful duplication of computer-related material, and (5) criminal possession of computer-related material. What are the main differences between these five types of crime?
2. How does New York law define "computer tampering"? Do you agree with the court in this case that "defendant's conduct constituted tampering within the intendment of the statute because it altered the computer programs at Kodak's State Street office and Kodak Park Complex by interrupting the telephone service to those two facilities"? Why or why not?
3. Why did the court not accept Versaggi's offered defense that he could not be found "guilty of altering [computer] programs because he did not change them; he merely activated existing instructions which commanded the computers to shut down"? Do you think that such a defense should have been acceptable? Why or why not?

NOTES

1. Cynthia Manson and Charles Ardai, *Future Crime: An Anthology of the Shape of Crime to Come* (New York: Donald I. Fine, 1992), p. ix.
2. United States Code, Title 18, Section 1028(a)(7).
3. Louis B. Schwartz, "Theft," in Sandord Kadish (ed.), *The Encyclopedia of Crime and Justice*, Vol. 4 (New York: Macmillian Library Reference, 1983). pp. 1537–1551.

4. American Law Institute, *Model Penal Code and Commentaries,* comment to section 223.1 at 127-132 (1980).

5. Ibid.

6. East's *Pleas of the Crown* 553 (1803).

7. *Rex* v. *Wheatly,* 97 E.R. 746 (1761).

8. Rollin M. Perkins and Ronald N. Boyce, *Criminal Law,* 3rd ed. (Mineola, NY: The Foundation Press, 1982), p. 289.

9. Schwartz, "Theft," p. 1537.

10. The statute also effectively eliminates any common law vestiges of the classification of dogs as "base" animals.

11. *State* v. *Jackson,* 11 S.E.2d 149 (N.C. 1940).

12. Texas Penal Code, Section 28.01(3).

13. Model Penal Code, Section 223.0(6).

14. *Thompson* v. *State,* 10 So. 520 (Ala. 1891).

15. *Commonwealth* v. *Tluchak,* 70 A.2d. 657 (Pa. 1950).

16. *Carrier's Case,* Y.B. Rasch. 13 Edw. IV, f. 9, pl. 5 (Eng. 1473).

17. Frances Robles, "Truck Crash Turns I-95 into Road to Riches," *The Miami Herald,* January 9, 1997.

18. Ibid.

19. Model Penal Code, Section 223.5.

20. *State* v. *Jones,* 65 N.C. 395 (1871).

21. Ibid., pp. 297, 298.

22. Although not "larceny," other laws might criminalize such behavior.

23. Model Penal Code, Section 223.9.

24. Donald Cressy, *Other People's Money* (Belmont, CA: Wadsworth, 1953).

25. The material for this box was adapted from Cliff Roberson, *Preventing Employee Misconduct: A Self-Defense Manual for Business* (Lexington, MA: Lexington Books, 1986).

26. *United States* v. *Nelson,* 227 F.2d 72 (D.C. Cir. 1955).

27. See, for example, California Penal Code, Section 475.

28. See, for example, the Texas Penal Code, Section 32.22.

29. *State* v. *George,* 173 S.W. 1077 (Mo. 1915).

30. *People* v. *Taylor,* 4 Cal. App. 2d 214 (1935).

31. *State* v. *Harrington,* 260 A.2d 692 (Vt. 1970).

32. Model Penal Code, Section 223.4.

33. Stephen A. Saltzburg, John L. Diamond, Kit Kinports, and Thomas H. Morawetz, *Criminal Law: Cases and Materials* (Charlottesville, VA: Michie, 1994), p. 562.

34. Ibid.

35. California Attorney General's Office, press release, July 7, 2000.

36. Prepared Statement of the Federal Trade Commission on Identity Theft made before the Subcommittee on Technology, Terrorism, and Government Information of the Committee on the Judiciary of the United States Senate, Washington, D.C., March 7, 2000, from which some of the wording in this section is taken.

37. Ibid.

38. Ibid.

39. United States Code, Title 18, Section 1028(a)(7).

40. Ibid.

41. *State* v. *Sorenson,* 138 N.W. 411 (Iowa 1912).

42. *State* v. *Hill,* 520 P.2d 946 (Wash. App. 1974), citing *State* v. *Rosencrans,* 167 P.2d 170, 172 (Wash. 1946).

43. *Rolland* v. *Commonwealth,* 82 Pa. 306 (1876).

44. John S. Baker, Jr., Daniel H. Benson, Robert Force, and B. J. George, Jr., *Hall's Criminal Law: Cases and Materials,* 5th ed. (Charlottesville, VA: Michie, 1993), p. 496, citing *Lawson* v. *Commonwealth,* 169 S.W. 587 (Ky. 1914), and *People* v. *Toland,* 111 N.E. 760 (N.Y. 1916). See also *Rolland,* 324 (1876).

45. *Smith* v. *State,* 362 P.2d 1071 (Alaska 1961).

46. *State* v. *Gonzales,* 905 S.W.2d 4 (Tex. App. Eastland 1995).

47. *Mattox* v. *State,* 101 N.E. 1009 (Ind. 1913).

48. *Regina* v. *Davis,* 6 Cox Crim. Cas. 369 (1854).

49. *State* v. *Hudson,* 430 P.2d 386 (N.M. 1967).

50. *Henderson* v. *State,* 86 So. 439 (Fla. 1920).

51. *People* v. *Blair,* 288 N.E.2d 443 (Ill. 1952).

52. American Law Institute, *Model Penal Code and Commentaries,* Part II, Section 221.1 (1980).

53. Texas Penal Code, Section 30.05.

54. Steve Miletich, no title, *Seattle Post-Intelligencer,* via Simon and Schuster NewsLink online, May 21, 1997.

55. Some of the materials in this section are adapted from the Electronic Frontier Foundation World Wide Web site, http://www.eff.org.

56. *Hancock* v. *State,* 402 S.W.2d 906, 18 A.L.R. 3d 1113 (Tex. Crim. 1966).

57. *Lund* v. *Commonwealth,* 217 Va. 688, 232 S.E.2d 745 (1977).

58. *Ward* v. *Superior Court,* 3 Computer Law Serv. Rep. 206 (Cal. Super Ct. 1972).

59. *People* v. *Weg,* 113 Misc.2d 1017, 450 N.Y.S.2d 957 (N.Y. City Crim. Ct. 1982).

60. Electronic Frontier Foundation World Wide Web site, http://www.eff.org.

61. Public Law no. 98-473, Title II, Section 2102(a), October 12, 1984.

62. 18 U.S.C. 1029.

63. Public Law 104-294.

64. Public Law 105-147, 111 Stat. 2678 (1997).

65. For a good discussion of the development of computer crime laws, see Richard C. Hollinger and Lonn Lanza-Kaduce, "The Process of Criminalization: The Case of Computer Crime Laws," *Criminology,* Vol. 26 (1988), p. 101.

66. See, for example, the Alabama Computer Crime Act, Ala. Code Sections 13-A-8-100 through 103; the Florida Computer Crimes Act, Fla. Stat. Sections 815.01 through 815.07; the Illinois Computer Crime Prevention Law, Ill. Rev. Stat., Ch. 38, Section 5/16D-1 to 5/16D-7.

67. See Ohio Rev. Code Ann., Sections 2913.01, 2913.81, and Ohio Rev. Code Ann., Section 2901.01 (m)(10).

68. Visit the Electronic Frontier Foundation on the Web at http://www.eff.org.

69. Illinois Revised Statutes, Chapter 38, Section 5/16D-3 (a)(4).

70. California Penal Code, Section 502 (b)(10).

71. Title, XXIX, Sec. 290001. Computer Abuse Amendments Act of 1994.

72. See, for example, Illinois Revised Statutes, Chapter 38, Section 5/16D-3 (a)(4), from which the elements used in our definition of "computer tampering" are derived.

73. Adapted from The Computer Crime and Intellectual Property Section of the Criminal Division of the U.S. Department of Justice home page. Posted at http://www.cybercrime.gov.

74. Adapted from the FBI's Washington Field Office Infrastructure Protection and Computer Intrusion Squad home page. Posted at http://www.fbi.gov/programs/ipcis/ipcis.htm.

75. The President's Working Group on Unlawful Conduct on the Internet, *The Electronic Frontier: The Challenge of Unlawful Conduct Involving the Use of the Internet* (Washington, D.C.: The White House, 2000). Posted at http://www.usdoj.gov/ criminal/cybercrime/unlawful.htm.

76. Ibid.

77. Ibid.

78. Ibid.

79. Georgia Code, Section 16-9-94.

11

Offenses Against Public Order and the Administration of Justice

One declares so many things to be a crime that it becomes impossible for men to live without breaking laws.

—Ayn Rand (1905–1982), *Atlas Shrugged*

The criminal law is society's most destructive and intrusive form of intervention.

—Law Reform Commission of Canada (1977)

Vulgar statements directed at police officers . . . [are] not sufficient to constitute disorderly conduct.
—*People* v. *Stephen*, 153 Misc. 2d 382, 581 N.Y.S.2d 981 (N.Y. Crim. Ct. 1992)

CHAPTER OUTLINE

AFTER READING THIS CHAPTER YOU SHOULD:

▷ Appreciate the general nature of social order offenses and know the three fundamental types of social order offenses.

▷ Understand the nature of offenses classified as those against the public order and safety.

▷ Know what constitutes breach of peace and disorderly conduct.

▷ Understand how alcohol offenses are regulated.

▷ Know the two common types of DUI offenses.

▷ Be able to define and distinguish between rout, riot, and unlawful assembly.

▷ Be able to describe the shortcomings of traditional laws against vagrancy.

▷ Be able to list the deadly weapons crimes.

▷ Be able to list and describe crimes against the administration of government.

INTRODUCTION

On October 30, 1991, at about 4 o'clock in the morning, New York City Police Officer William McGill was on patrol at the corner of 150th Street and Broadway. While walking by a store that was still open, Officer McGill observed a young man whom he later learned was named Paul Stephen. Stephen was standing in the store and, as the officer walked by, Stephen clutched his genital area with his hands, and yelled, "F—you! If you were in jail, I'd f—you! You'd be my bitch. . . ." Stephen followed the officer out into the street repeating the statements, and yelling: "If you didn't have that gun and badge, I'd kick your ass, I'd kill you!" A crowd of approximately fifteen to twenty people gathered and joined the defendant yelling, "Yeah, f—the police!"[1]

Officer McGill decided to arrest Stephen for disorderly conduct. While the officer was attempting to restrain Stephen, the defendant struggled violently, flailing his arms, twisting and turning his body, and butting the officer in the chest with his head.

Stephen was jailed for a short while. When he appeared in court, his attorney argued that his conduct was protected under the U.S. Constitution's First Amendment guarantees of free speech, and by Article I, Section 8, of the New York State Constitution. A portion of the trial court's opinion is reproduced in the paragraphs that follow[2]:

... It has long been recognized that the guarantees of freedom of expression under the First and Fourteenth Amendments of the Federal Constitution are not absolute and do not prevent States from punishing certain "well-defined and narrowly limited classes of speech. . . ." Where words present a clear and present danger of inciting those listening to lawless action, they are not entitled to constitutional protections and may be punished. . . .

In this case, there is no indication that either defendant or any member of the crowd was armed or preparing to lay hands upon the officer. Accordingly, defendant's statements are protected speech and do not fall within the incitement exception to the First Amendment. . . .

The second class of unprotected speech relevant to this case is that category of speech constituting "fighting words," words "which by their very utterance inflict injury or tend to incite an immediate breach of the peace," or which are likely to provoke the average person to retaliation. (*Chaplinsky v. New Hampshire, supra*, 315 U.S. at 572, 62 S. Ct. at 769). The People contend that defendant's words to the officer fall squarely within this class of actionable conduct.

While the original *Chaplinsky* formulation of "fighting words" may have given some impression of establishing a category of words which could be proscribed regardless of the context in which they were used, developing First Amendment doctrine in the half century since *Chaplinsky* was decided has continually resorted to analyzing provocative expression contextually. . . . Thus, whether particular speech constitutes "fighting words" cannot be determined outside of the context in which the speech occurs.

In the context within which these words were uttered, defendant's remarks, even with the accompanying gestures, could not be said to have a direct tendency to provoke the police officer to retaliate with acts of violence or other breach of the peace. No reasonable person witnessing the situation would have thought it likely that the police officer would have been driven to attack defendant as a direct consequence of his comments.

Moreover, the Supreme Court has held that the "fighting words" doctrine applies more narrowly to police officers, as police officers are trained and expected to exercise more restraint in response to provocation than do other citizens. (*City of Houston v. Hill*, 482 U.S. 451, 107 S. Ct. 2502, 96 L. Ed. 2d 398 [1987]). One of the reasons we expect the police to be less sensitive to provocation, according to the Supreme Court, is because: "[t]he freedom of individuals verbally to oppose or challenge police action without thereby risking arrest is one of the principal characteristics by which we distinguish a free nation from a police state. . . ." Thus, even if reasonable civilians might have been provoked into retaliatory action by defendant's comments, one could expect that a trained police officer would remain calm (as he apparently did). Thus, defendant's remarks, while odious, do not come within the small class of "fighting words" for which the government may mete out punishment. . . .

As defendant's threatening comments and gestures did not present a clear and present danger of either of these types of immediate harm, and amounted to pure, protected speech, this prosecution infringes defendant's rights of free expression under the First and Fourteenth Amendments of the Federal Constitution. Accordingly, the motion to dismiss the charge of Penal Law Section 240.20(1) on Federal Constitutional grounds is granted.

Defendant next argues that because the officer lacked authority to arrest him for disorderly conduct, the resisting arrest charge must be dismissed as facially insufficient. . . . In this case, assuming the facts stated in the accusatory instrument to be true, the officer arrested the defendant for exercising his constitutional rights to express his views regarding members of the police department, albeit in an extremely derisive way. Because on these facts, no violation of disorderly conduct occurred, the officer was not authorized to arrest the defendant. . . . As the officer was not authorized to make an arrest at the time the defendant struggled with the officer, an essential element of resisting arrest is lacking. . . . Accordingly, the charge of resisting arrest is dismissed for facial insufficiency.

Web Extra! 11–1

City of Houston v. *Hill* (1987)

Although the preservation of liberty depends in part upon the maintenance of social order, the First Amendment requires that officers and municipalities respond with restraint in the face of verbal challenges to police action, since a certain amount of expressive disorder is inevitable in a society committed to individual freedom and must be protected if that freedom would survive.

—Justice William J. Brennan,
writing for the majority
City of Houston v. *Hill*,
482 U.S. 451 [1987]

CRIMES AGAINST PUBLIC ORDER

This chapter and the one that follows (Chapter 12) discuss crimes against the social order. Between the two chapters, three categories of social order crimes are discussed: (1) crimes against public order and safety, which include disorderly conduct, breach of peace, unlawful fighting, and so on; (2) crimes against justice and the administration of government, including treason and perjury, and; (3) crimes against public decency and morality, including obscenity, prostitution, sodomy, and other sex-related offenses. Our discussion of social order offenses begins in this chapter with discussion of crimes against the public order and safety and continues on to include crimes against the administration of justice. The final category of social order crimes, those committed against public morality, is discussed in Chapter 12.

Public order offenses are those that disturb or invade society's peace and tranquillity. Public order offenses include the following: breach of peace (sometimes called "disturbing the peace"), disorderly conduct, fighting, affray (fighting in public), vagrancy, loitering, (illegally) carrying weapons, keeping a disorderly (or "bawdy") house, public intoxication (whether by alcohol or other controlled substances), disturbance of public assembly, inciting to riot, rioting, unlawful assembly, rout, obstructing public passage, and others. Laws criminalizing such activity rest on the assumption that public order is inherently valuable and should be maintained—and that disorder is not to be tolerated and should be reduced, when it occurs, through application of the criminal law. This modern-day assumption derives from an early English common law principle, which held that anyone intentionally violating the peace decreed by the King, and desired by him for all of his subjects throughout the realm, could be called to answer to the King's representatives.

PUBLIC ORDER OFFENSE
an act that is wilfully and unlawfully committed and that disturbs public peace or tranquillity. Included are offenses such as fighting, breach of peace, disorderly conduct, vagrancy, loitering, unlawful assembly, public intoxication, obstructing public passage, and (illegally) carrying weapons.

Breach of Peace and Disorderly Conduct

As some authors[3] point out, all crimes, when viewed from a philosophical perspective, are breaches of peace and disruptions of public order. A murder, for example, victimizes not only the individual killed but also violates the orderliness of social interaction and lessens the overall integrity of the social order. Some crimes, however, do not just *theoretically* disturb public tranquillity but are themselves *actual* disturbances of public tranquillity or cause such disturbances—and these are the crimes that concern us here.

Under common law, **breach of peace** was the term used to describe any unlawful activity that unreasonably disturbed the peace and tranquillity of the community. Breach of peace, as the phrase is used today, is "a flexible term, occasionally defined by statute, for a violation of public order; [or] an act calculated to disturb the public peace."[5] Breach of peace can also be defined as "a public offense done by violence, or one causing or likely to cause an immediate disturbance of public order."[6] The term itself "embraces a great variety of conduct destroying or menacing public order and tranquillity. It includes not only violent acts, but acts and words likely to produce violence in others."[7]

All jurisdictions have statutes that prohibit conduct likely to cause breaches of the public peace. At common law, the main thrust of strictures against breach of peace was to discourage acts that were not otherwise deemed criminal but that tended to disturb the peace and tranquillity of the community. As Blackstone observed, "Peace is the very end and foundation of civil society."[8] Contemporary statutes build on the common law emphasis on public tranquillity, and specifically prohibit disorderly conduct, unlawful fighting, challenging a person to fight, the

BREACH OF PEACE
any unlawful activity that unreasonably disturbs the peace and tranquillity of the community. Also, "an act calculated to disturb the public peace."[4]

Mooning the public during spring break in Key Biscayne, Florida. Public order offenses are those that disturb or invade society's peace and tranquillity. (Photo by A. Ramey, courtesy of PhotoEdit.)

use of "fighting words," and so on. Certain types of conduct may be considered a "breach of peace" in one jurisdiction, but be called "disorderly conduct" in another. Accordingly, there is significant overlap between the two offenses, as will be obvious from our discussion in this section. The California breach of peace statute is reproduced in a Law on the Books box in this section.

The California statute contains the phrase "offensive words," referring to the use of fighting words. **Fighting words,** as the story that opens this chapter points out, are utterances that are intended to provoke the person(s) at whom they are directed. Impugning another's parentage provides an oft-cited example of fighting words. Fighting words are not protected by the free speech clause of the First Amendment to the U.S. Constitution, a position made clear by the U.S. Supreme Court in the case of *Chaplinsky* v. *New Hampshire*.[9] In *Chaplinsky*, the Court ruled that "it is well understood that the right of free speech is not absolute at all times and under all circumstances. There are certain well-defined and narrowly limited classes of speech, the prevention and punishment of which have never been thought to raise any Constitutional problem. These include the lewd and obscene, the profane, the libelous, and the insulting or 'fighting' words—those which by their very utterance inflict injury or tend to incite an immediate breach of the peace." As the Court explained, "It has been well observed that such utterances are no essential part of any exposition of ideas, and are of such slight social value as a step to truth that any benefit that may be derived from them is clearly outweighed by the social interest in order and morality." In short, the Court was saying that the use of "epithets or personal abuse is not in any proper sense communication of information or opinion safeguarded by the Constitution," and may be punished as a criminal act.

While breach of peace is a general term, **disorderly conduct** refers to specific, purposeful, and unlawful behavior that tends to cause public inconvenience, annoyance, or alarm. Because there was no disorderly conduct crime at common law, the modern-day crime of disorderly conduct has been created by statute. One of the constitutional problems associated with attempting to outlaw disorderly conduct, however, is accurately describing just what forms of behavior constitute the offense. At least one court has observed that disorderly conduct is "A term of loose and indefinite meaning (except as defined by statutes), but signifying generally

---

FIGHTING WORDS

words which, by their very utterance, inflict injury or tend to incite an immediate breach of peace. Fighting words are not protected by the free speech clause of the First Amendment to the U.S. Constitution.

DISORDERLY CONDUCT

specific, purposeful, and unlawful behavior that tends to cause public inconvenience, annoyance, or alarm.

any behavior that is contrary to law, and more particularly such as tends to disturb the peace or decorum, scandalize the community, or shock the public sense of morality."[10]

LAW ON THE BOOKS

"CRIMES AGAINST THE PUBLIC PEACE" AND "DISORDERLY CONDUCT" UNDER CALIFORNIA LAW.

Compare with Model Penal Code, Section 250.2

CALIFORNIA PENAL CODE

Section 415. Any of the following persons shall be punished by imprisonment in the county jail for a period of not more than 90 days, a fine of not more than four hundred dollars ($400), or both such imprisonment and fine:

1. Any person who unlawfully fights in a public place or challenges another person in a public place to fight.

2. Any person who maliciously and wilfully disturbs another person by loud and unreasonable noise.

3. Any person who uses offensive words in a public place which are inherently likely to provoke an immediate violent reaction.

Section 415.5 (a). Any person who:

1. unlawfully fights within any building or upon the grounds of any school, community college, university, or state university or challenges another person within any building or upon the grounds to fight, or

2. maliciously and wilfully disturbs another person within any of these buildings or upon the grounds by loud and unreasonable noise, or

3. uses offensive words within any of these buildings or upon the grounds which are inherently likely to provoke an immediate violent reaction is guilty of a misdemeanor punishable by a fine not exceeding four hundred dollars ($400) or by imprisonment in the county jail for a period of not more than ninety days, or both.

Section 647. Every person who commits any of the following acts is guilty of disorderly conduct, a misdemeanor:

   a. Who solicits anyone to engage in or who engages in lewd or dissolute conduct in any public place or in any place open to the public or exposed to public view.

   b. Who solicits or who agrees to engage in or who engages in any act of prostitution. A person agrees to engage in an act of prostitution when, with specific intent to so engage, he or she manifests an acceptance of an offer or solicitation to so engage, regardless of whether the offer or solicitation was made by a person who also possessed the specific intent to engage in prostitution. No agreement to engage in an act of prostitution shall constitute a violation of this subdivision unless some act, in addition to the agreement, is done within this state in furtherance of the commission of an act of prostitution by the person agreeing to engage in that act. As used in this subdivision, "prostitution" includes any lewd act between persons for money or other consideration.

   c. Who accosts other persons in any public place or in any place open to the public for the purpose of begging or soliciting alms.

   d. Who loiters in or about any toilet open to the public for the purpose of engaging in or soliciting any lewd or lascivious or any unlawful act.

   e. Who loiters or wanders upon the streets or from place to place without apparent reason or business and who refuses to identify himself or herself and to account for his or her presence when requested by any peace officer to do so, if the surrounding circumstances would indicate to a reasonable person that the public safety demands this identification.

   f. Who is found in any public place under the influence of intoxicating liquor, any drug, controlled substance, toluene, or any combination of any intoxicating liquor, drug, controlled substance, or toluene, in such a condition that he or she is unable to exercise care

(continued)

LAW ON THE BOOKS

for his or her own safety or the safety of others, or by reason of his or her being under the influence of intoxicating liquor, any drug, controlled substance, toluene, or any combination of any intoxicating liquor, drug, or toluene, interferes with or obstructs or prevents the free use of any street, sidewalk, or other public way. . . .

h. Who loiters, prowls, or wanders upon the private property of another, at any time, without visible or lawful business with the owner or occupant. As used in this subdivision, "loiter" means to delay or linger without a lawful purpose for being on the property and for the purpose of committing a crime as opportunity may be discovered.

i. Who, while loitering, prowling, or wandering upon the private property of another, at any time, peeks in the door or window of any inhabited building or structure, without visible or lawful business with the owner or occupant.

j. Who lodges in any building, structure, vehicle, or place, whether public or private, without the permission of the owner or person entitled to the possession or in control of it.

k. Anyone who looks through a hole or opening, into, or otherwise views, by means of any instrumentality, including, but not limited to, a periscope, telescope, binoculars, camera, or camcorder, the interior of a bathroom, changing room, fitting room, dressing room, or tanning booth, or the interior of any other area in which the occupant has a reasonable expectation of privacy, with the intent to invade the privacy of a person or persons inside. This subdivision shall not apply to those areas of a private business used to count currency or other negotiable instruments. . . .

Fighting and Affray

AFFRAY
the fighting of persons in a public place to the terror of the people.[11]

One form of disorderly conduct that is often described by statute is unlawful public fighting. While some fights may be officially sanctioned, as in the case of regulated sporting events, spontaneous and unregulated physical altercations that occur in a place open to public view constitute disorderly conduct. Many jurisdictions have statutes outlawing **affray,** which can be defined as "the fighting of persons in a public place to the terror of the people."[12] The term affray derives from the word "afraid," and means an altercation that tends to alarm the community.

PRIZE FIGHTING
unlawful public fighting undertaken for the purpose of winning an award or a prize.

Fighting is a mutual event and thus differs from assault. If one person attacks another, the attacker may be guilty of assault, since the accosted person may be an innocent victim. But when two people willingly and publicly fight one another, both are guilty of the crime of affray. **Prize fighting,** which is unlawful public fighting undertaken for the purpose of winning an award or a prize, is specifically contravened by statute in many jurisdictions. Participants in boxing matches that occur under public auspices, however, are exempted from prosecution—so long as they follow the rules of the game.

Public Intoxication

Alcohol abuse is commonplace in American society today. The problem, however, is not new to modern times. Records show that the early Puritans who came to this country in the 1600s, for example, stocked their ship, the *Arabella,* with ten thousand gallons of wine and forty-two tons of beer, but only eleven tons of water.[13]

Those who study the history of alcohol use in this country note that seventeenth-century and eighteenth-century America were "notable for the amount of alcoholic beverages consumed. . . . Liquor was food, medicine, and social lubricant, and even such a Puritan divine as Cotton Mather called it the 'good creature of God.' It flowed freely at weddings, christenings and funerals, at the building of churches, the installation of pews, and the ordination of ministers. . . . The tavern was a key institution in every town, the center of social and political life, and all varieties of drink were available. Americans drank wine, beer, cider, and distilled spirits, especially rum. They drank at home, at work, and while traveling; they drank morning, noon, and night. And they got drunk."[14]

Although drinking was accepted, habitual drunkenness was not. During the colonial period, for example, many towns circulated lists of common drunkards, and innkeepers who sold liquor to them could be fined. "In general, however, drunkards as a group or class of deviants were not especially problematic for colonial Americans."[15]

In the early 1830s, the Temperance Movement began in the United States and quickly grew—culminating in 1919 in the Eighteenth Amendment to the U.S. Constitution, and ushering in the era of Prohibition. Prohibition ended in 1933, with passage of the Twenty-first Amendment, leaving state and local governments to establish statutory controls over the behavior of those who consumed too much alcohol.

Our contemporary view of drunkenness builds on earlier American conceptions, and "translates the behavioral description of the habitual drunkard into . . . [that of] the alcoholic."[16] But the understanding we have of the drunkard is not the understanding of the seventeenth and eighteenth centuries. In that early view, the drunkard's sin was the love of "excess" drink to the point of drunkenness, and drunkenness was seen as the result of individual choice.

From a theoretical viewpoint, the modern understanding of problem drinking is framed in terms of the alcoholic—or a person who cannot consistently choose whether he or she will drink or not. The alcoholic is seen as essentially powerless, and suffering from the disease of alcoholism. "The core of the disease concept [is] the idea that habitual drunkards are alcohol addicts, persons who have lost control over their drinking and who must abstain entirely from alcohol. . . ."[17] The idea that alcoholism is a disease was officially endorsed by the American Medical Association in 1956.

Statistically speaking, about 7 percent of the population ages eighteen and older (about 14 million Americans) have problems with drinking, including 8.1 million people who are alcoholic. Almost three times as many men (9.8 million) as women (3.9 million) are problem drinkers, and prevalence is highest for both sexes in the eighteen to twenty-nine age group.[18] Moreover, about 43 percent of all adults in the United States, or 76 million people, have been exposed to alcoholism in the family. These people grew up with or married an alcoholic or problem drinker or had a blood relative who was at some time an alcoholic or problem drinker.[19] Young people are also affected by the ready availability of alcoholic beverages. For example, 63 percent of high school seniors report that they have been drunk, and nearly 30 percent say that have had five or more drinks in a row during the last two weeks.[20] Finally, the economic cost of alcoholism and alcohol-related problems is estimated to be around $100 billion per year, with most of the cost coming in the form of reduced or lost productivity and medical and other costs associated with premature death.[21]

Alcohol and Drug Laws

A few decades ago, the two most common crimes involving alcohol were public drunkenness and **driving while intoxicated** (DWI). While both crimes are still quite common, DWI ordinances have generally been expanded to encompass the operation of a motor vehicle while under the influence of drugs. Hence, **driving under**

DRIVING WHILE INTOXICATED (DWI)
unlawfully operating a motor vehicle while under the influence of alcohol.

DRIVING UNDER THE INFLUENCE (DUI)
unlawfully operating a motor vehicle while under the influence of alcohol or drugs.

the influence (DUI) is an offense which can be committed by a person under the influence of either alcohol or drugs.

In most jurisdictions, there are two separate crimes within the driving under the influence (DUI) category. The first type of DUI is the crime of driving while under the influence of alcohol or drugs. DUI occurs whenever a person operates a motor vehicle while under the influence of alcohol or drugs, and the blood alcohol level of the individual is immaterial as long as the individual's ability to operate a motor vehicle is impaired. The second type of DUI is the crime of operating a motor vehicle with a blood alcohol level specified by statute to be at or above a certain level. The second form of statutory DUI does not require that the individual's driving skills be impaired, but only that his or her blood alcohol level has reached a certain measurable level. In recognition of this distinction, some jurisdictions have modified their statutes to include the phrase "driving with an unlawful blood alcohol level" (or DUBAL). The normal blood alcohol level for most DUBAL crimes is generally set by law as either 0.10 percent or 0.08 percent (of alcohol content of blood by volume), with a lower level usually specified for operating an aircraft or boat.

A few jurisdictions use blood alcohol level tests only to establish a presumption that a person has been operating a vehicle while under the influence of alcohol. In those jurisdictions, evidence may be admitted as to the effect that a certain level of blood alcohol is likely to have had on the defendant. Another variation, used in a few jurisdictions, considers blood alcohol levels below 0.06 percent to establish the presumption that a person was not under the influence of alcohol; levels of 0.07 percent to 0.1 percent to establish a presumption that the driver was under the influence; and levels of over 0.1 percent as irrefutable evidence that the person was under the influence of alcohol.

Some jurisdictions, such as California, have statutorily established a third type of DUI, which involves the operation of a motor vehicle by a person who is addicted to the use of any drug, unless the person is on an approved drug maintenance program.[22] Most jurisdictions make it a crime for a juvenile to operate a motor vehicle, boat, or airplane with any trace of alcohol in his or her blood. Others use a level of 0.05 percent for juveniles. Generally, a person's first DUI conviction is counted as a misdemeanor, with subsequent offenses becoming felonies.

As with all statutes, some terminology is specific to DUI statutes. The term "under the influence" means, for example, that "alcohol or drugs or a combination thereof have so affected the nervous system, the brain, or muscles as to impair to an appreciable degree the ability of the person to operate a motor vehicle in an ordinary and cautious manner."[23] "Driving," for purposes of DUI statutes, generally requires some intentional movement of the driver's vehicle. The movement may be as simple as coasting down a hill or pedaling a "moped." A movement of a vehicle over a distance of a few feet has been held sufficient to constitute "driving." The definition of "motor vehicles" generally includes animal-drawn vehicles, go-carts, forklifts, snowmobiles, bulldozers, mopeds, and mobile cranes.[24] Almost all jurisdictions, however, also have statutes that prohibit operating an aircraft, boat, or locomotive while under the influence of alcohol or drugs. The operator or "driver" is usually defined as the person who "drives," or is in actual physical control of the vehicle.

Most jurisdictions provide for the administrative suspension of a DUI defendant's driver's license for refusal to take a test for the physical presence of alcohol. In California, for example, prior to asking a driver to submit to a chemical test, arresting officers must advise the person that refusal to submit to, or failure to complete, a chemical test for the presence of alcohol in the body will result in suspension or revocation of the person's driver's license and mandatory imprisonment upon conviction of DUI. Suspects are also advised that a refusal to take, or a failure to complete, such a test may be used in court as evidence that the driver was driving while under the influence. Defendants are similarly told that they have no right to consult with an attorney before taking the test or before making a choice of which test to take (Breathalyzer, blood analysis, or urinalysis).[25]

Public drunkenness is the second most common alcohol-related offense. To constitute the crime of **public drunkenness,** one must, while in a public place, be in a state of intoxication to such a degree that one is unable to care for oneself. It is not, however, a crime in most jurisdictions to be intoxicated in a private place, as in one's home. Some jurisdictions have established the statutory crime of being *drunk and disorderly.* As the name implies, this crime generally requires that the person be both drunk and disorderly for the offense to occur.

PUBLIC DRUNKENNESS
the offense of being in a state of intoxication in a place accessible to the public.

Riot and Unlawful Assembly

In most jurisdictions, an **unlawful assembly** is when three or more persons assemble for the purposes of doing an unlawful act, or a lawful act in a violent, boisterous, or tumultuous manner.[26] Unlawful assembly is a specific intent crime and therefore requires that those persons assembled must intend to commit an unlawful act or a lawful act in a prohibited manner.

A **rout,** which provides the root for the word "route," can be described as the preparatory stage of a riot.[27] A rout is when an unlawful assembly makes an attempt to advance toward the commission of an act that would be a riot. The difference between an unlawful assembly and a rout is that a rout requires both an unlawful assembly and an overt act. A **riot** is the culmination of unlawful assembly and rout and can be defined as a tumultuous disturbance of the peace by three or more persons assembled of their own authority.[29] The federal Anti-Riot Act of 1968 provides the following definition:

UNLAWFUL ASSEMBLY
a gathering of three or more persons for the purposes of doing an unlawful act, or for the purpose of doing a lawful act in a violent, boisterous, or tumultuous manner.

ROUT
the preparatory stage of a riot.

RIOT
a tumultuous disturbance of the peace by three or more persons assembled of their own authority.[28]

> the term 'riot' means a public disturbance involving: (1) an act or acts of violence by one or more persons, part of an assemblage of three or more persons, which act or acts shall constitute a clear and present danger of, or shall result in, damage or injury to the property of any other person or to the person of any other individual or (2) a threat or threats of the commission of an act or acts of violence by one or more persons part of an assemblage of three or more persons having, individually or collectively, the ability of immediate execution of such threat or threats, where the performance of the threatened act or acts of violence would constitute a clear and present danger of, or would result in, damage or injury to the property of any other person or to the person of any other individual.[30]

The federal Anti-Riot Act makes it illegal for any person to travel between states or to enter the country, or to use "any facility of interstate or foreign commerce" (such as the mail, telephones, radio, fax machines, the Internet, or television) to incite, organize, promote, encourage, participate in, or carry on a riot. As the wording of the act indicates, to constitute a riot, there must be at least *threats* to use force or violence, and the threats or use of force must actually disturb the peace. Public peace is considered "disturbed" when the actions of the group excite terror, alarm, and consternation in the neighborhood.[31]

As noted earlier, unlawful assembly, rout, and riot all require a common purpose by three or more persons. The requirement of *three* or more persons stems from common law, although some states (such as California, whose statutes on unlawful assemblies, routs, and riots are reproduced in the Law on the Books box on page 438) have statutorily reduced the required number of participating individuals to two. In any case, a single individual, acting alone, cannot commit these offenses. However, a single individual, acting alone, can commit the crime of urging or **inciting a riot.** Inciting a riot is the use of words or other means intended and calculated to provoke a riot. To establish the crime of urging or inciting a riot, the prosecution must prove that the defendant's acts or conduct were done with the intent to cause a riot.

INCITING A RIOT
the use of words or other means intended and calculated to provoke a riot.

LYNCHING
the taking, by means of riot, any person from the lawful custody of any peace officer.

Although rarely seen today, the crime of **lynching** is defined as the taking by means of riot any person from the lawful custody of any peace officer. Any participation in the lynching is sufficient to constitute the offense. The taking of the person from a lawful custody is the gist of the crime of lynching. Although "lynching" has come to mean a "hanging" in common parlance, there is no lawful requirement that the person taken be harmed nor is intended harm required by the law. Because lynching requires that the taking of the person be by means of a riot, lynching is not a crime that a single individual, acting alone, can commit. The crime of **rescuing a prisoner,** however, which has been codified in some jurisdictions, may be committed by a single individual, acting alone. The crime of rescuing a prisoner is committed when any person or persons rescues or attempts to rescue any person being held in lawful custody.

RESCUING A PRISONER
a crime that is committed when any person or persons rescues or attempts to rescue any person being held in lawful custody.

DISTURBANCE OF PUBLIC ASSEMBLY
a crime that occurs when any person(s) acts(s) unlawfully at a public gathering collected for a lawful purpose in such a way as to purposefully disturb the gathering.

Another "group" offense against the public order is **disturbance of public assembly,** sometimes termed "disturbing a public or religious meeting." The crime occurs when any person acts, or persons act, unlawfully at a public gathering collected for a lawful purpose in such a way as to purposefully disturb the gathering. Disturbing public meetings is a statutory crime in most jurisdictions and generally involves the *wilful* disturbance of a public or religious meeting without legal authority.

LAW ON THE BOOKS

"RIOTS," "ROUTS," AND "UNLAWFUL ASSEMBLIES" UNDER CALIFORNIA LAW.
Compare with Model Penal Code, Section 250.1

CALIFORNIA PENAL CODE

Section 403. Every person who, without authority of law, wilfully disturbs or breaks up any assembly or meeting that is not unlawful in its character, other than an assembly or meeting referred to in Section 302 of the Penal Code or Section 18340 of the Elections Code, is guilty of a misdemeanor.

Section 404. a. Any use of force or violence, disturbing the public peace, or any threat to use force or violence, if accompanied by immediate power of execution, by two or more persons acting together, and without authority of law, is a riot.

b. As used in this section, disturbing the public peace may occur in any place of confinement. Place of confinement means any state prison, county jail, industrial farm, or road camp, or any city jail, industrial farm, or road camp, or any juvenile hall, juvenile camp, juvenile ranch, or juvenile forestry camp.

Section 404.6. Every person who with the intent to cause a riot does an act or engages in conduct which urges a riot, or urges others to commit acts of force or violence, or the burning or destroying of property, and at a time and place and under circumstances which produce a clear and present and immediate danger of acts of force or violence or the burning or destroying of property, is guilty of a misdemeanor punishable by a fine not exceeding one thousand dollars ($1,000), or by imprisonment in a county jail not exceeding one year, or by both that fine and imprisonment.

Section 405. Every person who participates in any riot is punishable by a fine not exceeding one thousand dollars, or by imprisonment in a county jail not exceeding one year, or by both such fine and imprisonment.

Section 405a. The taking by means of a riot of any person from the lawful custody of any peace officer is a lynching.

Section 405b. Every person who participates in any lynching is punishable by imprisonment in the state prison for two, three, or four years.

(continued)

LAW ON THE BOOKS

Section 406. Whenever two or more persons, assembled and acting together, make any attempt or advance toward the commission of an act which would be a riot if actually committed, such assembly is a rout.

Section 407. Whenever two or more persons assemble together to do an unlawful act, or do a lawful act in a violent, boisterous, or tumultuous manner, such assembly is an unlawful assembly.

Section 408. Every person who participates in any rout or unlawful assembly is guilty of a misdemeanor.

Section 409. Every person remaining present at the place of any riot, rout, or unlawful assembly, after the same has been lawfully warned to disperse, except public officers and persons assisting them in attempting to disperse the same, is guilty of a misdemeanor.

Vagrancy and Loitering

At common law, **vagrancy** was the act of going about from place to place by a person without visible means of support, who was idle, and who, though able to work for his or her maintenance, refused to do so, but lived without labor or on the charity of others.[33] As such, the common law crime of vagrancy made it an offense simply to wander from place to place without any visible means of support. It focused on the idle and those avoiding work. Later English statutes required all able-bodied men to work. One English court explained the history of vagrancy laws as follows: "The early Vagrancy Acts came into being under peculiar conditions utterly different to those of the present time. From the time of the Black Death in the middle of the fourteenth century till the middle of the seventeenth century, and indeed, although in diminishing degree, right down to the reform of the Poor Law in the first half of the nineteenth century, the roads of England were crowded with masterless men and their families, who had lost their former employment through a variety of causes, had no means of livelihood, and had taken to a vagrant life. The main causes were the gradual decay of the feudal system under which the labouring classes had been anchored to the soil, the economic slackening of the legal compulsion to work for fixed wages; the break up of the monasteries in the reign of Henry VIII, and the consequent disappearance of the religious orders which had previously administered a kind of 'public assistance' in the form of lodging, food and alms; and, lastly, the economic changes brought about by the Enclosure Acts. Some of these people were honest labourers who had fallen upon evil days, others were the 'wild rogues,' so common in Elizabethan times and literature, who had been born to a life of idleness and had no intention of following any other. It was they and their confederates who formed themselves into the notorious 'brotherhood of beggars,' which flourished in the 16th and 17th centuries. They were a definite and serious menace to the community, and it was chiefly against them and their kind that the harsher provisions of the vagrancy laws of the period were directed."[34]

Seen in these terms, a **vagrant** (also called a **vagabond**) was "a wanderer; an idle person who, being able to maintain himself by lawful labor, either refuses to work or resorts to unlawful practices, e.g., begging, to gain a living."[36] The term "common vagrant" was often applied at common law to distinguish one whose condition or mode of life was that of a vagrant, from one who might be temporarily vagrant.

VAGRANCY
under common law, the act of going about from place to place by a person without visible means of support, who was idle, and who, though able to work for his or her maintenance, refused to do so and lived without labor or on the charity of others.[32]

VAGRANT
also **vagabond**; a wanderer; an idle person who, being able to maintain himself by lawful labor, either refuses to work or resorts to unlawful practices, e.g., begging, to gain a living.[35]

Early American laws against vagrancy were based on their English counterparts, as well as on strong cultural beliefs in the efficacy of a work ethic and fears that idleness would lead to crime. North Carolina law of three decades ago, for example, classified as vagrants:

> (1) Persons wandering or strolling about in idleness who are able to work and have no property to support them. (2) Persons leading an idle immoral or profligate life, who have no property to support them and who are able to work and do not work. (3) All persons able to work having no property to support them and who have not some visible and known means of a fair, honest, and reputable livelihood. (4) Persons having a fixed abode who have no visible property to support them and who live by stealing or by trading in, bartering for, or buying stolen property. (5) Professional gamblers living in idleness. (6) All able-bodied men having no visible means of support who shall live in idleness upon the wages or earnings of their mother, wife, or minor children, except of male children over eighteen years old. (7) Keepers and inmates of bawdy houses, assignation houses, lewd and disorderly houses, and other places where illegal sexual intercourse is habitually carried on: Provided, that nothing here is intended or shall be construed as abolishing the crime of keeping a bawdy house, or lessening the punishment by law for such crime. . . ."[37]

When common law vagrancy was enacted into law in the United States, vagrancy statutes were often successfully attacked as being vague and overbroad and as encouraging "arbitrary enforcement by failing to describe with sufficient particularity what a suspect must do in order to satisfy the statute."[38] Some authors have observed that "[s]tatutory language was intentionally rather vague, presumably to allow police broad discretion to arrest persons they deemed undesirable to the community."[39] Although vagrancy had often been described (in early vagrancy statutes) as being "an act," the truth of the matter was that one could be a vagrant by doing nothing at all. In terms of such laws, the less one did, it could be argued, the better vagrant one became. Hence, vagrancy, as defined by early laws, was really a **status** rather than an activity, and while one could be a vagrant, it was difficult to conceive of anyone committing vagrancy. As we have observed earlier in this text, generally speaking, to be something is not a crime, although to do something may be. Hence, to be a vagrant cannot be criminal, although the less one does the more vagrant one may appear to be.

STATUS
a person's state of being.

As a result of such flaws, most vagrancy statutes were eventually invalidated by state courts—and by the U.S. Supreme Court which, in the 1972 case of *Papachristou* v. *City of Jacksonville*,[40] held that many traditionally worded vagrancy statutes were void for vagueness because they failed "to give a person of ordinary intelligence fair notice that his contemplated conduct is forbidden by the statute and because [they] encourage arbitrary and erratic arrests and convictions." The Jacksonville city ordinance voided by the Supreme Court in 1972 read as follows: "Rogues and vagabonds, or dissolute persons who go about begging; common gamblers, persons who use juggling or unlawful games or plays, common drunkards, common night walkers, thieves, pilferers or pickpockets, traders in stolen property, lewd, wanton and lascivious persons, keepers of gambling places, common railers and brawlers, persons wandering or strolling around from place to place without any lawful purpose or object, habitual loafers, disorderly persons, persons neglecting all lawful business and habitually spending their time by frequenting houses of ill fame, gaming houses, or places where alcoholic beverages are sold or served, persons able to work but habitually living upon the earnings of their wives or minor children shall be deemed vagrants and, upon conviction in the Municipal Court shall be punished as provided for class D offenses."[41] At the time, class D offenses were punishable by ninety days imprisonment, a $500 fine, or both.

Web Extra! 11–2
Kolender v. *Lawson*
(1983)

A little more than a decade later, in *Kolender* v. *Lawson*,[42] the U.S. Supreme Court found a California statute, which prohibited loitering, or wandering about without apparent reason or business and refusing to identify oneself when asked to do so by police, unconstitutional because it vested too much discretionary power in the hands of the police.

States that today retain vagrancy statutes have typically rephrased their description of the crime to require some specific form of behavior. The California vagrancy statute, for example, which is reprinted below, couches vagrancy in terms of **loitering,** which it says "means to delay, to linger, or to idle about a school or public place without lawful business for being present." By specifying the circumstances under which loitering could occur, legislatures have sought to de-emphasize a person's *status* as a determinant of criminality.

LOITERING

the act of delaying or lingering or to idle about without lawful business for being present.

LAW ON THE BOOKS

"VAGRANCY" UNDER CALIFORNIA LAW.
CALIFORNIA PENAL CODE

Section 653(g). Every person who loiters about any school or public place at or near which children attend or normally congregate and who remains at any school or public place at or near which children attend or normally congregate, or who reenters or comes upon a school or place within seventy-two hours, after being asked to leave by the chief administrative official of that school or, in the absence of the chief administrative official, the person acting as the chief administrative official, or by a member of the security patrol of the school district who has been given authorization, in writing, by the chief administrative official of that school to act as his or her agent in performing this duty, or a city police officer, or sheriff or deputy sheriff, or Department of the California Highway Patrol peace officer is a vagrant, and is punishable by a fine of not exceeding one thousand dollars ($1,000) or by imprisonment in the county jail for not exceeding six months, or by both the fine and the imprisonment.

As used in this section, "loiter" means to delay, to linger, or to idle about a school or public place without lawful business for being present.

LAW IN PRACTICE

SHOULD HOMELESSNESS BE CRIMINALIZED?

In the past, laws against vagrancy often criminalized the status of persons who were idle and without visible means of support. Vagrancy laws were predicated on the strong work ethic characteristic of Western society. They also attempted to prevent crimes—such as theft—that were frequently associated with idleness. Today, few such laws remain on the books, having been found vague, overbroad, or unconstitutional by virtue of the fact that they criminalized a "status," or way of being, rather than any particular form of behavior. Even so, vagrant persons remain—although the term "homeless" is now often applied to them.

Homelessness has become a problem, not only for the people who occupy that status, but for many American cities and towns who are unsure of how to deal with what is sometimes a huge (and expanding) homeless population. Because of its pleasant year-round weather, San Francisco, California, has attracted large numbers of homeless persons. Reprinted in this box are excerpts from the 1995 "Platform Papers" of San Francisco mayoral candidate Ben Hom. Hom proposed recriminalizing vagrancy, but he received only 3 percent of the votes cast for mayor in the election, which was held on November 7, 1995.

(continued)

LAW IN PRACTICE

"Controlling Vagrancy," Position Paper of 1995 San Francisco Mayoral Candidate, Ben Hom.

IDENTIFYING THE PROBLEM

"Vagrant" is defined by Webster as "one who has no established residence and wanders idly from place to place without lawful or visible means of support."

To "panhandle" is defined: "to stop people on the street and ask for food or money; to accost on the street and beg from."

"Bum" is described as "one who sponges off others and avoids work . . . with no settled residence or means of support."

"Homeless," on the other hand, is defined as "having no home or permanent place of residence."

San Franciscans have homogenized the population that roams our streets and parks into one category, "the homeless." We have arbitrarily combined the economically displaced, the mentally ill, teenage runaways, parolees, drug addicts, alcoholics, unemployed veterans, and the elderly without families, all of whom have one thing in common. We call them "the homeless." Is it any wonder that we have been unable to control, let alone solve, the problem?

Because we confuse the definitions, and don't make distinctions, our feelings about this population have become polarized and extreme. When we encounter the physically disabled, veterans, or women with children begging on the street, our reaction is one of compassion. Conversely, if our experience has been with public drunks who urinate or pass out on our doorsteps, then our reaction is disgust and outrage. Unfortunately, our public policy has been driven by these emotional reactions, rather than by objective perception and analysis. So-called solutions have been no more than political reactions to constituent impressions, whether these impressions are based on reality or not. As Mayor, I will end this confusion, once and for all.

There can be no solution to the "homeless" problem. There will always be economically disadvantaged people requiring affordable housing. There are many actions that can be taken to provide more affordable housing, such as relaxing zoning controls, legalizing in-law apartments, re-

examining the merits of rent control, streamlining the building permit process, and providing decent public housing. But housing supply can never completely meet the demand of such a desirable place to live as San Francisco. We must face that fact, and do the best that we can.

On the other hand, the problem of the vagrants, panhandlers, and bums who plague our neighborhoods and commercial districts can be controlled, if there is the political will to do it.

VAGRANCY: Homeless advocates would have us believe that the homeless are just like you and me, except that they lack a roof over their head. This ludicrous assertion is simply NOT TRUE!! The fact is that seven out of ten homeless adults have been institutionalized, at some time in their lives, in a mental hospital, detoxification center, jail, or prison. Most studies of the homeless show that one-third are seriously mentally ill, one-third substance abusers, and one-third in economic or personal crisis. One study done in California in 1987 concluded that seven out of ten homeless people were substance abusers. The "Polaris" study of the Trans-Bay terminal homeless population from two years ago found over three-quarters of the bus terminal residents to be mentally ill and/or substance abusers. In other words, merely providing housing will not solve the problems of over two-thirds of the homeless population. Vagrants are vagrants because they either don't know how, or can't, or choose not to, live like the rest of us.

San Francisco has become a magnet for vagrants from all over the country. Our weather is comparatively good for living on the street, our general assistance payments are high, and most of our politicians have a welcoming, politically correct attitude of tolerance. As a result, we take vagrancy on our streets for granted. It isn't until we travel to another city that we recognize the problem for what it is. Other cities have addressed the problem and controlled it. Seattle's problem decreased when generous cash payments were lessened and replaced with mandatory assignments to drug and alcohol detox centers. In Washington, D.C., police admonish and may cite citizens who give money to panhandlers. But in San Francisco, we provide hotel rooms, free bus rides, free medical care, and the highest general assistance payments in the Bay Area. The laws of supply and demand have infested downtown, our neighborhoods, and our parks with an ever-growing population which threatens to eventually bankrupt our city and destroy our quality of life.

San Francisco represents only 12 percent of the population of the nine Bay Area counties, but we bear nearly 40 percent of the Bay Area's general assistance (GA) disbursements. The problem is only worsening. In the past five years, our GA rolls have risen from 8,000 to 12,000, with a correspondingly increased demand on our public safety and health resources.

Providing for our vagrant population is very expensive and goes well beyond general assistance checks. According to the September 1, 1995, San Francisco Examiner:

"The latest spending figures are not available, but in 1993–94, the City spent roughly $56 million—$39 million from the general fund, $14.6 million in federal money, and $2.4 million in state funds—on homeless programs, according to the mayor's office. Another $20 million came from the private sector."

When calculating costs, we must also include lost revenue when neighborhood businesses suffer losses or close because their patrons are accosted by panhandlers, or when major corporations decide to locate elsewhere because of the high taxes necessitated by generous social programs, or when tourists and conventions choose to tour and meet in more hospitable, safe, and pleasant cities.

We must re-examine how we're spending our money. The number of vagrants on the street, estimated to be from 6,000 to 10,000, is not decreasing, but increasing. Increased social service funding has not worked. . . .

We have traveled in the wrong direction for far too long. We must face the reality that vagrancy is against the law and proceed accordingly with formulating public policy. The public has a right to the enjoyment of public spaces set aside and maintained with tax dollars. Illegal camping, drinking alcohol, and taking drugs in public, publicly relieving oneself, begging, public sex, shouting obscenities, lurking threateningly, and creating public messes and nuisances are not constitutionally protected. Nor is such perverse behavior permitted by local laws. People do not have the right to live on our streets or in our parks. Proliferation of vagrancy is a problem of law enforcement and should be dealt with accordingly.

BEN L. HOM'S STRATEGY FOR VAGRANT CONTROL:

As Mayor, I will send an immediate signal that San Francisco is no longer hospitable to vagrants. . . .

Law enforcement will play a primary role in my strategy. Laws against vagrancy will be enforced without exception. Our police personnel are not social service providers nor should they be. Vagrants will be removed, not simply told to move on to another neighborhood. Aggressive panhandlers will be arrested, as will the intoxicated, and other public nuisances.

I will expand the opportunities for private security patrols in commercial and residential districts to supplement police services. A security presence will further serve to discourage vagrancy downtown and in our neighborhoods.

No other candidate for Mayor, or the current Mayor, has the courage to place our rights above the rights of those who are on the public dole. I will never be an apologist for present or past failed systems, as are my opponents. Their compassion is for the "homeless." Mine is for you, the beleaguered taxpayer.

A message must be sent to the vagrants of this city, and elsewhere, that panhandlers and bums will no longer be permitted to destroy the quality of life for hard-working taxpayers and their families, and that the free ride is over in San Francisco. I pledge to do so as your Mayor.

What Do *You* Think?

1. Do you agree with Hom's portrayal of the homeless? Why or why not?

2. Do you agree with Hom's views on vagrancy? Why or why not?

3. Do you agree that "people do not have the right to live on our streets or in our parks"? Why or why not?

4. Do you agree that "proliferation of vagrancy is a problem of law enforcement and should be dealt with accordingly"? Why or why not?

SOURCE: Ben Hom, "Controlling Vagrancy," Platform Paper, 1995. Reprinted with permission.

Weapons Carrying

At common law, riding or going about in public armed with a dangerous weapon was a misdemeanor. The display of weapons was regarded as alarming to the general populace and came to be classified as an "offense against the public peace." It was, however, generally accepted that men of "quality" (i.e., the nobility and the landed gentry) could lawfully carry and display weapons (such as swords, daggers, and handguns), while lower class persons were barred from such displays—apparently on the theory that the armed poor were dangerous, while the armed rich were merely protecting their property and their persons.

Web Extra! 11–3
Britannica online:
Vagrancy

In the United States today, gun control has become a controversial topic. Some individuals and groups, such as the National Rifle Association, argue that American citizens have a fundamental right to own firearms. Arguments in support of the right to own or carry weapons are often based on the Second Amendment to the U.S. Constitution, which reads, "A well-regulated militia, being necessary to the security of a free State, the right of the people to keep and bear arms, shall not be infringed." Others, however, say that the individual ownership of handguns, rifles, shotguns, and other similar weapons, has no place in a civilized society such as ours. They argue that the Second Amendment is merely a restriction on the actions of the federal Congress—and that states are free to regulate or limit gun ownership as they see fit.

CONCEALED WEAPON

a weapon that is carried on or near one's person and is not discernible by ordinary observation.

All states have, in fact, passed a variety of laws intended to control gun ownership and possession, as well as the possession of weapons of "mass destruction"—such as explosives, "heavy weapons," and so forth. The thrust of most substantive weapons laws in this country is against the carrying of concealed weapons. A **concealed weapon** is one that is carried on or near one's person and is not discernible by ordinary observation. In recent years, however, and in response to growing crime rates and citizen's fears of victimization, a number of states have enacted laws permitting the carrying of concealed weapons by citizens meeting certain licensing requirements. Such requirements typically include handgun training and background checks or a demonstrated need to carry a weapon for protection.

Laws regulating weapons possession and the purchase of handguns, rifles, and shotguns vary greatly from state to state. Moreover, many municipalities have enacted local ordinances even more restrictive than the laws of the states in which they are located. Most state gun control statutes: (1) outlaw concealed weapons; (2) limit access to, or ownership of, handguns; (3) severely restrict ownership of modified shotguns and rifles, such as those which have been "sawed-off"; and (4) criminalize possession of high explosives and weapons of "mass destruction." Most states also have laws that make it a crime to carry guns on school property, as well as laws controlling the possession of guns by an underage person and laws making it unlawful to discharge a firearm under a variety of circumstances. Many state codes go to considerable lengths in describing persons to whom handgun and weapons laws do not apply—such as law enforcement officers, correctional personnel, military personnel, and so forth. A comprehensive box in this chapter provides a summarized version of Georgia laws regulating handguns, explosives, and other such weapons.

Federal Gun Control Laws The so-called "Brady Law" may be the most significant federal gun control legislation passed to date. The Brady Law—formally called the Brady Handgun Violence Prevention Act[43]—is named after former President Ronald Reagan's White House press secretary, James Brady, who was shot in the head during John Hinckley's attempted assassination of Reagan in 1981. The Brady Law, signed by President Clinton in 1994, provides for a five-day waiting period before the purchase of a handgun,[44] and for the establishment of a national instant criminal background check system to be contacted by firearms dealers before the transfer of any handgun. An original provision of the law required that until the instant background checking system could be established, licensed gun dealers were to notify the chief law enforcement officer in their area of all applications to purchase a handgun. In 1997, however, in the combined cases of *Printz* v. *United States* (1997)[45] and *Mack* v. *United States* (1997),[46] the U.S. Supreme Court held that to impose such a requirement on local law enforcement officers was unconstitutional. Under the constitutional principle of dual sovereignty, said the Court, the "Framers of the Constitution rejected the concept of a central government that would act upon and through the States, and instead designed a system in which the State and Federal Governments would exercise concurrent authority over the people." Under the dual sovereignty principle, the justices held, the federal government is prohibited from exercising direct control over state officers. Were it to be able to do so, said the Court, "the Federal Government's power would be augmented immeasurably and impermissibly. . . ." Writing for the majority, Justice Scalia noted that "the Court's jurisprudence makes clear that the Federal Government may not compel the States to enact or administer a federal regulatory program."

Although the cooperation of local law enforcement officers in conducting background checks can no longer be required, the general thrust of the Brady Law remains in effect. Once the mandated national instant criminal background check system, called Instacheck, is in place, a licensed importer, licensed manufacturer, or licensed dealer will be required to verify the identity of the applicant using a valid photo ID (such as a driver's license) and to contact the system in order to receive a unique identification number authorizing the purchase before transfer of the handgun is made. Three years after the Brady Law went into effect, the Justice Department noted that the law had blocked gun sales to 186,000 criminals and others not allowed to buy firearms under its provisions.[47]

The Violent Crime Control and Law Enforcement Act of 1994 further regulated the sale of weapons within the United States, banning the manufacture of nineteen military-style assault weapons, including those with specific combat features, such as high-capacity ammunition clips that are capable of holding more than ten rounds. The act also specifically prohibited the sale or transfer of a gun to a juvenile, as well as the possession of a gun by a juvenile, and it prohibited gun sales to, and possession by, persons subject to family violence restraining orders.

Some years earlier, in the Gun-Free School Zones Act of 1990,[48] Congress made it a federal offense "for any individual knowingly to possess a firearm at a place that the individual knows, or has reasonable cause to believe, is a school zone."[49] The law was passed to assuage parents' concerns that their children might be in mortal danger due to the presence of guns in the hands of school-aged children and interlopers on school property.

In 1995, however, in a blow to federal efforts at gun control, the U.S. Supreme Court agreed with a lower court ruling that dismissed charges against a twelfth-grade student who had carried a concealed .38-caliber handgun and five bullets into the Edison High School in San Antonio, Texas. The student had been charged with violating the federal Gun-Free School Zones Act. Arguing that the federal government has the power to control commerce between the states (based on Article I, Section 8, Clause 3, of the U.S. Constitution, which delegates to Congress the power "[t]o regulate Commerce with foreign Nations, and among the several States, and with the Indian Tribes"), government lawyers told the Court that it was necessary for the federal government to take steps intended to control violence in schools because "the occurrence of violent crime in school zones" has brought about a "decline in the quality of education" that "has an adverse impact on interstate commerce and the foreign commerce of the United States."

While the Court agreed that this was a rational conclusion, it ruled that education, in the context of the law, was a local and not a national concern. Hence, said

Web Extra! 11–4

National Rifle
Association

Web Extra! 11–5

Center to Prevent
Handgun Violence

Web Extra! 11–6

CNN: Guns under fire

the Justices, "To uphold the Government's contentions here, we would have to pile inference upon inference in a manner that would bid fair to convert congressional authority under the Commerce Clause to a general police power of the sort retained by the States."[50]

LAW ON THE BOOKS

"DEADLY WEAPONS CRIMES" AS DEFINED BY THE STATE OF GEORGIA.

GEORGIA CODE

Section 16-11-121. As used in this part, the term:

1. "Dangerous weapon" means any weapon commonly known as a "rocket launcher," "bazooka," or "recoilless rifle" which fires explosive or nonexplosive rockets designed to injure or kill personnel or destroy heavy armor, or similar weapon used for such purpose. The term shall also mean a weapon commonly known as a "mortar" which fires high explosive from a metallic cylinder and which is commonly used by the armed forces as an antipersonnel weapon or similar weapon used for such purpose. The term shall also mean a weapon commonly known as a "hand grenade" or other similar weapon which is designed to explode and injure personnel or similar weapon used for such purpose. . . .

Section 16-11-122. No person shall have in his possession any sawed-off shotgun, sawed-off rifle, machine gun, dangerous weapon, or silencer except as provided in Code Section 16-11-124.

Section 16-11-123. A person commits the offense of unlawful possession of firearms or weapons when he knowingly has in his possession any sawed-off shotgun, sawed-off rifle, machine gun, dangerous weapon, or silencer, and, upon conviction thereof, he shall be punished by imprisonment for not less than one nor more than five years.

Section 16-11-126.

a. A person commits the offense of carrying a concealed weapon when such person knowingly has or carries about his or her person, unless in an open manner and fully exposed to view, any bludgeon, metal knuckles, firearm, knife designed for the purpose of offense and defense, or any other dangerous or deadly weapon or instrument of like character outside of his or her home or place of business, except as permitted under this Code section.

b. Upon conviction of the offense of carrying a concealed weapon, a person shall be punished as follows:

   (1) For the first offense, he or she shall be guilty of a misdemeanor; and

   (2) For the second offense, and for any subsequent offense, he or she shall be guilty of a felony and, upon conviction thereof, shall be imprisoned for not less than one year and not more than five years. . . .

Section 16-11-127.

a. Except as provided in Code Section 16-11-127.1, a person is guilty of a misdemeanor when he carries to or while at a public gathering any explosive compound, firearm, or knife designed for the purpose of offense and defense.

b. For the purpose of this Code section, "public gathering" shall include, but shall not be limited to, athletic or sporting events, churches or church functions, political rallies or functions, publicly owned or operated buildings, or establishments at which alcoholic beverages are sold for consumption on the premises.

c. This Code section shall not apply to competitors participating in organized sport shooting events. Law enforcement officers, peace officers retired from state or federal law enforcement agencies, judges, magistrates, solicitors-general, and district attorneys may carry pistols in publicly owned or operated buildings.

Section 16-11-127.1. . . . b. Except as otherwise provided in subsection (c) of this Code section, it shall be unlawful for any person to carry to or to possess or have under such person's

(continued)

LAW ON THE BOOKS

control while within a school safety zone or at a school building, school function, or school property or on a bus or other transportation furnished by the school any weapon or explosive compound, other than fireworks the possession of which is regulated by Chapter 10 of Title 25. Any person who violates this subsection shall be guilty of a felony and, upon conviction thereof, be punished by a fine of not more than ten thousand dollars ($10,000), by imprisonment for not less than two nor more than ten years, or both. A juvenile who violates this subsection shall be subject to the provisions of Code Section 15-11-37. . . .

Section 16-11-130. a. Code Sections 16-11-126 through 16-11-128 shall not apply to or affect any of the following persons if such persons are employed in the offices listed below or when authorized by federal or state law, regulations, or order:

  (1) Peace officers;
  (2) Wardens, superintendents, and keepers of correctional institutions, jails, or other institutions for the detention of persons accused or convicted of an offense;
  (3) Persons in the military service of the state or of the United States;
  (4) Persons employed in fulfilling defense contracts with the government of the United States or agencies thereof when possession of the weapon is necessary for manufacture, transport, installation, and testing under the requirements of such contract;
  (5) District attorneys, investigators employed by and assigned to a district attorney's office, and assistant district attorneys;
  (6) State court solicitors-general; investigators employed by and assigned to a state court solicitor-general's office; assistant state court solicitors-general; the corresponding personnel of any city court expressly continued in existence as a city court pursuant to Article VI, Section X, Paragraph I, subparagraph (5) of the Constitution; and the corresponding personnel of any civil court expressly continued as a civil court pursuant to said provision of the Constitution;
  (7) Those employees of the State Board of Pardons and Paroles when specifically designated and authorized in writing by the members of the State Board of Pardons and Paroles to carry a weapon;
  (8) The Attorney General and those members of his or her staff whom he or she specifically authorizes in writing to carry a weapon;
  (9) Chief probation officers, probation officers, intensive probation officers, and surveillance officers employed by and under the authority of the Department of Corrections pursuant to Article 2 of Chapter 8 of Title 42, known as the "State-wide Probation Act," when specifically designated and authorized in writing by the director of Division of Probation;
  (10) Public safety directors of municipal corporations;
  (11) Explosive ordnance disposal technicians, as such term is defined by Code Section 16-7-80, and persons certified as provided in Code Section 35-8-13 to handle animals trained to detect explosives, while in the performance of their duties;
  (12) State and federal trial and appellate judges;
  (13) United States Attorneys and Assistant United States Attorneys;
  (14) County medical examiners and coroners and their sworn officers employed by county government; and
  (15) Clerks of the superior courts. . . .
 b. Notwithstanding any other provisions of this part and except as otherwise provided in this Code section, it shall be unlawful for any person under the age of eighteen to possess or have under such person's control a pistol or revolver. A person convicted of a first violation of this subsection shall be guilty of a misdemeanor and shall be punished by a fine not to exceed one thousand dollars ($1,000) or by imprisonment for not more than 12 months, or both. A person convicted of a second or subsequent violation of this subsection shall be guilty of a felony and shall be punished by a fine not to exceed five thousand dollars ($5,000) or by imprisonment for not less than one nor more than three years, or both.

(continued)

LAW ON THE BOOKS

c. Except as otherwise provided in subsection (d) of this Code section, the provisions of subsection (b) of this Code section shall not apply to:

  (1) Any person under the age of eighteen years who is:

    (A) Attending a hunter education course or a firearms safety course;

    (B) Engaging in practice in the use of a firearm or target shooting at an established range authorized by the governing body of the jurisdiction where such range is located;

    (C) Engaging in an organized competition involving the use of a firearm or participating in or practicing for a performance by an organized group under 26 U.S.C. Section 501(c)(3) which uses firearms as a part of such performance;

    (D) Hunting or fishing pursuant to a valid license if such person has in his or her possession such a valid hunting or fishing license if required; is engaged in legal hunting or fishing; has permission of the owner of the land on which the activities are being conducted; and the pistol or revolver, whenever loaded, is carried only in an open and fully exposed manner; or

    (E) Traveling to or from any activity described in subparagraphs (A) through (D) of this paragraph if the pistol or revolver in such person's possession is not loaded;

  (2) Any person under the age of eighteen years who is on real property under the control of such person's parent, legal guardian, or grandparent and who has the permission of such person's parent or legal guardian to possess a pistol or revolver; or

  (3) Any person under the age of eighteen years who is at such person's residence and who, with the permission of such person's parent or legal guardian, possesses a pistol or revolver for the purpose of exercising the rights authorized in Code Section 16-3-21 or 16-3-23.

d. Subsection (c) of this Code section shall not apply to any person under the age of 18 years who has been convicted of a forcible felony or forcible misdemeanor, as defined in Code Section 16-1-3, or who has been adjudicated delinquent under the provisions of Article 1 of Chapter 11 of Title 15 for an offense which would constitute a forcible felony or forcible misdemeanor, as defined in Code Section 16-1-3, if such person were an adult.

Section 16-11-134. a. It shall be unlawful for any person to discharge a firearm while:

  (1) Under the influence of alcohol or any drug or any combination of alcohol and any drug to the extent that it is unsafe for the person to discharge such firearm except in the defense of life, health, and property;

  (2) The person's alcohol concentration is 0.08 grams [i.e., mg/dL] or more at any time while discharging such firearm or within three hours after such discharge of such firearm from alcohol consumed before such discharge ended; or

  (3) Subject to the provisions of subsection (b) of this Code section, there is any amount of marijuana or a controlled substance, as defined in Code Section 16-13-21, present in the person's blood or urine, or both, including the metabolites and derivatives of each or both without regard to whether or not any alcohol is present in the person's breath or blood.

b. The fact that any person charged with violating this Code section is or has been legally entitled to use a drug shall not constitute a defense against any charge of violating this Code section; provided, however, that such person shall not be in violation of this Code section unless such person is rendered incapable of possessing or discharging a firearm safely as a result of using a drug other than alcohol which such person is legally entitled to use.

c. Any person convicted of violating subsection (a) of this Code section shall be guilty of a misdemeanor of a high and aggravated nature.

Report: Most States Lack 'Basic Gun Laws'

Group Calls for Standard Rules Across Country

WASHINGTON—An advocacy group says that most states do little to regulate gun ownership, with the vast majority lacking even "basic gun laws."

A report issued by the Open Society Institute's Center on Crime, Communities and Culture found Massachusetts has the most stringent gun control laws, followed closely by Hawaii.

California, Connecticut and Maryland rounded out the top five. States with the fewest gun control laws included Maine, at the bottom, Louisiana, Alaska, Texas and Montana. Overall, the group concluded that 42 states had almost no regulation.

The group assigned each state a number based on whether it had passed 30 different gun laws. The most heavily weighed law, a statewide registration system for handguns, was worth seven points. Assault-weapon bans and "junk gun" bans were each worth six points.

On the other hand, states that passed laws to protect the gun industry from lawsuits lost a point. Similarly, states that passed laws preventing local governments from passing their own gun control laws lost four points.

Traditional black-market sources

The institute calls for states to reach a standard of strong gun control measures, saying that states with lax gun laws have traditionally served as sources of black-market guns sold in states with stringent regulations.

Vermont, which scored minus five on the scale, for example, lies just 192 miles from New York City, which has stringent regulations and is in the state with the eighth-most aggressive gun codes. Law enforcement officials in New York City have long said that many of the illegal guns on their streets were bought legally elsewhere.

"There's a great deal of reasons and legislative reasons why a state has a much more difficult time to progress on these laws, which we're now seeing are a problem for all other states, since a given state is only as strong as the neighboring states when it comes to gun laws," said Gil Kline, a spokesman for the Open Society Institute.

In Massachusetts, the only state to both license gun owners and register individual weapons, gun control advocates praised the report.

"We simply regulate guns and gun ownership, and gun manufacturing and gun distribution like we regulate cars or any potentially dangerous product," said John Rosenthal, a Boston real estate developer and the founder of Stop Handgun Violence, a grass-roots gun control group. "It's just common sense."

Building support for stricter measures

By examining laws in place on how guns are bought and sold, the study's authors hope to create support for measures such as licensing and registration, purchase limits and waiting periods, even for private sales.

These gun control methods can prevent legally bought guns from ending up in the hands of criminals, Kline said.

Thirty percent to forty percent of all criminal guns traced by the federal government were sold new by a licensed dealer less than three years before they were seized, according to statistics from the U.S. Bureau of Alcohol, Tobacco and Firearms cited in the report.

"The major problem is the shift of guns from legal hands to illegal hands," Kline said. "If we instituted registration and licensing, we could track it."

The Second Amendment

But to many gun owners, licensing gun owners and registering guns represents a serious infringement of Second Amendment rights and an invitation to government tyranny.

The Gun Owners Action League of Massachusetts is suing to overturn the state's two restrictions. The group says the laws are being applied unfairly, anyway, with licensing restrictions varying by town.

"It would strictly come up to the political aspirations of the police chief or what his policy is for his town," said Steve Ruel, spokesman for the Gun Owners Action League.

"So we get calls from people out of state asking, 'Well, what town should I move to? Who is politically motivated, who is doing the right thing?' "

Critics faulted the study for not comparing each state's strength of gun control laws with its crime rate.

Evidence seems mixed

"To me, you can ask a librarian to list the various state laws," said John Lott, a professor at Yale Law School and a supporter of gun owner rights. "If you're going to argue that stricter gun control laws are good, there's got to be evidence for it."

Lott has written that widespread gun ownership can actually deter criminals. Rosenthal, on the other hand, called Massachusetts, with its strict laws, one of the safest states in the country.

In fact, the evidence is mixed. Massachusetts is the 10th-safest state, according to FBI numbers for 1997, the latest year for which state-by-state crime statistics were available. But that same year, Hawaii was the eighth-most dangerous state.

(continued)

Report: Most States Lack 'Basic Gun Laws'

Group Calls for Standard Rules Across Country

States with stringent gun control laws fall at both the high and low end for crime rates. States with loose gun control laws also experienced a wide variation in crime rates.

Crucial cultural differences
Kline argued that other industrialized Western nations, which have strict gun control laws, have very low rates of gun violence when compared to the United States overall.

But another critic said this comparison ignored crucial cultural differences. Americans are just a more violent people, whether armed with guns or not, said John Velleco, a spokesman for the Gun Owners of America, an advocacy group based in Springfield, Va.

"We're a different society," Velleco said. "It would be ridiculous to argue that we don't have a problem in this culture, but the problem isn't that we have not enough gun laws. The problem is we have too many gun laws, and we're disarming the good people."

Source: Hans H. Chen, "Most States Lack 'Basic Gun Laws'; Group Calls for Standard Rules Across Country," APB News. April 14, 2000. Reprinted with permission.

Lawsuits Against Gun Manufacturers Beginning in 1999, a number of cities and counties filed lawsuits against gun manufacturers, alleging product liability and negligence against members of the firearms industry. They sought to recover damages for the manufacture, sale, marketing, promotion, and distribution of guns that were said to be unreasonably dangerous and negligently designed.[51] Although these complaints were civil in nature (and not criminal), they are relevant here because they represented efforts by local municipalities to control gun-related crime and violence within their borders.

These complaints sought to recover from firearms manufacturers and distributors the costs incurred in providing police, emergency, court, prison, and other related services in connection with shootings that are homicidal, suicidal, or accidental. Cities also sought damages for alleged declines in property values in areas ridden by gun crime, and asked the courts to require gun manufacturers to change the methods by which they design, distribute, and advertise their products. Cities also alleged that firearm trade associations and gun manufacturers are negligent because they cooperate with one another to avoid developing and implementing safety features and to inadequately warn users of the risks of guns. Although some of the suits filed by cities were dismissed by courts which held that the issues raised could only be properly addressed by legislatures,[52] some are still pending as of this writing.

On June 26, 2000, the state of New York became the first state to sue gun manufacturers and wholesalers. A complaint filed by New York State Attorney General Eliot Spitzer alleged that gun manufacturers and wholesalers "have created, contributed to, and maintained a statutory and a common law public nuisance" through the sale of guns within New York State. The lawsuit claimed "that defendants' conduct or omissions with respect to . . . manufacturing and marketing operations have: offended, interfered with, or caused damage to the public in the exercise of rights common to all in a manner such as to offend public morals, interfere with the use by the public of a public place, or endanger or injure the property, health, safety, or comfort of a considerable number of persons." The suit asked the court to order gun manufacturers to "abate the nuisance they have created," and "to cease contributing to and maintaining the nuisance within the State of New York." The suit, whose outcome is pending as of this writing, builds on: (1) the fact that New York State statutes declare any unlawfully possessed, transported, or disposed of gun to be a nuisance,[53] (2) the number of firearms-related deaths in the state,

(3) findings by the federal Bureau of Alcohol, Tobacco and Firearms that many firearms fall into the hands of criminals, and (4) the state's allegation that manufacturers have upped the production of specific types of firearms to meet the demands of criminals for those kinds of weapons. Portions of the New York complaint are reproduced in the Law in Practice box below.

City, county, and state efforts to sue gun manufacturers, distributors, and trade associations have found encouragement in the recently successful efforts of states to recover damages against the tobacco industry. Suits against cigarette manufacturers claimed the conduct of those manufacturers was irresponsible and that such conduct increased the risk of tobacco-related diseases. In a similar fashion, today's lawsuits against the gun industry grew out of a growing belief that industry representatives have conducted themselves in such a way as to increase the risk of gun violence by deceptively marketing and negligently distributing unreasonably dangerous guns.

LAW IN PRACTICE

WHAT IS THE LEGAL BASIS FOR STATE LAWSUITS AGAINST GUN MANUFACTURERS?

On June 26, 2000, New York became the first state to sue gun manufacturers and wholesalers for their alleged misdeeds in contributing to gun-related violence throughout the state. Excerpts from the state's filing are reproduced in this box.

II. Defendants have created, contributed to, and maintained a statutory and a common law public nuisance.

A. ILLEGALLY POSSESSED HANDGUNS ARE A NUISANCE BY STATUTE IN NEW YORK STATE.

47. New York State, by statute, has declared any unlawfully possessed, transported or disposed of gun to be a nuisance: "Any weapon, instrument, appliance or substance specified in article two hundred sixty-five, when unlawfully possessed, manufactured, transported or disposed of, or when utilized in the commission of an offense, is hereby declared a nuisance." Penal Law § 400.05(1).

48. Among other provisions restricting the sale and use of firearms, article 265 of the New York State Penal law makes it a crime to possess a pistol or revolver without a duly issued license,

and a crime to possess a loaded firearm with intent to use it unlawfully against another. Penal Law §§ 265.01(1), 265.20(3), 265.03.

49. In enacting Penal Law § 400.05 the Legislature deemed the existence of the nuisance involving unlawful guns so dangerous to the public that any official coming into possession of an unlawfully possessed handgun is directed either to destroy it or to "render the same or cause it to be rendered ineffective and useless for its intended purpose and harmless to human life." Penal Law § 400.05(2).

50. The size of the nuisance is significant. In 1997, for example, New York State law enforcement agencies confiscated over 8,340 handguns in the course of investigating or solving crimes in New York State. This figure, however, represents only the successes, those cases in which law enforcement actually confiscated the unlawful guns. The size of the actual public nuisance—unlawful guns at large—remains far greater.

B. ILLEGALLY POSSESSED HANDGUNS ARE A PUBLIC NUISANCE AT COMMON LAW.

51. In addition to being a nuisance by statute, illegally possessed handguns in New York State,

(continued)

LAW IN PRACTICE

both individually and as a pool, also comprise a common law public nuisance. That the presence of unlicensed lethal and illegal devices endangers the health and safety of a significant portion of the population is demonstrated by, among other things, the number of deaths and injuries firearms cause in New York State. In 1997, there were 1,234 firearm-related deaths in New York State. Of these deaths, 709 were homicides, 486 were suicides, and 39 were unintentional and intent unknown. In 1996, firearms killed 1,428 New Yorkers. Of these deaths, 874 were homicides, 488 were suicides, 38 were unintentional, and 10 were of undetermined intent and circumstances. In 1995, 1,638 New Yorkers were killed by a firearm. Of these deaths, 1,052 were homicides, 522 were suicides, and 39 were unintentional shootings. About three-quarters involved handguns. For every death, there were approximately another three or four nonfatal injuries.

52. Illegal handguns in New York State cause harm above and beyond actual physical wounds. The presence of illegal handguns impairs residents' ability to use public spaces. In locations around the state, parents do not allow their children to use public playgrounds or to walk home from school alone because they fear gunfire may erupt.

53. Together, the actual and threatened harm posed by unlawfully possessed handguns offends, interferes with, or causes damage to the public in the exercise of rights common to all in a manner such as to offend public morals, interfere with the use by the public of a public place, or endanger or injure the property, health, safety, or comfort of a considerable number of persons.

C. DEFENDANTS' CONDUCT AND OMISSIONS HAVE CREATED, MAINTAINED, AND CONTRIBUTED TO THIS PUBLIC NUISANCE.

54. The defendant manufacturers design, manufacture, and distribute handguns in a manner that creates, maintains, and contributes to the public nuisance. The defendant wholesalers purchase and resell the handguns in a manner

that creates, maintains, and contributes to the public nuisance.

55. While on notice of ATF's trace requests and of the movement of guns into crime, the defendant manufacturers make design, production, and marketing choices:

56. First, manufacturers determine the volume of guns they produce. With knowledge of the demand for illegal guns, manufacturers produce and seek to profit from the sale of a sufficient volume of guns to meet that demand.

57. Second, manufacturers choose which features will or will not be included in a model, and how many of each model they will produce and sell. Because of manufacturers' receipt of trace requests, each manufacturing decision—including decisions about whether to discontinue certain models or eliminate features that make models attractive to criminals—is made against the background of the manufacturers' actual knowledge of which of their models appear most often in crimes.

58. Certain makes and models of guns particularly appeal to illegal owners. The factors that make these specific guns attractive to criminals include, among others, styling, concealability, and low cost. To attain these characteristics, defendant manufacturers often make engineering decisions that sacrifice accuracy, durability, reliability, and safety.

59. Manufacturers also determine the wholesalers to whom they sell guns. Notwithstanding notice, through trace requests and otherwise, that a disproportionate number of crime guns are associated with particular wholesalers, manufacturers continue to supply guns to those wholesalers.

60. As the link in the distribution chain that sells to retailers, wholesalers likewise make a series of decisions that affect the volume of illegal guns in New York State. Because of ATF trace requests, wholesalers, like manufacturers, are on actual and constructive notice of which of the guns they

(continued)

LAW IN PRACTICE

have sold were used in crimes, and to whom they had sold those guns. Each commercial decision that wholesalers make is, thus, made against a background of actual and constructive notice. Because they know both the make and model of each gun that ATF traces through them and the total number of those models that they sell, wholesalers know precisely which of the models that they choose to carry are disproportionately used in crime.

61. In addition to which models to carry, wholesalers also choose the retailers to which they sell. As they make this choice, wholesalers are on actual notice—through ATF inquiries—of how many traced crime guns they previously sold to each retailer. Because they also know how many total guns they have sold to each retailer, they are on actual and constructive notice of

which of their retailers sell disproportionate numbers of guns that are used in crime.

62. In sum, defendants know that a significant portion of their guns become crime guns, but turn a blind eye so as to increase their profits, at the cost of many human lives and much human suffering. . . .

What Do *You* Think?

1. Should gun manufacturers and distributors be held accountable for gun-related violence and deaths? Why or why not?

2. Does the state's complaint make convincing arguments about the role gun manufacturers and dealers have played in contributing to gun-related violence and deaths? Why or why not?

CRIMINAL LAW IN THE NEWS

States Faulted on Gun Safety Measures

Report Says Many Don't Do Enough to Protect Kids

WASHINGTON—Just as the school year begins, a gun control advocacy group is failing seven states for missing opportunities aimed at keeping children safe from firearms.

In its fourth annual report card rating the country's state gun laws, Handgun Control Inc. slapped failing grades on seven states for having few "gun safety" measures on the books.

The ratings overall were harsher this year than in the previous report card—21 states received D grades, three more than in 1999.

Handgun Control spokeswoman Nancy Hwa said some states received lower grades than they did last year.

"The greatest reason for the grades that declined is probably missed op-

portunities more than anything else," she said, referring to legislatures that axed new proposals for state gun restrictions.

Kentucky gets F-minus

Hwa also faulted many states for concealed-carry weapon laws that allow guns to be hidden on a person. She said Kentucky was even given a first-ever F-minus for allowing wider latitude in its existing carry law, which now allows concealed weapons in churches.

In a statement, Handgun Control Chairman Sarah Brady also slammed Colorado and Georgia for not passing stiffer gun control laws last year, which she said was appropriate in the aftermath of high-profile school shootings in those states.

Brady is the wife of former Reagan Press Secretary James Brady, who was shot and seriously injured in an assassination attempt in 1981. Both have lobbied for the nation's toughest gun laws passed to date, including the 1993 "Brady Bill" requiring background checks on over-the-counter firearms purchases.

NRA: concealed weapon states are safer

National Rifle Association spokeswoman Kelly Whitley said the Handgun Control report card used misguided logic.

"They are basing these grades solely on the number of strict gun laws each state has," she said. "What the grades should really be based on

(continued)

CRIMINAL LAW IN THE NEWS

States Faulted on Gun Safety Measures

Report Says Many Don't Do Enough to Protect Kids

is how effective these laws are at stopping violent crime and accidents with firearms."

Whitley also faulted the gun control advocates for their stand on concealed weapons.

"They lower the grade for states that have concealed-carry laws, but we find through research that in states that do have concealed-carry laws, the violent crime rate has dropped," she said, citing the decrease in violent crime in Florida since passing its version of the law in 1994.

"We can always do more"

The home states of President George W. Bush of Texas and former Vice President Al Gore, who was once a U.S. senator from Tennessee, each received Ds. The two southern states have laws that allow concealed weapons and laws that attempt to prevent cities from suing gun manufacturers.

The governors in states that received failing marks either declined to comment on the report or did not return phone calls.

Larry Fasbender, deputy director of Montana's Department of Justice, said the state's F didn't surprise him.

"We can always do more to prevent kids from getting killed by guns, or getting injured by them," Fasbender said. "Montana does not have the greatest record in the world, as far as legislation in that regard."

But, he said the Handgun Control report card failed to give Montana officials any credit for trying—without success—to pass a law that would ban guns from school grounds.

Fasbender also took exception to the criticism by the group over Montana's concealed weapons provision, since it involves a criminal background check and is only issued at the discretion of law enforcement.

Maryland gets an A+

Maryland received the highest grade this year, an A+ due in large part to the successful efforts of Gov. Parris Glendening to pass a slew of gun measures that puts trigger locks on new firearms sold and subjects those weapons to ballistic tests prior to sale.

"The governor is very pleased with getting that grade,." said Michelle Byrnie, Glendening spokesman. "He believes other states will follow Maryland's lead because this is a common sense approach to making guns safer."

Source: James Gordon Meek, "States Faulted on Gun Safety Measures; Report Says Many Don't Do Enough to Protect Kids," APB News. August 31, 2000. Reprinted with permission.

CRIMES AGAINST THE ADMINISTRATION OF GOVERNMENT

A second class of social order offense is that of crimes against the administration of government. Offenses in this category include treason, misprision of treason, rebellion, espionage, sedition, perjury, subornation of perjury, false swearing, bribery, contempt, obstruction of justice, resisting arrest, escape, and misconduct in office. We discuss each of these types of offenses in the pages that follow.

Treason

TREASON

violation of allegiance toward one's country or sovereign, esp., the betrayal of one's own country by waging war against it or by consciously and purposely acting to aid its enemies.[54]

Treason can be defined as the attempt to overthrow the government of the society of which one is a member. At early common law it was considered "high treason" to kill the king or to promote a revolt in the kingdom. Treason under common law was neither a felony nor misdemeanor, but thought to be in a class by itself. Much the same is true today, and treason is the only crime specifically mentioned in the U.S. Constitution—which says that: "Treason against the United States, shall consist only in levying War against them, or in adhering to their Enemies, giving them

Aid and Comfort."[55] Federal statutes use wording similar to the Constitution, and say: "Whoever, owing allegiance to the United States, levies war against them or adheres to their enemies, giving them aid and comfort within the United States or elsewhere, is guilty of treason and shall suffer death, or shall be imprisoned not less than five years and fined under this title but not less than ten thousand dollars ($10,000); and shall be incapable of holding any office under the United States."[56] Because treason is a breach of allegiance, a person who has lost or renounced his American citizenship cannot commit treason against the United States.[57]

The crime of treason requires some overt act such as affirmative encouragement of the enemy. Disloyal thoughts alone are not sufficient to constitute treason. In addition, treason is a specific intent offense and conviction for treason requires that the defendant must have intended to betray the government. If the defendant acts with knowledge that his or her conduct will benefit the enemy, specific intent can be demonstrated. The U.S. Constitution stipulates that "No Person shall be convicted of Treason unless on the Testimony of two Witnesses to the same overt Act, or on Confession in open Court."[58]

Treason is also a crime under the laws of most states. Some states, like California, have legislatively created the crime of treason, while in others the crime is constitutionally defined. Florida's constitution, for example, which mirrors wording in the U.S. Constitution, says that: "Treason against the state shall consist only in levying war against it, adhering to its enemies, or giving them aid and comfort, and no person shall be convicted of treason except on the testimony of two witnesses to the same overt act or on confession in open court."[59]

Misprision of treason is the concealment or nondisclosure of the known treason of another. It is punishable under federal law and under the laws of most states. **Rebellion** consists of "deliberate, organized resistance, by force and arms, to the laws or operations of the government, committed by a subject."[61] Under federal law, rebellion is committed when a person incites or engages in any rebellion against the United States.[62] A related crime is that of advocating the overthrow of government. Federal law prohibits knowingly or wilfully advocating the overthrow or destruction of the government of the United States or of any state.[63] It is also an offense in many jurisdictions to advocate, teach, or aid and abet **criminal syndicalism.** Criminal syndicalism consists of advocating the use of unlawful acts as a means of accomplishing a change in industrial ownership, or to control political change.[65]

Related to treason is the crime of **espionage,** or spying for a foreign government. Espionage is defined under the federal Espionage Act[66] as "gathering, transmitting or losing" information or secrets related to the national defense with the intent or the reasonable belief that such information will be used against the United States.

Espionage against the United States did not end with the Cold War. In 1994, for example, CIA agent Aldrich Hazen Ames and his wife, Rosario, were arrested and charged with conspiracy to commit espionage in a plot to sell U.S. government secrets to the Russian KGB. The Ames couple apparently told their Russian handlers of CIA operatives within the former Soviet Union and revealed the extent of American knowledge of KGB plans. Their activities had gone undetected for nearly a decade. Following arrest, the Ames couple pleaded guilty to charges of espionage and tax fraud. Aldrich Ames was sentenced to life in prison; his wife received a five-year term. Two years later, in 1996, CIA station chief Harold Nicholson was arrested as he was preparing to leave Washington's Dulles Airport—allegedly on his way to meet his Russian handlers. Nicholson is the highest ranking CIA employee to ever be charged with espionage. Also in 1996, forty-three-year-old Earl Edwin Pitts, a thirteen-year FBI veteran, was taken into custody at the FBI academy in Quantico, Virginia, and arraigned on charges of attempted espionage and conspiracy.[67] Pitts was charged with spying for the Russians and is said to have turned over lists of Russian agents within the United States who had been compromised. Nicholson and Pitts pled guilty to espionage charges in early 1997.[68] Both were sentenced to lengthy prison terms.

MISPRISION OF TREASON
the concealment or nondisclosure of the known treason of another.

REBELLION
deliberate, organized resistance, by force and arms, to the laws or operations of the government, committed by a subject.[60]

CRIMINAL SYNDICALISM
advocating the use of unlawful acts as a means of accomplishing a change in industrial ownership, or to control political change.[64]

ESPIONAGE
the unlawful act of spying for a foreign government.

SEDITION

a crime that consists of a communication or agreement intended to defame the government or to incite treason.

Finally, the crime of **sedition** consists of a communication or agreement intended to defame the government or to incite treason. Under federal law, the crime of seditious conspiracy is described as follows: "If two or more persons in any State or Territory, or in any place subject to the jurisdiction of the United States, conspire to overthrow, put down, or to destroy by force the Government of the United States, or to levy war against them, or to oppose by force the authority thereof, or by force to prevent, hinder, or delay the execution of any law of the United States, or by force to seize, take, or possess any property of the United States contrary to the authority thereof, they shall each be fined under this title or imprisoned not more than twenty years, or both."[69]

Perjury and Contempt

PERJURY

the wilful giving of false testimony under oath in a judicial proceeding; also, false testimony given under any lawfully administered oath.

At common law, **perjury** was the wilful giving of false testimony under oath in a judicial proceeding. Most jurisdictions have enlarged the conduct prohibited under the crime of perjury to include any false testimony given under any lawfully administered oath. Accordingly, perjury may be committed if false testimony or a false statement is made under oath before any body that has lawful authority to administer an oath to witnesses who appear before it. Pennsylvania law, for example, says: "A person is guilty of perjury, a felony of the third degree, if in any official proceeding he makes a false statement under oath or equivalent affirmation, or swears or affirms the truth of a statement previously made, when the statement is material and he does not believe it to be true."[70] Jurisdictions which have broadened the law of perjury sometimes call the offense **false swearing.**

To constitute perjury or false swearing, however, the false statement, as noted by the Pennsylvania law cited above, must be material. That is, a false statement made under oath that concerns a matter which has no bearing on the proceedings at hand is not perjury. Pennsylvania law, for example, says: "Falsification is material, regardless of the admissibility of the statement under rules of evidence, if it could have affected the course or outcome of the proceeding. It is no defense that the declarant mistakenly believed the falsification to be immaterial. Whether a falsification is material in a given factual situation is a question of law."[71]

Common law required that perjury be proven by the testimony of at least two witnesses. Most jurisdictions have relaxed this rule and allow a perjury conviction to be obtained by the testimony of a single witness if supplemented by other indirect evidence. Jurisdictions are divided, however, as to whether retraction of perjured testimony is a defense. Many hold that it is a defense if the witness retracts his or her statement in the same proceedings and before the falsity has been discovered. In other jurisdictions, retraction is only a matter in mitigation.

SUBORNATION OF PERJURY

unlawfully procuring another to commit perjury.

Subornation of perjury occurs when a person procures another to commit perjury. Federal law, for example, reads: "Whoever procures another to commit any perjury is guilty of subornation of perjury, and shall be fined under this title or imprisoned not more than five years, or both."[72] To commit this crime, the defendant must have known that the testimony to be given by a witness would be false, and the defendant must have caused the witness to actually give the false testimony.[73] An attorney, for example, who calls a witness whom the attorney knows will commit perjury is guilty of subornation of perjury in some jurisdictions. In other jurisdictions, he or she would be considered to be a principle under the law of principles and thus guilty of perjury.

CRIMINAL CONTEMPT

deliberate conduct calculated to obstruct or embarrass a court of law. Also, conduct intended to degrade the role of a judicial officer in administering justice.

Criminal contempt consists of deliberate conduct calculated to obstruct or embarrass a court of law, or conduct intended to degrade the role of a judicial officer in administering justice. Criminal contempt harms the judicial process itself. Criminal contempt differs from civil contempt in that criminal conduct is a violation of

Former CIA station chief Harold Nicholson, the highest ranking CIA employee ever to be charged with espionage. Nicholson was accused of spying for the Russians and pled guilty to espionage charges in early 1997. He was sentenced to a lengthy prison term. (Photo courtesy of AP/Wide World Photos.)

criminal law[74] (i.e., of common law, and the statutory criminal law of most jurisdictions), whereas civil contempt is a sanction available to a court that can be imposed on a person who is recalcitrant to meet the court's lawful demands made on behalf of another party. Violating a court order to pay alimony, for example, may lead to a civil contempt charge, while being verbally abusive within the courtroom might constitute criminal contempt. In addition, two types of criminal contempt can be distinguished: (1) direct contempt, which consists of acts committed in the presence of the court, and (2) indirect contempt, which consists of acts committed outside of the court's presence. Direct contempt might consist, for example, of a physical assault on a judge while a hearing or trial is in progress. Indirect contempt might involve actions by a juror outside of the courtroom that are contrary to the court's instructions—such as discussing the case with family or friends when ordered not to do so and before the case has been concluded.

Although it is generally recognized that both forms of contempt are crimes, instances of direct contempt are usually dealt with summarily. That is, the judge in whose court the contempt occurs informs the "contemnor" of the contempt accusation and asks him or her why he or she should not be found guilty of contempt. Lacking a satisfactory answer, the court will enter a judgment against the offender and impose punishment. Individuals charged with indirect contempt must be afforded an opportunity to prepare a defense and may be represented by counsel.

Obstruction of Justice

Obstruction of justice, or the attempt to interfere with the administration of public justice, was a misdemeanor under common law. Today, obstruction of justice is statutorily defined by both the states and the federal government, and may be either a felony or misdemeanor, depending on the seriousness of the offense. As with common law, the statutory crime of obstruction of justice might involve jury tampering; interfering with the activities of an officer of the law or of the court; tampering or

OBSTRUCTION OF JUSTICE
an unlawful attempt to interfere with the administration of the courts, the judicial system, or law enforcement officers, or with the activities of those who seek justice in a court or whose duties involve the administration of justice.

suppressing evidence; threatening witnesses; or bribing judges, jurors, or witnesses. Additionally, some states have made it a crime to refuse to render aid to law enforcement personnel in the official performance of their duties, or to give false or misleading evidence to investigators. Many states have also created the crimes of "endeavoring to obstruct justice" and "conspiring to obstruct justice."

Obstruction of justice may involve activities such as picketing or parading, or the use of sound amplifiers with intent to disrupt or influence judges, jurors, or witnesses. Section 1507 of the federal criminal code says, for example: "Whoever, with the intent of interfering with, obstructing, or impeding the administration of justice, or with the intent of influencing any judge, juror, witness, or court officer, in the discharge of his duty, pickets or parades in or near a building housing a court of the United States, or in or near a building or residence occupied or used by such judge, juror, witness, or court officer, or with such intent uses any sound-truck or similar device or resorts to any other demonstration in or near any such building or residence, shall be fined under this title or imprisoned not more than one year, or both."[75]

RESISTING ARREST

the crime of obstructing or opposing a peace officer who is making an arrest.

The most common form of obstruction of justice is **resisting arrest.** All states make it a crime to resist a lawful arrest. Some even require that a person submit to arrest by a police officer who is carrying out his duties, even though the arrest may be unlawful (the offense of resisting unlawful arrest is discussed in Chapter 5 as a separate topic). Oregon law, for example, says that: "A person commits the crime of resisting arrest if the person intentionally resists a person known by the person to be a peace officer in making an arrest."[76] Some states, like North Carolina, employ more generic statutes that take the focus off of arrest and place it on resisting any public officer in the performance of his or her duties. North Carolina law, for example, says: "If any person shall wilfully and unlawfully resist, delay or obstruct a public officer in discharging or attempting to discharge a duty of his office, he shall be guilty of a Class 2 misdemeanor."[77]

LAW ON THE BOOKS

"RESISTING ARREST" UNDER OHIO LAW.

Compare with Model Penal Code, Section 242.2

OHIO REVISED CODE

Section 2921.33

(A) No person, recklessly or by force, shall resist or interfere with a lawful arrest of the person or another.

(B) No person, recklessly or by force, shall resist or interfere with a lawful arrest of the person or another person and, during the course of or as a result of the resistance or interference, cause physical harm to a law enforcement officer.

C) No person, recklessly or by force, shall resist or interfere with a lawful arrest of the person or another person if either of the following applies:

(1) The offender, during the course of or as a result of the resistance or interference, recklessly causes physical harm to a law enforcement officer by means of a deadly weapon;

(2) The offender, during the course of the resistance or interference, brandishes a deadly weapon.

(D) Whoever violates this section is guilty of resisting arrest. A violation of division (A) of this section is a misdemeanor of the second degree. A violation of division (B) of this section is a misdemeanor of the first degree. A violation of division (C) of this section is a felony of the fourth degree.

(E) As used in this section, "deadly weapon" has the same meaning as in section 2921.11 of the Revised Code.

Escape

Under common law, prisoners who left lawful custody without permission committed the crime of **escape.** If force was used in the escape, the offense was termed "prison break" or "breach of prison." While all jurisdictions have enacted statutes criminalizing escape, some state statutes apply only to persons who leave correctional custody without permission, while others apply as well to persons who leave the custody of law enforcement personnel. Generally, escape laws require intent on the part of escapees, but even where they don't the courts have typically held that intent is a necessary element of the crime of escape. Otherwise it would be possible to imagine, for example, the arrest and conviction of a sleeping work crew prisoner inadvertently left behind by authorities when they returned to prison.

Some jurisdictions make it lawful for prisoners to escape if they are under extreme duress or facing threats. Hence, a prisoner who believes he is about to be murdered or raped by other inmates might lawfully escape in order to avoid being attacked. If such were to happen, however, the law would likely require that he turn himself in to authorities as soon as possible.

All jurisdictions make it illegal for anyone to help with an escape. Visitors to penal institutions, for example, may be guilty of the crime of aiding escape if they smuggle items into the facility that might be used in an escape attempt. Inmates who provide other prisoners with the tools or other means needed for an escape may also be charged with aiding or facilitating escape, as may correctional personnel who assist inmates to escape.

ESCAPE
the unlawful leaving of official custody or confinement without permission, or the failure to return to custody or confinement following an official temporary leave.

LAW ON THE BOOKS

"ESCAPE" UNDER OHIO LAW.

Compare with Model Penal Code, Section 246.6

OHIO REVISED CODE

Section 2921.34.

(A) (1) No person, knowing the person is under detention or being reckless in that regard, shall purposely break or attempt to break the detention, or purposely fail to return to detention, either following temporary leave granted for a specific purpose or limited period, or at the time required when serving a sentence in intermittent confinement.

(2) No person who is sentenced to a prison term pursuant to division (A)(3) of section 2971.03 of the Revised Code as a sexually violent predator, for whom the requirement that the entire prison term be served in a state correctional institution has been modified pursuant to section 2971.05 of the Revised Code, and who, pursuant to that modification, is restricted to a geographic area, knowing that the person is under a geographic restriction or being reckless in that regard, shall purposely leave the geographic area to which the restriction applies or purposely fail to return to that geographic area following a temporary leave granted for a specific purpose or for a limited period of time.

(B) Irregularity in bringing about or maintaining detention, or lack of jurisdiction of the committing or detaining authority, is not a defense to a charge under this section if the detention is pursuant to judicial order or in a detention facility. In the case of any other detention, irregularity or lack of jurisdiction is an affirmative defense only if either of the following occurs:

(1) The escape involved no substantial risk of harm to the person or property of another.

(2) The detaining authority knew or should have known there was no legal basis or authority for the detention.

(continued)

LAW ON THE BOOKS

(C) Whoever violates this section is guilty of escape.

  (1) If the offender, at the time of the commission of the offense, was under detention as an alleged or adjudicated delinquent child or unruly child and if the act for which the offender was under detention would not be a felony if committed by an adult, escape is a misdemeanor of the first degree.

  (2) If the offender, at the time of the commission of the offense, was under detention in any other manner or was a sexually violent predator for whom the requirement that the entire prison term imposed pursuant to division (A)(3) of section 2971.03 of the Revised Code be served in a state correctional institution has been modified pursuant to section 2971.05 of the Revised Code, escape is one of the following:

    (a) A felony of the second degree, when the most serious offense for which the person was under detention or adjudicated a sexually violent predator is aggravated murder, murder, or a felony of the first or second degree or, if the person was under detention as an alleged or adjudicated delinquent child, when the most serious act for which the person was under detention would be aggravated murder, murder, or a felony of the first or second degree if committed by an adult;

    (b) A felony of the third degree, when the most serious offense for which the person was under detention or adjudicated a sexually violent predator is a felony of the third, fourth, or fifth degree or an unclassified felony or, if the person was under detention as an alleged or adjudicated delinquent child, when the most serious act for which the person was under detention would be a felony of the third, fourth, or fifth degree or an unclassified felony if committed by an adult;

    (c) A felony of the fifth degree, when any of the following applies:

      (i) The most serious offense for which the person was under detention is a misdemeanor.

      (ii) The person was found not guilty by reason of insanity, and the person's detention consisted of hospitalization, institutionalization, or confinement in a facility under an order made pursuant to or under authority of section 2945.40, 2945.401, or 2945.402 of the Revised Code.

    (d) A misdemeanor of the first degree, when the most serious offense for which the person was under detention is a misdemeanor and when the person fails to return to detention at a specified time following temporary leave granted for a specific purpose or limited period or at the time required when serving a sentence in intermittent confinement.

Misconduct in Office and Bribery

MISCONDUCT IN OFFICE

acts that a public office holder: (1) has no right to perform, (2) performs improperly, or (3) fails to perform in the face of an affirmative duty to act.

A public official who, under color of law or in his or her official capacity, acts in such a way as to exceed the bounds of his or her office, may be guilty of **misconduct in office.** The term "misconduct in office" includes acts "which the office holder had no right to perform, acts performed improperly, and failure to act in the face of an affirmative duty to act."[78] Doing that which the office holder has no right to do is called *malfeasance. Misfeasance* refers to official acts performed improperly, and *nonfeasance* describes failing to do that which should be done.

BRIBERY

the offense of giving or receiving a gift or reward intended to influence a person in the exercise of a judicial or public duty.[79]

Misconduct can sometimes be the result of bribery. **Bribery** consists of "the offense of giving or receiving a gift or reward intended to influence a person in the exercise of a judicial or public duty."[80] As the definition notes, both the act of giving, and the act of taking can constitute bribery—and a person who offers a bribe is just as guilty of the crime of bribery as the one who accepts it. The crime of bribery concerns only *official* acts, and no crime occurs when merely personal actions outside of

LAW ON THE BOOKS

"BRIBERY" UNDER PENNSYLVANIA LAW.

Compare with Model Penal Code, Sections 240.0 - 240.7

PENNSYLVANIA CODE

Title 18, Sec. 4701. Bribery in official and political matters.
   a. Offenses defined.—A person is guilty of bribery, a felony of the third degree, if he offers, confers, or agrees to confer upon another, or solicits, accepts, or agrees to accept from another:
      (1) any pecuniary benefit as consideration for the decision, opinion, recommendation, vote or other exercise of discretion as a public servant, party official, or voter by the recipient;
      (2) any benefit as consideration for the decision, vote, recommendation, or other exercise of official discretion by the recipient in a judicial, administrative, or legislative proceeding; or
      (3) any benefit as consideration for a violation of a known legal duty as public servant or party official.
   b. Defenses prohibited.—It is no defense to prosecution under this section that a person whom the actor sought to influence was not qualified to act in the desired way whether because he had not yet assumed office, had left office, or lacked jurisdiction, or for any other reason.

the official sphere are influenced by a bribe. Hence, under the laws of most jurisdictions, only public office holders, state officials, or state employees acting in some official capacity can be found guilty of accepting bribes. Bribes may be offered (to a jailer, for example) in an attempt to win the release of a prisoner, (to a judge or juror) to ensure the acquittal of a defendant in a criminal trial, (to a judge or juror) to insure a verdict in a civil hearing or civil trial, (to an elections official) to win or influence an election, (to a government decision maker) to win a government contract, (to a legislator) to gain passage of a favored bill or law, and for other reasons. The Pennsylvania bribery law is reproduced in the Law on the Books box above.

SUMMARY

- This chapter discusses crimes against public order and safety, and crimes against justice and the administration of government. Both types of offenses can be generally classified as "social order" crimes. A third category of social order crime, offenses against public decency and morality, is discussed in the next chapter.
- Public order offenses are those that disturb or invade society's peace and tranquillity. They include the following: breach of peace, disorderly conduct, fighting, affray, vagrancy, loitering, carrying weapons, keeping a disorderly house, public intoxication, disturbance of public assembly, inciting to riot, rioting, unlawful assembly, rout, obstructing public passage, and others.
- Laws criminalizing public order offenses rest on the assumption that public order is inherently valuable and should be maintained—and that disorder is not to be tolerated and should be reduced, when it occurs, through application of the criminal law.

- Some court decisions have focused specifically on "fighting words," or those utterances that are an affront to the public peace and which are intended to provoke the person(s) at whom they are directed. According to the U.S. Supreme Court, fighting words are not protected under free speech constitutional guarantees.

- Public intoxication is a common offense, and many people are arrested annually for driving while intoxicated (DWI) or driving under the influence (DUI).

- Vagrancy, a crime at common law, has been largely recast today in terms of loitering. Traditional vagrancy laws often ran afoul of the constitutional prohibition against vagueness because they criminalized a person's status rather than conduct.

- A special category of public order offense is that of weapons carrying. Considerable debate exists within the United States today over the issue of gun control, with persuasive arguments being advanced on both sides of the controversy.

- A final class of social order offense discussed in this chapter is that of crimes against the administration of government. Offenses in this category include treason, misprision of treason, rebellion, espionage, sedition, perjury, subornation of perjury, false swearing, bribery, contempt, obstruction of justice, resisting arrest, escape, and misconduct in office.

QUESTIONS FOR DISCUSSION

1. What are the three categories of social order crimes described in this chapter? How do they differ? With which forms is this chapter most concerned?

2. What are "fighting words"? How can fighting words be distinguished from protected forms of speech?

3. What is vagrancy? Why have traditional laws against vagrancy been held unconstitutional?

4. Should the possession of handguns be regulated? Why or why not?

5. Explain the differences between rout, riot, and unlawful assembly.

6. What is the difference between treason and espionage?

7. Explain the differences between perjury, bribery, and contempt. How does criminal contempt differ from civil contempt?

LEGAL RESOURCES ON THE WORLD WIDE WEB

A number of courts now offer Web sites containing information on court structure, administrative procedures, and coming changes in court procedure. A few of those sites are listed here.

California Courts and Judicial System
http://www.courtinfo.ca.gov
Home page of the California judicial branch.

Conference of State Court Administrators (COSCA)
http://cosca.ncsc.dni.us
COSCA was organized in 1953 and is dedicated to the improvement of state court systems. Its membership consists of the state court administrator in each of the fifty states, the District of Columbia, Puerto Rico, American Samoa, and the Virgin Islands.

Courts Net
http://www.courts.net
A site that provides directory listings for courts across the United States.

Federal Judiciary
http://www.uscourts.gov
Home page of the Administrative Office of the U.S. Courts.

JOSHUA: The Florida Court System
http://www.flcourts.org
JOSHUA is a statewide information system serving Florida's judiciary.

National Center for State Courts
http://www.ncsc.dni.us
The National Center for State Courts is an independent, nonprofit organization dedicated to the improvement of justice.

U.S. Court of Appeals for the Armed Forces
http://www.armfor.uscourts.gov
Appellate court empowered to review court-martial cases.

U.S. Court of Appeals, First Circuit
http://www.ca1.uscourts.gov/opinions.main.php

U.S. Court of Appeals, Second Circuit
http://www.law.pace.edu/lawlib/legal/us-legal/judiciary/second-circuit

U.S. Court of Appeals, Third Circuit
http://pacer.ca3.uscourts.gov

U.S. Court of Appeals, Fourth Circuit
http://www.law.emory.edu/4circuit

U.S. Court of Appeals, Fifth Circuit
http://www.ca5.uscourts.gov

U.S. Court of Appeals, Sixth Circuit
http://pacer.ca6.uscourts.gov/opinions/main.php

U.S. Court of Appeals, Seventh Circuit
http://www.ca7.uscourts.gov

U.S. Court of Appeals, Eighth Circuit
http://www.ca8.uscourts.gov/index.html

U.S. Court of Appeals, Ninth Circuit
http://www.ca9.uscourts.gov

U.S. Court of Appeals, Tenth Circuit
http://www.kscourts.org/ca10

U.S. Court of Appeals, Eleventh Circuit
http://www.ca11.uscourts.gov/opinions.htm

U.S. Court of Appeals, D.C. Circuit
http://www.cadc.uscourts.gov

U.S. Court of Appeals, Federal Circuit
http://www.fedcir.gov

U.S. Supreme Court
http://www.supremecourtus.gov
Round-the-clock access to the U.S. Supreme Court. This site provides public access to the Court's decisions, argument calendar, schedules, rules, visitors' guides, building photos, and bar admission forms. Although dockets have also been available by phone, this is the first venture onto the Internet for the nation's highest court. It has decision texts available online by noon on the day they are announced (which always occurs at 10 A.M. ET).

Check the *Criminal Law Today* Web site for URLs that may have changed.

SUGGESTED READINGS AND CLASSIC WORKS

Jeffery S. Adler, "A Historical Analysis of the Law of Vagrancy," *Criminology,* Vol. 27 (May 1989), p. 209.

William J. Chambliss, *Crime and the Legal Process* (New York: McGraw Hill, 1969).

Joel Feinberg, *The Moral Limits of the Criminal Law* (New York: Oxford University Press, 1986).

Wayne R. Lapierre, *Guns, Crime, and Freedom* (Washington, D.C.: Regnery Publishing, 1994).

Lee Nisbet, Ed. *The Gun Control Debate: You Decide* (Amherst, NY: Prometheus Books, 1991).

Steven Vago, *Law and Society,* 4th ed. (Upper Saddle River, NJ: Prentice Hall, 1994).

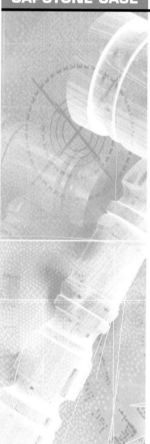

CAPSTONE CASE

WHEN DO OFFENSIVE WORDS ADDRESSED BY ONE PERSON TO ANOTHER IN A PUBLIC PLACE EXCEED THE LIMITS OF THE FREE SPEECH GUARANTEE OF THE FIRST AMENDMENT TO THE U.S. CONSTITUTION AND INCUR CRIMINAL LIABILITY FOR ONE WHO SPEAKS THEM?

Chaplinsky v. *New Hampshire*
U.S. Supreme Court, 1942
315 U.S. 568

Mr. Justice Murphy delivered the opinion of the Court.

Appellant, a member of the sect known as Jehovah's Witnesses, was convicted in the municipal court of Rochester, New Hampshire, for violation of Chapter 378, Section 2, of the Public Laws of New Hampshire: "No person shall address any offensive, derisive or annoying word to any other person who is lawfully in any street or other public place, nor call him by any offensive or derisive name, nor make any noise or exclamation in his presence and hearing with intent to deride, offend or annoy him, or to prevent him from pursuing his lawful business or occupation."

The complaint charged that appellant, "with force and arms, in a certain public place in said city of Rochester, to-wit, on the public sidewalk on the easterly side of Wakefield Street, near unto the entrance of the City Hall, did unlawfully repeat the words following, addressed to the complainant, that is to say, "You are a God damned racketeer" and "a damned Fascist and the whole government of Rochester are Fascists or agents of Fascists," the same being offensive, derisive and annoying words and names.

Upon appeal, there was a trial *de novo* of appellant before a jury in the Superior Court. He was found guilty, and the judgment of conviction was affirmed by the Supreme Court of the State. 91 N.H. 310, 18 A.2d 754.

By motions and exceptions, appellant raised the questions that the statute was invalid under the Fourteenth Amendment of the Constitution of the United States in that it placed an unreasonable restraint on freedom of speech, freedom of the press, and freedom of worship, and because it was vague and indefinite. These contentions were overruled, and the case comes here on appeal.

There is no substantial dispute over the facts. Chaplinsky was distributing the literature of his sect on the streets of Rochester on a busy Saturday afternoon. Members of the local citizenry complained to the City Marshal, Bowering, that Chaplinsky was denouncing all religion as a "racket." Bowering told them that Chaplinsky was lawfully engaged, and then warned Chaplinsky that the crowd was getting restless. Some time later, a disturbance occurred and the traffic officer on duty at the busy intersection started with Chaplinsky for the police station, but did not inform him that he was under arrest or that he was going to be arrested. On the way, they encountered Marshal Bowering, who had been advised that a riot was under way and was therefore hurrying to the scene. Bowering repeated his earlier warning to Chaplinsky, who then addressed to Bowering the words set forth in the complaint.

Chaplinsky's version of the affair was slightly different. He testified that, when he met Bowering, he asked him to arrest the ones responsible for the disturbance. In reply, Bowering cursed him and told him to come along. Appellant admitted that he said the words charged in the complaint, with the exception of the name of the Deity.

Over appellant's objection, the trial court excluded, as immaterial, testimony relating to appellant's mission "to preach the true facts of the Bible," his treatment at the hands of the crowd, and the alleged neglect of duty on the part of the police. This action was approved by the court below, which held that neither provocation nor the truth of the utterance would constitute a defense to the charge.

It is now clear that "Freedom of speech and freedom of the press, which are protected by the First Amendment from infringement by Congress, are among the fundamental personal rights and liberties which are protected by the Fourteenth Amendment from invasion by state action." *Lovell* v. *Griffin,* 303 U.S. 444, 450. Freedom of worship is similarly sheltered. *Cantwell* v. *Connecticut,* 310 U.S. 296, 303.

Appellant assails the statute as a violation of all three freedoms, speech, press and worship, but only an attack on the basis of free speech is warranted. The spoken, not the written, word is involved. And we cannot conceive that cursing a public officer is the exercise of religion in any sense of the term. But even if the activities of the appellant, which preceded the incident, could be viewed as religious in character, and therefore entitled to the protection of the Fourteenth Amendment, they would not cloak him with immunity from the legal consequences for concomitant acts committed in violation of a valid criminal statute. We turn, therefore, to an examination of the statute itself.

Allowing the broadest scope to the language and purpose of the Fourteenth Amendment, it is well understood that the right of free speech is not absolute at all times and under all circumstances. There are certain well-defined and narrowly limited classes of speech, the prevention and punishment of which have never been thought to raise any Constitutional problem. These include the lewd and obscene, the profane, the libelous, and the insulting or "fighting" words—those which, by their very utterance, inflict injury or tend to incite an immediate breach of the peace. It has been well observed that such utterances are no essential part of any exposition of ideas and are of such slight social value as a step to truth that any benefit that may be derived from them is clearly outweighed by the social interest in order and morality.

"Resort to epithets or personal abuse is not in any proper sense communication of information or opinion safeguarded by the Constitution, and its punishment as a criminal act would raise no question under that instrument." *Cantwell* v. *Connecticut,* 310 U.S. 296, 309–310.

The state statute here challenged comes to us authoritatively construed by the highest court of New Hampshire. It has two provisions—the first relates to words or names addressed to another in a public place; the second refers to noises and

exclamations. The court said: "The two provisions are distinct. One may stand separately from the other. Assuming, without holding, that the second were unconstitutional, the first could stand if constitutional."

We accept that construction of severability and limit our consideration to the first provision of the statute.

On the authority of its earlier decisions, the state court declared that the statute's purpose was to preserve the public peace, no words being "forbidden except such as have a direct tendency to cause acts of violence by the persons to whom, individually, the remark is addressed." It was further said: "The word 'offensive' is not to be defined in terms of what a particular addressee thinks. . . . The test is what men of common intelligence would understand would be words likely to cause an average addressee to fight. . . . The English language has a number of words and expressions which, by general consent, are 'fighting words' when said without a disarming smile. . . . [S]uch words, as ordinary men know, are likely to cause a fight. So are threatening, profane, or obscene revilings. Derisive and annoying words can be taken as coming within the purview of the statute as heretofore interpreted only when they have this characteristic of plainly tending to excite the addressee to a breach of the peace. . . . The statute, as construed, does no more than prohibit the face-to-face words plainly likely to cause a breach of the peace by the addressee, words whose speaking constitutes a breach of the peace by the speaker—including 'classical fighting words,' words in current use less 'classical' but equally likely to cause violence, and other disorderly words, including profanity, obscenity, and threats."

We are unable to say that the limited scope of the statute as thus construed contravenes the Constitutional right of free expression. It is a statute narrowly drawn and limited to define and punish specific conduct lying within the domain of state power, the use in a public place of words likely to cause a breach of the peace. Cf. *Cantwell* v. *Connecticut,* 310 U.S. 296, 311; *Thornhill* v. *Alabama,* 310 U.S. 88, 105. This conclusion necessarily disposes of appellant's contention that the statute is so vague and indefinite as to render a conviction thereunder a violation of due process. A statute punishing verbal acts, carefully drawn so as not unduly to impair liberty of expression, is not too vague for a criminal law. Cf. *Fox* v. *Washington* 236 U.S. 273, 277.

Nor can we say that the application of the statute to the facts disclosed by the record substantially or unreasonably impinges upon the privilege of free speech. Argument is unnecessary to demonstrate that the appellations "damned racketeer" and "damned Fascist" are epithets likely to provoke the average person to retaliation and thereby cause a breach of the peace.

The refusal of the state court to admit evidence of provocation and evidence bearing on the truth or falsity of the utterances is open to no Constitutional objection. Whether the facts sought to be proved by such evidence constitute a defense to the charge, or may be shown in mitigation, are questions for the state court to determine. Our function is fulfilled by a determination that the challenged statute, on its face and as applied, does not contravene the Fourteenth Amendment.

Affirmed.

[footnotes omitted]

WHAT DO *YOU* THINK?
1. Do you think that the language used by Chaplinsky was obscene? Why or why not?
2. Do you believe that all manner of speech should be protected by the First Amendment? If not, what limits would you put on such protections?
3. What are "fighting words"? Why are "fighting words" not protected by the First Amendment? Do you think they should be? Why or why not?

ONE CONSTITUTIONAL REQUIREMENT OF A VALID CRIMINAL STATUTE IS THAT IT BE WORDED CONCISELY ENOUGH FOR PEOPLE TO KNOW WHEN THEIR BEHAVIOR IS IN VIOLATION OF THE LAW. OTHERWISE, AS THIS EXAMPLE OF VAGRANCY LAW SHOWS, THE STATUTE MAY BE HELD TO BE "VOID FOR VAGUENESS."

CAPSTONE CASE

Papachristou v. *City of Jacksonville*
U.S. Supreme Court, 1972
405 U.S. 156

Mr. Justice Douglas delivered the opinion of the Court.

This case involves eight defendants who were convicted in a Florida municipal court of violating a Jacksonville, Florida, vagrancy ordinance. Their convictions were affirmed by the Florida Circuit Court in a consolidated appeal, and their petition for *certiorari* was denied by the District Court of Appeal on the authority of *Johnson* v. *State,* 202 So. 2d 82. The case is here on a petition for *certiorari,* which we granted. For reasons which will appear, we reverse.

At issue are five consolidated cases. Margaret Papachristou, Betty Calloway, Eugene Eddie Melton, and Leonard Johnson were all arrested early on a Sunday morning, and charged with vagrancy—"prowling by auto." Jimmy Lee Smith and Milton Henry were charged with vagrancy—"vagabonds." Henry Edward Heath and a codefendant were arrested for vagrancy—"loitering" and "common thief." Thomas Owen Campbell was charged with vagrancy—"common thief." Hugh Brown was charged with vagrancy—"disorderly loitering on street" and "disorderly conduct—resisting arrest with violence."

The facts are stipulated. Papachristou and Calloway are white females. Melton and Johnson are black males. Papachristou was enrolled in a job-training program sponsored by the State Employment Service at Florida Junior College in Jacksonville. Calloway was a typing and shorthand teacher at a state mental institution located near Jacksonville. She was the owner of the automobile in which the four defendants were arrested. Melton was a Vietnam war veteran who had been released from the Navy after nine months in a veterans' hospital. On the date of his arrest, he was a part-time computer helper while attending college as a full-time student in Jacksonville. Johnson was a tow-motor operator in a grocery chain warehouse and was a lifelong resident of Jacksonville.

At the time of their arrest, the four of them were riding in Calloway's car on the main thoroughfare in Jacksonville. They had left a restaurant owned by Johnson's uncle, where they had eaten, and were on their way to a nightclub. The arresting officers denied that the racial mixture in the car played any part in the decision to make the arrest. The arrest, they said, was made because the defendants had stopped near a used-car lot which had been broken into several times. There was, however, no evidence of any breaking and entering on the night in question.

Of these four charged with "prowling by auto," none had been previously arrested except Papachristou, who had once been convicted of a municipal offense.

Jimmy Lee Smith and Milton Henry (who is not a petitioner) were arrested between 9 and 10 A.M. on a weekday in downtown Jacksonville, while waiting for a friend who was to lend them a car so they could apply for a job at a produce company. Smith was a part-time produce worker and part-time organizer for a Negro political group. He had a common law wife and three children supported by him and his wife. He had been arrested several times, but convicted only once. Smith's companion, Henry, was an 18-year-old high school student with no previous record of arrest.

This morning, it was cold, and Smith had no jacket, so they went briefly into a dry cleaning shop to wait, but left when requested to do so. They thereafter walked back and forth two or three times over a two-block stretch looking for their friend. The store owners, who apparently were wary of Smith and his companion, summoned two police officers, who searched the men and found neither had a weapon. But they were arrested because the officers said they had no identification and because the officers did not believe their story.

Heath and a codefendant were arrested for "loitering" and for "common thief." Both were residents of Jacksonville, Heath having lived there all his life and being employed at an automobile body shop. Heath had previously been arrested, but his codefendant had no arrest record. Heath and his companion were arrested when they drove up to a residence shared by Heath's girlfriend and some other girls. Some police officers were already there in the process of arresting another man. When Heath and his companion started backing out of the driveway, the officers signaled to them to stop and asked them to get out of the car, which they did. Thereupon they and the automobile were searched. Although no contraband or incriminating evidence was found, they were both arrested, Heath being charged with being a "common thief" because he was reputed to be a thief. The codefendant was charged with "loitering" because he was standing in the driveway, an act which the officers admitted was done only at their command.

Campbell was arrested as he reached his home very early one morning and was charged with "common thief." He was stopped by officers because he was traveling at a high rate of speed, yet no speeding charge was placed against him.

Brown was arrested when he was observed leaving a downtown Jacksonville hotel by a police officer seated in a cruiser. The police testified he was reputed to be a thief, narcotics pusher, and generally opprobrious character. The officer called Brown over to the car, intending at that time to arrest him unless he had a good explanation for being on the street. Brown walked over to the police cruiser, as commanded, and the officer began to search him, apparently preparatory to placing him in the car. In the process of the search, he came on two small packets, which were later found to contain heroin. When the officer touched the pocket where the packets were, Brown began to resist. He was charged with "disorderly loitering on street" and "disorderly conduct—resisting arrest with violence." While he was also charged with a narcotics violation, that charge was *nolled.*

Jacksonville's ordinance and Florida's statute were "derived from early English law," *Johnson* v. *State,* 202 So. 2d at 854, and employ "archaic language" in their definitions of vagrants. *Id.* at 855. The history is an often-told tale. The breakup of feudal estates in England led to labor shortages which, in turn, resulted in the Statutes of Laborers, designed to stabilize the labor force by prohibiting increases in wages and prohibiting the movement of workers from their home areas in search of improved conditions. Later, vagrancy laws became criminal aspects of the poor laws. The series of laws passed in England on the subject became increasingly severe. But "the theory of the Elizabethan poor laws no longer fits the facts," *Edwards* v. *California,* 314 U.S. 160, 174. The conditions which spawned these laws may be gone, but the archaic classifications remain.

This ordinance is void for vagueness, both in the sense that it "fails to give a person of ordinary intelligence fair notice that his contemplated conduct is forbidden by the statute," *United States* v. *Harriss,* 347 U.S. 612, 617, and because it encourages arbitrary and erratic arrests and convictions. *Thornhill* v. *Alabama,* 310 U.S. 88; *Herndon* v. *Lowry,* 301 U.S. 242.

Living under a rule of law entails various suppositions, one of which is that "[all persons] are entitled to be informed as to what the State commands or forbids." *Lanzetta* v. *New Jersey,* 306 U.S. 451, 453.

Lanzetta is one of a well recognized group of cases insisting that the law give fair notice of the offending conduct. See *Connally* v. *General Construction Co.,* 269 U.S.

385, 391; *Cline* v. *Frink Dairy Co.,* 274 U.S. 445; *United States* v. *Cohen Grocery Co.,* 255 U.S. 81. In the field of regulatory statutes governing business activities, where the acts limited are in a narrow category, greater leeway is allowed. *Boyce Motor Lines, Inc.* v. *United States,* 342 U.S. 337; *United States* v. *National Dairy Products Corp.,* 372 U.S. 29; *United States* v. *Petrillo,* 332 U.S. 1.

The poor among us, the minorities, the average householder, are not in business and not alerted to the regulatory schemes of vagrancy laws; and we assume they would have no understanding of their meaning and impact if they read them. Nor are they protected from being caught in the vagrancy net by the necessity of having a specific intent to commit an unlawful act. See *Screws* v. *United States,* 325 U.S. 91; *Boyce Motor Lines, Inc.* v. *United States, supra.*

The Jacksonville ordinance makes criminal activities which, by modern standards, are normally innocent. "Nightwalking" is one. Florida construes the ordinance not to make criminal one night's wandering, *Johnson* v. *State,* 202 So. 2d at 855, only the "habitual" wanderer or, as the ordinance describes it, "common nightwalkers." We know, however, from experience that sleepless people often walk at night, perhaps hopeful that sleep-inducing relaxation will result.

Luis Munoz-Marin, former Governor of Puerto Rico, commented once that "loafing" was a national virtue in his Commonwealth, and that it should be encouraged. It is, however, a crime in Jacksonville.

"[P]ersons able to work but habitually living upon the earnings of their wives or minor children"—like habitually living "without visible means of support"—might implicate unemployed pillars of the community who have married rich wives.

"[P]ersons able to work but habitually living upon the earnings of their wives or minor children" may also embrace unemployed people out of the labor market, by reason of a recession or disemployed by reason of technological or so-called structural displacements.

Persons "wandering or strolling" from place to place have been extolled by Walt Whitman and Vachel Lindsay. The qualification "without any lawful purpose or object" may be a trap for innocent acts. Persons "neglecting all lawful business and habitually spending their time by frequenting . . . places where alcoholic beverages are sold or served" would literally embrace many members of golf clubs and city clubs.

Walkers and strollers and wanderers may be going to or coming from a burglary. Loafers or loiterers may be "casing" a place for a holdup. Letting one's wife support him is an intra-family matter, and normally of no concern to the police. Yet it may, of course, be the setting for numerous crimes.

The difficulty is that these activities are historically part of the amenities of life as we have known them. They are not mentioned in the Constitution or in the Bill of Rights. These unwritten amenities have been, in part, responsible for giving our people the feeling of independence and self-confidence, the feeling of creativity. These amenities have dignified the right of dissent, and have honored the right to be nonconformists and the right to defy submissiveness. They have encouraged lives of high spirits, rather than hushed, suffocating silence.

They are embedded in Walt Whitman's writings, especially in his "Song of the Open Road." They are reflected, too, in the spirit of Vachel Lindsay's "I Want to Go Wandering," and by Henry D. Thoreau.

This aspect of the vagrancy ordinance before us is suggested by what this Court said in 1876 about a broad criminal statute enacted by Congress: "It would certainly be dangerous if the legislature could set a net large enough to catch all possible offenders, and leave it to the courts to step inside and say who could be rightfully detained, and who should be set at large." *United States* v. *Reese,* 92 U.S. 214, 221.

While that was a federal case, the due process implications are equally applicable to the States and to this vagrancy ordinance. Here, the net cast is large, not to give the courts the power to pick and choose, but to increase the arsenal of the police. In *Winters* v. *New York,* 333 U.S. 507, the Court struck down a New York statute

that made criminal the distribution of a magazine made up principally of items of criminal deeds of bloodshed or lust so massed as to become vehicles for inciting violent and depraved crimes against the person. The infirmity the Court found was vagueness—the absence of "ascertainable standards of guilt" (*id.* at 515) in the sensitive First Amendment area. Mr. Justice Frankfurter dissented. But concerned as he, and many others, had been over the vagrancy laws, he added: "Only a word needs to be said regarding *Lanzetta* v. *New Jersey,* 306 U.S. 451. The case involved a New Jersey statute of the type that seek to control 'vagrancy.' These statutes are in a class by themselves, in view of the familiar abuses to which they are put. . . . Definiteness is designedly avoided so as to allow the net to be cast at large, to enable men to be caught who are vaguely undesirable in the eyes of police and prosecution, although not chargeable with any particular offense. In short, these 'vagrancy statutes' and laws against 'gangs' are not fenced in by the text of the statute or by the subject matter so as to give notice of conduct to be avoided." *Id.* at 540.

Where the list of crimes is so all-inclusive and generalized as the one in this ordinance, those convicted may be punished for no more than vindicating affronts to police authority: "The common ground which brings such a motley assortment of human troubles before the magistrates in vagrancy-type proceedings is the procedural laxity which permits 'conviction' for almost any kind of conduct and the existence of the House of Correction as an easy and convenient dumping-ground for problems that appear to have no other immediate solution." Foote, "Vagrancy-Type Law and Its Administration," 104 U.Pa.L.Rev. 603, 631.

Another aspect of the ordinance's vagueness appears when we focus not on the lack of notice given a potential offender, but on the effect of the unfettered discretion it places in the hands of the Jacksonville police. Caleb Foote, an early student of this subject, has called the vagrancy-type law as offering "punishment by analogy." *Id.* at 609. Such crimes, though long common in Russia, are not compatible with our constitutional system. We allow our police to make arrests only on "probable cause," a Fourth and Fourteenth Amendment standard applicable to the States as well as to the Federal Government. Arresting a person on suspicion, like arresting a person for investigation, is foreign to our system, even when the arrest is for past criminality. Future criminality, however, is the common justification for the presence of vagrancy statutes. See Foote, *supra,* at 625. Florida has, indeed, construed her vagrancy statute "as necessary regulations," *inter alia,* "to deter vagabondage and prevent crimes." *Johnson* v. *State,* 202 So. 2d 852; *Smith* v. *State,* 239 So. 2d 250, 251.

A direction by a legislature to the police to arrest all "suspicious" persons would not pass constitutional muster. A vagrancy prosecution may be merely the cloak for a conviction which could not be obtained on the real but undisclosed grounds for the arrest. *People* v. *Moss,* 309 N.Y. 429, 131 N.E.2d 717. But as Chief Justice Hewart said in *Frederick Dean,* 18 Crim. App. 133, 134 (1924): "It would be in the highest degree unfortunate if, in any part of the country, those who are responsible for setting in motion the criminal law should entertain, connive at, or coquette with the idea that, in a case where there is not enough evidence to charge the prisoner with an attempt to commit a crime, the prosecution may, nevertheless, on such insufficient evidence, succeed in obtaining and upholding a conviction under the Vagrancy Act, 1824."

Those generally implicated by the imprecise terms of the ordinance—poor people, nonconformists, dissenters, idlers—may be required to comport themselves according to the lifestyle deemed appropriate by the Jacksonville police and the courts. Where, as here, there are no standards governing the exercise of the discretion granted by the ordinance, the scheme permits and encourages an arbitrary and discriminatory enforcement of the law. It furnishes a convenient tool for "harsh and discriminatory enforcement by local prosecuting officials, against particular groups deemed to merit their displeasure." *Thornhill* v. *Alabama,* 310 U.S. 88, 97–98. It results

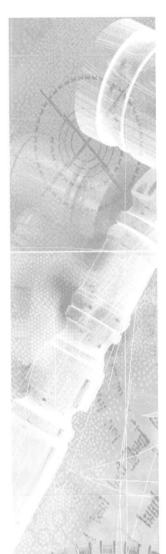

in a regime in which the poor and the unpopular are permitted to "stand on a public sidewalk . . . only at the whim of any police officer." *Shuttlesworth* v. *Birmingham*, 382 U.S. 87, 90. Under this ordinance, "[I]f some carefree type of fellow is satisfied to work just so much, and no more, as will pay for one square meal, some wine, and a flophouse daily, but a court thinks this kind of living subhuman, the fellow can be forced to raise his sights or go to jail as a vagrant." Amsterdam, Federal Constitutional Restrictions on the Punishment of Crimes of Status, Crimes of General Obnoxiousness, Crimes of Displeasing Police Officers, and the Like, 3 Crim. L. Bull. 205, 226 (1967).

A presumption that people who might walk or loaf or loiter or stroll or frequent houses where liquor is sold, or who are supported by their wives or who look suspicious to the police are to become future criminals is too precarious for a rule of law. The implicit presumption in these generalized vagrancy standards—that crime is being nipped in the bud—is too extravagant to deserve extended treatment. Of course, vagrancy statutes are useful to the police. Of course, they are nets, making easy the roundup of so-called undesirables. But the rule of law implies equality and justice in its application. Vagrancy laws of the Jacksonville type teach that the scales of justice are so tipped that even-handed administration of the law is not possible. The rule of law, evenly applied to minorities as well as majorities, to the poor as well as the rich, is the great mucilage that holds society together.

The Jacksonville ordinance cannot be squared with our constitutional standards and is plainly unconstitutional.

Reversed.

[footnotes omitted]

WHAT DO *YOU* THINK?

1. In this case, defendant Heath was charged with being a "common thief" because he was reputed to be a thief. A codefendant was charged with "loitering" because he was standing in a driveway. Charges brought against these defendants derived from Elizabethan poor laws, which, according to a case cited by the court in this decision, "no longer fits the facts." Do you agree that laws against being a "common thief" and "loitering" may not be applicable in today's legal and social environment? Why or why not?
2. The court says that Jacksonville's vagrancy statute was too vague. What aspect of the law made it appear vague?

CAN A STATE MAKE IT A CRIME FOR AN ALCOHOLIC TO BE FOUND INTOXICATED IN A PUBLIC PLACE? (THIS CASE REFERENCES *ROBINSON* V. *CALIFORNIA*, WHICH IS FOUND IN CHAPTER 12.)

CAPSTONE CASE

Powell v. *Texas*
U.S. Supreme Court, 1968
392 U.S. 514

Mr. Justice Marshall announced the judgment of the Court and delivered an opinion in which the Chief Justice, Mr. Justice Black, and Mr. Justice Harlan join.

In late December 1966, appellant was arrested and charged with being found in a state of intoxication in a public place, in violation of Texas Penal Code, Art. 477 (1952), which reads as follows: "Whoever shall get drunk or be found in a state of intoxication in any public place, or at any private house except his own, shall be fined not exceeding one hundred dollars."

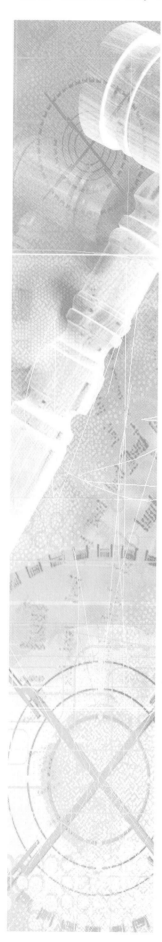

Appellant was tried in the Corporation Court of Austin, Texas, found guilty, and fined twenty dollars. He appealed to the County Court at Law No. 1 of Travis County, Texas, where a trial *de novo* was held. His counsel urged that appellant was "afflicted with the disease of chronic alcoholism," that "his appearance in public [while drunk was] . . . not of his own volition," and therefore that to punish him criminally for that conduct would be cruel and unusual, in violation of the Eighth and Fourteenth Amendments to the United States Constitution.

The trial judge in the county court, sitting without a jury, made certain findings of fact, *infra,* at 521, but ruled as a matter of law that chronic alcoholism was not a defense to the charge. He found appellant guilty, and fined him $50. There being no further right to appeal within the Texas judicial system, appellant appealed to this Court; we noted probable jurisdiction.

The principal testimony was that of Dr. David Wade, a Fellow of the American Medical Association, duly certified in psychiatry. His testimony consumed a total of seventeen pages in the trial transcript. Five of those pages were taken up with a recitation of Dr. Wade's qualifications. In the next twelve pages, Dr. Wade was examined by appellant's counsel, cross-examined by the State, and re-examined by the defense, and those twelve pages contain virtually all the material developed at trial which is relevant to the constitutional issue we face here. Dr. Wade sketched the outlines of the "disease" concept of alcoholism; noted that there is no generally accepted definition of "alcoholism"; alluded to the ongoing debate within the medical profession over whether alcohol is actually physically "addicting" or merely psychologically "habituating"; and concluded that in either case a "chronic alcoholic" is an "involuntary drinker," who is "powerless not to drink," and who "loses his self-control over his drinking." He testified that he had examined appellant, and that appellant is a "chronic alcoholic," who "by the time he has reached [the state of intoxication] . . . is not able to control his behavior, and [who] . . . has reached this point because he has an uncontrollable compulsion to drink." Dr. Wade also responded in the negative to the question whether appellant has "the willpower to resist the constant excessive consumption of alcohol." He added that in his opinion jailing appellant without medical attention would operate neither to rehabilitate him nor to lessen his desire for alcohol.

On cross-examination, Dr. Wade admitted that when appellant was sober he knew the difference between right and wrong, and he responded affirmatively to the question whether appellant's act of taking the first drink in any given instance when he was sober was a "voluntary exercise of his will." Qualifying his answer, Dr. Wade stated that "these individuals have a compulsion, and this compulsion, while not completely overpowering, is a very strong influence, an exceedingly strong influence, and this compulsion coupled with the firm belief in their mind that they are going to be able to handle it from now on causes their judgment to be somewhat clouded."

Appellant testified concerning the history of his drinking problem. He reviewed his many arrests for drunkenness; testified that he was unable to stop drinking; stated that when he was intoxicated he had no control over his actions and could not remember them later, but that he did not become violent; and admitted that he did not remember his arrest on the occasion for which he was being tried. On cross-examination, appellant admitted that he had had one drink on the morning of the trial and had been able to discontinue drinking. In relevant part, the cross-examination went as follows:

"Q. You took that one at eight o'clock because you wanted to drink?
"A. Yes, sir.
"Q. And you knew that if you drank it, you could keep on drinking and get drunk?
"A. Well, I was supposed to be here on trial, and I didn't take but that one drink.

"Q. You knew you had to be here this afternoon, but this morning you took one drink and then you knew that you couldn't afford to drink any more and come to court; is that right?

"A. Yes, sir, that's right.

"Q. So you exercised your will power and kept from drinking anything today except that one drink?

"A. Yes, sir, that's right.

"Q. Because you knew what you would do if you kept drinking, that you would finally pass out or be picked up?

"A. Yes, sir.

"Q. And you didn't want that to happen to you today?

"A. No, sir.

"Q. Not today?

"A. No, sir.

"Q. So you only had one drink today?

"A. Yes, sir."

On redirect examination, appellant's lawyer elicited the following:

"Q. Leroy, isn't the real reason why you just had one drink today because you just had enough money to buy one drink?

"A. Well, that was just give to me.

"Q. In other words, you didn't have any money with which you could buy any drinks yourself?

"A. No, sir, that was give to me.

"Q. And that's really what controlled the amount you drank this morning, isn't it?

"A. Yes, sir.

"Q. Leroy, when you start drinking, do you have any control over how many drinks you can take?

"A. No, sir."

Evidence in the case then closed. The State made no effort to obtain expert psychiatric testimony of its own, or even to explore with appellant's witness the question of appellant's power to control the frequency, timing, and location of his drinking bouts, or the substantial disagreement within the medical profession concerning the nature of the disease, the efficacy of treatment, and the prerequisites for effective treatment. It did nothing to examine or illuminate what Dr. Wade might have meant by his reference to a "compulsion" which was "not completely overpowering," but which was "an exceedingly strong influence," or to inquire into the question of the proper role of such a "compulsion" in constitutional adjudication. Instead, the State contented itself with a brief argument that appellant had no defense to the charge because he "is legally sane and knows the difference between right and wrong."

Following this abbreviated exposition of the problem before it, the trial court indicated its intention to disallow appellant's claimed defense of "chronic alcoholism." Thereupon defense counsel submitted, and the trial court entered, the following "findings of fact": "(1) That chronic alcoholism is a disease which destroys the afflicted person's will power to resist the constant, excessive consumption of alcohol. (2) That a chronic alcoholic does not appear in public by his own volition but under a compulsion symptomatic of the disease of chronic alcoholism. (3) That Leroy Powell, defendant herein, is a chronic alcoholic who is afflicted with the disease of chronic alcoholism."

Whatever else may be said of them, those are not "findings of fact" in any recognizable, traditional sense in which that term has been used in a court of law; they are the premises of a syllogism transparently designed to bring this case within the scope of this Court's opinion in *Robinson v. California,* 370 U.S. 660 (1962). Nonetheless, the

dissent would have us adopt these "findings" without critical examination; it would use them as the basis for a constitutional holding that "a person may not be punished if the condition essential to constitute the defined crime is part of the pattern of his disease and is occasioned by a compulsion symptomatic of the disease." The difficulty with that position, as we shall show, is that it goes much too far on the basis of too little knowledge. In the first place, the record in this case is utterly inadequate to permit the sort of informed and responsible adjudication which alone can support the announcement of an important and wide-ranging new constitutional principle. We know very little about the circumstances surrounding the drinking bout which resulted in this conviction, or about Leroy Powell's drinking problem, or indeed about alcoholism itself. The trial hardly reflects the sharp legal and evidentiary clash between fully prepared adversary litigants which is traditionally expected in major constitutional cases. The State put on only one witness, the arresting officer. The defense put on three—a policeman who testified to appellant's long history of arrests for public drunkenness, the psychiatrist, and appellant himself.

Furthermore, the inescapable fact is that there is no agreement among members of the medical profession about what it means to say that "alcoholism" is a "disease." One of the principal works in this field states that the major difficulty in articulating a "disease concept of alcoholism" is that "alcoholism has too many definitions and disease has practically none." This same author concludes that "a disease is what the medical profession recognizes as such." In other words, there is widespread agreement today that "alcoholism" is a "disease," for the simple reason that the medical profession has concluded that it should attempt to treat those who have drinking problems. There the agreement stops. Debate rages within the medical profession as to whether "alcoholism" is a separate "disease" in any meaningful biochemical, physiological, or psychological sense, or whether it represents one peculiar manifestation in some individuals of underlying psychiatric disorders. Nor is there any substantial consensus as to the "manifestations of alcoholism." E. M. Jellinek, [*The Disease Concept of Alcoholism* (1960)] one of the outstanding authorities on the subject, identifies five different types of alcoholics which predominate in the United States, and these types display a broad range of different and occasionally inconsistent symptoms. Moreover, wholly distinct types, relatively rare in this country, predominate in nations with different cultural attitudes regarding the consumption of alcohol.

Even if we limit our consideration to the range of alcoholic symptoms more typically found in this country, there is substantial disagreement as to the manifestations of the "disease" called "alcoholism." Jellinek, for example, considers that only two of his five alcoholic types can truly be said to be suffering from "alcoholism" as a "disease," because only these two types attain what he believes to be the requisite degree of physiological dependence on alcohol. He applies the label "gamma alcoholism" to "that species of alcoholism in which (1) acquired increased tissue tolerance to alcohol, (2) adaptive cell metabolism . . ., (3) withdrawal symptoms and 'craving,' i. e., physical dependence, and (4) loss of control are involved." A "delta" alcoholic, on the other hand, "shows the first three characteristics of gamma alcoholism as well as a less marked form of the fourth characteristic—that is, instead of loss of control there is inability to abstain." Other authorities approach the problems of classification in an entirely different manner and, taking account of the large role which psycho-social factors seem to play in "problem drinking," define the "disease" in terms of the earliest identifiable manifestations of any sort of abnormality in drinking patterns.

Dr. Wade appears to have testified about appellant's "chronic alcoholism" in terms similar to Jellinek's "gamma" and "delta" types, for these types are largely defined, in their later stages, in terms of a strong compulsion to drink, physiological dependence, and an inability to abstain from drinking. No attempt was made in the court below, of course, to determine whether Leroy Powell could in fact properly be diagnosed as a "gamma" or "delta" alcoholic in Jellinek's terms. The focus at the trial, and in the dissent here, has been exclusively upon the factors of loss of control and inability to abstain. Assuming that it makes sense to compartmentalize in this manner the diagnosis of such a formless "disease," tremendous gaps in our knowledge remain, which the record in this case does nothing to fill.

The trial court's "finding" that Powell "is afflicted with the disease of chronic alcoholism," which "destroys the afflicted person's will power to resist the constant, excessive consumption of alcohol" covers a multitude of sins. Dr. Wade's testimony that appellant suffered from a compulsion which was an "exceedingly strong influence," but which was "not completely overpowering" is at least more carefully stated, if no less mystifying. Jellinek insists that conceptual clarity can only be achieved by distinguishing carefully between "loss of control" once an individual has commenced to drink and "inability to abstain" from drinking in the first place. Presumably a person would have to display both characteristics in order to make out a constitutional defense, should one be recognized. Yet the "findings" of the trial court utterly fail to make this crucial distinction, and there is serious question whether the record can be read to support a finding of either loss of control or inability to abstain.

Dr. Wade did testify that once appellant began drinking he appeared to have no control over the amount of alcohol he finally ingested. Appellant's own testimony concerning his drinking on the day of the trial would certainly appear, however, to cast doubt upon the conclusion that he was without control over his consumption of alcohol when he had sufficiently important reasons to exercise such control. However that may be, there are more serious factual and conceptual difficulties with reading this record to show that appellant was unable to abstain from drinking. Dr. Wade testified that when appellant was sober, the act of taking the first drink was a "voluntary exercise of his will," but that this exercise of will was undertaken under the "exceedingly strong influence" of a "compulsion" which was "not completely overpowering." Such concepts, when juxtaposed in this fashion, have little meaning.

Moreover, Jellinek asserts that it cannot accurately be said that a person is truly unable to abstain from drinking unless he is suffering the physical symptoms of withdrawal. There is no testimony in this record that Leroy Powell underwent withdrawal symptoms either before he began the drinking spree which resulted in the conviction under review here, or at any other time. In attempting to deal with the alcoholic's desire for drink in the absence of withdrawal symptoms, Jellinek is reduced to unintelligible distinctions between a "compulsion" (a "psychopathological phenomenon" which can apparently serve in some instances as the functional equivalent of a "craving" or symptom of withdrawal) and an "impulse" (something which differs from a loss of control, a craving, or a compulsion, and to which Jellinek attributes the start of a new drinking bout for a "gamma" alcoholic). Other scholars are equally unhelpful in articulating the nature of a "compulsion."

It is one thing to say that if a man is deprived of alcohol his hands will begin to shake, he will suffer agonizing pains, and ultimately he will have hallucinations; it is quite another to say that a man has a "compulsion" to take a drink, but that he also retains a certain amount of "free will" with which to resist. It is simply impossible, in the present state of our knowledge, to ascribe a useful meaning to the latter statement. This definitional confusion reflects, of course, not merely the undeveloped state of the psychiatric art but also the conceptual difficulties inevitably attendant upon the importation of scientific and medical models into a legal system generally predicated upon a different set of assumptions. Despite the comparatively primitive state of our knowledge on the subject, it cannot be denied that the destructive use of alcoholic beverages is one of our principal social and public health problems. The lowest current informed estimate places the number of "alcoholics" in America (definitional problems aside) at 4 million and most authorities are inclined to put the

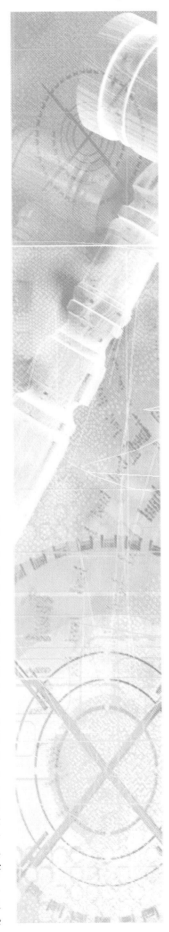

figure considerably higher. The problem is compounded by the fact that a very large percentage of the alcoholics in this country are "invisible"—they possess the means to keep their drinking problems secret, and the traditionally uncharitable attitude of our society toward alcoholics causes many of them to refrain from seeking treatment from any source. Nor can it be gainsaid that the legislative response to this enormous problem has in general been inadequate.

There is as yet no known generally effective method for treating the vast number of alcoholics in our society. Some individual alcoholics have responded to particular forms of therapy with remissions of their symptomatic dependence upon the drug. But just as there is no agreement among doctors and social workers with respect to the causes of alcoholism, there is no consensus as to why particular treatments have been effective in particular cases and there is no generally agreed-upon approach to the problem of treatment on a large scale. Most psychiatrists are apparently of the opinion that alcoholism is far more difficult to treat than other forms of behavioral disorders, and some believe it is impossible to cure by means of psychotherapy; indeed, the medical profession as a whole, and psychiatrists in particular, have been severely criticized for the prevailing reluctance to undertake the treatment of drinking problems. Thus it is entirely possible that, even were the manpower and facilities available for a full-scale attack upon chronic alcoholism, we would find ourselves unable to help the vast bulk of our "visible"—let alone our "invisible"—alcoholic population.

However, facilities for the attempted treatment of indigent alcoholics are woefully lacking throughout the country. It would be tragic to return large numbers of helpless, sometimes dangerous, and frequently unsanitary inebriates to the streets of our cities without even the opportunity to sober up adequately, which a brief jail term provides. Presumably no State or city will tolerate such a state of affairs. Yet the medical profession cannot, and does not, tell us with any assurance that, even if the buildings, equipment, and trained personnel were made available, it could provide anything more than slightly higher-class jails for our indigent habitual inebriates. Thus we run the grave risk that nothing will be accomplished beyond the hanging of a new sign—reading "hospital"—over one wing of the jailhouse.

One virtue of the criminal process is, at least, that the duration of penal incarceration typically has some outside statutory limit; this is universally true in the case of petty offenses, such as public drunkenness, where jail terms are quite short on the whole. "Therapeutic civil commitment" lacks this feature; one is typically committed until one is "cured." Thus, to do otherwise than affirm might subject indigent alcoholics to the risk that they may be locked up for an indefinite period of time under the same conditions as before, with no more hope than before of receiving effective treatment and no prospect of periodic "freedom."

Faced with this unpleasant reality, we are unable to assert that the use of the criminal process as a means of dealing with the public aspects of problem drinking can never be defended as rational. The picture of the penniless drunk propelled aimlessly and endlessly through the law's "revolving door" of arrest, incarceration, release, and re-arrest is not a pretty one. But before we condemn the present practice across-the-board, perhaps we ought to be able to point to some clear promise of a better world for these unfortunate people. Unfortunately, no such promise has yet been forthcoming. If, in addition to the absence of a coherent approach to the problem of treatment, we consider the almost complete absence of facilities and manpower for the implementation of a rehabilitation program, it is difficult to say in the present context that the criminal process is utterly lacking in social value. This Court has never held that anything in the Constitution requires that penal sanctions be designed solely to achieve therapeutic or rehabilitative effects, and it can hardly be said with assurance that incarceration serves such purposes any better for the general run of criminals than it does for public drunks.

Ignorance likewise impedes our assessment of the deterrent effect of criminal sanctions for public drunkenness. The fact that a high percentage of American alcoholics conceal their drinking problems, not merely by avoiding public displays of intoxication but also by shunning all forms of treatment, is indicative that some powerful deterrent operates to inhibit the public revelation of the existence of alcoholism. Quite probably this deterrent effect can be largely attributed to the harsh moral attitude which our society has traditionally taken toward intoxication and the shame which we have associated with alcoholism. Criminal conviction represents the degrading public revelation of what Anglo-American society has long condemned as a moral defect, and the existence of criminal sanctions may serve to reinforce this cultural taboo, just as we presume it serves to reinforce other, stronger feelings against murder, rape, theft, and other forms of antisocial conduct.

Obviously, chronic alcoholics have not been deterred from drinking to excess by the existence of criminal sanctions against public drunkenness. But all those who violate penal laws of any kind are by definition undeterred. The long-standing and still-raging debate over the validity of the deterrence justification for penal sanctions has not reached any sufficiently clear conclusions to permit it to be said that such sanctions are ineffective in any particular context or for any particular group of people who are able to appreciate the consequences of their acts. Certainly no effort was made at the trial of this case, beyond a monosyllabic answer to a perfunctory one-line question, to determine the effectiveness of penal sanctions in deterring Leroy Powell in particular or chronic alcoholics in general from drinking at all or from getting drunk in particular places or at particular times. Appellant claims that his conviction on the facts of this case would violate the Cruel and Unusual Punishment Clause of the Eighth Amendment as applied to the States through the Fourteenth Amendment. The primary purpose of that clause has always been considered, and properly so, to be directed at the method or kind of punishment imposed for the violation of criminal statutes; the nature of the conduct made criminal is ordinarily relevant only to the fitness of the punishment imposed. See, e. g., *Trop* v. *Dulles*, 356 U.S. 86 (1958); *Louisiana ex rel. Francis* v. *Resweber*, 329 U.S. 459 (1947); *Weems* v. *United States*, 217 U.S. 349 (1910).

Appellant, however, seeks to come within the application of the Cruel and Unusual Punishment Clause announced in *Robinson* v. *California*, 370 U.S. 660 (1962), which involved a state statute making it a crime to "be addicted to the use of narcotics." This Court held there that "a state law which imprisons a person thus afflicted [with narcotic addiction] as a criminal, even though he has never touched any narcotic drug within the State or been guilty of any irregular behavior there, inflicts a cruel and unusual punishment. . . ." *Id.*, at 667.

On its face the present case does not fall within that holding, since appellant was convicted, not for being a chronic alcoholic, but for being in public while drunk on a particular occasion. The State of Texas thus has not sought to punish a mere status, as California did in *Robinson*; nor has it attempted to regulate appellant's behavior in the privacy of his own home. Rather, it has imposed upon appellant a criminal sanction for public behavior which may create substantial health and safety hazards, both for appellant and for members of the general public, and which offends the moral and esthetic sensibilities of a large segment of the community. This seems a far cry from convicting one for being an addict, being a chronic alcoholic, being "mentally ill, or a leper. . . ." *Id.* at 666.

Robinson so viewed brings this Court but a very small way into the substantive criminal law. And unless *Robinson* is so viewed it is difficult to see any limiting principle that would serve to prevent this Court from becoming, under the aegis of the Cruel and Unusual Punishment Clause, the ultimate arbiter of the standards of criminal responsibility, in diverse areas of the criminal law, throughout the country.

It is suggested in dissent that *Robinson* stands for the "simple" but "subtle" principle that "[c]riminal penalties may not be inflicted upon a person for being in a

condition he is powerless to change." Post, at 567. In that view, appellant's "condition" of public intoxication was "occasioned by a compulsion symptomatic of the disease" of chronic alcoholism, and thus, apparently, his behavior lacked the critical element of *mens rea*. Whatever may be the merits of such a doctrine of criminal responsibility, it surely cannot be said to follow from *Robinson*. The entire thrust of *Robinson's* interpretation of the Cruel and Unusual Punishment Clause is that criminal penalties may be inflicted only if the accused has committed some act, has engaged in some behavior, which society has an interest in preventing, or perhaps in historical common law terms, has committed some *actus reus*. It thus does not deal with the question of whether certain conduct cannot constitutionally be punished because it is, in some sense, "involuntary" or "occasioned by a compulsion."

Likewise, as the dissent acknowledges, there is a substantial definitional distinction between a "status," as in *Robinson*, and a "condition," which is said to be involved in this case. Whatever may be the merits of an attempt to distinguish between behavior and a condition, it is perfectly clear that the crucial element in this case, so far as the dissent is concerned, is whether or not appellant can legally be held responsible for his appearance in public in a state of intoxication. The only relevance of *Robinson* to this issue is that because the Court interpreted the statute there involved as making a "status" criminal, it was able to suggest that the statute would cover even a situation in which addiction had been acquired involuntarily. That this factor was not determinative in the case is shown by the fact that there was no indication of how Robinson himself had become an addict. Ultimately, then, the most troubling aspects of this case, were *Robinson* to be extended to meet it, would be the scope and content of what could only be a constitutional doctrine of criminal responsibility. In dissent it is urged that the decision could be limited to conduct which is "a characteristic and involuntary part of the pattern of the disease as it afflicts" the particular individual, and that "[i]t is not foreseeable" that it would be applied "in the case of offenses such as driving a car while intoxicated, assault, theft, or robbery." Post, at 559, n. 2. That is limitation by fiat. In the first place, nothing in the logic of the dissent would limit its application to chronic alcoholics. If Leroy Powell cannot be convicted of public intoxication, it is difficult to see how a State can convict an individual for murder, if that individual, while exhibiting normal behavior in all other respects, suffers from a "compulsion" to kill, which is an "exceedingly strong influence," but "not completely overpowering." Even if we limit our consideration to chronic alcoholics, it would seem impossible to confine the principle within the arbitrary bounds which the dissent seems to envision.

It is not difficult to imagine a case involving psychiatric testimony to the effect that an individual suffers from some aggressive neurosis which he is able to control when sober; that very little alcohol suffices to remove the inhibitions which normally contain these aggressions, with the result that the individual engages in assaultive behavior without becoming actually intoxicated; and that the individual suffers from a very strong desire to drink, which is an "exceedingly strong influence" but "not completely overpowering." Without being untrue to the rationale of this case, should the principles advanced in dissent be accepted here, the Court could not avoid holding such an individual constitutionally unaccountable for his assaultive behavior.

Traditional common law concepts of personal accountability and essential considerations of federalism lead us to disagree with appellant. We are unable to conclude, on the state of this record or on the current state of medical knowledge, that chronic alcoholics in general, and Leroy Powell in particular, suffer from such an irresistible compulsion to drink and to get drunk in public that they are utterly unable to control their performance of either or both of these acts and thus cannot be deterred at all from public intoxication. And in any event this Court has never articulated a general constitutional doctrine of *mens rea*.

We cannot cast aside the centuries-long evolution of the collection of interlocking and overlapping concepts which the common law has utilized to assess the moral accountability of an individual for his antisocial deeds. The doctrines of *actus reus, mens rea,* insanity, mistake, justification, and duress have historically provided the tools for a constantly shifting adjustment of the tension between the evolving aims of the criminal law and changing religious, moral, philosophical, and medical views of the nature of man. This process of adjustment has always been thought to be the province of the States.

Nothing could be less fruitful than for this Court to be impelled into defining some sort of insanity test in constitutional terms. Yet, that task would seem to follow inexorably from an extension of *Robinson* to this case. If a person in the "condition" of being a chronic alcoholic cannot be criminally punished as a constitutional matter for being drunk in public, it would seem to follow that a person who contends that, in terms of one test, "his unlawful act was the product of mental disease or mental defect," *Durham* v. *United States,* 94 U.S. App. D.C. 228, 241, 214 F.2d 862, 875 (1954), would state an issue of constitutional dimension with regard to his criminal responsibility had he been tried under some different and perhaps lesser standard, e.g., the right-wrong test of *M'Naughten's* case. The experimentation of one jurisdiction in that field alone indicates the magnitude of the problem. . . . But formulating a constitutional rule would reduce, if not eliminate, that fruitful experimentation, and freeze the developing productive dialogue between law and psychiatry into a rigid constitutional mold. It is simply not yet the time to write into the Constitution formulas cast in terms whose meaning, let alone relevance, is not yet clear either to doctors or to lawyers.

Affirmed.

[footnotes omitted]

WHAT DO *YOU* THINK?
1. Do you agree with the majority opinion that an alcoholic may be punished for public drunkenness?
2. What are the differences between this case and *Robinson* v. *California* (discussed in Chapter 12), where the state could not punish a person for being addicted? Which opinion do you most agree with? Why?
3. The medical and scientific premises of the defense position has been questioned by many experts. Do you consider alcoholism a disease? Explain your answer.
4. In your opinion, does punishing alcoholics violate the prohibition against cruel and unusual punishments contained in the U.S. Constitution? Why or why not?

NOTES

1. *People* v. *Stephen,* 153 Misc. 2d 382, 581 N.Y.S.2d 981 (1992).
2. Ibid.
3. Rollins M. Perkins and Ronald N. Boyce, *Criminal Law,* 3rd ed. (Mineola, NY: Foundation Press, 1982), p. 477.
4. Wesley Gilmer, *The Law Dictionary,* 6th ed. (Cincinnati, OH: Anderson, 1986), p. 54.
5. Ibid.
6. Ibid.
7. *Cantwell* v. *Connecticut,* 310 U.S. 296, 308, 60 S. Ct. 900 (1940).
8. Sir William Blackstone, *Commentaries on the Laws of England,* Vol. 1 (Oxford: Clarendon Press, 1765), p. 349.

9. *Chaplinsky* v. *New Hampshire,* 315 U.S. 568 (1942).

10. *State* v. *Cherry,* 173 N.W.2d 887, 888 (Neb. 1970).

11. Gilmer, *The Law Dictionary,* p. 19.

12. Ibid.

13. H. Lee, *How Dry Were We: Prohibition Revisited* (Upper Saddle River, NJ: Prentice Hall, 1963).

14. Levine, Harry G. "The Discovery of Addiction: Changing Conceptions of Habitual Drunkenness in America." *Journal of Studies on Alcohol,* Vol. 15 (1979), pp. 493–506.

15. Ibid.

16. Ibid.

17. Stanton Peele, "The Cultural Context of Psychological Approaches to Alcoholism: Can We Control the Effects of Alcohol?" *American Psychologist,* Vol. 39 (1984), pp. 1137–1351.

18. NIAAA, *Alcohol Health & Research World,* Vol. 18, no. 3 (1994), pp. 243, 245.

19. National Center For Health Statistics, Advance Data, USDHHS, No. 205, September 30, 1991, p. 1.

20. L. D. Johnston *et al.,* "Monitoring the Future," Institute for Social Research, University of Michigan, December, 1994.

21. NIAAA, *Alcohol Health & Research World,* Vol. 17, No. 2 (1993), p. 133.

22. California Penal Code, Section 23152 (c).

23. *People* v. *Byrd,* 125 Ca. 3d 1054 (1985).

24. *People* v. *Jordan,* 75 Ca. 3d Supp. 1 (1979).

25. California Penal Code, Section 23157.

26. The need for "three or more persons" emanates from traditional common law, although the number required by statute in some jurisdictions may be "two or more persons."

27. Derald D. Hunt, *California Criminal Law Manual,* 8th ed. (Edina, MN: Burgess Publishing, 1996).

28. Gilmer, *The Law Dictionary,* p. 293.

29. Ibid.

30. 18 U.S.C.A., Section 210(a)(1).

31. California Penal Code, Sections 404 and 406.

32. Adapted from Joseph R. Nolan and Jacqueline M. Nolan-Haley, *Black's Law Dictionary: Definitions of the Terms and Phrases of American and English Jurisprudence, Ancient and Modern,* 6th ed. (St. Paul, MN: West Publishing Co., 1990), p. 1549.

33. Ibid.

34. *Ledwith* v. *Roberts,* 1 K.B. 232, 271 (1937).

35. Gilmer, *The Law Dictionary,* p. 334.

36. Ibid.

37. North Carolina General Statutes, Article 43, Section 14-336 (1969).

38. *Papachristou* v. *City of Jacksonville,* 405 U.S. 156 (1972).

39. John M. Scheb and John M. Scheb, II, *American Criminal Law* (St. Paul, MN: West Publishing Co., 1996), p. 284.

40. Ibid.

41. City of Jacksonville (Florida) Ordinance Code § 257 (rescinded).

42. *Kolender* v. *Lawson,* 461 U.S. 353 (1983).

43. 18 U.S.C., Section 922.

44. The five-day waiting period will be phased out after a planned national instant background checking system becomes fully operational.

45. *Printz* v. *United States*, 521 U.S. 98 (1997).

46. *Mack* v. *United States*, 521 U.S. 98 (1997). Combined with *Printz* v. *U.S.*, op. cit.

47. "Brady Bill Backers Hail 3rd Anniversary Friday," Reuters wire services, February 28, 1997.

48. 18 U.S.C., Section 922.

49. 18 U.S.C., Section 922(q)(1)(A)(1988 ed., Supp. V).

50. *United States* v. *Lopez,* 115 S. Ct. 1624 (1995).

51. See Firearms Litigation Clearinghouse, "Firearms Litigation: Current Cases— Atlanta." Posted at http://www.firearmslitigation.org/cases/atlanta.html, from which some of the wording in this section is adapted.

52. See, for example, *City of Cincinnati* v. *Beretta U.S.A., Corp., et al,* Court of Common Pleas, Hamilton County (Ohio), October 7, 1999. Case No. A9902369.

53. New York Penal Law, Section 4005.05(1).

54. *The American Heritage Dictionary and Electronic Thesaurus* (New York: Houghton Mifflin, 1987).

55. U.S. Constitution, Article 3, Section 3, Clause 1.

56. 18 U.S.C., Section 2381.

57. *Kawakita* v. *United States,* 343 U.S. 717 (1952).

58. Article III, Section 3.

59. Florida Constitution, Section 20.

60. *Crashley* v. *Press Publishing Company,* 74 App. Div. 118, 77 N.Y.S. 711.

61. Ibid.

62. 18 U.S.C., Section 2383.

63. 18 U.S.C., Section 2385.

64. California Penal Code, Sections 11400-01.

65. Ibid.

66. 18 U.S.C., Section 793.

67. Steven Komarow, "FBI Agent Is Accused of Spying for Russians," *USA Today,* December 19, 1996, p. 1A.

68. "Ex-CIA Officer Pleads Guilty to Spying," Reuters wire services, March 4, 1997.

69. 18 U.S.C., Section 2384.

70. Pennsylvania Code, Title 18, Section 4902(a).

71. Pennsylvania Code, Title 18, Section 4902(b).

72. 18 U.S.C., Section 1622.

73. *Niehoff* v. *Sahagin,* 103 A.2d 211 (Me. 1954).

74. See *Bloom* v. *Illinois,* 391 U.S. 194, 88 S. Ct. 1477 (1968).

75. U.S. Code, Title 18, Section 1507.

76. Oregon Revised Statutes, Section 162.315(1).

77. North Carolina General Statutes, Chapter 14, Section 223.

78. Nolan and Nolan-Haley, *Black's Law Dictionary,* p. 999.

79. Gilmer, *The Law Dictionary,* p. 54.

80. Ibid.

12

Offenses Against Public Morality

Whatever differences of opinion may exist as to the extent and boundaries of the police power . . . there seems to be no doubt that it does extend to . . . the preservation of good order and the public morals.
—Boston Beer Co. v. Massachusetts, 97 U.S. 25, 33, 24 L. Ed. 989 (1878)

We do not allow a leper to live in our midst of his own volition, and the unfortunate woman, living in a respectable neighborhood and plying her terrible trade, is a leprous sore on the community which will fester until it leavens others with its dreadful poison.
—Mrs. C. M. Weymann, secretary of the Women's Legislative Council, describing Sacramento (CA) prostitutes in 1913[1]

CHAPTER OUTLINE

AFTER READING THIS CHAPTER YOU SHOULD:

▷ Be able to enumerate the crimes against public decency and morality.

▷ Be able to define prostitution and associated offenses.

▷ Understand the requirements for material to be considered obscene.

▷ Know what is meant by a "crime against nature."

▷ Understand the difference between bigamy and polygamy.

▷ Understand the legal nature of controlled substances, and know how drugs are regulated.

▷ Be able to explain forfeiture and describe how it is useful in the fight against drugs.

▷ Be able to critique laws regulating public morality.

INTRODUCTION

A few years ago, the city of Erie, Pennsylvania, enacted an ordinance making it an offense to knowingly or intentionally appear in public in a "state of nudity." At the time, a company known as "Pap's A. M." operated an Erie nightclub called "Kandyland." Kandyland featured totally nude erotic dancing by women. To comply with the new ordinance, Kandyland dancers were forced to change their dance routines by wearing "pasties" and a "G-string." Pap's sought to overturn the ordinance, and filed suit against Erie and city officials. Initially, a Pennsylvania court struck down the city ordinance as unconstitutional, but a state appellate court reversed the decision. The Pennsylvania Supreme Court, in turn, reversed the decision of the appellate court, finding that the ordinance's public nudity sections violated Pap's First Amendment right to freedom of expression. The Pennsylvania Supreme Court held that nude dancing is a form of expressive conduct entitled to protection under the First Amendment, and reasoned that the Erie ordinance impacted "negatively on the erotic message of the dance."[2]

The city appealed to the U.S. Supreme Court,[3] which, in March 2000, overturned the decision by Pennsylvania's high court. The Court allowed that "nude dancing . . . is expressive conduct that falls within the outer ambit of the First Amendment's

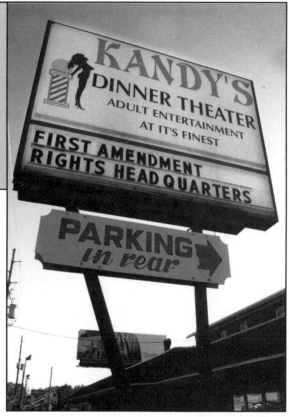

The Kandyland Club in Erie, Pennsylvania. Kandyland, a club featuring nude female dancers, became the focus of a 2000 U.S. Supreme Court case. The Court decided that while nude dancing might be expressive conduct that comes under First Amendment protections, it can also be subject to regulation because of its "negative secondary effects." (Photo by Gene J. Puskar, courtesy of AP/Wide World Photos.)

protection." However, the justices said, the purpose the city had in mind when enacting the ordinance was unrelated to the suppression of expressive conduct, but was aimed instead at the "negative secondary effects" of such dancing. Negative secondary effects include crime, lowered property values, the potential for substance abuse in the vicinity of the bar, and other undesirable consequences "caused by the presence of adult entertainment establishments like Kandyland. . . ." Moreover, said the Court, the ordinance "does not target nudity that contains an erotic message; rather, it bans all public nudity, regardless of whether that nudity is accompanied by expressive activity." The Court concluded by saying that "even if Erie's public nudity ban has some minimal effect on the erotic message by muting that portion of the expression that occurs when the last stitch is dropped, the dancers at Kandyland and other such establishments are free to perform wearing pasties and G-strings. Any effect on the overall expression is therefore [minimal]." An official summary of the Court's decision can be seen in a Capstone Case at the end of this chapter.

CRIMES AGAINST PUBLIC DECENCY AND MORALITY

While most crimes have specific and identifiable *individual* victims, some crimes do not. Such offenses fall into a category of social order offenses called "crimes against public decency and morality."

Legal strictures against behavior that negatively impacts public decency and morality originated in medieval days, when secular rulers and church leaders became concerned with institutionalizing accepted notions of good and evil—and especially with controlling human sexual behavior to have it conform to existing notions of propriety. At that time, authorities were mostly concerned with crimes of adultery and prostitution. Morals offenses, as in the example that opened this chapter, are often identified by municipal codes, although many have also been codified in state statutes.

Crimes against public decency and morality are sometimes termed **victimless crimes** by virtue of the fact that they generally involve willing participants. The key to understanding the meaning of the term "victimless crimes" is to recognize that while the behavior of those involved in such crimes may violate the criminal law, it is, in almost all cases, consensual behavior which is freely engaged in by all of the parties involved. Persons committing the act of prostitution, for example, are willing—even eager—participants in the crime. The same is true for those participating in drug sales, drug purchases, drug use, gambling, and so on. Hence, we can define a victimless crime as an offense committed against the social values and interests represented in and protected by the criminal law *and* in which parties to the offense willingly participate. In short, victimless crimes are those with willing participants.

Crimes against public decency and morality typically include not only prostitution, drug use, and gambling, but also pornography, obscenity, and various other consensual sex offenses—such as bestiality, homosexuality, sodomy, deviate sexual relations, oral sexual performance, lewdness, indecency, seduction, fornication, adultery, bigamy, and so on. Although they do not have readily identifiable *complaining* victims, it is important to recognize that persons not directly involved in such offenses may still see themselves as victimized by the activity. The spouses of men who visit prostitutes, for example, are victims of prostitution in the sense that they may be exposed to sexually transmitted diseases, the marriage bond may be weakened by the husband's criminal activity, and the affected families may have fewer financial resources as a result of the man's expenditures for illicit sexual services. Moreover, because prostitution (and other such crimes) lowers the moral quality of life for everyone even tangentially related to the parties involved in the crime, and because it demeans the status of women in society, the offense is not without arguable victims.

VICTIMLESS CRIME
an offense committed against the social values and interests represented in and protected by the criminal law *and* in which parties to the offense willingly participate.

Prostitution

In July 1995, English movie star Hugh Grant was arrested in Hollywood, California, for felonious fellatious activity with prostitute Divine Brown.[4] While some of Grant's fans asked, "Why would he do such a thing?," others asked, "Why not?" Three weeks later, when Grant made an appearance on NBC's *Tonight* show, female fans lined the streets with signs reading: "We forgive you, Hugh!"[5]

Prostitution is sometimes said to be the world's "oldest profession." In early England, it was an ecclesiastical crime (that is, one coming under church jurisdiction rather than the jurisdiction of lay courts), and not a common law offense. In the early American colonies, the Protestant ethic greatly influenced criminal law as it developed, and quickly led to a definition of prostitution as a criminal offense. At the federal level, the Mann Act,[6] also known as the "White Slave Traffic Act," was passed in 1910 and prohibited the interstate transportation of "any woman or girl" for "an immoral purpose." The "moral purity movement" of the early twentieth century, whose members were influential in seeing the Mann Act passed into law, led to the enactment of a series of "Red Light Abatement Acts" in many western states during the period 1914 to 1920. Today, prostitution is a crime in all states except Nevada—where the legal status of acts of prostitution is determined on a county-by-county basis.

> I was naughty. I wasn't bad. Bad is hurting people, doing evil. Naughty is not hurting anyone. Naughty is being amusing.
>
> —Sydney Biddle Barrows, the "Mayflower Madam" (1986)

North Carolina law defines **prostitution** as "the offering or receiving of the body for sexual intercourse for hire [as well as] the offering or receiving of the body for indiscriminate sexual intercourse without hire."[7] Georgia law, on the other hand, limits the crime of prostitution to sexual intercourse for hire. Georgia law reads, "A person commits the offense of prostitution when he performs or offers or consents to perform an act of sexual intercourse for money."[8] Many states substitute the term "sexual act" or "sexual conduct" for "sexual intercourse," or interpret the term "sexual intercourse" to mean any overt sexual activity. As both the North Carolina and Georgia definitions indicate, however, a conviction for prostitution does not require that the sexual act in question actually take place. An offer to perform the act, or consent to do so, is sufficient to constitute prostitution. **Soliciting prostitution** is the act of asking, enticing, or requesting another to commit the crime of prostitution. In most situations, of course, voluntary sexual intercourse between consenting adults is not a crime. It is primarily the act of solicitation and payment for sexual services that violates the criminal law.[9]

Generally speaking, the elements of the crime of prostitution are:

- engaging in or offering to perform,
- a sexual act,
- for hire.

Prostitutes can be of either gender, and in most states both the prostitute and his or her customer can be found guilty of prostitution.

The crime of **promoting prostitution** is a statutory offense in almost all jurisdictions. It is intended to punish persons who profit or attempt to profit by using others to engage in prostitution. Generally, the following acts constitute the crime of promoting prostitution: (1) owning, controlling, managing, supervising, or otherwise keeping a house of prostitution; (2) procuring a person for a house of prostitution; (3) encouraging, inducing, or otherwise purposely causing another to become or remain a prostitute; (4) soliciting a person to patronize a prostitute; (5) procuring a prostitute for another; or (6) transporting a person with the purpose of promoting that person's involvement in prostitution.[11]

Other offenses are associated with the crime of prostitution. A person having or exercising control over the use of any place or conveyance which would offer seclusion or shelter for the practice of prostitution commits the offense of **keeping a place of prostitution** when he or she knowingly grants or permits the use of such place for the purpose of prostitution.[12] At common law, a place of prostitution was known as a "bawdy house," and the term is still used in some states today. Both owner and keeper of a bawdy house were guilty of a misdemeanor under the common law.

According to contemporary Georgia law, "A person commits the offense of **pimping** when he performs any of the following acts: (1) offers or agrees to procure a prostitute for another; (2) offers or agrees to arrange a meeting of persons for the purpose of prostitution; (3) directs another to a place knowing such direction is for the purpose of prostitution; (4) receives money or other thing of value from a prostitute, without lawful consideration, knowing it was earned in whole or in part from prostitution; or (5) aids or abets, counsels, or commands another in the commission of prostitution or aids or assists in prostitution where the proceeds or profits derived therefrom are to be divided on a pro rata basis."[13] Similarly, "a person commits the offense of **pandering** when he or she solicits a person to perform an act of prostitution or when he or she knowingly assembles persons at a fixed place for the purpose of being solicited by others to perform an act of prostitution."[14]

A number of jurisdictions have also enacted special laws criminalizing "massage parlor" activities akin to prostitution. Georgia law, for example, says: "(a) A person, including a masseur or masseuse, commits the offense of masturbation for hire when he erotically stimulates the genital organs of another, whether resulting in orgasm or not, by manual or other bodily contact exclusive of sexual intercourse or by instrumental manipulation for money or the substantial equivalent thereof. (b) A person committing the offense of masturbation for hire shall be guilty of a misdemeanor."[15]

Web Extra! 12–1

Roth v. *U.S.* (1957)

Pornography, Obscenity, and Lewdness

The word "obscenity" comes from the Latin word *caenum* (filth), and the word "pornography" is taken from the Greek word *porne* (prostitute). All jurisdictions have laws that punish the sale, possession, and distribution of obscene material, and most have statutes defining lewdness or public indecency.

Pornography can be defined as "the depiction of sexual behavior in such a way as to excite the viewer sexually."[17] Obscenity is a bit more difficult to define. Generally speaking, **obscenity** can be defined as: "That which appeals to the prurient interest and lacks serious literary, artistic, political or scientific value."[19] In 1957, in the case of *Roth* v. *United States*,[20] the U.S. Supreme Court was careful to distinguish between "sex" and "obscenity," while holding that obscenity was not constitutionally protected under First Amendment free speech guarantees.

In 1973, the Court, in the case of *Miller* v. *California*,[21] held that to be obscene, and thus not protected by the Free Speech Clause of the U.S. Constitution, objectionable material must meet all of the following requirements:

1. the average person, applying contemporary community standards, would find that the work, taken as a whole, appeals to the prurient interest;

2. the work depicts or describes, in a patently offensive way, sexual conduct specifically defined by the applicable statute; and

3. the work, taken as a whole, lacks serious literary, artistic, political, or scientific value.

Building on the *Roth* and *Miller* decisions, modern California law defines obscene matter as "matter, taken as a whole, that to the average person, applying contemporary statewide standards, appeals to the prurient interest, that, taken as a whole, depicts or describes sexual conduct in a patently offensive way, and that, taken as a whole, lacks serious literary, artistic, political, or scientific value."[22] As used in the definition, **prurient interest** means "[o]bsession with lascivious and immoral matters."[23]

While the production, mailing, and sale of obscene material may be subject to criminal sanctions, the U.S. Supreme Court has made it clear that overarching issues of privacy protect a person's right to read or view such materials within the confines of his or her own home. In the 1969 case of *Stanley* v. *Georgia*,[24] for example, the Court stated: "Whatever may be the justification for other statutes regulating obscenity, we do not think they reach into the privacy of one's own home. If the first amendment means anything, it means a State has no business telling a man, sitting alone in his own home, what books he may read or what films he may watch." The "right of privacy," however, does not protect the public exhibition of obscene matter, nor the involvement of minors.[25]

One special area of recent concern in pornography legislation is the sexual exploitation of children, or **child pornography**. California law, for example, reads: "A person is guilty of sexual exploitation of a child if he or she knowingly develops, duplicates, prints, or exchanges any representation of information, data, or image, including, but not limited to, any film, filmstrip, photograph, negative, slide, photocopy, videotape, video laser disc, computer hardware, computer software, computer floppy disc, data storage media, CD-ROM, or computer-generated equipment

PORNOGRAPHY
the depiction of sexual behavior in such a way as to excite the viewer sexually.[16]

OBSCENITY
that which appeals to the prurient interest and lacks serious literary, artistic, political, or scientific value.[18]

> Pornography is the undiluted essence of anti-female propaganda.
>
> —Susan Brownmiller
> (*Against Our Will*, 1975)

PRURIENT INTEREST
a morbid interest in sex; an obsession with lascivious and immoral matters.

Web Extra! 12–2

Miller v. *California* (1973)

CHILD PORNOGRAPHY
the depiction of sexual behavior involving children.

LEWD
obscene. Also, obscene behavior (lewdness).

LASCIVIOUS
that which is obscene or lewd, or which tends to cause lust.

INDECENT EXPOSURE
public indecency. The wilful exposure of the private parts of one person to the sight of another person in a public place with the intent to arouse or gratify sexual desires. Also, the commission, in a place accessible to the public, of (1) an act of sexual intercourse; (2) a lewd exposure of the sexual organs; (3) a lewd appearance in a state of partial or complete nudity; or (4) a lewd caress or indecent fondling of the body of another person.

or any other computer-generated image that contains or incorporates in any manner, any film or filmstrip that depicts a person under the age of eighteen years engaged in an act of sexual conduct."[26] Title XVI ("Child Pornography") of the federal Violent Crime Control and Law Enforcement Act of 1994 sets penalties for international trafficking in child pornography. The law reads: "A person who, outside the United States, employs, uses, persuades, induces, entices, or coerces any minor to engage in, or who has a minor assist any other person to engage in, or who transports any minor with the intent that the minor engage in any sexually explicit conduct for the purpose of producing any visual depiction of such conduct, intending that the visual depiction will be imported into the United States or into waters within twelve miles of the coast of the United States, shall be . . . fined under this title, imprisoned not more than ten years, or both. . . ."[27] A second conviction is punishable by up to twenty years in prison. Pornography involving children is also controlled by the Child Protection Act of 1984, which makes it a crime to knowingly receive through the mail a "visual depiction [involving] a minor engaging in sexually explicit conduct. . . ." (See the Capstone Case of *Jacobsen* v. *United States* in Chapter 6).

In 1982, in the case of *New York* v. *Ferber*,[28] the U.S. Supreme Court held that a New York law against the distribution of child pornography was valid even though the material in question didn't appeal to the prurient interest of the average person and was not displayed in what could be regarded as a patently offensive manner.

An emerging area of concern is the availability of pornography via the Internet. In 1997, the U.S. Supreme Court found key provisions of the Communications Decency Act of 1996 (CDA)[29] unconstitutional because they unduly prohibited free speech. The law, Title V of the Telecommunications Act of 1996,[30] criminalized the activities of anyone making indecent or patently offensive words or pictures accessible by children online. In striking down key provisions of the CDA, the Court, in the case of *Reno* v. *ACLU* (1997),[31] found it impossible to broadly curtail the access of minors to indecent material on the Internet without unduly limiting free speech guarantees. Justice John Paul Stevens, speaking for the majority, wrote: "It is true that we have repeatedly recognized the governmental interest in protecting children from harmful materials. But that interest does not justify an unnecessarily broad suppression of speech addressed to adults." The Court also noted the availability of parental control software, which has proliferated throughout the technological marketplace and lessened the pressure for government action to regulate the availability of material on the Internet.

Similar to laws against pornography and obscenity are strictures against **lewdness.** Whereas pornography refers to some *thing* that is obscene, lewdness refers to *behavior* that is obscene. Lewd behavior consists of intimate activity by a single individual where such activity is intended to be sexually arousing. A lewd act might be captured on videotape, causing the tape to be classified as pornography. New Jersey defines "lewd acts" to "include the exposing of the genitals for the purpose of arousing or gratifying the sexual desire of the actor or of any other person."[32] At common law it was a misdemeanor for persons to intentionally expose their private parts in a public place—and most of today's laws follow in this tradition.

Lewd behavior is sometimes also termed "lasciviousness." **Lascivious** means that which is obscene or lewd, or which tends to cause lust. Lewd and lascivious conduct is sometimes also termed "public indecency," or **indecent exposure.** Georgia law, for example, provides that: "A person commits the offense of public indecency when he or she performs any of the following acts in a public place: (1) An act of sexual intercourse; (2) A lewd exposure of the sexual organs; (3) A lewd appearance in a state of partial or complete nudity; or (4) A lewd caress or indecent fondling of the body of another person."[33] The New Jersey statute on lewdness, which takes a somewhat different approach, follows.

Many parents have become concerned that growing use of the World Wide Web, combined with the indiscriminate availability of a wide variety of materials via the Internet, may expose young children to pornography. In 1997, the U.S. Supreme Court held that portions of the Communications Decency Act of 1996 improperly limited free speech. The Court struck down provisions of the law that would have regulated the access of minors to indecent material on the Internet. (Photo courtesy of Silver Burdett Ginn.)

CRIMINAL LAW IN THE NEWS

Cops: Man Peddled Teen Sex on Net

Allegedly Delivered Girls to Fla. Hotels and Homes

PALM BEACH GARDENS, Fla.—A 27-year-old man is scheduled to appear in Palm Beach County Court Thursday to answer charges he ran a teen prostitution ring on the Internet, peddling the services of runaway girls as young as 14.

Ryan Jay Quinn of Palm Beach Gardens is being held without bail in Palm Beach County Jail pending his court appearance, police said.

Quinn was arrested last Thursday and charged with 10 counts of procuring minors for prostitution, one count of conspiracy to procure minors for prostitution and one count of deriving support from the proceeds of prostitution, according to Palm Beach Gardens police.

Girls were runaways

He is accused of using about 10 girls between the ages of 14 and 17 in the ring, police said. The girls are runaways or troubled girls who live at home, police said.

Quinn ran the prostitution ring while he was unable to work as a photographer after being injured in a car accident, police said. He is reported to have earned at least $53,000 between February and October 1998.

Quinn, who was arrested following a tip from an informant, ran the prostitution network by using a Web site, police said. He is accused of driving the girls to customers at their homes or hotels throughout Florida.

Five accomplices sought

One deal he allegedly worked on, but which fell through, involved a man who claimed to be a Saudi Arabian prince who was interested in procuring five girls from Quinn.

Quinn allegedly was assisted by five people who recruited girls and customers, police said. The accomplices are facing arrest.

Source: Richard Zitrin, "Cops: Man Peddled Teen Sex on Net; Allegedly Delivered Girls to Fla. Hotels and Homes," APB News. February 16, 1999. Reprinted with permission.

LAW ON THE BOOKS

"LEWDNESS" UNDER NEW JERSEY LAW.
Compare with Model Penal Code, Section 251.1

NEW JERSEY CODE
Section 14-4

a. A person commits a disorderly persons offense if he does any flagrantly lewd and offensive act which he knows or reasonably expects is likely to be observed by other nonconsenting persons who would be affronted or alarmed.

b. A person commits a crime of the fourth degree if:

(1) He exposes his intimate parts for the purpose of arousing or gratifying the sexual desire of the actor or of any other person under circumstances where the actor knows or reasonably expects he is likely to be observed by a child who is less than thirteen years of age where the actor is at least four years older than the child.

(2) He exposes his intimate parts for the purpose of arousing or gratifying the sexual desire of the actor or of any other person under circumstances where the actor knows or reasonably expects he is likely to be observed by a person who because of mental disease or defect is unable to understand the sexual nature of the actor's conduct.

c. As used in this section: "lewd acts" shall include the exposing of the genitals for the purpose of arousing or gratifying the sexual desire of the actor or of any other person.

Other Consensual Sex Offenses

FORNICATION
voluntary sexual intercourse between two persons, one of whom is unmarried.

ADULTERY
sexual intercourse that occurs between a male and a female, at least one of whom is married to someone else.

CRIME AGAINST NATURE
a general term that can include homosexual or heterosexual acts of anal intercourse, oral intercourse, and bestiality and that may even apply to heterosexual intercourse in "positions" other than the generally accepted "missionary" position.

BESTIALITY
sexual relations with animals.

Although they may strike anyone with modern sensibilities as "strange" or outdated, laws against **fornication** and **adultery** continue to exist in many states. Holdovers from an earlier age, many such laws were passed in the late nineteenth or early twentieth centuries, when a strong family and sexual chastity were highly valued. As a result, many consensual sex offenses are still termed "offenses against the family."

Contemporary Georgia law, for example, says that: "An unmarried person commits the offense of fornication when he voluntarily has sexual intercourse with another person and, upon conviction thereof, shall be punished as for a misdemeanor."[34] As the law indicates, fornication can only be committed by an unmarried person. Sexual intercourse that occurs between a male and a female, at least one of whom is married to someone else, is adultery. In the words of the Official Code of Georgia, "A married person commits the offense of adultery when he voluntarily has sexual intercourse with a person other than his spouse and, upon conviction thereof, shall be punished as for a misdemeanor."[35]

In many jurisdictions, consensual sex offenses also include the crimes of homosexuality, bestiality, sodomy, and buggery. Homosexual behavior may be as old as humankind. Although legal in some jurisdictions today, the practice of homosexuality was against the law in this country in most places for many years.

Homosexuality has been traditionally viewed as unnatural sexual behavior, and was frequently termed a **crime against nature.** Crime against nature, however, is also a general term that can include homosexual or heterosexual acts of anal intercourse, oral intercourse, and **bestiality** (sexual relations with animals), and that may even apply to heterosexual intercourse in "positions" other than the generally accepted "missionary" position.

Concerning bestiality, Georgia law says, "A person commits the offense of bestiality when he performs or submits to any sexual act with an animal involving the sex organs of the one and the mouth, anus, penis, or vagina of the other."[36] Bestiality under Georgia law is punishable "by imprisonment for not less than one nor more than five years."[37]

Because crime against nature was long considered an unspeakable crime, statutes rarely provided any precise definition of the activity they outlawed. The Rhode Island law titled "Abominable and detestable crime against nature," for example, reads: "Every person who shall be convicted of the abominable and detestable crime against nature, either with mankind or with any beast, shall be imprisoned not exceeding twenty (20) years nor less than seven (7) years."[38] Idaho law is similar, and says, "Every person who is guilty of the infamous crime against nature, committed with mankind or with any animal, is punishable by imprisonment in the state prison not less than five (5) years."[39] The Idaho Penal Code goes on to say that, "Any sexual penetration, however slight, is sufficient to complete the crime against nature."[40] The lack of precise statutory definition of crimes against nature has strong historical precedent. Blackstone's *Commentaries on the Laws of England,* for example, said that "the very mention of [such offense] is a disgrace to human nature" and referred to crime against nature as "a crime not fit to be named."

Where statutory interpretations are lacking, courts have generally offered definitions of "the crime against nature." One North Carolina court, for example, held that, "The crime against nature is sexual intercourse contrary to the order of nature. It includes acts with animals and acts between humans per anum and per os."[41] Another ruled that, "Crime against nature embraces sodomy, buggery, and bestiality, as those offenses were known and defined at common law."[42] Some definitions have been less specific. In 1965, one Southern court ruled that, "Conduct declared criminal by this section [crime against nature] is sexual intercourse contrary to the order of nature."[43] In prosecutions brought under crime against nature statutes, courts have often held that, "In charging the offense of crime against nature, because of its vile and degrading nature, there has been some laxity of the strict rules of pleading. It has never been the usual practice to describe the particular manner or the details of the commission of the act."[44]

States use a variety of terms in describing what may be homosexual behavior or deviant sexual intercourse. South Carolina, for example, criminalizes the "abominable crime of **buggery.**" Although South Carolina provides no further statutory definition of the offense, buggery has generally been understood to mean anal intercourse. Some states, such as Minnesota, have laws against **sodomy.** Minnesota's anti-sodomy law reads: "Definition. 'Sodomy' means carnally knowing any person by the anus or by or with the mouth. . . . Whoever . . . voluntarily engages in or submits to an act of sodomy with another may be sentenced to imprisonment for not more than one year or to payment of a fine of not more than three thousand dollars ($3,000), or both."[45]

In *Bowers* v. *Hardwick,*[46] a 1986 case involving homosexual behavior, the U.S. Supreme Court upheld Georgia's law against sodomy, even though the act occurred in the privacy of an individual's home. The case has often been cited as supporting legislation that prohibits deviant heterosexual and/or homosexual conduct in private between consenting adults. Twelve years after *Bowers,* however, Georgia's supreme court, in the case of *Powell* v. *State,*[47] invalidated Georgia's statutory sodomy prohibition, holding that it violated rights to privacy guaranteed under the state's constitution. The contrasting opinions in both *Bowers* and *Powell* are summarized as Capstone Cases at the end of this chapter.

Laws against consensual adult homosexual behavior are currently being openly challenged on a number of fronts. Such laws were once on the books of all fifty states, but now exist in only nineteen states and Puerto Rico. Between 1960 and 1980, twenty-three states actively repealed sodomy laws. Laws in a number of other states have been struck down. One of the leaders in the fight to invalidate or repeal laws that criminalize consensual adult homosexual behavior is the American Civil

If the First Amendment means anything, it means that a state has no business telling a man, sitting alone in his own house, what books he may read or what films he may watch.

—Justice Thurgood Marshall
Stanley v. *Georgia*, 394 U.S. 557 (1969)

Web Extra! 12–3
ACLU's Lesbian and Gay Rights Project

BUGGERY
a term that has generally been understood to mean anal intercourse.

SODOMY
carnal knowledge of any person by the anus or by or with the mouth.

Liberties Union (ACLU). Through its National Lesbian and Gay Rights Project, the ACLU recently brought suit in Maryland, Puerto Rico, and other jurisdictions claiming that sodomy laws that target homosexuals unduly single out gay men and lesbian women for punishment. Other suits by the project target civil laws that deny the right to privacy and equal protection of the law to those who choose to live homosexual lifestyles.

Table 12.1 lists the status of laws against deviate sexual activity (sodomy, crime against nature, etc.) in the fifty states. Note that while many of the laws listed in the table appear to target homosexual activity, many of them also apply to heterosexual intercourse performed in what has been legislatively defined as an unacceptable fashion.

BIGAMY

the crime of marrying one person while still legally married to another person.

Bigamy is the crime of marrying one person while still legally married to another person. Bigamy is categorized as a crime against the family. While not a crime at early common law, bigamy was an ecclesiastical offense (or crime against the church). In 1603, the British Parliament declared bigamy a capital offense. Under the Model Penal Code and the laws of many states, it is a misdemeanor.

Generally, the crime of bigamy is not committed if a person marries without divorcing from a prior spouse if the defendant's wife or husband has been absent for an extended period (generally about seven years), and the defendant honestly believes the husband or wife is dead—or if there was a judgment of divorce or dissolution that was later declared void. Bigamy does not necessarily fall into the category of "victimless" crimes, since the second spouse of one who is already legally married may be unaware of the previous marriage. Even so, as one court recently held: "At common law and under this section bigamy is an offense against society rather than against the lawful spouse of the offender."[48]

POLYGAMY

having more than one wife or husband at the same time.

Some jurisdictions have also created the companion crime of "marrying the spouse of another." As the name implies, this offense occurs when a person knowingly and wilfully marries the husband or wife of another. Another offense, **polygamy,** is the marrying of, or cohabiting with, more than one spouse at a time in the purported exercise of the right of plural marriage. In most jurisdictions, polygamy is a felony.

INCEST

unlawful sexual intercourse with a relative through blood or marriage.

Incest, another sexually defined offense, consists of unlawful sexual intercourse with a relative through blood or marriage, such as one's brother, sister, mother, or father. One court defined incest as "sexual intercourse within or outside the bonds of marriage between persons related within certain prohibited degrees."[49] While strong religious and social taboos have traditionally existed against incestuous behavior, a number of recent movies, including *Lone Star* (1996), *The House of Yes* (1997), *This World* (1997), *Then the Fireworks* (1997), and *The Locusts* (1997), have tended to popularize, and even glamorize, acts of consensual incest. Kathryn Harrison's memoir for Random House, *The Kiss,* also reveals details of an incestuous but consensual affair between daughter (over age twenty) and father. In contrast, David Beatty, acting executive director of the National Victims Center, sees the use of incest as entertainment as troublesome, particularly when it is presented as morally neutral. "In most cases when you're talking about incest, there is nothing romantic about it," says Beatty. "What you're talking about is two victims. If we start accepting incest as a literary motif, we lose public outrage, and when we lose that, we start to condone it. I find it very troubling."[50]

Incest is sometimes termed "prohibited sexual contact." While many cases of incest are consensual, others are not, and can involve child sexual abuse or other, more serious crimes. Georgia's incest law reads as follows: "A person commits the offense of incest when he engages in sexual intercourse with a person to whom he knows he is related either by blood or by marriage as follows: (1) Father and daughter or stepdaughter; (2) Mother and son or stepson; (3) Brother and sister of the whole blood or of the half blood; (4) Grandparent and grandchild; (5) Aunt and nephew; or (6) Uncle and niece."[51] The law also stipulates that, "A person convicted

TABLE 12.1

UNITED STATES SODOMY LAWS BY JURISDICTION

State	Statute	Offense Title	Penalty	Special Considerations
ALABAMA	13A-6-65	Sexual Misconduct	1 year/$2,000	Does not apply to married couples
ALASKA	Repealed effective 1980			
ARIZONA	13-1411	Crime Against Nature (anal intercourse)	30 days/$500	
	13-1412	Lewd and Lascivious Acts	30 days/$500	
ARKANSAS	5-14-111	Sodomy	1 year/$1,000	Same sex only
CALIFORNIA	Repealed effective 1976			
COLORADO	Repealed effective 1972			
CONNECTICUT	Repealed effective 1971			
DELAWARE	Repealed effective 1973			
FLORIDA	800.02	Unnatural/Lascivious Acts	60 days/$500	
GEORGIA[1]				
HAWAII	Repealed effective 1973			
IDAHO	18-6605	Crime Against Nature	5 years to life	
ILLINOIS	Repealed effective 1962			
INDIANA	Repealed effective 1977			
IOWA	Repealed effective 1978			
KANSAS	21-3505	Sodomy	6 months/ $1,000	Same sex only
KENTUCKY[2]				
LOUISIANA	14.89	Crime Against Nature	5 years/$2,000	
MAINE	Repealed effective 1976			
MARYLAND	Invalidated (1998) and repealed (1999)			
MASSACHUSETTS	272-34	Crime Against Nature	20 years	Not applicable to private consensual adult behavior (*Commonwealth* v. *Balthazar*, 1974).
	272-35	Unnatural and Lascivious Acts	5 years/ $100–$1,000	
MICHIGAN	750.158	Crime Against Nature	15 years	
MINNESOTA	609.293	Sodomy	1 year/$3,000	
MISSISSIPPI	97-29-59	Unnatural Intercourse	10 years	
MISSOURI	566.090	Sexual Misconduct	1 year/$1,000	Same sex only
MONTANA	45-5-505	Deviate Sexual Conduct	10 years/ $50,000	Same sex only
NEBRASKA	Repealed effective 1978			
NEVADA	Repealed effective 1993			
NEW HAMPSHIRE	Repealed effective 1975			
NEW JERSEY	Repealed effective 1979			
NEW MEXICO	Repealed effective 1975			
NEW YORK[3]				
NORTH CAROLINA	14-177	Crime Against Nature	10 years/ discretionary fine	
NORTH DAKOTA	Repealed effective 1975			
OHIO	Repealed effective 1974			
OKLAHOMA	21-886	Crime Against Nature	10 years	
OREGON	Repealed effective 1972			
PENNSYLVANIA[4]				
RHODE ISLAND	Repealed effective 1998			
SOUTH CAROLINA	16-15-120	Buggery	5 years/$500	
SOUTH DAKOTA	Repealed effective 1977			
TENNESSEE[5]				
TEXAS	25-02	Deviate Sexual Intercourse	Third-degree felony	
UTAH	76-5-403	Sodomy	6 months/ $1,000	
VERMONT	Repealed effective 1977			
VIRGINIA	18.2-361	Crime Against Nature	5 to 20 years	
WASHINGTON	Repealed effective 1976			
WEST VIRGINIA	Repealed effective 1976			
WISCONSIN	Repealed effective 1983			
WYOMING	Repealed effective 1977			

[1]Held unconstitutional by state supreme court in 1998, *Powell* v. *State*.
[2]Held unconstitutional by state supreme court in 1992, *Commonwealth* v. *Wasson*.
[3]Held unconstitutional by state supreme court in 1980, *People* v. *Onofre*.
[4]Held unconstitutional by state supreme court in 1980, *Commonwealth* v. *Bonadio*.
[5]Invalidated by Tennessee Court of Appeals in 1996, *Campbell* v. *Sundquist*.

LAW ON THE BOOKS

"BIGAMY" UNDER THE CALIFORNIA CODE.

Compare with Model Penal Code, Section 230.1

CALIFORNIA PENAL CODE

Section 281

a. Every person having a husband or wife living, who marries any other person, except in the cases specified in Section 282, is guilty of bigamy.

b. Upon a trial for bigamy, it is not necessary to prove either of the marriages by the register, certificate, or other record evidence thereof, but the marriages may be proved by evidence which is admissible to prove a marriage in other cases; and when the second marriage took place out of this state, proof of that fact, accompanied with proof of cohabitation thereafter in this state, is sufficient to sustain the charge.

Section 282. Section 281 does not extend to any of the following:

a. To any person by reason of any former marriage whose husband or wife by such marriage has been absent for five successive years without being known to such person within that time to be living.

b. To any person by reason of any former marriage which has been pronounced void, annulled, or dissolved by the judgment of a competent court.

Section 283. Bigamy is punishable by a fine not exceeding ten thousand dollars ($10,000) or by imprisonment in a county jail not exceeding one year or in the state prison.

of the offense of incest shall be punished by imprisonment for not less than one nor more than 20 years."

Until recently,[52] *seduction* statutes in some jurisdictions made it a crime for a man to seduce a "virtuous and innocent young woman, upon promise of marriage."[53] Marriage between the parties was generally a bar to prosecution. As one court explained, "To convict the defendant of seduction, it is incumbent upon the State to satisfy the jury beyond a reasonable doubt of every element essential to the offense. The three elements are: (1) The innocence and virtue of the prosecutrix; (2) the promise of marriage; and (3) the carnal intercourse induced by such promise. . . . If any one of these elements is lacking there can be no seduction."[54] Another court held that "deceit is the very essence of this offense,"[55] while yet another said, "The promise of marriage alone makes the seduction criminal."[56]

Although growing gender equality has largely eliminated criminal sanctions associated with such activity, some states still permit claims for civil damages when seduction occurs. Georgia law, for example, says: "The seduction of a daughter, unmarried and living with her parent, whether followed by pregnancy or not, shall give a right of action to the father or to the mother if the father is dead, or absent permanently, or refuses to bring an action. No loss of services need be alleged or proved. The seduction is the gist of the action, and in well-defined cases exemplary damages shall be granted."[57] Under Georgia law, civil compensation may be available in seduction cases even when no promise of marriage was made.

Gambling and Gaming

Gambling is sometimes categorized under the heading "organized crime and vice offenses." We treat it here as an offense against morality because it has all of the characteristics of such an offense—although it may also frequently be associated with organized criminal activity. **Gambling** can be defined as the wagering of money, or of some other thing of value, on the outcome or occurrence of an event. It is illegal where made so by law. Gambling is sometimes called **gaming**, in recognition of the fact that it may involve games of chance—that is, contests or events whose outcomes are determined at least in part by luck or chance.

Gambling was not a crime at common law unless conducted in such a manner that it constituted a public nuisance. Today, games of chance, including those based upon lotteries as well as those making use of slot machines, are regulated in all jurisdictions, and violations of those regulations constitute the statutory crime of gambling. The laws of U.S. jurisdictions vary considerably, however, as to what constitutes illegal gambling. North Carolina law, for example, says, "If any person plays at any game of chance at which any money, property, or other thing of value is bet, whether the same be in stake or not, both those who play and those who bet thereon shall be guilty of a misdemeanor."[58] North Carolina is among those states having no officially sanctioned "state lottery." States which have stringent anti-gaming laws generally also usually have statutes making it illegal to keep or own slot machines (unless disabled), "punchboards," gaming tables, and other gambling accouterments.

In the state of Nevada, on the other hand, many games of chance—such as blackjack, poker, and "shooting dice,"—are authorized but strictly regulated and closely controlled. In a number of other jurisdictions, only state-run lotteries are permitted. Some states allow on-track participants to bet on dog and horse races, while in others no gambling or lottery of any type is allowed (although exceptions are frequently made for church raffles, bingo games, and fund-raisers sponsored by non-profit organizations). Under federal law, Native Americans are allowed to conduct games of chance on Indian reservations that are recognized by the U.S. government as independent jurisdictions. As a general rule, however, it is fair to conclude that in most jurisdictions any form of gambling not specifically authorized by statute is considered illegal. Although state laws regulating gambling vary considerably, the following box provides an excerpt from the Georgia Constitution concerning gambling.

Celebration at a blackjack table in Las Vegas. While most forms of gaming are illegal in U.S. jurisdictions, the state of Nevada authorizes and oversees the operation of numerous highly successful gambling casinos. (Photo by James Marshall, courtesy of Corbis.)

LAW ON THE BOOKS

GEORGIA REGULATES "GAMBLING" BY CONSTITUTIONAL PROVISIONS.

Georgia Constitution

Article I, Paragraph VIII. Lotteries and nonprofit bingo games.

a. Except as herein specifically provided in this Paragraph VIII, all lotteries, and the sale of lottery tickets, and all forms of pari-mutuel betting and casino are hereby prohibited; and this prohibition shall be enforced by penal laws.

b. The General Assembly may by law provide that the operation of a nonprofit bingo game shall not be a lottery and shall be legal in this state. The General Assembly may by law define a nonprofit bingo game and provide for the regulation of nonprofit bingo games.

c. The General Assembly may by law provide for the operation and regulation of a lottery or lotteries by or on behalf of the state and for any matters relating to the purposes or provisions of this subparagraph. Proceeds derived from the lottery or lotteries operated by or on behalf of the state shall be used to pay the operating expenses of the lottery or lotteries, including all prizes, without any appropriation required by law, and for educational programs and purposes as hereinafter provided. . . .

d. On and after January 1, 1995, the holding of raffles by nonprofit organizations shall be lawful and shall not be prohibited by any law enacted prior to January 1, 1994. Laws enacted on or after January 1, 1994, however, may restrict, regulate, or prohibit the operation of such raffles.

Several federal statutes also restrict gambling, including: (1) 18 U.S.C. 1955, which prohibits illegal gambling on federally controlled property that is in violation of the local or state law; (2) 18 U.S.C. 1084, which prohibits the interstate transmission by wire communications of wagering information by persons engaged in illegal betting; (3) 18 U.S.C. 1952, which prohibits similar activities using the U.S. Postal Service; and (4) 18 U.S.C. 1953, which regulates the interstate transportation of gambling devices. A federal study of gambling, conducted some years ago, came to the conclusion that: (1) illegal gambling is a growing industry in the United States; (2) the legalization of commercial gambling has not reduced illegal gambling; and (3) social gambling has generally been decriminalized by society.[59]

Controlled Substances

DRUG
a generic term applicable to a wide variety of substances having any physical or psychotropic effect on the human body.

The word **drug** is a generic term applicable to a wide variety of substances having any physical or psychotropic effect on the human body. Over the years drugs have been defined by social convention. While today, for example, most everyone would agree that heroin and cocaine are "drugs," they were not always seen as such. Similarly, although alcohol, nicotine, and even caffeine probably fall into the "drug" category in the minds of most people today, their categorization as "drugs" is relatively recent—having occurred during the past two to three decades.[60]

Both the law and social convention make strong distinctions between drugs that are socially acceptable and those that are not. Some ingestible substances with profound effects on the body and mind are often not even thought of as drugs. Gasoline fumes, chemical vapors of many kinds, perfumes, certain vitamins, sugar-rich foods, and toxic chemicals may all have profound effects on the mind and body. Even so, most people do not view such substances as drugs, and these substances are rarely regulated by the criminal law. Hence, answers to the question of: "What is a drug?" depend to a large extent on the social definitions and conventions operative at a given time and in a given place.

An important distinction can be made between two major classes of drugs: (1) those which are biologically active and (2) those which are psychologically active. Psychotropic substances, or drugs that affect the mind, are said to have psychoactive properties. Bioactive substances, on the other hand, are drugs that affect the body. While bioactive drugs are subject to considerable regulation and control, most drug laws concern themselves with the manufacture, sale, and possession of psychoactive substances. The term **controlled substance** refers to specifically defined bioactive or psychoactive chemical substances that come under the purview of the criminal law. It is interesting to recognize that all of today's controlled substance laws are the result of legislative action, because common law had nothing to say about drugs other than alcohol.

CONTROLLED SUBSTANCE
a specifically defined bioactive or psychoactive chemical substance that comes under the purview of the criminal law.

Drug Abuse Legislation Anti–drug abuse legislation in the United States dates back to around 1875, when the city of San Francisco enacted a statute prohibiting the smoking of opium.[61] A number of Western states were quick to follow the city's lead. The San Francisco law and many laws that came after it, however, clearly targeted Chinese immigrants and were rarely applied to other ethnic groups that may have been involved in the practice.

DRUG TERMINOLOGY

Drug: Any chemical substance defined by social convention as bioactive or psychoactive. Not all "drugs" are socially recognized as such, although those which are may not be well understood. Among recognized drugs, some are "legal" and readily available, while others are closely controlled.

Controlled substance: A specifically defined bioactive or psychoactive chemical substance that is proscribed by law.

Drug abuse: The frequent, overindulgent, or long-term use of a controlled substance in a way that creates problems in the user's life or in the lives of those with whom the user associates.

Psychological addiction: A craving for a specific drug that results from long-term substance abuse. People who are psychologically addicted use the drug in question as a "crutch" to deal with the events in their lives. Also referred to as psychological dependence.

Physical addiction: A biologically based craving for a specific drug, which results from frequent use of the substance. Also referred to as physical dependence.

Addict: Generally, someone who abuses drugs and is psychologically dependent, physically dependent, or both.

Soft drugs: Psychoactive drugs with relatively mild effects whose potential for abuse and addiction is substantially less than for the hard drugs. By social convention, soft drugs include marijuana, hashish, and some tranquilizers and mood elevators.

Hard drugs: Psychoactive substances with serious potential for abuse and addiction. By social convention, hard drugs include heroin, methaqualone (Quaaludes), sopors, LSD, mescaline, peyote, psilocybin, and MDA. Cocaine and its derivative, crack, along with methamphetamine (speed), are often placed in the hard drug category.

Recreational drug user: A person who uses drugs relatively infrequently and whose use occurs primarily among friends and within social contexts that define drug use as pleasurable. Most addicts began as recreational users.

SOURCE: *Criminal Justice Today: An Introductory Text for the Twenty-first Century,* 6th ed. by Frank Schmalleger. Copyright 2001. Adapted by permission of Prentice-Hall, Inc., Upper Saddle River, NJ.

EXHIBIT 12-A

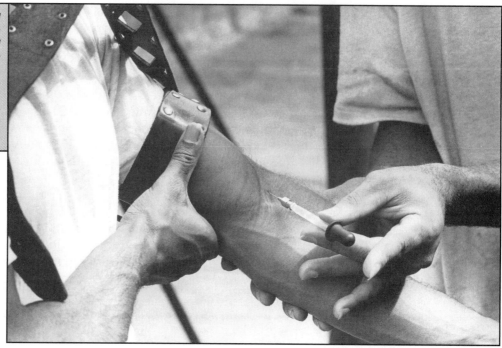

The continued and widespread illegal use of controlled substances results in many arrests throughout the United States each year and has filled the nation's prisons with drug offenders. Controlled substances are bioactive or psychoactive chemical substances that come under the purview of the criminal law. (Photo courtesy of Joel Gordon Photography.)

The first major piece of federal antidrug legislation came in 1914, with enactment of the Harrison Act. The Harrison Act required persons dealing in opium, morphine, heroin, cocaine, and specified derivatives of those drugs to register with the federal government and to pay a tax of one dollar per year. The only people permitted to register, however, were physicians, pharmacists, and members of the medical profession. Nonregistered drug traffickers faced a maximum fine of $2,000 and up to five years in prison.

Because the Harrison Act allowed physicians to prescribe controlled substances for the purpose of medical treatment, heroin addicts and other drug users could still legally purchase the drugs they needed. By 1920, however, court rulings had established that drug "maintenance" only prolonged addiction and did not qualify as "treatment."[62] The era of legally available heroin had ended.

By the 1930s government attention came to be riveted on marijuana. In 1937, at the urging of the Federal Bureau of Narcotics, Congress passed the Marijuana Tax Act. As the title of the law indicates, the Marijuana Tax Act placed a levy on cannabis—at the rate of $100 per ounce. Individuals who didn't pay the tax were subject to prosecution. With passage of the Boggs Act in 1951, however, marijuana, along with a number of other drugs, entered the class of federally prohibited controlled substances. The Boggs Act also removed heroin from the list of medically useful substances and required the removal, within 120 days after the act's passage, of any medicines containing heroin from pharmacies across the country.[63]

The Narcotic Control Act of 1956 increased penalties for drug trafficking and possession and made the sale of heroin to anyone under age eighteen a capital offense. By 1970 America's drug problem was clear to almost everyone, and legislators assumed a highly punitive approach to controlling drug abuse. Under President Nixon, legislation designed to encompass all aspects of drug abuse and to permit federal intervention at all levels of use was enacted. Termed the Comprehensive Drug Abuse Prevention and Control Act of 1970,[64] the bill still forms the basis of federal enforcement efforts today. Title II of the Comprehensive Drug Abuse Prevention and Control Act is the Controlled Substances Act (CSA). The CSA sets up five schedules that classify psychoactive drugs according to their degree of psychoactivity and abuse potential.[65] The five schedules are described below:

- **Schedule I controlled substances** have no established medical usage, cannot be used safely, and have great potential for abuse. Federal law requires that any research employing Schedule I substances be fully documented and that the substances themselves be stored in secure vaults. Included in this category are heroin, LSD, mescaline, peyote, methaqualone (Quaaludes), psilocybin, marijuana, and hashish, as well as other powerful drugs. Penalties for a first-offense possession and sale of Schedule I controlled substances under the federal Narcotic Penalties and Enforcement Act of 1986 range up to life imprisonment and a $10 million fine. Penalties increase for subsequent offenses.

- **Schedule II controlled substances** are defined as drugs with high abuse potential for which there is a currently accepted pharmacological or medical use. Most Schedule II substances are also considered to be addictive. Drugs that fall into this category include opium, morphine, codeine, cocaine, phencyclidine (PCP), and their derivatives. Certain other stimulants, such as methylphenidate (Ritalin) and phenmetrazine (Preludin), and a few barbiturates with high abuse potential also come under Schedule II. Legal access to Schedule II substances requires written nonrefillable prescriptions, vault storage, and thorough record keeping by vendors. Penalties for first-offense possession and sale of Schedule II controlled substances range up to twenty years imprisonment and a $5 million fine under the federal Narcotic Penalties and Enforcement Act. Penalties increase for subsequent offenses.

- **Schedule III controlled substances** involve lower abuse potential than do those in previous schedules. They are drugs with an accepted medical use but whose use may lead to a high level of psychological dependence or to moderate or low physical dependence. Schedule III substances include many of the drugs found in Schedule II, but in derivative or diluted form. Common low-dosage antidiarrheals, such as opium-containing paregoric, and cold medicines or pain relievers with low concentrations of codeine fall into this category. Anabolic steroids, whose abuse by professional athletes has come under increased scrutiny, were added to the list of Schedule III controlled substances by congressional action in 1991. Legitimate access to Schedule III drugs is through a doctor's prescription (written or oral) with refills authorized in the same manner. Maximum penalties associated with first-offense possession and sale of Schedule III controlled substances under federal law include five years imprisonment and fines of up to $1 million.

- **Schedule IV controlled substances** have a relatively low potential for abuse (when compared to higher schedules), are useful in established medical treatments, and involve only a limited risk of psychological or physical dependency. Depressants and minor tranquilizers, such as Valium, Librium, and Equanil, fall into this category, as do some stimulants. Schedule IV substances are medically available in the same fashion as Schedule III drugs. Maximum penalties associated with first-offense possession and sale of Schedule IV substances under federal law include three years in prison and fines of up to $1 million.

- **Schedule V controlled substances** are prescription drugs with a low potential for abuse, and with only a very limited possibility of psychological or physical dependence. Cough medicines (antitussives) and antidiarrheals containing small amounts of opium, morphine, or codeine are found in Schedule V. A number of Schedule V medicines may be purchased through retail vendors with only minimal controls or on the signature of the buyer (with some form of identification required). Maximum federal penalties for first-offense possession and sale of Schedule V substances include one year in prison and a $250,000 fine.

Because each of the federal schedules depends primarily on a drug's abuse potential, it is important to understand the phrase "potential for abuse." One state law says that potential for abuse "means that a substance has properties of a central nervous system stimulant or depressant or an hallucinogen that creates a substantial likelihood of its being: (a) Used in amounts that create a hazard to the user's health or the safety of the community; (b) Diverted from legal channels and distributed through illegal channels; or (c) Taken on the user's own initiative rather than on the basis of professional medical advice."[66] The law goes on to say that "[p]roof of potential for abuse can be based upon a showing that these activities are already taking place, or upon a showing that the nature and properties of the substance make it reasonable to assume that there is a substantial likelihood that such activities will take place, in other than isolated or occasional instances."[67]

DESIGNER DRUGS

chemical substances that have a potential for abuse similar to or greater than that for controlled substances, are designed to produce a desired pharmacological effect, and are produced to evade the controlling statutory provisions.

Pharmacologists, chemists, and botanists are constantly discovering and creating new drugs. Likewise, street-corner "chemists" in clandestine laboratories churn out inexpensive **designer drugs**—psychoactive substances with widely varying effects and abuse potential. Hence, the Controlled Substances Act also includes provisions for determining what newly developed drugs should be controlled and into which schedule they should be placed. Under the CSA, criteria for assigning a new drug to one of the existing schedules include: (1) the drug's actual or relative potential for abuse; (2) scientific evidence of the drug's pharmacological effects; (3) the state of current scientific knowledge regarding the substance; (4) its history and current pattern of abuse; (5) the scope, duration, and significance of abuse; (6) what, if any, risk there is to the public health; (7) the drug's psychic or physiological dependence liability; and (8) whether the substance is an immediate precursor of a substance already controlled.

In recent years a number of federal and state laws have been enacted to combat the growing popularity of so-called "date rape drugs" such as Rohypnol and GBH (gamma hydroxybutyric acid). GBH is popularly known as "Liquid X," "Georgia Home Boy," "Grievous Bodily Harm," and "Scoop."

Rohypnol (whose genetic name is flunitrazepam) is a powerful sedative manufactured by Hoffmann-LaRoche Pharmaceuticals. A member of the benzodiazepine family of depressants, it is legally prescribed in sixty-four countries for insomnia and as a preoperative anesthetic. Seven to ten times more powerful than Valium, and virtually tasteless, Rohypnol has become popular with some college students and with "young men [who] put doses of Rohypnol in women's drinks without their consent in order to lower their inhibitions."[68] As one woman who was sexually attacked while under the drug's influence said: "You know something is going on, but you can't do anything about it."[69] Available on the black market, Rohypnol dissolves easily in drinks and can leave anyone who consumes it either severely disoriented or unconscious for hours. The drug is variously known as "roples," "roche," "ruffles," "roofies," and "rophies" on the street.

Penalties for trafficking in flunitrazepam were increased under the Drug-Induced Rape Prevention and Punishment Act (DIRPPA) of 1996.[70] In January 2000, the federal Date Rape Prevention Drug Act (DRPDA) was signed into law.[71] The law amended the Controlled Substances Act by adding GBH to Schedule I, and ketamine (another abused general anesthetic often used as a party drug, and sometimes called "Special K") to Schedule III.

The Anti–Drug Abuse Act of 1988 In 1988, the federal Anti–Drug Abuse Act was passed into law. Under the law, penalties for "recreational" drug users were substantially increased,[72] and weapons purchases by suspected drug dealers became more difficult. The law also denied federal benefits to convicted drug offenders, ranging from loans (including student loans) to contracts and licenses.[73] Earned benefits, such as Social Security, retirement, and health and disability benefits were not affected by the legislation nor were welfare payments or existing public housing arrangements (although separate legislation does provide for termination of public housing tenancy for drug offenses). Under the law, civil penalties of up to $10,000 may be assessed against convicted "recreational" users for possession of even small amounts of drugs.

The 1988 legislation also included the possibility of capital punishment for drug-related murders. The killing of a police officer by offenders seeking to avoid apprehension or prosecution is specifically cited in the law as carrying a possible sentence of death—although other murders by major drug dealers also fall under the capital punishment provision.[74] On May 14, 1991, thirty-seven-year-old David Chandler, an Alabama marijuana kingpin, became the first person sentenced to die under the law.[75] Chandler had been convicted of ordering the murder of a police informant in 1990.

Other Federal Antidrug Legislation Other significant federal antidrug legislation exists in the form of the Crime Control Act of 1990 and the Violent Crime Control and Law Enforcement Act of 1994. The Crime Control Act of 1990 targeted drug crime through a number of initiatives. Specifically, it: (1) doubled the appropriations authorized for drug law enforcement grants to states and local communities; (2) enhanced drug control and education programs aimed at the nation's schools; (3) expanded specific drug enforcement assistance to rural states; (4) expanded regulation of precursor chemicals used in the manufacture of illegal drugs; (5) sanctioned anabolic steroids under the Controlled Substances Act; (6) included provisions to enhance control over international money laundering; (7) created "drug-free school zones" by enhancing penalties for drug offenses occurring in close proximity to schools; and (8) enhanced the ability of federal agents to seize property used in drug transactions or purchased with drug proceeds.

The Violent Crime Control and Law Enforcement Act of 1994 provided $245 million for rural anticrime and antidrug efforts; set aside $1.6 billion for direct funding to localities around the country for anticrime efforts, including drug treatment programs; budgeted $383 million for drug treatment programs for state and federal prisoners; created a treatment schedule for all drug-addicted federal prisoners; required postconviction drug testing of all federal prisoners on release; allocated $1 billion for drug court programs for nonviolent offenders with substance abuse problems; and mandated new, stiff penalties for drug crimes committed by gangs. The act also tripled penalties for using children to deal drugs near schools and playgrounds and enhanced penalties for drug dealing in "drug free zones" designated as those near playgrounds, schoolyards, video arcades, and youth centers. Finally, the law also expanded the federal death penalty to include offenders involved in large-scale drug trafficking and mandated life imprisonment for criminals convicted of three violent felonies or drug offenses.

State Level Antidrug Laws Antidrug laws at the state level show a surprising degree of uniformity. Such uniformity is due to the fact that almost all states have adopted some version of the Uniform Controlled Substances Act, which was proposed in 1972 by the National Conference of Commissioners on Uniform State Laws. The National Conference's Uniform Controlled Substances Act is similar to the federal Drug Abuse and Prevention Control Act in that it also groups controlled substances into five schedules. The schedules are quite similar to those under federal law.

Most jurisdictions have also categorized controlled substances into penalty groups, with penalties ranging from first-degree felonies to misdemeanors. The possession of drugs or substances listed in schedules I and II are generally felonies, and the possession of drugs or substances listed in schedules III to V may be either felonies or misdemeanors. Under the laws of most jurisdictions, the crime of possessing a controlled substance involves a person's possession or right to exercise control over a controlled substance; his or her knowledge of the presence of the controlled substance and of its nature as a controlled substance; and possession of a usable quantity of the controlled substance. Generally speaking, the elements of the offense of unlawful possession of a controlled substance are:

- possession (except as otherwise provided by law),
- of any controlled substance (as classified by law),
- unless upon the written prescription of a physician, dentist, podiatrist, or veterinarian licensed to prescribe such a drug.

Other than possession, jurisdictions generally criminalize the manufacture, sale, and purchase of a controlled substance. Florida law,[76] for example, says that "it is unlawful for any person to sell, manufacture, or deliver, or possess with intent to sell, manufacture, or deliver, a controlled substance." Similar to the laws of other states, Florida law also criminalizes the sale, manufacture, and possession with intent to sell or deliver a controlled substance "within one thousand feet of the real property comprising a public or private elementary, middle, or secondary school between the hours of 6 A.M. and 12 A.M.," and says "it is unlawful for any person to sell, manufacture, or deliver, or possess with intent to sell, manufacture, or deliver, a controlled substance in, on, or within two hundred feet of the real property comprising a public housing facility, within two hundred feet of the real property comprising a public or private college, university, or other postsecondary educational institution, or within two hundred feet of any public park." As in other states, Florida law also makes it "unlawful for any person to purchase, or possess with intent to sell, a controlled substance," except as allowed by law (i.e., with a license, through prescription, etc.). Finally, Florida law says that: "It is unlawful for any person to be in actual or constructive possession of a controlled substance unless such controlled substance was lawfully obtained from a practitioner or pursuant to a valid prescription or order of a practitioner while acting in the course of his professional practice or to be in actual or constructive possession of a controlled substance except as otherwise authorized by this chapter."

Most jurisdictions have also created special penalties for adults who sell drugs to juveniles, and for adults who employ juveniles in the illegal drug trade. Florida law, for example, says, "Except as authorized by this chapter, it is unlawful for any person eighteen years of age or older to deliver any controlled substance to a person under the age of eighteen years, or to use or hire a person under the age of eighteen years as an agent or employee in the sale or delivery of such a substance, or to use such person to assist in avoiding detection or apprehension for a violation of this chapter."

As in the case of federal law, most states have created special procedures for quickly adding individual designer drugs to controlled substance categories. Florida law, for example, describes designer drugs as "chemical substances which have a potential for abuse similar to or greater than that for substances controlled but which are designed to produce a desired pharmacological effect and to evade the controlling statutory provisions." Generally such new substances are officially untested, and it cannot be immediately determined whether they have useful medical or chemical purposes. Because designer drugs can be created more rapidly than they can be identified and controlled by legislative action, many states, like Florida, authorize their attorneys general to identify and classify any new substances that have a potential for abuse and to add such substances to existing schedules.[77]

PRECURSOR CHEMICALS

chemicals that may be used in the manufacture of a controlled substance.

Generally speaking, most states, like the federal government, also control the sale and possession of **precursor chemicals,** or those chemicals that may be used in the manufacture of a controlled substance. Similarly, most states have enacted antiparaphernalia laws similar to the Model Drug Paraphernalia Act, which prohibits possession, manufacture, delivery, or advertising of drug paraphernalia. Drug paraphernalia may include "bongs," hypodermic needles, "roach clips," crack pipes, and other specially described items normally used in the distribution and consumption of controlled substances.

CRIMINAL LAW IN THE NEWS

Meth Infants Called the New "Crack Babies"

Doctors See Spike as Drug's Popularity Rises

DES MOINES, Iowa—With an increasing number of methamphetamine-addicted babies in area hospitals, an Iowa doctor is concentrating her clinic's efforts on treating babies suffering from prenatal exposure to the drug.

Clinic founder Dr. Rizwan Shah made her first methamphetamine-baby discovery several years ago when a routine lab workup found the drug in the urine of an infant newly admitted to the Child and Infant Recovery Effort program at Blank Children's Hospital.

She said she had been seeing mostly "crack babies" since 1989, when her clinic first opened its doors to drug-exposed infants. Little did Dr. Shah suspect that this "meth baby" would be the first of many. "And 80 percent of our patients here are methamphetamine-exposed," Shah said.

Clinic doctors have now treated more than 300 meth babies, a reflection of a growing national trend. Though still the signature drug of the San Diego area, methamphetamine has become popular in other parts of the country as well, especially the West, the Southwest, the South and the Midwest.

"In the last three or four years, the Midwest has been inundated," said Tim Condon, associate director of the National Institute on Drug Abuse in Bethesda, MD. "We don't know if methamphetamine was always a problem in rural America or if we're just seeing more in rural America now."

Comparing drugs' effects

The question in the minds of many methamphetamine experts is: Will meth babies follow in the tragic footsteps of their drug-exposed predecessors? Shah is one of the few researchers in a position to compare the effects of both crack and meth.

"A crack cocaine high can last three hours, while a methamphetamine high can last for 12," Shah said. This is because methamphetamine breaks down more slowly—and it implies a longer fetal exposure to its damaging effects.

Like crack babies, meth babies tend to be born prematurely and are smaller than normal even when carried to term. Unlike crack babies, who are jittery from the start, meth babies go through three or four weeks of limpness, sleepiness and apparent depression.

"And they don't want to eat even though they were born small and need the calories," Shah said.

Meth babies show late irritability

Crack babies and meth babies experience shaking and tremors. Crack babies show this nervous irritability from birth, and it often resolves at eight, nine or 10 months of age, Shah said.

Meth babies become irritable starting at three to four weeks of age—"and from what we have seen here—the oldest meth children we have followed are now 6 years old—in some cases it is still present at age 5," Shah said.

Though they have many differences, the behaviors of crack and meth babies do parallel each other.

Dr. Ira Chasnoff, president and medical director of the National Association for Families and Addiction Research and Education, at first observed only a minimal impact on IQ from prenatal exposure to crack, but he now reports that behavioral problems are beginning to surface as the crack babies of the mid- to late '80s and '90s become the adolescents and pre-adolescents of today.

Biology or environment?

Though there are no hard statistics, psychologists and officials in treatment centers describe children with outbursts of screaming, hitting, attacks and tantrums. Likewise, as meth babies become meth children, they may show hyperactivity, attention disorders, learning disabilities and fits of rage.

The unanswered question is whether the behavior is the result of biology or environment. Most drug-exposed children come from unstable environments that would undoubtedly affect any child's mental state, officials said.

For example, about 68 percent of the children who enter the Child and Infant Recovery Effort program at Blank Children's Hospital have been taken from their parents and are already in foster care or with adoptive parents, officials said. One Swedish study compared meth kids in three different family situations: single foster placement, multiple foster placement (moving from place to place) and staying with the biological parents.

"The worst outcome for behavior was multiple placement, and the best was a stable, substance-free environment," Shah said. "This is, in effect, a treatment."

Source: Joan Lippert, "Meth Infants Called the New 'Crack Babies'; Doctors See Spike as Drug's Popularity Rises," APBNews. June 23, 2000. Reprinted with permission.

FORFEITURE

an enforcement strategy supported by federal statutes and some state laws that authorizes judges to seize "all monies, negotiable instruments, securities, or other things of value furnished or intended to be furnished by any person in exchange for a controlled substance . . . (and) all proceeds traceable to such an exchange."[78]

RICO

an acronym for a section of the federal Organized Crime Control Act known as the Racketeer Influenced Corrupt Organizations provision. Some states have passed their own RICO-like statutes.

Web Extra! 12–4

U.S. v. *Ursery* (1996)

Asset Forfeiture Forfeiture is an enforcement strategy that federal statutes and some state laws support—and one that bears special mention. Antidrug forfeiture statutes at both the state and federal level provide a special category of forfeiture laws. Such statutes authorize judges to seize "all monies, negotiable instruments, securities, or other things of value furnished or intended to be furnished by any person in exchange for a controlled substance . . . (and) all proceeds traceable to such an exchange."[79] Forfeiture statutes find a legal basis in the relation-back doctrine. The relation-back doctrine assumes that because the government's right to illicit proceeds relates back to the time they are generated, anything acquired through the expenditure of those proceeds also belongs to the government.[80]

The first federal laws to authorize forfeiture as a criminal sanction were both passed in 1970. They are the Continuing Criminal Enterprise statute, commonly called the CCE, and the Organized Crime Control Act. A section of the Organized Crime Control Act, known as the **RICO** statute (for Racketeer Influenced Corrupt Organizations), was designed to prevent criminal infiltration of legitimate businesses, and has since been extensively applied in federal drug smuggling cases. In 1978, Congress authorized *civil forfeiture* of any assets acquired through narcotics trafficking in violation of federal law. Many states modeled their own legislation after federal law and now have similar statutes.

Forfeiture statutes have provided considerable grist for the judicial mill. In 1993, in the case of *United States* v. *92 Buena Vista Ave.*,[81] for example, the U.S. Supreme Court established an "innocent owner defense" in forfeiture cases, whereby federal authorities were forbidden from seizing drug transaction assets that were later acquired by a new and innocent owner. In the same year, in the case of *Austin* v. *United States*,[82] the Court placed limits on the government's authority to use forfeiture laws against drug criminals, finding that seizures of property must not be excessive when compared to the seriousness of the offense charged. Otherwise, the justices wrote, the Eighth Amendment's ban on excessive fines could be contravened. The justices, however, refused to establish a rule by which excessive fines could be judged, saying, "[t]he Court declines to establish a test for determining whether a forfeiture is constitutionally 'excessive,' since prudence dictates that the lower courts be allowed to consider that question." The *Austin* ruling was supported by two other 1993 cases, *Alexander* v. *United States*[83] and *United States* v. *Real*.[84] In *Alexander*, the Court found that forfeitures under the RICO statute must be limited according to the rules established in *Austin*, while in *Real* the Court held that "[a]bsent exigent circumstances, the Due Process Clause requires the Government to afford notice and a meaningful opportunity to be heard before seizing real property subject to civil forfeiture."

In 1996, however, in a case which may have relevance for drug law enforcement, the U.S. Supreme Court upheld the seizure of private property used in the commission of a crime, even though the property belonged to an innocent owner not involved in the crime. The case, *Bennis* v. *Michigan*,[85] involved the government's taking of a wife's car used by her husband in procuring the services of a prostitute. In effect, the justices ruled, an innocent owner is not protected from criminal conviction-related property forfeiture.

Also in 1996, in the case of *United States* v. *Ursery*,[86] the U.S. Supreme Court rejected claims that civil forfeiture laws constitute a form of double jeopardy. In *Ursery*, the defendant's house had been seized by federal officials who claimed that it had been used to facilitate drug transactions. The government later seized other personal items owned by Ursery, saying that they had been purchased with the proceeds of drug sales and that Ursery had engaged in money laundering activities to hide the source of his illegal income. The court of appeals reversed Ursery's drug conviction and the forfeiture judgment, holding that the double jeopardy clause of the U.S. Constitution prohibits the government from both punishing a defendant for a criminal offense and forfeiting his property for that same offense in a separate civil proceeding. In reaffirming Ursery's conviction, however, the U.S. Supreme Court ruled that "a forfeiture [is] not barred by a prior criminal proceeding after applying a two-part test asking, first, whether Congress intended the particular forfeiture to be a remedial civil sanction or a criminal penalty, and, second, whether the forfeiture proceedings are so punitive in fact as to establish that they may not legitimately be viewed as civil in nature, despite any congressional intent to establish a civil remedial mechanism." The Court concluded that "civil forfeitures are neither 'punishment' nor criminal for purposes of the Double Jeopardy clause." In distinguishing civil forfeitures and criminal punishments, the majority opinion held that "Congress has long authorized the Government to bring parallel criminal actions and . . . civil forfeiture proceedings based upon the same underlying events . . ., and this Court consistently has concluded that the Double Jeopardy Clause does not apply to such forfeitures because they do not impose punishment."

Coming Changes in Drug Laws In 1996, voters in the state of California passed Proposition 215, known as "The Compassionate Use Act," which allows doctors to prescribe marijuana for medicinal purposes. About the same time, a similar measure passed in Arizona, and in November 1999, Maine voters passed a referendum permitting some sick people to use small amounts of marijuana. Twenty-six other states and the District of Columbia have now passed various laws and resolutions allowing therapeutic research programs involving the use of marijuana or asking the federal government to lift its ban on medical use of the drug.[87] Federal law enforcement agencies, however, have pointedly announced that they will continue to enforce federal antidrug laws prohibiting marijuana possession by citizens of *all* states. The agencies' stance spotlights an emerging policy issue: who controls America's drug policy—the states or the federal government? Also, in August 2000, the U.S. Supreme Court issued an emergency order stopping California marijuana-growing clubs from distributing the drug to those who are ill or in pain.[88] Many regard the ruling as a sign that the Court will soon overturn state laws permitting such practices.

However, if federal courts do not further intervene, the actions of voters in states like California, Maine, and Arizona, might eventually lead to the complete legalization of marijuana in those states. If so, this would create major differences in the drug policies of individual states and would lead to state laws that are substantially inconsistent with existing federal legislation. The thrust of voter-approved California Proposition 215 is contained in the following language taken from the proposition:

> (A) To ensure that seriously ill Californians have the right to obtain and use marijuana for medical purposes where that medical use is deemed appropriate and has been recommended by a physician who has determined that the person's health would benefit from the use of marijuana in the treatment of cancer, anorexia, AIDS, chronic pain, spasticity, glaucoma, arthritis, migraine, or any other illness for which marijuana provides relief.

> (B) To ensure that patients and their primary caregivers who obtain and use marijuana for medical purposes upon the recommendation of a physician are not subject to criminal prosecution or sanction.

Although the California law permits possession of marijuana for valid medicinal purposes, buying and selling the drug remain illegal throughout the state—meaning that legitimate users may have to grow their own supply or buy it on the black market. Arizona law requires prescribing physicians to write a scientific opinion explaining why the drug is appropriate for a specific patient and a supportive second opinion is required before the drug can be administered. In both states, the amount of marijuana that may be in a patient's possession at any given time is subject to state or local government regulation, while Maine sets that amount at 1.25 ounces.

A Critique of Laws Regulating Public Morality

A number of legal scholars have criticized the notion of crimes against public decency and morality—calling them "legal moralism"—and saying that they represent little more than attempts "to achieve conformity with private moral standards through use of the criminal law."[89] The well-known mid-twentieth century-legal theorist Sanford H. Kadish, for example, wrote of "the crisis of overcriminalization," in which attempts to legislate what should be issues of private morality have "been attended by grave consequences." Since crimes against public decency are consensual, says Kadish, the police, to obtain evidence, "are obliged to resort to behavior which tends to degrade and demean both themselves personally and law enforcement as an institution.[90] Because local officials may use moral crusades as a means of deflecting criticism of their own inept administrations, says Kadish, "these laws invite discriminatory enforcement against persons selected for prosecution on grounds unrelated to the evil against which these laws are purportedly addressed." Shutting down "massage parlors" or "bath houses," for example, may merely serve as a diversionary strategy in the political arena, while diverting enforcement resources from more critical areas. A war on drugs can be seen in the same light. "Our indiscriminate policy of using the criminal law against selling what people insist on buying has spawned large-scale, organized systems, often of national scope, comprising an integration of the stages of production and distribution of the illicit product on a continuous and thoroughly businesslike basis," says Kadish. "Not only are these organizations especially difficult for law enforcement to deal with; they have the unpleasant quality of producing other crimes as well. . . ." Kadish adds: "There is, finally, a cost of inestimable importance, one which tends to be a product of virtually all the misuses of the criminal law discussed in this paper. That is the substantial diversion of police, prosecutorial, and judicial time, personnel, and resources. At a time when the volume of crime is steadily increasing, the burden on law enforcement agencies is becoming more and more onerous. . . ."[91]

While the issues Kadish identifies are significant ones, American legislative history shows that law-making bodies across the country have generally assumed the authority to criminalize any conduct that they thought might be damaging to the health, safety, and morality of the community—sometimes even when such legislative restrictions were obviously in violation of constitutional protections. When a moral perspective becomes widely persuasive, even closely held constitutional principles may be modified. Our nation's experience with constitutional prohibitions on the manufacture, transportation, and sale of alcoholic beverages (alluded to earlier in this chapter) shows, for example, that legislative restrictions on morality are essentially arbitrary and may not always be workable. While one could argue that all laws—even those condemning murder, rape, and other violent crimes—are based on socially shared conceptualizations of morality, the real question that needs to be answered is: "How far into the private lives of citizens may government-sanctioned views of morality properly intrude?"

SUMMARY

- Crimes against public decency and morality constitute a third type of social order offense. The first two types, crimes against public order and safety and crimes against justice and the administration of government, were discussed in Chapter 11.

- Crimes against public decency and morality typically include not only prostitution, drug use, and gambling, but also pornography, obscenity, and various other consensual sex offenses—such as bestiality, homosexuality, sodomy, deviate sexual relations, oral sexual performance, lewdness, indecency, seduction, fornication, adultery, and bigamy.

- Crimes against public decency and morality are sometimes termed "victimless crimes" by virtue of the fact that they generally involve willing participants.

- Pornography is the depiction of sexual behavior in such a way as to excite the viewer sexually. Obscenity, a related term, can be defined as that which appeals to the prurient interest and lacks serious literary, artistic, political, or scientific value. Sex and obscenity are not synonymous, and obscenity is not constitutionally protected under First Amendment free speech guarantees.

- "Obscene matter" means material, taken as a whole, that to the average person, applying contemporary community standards, appeals to the prurient interest, that depicts or describes sexual conduct in a patently offensive way and that lacks serious literary, artistic, political, or scientific value. "Prurient interest" means a morbid interest in sex or an obsession with lascivious and immoral matters.

- An emerging concern in the area of crimes against public decency and morality is the availability of pornography via the Internet, and efforts by lawmakers (especially at the federal level) to restrict access to such materials.

- "Crime against nature" refers to intercourse contrary to the order of nature. It can include homosexual behavior, anal or oral intercourse, bestiality, and even heterosexual intercourse in "positions" other than those that are generally accepted.

- Drug use and abuse and lawfully controlled substances represent an area of special interest to many Americans today. Controlled substances are specifically defined as bioactive or psychoactive chemical substances that come under the purview of the criminal law.

- Under federal law and the laws of many states, controlled substances are classified according to five "schedules." Schedules are an attempt to categorize controlled substances according to their abuse potential.

- Laws regulating public morality have sometimes been criticized as contributing to a "crisis of overcriminalization." Overcriminalization refers to the idea that laws regulating public morality may result in a substantial diversion of police, prosecutorial, and judicial time, personnel, and resources.

QUESTIONS FOR DISCUSSION

1. What are "victimless crimes"? Do you agree that some crimes are truly "victimless"? Why or why not?

2. Should prostitution remain illegal in most jurisdictions? Why or why not?

3. Should homosexual behavior be considered a crime? Give reasons for your answer.

4. Should marijuana use be legalized under certain conditions? If so, what might those conditions be?

5. What is meant by the "crisis of overcriminalization"? Do you agree that such a crisis exists? Why or why not?

LEGAL RESOURCES ON THE WORLD WIDE WEB

A growing number of law journals and abstracting services are now available on the Web or via e-mail subscription. Representatives of such publications are the following:

Alabama Law Review
http://www.law.ua.edu/lawreview
Provides full-text reproductions of its articles via the Internet.

American University International Law Review
http://www.wcl.american.edu/pub/ilr/home.htm
An international law journal produced by law students at American University.

American University Law Review
http://www.wcl.american.edu/pub/journals/lawrev/aulrhome.htm
The oldest and the largest journal at the American University Washington College of Law. The range of articles *The Law Review* publishes is not limited to one particular area of law. Full text of some articles is available.

Cardozo Law Review
http://www.cardozo.yu.edu/cardlrev/index.html
An online version of the Cardozo Law Review, a student-edited publication of the Benjamin N. Cardozo School of Law at Yeshiva University. Full-text articles are provided.

Florida State University Law Review
http://www.law.fsu.edu/journals/lawreview/index.html
Published by the FSU College of Law, the journal provides Adobe PDF versions of its articles online.

Indiana Law Journal
http://www.law.indiana.edu/ilj/ilj.html
Published quarterly by students of the Indiana University School of Law–Bloomington. Full-text articles of selected volumes are available online.

Mercer Law Review
http://review.law.mercer.edu/issueindex.cfm
Published by students at the Walter F. George School of Law of Mercer University (Georgia). The full text of articles from recent issues is available online.

Murdoch University Electronic Journal of Law
http://www.murdoch.edu.au/elaw
An Australian law journal available entirely online.

New England Law Review
http://www.nesl.edu/lawrev/lawrev.htm
Published on the Web by the New England School of Law.

Stanford Law & Policy Review
http://www.stanford.edu/group/SLPR
An academic journal concentrating on issues of law and public policy, published twice a year by the law students of Stanford Law School.

Washington and Lee Law Review
http://www.wlu.edu/~lawrev
Published quarterly by students of the Washington and Lee University School of Law. Full-text articles are available online.

Web Journal of Current Legal Issues
http://www.webjcli.ncl.ac.uk
Published by the University of Newcastle upon Tyne, United Kingdom, in association with Blackstone Press, Ltd.

You can perform a full-text search of law journals on the Internet and of law journal abstracts via the University Law Review Project at http://www.lawreview.org. Visit the Coalition of Online Law Journals at http://www.urich.edu/~jolt/e-journals for information about additional online availability, and remember to check the *Criminal Law Today* Web site for URLs that may have changed.

SUGGESTED READINGS AND CLASSIC WORKS

Freda Adler, *Sisters in Crime: The Rise of the New Female Criminal* (New York: McGraw-Hill, 1975).

Attorney General's Commission on Pornography, *Final Report* (Washington, D.C.: U.S. Government Printing Office, 1986).

David L. Bazelon, The Morality of the Criminal Law, *Southern California Law Review,* Vol. 49 (1976), p. 385.

Edward Donnerstein, "Pornography and Violence Against Women," *Annals of the New York Academy of Sciences,* Vol. 347 (1980), p. 277.

Gilbert Geis, *Not the Law's Business: An Examination of Homosexuality, Abortion, Prostitution, Narcotics, and Gambling in the United States* (New York: Schocken Books, 1979).

Berl Kutchinsky, "The Effects of Easy Availability or Pornography on the Incidence of Sex Crimes," *Journal of Social Issues,* Vol. 29 (1973), p. 95.

Laura Myers, "Incest: No One Wants to Know," *Student Lawyer* (November 1980), p. 30.

Office of National Drug Control Policy, *The National Drug Control Strategy: 1997* (Washington, D.C.: U.S. Government Printing Office, 1997).

Edwin M. Schur and Hugo Adam Bedau, *Victimless Crimes: Two Sides of a Controversy* (Upper Saddle River, NJ: Prentice Hall, 1974).

Alexander T. Shulgin, *Controlled Substances: A Chemical and Legal Guide to the Federal Drugs Laws,* 2nd ed. (Berkeley, CA: Ronin Publishing, 1992).

IS NUDE DANCING A PROTECTED FORM OF FREE SPEECH UNDER THE FIRST AMENDMENT?

CAPSTONE CASE

City of Erie v. *Pap's A.M.*
U.S. Supreme Court, 2000
No. 98-1161 (Decided March 29, 2000)

SYLLABUS
NOTE: Where it is feasible, a syllabus (headnote) will be released, as is being done in connection with this case, at the time the opinion is issued. The syllabus constitutes no part of the opinion of the Court but has been prepared by the Reporter of Decisions for the convenience of the reader.

Erie, Pennsylvania, enacted an ordinance making it a summary offense to knowingly or intentionally appear in public in a "state of nudity." Respondent Pap's A. M. (hereinafter Pap's), a Pennsylvania corporation, operated "Kandyland," an Erie establishment featuring totally nude erotic dancing by women. To comply with

the ordinance, these dancers had to wear, at a minimum, "pasties" and a "G-string." Pap's filed suit against Erie and city officials, seeking declaratory relief and a permanent injunction against the ordinance's enforcement. The Court of Common Pleas struck down the ordinance as unconstitutional, but the Commonwealth Court reversed. The Pennsylvania Supreme Court in turn reversed, finding that the ordinance's public nudity sections violated Pap's right to freedom of expression as protected by the First and Fourteenth Amendments. The Pennsylvania court held that nude dancing is expressive conduct entitled to some quantum of protection under the First Amendment, a view that the court noted was endorsed by eight Members of this Court in *Barnes* v. *Glen Theatre, Inc.*, 501 U.S. 560. The Pennsylvania court explained that, although one stated purpose of the ordinance was to combat negative secondary effects, there was also an unmentioned purpose to "impact negatively on the erotic message of the dance." Accordingly, the Pennsylvania court concluded that the ordinance was related to the suppression of expression. Because the ordinance was not content neutral, it was subject to strict scrutiny. The court held that the ordinance failed the narrow tailoring requirement of strict scrutiny. After this Court granted *certiorari*, Pap's filed a motion to dismiss the case as moot, noting that Kandyland no longer operated as a nude dancing club, and that Pap's did not operate such a club at any other location. This Court denied the motion.

Held: The judgment is reversed, and the case is remanded.

533 Pa. 348, 719 A.2d 273, reversed and remanded.

Justice O'Connor, delivered the opinion of the Court with respect to Parts I and II, concluding that the case is not moot. A case is moot when the issues presented are no longer "live" or the parties lack a legally cognizable interest in the outcome. *County of Los Angeles* v. *Davis*, 440 U.S. 625, 631. Simply closing Kandyland is not sufficient to moot the case because Pap's is still incorporated under Pennsylvania law, and could again decide to operate a nude dancing establishment in Erie. Moreover, Pap's failed, despite its obligation to the Court, to mention the potential mootness issue in its brief in opposition, which was filed after Kandyland was closed and the property sold. See *Board of License Comm'rs of Tiverton* v. *Pastore*, 469 U.S. 238, 240. In any event, this is not a run of the mill voluntary cessation case. Here it is the plaintiff who, having prevailed below, seeks to have the case declared moot. And it is the defendant city that seeks to invoke the federal judicial power to obtain this Court's review of the decision. Cf. *ASARCO Inc.* v. *Kadish*, 490 U.S. 605, 617–618. The city has an ongoing injury because it is barred from enforcing the ordinance's public nudity provisions. If the ordinance is found constitutional, then Erie can enforce it, and the availability of such relief is sufficient to prevent the case from being moot. See *Church of Scientology of Cal.* v. *United States*, 506 U.S. 9, 13. And Pap's still has a concrete stake in the case's outcome because, to the extent it has an interest in resuming operations, it has an interest in preserving the judgment below. This Court's interest in preventing litigants from attempting to manipulate its jurisdiction to insulate a favorable decision from review further counsels against a finding of mootness. See, e.g., *United States* v. *W. T. Grant Co.*, 345 U.S. 629, 632. Pp. 5–7.

Justice O'Connor, joined by the Chief Justice, Justice Kennedy, and Justice Breyer, concluded in Parts III and IV that:

1. Government restrictions on public nudity such as Erie's ordinance should be evaluated under the framework set forth in *United States* v. *O'Brien*, 391 U.S. 367, for content-neutral restrictions on symbolic speech. Although being "in a state of nudity" is not an inherently expressive condition, nude dancing of the type at issue here is expressive conduct that falls within the outer ambit of the First Amend-

ment's protection. See, e.g., *Barnes, supra,* at 565–566 (plurality opinion). What level of scrutiny applies is determined by whether the ordinance is related to the suppression of expression. E.g., *Texas* v. *Johnson,* 491 U.S. 397, 403. If the governmental purpose in enacting the ordinance is unrelated to such suppression, the ordinance need only satisfy the "less stringent," intermediate *O'Brien* standard, e.g., *Johnson, supra,* at 403. If the governmental interest is related to the expression's content, however, the ordinance falls outside *O'Brien* and must be justified under the more demanding, strict scrutiny standard. *Johnson, supra,* at 403. An almost identical public nudity ban was held not to violate the First Amendment in *Barnes,* although no five Members of the Court agreed on a single rationale for that conclusion. The ordinance here, like the statute in *Barnes,* is on its face a general prohibition on public nudity. By its terms, it regulates conduct alone. It does not target nudity that contains an erotic message; rather, it bans all public nudity, regardless of whether that nudity is accompanied by expressive activity. Although Pap's contends that the ordinance is related to the suppression of expression because its preamble suggests that its actual purpose is to prohibit erotic dancing of the type performed at Kandyland, that is not how the Pennsylvania Supreme Court interpreted that language. Rather, the Pennsylvania Supreme Court construed the preamble to mean that one purpose of the ordinance was to combat negative secondary effects. That is, the ordinance is aimed at combating crime and other negative secondary effects caused by the presence of adult entertainment establishments like Kandyland and not at suppressing the erotic message conveyed by this type of nude dancing. See 391 U.S., at 382; see also *Boos* v. *Barry,* 485 U.S. 312, 321. The Pennsylvania Supreme Court's ultimate conclusion that the ordinance was nevertheless content based relied on Justice White's position in dissent in *Barnes* that a ban of this type *necessarily* has the purpose of suppressing the erotic message of the dance. That view was rejected by a majority of the Court in *Barnes,* and is here rejected again. Pap's argument that the ordinance is "aimed" at suppressing expression through a ban on nude dancing is really an argument that Erie also had an illicit motive in enacting the ordinance. However, this Court will not strike down an otherwise constitutional statute on the basis of an alleged illicit motive. *O'Brien, supra,* 391 U.S., at 382–383. Even if Erie's public nudity ban has some minimal effect on the erotic message by muting that portion of the expression that occurs when the last stitch is dropped, the dancers at Kandyland and other such establishments are free to perform wearing pasties and G-strings. Any effect on the overall expression is therefore *de minimis.* If States are to be able to regulate secondary effects, then such *de minimis* intrusions on expression cannot be sufficient to render the ordinance content based. See, e.g., *Clark* v. *Community for Creative Non-Violence,* 468 U.S. 288, 299. Thus, Erie's ordinance is valid if it satisfies the *O'Brien* test. Pp. 7–15.

2. Erie's ordinance satisfies *O'Brien*'s four-factor test. First, the ordinance is within Erie's constitutional power to enact because the city's efforts to protect public health and safety are clearly within its police powers. Second, the ordinance furthers the important government interests of regulating conduct through a public nudity ban and of combating the harmful secondary effects associated with nude dancing. In terms of demonstrating that such secondary effects pose a threat, the city need not conduct new studies or produce evidence independent of that already generated by other cities, so long as the evidence relied on is reasonably believed to be relevant to the problem addressed. *Renton* v. *Playtime Theatres, Inc.,* 475 U.S. 41, 51–52. Erie could reasonably rely on the evidentiary foundation set forth in *Renton* and *Young* v. *American Mini Theatres, Inc.,* 427 U.S. 50, to the effect that secondary effects are caused by the presence of even one adult entertainment establishment in a given neighborhood. See *Renton, supra,* at 51–52. In fact, Erie expressly relied on *Barnes* and its discussion of secondary effects, including its reference to *Renton* and *American Mini Theatres.* The evidentiary standard described in *Renton* controls here, and

Erie meets that standard. In any event, the ordinance's preamble also relies on the city council's express findings that "certain lewd, immoral activities carried on in public places for profit are highly detrimental to the public health, safety and welfare. . . ." The council members, familiar with commercial downtown Erie, are the individuals who would likely have had first-hand knowledge of what took place at and around nude dancing establishments there, and can make particularized, expert judgments about the resulting harmful secondary effects. Cf., e.g., *FCC* v. *National Citizens Comm. For Broadcasting*, 436 U.S. 775. The fact that this sort of leeway is appropriate in this case, which involves a content-neutral restriction that regulates conduct, says nothing whatsoever about its appropriateness in a case involving actual regulation of First Amendment expression. Also, although requiring dancers to wear pasties and G-strings may not greatly reduce these secondary effects, *O'Brien* requires only that the regulation further the interest in combating such effects. The ordinance also satisfies *O'Brien's* third factor, that the government interest is unrelated to the suppression of free expression, as discussed *supra*. The fourth *O'Brien* factor—that the restriction is no greater than is essential to the furtherance of the government interest—is satisfied as well. The ordinance regulates conduct, and any incidental impact on the expressive element of nude dancing is *de minimis*. The pasties and G-string requirement is a minimal restriction in furtherance of the asserted government interests, and the restriction leaves ample capacity to convey the dancer's erotic message. See, e.g., *Barnes, supra*, at 572. Pp. 15–21.

Justice Scalia, joined by Justice Thomas, agreed that the Pennsylvania Supreme Court's decision must be reversed, but disagreed with the mode of analysis that should be applied. Erie self-consciously modeled its ordinance on the public nudity statute upheld in *Barnes* v. *Glen Theatre, Inc.*, 501 U.S. 560, calculating (one would have supposed reasonably) that the Pennsylvania courts would consider themselves bound by this Court's judgment on a question of federal constitutional law. That statute was constitutional not because it survived some lower level of First Amendment scrutiny, but because, as a general law regulating conduct and not specifically directed at expression, it was not subject to First Amendment scrutiny at all. *Id.*, at 572 (Scalia, J., concurring in judgment). Erie's ordinance, too, by its terms prohibits not merely nude dancing, but the act—irrespective of whether it is engaged in for expressive purposes—of going nude in public. The facts that the preamble explains the ordinance's purpose, in part, as limiting a recent increase in nude live entertainment, that city council members in supporting the ordinance commented to that effect, and that the ordinance includes in the definition of nudity the exposure of devices simulating that condition, neither make the law any less general in its reach nor demonstrate that what the municipal authorities *really* find objectionable is expression rather than public nakedness. That the city made no effort to enforce the ordinance against a production of *Equus* involving nudity that was being staged in Erie at the time the ordinance became effective does not render the ordinance discriminatory on its face. The assertion of the city's counsel in the trial court that the ordinance would not cover theatrical productions to the extent their expressive activity rose to a higher level of protected expression simply meant that the ordinance would not be enforceable against such productions if the Constitution forbade it. That limitation does not cause the ordinance to be not generally applicable, in the relevant sense of being *targeted* against expressive conduct. Moreover, even if it could be concluded that Erie specifically singled out the activity of nude dancing, the ordinance still would not violate the First Amendment unless it could be proved (as on this record it could not) that it was the communicative character of nude dancing that prompted the ban. See *id.*, at 577. There is no need to identify "secondary effects" associated with nude dancing that Erie could properly seek to eliminate. The traditional power of government to foster good morals, and the acceptability of the traditional judgment that nude public dancing *itself* is immoral, have not been repealed by the First Amendment. Pp. 6–10.

WHAT DO *YOU* THINK?
1. While the complete logic of the Pennsylvania Supreme Court is not provided in this summary opinion, why do you think that court found nude dancing to be a protected form of expression? On what basis might such an argument be made?
2. Did the U.S. Supreme Court contradict the Pennsylvania Supreme Court's finding relative to the nature of nude dancing as expressive conduct? If not, then how did the U.S. Supreme Court reach a conclusion that was different from that of Pennsylvania's high court?

DOES THE U.S. CONSTITUTION CONFER A FUNDAMENTAL RIGHT ON HOMOSEXUALS TO ENGAGE IN SODOMY?

CAPSTONE CASE

Bowers v. *Hardwick*
U.S. Supreme Court, 1986
478 U.S. 186

In August, 1982, respondent Hardwick (hereafter respondent) was charged with violating the Georgia statute criminalizing sodomy by committing that act with another adult male in the bedroom of respondent's home. After a preliminary hearing, the District Attorney decided not to present the matter to the grand jury unless further evidence developed.

Respondent then brought suit in the Federal District Court, challenging the constitutionality of the statute insofar as it criminalized consensual sodomy. He asserted that he was a practicing homosexual, that the Georgia sodomy statute, as administered by the defendants, placed him in imminent danger of arrest, and that the statute for several reasons violates the Federal Constitution. The District Court granted the defendants' motion to dismiss for failure to state a claim, relying on *Doe* v. *Commonwealth's Attorney for the City of Richmond*, 403 F. Supp. 1199 (ED Va. 1975), which this Court summarily affirmed, 425 U.S. 901 (1976).

A divided panel of the Court of Appeals for the Eleventh Circuit reversed. 760 F.2d 1202 (1985). The court first held that, because *Doe* was distinguishable and, in any event, had been undermined by later decisions, our summary affirmance in that case did not require affirmance of the District Court. Relying on our decisions in *Griswold* v. *Connecticut*, 381 U.S. 479 (1965); *Eisenstadt* v. *Baird*, 405 U.S. 438 (1972); *Stanley* v. *Georgia*, 394 U.S. 557 (1969); and *Roe* v. *Wade*, 410 U.S. 113 (1973), the court went on to hold that the Georgia statute violated respondent's fundamental rights because his homosexual activity is a private and intimate association that is beyond the reach of state regulation by reason of the Ninth Amendment and the Due Process Clause of the Fourteenth Amendment. The case was remanded for trial, at which, to prevail, the State would have to prove that the statute is supported by a compelling interest and is the most narrowly drawn means of achieving that end.

Because other Courts of Appeals have arrived at judgments contrary to that of the Eleventh Circuit in this case, we granted the Attorney General's petition for *certiorari* questioning the holding that the sodomy statute violates the fundamental rights of homosexuals. We agree with petitioner that the Court of Appeals erred, and hence reverse its judgment.

This case does not require a judgment on whether laws against sodomy between consenting adults in general, or between homosexuals in particular, are wise or desirable. It raises no question about the right or propriety of state legislative decisions

to repeal their laws that criminalize homosexual sodomy, or of state court decisions invalidating those laws on state constitutional grounds. The issue presented is whether the Federal Constitution confers a fundamental right upon homosexuals to engage in sodomy, and hence invalidates the laws of the many States that still make such conduct illegal, and have done so for a very long time. The case also calls for some judgment about the limits of the Court's role in carrying out its constitutional mandate.

We first register our disagreement with the Court of Appeals and with respondent that the Court's prior cases have construed the Constitution to confer a right of privacy that extends to homosexual sodomy and, for all intents and purposes, have decided this case. The reach of this line of cases was sketched in *Carey* v. *Population Services International*, 431 U.S. 678, 685 (1977), *Pierce* v. *Society of Sisters*, 268 U.S. 510 (1925), and *Meyer* v. *Nebraska*, 262 U.S. 390 (1923), were described as dealing with childrearing and education; *Prince* v. *Massachusetts*, 321 U.S. 158 (1944), with family relationships; *Skinner* v. *Oklahoma ex rel. Williamson*, 316 U.S. 535 (1942), with procreation; *Loving* v. *Virginia*, 388 U.S. 1 (1967), with marriage; *Griswold* v. *Connecticut, supra*, and *Eisenstadt* v. *Baird, supra*, with contraception; and *Roe* v. *Wade*, 410 U.S. 113 (1973), with abortion. The latter three cases were interpreted as construing the Due Process Clause of the Fourteenth Amendment to confer a fundamental individual right to decide whether or not to beget or bear a child. *Carey* v. *Population Services International, supra*, at 688–689.

Accepting the decisions in these cases and the above description of them, we think it evident that none of the rights announced in those cases bears any resemblance to the claimed constitutional right of homosexuals to engage in acts of sodomy that is asserted in this case. No connection between family, marriage, or procreation, on the one hand, and homosexual activity, on the other, has been demonstrated, either by the Court of Appeals or by respondent. Moreover, any claim that these cases nevertheless stand for the proposition that any kind of private sexual conduct between consenting adults is constitutionally insulated from state proscription is unsupportable. Indeed, the Court's opinion in *Carey* twice asserted that the privacy right, which the *Griswold* line of cases found to be one of the protections provided by the Due Process Clause, did not reach so far. 431 U.S. at 688, n. 5, 694, n. 17.

Precedent aside, however, respondent would have us announce, as the Court of Appeals did, a fundamental right to engage in homosexual sodomy. This we are quite unwilling to do. It is true that, despite the language of the Due Process Clauses of the Fifth and Fourteenth Amendments, which appears to focus only on the processes by which life, liberty, or property are taken, the cases are legion in which those Clauses have been interpreted to have substantive content, subsuming rights that to a great extent are immune from federal or state regulation or proscription. Among such cases are those recognizing rights that have little or no textual support in the constitutional language. *Meyer, Prince,* and *Pierce* fall in this category, as do the privacy cases from *Griswold* to *Carey*.

Striving to assure itself and the public that announcing rights not readily identifiable in the Constitution's text involves much more than the imposition of the Justices' own choice of values on the States and the Federal Government, the Court has sought to identify the nature of the rights qualifying for heightened judicial protection. In *Palko* v. *Connecticut*, 302 U.S. 319, 325, 326 (1937), it was said that this category includes those fundamental liberties that are "implicit in the concept of ordered liberty," such that "neither liberty nor justice would exist if [they] were sacrificed." A different description of fundamental liberties appeared in *Moore* v. *East Cleveland*, 431 U.S. 494, 503 (1977) (opinion of POWELL, J.), where they are characterized as those liberties that are "deeply rooted in this Nation's history and tradition." *Id.* at 503 (POWELL, J.). See also *Griswold* v. *Connecticut*, 381 U.S. at 506.

It is obvious to us that neither of these formulations would extend a fundamental right to homosexuals to engage in acts of consensual sodomy. Proscriptions against that conduct have ancient roots. See generally Survey on the Constitutional Right to Privacy in the Context of Homosexual Activity, 40 U. Miami L. Rev. 521, 525 (1986). Sodomy was a criminal offense at common law, and was forbidden by the laws of the original 13 States when they ratified the Bill of Rights. In 1868, when the Fourteenth Amendment was ratified, all but 5 of the 37 States in the Union had criminal sodomy laws. In fact, until 1961, all 50 States outlawed sodomy, and today, 24 States and the District of Columbia continue to provide criminal penalties for sodomy performed in private and between consenting adults. See Survey, U. Miami L. Rev. *supra,* at 524, n. 9. Against this background, to claim that a right to engage in such conduct is "deeply rooted in this Nation's history and tradition" or "implicit in the concept of ordered liberty" is, at best, facetious.

Nor are we inclined to take a more expansive view of our authority to discover new fundamental rights imbedded in the Due Process Clause. The Court is most vulnerable and comes nearest to illegitimacy when it deals with judge-made constitutional law having little or no cognizable roots in the language or design of the Constitution. That this is so was painfully demonstrated by the face-off between the Executive and the Court in the 1930s, which resulted in the repudiation of much of the substantive gloss that the Court had placed on the Due Process Clauses of the Fifth and Fourteenth Amendments. There should be, therefore, great resistance to expand the substantive reach of those Clauses, particularly if it requires redefining the category of rights deemed to be fundamental. Otherwise, the Judiciary necessarily takes to itself further authority to govern the country without express constitutional authority. The claimed right pressed on us today falls far short of overcoming this resistance.

Respondent, however, asserts that the result should be different where the homosexual conduct occurs in the privacy of the home. He relies on *Stanley v. Georgia,* 394 U.S. 557 (1969), where the Court held that the First Amendment prevents conviction for possessing and reading obscene material in the privacy of one's home:

> *If the First Amendment means anything, it means that a State has no business telling a man, sitting alone in his house, what books he may read or what films he may watch. Id.* at 565.

Stanley did protect conduct that would not have been protected outside the home, and it partially prevented the enforcement of state obscenity laws; but the decision was firmly grounded in the First Amendment. The right pressed upon us here has no similar support in the text of the Constitution, and it does not qualify for recognition under the prevailing principles for construing the Fourteenth Amendment. Its limits are also difficult to discern. Plainly enough, otherwise illegal conduct is not always immunized whenever it occurs in the home. Victimless crimes, such as the possession and use of illegal drugs, do not escape the law where they are committed at home. *Stanley* itself recognized that its holding offered no protection for the possession in the home of drugs, firearms, or stolen goods. *Id.* at 568, n. 11. And if respondent's submission is limited to the voluntary sexual conduct between consenting adults, it would be difficult, except by fiat, to limit the claimed right to homosexual conduct while leaving exposed to prosecution adultery, incest, and other sexual crimes even though they are committed in the home. We are unwilling to start down that road.

Even if the conduct at issue here is not a fundamental right, respondent asserts that there must be a rational basis for the law, and that there is none in this case other than the presumed belief of a majority of the electorate in Georgia that homosexual sodomy is immoral and unacceptable. This is said to be an inadequate rationale to support the law. The law, however, is constantly based on notions of morality, and if all laws representing essentially moral choices are to be invalidated under the Due

Process Clause, the courts will be very busy indeed. Even respondent makes no such claim, but insists that majority sentiments about the morality of homosexuality should be declared inadequate. We do not agree, and are unpersuaded that the sodomy laws of some 25 States should be invalidated on this basis.

Accordingly, the judgment of the Court of Appeals is *Reversed.*

WHAT DO *YOU* THINK?

1. Why did the Court hold that to claim that a right to engage in such conduct is "deeply rooted in this Nation's history and tradition" or "implicit in the concept of ordered liberty" is, at best, facetious? Do you agree? Why or why not?
2. Why didn't the fact that most homosexual conduct occurs within the privacy of the home affect the Court's thinking?

DOES THE GEORGIA STATUTE CRIMINALIZING INTIMATE SEXUAL ACTS PERFORMED BY ADULTS IN PRIVATE AND WITHOUT FORCE IMPERMISSIBLY INFRINGE ON THE RIGHT OF PRIVACY GUARANTEED TO ALL GEORGIA CITIZENS BY THE STATE'S CONSTITUTION?

CAPSTONE CASE

Powell v. *State*
Georgia Supreme Court, 1998
270 Ga. 327, 510 S.E.2d 18

Anthony San Juan Powell was charged in an indictment with rape and aggravated sodomy in connection with sexual conduct involving him and his wife's 17-year-old niece in Powell's apartment. The niece testified that appellant had sexual intercourse with her and engaged in an act of cunnilingus without her consent and against her will. Powell testified and admitted he performed the acts with the consent of the complainant. In light of Powell's testimony, the trial court included in its jury charge instructions on the law of sodomy. The jury acquitted Powell of the rape and aggravated sodomy charges and found him guilty of sodomy, thereby establishing that the State did not prove beyond a reasonable doubt that the act was committed "with force and against the will" of the niece. See OCGA § 16-6-2 (a). Powell brings this appeal contending the statute criminalizing acts of sodomy committed by adults without force in private is an unconstitutional intrusion on the right of privacy guaranteed him by the Georgia Constitution. Powell also contends that the trial court erred when it offered the jury the opportunity to consider the unindicted charge of sodomy by *sua sponte* instructing the jury on the law of sodomy.

1. In keeping with the well-established principle that this Court will not decide a constitutional question if the appeal can be decided upon other grounds (*Bd. of Tax Assessors* v. *Tom's Foods*, 264 Ga. 309, 310 (444 SE2d 771) (1994)), we first address the non-constitutional issues raised by the appeal. The first issue is the sufficiency of the evidence. OCGA § 16-6-2 (a) defines sodomy as the performance of or submission to "any sexual act involving the sex organs of one person and the mouth or anus of another." Appellant's admission at trial that he placed his mouth upon the genitalia of his wife's niece, and the niece's testimony similarly describing appellant's conduct constitute sufficient evidence to authorize a rational trier of fact to conclude beyond a reasonable doubt that appellant committed sodomy. *Jackson* v. *Virginia*, 443 U.S. 307 (99 SC 2781, 61 LE2d 560) (1979); *Carter* v. *State*, 122 Ga. App. 21 (4) (176 SE2d 238) (1970), overruled on other grounds in *Hines* v. *State*, 173 Ga. App. 657 (2) (327 SE2d 786) (1985).

2. Appellant next contends that the trial court erred when, without request by the State or appellant, it instructed the jury on the law of sodomy and permitted the fact-finder to return a verdict on that included charge.

In *Stonaker v. State,* 236 Ga. 1, 2 (222 SE2d 354) (1976), this Court set forth rules "to clarify for the trial courts what must be charged and what may be charged and what need not be charged in the area of lesser included crimes in criminal trials." The second rule stated that the trial court could, "of [its] own volition and in [its] discretion, charge on a lesser crime of that included in the indictment and accusation." *Id.; Rodriguez v. State,* 211 Ga. App. 256 (2) (439 SE2d 510) (1993). Thus, when the evidence authorizes a charge on an offense included in the offense for which the defendant is being tried, the trial court is authorized to instruct the jury on the included offense *sua sponte. Alford v. State,* 200 Ga. App. 483, 484 (408 SE2d 497) (1991). Sodomy is an offense included in the crime of aggravated sodomy (*Stover v. State,* 256 Ga. 515 (2) (350 SE2d 577) (1986)), and the evidence summarized in Division 1 authorized a charge on the law of sodomy as an included offense. Accordingly, the trial court acted within the *Stonaker* framework when it exercised its discretion and instructed the jury on the included offense of sodomy.

3. Lastly, we address appellant's constitutional challenge to OCGA § 16-6-2 (a). In so doing, we are mindful that a solemn act of the General Assembly carries with it a presumption of constitutionality that is overturned only when it is established that the legislation "manifestly infringes upon a constitutional provision or violates the rights of the people . . . [Cit.]" *Miller v. State,* 266 Ga. 850 (2) (472 SE2d 74) (1996). Appellant contends that the statute criminalizing intimate sexual acts performed by adults in private and without force impermissibly infringes upon the right of privacy guaranteed all Georgia citizens by the Georgia Constitution.

The right of privacy has a long and distinguished history in Georgia. In 1905, this Court expressly recognized that Georgia citizens have a "liberty of privacy" guaranteed by the Georgia constitutional provision which declares that no person shall be deprived of liberty except by due process of law. *Pavesich v. New England Life Ins.,* 122 Ga. 190, 197 (50 SE 68) (1905). The *Pavesich* decision constituted the first time any court of last resort in this country recognized the right of privacy (Katz, The History of the Georgia Bill of Rights, 3 GSU L. Rev. 83, 118 (1986); *Gouldman-Taber Pontiac v. Zerbst,* 213 Ga. 682 (100 SE2d 881) (1957)), making this Court a pioneer in the realm of the right of privacy. *Bodrey v. Cape,* 120 Ga. App. 859, 866 (172 SE2d 643) (1969). See also *Cox Broadcasting Corp. v. Cohn,* 231 Ga. 60 (200 SE2d 127) (1973), *rev'd* 420 U.S. 469 (95 SC 1029, 43 LE2d 328) (1975), where this Court proudly noted that the right of privacy "was birthed by this court" in *Pavesich.* By the time the U.S. Supreme Court recognized the existence of a right of privacy in the U.S. Constitution (*Griswold v. Connecticut,* 381 U.S. 479 (85 SC 1678, 14 LE2d 510) (1965)), the Georgia courts had developed a rich appellate jurisprudence in the right of privacy. Today, Georgia recognizes the right of privacy as a fundamental constitutional right, "having a value so essential to individual liberty in our society that [its] infringement merits careful scrutiny by the courts." *Ambles v. State,* 259 Ga. 406 (2b) (383 SE2d 555) (1989).

In *Pavesich,* the Court found the right of privacy to be "ancient law," with "its foundation in the instincts of nature[,]" derived from "the Roman's conception of Justice" and natural law, making it immutable and absolute. *Id.,* at 194. The Court described the liberty interest derived from natural law as "embrac[ing] the right of man to be free in the enjoyment of the faculties with which he has been endowed by his Creator, subject only to such restraints as are necessary for the common good." *Id.,* at 195. "Liberty" includes "the right to live as one will, so long as that will does not interfere with the rights of another or of the public" (*id.,* at 196), and the individual is "entitled to a liberty of choice as to his manner of life, and neither an individual nor the public has the right to arbitrarily take away from him his liberty." *Id.,* at 197.

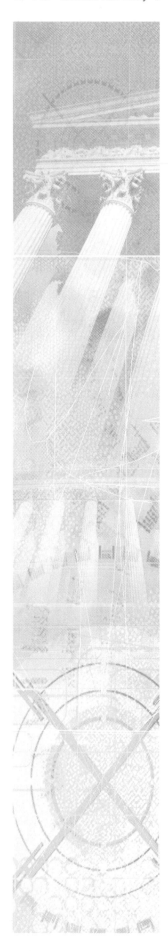

The *Pavesich* Court further recognized that the "right of personal liberty" also embraces "[t]he right to withdraw from the public gaze at such times as a person may see fit, when his presence in public is not demanded by any rule of law. . . ." *Id.* Stated succinctly, the Court ringingly endorsed the "right 'to be let alone' so long as [one] was not interfering with the rights of other individuals or of the public." *Id.*

In the ensuing years since *Pavesich* was decided and Georgia's right of privacy recognized, the Georgia appellate courts have expounded on the right of privacy, describing it as protection for the individual from unnecessary public scrutiny (*Athens Observer* v. *Anderson,* 245 Ga. 63 (263 SE2d 128) (1980)); as the right of the individual "to be free from . . . the publicizing of one's private affairs with which the public has no legitimate concern" (*Gouldman-Taber Pontiac* v. *Zerbst,* supra, 213 Ga. At 683); "the right to define one's circle of intimacy" (*Macon-Bibb County & c. Auth.* v. *Reynolds,* 165 Ga. App. 348, 350 (299 SE2d 594) (1983)); and the right "to be free of unwarranted interference by the public about matters [with] which the public is not necessarily concerned, or to be protected from any wrongful intrusion into an individual's private life which would outrage . . . a person of ordinary sensibilities." *Georgia Power Co.* v. *Busbin,* 149 Ga. App. 274 (6) (254 SE2d 146) (1979). This Court has determined that a citizen's right of privacy is strong enough to withstand a variety of attempts by the State to intrude in the citizen's life. In *Zant* v. *Prevatte,* 248 Ga. 832 (286 SE2d 715) (1982), the Court ruled that the State's assertion of a duty to protect a prisoner's health and its interest in preserving human life did not amount to the compelling state interest which could override a sane state prisoner's refusal to eat or submit to medical treatment for the effects of starvation. In *State of Georgia* v. *McAfee,* 259 Ga. 579 (385 SE2d 651) (1989), the Court again ruled that a citizen's constitutional right of privacy and liberty under which he refused medical treatment was not outweighted by any interest the State might have in the preservation of life. In *Harris* v. *Cox Enterprises,* 256 Ga. 299, 302 (348 SE2d 448) (1986), Georgia's strong public policy in favor of open government was required to bend in favor of the individual's right of privacy when matters about which the public had no legitimate concern were at issue. It is clear from the right of privacy appellate jurisprudence which emanates from *Pavesich* that the "right to be let alone" guaranteed by the Georgia Constitution is far more extensive that the right of privacy protected by the U.S. Constitution, which protects only those matters "deeply rooted in this Nation's history and tradition" or which are "implicit in the concept of ordered liberty. . . ." *Bowers* v. *Hardwick,* 478 U.S. 186, 191–92 (106 SC 2841, 92 LE2d 140) (1986).

While Georgia citizens' right to privacy is far-reaching, that is not to say that the individual's right to privacy is without limitation. The *Pavesich* court recognized that the right could be waived by the individual (122 Ga. At 199); could be subsumed when the individual was required to "perform public duties . . ." (*Id.,* at 196), and had to yield "in some particulars . . . to the right of speech and of the press." *Id.,* at 204. See also *Cox* v. *Brazo,* 165 Ga. App. 888 (303 SE2d 71) (1983) (individual has no right of privacy in information published by another when individual had publicized the information); *Cabaniss* v. *Hipsley,* 114 Ga. App. 367 (151 SE2d 496) (1966) (exotic dancer has no right of privacy in a photo which she had permitted others to use for publicity purposes); *Cummings* v. *Walsh Constr. Co.,* 561 F. Supp 872 (S. D. Ga. 1983) (under Georgia law, a supervisor does not violate a woman's right of privacy by telling co-workers of their affair when the woman had told other co-workers of the relationship). Nor will an individual's right of privacy serve as the basis for liability against one who publishes facts which are a matter of public record (*Reece* v. *Grissom,* 154 Ga. App. 194 (267 SE2d 839) (1980)), or against one who publishes photographs of the subject matter of a public investigation. *Waters* v. *Fleetwood,* 212 Ga. 161 (91 SE2d 344) (1956). See also *Tucker* v. *News Pub. Co.,* 197 Ga. App. 85 (1) (397 SE2d 499) (1990) (publication of information connected with a matter of public interest or a public investigation does not violate the right of privacy). Through the appeals of defendants convicted of sexual assault who have asserted the constitutional right of privacy on appeal, we have ruled that a defendant may not success-fully assert a privacy right when the acts are committed: in a public place (*Stover* v. *State, supra,* 256 Ga. 515 (1)); in exchange for money (*Ray* v. *State,* 259 Ga. 868 (3) (389 SE2d 326) (1990)); or with those legally incapable of consenting to sexual acts. *Id.;* Richardson v. *State,* 256 Ga. 746 (2) (353 SE2d 342) (1987).

Today, we are faced with whether the constitutional right of privacy screens from governmental interference a non-commercial sexual act that occurs without force in a private home between persons legally capable of consenting to the act. While *Pavesich* and its progeny do not set out the full scope of the right of privacy in con-nection with sexual behavior, it is clear that consensual sexual behavior conducted in private between adults is covered by the principles espoused in *Pavesich* since such behavior between adults in private is recognized as a private matter by "[a]ny person whose intellect is in a normal condition. . . ." *Pavesich, supra,* at 194. Adults who "withdraw from the public gaze" (*id.,* at 196) to engage in private consensual sexual behavior are exercising a right "embraced within the right of personal lib-erty." *Id.* We cannot think of any other activity that reasonable persons would rank as more private and more deserving of protection from governmental interference than consensual, private, adult sexual activity. See *Gryczan* v. *State,* 942 P2d 112 (Mont. 1997); *Campbell* v. *Sundquist,* 926 SW2d 250 (Tn. App. 1996); *State* v. *Morales,* 826 SW2d 201 (Tex. App. 1992), *rev'd on other grounds,* 869 SW2d 941 (Tex. 1994). We conclude that such activity is at the heart of the Georgia Constitution's protection of the right of privacy.

Having determined that appellant's behavior falls within the area protected by the right of privacy, we next examine whether the government's infringement upon that right is constitutionally sanctioned. As judicial consideration of the right to pri-vacy has developed, this Court has concluded that the right of privacy is a funda-mental right (*Ambles* v. *State, supra,* 259 Ga. 406 (b)) and that a government-imposed limitation on the right to privacy will pass constitutional muster if the limitation is shown to serve a compelling state interest and to be narrowly tailored to effectuate only that compelling interest. *Phagan* v. *State,* 268 Ga. 272 (1) (486 SE2d 876) (1997); *Zant* v. *Prevatte, supra,* 248 Ga. At 833–34. But see *Christenson* v. *State,* 266 Ga. 474 (2) (a) (468 SE2d 188) (1996), where the Court's plurality opinion employed the "legit-imate state interest" yardstick to measure the State's limitation on the defendant's asserted right of privacy. Implicit in our decisions curtailing the assertion of a right to privacy in sexual assault cases involving sexual activity taking place in public, performed with those legally incapable of giving consent, performed in exchange for money, or performed with force and against the will of a participant, is the de-termination that the State has a role in shielding the public from inadvertent expo-sure to the intimacies of others, in protecting minors and others legally incapable of consent from sexual abuse, and in preventing people from being forced to submit to sex acts against their will. The State fulfills its role in preventing sexual assaults and shielding and protecting the public from sexual acts by the enactment of crim-inal statutes prohibiting such conduct: OCGA § 16-6-1 (rape); § 16-6-2(a) (aggra-vated sodomy); § 16-6-3 (statutory rape); § 16-6-4 (child molestation and aggravated child molestation); § 16-6-5 (enticing a child for immoral purposes); § 16-6-5.1 (sex-ual assault of prisoners, the institutionalized, and the patients of psychotherapists); § 16-6-6 (bestiality); § 16-6-7 (sexual assault of a dead human being); § 16-6-8 (pub-lic indecency); §§ 16-6-9-12 (prostitution, pimping, pandering); and § 16-6-15 (solic-itation of sodomy), § 16-6-16 (masturbation for hire), and by the vigorous enforce-ment of those laws through the arrest and prosecution of offenders. In light of the existence of these statutes, the sodomy statute's *raison d'etre* can only be to regulate the private sexual conduct of consenting adults, something which Georgians' right of privacy puts beyond the bounds of government regulation.

Citing *Christensen, supra,* 266 Ga. 474, the State reminds us that the plurality de-cision therein held that the proscription against sodomy was a valid exercise of the

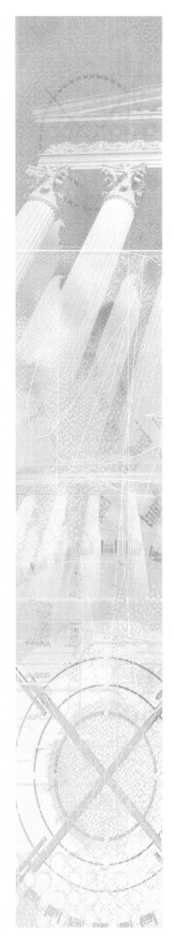

State's police power in furtherance of the public's moral welfare, and that the Georgia Constitution did not deny the General Assembly the right to prohibit such conduct. "Police power" is the governing authority's ability to legislate for the protection of the citizens' lives, health, and property, and to preserve good order and public morals. *Hayes v. Howell,* 251 Ga. 580 (2b) (308 SE2d 170) (1983); *Ward v. State,* 188 Ga. App. 373 (1) (373 SE2d 65) (1988). "To justify the State in thus interposing its authority in behalf of the public, it must appear, first that the interests of the public generally . . . require such interference; and second, that the means are reasonably necessary for the accomplishment of the purpose, and not unduly oppressive upon individuals." *Lawton v. Steele,* 152 U.S. 133, 137 (14 SC 499, 38 LE 385) (1984). Stated another way, the legislation must serve a public purpose and the means adopted to achieve the purpose must be reasonably necessary for the accomplishment of the purpose and not unduly oppressive upon the persons regulated. *Cannon v. Coweta County,* 260 Ga. 56 (2) (389 SE2d 329) (1990). In recent years, legislative bodies in Georgia have exercised the "police power" to combat the negative effects of the combination of alcohol and nude dancing (*Goldrush v. City of Marietta,* 267 Ga. 683 (482 SE2d 347) (1997)); to limit land usage through zoning restrictions (*Cannon v. Coweta County, supra,* 260 Ga. 56); to regulate the health professions (*Foster v. Ga. Bd. of Chiropractic Exam.,* 257 Ga. 409 (14) (359 SE2d 877) (1987); and to impose reasonable regulations on the establishment and operation of cemeteries. *Arlington Cem. v. Bindig,* 212 Ga. 698 (2) (95 SE2d 378) (1956). That the legislative body has determined that it is properly exercising its police powers "is not final or conclusive, but is subject to the supervision of the courts." *Lawton v. Steele, supra,* 152 U.S. at 137. Thus, the suggestion that OCGA § 16-6-2 is a valid exercise of the police power requires us to consider whether it benefits the public generally without unduly oppressing the individual. Since, as determined earlier, the only possible purpose for the statute is to regulate the private conduct of consenting adults, the public gains no benefit, and the individual is unduly oppressed by the invasion of the right to privacy. Consequently, we must conclude that the legislation exceeds the permissible bounds of the police power. See *Commonwealth v. Bonadio,* 415 A2d 47, 49–50 (Pa. 1980).

The State also maintains that the furtherance of "social morality," giving "due regard to the collective will of the citizens of Georgia," is a constitutional basis for legislative control of the non-commercial, unforced, private sexual activity of those legally capable of consenting to such activity. It is well within the power of the legislative branch to establish public policy through legislative enactment. It is also without dispute that oftentimes the public policy so established and the laws so enacted reflect the will of the majority of Georgians as well as the majority's notion of morality. However, "it does not follow . . . that simply because the legislature has enacted as law what may be a moral choice of the majority, the courts are, thereafter, bound to simply acquiesce." *Gryczan v. State, supra,* 942 P2d at 125 (where the Supreme Court of Montana ruled that private consensual, noncommercial sexual conduct is protected by Montana's constitutional right of individual privacy). "Social morality legislation," like any legislative enactment, is subject to the scrutiny of the judicial branch under our tripartite system of "checks and balances." See *Cantrell v. State of Ga.,* 129 Ga. App. 465 (200 SE2d 163) (1973).

In undertaking the judiciary's constitutional duty, it is not the prerogative of members of the judiciary to base decisions on their personal notions of morality. Indeed, if we were called upon to pass upon the propriety of the conduct herein involved, we would not condone it. Rather, the judiciary is charged with the task of examining a legislative enactment when it is alleged to impinge upon the freedoms and guarantees contained in the Georgia Bill of Rights and the U.S. Constitution, and scrutinizing the law, the interests it promotes, and the means by which it seeks to achieve those interests, to ensure that the law meets constitutional standards. While many believe that acts of sodomy, even those involving consenting adults, are morally reprehensible, this repugnance alone does not create a compelling justification for state regulation of the activity. *Post v. State,* 715 P2d 1105, 1109 (Okla. Cr. App.), *cert. denied* 479 U.S. 890 (107 SC 290, 93 LE2d 264) (1986) (where the Oklahoma appellate court held that a statute violated the federal right of privacy when applied to "non-violent consensual activity between adults in private.") See also *Campbell v. Sundquist, supra,* 926 SW2d at 266; *Commonwealth v. Wasson, supra,* 842 SW2d at 498; *Commonwealth v. Bonadio, supra,* 415 A2d at 50 (where appellate courts in Tennessee, Kentucky, and Pennsylvania concluded that "no sufficient state interest justifies legislation of norms simply because a particular belief is followed by a number of people, or even a majority.") We agree with our fellow jurists that legislative enactments setting "social morality" are not exempt from judicial review testing their constitutional mettle.

We conclude that OCGA § 16-6-2, insofar as it criminalizes the performance of private, non-commercial acts of sexual intimacy between persons legally able to consent, "manifestly infringes upon a constitutional provision" (*Miller v. State, supra,* 266 Ga. 850 (2)) which guarantees to the citizens of Georgia the right of privacy. Appellant was convicted for performing an unforced act of sexual intimacy with one legally capable of consenting thereto in the privacy of his home. Accordingly, appellant's conviction for such behavior must be reversed.

Judgment reversed. All the Justices concur, except Carley, J., who Dissents.

WHAT DO *YOU* THINK?

1. The Georgia court says that the understanding of privacy inherent in natural law means "embracing the right of man to be free in the enjoyment of the faculties with which he has been endowed by his Creator, subject only to such restraints as are necessary for the common good." How does this notion relate to natural law understandings of personal "liberty" as expressed in this opinion?
2. Do you agree with the court's observation that "While many believe that acts of sodomy, even those involving consenting adults, are morally reprehensible, this repugnance alone does not create a compelling justification for state regulation of the activity"? Why or why not?
3. What does the court mean when it says: "While Georgia citizens' right to privacy is far-reaching, that is not to say that the individual's right to privacy is without limitation"? What might those limitations be?

DOES THE SENDING OF OBSCENE MATERIAL OVER THE INTERNET CONSTITUTE THE TRANSPORTATION OF OBSCENE MATERIAL IN INTERSTATE COMMERCE?

CAPSTONE CASE

United States v. *Thomas*
U.S. Sixth Circuit Court of Appeals, 1996
74 F.3d 701

Defendants Robert and Carleen Thomas appeal their convictions and sentences for violating 18 U.S.C. 1462 and 1465, federal obscenity laws, in connection with their operation of an electronic bulletin board. For the following reasons, we AFFIRM Robert and Carleen Thomas' convictions and sentences.

Robert Thomas and his wife Carleen Thomas began operating the Amateur Action Computer Bulletin Board System ("AABBS") from their home in Milpitas, California, in February 1991. The AABBS was a computer bulletin board system that operated by using telephones, modems, and personal computers. Its features included e-mail, chat lines, public messages, and files that members could access, transfer, and download to their own computers and printers. Information loaded

onto the bulletin board was first converted into binary code, i.e., 0's and 1's, through the use of a scanning device. After purchasing sexually explicit magazines from public adult book stores in California, Defendant Robert Thomas used an electronic device called a scanner to convert pictures from the magazines into computer files called Graphic Interchange Format files or "GIF" files. The AABBS contained approximately 14,000 GIF files. Mr. Thomas also purchased, sold, and delivered sexually explicit videotapes to AABBS members. Customers ordered the tapes by sending Robert Thomas an e-mail message, and Thomas typically delivered them by use of the United Parcel Service ("U.P.S.").

Persons calling the AABBS without a password could view the introductory screens of the system, which contained brief, sexually explicit descriptions of the GIF files and adult videotapes that were offered for sale. Access to the GIF files, however, was limited to members who were given a password after they paid a membership fee and submitted a signed application form that Defendant Robert Thomas reviewed. The application form requested the applicant's age, address, and telephone number and required a signature.

Members accessed the GIF files by using a telephone, modem, and personal computer. A modem located in the Defendants' home answered the calls. After they established membership by typing in a password, members could then select, retrieve, and instantly transport GIF files to their own computer. A caller could then view the GIF file on his computer screen and print the image out using his printer. The GIF files contained the AABBS name and access telephone number; many also had "Distribute Freely" printed on the image itself.

In July 1993, a United States Postal Inspector, Agent David Dirmeyer ("Dirmeyer"), received a complaint regarding the AABBS from an individual who resided in the Western District of Tennessee. Dirmeyer dialed the AABBS telephone number. As a nonmember, he viewed a screen that read "Welcome to AABBS, the Nastiest Place On Earth" and was able to select various "menus" and read graphic descriptions of the GIF files and videotapes that were offered for sale.

Subsequently, Dirmeyer used an assumed name and sent in fifty-five dollars along with an executed application form to the AABBS. Defendant Robert Thomas called Dirmeyer at his undercover telephone number in Memphis, Tennessee, acknowledged receipt of his application, and authorized him to log-on with his personal password. Thereafter, Dirmeyer dialed the AABBS telephone number, logged-on, and using his computer/modem in Memphis, downloaded the GIF files listed in counts 2–7 of the Defendants' indictments. These GIF files depicted images of bestiality, oral sex, incest, sadomasochistic abuse, and sex scenes involving urination. Dirmeyer also ordered six sexually explicit videotapes from the AABBS and received them via U.P.S. at a Memphis, Tennessee, address. Dirmeyer also had several e-mail and chat-mode conversations with Defendant Robert Thomas.

On January 10, 1994, a search warrant was issued by a U.S. Magistrate Judge for the Northern District of California. The AABBS location was subsequently searched, and the Defendants' computer system was seized. On January 25, 1994, a federal grand jury for the Western District of Tennessee returned a twelve-count indictment charging Defendants Robert and Carleen Thomas with the following criminal violations: one count under 18 U.S.C. 1662 for conspiracy to violate federal obscenity laws—18 U.S.C. 1465, 1465 (count 1); six counts under 18 U.S.C. 1465 for knowingly using and causing to be used a facility and means of interstate commerce—a combined computer/telephone system—for the purpose of transporting obscene, computer-generated materials (the GIF files) in interstate commerce (counts 2-7); three counts under 18 U.S.C. 1462 for shipping obscene videotapes via U.P.S. (counts 8-10); one count of causing the transportation of materials depicting minors engaged in sexually explicit conduct in violation of 18 U.S.C. 2252(a)(1) as to Mr. Thomas only (count 11); and one count of forfeiture under 18 U.S.C. 1467 (count 12).

Both Defendants were represented by the same retained counsel, Mr. Richard Williams of San Jose, California. They appeared twice in federal district court for the Northern District of California, San Jose division, before being arraigned on March 15, 1994, in federal court in Memphis, Tennessee. They did not retain local counsel for the Tennessee criminal prosecution. Both Defendants were tried by a jury in July, 1994. Defendant Robert Thomas was found guilty on all counts except count 11 (child pornography). Defendant Carleen Thomas was found guilty on counts 1-10. The jury also found that the Defendants' interest in their computer system should be forfeited to the United States. Robert and Carleen Thomas were sentenced on December 2, 1994, to 37 and 30 months of incarceration, respectively. They filed their notices of appeal on December 9, 1994.

Defendants contend that their conduct, as charged in counts 1-7 of their indictments, does not constitute a violation of 18 U.S.C. 1465. This presents a question of statutory interpretation, a matter of law, and is reviewed by this court under a *de novo* [new] standard. *United States* v. *Hans*, 921 F.2d 81, 82 (6th Cir. 1990).

Defendants' challenge to their convictions under counts 1–7 rests on two basic premises: (1) Section 1465 does not apply to intangible objects like the computer GIF files at issue here.

> *Whoever knowingly transports in interstate or foreign commerce for the purpose of sale or distribution, or knowingly travels in interstate commerce, or uses a facility or means of interstate commerce for the purpose of transporting obscene material in interstate or foreign commerce, any obscene, lewd, lascivious, or filthy book, pamphlet, picture, film, paper, letter, writing, print, silhouette, drawing, figure, image, cast, phonograph recording, electrical transcription or other article capable of producing sound or any other matter of indecent or immoral character, shall be fined under this title or imprisoned not more than five years, or both.*
>
> *The transportation as aforesaid of two or more copies of any publication or two or more of any article of the character described above, or a combined total of five such publications and articles, shall create a presumption that such publications or articles are intended for sale or distribution, but such presumption is rebuttable. 42 U.S.C. 1465.*

[A]nd (2) Congress did not intend to regulate computer transmissions such as those involved here because 18 U.S.C. 1465 does not expressly prohibit such conduct.

In support of their first premise, Defendants cite a Tenth Circuit dial-a-porn decision which holds that 18 U.S.C. 1462 and 1465 prohibit the interstate transportation of tangible objects; not intangible articles like pre-recorded telephone messages. See *United States* v. *Carlin Commun., Inc.*, 815 F.2d 1367, 1371 (10th Cir. 1987). Defendants claim *Carlin* is controlling because transmission of the GIF files at issue under counts 1–7 involved an intangible string of 0's and 1's which became viewable images only after they were decoded by an AABBS member's computer. We disagree.

The subject matter in Carlin—telephonic communication of pre-recorded sexually suggestive comments or proposals—is inherently different from the obscene computer-generated materials that were electronically transmitted from California to Tennessee in this case. Defendants erroneously conclude that the GIF files are intangible, and thus outside the scope of Section 1465, by focusing solely on the manner and form in which the computer-generated images are transmitted from one destination to another. *United States* v. *Gilboe*, 684 F.2d 235 (2nd Cir. 1982), *cert. denied*, 459 U.S. 1201 (1983), illustrates this point.

In *Gilboe*, the Second Circuit rejected the argument that the defendant's transmission of electronic impulses could not be prosecuted under a criminal statute prohibiting the transportation of money obtained by fraud. The *Gilboe* court reasoned

that: [e]lectronic signals in this context are the means by which funds are transported. The beginning of the transaction is money in one account and the ending is money in another. The manner in which the funds were moved does not affect the ability to obtain tangible paper dollars or a bank check from the receiving account. The same rationale applies here. Defendants focus on the means by which the GIF files were transferred rather than the fact that the transmissions began with computer-generated images in California and ended with the same computer-generated images in Tennessee. The manner in which the images moved does not affect their ability to be viewed on a computer screen in Tennessee or their ability to be printed out in hard copy in that distant location.

The record does not support Defendants' argument that they had no knowledge, intent, or expectation that members of their AABBS would download and print the images contained in their GIF files. They ran a business that advertised and promised its members the availability and transportation of the sexually explicit GIF files they selected. In light of the overwhelming evidence produced at trial, it is spurious for Defendants to claim now that they did not intend to sell, disseminate, or share the obscene GIF files they advertised on the AABBS with members outside their home and in other states.

We also disagree with Defendants' corollary position, raised at oral argument, that they were prosecuted under the wrong statute and that their conduct, if criminal at all, falls within the prohibitions under 47 U.S.C. 223(b) (1) "Whoever knowingly within the United States, by means of telephone, (A) makes (directly or by recording device) any obscene communication for commercial purposes to any person, regardless of whether the maker of such communication placed the call; or (B) permits any telephone facility under such person's control to be used for an activity prohibited by subparagraph (A), shall be fined in accordance with Title 18, or imprisoned not more than two years, or both," rather than 18 U.S.C. 1465. As recognized by the Supreme Court, Section 223(b) of the Communications Act of 1934, was drafted and enacted by Congress in 1982 "explicitly to address 'dial-a-porn.' " *Sable Communications of Cal., Inc.* v. *F.C.C.*, 492 U.S. 115, 120-121 (1989).

Congress amended Section 223(b) in 1988 to impose a total ban "on dial-a-porn, making it illegal for adults, as well as children, to have access to sexually-explicit messages" that are indecent or obscene. *Id.* at 122-123. 47 U.S.C. 223(b) addresses commercial dial-a-porn operations that communicate sexually-explicit telephone messages; not commercial computer bulletin boards that use telephone facilities for the purpose of transmitting obscene, computer-generated images to approved members.

Defendants' second premise, that Congress did not intend to regulate computer transmissions because the statute does not expressly prohibit such conduct, is faulty as well. We have consistently recognized that when construing federal statutes, our duty is to "construe the language so as to give effect to the intent of Congress." *United States* v. *Underhill*, 813 F.2d 105, 111 (6th Cir.), *cert. denied*, 482 U.S. 906 (1987) (quoting *United States* v. *American Trucking Associations, Inc.*, 310 U.S. 534, 542-44 (1940)). The Supreme Court observed this principle when it rejected an argument similar to one Defendants raise here, i.e., that Congress could not possibly have intended to include conduct not expressly prohibited in the statute. See *United States* v. *Alpers*, 338 U.S. 680 (1950).

In *United States* v. *Alpers,* the Supreme Court considered the question whether obscene phonograph records—at the time, a novel means of transmitting obscenity—came within the prohibition of 18 U.S.C. 1462. Initially, the Court acknowledged that criminal statutes are to be strictly construed and that "no offense may be created except by the words of Congress used in their usual and ordinary way." *Id.* at 681. The Court emphasized, however, that Congress' intent is the most important determination and statutory language is not to be construed in a manner that would defeat that intent. Applying those principles, the Court held that the rule of *ejusdem generis* should not be "employed to render general words meaningless" or "be used to defeat the obvious purpose of legislation." It recognized that "[t]he obvious purpose of [Section 1462] was to prevent the channels of interstate commerce from being used to disseminate" any obscene matter. *Id.* at 683. The Court further recognized that Section 1462 "is a comprehensive statute, which should not be constricted by a mechanical rule of construction." *Id.* at 684. Accordingly, the Court rejected the defendant's argument that the general words "other matter of indecent character" could not be interpreted to include objects comprehensible by hearing (phonographic recordings) rather than sight; an argument similar to the tangible/intangible one raised here, and held that obscene records fell within the scope of the criminal statute. In reaching its decision, the *Alpers* Court found that the legislative history of Section 1462 did not support defendant's sight/sound distinction. It was not persuaded that Congress' amendment of Section 1462 to add motion picture films to the list of prohibited materials "evidenced an intent that obscene matter not specifically added was without the prohibition of the statute." *Id.* Rather, the Court concluded that the amendment evidenced Congress' preoccupation "with making doubly sure that motion-picture film was within the Act, and was concerned with nothing more or less." We are similarly unpersuaded by Defendants' arguments that the absence of the words "including by computer" in Section 1465, despite Congress' addition of those words in other legislation, is evidence of its intent not to criminalize conduct, such as Defendants', that falls within the plain language and intent of Section 1465.

Furthermore, under similar facts, the U.S. Air Force Court of Criminal Appeals recently considered 1465's plain language and its intended purpose. In *United States v. Maxwell*, 42 M.J. 568, 1995 WL 259269 (A.F. Ct. Crim. App. 1995), a defendant was charged with violating Section 1465 because he had transmitted obscene visual images electronically through the use of an online computer service. He argued that since the statute is silent concerning computer transmissions, such transmissions were not to be included within the terms "transporting obscene materials in interstate or foreign commerce." The court observed that well-established principles of statutory construction require a court to look first to the statute's plain language. *Maxwell*, 1995 WL 259269 at *10 (citing *Rubin* v. *United States*, 449 U.S. 424, 430 (1981)). Applying that principle, the *Maxwell* court concluded that the defendant's conduct fell within the plain language of Section 1465. Specifically, the court held: [t]he use of the terms "transports," "distribution," "picture," "image" and "electrical transcription" leads us to the inescapable conclusion the statute is fully applicable to the activities engaged in by applicant. . . . It is clear Congress intended to stem the transportation of obscene material in interstate commerce regardless of the means used to effect that end. *Maxwell*, 1995 WL 259269 at *10.

Likewise, we conclude that Defendants' conduct here falls within the plain language of Section 1465. Moreover, our interpretation of Section 1465 is consistent with Congress' intent to legislate comprehensively the interstate distribution of obscene materials.

Defendants also challenge venue in the Western District of Tennessee for counts 2–7 of their indictments. They argue that even if venue was proper under count 1 (conspiracy) and counts 8–10 (videotapes sent via U.P.S.), counts 2–7 (GIF files) should have been severed and transferred to California because Defendants did not cause the GIF files to be transmitted to the Western District of Tennessee. Rather, Defendants assert, it was Dirmeyer, a government agent, who, without their knowledge, accessed and downloaded the GIF files and caused them to enter Tennessee. We disagree. To establish a Section 1465 violation, the Government must prove that a defendant knowingly used a facility or means of interstate commerce for the purpose of distributing obscene materials. Contrary to Defendants' position, Section

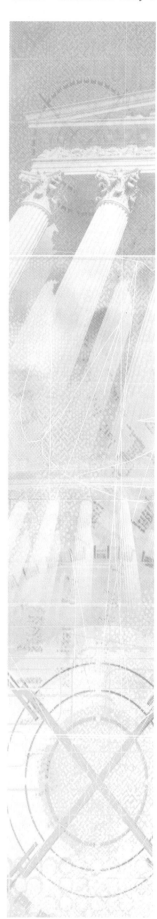

1465 does not require the Government to prove that Defendants had specific knowledge of the destination of each transmittal at the time it occurred.

"Venue lies in any district in which the offense was committed," and the Government is required to establish venue by a preponderance of the evidence. *United States v. Beddow,* 957 F.2d 1330, 1335 (6th Cir. 1992) (quoting *United States v. Williams,* 788 F.2d 1213, 1215 (6th Cir. 1986)). This court examines the propriety of venue by taking "into account a number of factors—the site of the defendant's acts, the elements and nature of the crime, the locus of the effect of the criminal conduct, and the suitability of each district for accurate fact finding. . . ." Section 1465 is an obscenity statute, and federal obscenity laws, by virtue of their inherent nexus to interstate and foreign commerce, generally involve acts in more than one jurisdiction or state. Furthermore, it is well-established that "there is no constitutional impediment to the government's power to prosecute pornography dealers in any district into which the material is sent." *United States v. Bagnell,* 679 F.2d 826, 830 (11th Cir. 1982), *cert. denied,* 460 U.S. 1047 (1983); *United States v. Peraino,* 645 F.2d 548, 551 (6th Cir. 1981). Thus, the question of venue has become one of legislative intent. *Bagnell,* 679 F.2d at 830.

The *Bagnell* court examined both 1462 and 1465 and found that each statute established a continuing offense within the venue provisions of 18 U.S.C. 3237(a) "that occur[s] in every judicial district which the material touches." *Id.* at 830. This court likewise recognized that venue for federal obscenity prosecutions lies "in any district from, through, or into which the allegedly obscene material moves." *Peraino,* 645 F.2d at 551 (citing 18 U.S.C. 3237).

Substantial evidence introduced at trial demonstrated that the AABBS was set up so members located in other jurisdictions could access and order GIF files which would then be instantaneously transmitted in interstate commerce. Moreover, AABBS materials were distributed to an approved AABBS member known to reside in the Western District of Tennessee. Specifically, Defendant Robert Thomas knew of, approved, and had conversed with an AABBS member in that judicial district who had his permission to access and copy GIF files that ultimately ended up there. Some of these GIF files were clearly marked "Distribute Freely." In light of the above, the effects of the Defendants' criminal conduct reached the Western District of Tennessee, and that district was suitable for accurate fact-finding. Accordingly, we conclude venue was proper in that judicial district.

Defendants further argue that their convictions under counts 1–7 of their indictments violate their First Amendment rights to freedom of speech. As the Supreme Court noted in *Bose,* when constitutional facts are at issue, this court has a duty to conduct an independent review of the record "both to be sure that the speech in question actually falls within the unprotected category and to confine the perimeters of any unprotected category within acceptably narrow limits in an effort to ensure that protected expression will not be inhibited." *Bose Corp.* v. *Consumers Union of United States, Inc.,* 466 U.S. 485, 505 (1984).

Defendants rely on *Stanley* v. *Georgia,* 394 U.S. 557 (1969), and argue they have a constitutionally protected right to possess obscene materials in the privacy of their home. They insist that the GIF files containing sexually-explicit material never left their home. Defendants' reliance on *Stanley* is misplaced.

The Supreme Court has clarified that *Stanley* "depended not on any First Amendment Right to purchase or possess obscene materials, but on the right to privacy in the home." *United States* v. *Twelve 200-Ft. Reels of Super 8mm. Film,* 413 U.S. 123, 126 (1973). It has also recognized that the right to possess obscene materials in the privacy of one's home does not create "a correlative right to receive it, transport it, or distribute it" in interstate commerce even if it is for private use only. Nor does it create "some zone of constitutionally protected privacy [that] follows such material when it is moved outside the home area." *United States* v. *Orito,* 413 U.S. 139, 141 (1973); see also *Twelve 200-Ft. Reels,* 413 U.S. at 128.

Defendants went beyond merely possessing obscene GIF files in their home. They ran a business that advertised and promised its members the availability and transportation of the sexually explicit GIF files they selected. In light of the overwhelming evidence produced at trial, it is spurious for Defendants to claim now that they did not intend to sell, disseminate, or share the obscene GIF files they advertised on the AABBS with members outside their home and in other states.

In *Miller v. California,* 413 U.S. 15 (1973), the Supreme Court set out a three-prong test for obscenity. It inquired whether (1) " 'the average person applying contemporary community standards' would find that the work, taken as a whole, appeals to the prurient interest"; (2) it "depicts or describes, in a patently offensive way, sexual conduct specifically defined by applicable state law"; and (3) "the work, taken as a whole, lacks serious literary, artistic, political, or scientific value." *Id.* at 24.

Under the first prong of the *Miller* obscenity test, the jury is to apply "contemporary community standards." Defendants acknowledge the general principle that, in cases involving interstate transportation of obscene material, juries are properly instructed to apply the community standards of the geographic area where the materials are sent. *Miller,* 413 U.S. at 15, 30–34. Nonetheless, Defendants assert that this principle does not apply here for the same reasons they claim venue was improper. As demonstrated above, this argument cannot withstand scrutiny. The computer-generated images described in counts 2–7 were electronically transferred from Defendants' home in California to the Western District of Tennessee. Accordingly, the community standards of that judicial district were properly applied in this case.

Issues regarding which community's standards are to be applied are tied to those involving venue. It is well-established that: [v]enue for federal obscenity prosecutions lies "in any district from, through, or into which" the allegedly obscene material moves, according to 18 U.S.C. 3237. This may result in prosecutions of persons in a community to which they have sent materials which [are] obscene under that community's standards though the community from which it is sent would tolerate the same material. *United States v. Peraino,* 645 F.2d 548, 551 (6th Cir. 1981). Prosecutions may be brought either in the district of dispatch or the district of receipt, *Bagnell,* 679 F.2d at 830–31, and obscenity is determined by the standards of the community where the trial takes place. See *Miller,* 413 U.S. at 15, 30–34; *Hamling v. United States,* 418 U.S. 87, 105–6 (1974); *Sable,* 492 U.S. at 125. Moreover, the federal courts have consistently recognized that it is not unconstitutional to subject interstate distributors of obscenity to varying community standards. *Hamling,* 418 U.S. at 106; *United States v. Sandy,* 605 F.2d 210, 217 (6th Cir.), *cert. denied,* 444 U.S. 984 (1979).

Defendants . . . argue that the computer technology used here requires a new definition of community, i.e., one that is based on the broad-ranging connections among people in cyberspace rather than the geographic locale of the federal judicial district of the criminal trial. Without a more flexible definition, they argue, there will be an impermissible chill on protected speech because BBS operators cannot select who gets the materials they make available on their bulletin boards. Therefore, they contend, BBS operators like Defendants will be forced to censor their materials so as not to run afoul of the standards of the community with the most restrictive standards.

Defendants' First Amendment issue, however, is not implicated by the facts of this case. This is not a situation where the bulletin board operator had no knowledge or control over the jurisdictions where materials were distributed for downloading or printing. Access to the Defendants' AABBS was limited. Membership was necessary and applications were submitted and screened before passwords were issued and materials were distributed. Thus, Defendants had in place methods to limit user access in jurisdictions where the risk of a finding of obscenity was greater than that in California. They knew they had a member in Memphis; the member's address and local phone number were provided on his application form. If Defendants did not wish to subject themselves to liability in jurisdictions with less

tolerant standards for determining obscenity, they could have refused to give passwords to members in those districts, thus precluding the risk of liability.

This result is supported by the Supreme Court's decision in *Sable Communications of Cal., Inc. v. F.C.C.* where the Court rejected Sable's argument that it should not be compelled to tailor its dial-a-porn messages to the standards of the least tolerant community. 492 U.S. 115, 125–26 (1989). The Court recognized that distributors of allegedly obscene materials may be subjected to the standards of the varying communities where they transmit their materials, citing *Hamling*, and further noted that Sable was "free to tailor its messages, on a selective basis, if it so chooses, to the communities it chooses to serve." *Id.* at 125. The Court also found no constitutional impediment to forcing Sable to incur some costs in developing and implementing a method for screening a customer's location and "providing messages compatible with community standards." *Id.*

Thus, under the facts of this case, there is no need for this court to adopt a new definition of "community" for use in obscenity prosecutions involving electronic bulletin boards. This court's decision is guided by one of the cardinal rules governing the federal courts, i.e., never reach constitutional questions not squarely presented by the facts of a case. *Brockett* v. *Spokane Arcades, Inc.*, 472 U.S. 491, 502 (1985).

. . . We next address the Defendants' argument that the district court erred when it instructed the jury that the government was not required to present expert testimony regarding the prurient appeal of the materials at issue here.

. . . [The jury was instructed as follows:] You have heard testimony from an expert witness presented on behalf of the defendants. An expert is allowed to express his opinion on those matters about which he has special knowledge and training. Expert testimony is presented to you on the theory that someone [who] is experienced in the field can assist you in understanding the evidence or in reaching an independent decision on the facts. There is no requirement, however, that expert testimony be presented in an obscenity case.

The government need not produce expert evidence that the materials are obscene, but may rely on the computer generated images and videotapes themselves for its argument that the materials are obscene. Under the first prong of the Miller obscenity test, the jury must consider whether the allegedly obscene material "appeals to the prurient interest." *Miller*, 413 U.S. at 24.

The computer-generated images and videotapes involved here portrayed bestiality, incest, rape, and sex scenes involving defecation, urination, and sadomasochistic abuse. Defendants argue that the Government is required to present expert testimony when sexually explicit material is directed at a deviant group. We disagree. Neither the United States Supreme Court nor this court has adopted any such per se rule. The Supreme Court has consistently recognized that "[e]xpert testimony is not necessary to enable the jury to judge the obscenity of material which . . . has been placed into evidence." *Hamling* v. *United States*, 418 U.S. 87, 100 (1974) (citing *Paris Adult Theatre I* v. *Slaton*, 413 U.S. 49, 56 (1973), *Kaplan* v. *California*, 413 U.S. 115, 120-21 (1973), *Ginzburg* v. *United States*, 383 U.S. 463, 465 (1966)). In *Paris Adult Theatre I*, the Court observed that the allegedly obscene materials, "obviously, are the best evidence of what they represent" and have been consistently recognized as "sufficient in themselves for the determination of the question." 413 U.S. at 56 (quoting *Ginzburg*, 383 U.S. at 465). The *Paris I* Court further elaborated that: [t]his is not a subject that lends itself to the traditional use of expert testimony. Such testimony is usually admitted for the purpose of explaining to lay jurors what they otherwise could not understand. No such assistance is needed by jurors in obscenity cases; indeed the "expert witness" practices employed in these cases have often made a mockery out of the otherwise sound concept of expert testimony. . . .

For the foregoing reasons, this court AFFIRMS Robert and Carleen Thomas' convictions and sentences.

WHAT DO *YOU* THINK?

1. Do you agree that the statute in question applies to computer-generated and transmitted information?
2. Should the government be required to present expert witnesses to establish that the material in question is obscene? Is this a question that juries can decide on their own? How are jury members aware of "community standards"?
3. If the community standards are different in Milpitas, California, from Memphis, Tennessee, why should the defendants be held accountable for the standards in Memphis and not those in the location where the material was transmitted?
4. Are you satisfied with the test for obscenity? In what manner, if any, would you change the standards?

CAN DRUG ADDICTION PROPERLY BE REGARDED AS AN "ILLNESS"? IF SO, CAN IT BE A CRIME?

CAPSTONE CASE

Robinson v. *California*
U.S. Supreme Court, 1962
370 U.S. 660

Mr. Justice Stewart delivered the opinion of the Court.

A California statute makes it a criminal offense for a person to "be addicted to the use of narcotics." This appeal draws into question the constitutionality of that provision of the state law, as construed by the California courts in the present case.

The appellant was convicted after a jury trial in the Municipal Court of Los Angeles. The evidence against him was given by two Los Angeles police officers. Officer Brown testified that he had had occasion to examine the appellant's arms one evening on a street in Los Angeles some four months before the trial. The officer testified that at that time he had observed "scar tissue and discoloration on the inside" of the appellant's right arm and "what appeared to be numerous needle marks and a scab which was approximately three inches below the crook of the elbow" on the appellant's left arm. The officer also testified that the appellant, under questioning, had admitted to the occasional use of narcotics.

Officer Lindquist testified that he had examined the appellant the following morning in the Central Jail in Los Angeles. The officer stated that at that time he had observed discolorations and scabs on the appellant's arms, and he identified photographs which had been taken of the appellant's arms shortly after his arrest the night before. Based on more than ten years of experience as a member of the Narcotic Division of the Los Angeles Police Department, the witness gave his opinion that "these marks and the discoloration were the result of the injection of hypodermic needles into the tissue [and] into the vein that [were] not sterile." He stated that the scabs were several days old at the time of his examination and that the appellant was neither under the influence of narcotics nor suffering withdrawal symptoms at the time he saw him. This witness also testified that the appellant had admitted using narcotics in the past.

The appellant testified in his own behalf, denying the alleged conversations with the police officers and denying that he had ever used narcotics or been addicted to their use. He explained the marks on his arms as resulting from an allergic condition contracted during his military service. His testimony was corroborated by two witnesses.

The trial judge instructed the jury that the statute made it a misdemeanor for a person "either to use narcotics, or to be addicted to the use of narcotics.... That portion of the statute referring to the 'use' of narcotics is based upon the 'act' of using. That portion of the statute referring to 'addicted to the use' of narcotics is based

upon a condition or status. They are not identical. . . . To be addicted to the use of narcotics is said to be a status or condition, and not an act. It is a continuing offense, and differs from most other offenses in the fact that [it] is chronic, rather than acute; that it continues after it is complete, and [that it] subjects the offender to arrest at any time before he reforms. The existence of such a chronic condition may be ascertained from a single examination if the characteristic reactions of that condition be found present."

The judge further instructed the jury that the appellant could be convicted under a general verdict if the jury agreed either that he was of the "status" or had committed the "act" denounced by the statute. "All that the People must show is either that the defendant did use a narcotic in Los Angeles County, or that, while in the City of Los Angeles, he was addicted to the use of narcotics. . . ."

Under these instructions, the jury returned a verdict finding the appellant "guilty of the offense charged." An appeal was taken to the Appellate Department of the Los Angeles County Superior Court, "the highest court of a State in which a decision could be had" in this case. 28 U.S.C. 1257. See *Smith* v. *California,* 361 U.S. 147, 149; *Edwards* v. *California,* 314 U.S. 160, 171. Although expressing some doubt as to the constitutionality of "the crime of being a narcotic addict," the reviewing court, in an unreported opinion affirmed the judgment of conviction, citing two of its own previous unreported decisions which had upheld the constitutionality of the statute. We noted probable jurisdiction of this appeal, 368 U.S. 918, because it squarely presents the issue whether the statute as construed by the California courts in this case is repugnant to the Fourteenth Amendment of the Constitution.

The broad power of a State to regulate the narcotic drugs traffic within its borders is not here in issue. More than forty years ago, in *Whipple* v. *Martinson,* 256 U.S. 41, this Court explicitly recognized the validity of that power: "There can be no question of the authority of the state in the exercise of its police power to regulate the administration, sale, prescription, and use of dangerous and habit-forming drugs. . . . The right to exercise this power is so manifest in the interest of the public health and welfare that it is unnecessary to enter upon a discussion of it beyond saying that it is too firmly established to be successfully called in question." 256 U.S. at 45.

Such regulation, it can be assumed, could take a variety of valid forms. A State might impose criminal sanctions, for example, against the unauthorized manufacture, prescription, sale, purchase, or possession of narcotics within its borders. In the interest of discouraging the violation of such laws, or in the interest of the general health or welfare of its inhabitants, a State might establish a program of compulsory treatment for those addicted to narcotics. Such a program of treatment might require periods of involuntary confinement. And penal sanctions might be imposed for failure to comply with established compulsory treatment procedures. Cf. *Jacobson* v. *Massachusetts,* 197 U.S. 11. Or a State might choose to attack the evils of narcotics traffic on broader fronts also—through public health education, for example, or by efforts to ameliorate the economic and social conditions under which those evils might be thought to flourish. In short, the range of valid choice which a State might make in this area is undoubtedly a wide one, and the wisdom of any particular choice within the allowable spectrum is not for us to decide. Upon that premise we turn to the California law in issue here.

It would be possible to construe the statute under which the appellant was convicted as one which is operative only upon proof of the actual use of narcotics within the State's jurisdiction. But the California courts have not so construed this law. Although there was evidence in the present case that the appellant had used narcotics in Los Angeles, the jury [members] were instructed that they could convict him even if they disbelieved that evidence. The appellant could be convicted, they were told, if they found simply that the appellant's "status" or "chronic condition" was that of being "addicted to the use of narcotics." And it is impossible to know from the jury's verdict that the defendant was not convicted upon precisely such a finding.

The instructions of the trial court, implicitly approved on appeal, amounted to "a ruling on a question of state law that is as binding on us as though the precise words had been written" into the statute. *Terminiello* v. *Chicago,* 337 U.S. 1, 4. "We can only take the statute as the state courts read it." *Id.* at 6. Indeed, in their brief in this Court, counsel for the State have emphasized that it is "the proof of addiction by circumstantial evidence . . . by the tell-tale track of needle marks and scabs over the veins of his arms that remains the gist of the section."

This statute, therefore, is not one which punishes a person for the use of narcotics, for their purchase, sale, or possession, or for antisocial or disorderly behavior resulting from their administration. It is not a law which even purports to provide or require medical treatment. Rather, we deal with a statute which makes the "status" of narcotic addiction a criminal offense, for which the offender may be prosecuted "at any time before he reforms." California has said that a person can be continuously guilty of this offense, whether or not he has ever used or possessed any narcotics within the State, and whether or not he has been guilty of any antisocial behavior there.

It is unlikely that any State at this moment in history would attempt to make it a criminal offense for a person to be mentally ill, or a leper, or to be afflicted with a venereal disease. A State might determine that the general health and welfare require that the victims of these and other human afflictions be dealt with by compulsory treatment, involving quarantine, confinement, or sequestration. But, in the light of contemporary human knowledge, a law which made a criminal offense of such a disease would doubtless be universally thought to be an infliction of cruel and unusual punishment in violation of the Eighth and Fourteenth Amendments. See *Francis* v. *Resweber,* 329 U.S. 459.

We cannot but consider the statute before us as of the same category. In this Court, counsel for the State recognized that narcotic addiction is an illness. Indeed, it is apparently an illness which may be contracted innocently or involuntarily. We hold that a state law which imprisons a person thus afflicted as a criminal, even though he has never touched any narcotic drug within the State or been guilty of any irregular behavior there, inflicts a cruel and unusual punishment in violation of the Fourteenth Amendment. To be sure, imprisonment for ninety days is not, in the abstract, a punishment which is either cruel or unusual. But the question cannot be considered in the abstract. Even one day in prison would be a cruel and unusual punishment for the "crime" of having a common cold.

We are not unmindful that the vicious evils of the narcotics traffic have occasioned the grave concern of government. There are, as we have said, countless fronts on which those evils may be legitimately attacked. We deal in this case only with an individual provision of a particularized local law as it has so far been interpreted by the California courts.

Reversed.

[footnotes omitted]

WHAT DO *YOU* THINK?

1. What is the difference between using a drug and being a drug user? Why is such a distinction important from a legal point of view?
2. Do you agree with the Court that being a drug addict should be considered a "status" of the same sort as being mentally ill, being a leper, or being afflicted with cancer? Why or why not?
3. Although a person does not choose to be sick, or mentally ill, does he (or she) choose to use drugs and (therefore) to become a drug addict? Could one make an argument for a plausible distinction between these two kinds of statuses? If so, what might that argument be?
4. How does this case compare with *Powell* v. *Texas* (a Chapter 11 Capstone Case)? What are the crucial differences between these two cases (if any)?

NOTES

1. "Club Women Urge Segregation: See No Other Sane Recourse," *The Sacramento Bee,* January 15, 1913, p. 1.

2. *Pap's* v. *Erie,* 553 Pa. 348, 719 A.2d 273.

3. *City of Erie* v. *Pap's A. M.,* U.S. Supreme Court, No. 98-1161 (Decided March 29, 2000).

4. Fellatio may be felonious even when consensual.

5. *Time,* July 24, 1995, p. 58.

6. 18 U.S.C.A., Section 2421.

7. General Statutes of North Carolina, 14-203.

8. Official Code of Georgia Annotated, 16-6-9.

9. Note, however, that North Carolina law (and the laws of some other states) makes "indiscriminate sexual intercourse" a crime—even when no money changes hands.

10. Model Penal Code, Section 251.2(2).

11. Ibid.

12. Official Code of Georgia Annotated, 16-6-10.

13. Ibid., 16-6-11.

14. Ibid., 16-6-12.

15. Ibid., 16-6-16.

16. William Kornblum and Joseph Julian, *Social Problems,* 8th ed. (Upper Saddle River, NJ: Prentice Hall, 1995), p. 115.

17. Ibid.

18. David R. Simon, *The American Standard Law Dictionary,* 1995 (via Cybernation online, http://www.e-legal.com).

19. Ibid.

20. *Roth* v. *United States,* 354 U.S. 476 (1957).

21. *Miller* v. *California,* 413 U.S. 15 (1973).

22. California Penal Code, Section 311(a).

23. Ibid.

24. *Stanley* v. *Georgia,* 394 U.S. 557 (1969).

25. *Paris Adult Theatre* v. *Slaton,* 413 U.S. 49 (1973).

26. California Penal Code, Section 311.3(a).

27. Violent Crime Control and Law Enforcement Act of 1994, Title XVI, Section 160001, Subsection 2258.

28. *New York* v. *Ferber,* 458 U.S. 747 (1982).

29. 47 U.S.C.A., Section 223(a)(1)(B)(ii)(Supp. 1997).

30. Public Law 104-104, 110 Statute 56.

31. *Reno* v. *ACLU,* 521 U.S. 844 (1997).

32. New Jersey Code of Criminal Justice, Section 14-4.

33. Official Code of Georgia Annotated, 16-6-8.

34. Ibid., 16-6-18.

35. Ibid., 16-6-19.

36. Ibid., 16-6-6.

37. Ibid.

38. Rhode Island, Section 11-10-1.

39. Idaho Penal Code, Section 18-6605.

40. Ibid., Section 18-6606.

41. *State* v. *Chance*, 3 N.C. App. 459, 165 S.E.2d 31 (1969).

42. *State* v. *Stokes*, 1 N.C. App. 245, 161 S.E.2d 53 (1968).

43. *State* v. *Whittemore*, 255 N.C. 583, 122 S.E.2d 396 (1961).

44. *Stokes*, 1 N.C. App. 245, 161 S.E.2d 53.

45. Minnesota Statutes, 609.293 (Sodomy).

46. *Bowers* v. *Hardwick*, 478 U.S. 186 (1986).

47. *Powell* v. *State*, 270 Ga. 327, 510 S.E.2d 18, 1998.

48. *State* v. *Williams*, 220 N.C. 445, 17 S.E.2d 769 (1941).

49. *Haller* v. *State*, 232 S.W.2d 829 (Ark. 1950).

50. Karen De Witt, "Incest as a Selling Point," *The New York Times* News Service, March 30, 1997.

51. Official Code of Georgia Annotated, 16-6-22.

52. Most seduction statutes were rescinded or invalidated by court decree during the 1970s or 1980s.

53. General Statutes of North Carolina, 14-180.

54. *State* v. *Smith*, 223 N.C. 199, 25 S.E.2d 619 (1943).

55. *State* v. *Crowell*, 116 N.C. 1052, 21 S.E. 502 (1895).

56. *State* v. *Whitley*, 141 N.C. 823, 53 S.E. 820 (1906).

57. Official Code of Georgia Annotated, 51-1-16.

58. North Carolina General Statutes, 14-292.

59. G. R. Blakey and H. A. Kurland, "Development of Federal Law on Gambling," *Cornell L. Rev.*, Vol. 63 (1978), p. 923.

60. Some of the materials in this section have been adapted from *Criminal Justice Today: An Introductory Text for the Twenty-first Century*, by Frank Schmalleger. Copyright 1999. Adapted by permission of Prentice-Hall, Inc., Upper Saddle River, NJ.

61. The President's Commission on Organized Crime, *Organized Crime Today* (Washington, D.C.: U.S. Government Printing Office, 1986).

62. *Webb* v. *United States*, 249 U.S. 96, 63 L. Ed. 497, 39 S. Ct. 217 (1919).

63. Drug Enforcement Administration, *Drug Enforcement: The Early Years* (Washington, D.C.: DEA, December 1980), p. 41.

64. 21 U.S.C., Section 801 *et seq.*

65. For a good summary of the law, see Drug Enforcement Administration, *Drugs of Abuse*, Web posted at http://usdoj.gov/dea/concern/abuse/contents.htm

66. Florida Statutes, Section 893.02

67. Ibid.

68. "Rophies" Reported Spreading Quickly Throughout the South," *Drug Enforcement Report*, June 23, 1995, pp. 1–5.

69. Jodi S. Cohen, "Drug May Be Used in Sexual Assaults," *USA Today*, June 20, 1996, p. 2A.

70. Public Law 104-3305

71. Public Law 106-172.

72. This provision became effective on September 1, 1989.

73. "Congress Gives Final OK to Major Antidrug Bill," *Criminal Justice Newsletter,* Vol. 19, No. 21 (November 1, 1988), pp. 1–4.

74. Ibid., p. 2

75. "Drug Lord Sentenced to Death," *USA Today,* May 15, 1991, p. 3A.

76. Florida Statutes, Section 893.13

77. Most states also permit the attorney general to remove a substance previously added to a schedule if he or she finds that the substance does not meet the requirements for inclusion in that schedule.

78. 21 U.S.C., Section 881 (a) (6).

79. Ibid.

80. Michael Goldsmith, *Civil Forfeiture: Tracing the Proceeds of Narcotics Trafficking* (Washington, D.C.: Police Executive Research Forum, 1988), p. 3.

81. *United States* v. *92 Buena Vista Ave.,* 113 S. Ct. 1126, 122 L. Ed. 2d 469 (1993).

82. *Austin* v. *United States,* 113 S. Ct. 2801, 15 L. Ed. 2d 448 (1993).

83. *Alexander* v. *United States,* 113 S. Ct. 2766, 125 L. Ed. 2d 441 (1993).

84. *United States* v. *James Daniel Good Real Property,* 114 S. Ct. 492, 126 L. Ed. 2d 490 (1993).

85. *Bennis* v. *Michigan,* 116 S. Ct. 1560, 134 L. Ed. 2d 661 (1996).

86. *United States* v. *Ursery,* 116 S. Ct. 2135, 135 L. Ed. 2d 549 (1996).

87. *Newsweek,* February 3, 1997, pp. 20–23.

88. *U.S.* v. *Oakland Cannabis Buyers Cooperative,* 00-151 (August 29, 2000).

89. Stanford H. Kadish, "The Crisis of Overcriminalization," *The Annals of the American Academy of Political and Social Science,* Vol. 374 (1967), p. 157.

90. Ibid.

91. Ibid.

13

Victims and the Law

Justice, though due to the accused, is due to the accuser also.
—Justice Benjamin Cardozo, *Snyder v. Massachusetts*, 291 U.S. 97, 122 (1934)

Let victim rights ring across America.
                    —National Organization for Victim Assistance (NOVA)[1]

CHAPTER OUTLINE

KEY CONCEPTS

Crime Index

Golden Age of the Victim

hidden costs of crime

National Center for Victims
of Crime (NCVC)

National Crime
Victimization Survey
(NCVS)

National Organization for
Victim Assistance (NOVA)

Office for Victims of Crime
(OVC)

Part I offenses

Part II offenses

postcrime victimization

right of allocution

"Son of Sam" laws

Uniform Crime Reports
(UCR)

victim

victim impact statement

victim/witness assistance
programs

Victims of Crime Act
(VOCA)

victims' rights

AFTER READING THIS CHAPTER YOU SHOULD:

▷ Be able to define the term "victim."

▷ Appreciate the status of victims throughout history.

▷ Appreciate the personal, economic, and "hidden costs" of crime to victims and to society as a
whole.

▷ Understand the needs of victims and appreciate the types of programs that have been established to meet them.

▷ Understand federal, state, and local initiatives in the area of victims' legislation.

▷ Describe efforts by the states and by the federal government to develop victims' rights constitutional amendments.

▷ Be familiar with "Son of Sam" legislation and know its purpose.

▷ Know the purpose and history of victim impact statements.

▷ Know the difference between "restitution" and "restorative justice."

INTRODUCTION

Around 9:45 A.M. on August 24, 2000, an intruder broke into the Merced, California, home of John and Tephanie Carpenter.[2] At home were the couple's five children, Anna, 13; Vanessa, 11; Jessica Lynne, 14; Ashley, 9; and John William, 8. The parents were out of the house—the father at work; the mother running errands.

The intruder, twenty-seven-year-old Jonathon David Bruce, was a stranger to the family, but had a hatred of children. Bruce picked up a short handled spading fork from the family garden, entered the house naked, and surprised the children—attacking them as they slept or watched television. Before the attack ended, little John William and Ashley were dead. More than 100 stab wounds covered Ashley's body, while John William died from over 40 wounds. The older children managed to flee, and ran to a neighbor's house to call 911. "Somebody's in my house that I don't know; they're stabbing my brother and sister with a pitchfork," fourteen-year-old Jessica Lynne Carpenter cried to an emergency dispatcher moments after escaping the attack with her two sisters. "I don't know who it is. I just woke up and he was in the house."[3]

> No more essential duty of government exists than the protection of the lives of its people. Fail in this, and we fail in everything.
>
> *Harper's* magazine (July 1984)

Twenty-seven-year-old Jonathon David Bruce. In August 2000, Bruce broke into a house in Merced, California, and attacked five children who were home alone. Two of the children were stabbed to death before police arrived and killed Bruce. (Photo by Merced Sun Star/Merced County Sheriff's Office, courtesy of AP/Wide World Photos.)

When police arrived, Bruce was sprayed with mace, but still charged at officers with the spading fork. He was shot thirteen times and died at the scene.

A senseless tragedy, the attack on the Carpenter children, serves as an example that no one is safe from crime. Nonetheless, John William and Ashley Carpenter were unusual victims of violent crimes. Both were children from a middle-class family who died at the hands of a stranger. Surveys of crime victims, such as the **National Crime Victimization Survey (NCVS),** which will be discussed later in this chapter, show that males, the poor, members of racial minorities, and young adults are more likely to be victimized than are others. Before we can meaningfully discuss victims' issues or crime statistics, however, it is necessary to clarify the term "victim."

NATIONAL CRIME VICTIMIZATION SURVEY (NCVS)
a survey, conducted annually by the Bureau of Justice Statistics (BJS), that provides data on surveyed households that report they were affected by crime.

Web Extra! 13–1
Center for Crime Victims' Rights, Remedies, and Resources

VICTIM
any individual against whom an offense has been committed. Or, for certain procedural purposes, a parent or legal guardian if the victim is below the age of eighteen years or is incompetent. Also, one or more family members or relatives designated by the court if the victim is deceased or incapacitated.

WHO IS A VICTIM?

The concept of a "victim" is foreign to civil law, which speaks, instead, in terms of persons who have been injured or wronged. The word "victim" denotes someone who has been harmed through the kind of activity proscribed by the criminal law.[4]

While everyone has an intuitive appreciation of what it means to be a victim, the term "crime victim" can be more formally defined. The Violent Crime Control and Law Enforcement Act of 1994, for example, says that the word **victim** "means any individual against whom an offense has been committed. . . ."[5] For certain purposes, however, federal law expands the term to include "a parent or legal guardian if the victim is below the age of eighteen years or incompetent" and "one or more family members or relatives designated by the court if the victim is deceased or incapacitated."

A federal Bureau of Prisons (BOP) policy directive defines the term "victim" as "someone who suffers direct or threatened physical, emotional, or financial harm as

LAW ON THE BOOKS

THE CONCEPT OF A "VICTIM" UNDER ALASKA LAW.
ALASKA STATUTES

Section 12.55.185. Definitions. In this chapter, unless the context requires otherwise, "victim" means:

    A. a person against whom an offense has been perpetrated;

    B. one of the following, not the perpetrator, if the person specified in (A) of this paragraph is a minor, incompetent, or incapacitated:

        i. an individual living in a spousal relationship with the person specified in (A) of this paragraph; or

        ii. a parent, adult child, guardian, or custodian of the person;

    C. one of the following, not the perpetrator, if the person specified in (A) of this paragraph is dead:

        i. a person living in a spousal relationship with the deceased before the deceased died;

        ii. an adult child, parent, brother, sister, grandparent, or grandchild of the deceased; or

        iii. any other interested person, as may be designated by a person having authority in law to do so.

the result of the commission of a crime." According to the BOP, "the term 'victim' also includes the immediate family of a minor or homicide victim."[6] An even more elaborate definition of the term victim is described in the Law on the Books feature above.

A SHORT HISTORY OF THE VICTIM

Throughout much of early human history, victims had few, if any, "official" support mechanisms. Nonetheless, early social norms generally supported the actions of victims who, before the emergence of organized law enforcement and formal judicial systems, were able to exact revenge on those who had victimized them. Such early victims typically sought the support of friends and family members in hunting down and punishing the perpetrator. Moreover, early tribal codes generally required victims' families to care for the needs of victims or their survivors. This early period in history, during which victims took an active role in determining the fate of offenders and the care of victims was socially mandated, has been termed the **"Golden Age of the Victim."** The Golden Age lent a sense of closure to the victimization experience and had the effect of making victims feel "whole again."

Eventually, however, crimes came to be seen as offenses against society, and the needs of the victim were largely forgotten. By the late Middle Ages in England, the concept of "King's Peace" had emerged, under which all offenses were seen as violations of laws decreed by the monarch. Under the King's Peace, it became the duty of local officials, including sheriffs and constables, to apprehend offenders and to arrange for their trial and punishment. As a consequence, victims were effectively removed from any direct involvement in deciding the offender's fate. From that point onward, in the Western legal tradition, victims were expected only to provide evidence of a crime and to testify against those who had offended them. Society's moral responsibility toward making victims "whole again" was largely forgotten, and victims as a class were moved to the periphery of the justice process. Victim-centered

GOLDEN AGE OF THE VICTIM
an historical epoch during which victims had well-recognized rights, including a personal say in imposing punishments on apprehended offenders.

The mugger who is arrested is back on the street before the police officer; but the person mugged may not be back on the street for a long time, if ever.

—Mario Cuomo (April 1985)

justice had become translated into state-centered justice, under which the victim played a mere token role as the personal target of criminal activity.

The situation remained relatively unchanged until the 1960s, when a renewed interest in victims led to a resurgence of efforts meant to assist them. Popular sentiments were soon translated into a flurry of laws designed to provide compensation to victims of violent crimes. The first modern victim compensation statute was adopted by New Zealand in 1963. Known as the Criminal Injuries Compensation Act, it provided a mechanism for claims to be filed by victims of certain specified violent crimes. Under the law, a three-member New Zealand government board was created with the authority to make awards to victims. A year later, partially in response to a movement led by victim rights advocate Margaret Fry, Great Britain passed a similar law. In 1965, California passed the first American legislation intended to assist victims of crime. About the same time, the New York city council passed a "good Samaritan" statute designed to pay up to $4,000 to persons suffering physical injuries while going to the aid of others being victimized by crime. Many states then joined the victim compensation bandwagon, and today all fifty states and the District of Columbia have passed legislation providing for monetary payments to crime victims—although legislatures have rarely funded programs at levels that would pay all requests.

Modern state victim compensation programs require applicants to meet certain eligibility requirements, and most set award maximums. A number of states set minimum loss limits (similar to "deductibles provisions" in insurance policies) and have established a "needs test," whereby only financially needy crime victims are eligible for compensation. Likewise, some states deny awards to family members of the offender, as in the case where a son assaults a father. All states provide for the possibility of payment for medical assistance, lost wages, and living expenses. However, victims who are responsible in some significant way for their own victimization are generally not eligible for reimbursement under existing laws.

In California, for example, qualifying victims of crime may receive financial assistance for losses resulting from a crime when these losses cannot be reimbursed by other sources. The State Board of Control's Victims of Crime Program administers California's Crime Victim Compensation Program. Under California law, victims of crime or their survivors may be eligible for financial reimbursement for: (1) medical and hospital expenses, (2) loss of wages and support, (3) funeral and burial expenses, (4) professional counseling, and (5) job retraining or rehabilitation. California law requires that applications from adult victims be filed within one year of the date of the crime, while applications resulting from a crime against a minor must be filed before the minor's nineteenth birthday.

The Philosophy of Victim Compensation

Victim compensation programs find their philosophical underpinnings in seven different schools of thought. They are[7]: (1) strict liability theory, which claims that compensation is due victims because the social contract between victim and society (specifically, the government, which has a duty to safeguard its citizens) has been broken by the experience of victimization; (2) government negligence theory, which holds that the government was negligent for allowing harm and should make appropriate forms of compensation; (3) equal protection theory, which says that compensation should serve to ameliorate imbalances in society, including the huge variation in crime risk faced by citizens living in different parts of the nation and under different social conditions; (4) humanitarian theory, which advocates compensation because of the suffering victims undergo; (5) social welfare theory, which says that victims should be compensated if they are in need; (6) crime prevention theory, which holds that compensation programs encourage more citizens to report crime, thereby resulting in more effective law-enforcement programs; and (7) political motives theory, which says that victim compensation is in vogue with the voting public and that any politician desiring continued election must inevitably support the concept.

Victims' Assistance Programs Today

Victims experience many hardships extending beyond their original victimization, including the trauma of testifying, uncertainty about their role in the justice process, lost time at work, trial delays, fear of retaliation by the defendant, and a general lack of knowledge about what is expected of them as the wheels of justice grind forward. Problems that follow from initial victimization are referred to as **postcrime victimization,** or **secondary victimization.** Police, employer, and spousal insensitivity can all exacerbate the difficulties crime victims face. Even hospitals that charge high fees for medical records and social service agencies that swamp applicants in a plethora of forms can contribute to the victim's sense of continuing victimization.

In recent years a number of victims' assistance programs, designed to provide comfort and assistance to victims of crime, have developed across the nation. The earliest of these programs began as grass-roots movements designed to counsel victims of rape. In 1975, a national survey[8] identified only twenty-three victims' assistance programs in the United States. By 1986, the number had grown to over six hundred, and estimates today place the number of such programs at more than one thousand. Some authors have drawn a distinction between victim service programs, which emphasize therapeutic counseling, and **victim/witness assistance programs,** which provide a wide array of services.

Most victim/witness assistance programs are small and are staffed by local volunteers. They typically counsel victims and witnesses, orient them to the justice process, and provide a variety of other services, such as transportation to court, child care during court appearances, and referrals to social service agencies when additional assistance is needed. A recent survey[9] found that most such organizations explain the court process to victims (71.2 percent of all organizations surveyed), make referrals to other agencies (68.4 percent), provide court escorts (65.2 percent), help victims complete victim compensation forms (64.1 percent), attempt to educate the public as to the needs of victims (60.9 percent), advocate with employers on behalf of victims (60.3 percent), and provide transportation to court (59.2 percent).

Victims' assistance programs in California, for example, are eligible to receive funding through the Office of Criminal Justice Planning from the state's Victim-Witness Assistance Fund if they provide *all* of the following services[10]: (1) crisis intervention; (2) emergency assistance (i.e., directly or indirectly providing food, housing, clothing, and, when necessary, cash); (3) resource and referral counseling to agencies within the community that are appropriate to meet the victim's needs; (4) direct counseling of the victim on problems resulting from the crime; (5) assistance in the processing, filing, and verifying of claims filed by victims; (6) assistance in obtaining the return of a victim's property held as evidence by law enforcement agencies; (7) orientation to the criminal justice system; (8) court escort; (9) presentations to and training of criminal justice system agencies; (10) public presentations and publicity; (11) the monitoring of appropriate court cases to keep victims and witnesses apprised of the progress and outcome of their case; (12) notification to friends, relatives, and employers of the occurrence of the crime and the victim's condition, upon request of the victim; (13) notification to the employer of the victim or witness, if

POSTCRIME VICTIMIZATION
also **secondary victimization;** problems that follow from initial victimization, such as the loss of employment, inability to pay medical bills, insensitivity of family members, etc.

VICTIM/WITNESS ASSISTANCE PROGRAMS
service organizations that work to provide comfort and assistance to victims of crime and to witnesses.

Web Extra! 13–2

National Organization for Victim Assistance (NOVA)

requested by the victim or witness, informing the employer that the employee was a victim of, or witness to, a crime and asking the employer to minimize any loss of pay or other benefits that may result because of the crime or the employee's participation in the criminal justice system; and (14) upon request of the victim, assisting in obtaining restitution for the victim, in ascertaining the victim's economic loss, and in providing the probation department, district attorney, and court with information relevant to his or her losses prior to the imposition of sentence.

To meet the state's nondiscrimination guidelines, California victims' assistance programs that receive state funding must also provide: (1) translation services for non-English-speaking or hearing-impaired victims and witnesses; (2) follow-up contact to determine whether the client(s) received the necessary assistance; (3) field visits to a client's home, place of business, or other location, whenever necessary to provide services; (4) service to victims and witnesses of all types of crime; (5) volunteer participation to encourage community involvement; and (6) services for elderly victims of crime, appropriate to their special needs.

Two large nonprofit public groups that serve the needs of victims on a national scale are the National Organization for Victim Assistance **(NOVA)** and the National Center for Victims of Crime **(NCVC).** Both are located in the Washington, D.C., area and provide leadership in victim education, lobby the federal Congress, and hold conferences and workshops designed to assist local victim/witness assistance programs.

Founded in 1975, NOVA is a private, nonprofit, umbrella organization working on behalf of victims of crime and disaster. NOVA is guided by four official purposes: (1) to serve as a national advocate in support of victim rights and services, (2) to provide direct services to victims, (3) to be an educational resource providing support to victim assistance professionals, and (4) to be of service to its members. NOVA's avowed central focus is to educate policy makers about victim rights.

Begun in December of 1985, the NCVC has as its mission: (1) to serve as a national resource center for victims and their advocates; (2) to establish training programs and other self-help opportunities to help victims and their advocates deal effectively with the judicial system, understand victims' rights, seek reparation, and cope with grief; and (3) to encourage and promote research concerning victims of violent crime through the establishment of a national databank and resource library.[11] The NCVC is a nonprofit organization with offices in Arlington, Virginia, and New York City. The center maintains a comprehensive library and a national

NOVA

an acronym for the National Organization for Victim Assistance.

NCVC

an acronym for the National Center for Victims of Crime.

Victims have won many rights in recent years. Here, a victim testifies at a parole hearing for an assailant, seeking to prevent his release. (Photo by Peter A. O'Boyle, courtesy of South Carolina Department of Probation, Parole and Pardon Services.)

Reaching Out to Crime Victims

Feds Plan Automatic Notification of Changes in Case

WASHINGTON—By the end of 2001, all federal crime victims will be offered automatic notification about developments in their cases—including when an offender will be released—under a new system modeled after the successful state crime victims notification program.

The Justice Department this week awarded a contract to a Virginia firm to develop the National Victim of Crime Notification System (VNS) that for the first time will allow victims registered with the agency to receive all developments in their cases.

"It will allow the Justice Department and the other initial entities, the FBI and the Bureau of Prisons to provide 24-hour notification of the status of offenders by every means of communication from snail mail to cell phone and fax," said Gerald David, program director for GRC International, the AT&T-owned information technology company that received the contract.

Currently each department operates independent systems that track offenders and notify victims individually. The new automated system will allow the agencies to integrate case information, and computers will handle the notification process. In addition, victims will be able to call a toll-free number to receive information on their cases.

"There will be a seamless transition from arrest through the court system to incarceration and release," David said.

Complex coordination efforts

In 1996, President Clinton directed Attorney General Janet Reno to adopt a nationwide victim notification system

and $8 million was set aside to develop and implement the program, said Kurt Shernuk, an assistant U.S. attorney and the project director for the Justice Department.

"The system will improve the notification methods we have," he said. "Right now people are responsible for generating a letter or picking up the phone, which will still be done, but this will enhance the ways we can provide the information."

Shernuk said the project is taking five years to bring on line because of the complex coordination efforts among the three federal departments which each operate on an independent computer system.

"If a case came to [the Justice Department] from the FBI, we would have to rekey that information in the computers," he said.

Victims "not dependent on a person"

"Although the total federal caseload is smaller than the state or local jurisdictions, some federal cases, such as fraud, can have thousands of victims," Shernuk said.

Victims' rights advocates applauded the system, saying it will help victims in potentially violent federal crimes such as kidnapping, interstate stalking and Internet sex offenses.

"I like the concept of automated notification," said Carol Dorris, public policy staff attorney for the National Center for Victims of Crime. "That way, victims are not dependent on a person [to notify them]."

"Any information, that's what victims want to know," said Ellen Halbert, director of the victim/witness di-

vision of the Travis County, Texas, District Attorney's Office. "Where the offender is at the moment is at the top of the list."

System used in 35 states

All states have legislation requiring the creation of a victim notification system, but the scope of the information released and how it is released varies widely, Dorris said.

"There is a lack of services in rural areas," Dorris said. "Even if the funding is there they don't have an advocate who knows it's there or people who are aware and can implement it."

The federal system will be based in the Louisville, Ky., facility where Appris Inc., the nation's leading provider of victim notification software to states and local jurisdictions, is housed.

Formerly known as The VINE—or Victim Information and Notification Everyday—Company, Appris software serves 750 communities in 35 states.

Could help healing process

Halbert, a victim of rape and attempted murder, said had she been a victim of a less violent attack she would want regular notices about her case.

"I was attacked in 1986 and he got life, which meant 20 years, so he will not be eligible until 2006," she said. "If he had not gotten a long sentence it would have been beneficial to the healing process to know I could call a number and know where he was."

Source: Amy Worden, "Reaching Out to Crime Victims; Feds Plan Automatic Notification of Changes in Case," APB News. August 4, 2000. Reprinted with permission.

computer database collection of victim-related legislation. The database contains more than 27,000 statutes of relevance to violence, victimization, and other victim-related criminal justice issues in all fifty states and at the federal level.

VICTIMS' RIGHTS LEGISLATION

Legislative milestones in the American **victims' rights** movement include the federal Victim and Witness Protection Act of 1982, which was enacted "to enhance and protect the necessary role of crime victims and witnesses in the criminal justice process." Other federal legislation of importance to victims includes the Victims of Crime Act of 1984, the Violence Against Women Act of 1994 (part of the Violent Crime Control and Law Enforcement Act of 1994), the Victims' Rights and Restitution Act, and the Child Victims' Bill of Rights of 1990.

Perhaps the most significant victims' legislation to date, the 1984 Victims of Crime Act **(VOCA),** resulted from recommendations made in 1982 by the President's Task Force on Victims of Crime. VOCA established a federal crime victim compensation fund, which provides payments for medical expenses attributable to a physical injury, loss of wages, and funeral expenses resulting from "a compensable crime." The fund is administered through the federal Office for Victims of Crime **(OVC)**—another VOCA product—which began operations in 1985. Since its beginnings, OVC has served as the federal government's focal point for all issues affecting crime victims across the nation. Today, OVC is one of five agencies within the U.S. Department of Justice's Office of Justice Programs. OVC offers a broad range of programs and activities designed to help crime victims cope with the personal and financial problems that result from victimization.

OVC also plays a pivotal leadership role in the victims movement. The office supplements, reinforces, and encourages the expansion of state compensation and assistance programs throughout the country. OVC administers VOCA funding to all populations affected by victimization, including underserved populations, such as sexually exploited children and victims residing on remote Indian reservations. The office also awards grants to sponsor training and technical assistance on cutting edge substantive issues of interest to victim advocates as well as to criminal justice system personnel who regularly interact with victims. OVC's leadership role at the federal level encompasses activities designed to draw public attention to the needs of crime victims, and to promote victim rights through legislation and public policy.

OVC operates the Office for Victims of Crime Resource Center, a component of the National Criminal Justice Reference Service (NCJRS). The OVC Resource Center provides victim-related information on such issues as domestic violence, child abuse, elderly victims, bias-related violence, victim rights, and victim compensation to practitioners, policy makers, researchers, crime victims, and other interested parties. The resource center collects, maintains, and disseminates information about national, state, and local victim-related organizations and about state programs that receive funds authorized by the VOCA.

The Violent Crime Control and Law Enforcement Act of 1994 contained significant victims' rights legislation, although the full effects of the new law have yet to be felt. The act, which was the culmination of six years of bipartisan work in the United States Congress, was the largest crime bill in the nation's history. It provides funding for 100,000 new police officers, $9.7 billion in funding for prisons, and $6.1 billion in funding for prevention programs. The 1994 crime bill also provides $2.6 billion in additional funding for the FBI, Drug Enforcement Administration (DEA), Immigration and Naturalization Service (INS), United States Attorneys, Treasury Department, and other Justice Department components, as well as the federal courts.

Some of the most significant victims' rights provisions of the Violent Crime Control and Law Enforcement Act of 1994 include: (1) the Violence Against Women Act, which provides financial support for police, prosecutors, and victims' services in cases involving sexual violence or domestic abuse; (2) a **"right of allocution"** provision, permitting victims of federal violent and sex crimes to speak at the sentencing of their assailants; (3) a requirement that federal sex offenders and child molesters pay restitution to their victims; (4) increased penalties for frauds perpetrated against older victims; and (5) enhanced funding for the federal Crime Victims' Fund (established under the Victims of Crime Act of 1984), and the victim-support programs funded by it.

RIGHT OF ALLOCUTION
a statutory provision permitting crime victims to speak at the sentencing of convicted offenders. A federal right of allocution was established for victims of federal violent and sex crimes under the Violent Crime Control and Law Enforcement Act of 1994.

The Growth of Victims' Rights

When the victims' movement began, the idea of legal rights for victims of crime was a novel idea. At the time, victims advocates built a platform of victims' rights on six principles. Those principles declared that:

- Victims and witnesses have a right to protection from intimidation and harm.
- Victims and witnesses have a right to be informed concerning the criminal justice process.
- Victims and witnesses have a right to reparations.
- Victims and witnesses have a right to preservation of property and employment.
- Victims and witnesses have a right to due process in criminal court proceedings.
- Victims and witnesses have a right to be treated with dignity and compassion.

The rights of victims have advanced considerably since the 1970s, and more than thirty states have enacted legislation or modified their constitutions in recognition of victims' rights. Some states, like California, have done both. Victims' rights provisions of the California Penal Code are reproduced in an accompanying Law on the Books box. The California victims' rights constitutional amendment can also be found in a box in this chapter.

A key focus of victims' rights advocates today is on passage of a federal constitutional amendment.[12] One organization that is central to the push for such an amendment is the National Victims' Constitutional Amendment Network, also known as Victims' CAN (or NVCAN). On January 19, 1999, in collaboration with NVCAN and other victims' rights supporters, Senators Jon Kyl and Dianne Feinstein introduced Senate Joint Resolution 3. The resolution called for congressional endorsement of a victims' rights amendment to the U.S. Constitution.[13] According to Kyl and Feinstein, in speaking about an earlier, similar version of the resolution, "Extending basic rights to victims will not take away any right of the accused. It will merely give courts the ability to balance legitimate interests. This can only be accomplished by giving victims constitutionally protected rights equal in weight to those of the accused."[14]

Not everyone thinks a victims' rights amendment to the constitution is a good idea, however. Elisabeth Semel, a San Diego attorney and member of the National Association of Criminal Defense Lawyers, said of an earlier version of the resolution: "We have a constitutional system that is intended to be out of balance—that's what the presumption of innocence is all about. The proposed amendment," says Semel, "would have an impact at a stage when someone merely is accused of a crime, not convicted of one."[15]

LAW ON THE BOOKS

"RIGHTS OF CRIME VICTIMS" UNDER CALIFORNIA LAW.
CALIFORNIA PENAL CODE

Section 679. In recognition of the civil and moral duty of victims and witnesses of crime to fully and voluntarily cooperate with law enforcement and prosecutorial agencies, and in further recognition of the continuing importance of this citizen cooperation to state and local law enforcement efforts and the general effectiveness and well-being of the criminal justice system of this state, the Legislature declares its intent, in the enactment of this title, to ensure that all victims and witnesses of crime are treated with dignity, respect, courtesy, and sensitivity. It is the further intent that the rights enumerated in Section 679.02 relating to victims and witnesses of crime are honored and protected by law enforcement agencies, prosecutors, and judges in a manner no less vigorous than the protections afforded criminal defendants. It is the intent of the Legislature to add to Section 679.02 references to new rights as or soon after they are created. The failure to enumerate in that section a right which is enumerated elsewhere in the law shall not be deemed to diminish the importance or enforceability of that right.

Section 679.01. As used in this title, the following definitions shall control:

a. "Crime" means an act committed in this state which, if committed by a competent adult, would constitute a misdemeanor or felony.

b. "Victim" means a person against whom a crime has been committed.

c. "Witness" means any person who has been or is expected to testify for the prosecution, or who, by reason of having relevant information, is subject to call or likely to be called as a witness for the prosecution, whether or not any action or proceeding has yet been commenced.

Section 679.02. (a) The following are hereby established as the statutory rights of victims and witnesses of crimes:

1. To be notified as soon as feasible that a court proceeding to which he or she has been subpoenaed as a witness will not proceed as scheduled, provided the prosecuting attorney determines that the witness' attendance is not required.

2. Upon request of the victim or a witness, to be informed by the prosecuting attorney of the final disposition of the case, as provided by Section 11116.10.

3. For the victim, the victim's parents or guardian if the victim is a minor, or the next of kin of the victim if the victim has died, to be notified of all sentencing proceedings, and of the right to appear, to reasonably express his or her views, and to have the court consider his or her statements, as provided by Section 1191.1.

4. For the victim, the victim's parents or guardian if the victim is a minor, or the next of kin of the victim if the victim has died, to be notified of all juvenile disposition hearings in which the alleged act would have been a felony if committed by an adult, and of the right to attend and to express his or her views, as provided by Section 656.2 of the Welfare and Institutions Code.

5. Upon request by the victim, or the next of kin of the victim if the victim has died, to be notified of any parole eligibility hearing and of the right to appear, to reasonably express his or her views, and to have his or her statements considered, as provided by Section 3043 of this code and by Section 1767 of the Welfare and Institutions Code.

6. Upon request by the victim, or the next of kin of the victim if the crime was a homicide, to be notified of an inmate's placement in a reentry or work furlough program, or notified of the inmate's escape as provided by Section 11155.

7. To be notified that he or she may be entitled to witness fees and mileage, as provided by Section 1329.1.

8. For the victim, to be provided with information concerning the victim's right to civil recovery and the opportunity to be compensated from the Restitution Fund pursuant to Chapter 5 (commencing with Section 13959) of Part 4 of Division 3 of Title 2 of the Government Code and Section 1191.2 of this code.

9. To the expeditious return of his or her property which has allegedly been stolen or embezzled, when it is no longer needed as evidence, as provided by Chapter 12 (commencing with Section 1407) and Chapter 13 (commencing with Section 1417) of Title 10 of Part 2.

10. To an expeditious disposition of the criminal action.

(continued)

LAW ON THE BOOKS

11. To be notified, if applicable, in accordance with Sections 679.03 and 3058.8 if the defendant is to be placed on parole.

12. To be notified by the district attorney's office where the case involves a violent felony, as defined in subdivision (c) of Section 667.5, or in the event of a homicide, the victim's next of kin, of a pending pretrial disposition before a change of plea is entered before a judge. . . .

Section 679.03. (a) With respect to the conviction of a defendant involving a violent offense, as defined in subdivision (b) of Section 12021.1, the county district attorney, probation department, and victim-witness coordinator shall confer and establish an annual policy within existing resources to decide which one of their agencies shall inform each witness involved in the conviction who was threatened by the defendant following the defendant's arrest and each victim or next of kin of the victim of that offense of the right to request and receive a notice pursuant to Section 3058.8. If no agreement is reached, the presiding judge shall designate the appropriate county agency or department to provide this notification.

b. The Department of Corrections shall supply a form to the agency designated pursuant to subdivision (a) in order to enable persons specified in subdivision (a) to request and receive notification from the department of the release, escape, or death of the violent offender. That agency shall give the form to the victim, witness, or next of kin of the victim for completion, explain to that person or persons the right to be so notified, and forward the completed form to the department. The department or the Board of Prison Terms is responsible for notifying all victims, witnesses, or next of kin of victims who request to be notified of a violent offender's release, as provided by Section 3058.8.

c. All information relating to any person receiving notice pursuant to subdivision (b) shall remain confidential and is not subject to disclosure pursuant to the California Public Records Act (Chapter 3.5 [commencing with Section 6250] of Title 7 of Division 1 of the Government Code).

Section 679.04. A victim of sexual assault, as defined in subdivisions (a) and (b) of Section 11165.1, or spousal rape has the right to have advocates present at any evidentiary, medical, or physical examination or interview by law enforcement authorities or defense attorneys. As used in this section, "advocates" means a sexual assault victim counselor, as defined in Section 1035.2 of the Evidence Code, and at least one additional support person chosen by the victim.

LAW IN PRACTICE

IS AN AMENDMENT TO THE CONSTITUTION OF THE UNITED STATES NEEDED TO PROTECT THE RIGHTS OF CRIME VICTIMS?

106th Congress
1st Session
S. J. RES. 3

Proposing an amendment to the Constitution of the United States to protect the rights of crime victims.

IN THE SENATE OF THE UNITED STATES, JANUARY 19, 1999.

Mr. KYL (for himself, Mrs. FEINSTEIN, Mr. BIDEN, Mr. GRASSLEY, Mr. INOUYE, Mr. DEWINE,

Ms. LANDRIEU, Ms. SNOWE, Mr. LIEBERMAN, Mr. MACK, Mr. CLELAND, Mr. COVERDELL, Mr. SMITH of New Hampshire, Mr. SHELBY, Mr. HUTCHINSON, Mr. HELMS, Mr. FRIST, Mr. GRAMM, Mr. LOTT, and Mrs. HUTCHISON) introduced the following joint resolution; which was read twice and referred to the Committee on the Judiciary.

JOINT RESOLUTION: Proposing an amendment to the Constitution of the United States to protect the rights of crime victims.

(continued)

LAW IN PRACTICE

Resolved by the Senate and House of Representatives of the United States of America in Congress assembled (two-thirds of each House concurring therein), that the following article is proposed as an amendment to the Constitution of the United States, which shall be valid for all intents and purposes as part of the Constitution when ratified by the legislatures of three-fourths of the several States within seven years from the date of its submission by the Congress:

ARTICLE

SECTION 1. A victim of a crime of violence, as these terms may be defined by law, shall have the rights:

—*to reasonable notice of, and not to be excluded from, any public proceedings relating to the crime;*

—*to be heard, if present, and to submit a statement at all such proceedings to determine a conditional release from custody, an acceptance of a negotiated plea, or a sentence;*

—*to the foregoing rights at a parole proceeding that is not public, to the extent those rights are afforded to the convicted offender;*

—*to reasonable notice of a release or escape from custody relating to the crime;*

—*to consideration of the interest of the victim that any trial be free from unreasonable delay;*

—*to an order of restitution from the convicted offender;*

—*to consideration for the safety of the victim in determining any conditional release from custody relating to the crime; and*

—*to reasonable notice of the rights established by this article.*

SECTION 2. Only the victim or the victim's lawful representative shall have standing to assert the rights established by this article. Nothing in this article shall provide grounds to stay or continue any trial, reopen any proceeding or invalidate any ruling, except with respect to conditional release or restitution or to provide rights guaranteed by this article in future proceedings, without staying or continuing a trial. Nothing in this article shall give rise to or authorize the creating of a claim for damages against the United States, a State, a political subdivision, or a public officer or employee.

SECTION 3. The Congress shall have the power to enforce this article by appropriate legislation. Exceptions to the rights established by this article may be created only when necessary to achieve a compelling interest.

SECTION 4. This article shall take effect on the 180th day after the ratification of this article. The right to an order of restitution established by this article shall not apply to crimes committed before the effective date of this article.

SECTION 5. The rights and immunities established by this article shall apply in Federal and State proceedings, including military proceedings to the extent that the Congress may provide by law, juvenile justice proceedings, and proceedings in the District of Columbia and any commonwealth, territory, or possession of the United States.

What Do *You* Think?

1. Do you believe that crime victims are entitled to "rights" at least equal to those of criminals? Why or why not?

2. Do you believe that an amendment to the U.S. Constitution is necessary to protect and guarantee the rights of crime victims? Why or why not?

3. Study the wording of the proposed victims' rights constitutional amendment in this box. Are there any changes that you might make to the wording? If so, what might they be? Why do you think such changes are necessary?

LAW IN PRACTICE

THE CALIFORNIA VICTIMS' RIGHTS CONSTITUTIONAL AMENDMENT

California is one of twenty states that have enacted a crime victims' constitutional amendment. Proposition 8, popularly known as "the crime victims' bill of rights," was ratified by the state's voters in 1982. The amendment reads as follows:

ARTICLE I, SECTION 28. VICTIMS' BILL OF RIGHTS.

(a) The People of the State of California find and declare that the enactment of comprehensive provisions and laws ensuring a bill of rights for victims of crime, including safeguards in the criminal justice system to fully protect those rights, is a matter of grave statewide concern. The rights of victims pervade the criminal justice system, encompassing not only the right to restitution from the wrongdoers for financial losses suffered as a result of criminal acts, but also the more basic expectation that persons who commit felonious acts causing injury to innocent victims will be appropriately detained in custody, tried by the courts, and sufficiently punished so that the public safety is protected and encouraged as a goal of highest importance. Such public safety extends to public primary, elementary, junior high, and senior high school campuses, where students and staff have the right to be safe and secure in their persons.

To accomplish these goals, broad reforms in the procedural treatment of accused persons and the disposition and sentencing of convicted persons are necessary and proper as deterrents to criminal behavior and to serious disruption of people's lives.

(b) Restitution. It is the unequivocal intention of the People of the State of California that all persons who suffer losses as a result of criminal activity shall have the right to restitution from the persons convicted of the crimes for losses they suffer.

Restitution shall be ordered from the convicted persons in every case, regardless of the sentence or disposition imposed, in which a crime victim suffers a loss, unless compelling and extraordinary reasons exist to the contrary. The Legislature shall adopt provisions to implement this section during the calendar year following adoption of this section.

(c) Right to Safe Schools. All students and staff of public primary, elementary, junior high, and senior high schools have the inalienable right to attend campuses which are safe, secure and peaceful.

(d) Right to Truth-in-Evidence. Except as provided by statute hereafter enacted by a two-thirds vote of the membership in each house of the Legislature, relevant evidence shall not be excluded in any criminal proceeding, including pretrial and post conviction motions and hearings, or in any trial or hearing of a juvenile for a criminal offense, whether heard in juvenile or adult court. Nothing in this section shall affect any existing statutory rule of evidence relating to privilege or hearsay, or Evidence Code, Sections 352, 782, or 1103. Nothing in this section shall affect any existing statutory or constitutional right of the press.

(e) Public Safety Bail. A person may be released on bail by sufficient sureties, except for capital crimes when the facts are evident or the presumption great. Excessive bail may not be required. In setting, reducing, or denying bail, the judge or magistrate shall take into consideration the protection of the public, the seriousness of the offenses charged, the previous criminal record of the defendant, and the probability of his or her appearing at the trial or hearing of the case. Public safety shall be the primary consideration.

A person may be released on his or her own recognizance in the court's discretion, subject to the same factors considered in setting bail. However, no person charged with the commission of any serious felony shall be released on his or her own recognizance.

Before any person arrested for a serious felony may be released on bail, a hearing may be held

(continued)

LAW IN PRACTICE

before the magistrate or judge, and the prosecuting attorney shall be given notice and reasonable opportunity to be heard on the matter. When a judge or magistrate grants or denies bail or release on a person's own recognizance, the reasons for that decision shall be stated in the record and included in the court's minutes.

(f) Use of Prior Convictions. Any prior felony conviction of any person in any criminal proceeding, whether adult or juvenile, shall

subsequently be used without limitation for purposes of impeachment or enhancement of sentence in any criminal proceeding. When a prior felony conviction is an element of any felony offense, it shall be proved to the trier of fact in open court.

(g) As used in this article, the term "serious felony" is any crime defined in Penal Code, Section 1192.7(c).

"Son of Sam" Laws

"SON OF SAM" LAWS
also known as **notoriety-for-profit laws;** statutes that provide support for the rights of victims by denying convicted offenders the opportunity to further capitalize on their crimes. Son of Sam laws set the stage for civil action against infamous offenders who might otherwise profit from the sale of their "story."

Notoriety-for-profit statutes, also called **"Son of Sam" laws,** provide additional support for the rights of victims. Notoriety-for-profit laws are intended to deny convicted offenders the opportunity to further capitalize on their crimes. The laws work by setting the stage for civil action against infamous offenders who might otherwise profit from the sale of their "story." A few state laws, such as the one in California, also target the sale of memorabilia associated with crimes. Most such laws hold potential profits in an escrow account, allowing victims or their survivors the time necessary to file suit.

In 1977, New York became the first state to enact a Son of Sam law.[16] The original New York statute was developed in response to efforts by convicted serial killer David Berkowitz to profit from the sale of his life's story. (Berkowitz took the name "Son of Sam" because of the way in which he "heard" instructions in his head telling him whom to kill.) The New York law required that publishers turn over proceeds of a convict's book to an escrow account for the benefits of any victim. The law defined "person convicted of a crime" to include "any person who has voluntarily and intelligently admitted the commission of a crime for which such person is not prosecuted."

Notoriety-for-profit laws exist today in forty-three states. The federal government also has such a law. Generally, such statutes apply to any convicted felon and provide that when an offender enters into a contract to receive profits from the recounting of his or her crime(s)—as in a book, movie, television show, or other depiction of the crime(s)—all profits, which would otherwise be paid to the offender, must instead be held for the benefit of the offender's victims. In some cases, media proceeds that would otherwise be payable to the offender must be contributed to the state's victim compensation fund.

Son of Sam laws are predicated on the belief that permitting violent criminals to profit from a retelling of their crimes in the mass media is fundamentally offensive to society's sense of propriety.[17] Profiteering is made especially repugnant by the fact that victims often continue to suffer financially and are sometimes forced to endure added emotional pain from publicity following their victimization.

The need for notoriety-for-profit laws was explained succinctly by California state Senator Charles Calderon, chairman of that state's Senate Judiciary Committee. "There used to be a saying: 'If you do the crime, you do the time,' " said Calderon. "Now it's 'If you do the crime, you do prime time.' "[18]

Son of Sam laws, although widespread, have been challenged under the First Amendment's guarantee of the right to freedom of expression. In 1991, the U.S. Supreme Court, in the case of *Simon & Schuster, Inc.* v. *New York Crime Victims Board*,[19] found New York's original notoriety-for-profit law unconstitutional. The Court held that the New York law was overly broad and could have been applied to a wide array of authors—including many whom the law obviously did not intend to target. Attorneys for Simon and Schuster pointed out that historical figures as diverse as Saint Augustine, Malcolm X, and Henry David Thoreau could have had profits from their writings escrowed in the state of New York because of misdeeds they admitted committing.

Following that 1991 case, new legislation—intended to overcome the Court's objections—was enacted by New York and several other states. Key provisions of the revised New York law specify that: (1) sanctions apply to any economic benefit an offender may derive from crime, not just to proceeds from the sale of an offender's story; (2) once notified of pending financial payments to an offender, victims have three years in which to obtain a civil judgment for damages; and (3) the state's Crime Victim Compensation Board can freeze and seize all profits before victims have the opportunity to sue. Other states have amended their notoriety-for-profit laws to include provisions designating all profits derived from the offender's criminal activities as subject to attachment; or by making their laws applicable only to literary or media works depicting violent crimes of which the offender was convicted.

Procedures required for compensation under Son of Sam laws vary from state to state. In most states, the victim must sue the offender in civil court and obtain a judgment for damages before being eligible to file a claim against the offender's potential profits. In other states, claims may be made through the state's victim compensation

LAW ON THE BOOKS

ALASKA'S "SON OF SAM" STATUTE.

ALASKA STATUTES

Section 12.61.020. Money received as the result of the commission of a crime.

a. Every person contracting with an offender with respect to the reenactment of the offender's crime by way of a movie, book, magazine article, radio, or television presentation, live entertainment of any kind, or from the expression of the offender's thoughts, feelings, opinions, or emotions regarding the crime, shall pay to the state any money that would otherwise be owing to the offender.

b. A claim by a victim arising out of an order of restitution under AS 12.55.045, or a judgment in a civil action against an offender for damages resulting from a crime is a superior claim for money that would otherwise be paid to the state under (a) of this section.

c. Notwithstanding other statutory limitations, a civil action by a victim against an offender for damages resulting from the commission of the crime, must be commenced within ten years of the date of the crime, or the date of the discovery of the perpetrator of the crime if the perpetrator is unknown on the date of the commission of the crime.

d. For the purposes of this section, if the offender has not been convicted, proof of the commission of a crime must be established by a preponderance of the evidence.

e. In this section

1. "offender" means a person who has committed a crime in this state, whether or not the person has been convicted of the crime, or that person's representative or assignee. . . .

program. Some states require that the offender be convicted before his or her profits can be frozen, while other states provide for the attachment of profits upon indictment or at some other preliminary stage in the criminal justice process. If found not guilty, however, all funds are usually returned to the person acquitted.

Victim Impact Statements

VICTIM IMPACT STATEMENT
the in-court use of victim- or survivor-supplied information by sentencing authorities wishing to make an informed sentencing decision. Also, a written document that describes the losses, suffering, and trauma experienced by the crime victim or by victim's survivors. In jurisdictions where victim impact statements are used, judges are expected to consider them in arriving at an appropriate sentence for the offender.

Another result of the victim rights movement has been an ongoing call for the use of **victim impact statements** prior to the sentencing of convicted offenders. Victim impact statements generally take the form of written documents that describe the losses, suffering, and trauma experienced by crime victims or by surviving family members. Jurisdictions that have laws supporting the use of victim impact statements expect judges to consider them in arriving at an appropriate sanction for the offender.

The drive to include victim impact statements in sentencing decisions, already mandated in federal courts by the 1982 Victim and Witness Protection Act, was substantially enhanced by the "right of allocution" provision of the Violent Crime Control and Law Enforcement Act of 1994. That law requires that "if sentence is to be imposed for a crime of violence or sexual abuse," in a federal court, the court must "address the victim personally if the victim is present at the sentencing hearing and determine if the victim wishes to make a statement or present any information in relation to the sentence."[20]

Additional wording in the 1994 law made clear that "[i]t is the sense of the Senate that (1) the law of a State should provide for a victim's right of allocution at a sentencing hearing and at any parole hearing if the offender has been convicted of a crime of violence or sexual abuse; [and] (2) such a victim should have an opportunity equivalent to the opportunity accorded to the offender to address the sentencing court or parole board and to present information in relation to the sentence imposed or to the early release of the offender."[21]

Approximately twenty states now have laws that permit direct victim involvement at the sentencing phase of criminal trials, and all fifty states and the District of

Columbia "allow for some form of submission of a victim impact statement either at the time of sentencing or to be contained in the presentence investigation reports" made by court officers.[22] Where written victim impact statements are not available, courts may invite the victim to testify directly prior to sentencing.

Hearing from victims, however, does not guarantee that a sentencing court will sympathize with them. A recent study of victim impact statements found, for example, that sentencing decisions were rarely influenced by them. In the words of the study: "These statements did not produce sentencing decisions that reflected more clearly the effects of crime on victims. Nor did we find much evidence that—with or without impact statements—sentencing decisions were influenced by our measures of the effects of crime on victims, once the charge and the defendant's prior record were taken into account.[23] The authors concluded that victim impact statements have little effect on courts because judges and other "officials have established ways of making decisions which do not call for explicit information about the impact of crime on victims."

The Constitutionality of Victim Impact Statements Victim impact statements met a significant constitutional challenge in 1987 in the case of *Booth* v. *Maryland*.[24] The case involved Irvin Bronstein, age 78, and his wife Rose, age 75, who were both robbed and brutally murdered in their home in Baltimore, Maryland, in 1983. Arrested were John Booth and Willie Reid, acquaintances of the Bronsteins, who were caught stealing to support heroin habits. Booth and Reid were both convicted of murdering the Bronsteins. Booth, however, decided to allow the jury (rather than the judge) to set his sentence. The jury considered, as required by state law, a victim impact statement that was part of a presentence report prepared by probation officers. The victim impact statement used in the case was a powerful one, describing the wholesome personal qualities of the Bronsteins and the emotional suffering their children had experienced as a result of the murders.

Booth received a death sentence, but appealed—with his appeal eventually reaching the U.S. Supreme Court. The Court overturned his sentence, reasoning that victim impact statements, at least in capital cases, violate the Eighth Amendment's ban on cruel and unusual punishments. In a close (5-to-4) decision, the majority held that information in victim impact statements leads to the risk that the death penalty might be imposed in an arbitrary and capricious manner.

In 1991, however, in what was to be a complete about-face, the U.S. Supreme Court in the case of *Payne* v. *Tennessee*,[25] recanted the *Booth* ruling, explaining that it had been based on "a misreading of precedent."[26] Like *Booth,* the *Payne* case began with a 1987 double murder. In this case, a twenty-eight-year-old mother and two-year-old daughter were stabbed to death in Millington, Tennessee.[27] A second child, three-year-old Nicholas Christopher, himself severely wounded in the incident, witnessed the deaths of his mother and young sister. In a trial following the killings, the prosecution established that Pervis Tyrone Payne, a twenty-year-old retarded man, had killed the mother and child after the woman resisted his sexual advances. Payne was convicted of both murders. At the sentencing phase of the trial, Mary Zvolanek, Nicholas's grandmother, testified that the boy continued to cry out daily for his dead sister, and Payne received two death sentences.

Interestingly, by this time *Booth* had already been decided, and might have been used by a Tennessee appellate court to overturn Payne's conviction or to send his case back to a lower court for resentencing. Nonetheless, Payne's conviction was upheld by the Tennessee Supreme Court in an opinion that then-Justice Thurgood Marshall said did little to disguise the Tennessee court's contempt for the High Court's majority opinion in *Booth.*

This time, however, due largely to an increasingly conservative majority, the U.S. Supreme Court agreed with the Tennessee justices, holding that "[v]ictim impact evidence is simply another form or method of informing the sentencing authority about the specific harm caused by the crime in question, evidence of a general type long considered by sentencing authorities." Chief Justice Rehnquist wrote for the majority: "[c]ourts have always taken into consideration the harm done by the defendant in imposing sentence." In a concurring opinion, Justice Antonin Scalia rejected the earlier ruling in *Booth*, saying that it "significantly harms our criminal justice system. . . ." *Booth*, said Scalia, had been decided with "plainly inadequate rational support."

VICTIM STATISTICS

Web Extra! 13–4

Uniform Crime Reports

UNIFORM CRIME REPORTS (UCR)
a summation of crime statistics tallied annually by the Federal Bureau of Investigation (FBI) and consisting primarily of data on crimes reported to the police and of arrests.

It is difficult to know precisely how much crime is committed yearly in the United States. On the one hand, many crimes go unreported. On the other, victims may describe their victimization experiences in terms that do not readily fit statistical categories used for determining "official" counts of crime. In addition, a number of false reports are filed, while "real" victims sometimes hesitate to report their victimization.

In an effort to measure the extent of criminal victimization throughout the nation, two major surveys provide annual crime statistics for the United States. They are: (1) the Federal Bureau of Investigation's **Uniform Crime Reports (UCR)** and National Incident-Based Reporting System (NIBRS), which collect data from police departments across the country about the number of crimes reported or known to the police; and (2) the Bureau of Justice Statistics' survey of households, better known as the National Crime Victimization Survey (NCVS), which is based on victim self-reports that are made to survey interviewers, and therefore information about crimes not known to the police is obtained. Hence, the NCVS typically uncovers more criminal activity than the UCR. Even so, the NCVS still probably underestimates the total number of crimes occurring in the country, especially those regarding gunshot and knife assaults, domestic violence, and rape. Undercounting may be due to fear of reprisals, the reluctance of victims to speak to "officials," and the general unavailability of many victims.

Comparisons between the UCR and the NCVS can be difficult. For one thing, the NCVS excludes many crimes that are counted by the UCR. Not measured by the NCVS, for example, are murder (since murder victims cannot self-report), arson, drunk driving, child abuse and neglect, and crimes against children under age twelve. Also, the NCVS survey sample of U.S. households largely omits the homeless and others not attached to traditional households.

Web Extra! 13–5

The NIBRS Project

The National Crime Victimization Survey

Web Extra! 13–6

NCVS data

For all of its shortcomings, the NCVS is the government's primary source of information about criminal victimization. Twice each year, data are obtained from a nationally representative sample (roughly 50,000 households, comprising about 100,000 persons) on the frequency, characteristics, and consequences of criminal victimization throughout the United States. In order to collect NCVS information, the Bureau of Justice Statistics annually polls people over age twelve about rape, robbery, assault, larceny, burglary, and motor vehicle theft. Partly because of the difficulty in obtaining certain kinds of information in a survey format, the NCVS does not collect data on certain crime categories (such as child abuse and drug abuse) and inevitably undercounts others (such as rape and domestic violence). Nonetheless,

NCVS data consistently show that about 63 percent of all crimes are never brought to official attention.

NCVS findings report the likelihood of victimization by rape, sexual assault, robbery, assault, theft, household burglary, and motor vehicle theft for the population as a whole, as well as for special segments of the population, such as women, the elderly, members of various racial groups, city dwellers, and other groups. As such, the NCVS provides the largest national forum for victims to describe the impact of crime and the social and physical characteristics of violent offenders. Nearly 29 million crimes were documented by the NCVS program during 1999, the latest year for which data are available. The total consisted of 7.4 million violent crimes and another 21.1 million property crimes.[28]

NCVS Findings—Violent Crime NCVS data have been gathered since 1973. They paint a vivid picture of crime in America, and show that males, blacks, Hispanics, the young, the poor, and inner city dwellers are the most vulnerable to crimes of violence. Moreover, except for rape and sexual assault, every violent crime victimization rate for males is higher than for females. Males are about twice as likely as females to experience robbery and aggravated assault. However, there are, on average, 3 rapes or sexual assaults per 1,000 females age twelve or older, compared to 0.4 rapes per 1,000 males. Almost two-thirds of victims of completed rapes do not report the crime to the police. Two-thirds of the victims of rape or sexual assault know their assailants.

Blacks are more likely than whites or persons of other races (i.e., Asians or Native Americans) to be victims of robbery or aggravated assault. In 1999 there were 10.6 aggravated assaults per 1,000 black persons; 6.2 per 1,000 whites; and 5.7 per 1,000 persons in other racial categories. Victimization rates for rape/sexual assault were not significantly different among the three racial groups.

NCVS findings indicate that 53 percent of persons victimized by violence do not know their assailants. According to the NCVS, almost eight out of ten robberies are committed by strangers, compared to just three out of ten rapes and sexual assaults. Just over half of all rapes and sexual assaults are committed by people either well known or casually known to the victim. In three out of ten incidents of violent crimes, offenders use or threaten to use a weapon.

NCVS data show that teenagers and young adults are more likely to become victims of violent crime than are older persons. Persons aged sixteen to nineteen are about thirty times more likely than persons age sixty-five or older to be victimized by assault. Almost half of all victims of violence are under age twenty-five. About a third are ages twelve to nineteen.

According to the NCVS, persons from households with lower incomes are more vulnerable to violent crime than those from higher income households. Persons with household incomes of less than $15,000 per year have significantly higher violent crime rates for all categories of violent crime when compared with those who have household incomes of $15,000 or more per year. They are three times more likely to be raped or sexually assaulted; twice as likely to be robbed; and one and one-half times more likely to be victims of an aggravated assault. Almost a quarter of all violent victimizations result in an injury to the victim.

NCVS Findings—Property Crime According to the NCVS, minorities, urban dwellers, and those who rent their homes experience the highest rates of property crime. Black households suffer higher rates of property victimization for all types of property crime than do white households (approximately 250 versus 190 per 1,000 households, respectively). Hispanic households have a significantly higher rate of property crime victimization than non–Hispanics (approximately 240 incidents per 1,000 households).

Households earning $75,000 or more annually have a theft rate about 50 percent higher than those households earning less than $75,000 annually. Households earning under $75,000 a year suffer almost twice the rate of household burglary compared to those with the highest annual earnings. Place of residence also correlates with rates of reported victimization. City residents experience higher rates of property crime (approximately 256 per 1,000 households) than either suburban residents (181) or rural area dwellers (160). Similarly, renters have significantly higher property crime rates than do home owners.

NCVS Findings—Crime Trends Between 1973 and 1994, violent crime victimization rates fluctuated.[29] Since 1994, however, declines in violent crime rates have been constant. Between 1994 and 1995, between 1995 and 1996, and again between 1998 and 1999, 10 percent reductions in the violent crime rate occurred.

Robbery trends during the last twenty-seven years have paralleled overall violent crime trends. Robbery rates fell from 1974 to 1978, then increased until 1981. Between 1981 and 1985 the rate rose slowly until 1994, and since then has decreased to around 7 robberies per 1,000 persons.

Starting in 1974 the rate of aggravated assault declined, with some interruptions, until the mid-1980s. After a few years of minimal change in both directions, the aggravated assault rate increased from 1990 to 1993. Since that time, the aggravated assault rate has fallen steadily.

Simple assault, the most common form of violent crime measured by the NCVS, increased from 1974 to 1977, remained stable until 1979, then declined until 1989. Between 1990 and 1991, simple assault rates returned to the peak levels found during the late 1970s. Between 1991 and 1994, the rates rose to the highest levels ever recorded, 32 victimizations per 1,000 persons. Since 1994, however, simple assault rates have fallen to their lowest level—approximately 21 simple assaults per 1,000 persons.

The overall property crime rate has declined since 1974. After a period of slow decline that was interrupted by a brief increase from 1980 to 1981, the burglary rate fell each year through the rest of the period. The 1999 household burglary rate was about a third that of the adjusted rate of 1973 (34 burglaries per 1,000 households).

Despite some periods of increases, the motor vehicle theft rate declined from 1973 through 1999. The 1999 rates were nearly half those seen in 1973 (10 versus 19 motor vehicle thefts per 1,000 households). In general, between 1973 and 1985, motor vehicle theft rates fell. From 1985 through 1991, motor vehicle theft rates increased markedly, peaking in 1991. Between 1992 and 1994, motor vehicle theft rates remained stable, then began to decline.

Thefts increased between 1973 and 1974, then remained stable until 1977. Since then the theft rate has declined steadily.

Violence Against Women

Violence against women first came to be viewed as a serious social problem in the early 1970s, in part because of the reemergence of the women's movement. In unprecedented numbers, scholars trained in such diverse disciplines as philosophy, literature, law, and sociology began to examine violence against women in the context of a feminist ideology.[30] One result of this heightened interest in women's victimization was the creation of the federal Violence Against Women Office; another was initiation of a National Violence Against Women (NVAW) Survey.

The NVAW Survey also gathers information on men's victimization. Using a definition of rape that includes forced vaginal, oral, and anal sex, the survey found that one of six U.S. women have experienced an attempted or completed rape as a child and/or an adult. Specifically, 18 percent of surveyed women said they experienced a completed or attempted rape at some time in their lives. The survey also found that 0.3 percent of surveyed women said they experienced a completed or attempted rape in the previous twelve months. These estimates equate to approximately 302,100 women who are forcibly raped each year in the United States.

Because some rape victims experienced more than one rape in the twelve months preceding the survey, the incidence of rape (number of separate victimizations) exceeded the prevalence of rape (number of rape victims). Specifically, women who were raped in the previous twelve months averaged 2.9 rapes. According to survey estimates, approximately 876,100 rapes were perpetrated against women in the United States during the twelve months preceding the survey.

The annual rape victimization estimates generated by the NVAW Survey are higher than comparable victimization estimates generated by the National Crime Victimization Survey. However, direct comparisons between the NVAW Survey and the NCVS are difficult to make because the two surveys differ substantially with respect to methodological issues.

The survey also found that women experience significantly more partner violence than men do: 25 percent of surveyed women, compared with 8 percent of surveyed men, said they were raped and/or physically assaulted by a current or former spouse, cohabiting partner, or date in their lifetime; 1.5 percent of surveyed women and 0.9 percent of surveyed men said they were raped and/or physically assaulted by such a perpetrator in the previous twelve months. Women were also found much more likely to be injured by intimate partners.

Generally speaking, the NVAW Survey shows that violence against women is primarily partner violence. Seventy-six percent of the women who were raped and/or physically assaulted since age eighteen were assaulted by a current or former husband, cohabiting partner, or date, compared with 18 percent of surveyed men.

Using a definition of stalking that requires the victim to feel a high level of fear, the survey found that stalking is more prevalent than previously thought: 8 percent of surveyed women and 2 percent of surveyed men said they were stalked at some time in their life. One percent of surveyed women and 0.4 percent of surveyed men said they were stalked in the previous twelve months.

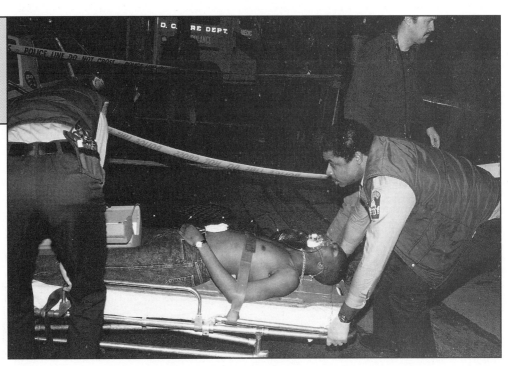

Young black males are more likely to be victims of violent crime than are members of any other group. Here, a shooting victim receives help from emergency personnel. (Photo by M. Reinstein, courtesy of The Image Works.)

Young Black Male Victims

According to data from both the UCR and the NCVS, black males ages twelve to twenty-four experience violent crime at a rate significantly higher than the rates for other population groups. According to the NCVS, black males ages sixteen to nineteen are particularly at risk and have violent victimization rates double that of white males and three times that of white females in the same age range.[31] While black males between the ages of sixteen and twenty-four comprise only about 1 percent of the population age twelve and over, they suffer 5 percent of all NCVS-reported violent victimizations. Moreover, while the rate of violent victimizations experienced by young white males has remained relatively constant during the past decade, it has increased substantially among young black males. Generally speaking, black men age sixteen to nineteen sustain one violent crime for every two or three persons annually.

Handgun violence is especially prevalent in the violent victimization of young black males. NCVS data show that for victimizations involving a weapon, among male victims age sixteen to nineteen, 50 percent of black victims and 22 percent of white victims face a handgun. The average rate of handgun victimizations per 1,000 black males age sixteen to nineteen is 39.7—or four times the rate for white males. The rate of handgun victimization by race is even more striking when other age categories are considered, as Table 13.1 shows.

> Black males age twelve to twenty-four [are] almost fourteen times as likely to be homicide victims as [are] members of the general population.
>
> —Bureau of Justice Statistics

TABLE 13.1

AVERAGE ANNUAL RATE OF HANDGUN VICTIMIZATION*

Age of Victim (Years)	Male Victims		Female Victims	
	White	Black	White	Black
12–15	3.1	14.1	2.1	4.7
16–19	9.5	39.7	3.6	13.4
20–24	9.2	29.4	3.5	9.1
25–34	4.9	12.3	2.1	9.0
35–49	2.7	8.7	1.4	3.3
50–64	1.2	3.5	0.7	1.6
65 or older	0.6	3.7	0.2	2.3

*Rates per 1,000 persons age twelve or older in each specified category of the population. Rates do not include murder or nonnegligent manslaughter committed with handguns.
SOURCE: Bureau of Justice Statistics, *National Crime Victimization Survey*, average of years 1987–1998.

NCVS data do not include information on homicide, since victim self-reports are impossible in homicide cases. The FBI's Uniform Crime Reports, however, show that although black males ages twelve to twenty-four comprise 1.3 percent of the population, they suffer 17.2 percent of all single-victim homicides. This translates into a homicide rate of 114.9 per 100,000 black males in the twelve to twenty-four age range—a rate almost fourteen times higher than that of the general population.

Elderly Victims

Persons aged sixty-five or older have the lowest victimization rates for all types of crime.[32] Although those aged sixty-five or older comprise about 14 percent of all persons interviewed in the NCVS, they report less than 2 percent of all victimizations. In a given year, according to NCVS data, persons aged sixty-five or older living in the United States experience about 2.7 million criminal victimizations.

Not only are victimization rates among the elderly low, they are declining. During the past twenty years, the lowest rate of violent crime against the elderly was recorded in 1990, at 3.5 violent victimizations per 1,000 persons age sixty-five or older. The 1990 rate was 61 percent lower than the 9 crimes per 1,000 persons in 1974—the peak year for reports of victimization of the elderly. The 1999 violent victimization rate of elderly persons was 3.8 per 1,000.

As Table 13.2 shows, the violent crime rate is nearly eighteen times higher for persons under age twenty-five than for persons over sixty-five. The rate for robbery, one of the crimes of violence, for those under age twenty-five is nearly six times higher than for those age sixty-five or older.

TABLE 13.2

NUMBER OF VICTIMIZATIONS PER 1,000 PERSONS OR HOUSEHOLDS

Age (years)	Number of Crimes per 1,000	
	Violent Crime	Property Crime
12–24	89	409
25–49	39	295
50–64	17	196
65 or older	5	96

SOURCE: Patsy A. Klaus, *Crimes Against Persons 65 or Older, 1992–97* (Washington, D.C.: Bureau of Justice Statistics, 2000).

As for personal crime victimizations, persons over the age of sixty-five are significantly less likely to become victims of all forms of household crime than younger age groups. Personal larceny with contact (purse snatching and pocket picking) is an exception. Those who are sixty-five or older are about as likely as those under age sixty-five to be victims of personal larceny with contact.

The elderly, however, appear to be particularly susceptible to crimes motivated by economic gain. Such crimes include robbery and personal theft, as well as the household crimes of larceny, burglary, and motor vehicle theft. Like the general population, the elderly are most susceptible to household crimes and least susceptible to violent crimes. Unlike younger victims of violence, however, elderly victims of violence are about as likely to be robbed as assaulted. Robberies comprise 38 percent of the violent crimes committed against the elderly but account for only 20 percent of the violence experienced by persons younger than age sixty-five.

Violent offenders injure about a third of all victims, and elderly victims of violent crime are more likely than younger victims to suffer a serious injury. Among violent crime victims age sixty-five or older, 9 percent suffer serious injuries like broken bones and loss of consciousness. By comparison, 5 percent of younger victims suffer similar injuries. In addition, when injured, almost half of all older victims (but only a fourth of younger ones) receive medical care in a hospital.

Most victims of violent crime are attacked by a stranger rather than by a relative or someone whom the victim knows. However, elderly violent crime victims are more likely than younger victims to face assailants who are strangers. Robbery victims age sixty-five or older are especially more likely than younger victims to be vulnerable to offenders whom they do not know.

Similarly, elderly victims of violent crime are almost twice as likely as younger victims to be raped, robbed, or assaulted at or near their home. Half of the elderly victims of violence and a quarter of those under age sixty-five are victimized at or near their home. The vulnerability of the elderly to violent crime at or near the home may reflect the lifestyle of the elderly, which typically involves more time spent at home and may mean living alone.

About 38 percent of elderly victims of violent crime (compared to 35 percent of younger victims) report facing an armed offender. When facing an armed offender, older victims are somewhat more likely to face an offender with a gun (41 percent versus 36 percent). Most victims of violent crime, regardless of age, face lone assailants, but about half the robbery victims age sixty-five or older are accosted by multiple robbers (a substantially greater figure than for those under sixty-five). In cases of aggravated assault, the reverse is true (younger victims of aggravated assault are more likely than older victims to face multiple offenders).

Elderly victims are less likely than younger victims to act to protect themselves during a violent crime. Victims age sixty-five or older take self-protective measures during 58 percent of victimizations, compared with 73 percent of younger victims who take such action. Moreover, older victims are less likely to use physical force against offenders (such as attacking or chasing an offender or offering physical resistance). Those persons age sixty-five or older who do protect themselves typically use nonviolent means, including arguing or reasoning with the offender, screaming, or running away.

Elderly victims of robbery and personal theft are more likely than younger victims to report victimization to the police. Seven out of ten elderly victims (versus five out of ten victims under age sixty-five) report a robbery or attempted robbery to the police. No measurable difference, however, distinguishes older from younger victims in reporting aggravated assault or household crimes to the police.

Among the elderly, NCVS data show that certain groups are generally more likely to be victimized than others. Elderly men generally have higher victimization rates than elderly women. Elderly women, however, have higher rates of personal larceny with contact, such as purse snatching. The elderly aged sixty-five to seventy-four have higher rates of victimization than those age seventy-five or older. Elderly blacks are more likely than elderly whites to be crime victims. However, rates of personal larceny that do not involve contact between the victim and offender are higher for whites.

The elderly with the lowest incomes experience higher violence rates than do others. Elderly persons with the highest family incomes experience the highest rates of personal theft or household crime. Similarly, elderly persons who are either separated or divorced have the highest rates of victimization for all types of crime, and elderly residents living in cities have higher rates of victimization for all types of crime than do others in the same age group. Elderly renters are more likely than homeowners to experience both violence and personal theft. However, elderly homeowners are more likely than renters to be victims of household crime.

PART I OFFENSES
that group of offenses, also called **major crimes** or **index offenses,** for which the Uniform Crime Reports publishes counts of reported instances, and which consists of murder, rape, robbery, aggravated assault, burglary, larceny, auto theft, and arson.

PART II OFFENSES
a group of nineteen "lesser crimes" including forgery, fraud, embezzlement, vandalism, prostitution, drug abuse violations, etc., which are reported in the FBI's Uniform Crime Reports. Part II offenses are counted only in terms of arrests (rather than as reported crimes).

The Uniform Crime Reports

The Uniform Crime Reporting (UCR) program has been in existence since the early 1930s. The program gathers statistics on crimes that are reported to the police and on arrests for two major crime categories called **Part I offenses** and **Part II offenses.** By programmatic definition, Part I offenses consist of eight major crimes: murder, rape, robbery, aggravated assault, burglary, auto theft, larceny, and arson. Part I offenses are further subdivided into **violent crimes** (also called personal crimes) and **property crimes.** Violent crimes include murder, forcible rape, and robbery, while burglary, auto theft, larceny, and arson comprise the "property crime" category. Statistics on Part I offenses, reported as "crimes known to the police," are derived from victim's calls to the police or from crimes discovered by the police (such as murder). The UCR **Crime Index** is a rate-based measure that sums the total of all Part I offenses divided by the total population. 1999 crime statistics, for example, showed that 11.6 million Crime Index offenses were reported to law enforcement in a rate of 4,267 offenses for every 100,000 U.S. inhabitants.

Part II offenses, which consist of nineteen lesser crimes, including forgery, fraud, embezzlement, vandalism, prostitution, and drug abuse violations, are counted only in terms of arrests. In 1999, for example, law enforcement agencies across the country made an estimated 14 million arrests for all criminal infractions, excluding traffic violations. The highest arrest counts were for driving under the influence and drug abuse violations—1.5 million each. Arrests for simple assaults and larceny theft followed, at 1.3 and 1.2 million arrests, respectively. Relating the number of arrests to the total U.S. population, the rate of arrest for 1999 was 5,317 per every 100,000 members of the population.

UCR statistics on Part I offenses show that 15,533 murders were committed in 1999—a 9 percent lower total than in 1998. The murder rate was 5.7 per 100,000 inhabitants. Seventy-six percent of murder victims in 1999 were males, and 88 percent were persons age eighteen years or older. By race, 47 percent of victims were black and 50 percent were white. Based on arrest data, 90 percent of murder assailants were males, and 90 percent were age eighteen years or older. Fifty percent of murder suspects were black and 47 percent were white. Fifty-two percent of murder victims were slain by strangers or by unknown persons. Among female murder victims in 1999, 32 percent were killed by husbands or boyfriends, while 3 percent of male victims were slain by wives or girlfriends. By circumstance, 30 percent of all murders resulted from arguments and 17 percent from felonious activities, such as robbery, arson, and burglary. Firearms were the weapons used in approximately seven out of every ten murders reported during 1999.

A total of 89,107 forcible rapes were reported to law enforcement agencies across the country during 1999—the lowest number since 1989. The 1999 count was 4.3 percent lower than in 1998. By definition, victims of forcible rape in the Uniform Crime Reporting Program, are always female, and in 1999, an estimated 65 of every 100,000 females in the country were rape victims. Two-thirds of all rapes in 1999 were committed by someone acquainted with, known to, or related to the victim. Similarly, two-thirds of all rapes occurred in the evening or at night, and about six in ten occurred in the victim's or someone else's home. Offenders had a weapon in 16 percent of all rape victimizations.[33]

In 1999, law enforcement agencies recorded 409,670 robberies, for a rate of 150 robberies per 100,000 population nationwide. The volume of robbery was down 8.4 percent from the 1998 total; and from 1998 to 1999, robbery rates per 100,000 inhabitants declined in all regions of the country. Monetary loss attributed to property stolen in connection with robberies was estimated at $463 million. Bank robberies resulted in the highest average losses, i.e., $4,552 per offense; convenience store robberies the lowest, or $620 per reported offense. Robberies on streets or highways accounted for almost half (48 percent) of the offenses in this category. In 1999, robberies committed with firearms accounted for 40 percent of the robbery total. Robberies committed through the use of strong-arm tactics accounted for 42 percent of the total. A third of robbery victims were injured as a result of the incident.

Aggravated assaults reported under the UCR totaled 916,383 in 1999. Aggravated assaults comprised 64 percent of all violent crimes reported in 1999. On average, there were 336 victims of aggravated assault for every 100,000 people nationwide in 1999. In 1999, 35 percent of all aggravated assaults were committed with blunt objects or other dangerous weapons. Personal weapons, such as hands, fists, and feet, were used in 29 percent of such assaults; firearms in 18 percent; and knives or cutting instruments in the remainder. Strangers committed about 60 percent of all aggravated assaults, while the assailant was known to the victim in about 40 percent of assaults.

The total number of burglaries reported under the UCR program in 1999 was 2.1 million, for a rate of 770 burglaries per every 100,000 U.S. inhabitants. Two out of every three reported burglaries were residential in nature. Sixty-four percent of all burglaries involved forcible entry, and 53 percent occurred during daylight hours. The total value of all property stolen during burglaries was estimated at $3.1 billion in 1999.

Larceny-theft, with a reported total of 6.9 million offenses, comprised 60 percent of all Crime Index offenses in 1999. The total dollar loss to victims of theft nationwide was $4.7 billion. The average value of property stolen was $678 per incident. Thefts of motor vehicle parts made up the largest portion of reported larcenies, or 36 percent.

Slightly fewer than 1.2 million motor vehicles were reported stolen in 1999. The estimated value of motor vehicles stolen nationwide was $7 billion, for an average of $6,104 per vehicle.

A total 66,326 arson offenses were reported in 1999. As in previous years, structures were the most frequent targets of arsonists in 1999, comprising 45 percent of all reported incidents. Residential property was involved in 28 percent of structural arsons during the year, and 19 percent of arsons were directed at single-family dwellings. In 1999, the monetary value of property damaged due to arson averaged $10,882 per offense. Of the arsons cleared during the year, 54 percent involved only young people under the age of eighteen, a higher percentage of juvenile involvement than for any other Index Crime.

THE COSTS OF CRIMINAL VICTIMIZATION

Neither the UCR nor the NCVS attempt to measure crime costs and consequences comprehensively nor do they attempt to document and assess crime-induced permanent disability and mental health treatment costs, which would cover such intangibles as the pain, suffering, fear, and lost quality of life that victimization brings. A recent two-year multidisciplinary research effort by the Bureau of Justice Statistics (BJS),[34] however, did just that.

As a result of the survey, BJS estimates place the tangible costs of personal crime in the United States at approximately $105 billion annually, including medical expenses, lost earnings, and public program costs related to victim assistance. Such tangible losses, however, do not account for the full impact of crime on victims, according to BJS, because they ignore pain, suffering, and lost quality of life. When dollar estimates of such **hidden costs of crime** are made, costs to victims increase to an estimated $450 billion annually. Violent crime (including drunk driving and arson) accounts for $426 billion of the total, and property crime another $24 billion. According to BJS, several "yardsticks" put such estimated costs into context:

HIDDEN COSTS OF CRIME

the intangible impact of crime on victims, including such difficult-to-measure aspects of the victimization experience as pain, suffering, and decreased quality of life.

- Violent crime accounts for 3 percent of U.S. medical spending and for 14 percent of injury-related medical spending.

- Violent crime results in wage losses equivalent to 1 percent of American earnings annually.

- Violent crime is a significant factor in mental health care usage. As much as 10 to 20 percent of mental health care expenditures in the United States may be attributable to crime, primarily for victims treated as a result of their victimization. About half of these expenditures are for child abuse victims who are receiving treatment for abuse experienced years earlier. These estimates do not include any treatment for perpetrators of violence.

- Personal crime reduces the average American's quality of life annually by 1.8 percent. Violence alone causes a 1.7 percent loss. These estimates, according to study authors, are conservative because they include only costs to victimized households and ignore the broader impact of crime-induced fear on our society.

Behind the dollar figures assigned by researchers lies the social toll exacted by crime. Social costs consist of adverse emotional and psychological effects that can have far-reaching consequences for crime victims. Translating them into dollar figures, says BJS, "borrows from the approach of the civil law damage suit and helps illustrate just how profound these effects can be."

Although the BJS authors recognize that "placing a dollar value on the suffering resulting from violent crime may seem cold and impersonal" to some, "such information is useful in the public policy arena." Without a common measure to compare various crimes, say the authors, "it is difficult to assess the merits of criminal justice or victim assistance programs." For example, "the aggregate out-of-pocket costs of rape are about $7.5 billion, roughly equal to the out-of-pocket costs to burglary victims and less than the approximately $9 billion cost to larceny victims. Yet the crimes of burglary and larceny have much less severe psychological effects on victims. When pain, suffering, and lost quality of life are quantified, the cost of rape—$127 billion—dwarfs the estimated costs of either burglary or larceny."

As the authors observe, the "complete characterization of criminal victimization costs can be an important tool in formulating criminal justice policy." Identifying and quantifying costs and consequences of victimization may be helpful both in characterizing the crime problem and in examining ways to address it, while ignoring the nonmonetary benefits of crime reduction can lead to a misallocation of resources. For example, say the study authors, "suppose that an additional year of incarceration for a rape offender would prevent one additional rape incident. Considering only tangible, out-of-pocket costs, the average rape (or attempted rape) costs $5,100—less than the $15,000 to $20,000 annual cost of a prison cell. The bulk of these expenses are medical and mental health care costs to victims. However, if rape's effect on the victim's quality of life is quantified, the average rape costs $87,000—many times greater than the cost of prison."

Another example cited by study authors are early release-from-prison programs. "When offenders are kept in prison," says the report, "there is no cost to individual victims during the incapacitation period. By contrast, when an offender who is released early (to avoid the high cost of incarceration) commits a crime, the costs are shifted to the victim. The high cost the victim must pay highlights the importance of ensuring public safety in designing early release programs."

RESTITUTION

The 1982 President's Task Force on Victims of Crime recognized the inequitable financial consequences that often follow criminal victimization with these words: "It is simply unfair that victims should have to liquidate their assets, mortgage their homes, or sacrifice their health or education or that of their children while the offender escapes responsibility for the financial hardship he has imposed. It is unjust that a victim should have to sell his car to pay bills while the offender drives to his probation appointments. The victim may be placed in a financial crisis that will last a lifetime. If one of the two must go into debt, the offender should do so."[35] The report recommended that legislation be passed requiring restitution (defined in Chapter 12) in all criminal cases. The report also suggested that mandates be established requiring judges to order that convicted offenders be required to pay restitution in cases where victims have suffered financially, unless compelling reasons to the contrary could be demonstrated.

A year later, the American Bar Association, in its *Guidelines for Fair Treatment of Crime Victims and Witnesses,* recommended that "victims of a crime involving economic loss, loss of earnings, or [loss of] earning capacity should be able to expect the sentencing body to give priority consideration to restitution as a condition of probation.[36]

The President's Task Force and the ABA were both recognizing growing sentiment, brought about throughout the nation by the burgeoning victims' rights movement of the 1970s, in support of offender restitution. Although offenders in times past were often required to make restitution payments to their victims, the development of the concept of King's Peace (discussed earlier) and the associated vision of crime as an offense against society (rather than as primarily a violation of the individual) led to the abandonment of mandated offender restitution—and its replacement with fines paid to government authorities.

One of the original proponents of restitution as a sentencing philosophy was criminologist Stephen Schafer. Schafer, who wrote the book *The Victim and His Criminal*[37] in 1968, discussed three types of restitution: (1) compensatory fines, which can be imposed in addition to other court-ordered punishments and which compensate the victim for the actual amount of loss; (2) double or treble damages, in which offenders are required, as punishment, to pay the victim back more than the amount of the original injury; and (3) restitution in lieu of other punishment, where the offender discharges any criminal responsibility by compensating the victim. The latter form of restitution imposes no other criminal penalties if the offender meets his or her restitution obligations.

Restitution differs considerably in nature from government-sponsored victim assistance. Although both may result in financial payments to victims, court-ordered offender restitution is a sentencing option that forces the offender to assume at least some financial responsibility for crime committed. Restitution advocates argue that criminal offenders should be required to shoulder a substantial portion of the financial burden required to make victims whole again. Requiring offenders to make restitution payments, they say, helps restore victims to their previous condition of "wholeness" and also places at least partial responsibility for the process back on offenders who caused the loss of "wholeness" to begin with. Advocates of court-ordered restitution, which works through fines and garnishments, claim that, as a sentence, restitution benefits everyone because it lessens society's share of the financial costs of assisting victims and because it enhances the sense of social and individual responsibility that convicted offenders are made to experience.

The Restoration Movement

The change in perspective that the American system of justice underwent in the 1970s and 1980s meant that restitution was no longer seen "solely as a punitive or rehabilitative measure," but came to be understood "as a matter of justice to crime victims. . . ."[38] A maturing of the victims movement led to development of the concept of restoration, which was built on a restorative justice model.[39] Restorative justice (defined and discussed more fully in Chapter 12) builds on restitution and other sentencing strategies to benefit all parties impacted by the criminal event—i.e., the victim, society, and the offender.

A recent report by the U.S. Department of Justice explains restoration this way: "Crime was once defined as a 'violation of the State.' This remains the case today, but we now recognize that crime is far more. It is—among other things—a violation of one person by another. While retributive justice may address the first type of violation adequately, restorative justice is required to effectively address the later. . . . Thus (through restorative justice) we seek to attain a balance between the legitimate needs of the community, the . . . offender, and the victim.[40]

Vermont began a Sentencing Options Program in 1995 built around the concept of reparative probation. The Vermont program provides an example of how the restorative justice model can be put into practice. According to state officials, the Vermont reparative options program, which "requires the offender to make reparations to the victim and to the community, marks the first time in the United States that the restorative justice model has been embraced by a state department of corrections and implemented on a statewide scale."[41] Vermont's reparative program builds on "community reparative boards," consisting of five or six citizens from the community where the crime was committed, and requires face-to-face public meetings between the offender and board representatives. Keeping in mind the program's avowed goals of "making the victim(s) whole again" and having the offender "make amends to the community," board members determine the specifics of the offender's sentence. Options include restitution, community service, victim–offender mediation, victim empathy programs, driver improvement courses, and similar programs. Some advocates of the restoration philosophy of sentencing point out that restitution payments and work programs that benefit the victim may also have the added benefit of rehabilitating the offender. The hope is that such sentences can teach offenders personal responsibility through structured financial obligations, job requirements, regularly scheduled payments, and the like.

One proponent of the restorative justice model points out that a central question still needing to be answered is: "Who or what is restored?" According to John V. Wilmerding, "while various groups embracing different perspectives may say that using the term restorative justice implies that victims, communities, offenders, or even the entire 'trinity' of these benefit from 'restoration,' in fact none of these interpretations suffices completely, for each is vulnerable to criticisms from those with differing opinions or felt philosophical loyalties." A better answer to the question of "Who or what is restored?" says Wilmerding, is "equity." Wilmerding writes: "Heralded in antiquity, crystallized in the major religious philosophies, and brought to bear upon practical social theory during the American Revolution was the premise that a cardinal component of justice is equity, and that some kinds of processes are uniquely suited to restoring equity. And while some of these justice processes might also be said to foster the conservation and even the creation of equity, it may be posited that the restoration of equity is indeed the most important central calling within the modern compensatory trend popularly known as restorative justice."[42] As a consequence of such thinking, Wilmerding suggests use of the term "equity restorative justice" in place of "restorative justice."

SUMMARY

- A victim is any person against whom an offense has been committed. For certain procedural purposes, a parent or legal guardian is considered to be the victim if the actual victim is below the age of eighteen years or is incompetent. A victim may also be one or more family members or relatives designated by the court if the actual victim is deceased or incapacitated.
- During the "Golden Age of the Victim," which blossomed a few hundred years ago in England, victims had well-recognized rights, including a personal say in imposing punishments on apprehended offenders.

- An international rebirth of the "Golden Age" began during the 1960s, when a renewed interest in victims worldwide led to a resurgence of efforts intended to assist them.

- Victim compensation programs are part of the new "Golden Age" and exist in many states to help pay the medical and other costs associated with the victimization experience.

- During the past two decades a flurry of victims' rights legislation has been passed by state governments and by the federal government. The most significant victims' legislation to date has been the 1984 federal Victims of Crime Act (VOCA), which established a federal crime victim compensation fund and the federal Office for Victims of Crime (OVC).

- A key focus of victims' rights advocates today is on passage of a federal constitutional amendment, which proponents claim would give victims and offenders equal standing in criminal proceedings.

- "Son of Sam" laws, also known as notoriety-for-profit laws, provide additional support for the rights of victims by denying convicted offenders the opportunity to further capitalize on their crimes. Such laws set the stage for civil action against infamous offenders who might otherwise profit from the sale of their "story" to media representatives or from the sale of crime memorabilia.

- Victim impact statements, which are supported by laws in many states and (for certain crimes) under federal jurisdiction, provide for the in-court use of victim- or survivor-supplied information by sentencing authorities wishing to make an informed sentencing decision. A federal "right of allocution" permits victims to make in-court statements during the sentencing of offenders who have committed violent or sex crimes.

- Statistics describing the extent of crime in the United States are available from two major sources: the Bureau of Justice Statistics, which publishes the annual National Crime Victimization Survey (NCVS); and the FBI, which publishes the annual Uniform Crime Reports (UCR).

- The NCVS depends primarily on victim self-reports made to surveyors, while the UCR gathers data on reported crimes and on arrests from police departments nationwide.

- Crime surveys show that while the incidence of crime rose after the 1960s, crime rates today are declining in most categories for which information is gathered.

- Crime surveys, while they measure the extent of crime commission, do not measure the costs of crime to victims and to society as a whole. Moreover, when such hidden costs as the pain and suffering experienced by victims are considered, even official estimates of dollar losses do not approach the true cost of crime.

- Court-ordered restitution is one method by which victims can recoup some of the costs of victimization. Restitution supports the restorative justice model, which holds that it is necessary to attain a balance between the legitimate needs of the community, the offender, and the victim.

QUESTIONS FOR DISCUSSION

1. Do you believe that the definition of the term "victim" offered by this chapter is adequate? Why or why not?

2. How did the status of crime victims during the historical "Golden Age of the Victim" differ from the status of victims today? Discuss how a changed view of the nature of crime has impacted the status of victims.

3. What is meant by "victims' rights?" Should today's crime victims have more rights? Why or why not?

4. Do you believe that a victims' rights amendment to the U.S. Constitution is needed to balance the rights of crime victims with those of suspects? Why or why not?

5. If you were a sentencing judge hearing or reading a victim impact statement, what kinds of information would you like it to contain?

6. List the "hidden costs of crime." How many different "costs" can you think of?

LEGAL RESOURCES ON THE WORLD WIDE WEB

A growing number of victims' organizations have created sites on the World Wide Web. Some of the better known are listed here.

Center for Crime Victims' Rights, Remedies and Resources
http://www.newhaven.edu/UNH/ShowcaseSites/CenterStudyCrimeVictims.html
The School of Public Safety and Professional Studies of the University of New Haven is home to the Center for the Study of Crime Victims Rights, Remedies, and Resources. The center assists crime victims through educational, training, and technical assistance.

National Center for Victims of Crime (formerly the National Victim Center)
http://www.nvc.org
Extensive online resource for victim information and advocacy. Contains many links and information about the organization's advocacy efforts.

National Crime Victims Research and Treatment Center
http://www.musc.edu/cvc
A Web site that works to foster "better understanding of the impact of criminal victimization on adults, children and their families." Contains information about the center and its work as well as links to related sites.

National Organization for Victim Assistance (NOVA)
http://www.try-nova.org
NOVA is a private, nonprofit organization of victim and witness assistance programs and practitioners, criminal justice agencies and professionals, mental health professionals, researchers, former victims and survivors, and others who are committed to the recognition and implementation of victims' rights and services.

National Victims Constitutional Amendment Network (NVCAN)
http://www.nvcan.org
NVCAN supports the adoption of a U.S. constitutional amendment recognizing the fundamental rights of crime victims to be treated with dignity, fairness, and respect by the criminal justice system.

Office for Victims of Crime (OVC)
http://www.ojp.usdoj.gov/ovc
A U.S. Department of Justice site with information about crime victims and resources for crime victims. Contains an extensive collection of links to relevant information.

Victim Offender Mediation Association (VOMA)
http://www.igc.org/voma
VOMA's purpose is to develop and implement a program of public information and education in the field of victim offender mediation and reconciliation programs.

Check the *Criminal Law Today* Web site for URLs that may have changed.

SUGGESTED READINGS AND CLASSIC WORKS

Robert B. Coates, Boris Kalanj, and Mark S. Umbreit, *Victim Meets Offender: The Impact of Restorative Justice and Mediation* (Monsey, NY: Willow Tree Press, 1994).

Gwynn Davis, *Making Amends: Mediation and Reparation in Criminal Justice* (New York: Routledge, 1992).

Robert C. Davis, Arthur J. Lurigio, and Wesley Skogan (Eds.), *Victims of Crime*, 2nd ed. (Newbury Park, CA: Sage, 1996).

Ezzat A. Fattah (Ed.), *From Crime Policy to Victim Policy: Reorienting the Justice System* (New York: St. Martin's Press, 1986).

Ezzat A. Fattah, *The Plight of Crime Victims in Modern Society* (New York: St. Martin's Press, 1989).

George P. Fletcher, *With Justice for Some* (Reading, MA: Addison-Wesley, 1995).

John Hagan, *Victims Before the Law: The Organizational Domination of Criminal Law* (Toronto: Butterworth, 1983).

Marilyn D. McShane and Frank P. Williams III (Eds.), *Victims of Crime and the Victimization Process*, reprint ed. (New York: Garland, 1997).

Shelley Neiderbach, *Invisible Wounds: Crime Victims Speak* (Binghamton, NY: Haworth Press, 1986).

Valiant Poliny, *A Public Policy Analysis of the Emerging Victims' Rights Movement* (San Francisco: Austin & Winfield, 1995).

Albert R. Roberts, *Helping Crime Victims: Research, Policy, and Practice* (Newbury Park, CA: Sage, 1990).

Stephen Schafer, *Compensation and Restitution to Victims of Crime*, 2nd ed. (Montclair, NJ: Patterson Smith, 1970).

Emilio C. Viano (Ed.), *Critical Issues in Victimology: International Perspectives* (New York: Springer, 1992).

Frank J. Weed, *Certainty of Justice: Reform in the Crime Victim Movement* (Hawthorne, NY: Aldine De Gruyter, 1995).

Marlene A. Young, *Victim Assistance: Frontiers and Fundamentals* (Dubuque, IA: Kendall Hunt, 1993).

Marlene A. Young and John H. Stein (Eds.), *2001: The Next Generation in Victim Assistance* (Dubuque, IA: Kendall Hunt, 1994).

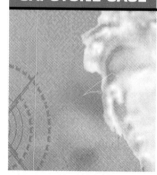

CAPSTONE CASE

THE CONSTITUTIONALITY OF NOTORIETY-FOR-PROFIT LAWS: DOES A PERSON WHO COMMITS A CRIME HAVE A RIGHT TO LATER PROFIT FROM IT?

Simon & Schuster, Inc. v. *The New York State Crime Victims Board*
U.S. Supreme Court, 1991
502 U.S. 105

OPINION
New York's "Son of Sam" law requires that an accused or convicted criminal's income from works describing his crime be deposited in an escrow account. These funds are then made available to the victims of the crime and the criminal's other creditors. We consider whether this statute is consistent with the First Amendment.

BACKGROUND: In the summer of 1977, New York was terrorized by a serial killer popularly known as the Son of Sam. The hunt for the Son of Sam received considerable publicity, and by the time David Berkowitz was identified as the killer and apprehended, the rights to his story were worth a substantial amount. Berkowitz's chance to profit from his notoriety while his victims and their families remained uncompensated did not escape the notice of New York's Legislature. The State quickly enacted the statute at issue, N.Y. Exec. Law § 632-a (McKinney 1982 and Supp. 1991).

The statute was intended to "ensure that monies received by the criminal under such circumstances shall first be made available to recompense the victims of that crime for their loss and suffering." Assembly Bill Memorandum Re: A 9019, July 22, 1977, reprinted in Legislative Bill Jacket, 1977 N.Y. Laws, ch. 823. As the author of the statute explained, "It is abhorrent to one's sense of justice and decency that an individual . . . can expect to receive large sums of money for his story once he is captured—while five people are dead, [and] other people were injured as a result of his conduct." Memorandum of Senator Emanuel R. Gold, reprinted in New York State Legislative Annual, 1977, p. 267.

The Son of Sam law, as later amended, requires any entity contracting with an accused or convicted person for a depiction of the crime to submit a copy of the contract to respondent Crime Victims Board, and to turn over any income under that contract to the Board. This requirement applies to all such contracts in any medium of communication:

"Every person, firm, corporation, partnership, association, or other legal entity contracting with any person or the representative or assignee of any person, accused or convicted of a crime in this state, with respect to the reenactment of such crime, by way of a movie, book, magazine article, tape recording, phonograph record, radio or television presentation, live entertainment of any kind, or from the expression of such accused or convicted person's thoughts, feelings, opinions, or emotions regarding such crime, shall submit a copy of such contract to the board and pay over to the board any moneys which would otherwise, by terms of such contract, be owing to the person so accused or convicted or his representatives." N.Y. Exec. Law § 632-a(1) (McKinney 1982).

The Board is then required to deposit the payment in an escrow account "for the benefit of and payable to any victim . . . provided that such victim, within five years of the date of the establishment of such escrow account, brings a civil action in a court of competent jurisdiction and recovers a money judgment for damages against such [accused or convicted] person or his representatives." *Ibid.* After five years, if no actions are pending, "the board shall immediately pay over any moneys in the escrow account to such person or his legal representatives." § 632-a(4). This five-year period in which to bring a civil action against the convicted person begins to run when the escrow account is established, and supersedes any limitations period that expires earlier. § 632-a(7).

Subsection (8) grants priority to two classes of claims against the escrow account. First, upon a court order, the Board must release assets "for the exclusive purpose of retaining legal representation." 632-a(8). In addition, the Board has the discretion, after giving notice to the victims of the crime, to "make payments from the escrow account to a representative of any person accused or convicted of a crime for the necessary expenses of the production of the moneys paid into the escrow account." *Ibid.* This provision permits payments to literary agents and other such representatives. Payments under subsection (8) may not exceed one-fifth of the amount collected in the account. *Ibid.*

Claims against the account are given the following priorities: (a) payments ordered by the Board under subsection (8); (b) subrogation claims of the State for payments made to victims of the crime; (c) civil judgments obtained by victims of the crime; and (d) claims of other creditors of the accused or convicted person, including state and local tax authorities. § 632-a(11) (McKinney Supp. 1991).

Subsection (10) broadly defines "person convicted of a crime" to include "any person convicted of a crime in this state either by entry of a plea of guilty or by conviction after trial and any person who has voluntarily and intelligently admitted the commission of a crime for which such person is not prosecuted." § 632-a(10)(b) (emphasis added). Thus a person who has never been accused or convicted of a crime in the ordinary sense, but who admits in a book or other work to having committed a crime, is within the statute's coverage.

As recently construed by the New York Court of Appeals, however, the statute does not apply to victimless crimes. *Children of Bedford, Inc.* v. *Petromelis*, 77 N.Y.2d 713, 726, 573 N.E.2d 541, 548 (1991).

The Son of Sam law supplements pre-existing statutory schemes authorizing the Board to compensate crime victims for their losses, see N.Y. Exec. Law § 631 (McKinney 1982 and Supp. 1991), permitting courts to order the proceeds of crime forfeited to the State, see N.Y. Civ. Prac. Law §§ 1310–1352 (McKinney Supp. 1991), providing for orders of restitution at sentencing, N.Y. Penal Law § 60.27 (McKinney 1987); and affording prejudgment attachment procedures to ensure that wrongdoers do not dissipate their assets, N.Y. Civ. Prac. Law §§ 6201–6226 (McKinney 1980 and Supp. 1991). The escrow arrangement established by the Son of Sam law enhances these provisions only insofar as the accused or convicted person earns income within the scope of § 632-a(1).

Since its enactment in 1977, the Son of Sam law has been invoked only a handful of times. As might be expected, the individuals whose profits the Board has sought to escrow have all become well known for having committed highly publicized crimes. These include Jean Harris, the convicted killer of "Scarsdale Diet" Doctor Herman Tarnower; Mark David Chapman, the man convicted of assassinating John Lennon; and R. Foster Winans, the former Wall Street Journal columnist convicted of insider trading. Ironically, the statute was never applied to the Son of Sam himself; David Berkowitz was found incompetent to stand trial, and the statute at that time applied only to criminals who had actually been convicted. N.Y. Times, Feb. 20, 1991, p. B8, col. 4. According to the Board, Berkowitz voluntarily paid his share of the royalties from the book *Son of Sam*, published in 1981, to his victims or their estates. Brief for Respondents 8, n. 13.

This case began in 1986, when the Board first became aware of the contract between petitioner Simon & Schuster and admitted organized crime figure Henry Hill.

Looking back from the safety of the Federal Witness Protection Program, Henry Hill recalled: "At the age of twelve my ambition was to be a gangster. To be a wiseguy. To me, being a wiseguy was better than being president of the United States." N. Pileggi, *Wiseguy: Life in a Mafia Family* 19 (1985) (hereinafter *Wiseguy*). Whatever one might think of Hill, at the very least it can be said that he realized his dreams. After a career spanning twenty-five years, Hill admitted engineering some of the most daring crimes of his day, including the 1978–1979 Boston College basketball point-shaving scandal, and the theft of $6 million from Lufthansa Airlines in 1978, the largest successful cash robbery in American history. *Wiseguy* 9. Most of Hill's crimes were more banausic: He committed extortion, he imported and distributed narcotics, and he organized numerous robberies.

Hill was arrested in 1980. In exchange for immunity from prosecution, he testified against many of his former colleagues. Since his arrest, he has lived under an assumed name in an unknown part of the country.

In August 1981, Hill entered into a contract with author Nicholas Pileggi for the production of a book about Hill's life. The following month, Hill and Pileggi signed a publishing agreement with Simon and Schuster. Under the agreement, Simon and Schuster agreed to make payments to both Hill and Pileggi. Over the next few years, according to Pileggi, he and Hill "talked at length virtually every single day, with not more than an occasional Sunday or holiday skipped. We spent more than three hundred hours together; my notes of conversations with Henry occupy more than six linear file feet." App. 27. Because producing the book required such a substantial investment of time and effort, Hill sought compensation. *Ibid.*

The result of Hill and Pileggi's collaboration was *Wiseguy*, which was published in January 1986. The book depicts, in colorful detail, the day-to-day existence of organized crime, primarily in Hill's first-person narrative. Throughout *Wiseguy*, Hill frankly admits to having participated in an astonishing variety of crimes. He discusses, among other things, his conviction for extortion and the prison sentence he served. In one portion of the book, Hill recounts how members of the Mafia received preferential treatment in prison:

> *The dorm was a separate three-story building outside the wall, which looked more like a Holiday Inn than a prison. There were four guys to a room, and we had comfortable beds and private baths. There were two dozen rooms on each floor, and each of them had mob guys living in them. It was like a wiseguy convention—the whole Gotti crew, Jimmy Doyle and his guys, Ernie Boy Abbamonte and Joe Crow Delvecchio, Vinnie Aloi, Frank Cotroni.*
>
> *It was wild. There was wine and booze, and it was kept in bath-oil or after-shave jars. The hacks in the honor dorm were almost all on the take, and even though it was against the rules, we used to cook in our rooms. Looking back, I don't think Paulie went to the general mess five times in the two and a half years he was there. We had a stove and pots and pans and silverware stacked in the bathroom. We had glasses and an ice-water cooler where we kept the fresh meats and cheeses. When there was an inspection, we stored the stuff in the false ceiling, and once in a while, if it was confiscated, we'd just go to the kitchen and get new stuff.*
>
> *We had the best food smuggled into our dorm from the kitchen. Steaks, veal cutlets, shrimp, red snapper. Whatever the hacks could buy, we ate. It cost me two, three hundred a week. Guys like Paulie spent five hundred to a thousand bucks a week. Scotch cost thirty dollars a pint. The hacks used to bring it inside the walls in their lunch pails. We never ran out of booze, because we had six hacks bringing it in six days a week. Depending on what you wanted and how much you were willing to spend, life could be almost bearable.* Wiseguy 150–151.

Wiseguy was reviewed favorably: The Washington Post called it an "amply detailed and entirely fascinating book that amounts to a piece of revisionist history," while New York Daily News columnist Jimmy Breslin named it "the best book on crime in America ever written." App. 5. The book was also a commercial success: Within nineteen months of its publication, more than a million copies were in print. A few years later, the book was converted into a film called *Goodfellas*, which won a host of awards as the best film of 1990.

From Henry Hill's perspective, however, the publicity generated by the book's success proved less desirable. The Crime Victims Board learned of *Wiseguy* in January 1986, soon after it was published.

On January 31, the Board notified Simon and Schuster: "It has come to our attention that you may have contracted with a person accused or convicted of a crime for the payment of monies to such person." App. 86. The Board ordered Simon and Schuster to furnish copies of any contracts it had entered into with Hill, to provide the dollar amounts and dates of all payments it had made to Hill, and to suspend all payments to Hill in the future. Simon and Schuster complied with this order. By that time, Simon and Schuster had paid Hill's literary agent $96,250 in advances and royalties on Hill's behalf and was holding $27,958 for eventual payment to Hill.

The Board reviewed the book and the contract, and on May 21, 1987, issued a Proposed Determination and Order. The Board determined that *Wiseguy* was covered by § 632-a of the Executive Law, that Simon and Schuster had violated the law by failing to turn over its contract with Hill to the Board and by making payments to

Hill, and that all money owed to Hill under the contract had to be turned over to the Board to be held in escrow for the victims of Hill's crimes. The Board ordered Hill to turn over the payments he had already received, and ordered Simon and Schuster to turn over all money payable to Hill at the time or in the future.

Simon and Schuster brought suit in August 1987, under 42 U.S.C. § 1983, seeking a declaration that the Son of Sam law violates the First Amendment and an injunction barring the statute's enforcement. After the parties filed cross-motions for summary judgment, the District Court found the statute consistent with the First Amendment. 724 F. Supp. 170 (S.D.N.Y. 1989). A divided Court of Appeals affirmed. *Simon and Schuster, Inc.* v. *Fischetti*, 916 F.2d 777 (2d Cir. 1990).

Because the Federal Government and most of the States have enacted statutes with similar objectives, see 18 U.S.C. § 3681; Note, *Simon and Schuster, Inc.* v. *Fischetti: Can New York's Son of Sam Law Survive First Amendment Challenge?*, 66 Notre Dame L. Rev. 1075, 1075, n. 6 (1991) (listing state statutes), the issue is significant and likely to recur. We accordingly granted certiorari, 498 U.S. (1991), and we now reverse.

REASONING: A statute is presumptively inconsistent with the First Amendment if it imposes a financial burden on speakers because of the content of their speech. *Leathers* v. *Medlock*, 499 U.S. (1991) (slip op., at 6–7). As we emphasized in invalidating a content-based magazine tax, "official scrutiny of the content of publications as the basis for imposing a tax is entirely incompatible with the First Amendment's guarantee of freedom of the press." *Arkansas Writers' Project, Inc.* v. *Ragland*, 481 U.S. 221, 230 (1987).

This is a notion so engrained in our First Amendment jurisprudence that last Term we found it so "obvious" as to not require explanation. *Leathers, supra,* at (slip op., at 7). It is but one manifestation of a far broader principle: "Regulations which permit the Government to discriminate on the basis of the content of the message cannot be tolerated under the First Amendment." *Regan* v. *Time, Inc.*, 468 U.S. 641, 648-649 (1984). See also *Police Dept. of Chicago* v. *Mosley*, 408 U.S. 92, 95 (1972). In the context of financial regulation, it bears repeating, as we did in *Leathers*, that the Government's ability to impose content-based burdens on speech raises the specter that the Government may effectively drive certain ideas or viewpoints from the marketplace. 499 U.S. at (slip op., at 8). The First Amendment presumptively places this sort of discrimination beyond the power of the Government. As we reiterated in *Leathers*, " 'The constitutional right of free expression is . . . intended to remove governmental restraints from the arena of public discussion, putting the decision as to what views shall be voiced largely into the hands of each of us . . . in the belief that no other approach would comport with the premise of individual dignity and choice upon which our political system rests.' " *Id.* at (slip op., at 8) (quoting *Cohen* v. *California*, 403 U.S. 15, 24 [1971]).

The Son of Sam law is such a content-based statute. It singles out income derived from expressive activity for a burden the State places on no other income, and it is directed only at works with a specified content. Whether the First Amendment "speaker" is considered to be Henry Hill, whose income the statute places in escrow because of the story he has told, or Simon and Schuster, which can publish books about crime with the assistance of only those criminals willing to forgo remuneration for at least five years, the statute plainly imposes a financial disincentive only on speech of a particular content.

The Board tries unsuccessfully to distinguish the Son of Sam law from the discriminatory tax at issue in Arkansas Writers' Project. While the Son of Sam law escrows all of the speaker's speech-derived income for at least five years, rather than taxing a percentage of it outright, this difference can hardly serve as the basis for disparate treatment under the First Amendment. Both forms of financial burden operate as disincentives to speak; indeed, in many cases it will be impossible to discern in advance which type of regulation will be more costly to the speaker.

The Board next argues that discriminatory financial treatment is suspect under the First Amendment only when the legislature intends to suppress certain ideas. This assertion is incorrect; our cases have consistently held that "illicit legislative intent is not the sine qua non of a violation of the First Amendment." *Minneapolis Star and Tribune Co. v. Minnesota Comm'r of Revenue,* 460 U.S. 575, 592 (1983). Simon and Schuster need adduce "no evidence of an improper censorial motive." *Arkansas Writers' Project, supra,* at 228. As we concluded in *Minneapolis Star,* "we have long recognized that even regulations aimed at proper governmental concerns can restrict unduly the exercise of rights protected by the First Amendment." 460 U.S. at 592.

Finally, the Board claims that even if the First Amendment prohibits content-based financial regulation specifically of the media, the Son of Sam law is different, because it imposes a general burden on any "entity" contracting with a convicted person to transmit that person's speech. Cf. *Cohen v. Cowles Media Co.,* 501 U.S. (slip op., at 6) (1991) ("Enforcement of . . . general laws against the press is not subject to stricter scrutiny than would be applied to enforcement against other persons or organizations"). This argument falters on both semantic and constitutional grounds. Any "entity" that enters into such a contract becomes by definition a medium of communication, if it wasn't one already. In any event, the characterization of an entity as a member of the "media" is irrelevant for these purposes. The Government's power to impose content-based financial disincentives on speech surely does not vary with the identity of the speaker.

The Son of Sam law establishes a financial disincentive to create or publish works with a particular content. In order to justify such differential treatment, "the State must show that its regulation is necessary to serve a compelling state interest and is narrowly drawn to achieve that end." *Arkansas Writers' Project,* 481 U.S. at 231.

The Board disclaims, as it must, any state interest in suppressing descriptions of crime out of solicitude for the sensibilities of readers. See Brief for Respondents 38, n. 38. As we have often had occasion to repeat, "The fact that society may find speech offensive is not a sufficient reason for suppressing it. Indeed, if it is the speaker's opinion that gives offense, that consequence is a reason for according it constitutional protection." *Hustler Magazine, Inc. v. Falwell,* 485 U.S. 46, 55 (1988) (quoting *FCC v. Pacifica Foundation,* 438 U.S. 726, 745 (1978)). "If there is a bedrock principle underlying the First Amendment, it is that the Government may not prohibit the expression of an idea simply because society finds the idea itself offensive or disagreeable." *United States v. Eichman,* 496 U.S. (slip op., at 8) (1990) (quoting *Texas v. Johnson,* 491 U.S. 397, 414 (1989)). The Board thus does not assert any interest in limiting whatever anguish Henry Hill's victims may suffer from reliving their victimization.

There can be little doubt, on the other hand, that the State has a compelling interest in ensuring that victims of crime are compensated by those who harm them. Every State has a body of tort law serving exactly this interest. The State's interest in preventing wrongdoers from dissipating their assets before victims can recover explains the existence of the State's statutory provisions for prejudgment remedies and orders of restitution. See N.Y. Civ. Prac. Law §§ 6201–6226 (McKinney 1980 and Supp. 1991); N.Y. Penal Law § 60.27 (McKinney 1987). We have recognized the importance of this interest before, in the Sixth Amendment context. See *Caplin and Drysdale, Chartered v. United States,* 491 U.S. 617, 629 (1989).

The State likewise has an undisputed compelling interest in ensuring that criminals do not profit from their crimes. Like most if not all States, New York has long recognized the "fundamental equitable principle," *Children of Bedford v. Petromelis,* 77 N.Y.2d at 727, 573 N.E.2d at 548, that "no one shall be permitted to profit by his

own fraud, or to take advantage of his own wrong, or to found any claim upon his own iniquity, or to acquire property by his own crime." *Riggs* v. *Palmer*, 115 N.Y. 506, 511–512, 22 N.E. 188, 190 (1989). The force of this interest is evidenced by the State's statutory provisions for the forfeiture of the proceeds and instrumentalities of crime. See N.Y. Civ. Prac. Law §§ 1310-1352 (McKinney Supp. 1991).

The parties debate whether book royalties can properly be termed the profits of crime, but that is a question we need not address here. For the purposes of this case, we can assume without deciding that the income escrowed by the Son of Sam law represents the fruits of crime. We need only conclude that the State has a compelling interest in depriving criminals of the profits of their crimes, and in using these funds to compensate victims.

The Board attempts to define the State's interest more narrowly, as "ensuring that criminals do not profit from storytelling about their crimes before their victims have a meaningful opportunity to be compensated for their injuries." Brief for Respondents 46. Here the Board is on far shakier ground. The Board cannot explain why the State should have any greater interest in compensating victims from the proceeds of such "storytelling" than from any of the criminal's other assets. Nor can the Board offer any justification for a distinction between this expressive activity and any other activity in connection with its interest in transferring the fruits of crime from criminals to their victims. Thus even if the State can be said to have an interest in classifying a criminal's assets in this manner, that interest is hardly compelling.

We have rejected similar assertions of a compelling interest in the past. In *Arkansas Writers' Project* and *Minneapolis Star*, we observed that while the State certainly has an important interest in raising revenue through taxation, that interest hardly justified selective taxation of the press, as it was completely unrelated to a press/non-press distinction. *Arkansas Writers' Project, supra,* at 231; *Minneapolis Star,* 460 U.S. at 586. Likewise, in *Carey* v. *Brown*, 447 U.S. 455, 467–469 (1980), we recognized the State's interest in preserving privacy by prohibiting residential picketing, but refused to permit the State to ban only nonlabor picketing. This was because "nothing in the content-based labor-nonlabor distinction has any bearing whatsoever on privacy." *Id.* at 465. Much the same is true here. The distinction drawn by the Son of Sam law has nothing to do with the State's interest in transferring the proceeds of crime from criminals to their victims.

Like the government entities in the above cases, the Board has taken the effect of the statute and posited that effect as the State's interest. If accepted, this sort of circular defense can sidestep judicial review of almost any statute, because it makes all statutes look narrowly tailored. As Judge Newman pointed out in his dissent from the opinion of the Court of Appeals, such an argument "eliminates the entire inquiry concerning the validity of content-based discriminations. Every content-based discrimination could be upheld by simply observing that the state is anxious to regulate the designated category of speech." 916 F.2d at 785 (Newman, J., dissenting).

In short, the State has a compelling interest in compensating victims from the fruits of the crime, but little if any interest in limiting such compensation to the proceeds of the wrongdoer's speech about the crime. We must therefore determine whether the Son of Sam law is narrowly tailored to advance the former, not the latter, objective.

As a means of ensuring that victims are compensated from the proceeds of crime, the Son of Sam law is significantly overinclusive. As counsel for the Board conceded at oral argument, the statute applies to works on any subject, provided that they express the author's thoughts or recollections about his crime, however tangentially or incidentally. See Tr. of Oral Arg. 30, 38; see also App. 109. In addition, the statute's broad definition of "person convicted of a crime" enables the Board to escrow the income of any author who admits in his work to having committed a crime, whether or not the author was ever actually accused or convicted. § 632-a(10)(b).

These two provisions combine to encompass a potentially very large number of works. Had the Son of Sam law been in effect at the time and place of publication, it would have escrowed payment for such works as *The Autobiography of Malcolm X*, which describes crimes committed by the civil rights leader before he became a public figure; *Civil Disobedience*, in which Thoreau acknowledges his refusal to pay taxes and recalls his experience in jail; and even the *Confessions of Saint Augustine*, in which the author laments "my past foulness and the carnal corruptions of my soul," one instance of which involved the theft of pears from a neighboring vineyard. See A. Haley & Malcolm X, *The Autobiography of Malcolm X* 108–125 (1964); H. Thoreau, *Civil Disobedience* 18–22 (1849, reprinted 1969); *The Confessions of Saint Augustine* 31, 36–37 (Franklin Library ed. 1980). Amicus Association of American Publishers, Inc., has submitted a sobering bibliography listing hundreds of works by American prisoners and ex-prisoners, many of which contain descriptions of the crimes for which the authors were incarcerated, including works by such authors as Emma Goldman and Martin Luther King, Jr. A list of prominent figures whose autobiographies would be subject to the statute if written is not difficult to construct: The list could include Sir Walter Raleigh, who was convicted of treason after a dubiously conducted 1603 trial; Jesse Jackson, who was arrested in 1963 for trespass and resisting arrest after attempting to be served at a lunch counter in North Carolina; and Bertrand Russell, who was jailed for seven days at the age of 89 for participating in a sit-down protest against nuclear weapons. The argument that a statute like the Son of Sam law would prevent publication of all of these works is hyperbole—some would have been written without compensation—but the Son of Sam law clearly reaches a wide range of literature that does not enable a criminal to profit from his crime while a victim remains uncompensated.[1]

Should a prominent figure write his autobiography at the end of his career, and include in an early chapter a brief recollection of having stolen (in New York) a nearly worthless item as a youthful prank, the Board would control his entire income from the book for five years, and would make that income available to all of the author's creditors, despite the fact that the statute of limitations for this minor incident had long since run. That the Son of Sam law can produce such an outcome indicates that the statute is, to say the least, not narrowly tailored to achieve the State's objective of compensating crime victims from the profits of crime.

FINDING: The Federal Government and many of the States have enacted statutes designed to serve purposes similar to that served by the Son of Sam law. Some of these statutes may be quite different from New York's, and we have no occasion to determine the constitutionality of these other laws. We conclude simply that in the Son of Sam law, New York has singled out speech on a particular subject for a financial burden that it places on no other speech and no other income. The State's interest in compensating victims from the fruits of crime is a compelling one, but the Son of Sam law is not narrowly tailored to advance that objective. As a result, the statute is inconsistent with the First Amendment.

The judgment of the Court of Appeals is accordingly Reversed.

Footnote

1. Because the Son of Sam law is so overinclusive, we need not address the Board's contention that the statute is content-neutral under our decisions in *Ward* v. *Rock Against Racism*, 491 U.S. 781 (1989), and *Renton* v. *Playtime Theaters, Inc.*, 475 U.S. 41 (1986). In these cases, we determined that statutes were content-neutral where they were intended to serve purposes unrelated to the content of the regulated speech, despite their incidental effects on some speakers but not others. Even under *Ward* and *Renton*, however, regulations must be "narrowly tailored" to advance the interest asserted by the State. *Ward, supra*, at 798; *Renton, supra*, at 52. A regulation is not "narrowly tailored"—even under the more lenient tailoring standards applied in *Ward* and

Renton—where, as here, "a substantial portion of the burden on speech does not serve to advance [the State's content-neutral] goals." *Ward, supra,* at 799. Thus whether the Son of Sam law is analyzed as content-neutral under *Ward* or content-based under *Leathers,* it is too overinclusive to satisfy the requirements of the First Amendment. And, in light of our conclusion in this case, we need not decide whether, as Justice Blackmun suggests, the Son of Sam law is underinclusive as well as overinclusive. Nor does this case present a need to address Justice Kennedy's discussion of what is a longstanding debate, see G. Gunther, *Constitutional Law* 1069–1070 (12th ed. 1991), on an issue which the parties before us have neither briefed nor argued.

WHAT DO *YOU* THINK?

1. Henry Hill's financial relationship with Simon and Schuster was the subject of the case described in this section. From what crimes did Hill intend to profit? How did he intend to profit?
2. What was the significance of this case for notoriety-for-profit laws? On what basis did the Court find the New York law unconstitutional?
3. Do you agree with the Court's conclusion that "[h]ad the Son of Sam law been in effect at the time and place of publication, it would have escrowed payment for such works as *The Autobiography of Malcolm X . . . , Civil Disobedience . . . ,* and even the *Confessions of Saint Augustine. . . .*"?
4. How might new notoriety-for-profit laws be written (or existing ones revised) so as to make them acceptable under U.S. Supreme Court scrutiny?

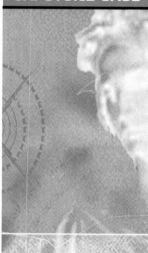

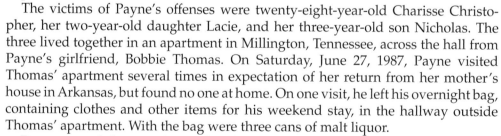

CAPSTONE CASE

ARE VICTIM IMPACT STATEMENTS ALLOWABLE AT THE SENTENCING PHASE OF TRIAL?

Payne v. *Tennessee*
U.S. Supreme Court, 1991
501 U.S. 808

OPINION

In this case we reconsider our holdings in *Booth* v. *Maryland,* 482 U.S. 496 (1987), and *South Carolina* v. *Gathers,* 490 U.S. 805 (1989), that the Eighth Amendment bars the admission of victim impact evidence during the penalty phase of a capital trial.

The petitioner, Pervis Tyrone Payne, was convicted by a jury on two counts of first-degree murder and one count of assault with intent to commit murder in the first degree. He was sentenced to death for each of the murders, and to thirty years in prison for the assault.

The victims of Payne's offenses were twenty-eight-year-old Charisse Christopher, her two-year-old daughter Lacie, and her three-year-old son Nicholas. The three lived together in an apartment in Millington, Tennessee, across the hall from Payne's girlfriend, Bobbie Thomas. On Saturday, June 27, 1987, Payne visited Thomas' apartment several times in expectation of her return from her mother's house in Arkansas, but found no one at home. On one visit, he left his overnight bag, containing clothes and other items for his weekend stay, in the hallway outside Thomas' apartment. With the bag were three cans of malt liquor.

Payne passed the morning and early afternoon injecting cocaine and drinking beer. Later, he drove around the town with a friend in the friend's car, each of them taking turns reading a pornographic magazine. Sometime around 3 P.M., Payne returned to the apartment complex, entered the Christophers' apartment, and began making sexual advances towards Charisse. Charisse resisted and Payne became violent. A neighbor who resided in the apartment directly beneath the Christophers heard Charisse screaming, " 'Get out, get out,' as if she were telling the children to leave." The noise briefly subsided and then began, "horribly loud." The neighbor called the police after she heard a "blood curdling scream" from the Christopher apartment. Brief for Respondent.

When the first police officer arrived at the scene, he immediately encountered Payne who was leaving the apartment building, so covered with blood that he appeared to be "sweating blood." The officer confronted Payne, who responded, " 'I'm the complainant.' " *Id.* at 3–4. When the officer asked, " 'What's going on up there?' " Payne struck the officer with the overnight bag, dropped his tennis shoes, and fled.

Inside the apartment, the police encountered a horrifying scene. Blood covered the walls and floor throughout the unit. Charisse and her children were lying on the floor in the kitchen. Nicholas, despite several wounds inflicted by a butcher knife that completely penetrated through his body from front to back, was still breathing. Miraculously, he survived, but not until after undergoing seven hours of surgery and a transfusion of 1700 cc's of blood—400 to 500 cc's more than his estimated normal blood volume. Charisse and Lacie were dead.

Charisse's body was found on the kitchen floor on her back, her legs fully extended. She had sustained 42 direct knife wounds and 42 defensive wounds on her arms and hands. The wounds were caused by 41 separate thrusts of a butcher knife. None of the 84 wounds inflicted by Payne were individually fatal; rather, the cause of death was most likely bleeding from all of the wounds.

Lacie's body was on the kitchen floor near her mother. She had suffered stab wounds to the chest, abdomen, back, and head. The murder weapon, a butcher knife, was found at her feet. Payne's baseball cap was snapped on her arm near her elbow. Three cans of malt liquor bearing Payne's fingerprints were found on a table near her body, and a fourth empty one was on the landing outside the apartment door.

Payne was apprehended later that day hiding in the attic of the home of a former girlfriend. As he descended the stairs of the attic, he stated to the arresting officers, "Man, I ain't killed no woman." According to one of the officers, Payne had "a wild look about him. His pupils were contracted. He was foaming at the mouth, saliva. He appeared to be very nervous. He was breathing real rapid." He had blood on his body and clothes and several scratches across his chest. It was later determined that the blood stains matched the victims' blood types. A search of his pockets revealed a packet containing cocaine residue, a hypodermic syringe wrapper, and a cap from a hypodermic syringe. His overnight bag, containing a bloody white shirt, was found in a nearby dumpster.

At trial, Payne took the stand and, despite the overwhelming and relatively uncontroverted evidence against him, testified that he had not harmed any of the Christophers. Rather, he asserted that another man had raced by him as he was walking up the stairs to the floor where the Christophers lived. He stated that he had gotten blood on himself when, after hearing moans from the Christophers' apartment, he had tried to help the victims. According to his testimony, he panicked and fled when he heard police sirens and noticed the blood on his clothes. The jury returned guilty verdicts against Payne on all counts.

During the sentencing phase of the trial, Payne presented the testimony of four witnesses: his mother and father, Bobbie Thomas, and Dr. John T. Huston, a clinical psychologist specializing in criminal court evaluation work. Bobbie Thomas testified that she met Payne at church, during a time when she was being abused by her husband. She stated that Payne was a very caring person, and that he devoted much time and attention to her three children, who were being affected by her marital difficulties. She said that the children had come to love him very much and would miss him, and that he "behaved just like a father that loved his kids." She asserted that he did not drink, nor did he use drugs, and that it was generally inconsistent with Payne's character to have committed these crimes.

Dr. Huston testified that, based on Payne's low score on an IQ test, Payne was "mentally handicapped." Huston also said that Payne was neither psychotic nor schizophrenic and that Payne was the most polite prisoner he had ever met. Payne's parents testified that their son had no prior criminal record and had never been arrested. They also stated that Payne had no history of alcohol or drug abuse, he worked with his father as a painter, he was good with children, and that he was a good son.

The State presented the testimony of Charisse's mother, Mary Zvolanek. When asked how Nicholas had been affected by the murders of his mother and sister, she responded: "He cries for his mom. He doesn't seem to understand why she doesn't come home. And he cries for his sister Lacie. He comes to me many times during the week and asks me, Grandmama, do you miss my Lacie. And I tell him yes. He says, I'm worried about my Lacie." App. 30.

In arguing for the death penalty during closing argument, the prosecutor commented on the continuing effects of Nicholas' experience, stating: "But we do know that Nicholas was alive. And Nicholas was in the same room. Nicholas was still conscious. His eyes were open. He responded to the paramedics. He was able to follow their directions. He was able to hold his intestines in as he was carried to the ambulance. So he knew what happened to his mother and baby sister." *Id.* at 9. "There is nothing you can do to ease the pain of any of the families involved in this case. There is nothing you can do to ease the pain of Bernice or Carl Payne, and that's a tragedy. There is nothing you can do basically to ease the pain of Mr. and Mrs. Zvolanek, and that's a tragedy. They will have to live with it the rest of their lives. There is obviously nothing you can do for Charisse and Lacie Jo. But there is something that you can do for Nicholas.

"Somewhere down the road Nicholas is going to grow up, hopefully. He's going to want to know what happened. And he is going to know what happened to his baby sister and his mother. He is going to want to know what type of justice was done. He is going to want to know what happened. With your verdict, you will provide the answer." *Id.* at 12.

In the rebuttal to Payne's closing argument, the prosecutor stated: "You saw the videotape this morning. You saw what Nicholas Christopher will carry in his mind forever. When you talk about cruel, when you talk about atrocious, and when you talk about heinous, that picture will always come into your mind, probably throughout the rest of your lives. . . .

". . . No one will ever know about Lacie Jo because she never had the chance to grow up. Her life was taken from her at the age of two years old. So, no there won't be a high school principal to talk about Lacie Jo Christopher, and there won't be anybody to take her to her high school prom. And there won't be anybody there—there won't be her mother there or Nicholas' mother there to kiss him at night. His mother will never kiss him good night or pat him as he goes off to bed, or hold him and sing him a lullaby. . . .

". . . [Petitioner's attorney] wants you to think about a good reputation, people who love the defendant and things about him. He doesn't want you to think about the people who love Charisse Christopher, her mother and daddy who loved her. The people who loved little Lacie Jo, the grandparents who are still here. The brother who mourns for her every single day and wants to know where his best little playmate is. He doesn't have anybody to watch cartoons with him, a little one. These are the things that go into why it is especially cruel, heinous, and atrocious, the burden that that child will carry forever." *Id.* at 13-15.

The jury sentenced Payne to death on each of the murder counts. The Supreme Court of Tennessee affirmed the conviction and sentence. 791 S.W.2d 10 (1990). The court rejected Payne's contention that the admission of the grandmother's testimony and the State's closing argument constituted prejudicial violations of his rights under the Eighth Amendment as applied in *Booth* v. *Maryland*, 482 U.S. 496

(1987), and *South Carolina* v. *Gathers*, 490 U.S. 805 (1989). The court characterized the grandmother's testimony as "technically irrelevant," but concluded that it "did not create a constitutionally unacceptable risk of an arbitrary imposition of the death penalty and was harmless beyond a reasonable doubt." 791 S.W.2d at 18. The court determined that the prosecutor's comments during closing argument were "relevant to [Payne's] personal responsibility and moral guilt." *Id.* at 19. The court explained that "when a person deliberately picks a butcher knife out of a kitchen drawer and proceeds to stab to death a twenty-eight-year-old mother, her two-and-one-half-year-old daughter, and her three-and-one-half-year-old son, in the same room, the physical and mental condition of the boy he left for dead is surely relevant in determining his 'blameworthiness.' " The court concluded that any violation of Payne's rights under *Booth* and *Gathers* "was harmless beyond a reasonable doubt." *Ibid.* We granted certiorari, 498 U.S. (1991), to reconsider our holdings in *Booth* and *Gathers* that the Eighth Amendment prohibits a capital sentencing jury from considering "victim impact" evidence relating to the personal characteristics of the victim and the emotional impact of the crimes on the victim's family.

In *Booth*, the defendant robbed and murdered an elderly couple. As required by a state statute, a victim impact statement was prepared based on interviews with the victims' son, daughter, son-in-law, and granddaughter. The statement, which described the personal characteristics of the victims, the emotional impact of the crimes on the family, and set forth the family members' opinions and characterizations of the crimes and the defendant, was submitted to the jury at sentencing. The jury imposed the death penalty. The conviction and sentence were affirmed on appeal by the State's highest court.

This Court held by a five-to-four vote that the Eighth Amendment prohibits a jury from considering a victim impact statement at the sentencing phase of a capital trial. The Court made clear that the admissibility of victim impact evidence was not to be determined on a case-by-case basis, but that such evidence was per se inadmissible in the sentencing phase of a capital case except to the extent that it "related directly to the circumstances of the crime." 482 U.S. at 507, n. 10. In *Gathers*, decided two years later, the Court extended the rule announced in *Booth* to statements made by a prosecutor to the sentencing jury regarding the personal qualities of the victim. The *Booth* Court began its analysis with the observation that the capital defendant must be treated as a " 'uniquely individual human being,' " 482 U.S. at 504 (quoting *Woodson* v. *North Carolina*, 428 U.S. 280, 304 (1976)), and therefore the Constitution requires the jury to make an individualized determination as to whether the defendant should be executed based on the " 'character of the individual and the circumstances of the crime.' " 482 U.S. at 502 (quoting *Zant* v. *Stephens*, 462 U.S. 862, 879 (1983). The Court concluded that while no prior decision of this Court had mandated that only the defendant's character and immediate characteristics of the crime may constitutionally be considered, other factors are irrelevant to the capital sentencing decision unless they have "some bearing on the defendant's 'personal responsibility and moral guilt.' " 482 U.S. at 502 (quoting *Enmund* v. *Florida*, 458 U.S. 782, 801 (1982). To the extent that victim impact evidence presents "factors about which the defendant was unaware, and that were irrelevant to the decision to kill," the Court concluded, it has nothing to do with the "blameworthiness of a particular defendant." 482 U.S. at 504, 505. Evidence of the victim's character, the Court observed, "could well distract the sentencing jury from its constitutionally required task [of] determining whether the death penalty is appropriate in light of the background and record of the accused and the particular circumstances of the crime." The Court concluded that, except to the extent that victim impact evidence relates "directly to the circumstances of the crime," *id.* at 507, and n. 10, the prosecution may not introduce such evidence at a capital sentencing hearing because "it creates an impermissible risk that the capital sentencing decision will be made in an arbitrary manner." *Id.* at 505.

Booth and *Gathers* were based on two premises: that evidence relating to a particular victim or to the harm that a capital defendant causes a victim's family do not in general reflect on the defendant's "blameworthiness," and that only evidence relating to "blameworthiness" is relevant to the capital sentencing decision. However, the assessment of harm caused by the defendant as a result of the crime charged has understandably been an important concern of the criminal law, both in determining the elements of the offense and in determining the appropriate punishment. Thus, two equally blameworthy criminal defendants may be guilty of different offenses solely because their acts cause differing amounts of harm. "If a bank robber aims his gun at a guard, pulls the trigger, and kills his target, he may be put to death. If the gun unexpectedly misfires, he may not. His moral guilt in both cases is identical, but his responsibility in the former is greater." *Booth*, 482 U.S. at 519 (SCALIA, J., dissenting). The same is true with respect to two defendants, each of whom participates in a robbery, and each of whom acts with reckless disregard for human life; if the robbery in which the first defendant participated results in the death of a victim, he may be subjected to the death penalty, but if the robbery in which the second defendant participates does not result in the death of a victim, the death penalty may not be imposed. *Tison* v. *Arizona*, 481 U.S. 137, 148 (1987). The principles which have guided criminal sentencing—as opposed to criminal liability—have varied with the times. The book of Exodus prescribes the *Lex talionis*, "An eye for an eye, a tooth for a tooth." Exodus 21: 22–23. In England and on the continent of Europe, as recently as the 18th century, crimes which would be regarded as quite minor today were capital offenses. Writing in the 18th century, the Italian criminologist Cesare Beccaria advocated the idea that "the punishment should fit the crime." He said that "we have seen that the true measure of crimes is the injury done to society." J. Farrer, *Crimes and Punishments*, 199 (London, 1880).

Gradually the list of crimes punishable by death diminished, and legislatures began grading the severity of crimes in accordance with the harm done by the criminal. The sentence for a given offense, rather than being precisely fixed by the legislature, was prescribed in terms of a minimum and a maximum, with the actual sentence to be decided by the judge. With the increasing importance of probation, as opposed to imprisonment, as a part of the penological process, some States, such as California, developed the "indeterminate sentence," where the time of incarceration was left almost entirely to the penological authorities rather than to the courts. But more recently the pendulum has swung back. The Federal Sentencing Guidelines, which went into effect in 1987, provided for very precise calibration of sentences, depending upon a number of factors. These factors relate both to the subjective guilt of the defendant and to the harm caused by his acts.

Wherever judges in recent years have had discretion to impose sentence, the consideration of the harm caused by the crime has been an important factor in the exercise of that discretion:

"The first significance of harm in Anglo-American jurisprudence is, then, as a prerequisite to the criminal sanction. The second significance of harm—one no less important to judges—is as a measure of the seriousness of the offense and therefore as a standard for determining the severity of the sentence that will be meted out." S. Wheeler, K. Mann, and A. Sarat, *Sitting in Judgment: The Sentencing of White-Collar Criminals* 56 (1988).

Whatever the prevailing sentencing philosophy, the sentencing authority has always been free to consider a wide range of relevant material. *Williams* v. *New York*, 337 U.S. 241 (1949). In the federal system, we observed that "a judge may appropriately conduct an inquiry broad in scope, largely unlimited as to the kind of information he may consider, or the source from which it may come." *United States* v. *Tucker*, 404 U.S. 443, 446 (1972). Even in the context of capital sentencing, prior to *Booth* the joint opinion of Justices Stewart, Powell, and Stevens in *Gregg* v. *Georgia*, 428 U.S. 153, 203-204 (1976), had rejected petitioner's attack on the Georgia statute because of the "wide scope of evidence and argument allowed at pre-sentence hearings." . . .

Booth reasoned that victim impact evidence must be excluded because it would be difficult, if not impossible, for the defendant to rebut such evidence without shifting the focus of the sentencing hearing away from the defendant, thus creating a " 'mini-trial' on the victim's character." *Booth, supra,* at 506–507. In many cases the evidence relating to the victim is already before the jury at least in part because of its relevance at the guilt phase of the trial. But even as to additional evidence ad-mitted at the sentencing phase, the mere fact that for tactical reasons it might not be prudent for the defense to rebut victim impact evidence makes the case no different than others in which a party is faced with this sort of a dilemma. As we explained in rejecting the contention that expert testimony on future dangerousness should be excluded from capital trials, "the rules of evidence generally extant at the federal and state levels anticipate that relevant, unprivileged evidence should be admitted and its weight left to the factfinder, who would have the benefit of cross examina-tion and contrary evidence by the opposing party." *Barefoot* v. *Estelle,* 463 U.S. 880, 898 (1983). Payne echoes the concern voiced in Booth's case than the admission of victim impact evidence permits a jury to find that defendants whose victims were assets to their community are more deserving of punishment that those whose vic-tims are perceived to be less worthy. *Booth, supra,* at 506, n. 8. As a general matter, however, victim impact evidence is not offered to encourage comparative judg-ments of this kind—for instance, that the killer of a hardworking, devoted parent deserves the death penalty, but that the murderer of a reprobate does not. It is de-signed to show instead each victim's "uniqueness as an individual human being," whatever the jury might think the loss to the community resulting from his death might be. The facts of *Gathers* are an excellent illustration of this: the evidence showed that the victim was an out-of-work, mentally handicapped individual, per-haps not, in the eyes of most, a significant contributor to society, but nonetheless a murdered human being.

Under our constitutional system, the primary responsibility for defining crimes against state law, fixing punishments for the commission of these crimes, and es-tablishing procedures for criminal trials rests with the States. The state laws re-specting crimes, punishments, and criminal procedure are of course subject to the overriding provisions of the United States Constitution. Where the State imposes the death penalty for a particular crime, we have held that the Eighth Amendment imposes special limitations upon that process. . . .

"Within the constitutional limitations defined by our cases, the States enjoy their traditional latitude to prescribe the method by which those who commit murder should be punished." *Blystone* v. *Pennsylvania,* 494 U.S. 299, 309 (1990). The States re-main free, in capital cases, as well as others, to devise new procedures and new remedies to meet felt needs. Victim impact evidence is simply another form or method of informing the sentencing authority about the specific harm caused by the crime in question, evidence of a general type long considered by sentencing au-thorities. We think the *Booth* Court was wrong in stating that this kind of evidence leads to the arbitrary imposition of the death penalty. In the majority of cases, and in this case, victim impact evidence serves entirely legitimate purposes. In the event that evidence is introduced that is so unduly prejudicial that it renders the trial fun-damentally unfair, the Due Process Clause of the Fourteenth Amendment provides a mechanism for relief. See *Darden* v. *Wainwright,* 477 U.S. 168, 179–183 (1986). Courts have always taken into consideration the harm done by the defendant in imposing sentence, and the evidence adduced in this case was illustrative of the harm caused by Payne's double murder.

We are now of the view that a State may properly conclude that for the jury to as-sess meaningfully the defendant's moral culpability and blameworthiness, it should have before it at the sentencing phase evidence of the specific harm caused

by the defendant. "The State has a legitimate interest in counteracting the mitigating evidence which the defendant is entitled to put in, by reminding the sentencer that just as the murderer should be considered as an individual, so too the victim is an individual whose death represents a unique loss to society and in particular to his family." *Booth*, 482 U.S. at 517 (WHITE, J., dissenting) (citation omitted). By turning the victim into a "faceless stranger at the penalty phase of a capital trial," *Gathers*, 490 U.S. at 821 (O'CONNOR, J., dissenting), *Booth* deprives the State of the full moral force of its evidence and may prevent the jury from having before it all the information necessary to determine the proper punishment for a first-degree murder.

The present case is an example of the potential for such unfairness. The capital sentencing jury heard testimony from Payne's girlfriend that they met at church, that he was affectionate, caring, kind to her children, that he was not an abuser of drugs or alcohol, and that it was inconsistent with his character to have committed the murders. Payne's parents testified that he was a good son, and a clinical psychologist testified that Payne was an extremely polite prisoner and suffered from a low IQ. None of this testimony was related to the circumstances of Payne's brutal crimes. In contrast, the only evidence of the impact of Payne's offenses during the sentencing phase was Nicholas' grandmother's description—in response to a single question—that the child misses his mother and baby sister. Payne argues that the Eighth Amendment commands that the jury's death sentence must be set aside because the jury heard this testimony. But the testimony illustrated quite poignantly some of the harm that Payne's killing had caused; there is nothing unfair about allowing the jury to bear in mind that harm at the same time as it considers the mitigating evidence introduced by the defendant. The Supreme Court of Tennessee in this case obviously felt the unfairness of the rule pronounced by *Booth* when it said "it is an affront to the civilized members of the human race to say that at sentencing in a capital case, a parade of witnesses may praise the background, character and good deeds of Defendant (as was done in this case), without limitation as to relevancy, but nothing may be said that bears upon the character of, or the harm imposed, upon the victims." 791 S.W.2d at 19.

In *Gathers*, as indicated above, we extended the holding of *Booth* barring victim impact evidence to the prosecutor's argument to the jury. Human nature being what it is, capable lawyers trying cases to juries try to convey to the jurors that the people involved in the underlying events are, or were, living human beings, with something to be gained or lost from the jury's verdict. Under the aegis of the Eighth Amendment, we have given the broadest latitude to the defendant to introduce relevant mitigating evidence reflecting on his individual personality, and the defendant's attorney may argue that evidence to the jury. Petitioner's attorney in this case did just that. For the reasons discussed above, we now reject the view—expressed in *Gathers*—that a State may not permit the prosecutor to similarly argue to the jury the human cost of the crime of which the defendant stands convicted. We reaffirm the view expressed by Justice Cardozo in *Snyder* v. *Massachusetts*, 291 U.S. 97, 122 (1934): "Justice, though due to the accused, is due to the accuser also. The concept of fairness must not be strained till it is narrowed to a filament. We are to keep the balance true."

We thus hold that if the State chooses to permit the admission of victim impact evidence and prosecutorial argument on that subject, the Eighth Amendment erects no per se bar. A State may legitimately conclude that evidence about the victim and about the impact of the murder on the victim's family is relevant to the jury's decision as to whether or not the death penalty should be imposed. There is no reason to treat such evidence differently than other relevant evidence is treated.

Payne and his amicus argue that despite these numerous infirmities in the rule created by *Booth* and *Gathers*, we should adhere to the doctrine of *stare decisis* and stop short of overruling those cases. *Stare decisis* is the preferred course because it promotes the evenhanded, predictable, and consistent development of legal principles, fosters reliance on judicial decisions, and contributes to the actual and per-

ceived integrity of the judicial process. See *Vasquez* v. *Hillery,* 474 U.S. 254, 265–266 (1986). Adhering to precedent "is usually the wise policy, because in most matters it is more important that the applicable rule of law be settled than it be settled right." *Burnet* v. *Coronado Oil & Gas Co.,* 285 U.S. 393, 406 (1932) (Brandeis, J., dissenting). Nevertheless, when governing decisions are unworkable or are badly reasoned, "this Court has never felt constrained to follow precedent." *Smith* v. *Allwright,* 321 U.S. 649, 665 (1944). *Stare decisis* is not an inexorable command; rather, it "is a principle of policy and not a mechanical formula of adherence to the latest decision." *Helvering* v. *Hallock,* 309 U.S. 106, 119 (1940). This is particularly true in constitutional cases, because in such cases "correction through legislative action is practically impossible." *Burnet* v. *Coronado Oil & Gas Co., supra,* at 407 (Brandeis, J., dissenting). Considerations in favor of stare decisis are at their acme in cases involving property and contract rights, where reliance interests are involved, see *Swift & Co.* v. *Wickham,* 382 U.S. 111, 116 (1965); *Oregon ex rel. State Land Board* v. *Corvallis Sand & Gravel Co.,* 429 U.S. 363 (1977); *Burnet* v. *Coronado Oil & Gas Co., supra,* at 405-411 (Brandeis, J., dissenting); *United States* v. *Title Ins. Co.,* 265 U.S. 472 (1924); The *Genesee Chief* v. *Fitzhugh,* 12 How. 443, 458 (1852), the opposite is true in cases such as the present one involving procedural and evidentiary rules.

Applying these general principles, the Court has during the past twenty terms overruled in whole or in part thirty-three of its previous constitutional decisions. *Booth* and *Gathers* were decided by the narrowest of margins, over spirited dissents challenging the basic underpinnings of those decisions. They have been questioned by members of the Court in later decisions, and have defied consistent application by the lower courts. See *Gathers,* 490 U.S. at 813 (O'CONNOR, J., dissenting); *Mills* v. *Maryland,* 486 U.S. 367, 395–396 (1988) (REHNQUIST, C. J., dissenting). See also *State* v. *Huertas,* 51 Ohio St. 3d 22, 33, 553 N.E. 2d 1058, 1070 (1990) ("The fact that the majority and two dissenters in this case all interpret the opinions and footnotes in *Booth* and *Gathers* differently demonstrates the uncertainty of the law in this area") (Moyer, C. J., concurring). Reconsidering these decisions now, we conclude for the reasons heretofore stated, that they were wrongly decided and should be, and now are, overruled.[1] We accordingly affirm the judgment of the Supreme Court of Tennessee.

Affirmed.

[selected footnotes omitted]

Footnote

1. Our holding today is limited to the holdings of *Booth* v. *Maryland,* 482 U.S. 496 (1987), and *South Carolina* v. *Gathers,* 490 U.S. 805 (1989), that evidence and argument relating to the victim and the impact of the victim's death on the victim's family are inadmissible at a capital sentencing hearing. *Booth* also held that the admission of a victim's family members' characterizations and opinions about the crime, the defendant, and the appropriate sentence violates the Eighth Amendment. No evidence of the latter sort was presented at the trial in this case.

WHAT DO *YOU* THINK?

1. In two cases (*Booth* v. *Maryland* and *South Carolina* v. *Gathers*) that were decided before the one described here, the U.S. Supreme Court held that victim impact statements were unconstitutional. On what basis did the Court reach those decisions?
2. How does the Court's holding in *Payne* differ from its decisions in *Booth* and *Gathers?* Why did the Court change its opinion?
3. What do you think of the Court's comment on the significance of *stare decisis* in cases such as *Payne?* Does the Court's interpretation of *stare decisis* significantly weaken the integrity of that principle? Why or why not?
4. Consider *Booth, Gathers,* and *Payne.* In your opinion, which case appears to offer the most reasonable constitutional interpretation of the role of victim impact statements during the sentencing phase of trial? Why?

NOTES

1. Slogan for Victim Rights Week, 1997. See NOVA's WWW home page at http://www.access.digex.net/~nova.

2. Kimi Yoshino, "Children's Wounds Detailed," *The Fresno Bee*, August 20, 2000. Posted at http:www.fresnobee.com/localnews/story/0,1724,190173,00.html.

3. "Pitchfork Attacker Kills Kid," *The Fresno Bee*, August 24, 2000, p. A1.

4. As found in Stephen A. Saltzburg, John L. Diamond, Kit Kinports, and Thomas H. Morawetz, *Criminal Law: Cases and Materials* (Charlottesville, VA: Michie, 1994), p. 38.

5. Violent Crime Control and Law Enforcement Act of 1994, Title XXIII, Section 230101.

6. Federal Bureau of Prisons, Directive 1490.03.

7. Robert Elias, *Victims of the System: Crime Victims and Compensation in American Politics and Criminal Justice* (New Brunswick, NJ: Transaction, 1983), pp. 24–26.

8. Albert R. Roberts, *Helping Crime Victims* (Newbury Park, CA: Sage, 1990).

9. Ibid., p. 31.

10. California Penal Code, Section 13835.4.

11. National Center for Victims of Crime World Wide Web site, http://www.ncvc.org.

12. It takes a two-thirds vote by each chamber of Congress to send a proposed amendment to the states, where ratification by thirty-eight legislatures is required.

13. Sen. J. Res. 3 was an amended version of SJR 65, which Senators Kyl and Feinstein introduced on September 30, 1996.

14. Richard Carelli, "Victims' Rights," Associated Press online, northern edition, October 18, 1996.

15. Ibid.

16. Some of the material in this section is adapted from Infolink, National Center for Victims of Crime online: http://www.ncvc.org.

17. See James Stark and Howard W. Goldstein, *The Rights of Crime Victims* (New York: Bantam Books, 1985).

18. "Trial and Error: Ten Things the O.J. Simpson Case Has Taught Us—For Better or Worse—About the Criminal Justice System," KQED's WWW home page, January 18, 1997.

19. *Simon & Schuster, Inc.* v. *New York Crime Victims Board*, 112 S. Ct. 501 (1992).

20. Violent Crime Control and Law Enforcement Act of 1994, Title XXIII, Subtitle A, Section 230101.

21. Violent Crime Control and Law Enforcement Act of 1994, Title XXIII, Subtitle A, Section 230102.

22. National Center for Victims of Crime/Mothers Against Drunk Driving/American Prosecutors Research Institute, *Impact Statements: A Victim's Right to Speak: A Nation's Responsibility to Listen*, July 1994.

23. Robert C. Davis and Barbara E. Smith, "The Effects of Victim Impact Statements on Sentencing Decisions: A Test in an Urban Setting," *Justice Quarterly*, Vol. 11, no. 3 (September 1994), pp. 453–469.

24. *Booth* v. *Maryland*, 107 S. Ct. 2529 (1987).

25. *Payne* v. *Tennessee*, 501 U.S. 808 (1991).

26. "Supreme Court Closes Term with Major Criminal Justice Rulings," *Criminal Justice Newsletter,* Vol. 22, no. 13 (July 1, 1991), p. 2.

27. See "What Say Should Victims Have?" *Time,* May 27, 1991, p. 61.

28. *Criminal Victimization 1999* (Washington, D.C.: Bureau of Justice Statistics, 2000).

29. The information, and some of the wording, in this section is taken from *Criminal Victimization 1999, Changes 1998–99 with Trends 1993–99* (Washington, D.C.: Bureau of Justice Statistics, 2000).

30. Much of the information, and some of the wording, in this section is taken from Patricia Tjaden and Nancy Thoennes, *Prevalence, Incidence, and Consequences of Violence Against Women: Findings from the National Violence Against Women Survey* (Washington, D.C.: Bureau of Justice Statistics, 1998).

31. Lisa D. Bastian and Bruce M. Taylor, "Young Black Male Victims: National Crime Victimization Survey," A BJS Crime Data Brief (Washington, D.C.: Bureau of Justice Statistics, 1994).

32. Data in this section come from "Elderly Crime Victims: National Crime Victimization Survey," (Washington, D.C.: Bureau of Justice Statistics, March 1994) and Patsy A. Klaus, *Crimes Against Persons Age 65 or Older* (Washington, D.C.: Bureau of Justice Statistics, Revised Jan. 2000).

33. Data in this section come from Federal Bureau of Investigation, *Crime in the United States, 1999* (Washington, D.C.: USGPO, 2000).

34. Ted R. Miller, Mark A. Cohen, and Brian Wierseman, *Victim Costs and Consequences: A New Look* (Washington, D.C.: Bureau of Justice Statistics, 1996).

35. The President's Task Force on Victims of Crime, *Final Report* (Washington, D.C.: U.S. Government Printing Office, 1982).

36. *Guidelines for Fair Treatment of Crime Victims and Witnesses* (Chicago: American Bar Association, 1983), p. 22.

37. Stephen Schafer, *The Victim and His Criminal: A Study in Functional Responsibility* (New York: Random House, 1968).

38. Susan Hillenbrand, "Restitution and Victim Rights in the 1980s," in Arthur J. Lurigio, Wesley G. Skogan, and Robert C. Davis (Eds.), *Victims of Crime: Problems, Policies and Programs* (Newbury Park, CA: Sage, 1990), p. 192.

39. Restorative justice is sometimes also termed "community justice" or "relational justice."

40. Gordon Bazemore and Mark S. Umbreit, *Balanced and Restorative Justice: Program Summary* (Washington, D.C.: OJJDP, October 1994), foreword.

41. E-mail communications with the Office of Reparative Programs, Department of Corrections, State of Vermont, July 3, 1995.

42. John Wilmerding, "Toward a Campaign for Equity-Restorative Justice," e-mail communication, January 3, 1997.

14

Punishment and Sentencing

We will not punish a man because he hath offended, but that he may offend no more; nor does punishment ever look to the past, but to the future; for it is not the result of passion, but that the same thing be guarded against in time to come.

—Seneca (3 B.C.–A.D. 65)

Punishment, that is justice for the unjust.

—Saint Augustine (A.D. 345–430)

AFTER READING THIS CHAPTER YOU SHOULD:

▷ Know what "sentencing" is.

▷ Be able to identify and distinguish between the five purposes of criminal punishment.

▷ Understand the emerging notion of restorative justice, and know the difference between retributive and restorative justice.

▷ Be familiar with the history and purpose of "three-strikes" legislation, especially as enacted in California.

▷ Understand the legal requirements for an offense to be classified as a hate crime.

▷ Be able to summarize arguments for and against capital punishment.

INTRODUCTION

This chapter describes the purposes of criminal punishment and the sentencing of offenders. **Sentencing** is the last, or culminating, stage of a criminal trial. It can be defined as the process through which a sentencing authority imposes a lawful punishment or other sanction on a person convicted of violating the criminal law. The great Christian author C. S. Lewis, writing about the justice system, once penned these words: "It is only as deserved or undeserved that a sentence can be just or unjust." As you read through the following chapter-opening story, which is taken directly from a 1993 opinion of the Utah Supreme Court in the case of *State* v. *Wood*,[1] ask yourself just what kind of punishment, if any, might be "deserved" in this case.

On October 25, 1988, Lance Conway Wood, newly released from the Utah State Prison, moved into the Cedar City (Utah) two-bedroom apartment of his girlfriend, Brenda Stapely, and her roommate, Paula Jones. Soon after, Michael Archuleta, also just released from prison, moved into the same apartment to be with his girlfriend, Paula Jones. Wood and Archuleta had known each other in prison.

SENTENCING
the process through which a sentencing authority imposes a lawful punishment or other sanction on a person convicted of violating the criminal law.

Web Extra! 14–1
Britannica online: objectives of punishment

On November 21, 1988, Wood and Archuleta purchased soft drinks at a local convenience store. After adding whiskey to their drinks, the two men engaged in a conversation with Gordon Church, who was seated in his car in a nearby parking lot. Church drove Wood and Archuleta up and down Main Street and then up Cedar Canyon. After returning to Cedar City, Church left Wood and Archuleta at their apartment complex.

Wood and Archuleta walked to the apartment of Anthony Sich, who lived above the apartment rented to Stapely and Jones. Wood told Sich that he was going into the mountains and asked if he could borrow a pair of gloves. Sich sent Wood to retrieve the gloves from his car, and while Wood was outside, Church returned and invited him and Archuleta to go for another drive.

Church drove Wood and Archuleta back to Cedar Canyon and pulled off the road. Wood and Archuleta exited the car first and began to walk down a path. Archuleta told Wood that he wanted to rob Church, and Wood acquiesced. Church overtook the two men, and the three continued walking up the trail. As the men started back down the trail toward the car, Archuleta grabbed Church and put a knife to his neck. Although Wood attempted to stop Archuleta by grabbing his arm, Archuleta made a surface cut on Church's neck. Church broke free and ran, but Archuleta chased after and tackled him, again putting the knife to his neck and threatening to kill him. Archuleta cut Church's throat again so that the two cuts formed an "X" on the front of Church's neck.

Archuleta bent Church forward over the hood of the car and, with the knife still at Church's throat, had anal intercourse with him. At Church's request, Archuleta used a condom. Archuleta then turned to Wood, who was standing by the trunk of the car, and asked if he "wanted any." Wood declined. Archuleta went to the trunk of the car and opened it. He told Wood that he was looking for something with which he could bind Church. Wood removed a spare tire and a fan from the trunk, while Archuleta retrieved tire chains and battery cables. Wood remained at the rear of the car, while Archuleta returned to the front, where he wrapped the tire chains around Church. Archuleta also fastened the battery cable clamps to Church's genitals. Wood maintained before and at trial that he removed the clamps from Church as soon as he realized what Archuleta had done.

Archuleta led Church to the rear of the car and forced him into the trunk. Wood and Archuleta replaced the spare tire and fan and drove to a truck stop near Cedar City where they purchased gas. They continued north on Interstate 15 until they reached the Dog Valley exit. They parked along a deserted dirt road where Archuleta told Wood, "You know we have to kill him."

Archuleta removed Church from the trunk and attempted to kill him by breaking his neck. When that failed, Church suffered several blows to the head with a tire iron and a jack. The tire iron was then shoved and kicked so far into Church's rectum that it pierced his liver. A state medical examiner testified that the cause of death was injuries to the head and skull due to a blunt force and the internal injuries caused by the tire iron inserted into Church's rectum.

Wood told police that he waited inside the car while Archuleta killed Church. Evidence adduced at trial, however, showed that Wood's pants and jacket were splattered with blood in a cast-off pattern indicating that Wood was within two or three feet of Church, who was on the ground during the beating, and that Wood was facing Church when the blows were struck. A blood spot appeared on the back of Archuleta's jacket, and Wood's shoes bore a transfer or contact blood stain caused by contact with a bloody object. Investigators found strands of human hair consistent with Church's hair wrapped around Wood's shoelaces. The injuries to Church's lower jaw were consistent with being kicked by someone wearing Wood's shoes. Three paired lesions on Church's back were caused by a dull-tipped instrument, such as the red-handled side cutters found in the pocket of Wood's jeans.

Web Extra! 14–2

Britannica online: effectiveness of punishment

After Church died, Wood and Archuleta dragged his body to some nearby trees, where they covered it with branches. They swept their path with branches on the way back to the car to conceal any footprints. With Wood at the wheel, the pair again drove north on I-15 and abandoned Church's car in Salt Lake City.

Wood called his friend Christy Worsfold and asked if he and Archuleta could come to her apartment for a few minutes. When the men arrived at the apartment, Worsfold immediately noticed that Archuleta's pants were caked with blood. Wood explained that they had been rabbit hunting the night before, their car had broken down, and they had hitchhiked to Salt Lake. The two men then went to a thrift store, where Archuleta bought some clean pants, and Archuleta repeated the rabbit hunting story to the store clerk.

Archuleta discarded his bloody jeans in a drainage ditch near the 45th South on-ramp to I-15 in Salt Lake County. He and Wood then went into a nearby Denny's restaurant, where Wood left the gloves he had borrowed from Sich. After eating, the two hitchhiked as far as the Draper exit, where Archuleta pulled out Church's wallet, scattered its contents, and handed the wallet to Wood. They next hitchhiked to Salem, where they visited Archuleta's father. From there, they hitchhiked to Cedar City, arriving at about 11:30 P.M.

Wood immediately went upstairs to Sich's apartment and told him about the murder. When Sich advised him to contact the police, Wood responded, "[M]aybe I could get some kind of federal protection." Sich and Wood walked to a local convenience store, where Wood called Brenda Stapely, who was in Phoenix, and told her that Archuleta had killed someone. Stapely contacted John Graff, Wood's parole officer, and told him to call Wood at the store. Graff called Wood and arranged to meet him at the convenience store. Just before Graff's arrival with the police, Wood discarded Church's wallet.

Wood and Sich accompanied Graff and a police officer to the corrections department office, where Wood recounted the events of the previous night. The police arrested Archuleta for the murder and, after several interviews with Wood, also charged Wood with murder in the first degree, aggravated sexual assault, object rape, forcible sexual abuse, aggravated kidnapping, aggravated assault, and possession of a stolen vehicle. . . . Wood was tried by a jury for first-degree murder, aggravated sexual assault, and aggravated kidnapping. The jury found him guilty on all three counts. Because the jury could not reach a unanimous verdict as to the death penalty, the court imposed a life sentence for first-degree murder and two consecutive mandatory minimum sentences of ten years to life for aggravated sexual assault and aggravated kidnapping.[2]

As we asked at the start of this chapter: Would you say that the punishment imposed on Wood was appropriate? Might some other punishment have been "deserved"? You may be interested to know that, in this case, the Utah Supreme Court upheld Wood's conviction and sentence.

SENTENCING RATIONALES

Web Extra! 14–3
Britannica online:
crime and
punishment

One fundamental way of distinguishing crimes from violations of the civil law, or torts, is to recognize that crimes are subject to punishment. As one legal scholar says, "[t]he best candidate for a conceptual proposition about the criminal law is that the infliction of 'punishment' is sufficient to render a legal process criminal in nature." As George P. Fletcher says, "[a]s a test for when processes are criminal, the Supreme Court unhesitatingly invokes the concept of 'punishment' as the relevant criterion."[3] Hence, whatever name given to a statute by a legislature (i.e., "criminal," "civil," or "administrative"), if punishment is associated with violation of the law, the Court has ruled that constitutional guarantees of due process must apply.

The need to assign blame and the need to punish wrongdoers may be fundamental human qualities. Hence, criminal law itself may be rooted in deep moral and psychological principles basic to the human way of life. Within this context, it is important to realize that punishment, as a mechanism of the criminal law, can be distinguished from other attempts to discourage undesirable conduct—such as taxes, licensing requirements, civil liability, and administrative regulations. H. L. A. Hart[4] identifies five distinguishing features of criminal punishment, which set it apart from other sanctions. Those five features are:

1. It must involve pain or other consequences normally considered unpleasant.
2. It must be for an offense against legal rules.
3. It must be of an actual or supposed offender for his offense.
4. It must be intentionally administered by human beings other than the offender.
5. It must be imposed and administered by an authority constituted by a legal system against which the offense is committed.

More important, perhaps, than any definition of punishment is the *purpose* of punishment under criminal law. Lewis' notion of *punishment as deserved,* alluded to at the start of this chapter, underlies the purpose of most criminal punishments and supports what is today called the **just deserts** philosophy. Just deserts is a popular model of criminal sentencing that holds that criminal offenders deserve the punishment they receive at the hands of the state and suggests that punishments should be appropriate to the type and severity of crime committed. While at first glance the just deserts philosophy may appeal to common sense, it is important to realize that punishment is not the only goal of sentencing. The five primary sentencing rationales operative in American criminal justice today are:

1. Retribution
2. Deterrence
3. Rehabilitation
4. Restoration
5. Incapacitation.

Each is discussed in the following pages.

Retribution

One goal of criminal sentencing is retribution. **Retribution** is the most punishment-oriented of all sentencing goals and underlies the just deserts philosophy. As one writer observes, "[t]he distinctive aspect of retributivism is that the moral desert of an offender is a *sufficient* reason to punish him or her. . . . Retributivism is a very straightforward theory of punishment: We are justified in punishing because and only because offenders deserve it."[5] Still, retribution may call for even harsher punishments than those which are merely "deserved." The purpose of retribution is to "get back" at the offender by meting out a punishment that is in some primal way satisfying to the social group and to the victim or his or her survivors.

In older times, even minor offenses could be severely punished. The punishment for simple theft, for example, could be death—a sanction often imposed on the spot, before a pursuing mob, once the offender had been caught. Hence, the Old Testament dictum of an "eye for an eye, a tooth for a tooth" may have been intended to reduce the severity of punishment, bringing it in line with what was deserved. Pun-

JUST DESERTS
a model of criminal sentencing, which holds that criminal offenders deserve the punishment they receive at the hands of the state and suggests that punishments should be appropriate to the type and severity of crime committed.

Web Extra! 14–4
National Association of Sentencing Advocates

RETRIBUTION
the act of taking revenge on a criminal perpetrator. Also, the most punishment-oriented of all sentencing goals, which claims that we are justified in punishing offenders because they deserve it.

ishments imposed by today's criminal law generally consist of imprisonment, fines, probation, or some combination of the three—although death remains an option for some especially serious crimes in a large number of American jurisdictions.

Central to an understanding of retribution as a sentencing philosophy is recognition of the fact that it holds offenders responsible for their behavior and supports the view that law violators freely choose their illegal courses of action.

Some legal philosophers, however, have suggested that punishment should never be based solely on retributive sentiments. Jeremy Bentham, for example, whose writings have substantially influenced American jurisprudence, suggested that "punishment ought not be inflicted . . . where it must be inefficacious: where it cannot act so as to prevent the mischief."[6]

Deterrence

A second goal of criminal sentencing is deterrence. Deterrence, like retribution, also depends on the imposition of punishment—although for a different purpose. Under the philosophy of deterrence, punishment is seen as a powerful inhibitor, capable of keeping behavior in line. Two types of deterrence can be identified: specific and general. **Specific deterrence** is intended to deter the individual sentenced to punishment from committing future offenses. A burglar sentenced to a number of years in prison, for example, may find the lack of freedom such a painful experience that he or she refrains from committing any new crimes once released. **General deterrence,** on the other hand, uses punishment as an example to others who may be contemplating breaking the law. Hence, the burglar sentenced to prison stands as an example to associates that they, too, may face a similar fate if they choose the same course of action.

Critics of deterrence say that there is little evidence that punishment deters criminal behavior. In fact, say critics, many criminals seem to commit one offense after another, a fact that calls into question the efficacy of deterrence as a sentencing philosophy. Other writers argue, however, that, "If I interview a thousand prisoners, I collect information about a thousand men in whose cases general prevention has failed. But I cannot infer from this data that general prevention is ineffective in the cases of all those who have not committed crimes."[7] In other words, although deterrent effects may be difficult to measure, that doesn't mean that they don't exist.

Still other researchers have found that for deterrence to be effective, punishment needs to be both swift and certain.[8] Delayed punishment, or punishments that may or may not be imposed, seem to lessen the deterrent effects of any efforts intended to reduce criminal activity. Severity of punishment may also be important as a deterrent effect, but severe punishments may be more significant deterrents of minor offenses than of major ones. Hence, the swift and certain imposition of capital punishment on traffic offenders would theoretically serve as a strong deterrent to others inclined to violate posted speed limits, although the threat of capital punishment (especially a threat that is vague and whose imposition is often delayed) may not do much to reduce the murder rate.

Rehabilitation

Rehabilitation, also a goal of criminal sentencing, is quite different in its purpose than deterrence or retribution. The purpose of rehabilitation is to reform criminal offenders, restoring them to productive lives within the community. Rehabilitation

DETERRENCE
a goal of criminal sentencing that seeks to prevent others from committing crimes similar to the one for which an offender is being sentenced.

SPECIFIC DETERRENCE
a goal of criminal sentencing that seeks to prevent a particular offender from engaging in repeat criminality.

GENERAL DETERRENCE
a goal of criminal sentencing that seeks to prevent others from committing crimes similar to the one for which a particular offender is being sentenced by making an example of the person sentenced.

REHABILITATION
the attempt to reform a criminal offender. Also, the state in which a reformed offender is said to be.

programs, which may also involve a punishment component (since punishment *can* result in behavioral change), often include job or skills training, educational course work leading to high school completion, counseling, and psychological treatment. From the point of view of rehabilitation, the nature of the criminal offense is of less significance than the supposed likelihood of reforming the offender—except insofar as the offense committed provides a clue to the need for specific rehabilitative strategies.

The term "rehabilitation," although widely used, may be something of a misnomer, since it literally means to return a person (or thing) to a former state. A criminal offender's "former state" may, of course, not have been a desirable one from the point of view of those stressing rehabilitation, because many offenders grew up in crime-prone areas and may have been inculcated early in life with values that easily led to law-violating behavior. Hence, a more appropriate term for what advocates of rehabilitation have in mind might be "resocialization," a word sometimes associated with the process of "rehabilitation."

Although hopes for the successful rehabilitation of offenders ran high for two or three decades after World War II, studies of recidivism rates among released prisoners dispelled the notion that rehabilitation could be easily achieved. Recidivism refers to the rate at which formerly adjudicated offenders return to crime. It is more formally expressed as the rate at which released prisoners are reconvicted of new offenses during a specified period of time following release—often five years. One of the best known studies of recidivism rates was conducted by Robert Martinson in the early 1970s. Martinson surveyed 231 studies evaluating correctional treatment programs between the years 1945 and 1967, and his report, published in 1974,[9] proclaimed the failure of rehabilitative efforts. Martinson's findings, which showed recidivism rates of between 70 and 90 percent, led to development of the "nothing works doctrine," a perspective on criminal sentencing that held that efforts at rehabilitation were doomed to failure.

Richard Allen Davis, the convicted killer of twelve-year-old Polly Klaas, makes an obscene gesture for the camera. Davis, convicted of the killing in 1996, was sentenced to death. His extensive criminal record at the time of the Klaas killing led California to pass the nation's first 'three strikes and you're out' law. (Photo by John Burgess/Reuters, courtesy of Archive Photos.)

Restoration

Restoration, the third goal of criminal sentencing, emphasizes the emotional and financial cost of crime to its victims and seeks to restore crime victims to a state akin to that which they were in prior to victimization. **Restoration** is a sentencing goal that seeks to make victims and the community "whole again." It frequently builds on the use of fines, restitution, and community service—forms of punishment that may be imposed on offenders by a sentencing judge. Court-ordered **restitution** requires convicted offenders to repay their victims, through an agency of the court, such as the clerk of courts office. Restitution payments, like fines, may be collected on an installment basis, as arranged by the court. Court-ordered restitution became an option under federal law with passage of the 1982 Victim and Witness Protection Act, which permits federal courts to impose restitution as part of a sentence.

Although restoration has been a goal of sentencing for many years, emphasis today is on the notion of **restorative justice,** a concept that identifies a triad of needs: (1) the need to compensate victims, (2) the need to place appropriate responsibility on the criminal offender, and (3) the need to attempt reintegration of the offender with the community. A recent report on "restorative justice" by the U.S. Department of Justice explains the term this way: "Crime was once defined as a 'violation of the state.' This remains the case today, but we now recognize that crime is far more. It is—among other things—a violation of one person by another. While retributive justice may address the first type of violation adequately, restorative justice is required to effectively address the latter. . . . Thus, (through restorative justice) we seek to attain a balance between the legitimate needs of the community, the . . . offender, and the victim."[10] Some of the most significant differences between restorative and retributive justice are listed in Table 14.1.

RESTORATION
a sentencing goal that seeks to make victims and the community "whole again."

RESTITUTION
a court requirement that an alleged or convicted offender pay money or provide services to the victim of the crime or provide services to the community.

RESTORATIVE JUSTICE
a sentencing model that builds on restitution and community participation in an attempt to make the victim "whole again."

Web Extra! 14–5
Center for Restorative Justice and Peacemaking

TABLE 14.1

DIFFERENCES BETWEEN RESTORATIVE AND RETRIBUTIVE JUSTICE

Retributive Justice	Restorative Justice
Crime is an act against the state, a violation of a law, an abstract idea.	Crime is an act against another person or the community.
The criminal justice system controls crime.	Crime control lies primarily in the community.
Offender accountability is defined as taking punishment.	Accountability is defined as assuming responsibility and taking action to repair harm.
Crime is an individual act with individual responsibility.	Crime has both individual and social dimensions of responsibility.
Victims are peripheral to the process.	Victims are central to the process of resolving a crime.
The offender is defined by deficits.	The offender is defined by the capacity to make reparation.
Emphasis on adversarial relationship.	Emphasis on dialogue and negotiation.
Imposition of pain to punish and deter/prevent.	Restitution as a means of restoring both parties; goal of reconciliation/restoration.
Community on sidelines, represented abstractly by state.	Community as facilitator in restorative process.
Response focused on offender's past behavior.	Response focused on harmful consequences of offender's behavior; emphasis on the future and on reparation.
Dependence on proxy professionals.	Direct involvement by both the offender and the victim.

SOURCE: Adapted from Gordon Bazemore and Mark S. Umbreit, *Balanced and Restorative Justice: Program Summary* (Washington, D.C.: Office of Juvenile Justice and Delinquency Prevention, October 1994), p. 7.

Incapacitation

A final sentencing philosophy can be found in incapacitation. **Incapacitation** is a strategy that makes use of imprisonment or some other sentencing option to reduce the likelihood that an offender will be capable of committing future offenses. As one writer says, "[I]ncapacitation is founded on the basic premise that those who are removed from a community, particularly through incarceration, cannot victimize society during a time of physical separation."[11]

In modern guise, incapacitation was embodied in **habitual offender** statutes that were passed in many states during the 1940s and 1950s and were recommended in the 1973 report of the National Advisory Commission on Criminal Justice Standards and Goals. The commission advised that "[s]tate penal code revisions should contain separate provisions for sentencing offenders when, in the interest of public protection, it is considered necessary to incapacitate them for substantial periods of time." The report went on to define a dangerous offender as "a person over twenty-one years of age whose criminal conduct is found by the court to be characterized by: (a) a pattern of repetitive behavior which poses a serious threat to the safety of others, (b) a pattern of persistent aggressive behavior with heedless indifference to the consequences, or (c) a particularly heinous offense involving the threat or infliction of serious bodily harm."

In a similar vein, federal sentencing guidelines say that defendants can be counted as **career offenders** if: (1) they were at least eighteen years old at the time of the instant offense, (2) the instant offense of conviction is a felony that is either a crime of violence or a controlled substance offense, [and] (3) they have at least two prior felony convictions of either a crime of violence or a controlled substance offense." In 1990, the category of armed career criminal was added to federal sentencing guidelines, subjecting persons who fall into that category to some of the most severe sanctions available under federal law.

As a consequence of efforts at incapacitation, prisons throughout the United States found themselves being used during the 1980s as warehouses for huge numbers of prisoners that judges and paroling authorities were reluctant to release onto the nation's streets. The trend toward warehousing, which continues today, can be seen in **three-strikes legislation,** which mandates long prison sentences for offenders who are convicted of a third felony offense.

California has one of the nation's toughest three-strikes laws (described in Exhibit 14–A), requiring life sentences for "three-time losers." Shortly after passage, however, California's three-strike law was called into question by a California Supreme Court ruling,[12] which held that judges could disregard prior convictions at sentencing when they believed that a mandatory life prison sentence would be unwarranted. In 1997, however, the California Supreme Court ruled that a three-strikes defendant could be punished under the law for past juvenile convictions for violent felonies.[13] Specifically, the court held that prior adjudication of a delinquent offender sixteen years of age or older, for an offense that would count as a strike if it were the result of an adult conviction, could count as a strike once that person attained adult status under state law (i.e., age eighteen).

In further refinements to the applicability of the state's three-strikes law, the California Supreme Court ruled in 1998 that a single criminal act involving multiple charges could count as more than one felony offense for purposes of the law.[14] Also in 1998 the state's Supreme Court put limits on judges' discretion in exempting repeat offenders from receiving lengthy sentences under the three-strikes law. The court ruled that a defendant whose past and present conduct showed him or her to be within "the spirit of the three-strikes law" must be given the full sentence required by the statute.[15] In 1998, in further support of California's law, the U.S. Supreme Court upheld a provision of the statute that doubles prison sentences for

A crowded cell at the Massachusetts Correctional Institute. Incapacitation is one of five primary sentencing rationales operative in American criminal justice today. Incapacitation, which is usually achieved through the use of imprisonment, seeks to reduce the likelihood that convicted offenders will be capable of continued law violation. (Photo courtesy of AP/Wide World Photos.)

a second strike, saying that the sentencing requirement does not violate double jeopardy provisions of the U.S. Constitution.[16]

A year later, in 1999, the U.S. Supreme Court refused to hear the case of Michael Wayne Riggs who was caught stealing vitamin pills from a California supermarket and sentenced to twenty-five years in prison based on a record of drug crimes, robbery, and other felonies. Many saw the Court's refusal to hear the case as an endorsement of California's three-strikes sentencing scheme.[17]

On March 7, 2000, California voters passed Proposition 21, broadening legal categories for determining what felonies can "count" under that state's three-strikes law. As a result of the change, violent and serious felonies now officially include gang-related felonies and conspiracies under California law.

As a sentencing strategy, incapacitation works best when it selectively incapacitates those most likely to commit repeat offenses. Hence, three-strikes and other similar "get tough on crime" policies represent a philosophy of **selective incapacitation** under which only the most dangerous offenders are separated from society for long periods of time.

Incapacitation that makes use of imprisonment can be very costly. Proponents of California's three-strikes legislation, however, argue that increased prison costs are a small price to pay for substantial reductions in crime rates. Reduced rates of crime, they say, will quickly translate into substantial savings in the social costs associated with crime. In 1996, for example, California's then-Governor Pete Wilson said that the state's three-strikes law had reduced crime, kept potential repeat offenders out of the state, and saved millions of dollars in costs associated with crime.[18] The governor cited a report released by the California Department of Corrections, which concluded that, over the first two years of the program's existence,

SELECTIVE INCAPACITATION
a sentencing strategy that imprisons or otherwise removes from society a select group of offenders—especially those considered to be most dangerous.

three-strikes sentences had resulted in the incarceration of 1,342 additional offenders and had increased the cost to taxpayers for new prison beds by $41 million. In contrast, said Wilson, social costs associated with new crimes had been reduced by $150 million during the same time period. Imprisonment of another 14,497 offenders on second-strike convictions, the governor added, prevented them from committing more than $1.7 billion in crime each year.[19]

While lengthy prison terms may sound retributive, it is important to remember that a sentencing philosophy of incapacitation requires only restraint and not punishment. Hence, sentencing options that make use of home confinement, the electronic monitoring of offenders at home and at work, and other methods of restricting an offender's movements could all come under the rubric of incapacitation. Realistically, however, retributive influences are being increasingly brought to bear on incarcerated populations. A number of states, for example, have limited prisoner access to weightlifting equipment, curtailed furlough programs, and reduced opportunities for prison-based entertainment, including restrictions on the availability of television sets and limitations on programming. Hence, a mix of efforts directed at both incapacitation and retribution—with a built-in smattering of hopes for both deterrent and rehabilitative effects—tends to characterize American sentencing philosophy today.

EXHIBIT 14–A

CALIFORNIA'S ORIGINAL "THREE-STRIKES" LAW

On March 7, 1994, California Governor Pete Wilson signed into law what had been General Assembly Bill No. 971, an independently formulated three-strikes provision, which had been amended to conform to the language of a then-popular get-tough-on-crime initiative. The law was incorporated into the California Penal Code as subdivisions b through i of Section 667. It took effect as an "urgency measure" on the day it was signed.

The initiative after which the law was modeled was later approved by California voters (on November 8, 1994). Known as Proposition 184, the "Three Strikes and You're Out" initiative had been inspired by the 1993 killing of twelve-year-old Polly Klaas. Klaas had been kidnapped from a slumber party at her home and murdered by an ex-con named Richard Allen Davis. Davis was convicted of the murder after investigators discovered that his life had been a litany of criminal activity. After passage, Proposition 184 was codified as Section 1170.12 of the California Penal Code and took effect on November 9, 1994. Proposition 184 effectively endorsed Section 667 of the California Penal Code. Although it was incorporated into the code as a separate provision, there is no conflict between the two California three-strikes provisions, which are, in fact, quite similar. Relevant portions of Penal Code Section 1170.12 are reproduced below.

CALIFORNIA PENAL CODE, SECTION 1170.12
ALSO KNOWN AS PROPOSITION 184 (EFFECTIVE NOVEMBER 9, 1994)

a. Notwithstanding any other provision of law, if a defendant has been convicted of a felony and it has been pled and proved that the defendant has one or more prior felony convictions, as defined in subdivision (b), the court shall adhere to each of the following:

  1. There shall not be an aggregate term limitation for purposes of consecutive sentencing for any subsequent felony conviction.

  2. Probation for the current offense shall not be granted, nor shall execution or imposition of the sentence be suspended for any prior offense.

  3. The length of time between the prior felony conviction and the current felony conviction shall not affect the imposition of sentence.

(continued)

EXHIBIT 14-A

4. There shall not be a commitment to any other facility other than the state prison. . . .

5. If there is a current conviction for more than one felony count not committed on the same occasion, and not arising from the same set of operative facts, the court shall sentence the defendant consecutively on each count pursuant to this section.

6. If there is a current conviction for more than one serious or violent felony as described in paragraph (b) of this subdivision, the court shall impose the sentence for each conviction consecutive to the sentence for any other conviction for which the defendant may be consecutively sentenced in the manner prescribed by law.

7. Any sentence imposed pursuant to this section will be imposed consecutive to any other sentence which the defendant is already serving, unless otherwise provided by law.

b. Notwithstanding any other provision of law and for the purposes of this section, a prior conviction of a felony shall be defined as:

1. Any offense defined in subdivision (c) of Section 667.5 as a violent felony or any offense defined in subdivision (c) of Section 1192.7 as a serious felony in this state. The determination of whether a prior conviction is a prior felony conviction for purposes of this section shall be made upon the date of that prior conviction and is not affected by the sentence imposed unless the sentence automatically, upon the initial sentencing, converts the felony to a misdemeanor. None of the following dispositions shall affect the determination that a prior conviction is a prior felony for purposes of this section:

   A. The suspension of imposition of judgment or sentence.

   B. The stay of execution of sentence.

   C. The commitment to the State Department of Health Services as a mentally disordered sex offender following a conviction of a felony.

   D. The commitment to the California Rehabilitation Center or any other facility whose function is rehabilitative diversion from the state prison.

2. A conviction in another jurisdiction for an offense that, if committed in California, is punishable by imprisonment in the state prison. A prior conviction of a particular felony shall include a conviction in another jurisdiction for an offense that includes all of the elements of the particular felony as defined in subdivision (c) of Section 667.5 or subdivision (c) of Section 1192.7. . . .

c. For purposes of this section, and in addition to any other enhancements or punishment provisions which may apply, the following shall apply where a defendant has a prior felony conviction:

1. If a defendant has one prior felony conviction that has been pled and proved, the determinate term or minimum term for an indeterminate term shall be twice the term otherwise provided as punishment for the current felony conviction.

2. (A) If a defendant has two or more prior felony convictions, as defined in paragraph (1) of subdivision (b), that have been pled and proved, the term for the current felony conviction shall be an indeterminate term of life imprisonment with a minimum term of the indeterminate sentence calculated as the greater of (i) three times the term otherwise provided as punishment for each current felony conviction subsequent to the two or more prior felony convictions, or (ii) twenty-five years or (iii) the term determined by the court pursuant to Section 1170 for the underlying conviction, including any enhancement applicable under Chapter 4.5 (commencing with Section 1170) of Title 7 of Part 2, or any period prescribed by Section 190 or 3046. (B) The indeterminate term described in subparagraph (A) of paragraph (2) of this subdivision shall be served consecutive to any other term of imprisonment for which a consecutive term may be imposed by law. Any other term imposed subsequent to any indeterminate term described in subparagraph (A) of paragraph (2) of this subdivision shall not be merged therein but shall commence at the time the person would otherwise have been released from prison.

d. (1) Notwithstanding any other provision of law, this section shall be applied in every case in which a defendant has a prior felony conviction as defined in this section. The prosecuting attorney shall plead and prove each prior felony conviction except as provided in paragraph (2). (2) The prosecuting attorney may move to dismiss or strike a prior felony conviction allegation in the furtherance of justice pursuant to Section 1385, or if there is insufficient evidence to prove the prior conviction. If upon the satisfaction of the court that there is insufficient evidence to prove the prior felony conviction, the court may dismiss or strike the allegation.

e. Prior felony convictions shall not be used in plea bargaining, as defined in subdivision (b) of Section 1192.7. The prosecution shall plead and prove all known prior felony convictions and shall not enter into any agreement to strike or seek the dismissal of any prior felony conviction allegation except as provided in paragraph (2) of subdivision (d).

LAW IN PRACTICE

CAN SENTENCES REQUIRED UNDER SOME MANDATORY SENTENCING SCHEMES BE SO GROSSLY DISPROPORTIONATE TO THE OFFENSE INVOLVED THAT THEY VIOLATE THE EIGHTH AMENDMENT?

Riggs v. *California*
119 S. Ct. 890, 142 L. Ed. 2d 789
United States Supreme Court, 1999

ON PETITION FOR WRIT OF CERTIORARI TO THE COURT OF APPEAL OF CALIFORNIA, FOURTH APPELLATE DISTRICT.

The petition for a writ of *certiorari* is denied.

Opinion of Justice Stevens, with whom Justice Souter and Justice Ginsburg join, respecting the denial of the petition for a writ of *certiorari.*

This *pro se* petition for *certiorari* raises a serious question concerning the application of California's "three strikes" law, Cal. Penal Code Ann. §667 (West Supp. 1998), to petty offenses.

In 1995, petitioner stole a bottle of vitamins from a supermarket. The California Court of Appeal described his offense as "a petty theft motivated by homelessness and hunger." App. to Pet. for Cert. at 12. If this had been petitioner's first offense, it would have been treated as a misdemeanor punishable by a fine or a jail sentence of six months or less. See Cal. Penal Code Ann. §490 (West 1988). Because of petitioner's prior record, however, the trial Judge was authorized, and perhaps even required, to treat the crime as a felony. See Cal. Penal Code Ann. §666 (West Supp. 1998); *People* v. *Terry,* 47 Cal. App. 4th 329, 54 Cal. Rptr. 2d 769 (1996); *People* v. *Dent,* 38 Cal. App. 4th 1726, 45 Cal. Rptr. 2d 746 (1995). Having elevated the character of the offense, the Judge was then compelled to apply the mandatory sentencing provisions of the three-strikes law and to impose a minimum sentence of 25 years to life imprisonment. See Cal. Penal Code Ann. §667(e)(2)(A) (West Supp. 1998) (requiring that persons convicted of a "felony" who have two prior qualifying felony convictions be so sentenced). Petitioner asks us to decide that this sentence is so "grossly disproportionate" to his crime that it violates the Eighth Amendment. See *Harmelin* v.

Michigan, 501 U.S. 957, 1001 (1991) (Kennedy, J., Concurring in part and Concurring in judgment).

This question is obviously substantial, particularly since California appears to be the only State in which a misdemeanor could receive such a severe sentence. See *id.,* at 1004–1005 (opinion of Kennedy, J.); *Solem* v. *Helm,* 463 U.S. 277, 291 (1983). While this Court has traditionally accorded to state legislatures considerable (but not unlimited) deference to determine the length of sentences "for crimes concededly classified and classifiable as felonies," *Rummel* v. *Estelle,* 445 U.S. 263, 274 (1980), petty theft does not appear to fall into that category. Furthermore, petty theft has many characteristics in common with the crime for which we invalidated a life sentence in *Solem,* uttering a "no account" check for $100. "It involve[s] neither violence nor [the] threat of violence to any person"; the amount of money involved is relatively small; and the State treats the crime as a felony (here, only under certain circumstances) pursuant to a unique quirk in state law. 463 U.S., at 296, and n. 20.

Nevertheless, there are valid reasons for not issuing the writ in this case. Neither the California Supreme Court nor any federal tribunal has yet addressed the question. Given the fact that a defendant's prior criminal record may play a dual role in the enhancement scheme—first converting the misdemeanor into a felony, and then invoking the provisions of the three-strikes law—there is some uncertainty about how our cases dealing with the punishment of recidivists should apply. We have of course held that "a State is justified in punishing a recidivist more severely than it punishes a first offender." *Id.,* at 296. But in order to avoid double jeopardy concerns, we have repeatedly emphasized that under recidivist sentencing schemes "the enhanced punishment imposed for the [present] offense 'is not to be viewed as . . . [an] additional penalty for the earlier crimes,' but instead as 'a stiffened penalty for the latest crime, which is considered to be an

(continued)

LAW IN PRACTICE

aggravated offense because a repetitive one.' " *Witte* v. *United States*, 515 U.S. 389, 400 (1995) (quoting *Gryger* v. *Burke*, 334 U.S. 728, 732 (1948)). See also *Moore* v. *Missouri*, 159 U.S. 673, 677 (1895) (under a recidivist statute, "the accused is not again punished for the first offence" because " 'the punishment is for the last offence committed, and it is rendered more severe in consequence of the situation into which the party had previously brought himself' "). It is thus unclear how, if at all, a defendant's criminal record beyond the requisite two prior "strikes"—petitioner in this case has eight prior felony convictions—affects the constitutionality of his sentence, especially when the State "double counts" the defendant's recidivism in the course of imposing that punishment. Cf. *Solem*, 463 U.S., at 298–299; *Rummel*, 445 U.S., at 274, n. 11.

The denial of this petition for *certiorari*, as always, does not constitute a ruling on the merits. Moreover, since petitioner is asking us to apply a settled rule of Eighth Amendment law, rather than to fashion a new rule, his claim may be asserted in federal court by way of an application for a writ of *habeas corpus*. See *Spencer* v. *Georgia*, 500 U.S. 960, 960 (1991) (Kennedy, J., Concurring in the denial of *certiorari*). It is therefore prudent for this

Court to await review by other courts before addressing the issue. Cf. *McCray* v. *New York*, 461 U.S. 961 (1983) (opinion of Stevens, J., respecting denial of *certiorari*).

DISSENTING OPINION OF JUSTICE BREYER

Justice Breyer, Dissenting from the denial of the petition for a writ of certiorari. I agree with Justice Stevens that this petition for certiorari raises a serious question concerning the application of a "three-strikes" law to what is in essence a petty offense. I believe it appropriate to review that question in this case and would grant the writ of *certiorari*.

What Do *You* Think?

1. Do you believe that California's three-strikes law sometimes unfairly punishes relatively minor crimes? Why or why not?
2. Why did the Court deny *certiorari* in this case?
3. Is it likely that a similar case may be accepted by the Court in the future? If so, on what grounds?
4. If a similar case is heard by the full Court in the future, what do you predict the outcome will be? Why?

Web Extra! 14–6

Britannica online: mitigating circumstances

IMPOSING CRIMINAL SANCTIONS

At the start of this chapter, we said that sentencing is the process through which a *sentencing authority* imposes a lawful punishment or other sanction on a person convicted of violating the criminal law. In almost all cases, the sentencing authority is a judge, although in some jurisdictions and for certain types of crimes, juries may be called on to recommend an appropriate sentence.

Until recently, judges in most U.S. jurisdictions had considerably more leeway in sentencing decisions than they do today. As little as thirty years ago, most jurisdictions in the United States followed the practice of indeterminate sentencing. An **indeterminate sentence** is "a type of sentence to imprisonment where the commitment, instead of being for a specified single time quantity, such as three years, is for a range of time, such as two to five years, or five years maximum and zero minimum."[21] Like other sentences, indeterminate sentences for multiple offenses could be imposed either concurrently or consecutively. A **consecutive sentence** is "one of two or more sentences imposed at the same time, after conviction for more than one

INDETERMINATE SENTENCE

a relatively unspecific term of incarceration referring to a minimum and maximum time to be served (such as a term of imprisonment of "from one to ten years").[20]

CONSECUTIVE SENTENCE

one of two or more sentences imposed at the same time, after conviction for more than one offense, and served in sequence with the other sentences.

CONCURRENT SENTENCE

one of two or more sentences imposed at the same time after conviction for more than one offense and to be served simultaneously.[23]

DETERMINATE SENTENCE

also **presumptive** or **fixed sentence;** a fixed term of incarceration specified by law.

PROPORTIONALITY

a sentencing principle that holds that the severity of sanctions should bear a direct relationship to the seriousness of the crime committed.

EQUITY

a sentencing principle, based on concerns with social equality, which holds that similar crimes should be punished with the same degree of severity, regardless of the social or personal characteristics of offenders.

SOCIAL DEBT

a sentencing principle that objectively counts an offender's criminal history in sentencing decisions.

AGGRAVATING FACTORS

circumstances relating to the commission of a crime that cause its gravity to be greater than that of the average instance of the given type of offense.[25] Also, those elements of an offense or of an offender's background that could result in a harsher sentence under the determinate sentencing model than would otherwise be called for by sentencing guidelines.

MITIGATING FACTORS

circumstances surrounding the commission of a crime that do not in law justify or excuse the act but that in fairness may be considered as reducing the blameworthiness of the defendant.[27] Also, those elements of an offense or of an offender's background that could result in a lesser sentence under the determinate sentencing model than would otherwise be called for by sentencing guidelines.

offense, and which is served in sequence with the other sentences."[22] That is, consecutive sentences are served one after the other. Conversely, a **concurrent sentence** is one which is served at the same time another sentence is being served.

Indeterminate sentences were the rule throughout most of the United States for well over a hundred years. They were imposed in the belief that an offender facing a flexible sentence would be motivated to *earn* an early release from confinement through good behavior. Under the indeterminate model, the inmate's behavior while incarcerated is the primary determinant of the amount of time served. Hence, inherent in indeterminate sentencing strategies is the hope of rehabilitation through self-motivation.

As disappointment with the rehabilitative ideal grew, however, many states and the federal government increasingly switched to determinate sentencing approaches. In 1978, California, a bellwether state, joined the determinate sentencing bandwagon with passage of the California Determinate Sentencing Act. A **determinate sentence** sets a single standard "time quantity"[24] of imprisonment. In determinate sentencing, jurisdictions judges have little leeway in imposing sentences, and criminal law violators are sentenced to predetermined punishments generally set by law. The California law, for example, allows judges to impose a short, average-length, or long sentence for each offense of which a defendant is convicted. Judges must, however, impose the average-term sentence, unless extenuating circumstances indicate that either the shorter or longer sentence is more appropriate. Any deviation from the standard sentence requires judges to explain in writing, and for the record, why that deviation was made. Imposition of a long-term sentence requires judges in California to hold a formal fact-finding hearing before sentence is passed.

Another reason for the growth of determinate sentencing schemes, which are also variously termed "fixed," "mandatory," and "structured" sentencing, was a felt need to ensure three fundamental sentencing principles: proportionality, equity, and social debt. **Proportionality** refers to the belief that the severity of sanctions should bear a direct relationship to the seriousness of the crime committed. Hence, under the principle of proportionality, offenders committing similar crimes should receive similar sentences. Under indeterminate sentencing practices, however, two offenders who commit virtually the same offense, but come before different judges, may receive very different sentences, resulting in sentencing disparities and felt inequities. Hence, the notoriety of "hanging judges," who imposed strict punishments on convicted offenders, is often contrasted with the leniency of "soft" judges, who could be depended upon to "go easy" on those who stood before them. Sentencing **equity,** a related concept, is based on a concern with social equality and means that similar crimes should be punished with the same degree of severity, regardless of the social or personal characteristics of offenders. According to the equity principle, extralegal factors, such as gender, race, financial status, age, physical appearance, education, and so forth, should not influence sentencing decisions. Finally, the principle of **social debt,** which counts an offender's criminal history in sentencing decisions, should be objectively recognized in any sentencing decision.

Determinate sentencing incorporates the principles of proportionality, equity, and social debt by standardizing sentences according to offense severity and criminal history. In determinate sentencing jurisdictions, judicial deviation from determinate sentencing standards, while possible, typically must be predicated on a finding by the judge of specific aggravating or mitigating factors enumerated by sentencing laws. **Aggravating factors** are "circumstances relating to the commission of a crime which cause its gravity to be greater than that of the average instance of the given type of offense."[26] Conversely, **mitigating factors** are "circumstances surrounding the commission of a crime which do not in law justify or excuse the act, but which in fairness may be considered as reducing the blameworthiness of the defendant."[28] A list of typical aggravating and mitigating factors is provided in Exhibit 14–B.

EXHIBIT 14-B

AGGRAVATING AND MITIGATING FACTORS

Listed here are some typical aggravating and mitigating factors that judges may take into consideration in arriving at sentencing decisions in determinate sentencing jurisdictions.

AGGRAVATING FACTORS

- The defendant induced others to participate in the commission of the offense.

- The offense was especially heinous, atrocious, or cruel.

- The defendant was armed with or used a deadly weapon at the time of the crime.

- The offense was committed for the purpose of avoiding or preventing a lawful arrest or effecting an escape from custody.

- The offense was committed for hire.

- The offense was committed against a present or former law enforcement officer or correctional officer while engaged in the performance of official duties or because of the past exercise of official duties.

- The defendant took advantage of a position of trust or confidence to commit the offense.

MITIGATING FACTORS

- Defendant has no record of criminal convictions punishable by more than sixty days of imprisonment.

- The defendant has made substantial or full restitution.

- The defendant has been a person of good character or has had a good reputation in the community.

- The defendant aided in the apprehension of another felon or testified truthfully on behalf of the prosecution.

- The defendant acted under strong provocation, or the victim was a voluntary participant in the criminal activity or otherwise consented to it.

- The offense was committed under duress, coercion, threat, or compulsion, which was insufficient to constitute a defense but significantly reduced the defendant's culpability.

- The defendant was suffering from a mental or physical condition that was insufficient to constitute a defense but significantly reduced culpability for the offense.

Web Extra! 14–7

The Sentencing Project

Federal Sentencing Practices

The movement toward determinate sentencing was led by the federal government, which in 1984 passed the Sentencing Reform Act.[29] The act established the U.S. Sentencing Commission under the leadership of judge William W. Wilkins, Jr., and mandated the development of determinate sentencing guidelines. Guidelines developed by the commission took effect on November 1, 1987, and combined the seriousness of an offense with an offender's past criminal record in computing the length of prison time to which a federal court should sentence a convicted offender.

Federal sentencing guidelines are built around a table containing forty-three rows, each corresponding to one offense level. Penalties associated with each level overlap those of levels above or below in order to discourage unnecessary litigation. A person charged with a crime involving $11,000, for example, on conviction is unlikely to receive a penalty substantially greater than if the amount involved had been somewhat less than $10,000—a sharp contrast to the old system. A change of six levels roughly doubles the sentence imposed under the guidelines, regardless of the level at which one starts.

The federal sentencing table, which is reproduced in Table 14.2, contains six columns, corresponding to the criminal history category into which an offender falls. Criminal history categories are determined on a point basis. Offenders earn points through previous convictions. Each prior sentence of imprisonment for more than one year and one month counts as three points. Two points are assigned for each prior prison sentence over six months, or if the defendant committed the offense while on probation, parole, or work release. The system also assigns points for other types of previous convictions and for offenses committed less than two years after release from imprisonment. Points are added to determine the criminal history category into which an offender falls. Thirteen points or more are required for the highest category. At each offense level, sentences in the highest criminal history category are generally two to three times as severe as for the lowest category.

Defendants may also move into the highest criminal history category (number VI) by being designated career offenders. Under the sentencing guidelines, a defendant is a career offender if "(1) the defendant was at least eighteen years old at the time of the . . . offense, (2) the . . . offense is a crime of violence or trafficking in a controlled substance, and (3) the defendant has at least two prior felony convictions of either a crime of violence or a controlled substance offense."[30]

While based on determinate principles, current federal sentencing practices continue to reflect the traditional goals of sentencing. Federal law, for example, specifies that: "The court, in determining the particular sentence to be imposed, shall consider . . . the need for the sentence imposed: (A) to reflect the seriousness of the offense, to promote respect for the law, and to provide just punishment for the offense; (B) to afford adequate deterrence to criminal conduct; (C) to protect the public from further crimes of the defendant; and (D) to provide the defendant with needed educational or vocational training, medical care, or other correctional treatment in the most effective manner. . . ."[31]

In 1989, in the case of *Mistretta* v. *United States*,[32] the constitutionality of federal sentencing guidelines was tested. Mistretta, a federal prisoner, argued that Congress had overstepped its bounds in creating the U.S. Sentencing Commission and assigning to the commission the power to determine federal sentencing practices. Mistretta's claim was built on the doctrine of nondelegation, which holds that a clause in the U.S. Constitution mandates that no branch of government can engage in the excessive assignment of its discretionary powers to another agency. The Court, however, rejected Mistretta's argument, saying that, in a complex society, "Congress cannot do its job absent an ability to delegate power under broad general directives." Congress, concluded the Court, is not excessive in its delegation of authority if it is sufficiently precise in its assignment of responsibilities to external agencies.

TABLE 14.2

THE FEDERAL SENTENCING TABLE (SENTENCES SHOWN IN MONTHS)

Offense level	CRIMINAL HISTORY CATEGORY					
	I 0 or 1	II 2 or 3	III 4, 5, 6	IV 7, 8, 9	V 10, 11, 12	VI 13 or More
1	0–1	0–2	0–3	0–4	0–5	0–6
2	0–2	0–3	0–4	0–5	0–6	0–7
3	0–3	0–4	0–5	0–6	2–8	3–9
4	0–4	0–5	0–6	2–8	4–10	6–12
5	0–5	0–6	1–7	4–10	6–12	9–15
6	0–6	1–7	2–8	6–12	9–15	12–18
7	1–7	2–8	4–10	8–14	12–18	15–21
8	2–8	4–10	6–12	10–16	15–21	18–24
9	4–10	6–12	8–14	12–18	18–24	21–27
10	6–12	8–14	10–16	15–21	21–27	24–30
11	8–14	10–16	12–18	18–24	24–30	27–33
12	10–16	12–18	15–21	21–27	27–33	30–37
13	12–18	15–21	18–24	24–30	30–37	33–41
14	15–21	18–24	21–27	27–33	33–41	37–46
15	18–24	21–27	24–30	30–37	37–46	41–51
16	21–27	24–30	27–33	33–41	41–51	46–57
17	24–30	27–33	30–37	37–46	46–57	51–63
18	27–33	30–37	33–41	41–51	51–63	57–71
19	30–37	33–41	37–46	46–57	57–71	63–78
20	33–41	37–46	41–51	51–63	63–78	70–87
21	37–46	41–51	46–57	57–71	70–87	77–96
22	41–51	46–57	51–63	63–78	77–96	84–105
23	46–57	51–63	57–71	70–87	84–105	92–115
24	51–63	57–71	63–78	77–96	92–115	100–125
25	57–71	63–78	70–87	84–105	100–125	110–137
26	63–78	70–87	78–97	92–115	110–137	120–150
27	70–87	78–97	87–108	100–125	120–150	130–162
28	78–97	87–108	97–121	110–137	130–162	140–175
29	87–108	97–121	108–135	121–151	140–175	151–188
30	97–121	108–135	121–151	135–168	151–188	168–210
31	108–135	121–151	135–168	151–188	168–210	188–235
32	121–151	135–168	151–188	168–210	188–235	210–262
33	135–168	151–188	168–210	188–235	210–262	235–293
34	151–188	168–210	188–235	210–262	235–293	262–327
35	168–210	188–235	210–262	235–293	262–327	292–365
36	188–235	210–262	235–293	262–327	292–365	324–405
37	210–262	235–293	262–327	292–365	324–405	360–life
38	235–293	262–327	292–365	324–405	360–life	360–life
39	262–327	292–365	324–405	360–life	360–life	360–life
40	292–365	324–405	360–life	360–life	360–life	360–life
41	324–405	360–life	360–life	360–life	360–life	360–life
42	360–life	360–life	360–life	360–life	360–life	360–life
43	life	life	life	life	life	life

SOURCE: U.S. Sentencing Commission, *Federal Sentencing Guideline Manual* (Washington, D.C.: U.S. Government Printing Office, 1987), p. 210.

Truth in Sentencing

The 1984 Federal Comprehensive Crime Control Act, which adopted determinate sentencing for nearly all federal offenders, also addressed the issue of honesty in sentencing. Under the old federal system, a sentence of ten years in prison might actually have meant only a few years spent behind bars before the offender was released. On average, good-time credits and parole reduced time served to about one-third of actual sentences.[33] Similar sentencing practices in most states reflected the federal model. While sentence reductions may have benefited offenders, they often outraged victims who felt betrayed by the sentencing process and viewed it as misleading at best and dishonest at worst.

The federal emphasis on honesty in sentencing was emulated by many states, creating a "what you get is what you serve" sentencing environment. The idea that sentences that are imposed should closely match the time inmates actually serve is called **truth in sentencing.** Truth in sentencing, described more formally as "a close correspondence between the sentence imposed upon those sent to prison and the time actually served prior to prison release,"[35] has become an important policy focus of many state legislatures and the federal congress. The Violent Crime Control and Law Enforcement Act of 1994, for example, set aside $4 billion in federal prison construction funds, called "Truth in Sentencing Incentive Funds," for states which adopt truth in sentencing laws guaranteeing that certain violent offenders will serve at least 85 percent of their sentences. A recent study found that, given the current situation in most states, meeting federal truth in sentencing requirements would increase the time actually spent in prison for the average prison-bound offender by almost 50 percent.[36]

Some states have chosen to approach "truth in sentencing" another way. In 1994, for example, the New Jersey Supreme Court imposed a "truth in sentencing" rule on New Jersey judges which, although it doesn't require lengthened sentences, mandates that judges publicly disclose how much time a convicted defendant is likely to spend behind bars. The New Jersey court held that lower criminal court judges must "inform the public of the actual period of time" a defendant is likely to spend imprisoned. Judges must also state when a defendant could get out of prison on good behavior.[37]

TRUTH IN SENTENCING

a close correspondence between the sentence imposed on those sent to prison and the time actually served prior to prison release.[34]

Determinate Sentencing Under Attack

In sentencing practices, as in most walks of life, the pendulum swings both ways. Although determinate sentencing is now the ascendant philosophy in the federal and in many state jurisdictions, it has recently come under attack by those who claim that determinate sentencing practices unfairly eliminate the discretion of sentencing authorities and that such practices do not sufficiently distinguish among offenders according to the degree of blameworthiness of their crimes or the moral character of individual offenders. At a U.S. Sentencing Commission hearing held in Denver, Colorado, a few years ago for example, witnesses testified that current federal sentencing practices have led to injustices by eliminating the ability of most judges to consider individual circumstances in cases that come before them. U.S. District Court Judge Lewis Babcock of Denver said that, as a result of current practices, "we have dehumanized the sentencing process."[38] Federal guidelines have created an "assembly line system" for dispensing justice that is "rigid and mechanical" said Richard Miklic, the chief federal probation officer in Colorado.[39]

Supporters of the federal system, on the other hand, claimed that it has brought uniformity to the criminal justice system and has eliminated "the luck of the draw" by reducing the impact of varying judicial personalities, regional sentiments, and other random factors on sentencing decisions.

PLEA BARGAINING

Many sentences are imposed as a result of bargained pleas; that is, as the result of agreements among the prosecutor, defense attorney, and court as to what an appropriate sentence might be for an offender who pleads guilty. Fully 80 to 90 percent of sentences in some jurisdictions result from **plea bargaining.**[40] In a study of thirty-seven big-city prosecutors,[41] the Bureau of Justice Statistics found that for every one hundred adults arrested on a felony charge, half were eventually convicted of either a felony or a misdemeanor. Of all convictions, 94 percent were the result of a plea. Only 6 percent of convictions were the product of a criminal trial.

Plea bargaining circumvents the trial process and dramatically reduces the time required for the resolution of a criminal case. As such, it greatly increases the number of criminal cases that can be processed by a court. Without plea bargaining, most criminal courts would become mired in the legal formalities required by trials, and case backlogs would increase substantially. Some say that plea bargaining is the criminal process equivalent to the out-of-court settlement of civil process.

It is important to realize that bargained pleas do not always bear a close relationship to the crimes originally charged. Many plea negotiations turn on the acceptability of an anticipated sentence rather than on a close relationship between the charge and the plea. The nature of the plea entered may be based more on the punishment likely to be associated with it, than on any felt need to accurately describe the criminal offense in which the defendant was involved.[42] This is especially true where a defendant may be concerned with minimizing the socially stigmatizing impact of the offense. A charge of "indecent liberties," for example, in which the defendant is accused of sexual misconduct, may be pled out as assault. Such a plea, which takes advantage of the fact that "indecent liberties" can be thought of as a form of sexual assault, would effectively disguise the true nature of the offense while still allowing the court to impose what many might see as appropriate punishment.

The U.S. Supreme Court has held that a guilty plea constitutes conviction.[43] The Court has also given its consent to the informal decision-making processes of bargained pleas. In the case of *Brady* v. *United States*,[44] the court reasoned that such pleas were acceptable if they were voluntarily and knowingly made. A year later, in *Santobello* v. *New York* (1971),[45] the High Court ruled that plea bargaining is an important and necessary component of the American system of justice. In the words of the Court, "The disposition of criminal charges by agreement between the prosecutor and the accused, sometimes loosely called 'plea bargaining,' is an essential component of the administration of justice. Properly administered, it is to be encouraged. If every criminal charge were subjected to a full-scale trial, the States and the Federal Government would need to multiply by many times the number of judges and court facilities."[46]

To validate a negotiated plea, judicial consent is required. Judges are often likely to accept pleas that are the result of a bargaining process because such pleas reduce the workload of the court. Although few judges are willing to guarantee a sentence before a plea is entered, most prosecutors and criminal trial lawyers know what sentences to expect from typical pleas.

After a guilty plea has been entered, it may be withdrawn with the consent of the court. In the case of *Henderson* v. *Morgan* (1976),[47] for example, the U.S. Supreme Court permitted a defendant to withdraw a plea of guilty nine years after it had

PLEA BARGAINING
the process of negotiating an agreement among defendant, prosecutor, and the court as to what an appropriate plea and associated sentence should be in a given case.

If criminals wanted to grind justice to a halt, they could do it by banding together and all pleading not guilty.

—Dorothy Wright Wilson, former dean, University of Southern California Law Center been given. In *Henderson,* the defendant had originally entered a plea of guilty to second-degree murder, but attempted to withdraw it before sentencing. Reasons for wanting to withdraw the plea included the defendant's belief that he had not been completely advised as to the nature of the charge or the sentence he might receive as a result of the plea.

Recent Supreme Court decisions, however, have enhanced the prosecutor's authority in the bargaining process by declaring that negotiated pleas cannot be capriciously withdrawn by defendants.[48] Other rulings have supported discretionary actions by prosecutors, in which sentencing recommendations were retracted even after bargains had been struck.[49] Some lower court cases have upheld the government's authority to withdraw from a negotiated plea when the defendant fails to live up to certain conditions.[50] Conditions may include requiring the defendant to provide information on other criminal involvement, criminal cartels, the activities of smugglers, and so on.

Plea bargains, because they circumvent the trial process, hold the possibility of abuse by prosecutors, defense attorneys, and judges who are more interested in a speedy resolution of cases than they are in seeing justice done. Carried to the extreme, plea bargaining may result in defendants being convicted of crimes they did not commit. Although it probably happens only rarely, it is conceivable that innocent defendants (especially those with prior criminal records) who—for whatever reason—think a jury will convict them may plead guilty to lessened charges in order to avoid a trial. In an effort to protect defendants against hastily arranged pleas, the Federal Rules of Criminal Procedure require judges to: (1) inform the defendant of the various rights he or she is surrendering by pleading guilty, (2) determine that the plea is voluntary, (3) require disclosure of any plea agreements, and (4) make sufficient inquiry to ensure there is a factual basis for the plea.[51]

TRADITIONAL SENTENCING OPTIONS

Sentencing is fundamentally a risk management strategy designed to protect the public while serving the ends of rehabilitation, deterrence, retribution, and restoration. Because the goals of sentencing are difficult to agree on, so too are sanctions. Lengthy prison terms do little for rehabilitation, while community release programs can hardly protect the innocent from offenders bent on continuing criminality. Assorted sentencing philosophies continue to permeate state-level judicial systems. Each state has its own sentencing laws, and frequent revisions of those statutes are not uncommon. Because of huge variations from one state to another in the laws and procedures that control the imposition of criminal sanctions, sentencing has been called "the most diversified part of the Nation's criminal justice process."[52] There is at least one common ground, however, that can be found in the four traditional sanctions that continue to dominate the thinking of most legislators and judges when dealing with the criminal law. The four traditional sanctions are:

- Imprisonment
- Probation
- Fines
- Death.

Fines, imprisonment, and probation are sanctions that are generally available to judges in most indeterminate sentencing jurisdictions. The option selected typically depends on the severity of the offense and the judge's best guess as to the likelihood of future criminal involvement on the part of the defendant. Sometimes two or more options are combined, as when an offender might be fined and also sentenced to prison, or placed on probation and also fined in support of restitution payments. **Probation** is actually a sentence of imprisonment that is deferred. It is granted through a judgment suspending the prison sentence imposed on a convicted offender, and the offender's continued freedom is conditioned on his or her meeting certain behavioral requirements, such as avoiding future law violations.

Jurisdictions that operate under determinate sentencing guidelines generally limit a judge's choice to only one option and often specify the extent to which that option can be applied. Dollar amounts of fines, for example, are rigidly set, and prison terms are specified for each type of offense. The death penalty remains an option in a fair number of jurisdictions—both determinate and indeterminate—but only for a highly select group of offenders.

Recently, the Bureau of Justice Statistics reported on the sentencing practices of state felony courts.[53] Highlights of the study, using data gathered by the National Judicial Reporting Program, showed that state courts annually convict about 1 million persons of felonies. Of these:

- Thirty-eight percent are sentenced to active prison terms.
- Thirty-one percent receive jail sentences, usually involving less than a year's confinement.
- Thirty-one percent are sentenced to probation (often with fines or other special conditions).
- The average prison sentence imposed on convicted felons is five years and three months.
- The average amount of time served in confinement for felons receiving active sentences will average about two years and four months before release, as a result of considerations for good time and other credits.

The same survey revealed that 39 percent of those convicted in state courts of drug trafficking offenses were sentenced to prison. Twenty-seven percent of drug trafficking convictions, however, resulted in probation, while 33 percent of convicted traffickers were sent to local jails for brief terms of imprisonment. Although the number of active sentences handed out to felons may seem low to some, the number of criminal defendants receiving active prison time has increased dramatically over time. When viewed historically, statistics reveal that court-ordered prison commitments have increased nearly eightfold in the past thirty years.

HATE CRIMES

Hate crimes can be defined as criminal offenses in which the defendant's conduct was motivated by hatred, bias, or prejudice, based on the actual or perceived race, color, religion, national origin, ethnicity, gender, or sexual orientation of another individual or group of individuals.[54] A more extensive definition can be found in the California Penal Code, which says that: "Hate crimes . . . means any act of intimidation, harassment, physical force, or the threat of physical force directed against any person, or family, or their property or advocate, motivated either in whole or in part by the hostility to the real or perceived ethnic background, national origin, religious belief, gender, age, disability, or sexual orientation, with the intention of causing fear and intimidation."[55] Hate crimes are not separate offenses, however, and it is important to realize that many types of felonies can be prosecuted as hate crimes.

Hate crime laws, which have developed during the past decade or two, simply enhance or increase the penalties associated with serious offenses that fall into the

PROBATION
a sentence of imprisonment that is suspended. Also, the conditional freedom granted by a judicial officer to an adjudicated or adjudged adult or juvenile offender, as long as the person meets certain conditions of behavior.

HATE CRIMES
criminal offenses in which the defendant's conduct was motivated by hatred, bias, or prejudice, based on the actual or perceived race, color, religion, national origin, ethnicity, gender, or sexual orientation of another individual or group of individuals; sometimes called **bias crimes.**

"hate crimes" category. At the federal level, the Hate Crimes Sentencing Enhancement Act of 1994[56] is typical of such legislation. The act provides for enhanced sentences where a federal offense is determined to be a hate crime.

The federal Hate Crime Statistics Act, signed into law by then-President Bush in April 1990, mandates an annual statistical tally of hate crimes throughout the country. Data collection under the law began in January 1991. Yearly statistics show approximately 10,000 reported instances of hate crimes, including about a dozen murders. Most hate crimes (approximately 65 percent) appear to be motivated by racial bias, while religious hatred (15 percent), and sexual orientation (12 percent) account for most of the remainder.[57] Many hate crimes that are reported fall into the category of "intimidation," although vandalism, simple assault, and aggravated assault also account for a fair number of hate crime offenses. Notable in recent years has been a spate of church burnings throughout the south where congregations have been predominantly African-American. A few robberies and rapes are also classified under the hate crime umbrella in any given year. Hate crimes are sometimes also called **bias crimes.** One form of bias crime that bears special mention is homophobic homicide. Homophobic homicide is a term that refers to the murder of homosexuals by those opposed to their lifestyles.

Some hate crimes are committed by organized hate groups. According to the Intelligence Project of the Southern Poverty Law Center, 457 organized hate groups operated in the United States in 1999.[58] Another 523 so-called "patriot" organizations, many with separatist leanings based on race or ethnicity, existed throughout the country.

Some hate crime laws have not passed constitutional muster, often because they have run afoul of First Amendment concerns over free speech. In 1992, for example, in the case of *R.A.V. v. City of St. Paul,*[59] the U.S. Supreme Court invalidated a St. Paul, Minnesota, city ordinance designed to prevent the bias-motivated display of symbols or objects, such as Nazi swastikas or burning crosses. Also in 1992, in the case of *Forsyth County, Ga. v. Nationalist Movement,*[60] the Court held that a county requirement regulating parades was unconstitutional because it also regulated freedom of speech—in this case a plan by an affiliate of the Ku Klux Klan to parade in opposition to a Martin Luther King birthday celebration.

Some writers[61] have noted that statutes intended to control hate crimes may contravene constitutional guarantees if they: (1) are too vague, (2) criminalize thought more than action, (3) attempt to control what would otherwise be free speech, and (4) deny equal protection of the laws to those who wish to express their personal biases.

Examples of effective hate crime legislation can be found in a Wisconsin law that increases penalties for most crimes when the offender "Intentionally selects the person against whom the crime . . . is committed or selects the property that is damaged or otherwise affected by the crime . . . in whole or in part because of the actor's belief or perception regarding the race, religion, color, disability, sexual orientation, national origin or ancestry of that person or the owner or occupant of that property, whether or not the actor's belief or perception was correct."[62] Wisconsin's penalty-enhancement statute was upheld in the 1993 case of *Wisconsin v. Mitchell.*[63] In that case, the United States Supreme Court held that Mitchell, a black man whose severe beating of a white boy was racially motivated, could be punished with additional severity as permitted by Wisconsin law because he acted out of "race hatred." The Court called the assault "conduct unprotected by the First Amendment" and upheld the Wisconsin statute saying, "[since] the statute has no 'chilling effect' on free speech, it is not unconstitutionally overbroad."

In 2000, however, the Supreme Court, in the case of *Apprendi v. New Jersey,*[64] struck down a New Jersey law that allowed judges to sentence offenders to longer prison terms for crimes motivated by racism or other bias. The law did *not* require

Web Extra! 14–8
Center for the Study of Hate and Extremism

Web Extra! 14–9
Southern Poverty Law Center

that prosecutors prove to a jury that an offense was a "hate crime" under state law. As this book goes to press, the New Jersey legislature is working to amend the relevant statute to require juries in such cases to make a determination as to whether discriminatory intent was central to the offense following a finding of guilt and prior to the imposition of a sentence.

LAW ON THE BOOKS

CALIFORNIA'S "HATE CRIME" STATUTE.
CALIFORNIA PENAL CODE

Section 422.6.

(a) No person, whether or not acting under color of law, shall by force or threat of force, wilfully injure, intimidate, interfere with, oppress, or threaten any other person in the free exercise or enjoyment of any right or privilege secured to him or her by the Constitution or laws of this state or by the Constitution or laws of the United States because of the other person's race, color, religion, ancestry, national origin, disability, gender, or sexual orientation, or because he or she perceives that the other person has one or more of those characteristics.

(b) No person, whether or not acting under color of law, shall knowingly deface, damage, or destroy the real or personal property of any other person for the purpose of intimidating or interfering with the free exercise or enjoyment of any right or privilege secured to the other person by the Constitution or laws of this state or by the Constitution or laws of the United States, because of the other person's race, color, religion, ancestry, national origin, disability, gender, or sexual orientation, or because he or she perceives that the other person has one or more of those characteristics.

(c) Any person convicted of violating subdivision (a) or (b) shall be punished by imprisonment in a county jail not to exceed one year, or by a fine not to exceed five thousand dollars ($5,000), or by both that imprisonment and fine, and the court shall order the defendant to perform a minimum of community service, not to exceed 400 hours, to be performed over a period not to exceed 350 days, during a time other than his or her hours of employment or school attendance. However, no person shall be convicted of violating subdivision (a) based upon speech alone, except upon a showing that the speech itself threatened violence against a specific person or group of persons and that the defendant had the apparent ability to carry out the threat.

Section 422.7. Except in the case of a person punished under Section 422.6, any crime which is not made punishable by imprisonment in the state prison shall be punishable by imprisonment in the state prison or in a county jail not to exceed one year, by a fine not to exceed ten thousand dollars ($10,000), or by both that imprisonment and fine, if the crime is committed against the person or property of another for the purpose of intimidating or interfering with that other person's free exercise or enjoyment of any right secured to him or her by the Constitution or laws of this state or by the Constitution or laws of the United States and because of the other person's race, color, religion, ancestry, national origin, disability, gender, or sexual orientation, or because the defendant perceives that the other person has one or more of those characteristics, under any of the following circumstances, which shall be charged in the accusatory pleading:

(a) The crime against the person of another either includes the present ability to commit a violent injury or causes actual physical injury.

(b) The crime against property causes damage in excess of five hundred dollars ($500).

(c) The person charged with a crime under this section has been convicted previously of a violation of subdivision (a) or (b) of Section 422.6, or has been convicted previously of a conspiracy to commit a crime described in subdivision (a) or (b) of Section 422.6.

Section 422.75.

(a) Except in the case of a person punished under Section 422.7, a person who commits a felony or attempts to commit a felony because of the victim's race, color, religion,

(continued)

LAW ON THE BOOKS

nationality, country of origin, ancestry, disability, gender, or sexual orientation, or because he or she perceives that the victim has one or more of those characteristics, shall receive an additional term of one, two, or three years in the state prison, at the court's discretion.

(b) Except in the case of a person punished under Section 422.7 or subdivision (a) of this section, any person who commits a felony or attempts to commit a felony against the property of a public agency or private institution, including a school, educational facility, library or community center, meeting hall, place of worship, or offices of an advocacy group, or the grounds adjacent to, owned, or rented by the public agency or private institution, because the property of the public agency or private institution is identified or associated with a person or group of an identifiable race, color, religion, nationality, country of origin, ancestry, gender, disability, or sexual orientation, shall receive an additional term of one, two, or three years in the state prison, at the court's discretion.

(c) Except in the case of a person punished under Section 422.7 or subdivision (a) or (b) of this section, any person who commits a felony, or attempts to commit a felony, because of the victim's race, color, religion, nationality, country of origin, ancestry, gender, disability, or sexual orientation, or because he or she perceives that the victim has one or more of those characteristics, and who voluntarily acted in concert with another person, either personally or by aiding and abetting another person, shall receive an additional two, three, or four years in the state prison, at the court's discretion.

(d) For the purpose of imposing an additional term under subdivision (a) or (c), it shall be a factor in aggravation that the defendant personally used a firearm in the commission of the offense. Nothing in this subdivision shall preclude a court from also imposing a sentence enhancement pursuant to Section 12022.5, 12022.53, or 12022.55, or any other law.

(e) A person who is punished pursuant to this section also shall receive an additional term of one year in the state prison for each prior felony conviction on charges brought and tried separately in which it was found by the trier of fact or admitted by the defendant that the crime was committed because of the victim's race, color, religion, nationality, country of origin, ancestry, disability, gender, or sexual orientation, or that the crime was committed because the defendant perceived that the victim had one or more of those characteristics. This additional term shall only apply where a sentence enhancement is not imposed pursuant to Section 667 or 667.5.

(f) Any additional term authorized by this section shall not be imposed unless the allegation is charged in the accusatory pleading and admitted by the defendant or found to be true by the trier of fact.

(g) Any additional term imposed pursuant to this section shall be in addition to any other punishment provided by law.

(h) Notwithstanding any other provision of law, the court may strike any additional term imposed by this section if the court determines that there are mitigating circumstances and states on the record the reasons for striking the additional punishment.

(i)(1) "Because of" means that the bias motivation must be a cause in fact of the offense, whether or not other causes also exist. When multiple concurrent motives exist, the prohibited bias must be a substantial factor in bringing about the particular result.

(2) This subdivision does not constitute a change in, but is declaratory of, existing law under *In Re M.S.* (1995) 10 Cal. 4th 698 and *People* v. *Superior Court* (Aishman) (1995) 10 Cal. 4th 735.

Section 422.76. For purposes of Section 186.21, subdivisions (a) and (b) of Section 422.6, Section 422.7, subdivisions (a), (b), (c), and (e) of Section 422.75, Sections 1170.75 and 11410, paragraph (9) of subdivision (b) of Section 11413, Section 13023, subdivision (c) of Section 13519.4, and subdivision (a) of Section 13519.6, "gender" means the victim's actual sex or the defendant's perception of the victim's sex, and includes the defendant's perception of the victim's identity, appearance, or behavior, whether or not that identity, appearance, or behavior is different from that traditionally associated with the victim's sex at birth.

Section 422.8. Except as otherwise required by law, nothing in this title shall be construed to prevent or limit the prosecution of any person pursuant to any provision of law.

CAPITAL PUNISHMENT

The last of the four traditional sanctions—although by far the least commonly used—is **capital punishment,** or a sentence of death. A death sentence is, of course, the most extreme sentencing option available in the United States today. In 1995, the state of New York reinstated the death penalty after a thirty-year hiatus, and today thirty-eight states and the federal government make capital punishment an option when serious crimes are committed. Approximately 3,800 death row inmates languish in the nation's prisons, while around 100 executions are carried out yearly. The number of annual executions has been steadily rising as changes in the law and recent Supreme Court decisions have facilitated an increasing rate of legal death.

Capital punishment, as a sentencing possibility, was absent from federal law for a number of years prior to its reestablishment under the 1988 Anti–Drug Abuse Act, which included the possibility of capital punishment for drug-related murders. The 1994 Federal Violent Crime Control and Law Enforcement Act dramatically raised the number of crimes punishable by death under federal jurisdiction to around sixty distinct offenses. Candidates for death under the 1994 act are those who commit first-degree murder, espionage, kidnapping in which death results, murder of a foreign official, bank robbery in which death results, hostage taking resulting in death, murder for hire, genocide, car-jacking that leads to death, "civil rights murders," the murder of federal law enforcement officials, foreign murder of U.S. nationals, sexual abuse resulting in death, sexual exploitation of children resulting in death, the murder of state or local officials (to include state and local law enforcement officers and state correctional officers), murder by an escaped prisoner, the murder of federal witnesses or of court officers or jurors, and shipboard violence or violence at international airports resulting in death. A subsection of the 1994 Federal Violent Crime Control and Law Enforcement Act,[65] entitled the Drive By Shooting Prevention Act of 1994, specifies that "[a] person who, in furtherance or to escape detection of a major drug offense and with the intent to intimidate, harass, injure, or maim, fires a weapon into a group of two or more persons and who, in the course of such conduct, kills any person shall, if the killing . . . is a first-degree murder . . . be punished by death or imprisonment for any term of years or for life, fined under this title, or both. . . ." Similarly, the Violent Crime Control Act also states that "[a] person who, while confined in a Federal correctional institution under a sentence for a term of life imprisonment, commits the murder of another shall be punished by death or by life imprisonment."

Capital punishment can be analyzed from three quite different points of view: (1) a legal perspective, which includes constitutional issues; (2) a philosophical, moral, and ethical perspective; and (3) via empirical analysis of data on deterrence, public opinion, and so on.

While our emphasis in this textbook is on the criminal law, philosophical considerations of the morality of capital punishment and empirical studies of death penalty efficacy are important issues in their own right. In 2000, for example, Governor George Ryan suspended executions in Illinois and called for an examination of the fairness of capital punishment after discovering that more death row inmates had been found innocent and released than had been executed since Illinois returned to the use of capital punishment in 1977. In fact, seventy-five men and women have been released from U.S. death rows since 1972, after proof of their innocence was substantiated;[66] and an analysis of every capital conviction and appeal over a twenty-two-year period published in 2000 by Columbia Law School Professor James Liebman found an extremely high rate of prejudicial error in the American capital punishment system.[67] Liebman found serious reversible errors in nearly seven out of every ten capital cases.

CAPITAL PUNISHMENT
the imposition of a sentence of death.

Death is not only an unusually severe punishment, unusual in its pain, in its finality, and in its enormity, but it serves no penal purpose more effectively than a less severe punishment.

—Justice William J. Brennan, dissenting *Gregg* v. *Georgia*, 428 U.S. 153 (1976)

New forensic technologies, like DNA testing, have finally made it possible to definitively prove or disprove innocence in many cases. In 2000, in recognition of the power that DNA testing holds to exonerate the innocent, Senator Patrick Leahy (D–VT) and Representatives Ray LaHood (R–IL) and William Delahunt (D–MA) introduced legislation in Congress known as the Innocence Protection Act.[68] The legislation, which had not been enacted by the time this book went to press, would allow prisoners on death row to request DNA testing on evidence of relevance to their case that is in the government's possession.

CRIMINAL LAW IN THE NEWS

Texas Defense Lawyers Rip Death Penalty

Study Claims Misconduct, Racism Rampant in System

AUSTIN, Texas—Lawyers who represent the state's death row inmates this week joined civil rights groups and some politicians in calling for a halt to executions because of what they say are widespread abuses in the system, including racial bias and incompetent attorneys.

In a report released Monday, the Texas Defender Service, a nonprofit group of lawyers who represent condemned inmates, also accused police and prosecutors of misconduct and criticized the use of testimony from so-called "killer shrinks" to persuade juries to issue death sentences.

The service said in its report, *A State of Denial: Texas Justice and the Death Penalty,* that the capital punishment process "raises profound questions about the fairness of how and when the death penalty is applied."

But a spokeswoman for Gov. George W. Bush defended capital punishment, saying the system ensured that no innocent defendants were executed.

"In Texas, there are multiple checks and balances, including years and years of reviews by 22 judges in at least eight separate appeals, to ensure that an innocent person is not put to death," said Linda Edwards, a spokeswoman for Bush.

"Biased" arguments

The study paints an ugly picture of the capital punishment system in Texas—a system allegedly filled with psychia-

trists specializing in the prediction of the future dangerousness of convicted killers, scheming prosecutors and racial bias that sends more blacks to the death house than whites.

Despite the almost constant condemnations from human rights groups and defense lawyers over the years, executions in Texas show no sign of slackening. Courts so far have found the arguments lacking. With six more executions scheduled this year, Texas could set a new record for the number of condemned inmates put to death.

The pro-death penalty criminal justice group, Justice for All, said it was not buying the claims by the Texas Defender Service, arguing that these are the same old and "biased" arguments that have been consistently rejected by the courts.

"From my perspective, we've degraded the issue from guilt or innocence into 'Is your attorney slick enough to get you off,' " Dianne Clements, president of Justice for All, told APBnews.com. "So, if they don't get you off, you had an attorney that was not competent."

But Jim Marcus, executive director of the Defender Service, said that while those in favor of the death penalty are attacking the report because defense lawyers wrote it, no one is questioning the facts.

"The report has verified, objective information," Marcus said. "People keep referring to the checks and bal-

ances in the system. The facts speak for themselves. There are too many instances of misconduct, too much racial bias and too many instances where the safety value is broken."

Report findings

Highlights of the Defenders Service report include:

- In 41 cases reviewed by the service, prosecutors or police allegedly provided false or misleading testimony, hid evidence or used unreliable evidence through sources such as a "jailhouse snitch." The report also cites several examples of alleged misconduct and states that police and prosecutors are caught in a "vice of political pressure" to solve capital cases, sometimes using flimsy evidence and fabricated testimony to gain convictions.

- The report claims a common prosecution tactic is to fool juries by using phony experts. In 121 death penalty cases it reviewed, the Defender Service said "expert psychiatrists testified at the penalty phase of the trial that the convicted killer would be a danger in the future."

But according to the report, the testimony of these psychiatrists, or "killer shrinks," was based on hypothetical questions regarding "future dangerousness." The Defender Service accuses these psychiatrists of either not interviewing the defendant or talking with him or her for a short

(continued)

Texas Defense Lawyers Rip Death Penalty

Study Claims Misconduct, Racism Rampant in System

time. According to Texas law, future dangerousness must be proved to determine whether a convicted killer receives a death sentence.

• In 79 percent of post-conviction death penalty appeals, initial appellate judges affirmed the death sentences without bothering to conduct hearings.

• More death sentences are given to blacks convicted of killing whites than are given to whites convicted of slaying blacks. The Defender Service said there was a "clear pattern of disparity" between the two groups, but that more data must be analyzed.

• The study found that the death penalty is used most often to punish those convicted of murdering white women—a group the report calls the least likely to be killed.

• The study cites some cases in which lawyers slept through capital murder trials, ignored obvious exculpatory evidence, were disciplined for ethical lapses or used drugs or alcohol while representing a poor capital defendant at trial.

In one case, a lawyer allegedly took cocaine and drank during his client's trial for capital murder, and in another, the attorney only put in 85 hours of work on the entire capital murder case. The American Bar Association reports preparation for a capital case should take a lawyer at least 1,000 hours.

• The report also cited surveys done by the state bar association indicating that trial court judges routinely appoint attorneys who are their personal friends or contribute to the judge's re-election campaign to represent capital defendants.

A system under attack

In recent years, the death penalty process in Texas has come under constant attack. The State Bar of Texas and the Texas Civil Rights Project, a nonprofit group that works to protect civil rights issues in Texas, have called for a moratorium.

But pro-death penalty groups say the system is working fine.

Dudley Sharp, of Justice for All, said with only about 15 percent of death penalty verdicts in Texas overturned by the state and federal courts, it proves that arguments of racial bias, incompetence by attorneys or innocence are not holding water.

He said the study is "laughable" because it represents the views of criminal defense lawyers, not objective observers.

"They are totally overblown and do not reflect the reality of the system. . . . Are there individual cases where Texas could have done a better job? Of course. That exists in every state. . . . Attorneys don't like their claims being rejected. That's when they go to the court of public opinion," Sharp said.

But Marcus counters that "Draconian" limitations on federal review of death penalty sentences and elected state judges who do not want to overturn the cases are the real reasons so few convictions are reversed in Texas.

He said that most death penalty cases—including the ones in which lawyers have slept through the trial—are overturned at the federal court level.

Congressman calls for moratorium

The barrage of criticism leveled at the Texas death penalty system has even led some of its supporters to demand a moratorium on executions so the process could be studied.

U.S. Rep. Ciro D. Rodriguez, who favors the death penalty, is backing legislation in Congress calling for a national moratorium on executions.

"We don't see a problem with taking a break to make sure the system is done right," Rodriguez, a Democrat, told APBnews.com.

A "runaway train"

Sam Millsap, a former district attorney in Bexar County who sent several men to death row in the mid-1980s, also is asking for a moratorium, calling the system a "runaway train."

"The situation that exists today in Texas can only be described as embarrassing," he said.

Before another person is sent to death row or executed, the state must make the post-trial review process fairer for poor defendants, he said.

Record-setting pace

Under the Bush administration, 145 people have been executed in Texas. Since 1982, the state has executed 232 people—by far the highest number in the nation.

Texas sent 37 people to its death house at Huntsville State Prison in 1997, the most in the state's history. But with 33 convicted killers executed so far in 2000 and six others scheduled before the end of the year, Texas could break its own record. The state has 446 convicted murderers on death row.

Millsap said he doubted that things would change quickly in Texas, or that the latest report would suddenly shift public opinion.

"The attitude among far too many people is that maybe the guy didn't commit the crime, but he's a bad son of a bitch and ought to be executed, anyway," Millsap said.

Source: Robert Anthony Phillips, "Texas Defense Lawyers Rip Death Penalty; Study Claims Misconduct, Racism Rampant in System," APB News. October 18, 2000. Reprinted with permission.

The Courts and Capital Punishment

Among death penalty cases decided by the U.S. Supreme Court, one of the earliest was *Wilkerson* v. *Utah* (1878),[69] which questioned shooting as a method of execution and raised Eighth Amendment claims that firing squads constituted a form of cruel and unusual punishment. The Court disagreed, however, contrasting the relatively civilized nature of firing squads with the many forms of torture often associated with capital punishment around the time the Bill of Rights was written. Similarly, electrocution found acceptance as a permissible form of execution in *In re Kemmler* (1890).[70] In *Kemmler*, the Court defined cruel and unusual methods of execution as follows: "Punishments are cruel when they involve torture or a lingering death; but the punishment of death is not cruel, within the meaning of that word as used in the Constitution. It implies there something inhuman and barbarous, something more than the mere extinguishing of life."[71] Almost sixty years later, the Court ruled that a second attempt at the electrocution of a convicted person, when the first did not work, did not violate the Eighth Amendment.[72] The Court reasoned that the initial failure was the consequence of accident or unforeseen circumstances and not the result of an effort on the part of executioners to be intentionally cruel.

In 1971, in the case of *McGautha* v. *California*,[73] the Court rejected a defendant's claim that the due process clause of the Constitution prohibited "committing to the untrammeled discretion of the jury the power to pronounce life or death in capital cases." In effect, in *McGautha*, the Court upheld the power of juries to make decisions regarding life and death.

However, only one year later, in 1972, in the landmark case of *Furman* v. *Georgia*,[74] the Court ruled that "evolving standards of decency"[75] necessitated a reconsideration of Eighth Amendment guarantees. In a five-to-four ruling, with no majority opinion,[76] the *Furman* decision invalidated Georgia's death penalty statute on the basis that it allowed a jury *unguided* discretion in the imposition of a capital sentence. The majority of justices concluded that the Georgia statute, which permitted a jury to simultaneously decide issues of guilt or innocence while it weighed sentencing options, permitted an arbitrary and capricious application of the death penalty. The *Furman* case had the effect of striking down every death penalty statute then in existence, while it did little to provide clear guidance to states interested in reestablishing the practice of capital punishment.

> We are concerned here only with the imposition of capital punishment for the crime of murder, and when a life has been taken deliberately by the offender, we cannot say that the punishment is invariably disproportionate to the crime. It is an extreme sanction suitable to the most extreme of crimes.
>
> —Justice Potter Stewart
> *Gregg* v. *Georgia*, 428 U.S. 153 (1976)

Following *Furman*, states that reenacted death penalty laws did so in one of two ways: they either imposed mandatory death sentences for certain types of crimes, or they created a two-step procedure whereby the determination of guilt was separated from the penalty phase of a criminal trial. In 1976, in the case of *Woodson* v. *North Carolina*,[77] a law requiring the death penalty for specific crimes was overturned. In *Woodson*, the Court held that "the fundamental respect for humanity underlying the Eighth Amendment . . . requires consideration of the character and record of the individual offender and the circumstances of the particular offense."

Also in 1976, however, in the case of *Gregg* v. *Georgia*, the Court approved Georgia's newly developed two-step trial procedure.[78] In that case, the Court upheld the two-stage procedural requirements as necessary for ensuring the separation of the highly personal information needed in sentencing decisions from the kinds of information reasonably permissible in jury trials where issues of guilt or innocence alone are being decided. As a consequence of *Gregg*, death penalty trials in most jurisdictions today involve two stages. In the first stage, guilt or innocence is decided. If the defendant is convicted of a crime for which execution is possible, a second (or "penalty") phase ensues. The penalty phase generally permits the introduction of new evidence that may have been irrelevant to the question of guilt but which may be relevant to punishment, such as drug use or childhood abuse. While in most death penalty jurisdictions juries determine the punishment, the trial judge sets the sentence in the second phase of capital murder trials in Arizona, Idaho, Montana, and Nebraska. Alabama, Delaware, Florida, and Indiana allow juries only to recommend a sentence to the judge.

Decisions following *Gregg* set limits on the use of death as a penalty for all but the most severe crimes. In the case of *Coker* v. *Georgia* (1977),[79] for example, the Court struck down a state law imposing the death penalty for the rape of an adult woman, concluding that capital punishment under such circumstances would be "grossly disproportionate" to the crime committed. Somewhat later, in *Edmund* v. *Florida* (1982),[80] the Court overturned the death sentence of an individual convicted of felony murder, ruling that the Constitution forbids executing a defendant "who does not himself kill, attempt to kill, or intend that a killing take place or that lethal force be employed." In *Edmund,* the defendant was a getaway-car driver whose accomplices committed murder while he waited in the vehicle. In 1987, in *Tison* v. *Arizona,*[81] a divided Court held that felony murder rules might lead to death sentences when defendants "could have foreseen that lethal force might be used" in a crime, even though they were not the ones to employ it.

In two 1990 rulings, *Blystone* v. *Pennsylvania* and *Boyde* v. *California,* the Court upheld state statutes that had been interpreted to require death penalties where juries find a lack of mitigating factors to offset aggravating circumstances. Similarly, in the 1990 case of R. Gene Simmons, an Arkansas mass murderer convicted of killing sixteen relatives during a 1987 shooting rampage, the Court granted inmates under sentence of death the right to waive appeals. Before the *Simmons* case, any interested party could file a brief on behalf of condemned persons—with or without their consent.

Although capital punishment is not unconstitutional, long delays associated with its imposition may be. In 1998, in a case which the U.S. Supreme Court refused to hear, but where an execution had been delayed for twenty-three years, Justice Stephen Breyer observed that "twenty-three years under sentence of death is unusual—whether one takes as a measuring rod current practice or the practice in this country and in England at the time our Constitution was written."[82] Breyer noted that his concern arose from the fact that the defendant "has experienced that delay because of the State's own faulty procedures and not because of frivolous appeals on his own part."

Limits on Death Row Appeals

The federal Constitution allows people who are in custody to challenge the legality of their confinement by seeking a writ of **habeas corpus.** *Habeas corpus* is a Latin term that literally means "you have the body," and a writ of *habeas corpus* is an order requiring a prisoner to be brought before a court for the purpose of determining the legality of the prisoner's detention.

Also known as "the Great Writ," *habeas corpus* has been interpreted to mean that death row prisoners and other state inmates whose convictions have been upheld by state appellate courts can petition federal court in order to argue that their rights were violated at trial.

In a move to reduce delays in the carrying out of death sentences, the U.S. Supreme Court, in the case of *McCleskey* v. *Zandt* (1991),[83] limited the number of appeals a condemned person may bring to the courts. Saying that repeated filings for the sole purpose of delay promotes "disrespect for the finality of convictions" and "disparages the entire criminal justice system," the Court established a two-pronged criterion for future appeals. According to *McCleskey,* in any petition beyond the first, filed with a federal court, capital defendants must demonstrate:

HABEAS CORPUS
literally, "you have the body"; a writ challenging the legality of incarceration; or a writ ordering a prisoner to be brought before a court to determine the legality of the prisoner's detention.

Web Extra! 14–12
Capital Defense Network

(1) good cause why the claim now being made was not included in the first filing and (2) how the absence of that claim may have harmed the petitioner's ability to mount an effective defense. Two months later, the Court reinforced *McCleskey,* when it ruled, in *Coleman* v. *Thompson,*[84] that state prisoners could not cite "procedural default," such as a defense attorney's failure to meet a state's filing deadline for appeals, as the basis for an appeal to federal court.

In 1995, in the case of *Schlup* v. *Delo,*[85] the Court continued to define standards for continued appeals from death row inmates under federal jurisdiction, ruling that before appeals based on claims of new evidence can be heard, "a petitioner must show that, in light of the new evidence, it is more likely than not that no reasonable juror would have found him guilty beyond a reasonable doubt."[86] A "reasonable juror" was defined as one who "would consider fairly all of the evidence presented and would conscientiously obey the trial court's instructions requiring proof beyond a reasonable doubt."

In 1996, a unanimous Supreme Court upheld a provision of the Antiterrorism and Effective Death Penalty Act of 1996 that sharply restricts appeals by death row prisoners and other convicts. Provisions of the antiterrorism legislation deny a second federal *habeas* appeal for most death row inmates who claim violations of their constitutional rights. The law, however, does allow prisoners to petition the Supreme Court directly during their first round of appeals but requires that additional appeals be approved by a three-judge U.S. appeals court panel before they can make their case to a trial court. Specifically, Title I of the Antiterrorism and Effective Death Penalty Act of 1996 requires dismissal of a claim presented in a state prisoner's second or successive federal *habeas* application if that claim was also presented in a prior application; compels dismissal of a claim that was not presented in a prior federal application, unless certain conditions apply; and creates a gate-keeping mechanism whereby the prospective applicant files in the court of appeals a motion for leave to file a second or successive *habeas* application in the district court, and a three-judge panel determines whether the application makes a *prima facie* showing that it satisfies the requirements of the law. Under the law, the panel's decisions cannot be appealed to the Supreme Court.

The 1996 case, *Felker* v. *Turpin,*[87] involved Ellis Wayne Felker, 47, a Georgia inmate who had been scheduled to die for the 1981 rape and murder of a nineteen-year-old college student. Felker challenged the new law, claiming that it unconstitutionally restricted the jurisdiction of the U.S. Supreme Court and improperly suspended his ability to file *habeas corpus* applications with the Court. The Court ruled, however, that the law does not improperly limit the Supreme Court's ability to consider successive appeals by inmates challenging their convictions or sentences. "We hold that the act does not preclude this court from entertaining an application for *habeas corpus* relief, although it does affect the standards governing the granting of such relief," Chief Justice Rehnquist wrote in the opinion issued by the Court. Justice Rehnquist went on to describe the new restrictions as part of a recent trend independently initiated by the Court and aimed at preventing abuses. "The added restrictions which the act places on second *habeas* petitions are well within the compass of this evolutionary process and we hold that they do not amount to a 'suspension' of the writ," Rehnquist said.

Cruel and Unusual Punishments

While the majority of justices on the U.S. Supreme Court in recent years have seemed largely convinced of the constitutionality of a sentence of death, a few have viewed capital punishment as a barbarous punishment that has no place in civilized society. In 1994, for example, Justice Harry A. Blackmun spoke out against capital punishment in a Texas case.[88] In a dissenting opinion, Blackmun wrote: "From this day forward, I no longer shall tinker with the machinery of death. . . . Rather than continue to coddle the Court's delusion that the desired level of fairness has been achieved . . . I feel morally and intellectually obligated simply to concede that the death penalty experiment has failed. . . . The basic question—does the system accurately and consistently determine which defendants 'deserve' to die?—cannot be answered in the affirmative." In response to Blackmun's objections, Justice Antonin Scalia said that Blackmun missed the mark because his "explanation often refers to 'intellectual, moral, and personal' perceptions, but never to the text and tradition of the Constitution. It is the latter rather than the former," wrote Scalia, "that ought to control." Mention of capital crimes in the Fifth Amendment[89] is sufficient evidence, argued Scalia, that the Constitution permits imposition of the penalty of death under appropriate circumstances.

> In order for a punishment to constitute cruel or unusual punishment, it must involve torture or a lingering death, or the infliction of unnecessary and wanton pain.
>
> —Supreme Court of Florida, *Jones* v. *Butterworth* (1997)

CRIMINAL LAW IN THE NEWS

Grandmothers at Odds as Execution Date Nears

Take Opposing Views on Fate of Young Girl's Killer

OKLAHOMA CITY—Johnnie Cabrera said a prayer for the man who killed her grandchild after learning that an execution date had been set for him and promised to attend a clemency hearing to ask that his life be spared.

Judy Busch said she was both happy and sad that the execution date had been set, and that she would like her granddaughter's killer to be able to see her face as he is executed at Oklahoma State Penitentiary.

Floyd Allen Medlock, whose murder of a 9-year-old girl made bitter enemies of her grandmothers and caused them to come down on opposite sides of the death penalty issue, is to be executed on Jan. 16, 2001.

Medlock, 31, confessed to killing Katherine Ann Busch in 1990. Since the slaying, the child's grandmothers, Busch and Cabrera, have become leaders and activists on opposite sides of the death penalty issue.

Busch, 56, the child's paternal grandmother, counsels families of homicide victims for the Oklahoma City Police Department and is a death penalty supporter. Cabrera, 63, Katherine's maternal grandmother, is the leader of the Oklahoma City chapter of the state Coalition to Abol-ish the Death Penalty and frequently stands vigil outside the governor's mansion when executions take place.

"I want to know why he did it"
Cabrera said that she planned to meet with Medlock at the penitentiary before he is executed and ask the Oklahoma Probation and Parole Board, which hears clemency petitions, to spare his life. The clemency hearing has not yet been scheduled. She said Medlock agreed to the meeting and his lawyer is trying to arrange it.

"I don't know what I'll say [to Medlock]," Cabrera told APBnews.com. "Whatever comes into my heart. I want to know why he did it, whether he is really remorseful. I don't know why it's important. I just feel that it's very important for me to do this."

The Oklahoma Department of Corrections said it has yet to receive a request from Cabrera to meet with Medlock. The department said such a request would have to be approved by the prison warden.

If Medlock is executed, Cabrera will join members of the state's anti-death penalty coalition standing vigil outside the governor's mansion, she said.

Scott Braden, Medlock's appeals lawyer, refused comment.

Elation and sadness
Busch said she had mixed emotions about Medlock getting a date with death.

"Part of me was elated that we finally are getting this behind us, and there was a part of me that thought 'Someone else is getting a call that they are going to die,' " Busch said. "It's a difficult situation. I guess I care more about life than he did. That's why he's dying. He did not have a regard for life when he killed Kathy."

Busch said that she was undecided whether she would witness Medlock's execution because the condemned man will not be able to see Busch's face.

"I want him to see us," Busch said. "He was the last person Kathy saw. I want to make sure we are the last people he sees."

Jerry Massie, spokesman for the corrections department, said state law would have to be changed to allow the condemned to see the victim's family members while being executed.

The current law requires the families to be separated from the state and

(continued)

CRIMINAL LAW IN THE NEWS

Grandmothers at Odds as Execution Date Nears

Take Opposing Views on Fate of Young Girl's Killer

media witnesses, Massie said. A one-way glass in the death chamber allows the families to see the execution, but the condemned cannot see them.

Five executions set
Oklahoma has scheduled five executions—including Medlock's—for January 2001.

Included in the group is Wanda Jean Allen, 42, who shot her lesbian lover to death outside a police station in Oklahoma City. The dispute stemmed from an argument over a welfare check, prosecutors stated. If she dies by lethal injection, she will become the first woman executed in Oklahoma since it became a state in 1907.

Allen had previously received a four-year prison sentence on a manslaughter charge in connection with the 1981 shooting death of another woman, the Department of Corrections said.

The state has executed 11 convicted killers this year, six in 1999 and four in 1998.

Gerald Adams, spokesman for the Oklahoma attorney general's office, said the reason for the high number of executions has to do with the Supreme Court and state and federal legislative reforms speeding up the appeals process.

Adams said the five people scheduled to go to the death house in January had their cases reviewed by the Supreme Court, and when the high court dismissed them, new execution dates were set.

Adams said that there is "no question" that the number of executions in Oklahoma will increase in the coming years.

Says inner voice made him kill
Medlock lived in the same apartment complex as Katherine and her mother did in the city of Yukon, located outside of Oklahoma City. Medlock told police that the child knocked on his door and asked for something to eat.

Once the girl was inside his apartment, Medlock claimed a sadistic inner personality, whom he called "Charlie," told him to kill her. He grabbed the girl, pushed her head into a toilet and stabbed her in the back of the neck with a knife. He then attempted to sexually assault the child before tossing her body in a nearby dumpster.

The next day, following the discovery of Katherine's body, Medlock called police and told them he was the man they were looking for. He later said that he feared he would kill again.

After pleading guilty to the murder, defense lawyers tried to convince a judge that the chubby, baby-faced Medlock suffered from a multiple personality disorder caused by years of abuse by his parents.

Grandmothers become enemies
The issue of whether Medlock should spend the rest of his life in prison or be executed has turned Busch and Cabrera against each other. Busch said she became angry when Cabrera befriended Medlock's family during the trial. She also said that Cabrera did not love Katherine as much as she did.

Cabrera believes it is against "God's will" to execute a person. She also said that she had to let go of the hate she felt for Medlock in order to end the pain the murder had caused her. She has stated that she forgives the "evil" that Medlock did but has not forgotten that he murdered her grandchild.

The two women refuse to be in the same room together. Several years ago during an anti-death penalty rally at the state Capitol, Busch and Cabrera exchanged words, with Busch accusing Cabrera of using their murdered granddaughter's name to further the anti-death penalty cause.

Source: Robert Anthony Phillips, "Grandmothers at Odds as Execution Date Nears; Take Opposing Views on Fate of a Young Girl's Killer," APB News. October 11, 2000. Reprinted with permission.

More open to debate is the constitutionality of *methods* for the imposition of capital punishment. In a 1993 hearing, *Poyner* v. *Murray*,[90] the U.S. Supreme Court hinted at the possibility of reopening questions first raised in *Kemmler*. The case challenged Virginia's use of the electric chair as a form of cruel and unusual punishment. Syvasky Lafayette Poyner, who originally brought the case before the Court, lost his bid for a stay of execution and was electrocuted in March 1993.

Nonetheless, in *Poyner*, Justices Souter, Blackmun, and Stevens wrote: "The Court has not spoken squarely on the underlying issue since *In re Kemmler* . . . and the holding of that case does not constitute a dispositive response to litigation of the issue in light of modern knowledge about the method of execution in question." In a still more recent ruling, members of the Court questioned the constitutionality of hanging, suggesting that it may be a form of cruel and unusual punishment. In that case, *Campbell* v. *Wood* (1994), the defendant, Charles Campbell, raped a woman, got out of prison, and then came back and murdered her. His request for a stay of execution was denied since Washington State law (the state in which the murder occurred) offered Campbell a choice between various methods of execution and, therefore, an alternative to hanging. Similarly, in 1996, the Court upheld California's death penalty statute, which provides for lethal injection as the primary method of capital punishment in that state.[91] The constitutionality of the statute had been challenged by two death row inmates who claimed that a provision in the law that permitted condemned prisoners the choice of lethal gas in lieu of injection brought the statute within the realm of allowing cruel and unusual punishments.

Finally, in 2000, lawmakers in the state of Florida enacted legislation making lethal injection the state's preferred method of capital punishment. The action came after the U.S. Supreme Court agreed to hear claims that Florida's electric chair constituted a form of cruel and unusual punishment. Those claims arose following a series of botched Florida executions, including the 1997 execution of Pedro Medina during which foot-high flames shot from the condemned man's head, and the 1999 execution of 350-pound Allen Lee "Tiny" Davis, which caused blood to pour from Davis's mouth. After examining photographs taken during Davis' execution, Florida Supreme Court Justice Leander Shaw, Jr., concluded that "Davis . . . was brutally tortured to death by the citizens of Florida."[92] In an effort to show the brutality of the electric chair, Shaw put three especially gruesome posthumous photographs of Davis online. The images had been provided by the Florida Department of Corrections for use in a case before the Florida court concerning the constitutionality of electrocution. Davis was put to death for the 1982 murders of a pregnant Jacksonville woman and her two young daughters.

INTERMEDIATE SANCTIONS

While traditional sentencing options have included imprisonment, fines, probation, and—for very serious offenses—death, a significant number of innovative sentencing options, also called **alternative** or **intermediate sanctions,** have become available to judges in many jurisdictions during the past few decades. Intermediate sanctions—which may be imposed in lieu of other more traditional sanctions—include the use of split sentencing, shock probation and shock parole, shock incarceration, mixed sentencing, community service, home confinement, and intensive supervision.

A **split sentence** requires a convicted offender to serve a brief period of confinement in a local, state, or federal correctional facility, followed by a term of court-ordered probation. "Ninety days in jail, to be followed by a probationary term of two years," might be a typical split sentence. Split sentences are frequently imposed on youthful offenders who commit minor crimes in hopes that the threat of further sanctions might deter the person from additional law violation.

Shock probation is much like split sentencing in that the offender serves a relatively short period of time in correctional custody and is then released by court order. An important difference is that, under shock probation programs, an offender must *apply* for release after entering confinement and can never be sure whether his or her request will be granted. If it is, release may come as something of a shock to an offender who might otherwise be anticipating a relatively long prison term. *Shock parole* is similar in purpose and design to shock probation, the main difference being that release decisions made under shock probation programs are made by a judge, while such decisions under shock parole programs are made by a paroling authority, such as a state parole board.

INTERMEDIATE SANCTIONS
also **alternative sanctions;** the use of split sentencing, shock probation and parole, home confinement, shock incarceration, and community service in lieu of other, more traditional sanctions, such as imprisonment and fines. Intermediate sanctions are becoming increasingly popular as prisons become more crowded.

SPLIT SENTENCE
a sentence explicitly requiring the convicted person to serve a period of confinement in a local, state, or federal facility, followed by a period of probation.

SHOCK PROBATION
the practice of sentencing offenders to prison, allowing them to apply for probationary release, and enacting such release in surprise fashion. Offenders who receive shock probation may not be aware of the fact that they will be released on probation and may expect to spend a much longer time behind bars.

Shock incarceration, another form of alternative sanction, makes use of "boot camp" correctional programs that are intended to impress on youthful offenders the realities of prison life. Shock incarceration programs are modeled after military basic training and typically employ "drill sergeant"–type instructors selected for their ability to control and harass their charges. Such programs are highly regimented and make use of strict discipline, rigorous physical training, and hard labor in an effort to convince young offenders of the need to avoid future violations of the criminal law. While shock incarceration programs are generally of short duration (often only weeks or months), program "failures" may be moved into the general prison population and be ordered to serve longer terms of confinement.

Although most states allow judges to place offenders into shock incarceration settings, some jurisdictions delegate that authority to corrections officials. Two states, Louisiana and Texas, authorize judges and corrections personnel joint authority in the decision-making process.[93] Some states, such as Massachusetts, have begun to accept classes of female inmates into boot camp settings. The Massachusetts program, which first accepted women in 1993, requires inmates to spend nearly four months in the program.

A comprehensive 1995 study of boot camp prisons examined shock incarceration programs in eight states: Florida, Georgia, Illinois, Louisiana, New York, Oklahoma, South Carolina, and Texas. The study[94] found that boot camp programs are especially popular today because "they are . . . perceived as being tough on crime," and "have been enthusiastically embraced as a viable correctional option." The report concluded, however, that "the impact of boot camp programs on offender recidivism is at best negligible."

A **mixed sentence,** another alternative sentencing option, requires offenders to perform some type of community service along with brief periods of time in confinement—which is often served as weekends in jail. The community service component of mixed sentencing may require offenders to work a specified number of hours per week in government offices, clean public parks, wash police cars, or renovate state or county buildings. Offenders with special skills, such as nurses, physicians, or accountants, may be ordered to serve the community in a capacity in keeping with their abilities. Mixed sentencing is typically employed only with minor offenders, and there is considerable disagreement among justice professionals as to whether such punishment reduces recidivism, provides an effective deterrent, or rehabilitates offenders. Sometimes probationers are ordered to perform community service without having to serve time behind bars. **Community service** is a sentencing alternative that requires an offender to spend at least part of his or her time working for a public agency.

Intensive supervision, also called intensive probation supervision (IPS), is an alternative form of sentencing that imposes especially strict requirements on offenders sentenced to probation. Such requirements may include a mandatory curfew, required employment, routine and unannounced alcohol and drug testing, community service requirements, and frequent face-to-face meetings with probation officers. Some intensive probation supervision programs also include "prison awareness visits" during which individuals assigned to the program must tour correctional facilities in order to witness first-hand the unsavory conditions of confinement in a penal institution.

Home confinement, the last alternative sanction we shall discuss, has grown substantially in popularity in recent years. Home confinement, also called **house arrest,** requires that offenders be confined in their homes and sometimes makes use of electronic monitoring to insure they do not leave during the hours of confinement. Home confinement programs generally permit persons so sentenced to travel to and from work, medical appointments, or treatment programs. Participants sometimes wear ankle or arm bracelets that send out a signal, which can be monitored from equipment installed in their residences for that purpose. Some electronic monitoring devices are attached to an offender's telephone and require the confined individual to insert a device into a "reader" connected to the phone or to make some other predefined response to telephone calls intended to determine the offender's location.

House arrest can be an effective response to the rising cost of imprisonment. Estimates show that while imprisonment may cost taxpayers as much as $50,000 per year per offender, traditional home confinement programs cost only $1,500 to $7,000 per offender per year (depending on jurisdiction and the type of supervision employed), and electronic monitoring increases the cost of home confinement by about $1,000.[95] Advocates of house arrest argue that it is also socially cost effective,[96] because it provides no opportunity for the kinds of negative socialization that occur in prison.

Intermediate sanctions are generally available to relatively unthreatening, nonviolent, and first-time offenders. In 1994, California legislators reaffirmed their commitment to intermediate sanctions with passage of the Community-Based Punishment Act. The Act, passed alongside of the state's punitive three-strikes legislation, has as its goal the release of nonviolent offenders—a group that continues to comprise a majority of the California prison population.

SUMMARY

- This chapter describes criminal sentencing. Sentencing is the process through which a sentencing authority imposes a lawful punishment or other sanction on a person convicted of violating the criminal law.

- One fundamental way of distinguishing crimes from violations of the civil law, or torts, is to recognize that crimes are subject to punishment. When criminal punishment is associated with violation of the law, the U.S. Supreme Court has ruled that constitutional guarantees of due process must apply.

- A felt need for retribution, as a goal of criminal sentencing, may be fundamental to the human condition. In its present guise, retribution is found in the just deserts philosophy, which holds that criminal offenders deserve the punishment they receive at the hands of the state and which suggests that punishments should be appropriate to the type and severity of crime committed.

- Other goals of criminal sentencing include deterrence, rehabilitation, restoration, and incapacitation.

- Three-strikes laws and habitual offender statutes, which are built on a policy of selective incapacitation, reflect a growing society-wide emphasis on both retribution and deterrence.

- Restoration, a sentencing goal that seeks to make victims and the community "whole again," frequently builds on the practice of restitution and embodies many of the principles of restorative justice.

- Two major approaches to sentencing are found in the indeterminate and determinate models. An indeterminate sentence is a type of sentence to imprisonment where the commitment, instead of being for a specified single time quantity, such as three years, is for a range of time, such as two to five years, or five years maximum and zero minimum. A determinate sentence sets a single standard "time quantity" of imprisonment.

- Determinate sentencing schemes typically take into consideration both aggravating and mitigating factors in reaching sentencing decisions. Aggravating factors are circumstances relating to the commission of a crime that cause its gravity to be greater than that of the average instance of the given type of offense. Conversely, mitigating factors are circumstances surrounding the commission of a crime that do not in law justify or excuse the act but which in fairness may be considered as reducing the blameworthiness of the defendant.

- A recent movement toward "truth in sentencing" at both the state and federal levels has tended to ensure that sentences that are imposed closely match the time inmates actually serve in prison.

- Traditional sentencing options have generally included imprisonment, probation, fines, and death. Studies show that 44 percent of sentenced felons receive active prison terms.

- Hate crime laws, which have developed during the past 20 years, increase the penalties associated with bias crimes.

- The U.S. Supreme Court has created an environment in which capital punishment remains a viable sentencing option for especially heinous crimes, such as murder, in which mitigating factors are lacking. Death sentences today are usually imposed via a two-step process, which first determines a defendant's guilt and later decides the sentence.

- *Habeas corpus* appeals are used by death row prisoners and other state inmates whose convictions have been upheld by state appellate courts to petition federal courts in order to argue that their rights were violated at trial. Recent initiatives in both federal law and U.S. Supreme Court precedents, however, have had the effect of limiting *habeas* opportunities.

QUESTIONS FOR DISCUSSION

1. What are the purposes of criminal sentencing? What sentencing strategies are most closely associated with each sentencing purpose?

2. List each of the purposes of criminal sentencing. How is each purpose served by indeterminate sentencing? By determinate sentencing? Which sentencing model (determinate or indeterminate) is most appropriate today? Why?

3. Do you believe that three-strikes laws can be an effective deterrent to crime? Why or why not? Are three-strikes laws economically efficient? Why or why not?

4. What is restorative justice? How does it differ in purpose from retribution as a purpose of criminal punishment? How does restorative justice build on restitution?

5. Do you believe that capital punishment should continue to remain a viable sentencing option for especially heinous crimes? Why or why not?

6. Do you think that opportunities for *habeas corpus* appeals should be limited? Why or why not?

LEGAL RESOURCES ON THE WORLD WIDE WEB

A number of Internet sites provide information about criminal sentencing and capital punishment. Some of the more comprehensive sites are listed here.

ACLU's Death Penalty Page
http://www.aclu.org/issues/death/hmdp.html
The ACLU's Execution Watch page offers comprehensive resources on activism against the death penalty in the United States. It includes a link to the ACLU's death penalty briefing paper and the ACLU Abolitionist.

Amnesty International—Death Penalty Information
http://www.derechos.org/dp
This site lists all the countries that currently retain the death penalty.

Cornell Law School Death Penalty Project
http://www.lawschool.cornell.edu/lawlibrary/death/default.htm
The project, which began in 1997, is composed of several elements, including a capital punishment clinic, a commitment to provide continuing education programs for capital defense attorneys, and the active collection and study of data in this field.

Death Penalty Information Center (DPIC)
http://www.deathpenaltyinfo.org
This site contains a wealth of information on the death penalty, including current law, statistics, and historical information.

The Sentencing Project
http://www.sentencingproject.org
The Sentencing Project is an independent source of criminal justice policy analysis, data, and program information for the public and policy makers.

U.S. Sentencing Commission
http://www.ussc.gov
Home page of the U.S. Sentencing Commission, whose guidelines provide federal judges with clear direction for the sentencing of defendants in their courts.

Check the *Criminal Law Today* Web site for URLs that may have changed.

SUGGESTED READINGS AND CLASSIC WORKS

Peter de Graaff, "The Poverty of Punishment," *Current Issues in Criminal Justice,* Vol. 5, no. 1 (July 1993), pp. 13–28.

Jan Gorecki, *Capital Punishment: Criminal Law and Social Evolution* (New York: Columbia University Press, 1983).

Michael J. Gorr and Sterling Harwood (Eds.), *Controversies in Criminal Law: Philosophical Essays on Responsibility and Procedure* (Boulder, CO: Westview Press, 1992).

Douglas N. Husak, *Philosophy of Criminal Law* (Totowa, NJ: Rowman & Littlefield, 1987).

Sanford H. Kadish, *Blame and Punishment: Essays in the Criminal Law* (New York: Macmillan Publishing, 1987).

Steven Shavell, *Criminal Law and Optimal Use of Nonmonetary Sanctions as a Deterrent* (Cambridge, MA: Harvard Law School, 1985).

Franklin E. Zimring and Gordon Hawkins, *Capital Punishment and the American Agenda* (New York: Cambridge University Press, 1989).

WHAT FACTORS SHOULD A JURY CONSIDER IN DETERMINING IF THE DEATH PENALTY IS THE APPROPRIATE SENTENCE IN A CAPITAL PUNISHMENT CASE?

CAPSTONE CASE

Weeks v. *Angelone*
U.S. Supreme Court (2000)
No. 99-5746

Chief Justice Rehnquist delivered the opinion of the Court.

This case presents the question whether the Constitution is violated when a trial judge directs a capital jury's attention to a specific paragraph of a constitutionally sufficient instruction in response to a question regarding the proper consideration of mitigating circumstances. We hold that it is not and that *habeas* relief is barred by 28 U.S.C. §§ 2254(d) (1994 ed., Supp. III).

Petitioner Lonnie Weeks, Jr., was riding from Washington, D.C., to Richmond, Virginia, as a passenger in a car driven by his uncle, Lewis Dukes. Petitioner had stolen the vehicle in a home burglary earlier in the month. The two sped past the marked car of Virginia State Trooper Jose Cavazos, who was monitoring traffic. Trooper Cavazos activated his emergency lights and took chase. After passing other vehicles on the highway shoulder, Dukes stopped on an exit ramp. Trooper Cavazos approached the driver's side of the stolen vehicle on foot. Upon the trooper's request, Dukes alighted and stood near the rear of the car. Trooper Cavazos, still standing near the driver's side, asked petitioner to step out as well. As Weeks stepped out on the passenger's side, he carried a 9-millimeter semiautomatic pistol loaded with hollow-point bullets. Petitioner proceeded to fire six bullets at the trooper, two of which entered his body near the right and left shoulder straps of his protective vest, and four of which entered his forearms and left wrist. Trooper Cavazos died within minutes.

Petitioner was arrested the next morning. During routine questioning about his physical and mental state by classification officers, petitioner confessed, indicating that he was considering suicide because he shot the trooper. Petitioner also voluntarily wrote a letter to a jail officer admitting the killing and expressing remorse.

Petitioner was tried in the Circuit Court for Prince William County, Virginia, in October 1993. After the jury had found him guilty of capital murder, a 2-day penalty phase followed. In this proceeding the prosecution sought to prove two aggravating circumstances: that Weeks "would commit criminal acts of violence that would constitute a continuing serious threat to society" and that his conduct was "outrageously or wantonly vile, horrible or inhuman, in that it involved depravity of mind or aggravated battery." During the penalty phase, the defense presented 10 witnesses, including petitioner, in mitigation.

The jury retired at 10:40 A.M. on the second day to begin deliberations. At around noon, the judge informed counsel that the jury had asked the following question:

> *"Does the sentence of life imprisonment in the State of Virginia have the possibility of parole, and if so, under what conditions must be met to receive parole?"*

The judge responded to the jury's question as follows:

> *"You should impose such punishment as you feel is just under the evidence, and within the instructions of the Court. You are not to concern yourselves with what may happen afterwards."*

The prosecution agreed with the judge's response and defense counsel objected. At 12:40 P.M., court reconvened and the judge told the jurors that there would be a one-hour luncheon recess and that they could go to lunch or continue deliberations, as a juror had apparently informed the bailiff that they might be interested in working through lunch. At 12:45 P.M., the jury retired from the courtroom. At 3:15 P.M., the judge informed counsel that he had received the following written question from the jury:

> *"If we believe that Lonnie Weeks, Jr. is guilty of at least 1 of the alternatives, then is it our duty as a jury to issue the death penalty? Or must we decide (even though he is guilty of one of the alternatives) whether or not to issue the death penalty, or one of the life sentences? What is the Rule? Please clarify?"*

The judge wrote the following response: "See second paragraph of Instruction #2 (Beginning with 'If you find from . . .')." *Ibid.* The judge explained to counsel his answer to the jury's question:

"In instruction number 2 that was given to them, in the second paragraph, it reads, 'If you find from the evidence that the Commonwealth has proved, beyond a reasonable doubt, either of the two alternatives, and as to that alternative, you are unanimous, then you may fix the punishment of the defendant at death, or if you believe from all the evidence that the death penalty is not justified, then you shall fix the punishment of the defendant at imprisonment for life, or imprisonment for life with a fine not to exceed $100,000.'

"I don't believe I can answer the question any clearer than the instruction, so what I have done is referred them to the second paragraph of instruction number 2, and I told them beginning with, 'If you find from,' et cetera, et cetera, for them to read that paragraph."

The prosecution stated that the judge's solution was appropriate. Defense counsel disagreed, and stated:

"Your Honor, we would ask that Your Honor instruct the jury that even if they find one or both of the mitigating factors—I'm sorry, the factors that have been proved beyond a reasonable doubt, that they still may impose a life sentence, or a life sentence plus a fine."

Defense counsel asked that his objection be noted.

More than two hours later, the jury returned. The clerk read its verdict:

"[W]e the jury, on the issue joined, having found the defendant Lonnie Weeks, Jr., guilty of capital murder, and having unanimously found that his conduct in committing the offense is outrageously or wantonly vile, horrible or inhumane, in that it involved depravity of mind and or aggravated battery, and having considered the evidence in mitigation of the offense, unanimously fix his punishment at death. . . ." Id., at 225 (emphasis added).

The jurors were polled and all responded affirmatively that the foregoing was their verdict in the case.

Petitioner presented 47 assignments of error in his direct appeal to the Virginia Supreme Court, and the assignment of error respecting the judge's answering the jury's question about mitigating circumstances was number 44. The Virginia Supreme Court affirmed petitioner's conviction and sentence, holding that the claims petitioner advances here lack merit. 248 Va. 460, 465–466, 476–477, 450 S.E.2d 379, 383, 390 (1994), *cert. denied*, 516 U.S. 829 (1995). The Virginia Supreme Court dismissed petitioner's state *habeas* petition as jurisdictionally barred on timeliness grounds. The District Court denied petitioner's request for federal *habeas* relief, and the Court of Appeals for the Fourth Circuit denied a certificate of appealability and dismissed his petition. 176 F.3d 249 (1999). We granted *certiorari*, 527 U.S. __ (1999), and now affirm.

Petitioner relies heavily on our decisions in *Bollenbach* v. *United States*, 326 U.S. 607 (1946), and *Eddings* v. *Oklahoma*, 455 U.S. 104 (1982). *Bollenbach* involved a supplemental instruction by the trial court following an inquiry from the jury—in that respect it is like the present case—but the instruction given by the trial court in *Bollenbach* was palpably erroneous. 326 U.S., at 611. In this respect it is quite unlike the present case. *Eddings* arose out of a bench trial in a capital case, and this Court reversed a sentence of death because the trial judge had refused to consider mitigating evidence: "[I]t was as if the trial judge had instructed a jury to disregard the mitigating evidence Eddings proffered on his behalf." 455 U.S., at 114.

Here the trial judge gave no such instruction. On the contrary, he gave the instruction that we upheld in *Buchanan* v. *Angelone*, 522 U.S. 269 (1998), as being sufficient to allow the jury to consider mitigating evidence. And in addition, he gave a specific instruction on mitigating evidence—an instruction that was not given in *Buchanan*—in which he told the jury that "[y]ou must consider a mitigating circumstance if you find there is evidence to support it." Even the dissenters in

Buchanan said that the ambiguity that they found in the instruction there given would have been cleared up by "some mention of mitigating evidence anywhere in the instructions." *Id., at 283.*

In *Buchanan,* we considered whether the Eighth Amendment required that a capital jury be instructed on particular mitigating factors. Buchanan's jury was given precisely the same Virginia pattern capital instruction that was given to Weeks' jury. See *id.,* at 272, and n. 1. We noted that our cases have established that the sentencer may not be precluded from considering, and may not refuse to consider, any constitutionally relevant mitigating evidence, and that the State may structure the jury's consideration of mitigation so long as it does not preclude the jury from giving effect to it. *Id.,* at 276. We further noted that the "standard for determining whether jury instructions satisfy these principles was 'whether there is a reasonable likelihood that the jury has applied the challenged instruction in a way that prevents the consideration of constitutionally relevant evidence.' " *Ibid.* (quoting *Boyde* v. *California,* 494 U.S. 370, 380 (1990)). But, we stated that we have never held that the State must structure in a particular way the manner in which juries consider mitigating evidence. 522 U.S., at 276. We concluded that the Virginia pattern jury instruction at issue there, and again at issue here, did not violate those principles:

> *"The instruction did not foreclose the jury's consideration of any mitigating evidence. By directing the jury to base its decision on 'all the evidence,' the instruction afforded jurors an opportunity to consider mitigating evidence. The instruction informed the jurors that if they found the aggravating factor proved beyond a reasonable doubt then they 'may fix' the penalty at death, but directed that if they believed that all the evidence justified a lesser sentence then they 'shall' impose a life sentence. The jury was thus allowed to impose a life sentence even if it found the aggravating factor proved." Id., at 277.*

But, as noted above, the jury in this case also received an explicit direction to consider mitigating evidence—an instruction that was not given to the jury in *Buchanan.* Thus, so far as the adequacy of the jury instructions is concerned, their sufficiency here follows *a fortiori* from *Buchanan.*

Given that petitioner's jury was adequately instructed, and given that the trial judge responded to the jury's question by directing its attention to the precise paragraph of the constitutionally adequate instruction that answers its inquiry, the question becomes whether the Constitution requires anything more. We hold that it does not.

A jury is presumed to follow its instructions. *Richardson* v. *Marsh,* 481 U.S. 200, 211 (1987). Similarly, a jury is presumed to understand a judge's answer to its question. See, e.g., *Armstrong* v. *Toler,* 11 Wheat. 258, 279 (1826) (opinion of Marshall, C. J.). Weeks' jury did not inform the court that after reading the relevant paragraph of the instruction, it still did not understand its role. See *ibid.* ("Had the jury desired further information, they might, and probably would, have signified their desire to the court. The utmost willingness was manifested to gratify them, and it may fairly be presumed that they had nothing further to ask.") To presume otherwise would require reversal every time a jury inquires about a matter of constitutional significance, regardless of the judge's answer.

Here the presumption gains additional support from several empirical factors. First and foremost, each of the jurors affirmed in open court the verdict which included a finding that they had "considered the evidence in mitigation of the offense." It is also significant, we think, that the jurors deliberated for more than two hours after receiving the judge's answer to their question. Over 4 1/2 hours after the jury retired to begin deliberations, the jury asked the question at issue. Again, the question was:

> *"If we believe that Lonnie Weeks, Jr. is guilty of at least 1 of the alternatives, then is it our duty as a jury to issue the death penalty? Or must we decide*

(even though he is guilty of one of the alternatives) whether or not to issue the death penalty, or one of the life sentences? What is the Rule? Please clarify?"

The question indicates that at that time it was asked, the jury had determined that the prosecution had proved one of the two aggravating factors beyond a reasonable doubt. More than two hours passed between the judge directing the jury's attention to the appropriate paragraph of the instruction that answered its question and the jury returning its verdict. We cannot, of course, know for *certain* what transpired during those two hours. But the most likely explanation is that the jury was doing exactly what it was instructed to do: that is, weighing the mitigating circumstances against the aggravating circumstance that it found to be proved beyond a reasonable doubt. If, after the judge's response to its question, the jury thought that it was required to give the death penalty upon finding of an aggravating circumstance, it is unlikely that the jury would have consumed two more hours in deliberation. This particular jury demonstrated that it was not too shy to ask questions, suggesting that it would have asked another if it felt the judge's response unsatisfactory. Finally, defense counsel specifically explained to the jury during closing argument that it could find both aggravating factors proven and still not sentence Weeks to death. Thus, once the jury received the judge's response to its question, it had not only the text of the instruction we approved in *Buchanan,* but also the additional instruction on mitigation, see n. 2, *supra,* and its own recollection of defense counsel's closing argument for guidance. At best, petitioner has demonstrated only that there exists a slight *possibility* that the jury considered itself precluded from considering mitigating evidence. Such a demonstration is insufficient to prove a constitutional violation under *Boyde,* which requires the showing of a reasonable *likelihood* that the jury felt so restrained.

It also appears that petitioner's attorneys did not view the judge's answer to the jury's question as a serious flaw in the trial at that time. Petitioner's attorney made an oral motion to set aside the sentence after the verdict of death was received, and did not even mention this incident in his motion. And the low priority and space which his counsel assigned to the point on his appeal to the Supreme Court of Virginia suggests that the present emphasis has some of the earmarks of an afterthought.

Because petitioner seeks a federal writ of *habeas corpus* from a state sentence, we must determine whether 28 U.S.C. §§ 2254(d) precludes such relief. The Court of Appeals below held that it did. 176 F.3d, at 261. We agree. Section 2254(d) prohibits federal *habeas* relief on any claim "adjudicated on the merits in State court proceedings," unless that adjudication resulted in a decision that was "contrary to, or involved an unreasonable application of, clearly established Federal law, as determined by the Supreme Court of the United States." 28 U.S.C. §§ 2254(d) and (1) (1994 ed., Supp. III). For the reasons stated above, it follows *a fortiori* that the adjudication of the Supreme Court of Virginia affirming petitioner's conviction and sentence was neither "contrary to," nor did it involve an "unreasonable application of," any of our decisions.

The judgment of the Court of Appeals is AFFIRMED.

DISSENTING OPINION
Justice Stevens, with whom Justice Ginsburg and Justice Breyer join, and with whom Justice Souter joins with respect to all but Part I, dissenting.

Congress has directed us to apply "clearly established Federal law" in the exercise of our *habeas corpus* jurisdiction. The clearly established rule that should govern the disposition of this case also emphasizes the importance of clarity—clarity in the judge's instructions when there is a reasonable likelihood that the jury may misunderstand the governing rule of law. In this case, as in *Boyde* v. *California,* 494 U.S. 370,

380 (1990), we are confronted with a claim that an instruction, though not erroneous, is sufficiently ambiguous to be "subject to an erroneous interpretation." In *Boyde,* we held that "the proper inquiry in such a case is whether there is a reasonable likelihood that the jury has applied the challenged instruction in a way that prevents the consideration of constitutionally relevant evidence." *Ibid.*

The record in this case establishes, not just a "reasonable likelihood" of jury confusion, but a virtual certainty that the jury did not realize that there were two distinct legal bases for concluding that a death sentence was not "justified." The jurors understood that such a sentence would not be justified unless they found at least one of the two alleged aggravating circumstances. Despite their specific request for enlightenment, however, the judge refused to tell them that *even if* they found one of those circumstances, they did not have a "duty as a jury to issue the death penalty." App. 217.

Because the Court creatively suggests that petitioner's claim has "the earmarks of an afterthought," *ante,* at 10, it is appropriate to note that his trial counsel specifically and repeatedly argued that both the instructions and the verdict forms were inadequate because " 'the jury has to be instructed that . . . even if they find aggravating factors beyond a reasonable doubt, . . . they can still give effect to the evidence in mitigation by sentencing the defendant to life, as opposed to death.' " App. 178. See also *id.,* at 179, 180, 185–186, 223.

Four different aspects of the record cumulatively provide compelling support for the conclusion that this jury did not understand that the law authorized it "not to issue the death penalty" even though it found petitioner "guilty of at least 1" aggravating circumstance. *Id.,* at 217. Each of these points merits separate comment: (1) the text of the instructions; (2) the judge's responses to the jury's inquiries; (3) the verdict forms given to the jury; and (4) the court reporter's transcription of the polling of the jury.

I

Because the prosecutor in this case relied on two separate aggravating circumstances, the critical instruction given in this case differed from that given and upheld by this Court in *Buchanan* v. *Angelone,* 522 U.S. 269 (1998). The Weeks instructions contain a longer description of the ways in which the jury would be justified in imposing the death penalty; this made it especially unlikely that the jury would understand that it could lawfully impose a life sentence by either (1) refusing to find an aggravator, or (2) concluding that even if it found an aggravator, the mitigating evidence warranted a life sentence. The point is best made by quoting the instruction itself:

> *Before the penalty can be fixed at death, the Commonwealth must prove beyond a reasonable doubt, at least one of the following two alternatives: one, that, after consideration of his history and background, there is a probability that he would commit criminal acts of violence that would constitute a continuing serious threat to society, or two; that his conduct in committing the offense was outrageously or wantonly vile, horrible, or inhumane, in that it involved depravity of mind and aggravated battery to the victim, beyond the minimum necessary to accomplish the act of murder.*
>
> *If you find from the evidence that the Commonwealth has proved beyond a reasonable doubt, either of the two alternatives, and as to that alternative you are unanimous, then you may fix the punishment of the defendant at death; or, if you believe from all the evidence that the death penalty is not justified, then you shall fix the punishment of the defendant at life imprisonment, or imprisonment for life and a fine of a specific amount, but not more than $100,000.*

The first paragraph and the first half of the second are perfectly clear. They unambiguously tell the jury: "In order to justify the death penalty, you must find an aggravating circumstance." The second clause in the second paragraph is, however, ambiguous. It could mean either:

> *(1) even if you find one of the two aggravating alternatives, if you believe from all the evidence that the death penalty is not justified because the mitigating evidence outweighs the aggravating evidence, then you shall fix the punishment [at life]; or*

> *(2) if you believe from all the evidence that the death penalty is not justified because neither of the aggravating circumstances has been proven beyond a reasonable doubt, then you shall fix the punishment [at life].*

It is not necessary to reiterate Justice Breyer's reasons for believing that the latter message is the one a non-lawyer would be most likely to receive. See *Buchanan*, 522 U.S., at 281–284 (dissenting opinion). Nor is it necessary to disagree with the Court's view in *Buchanan* that trained lawyers and logicians could create a "simple decisional tree" that would enable them to decipher the intended meaning of the instruction, see *id.*, at 277–278, n. 4, to identify a serious risk that this jury failed to do so.

That risk was magnified by the fact that the instructions did not explain that there were two reasons why mitigating evidence was relevant to its penalty determination. The instructions did make it clear that mitigating evidence concerning the history and background of the defendant should be considered when deciding *whether* either aggravating circumstance had been proved. The instructions did not, however, explain that mitigating evidence could serve another purpose—to provide a lawful justification for a life sentence *even if* the jury found at least one aggravating circumstance. Indeed, given the fact that the first task assigned to the jury was to decide whether "*after consideration of his history and background*, there is a probability that he would commit criminal acts of violence that would constitute a continuing serious threat to society," App. 192–193 (emphasis added), it would have been reasonable for the jury to infer that his history and background were only relevant to the threshold question whether an aggravator had been proved.

It is of critical importance in understanding the jury's confusion that the instructions failed to inform the jury that mitigating evidence serves this dual purpose.

II

The jurors had a written copy of the judge's instructions with them in the jury room during their deliberations. The fact that the jurors submitted the following written inquiry to the trial judge after they had been deliberating for several hours demonstrates both that they were uncertain about the meaning of the ambiguous clause that I have identified, and that their uncertainty had not been dissipated by their recollection of anything said by counsel:

> *"If we believe that Lonnie Weeks, Jr. is guilty of at least 1 of the alternatives, then is it our duty as a jury to issue the death penalty? Or must we decide (even though he is guilty of one of the alternatives) whether or not to issue the death penalty, or one of the life sentences? What is the Rule? Please clarify."*

The only portion of the written instructions that could possibly have prompted this inquiry is the second half of the second paragraph of the instruction quoted above. The fact that the jurors asked this question about that instruction demonstrates beyond peradventure that the instruction had confused them. There would have been no reason to ask the question if they had understood the instruction to authorize a life sentence even though they found that an aggravator had been proved.

Although it would have been easy to do so, the judge did not give the jurors a straightforward categorical answer to their simple question; he merely told them to re-examine the portion of the instructions that they, in effect, had already said they

did not understand. The text of their question indicates that they believed that they had a duty "to issue the death penalty" if they believed that "Weeks is guilty of at least 1 of the alternatives." *Ibid.* Without a simple, clear-cut statement from the judge that that belief was incorrect, there was surely a reasonable likelihood that they would act on that belief.

Instead of accepting a commonsense interpretation of the colloquy between the jury and the judge, the Court first relies on a presumption that the jury understood the instruction (a presumption surely rebutted by the question itself), and then presumes that the jury must have understood the judge's answer because it did not repeat its question after re-reading the relevant paragraph, and continued to deliberate for another two hours. But if the jurors found it necessary to ask the judge what that paragraph meant in the first place, why should we presume that they would find it any less ambiguous just because the judge told them to read it again? It seems to me far more likely that the reason they did not ask the same question a second time is that the jury believed that it would be disrespectful to repeat a simple, unambiguous question that the judge had already refused to answer directly. The fact that it had previously asked the judge a different question—also related to the effect of a sentencing decision—that he had also refused to answer would surely have tended to discourage a repetition of the question about the meaning of his instructions.

By the Court's logic, a rather exceptionally assertive jury would have to question the judge at least twice and maybe more on precisely the same topic before one could find it no more than "reasonably likely" that the jury was confused. But given the Court's apt recognition that we cannot, of course, actually know what occupied the jury during its final deliberations and in light of the explanation I have just offered, it is at the very least equally likely that the two hours of deliberation following the judge's answer were devoted to continuing debate about the *same* instruction, as they were to weighing aggravating and mitigating evidence (having been magically satisfied by the repetition of the instruction that had not theretofore answered its question).

When it comes to the imposition of the death penalty, we have held repeatedly that justice and "the fundamental respect for humanity underlying the Eighth Amendment" require jurors to give full effect to their assessment of the defendant's character, circumstances, and individual worth. *Eddings* v. *Oklahoma*, 455 U.S. 104, 112 (1982). In this context, even if one finds the explanations of the jury's conduct here in equipoise, a 50–50 chance that the jury has not carried out this mandate seems to me overwhelming grounds for reversal.

Other than the Court's reliance on inapplicable presumptions and speculation, there is no reason to believe that the jury understood the judge's answer to its question. As we squarely held in *Boyde*, the "defendant need not establish that the jury was more likely than not to have been impermissibly inhibited by the instruction," to satisfy the clearly established "reasonable likelihood" standard. 494 U.S., at 380. The Court's application of that standard in this case effectively drains it of meaning.

III

The judge provided the jury with five verdict forms, three of which provided for the death penalty and two for a life sentence. Three death forms were appropriate because the death penalty might be justified by a finding that the first, the second, or both aggravating circumstances had been proved. One would expect the two life forms to cover the two alternatives, first that no aggravator had been proved, and second that despite proof of at least one aggravator, the mitigating circumstances warranted a life sentence. But that is not why there were two forms; neither referred to the possibility of a life sentence if an aggravator had been proved. Rather, the two life alternatives merely presented the jury with a choice between life plus a fine and a life sentence without a fine.

The first form read as follows:

> *We, the jury, on the issue joined, having found the defendant, LONNIE WEEKS, JR., GUILTY of CAPITAL MURDER and having unanimously found after consideration of his history and background that there is a probability that he would commit criminal acts of violence that would constitute a continuing serious threat to society, and having considered the evidence in mitigation of the offense, unanimously fix his punishment at death.*

The jury ultimately refused to select this first form, which would have indicated a finding that there was a probability that petitioner would commit additional crimes that would constitute a serious threat to society. In doing so, it unquestionably gave weight to the unusually persuasive mitigating evidence offered by the defense—evidence that included not only petitioner's personal history but his own testimony describing the relevant events and his extreme remorse. As I explained above, the fact that the jury recognized the relevance of the mitigating "history and background" evidence to the question whether the aggravator had been proved, sheds no light on the question whether it understood that such evidence would also be relevant on the separate question whether a life sentence would be appropriate even if Weeks was "guilty of at least 1 of the alternatives."

The jury's refusal to find that petitioner would constitute a continuing threat to society also explains why it did not use the second form, which covered the option of a death penalty supported by both aggravators. The choice then, was between the third alternative, which included a finding that the second aggravator had been proved, and the fourth or fifth alternatives, neither of which included any such finding. Despite the fact that trial counsel had expressly objected to the verdict forms because they "do not expressly provide for a sentence of life imprisonment, upon finding beyond a reasonable doubt, on one or both of the aggravating factors," the judge failed to use forms that would have answered the question that the jury asked during its deliberations.

The ambiguity of the forms also helps further explain why the Court is wrong in its speculation as to the jury's final hours of deliberation following the judge's response to its question. The Court postulates that before the jury asked whether it had a duty to issue the death penalty "[i]f we believe that Lonnie Weeks, Jr. is guilty of at least 1 of the alternatives," the jury had already so decided. Thus, the remaining hours of deliberation must have been spent weighing the mitigating circumstances against the aggravating circumstance. Of course, the text of the question, which used the word "if" rather than the word "since," does not itself support that speculation. More important, however—inasmuch as we cannot know for certain what transpired during those deliberations—is the fact that after it eliminated the first two verdict options, the remaining forms identified a choice between a death sentence based on a guilty finding on "1 of the alternatives" and a life sentence without any such finding. In my judgment, it is thus far more likely that the conscientious jurors were struggling with the question whether the mitigating evidence not only precluded a finding that petitioner was a continuing threat to society, but also precluded a finding "that his conduct in committing the offense is outrageously or wantonly vile, horrible or inhuman in that it involved depravity of mind and/or aggravated battery." App. 228. And that question was answered neither by the instruction itself, nor by the judge's reference to the instruction again, nor, we now see, by the text of the jury forms with which the jury was finally faced.

IV

The Court repeatedly emphasizes the facts that the jury was told to consider the mitigating evidence and that the verdict forms expressly recite that the jury had given consideration to such evidence. As its refusal to find the first aggravator indicates, the jury surely did consider that evidence and presumably credited the testimony

of petitioner and the other defense witnesses. But, as I have explained, there is a vast difference between considering that evidence as relevant to the question whether either aggravator had been established, and assuming that the jurors were sufficiently sophisticated to understand that it would be lawful for them to rely on that evidence as a basis for a life sentence even if they found the defendant "guilty of at least 1 of the alternatives." For that reason, the Court's reliance on the fact that the jurors affirmed their verdict when polled in open court is misplaced.

The most significant aspect of the polling of the jury is a notation by the court reporter that is unique. (At least I do not recall seeing a comparable notation in any of the transcripts of capital sentencing proceedings that I have reviewed during the past 24-plus years.) The transcript states that, as they were polled, "a majority of the jury members [were] in tears." Given the unusually persuasive character of the mitigating evidence including petitioner's own testimony, it is at least "reasonable" to infer that the conscientious jury members performed what they regarded as their duty under the law, notwithstanding a strong desire to spare the life of Lonnie Weeks. Tragically, there is a "reasonable likelihood" that they acted on the basis of a misunderstanding of that duty.

I respectfully dissent.

WHAT DO *YOU* THINK?
1. What did state law require the jury to consider in deciding whether death was the appropriate punishment in this case?
2. What is the basic disagreement between the majority and dissenting opinions?
3. Which opinion do you agree with? Why?
4. The phrase "polling the jury" refers to the practice of asking each jury member after the verdict has been announced, if the announced verdict was in fact the unanimous verdict of the jury. Does the fact that the jury was "in tears" during the polling indicate that members of the jury were not pleased with their verdict?
5. Had the judge further explained to the jury the meaning of his instructions, would he have eliminated several important issues in this case? If so, which ones?

NOTES

1. *State* v. *Wood*, 868 P.2d 70 (Utah 1993).
2. Wording taken from the opinion of the Utah Supreme Court, *State* v. *Wood*, 868 P.2d 70 (1993).
3. George P. Fletcher, *Rethinking Criminal Law* (Boston: Little, Brown, 1978), p. 408.
4. H. L. A. Hart, *Punishment and Responsibility* (New York: Oxford 1968).
5. Michael S. Moore, "The Moral Worth of Retribution," in F. Schoeman (Ed.), *Responsibility, Character and Emotions: New Essays in Moral Psychology* (Cambridge: Cambridge University Press, 1987).
6. Jeremy Bentham, *An Introduction to the Principles of Morals and Legislation* (1789), reprinted by Clarendon Press, 1996.
7. J. Andenaes, "The General Preventive Effects of Punishment," *University of Pennsylvania Law Review*, Vol. 114, (1966), pp. 955–957.
8. See, for example, Franklin Zimring and Gordon Hawkins, *Deterrence: The Legal Threat in Crime Control* (Chicago: University of Chicago Press, 1973).
9. Robert Martinson, "What Works: Questions and Answers About Prison Reform," *Public Interest*, No. 35 (1974), pp. 22–54.

10. Gordon Bazemore and Mark S. Umbreit, *Balanced and Restorative Justice: Program Summary* (Washington, D.C.: Office of Juvenile Justice and Delinquency Prevention, October 1994), foreword.

11. John S. Baker, Jr., Daniel H. Benson, Robert Force, and B. J. George, Jr., *Hall's Criminal Law: Cases and Materials,* 5th ed. (Charlottesville, VA: Michie, 1993), p. 842.

12. *People* v. *Superior Court of San Diego (Romero),* 13 Cal. 4th 497 (1996).

13. *People* v. *Davis,* 15 Cal. 4th 1096, 1103 (1997). See also *People* v. *Garcia,* 21 Cal. 4th 1 (1999).

14. *People* v. *Benson,* 18 Cal. 4th 24 (1998).

15. *People* v. *Williams,* 17 Cal. 4th 148 (1998).

16. *Monge* v. *California,* 118 S. Ct. 2246 (1998).

17. *Riggs* v. *California,* 119 S. Ct. 890 (1999), *cert. denied.*

18. "Wilson Praises '3 Strikes' Law," United Press online, March 6, 1996.

19. For a detailed survey of the impact of three-strikes legislation on the California justice system, see Board of Corrections, *'Three Strikes, You're Out': Impact on California's Criminal Justice System and Options for Ongoing Monitoring* (Sacramento, CA: Board of Corrections, September 1996).

20. Bureau of Justice Statistics, *Dictionary of Criminal Justice Data Terminology,* 2nd ed. (Washington, D.C.: U.S. Department of Justice, 1981), p. 46.

21. Ibid., p. 107.

22. Ibid., p. 46.

23. Ibid.

24. Ibid., p. 107.

25. Ibid., p. 15.

26. Ibid.

27. Ibid., p. 16.

28. Ibid.

29. Public Law 98-473 (1984).

30. U.S. Sentencing Commission, *Federal Sentencing Guidelines Manual* (Washington, D.C.: U.S. Government Printing Office, 1987), p. 207.

31. 18 U.S.C. 3553.

32. *Mistretta* v. *United States,* 488 U.S. 361, 371 (1989).

33. U.S. Sentencing Commission, *Federal Sentencing Guidelines Manual,* p. 2.

34. Lawrence A. Greenfeld, "Prison Sentences and Time Served for Violence," Bureau of Justice Statistics, *Selected Findings,* No. 4 (April 1995).

35. Ibid.

36. Ibid.

37. Thomas Martello, "Truth in Sentencing," Associated Press, northern edition, April 26, 1994.

38. "Federally Mandated Sentences Come Under Attack," Reuters online, August 12, 1996.

39. Ibid.

40. Barbara Boland and Ronald Sones, *Prosecution of Felony Arrests, 1981* (Washington, D.C.: Bureau of Justice Statistics, 1986). See also U.S. Department of Justice, Bureau of Justice Statistics, *The Prosecution of Felony Arrests* (Washington, D.C.: U.S. Government Printing Office, 1983).

41. Barbara Boland, Wayne Logan, Ronald Sones, and William Martin, *The Prosecution of Felony Arrests, 1982* (Washington, D.C.: U.S. Government Printing Office, May 1988).

42. For a now-classic discussion of such considerations, see David Sudnow, "Normal Crimes: Sociological Features of the Penal Code in a Public Defender Office," *Social Problems*, Vol. 12 (1965), p. 255.

43. *Kercheval v. United States*, 274 U.S. 220, 223, 47 S.Ct. 582, 583 (1927); *Boykin v. Alabama*, 395 U.S. 238 (1969); and *Dickerson v. New Banner Institute, Inc.*, 460 U.S. 103 (1983).

44. *Brady v. United States*, 397 U.S. 742 (1970).

45. *Santobello v. New York*, 404 U.S. 257 (1971).

46. Ibid.

47. *Henderson v. Morgan*, 426 U.S. 637 (1976).

48. *Santobello v. New York*.

49. *Mabry v. Johnson*, 467 U.S. 504 (1984).

50. *United States v. Baldacchino*, 762 F.2d 170 (1st Cir. 1985); *United States v. Reardon*, 787 F.2d 512 (10th Cir. 1986); and *United States v. Donahey*, 529 F.2d 831 (11th Cir. 1976).

51. *Federal Rules of Criminal Procedure*, No. 11.

52. *Report to the Nation on Crime and Justice*, 2nd ed. (Washington, D.C.: U.S. Department of Justice, 1988), p. 90.

53. Judi M. Brown and Patrick A. Langan, *Felony Sentences in the U.S., 1996* (Washington, D.C.: Bureau of Justice Statistics, January 1999).

54. H.R. 4797, 102d Cong. 2d Sess. (1992).

55. California Penal Code, Section 13519.6.

56. Violent Crime Control and Law Enforcement Act of 1994, Section 280003.

57. FBI, *Uniform Crime Reports, 1999* (Washington, D.C.: U.S. Government Printing Office, 2000).

58. As reported in State of New Jersey Commission of Investigation and Attorney General of New Jersey, *Computer Crime: A Joint Report* (Trenton, NJ: New Jersey State Government, June 2000). Posted at http://www.state.nj.us/sci.

59. *R.A.V. v. City of St. Paul, Minn.*, 112 S. Ct. 2538 (1992).

60. *Forsyth County, Ga. v. Nationalist Movement*, 112 S. Ct. 2395 (1992).

61. John Kleinig, "Penalty Enhancements for Hate Crimes," *Criminal Justice Ethics* (Summer/Fall 1992), pp. 3–6.

62. Wisconsin Statutes, Chapter 939, Section 645(1)(b).

63. *Wisconsin v. Mitchell*, 508 U.S. 47 (1993).

64. *Apprendi v. New Jersey*, No. 99-478 (June 26, 2000).

65. Violent Crime Control and Law Enforcement Act of 1994, Section 60008.

66. Amnesty International, "Fatal Flaws: Innocence and Death Penalty in the USA," February 10, 2001. Posted at http://www.amnestyusa.org/rightsforall/dp/innocence/innocent-2.html.

67. James S. Lieberman, Jeffrey Fagan, and Valerie West, "A Broken System: Error Rates in Capital Cases, 1973–1995," *Texas Law Review*, October 2000.

68. S. 2690/H.R. 4167 (2000).

69. *Wilkerson v. Utah*, 99 U.S. 130 (1878).

70. *In re Kemmler*, 136 U.S. 436 (1890).

71. Ibid., p. 447.

72. *Louisiana ex rel. Francis v. Resweber,* 329 U.S. 459 (1947).

73. *McGautha v. California,* 402 U.S. 183 (1971).

74. *Furman v. Georgia,* 408 U.S. 238 (1972).

75. A position first ascribed to in *Trop v. Dulles,* 356 U.S. 86 (1958).

76. Each justice filed a separate opinion.

77. *Woodson v. North Carolina,* 428 U.S. 280 (1976).

78. *Gregg v. Georgia,* 428 U.S. 153 (1976).

79. *Coker v. Georgia,* 433 U.S. 584 (1977).

80. *Edmund v. Florida,* 458 U.S. 782 (1982).

81. *Tison v. Arizona,* 481 U.S. 137 (1987).

82. *Elledge v. Florida,* No. 98-5410 (1998).

83. *McCleskey v. Zandt,* 499 U.S. 467, 493-494 (1991).

84. *Coleman v. Thompson,* 501 U.S. 722, 729 (1991).

85. *Schlup v. Delo,* 513 U.S. 298 (1995).

86. Some Supreme Court watchers have concluded that *Schlup v. Delo* constitutes a relaxation of previous doctrine, under which the Court required prisoners to show "clear and convincing evidence" why their cases should be heard.

87. *Felker v. Turpin, Warden,* 519 U.S. 589 (1996).

88. Quotations in this paragraph are taken from opinions in the 1994 U.S. Supreme Court case of *Callins v. Collins,* in which *certiorari* was denied.

89. Which says that no person "shall be deprived of life . . . without due process of law."

90. *Syvasky Lafayette Poyner v. Edward W. Murray, Ellis B. Wright, Jr.,* and *John Doe,* No. 92-7944. Decided May 17, 1993 (*certiorari* denied).

91. *Director Gomez et al. v. Fierro and Ruiz,* 519 U.S. 918 (1996).

92. *Provenzano v. State,* 744 So. 2d 413, 440 (Fla. 1999).

93. *Multisite Evaluation of Shock Incarceration* (Washington, D.C.: National Institute of Justice, 1995).

94. Ibid.

95. Joan Petersilia, "House Arrest," *Crime File Study Guide* (Washington, D.C.: National Institute of Justice, 1988).

96. *BI Home Escort: Electronic Monitoring System,* advertising brochure, BI Incorporated, Boulder, CO (no date).

Appendix A:

THE CONSTITUTION OF THE UNITED STATES OF AMERICA

WE THE PEOPLE of the United States, in Order to form a more perfect Union, establish Justice, insure domestic Tranquility, provide for the common defence, promote the general Welfare, and secure the Blessings of Liberty to ourselves and our Posterity, do ordain and establish this CONSTITUTION for the United States of America.

ARTICLE I.

SECTION 1. All legislative Powers herein granted shall be vested in a Congress of the United States, which shall consist of a Senate and House of Representatives.

SECTION 2. The House of Representatives shall be composed of Members chosen every second Year by the People of the several States, and the Electors in each State shall have the Qualifications requisite for Electors of the most numerous Branch of the State Legislature.

No Person shall be a Representative who shall not have attained to the Age of twenty-five Years, and been seven Years a Citizen of the United States, and who shall not, when elected, be an Inhabitant of that State in which he shall be chosen.

Representatives and direct Taxes shall be apportioned among the several States which may be included within this Union, according to their respective Numbers, which shall be determined by adding to the whole Number of free Persons, including those bound to Service for a Term of Years, and excluding Indians not taxed, three fifths of all other Persons. The actual Enumeration shall be made within three Years after the first Meeting of the Congress of the United States, and within every subsequent Term of ten Years, in such Manner as they shall by Law direct. The Number of Representatives shall not exceed one for every thirty Thousand, but each State shall have at Least one Representative; and until such enumeration shall be made, the State of New Hampshire shall be entitled to chuse three, Massachusetts eight, Rhode-Island and Providence Plantations one, Connecticut five, New York six, New Jersey four, Pennsylvania eight, Delaware one, Maryland six, Virginia ten, North Carolina five, South Carolina five, and Georgia three.

When vacancies happen in the representation from any State, the Executive Authority thereof shall issue Writs of Election to fill such Vacancies.

The House of Representatives shall chuse their Speaker and other Officers; and shall have the sole Power of Impeachment.

SECTION 3. The Senate of the United States shall be composed of two Senators from each State, chosen by the Legislature thereof for six Years; and each Senator shall have one Vote.

Immediately after they shall be assembled in Consequence of the first Election, they shall be divided as equally as may be into three Classes. The Seats of the Senators of the first Class shall be vacated at the Expiration of the second Year, of the second Class at the Expiration of the fourth Year, and of the third Class at the Expiration of the sixth Year, so that one third may be chosen every second Year; and if Vacancies happen by Resignation, or otherwise, during the recess of the Legislature of any State, the Executive thereof may make temporary Appointments until the next Meeting of the Legislature, which shall then fill such Vacancies.

No Person shall be Senator who shall not have attained to the Age of thirty Years, and been nine Years a Citizen of the United States, and who shall not, when elected, be an Inhabitant of that State for which he shall be chosen.

The Vice President of the United States shall be President of the Senate, but shall have no Vote, unless they be equally divided.

The Senate shall chuse their other Officers, and also a President pro tempore, in the absence of the Vice President, or when he shall exercise the Office of President of the United States.

The Senate shall have the sole Power to try all Impeachments. When sitting for that Purpose, they shall be on Oath or Affirmation. When the President of the United States is tried, the Chief Justice shall preside: And no Person shall be convicted without the Concurrence of two thirds of the Members present.

Judgment in Cases of Impeachment shall not extend further than to removal from Office, and disqualification to hold and enjoy any Office of honor, Trust, or Profit under the United States: but the Party convicted shall nevertheless be liable and subject to Indictment, Trial, Judgment and Punishment, according to Law.

SECTION 4. The Times, Places and Manner of holding Elections for Senators and Representatives, shall be prescribed in each State by the Legislature thereof; but the Congress may at any time by Law make or alter such Regulations, except as to the Place of chusing Senators.

The Congress shall assemble at least once in every Year, and such Meeting shall be on the first Monday in December, unless they shall by law appoint a different Day.

SECTION 5. Each House shall be the Judge of the Elections, Returns and Qualifications of its own Members, and a Majority of each shall constitute a Quorum to do Business; but a smaller Number may adjourn from day to day, and may be authorized to compel the Attendance of absent Members, in such Manner, and under such Penalties as each House may provide.

Each House may determine the Rules of its Proceedings, punish its Members for disorderly Behaviour, and, with the Concurrence of two thirds, expel a Member.

Each House shall keep a Journal of its Proceedings, and from time to time publish the same, excepting such Parts as may in their Judgment require Secrecy; and the Yeas and Nays of the Members of either House on any question shall, at the Desire of one fifth of those Present, be entered on the journal.

Neither House, during the Session of Congress, shall, without the Consent of the other, adjourn for more than three days, nor to any other Place than that in which the two Houses shall be sitting.

SECTION 6. The Senators and Representatives shall receive a Compensation for their Services, to be ascertained by Law, and paid out of the Treasury of the United States. They shall in all Cases, except Treason, Felony and Breach of the Peace, be privileged from Arrest during their Attendance at the Session of their respective Houses, and in going to and returning from the same; and for any Speech or Debate in either House, they shall not be questioned in any other Place.

No Senator or Representative shall, during the Time for which he was elected, be appointed to any civil Office under the Authority of the United States, which shall have been created, or the Emoluments whereof shall have been encreased during such time; and no Person holding any Office under the United States, shall be a Member of either House during his Continuance in Office.

SECTION 7. All Bills for raising Revenue shall originate in the House of Representatives; but the Senate may propose or concur with Amendments as on other Bills.

Every Bill which shall have passed the House of Representatives and the Senate, shall, before it become a Law, be presented to the President of the United States; If he approve he shall sign it, but if not he shall return it, with his Objections to that House in which it shall have originated, who shall enter the Objections at large on their Journal, and proceed to reconsider it. If after such Reconsideration two thirds of that House shall agree to pass the Bill, it shall be sent, together with the Objections, to the other House, by which it shall likewise be reconsidered, and if approved by two thirds of that House, it shall become a Law. But in all such Cases the Votes of both Houses shall be determined by Yeas and Nays, and the Names of the Persons voting for and against the Bill shall be entered on the Journal of each House respectively. If any Bill shall not be returned by the President within ten Days (Sundays excepted) after it shall have been presented to him, the Same shall be a Law, in like Manner as if he had signed it, unless the Congress by their Adjournment prevent its Return, in which Case it shall not be a Law.

Every Order, Resolution, or Vote to which the Concurrence of the Senate and House of Representatives may be necessary (except on a question of Adjournment) shall be presented to the President of the United States; and before the Same shall take Effect, shall be approved by him, or being disapproved by him, shall be repassed by two thirds of the Senate and House of Representatives, according to the Rules and Limitations prescribed in the Case of a Bill.

SECTION 8. The Congress shall have Power to lay and collect Taxes, Duties, Imposts and Excises, to pay the Debts and provide for the common Defence and general Welfare of the United States; but all Duties, Imposts and Excises shall be uniform throughout the United States;

To borrow Money on the credit of the United States;

To regulate Commerce with foreign Nations, and among the several States, and with the Indian Tribes;

To establish an uniform Rule of Naturalization, and uniform Laws on the subject of Bankruptcies throughout the United States;

To coin Money, regulate the Value thereof, and of foreign Coin, and fix the Standard of Weights and Measures;

To provide for the Punishment of counterfeiting the Securities and current Coin of the United States;

To establish Post Offices and post Roads;

To promote the Progress of Science and useful Arts, by securing for limited times to Authors and Inventors the exclusive Right to their respective Writings and Discoveries;

To constitute Tribunals inferior to the supreme Court;

To define and punish Piracies and Felonies committed on the high Seas, and Offences against the Law of Nations;

To declare War, grant Letters of Marque and Reprisal, and make Rules concerning Captures on Land and Water;

To raise and support Armies, but no Appropriation of Money to that Use shall be for a longer Term than two Years;

To provide and maintain a Navy;

To make Rules for the Government and Regulation of the land and naval Forces;

To provide for calling forth the Militia to execute the Laws of the Union, suppress Insurrections and repel Invasions;

To provide for organizing, arming, and disciplining the Militia, and for governing such Part of them as may be employed in the Service of the United States, reserving to the States respectively, the Appointment of the Officers, and the Authority of training the Militia according to the discipline prescribed by Congress;

To exercise exclusive Legislation in all Cases whatsoever, over such District (not exceeding ten Miles square) as may, by Cession of particular States, and the Acceptance of Congress, become the Seat of the Government of the United States, and to exercise like Authority over all Places purchased by the Consent of the Legislature of the State in which the Same shall be, for the Erection of Forts, Magazines, and Arsenals, dock-Yards, and other needful Buildings;—And

To make all Laws which shall be necessary and proper for carrying into Execution the foregoing Powers, and all other Powers vested by this Constitution in the Government of the United States, or in any Department or Officer thereof.

SECTION 9. The Migration or Importation of such Persons as any of the States now existing shall think proper to admit, shall not be prohibited by the Congress prior to the Year one thousand eight hundred and eight, but a Tax or duty may be imposed on such Importation, not exceeding ten dollars for each Person.

The privilege of the Writ of Habeas Corpus shall not be suspended, unless when in Cases of Rebellion or Invasion the public Safety may require it.

No Bill of Attainder or ex post facto Law shall be passed.

No Capitation, or other direct, Tax shall be laid, unless in Proportion to the Census or Enumeration herein before directed to be taken.

No Tax or Duty shall be laid on Articles exported from any State.

No Preference shall be given by any Regulation of Commerce or Revenue to the Ports of one State over those of another: nor shall Vessels bound to, or from, one State, be obliged to enter, clear, or pay Duties in another.

No Money shall be drawn from the Treasury, but in Consequence of Appropriations made by Law; and a regular Statement and Account of the Receipts and Expenditures of all public Money shall be published from time to time.

No Title of Nobility shall be granted by the United States: And no Person holding any Office of Profit or Trust under them, shall, without the Consent of the Congress, accept of any present, Emolument, Office, or Title, of any kind whatever, from any King, Prince, or foreign State.

SECTION 10. No State shall enter into any Treaty, Alliance, or Confederation; grant Letters of Marque and Reprisal; coin Money; emit Bills of Credit; make any Thing but gold and silver Coin a Tender in Payment of Debts; pass any Bill of Attainder, ex post facto Law, or Law impairing the Obligation of Contracts, or grant any Title of Nobility.

No State shall, without the consent of the Congress, lay any Imposts or Duties on Imports or Exports, except what may be absolutely necessary for executing its inspection Laws: and the net Produce of all Duties and Imposts, laid by any State on Imports or Exports, shall be for the Use of the Treasury of the United States; and all such Laws shall be subject to the Revision and Control of the Congress.

No State shall, without the Consent of Congress, lay any Duty of Tonnage, keep Troops, or Ships of War in time of Peace, enter into any Agreement or Compact with another State, or with a foreign Power, or engage in War, unless actually invaded, or in such imminent Danger as will not admit of delay.

ARTICLE II.

SECTION 1. The executive Power shall be vested in a President of the United States of America. He shall hold his Office during the Term of four Years, and, together with the Vice President, chosen for the same Term, be elected, as follows

Each State shall appoint, in such Manner as the Legislature thereof may direct, a Number of Electors, equal to the whole Number of Senators and Representatives to which the State may be entitled in the Congress: but no Senator or Representative, or Person holding an Office of Trust or Profit under the United States, shall be appointed an Elector.

The Electors shall meet in their respective States, and vote by Ballot for two persons, of whom one at least shall not be an Inhabitant of the same State with themselves. And they shall make a List of all the Persons voted for, and of the Number of Votes for each; which List they shall sign and certify, and transmit sealed to the Seat of the Government of the United States, directed to the President of the Senate. The President of the Senate shall, in the Presence of the Senate and House of Representatives, open all the Certificates, and the Votes shall then be counted. The Person having the greatest Number of Votes shall be the President, if such Number be a Majority of the whole Number of Electors appointed; and if there be more than one who have such Majority, and have an equal Number of Votes, then the House of Representatives shall immediately chuse by Ballot one of them for President; and if no Person have a Majority, then from the five highest on the List the said House shall in like Manner chuse the President. But in choosing the President, the Votes shall be taken by States, the Representation from each State having one Vote; A quorum for this Purpose shall consist of a Member or Members from two thirds of the States, and a Majority of all the States shall be necessary to a Choice. In every Case, after the Choice of the President, the Person having the greatest Number of Votes of the Electors shall be the Vice President. But if there should remain two or more who have equal Votes, the Senate shall chuse from them by Ballot the Vice President.

The Congress may determine the Time of chusing the Electors, and the Day on which they shall give their Votes; which Day shall be the same throughout the United States.

No person except a natural born Citizen, or a Citizen of the United States, at the time of Adoption of this Constitution, shall be eligible to the Office of President; neither shall any Person be eligible to that Office who shall not have attained to the Age of thirty five Years, and been fourteen Years a Resident within the United States.

In Case of the Removal of the President from Office, or of his Death, Resignation, or Inability to discharge the Powers and Duties of the said Office, the same shall devolve on the Vice President, and the Congress may by Law provide for the Case of Removal, Death, Resignation or Inability, both of the President and Vice President, declaring what Officer shall then act as President, and such Officer shall act accordingly, until the Disability be removed, or a President shall be elected.

The President shall, at stated Times, receive for his Services, a Compensation, which shall neither be encreased nor diminished during the Period for which he shall have been elected, and he shall not receive within that Period any other Emolument from the United States, or any of them.

Before he enter on the Execution of his Office, he shall take the following Oath or Affirmation:—"I do solemnly swear (or affirm) that I will faithfully execute the Office of President of the United States, and will to the best of my Ability, preserve, protect and defend the Constitution of the United States."

SECTION 2. The President shall be Commander in Chief of the Army and Navy of the United States, and of the Militia of the several States, when called into the actual Service of the United States; he may require the Opinion in writing, of the principal Officer in each of the executive Departments, upon any subject relating to the Duties of their respective Offices, and he shall have Power to grant Reprieves and Pardons for Offenses against the United States, except in Cases of Impeachment.

He shall have Power, by and with the Advice and Consent of the Senate, to make Treaties, provided two thirds of the Senators present concur; and he shall nominate, and by and with the Advice and Consent of the Senate, shall appoint Ambassadors, other public Ministers and Consuls, Judges of the supreme Court, and all other Officers of the United States, whose Appointments are not herein otherwise provided for, and which shall be established by Law: but the Congress may by Law vest the Appointment of such inferior Officers, as they think proper, in the President alone, in the courts of Law, and in the Heads of Departments.

The President shall have Power to fill up all Vacancies that may happen during the Recess of the Senate, by granting Commissions which shall expire at the End of their next Session.

SECTION 3. He shall from time to time give to the Congress Information of the State of the Union, and recommend to their Consideration such Measures as he shall judge necessary and expedient; he may, on extraordinary Occasions, convene both Houses, or either of them, and in Case of Disagreement between them, with Respect to the Time of Adjournment, he may adjourn them to such Time as he shall think proper; he shall receive Ambassadors and other public Ministers; he shall take Care that the Laws be faithfully executed, and Shall Commission all the Officers of the United States.

SECTION 4. The President, Vice President and all civil Officers of the United States, shall be removed from Office on Impeachment for, and Conviction of, Treason, Bribery, or other high Crimes and Misdemeanors.

ARTICLE III.

SECTION 1. The judicial Power of the United States, shall be vested in one supreme Court, and in such inferior Courts as the Congress may from time to time ordain and establish. The Judges, both of the supreme and inferior Courts, shall hold their Offices during good Behavior, and shall, at stated Times, receive for their Services, a Compensation, which shall not be diminished during their Continuance in Office.

SECTION 2. The judicial Power shall extend to all Cases, in Law and Equity, arising under this Constitution, the Laws of the United States, and Treaties made, or which shall be made, under their Authority;—to all Cases affecting Ambassadors, other public Ministers and Consuls;—to all Cases of admiralty and maritime Jurisdiction;—to Controversies to which the United States shall be a

Party;—to Controversies between two or more States;—between a State and Citizens of another State;—between citizens of different States;—between Citizens of the same State claiming Lands under Grants of different States, and between a State, or the Citizens thereof, and foreign States, Citizens or Subjects.

In all Cases affecting Ambassadors, other public Ministers and Consuls, and those in which a State shall be Party, the supreme Court shall have original Jurisdiction. In all the other Cases before mentioned, the supreme Court shall have appellate Jurisdiction, both as to Law and Fact, with such exceptions, and under such Regulations as the Congress shall make.

The Trial of all Crimes, except in Cases of Impeachment, shall be by Jury; and such Trial shall be held in the State where the said Crimes shall have been committed; but when not committed within any State, the Trial shall be at such Place or Places as the Congress may by Law have directed.

SECTION 3. Treason against the United States, shall consist only in levying War against them, or in adhering to their Enemies, giving them Aid and Comfort. No Person shall be convicted of Treason unless on the Testimony of two Witnesses to the same overt Act, or on Confession in open Court.

The Congress shall have Power to declare the Punishment of Treason, but no Attainder of Treason shall work Corruption of Blood, or Forfeiture except during the Life of the Person attainted.

ARTICLE IV.

SECTION 1. Full Faith and Credit shall be given in each State to the public Acts, Records, and judicial Proceedings of every other State. And the Congress may by general Laws prescribe the Manner in which such Acts, Records and Proceedings shall be proved, and the Effect thereof.

SECTION 2. The Citizens of each State shall be entitled to all Privileges and Immunities of Citizens in the several States.

A Person charged in any State with Treason, Felony, or other Crime, who shall flee from Justice, and be found in another State, shall on Demand of the executive Authority of the State from which he fled, be delivered up, to be removed to the State having Jurisdiction of the Crime.

No Person held to Service or Labour in one State, under the Laws thereof, escaping into another, shall, in Consequence of any Law or Regulation therein, be discharged from such Service or Labour, but shall be delivered up on Claim of the Party to whom such Service or Labour may be due.

SECTION 3. New States may be admitted by the Congress into this Union; but no new State shall be formed or erected within the Jurisdiction of any other State; nor any State be formed by the Junction of two or more States, or parts of States, without the Consent of the Legislatures of the States concerned as well as of the Congress.

The Congress shall have Power to dispose of and make all needful Rules and Regulations respecting the Territory or other Property belonging to the United States; and nothing in this Constitution shall be so construed as to Prejudice any Claims of the United States, or of any particular State.

SECTION 4. The United States shall guarantee to every State in this Union a Republican Form of Government, and shall protect each of them against Invasion; and on Application of the Legislature, or of the Executive (when the Legislature cannot be convened) against domestic Violence.

ARTICLE V.

The Congress, whenever two thirds of both Houses shall deem it necessary, shall propose Amendments to this Constitution, or, on the Application of the Legislatures of two thirds of the several States, shall call a Convention for proposing Amendments, which, in either Case, shall be valid to all Intents and Purposes, as Part of this Constitution, when ratified by the Legislatures of three fourths of the several States, or by Conventions in three fourths thereof, as the one or the other Mode of Ratification may be proposed by the Congress; Provided that no Amendment which may be made prior to the Year One thousand eight hundred and eight shall in any Manner affect the first and fourth Clauses in the Ninth Section of the first Article; and that no State, without its Consent, shall be deprived of its equal Suffrage in the Senate.

ARTICLE VI.

All Debts contracted and Engagements entered into, before the Adoption of this Constitution, shall be as valid against the United States under this Constitution, as under the Confederation.

This Constitution, and the Laws of the United States which shall be made in Pursuance thereof; and all Treaties made, or which shall be made, under the Authority of the United States, shall be the supreme Law of the Land; and the Judges in every State shall be bound thereby; any Thing in the Constitution or Laws of any State to the Contrary notwithstanding.

The Senators and Representatives before mentioned, and the Members of the several State Legislatures, and all executive and judicial Officers, both of the United States and of the several States, shall be bound by Oath or Affirmation, to support this Constitution; but no religious Test shall ever be required as a Qualification to any Office or public Trust under the United States.

ARTICLE VII.

The Ratification of the Conventions of nine States shall be sufficient for the Establishment of this Constitution between the States so ratifying the Same.

Articles in Addition to, and Amendment of, the Constitution of the United States of America, Proposed by Congress, and Ratified by the Legislatures of the Several States, Pursuant to the Fifth Article of the Original Constitution.

AMENDMENT I. (1791)

Congress shall make no law respecting an establishment of religion, or prohibiting the free exercise thereof; or abridging the freedom of speech, or of the press; or the right of the people peaceably to assemble, and to petition the Government for a redress of grievances.

AMENDMENT II. (1791)

A well regulated Militia, being necessary to the security of a free State, the right of the people to keep and bear Arms, shall not be infringed.

AMENDMENT III. (1791)

No Soldier shall, in time of peace be quartered in any house, without the consent of the Owner, nor in time of war, but in a manner to be prescribed by law.

AMENDMENT IV. (1791)

The right of the people to be secure in their persons, houses, papers, and effects, against unreasonable searches and seizures, shall not be violated, and no Warrants shall issue, but upon probable cause, supported by Oath or affirmation, and particularly describing the place to be searched, and the persons or things to be seized.

AMENDMENT V. (1791)

No person shall be held to answer for a capital, or otherwise infamous crime, unless on a presentment or indictment of a Grand Jury, except in cases arising in the land or naval forces, or in the Militia, when in actual service in time of War or public danger; nor shall any person be subject for the same offence to be twice put in jeopardy of life or limb; nor shall be compelled in any criminal case to be a witness against himself, nor be deprived of life, liberty, or property, without due process of law; nor shall private property be taken for public use, without just compensation.

AMENDMENT VI. (1791)

In all criminal prosecutions, the accused shall enjoy the right to a speedy and public trial, by an impartial jury of the State and district wherein the crime shall have been committed, which district shall have been previously ascertained by law, and to be informed of the nature and cause of the accusation; to be confronted with the witnesses against him; to have compulsory process for obtaining Witnesses in his favor, and to have the Assistance of Counsel for his defence.

AMENDMENT VII. (1791)

In Suits at common law, where the value in controversy shall exceed twenty dollars, the right of trial by jury shall be preserved, and no fact tried by a jury, shall be otherwise reexamined in any Court of the United States, than according to the rules of the common law.

AMENDMENT VIII. (1791)

Excessive bail shall not be required, nor excessive fines imposed, nor cruel and unusual punishments inflicted.

AMENDMENT IX. (1791)

The enumeration of the Constitution, of certain rights, shall not be construed to deny or disparage others retained by the people.

AMENDMENT X. (1791)

The powers not delegated to the United States by the Constitution, nor prohibited by it to the States, are reserved to the States respectively, or to the people.

AMENDMENT XI. (1798)

The Judicial power of the United States shall not be construed to extend to any suit in law or equity, commenced or prosecuted against one of the United States by Citizens of another State, or by Citizens or Subjects of any Foreign State.

AMENDMENT XII. (1804)

The Electors shall meet in their respective states and vote by ballot for President and Vice-President, one of whom, at least, shall not be an inhabitant of the same state with themselves; they shall name in their ballots the person voted for as President, and in distinct ballots the person voted for as Vice-President, and they shall make distinct lists of all persons voted for as President, and of all persons voted for as Vice-President, and of the number of votes for each, which lists they shall sign and certify, and transmit sealed to the seat of the government of the United States, directed to the President of the Senate;—The President of the Senate shall, in the presence of the Senate and House of Representatives, open all the certificates and the votes shall then be counted;—The person having the greatest number of votes for President, shall be the President, if such number be a majority of the whole number of Electors appointed; and if no person have such majority, then from the persons having the highest numbers not exceeding three on the list of those voted for as President, the House of Representatives shall choose immediately, by ballot, the President. But in choosing the President, the votes shall be taken by states, the representation from each state having one vote; a quorum for this purpose shall consist of a member or members from two-thirds of the states, and a majority of all the states shall be necessary to a choice. And if the House of Representatives shall not choose a President whenever the right of choice shall devolve upon them, before the fourth day of March next following, then the Vice-President shall act as President, as in the case of the death or other constitutional disability of the President. The person having the greatest number of votes as Vice-President, shall be the Vice-President, if such number be a majority of the whole number of Electors appointed, and if no person have a majority, then from the two highest numbers on the list, the Senate shall choose the Vice-President; a quorum for the purpose shall consist of two-thirds of the whole number of Senators, and a majority of the whole number shall be necessary to a choice. But no person constitutionally ineligible to the office of President shall be eligible to that of Vice-President of the United States.

AMENDMENT XIII. (1865)

SECTION 1. Neither slavery nor involuntary servitude, except as a punishment for crime whereof the party shall have been duly convicted, shall exist within the United States, or any place subject to their jurisdiction.

SECTION 2. Congress shall have power to enforce this article by appropriate legislation.

AMENDMENT XIV. (1868)

SECTION 1. All persons born or naturalized in the United States, and subject to the jurisdiction thereof, are citizens of the United States and of the State wherein they reside. No State shall make or enforce any law which shall abridge the privileges or immunities of citizens of the United States; nor shall any State deprive any person of life, liberty, or property, without due process of law; nor deny to any person within its jurisdiction the equal protection of the law.

SECTION 2. Representatives shall be apportioned among the several States according to their respective numbers, counting the whole number of persons in each State, excluding Indians not taxed. But when the right to vote at any election for the choice of electors for President and Vice-President of the United States, Representatives in Congress, the Executive and Judicial officers of a State, or the members of the Legislature thereof, is denied to any of the male inhabitants of such State, being twenty-one years of age, and citizens of the United States, or in any way abridged, except for participation in rebellion, or other crime, the basis of representation therein shall be reduced in the proportion which the number of such male citizens shall bear to the whole number of male citizens twenty-one years of age in such State.

SECTION 3. No person shall be a Senator or Representative in Congress, or elector of President and Vice-President, or hold any office, civil or military, under the United States, or under any State, who, having previously taken an oath, as a member of Congress, or as an officer of the United States, or as a member of any State legislature, or as an executive or judicial officer of any State, to support the Constitution of the United States, shall have engaged in insurrection or rebellion against the same, or given aid or comfort to the enemies thereof. But Congress may by a vote of two-thirds of each House, remove such disability.

SECTION 4. The validity of the public debt of the United States, authorized by law, including debts incurred for payment of pensions and bounties for services in suppressing insurrection or rebellion, shall not be questioned. But neither the United States nor any State shall assume or pay any debt or obligation incurred in aid of insurrection or rebellion against the United States, or any claim for the loss or emancipation of any slave; but all such debts, obligations and claims shall be held illegal and void.

SECTION 5. The Congress shall have power to enforce, by appropriate legislation, the provisions of this article.

AMENDMENT XV. (1870)

SECTION 1. The right of citizens of the United States to vote shall not be denied or abridged by the United States or by any State on account of race, color, or previous condition of servitude.

SECTION 2. The Congress shall have power to enforce this article by appropriate legislation.

AMENDMENT XVI. (1913)

The Congress shall have power to lay and collect taxes on incomes, from whatever source derived, without apportionment among the several States, and without regard to any census or enumeration.

AMENDMENT XVII. (1913)

The Senate of the United States shall be composed of two Senators from each State, elected by the people thereof, for six years; and each Senator shall have one vote. The electors in each State shall have the qualifications requisite for electors of the most numerous branch of the State legislatures.

When vacancies happen in the representation of any State in the Senate, the executive authority of such State shall issue writs of election to fill such vacancies: *Provided,* That the legislature of any State may empower the executive thereof to make temporary appointments until the people fill the vacancies by election as the legislature may direct.

This amendment shall not be so construed as to affect the election or term of any Senator chosen before it becomes valid as part of the Constitution.

AMENDMENT XVIII. (1919)

SECTION 1. After one year from the ratification of this article the manufacture, sale, or transportation of intoxicating liquors within, the importation thereof into, or the exportation thereof from the United States and all territory subject to the jurisdiction thereof for beverage purposes is hereby prohibited.

SECTION 2. The Congress and the several States shall have concurrent power to enforce this article by appropriate legislation.

SECTION 3. This article shall be inoperative unless it shall have been ratified as an amendment to the Constitution by the legislatures of the several States, as provided in the Constitution, within seven years from the date of the submission hereof to the States by the Congress.

AMENDMENT XIX. (1920)

The right of citizens of the United States to vote shall not be denied or abridged by the United States or by any State on account of sex.

Congress shall have power to enforce this article by appropriate legislation.

AMENDMENT XX. (1933)

SECTION 1. The terms of the President and Vice President shall end at noon on the 20th day of January, and the terms of Senators and representatives at noon on the 3d day of January, of the years in which such terms would have ended if this article had not been ratified; and the terms of their successors shall then begin.

SECTION 2. The Congress shall assemble at least once in every year, and such meeting shall begin at noon on the 3d day of January, unless they shall by law appoint a different day.

SECTION 3. If, at the time fixed for the beginning of the term of the President, the President elect shall have died, the Vice President elect shall become President. If a President shall not have been chosen before the time fixed for the beginning of his term, or if the President elect shall have failed to qualify, then the Vice President elect shall act as President until a President shall have qualified; and the Congress may by law provide for the case wherein neither a President elect nor a Vice President elect shall have qualified, declaring who shall then act as President, or the manner in which one who is to act shall be selected, and such person shall act accordingly until a President or Vice President shall have qualified.

SECTION 4. The Congress may by law provide for the case of the death of any of the persons from whom the House of Representatives may choose a President whenever the right of choice shall have devolved upon them, and for the case of the death of any of the persons from whom the Senate may choose a Vice President whenever the right of choice shall have devolved upon them.

SECTION 5. Sections 1 and 2 shall take effect on the 15th day of October following the ratification of this article.

SECTION 6. This article shall be inoperative unless it shall have been ratified as an amendment to the Constitution by the legislatures of three-fourths of the several States within seven years from the date of submission.

AMENDMENT XXI. (1933)

SECTION 1. The eighteenth article of amendment to the Constitution of the United States is hereby repealed.

SECTION 2. The transportation or importation into any State, Territory, or possession of the United States for delivery or use therein of intoxicating liquors, in violation of the laws thereof, is hereby prohibited.

SECTION 3. This article shall be inoperative unless it shall have been ratified as an amendment to the Constitution by conventions in the several States, as provided in the Constitution, within seven years from the date of the submission hereof to the States by the Congress.

AMENDMENT XXII. (1951)

SECTION 1. No person shall be elected to the office of the President more than twice, and no person who has held the office of President, or acted as President, for more than two years of a term to which some other person was elected president shall be elected to the office of the President more than once. But this Article shall not apply to any person holding office of President when this Article was proposed by the Congress, and shall not prevent any person who may be holding the office of President, or acting as President, during the term within which this Article becomes operative from holding the office of President or acting as President during the remainder of such term.

SECTION 2. The article shall be inoperative unless it shall have been ratified as an amendment to the Constitution by the legislatures of three-fourths of the several States within seven years from the date of its submission to the States by the Congress.

AMENDMENT XXIII. (1961)

SECTION 1. The District constituting the seat of Government of the United States shall appoint in such manner as the Congress may direct:

A number of electors of President and Vice President equal to the whole number of Senators and Representatives in Congress to which the District would be entitled if it were a State, but in no event more than the least populous State; they shall be in addition to those appointed by the States, but they shall be considered, for the purposes of the election of President and Vice President, to be electors appointed by a State; and they shall meet in the District and perform such duties as provided by the twelfth article of amendment.

SECTION 2. The Congress shall have power to enforce this article by appropriate legislation.

AMENDMENT XXIV. (1964)

SECTION 1. The right of citizens of the United States to vote in any primary or other election for President or Vice President, for electors for President or Vice President, or for Senator or Representative in Congress, shall not be denied or abridged by the United States or any State by reason of failing to pay any poll tax or other tax.

SECTION 2. The Congress shall have power to enforce this article by appropriate legislation.

AMENDMENT XXV. (1967)

SECTION 1. In case of the removal of the President from office or of his death or resignation, the Vice President shall become President.

SECTION 2. Whenever there is a vacancy in the office of the Vice President, the President shall nominate a Vice President who shall take office upon confirmation by a majority vote of both Houses of Congress.

SECTION 3. Whenever the President transmits to the President pro tempore of the Senate and the Speaker of the House of Representatives his written declaration that he is unable to discharge the powers and duties of his office, and until he transmits to them a written declaration to the contrary, such powers and duties shall be discharged by the Vice President as Acting President.

SECTION 4. Whenever the Vice President and a majority of either the principal officers of the executive departments or of such other body as Congress may by law provide, transmit to the President pro tempore of the Senate and the Speaker of the House of Representatives their written declaration that the President is unable to discharge the powers and duties of his office, the Vice President shall immediately assume the powers and duties of the office as Acting President.

Thereafter, when the President transmits to the President pro tempore of the Senate and the Speaker of the House of Representatives his written declaration that no inability exists, he shall resume the powers and duties of his office unless the Vice President and a majority of either the principal officers of the executive department or of such other body as Congress may by law provide, transmit within four days to the President pro tempore of the Senate and the Speaker of the House of Representatives their written declaration that the President is unable to discharge the powers and duties of his office. Thereupon Congress shall decide the issue, assembling within forty-eight hours for that purpose if not in session. If the Congress, within twenty-one days after receipt of the latter written declaration, or, if Congress is not in session, within twenty-one days after Congress is required to assemble, determines by two-thirds vote of both Houses that the President is unable to discharge the powers and duties of his office, the Vice President shall continue to discharge the same as Acting President; otherwise, the President shall resume the powers and duties of his office.

AMENDMENT XXVI. (1971)

SECTION 1. The right of citizens of the United States, who are eighteen years of age or older, to vote shall not be denied or abridged by the United States or by any State on account of age.

SECTION 2. The Congress shall have power to enforce this article by appropriate legislation.

AMENDMENT XXVII. (1992)

No law, varying the compensation for the services of the Senators and Representatives, shall take effect, until an election of Representatives shall have intervened.

Appendix B:

MODEL PENAL CODE EXCERPTS

PART I: General Provisions

ARTICLE 1.

SECTION 1.02. Purposes; Principles of Construction.

(1) The general purposes of the provisions governing the definition of offenses are:

    (a) to forbid and prevent conduct that unjustifiably and inexcusably inflicts or threatens substantial harm to individual or public interests;

    (b) to subject to public control persons whose conduct indicates that they are disposed to commit crimes;

    (c) to safeguard conduct that is without fault from condemnation as criminal;

    (d) to give fair warning of the nature of the conduct declared to constitute an offense;

    (e) to differentiate on reasonable grounds between serious and minor offenses.

(2) The general purposes of the provisions governing the sentencing and treatment of offenders are:

    (a) to prevent the commission of offenses;

    (b) to promote the correction and rehabilitation of offenders;

    (c) to safeguard offenders against excessive, disproportionate or arbitrary punishment;

    (d) to give fair warning of the nature of the sentences that may be imposed on conviction of an offense;

    (e) to differentiate among offenders with a view to a just individualization in their treatment;

    (f) to define, coordinate and harmonize the powers, duties and functions of the courts and of administrative officers and agencies responsible for dealing with offenders;

    (g) to advance the use of generally accepted scientific methods and knowledge in the sentencing and treatment of offenders;

    (h) to integrate responsibility for the administration of the correctional system in a State Department of Correction [or other single department or agency].

Source: Copyright 1985, *Model Penal Code and Commentaries,* parts I and II, by The American Law Institute. Reprinted with the permission of The American Law Institute.

(3) The provisions of the Code shall be construed according to the fair import of their terms but when the language is susceptible of differing constructions it shall be interpreted to further the general purposes stated in this Section and the special purposes of the particular provision involved. The discretionary powers conferred by the Code shall be exercised in accordance with the criteria stated in the Code and, insofar as such criteria are not decisive, to further the general purposes stated in this Section.

SECTION 1.03. Territorial Applicability.

(1) Except as otherwise provided in this Section, a person may be convicted under the law of this State of an offense committed by his own conduct or the conduct of another for which he is legally accountable if:

(a) either the conduct that is an element of the offense or the result that is such an element occurs within this State; or

(b) conduct occurring outside the State is sufficient under the law of this State to constitute an attempt to commit an offense within the State; or

(c) conduct occurring outside the State is sufficient under the law of this State to constitute a conspiracy to commit an offense within the State and an overt act in furtherance of such conspiracy occurs within the State; or

(d) conduct occurring within the State establishes complicity in the commission of, or an attempt, solicitation or conspiracy to commit, an offense in another jurisdiction that also is an offense under the law of this State; or

(e) the offense consists of the omission to perform a legal duty imposed by the law of this State with respect to domicile, residence or a relationship to a person, thing or transaction in the State; or

(f) the offense is based on a statute of this State that expressly prohibits conduct outside the State, when the conduct bears a reasonable relation to a legitimate interest of this State and the actor knows or should know that his conduct is likely to affect that interest.

SECTION 1.04. Classes of Crimes; Violations.

(1) An offense defined by this Code or by any other statute of this State, for which a sentence of [death or of] imprisonment is authorized, constitutes a crime. Crimes are classified as felonies, misdemeanors or petty misdemeanors.

(2) A crime is a felony if it is so designated in this Code or if persons convicted thereof may be sentenced [to death or] to imprisonment for a term that, apart from an extended term, is in excess of one year.

(3) A crime is a misdemeanor if it is so designated in this Code or in a statute other than this Code enacted subsequent thereto.

(4) A crime is a petty misdemeanor if it is so designated in this Code or in a statute other than this Code enacted subsequent thereto or if it is defined by a statute other than this Code that now provides that persons convicted thereof may be sentenced to imprisonment for a term of which the maximum is less than one year.

(5) An offense defined by this Code or by any other statute of this State constitutes a violation if it is so designated in this Code or in the law defining the offense or if no other sentence than a fine, or fine and forfeiture or other civil penalty is authorized upon conviction or if it is defined by a statute other than this Code that now provides that the offense shall not constitute a crime. A violation does not constitute a crime and conviction of a violation shall not

give rise to any disability or legal disadvantage based on conviction of a criminal offense.

(6) Any offense declared by law to constitute a crime, without specification of the grade thereof or of the sentence authorized upon conviction, is a misdemeanor.

(7) An offense defined by any statute of this State other than this Code shall be classified as provided in this Section and the sentence that may be imposed upon conviction thereof shall hereafter be governed by this Code.

SECTION 1.05. **All Offenses Defined by Statute; Application of General Provisions of the Code.**

(1) No conduct constitutes an offense unless it is a crime or violation under this Code or another statute of this State.

(2) The provisions of Part I of the Code are applicable to offenses defined by other statutes, unless the Code otherwise provides.

(3) This Section does not affect the power of a court to punish for contempt or to employ any sanction authorized by law for the enforcement of an order or a civil judgment or decree.

SECTION 1.06. **Time Limitations.**

(1) A prosecution for murder may be commenced at any time.

(2) Except as otherwise provided in this Section, prosecutions for other offenses are subject to the following periods of limitation:

(a) A prosecution for a felony of the first degree must be commenced within six years after it is committed;

(b) a prosecution for any other felony must be commenced within three years after it is committed;

(c) a prosecution for a misdemeanor must be commenced within two years after it is committed;

(d) a prosecution for a petty misdemeanor or a violation must be commenced within six months after it is committed.

(3) If the period prescribed in Subsection (2) has expired, a prosecution may nevertheless be commenced for:

(a) any offense a material element of which is either fraud or a breach of fiduciary obligation within one year after discovery of the offense by an aggrieved party or by a person who has legal duty to represent an aggrieved party and who is himself not a party to the offense, but in no case shall this provision extend the period of limitation otherwise applicable by more than three years; and

(b) any offense based upon misconduct in office by a public officer or employee at any time when the defendant is in public office or employment or within two years thereafter, but in no case shall this provision extend the period of limitation otherwise applicable by more than three years.

(4) An offense is committed either when every element occurs, or, if a legislative purpose to prohibit a continuing course of conduct plainly appears, at the time when the course of conduct or the defendant's complicity therein is terminated. Time starts to run on the day after the offense is committed.

(5) A prosecution is commenced either when an indictment is found [or an information filed] or when a warrant or other process is issued, provided that such warrant or process is executed without unreasonable delay.

(6) The period of limitation does not run:

    (a) during any time when the accused is continuously absent from the State or has no reasonably ascertainable place of abode or work within the State, but in no case shall this provision extend the period of limitation otherwise applicable by more than three years; or

    (b) during any time when a prosecution against the accused for the same conduct is pending in this State.

SECTION 1.12. Proof Beyond a Reasonable Doubt; Affirmative Defenses; Burden of Proving Fact When Not an Element of an Offense; Presumptions.

(1) No person may be convicted of an offense unless each element of such offense is proved beyond a reasonable doubt. In the absence of such proof, the innocence of the defendant is assumed.

(2) Subsection (1) of this Section does not:

    (a) require the disproof of an affirmative defense unless and until there is evidence supporting such defense; or

    (b) apply to any defense that the Code or another statute plainly requires the defendant to prove by a preponderance of evidence.

(3) A ground of defense is affirmative, within the meaning of Subsection (2)(a) of this Section, when:

    (a) it arises under a section of the Code that so provides; or

    (b) it relates to an offense defined by a statute other than the Code and such statute so provides; or

    (c) it involves a matter of excuse or justification peculiarly within the knowledge of the defendant on which he can fairly be required to adduce supporting evidence.

(4) When the application of the Code depends upon the finding of a fact that is not an element of an offense, unless the Code otherwise provides:

    (a) the burden of proving the fact is on the prosecution or defendant, depending on whose interest or contention will be furthered if the finding should be made; and

    (b) the fact must be proved to the satisfaction of the Court or jury, as the case may be.

(5) When the Code establishes a presumption with respect to any fact that is an element of an offense, it has the following consequences:

    (a) when there is evidence of the facts that give rise to the presumption, the issue of the existence of the presumed fact must be submitted to the jury, unless the Court is satisfied that the evidence as a whole clearly negatives the presumed fact; and

    (b) when the issue of the existence of the presumed fact is submitted to the jury, the Court shall charge that while the presumed fact must, on all the evidence, be proved beyond a reasonable doubt, the law declares that the jury may regard the facts giving rise to the presumption as sufficient evidence of the presumed fact.

(6) A presumption not established by the Code or inconsistent with it has the consequences otherwise accorded it by law.

SECTION 1.13. General Definitions.

In this Code, unless a different meaning plainly is required:

(1) "statute" includes the Constitution and a local law or ordinance of a political subdivision of the State;

(2) "act" or "action" means a bodily movement whether voluntary or involuntary;

(3) "voluntary" has the meaning specified in Section 2.01;

(4) "omission" means a failure to act;

(5) "conduct" means an action or omission and its accompanying state of mind, or, where relevant, a series of acts and omissions;

(6) "actor" includes, where relevant, a person guilty of an omission;

(7) "acted" includes, where relevant, "omitted to act";

(8) "person," "he" and "actor" include any natural person and, where relevant, a corporation or an unincorporated association;

(9) "element of an offense" means (i) such conduct or (ii) such attendant circumstances or (iii) such a result of conduct as

   (a) is included in the description of the forbidden conduct in the definition of the offense; or

   (b) establishes the required kind of culpability; or

   (c) negatives an excuse or justification for such conduct; or

   (d) negatives a defense under the statute of limitations; or

   (e) establishes jurisdiction or venue;

(10) "material element of an offense" means an element that does not relate exclusively to the statute of limitations, jurisdiction, venue, or to any other matter similarly unconnected with (i) the harm or evil, incident to conduct, sought to be prevented by the law defining the offense, or (ii) the existence of a justification or excuse for such conduct;

(11) "purposely" has the meaning specified in Section 2.02 and equivalent terms such as "with purpose," "designed" or "with design" have the same meaning;

(12) "intentionally" or "with intent" means purposely;

(13) "knowingly" has the meaning specified in Section 2.02 and equivalent terms such as "knowing" or "with knowledge" have the same meaning;

(14) "recklessly" has the meaning specified in Section 2.02 and equivalent terms such as "recklessness" or "with recklessness" have the same meaning;

(15) "negligently" has the meaning specified in Section 2.02 and equivalent terms such as "negligence" or "with negligence" have the same meaning;

(16) "reasonably believes" or "reasonable belief" designates a belief that the actor is not reckless or negligent in holding.

ARTICLE 2. GENERAL PRINCIPLES OF LIABILITY

SECTION 2.01. Requirement of Voluntary Act; Omission as Basis of Liability; Possession as an Act.

(1) A person is not guilty of an offense unless his liability is based on conduct that includes a voluntary act or the omission to perform an act of which he is physically capable.

(2) The following are not voluntary acts within the meaning of this Section;

    (a) a reflex or convulsion;

    (b) a bodily movement during unconsciousness or sleep;

    (c) conduct during hypnosis or resulting from hypnotic suggestion;

    (d) a bodily movement that otherwise is not a product of the effort or determination of the actor, either conscious or habitual.

(3) Liability for the commission of an offense may not be based on an omission unaccompanied by action unless:

    (a) the omission is expressly made sufficient by the law defining the offense; or

    (b) a duty to perform the omitted act is otherwise imposed by law.

(4) Possession is an act, within the meaning of this Section, if the possessor knowingly procured or received the thing possessed or was aware of his control thereof for a sufficient period to have been able to terminate his possession.

SECTION 2.02. General Requirements of Culpability.

(1) *Minimum Requirements of Culpability.* Except as provided in Section 2.05, a person is not guilty of an offense unless he acted purposely, knowingly, recklessly or negligently, as the law may require, with respect to each material element of the offense.

(2) *Kinds of Culpability Defined.*

    (a) *Purposely.* A person acts purposely with respect to a material element of an offense when:

        (i) if the element involves the nature of his conduct or a result thereof, it is his conscious object to engage in conduct of that nature or to cause such a result; and

        (ii) if the element involves the attendant circumstances, he is aware of the existence of such circumstances or he believes or hopes that they exist.

    (b) *Knowingly.* A person acts knowingly with respect to a material element of an offense when:

        (i) if the element involves the nature of his conduct or the attendant circumstances, he is aware that his conduct is of that nature or that such circumstances exist; and

        (ii) if the element involves a result of his conduct, he is aware that it is practically certain that his conduct will cause such a result.

    (c) *Recklessly.* A person acts recklessly with respect to a material element of an offense when he consciously disregards a substantial and unjustifiable risk that the material element exists or will result from his conduct. The risk must be of such a nature and degree that, considering the nature and purpose of the actor's conduct and the circumstances known to him, its disregard involves a gross deviation from the standard of conduct that a law-abiding person would observe in the actor's situation.

    (d) *Negligently.* A person acts negligently with respect to a material element of an offense when he should be aware of a substantial and unjustifiable risk that the material element exists or will result from his conduct. The risk must be of such a nature and degree that the actor's failure to perceive it, considering the nature and purpose of his conduct and the circumstances known to him, involves a gross deviation from the standard of care that a reasonable person would observe in the actor's situation.

(3) *Culpability Required Unless Otherwise Provided.* When the culpability sufficient to establish a material element of an offense is not prescribed by law, such element is established if a person acts purposely, knowingly or recklessly with respect thereto.

(4) *Prescribed Culpability Requirement Applies to All Material Elements.* When the law defining an offense prescribes the kind of culpability that is sufficient for the commission of an offense, without distinguishing among the material elements thereof, such provision shall apply to all the material elements of the offense, unless a contrary purpose plainly appears.

(5) *Substitutes for Negligence, Recklessness and Knowledge.* When the law provides that negligence suffices to establish an element of an offense, such element also is established if a person acts purposely, knowingly or recklessly. When reckless-ness suffices to establish an element, such element also is established if a person acts purposely or knowingly. When acting knowingly suffices to establish an element, such element also is established if a person acts purposely.

(6) *Requirement of Purpose Satisfied if Purpose Is Conditional.* When a particular pur-pose is an element of an offense, the element is established although such pur-pose is conditional, unless the condition negatives the harm or evil sought to be prevented by the law defining the offense.

(7) *Requirement of Knowledge Satisfied by Knowledge of High Probability.* When knowl-edge of the existence of a particular fact is an element of an offense, such knowl-edge is established if a person is aware of a high probability of its existence, unless he actually believes that it does not exist.

(8) *Requirement of Wilfulness Satisfied by Acting Knowingly.* A requirement that an offense be committed wilfully is satisfied if a person acts knowingly with respect to the material elements of the offense, unless a purpose to impose further requirements appears.

(9) *Culpability as to Illegality of Conduct.* Neither knowledge nor recklessness or negli-gence as to whether conduct constitutes an offense or as to the existence, mean-ing or application of the law determining the elements of an offense is an element of such offense, unless the definition of the offense or the Code so pro-vides.

(10) *Culpability as Determinant of Grade of Offense.* When the grade or degree of an offense depends on whether the offense is committed purposely, knowingly, recklessly or negligently, its grade or degree shall be the lowest for which the determinative kind of culpability is established with respect to any material ele-ment of the offense.

SECTION 2.03. Causal Relationship Between Conduct and Result; Diver-gence Between Result Designed or Contemplated and Actual Result or Between Probable and Actual Result.

(1) Conduct is the cause of a result when:

   (a) it is an antecedent but for which the result in question would not have occurred; and

   (b) the relationship between the conduct and result satisfies any additional causal requirements imposed by the Code or by the law defining the offense.

(2) When purposely or knowingly causing a particular result is an element of an offense, the element is not established if the actual result is not within the pur-pose or the contemplation of the actor unless:

(a) the actual result differs from that designed or contemplated, as the case may be, only in the respect that a different person or different property is injured or affected or that the injury or harm designed or contemplated would have been more serious or more extensive than that caused; or

(b) the actual result involves the same kind of injury or harm as that designed or contemplated and is not too remote or accidental in its occurrence to have a [just] bearing on the actor's liability or on the gravity of his offense.

(3) When recklessly or negligently causing a particular result is an element of an offense, the element is not established if the actual result is not within the risk of which the actor is aware or, in the case of negligence, of which he should be aware unless:

(a) the actual result differs from the probable result only in the respect that a different person or different property is injured or affected or that the probable injury or harm would have been more serious or more extensive than that caused; or

(b) the actual result involves the same kind of injury or harm as the probable result and is not too remote or accidental in its occurrence to have a [just] bearing on the actor's liability or on the gravity of his offense.

(4) When causing a particular result is a material element of an offense for which absolute liability is imposed by law, the element is not established unless the actual result is a probable consequence of the actor's conduct.

SECTION 2.04. Ignorance or Mistake.

(1) Ignorance or mistake as to a matter of fact or law is a defense if:

(a) the ignorance or mistake negatives the purpose, knowledge, belief, recklessness or negligence required to establish a material element of the offense; or

(b) the law provides that the state of mind established by such ignorance or mistake constitutes a defense.

(2) Although ignorance or mistake would otherwise afford a defense to the offense charged, the defense is not available if the defendant would be guilty of another offense had the situation been as he supposed. In such case, however, the ignorance or mistake of the defendant shall reduce the grade and degree of the offense of which he may be convicted to those of the offense of which he would be guilty had the situation been as he supposed.

(3) A belief that conduct does not legally constitute an offense is a defense to a prosecution for that offense based upon such conduct when:

(a) the statute or other enactment defining the offense is not known to the actor and has not been published or otherwise reasonably made available prior to the conduct alleged; or

(b) he acts in reasonable reliance upon an official statement of the law, afterward determined to be invalid or erroneous, contained in (i) a statute or other enactment; (ii) a judicial decision, opinion or judgment; (iii) an administrative order or grant of permission; or (iv) an official interpretation of the public officer or body charged by law with responsibility for the interpretation, administration or enforcement of the law defining the offense.

(4) The defendant must prove a defense arising under Subsection (3) of this Section by a preponderance of evidence.

SECTION 2.05. When Culpability Requirements Are Inapplicable to Violations and to Offenses Defined by Other Statutes; Effect of Absolute Liability in Reducing Grade of Offense to Violation.

(1) The requirements of culpability prescribed by Sections 2.01 and 2.02 do not apply to:

(a) offenses that constitute violations, unless the requirement involved is included in the definition of the offense or the Court determines that its application is consistent with effective enforcement of the law defining the offense; or

(b) offenses defined by statutes other than the Code, insofar as a legislative purpose to impose absolute liability for such offenses or with respect to any material element thereof plainly appears.

(2) Notwithstanding any other provision of existing law and unless a subsequent statute otherwise provides:

(a) when absolute liability is imposed with respect to any material element of an offense defined by a statute other than the Code and a conviction is based upon such liability, the offense constitutes a violation; and

(b) although absolute liability is imposed by law with respect to one or more of the material elements of an offense defined by a statute other than the Code, the culpable commission of the offense may be charged and proved, in which event negligence with respect to such elements constitutes sufficient culpability and the classification of the offense and the sentence that may be imposed therefore upon conviction are determined by Section 1.04 and Article 6 of the Code.

SECTION 2.06. Liability for Conduct of Another; Complicity.

(1) A person is guilty of an offense if it is committed by his own conduct or by the conduct of another person for which he is legally accountable, or both.

(2) A person is legally accountable for the conduct of another person when:

(a) acting with the kind of culpability that is sufficient for the commission of the offense, he causes an innocent or irresponsible person to engage in such conduct; or

(b) he is made accountable for the conduct of such other person by the Code or by the law defining the offense; or

(c) he is an accomplice of such other person in the commission of the offense.

(3) A person is an accomplice of another person in the commission of an offense if:

(a) with the purpose of promoting or facilitating the commission of the offense, he

(i) solicits such other person to commit it, or

(ii) aids or agrees or attempts to aid such other person in planning or committing it, or

(iii) having a legal duty to prevent the commission of the offense, fails to make proper effort so to do; or

(b) his conduct is expressly declared by law to establish his complicity.

(4) When causing a particular result is an element of an offense, an accomplice in the conduct causing such result is an accomplice in the commission of that offense if he acts with the kind of culpability, if any, with respect to that result that is sufficient for the commission of the offense.

(5) A person who is legally incapable of committing a particular offense himself may be guilty thereof if it is committed by the conduct of another person for which he is legally accountable, unless such liability is inconsistent with the purpose of the provision establishing his incapacity.

(6) Unless otherwise provided by the Code or by the law defining the offense, a person is not an accomplice in an offense committed by another person if:

(a) he is a victim of that offense; or

(b) the offense is so defined that his conduct is inevitably incident to its commission; or

(c) he terminates his complicity prior to the commission of the offense and

(i) wholly deprives it of effectiveness in the commission of the offense; or

(ii) gives timely warning to the law enforcement authorities or otherwise makes proper effort to prevent the commission of the offense.

(7) An accomplice may be convicted on proof of the commission of the offense and of his complicity therein, though the person claimed to have committed the offense has not been prosecuted or convicted or has been convicted of a different offense or degree of offense or has an immunity to prosecution or conviction or has been convicted.

SECTION 2.07. **Liability of Corporations, Unincorporated Associations and Persons Acting, or Under a Duty to Act, in Their Behalf.**

(1) A corporation may be convicted of the commission of an offense if:

(a) the offense is a violation or the offense is defined by a statute other than the Code in which a legislative purpose to impose liability on corporations plainly appears and the conduct is performed by an agent of the corporation acting in behalf of the corporation within the scope of his office or employment, except that if the law defining the offense designates the agents for whose conduct the corporation is accountable or the circumstances under which it is accountable, such provisions shall apply; or

(b) the offense consists of an omission to discharge a specific duty of affirmative performance imposed on corporations by law; or

(c) the commission of the offense was authorized, requested, commanded, performed or recklessly tolerated by the board of directors or by a high managerial agent acting in behalf of the corporation within the scope of his office or employment.

(2) When absolute liability is imposed for the commission of an offense, a legislative purpose to impose liability on a corporation shall be assumed, unless the contrary plainly appears.

(3) An unincorporated association may be convicted of the commission of an offense if:

(a) the offense is defined by a statute other than the Code that expressly provides for the liability of such an association and the conduct is performed by an agent of the association acting in behalf of the association within the scope of his office or employment, except that if the law defining the offense designates the agents for whose conduct the association is accountable or the circumstances under which it is accountable, such provisions shall apply; or

(b) the offense consists of an omission to discharge a specific duty of affirmative performance imposed on associations by law.

(4) As used in this Section:

    (a) "corporation" does not include an entity organized as or by a governmental agency for the execution of a governmental program;

    (b) "agent" means any director, officer, servant, employee or other person authorized to act in behalf of the corporation or association and, in the case of an unincorporated association, a member of such association;

    (c) "high managerial agent" means an officer of a corporation or an unincorporated association, or, in the case of a partnership, a partner, or any other agent of a corporation or association having duties of such responsibility that his conduct may fairly be assumed to represent the policy of the corporation or association.

(5) In any prosecution of a corporation or an unincorporated association for the commission of an offense included within the terms of Subsection (1)(a) or Subsection (3)(a) of this Section, other than an offense for which absolute liability has been imposed, it shall be a defense if the defendant proves by a preponderance of evidence that the high managerial agent having supervisory responsibility over the subject matter of the offense employed due diligence to prevent its commission. This paragraph shall not apply if it is plainly inconsistent with the legislative purpose in defining the particular offense.

(6) (a) A person is legally accountable for any conduct he performs or causes to be performed in the name of the corporation or an unincorporated association or in its behalf to the same extent as if it were performed in his own name or behalf.

    (b) Whenever a duty to act is imposed by law upon a corporation or an unincorporated association, any agent of the corporation or association having primary responsibility for the discharge of the duty is legally accountable for a reckless omission to perform the required act to the same extent as if the duty were imposed by law directly upon himself.

    (c) When a person is convicted of an offense by reason of his legal accountability for the conduct of a corporation or an unincorporated association, he is subject to the sentence authorized by law when a natural person is convicted of an offense of the grade and the degree involved.

SECTION 2.08. Intoxication.

(1) Except as provided in Subsection (4) of this Section, intoxication of the actor is not a defense unless it negatives an element of the offense.

(2) When recklessness establishes an element of the offense, if the actor, due to self-induced intoxication, is unaware of a risk of which he would have been aware had he been sober, such unawareness is immaterial.

(3) Intoxication does not, in itself, constitute mental disease within the meaning of Section 4.01.

(4) Intoxication that (a) is not self-induced or (b) is pathological is an affirmative defense if by reason of such intoxication the actor at the time of his conduct lacks substantial capacity either to appreciate its criminality [wrongfulness] or to conform his conduct to the requirements of law.

(5) *Definitions.* In this Section unless a different meaning plainly is required:

    (a) "intoxication" means a disturbance of mental or physical capacities resulting from the introduction of substances into the body;

    (b) "self-induced intoxication" means intoxication caused by substances that the actor knowingly introduces into his body, the tendency of which to cause intoxication he knows or ought to know, unless he introduces them pursuant to medical advice or under such circumstances as would afford a defense to a charge of crime;

(c) "pathological intoxication" means intoxication grossly excessive in degree, given the amount of the intoxicant, to which the actor does not know he is susceptible.

SECTION 2.09. Duress.

(1) It is an affirmative defense that the actor engaged in the conduct charged to constitute an offense because he was coerced to do so by the use of, or a threat to use, unlawful force against his person or the person of another, that a person of reasonable firmness in his situation would have been unable to resist.

(2) The defense provided by this Section is unavailable if the actor recklessly placed himself in a situation in which it was probable that he would be subjected to duress. The defense is also unavailable if he was negligent in placing himself in such a situation, whenever negligence suffices to establish culpability for the offense charged.

(3) It is not a defense that a woman acted on the command of her husband, unless she acted under such coercion as would establish a defense under this Section. [The presumption that a woman acting in the presence of her husband is coerced is abolished.]

(4) When the conduct of the actor would otherwise be justifiable under Section 3.02, this Section does not preclude such defense.

SECTION 2.10. Military Orders.

It is an affirmative defense that the actor, in engaging in the conduct charged to constitute an offense, does no more than execute an order of his superior in the armed services that he does not know to be unlawful.

SECTION 2.11. Consent.

(1) *In General.* The consent of the victim to conduct charged to constitute an offense or to the result thereof is a defense if such consent negatives an element of the offense or precludes the infliction of the harm or evil sought to be prevented by the law defining the offense.

(2) *Consent to Bodily Injury.* When conduct is charged to constitute an offense because it causes or threatens bodily injury, consent to such conduct or to the infliction of such injury is a defense if:

(a) the bodily injury consented to or threatened by the conduct consented to is not serious; or

(b) the conduct and the injury are reasonably foreseeable hazards of joint participation in a lawful athletic contest or competitive sport or other concerted activity not forbidden by law; or

(c) the consent establishes a justification for the conduct under Article 3 of the Code.

(3) *Ineffective Consent.* Unless otherwise provided by the Code or by the law defining the offense, assent does not constitute consent if:

(a) it is given by a person who is legally incompetent to authorize the conduct charged to constitute the offense; or

(b) it is given by a person who by reason of youth, mental disease or defect or intoxication is manifestly unable or known by the actor to be unable to make a reasonable judgment as to the nature or harmfulness of the conduct charged to constitute the offense; or

(c) it is given by a person whose improvident consent is sought to be prevented by the law defining the offense; or

(d) it is induced by force, duress or deception of a kind sought to be prevented by the law defining the offense.

SECTION 2.12. De Minimis Infractions.

The Court shall dismiss a prosecution if, having regard to the nature of the conduct charged to constitute an offense and the nature of the attendant circumstances, it finds that the defendant's conduct:

(1) was within a customary license or tolerance, neither expressly negatived by the person whose interest was infringed nor inconsistent with the purpose of the law defining the offense; or

(2) did not actually cause or threaten the harm or evil sought to be prevented by the law defining the offense or did so only to an extent too trivial to warrant the condemnation of conviction; or

(3) presents such other extenuations that it cannot reasonably be regarded as envisaged by the legislature in forbidding the offense.

The Court shall not dismiss a prosecution under Subsection (3) of this Section without filing a written statement of its reasons.

SECTION 2.13. Entrapment.

(1) A public law enforcement official or a person acting in cooperation with such an official perpetrates an entrapment if for the purpose of obtaining evidence of the commission of an offense, he induces or encourages another person to engage in conduct constituting such offense by either:

(a) making knowingly false representations designed to induce the belief that such conduct is not prohibited; or

(b) employing methods of persuasion or inducement that create a substantial risk that such an offense will be committed by persons other than those who are ready to commit it.

(2) Except as provided in Subsection (3) of this Section, a person prosecuted for an offense shall be acquitted if he proves by a preponderance of evidence that his conduct occurred in response to an entrapment. The issue of entrapment shall be tried by the Court in the absence of the jury.

(3) The defense afforded by this Section is unavailable when causing or threatening bodily injury is an element of the offense charged and the prosecution is based on conduct causing or threatening such injury to a person other than the person perpetrating the entrapment.

ARTICLE 3. GENERAL PRINCIPLES OF JUSTIFICATION

SECTION 3.01. Justification an Affirmative Defense; Civil Remedies Unaffected.

(1) In any prosecution based on conduct that is justifiable under this Article, justification is an affirmative defense.

(2) The fact that conduct is justifiable under this Article does not abolish or impair any remedy for such conduct that is available in any civil action.

SECTION 3.02. Justification Generally: Choice of Evils.

(1) Conduct that the actor believes to be necessary to avoid a harm or evil to himself or to another is justifiable, provided that:

  (a) the harm or evil sought to be avoided by such conduct is greater than that sought to be prevented by the law defining the offense charged; and

  (b) neither the Code nor other law defining the offense provides exceptions or defenses dealing with the specific situation involved; and

  (c) a legislative purpose to exclude the justification claimed does not otherwise plainly appear.

(2) When the actor was reckless or negligent in bringing about the situation requiring a choice of harms or evils or in appraising the necessity for his conduct, the justification afforded by this Section is unavailable in a prosecution for any offense for which recklessness or negligence, as the case may be, suffices to establish culpability.

SECTION 3.03. Execution of Public Duty.

(1) Except as provided in Subsection (2) of this Section, conduct is justifiable when it is required or authorized by:

  (a) the law defining the duties or functions of a public officer or the assistance to be rendered to such officer in the performance of his duties; or

  (b) the law governing the execution of legal process; or

  (c) the judgment or order of a competent court or tribunal; or

  (d) the law governing the armed services or the lawful conduct of war; or

  (e) any other provision of law imposing a public duty.

(2) The other sections of this Article apply to:

  (a) the use of force upon or toward the person of another for any of the purposes dealt with in such sections; and

  (b) the use of deadly force for any purpose, unless the use of such force is otherwise expressly authorized by law or occurs in the lawful conduct of war.

(3) The justification afforded by Subsection (1) of this Section applies:

  (a) when the actor believes his conduct to be required or authorized by the judgment or direction of a competent court or tribunal or in the lawful execution of legal process, notwithstanding lack of jurisdiction of the court or defect in the legal process; and

  (b) when the actor believes his conduct to be required or authorized to assist a public officer in the performance of his duties, notwithstanding that the officer exceeded his legal authority.

SECTION 3.04. Use of Force in Self-Protection.

(1) *Use of Force Justifiable for Protection of the Person.* Subject to the provisions of this Section and of Section 3.09, the use of force upon or toward another person is justifiable when the actor believes that such force is immediately necessary for the purpose of protecting himself against the use of unlawful force by such other person on the present occasion.

(2) *Limitations on Justifying Necessity for Use of Force.*

    (a) The use of force is not justifiable under this Section:

        (i) to resist an arrest that the actor knows is being made by a peace officer, although the arrest is unlawful; or

        (ii) to resist force used by the occupier or possessor of property or by another person on his behalf, where the actor knows that the person using the force is doing so under a claim of right to protect the property, except that this limitation shall not apply if:

            (A) the actor is a public officer acting in the performance of his duties or a person lawfully assisting him therein or a person making or assisting in a lawful arrest; or

            (B) the actor has been unlawfully dispossessed of the property and is making a re-entry or recaption justified by Section 3.06; or

            (C) the actor believes that such force is necessary to protect himself against death or serious bodily injury.

    (b) The use of deadly force is not justifiable under this Section unless the actor believes that such force is necessary to protect himself against death, serious bodily injury, kidnapping or sexual intercourse compelled by force or threat; nor is it justifiable if:

        (i) the actor, with the purpose of causing death or serious bodily injury, provoked the use of force against himself in the same encounter; or

        (ii) the actor knows that he can avoid the necessity of using such force with complete safety by retreating or by surrendering possession of a thing to a person asserting a claim of right thereto or by complying with a demand that he abstain from any action that he has no duty to take, except that:

            (A) the actor is not obliged to retreat from his dwelling or place of work, unless he was the initial aggressor or is assailed in his place of work by another person whose place of work the actor knows it to be; and

            (B) a public officer justified in using force in the performance of his duties or a person justified in using force in his assistance or a person justified in using force in making an arrest or preventing an escape is not obliged to desist from efforts to perform such duty, effect such arrest or prevent such escape because of resistance or threatened resistance by or on behalf of the person against whom such action is directed.

    (c) Except as required by paragraphs (a) and (b) of this Subsection, a person employing protective force may estimate the necessity thereof under the circumstances as he believes them to be when the force is used, without retreating, surrendering possession, doing any other act that he has no legal duty to do or abstaining from any lawful action.

(3) *Use of Confinement as Protective Force.* The justification afforded by this Section extends to the use of confinement as protective force only if the actor takes all reasonable measures to terminate the confinement as soon as he knows that he safely can, unless the person confined has been arrested on a charge of crime.

SECTION 3.05. Use of Force for the Protection of Other Persons.

(1) Subject to the provisions of this Section and of Section 3.09, the use of force upon or toward the person of another is justifiable to protect a third person when:

(a) the actor would be justified under Section 3.04 in using such force to protect himself against the injury he believes to be threatened to the person whom he seeks to protect; and

(b) under the circumstances as the actor believes them to be, the person whom he seeks to protect would be justified in using such protective force; and

(c) the actor believes that his intervention is necessary for the protection of such other person.

(2) Notwithstanding Subsection (1) of this Section:

(a) when the actor would be obliged under Section 3.04 to retreat, to surrender the possession of a thing or to comply with a demand before using force in self-protection, he is not obliged to do so before using force for the protection of another person, unless he knows that he can thereby secure the complete safety of such other person; and

(b) when the person whom the actor seeks to protect would be obliged under Section 3.04 to retreat, to surrender the possession of a thing or to comply with a demand if he knew that he could obtain complete safety by so doing, the actor is obliged to try to cause him to do so before using force in his protection if the actor knows that he can obtain complete safety in that way; and

(c) neither the actor nor the person whom he seeks to protect is obliged to retreat when in the other's dwelling or place of work to any greater extent than in his own.

SECTION 3.06. Use of Force for Protection of Property.

(1) *Use of Force Justifiable for Protection of Property.* Subject to the provisions of this Section and of Section 3.09, the use of force upon or toward the person of another is justifiable when the actor believes that such force is immediately necessary:

(a) to prevent or terminate an unlawful entry or other trespass upon land or a trespass against or the unlawful carrying away of tangible, movable property, provided that such land or movable property is, or is believed by the actor to be, in his possession or in the possession of another person for whose protection he acts; or

(b) to effect an entry or re-entry upon land or to retake tangible movable property, provided that the actor believes that he or the person by whose authority he acts or a person from whom he or such other person derives title was unlawfully dispossessed of such land or movable property and is entitled to possession, and provided, further, that:

(i) the force is used immediately or on fresh pursuit after such dispossession; or

(ii) the actor believes that the person against whom he uses force has no claim of right to the possession of the property and, in the case of land, the circumstances, as the actor believes them to be, are of such urgency that it would be an exceptional hardship to postpone the entry or re-entry until a court order is obtained.

(2) *Meaning of Possession.* For the purposes of Subsection (1) of this Section:

(a) a person who has parted with the custody of property to another who refuses to restore it to him is no longer in possession, unless the property is movable and was and still is located on land in his possession;

(b) a person who has been dispossessed of land does not regain possession thereof merely by setting foot thereon;

(c) a person who has a license to use or occupy real property is deemed to be in possession thereof except against the licensor acting under claim of right.

(3) *Limitations on Justifiable Use of Force.*

    (a) *Request to Desist.* The use of force is justifiable under this Section only if the actor first requests the person against whom such force is used to desist from his interference with the property, unless the actor believes that:

        (i) such request would be useless; or

        (ii) it would be dangerous to himself or another person to make the request; or

        (iii) substantial harm will be done to the physical condition of the property that is sought to be protected before the request can effectively be made.

    (b) *Exclusion of Trespasser.* The use of force to prevent or terminate a trespass is not justifiable under this Section if the actor knows that the exclusion of the trespasser will expose him to substantial danger of serious bodily injury.

    (c) *Resistance of Lawful Re-entry or Recaption.* The use of force to prevent an entry or re-entry upon land or the recaption of movable property is not justifiable under this Section, although the actor believes that such re-entry or recaption is unlawful, if:

        (i) the re-entry or recaption is made by or on behalf of a person who was actually dispossessed of the property; and

        (ii) it is otherwise justifiable under Subsection (1)(b) of this Section.

    (d) *Use of Deadly Force.* The use of deadly force is not justifiable under this Section unless the actor believes that:

        (i) the person against whom the force is used is attempting to dispossess him of his dwelling otherwise than under a claim of right to its possession; or

        (ii) the person against whom the force is used is attempting to commit or consummate arson, burglary, robbery or other felonious theft or property destruction and either:

            (A) has employed or threatened deadly force against or in the presence of the actor; or

            (B) the use of force other than deadly force to prevent the commission or the consummation of the crime would expose the actor or another in his presence to substantial danger of serious bodily injury.

(4) *Use of Confinement as Protective Force.* The justification afforded by this Section extends to the use of confinement as protective force only if the actor takes all reasonable measures to terminate the confinement as soon as he knows that he can do so with safety to the property, unless the person confined has been arrested on a charge of crime.

(5) *Use of Device to Protect Property.* The justification afforded by this Section extends to the use of a device for the purpose of protecting property only if:

    (a) the device is not designed to cause or known to create a substantial risk of causing death or serious bodily injury; and

    (b) the use of the particular device to protect the property from entry or trespass is reasonable under the circumstances, as the actor believes them to be; and

(c) the device is one customarily used for such a purpose or reasonable care is taken to make known to probable intruders the fact that it is used.

(6) *Use of Force to Pass Wrongful Obstructor.* The use of force to pass a person whom the actor believes to be purposely or knowingly and unjustifiably obstructing the actor from going to a place to which he may lawfully go is justifiable, provided that:

(a) the actor believes that the person against whom he uses force has no claim of right to obstruct the actor; and

(b) the actor is not being obstructed from entry or movement on land that he knows to be in the possession or custody of the person obstructing him, or in the possession or custody of another person by whose authority the obstructor acts, unless the circumstances, as the actor believes them to be, are of such urgency that it would not be reasonable to postpone the entry or movement on such land until a court order is obtained; and

(c) the force used is not greater than would be justifiable if the person obstructing the actor were using force against him to prevent his passage.

SECTION 3.07. Use of Force in Law Enforcement.

(1) *Use of Force Justifiable to Effect an Arrest.* Subject to the provisions of this Section and of Section 3.09, the use of force upon or toward the person of another is justifiable when the actor is making or assisting in making an arrest and the actor believes that such force is immediately necessary to effect a lawful arrest.

(2) *Limitations on the Use of Force.*

(a) The use of force is not justifiable under this Section unless:

(i) the actor makes known the purpose of the arrest or believes that it is otherwise known by or cannot reasonably be made known to the person to be arrested; and

(ii) when the arrest is made under a warrant, the warrant is valid or believed by the actor to be valid.

(b) The use of deadly force is not justifiable under this Section unless:

(i) the arrest is for a felony; and

(ii) the person effecting the arrest is authorized to act as a peace officer or is assisting a person whom he believes to be authorized to act as a peace officer; and

(iii) the actor believes that the force employed creates no substantial risk of injury to innocent persons; and

(iv) the actor believes that:

(A) the crime for which the arrest is made involved conduct including the use or threatened use of deadly force; or

(B) there is a substantial risk that the person to be arrested will cause death or serious bodily injury if his apprehension is delayed.

(3) *Use of Force to Prevent Escape from Custody.* The use of force to prevent the escape of an arrested person from custody is justifiable when the force could justifiably have been employed to effect the arrest under which the person is in custody, except that a guard or other person authorized to act as a peace officer is justified in using any force, including deadly force, that he believes to be immediately necessary to prevent the escape of a person from a jail, prison, or other institution for the detention of persons charged with or convicted of a crime.

(4) *Use of Force by Private Person Assisting an Unlawful Arrest.*

    (a) A private person who is summoned by a peace officer to assist in effecting an unlawful arrest, is justified in using any force that he would be justified in using if the arrest were lawful, provided that he does not believe the arrest is unlawful.

    (b) A private person who assists another private person in effecting an unlawful arrest, or who, not being summoned, assists a peace officer in effecting an unlawful arrest, is justified in using any force that he would be justified in using if the arrest were lawful, provided that (i) he believes the arrest is lawful, and (ii) the arrest would be lawful if the facts were as he believes them to be.

(5) *Use of Force to Prevent Suicide or the Commission of a Crime.*

    (a) The use of force upon or toward the person of another is justifiable when the actor believes that such force is immediately necessary to prevent such other person from committing suicide, inflicting serious bodily injury upon himself, committing or consummating the commission of a crime involving or threatening bodily injury, damage to or loss of property or a breach of the peace, except that:

        (i) any limitations imposed by the other provisions of this Article on the justifiable use of force in self-protection, for the protection of others, the protection of property, the effectuation of an arrest or the prevention of an escape from custody shall apply notwithstanding the criminality of the conduct against which such force is used; and

        (ii) the use of deadly force is not in any event justifiable under this Subsection unless:

            (A) the actor believes that there is a substantial risk that the person whom he seeks to prevent from committing a crime will cause death or serious bodily injury to another unless the commission or the consummation of the crime is prevented and that the use of such force presents no substantial risk of injury to innocent persons; or

            (B) the actor believes that the use of such force is necessary to suppress a riot or mutiny after the rioters or mutineers have been ordered to disperse and warned, in any particular manner that the law may require, that such force will be used if they do not obey.

    (b) The justification afforded by this Subsection extends to the use of confinement as preventive force only if the actor takes all reasonable measures to terminate the confinement as soon as he knows that he safely can, unless the person confined has been arrested on a charge of crime.

SECTION 3.08. **Use of Force by Persons with Special Responsibility for Care, Discipline or Safety of Others.**

    The use of force upon or toward the person of another is justifiable if:

(1) the actor is the parent or guardian or other person similarly responsible for the general care and supervision of a minor or a person acting at the request of such parent, guardian or other responsible person and:

    (a) the force is used for the purpose of safeguarding or promoting the welfare of the minor, including the prevention or punishment of his misconduct; and

    (b) the force used is not designed to cause or known to create a substantial risk of causing death, serious bodily injury, disfigurement, extreme pain or mental distress or gross degradation; or

(2) the actor is a teacher or a person otherwise entrusted with the care or supervision for a special purpose of a minor and:

    (a) the actor believes that the force used is necessary to further such special purpose, including the maintenance of reasonable discipline in a school, class or other group, and that the use of such force is consistent with the welfare of the minor; and

    (b) the degree of force, if it had been used by the parent or guardian of the minor, would not be unjustifiable under Subsection (1)(b) of this section; or

(3) the actor is the guardian or other person similarly responsible for the general care and supervision of an incompetent person and:

    (a) the force is used for the purpose of safeguarding or promoting the welfare of the incompetent person, including the prevention of his misconduct, or, when such incompetent person is in a hospital or other institution for his care and custody, for the maintenance of reasonable discipline in such institution; and

    (b) the force used is not designed to cause or known to create a substantial risk of causing death, serious bodily injury, disfigurement, extreme or unnecessary pain, mental distress, or humiliation; or

(4) the actor is a doctor or other therapist or a person assisting him at his direction and:

    (a) the force is used for the purpose of administering a recognized form of treatment that the actor believes to be adapted to promoting the physical or mental health of the patient; and

    (b) the treatment is administered with the consent of the patient or, if the patient is a minor or an incompetent person, with the consent of his parent or guardian or other person legally competent to consent in his behalf, or the treatment is administered in an emergency when the actor believes that no one competent to consent can be consulted and that a reasonable person, wishing to safeguard the welfare of the patient, would consent; or

(5) the actor is a warden or other authorized official of a correctional institution and:

    (a) he believes that the force used is necessary for the purpose of enforcing the lawful rules or procedures of the institution, unless his belief in the lawfulness of the rule or procedure sought to be enforced is erroneous and his error is due to ignorance or mistake as to the provisions of the Code, any other provision of the criminal law or the law governing the administration of the institution; and

    (b) the nature or degree of force used is not forbidden by Article 303 or 304 of the Code; and

    (c) if deadly force is used, its use is otherwise justifiable under this Article; or

(6) the actor is a person responsible for the safety of a vessel or an aircraft or a person acting at his direction and:

    (a) he believes that the force used is necessary to prevent interference with the operation of the vessel or aircraft or obstruction of the execution of a lawful order, unless his belief in the lawfulness of the order is erroneous and his error is due to ignorance or mistake as to the law defining his authority; and

    (b) if deadly force is used, its use is otherwise justifiable under this Article; or

(7) the actor is a person who is authorized or required by law to maintain order or decorum in a vehicle, train or other carrier or in a place where others are assembled, and:

(a) he believes that the force used is necessary for such purpose; and

(b) the force used is not designed to cause or known to create a substantial risk of causing death, bodily injury, or extreme mental distress.

SECTION 3.09. Mistake of Law as to Unlawfulness of Force or Legality of Arrest; Reckless or Negligent Use of Otherwise Justifiable Force; Reckless or Negligent Injury or Risk of Injury to Innocent Persons.

(1) The justification afforded by Sections 3.04 to 3.07, inclusive, is unavailable when:

(a) the actor's belief in the unlawfulness of the force or conduct against which he employs protective force or his belief in the lawfulness of an arrest that he endeavors to effect by force is erroneous; and

(b) his error is due to ignorance or mistake as to the provisions of the Code, any other provision of the criminal law or the law governing the legality of an arrest or search.

(2) When the actor believes that the use of force upon or toward the person of another is necessary for any of the purposes for which such belief would establish a justification under Sections 3.03 to 3.08 but the actor is reckless or negligent in having such belief or in acquiring or failing to acquire any knowledge or belief that is material to the justifiability of his use of force, the justification afforded by those Sections is unavailable in a prosecution for an offense for which recklessness or negligence, as the case may be, suffices to establish culpability.

(3) When the actor is justified under Sections 3.03 to 3.08 in using force upon or toward the person of another but he recklessly or negligently injures or creates a risk of injury to innocent persons, the justification afforded by those Sections is unavailable in a prosecution for such recklessness or negligence towards innocent persons.

SECTION 3.10. Justification in Property Crimes.

Conduct involving the appropriation, seizure or destruction of, damage to, intrusion on or interference with property is justifiable under circumstances that would establish a defense of privilege in a civil action based thereon, unless:

(1) the Code or the law defining the offense deals with the specific situation involved; or

(2) a legislative purpose to exclude the justification claimed otherwise plainly appears.

SECTION 3.11. Definitions.

In this Article, unless a different meaning plainly is required:

(1) "unlawful force" means force, including confinement, that is employed without the consent of the person against whom it is directed and the employment of which constitutes an offense or actionable tort or would constitute such offense or tort except for a defense (such as the absence of intent, negligence, or mental capacity; duress; youth; or diplomatic status) not amounting to a privilege to use the force. Assent constitutes consent, within the meaning of this Section, whether or not it otherwise is legally effective, except assent to the infliction of death or serious bodily injury.

(2) "deadly force" means force that the actor uses with the purpose of causing or that he knows to create a substantial risk of causing death or serious bodily

injury. Purposely firing a firearm in the direction of another person or at a vehicle in which another person is believed to be constitutes deadly force. A threat to cause death or serious bodily injury, by the production of a weapon or otherwise, so long as the actor's purpose is limited to creating an apprehension that he will use deadly force if necessary, does not constitute deadly force.

(3) "dwelling" means any building or structure, though movable or temporary, or a portion thereof, that is for the time being the actor's home or place of lodging.

ARTICLE 4. RESPONSIBILITY

SECTION 4.01. Mental Disease or Defect Excluding Responsibility.

(1) A person is not responsible for criminal conduct if at the time of such conduct as a result of mental disease or defect he lacks substantial capacity either to appreciate the criminality [wrongfulness] of his conduct or to conform his conduct to the requirements of law.

(2) As used in this Article, the terms "mental disease or defect" do not include an abnormality manifested only by repeated criminal or otherwise antisocial conduct.

SECTION 4.02. Evidence of Mental Disease or Defect Admissible When Relevant to Element of the Offense; Mental Disease or Defect Impairing Capacity as Ground for Mitigation of Punishment in Capital Cases.

(1) Evidence that the defendant suffered from a mental disease or defect is admissible whenever it is relevant to prove that the defendant did or did not have a state of mind that is an element of the offense.

(2) Whenever the jury or the Court is authorized to determine or to recommend whether or not the defendant shall be sentenced to death or imprisonment upon conviction, evidence that the capacity of the defendant to appreciate the criminality [wrongfulness] of his conduct or to conform his conduct to the requirements of law was impaired as a result of mental disease or defect is admissible in favor of sentence of imprisonment.

SECTION 4.03. Mental Disease or Defect Excluding Responsibility Is Affirmative Defense; Requirement of Notice; Form of Verdict and Judgment when Finding of Irresponsibility Is Made.

(1) Mental disease or defect excluding responsibility is an affirmative defense.

(2) Evidence of mental disease or defect excluding responsibility is not admissible unless the defendant, at the time of entering his plea of not guilty or within ten days thereafter or at such later time as the Court may for good cause permit, files a written notice of his purpose to rely on such defense.

(3) When the defendant is acquitted on the ground of mental disease or defect excluding responsibility, the verdict and the judgment shall so state.

SECTION 4.04. Mental Disease or Defect Excluding Fitness to Proceed.

No person who as a result of mental disease or defect lacks capacity to understand the proceedings against him or to assist in his own defense shall be tried, convicted or sentenced for the commission of an offense so long as such incapacity endures.

ARTICLE 5. INCHOATE CRIMES

SECTION 5.01. Criminal Attempt.

(1) *Definition of Attempt.* A person is guilty of an attempt to commit a crime if, acting with the kind of culpability otherwise required for commission of the crime, he:

  (a) purposely engages in conduct that would constitute the crime if the attendant circumstances were as he believes them to be; or

  (b) when causing a particular result is an element of the crime, does or omits to do anything with the purpose of causing or with the belief that it will cause such result without further conduct on his part; or

  (c) purposely does or omits to do anything that, under the circumstances as he believes them to be, is an act or omission constituting a substantial step in a course of conduct planned to culminate in his commission of the crime.

(2) *Conduct that May Be Held Substantial Step Under Subsection (1)(c).* Conduct shall not be held to constitute a substantial step under Subsection (1)(c) of this Section unless it is strongly corroborative of the actor's criminal purpose. Without negativing the sufficiency of other conduct, the following, if strongly corroborative of the actor's criminal purpose, shall not be held insufficient as a matter of law:

  (a) lying in wait, searching for or following the contemplated victim of the crime;

  (b) enticing or seeking to entice the contemplated victim of the crime to go to the place contemplated for its commission;

  (c) reconnoitering the place contemplated for the commission of the crime;

  (d) unlawful entry of a structure, vehicle or enclosure in which it is contemplated that the crime will be committed;

  (e) possession of materials to be employed in the commission of the crime, that are specially designed for such unlawful use or that can serve no lawful purpose of the actor under the circumstances;

  (f) possession, collection or fabrication of materials to be employed in the commission of the crime, at or near the place contemplated for its commission, if such possession, collection or fabrication serves no lawful purpose of the actor under the circumstances;

  (g) soliciting an innocent agent to engage in conduct constituting an element of the crime.

(3) *Conduct Designed to Aid Another in Commission of a Crime.* A person who engages in conduct designed to aid another to commit a crime that would establish his complicity under Section 2.06 if the crime were committed by such other person, is guilty of an attempt to commit the crime, although the crime is not committed or attempted by such other person.

(4) *Renunciation of Criminal Purpose.* When the actor's conduct would otherwise constitute an attempt under Subsection (1)(b) or (1)(c) of this Section, it is an affirmative defense that he abandoned his effort to commit the crime or otherwise prevented its commission, under circumstances manifesting a complete and voluntary renunciation of his criminal purpose. The establishment of such defense does not, however, affect the liability of an accomplice who did not join in such abandonment or prevention.

Within the meaning of this Article, renunciation of criminal purpose is not voluntary if it is motivated, in whole or in part, by circumstances, not present or apparent at the inception of the actor's course of conduct, that increase the probability of detection or apprehension or that make more difficult the accomplishment of the criminal purpose. Renunciation is not complete if it is motivated by a decision to postpone the criminal conduct until a more advantageous time or to transfer the criminal effort to another but similar objective or victim.

SECTION 5.02. Criminal Solicitation.

(1) *Definition of Solicitation.* A person is guilty of solicitation to commit a crime if with the purpose of promoting or facilitating its commission he commands, encourages or requests another person to engage in specific conduct that would constitute such crime or an attempt to commit such crime or would establish his complicity in its commission or attempted commission.

(2) *Uncommunicated Solicitation.* It is immaterial under Subsection (1) of this Section that the actor fails to communicate with the person he solicits to commit a crime if his conduct was designed to effect such communication.

(3) *Renunciation of Criminal Purpose.* It is an affirmative defense that the actor, after soliciting another person to commit a crime, persuaded him not to do so or otherwise prevented the commission of the crime, under circumstances manifesting a complete and voluntary renunciation of his criminal purpose.

SECTION 5.03. Criminal Conspiracy.

(1) *Definition of Conspiracy.* A person is guilty of conspiracy with another person or persons to commit a crime if with the purpose of promoting or facilitating its commission he:

(a) agrees with such other person or persons that they or one or more of them will engage in conduct that constitutes such crime or an attempt or solicitation to commit such crime; or

(b) agrees to aid such other person or persons in the planning or commission of such crime or of an attempt or solicitation to commit such crime.

(2) *Scope of Conspiratorial Relationship.* If a person guilty of conspiracy, as defined by Subsection (1) of this Section, knows that a person with whom he conspires to commit a crime has conspired with another person or persons to commit the same crime, he is guilty of conspiring with such other person or persons, whether or not he knows their identity, to commit such crime.

(3) *Conspiracy with Multiple Criminal Objectives.* If a person conspires to commit a number of crimes, he is guilty of only one conspiracy so long as such multiple crimes are the object of the same agreement or continuous conspiratorial relationship.

(4) *Joinder and Venue in Conspiracy Prosecutions.*

(a) Subject to the provisions of paragraph (b) of this Subsection, two or more persons charged with criminal conspiracy may be prosecuted jointly if:

(i) they are charged with conspiring with one another; or

(ii) the conspiracies alleged, whether they have the same or different parties, are so related that they constitute different aspects of a scheme of organized criminal conduct.

(b) In any joint prosecution under paragraph (a) of this Subsection:

(i) no defendant shall be charged with a conspiracy in any county [parish or district] other than one in which he entered into such conspiracy or in which an overt act pursuant to such conspiracy was done by him or by a person with whom he conspired; and

(ii) neither the liability of any defendant nor the admissibility against him of evidence of acts or declarations of another shall be enlarged by such joinder; and

(iii) the Court shall order a severance or take a special verdict as to any defendant who so requests, if it deems it necessary or appropriate to promote the fair determination of his guilt or innocence, and shall take any other proper measures to protect the fairness of the trial.

(5) *Overt Act.* No person may be convicted of conspiracy to commit a crime, other than a felony of the first or second degree, unless an overt act in pursuance of such conspiracy is alleged and proved to have been done by him or by a person with whom he conspired.

(6) *Renunciation of Criminal Purpose.* It is an affirmative defense that the actor, after conspiring to commit a crime, thwarted the success of the conspiracy, under circumstances manifesting a complete and voluntary renunciation of his criminal purpose.

(7) *Duration of Conspiracy.* For purposes of Section 1.06(4):

(a) conspiracy is a continuing course of conduct that terminates when the crime or crimes that are its object are committed or the agreement that they be committed is abandoned by the defendant and by those with whom he conspired; and

(b) such abandonment is presumed if neither the defendant nor anyone with whom he conspired does any overt act in pursuance of the conspiracy during the applicable period of limitation; and

(c) if an individual abandons the agreement, the conspiracy is terminated as to him only if and when he advises those with whom he conspired of his abandonment or he informs the law enforcement authorities of the existence of the conspiracy and of his participation therein.

SECTION 5.04. Incapacity, Irresponsibility or Immunity of Party to Solicitation or Conspiracy.

(1) Except as provided in Subsection (2) of this Section, it is immaterial to the liability of a person who solicits or conspires with another to commit a crime that:

(a) he or the person whom he solicits or with whom he conspires does not occupy a particular position or have a particular characteristic that is an element of such crime, if he believes that one of them does; or

(b) the person whom he solicits or with whom he conspires is irresponsible or has an immunity to prosecution or conviction for the commission of the crime.

(2) It is a defense to a charge of solicitation or conspiracy to commit a crime that if the criminal object were achieved, the actor would not be guilty of a crime under the law defining the offense or as an accomplice under Section 2.06(5) or 2.06(6)(a) or (6)(b).

SECTION 5.05. Grading of Criminal Attempt, Solicitation and Conspiracy; Mitigation in Cases of Lesser Danger; Multiple Convictions Barred.

(1) *Grading.* Except as otherwise provided in this Section, attempt, solicitation and conspiracy are crimes of the same grade and degree as the most serious offense that is attempted or solicited or is an object of the conspiracy. An attempt, solicitation or conspiracy to commit a [capital crime or a] felony of the first degree is a felony of the second degree.

(2) *Mitigation.* If the particular conduct charged to constitute a criminal attempt, solicitation or conspiracy is so inherently unlikely to result or culminate in the commission of a crime that neither such conduct nor the actor presents a public

danger warranting the grading of such offense under this Section, the Court shall exercise its power under Section 6.12 to enter judgment and impose sentence for a crime of lower grade or degree or, in extreme cases, may dismiss the prosecution.

(3) *Multiple Convictions.* A person may not be convicted of more than one offense defined by this Article for conduct designed to commit or to culminate in the commission of the same crime.

SECTION 5.06. Possessing Instruments of Crime; Weapons.

(1) *Criminal Instruments Generally.* A person commits a misdemeanor if he possesses any instrument of crime with purpose to employ it criminally. "Instrument of crime" means:

    (a) anything specially made or specially adapted for criminal use; or

    (b) anything commonly used for criminal purposes and possessed by the actor under circumstances that do not negative unlawful purpose.

(2) *Presumption of Criminal Purpose from Possession of Weapon.* If a person possesses a firearm or other weapon on or about his person, in a vehicle occupied by him, or otherwise readily available for use, it is presumed that he had the purpose to employ it criminally, unless:

    (a) the weapon is possessed in the actor's home or place of business;

    (b) the actor is licensed or otherwise authorized by law to possess such weapon; or

    (c) the weapon is of a type commonly used in lawful sport.

"Weapon" means anything readily capable of lethal use and possessed under circumstances not manifestly appropriate for lawful uses it may have; the term includes a firearm that is not loaded or lacks a clip or other component to render it immediately operable, and components that can readily be assembled into a weapon.

(3) *Presumptions as to Possession of Criminal Instruments in Automobiles.* If a weapon or other instrument of crime is found in an automobile, it is presumed to be in the possession of the occupant if there is but one. If there is more than one occupant, it is presumed to be in the possession of all, except under the following circumstances:

    (a) it is found upon the person of one of the occupants;

    (b) the automobile is not a stolen one and the weapon or instrument is found out of view in a glove compartment, car trunk, or other enclosed customary depository, in which case it is presumed to be in the possession of the occupant or occupants who own or have authority to operate the automobile;

    (c) in the case of a taxicab, a weapon or instrument found in the passengers' portion of the vehicle is presumed to be in the possession of all the passengers, if there are any, and, if not, in the possession of the driver.

SECTION 5.07. Prohibited Offensive Weapons.

A person commits a misdemeanor if, except as authorized by law, he makes, repairs, sells, or otherwise deals in, uses, or possesses any offensive weapon. "Offensive weapon" means any bomb, machine gun, sawed-off shotgun, firearm specially made or specially adapted for concealment or silent discharge, any blackjack, sandbag, metal knuckles, dagger, or other implement for the infliction of serious bodily injury that serves no common lawful purpose. It is a defense under this

Section for the defendant to prove by a preponderance of evidence that he possessed or dealt with the weapon solely as a curio or in a dramatic performance, or that he possessed it briefly in consequence of having found it or taken it from an aggressor, or under circumstances similarly negativing any purpose or likelihood that the weapon would be used unlawfully. The presumptions provided in Section 5.06(3) are applicable to prosecutions under this Section.

ARTICLE 6. AUTHORIZED DISPOSITION OF OFFENDERS

SECTION 6.01. Degrees of Felonies.

(1) Felonies defined by this Code are classified, for the purpose of sentence, into three degrees, as follows:

(a) felonies of the first degree;

(b) felonies of the second degree;

(c) felonies of the third degree.

A felony is of the first or second degree when it is so designated by the Code. A crime declared to be a felony, without specification of degree, is of the third degree.

(2) Notwithstanding any other provision of law, a felony defined by any statute of this State other than this Code shall constitute, for the purpose of sentence, a felony of the third degree.

SECTION 6.02. Sentence in Accordance with Code; Authorized Dispositions.

(1) No person convicted of an offense shall be sentenced otherwise than in accordance with this Article.

(2) The Court shall sentence a person who has been convicted of murder to death or imprisonment, in accordance with Section 210.6.

(3) Except as provided in Subsection (2) of this Section and subject to the applicable provisions of the Code, the Court may suspend the imposition of sentence on a person who has been convicted of a crime, may order him to be committed in lieu of sentence, in accordance with Section 6.13, or may sentence him as follows:

(a) to pay a fine authorized by Section 6.03; or

(b) to be placed on probation [, and, in the case of a person convicted of a felony or misdemeanor to imprisonment for a term fixed by the Court not exceeding thirty days to be served as a condition of probation]; or

(c) to imprisonment for a term authorized by Section 6.05, 6.06, 6.07, 6.08, 6.09, or 7.06; or

(d) to fine and probation or fine and imprisonment, but not to probation and imprisonment [, except as authorized in paragraph (b) of this Subsection].

(4) The Court may suspend the imposition of sentence on a person who has been convicted of a violation or may sentence him to pay a fine authorized by Section 6.03.

(5) This Article does not deprive the Court of any authority conferred by law to decree a forfeiture of property, suspend or cancel a license, remove a person from office, or impose any other civil penalty. Such a judgment or order may be included in the sentence.

SECTION 6.03. Fines.

A person who has been convicted of an offense may be sentenced to pay a fine not exceeding:

(1) $10,000, when the conviction is of a felony of the first or second degree;

(2) $5,000, when the conviction is of a felony of the third degree;

(3) $1,000, when the conviction is of a misdemeanor;

(4) $500, when the conviction is of a petty misdemeanor or a violation;

(5) any higher amount equal to double the pecuniary gain derived from the offense by the offender;

(6) any higher amount specifically authorized by statute.

SECTION 6.04. Penalties Against Corporations and Unincorporated Associations; Forfeiture of Corporate Charter or Revocation of Certificate Authorizing Foreign Corporation to Do Business in the State.

(1) The Court may suspend the sentence of a corporation or an unincorporated association that has been convicted of an offense or may sentence it to pay a fine authorized by Section 6.03.

(2) (a) The [prosecuting attorney] is authorized to institute civil proceedings in the appropriate court of general jurisdiction to forfeit the charter of a corporation organized under the laws of this State or to revoke the certificate authorizing a foreign corporation to conduct business in this State. The Court may order the charter forfeited or the certificate revoked upon finding

    (i) that the board of directors or a high managerial agent acting in behalf of the corporation has, in conducting the corporation's affairs, purposely engaged in a persistent course of criminal conduct and

    (ii) that for the prevention of future criminal conduct of the same character, the public interest requires the charter of the corporation to be forfeited and the corporation to be dissolved or the certificate to be revoked.

(b) When a corporation is convicted of a crime or a high managerial agent of a corporation, as defined in Section 2.07, is convicted of a crime committed in the conduct of the affairs of the corporation, the Court, in sentencing the corporation or the agent, may direct the [prosecuting attorney] to institute proceedings authorized by paragraph (a) of this Subsection.

PART II: Definition of Specific Crimes

Offenses Involving Danger to the Person

ARTICLE 210. CRIMINAL HOMICIDE

SECTION 210.0. Definitions.

In Articles 210–213, unless a different meaning plainly is required:

(1) "human being" means a person who has been born and is alive;

(2) "bodily injury" means physical pain, illness or any impairment of physical condition;

(3) "serious bodily injury" means bodily injury which creates a substantial risk of death or which causes serious, permanent disfigurement, or protracted loss or impairment of the function of any bodily member or organ;

(4) "deadly weapon" means any firearm or other weapon, device, instrument, material or substance, whether animate or inanimate, which in the manner it is used or is intended to be used is known to be capable of producing death or serious bodily injury.

SECTION 210.1 Criminal Homicide.

(1) A person is guilty of criminal homicide if he purposely, knowingly, recklessly or negligently causes the death of another human being.

(2) Criminal homicide is murder, manslaughter or negligent homicide.

SECTION 210.2 Murder.

(1) Except as provided in Section 210.3(1)(b), criminal homicide constitutes murder when:

(a) it is committed purposely or knowingly; or

(b) it is committed recklessly under circumstances manifesting extreme indifference to the value of human life. Such recklessness and indifference are presumed if the actor is engaged or is an accomplice in the commission of, or an attempt to commit, or flight after committing or attempting to commit robbery, rape or deviate sexual intercourse by force or threat of force, arson, burglary, kidnapping or felonious escape.

(2) Murder is a felony of the first degree [but a person convicted of murder may be sentenced to death, as provided in Section 210.6].

SECTION 210.3. Manslaughter.

(1) Criminal homicide constitutes manslaughter when:

(a) it is committed recklessly; or

(b) a homicide which would otherwise be murder is committed under the influence of extreme mental or emotional disturbance for which there is reasonable explanation or excuse. The reasonableness of such explanation or excuse shall be determined from the viewpoint of a person in the actor's situation under the circumstances as he believes them to be.

(2) Manslaughter is a felony of the second degree.

SECTION 210.4. Negligent Homicide.

(1) Criminal homicide constitutes negligent homicide when it is committed negligently.

(2) Negligent homicide is a felony of the third degree.

SECTION 210.5. Causing or Aiding Suicide.

(1) *Causing Suicide as Criminal Homicide.* A person may be convicted of criminal homicide for causing another to commit suicide only if he purposely causes such suicide by force, duress or deception.

(2) *Aiding or Soliciting Suicide as an Independent Offense.* A person who purposely aids or solicits another to commit suicide is guilty of a felony of the second degree if

his conduct causes such suicide or an attempted suicide, and otherwise of a misdemeanor.

SECTION 210.6. Sentence of Death for Murder; Further Proceedings to Determine Sentence.

(1) *Death Sentence Excluded.* When a defendant is found guilty of murder, the Court shall impose sentence for a felony of the first degree if it is satisfied that:

    (a) none of the aggravating circumstances enumerated in Subsection (3) of this Section was established by the evidence at the trial or will be established if further proceedings are initiated under Subsection (2) of this Section; or

    (b) substantial mitigating circumstances, established by the evidence at the trial, call for leniency; or

    (c) the defendant, with the consent of the prosecuting attorney and the approval of the Court, pleaded guilty to murder as a felony of the first degree; or

    (d) the defendant was under 18 years of age at the time of the commission of the crime; or

    (e) the defendant's physical or mental condition calls for leniency; or

    (f) although the evidence suffices to sustain the verdict, it does not foreclose all doubt respecting the defendant's guilt.

(2) *Determination by Court or by Court and Jury.* Unless the Court imposes sentence under Subsection (1) of this Section, it shall conduct a separate proceeding to determine whether the defendant should be sentenced for a felony of the first degree or sentenced to death. The proceeding shall be conducted before the Court alone if the defendant was convicted by a Court sitting without a jury or upon his plea of guilty or if the prosecuting attorney and the defendant waive a jury with respect to sentence. In other cases it shall be conducted before the Court sitting with the jury which determined the defendant's guilt or, if the Court for good cause shown discharges that jury, with a new jury empanelled for the purpose.

In the proceeding, evidence may be presented as to any matter that the Court deems relevant to sentence, including but not limited to the nature and circumstances of the crime, the defendant's character, background, history, mental and physical condition and any of the aggravating or mitigating circumstances enumerated in Subsections (3) and (4) of this Section. Any such evidence, not legally privileged, which the Court deems to have probative force, may be received, regardless of its admissibility under the exclusionary rules of evidence, provided that the defendant's counsel is accorded a fair opportunity to rebut such evidence. The prosecuting attorney and the defendant or his counsel shall be permitted to present argument for or against sentence of death.

The determination whether sentence of death shall be imposed shall be in the discretion of the Court, except that when the proceeding is conducted before the Court sitting with a jury, the Court shall not impose sentence of death unless it submits to the jury the issue whether the defendant should be sentenced to death or to imprisonment and the jury returns a verdict that the sentence should be death. If the jury is unable to reach a unanimous verdict, the Court shall dismiss the jury and impose sentence for a felony of the first degree.

The Court, in exercising its discretion as to sentence, and the jury, in determining upon its verdict, shall take into account the aggravating and mitigating circumstances enumerated in Subsections (3) and (4) and any other facts that it deems relevant, but it shall not impose or recommend sentence of death unless it finds one of the aggravating circumstances enumerated in Subsection (3) and further finds that there are no mitigating circumstances sufficiently substantial to call for leniency. When the issue is submitted to the jury, the Court shall so instruct and also shall inform the jury of the nature of the sentence of imprisonment that may be imposed, including its implication with respect to possible release upon parole, if the jury verdict is against sentence of death.

Alternative formulation of Subsection (2):

(2) *Determination by Court.* Unless the Court imposes sentence under Subsection (1) of this Section, it shall conduct a separate proceeding to determine whether the defendant should be sentenced for a felony of the first degree or sentenced to death. In the proceeding, the Court, in accordance with Section 7.07, shall consider the report of the presentence investigation and, if a psychiatric examination has been ordered, the report of such examination. In addition, evidence may be presented as to any matter that the Court deems relevant to sentence, including but not limited to the nature and circumstances of the crime, the defendant's character, background, history, mental and physical condition and any of the aggravating or mitigating circumstances enumerated in Subsections (3) and (4) of this Section. Any such evidence, not legally privileged, which the Court deems to have probative force, may be received, regardless of its admissibility under the exclusionary rules of evidence, provided that the defendant's counsel is accorded a fair opportunity to rebut such evidence. The prosecuting attorney and the defendant or his counsel shall be permitted to present argument for or against sentence of death.

The determination whether sentence of death shall be imposed shall be in the discretion of the Court. In exercising such discretion, the Court shall take into account the aggravating and mitigating circumstances enumerated in Subsections (3) and (4) and any other facts that it deems relevant but shall not impose sentence of death unless it finds one of the aggravating circumstances enumerated in Subsection (3) and further finds that there are no mitigating circumstances sufficiently substantial to call for leniency.

(3) *Aggravating Circumstances.*

(a) The murder was committed by a convict under sentence of imprisonment.

(b) The defendant was previously convicted of another murder or of a felony involving the use or threat of violence to the person.

(c) At the time the murder was committed the defendant also committed another murder.

(d) The defendant knowingly created a great risk of death to many persons.

(e) The murder was committed while the defendant was engaged or was an accomplice in the commission of, or an attempt to commit, or flight after committing or attempting to commit robbery, rape or deviate sexual intercourse by force or threat of force, arson, burglary or kidnapping.

(f) The murder was committed for the purpose of avoiding or preventing a lawful arrest or effecting an escape from lawful custody.

(g) The murder was committed for pecuniary gain.

(h) The murder was especially heinous, atrocious or cruel, manifesting exceptional depravity.

(4) *Mitigating Circumstances.*

(a) The defendant has no significant history of prior criminal activity.

(b) The murder was committed while the defendant was under the influence of extreme mental or emotional disturbance.

(c) The victim was a participant in the defendant's homicidal conduct or consented to the homicidal act.

(d) The murder was committed under circumstances which the defendant believed to provide a moral justification or extenuation for his conduct.

(e) The defendant was an accomplice in a murder committed by another person and his participation in the homicidal act was relatively minor.

(f) The defendant acted under duress or under the domination of another person.

(g) At the time of the murder, the capacity of the defendant to appreciate the criminality [wrongfulness] of his conduct or to conform his conduct to the requirements of law was impaired as a result of mental disease or defect or intoxication.

(h) The youth of the defendant at the time of the crime.

ARTICLE 212. KIDNAPPING AND RELATED OFFENSES; COERCION

SECTION 212.0 Definitions.

In this Article, the definitions given in Section 210.0 apply unless a different meaning plainly is required.

SECTION 212.1 Kidnapping.

A person is guilty of kidnapping if he unlawfully removes another from his place of residence or business, or a substantial distance from the vicinity where he is found, or if he unlawfully confines another for a substantial period in a place of isolation, with any of the following purposes:

(a) to hold for ransom or reward, or as a shield or hostage; or

(b) to facilitate commission of any felony or flight thereafter; or

(c) to inflict bodily injury on or to terrorize the victim or another; or

(d) to interfere with the performance of any governmental or political function.

Kidnapping is a felony of the first degree unless the actor voluntarily releases the victim alive and in a safe place prior to trial, in which case it is a felony of the second degree. A removal or confinement is unlawful within the meaning of this Section if it is accomplished by force, threat or deception, or, in the case of a person who is under the age of 14 or incompetent, if it is accomplished without the consent of a parent, guardian or other person responsible for general supervision of his welfare.

SECTION 212.2 Felonious Restraint.

A person commits a felony of the third degree if he knowingly:

(a) restrains another unlawfully in circumstances exposing him to risk of serious bodily injury; or

(b) holds another in a condition of involuntary servitude.

SECTION 212.3 False Imprisonment.

A person commits a misdemeanor if he knowingly restrains another unlawfully so as to interfere substantially with his liberty.

SECTION 212.4 Interference with Custody.

(1) *Custody of Children.* A person commits an offense if he knowingly or recklessly takes or entices any child under the age of 18 from the custody of its parent, guardian or other lawful custodian, when he has no privilege to do so. It is an affirmative defense that:

(a) the actor believed that his action was necessary to preserve the child from danger to its welfare; or

(b) the child, being at the time not less than 14 years old, was taken away at its own instigation without enticement and without purpose to commit a criminal offense with or against the child.

Proof that the child was below the critical age gives rise to a presumption that the actor knew the child's age or acted in reckless disregard thereof. The offense is a misdemeanor unless the actor, not being a parent or person in equivalent relation to the child, acted with knowledge that his conduct would cause serious alarm for the child's safety, or in reckless disregard of a likelihood of causing such alarm, in which case the offense is a felony of the third degree.

(2) *Custody of Committed Persons.* A person is guilty of a misdemeanor if he knowingly or recklessly takes or entices any committed person away from lawful custody when he is not privileged to do so. "Committed person" means, in addition to anyone committed under judicial warrant, any orphan, neglected or delinquent child, mentally defective or insane person, or other dependent or incompetent person entrusted to another's custody by or through a recognized social agency or otherwise by authority of law.

SECTION 212.5. Criminal Coercion.

(1) *Offense Defined.* A person is guilty of criminal coercion if, with purpose unlawfully to restrict another's freedom of action to his detriment, he threatens to:

(a) commit any criminal offense; or

(b) accuse anyone of a criminal offense; or

(c) expose any secret tending to subject any person to hatred, contempt or ridicule, or to impair his credit or business repute; or

(d) take or withhold action as an official, or cause an official to take or withhold action.

It is an affirmative defense to prosecution based on paragraphs (b), (c) or (d) that the actor believed the accusation or secret to be true or the proposed official action justified and that his purpose was limited to compelling the other to behave in a way reasonably related to the circumstances which were the subject of the accusation, exposure or proposed official action, as by desisting from further misbehavior, making good a wrong done, refraining from taking any action or responsibility for which the actor believes the other disqualified.

(2) *Grading.* Criminal coercion is a misdemeanor unless the threat is to commit a felony or the actor's purpose is felonious, in which cases the offense is a felony of the third degree.

ARTICLE 213. SEXUAL OFFENSES

SECTION 213.0. Definitions.

In this Article, unless a different meaning plainly is required:

criminal law: that body of rules and regulations that defines and specifies punishments for offenses of a public nature or for wrongs committed against the state or society; also called **penal law.**

criminal liability: the degree of blameworthiness assigned to a defendant by a criminal court and the concomitant extent to which the defendant is subject to penalties prescribed by the criminal law.

criminal mischief: the intentional or knowing damage or destruction of the tangible property of another.

criminal negligence: (1) behavior in which a person fails to reasonably perceive substantial and unjustifiable risks of dangerous consequences; (2) negligence of such a nature and to such a degree that it is punishable as a crime; or (3) flagrant and reckless disregard for the safety of others, or willful indifference to the safety and welfare of others.

criminal sexual conduct: a gender-neutral term that is applied today to a wide variety of sex offenses, including rape, sodomy, criminal sexual conduct with children, and deviate sexual behavior.

criminal simulation: the making of a false document or object that does not have any apparent legal significance.

criminal solicitation: the encouraging, requesting, or commanding of another person to commit a crime.

criminal syndicalism: advocating the use of unlawful acts as a means of accomplishing a change in industrial ownership or to control political change.[11]

criminal trespass: the entering or remaining on the property or in the building of another when entry was forbidden or, having received notice to depart, failing to do so.

criminalize: to make criminal. To declare an act or omission to be criminal or in violation of a law making it so.

criminally negligent homicide: homicide that results from criminal negligence.

culpable ignorance: the failure to exercise ordinary care to acquire knowledge of the law or of facts, which may result in criminal liability.

cybercrime: crime that employs computer technology as central to its commission, which could not occur without such technology. Another word for **computer crime.**

dangerous proximity test: a test for assessing attempts, under which a person is guilty of an attempt when his or her conduct comes dangerously close to success.

deadly force: force likely to cause death or great bodily harm.

defense: evidence and arguments offered by a defendant and his or her attorney(s) to show why that person should not be held liable for a criminal charge.

---

[11]California Penal Code, Sections 11400–01.

degree: the level of seriousness of an offense.

depraved heart murder: (1) unjustifiable conduct that is extremely negligent and results in the death of a human being, or (2) the killing of a human being with extreme atrocity.

designer drugs: chemical substances that have a potential for abuse similar to or greater than that for controlled substances, are designed to produce a desired pharmacological effect, and produced to evade the controlling statutory provisions.

determinate sentencing (also **presumptive** or **fixed sentencing**): a model for criminal punishment that sets one particular punishment, or length of sentence, for each specific type of crime. Under the model, for example, all offenders convicted of the same degree of burglary would be sentenced to the same length of time behind bars.

deterrence: a goal of criminal sentencing that seeks to prevent others from committing crimes similar to the one for which an offender is being sentenced.

deviate sexual intercourse: any contact between any part of the genitals of one person and the mouth or anus of another.

diminished capacity, also **diminished responsibility:** a defense based on claims of a mental condition, which may be insufficient to exonerate a defendant of guilt but that may be relevant to specific mental elements of certain crimes or degrees of crime.

disorderly conduct: specific, purposeful, and unlawful behavior that tends to cause public inconvenience, annoyance, or alarm.

distinguish: to argue or to find that a rule established by an earlier appellate court decision does apply to a case currently under consideration even though an apparent similarity exists between the cases.

disturbance of public assembly: a crime that occurs when any person(s) act(s) unlawfully at a public gathering collected for a lawful purpose in such a way as to purposefully disturb the gathering.

driving under the influence (DUI): unlawfully operating a motor vehicle while under the influence of alcohol or drugs. See also **driving while intoxicated** (DWI).

driving while intoxicated (DWI): unlawfully operating a motor vehicle while under the influence of alcohol. See also **driving under the influence** (DUI).

drug: a generic term applicable to a wide variety of substances having any physical or psychotropic effect on the human body.

DSM-IV: The fourth edition of the *Diagnostic and Statistical Manual of Mental Disorders,*[12] published by the American Psychiatric Association. The DSM-IV lists twelve major categories of mental disorder.

---

[12]American Psychiatric Association, *Diagnostic and Statistical Manual of Mental Disorders,* 4th ed. (Washington, D.C.: American Psychiatric Association, 1994).

due process of law: those procedures that effectively guarantee individual rights in the face of criminal prosecution; the due course of legal proceedings according to the rules and forms that have been established for the protection of private rights; formal adherence to fundamental rules for fair and orderly legal proceedings.

duress: or **compulsion,** a condition under which one is forced to act against one's will.

Durham **Rule:** also known as the **product rule,** holds that an accused is not criminally responsible if his or her unlawful act was the product of mental disease or mental defect.

effective consent: also termed **legal consent,** it is consent that has been obtained in a legal manner.

elements of crime: (1) the basic components of crime; (2) in a specific crime, the essential features of that crime as specified by law or statute.

embezzlement: the misappropriation of property already in possession of the defendant. Also, the unlawful conversion of the personal property of another, by a person to whom it has been entrusted by (or for) its rightful owner.

entrapment: an improper or illegal inducement to crime by agents of enforcement. Also, a defense that may be raised when such inducements occur.

equity: a sentencing principle, based on concerns with social equality, which holds that similar crimes should be punished with the same degree of severity, regardless of the social or personal characteristics of offenders.

escape: the unlawful leaving of official custody or confinement without permission, or the failure to return to custody or confinement following an official temporary leave.

espionage: the unlawful act of spying for a foreign government.

excusable homicide: killing in a manner that the criminal law does not prohibit. Also, homicide that may involve some fault, but which is not criminal homicide.

excuses: a category of legal defenses in which the defendant claims that some personal condition or circumstance at the time of the act was such that he or she should not be held accountable under the criminal law.

execution of public duty defense: a defense to a criminal charge (such as assault), which is often codified and which precludes the possibility of police officers and other public employees from being prosecuted when lawfully exercising their authority.

express consent: verbally expressed willingness to engage in a specified activity.

extortion: the taking of personal property by threat of future harm.

false arrest: see **false imprisonment.**

false imprisonment: the unlawful restraint of another person's liberty. Also, the unlawful detention of a person without his or her consent. Sometimes called **false arrest.**

false pretenses: knowingly and unlawfully obtaining title to, and possession of, the lawful property of another by means of deception, and with intent to defraud. Also known as **obtaining property by false pretenses.**

fellatio: oral stimulation of the penis.

felony: a serious crime, generally one punishable by death or by incarceration in a state or federal prison facility as opposed to a jail.

felony murder rule: a rule that establishes murder liability for a defendant if another person dies during the commission of certain felonies.

fighting words: words which, by their very utterance, inflict injury or tend to incite an immediate breach of the peace.

first-degree murder: any willful, deliberate, and premeditated killing.

fixtures: items that are permanently affixed to the land.

fleeing felon rule: a now-defunct law enforcement practice that permitted officers to shoot a suspected felon who attempted to flee from a lawful arrest.

forcible rape: rape that is accomplished against a person's will by means of force, violence, duress, menace, or fear of immediate and unlawful bodily injury to the victim.

forfeiture: an enforcement strategy supported by federal statutes and some state laws, which authorizes judges to seize "all monies, negotiable instruments, securities, or other things of value furnished or intended to be furnished by any person in exchange for a controlled substance . . . (and) all proceeds traceable to such an exchange."[13]

forgery: the making of a false written instrument or the material alteration of an existing genuine written instrument.

fornication: voluntary sexual intercourse between two persons, one of whom is unmarried.

gambling: the wagering of money, or of some other thing of value, on the outcome or occurrence of an event.

general deterrence: a goal of criminal sentencing that seeks to prevent others from committing crimes similar to the one for which a particular offender is being sentenced by making an example of the person sentenced.

general intent: that form of intent that can be assumed from the defendant's behavior. General intent refers to an actor's physical conduct.

general intent crimes: those particular forms of voluntary behavior that are prohibited by law.

Golden Age of the Victim: an historical epoch during which victims had well-recognized rights, including a personal say in imposing punishments on apprehended offenders.

gross negligence: conscious disregard of one's duties, resulting in injury or damage to another.

---

[13]21 U.S.C. §881 (a)(6).

guilty but mentally ill (GBMI): equivalent to a finding of "guilty," a GBMI verdict establishes that "the defendant, although mentally ill, was sufficiently in possession of his faculties to be morally blameworthy for his acts."[14]

habeas corpus: literally, "you have the body"; a writ challenging the legality of incarceration; or a writ ordering a prisoner to be brought before a court to determine the legality of the prisoner's detention.

habitual offender: a person sentenced under the provisions of a statute declaring that persons convicted of a given offense and shown to have previously been convicted of another specified offense(s) shall receive a more severe penalty than that for the current offense alone.

harm: also **resulting harm.** Loss, disadvantage, or injury or anything so regarded by the person affected, including loss, disadvantage, or injury to any other person in whose welfare he or she is interested.

hate crimes: those crimes in which the expression of hatred or bigotry toward minorities plays a central role.

hidden costs of crime: the intangible impact of crime on victims, including such difficult to measure aspects of the victimization experience as pain, suffering, and decreased quality of life.

home confinement: house arrest. Individuals ordered confined in their homes are sometimes monitored electronically to be sure they do not leave during the hours of confinement (absence from the home during working hours is often permitted).

homicide: the killing of a human being by the act, procurement, or omission of another human being.

identity theft: the unauthorized use of another individual's personal identity to fraudulently obtain money, goods, or services, to avoid the payment of debt, or to avoid criminal prosecution.

ignorance of fact: lack of knowledge of some fact relating to the subject matter at hand.

ignorance of the law: a lack of knowledge of the law or of the existence of a law relevant to a situation at hand.

impossibility: a defense to a charge of attempted criminal activity that claims either that the defendant could not have factually or legally committed the envisioned offense even if he or she had been able to carry through the attempt to do so. It is, for example, factually impossible to kill someone who is already dead.

incapacitation: the use of imprisonment or other means to reduce the likelihood that an offender will be capable of committing future offenses.

incest: unlawful sexual intercourse with a relative through blood or marriage.

---

[14]Ira Mickenberg, "A Pleasant Surprise: The Guilty But Mentally Ill Verdict Has Both Succeeded in Its Own Right and Successfully Preserved the Traditional Role of the Insanity Defense," *University of Cincinnati Law Review,* Vol. 55 (1987), pp. 943, 987–991.

inchoate crime: an unfinished crime that generally leads to another crime. Also, crimes that consist of actions that are steps toward another offense. Sometimes referred to as an anticipatory offense.

inciting a riot: the use of words or other means intended and calculated to provoke a riot.

incompetent to stand trial: a finding by a court that, as a result of a mental illness, defect, or disability, a defendant is unable to understand the nature and object of the proceeding against him or her or to assist in the preparation of his or her own defense.

indecent exposure: public indecency. Specifically, the willful exposure of the private parts of one person to the sight of another person in a public place with the intent to arouse or gratify sexual desires. Also, the commission, in a place accessible to the public, of (1) an act of sexual intercourse; (2) a lewd exposure of the sexual organs; (3) a lewd appearance in a state of partial or complete nudity; or (4) a lewd caress or indecent fondling of the body of another person.

indeterminate sentencing: a model of criminal punishment that builds on the use of general and relatively unspecific sentences (such as a term of imprisonment of "from one to ten years").

infancy: also **immaturity,** a defense that makes the claim that certain individuals should not be held criminally responsible for their activities by virtue of youth.

infraction: sometimes called a **summary offense;** a violation of a state statute or local ordinance punishable by a fine or other penalty, but not by incarceration.

inherently dangerous: an act or course of behavior (usually a felony), which, by its very nature, is likely to result in death or serious bodily harm to either the person involved in the behavior or to someone else.

insanity: an affirmative defense to a criminal charge; a social and legal term (rather than a medical one) that refers to "a condition which renders the affected person unfit to enjoy liberty of action because of the unreliability of his behavior with concomitant danger to himself and others."[15] Also, a finding by a court of law.

Insanity Defense Reform Act (IDRA): Part of the 1984 Crime Control and Prevention Act, the IRDA mandated a comprehensive overhaul of the insanity defense as it operated in the federal courts, making insanity an affirmative defense to be proved by the defendant by clear and convincing evidence and creating a special verdict of "not guilty by reason of insanity."

intangible property: property that has no intrinsic value but that represents something of value. Intangible personal property may include documents, deeds, records of ownership, promissory notes, stock certificates, computer software, and intellectual property.

intellectual property: a form of creative endeavor that can be protected through patent, copyright, trademark, or other legal means. Intellectual property includes proprietary knowledge, trade secrets, confidentiality

---

[15]Joseph R. Nolan and Jacqueline M. Nolan-Haley, *Black's Law Dictionary: Definitions of the Terms and Phrases of American and English Jurisprudence, Ancient and Modern,* 6th ed. (St. Paul, MN: West Publishing Co., 1990).

agreements, know-how, ideas, inventions, creations, technologies, processes, works of art and literature, and scientific discoveries or improvements.

intensive supervision: a form of probation supervision involving frequent face-to-face contacts between the probationary client and probation officers.

intentional action: that action which is undertaken volitionally to achieve some goal.

intermediate sanctions: also **alternative sanctions;** the use of split sentencing, shock probation and parole, home confinement, shock incarceration, and community service in lieu of other, more traditional sanctions, such as imprisonment and fines. Intermediate sanctions are becoming increasingly popular as prisons become more crowded.

involuntary intoxication: intoxication that is not willful.

involuntary manslaughter: an unintentional killing for which criminal liability is imposed, but which does not constitute murder. Also, the unintentional killing of a person during the commission of a lesser unlawful act, or the killing of someone during the commission of a lawful act, which nevertheless results in an unlawful death.

irresistible impulse test: a test for insanity that evaluates defense claims that, at the time the crime was committed, a mental disease or disorder prevented the defendant from controlling his or her behavior in keeping with the requirements of the law.

jural postulates: rules that, according to former Harvard Law School dean Roscoe Pound, reflect shared needs common to the members of society and form the basis of all law in advanced societies.

jurisdiction: (1) the geographical district or subject matter over which the authority of a government body, especially a court, extends; (2) the authority of a court to hear and decide an action or lawsuit.

jurisprudence: the philosophy of law; the science and study of the law.

jury instructions: directions given by a judge to a jury concerning the law of the case.

just deserts: a model of criminal sentencing that holds that criminal offenders deserve the punishment they receive at the hands of the state and suggests that punishments should be appropriate to the type and severity of crime committed.

justifiable homicide: (1) homicide which is permitted under the law; (2) a killing justified for the good of society; (3) the killing of another in self-defense when danger of death or serious bodily harm exists; (4) the killing of a person according to one's duties or out of necessity but without blame.

justifications: a category of legal defenses in which the defendant admits committing the act in question but claims it was necessary in order to avoid some greater evil.

juvenile offender: a child who violates the criminal law, or who commits a status offense. Also, a person subject to juvenile court proceedings because a statutorily defined event caused by the person was alleged to have occurred while his or her age was below the statutorily specified age limit of original jurisdiction of a juvenile court.

keeping a place of prostitution: knowingly granting or permitting the use of a place for the purpose of prostitution.

kidnapping: the unlawful and forcible removal of a person from his or her residence or place of business. Also, an aggravated form of false imprisonment that is accompanied by either a moving or secreting of the victim.

knowing behavior: action undertaken with awareness.

knowing possession: possession with awareness (of what one possesses).

larceny: the trespassory or wrongful taking and carrying away (asportation) of the personal property of another with intent to steal. Also, the wrongful taking of the personal property of another, with intent to steal.

lascivious: that which is obscene or lewd, or which tends to cause lust.

last act test: in the crime of attempt, a test that asks whether the accused had taken the last step or act toward commission of the offense and had performed all that he or she intended to do and was able to do in an attempt to commit the crime, but for some reason, the crime was not completed.

law: that which is laid down, ordained, or established . . . a body of rules of action or conduct prescribed by controlling authority, and having binding *legal* force.[16]

legal cause: a legally recognizable cause. The type of cause that is required to be demonstrated in court in order to hold an individual criminally liable for causing harm.

legal consent: see **effective consent.**

lewd: obscene. Also, obscene behavior **(lewdness).**

loitering: the act of delaying or lingering or to idle about without lawful business for being present.

looting: burglary committed within an affected geographical area during an officially declared state of emergency or during a local emergency resulting from an earthquake, fire, flood, riot, or other natural or man-made disaster.

lynching: the taking, by means of riot, of any person from the lawful custody of any peace officer.

***M'Naughten* Rule:** a rule for determining insanity that asks whether the defendant knew what he or she was doing, or whether he or she knew that what he or she was doing was wrong.

mala in se: acts that are regarded, by tradition and convention, as wrong in themselves.

mala prohibita: acts that are considered "wrongs" only because there is a law against them.

malice: a legal term that refers to the intentional doing of a wrongful act without just cause or legal excuse. In cases of homicide, the term means "an intention to kill."

---

[16]Ibid. Italics added.

malice aforethought: an "unjustifiable, inexcusable, and unmitigated person-endangering state of mind."[17]

manslaughter: the unlawful killing of a human being without malice. Manslaughter differs from murder in that malice and premeditation are lacking. See also **voluntary manslaughter** and **involuntary manslaughter.**

mayhem: intentional infliction of injury on another that causes the removal of, seriously disfigures, or impairs the function of a member or organ of the body.

mens rea: the specific mental state operative in the defendant at the time of a crime; a guilty mind.

mere possession: possession in which one may or may not be aware of what he or she possesses.

mere preparation: an act or omission that may be part of a series of acts or omissions constituting a course of conduct planned to culminate in the commission of a crime, but which fails to meet the requirements for a **substantial step.** Also, preparatory actions or steps taken toward the completion of a crime that are remote from the actual commission of the crime.

misconduct in office: acts that a public office holder (1) has no right to perform, (2) performs improperly, or (3) fails to perform in the face of an affirmative duty to act.

misdemeanor: a minor crime; an offense punishable by incarceration, usually in a local confinement facility, for a period of which the upper limit is prescribed by statute in a given jurisdiction, typically limited to a year or less.

misprision of felony: the failure to report a known crime; concealment of a crime.

misprision of treason: the concealment or nondisclosure of the known treason of another.

mistake of fact: misinterpretation, misunderstanding, or forgetfulness of a fact relating to the subject matter at hand; belief in the existence of a thing or condition that does not exist.

mistake of law: a misunderstanding or misinterpretation of the law relevant to a situation at hand.

mitigating factors: circumstances surrounding the commission of a crime that do not in law justify or excuse the act, but which in fairness may be considered as reducing the blameworthiness of the defendant.[18] Also, those elements of an offense or of an offender's background that could result in a lesser sentence under the determinate sentencing model than would otherwise be called for by sentencing guidelines.

mixed sentence: one that requires that a convicted offender serve weekends (or other specified periods of time) in a confinement facility (usually a jail), while undergoing probation supervision in the community.

---

[17]Rollin M. Perkins and Ronald N. Boyce, *Criminal Law,* 3rd ed. (Mineola, NY: Foundation Press, 1982), p. 75.
[18]Ibid, p. 16.

Model Penal Code: a model code of criminal laws intended to standardize general provisions of criminal liability, sentencing, defenses, and the definitions of specific crimes between and among the states. The Model Penal Code was developed by the American Law Institute.

moral enterprise: the activities of moral crusaders through which new laws are created.

moral entrepreneurs: those who work to enact desired legislation.

morals: ethical principles, or principles meant to guide human conduct and behavior; principles or standards of right and wrong.

morals offenses: a category of unlawful behavior that was originally created to protect the family and related social institutions. Included are crimes such as lewdness, indecency, sodomy, and other sex-related offenses, such as seduction, fornication, adultery, bigamy, pornography, obscenity, cohabitation, and prostitution.

mores: unwritten but generally known rules that govern serious violations of the social code.

motive: a person's reason for committing a crime.

murder: the unlawful killing of a human being, carried out with malice or planned in advance. According to common law, the killing of one human being by another with malice aforethought. See also **criminal homicide.**

National Crime Victimization Survey (NCVS): a survey that is conducted annually by the Bureau of Justice Statistics, which provides data on surveyed households that report they were affected by crime.

natural law: rules of conduct inherent in human nature and in the natural order that are thought to be knowable through intuition, inspiration, and the exercise of reason, without the need for reference to man-made laws.

NCVC: an acronym for the National Victims Center; now called the National Center for Victims of Crime.

necessity: a defense to a criminal charge that claims that it was necessary to commit some unlawful act in order to prevent or to avoid a greater harm.

negligent homicide: the killing of a human being by criminal negligence, or by the failure to exercise reasonable, prudent care. Also, a criminal offense committed by one whose negligence is the direct and proximate cause of another's death.

norms: unwritten rules that underlie and are inherent in the fabric of society.

not guilty by reason of insanity (NGRI): one of a number of possible verdicts in a criminal trial where the defense of insanity is raised. Other possible verdicts include "guilty" and "not guilty."

NOVA: an acronym for the National Organization for Victim Assistance.

obscenity: "that which appeals to the prurient interest and lacks serious literary, artistic, political, or scientific value."[19]

---

[19] David R. Simon, *The American Standard Law Dictionary,* 1995 (via Cybernation online, http://www.e-legal.com).

obstruction of justice: an unlawful attempt to interfere with the administration of the courts, the judicial system, or law enforcement officers, or with the activities of those who seek justice in a court or whose duties involve the administration of justice.

omission to act: an intentional or unintentional failure to act, which may impose criminal liability if a duty to act under the circumstances is specified by law.

ordinary negligence: the want of ordinary care, or negligence that could have been avoided if one had exercised ordinary, reasonable, or proper care.

outrageous government conduct: a kind of entrapment defense based on an objective criterion involving "the belief that the methods employed on behalf of the Government to bring about conviction cannot be countenanced."[20]

OVC: an acronym for the federal Office for Victims of Crime, established under the 1984 Victims of Crime Act (**VOCA**).

pandering: soliciting a person to perform an act of prostitution.

Part I offenses: that group of offenses, also called **major offenses** or **index offenses,** for which the Uniform Crime Reports (UCR) publish counts of reported instances and which consist of murder, rape, robbery, aggravated assault, burglary, larceny, auto theft, and arson.

Part II offenses: a group of nineteen "lesser crimes" including forgery, fraud, embezzlement, vandalism, prostitution, drug abuse violations, etc., which are reported in the FBI's Uniform Crime Reports (UCR). Part II offenses are counted only in terms of arrests (rather than as reported crimes).

parties to crime: all persons who take part in the commission of a crime, including those who aid and abet, and who are therefore criminally liable for the offense.

penal law: see **criminal law.**

perfect self-defense: a claim of self-defense that meets all of the generally accepted legal conditions for such a claim to be valid. Where deadly force is used, perfect self-defense requires that, in light of the circumstances, the defendant reasonably believed it to be necessary to kill the decedent to avert imminent death or great bodily harm, and the defendant was not the initial aggressor and was not responsible for provoking the fatal confrontation.

perjury: the willful giving of false testimony under oath in a judicial proceeding. Also, false testimony given under any lawfully administered oath.

personal crime: also called **violent crime;** a crime committed against a person, including (according to the FBI's UCR program) murder, rape, aggravated assault, and robbery.

personal property: anything of value that is subject to ownership that is not land or fixtures.

---

[20]Perkins and Boyce, *Criminal Law,* p. 1167.

personal trespass by computer: an offense in which a person uses a computer or computer network without authority and with the intent to cause physical injury to an individual.

physical proximity test: a test traditionally used under common law to determine whether a person was guilty of attempted criminal activity. The physical proximity test requires that the accused has it within his or her power to complete the crime almost immediately.

pimping: aiding, abetting, counseling, or commanding another in the commission of prostitution, or the act of procuring a prostitute for another.

plea bargaining: the process of negotiating an agreement among defendant, prosecutor, and the court as to what an appropriate plea and associated sentence should be in a given case.

plurality requirement: the logical and legal requirement that a conspiracy involves two or more parties.

police power: the authority of a state to enact and enforce a criminal statute.

polygamy: having more than one wife or husband at the same time.

pornography: "the depiction of sexual behavior in such a way as to excite the viewer sexually."[21]

post-crime victimization: also **secondary victimization;** problems that follow from initial victimization, such as the loss of employment, inability to pay medical bills, the insensitivity of family members, and others.

precursor chemicals: chemicals that may be used in the manufacture of a controlled substance.

premeditated murder: murder that was planned in advance (however briefly) and willfully carried out.

premeditation: the act of deliberating or meditating on, or planning, a course of action (i.e., a crime). For purposes of the criminal law, premeditation requires the opportunity for reflection between the time the intent to act is formed and the act is committed.

preponderance of the evidence: a standard for determining legal liability, which requires a probability of just over 50 percent that the defendant did what is claimed.

present ability: as used in assault statutes, a term meaning that the person attempting assault is physically capable of immediately carrying it out.

principal in the first degree: a person whose acts directly result in the criminal misconduct in question.

principal in the second degree: any person who was present at the crime scene and who aided, abetted, counseled, or encouraged the principal.

principle of legality: an axiom that holds that behavior cannot be criminal if no law exists that defines it as such.

---

[21]William Kornblum and Joseph Julian, *Social Problems*, 8th ed. (Upper Saddle River, NJ: Prentice Hall, 1995), p. 115.

prize fighting: unlawful public fighting undertaken for the purpose of winning an award or a prize.

probation: a sentence of imprisonment that is suspended. Also, the conditional freedom granted by a judicial officer to an adjudicated or adjudged adult or juvenile offender, as long as the person meets certain conditions of behavior.

probative value: the worth of any evidence to prove or disprove the facts at issue.

procedural law: that aspect of the law that specifies the methods to be used in enforcing substantive law.

product rule: see *Durham* **Rule.**

promoting prostitution: the statutory offense of (1) owning, controlling, managing, supervising, or otherwise keeping a house of prostitution; (2) procuring a person for a house of prostitution; (3) encouraging, inducing, or otherwise purposely causing another to become or remain a prostitute; (4) soliciting a person to patronize a prostitute; (5) procuring a prostitute for another; or (6) transporting a person with the purpose of promoting that person's involvement in prostitution.[22]

property crime: a crime committed against property, including (according to the FBI's UCR program) burglary, larceny, auto theft, and arson.

proportionality: a sentencing principle that holds that the severity of sanctions should bear a direct relationship to the seriousness of the crime committed.

prostitution: "the offering or receiving of the body for sexual intercourse for hire [as well as] the offering or receiving of the body for indiscriminate sexual intercourse without hire."[23] Some states limit the crime of prostitution to sexual intercourse for hire.

proximate cause: the primary or moving cause that plays a substantial part in bringing about injury or damage. It may be a first cause that sets in motion a string of events whose ultimate outcome is reasonably foreseeable.

prurient interest: a morbid interest in sex; an obsession with lascivious and immoral matters.

psycholegal error: "the mistaken belief that if we identify a cause for conduct, including mental or physical disorders, then the conduct is necessarily excused."[24]

public drunkenness: the offense of being in a state of intoxication in a place accessible to the public.

public order offense: an act that is willfully and unlawfully committed and that disturbs public peace or tranquillity. Included are offenses such as fighting, breach of peace, disorderly conduct, vagrancy, loitering, unlawful assembly, public intoxication, obstructing public passage, and (illegally) carrying weapons.

---

[22]Model Penal Code, Section 251.2(2).

[23]General Statutes of North Carolina, 14-203.

[24]Stephen J. Morse, "The 'New Syndrome Excuse Syndrome,' " *Criminal Justice Ethics* (Winter/Spring 1995), p. 7.

rape: in common law, unlawful sexual intercourse with a female without her consent. Today, rape statutes in a number of jurisdictions encompass unlawful sexual intercourse between members of the same gender.

rape shield laws: statutes intended to protect victims of rape by limiting a defendant's in-court use of a victim's sexual history.

real property: land and fixtures.

reasonable doubt: (in legal proceedings) an actual and substantial doubt arising from the evidence, from the facts or circumstances shown by the evidence, or from the lack of evidence.[25] Also, that state of the case, which after the entire comparison and consideration of all the evidence, leaves the minds of the jurors in such a condition that they cannot say they feel an abiding conviction of the truth of the charge.[26]

reasonable doubt standard: that standard of proof necessary for conviction in criminal trials.

reasonable force: a degree of force that is appropriate in a given situation and is not excessive. The minimum degree of force necessary to protect oneself, one's property, a third party, or the property of another in the face of a substantial threat.

reasonable person: a person who acts with common sense and who has the mental capacity of an average, normal, sensible human being. The reasonable person criterion requires that the assumptions and ideas on which a defendant acted must have been reasonable, in that the circumstances as they appeared to the defendant would have created the same beliefs in the mind of an ordinary person.

reasonable provocation: see **adequate provocation** and **adequate cause.**

rebellion: "deliberate, organized resistance, by force and arms, to the laws or operations of the government, committed by a subject."[27]

receiving stolen property: (1) knowingly taking possession of or control over property that has been unlawfully stolen from another; (2) the receiving of stolen property, knowing that it has been stolen.

reckless behavior: activity that increases the risk of harm.

rehabilitation: the attempt to reform a criminal offender. Also, the state in which a reformed offender is said to be.

renunciation (abandonment): the voluntary and complete abandonment of the intent and purpose to commit a criminal offense. Renunciation (abandonment) is a defense to a charge of attempted criminal activity.

rescuing a prisoner: a crime that is committed when any person or persons rescues or attempts to rescue any person being held in lawful custody.

resisting arrest: the crime of obstructing or opposing a peace officer who is making an arrest.

---

[25] *Victor* v. *Nebraska*, 114 S. Ct. 1239, 127 L. Ed. 2d 583 (1994).

[26] As found in California Jury Instructions.

[27] *Crashley* v. *Press Publishing Company*, 74 App. Div. 118, 77 N.Y.S. 711.

restitution: a court requirement that an alleged or convicted offender pay money or provide services to the victim of the crime or provide services to the community.

restoration: a sentencing goal that seeks to make victims and the community "whole again."

restorative justice: a sentencing model that builds upon restitution and community participation in an attempt to make the victim "whole again."

retreat rule: a rule operative in many jurisdictions, which requires that a person being attacked retreat to avoid the necessity of using force against the attacker, if retreat can be accomplished with "complete safety."

retribution: the act of taking revenge on a criminal perpetrator. Also, the most punishment-oriented of all sentencing goals, and one that claims that we are justified in punishing because offenders deserve it.

RICO: an acronym for a section of the federal Organized Crime Control Act known as the Racketeer Influenced Corrupt Organizations provision. Some states have passed their own RICO-like statutes.

right of allocution: a statutory provision permitting crime victims to speak at the sentencing of convicted offenders. A federal right of allocution was established for victims of federal violent and sex crimes under the Violent Crime Control and Law Enforcement Act of 1994.

riot: a tumultuous disturbance of the peace by three or more persons assembled of their own authority.[28]

robbery: the unlawful taking of property that is in the immediate possession of another by force or threat of force. Also, larceny from a person by violence, intimidation, or by placing the person in fear.

rout: the preparatory stage of a riot.

rule of law: also called the **supremacy of law;** the maxim that an orderly society must be governed by established principles and known codes, which are applied uniformly and fairly to all of its members.

scienter: knowledge; guilty knowledge.

second-degree murder: depending on jurisdiction, either (1) murders committed during the perpetration or attempted perpetration of an enumerated felony, such as arson, rape, robbery, and burglary, or (2) all murder not classified by statute as first degree.

sedition: a crime that consists of a communication or agreement intended to defame the government or to incite treason.

selective incapacitation: a sentencing strategy that imprisons or otherwise removes from society a select group of offenders—especially those considered to be most dangerous.

self-defense: a defense to a criminal charge that is based on the recognition that a person has an inherent right to self-protection and that to reasonably

---

[28]Gilmer, *The Law Dictionary,* p. 293.

defend oneself from unlawful attack is a "natural" response to threatening situations.

sentencing: the process through which a sentencing authority imposes a lawful punishment or other sanction on a person convicted of violating the criminal law.

sexual assault: a statutory crime that combines all sexual offenses into one offense (often with various degrees). It is broader than the common law crime of rape.

sexual battery: the unlawful touching of an intimate part of another person against that person's will and for the purpose of sexual arousal, gratification, or abuse.

sexual contact: any touching of the anus, breast, or any part of the genitals of another person with intent to arouse or gratify the sexual desire of any person.

shock incarceration: a sentencing option that makes use of "boot camp"–type prisons in order to impress on convicted offenders the realities of prison life.

shock probation: the practice of sentencing offenders to prison, allowing them to apply for probationary release, and enacting such release in surprise fashion. Offenders who receive shock probation may not be aware of the fact that they will be released on probation and may expect to spend a much longer time behind bars.

simple assault: see **assault.**

social debt: a sentencing principle that objectively counts an offender's criminal history in sentencing decisions.

sodomy: oral or anal copulation between persons of the same or different gender, or between a human being and an animal.

solicitation: see **criminal solicitation.**

soliciting prostitution: the act of asking, enticing, or requesting another to commit the crime of prostitution.

"Son of Sam" laws: also known as **notoriety-for-profit laws;** statutes that provide support for the rights of victims by denying convicted offenders the opportunity to further capitalize on their crimes. "Son of Sam" laws set the stage for civil action against infamous offenders who might otherwise profit from the sale of their "story."

specific deterrence: a goal of criminal sentencing that seeks to prevent a particular offender from engaging in repeat criminality.

specific intent: a thoughtful, conscious intention to perform a specific act to achieve a particular result.

specific intent crimes: literally, crimes that require a specific intent. Generally speaking, specific intent crimes involve a secondary purpose.

split sentence: a sentence explicitly requiring the convicted person to serve a period of confinement in a local, state, or federal facility followed by a period of probation.

spousal rape: the rape of one's spouse.

stalking: the intentional frightening of another through following, harassing, annoying, tormenting, or terrorizing activities.

stare decisis: the legal principle that requires that courts be bound by their own earlier decisions and by those of higher courts having jurisdiction over them regarding subsequent cases on similar issues of law and fact. The term literally means "standing by decided matters."

status: a person's state of being.

statutory law: law in the form of statutes or formal written strictures, made by a legislature or governing body with the power to make law.

statutory rape: sexual intercourse, whether consensual or not, with a person under the "age of consent," as specified by statute.

strict liability: liability without fault or intention. Strict liability offenses do not require *mens rea.*

strict liability crimes: violations of law for which one may incur criminal liability without fault or intention.

subornation of perjury: unlawfully procuring another to commit perjury.

substantial capacity test: a test developed by the American Law Institute and embodied in the Model Penal Code. The test holds that "a person is not responsible for criminal conduct if at the time of such conduct as a result of mental disease or defect he lacks substantial capacity either to appreciate the criminality [wrongfulness] of his conduct or to conform his conduct to the requirements of the law."[29]

substantial step: significant activity undertaken in furtherance of some goal. An act or omission that is a significant part of a series of acts or omissions constituting a course of conduct planned to culminate in the commission of a crime. Also, an important or essential step toward the commission of a crime that is considered as sufficient to constitute the crime of criminal attempt. A substantial step is conduct that is strongly corroborative of the actor's criminal purpose. According to one court, a substantial step is "behavior of such a nature that a reasonable observer, viewing it in context, could conclude beyond a reasonable doubt that it was undertaken in accordance with a design to violate the statute."

substantive criminal law: that part of the law that defines crimes and specifies punishments.

substantive law: that part of the law that creates and defines fundamental rights and duties.

sudden passion: (as in instances of **voluntary manslaughter**) passion directly caused by and rising out of provocation by the victim or of another acting with the victim, including the understanding that the passion arises at the time of the killing and is not solely the result of former provocation.

summary offense: see **infraction.**

---

[29]Model Penal Code, Section 4.01(1).

syndrome: "a complex of signs and symptoms presenting a clinical picture of a disease or disorder."[30]

syndrome-based defense: a defense predicated on, or substantially enhanced by, the acceptability of syndrome-related claims.

tangible property: property that has physical form and is capable of being touched, such as land, goods, jewelry, furniture, and so forth. Movable property that can be taken and carried away.

theft: a general term embracing a wide variety of misconduct by which a person is unlawfully deprived of his or her property.

theft of computer services: an offense in which a person willfully uses a computer or computer network with intent to obtain computer services without authority.

three-strikes legislation: statutory provisions that mandate lengthy prison terms for criminal offenders convicted of a third violent crime or felony.

tort: a private or civil wrong or injury. The "unlawful violation of a private legal right other than a mere breach of contract, express or implied."[31]

tort-feasor: an individual, business, or other legally recognized entity that commits a tort.

transferred intent: a legal construction by which an unintended act that results from intentional action undertaken in the commission of a crime may also be illegal.

treason: violation of allegiance toward one's country or sovereign, esp., the betrayal of one's own country by waging war against it or by consciously and purposely acting to aid its enemies.[32]

trespassory taking: for purposes of crimes of theft, a taking without the consent of the victim.

truth in sentencing: a close correspondence between the sentence imposed on those sent to prison and the time actually served prior to prison release.[33]

Uniform Crime Reports (UCR): a summation of crime statistics tallied annually by the Federal Bureau of Investigation (FBI), consisting primarily of data on crimes reported to the police and of arrests.

Uniform Determination of Death Act (UDDA): a standard supported by the American Medical Association, the American Bar Association, and by the National Conference of Commissioners on Uniform State Laws that provides that "an individual who has sustained either (1) irreversible cessation of circulatory and respiratory functions, or (2) irreversible cessation of all functions of the entire brain, including the brain stem, is dead."[34] The

---

[30]*Barron's Medical Dictionary for the Non-Professional.*

[31]General Statutes of Georgia, 51-1-1.

[32]*The American Heritage Dictionary and Electronic Thesaurus* (New York: Houghton Mifflin, 1987).

[33]Lawrence A. Greenfeld, "Prison Sentences and Time Served for Violence," *Bureau of Justice Statistics Selected Findings,* No. 4, April 1995.

[34]Uniform Determination of Death Act, Uniform Law Ann., Chapter 12 (1981 Supp.) p. 187.

UDDA provides a model for legislation and has been adopted in various forms by many states.

unlawful assembly: a gathering of three or more persons for the purposes of doing an unlawful act or for the purpose of doing a lawful act in a violent, boisterous, or tumultuous manner.

uttering: the offering, passing, or attempted passing of a forged instrument with knowledge that the document is false and with intent to defraud.

vagrancy: under common law, the act of going about from place to place by a person without visible means of support, who was idle, and who, though able to work for his or her maintenance, refused to do so, but lived without labor or on the charity of others.[35]

vagrant: also, **vagabond,** "a wanderer; an idle person who, being able to maintain himself by lawful labor, either refuses to work or resorts to unlawful practices, e.g., begging, to gain a living."[36]

vehicular homicide: the killing of a human being by the operation of a motor vehicle by another in a reckless manner likely to cause the death of, or great bodily harm to, another.

venue: the geographical location or place where a case may be prosecuted.

vicarious liability: the criminal liability of one party for the criminal acts of another party.

victim: any individual against whom an offense has been committed. Or, for certain procedural purposes, a parent or legal guardian if the victim is below the age of eighteen years or is incompetent. Also, one or more family members or relatives designated by the court if the victim is deceased or incapacitated.

victim impact statement: the in-court use of victim- or survivor-supplied information by sentencing authorities wishing to make an informed sentencing decision. Also, a written document that describes the losses, suffering, and trauma experienced by the crime victim or by the victim's survivors. In jurisdictions where victim impact statements are used, judges are expected to consider them in arriving at an appropriate sentence for the offender.

victimless crime: an offense committed against the social values and interests represented in and protected by the criminal law *and* in which parties to the offense willingly participate.

victims' rights: the fundamental right of victims to be equitably represented throughout the criminal justice process.

victim/witness assistance programs: service organizations that work to provide comfort and assistance to victims of crime and to witnesses.

VOCA: an acronym for the 1984 Victims of Crime Act.

---

[35] Adapted from Nolan and Nolan-Haley, *Black's Law Dictionary,* p. 1549.

[36] Gilmer, *The Law Dictionary,* p. 334.

void for vagueness: a constitutional principle that refers to a statute defining a crime that is so unclear that a reasonable person of at least average intelligence could not determine what the law purports to command or prohibit.

voluntary intoxication: willful intoxication; intoxication that is the result of personal choice. Voluntary intoxication includes the voluntary ingestion, injection, or taking by any other means of any intoxicating liquor, drug, or other substance.

voluntary manslaughter: the unlawful killing of a human being, without malice, which is done intentionally upon a sudden quarrel or in the heat of passion. Also, a killing committed without lawful justification, wherein the defendant acted under a sudden and intense passion resulting from adequate provocation.

Wharton's Rule: a rule applicable to conspiracy cases that holds that where the targeted crime by its very nature takes more than one person to commit, then there can be no conspiracy when no more than the number of persons required to commit the offense participate in it.

year and a day rule: a common law requirement that homicide prosecutions could not take place if the victim did not die within a year and a day from the time that the fatal act occurred.

Table of Cases

Subject Index

Amnesty International—Death Penalty Information
http://www.derechos.org/dp
This site lists all the countries that currently retain the death penalty.

Cornell Law School Death Penalty Project
http://www.lawschool.cornell.edu/lawlibrary/death/default.htm
The project, which began in 1997, is composed of several elements including a capital punishment clinic, a commitment to provide continuing education programs for capital defense attorneys, and the active collection and study of data in this field.

Death Penalty Information Center (DPIC)
http://www.deathpenaltyinfo.org
This site contains a wealth of information on the death penalty, including current law, statistics, historical information, and more.

The Sentencing Project
http://www.sentencingproject.org
The Sentencing Project is an independent source of criminal justice policy analysis, data, and program information for the public and policy makers.

U.S. Sentencing Commission
http://www.ussc.gov
Home page of the U.S. Sentencing Commission, whose guidelines provide federal judges with clear direction for the sentencing of defendants in their courts.

Law School Information

American Bar Association Approved Law Schools
http://www.abanet.org/legaled/approvedlawschools/approved.html
Includes 184 institutions searchable by state and via a clickable map.

Association of American Law Schools
http://www.aals.org/members.html
Provides a list of 162 member schools.

New York University School of Law
http://www.law.nyu.edu/library/lawsch.html
A directory of law school directories, including some of those listed here.

The Open Directory Project Law Schools List
http://dmoz.org/Reference/Education/Colleges_and_Universities/Post_Graduate_Education/Law_School/Law_Schools
Lists most law schools in the United States.

Rominger Legal Services Law School Directory
http://www.romingerlegal.com/lawschools.htm
An alphabetical listing of law schools. A state-by-state directory is also provided.

Washburn University School of Law, Law School Directory
http://www.washlaw.edu/lawschools.html
A thorough listing of American and foreign law schools.

The Washington, D.C., Regional Legal Directory
http://www.dclegal.com/us_law_schools.htm
Provides a nation-wide listing of law schools.

Law-Related Job Sites

Association of Trial Lawyers of America (ATLA)
http://www.atlanet.org/jobbank/openings.ht
The job bank at ATLA provides hundreds of listings at any one time.

Counsel Net
http://www.counsel.net/jobs
The career center at Counsel Net contains a series of free job posting boards for law firms and other businesses. An e-mail alert system, called JobAlert, notifies job hunters of legal jobs as they become available.

Emplawyer
http://www.emplawyernet.com
The site offers free career planning and contains a list of almost 6,000 law-related job openings.

Federal Judiciary Employment Opportunities
http://www.uscourts.gov/employment/opportunity.html
Includes information on a wide variety of federal government jobs in law-related fields.

Job Links for Lawyers
http://home.sprynet.com/~ear2ground
Not just for lawyers, this site provides jobs information for attorneys as well as law librarians, anyone in legal publishing, and those wanting to work in academia.

Law Info
http://jobs.lawinfo.com
The jobs page at Law Info allows attorneys and anyone involved with the law to post resumes, and it also provides a list of jobs offered.

Lawyer's Weekly
http://www.lawyersweeklyjobs.com
The careers section of *Lawyer's Weekly* online includes job postings for attorneys, paralegals, legal secretaries, and other legal fields and specialties.

Law-Related Professional Associations

American Bar Association (ABA)

http://www.abanet.org

The largest and most influential national association of attorneys. Information about the positions taken by the association and model rules of ethics are available at this site.

American Bar Association's Criminal Justice Section

http://www.abanet.org/crimjust/home.html

The mission of the ABA's Criminal Justice Section is to improve the criminal justice system. The site offers publications and press releases.

Association of Federal Defense Attorneys

http://www.afda.org

Members' Web site (though visitors are allowed) for attorneys that represent defendants in federal criminal actions.

Association of Trial Lawyers of America (ATLA)

http://www.atlanet.org

Web site of the largest national association of attorneys involved in criminal defense and personal injury litigation.

National Association of Criminal Defense Lawyers (NACDL)

http://www.criminaljustice.org

The preeminent organization in the United States advancing the mission of the nation's criminal defense lawyers to ensure justice and due process for persons accused of crime or other misconduct.

National Association of Sentencing Advocates (NASA)

http://www.sentencingproject.org/nasa

A professional membership organization of sentencing advocates and defense-based mitigation specialists.

National District Attorneys Association (NDAA)

http://www.ndaa.org

NDAA offers local prosecutors the opportunity to network with fellow prosecutors throughout the nation to enhance their knowledge and skills.

National Lawyers Association (NLA)

http://www.nla.org

A national bar association organized to improve the image of the legal profession, to advance legal institutions and respect for the law, and to educate the public on such matters.

Victims' Resources on the World Wide Web

Center for the Study of Crime Victims' Rights, Remedies, and Resources

http://www.newhaven.edu/UNH/ShowcaseSites/CenterStudyCrimeVictims.html

The School of Public Safety and Professional Studies of the University of New Haven is home to the Center for the Study of Crime Victims' Rights, Remedies, and Resources. The center assists crime victims through educational, training, and technical assistance.

National Center for Victims of Crime (formerly the National Victim Center)

http://www.nvc.org

Extensive on-line resource for victim information and advocacy. Contains many links and information about the organization's advocacy efforts.

National Crime Victims Research and Treatment Center

http://www.musc.edu/cvc

A Web site that works to foster "better understanding of the impact of criminal victimization on adults, children and their families." Contains information about the center and its work as well as links to related sites.

National Organization for Victim Assistance (NOVA)

http://www.try-nova.org

NOVA is a private, nonprofit organization of victim and witness assistance programs and practitioners, criminal justice agencies and professionals, mental health professionals, researchers, former victims and survivors, and others who are committed to the recognition and implementation of victims' rights and services.

National Victims' Constitutional Amendment Network (NVCAN)

http://www.nvcan.org

NVCAN supports the adoption of a U.S. Constitutional amendment recognizing the fundamental rights of crime victims to be treated with dignity, fairness, and respect by the criminal justice system.

Office for Victims of Crime (OVC)

http://www.ojp.usdoj.gov/ovc

A U.S. Department of Justice site with information about crime victims and resources for crime victims. Contains an extensive collection of links to relevant information.

Victim Offender Mediation Association (VOMA)

http://www.igc.org/voma

VOMA's purpose is to develop and implement a program of public information and education in the field of victim offender mediation and reconciliation programs.